GENERAL
PATTON

★ ★ ★ ★ ★

GENERAL PATTON

A Soldier's Life

★ ★ ★ ★ ★

STANLEY P. HIRSHSON

HarperCollins*Publishers*

HarperCollins books may be purchased for educational, business, or sales promotional use. For information, please write: Special Markets Department, Harper-Collins Publishers Inc., 10 East 53rd Street, New York, NY 10022.

FIRST EDITION

Maps by Scott G. Hirshson and Paul J. Pugliese
Designed by Joseph Rutt

Printed on acid-free paper

Library of Congress Cataloging-in-Publication Data is available upon request.
ISBN 0-06-000982-9
02 03 04 05 06 WBC/RRD 10 9 8 7 6 5 4 3 2 1

To the memory of my beloved parents and
the memory of Colonel Roger H. Nye

. . . for according to what the wise say, the art and beauty of historical composition is, to write the truth . . .

—Captain Bernal Diaz Del Castillo,
The True History of the Conquest of Mexico
(1568)

General Patton had trouble spelling, not, I believe, because he was dyslexic but because he first saw a printed page at the age of twelve. No matter what the reason, I have tried when quoting him to leave his words as he spelled them.

Contents

Illustrations follow page 362.

Maps

Preface

A reader of a volume this big is, I believe, entitled to know about its origins and why I think it differs from other biographies of General Patton. The book had its beginnings in 1990, when I was using the West Point library to research my biography of General William Tecumseh Sherman. Having worked for a decade on Sherman, I grew tired of spending day after day on him. Speaking to Gladys T. Calvetti of Special Collections and Colonel Roger H. Nye, the former head of the History Department at West Point, I found out that through Colonel Nye the library was acquiring the remaining documents the Patton family still possessed, including General Patton's vast library. Their friendship going back to their cadet days, when, Colonel Nye once told me, they were in the same squad, Colonel Nye and Major General George S. Patton IV were bringing carloads of material to West Point.

For about two years after that I drove up to West Point every day that I was not teaching, reading Sherman letters—the library had the two largest collections on microfilm—in the morning and General Patton's diary and letters in the afternoon. From 1992 or 1993 on, after I virtually completed working on Sherman, I spent all of my time on Patton. Almost every day when I was at West Point, Colonel Nye would come in about eleven o'clock. He had just finished the manuscript of his trailblazing study *The Patton Mind,* and we would exchange a few words, usually disagreeing about some aspect of Patton's life, such as whether he was dyslexic or whether the Sicilian campaign was marred by atrocities. We seldom agreed about anything. Yet the discussions never degenerated into arguments, chiefly, I always suspected, because we were both Columbia Ph.D.'s and bore an innate respect for each other's opinions and dignity. Colonel Nye often ended the discussion with the warning that someone else was studying General Patton's life. I never answered, for I was not especially concerned.

I did not care for a very good reason. Put simply, I take issue with the way previous biographies of Patton have been researched. Incomplete research has, in my opinion, led to interpretations that are at best dubious. I invite readers, to cite just a few examples, to compare my chapters on Patton's early life, on the conflict between tankers and infantrymen in the 1920s and 1930s, on Patton's failure to denazify Bavaria and on his loss of the Third Army, and on the struggle over the Patton diary and the movie with those in any other book. I especially invite a comparison of the footnotes.

As illustrations, I should like to mention a few of the sources that have been ignored. Among the most important is the Henry E. Huntington Library in San Marino, California. The Huntington possesses the vast correspondence of Patton's father, of his sister Nita, of his cousins the Browns, of his other cousins the Bannings, and of his maternal grandfather, Benjamin Davis Wilson. Equally vital are libraries in England. At the urging of my friend and colleague David Syrett, I made three trips to London, the last two of which the Research Foundation of the City University of New York helped finance. There I found the papers of Captain Basil H. Liddell Hart at King's College filled with material about Patton and numerous other American generals. Another forgotten source, the Yale University libraries, contain the papers of Henry L. Stimson, Hanson W. Baldwin, and, most importantly, John P. Marquand.

Especially puzzling has been the failure of historians to use government repositories, both here and in England. Available at the Public Record Office in Kew, London, are the two volumes on Allied plans of deception, many involving Patton. The Library of Congress contains numerous neglected collections, including the Nelson A. Miles Family Papers, the Robert P. Patterson Papers, the James W. Wadsworth Papers, the Everett S. Hughes Papers, and the Douglas Southall Freeman Papers. Second to none in importance are the documents in what I have called, as nearby road signs call it, National Archives II at College Park, Maryland, to which I made a dozen trips. In my opinion it is impossible to understand numerous phases of Patton's career without consulting the appropriate Record Groups at the Archives. I am convinced that scholars often shy away from the Archives because the work there is the most difficult, and often the most frustrating, imaginable.

I should also like to mention the government materials virtually impossible to get but often especially rewarding: trial records. The Judge Advocate General's Office at Falls Church, Virginia, has the records of the two soldiers court-martialed for atrocities in Sicily, and the branch of the National Archives at Waltham, Massachusetts, the records of the government's long and unfruitful suit against the Ayer family.

Finally, I found the Columbia University Library, with its vast oral history collection, a storehouse of information on World War II. After all, Dwight D. Eisenhower was once president of Columbia. The library also has the Walter L. Dorn Papers, essential to understanding Patton's career in Bavaria.

These and other collections greatly enhance our knowledge of General Patton's heritage and life. They provide insight into the slave trading of Patton's great-grandfather in Alabama and into the bravery and unhappiness of his paternal grandmother, widowed by the Civil War. They enable the historian to trace more closely Patton's relationship with his father, with his sister, and with his cousins, especially with Arvin Brown, Sr. They develop further the story of Patton's cadet days at West Point and the details of his brief flirtation with Kate Fowler, who became his and his wife's lifelong friend and whose son became his last aide. They trace in greater detail the conflict over tanks in the American and British armies from the 1920s to just before D-Day in Europe. They substantiate the hypothesis that Patton's concept of the warrior soul bore a direct relationship to his belief in reincarnation, the latter being Patton's way of controlling fear in battle. This, in turn, inspired Patton's many warlike speeches, delivered to fire up his troops. In Sicily these talks brought on the most controversial events of Patton's life, not the slappings but perhaps five massacres in two days.

Manuscripts and oral histories also shed light on events in Western Europe in 1944 and 1945: the breakout in Normandy, for which Patton often receives credit, even though General John S. Wood repeatedly asserted that he had nothing to do with it; the brilliant relief of Bastogne; and the disappointments in the drives for Metz and Houffalize.

Another important theme is Patton's relationship with the family of his wife, Beatrice Ayer Patton. Attaining wealth from patent medicines, the Ayer family also operated woolen mills whose workers lived in tenements under conditions condemned by Mrs. William Howard Taft and dozens of other prominent people of that day. The result was the

Lawrence, Massachusetts, strike, one of the bitterest in American history. After the death of his father, a reform Democrat, Patton seemed to adopt the Ayer family's attitude toward labor, race, and ethnicity. Such views led to his refusal, in the face of army directives, to denazify Bavaria and to his relief from command of the Third Army.

Demonstrating the fickleness of history, many important figures are now forgotten by the public. While researching and writing this book, I came away with respect not only for the famous generals and admirals who had to make so many decisions but also for their subordinates, who actually fought the Second World War. John S. Wood, Otto P. Weyland, Bradford G. Chynoweth, John Lesslie Hall, Jr., Robert W. Grow, Gilbert R. Cook, Geoffrey Keyes, and Holmes E. Dager, to name just a few, deserve better of history than they have received. I can only hope that this volume helps revive interest in some of them. Among the members of Patton's staff, James T. Quirk and Bernard S. Carter left wartime letters that are filled with acute observations. I grew to like each immensely.

Of the civilians in this story I found that my favorites were the wise and generous Arvin Browns, father and son, although I will never understand why as late as the 1940s the father endorsed racial covenants, and, much of the time, George S. Patton, Sr., so often a pillar of strength. I have often asked myself whether I would have had the courage to take on, as George Patton, Sr., did, the Southern Pacific Railroad, which controlled California politics for decades. The same can be said of the Arvin Browns and the movie studios. I also found interesting John P. Marquand, even though, clearly, he was unduly critical of Patton. For one thing, without realizing it, he demonstrated the unreliability of Charles R. Codman's memoir *Drive,* just as Dr. Donald E. Currier later showed the unreliability of Fred Ayer, Jr.'s *Before the Colors Fade.* Reading the drafts of Marquand's essay in the Beinecke Library at Yale, I concluded that he possessed the colorful though direct writing style that I have always admired but have probably never attained.

Acknowledgments

Working on a book that took me across both the United States and the Atlantic Ocean has reaffirmed what I have always believed. No groups are more generous with their time and energy than academicians and librarians. Wherever I have gone, I have been welcomed, and I should like to thank those who aided me.

To two friends who encouraged me from the start, I owe a great debt. My colleague David Syrett is in many ways the originator of this study. He urged me to undertake it, constantly asked about its progress, and, in the face of those who told me I would find nothing in Europe, repeatedly advised me to go to King's College of London and to the Public Record Office. My footnotes are testimony to his sagacious advice. Similarly, John Shelter encouraged me in so many ways that I can hardly list them. Living in Highland Falls, he helped make my numerous trips to West Point pleasant and profitable. As I progressed with the work, I discussed with him almost every phase of General Patton's life, always receiving the enlightened response that I have come to expect from him. This paragraph can hardly do justice to the help given me by these two friends, but it is at least an attempt.

In the dozen years that I have taken the forty-minute drive from northeastern New Jersey, where I live, to the West Point Library, I have received nothing but assistance and encouragement. Indeed, I consider those mentioned in this paragraph not archivists and librarians but dear friends who helped me, first with General Sherman and then with General Patton, in so many ways that I can only begin to state them. At Special Collections, Alan Aimone was always his cheerful, knowledgeable self. I can scarcely think of a topic about which I knew more than Alan does. He is really a researcher's dream. At the Archives, Suzanne Christoff has been equally cheerful and helpful. I remember the first day I ever drove up to West Point. Not knowing what to expect, I asked

Suzanne what she had on Sherman. She pulled out school records, demerit books, and other sources of which I never dreamed, immediately convincing me that the Archives was a gold mine of information on any West Point graduate. To list the other archivists and former archivists at Special Collections does not do them justice, but I can think of no other way of thanking them. Gladys Calvetti, Susan Lintelmann, Sheila Biles, Debbie McKeon-Pogue, Alicia Mauldin, and Judith Sibley are close friends of mine, and I wish publicly to express my fondness and warm regard for each of them.

At three hitherto unused archives, each of which possesses large amounts of material on General Patton, I received special treatment. The Huntington Library generously awarded me an Andrew W. Mellon Fellowship that enabled me to spend an entire summer reading the letters of Patton's father, sister, cousins, children, and, above all, grandmother. At the Huntington I was especially aided by Dr. Bill Frank, Kelli Ann Brown, Frances Rouse, Brita Mack, and Leona Schonfeld. Four fine historians who also happened to be at the library made my stay pleasanter. They are, in no particular order, J.J. Humphrey, Michael Green, Wang Xi, and Jim Long.

The second neglected source is the National Archives at College Park, Maryland, a huge repository containing most of the records of the Second World War. There four archivists helped me. Don Singer twice made available to me documents that others were using and had on reserve. John Taylor suggested to me several sources, including the Magic intercepts so frequently mentioned in this book. Stuart Cluny helped get the release of classified material. And a truly remarkable archivist, Rebecca L. Collier, who specializes in World War II, helped me find such documents as Walter L. Dorn's report to General Eisenhower, buried among piles of unrelated material. I am convinced that somewhere, somehow, several things I looked for but could not find have been destroyed. These include the Spofford Report on military government in Sicily and elsewhere, for which I searched a half dozen times. This, however, in no way detracts from the assistance given me at the Archives.

The third of the special repositories is the Liddell Hart Centre at King's College, where Kate O'Brien and the entire staff were invariably friendly and attentive. Many of the collections there are important, none more than the papers of the person for whom the library is named.

When, for example, playing a hunch, I asked for the container with the correspondence between Liddell Hart and General Wood, I received a large box with three or four hundred letters and clippings, many about Patton. The collection is so huge and so rich that I believe even Liddell Hart's biographers do not fully realize how many different subjects it touches.

Other librarians and archivists also aided me. They include Dr. Robert Sommers and Pamela A. Cheney of the United States Army Military History Institute at Carlisle Barracks; Mary B. Dennis, the Deputy Clerk of the Court, Judge Advocate General's Office, Falls Church, Virginia; Randy Sowell and Raymond M. Geselbracht of the Harry S. Truman Library; Cindy Worrell of the Herbert Hoover Library; Tod R. Walters of Texas A&M's Cushing Library; Carolyn A. Davis of the Syracuse University Library; Thomas E. Camden of the George C. Marshall Library; Thomas Betts and Thomas W. Branigan of the Dwight D. Eisenhower Library; Nancy Snedeker of the Franklin D. Roosevelt Library; Elizabeth Pauk of the Yale University Libraries; Stephen Walton of the Imperial War Museum in London; Jim Owens of the branch of the National Archives at Waltham, Massachusetts; and the entire staff of the Oral History Research Office and of Special Collections at the Columbia University Library, where I spent an entire summer reading reminiscences.

I also wish to thank several other people. My officemate, Philip Cannistraro, who directs the Calandra Italian-American Institute of the City University of New York, introduced me to Professor Joseph Salemi, who in turn related the details of the Canicatti massacres, which his father witnessed. Scott MacKenzie frequently discussed with me the career of General Jacob Devers, in whom he is passionately interested. And, at the Public Record Office in Kew, Professor Syrett introduced me to the accomplished historian Bradley F. Smith, who suggested that I use the two-volume manuscript history of Allied plans of deception, so frequently cited in this work.

It is a special pleasure to acknowledge the aid of relatives. During several of my trips to College Park, my sister-in-law and brother-in-law Debbye and Bruce Feldman put up with me, as did my nieces Marci and Staci. In the Midwest I had a similar experience. Returning from the Eisenhower Library in Abilene, I stopped off near Kansas City to visit my sister. There my two nephews, Thomas Moss and Richard

Chase, offered to see to it that I found the Truman Library. The next day, driving through a maze of streets, they took me past the Truman house to the library, which I never would have found without them. In a trip that seemed even more complicated, Tom also drove me to Fort Leavenworth. I am sure that, looking back, Tom and Richard will count the days they sat around while I went through documents as among the most boring they have ever spent, but I still appreciate their thoughtfulness.

Showing my age, I should like to acknowledge some people I have known for close to half a century. At Columbia, David Herbert Donald directed my doctoral dissertation, William E. Leuchtenburg was my second reader, and the late Herman Ausubel directed my master's essay. Each has done me so many favors over the years that words cannot express my indebtedness to them.

I should also like to mention the three other members of Professor Donald's first seminar. Ari Hoogenboom, Grady McWhiney, and Irwin Unger have always set an academic standard that it is almost impossible to reach. When I asked Irwin about getting an agent for the manuscript, he most generously recommended his, Alexander Hoyt, whom he then called. It has indeed been a privilege to know each of the three.

To the Timken Roller Bearing Company I owe a special thanks. In 1944 the firm sponsored a series of magnificent portraits of American military and naval leaders that appeared monthly in the *Saturday Evening Post*. The Timken Company most generously allowed me to reproduce the portrait of General Patton and use it for the book jacket.

At HarperCollins, I would like to thank my editor, Hugh Van Dusen, and assistant editor, David Semanki, as well as production editor Sue Llewellyn and copy editor Eleanor Mikucki, for their help throughout the production of *General Patton*. Working with them has been a pleasure.

Finally, I wish to acknowledge my wife, Janet, and son, Scott. They tolerated my verbal refighting of World War II and shared with me the defeats and triumphs accompanying research and writing. They provided the steadying hand that I often lacked. I am especially grateful to Scott for doing the maps. Finding most maps difficult to follow, we aimed at simplicity and clarity in the ones for this book.

SICILY, JULY 12, 1943, TO JULY 14, 1943

The place and time were Sicily just after the Allied landings of July 10, 1943. During the early days of the invasion, a series of events occurred that, if known to the outside world, probably would have led to the relief of Lieutenant General George S. Patton, Jr., the commander of the American Seventh Army; of Major General Lucian K. Truscott, Jr., who led the 3rd Infantry Division; and of Truscott's chief of staff, Colonel Don E. Carleton. Viewed from the perspective of over half a century, they constitute a regrettable episode in American military history.

The events go back to the month before the invasion, when Patton began addressing various segments of his army. Colonel Homer W. Jones, the judge advocate of the Seventh Army, described one of these, delivered at Patton's headquarters at Mostaganem in Algeria to his staff and division leaders.

> In his talk, General Patton, as I recall, told of some of the experiences he had had in Tunisia, or that he had known of where Germans had indicated they were offering to surrender and when our troops arrived, the Germans immediately shot them down. He did indicate in a situation of this sort, if the enemy waited until our troops were about to capture them, and immediately offered to surrender, that the American soldiers could not afford to take the chance—that it was too late, and they should kill them.

Upset, Jones suggested to Patton's chief of staff, General Hobart R. "Hap" Gay, that Patton clarify his comments, "otherwise, we might have remarks misinterpreted and have violations of international law."[1]

In a speech to the 45th Division, Patton spoke similarly. "General Patton made it very plain over there that we were to kill the enemy wherever we found him," remembered Captain Howard Cry of the division's 180th Regimental Combat Team. "He said to kill and to continue to kill and that the more we killed then the less we'd have to kill later and the better off the Division would be in the long run. . . . He did say that the more prisoners we took the more men we'd have to feed and not to fool around with prisoners. He said that there was only one good German and that was a dead one."[2]

Such remarks helped inspire two well-known massacres at Biscari airfield, which, along with the airfields at Comiso and Ponte Olivio, all in southeastern Sicily, constituted a prime American objective. In the first, Captain John T. Compton, who commanded Company C of the 180th, ordered a firing squad of about two dozen men to shoot forty or so snipers. In the second, Sergeant Horace T. West of Company A killed thirty-six prisoners, thirty-four Italians and two Germans, with a Thompson submachine gun. Both were tried by military courts. Using Patton's statements as his defense, Compton was acquitted. West, however, was found guilty and sentenced to life in prison. That November Compton, "going forward alone to investigate a white flag raised by the Germans," was shot and killed in Italy. The following November West was freed and returned to duty as a private.[3]

While the West and Compton cases have been fully explored, evidence exists of several other atrocities. Alexander Clifford of the *London Daily Mail* testified to at least two other incidents. After the Sicilian campaign ended, Clifford, whose reports appeared in such American papers as the *New York Times* and the *Washington Post,* described what he had seen to the British military analyst Basil H. Liddell Hart, who left a memorandum of their conversation. Clifford left no doubt about whom he blamed for what he saw.

Patton's bloodthirsty way of talking, and wording of his instructions, before the landing in Sicily, was taken too literally by the American troops of the 45th Division particularly. On or about the third day after the landing, Clifford visited the Comiso Airfield along with an American War Correspondent. There they saw a lorry-load of German prisoners brought in who, when they started to debus, were shot down by a heavy machine-gun turned on them.

All were killed except two or three, who were merely wounded. Clifford also saw a batch of about 60 Italian prisoners shot in the same way, after they had been brought in. Clifford and the American War Correspondent went off to Patton and protested. Patton then sent off orders to the Division to stop such killing.

Clifford subsequently discussed these incidents with Clark Lee, who during the Sicilian campaign covered the 45th Division for William Randolph Hearst's International News Service. Lee "told Clifford of several even worse American atrocities," presumably the shootings at Biscari.[4]

Truscott, Carleton, and Patton bore at least partial responsibility for the final atrocity. Unlike the four others, it involved civilians and took place in the central Sicilian town of Canicatti, which Truscott's 3rd Division entered at 3 P.M. on July 12. After the troops took the town, a riot supposedly broke out. Its cause, according to a report tucked away in a remote Record Group in the National Archives, was "a shortage of food." The disturbance "was only quelled with great difficulty by the 14 MPs who had been on continuous duty in that town since the occupation." The lieutenant colonel in charge of American Military Government "then reported the situation to the Chief of Staff of the 3rd Division who instructed him to shoot looters caught in the act, if necessary, to reestablish order." To help quiet things Colonel Charles R. Johnson of the 15th Infantry Regiment sent the lieutenant colonel a platoon of soldiers.

The remaining events rank with the most brutal of the campaign. As the lieutenant colonel told it, he followed a line of "fleeing carts" and "came upon a soap factory outside of which there was a large crowd obviously looting the place." Entering the grounds through a break in a wall, the Sicilians were filling buckets with liquid soap stored in shallow pits. The report in the National Archives gives the officer's version of what happened next.

Lt. Col.———and the infantry platoon endeavored to stop the looting and round up the looters. Their orders were disobeyed. Lt. Col.———then shot at some of the men in the crowd and the infantry rounded up others. Six were killed. Some of those who escaped may have been wounded.

An American soldier who witnessed the incident disagreed with this saccharine account. Arriving at the factory, the lieutenant colonel immediately ordered his MPs to shoot the Sicilians. When they froze, the officer fired his 45-caliber pistol twenty-one times into the crowd, emptying three clips and killing an unknown number of civilians. Those shot included a child, whose stomach was blown out.[5]

Acting on a loosely worded order that should never have been transmitted over the phone, the lieutenant colonel submitted a brief description of the atrocity. Amid the fighting, neither Carleton nor Truscott bothered to investigate it. Patton unquestionably never knew of it.

Who, then, was this general who, in his zeal for victory, created the atmosphere for such events? Recent historians have correctly called him "An Extraordinary Leader" who possessed "A Genius for War." On the one hand, the novelist John P. Marquand, who met Patton just after the capture of Sicily, dismissed him as "a tactless, high-strung, profane officer with a one-cell juvenile mind." Colonel Charles Poletti, the former lieutenant governor of New York, found him, on the other hand, "a very cultured fellow and I liked him."[6]

Such contradictory analyses are common. Colonel Redding Perry, who served as chief of staff of the 2d Armored Division, captured Patton's complexity: "The amazing thing about George was that he was just a bit of everything—brave and timid, tender and harsh, coarse and poetic, sacrilegious and religious—all the opposites mixed up into a really legendary, adorable character." As Colonel Roger H. Nye, a family friend, observed of Patton: "In his case, the historian is well advised to avoid choosing whether he was this or that—he was both." The son of a turn-of-the-century Progressive who despised robber barons and monopolists, Patton lived among and came to admire those his father detested. In turn, he looked down on numerous ethnic and social groups. Who and what motivated and influenced him? Was he a great general? What is Patton's story?[7]

One

GLASSELLS AND HEREFORDS, WILSONS AND PATTONS

(with Some Account of the Dyslexia Myth)

I

Exactly two months before the Japanese attacked Pearl Harbor, General Lesley J. McNair rated the army's "high commanders" for General George C. Marshall, the chief of staff. Of the seven corps commanders McNair endorsed, only one, Joseph W. Stilwell, attained fame in the coming conflict. One, Lloyd R. Fredendall, commanded at Kasserine Pass, perhaps the army's greatest debacle. McNair did just as miserably forecasting the future of the army's division commanders. He said of William H. Simpson, who later led an army: "untried but should do well." One of Simpson's classmates at West Point appeared as poorly to McNair. "Good," McNair, a dedicated infantryman, noted of George S. Patton, Jr., then the commander of the 2d Armored Division; "a division possibly his ceiling." Even more startling today was the last name on McNair's list of "others," an officer who lacked World War I combat experience, Dwight D. Eisenhower. Omitted entirely was Omar N. Bradley. "This is fascinating," Patton's son, himself a major general, wrote when he saw the list a half century later. "McNair's predictions were not too hot. Take notice of Ike at the bottom of the list—'an also ran.' "[1]

No American war produced more generals whose names are instantaneously recognizable than did the Second World War: Eisenhower, Bradley, Marshall, Stilwell, MacArthur, and Patton. Perhaps Patton has held the most fascination, for his fame stems solely from his skill and determination as a combat commander, not from service as an administrator or executive. Ambitious, controversial, and brilliant, he blazed brightest but for the shortest time. Just as war helped define him, he helped define it. As he often predicted, students of war today study his campaigns, and those who served under him led the American army for a quarter of a century.

At different times and to different people, General Patton appeared to be different things. To British general Sir Charles Richardson, who met him in Sicily in September 1943, Patton was more cowboy than anything else. "I was led by an ADC into a large room; in one corner, flags of the Allies, very large flags at that, were erected behind an enormous desk. A slim, elderly figure rose up, with pearl-handled revolver strapped to his hip, and greeted me in movietone accent. Was I at war, or was I in Hollywood, I wondered?"[2] Conversely, Patton's father considered him the heir to the traditions, military and otherwise, of the great Southern family from which he came. Patton himself lived and never felt uncomfortable in Massachusetts. In reality, he was an American, and it is hard to imagine any other nation producing a general exactly like him.

II

Pattons lived in Virginia throughout the eighteenth century. In 1755 Colonel James Patton, the head of the Augusta County militia, displayed all the family's impulsiveness. After the Shawnees massacred some settlers, James Patton gathered his troops and drove straight for the Indian encampment. On July 8, the day before General Edward Braddock's defeat by the French and Indians near Fort Duquesne, he marched into a trap and was never heard of again.[3]

Just before the Revolutionary War, Robert Patton, a Scotsman, came to the New World and settled in Fredericksburg, Virginia. About 1793 he married Anne Gordon Mercer, the only daughter of the Revolutionary War hero General Hugh Mercer, who was killed at the Battle of Princeton in 1777, and for whom the New Jersey county containing that town is named. Of their six children the most distinguished was John Mercer Patton, who lived from 1797 to 1858. He served in Congress from 1830 to 1838 and was for a short time the acting governor of

Virginia. John Mercer Patton and his wife, Margaret French Williams, in turn produced twelve children. They named the sixth, born on June 26, 1833, George Smith Patton.[4]

During his brief life George Smith Patton had two great loves: the military and Susan Thornton Glassell. A graduate in 1852 of the Virginia Military Institute, he practiced law in Charleston, Virginia, now West Virginia. He also led the county militia unit, the Kanawha Riflemen. "It was well trained and equipped," George Smith Patton's commander informed his son sixty years later, "all of which was due to your Fathers energy and genius. The Kanawha Riflemen was composed of the best young & old men in Charleston & the Valley. Many of them have become distinguished & all were engaged in developing the resources of the Valley. Your Father served with me in many engagements & I have never had a more efficient & gallant officer under my command." In 1859, when John Brown captured the federal arsenal at Harpers Ferry, the Kanawha Riflemen was among the units rushed into action to retake the place.[5]

In the fall of 1854 George Smith Patton, then twenty-one, met his other love, Susan Thornton Glassell, two years his junior. That November, from Richmond, Susan described the relationship to her cousin, Virginia Ring:

> You will be astonished when I tell you that to this individual I have given my entire heart. He is one of God's own noble men a work of his own hands. He is a son of Mr. M. Patton of this place. His name is George. I met with him last evening and liked him from the first moment that I saw him. . . . I have been engaged to him now rather more than six weeks, and every day develops some new and noble treat. . . . His hair is as black as a raven's wing with eyes of the same hue but oh my, so deep, so bright, and so full of *soul*. He is very fond of *fun* and we keep up a most incessant chatter.[6]

The Glassell family bore little of the luster of the Pattons. Originally from Virginia, Susan had grown up deep in Alabama in Greensboro, where her father, Andrew Glassell, Sr., engaged principally in hiring out his slaves to a Mr. Franklin Randolph. In January 1835, just after moving to Alabama, he urged his wife, Susan Thompson Thornton Glassell, to send her brother, Dr. William Thornton, there.

I would hire his negros [*sic*] at a much higher rate than the Kanawha price. I mean men, boys, girls & women without children (young negro children in this country are a great drawback to the services of the mother, & I do not hire them). There are many others in this country who will treat them well, give an exorbitant hire for such & if he could bring out a few of that description, they alone would support him, particularly as he could attend to their medical wants.

With cotton selling above fifteen cents a pound, both land and slaves were valuable in Alabama.[7]

A year later, again writing to his wife, who was visiting her family in Virginia, Andrew Glassell, Sr., repeated this theme.

I know of a great number of Gentlemen who intend to go into Va. for the purpose of purchasing negros.—I will therefore advise your brother to purchase his cook's husband as soon as possible.

Negro fellows will readily command here $800 & in Mississippi $900 & 1000, but say nothing about this, that property will rise still higher next fall. As the great demand for money on account of the late public sales of land has hitherto kept that property down, if *down* I can say.[8]

On October 18, 1836, Susan Thompson Thornton Glassell died. Her husband remained in Alabama, but their three children took different paths. Their daughter, Susan Thornton Glassell, spent much of her time with her mother's family in western Virginia. One son, William T. Glassell, became a naval officer, and the other, Andrew Glassell, Jr., migrated in 1852 to San Francisco, where he became a partner in the law firm of Glassell and Leigh.[9]

Prospering, the younger Andrew Glassell urged his father to bring the entire family to California. The weather was the best in the world, he boasted, making agriculture enormously profitable. And the gold seemed as if it would not run out for twenty years.

As to your objections on the ground that you would dislike to sell family negroes; that may be avoided—I observed that Sue and

Grandma were anxious to have Nelly and Betsy about them—Let them have them and such others as you would not sell; and dispose of the balance. If you could realize $12 or $15,000 and bring it to this place, I know that you could make it safer and more profitable than are the negroes in whom it is now invested, to say nothing of your own personal comfort and independence. The present high value of negroes is tenfold more precarious than the present value of property in California, to say nothing of the risk of their lives.[10]

Meantime, on November 8, 1855, Susan Glassell married George Smith Patton. Their first child, George William Patton, was born on September 30, 1856. "The Boy grows and begins to laugh & grow," Susan's grandmother, Eleanor B. Thornton, informed the elder Andrew Glassell when the baby was six weeks old.[11]

Like many a child, George William proved to be a handful. When he was fourteen months old, his mother described him as "a great large red faced rowdy boy. He is so wild and turbulent, never still one moment in the day."[12]

George's behavior did not discourage his parents from having other children. Two daughters, Ellen Thornton, nicknamed Nellie, and Susan, and a son, Andrew but called by his middle name, Glassell, completed the family.

In early 1861, visiting her brother-in-law, John Mercer Patton, and his wife, Sally Taylor Patton, Susan witnessed the turmoil over secession. "I have never in my wildest dreams," she informed her husband in late February, "could have imagined the foul corruption of this once glorious old state. My soul sickens when I think of her." While shopping, Susan ran into a woman abolitionist who praised President-elect Abraham Lincoln, predicted the end of slavery in Virginia, and said that Northerners would soon come to live there. "I was so much excited that I scarce know what I said. Grandma says my eye flashed fire, and that I was very rude to her, but I don't care if I was."[13]

On April 13, 1861, as a Virginia convention discussed secession, Susan heard cannons. She and her grandmother rushed down to the convention hall, where, she wrote her husband, she learned that Fort Sumter, the Union installation in Charleston harbor, had surrendered. At the convention Jubal A. Early, later a prominent Confederate general, rose and said that he for one regretted it very much. . . . The people of Richmond collected in the square, and after firing one hundred guns called for speeches from brother John and others, who addressed the crowd from the Capitol porch, and gave it to the convention right and left. Last night there was one of the grandest illuminations ever seen in these parts. Torch light processions, bon-fires, roman candles and every thing that could be gotten up on the spur of the moment. . . . The people are wild with excitement now, and the old fogies in the convention thoroughly scared out of their wits. . . . We are in the midst of the most dreadful times, and I feel that I must nerve my heart for the worst.[14]

Just before his death in 1927, George William Patton, then known as George Smith Patton, Sr., dictated his "A Child's Memory of the Civil War." He remembered that in the spring of 1861 the family moved to the Patton ancestral home, Spring Farm, near Culpeper Court House. "It was a long low rambling house with a veranda in front and detached kitchen and well beyond this the line of slave cabins." Several of his father's brothers were there: Robert Williams Patton, the eldest, a former naval officer, "but now old and no account"; Isaac Williams Patton, who had left the army and in 1855 married the daughter of a Louisiana sugar planter; and Waller Tazewell Patton, who practiced law in Culpeper and was a member of the state legislature and of the Richmond secession convention.[15]

When war broke out, the original George Smith Patton returned to Charleston and his army unit. His first action came at Scarry Creek, near Charleston, where a minié ball shattered the upper bone of his right arm. Captured by the Yankees, he refused to have his arm amputated. His son recalled that it healed, but his father never regained full use of it. "As illustrative of the poor surgery of the day I can remember seeing my father shaving one morning and of his asking my mother for a knitting needle with which he fished a piece of bone out of his wound. That was at least a year after he was hit."[16]

Returned to the Confederates in a prisoner exchange, George Smith Patton became the colonel of the 22d Virginia Infantry Regiment. Fighting in southwest Virginia, he was hit in the abdomen. General Henry Heth later told how he found the wounded colonel leaning against a tree writing a letter to his wife. Patton said he was "shot in the belly so it is over with me and I sent the doctor to look after men he can save." Heth then stuck his dirty finger into the hole and pulled out a ten-dollar gold piece. The ball had struck the coin, driving it into Patton's stomach. The colonel recovered.[17]

The child vividly recalled the nearby Battle of Dry Creek, where his father defeated his old friend, General William Woods Averell. Amputated arms and legs formed a huge pile, and the dead and wounded covered acres of ground. Helping to care for the wounded, Susan Patton fainted from the smell.[18]

The worst news came in September 1864. On about the twenty-third of the month the family physician brought Susan Patton a newspaper with an account of the Third Battle of Winchester. Among the prominent Confederate dead were General Robert E. Rodes and Colonels Archibald C. Godwin and George S. Patton. Wounded in the stomach by a piece of shrapnel, Patton at first began to recover. Taken to the house of his cousin Mary Williams in Winchester, he sat up and ate some peaches. Suddenly he developed a fever and died of gangrene several days after the fight.

The child remembered the loyalty of his father's slave. "His nigrow boy Peter (the same who his mother had given him at the start of the war) took his horse, saddle and saber and hiding in the woods by day and riding at night eluded the pickets and foragers of both armies and brought the horse etc safely to Uncle John's house at the Meadows."[19]

During the winter of 1864–1865, the family, the child remembered, stayed in Goochland County, in western Virginia, "in great want of food and clothing." Had John Mercer Patton "not sent us a steer all the way from the Meadows, driven by a nigger boy we would have starved but by corning the beef we managed to get along."[20]

III

With his sister widowed and in want, his brother jobless, and his father old and blind, Andrew Glassell, Jr., urged his family to join him in California. Having left San Francisco during the war, he had for a time operated a sawmill near Santa Cruz but had recently moved to Los Angeles, where he opened a law office with his boyhood friend, Alfred B. Chapman, a former Union officer. "You do not yet answer definitely to whether you all will come out or stay in Va.," Andrew wrote his brother William in June 1866, "and evidently exhibit much hesitation and shrinking from the pains and perils of the voyage out. . . . You all know, and I hope cannot doubt my sincerity in urging you to come out and live with me. It is my judgment that it would be best for all parties. Some facts however—in regard to the ability of Our Father & Sister & the children to undergo the journey . . . are better known to you than to me, and therefore so far as those facts affect your determination upon the move, I must leave them to your better judgment." Andrew considered the first of October the best time to start. To secure cheap accommodations the family should watch for a day when two steamers were leaving New York, for they would be in competition. Take quinine daily, Andrew advised, for he considered California "the tropics. . . . Your Money in my hands is loaned out at 1½ per cent per month in Mortgages—due next May. Sue's $800 is out also at the same rate. I am continuing to do well and improving in my practice here."[21]

With $600 from Andrew, the family began the migration to the West in early November. Arriving in New York at 5 A.M. on the ninth, Nellie and her mother walked up Broadway, "the former much delighted with the shop windows—prices of everything enormous." On the eleventh, Susan told her sister-in-law Sally Taylor Patton, the family sailed out of New York on the *Arizona*. William had a room to himself, George shared one with his grandfather, and Susan and "the three little ones" occupied a double cabin. Susan found few Southerners aboard. One of them, a Mr. McDonald, "told one lady that I was from the Confederacy at which information she raised her hands in horror." Among the Yankees were two generals. One was the evil James B. Fry, "whose countenance denotes relentless cruelty. I believe he was Provost Marshal General at one time during the War, and distinguished himself as a villain." The other, Rufus King, "with a more magnanimous face, has made several efforts to gain our good will. His wife seized George and told him that she was sure he had never been kissed by a Yankee and she wished to show him what a nice kiss she could bestow. He refused however most positively and said he never would kiss a Yankee at which she seemed highly amused, and asked if all the Southern boys were as smart as he."[22]

On the sixth of December the *Arizona* reached San Francisco. Busy in court, Andrew did not meet the ship, but numerous others did. The most emotional, Uncle John J. Williams, the brother of Susan's mother-in-law, was, Susan told Sally, "moved to tears when he embraced the children, they reminding him so forcibly of home and the dear ones in Va. . . . The splendor of everything quite amazed the poor half starved Confederates. Everything was so new and different from anything I had ever before seen. The customs, manners and habits so different that I felt I had been transferred to another world."

After spending ten days in San Francisco, the family sailed to San Pedro, the port for Los Angeles. Awaiting them was Andrew, "so little changed that I knew him at the distance of two hundred yards off. Not so with regard to me whom he declared he would never have known. He is not only the same in appearance but the same warm hearted affectionate brother that he was when he left Alabama nearly fourteen years ago." The new arrivals were staying in Andrew's house, which had nine rooms and a bathroom, but Susan hoped soon to begin teaching, for Andrew had seven children to take care of. "I am convinced from all I can observe that Brother lost very heavily in some of his speculations and has economised in his family to enable him to help me as he has done, and I am determined to put my shoulder to the wheel and do all in my power to avoid being a burden on him."[23]

Late that May, Susan wrote Sally about her school and her children.

I number eleven scholars now at three dollars a month, fifteen of which goes for rent. I am anxious to get enough to be able to send George to a good school. At the public school where he now is he learns nothing and I feel that it is so important for him to be getting forward. Nellie and Glassell I teach in my school but George is too large, and parents would object to sending me their daughters if he were there. . . . Susie is my sunshine indeed, and I think has a most affectionate and lovely temper. . . . I am so tired of oranges that I would not take the trouble to peel one to eat.[24]

Strong as Susan was, her life was drudgery. She got up at six, cleaned the schoolroom, and then prepared breakfast for her children. With the help of Nellie and Susie she cleaned the house until nine, when school began. School ended at four and supper was at five-thirty. After supper, Susan went for a walk, generally with her brother. "This," she told her husband's sister, Elisa Patton Gilmer, "is the general routine day after day and week after week."[25]

By early fall Susan had twenty-one students and added a Mrs. Smith to her staff to teach music and French. But brave as she was, she could not hide her grief. "This is the saddest time of all the year to me," she wrote Sally in late September, "and I feel like a stricken down woman when I remember the full blow that came upon me just three years ago, bloting out the light of life for me, and sending me and mine forth in the world homeless wanderers. May Gods will be done, and may He strengthen me in fighting lifes battles with an unfaltering heart, but Oh! strange and misterious are His ways. Surely we are groping in the dark." Two weeks later, attempting to console her cousin Virginia Ring on the death of her husband, Susan lamented: "My children are a great comfort to me, especially my youngest [Susie], yet were I called on tomorrow to leave this world, I should not regret it."[26]

Adding to Susan's unhappiness, she did not get along with her brother's wife, Lucy Toland. "As I told you before," she informed Sally,

> there is not a particle of congeniality between L. and my-self. That is no more her fault than mine, but it is a misfortune nevertheless, and causes me many heart aches. I hope my dear sister you will not hint these things to any one, of course brother John excepted, but I cant bear for my Brothers sake that it should be known. . . . I wish you could know my Brother. He is all that a fond sister could wish, and is willing to divide the last crust with me and mine.

In part, the trouble between the two may have stemmed from religion. Lucy was a devout Catholic, a belief that Susan, an Episcopalian, believed to be shallow. After going "for the first time in my life to the Romish Church," Susan related to Sally her horror: "I can not begin to express to you how I felt, but is [it] not strange how any sensible people can admire such performances and think them solemn or sacred?"[27]

IV

Despite the growth of her school, Susan Glassell Patton remained morose. "Life is so dreary without genial souls to commune with," she told Sally in May 1868.

But for the constant occupation I should die and yet I long for rest. . . . May God preserve you from all that I have suffered, and still suffer. It is useless my darling to conceal the fact that I am most unhappy. With every comfort of house, and food, there is the all important love and peace denied me. Who can be happy without these? I had rather live in a shanty of my own on the coarsest food, and do all my own work, than as I am now.

Susan hoped John Mercer Patton might be able to sell her husband's law books.

If he could get any thing for them I might put it with the little I have and buy myself a small house, even if it only had two rooms in it. Do not understand me as saying that I have not the love of my Brother, but he does not begin to know all I endure, nor is it a subject that even a sister can speak into the ear of a Brother. Do not I implore you mention these things to any one except brother John. . . . Today I feel so very miserable that I walked my room for an hour pressing my head between my hands trying to devise some means of escape, when suddenly I thought there might be some chance of selling the Law Books.[28]

The great change in Susan's life came later that year. Her husband's cousin George Hugh Smith—his mother and George Smith Patton's were sisters—arrived in California. At VMI he had been a year behind his cousin and during the war had served as the colonel of the 62d Virginia Infantry. Refusing to surrender to the Yankees, he immigrated to Mexico and from there went to California in 1868. "He never took the oath of allegiance to the United States," noted General Patton's daughter, Ruth Ellen, "but he was such a distinguished gentleman that the Federal agencies never bothered him." In California, Smith began spending much time near Susan. "I enjoy his company," Susan told Sally in December, "as it reminds me so of home and the dear ones in Va. He is employed in Brothers office at a salary of one hundred dollars a month with the privilege of studying California practice. I would not be surprised if Brother offers him a partnership in the firm of Glassell & Chapman at the end of six months, that is if he continues to like him as well as he does now."[29]

In the same letter Susan praised her oldest child. "George grows in body and mind astonishingly, and is thought by every one a very uncommon boy." In 1868 his mother was able to take him out of public school and enroll him in the Boys' Grammar School, run by Dr. Truman S. Rose. A former classmate remembered him as one of the three best students in the school, excelling in grammar, physiology, and oratory. Delivering a lecture on the circulation of the blood, he did so well that he seemed to be heading for a career in medicine, rather than for VMI and law.[30]

Events now moved swiftly. In 1870 Smith and Susan married. The union produced two children, a son, Eltinge, who was born in 1876 and died in 1887, and a daughter, Anne Ophelia, whose marriage in November 1890, strangely enough, helped shape General Patton's life.[31]

Meantime, young George Patton, who, out of reverence for his devoted stepfather, dropped the middle name of William and replaced it with Smith, followed the usual family course. With financial help from his uncle, John Mercer Patton, he attended VMI. Graduating in 1877, he remained there for a year teaching French. He then hoped to join an expedition to Egypt, but his mother, who needed his help, implored him to return home. As it turned out, the entire expedition was wiped out.

George then returned to California. The firm of Glassell and Chapman was now Glassell and Smith, Colonel Smith having become a partner in 1870 and Chapman having retired in 1879. "I am working hard and studying under Cousin Geo's direction," George Patton wrote Uncle John Mercer Patton in 1879. "He takes a kind and generous interest in my progress and great pains. He is one of the very best men I know." Admitted to the bar in 1880, George joined the family firm, now called Glassell, Smith, and Patton.[32]

Three years later Susan Patton developed breast cancer. Early in October 1883 her physician gave her four months to live. On November 16, 1883, she died. "Poor Mrs. Smith her suffering & agony are ended," noted Anne Wilson, General Patton's beloved Aunt Nannie. "We will miss her very much."[33]

V

The Pattons and Glassells formed one line of General Patton's heritage, the Wilsons and Herefords the other. Patton's maternal grandfather, Benjamin D. Wilson, was, during his lifetime, one of the most important men in California. Born in Nashville on December 1, 1811, he was told he could not survive in Tennessee's climate and in 1833 traveled west to Santa Fe. The turning point in his life came roughly a decade later. He arrived in California in November 1841 and in 1843 bought Rancho Jurupa, covering what is now Riverside, California. The next year he married sixteen-year-old Ramona Yorba, the daughter of the owner of the Santa Ana Rancho, which covered thirty leagues, roughly ninety miles, and adjoined Wilson's property.

For Wilson the Mexican War presented a problem. He had married into a Mexican family and owed his vast fortune to it. At first he remained neutral, but when Commodore Robert F. Stockton arrived in San Pedro Bay, he reluctantly accepted a captain's commission, serving in the California Battalion.

The death of his young wife on March 21, 1849, failed to stop Wilson. In 1851, after the City of Los Angeles was created, he served as its first mayor. Three years later he bought 120 acres of land in what became the heart of San Marino. On it he built a two-story adobe brick home with a wine cellar and a tile roof. Spending what was then the vast sum of $20,000, he surrounded it with thirty thousand raisin grape cuttings and eighteen hundred orange trees. He also grew olives, figs, pears, apples, apricots, nectarines, plums, cherries, almonds, and walnuts. He called the place Lake Vineyard Rancho.[34]

As time went on, Wilson added to his holdings. He bought Rancho San Pasqual, a fourteen-hundred-acre property that covered what became Pasadena, which Wilson used for his sheep corral before selling it to a commune from Indiana; Alhambra; San Gabriel; South Pasadena; Rosemead; and Altadena. Along with his son-in-law, James de Barth Shorb, who owned the five-hundred-acre San Marino Ranch, on which the Henry E. Huntington Library now sits, Wilson became one of the first Californians to ship oranges east. When high property taxes came along, he began to sell off his land, but he kept his beloved Lake Vineyard.[35]

After the death of Ramona, Margaret S. Hereford entered Wilson's life. If Wilson's first wife put him on the road to prosperity, Margaret's first husband, her cousin Thomas A. Hereford, dragged her down the opposite path. A physician unable to earn a living in his native Alabama, Hereford regaled his wife with dreams of riches trading in Santa Fe and Mexico. When, after enduring heartbreaking hardships, he failed at these ventures, he went to California, where his wife joined him in mid-1850. Then, on January 7, 1852, the sickly physician died, leaving his widow to support her small son. She became the governess of Wilson's two children and, according to family legend, taught them English. Attracted to each other, Wilson and Margaret married, each for the second time, in San Jose on February 1, 1853.[36]

The union of Wilson and Margaret Hereford produced two remarkably gentle and enlightened daughters, both born at Lake Vineyard Rancho. Anne Wilson, forever known as Nannie, arrived on July 6, 1858. Her devoted sister, Ruth, was born on April 28, 1861.

For the Wilson girls, growing up on a huge estate among Southern California's elite proved exciting. General Irvin McDowell, in charge of the army in California and a business associate of Wilson, visited often. So, too, did important politicians and businessmen like Governor George Stoneman, the Civil War cavalryman. To Lake Vineyard Rancho also came Wilson's close friend Phineas Banning, a state senator and brigadier general of the militia. Banning, "who operated a large string of coaches" and was involved with Wilson in railroad projects and in the development of the harbor at Wilmington, just below Los Angeles, "brought gay stage parties in those gay days when the Wilson family was renown[ed] for its hospitality and generosity." One newspaper said of Banning: "His heart is as big as his body, and this body is like an ox." He loved the title of general. Once, when one of his tugs blew a boiler and threw him into the water, some people on shore yelled: "Poor Banning." "Poor General," he yelled back.[37]

To the Wilson house also came the Pattons, who knew the Wilsons from almost their earliest days in California. After his return from Virginia and the death of Benjamin Wilson on March 9, 1878, George Patton constantly visited the Wilson sisters. "George Patton is a splendid talker," Nannie noted in her diary. "He is so smart & so well read. I have a great admiration for him." But George Patton, as his son would be, was sometimes impulsive and unpredictable. One day in 1882 he raced a companion home and forced his horse, Nannie recorded, to "gallop nearly all the way up the long hill—They are all teasing him about it saying the horse is ruined." Then, during the holidays late in 1883, George and his brother Glassell "were in a row in a saloon—& we felt badly about it, but it is hard for us to believe George Patton would do anything very wrong—he told us all about it tonight & it was all an accident that could not be helped."[38]

Like most young girls, the Wilson sisters thought about marriage. In 1882 Nannie bet George's sister, Susan, "that I will *not* be married inside of five (5) years. The penalty half a dozen pairs of six button kid gloves. Ruth makes the same bet."[39]

Susie Patton won her bet with Nannie, who never married. But her brother saw to it that she had to pay the one with Ruth. On the morning of Wednesday, December 10, 1884, George and Ruth married in the Church of Our Saviour, the church in San Gabriel that the Wilsons helped build and the Pattons attended. Best man was George Patton's close friend and business associate, the former British army captain Arthur J. Hutchinson, who would soon marry into the Patton family. After the wedding reception, the newlyweds took the train east on their honeymoon.[40]

Returning, the couple moved into the adobe house on Lake Vineyard Rancho. There, in the room in which Nannie and Ruth had first seen daylight, their first child, George S. Patton, Jr., till his death called Georgie, was born on November 11, 1885. On August 24, 1887, just after Ruth and George moved into their new house on the property, their second child arrived. Named Anne Wilson Patton, she forever bore the nickname Nita.[41]

From their birth Georgie and Nita were nurtured in this loving atmosphere by their parents and by their nurse, Mary Scally. In early 1888 George Patton described things to Nannie.

Ruth and the babies are well. The boy is growing and talks now remarkably well. He remarked the other day—when told to be careful or he would break his neck—"I don't want to break my neck—I wouldn't break it for any 'mount of money."

Mary had quite a sore throat—& the other night Ruth & I kept

both babies all night. We had a circus—had to take both in bed—
at the same time. The boy is fearful as a bed-fellow. I had just as
soon sleep with a mule.

Little "sister" is growing very pretty. She is stronger I think
than the boy was and nearly jumps out of your arms. She is the
best natured thing I ever saw—rarely cries—and is always ready
for a frolic.[42]

An intense individual who drove himself to the point of physical and
mental exhaustion—General Patton's mother-in-law later described
him "as made of goodness and fire"—George Patton molded his son
into a man's man. When Georgie was two, his father was prepared to
get him his own horse, but his mother thought he was too young. But
by the age of four Georgie was a competent rider, taking lessons first
from his godfather, Captain Hutchinson, who in 1888 had married
George Patton's cousin Sadie, and then from his father. The captain also
gave little Georgie his first English saddle. By his early teens Georgie
was so expert that on January 1, 1901, along with his friend Maurice
Phillips, he served as the standard-bearer in the Tournament of Roses
parade in Pasadena.[43]

Georgie also grew up with weapons. At the age of five he had his own
pistol. One day, while he was playing with it in his grandmother's room,
it went off. Luckily, Georgie only burned his finger. Even for a woman
who had made the long, dangerous trek from St. Louis to Southern California almost a half century before, such behavior was startling.[44]

With such friends as Ignacio "Nacho" Callahan, whose Mexican-Irish
father had come to California with Benjamin D. Wilson in 1841,
Georgie experienced an energetic childhood. "When we were about 8 or
10 years old and learning to ride," Nacho observed, "Georgie would not
be defeated. If a horse threw him, he'd get up and try again."

The two were in constant competition. "The only thing I could beat
him at was boxing," Nacho remembered. "He used to tell me 'Natcho,
do you have to keep hitting me on the nose—is that the only place you
can hit me?'" But Nacho was no match for Georgie with swords. "He
was ferocious, and that's where he had me."

Georgie, thin and blond, and Nacho, wiry and swarthy, roamed over
the eighteen-hundred-acre estate, covering much of what is today San
Marino and Pasadena, on ponies, Georgie's being a fat Shetland named

Peach Blossom. They played polo in the alfalfa field below the house, swam in and hunted ducks on what later became a mosquito-ridden swamp that had to be filled in with dirt from excavations at the nearby college, the predecessor of the California Institute of Technology, and got free rides by grabbing the tails of calves and hanging on as the terrified animals stormed off. Their favorite trick was to turn loose some of George Patton's forty or so horses and mules. "Then Mr. Patton would order us to round them up and we would spend the whole night out."

Georgie, Nita, and their friends, including the children of the elder Patton sister, Nellie Patton Brown, also played military games. "Was he a soldier in his boyhood," Nita once asked herself. "Yes," she answered, "from the time he could walk, and I, I was the defeated Army."[45]

VI

During the time his son was growing up, George Patton became a noted figure in Los Angeles. After serving two terms as the district attorney of Los Angeles County, he returned to the office of Glassell, Smith, and Patton, which Georgie frequently visited. Located in the old Temple Block, which was eventually razed to build a civic center, the offices were, Georgie noted, "dirty and their chief furnature was a letter book in a big press. There were no carpets and things were for utility rather than looks." For a while the partners allowed an impoverished acquaintance to sleep in the office. The Palace Saloon, the site of innumerable brawls and an occasional killing, ran through the building.[46]

The year 1890 brought the initial cementing of the families of Phineas Banning and Benjamin D. Wilson, a process George Patton, Jr., and his wife helped complete. On the twelfth of November George Patton's half sister, Anne Ophelia Smith, married Hancock Banning, the eldest of Phineas's sons. With his two brothers Hancock Banning already owned much of Wilmington, California, which his father had founded. In 1892 the brothers bought control of the island paradise twenty-six miles into the Pacific Ocean, Santa Catalina. In the latter venture George Patton also invested.[47]

With the Bannings, George Patton became the chief advocate of the development of San Pedro, directly across from Catalina, as the port for Los Angeles. In the fight he took on Collis P. Huntington's Southern

Pacific Railroad, later denounced in Frank Norris's *The Octopus,* which dominated California politics for decades. Sent to Washington by the Los Angeles Chamber of Commerce, Patton testified on the advantages of San Pedro before the Senate Committee on Harbors, several of whose members were associates of Huntington. A railroad line leading from San Pedro to the East would, he argued, be nearly five hundred miles shorter than the Southern Pacific's line from San Francisco. The road would have better grades and, being to the south, no interference from snow. "I was particularly polite but ruthlessly frank," Patton admitted to Shorb, who was married to Ruth and Nannie's half sister, "—and Mr. H. did not enjoy it. . . . My observation of Congress has considerably dampened my ambition in that direction. It is a terribly dead level of mediocrity & purely selfish ends seem to occupy all."[48]

In 1894 George Patton nonetheless accepted the Democratic nomination for Congress from California's Sixth Congressional District. Campaigning vigorously, he made Huntington and the Southern Pacific the chief issue. "My belief is," he said in one speech, "that the time has come when the people of California must shake from their limbs the shackles of the commercial slavery imposed upon them by this corporation or consent that hereafter they shall remain at sufferance upon territory owned by it." Like the Populists, then at the height of their influence in the West, George Patton advocated government ownership of the railroads.[49]

Called by the *Los Angeles Examiner* "the Stormy Petrel of the Democratic Party," George Patton became two years later a central figure in "the hottest fight ever made in Los Angeles." Again seeking the Democratic nomination for Congress, he and a conservative rival, L. J. Rose, engaged in a battle that lasted six weeks. The nominating convention moved from city to city—Sacramento, Fresno, Ventura, and Los Angeles—and for 152 ballots could decide on no one. Finally the convention selected a compromise candidate, Harry Patton (unrelated), a newspaperman who withdrew in favor of a Populist, who won.[50]

A true turn-of-the-century Progressive, George Patton saw American history as a struggle between the followers of Thomas Jefferson, who believed in democracy, and the followers of Alexander Hamilton, who favored an oligarchy of the wealthy. In a speech, "Progressive Democracy," he denounced "these self-styled Captains of Industry" who since the Civil War had managed "to absorb into their own hands the practical control of the wealth and credit of the greatest industrial civilization the world has yet seen." He pointed to Andrew Carnegie, who "in one short lifetime" had accumulated $500 million, and to John D. Rockefeller, who amassed "twice that sum. Yet these two are but the extreme types of a class in this country who, apparently blinded by impunity and drunk with power, imagine that the conditions which have existed in respect to their own cases can be indefinitely continued." Such people perverted democratic government.[51]

Equally dangerous to George Patton were two movements that he somehow tied together, the Oriental menace and women's suffrage. "Here in California," he wrote in a magazine article, "we occupy the position of the vanguard of Aryan civilization, and before our very eyes the Asiatic Titan stretches his great limbs after the sleep of centuries." Men, he reasoned, had produced this great Aryan culture. Why, then, should women be allowed to intrude?[52]

Along with such associates as Henry W. O'Melveny, who often served as the Patton lawyer; John S. McGroarty, the author of the magisterial work *California of the South,* which glorified the achievements of migrants from Dixie; and William Banning, George Patton was one of the leaders of the Men's League Opposed to Suffrage Extension of Los Angeles County. So vehement was Patton on the subject that Judge Henry C. Dillon, who had helped him campaign for Congress in the 1890s against the Southern Pacific, depicted "the handsome Mr. Patton" as standing "in front of the ballot box, swinging the club of brute force over the heads of the women who want to vote."[53]

VII

George Patton, Sr., possessed ideas on education that shaped his children's early lives. Believing that, like mankind itself, the human mind must evolve, he insisted that his son and daughter be educated in stages. The first emphasized nursery rhymes like "Hickory Dickory Dock." He next acquainted his children with stories that might scare ordinary youngsters, tales of fairies and of wicked witches, such as the queen in "Snow White." After several other stages, the children emerged onto the heights of learning: mythology, history, and the classics, all of which George Patton, Nannie, and others read to them long before they were able to read for themselves. The first game Nita remembered playing involved mythology. She was a horse dragging the body of the legendary Greek warrior Ajax, in reality a dead bird, around the walls of Troy. George Patton believed that to find "his own special channel" a child must progress through these stages. In later years, when peeved at Georgie's wife, he would point a finger at her and say: "You, Bea, settled down with the fairies."[54]

George Patton's ideas on education have led directly to the assertion by several historians that General Patton suffered from dyslexia, or developmental reading disabilities. Put simply, dyslexics see letters and numbers backward. Often highly intelligent, they have problems in school with reading and writing, numbers, coordination, memory, and sometimes deportment. They usually work slowly, have trouble following oral directions, and are incapable of reading aloud.[55]

Of these George S. Patton, Jr., possessed only an inability to spell correctly. Once he learned to read, he read incessantly. He wrote and spoke extensively, was never a deportment problem in school, and, as the dash and hurdles star on the army track team, showed superb coordination. He later organized and directed troops masterfully and, like few other generals, was able to visualize entire battlefields.

Dyslexia is hardly as common as some previous biographers of General Patton have asserted. In a study done for the National Association of School Psychologists, two University of Wisconsin psychologists put the school-age children who are dyslexic at between 3 and 6 percent, hardly the 20 percent offered by one historian.[56]

Why then did Patton never learn to spell? Two people who knew him well, Brigadier General Frank McCarthy, who served during World War II on General George C. Marshall's staff and later produced the movies *Patton* and *MacArthur*, and Colonel Paul D. Harkins, who served on Patton's staff and later became a four-star general, suggested the same explanation. "He received no formal education, and could neither read nor write until he was twelve," Harkins observed in a paper he compiled and sent to the historian Douglas Southall Freeman.

Even General Patton realized the weakness of his early education. In his youth John Singleton Mosby, the ex-Confederate cavalryman who for a time practiced law in California, regaled him with war stories. When he was seven, George Hugh Smith helped prepare him for soldiering by teaching him to read maps, interpret contour lines, and plot locations by grid coordinates. Never seeing a printed page, Georgie would lie sprawled on the window seat in the living room while his father or Aunt Nannie read to him. His father's favorites included the romantic novels of Sir Walter Scott, the epics of Homer, and the plays of William Shakespeare.[57]

Dressed in their fanciest clothes, Georgie and Nita began attending school on September 29, 1897. Nita enrolled in Miss Anna Orton's Classical School for Girls in Pasadena, and Georgie enrolled in Stephen Cutter Clark's Classical School for Boys at 39 South Euclid Avenue in Pasadena. His classmates included Thomas G. Bard, the son of the United States senator, and Charles B. Nordhoff, later the coauthor of the *Mutiny on the Bounty* trilogy.[58]

Scattered about the various collections at the Henry E. Huntington Library, Georgie Patton's report cards show several things. First of all, he did not consistently have trouble with mathematics, as those who call him dyslexic assert. During the term ending June 1898 he received a 76 in algebra recitation and an 84 in the examination. By December 1899 he had raised these grades to 79 and 91, only to fall back to a 68 in recitation for the term ending in December 1900. Second, Patton had no difficulty spelling words given to him, leading to the conclusion that his spelling troubles stemmed from learning to read and write six or seven years after his fellow students. During the June 1898 term, Patton received an 86 in spelling recitation and an 88 in the examination. In 1899 he was equally proficient, 80 and 92; and in 1900 he received an overall spelling grade of 89. His spelling grades, in fact, matched those in history, his great love, and exceeded those in English. Exceptionally well behaved and attentive, Georgie seldom missed school and received deportment grades of 96, 98, and 91.[59]

Meantime, the Pattons and the Bannings, now related by marriage, grew even closer. Just as Benjamin D. Wilson had invested with Phineas Banning, so George Patton was involved with Phineas's three sons: Hancock, married to George Patton's half sister; the lovable throwback to the Old West, Captain William; and Joseph Brent, who ended up marrying his first cousin and introducing Georgie to his future wife. George Patton was an investor when, in 1892, the brothers bought Santa Catalina.

For a decade thereafter Georgie and Nita spent summers on the island, first at the Metropole Hotel, then at the Patton cottage on Sumner Avenue, a wide, shady street in Avalon. For Georgie summers there resembled a dream. He rode horseback. With Jim Gardner, who ran the boats at Avalon and modestly advertised himself as the world record holder, he went fishing, developing enough skill during the summer of 1899 to catch a forty-five-pound yellowtail.[60]

But Georgie's chief passion proved to be sailing. With Nacho Callahan he engaged in wild escapades similar to those they performed on land at Lake Vineyard. The trip from San Clemente, along the California coast, to Catalina required a steam engine. "But my cousin George Patton, sailed down there in an eighteen-foot sloop with one of his ranch hands from San Marino, Callahan, and sailed back again," remembered Hancock Banning, Jr. "Which was a silly thing to do. But George could do things like that and get away with them. He always could. . . . It was an open cockpit boat. No cabin or anything else. They had two good bailing cans. His father made them take them."[61]

During the summer of 1902, fate, in the form of the Banning family, had its eyes on Georgie, spending the summer at the Patton cottage. Phineas Banning had an older brother, William Lowber Banning, a lawyer who, in search of better times, moved his three daughters, his son, and his wife from Wilmington, Delaware, to Minnesota. After serving in the Civil War, he became a railroad executive and as a politician was important enough to be the Democratic candidate for governor in 1876.[62]

Strangely enough, William Lowber Banning's daughters helped shape General Patton's life. One of them, Katherine Stewart Banning, fell in love with and married her first cousin, Joseph Brent Banning, after which she became a leading light in Los Angeles society. After visiting Avalon, Selena Gray Galt Ingram, whose husband was the superintendent of the Los Angeles division of the Southern Pacific, raved about Katherine, her sister May, and their mother—and about Ruth and Nannie: "Rob & I are both of the opinion that we never knew finer people than the Banning Bros. & their wives. Of course my special friends are Mrs. Joe & May—& their mother—& they are so sweet & so dear—& such splendid women! Mrs. Patton & Miss Wilson are so lovely too that we fell completely in love with them."[63]

During the summer of 1902 Katherine and Joseph invited the third sister, Ellen Banning Ayer, to spend the summer in the cottage just up the street from the Patton cottage. Although Katherine's life had been unusual and exciting up to that point, it could not compare with that of Ellen and Frederick C. Ayer and of Frederick's brother, James C. Ayer. A half century before, while an apprentice in an apothecary shop in Lowell, Massachusetts, James had developed Cherry Pectoral, a cough medicine. Americans literally gobbled up Cherry Pectoral, consuming a half million doses a day, second only to Lydia Pinkham's medicine for women. James and Frederick Ayer soon became kings of patent medicines, developing and marketing Ayer's Cathartic Pills, Extract of Sarsaparilla, the dandruff cure Comatone, Ague Care, Vigor, and Nose Spray. Advertisements for these products appeared in magazines and newspapers, on the sides of buildings, and in *Ayer's Almanac,* which sold millions of copies.[64]

Frederick Ayer was hardly the genial Sarsaparilla King his family liked to present to the world. In 1899 he formed the American Woolen Company of Lawrence, Massachusetts, whose practices rivaled those of the businessmen George Patton, Sr., denounced. In 1912, after the state reduced the work week, the company cut wages and increased rents in its deplorably filthy tenements. Led by the radical International Workers of the World, its workers began one of the bitterest strikes of the century. During the squabble the company, led by Ayer's son-in-law, William M. Wood, brought in Burns and Pinkerton agents to try to break up the strike. Perhaps with some sarcasm the sagacious George Patton, Sr., a Progressive, in 1904 described Ayer as "a very wealthy and prominent manufacturer of Boston and head of the American Wool Trust."[65]

The older he became the more unusual Frederick Ayer's story became. After the death of his first wife, Ayer visited his sister-in-law in St. Paul. Anxious to see him remarried, she introduced him to Ellen Banning, a would-be actress thirty-one years his junior. The two were married the next year. They took with them on their honeymoon the bride's sister May and Frederick's daughter, Ellen Wheaton Ayer, who in 1888 married Wood.

Summering with the California Bannings in 1902, the Ayers brought along their three children. The eldest, Beatrice Banning Ayer, had been born on January 12, 1886. She bore a striking resemblance to her Aunt Katherine, possessing the same small frame, nose, and cleft chin. From the beginning Georgie was attracted to Bea, who was pretty, intelligent, and vivacious, but he did not fall in love with her. In what was probably his first attempt at poetry, an alphabetical rhyming of events at Avalon, he wrote of her:

> *B is for Beatrice, who early one Morn*
> *Was deep in her "Logic," before it was dawn!*[66]

Even if Bea, only sixteen, and Georgie, then seventeen, did not immediately fall in love, the summer of 1902 brought the Ayer and Patton families together. George Patton had suggested a new process for curing olives, a procedure on which Ayer put his chemists to work. "It may surprise you to know that I voted and gave my influence for a democratic governor of our state," Ayer flattered Patton, an ardent Democrat, "and so you see you and I are in the same boat politically to some extent." That October Ellen Banning Ayer wished she could once again hear George Patton say: "Mrs. Ayer wont you have some Shasta lemonade?"[67]

In January 1903 Collis Huntington's nephew and heir, Henry E. Huntington, bought the Shorb estate, bordering on the Patton property. Selling his interest in the Southern Pacific, he appointed Patton the general manager of the Huntington properties, one of which, the San Gabriel Wine Company, bore the unusual motto *In Vino Veritas*: In Wine Truth. "I do not exactly like the name 'San Marinao,'" Huntington wrote Patton of the Shorb estate. "I have decided to change the name of Shorb Ranch to 'Los Robles' Ranch, which I think more appropriate; so I suggest that you have a sign drawn with 'LOS ROBLES' neatly printed on it put at the entrance of the place. It should not be over 3 or 4 feet long." Patton would later help persuade his friend to turn the place into a library, art gallery, and gardens, of which he served as president of the board of trustees.[68]

Georgie's future, meantime, presented a problem for his father. From childhood the boy had desired a military education, but having started school so late, he was behind those of his age. For six months during the 1901–1902 school year, George Patton hired Charles A. Stocking of Long Island to live in and help Georgie and Nita, who spelled somewhat better than her brother but punctuated just as poorly.[69]

Late in 1902, when he asked congressmen and senators about a West Point appointment for his son, George Patton met only disappointment. His friend Senator Francis G. Newlands of Nevada, an investor in the San Gabriel Wine Company, hesitated to appoint anyone not from his state, and even then a candidate must take "a competitive examination." Similarly, Congressman James McLachlan of Los Angeles reported that he had made the appointment over a year ago. "I did not know of the ambition of young Mr. Patton in the direction until a few weeks ago," he explained. "Had I known in time, I certainly would have given it favorable consideration."[70]

Uncertain, George Patton went from one idea to another. "It is possible that I may wish to send Georgie to the University of Arizona for a time," he informed his cousin John Mercer Patton, who taught at that college, in February 1903.

> He is well up now in Math but needs Latin & Languages—I wish you would write me fully as to the school—the accommodations as to rooming—& "grub"—terms &c &c. In fact as freely as you can in all particulars. Georgie has never been away from home & is in a way a pet—but all the same—I feel sure is a manly & OK boy—He is dead bent on West Point—and I have a possible chance for an appointment next year—I think it would be a good thing for him in every way to try Arizona—if he can at the same time prepare for the West Point Exam. He is now the advanced boy at Clarks— & being practically alone is not doing as well for himself as if he were with boys of his own age—Ruth & I feel that it might be an easy "break" for him in Arizona while you & Bruen are there. Can he enter at any time—i.e.—in the middle of term—Write me as fully as you can, & perhaps I will run down for a few days to talk it over with you.[71]

By the spring George Patton had different ideas. At the suggestion of his bishop, he thought of sending Georgie to Francis C. Woodman's School in Morristown, New Jersey, which prepared students for the service academies. "Allow me in the first place by way of introduction to say that my son is of good old American stock (Virginia)," he explained to Woodman.

> He is a direct descendant of John Washington—the original immigrant (and the grandfather of Geo. Washington). He is also the direct descendant of Gen. Hugh Mercer of the Revolutionary Army, who led the attack & was killed at Princeton. Intermediate

generations have all had a marked predilection for Military careers, and the ambition is strongly developed in him.

While I have no absolute assurance of getting him the West Point appointment to fall due June 1904, I have strong hopes of doing so, and am extremely anxious to have him ready if need be to pass a creditable competitive examination if it should come to that instead of an outright appointment. If while preparing himself for this he can enjoy the advantages of your school I shall be doubly pleased.

He has never attended but one school—That a private school in Pasadena conducted by a Harvard Graduate. He has passed through arithmetic, Algebra & Geometry and is I believe well up in these. He is also well up in English composition—and very well up indeed for history—In all these he would I believe be well fitted for your 6th Form. He has never studied any Greek or German at all—and only very little Latin and French. He is also a bad speller in English, and would need a little special attention in this particular. At the risk of trespassing upon your kindness—I am enclosing his last Exam papers on Roman History—written off hand at school under the usual regulations as to time &c—in order that you may more fairly estimate his requirements in the last particular.[72]

But instead of sending his son to Arizona or to Morristown, George Patton sent him to VMI, in Lexington. "He seems to be doing remarkably well," the elder Patton told George Hugh Smith in November 1903, after a typhoid epidemic closed the school for several weeks, "better than I anticipated. Up to the time of his leaving he stood first in Algebra and was doing well in his other studies, except Latin in which he is backward and in which he finds the course very difficult on account of the rapidity with which they go over the ground."[73]

At VMI Georgie's late start in school proved no handicap, for, as his father said, he ranked high during his first term. In a class of ninety-three, he stood second in both English and history, sixth in drawing, ninth in algebra, and, surprisingly, pulled himself up to tenth in Latin.[74]

Still, Georgie yearned for an appointment to West Point. Returning to the college in late November he grew angry at the success of others. "That fat Dunbar has an appointment to West Point," he complained about a classmate, "and *I* cadet Private Patton have not. Doesn't that show the rottiness of the government. I believe I will get 'Fat' to appoint me as his alternate for they are sure to kill him at the Point. I got a letter from Young Tom Bard yesterday but he did not even mention West Point. If I do get [an appointment] send a rush telegram."[75]

Since 1902 George Patton had been in touch with Senator Thomas R. Bard of California. But in early 1904, when Bard selected a commissioner to examine the candidates for appointment, Georgie faced a problem. If he left VMI, where he was doing well, for West Point, he would lose a year. The examination, moreover, was to be conducted in Los Angeles. Georgie would have to take all of February 1904 to cross the country, take the examination, and return to Virginia. Granting the son the month's furlough necessary, Major L. Harvie Strother, the commandant at VMI, informed the father: "George is doing well. He must have gained ten pounds or more. He seems to have the esteem and respect of all. Must resemble his *mother*."[76]

In his West Point papers, now in the academy's archives, young George Patton noted that, including himself, sixteen young men sought the nomination from Bard. Appearing before the examiner on February 15, 1904, he finished first and received the appointment. "You cannot know how proud we feel," George Patton informed his son,

> —and how gratified that you have won your first promotion in the battle of life. If you keep your head level—and work hard—avoiding the pitfalls of dissipation into which so many fall—you may look forward to an honorable career—as a soldier of your country. All signs seem to indicate that the world is about to enter one of those periods of war, that mark the transition from one stage to another in the march of progress.—It is the decree of Providence that our own country shall play a leading and probably a decisive part in the events which are to usher in the new era—You have in you good soldier blood—and the opportunity before you is one to inspire your earnest effort. Be honorable—brave—clean—and you will reap your merited reward.[77]

By mid-March only one obstacle remained before Georgie enrolled at West Point. "I have just at this moment *received* the acceptance of my certificate," the young man wrote to his father, and now it only remains for the government inspectors to examin this hundred and seventy pounds of meat (which forms the eartly cage of my imortal soul) and if they consider that I am sufficiently sound to be killed, I suppose that like the Christmas turkey I will be admitted to the mental fatning pen at the point. . . .

The study here is a lot harder than it was before I went away. The first week I got back I only got a 7.8 in geometry (the worst mark I ever got here) and that scared me so that I began to study hard and I have had no time to do anything else. I should have written but I kept putting it off. Well every thing is now settled and with the help of God and a vigorous use of your influence I have the appointment.[78]

Ordered to the Presidio in San Francisco for the physical examination, Georgie objected. He had already crossed the country once. Now he was being asked to do it a second time. Luckily Bard intervened with the secretary of war, and Patton was allowed to take the physical, which he passed, that May at Fort McHenry in Baltimore.[79]

VIII

When, on June 15, 1904, the day before plebe registration, the West Shore local from Weehawken, New Jersey, pulled into the dilapidated railroad station at West Point, it disgorged a father and a son. The father, ramrod straight, drew salutes from some of the cadets, who believed him to be a retired officer. The son, six feet one, was "a tall, well-built lad with blond hair and a determined look in his gray eyes." Georgie Patton had arrived at the school of his dreams.[80]

Having celebrated its hundredth anniversary, the institution was being transformed both physically and intellectually. After Congress appropriated $5.5 million the campus expanded southward, with barracks and stables for the artillery and cavalry troops, a new administration building, a new heating plant, and a new chapel.

Equally important was the conflict over curriculum. The academy's superintendent, Albert L. Mills, a first lieutenant to whom President William McKinley had taken a liking after he was shot in the head and lost an eye during the Spanish-American War, had questioned the value of the old curriculum, which stressed mathematics and science. Under Mills's successor, the crusty frontier fighter Major Hugh L. Scott, the curriculum was revised to give more emphasis to other subjects.[81] Unfortunately Patton would become one of the casualties, albeit not permanently, of the squabble that embittered members of the mathematics department.

Patton's entering class contained 148 men, but it was hardly among the more notable to attend the academy. Seven other VMI cadets, four of whom failed to graduate, entered with him. The most distinguished of these was Simon Bolivar Buckner, Jr., the son of the Confederate general, who as a lieutenant general was killed on Okinawa during the Second World War. Among members of the class Patton's closest friend eventually turned out to be someone who at the academy detested him, Everett S. Hughes, a font of gossip who in his personal papers in the Library of Congress left memoranda on Dwight D. Eisenhower's supposed romance with his chauffeur and Patton's with Bea's niece. Strangely enough, the two members of the entering class who became four-star generals had academic difficulties and did not graduate with the class. They were Patton and Courtney H. Hodges.[82]

For Patton the summer started out well enough. "We are in plebe camp at last," he told his father on July 10, "and it is raining but the tents are quite dry and nice." Patton was "tenting" with a comrade from VMI, Henry Fairfax Ayres, "a fine fellow his mother is one of the Fairfaxes of Virginia and he is strong for ancestors." Finding the discipline more lenient than at VMI, Georgie had already made friends with two third class cadets, Truman D. Thorp, a fellow Californian, and George F. Patton. "G. F.," he warned his father, "so be careful about my address." A week later he wrote: "The third class is having riding this year and yesterday one of them came and asked me for some of my 'foot-ease.' I suppose he wanted it for his bottom."[83]

By late July Patton demonstrated that he shared his father's sense of aristocracy and ambition. "Most of the men here are nice fellows," he conceded, "but very few indeed are born gentlemen in fact the only ones of that type are Southerners." When the yearlings, or sophomores, asked Patton what he hoped to become, he answered: "First, Adjutant of the Cadet Corps and then Chief of Staff of the Army, sir." Such brashness stunned the upper classmen. "Humility is the indispensable attribute of a good plebe," Patton's future tentmate in Mexico, General Hugh S. Johnson, later observed, "and humility in Georgie Patton is as inconceivable as hair on a frog's leg."[84]

While Georgie struggled with plebe camp, the women of the Ayer and Patton families grew closer. Early in the summer of 1904 George Patton escorted Ruth, Nita, and Nannie east, where they met Bea, her younger sister Mary Katherine, and their mother. The group then sailed for Europe. On September 17 the tourists returned, and the next day Ruth, Nita, and Nannie visited Georgie at West Point. "Seeing mama makes me feel like being a W. P. cadet is a dream and that I will awake at home or at VMI," George wrote his father. "I did not do so well last week in math but was much better in English. I have been perfect so far in drill regulations."[85]

By the end of October Patton's poor spelling and grammar were showing up in his work. "His spelling was about like George Washington's," Johnson noted, "but in knowledge of the poesy and history of all nations I have never seen his equal." Patton stood fourteenth in his class in drill regulations and fifty-fifth in mathematics, but he was 139th in English. "I cant imagine what makes me so rotten," he complained to his father, "for it is nearly the same stuff as I had last year and then I stood second in it. I changed instructors this week and that may be a good thing for my marks."[86]

Some of Patton's difficulty stemmed from his belief that West Point trained soldiers, rather than rounded men who became soldiers. A classmate and fellow Californian, Robert H. Fletcher, suggested to Patton that "if he were not such an avid reader of military history, strategy and tactics, he would have more time to study the subjects on which his class standing depended." Patton's friend George R. Goethals of New York, whose father had built the Panama Canal, told him the same thing. During their plebe year, he stood next to Patton in ranks and noticed that his friend never relaxed. Patton braced even when told to be "at ease." Living across the hall from Patton, Goethals, who ended up with the fourth highest average in the class, advised him: "See here, George. Your drill regs count only 15 points on graduation, whereas plebe math, where you are already shaky, counts 200. Put 80% of your drill reg time on math, you'll pass the drill regs easily anyhow, and will be almost sure to conquer math if you do." Patton ignored the advice.

He frequently told Goethals that he wanted to do three things at the academy: stand number one in drill regulations, become adjutant of the cadet corps in his last year there, and set an academy record in track.[87]

By November Patton could not hide his uncertainty. "I some times fear that I am one of those darned dreamers with a willing spirit but week flesh," he told his father, "a man who is always going to succeed but who never does. Should I be such an one it would have been far more merciful had I died ten years ago for I at least can imagine no more infernal hell than to be forced to live—a failure. If I ever seem to be degenerating into a commonplace American army officer please either nock me on the head or make me brace up."[88]

During his first term at West Point, Patton developed a new passion: fencing. Just before Christmas he was at the gym practicing with a classmate, Herman Kobbe, whose father was a general, when, accompanied by "a lot of ladies," in walked Alvin B. Barber, a first classman described by Patton as "West Point's crack fencer and second best in America." Barber asked the plebes to demonstrate fencing for the girls, a request the two could hardly refuse. "By mere accident," Patton related to his father, "I happened to nock the foil out of Kobbe's hand and then you should have heard them. I expect they thought I was master of the sword or something of the sort." Showman that he was, Patton then saluted Barber with "present-sword" and marched out.[89]

Spending time that might better have been used studying, Patton became a demon with the broadsword, taking delight at punishing those who opposed him. In March he bragged to his father that he now was one of the best swordsmen in his class. "It is lots of fun," he noted, "and I practice it as much as possible. . . . The other day I was fencing with a man who would not acknowledge my touches, though they nearly knocked him down. So I tried a dueling cut not supposed to be used in fencing on the right wrist. As a result he could not hold a pen for a day, but will probably be a better sport in the future." Another classmate who went through a similar experience with Patton said: "My most vivid recollection of him as cadet was at one of the classes in broadsword, when I, a frail mouse, was unfortunate enough to be opposite him. I was sore for a week."[90]

For Patton, Bea provided the highlight of the year. In 1905 Ellen Banning Ayer, desiring to move to a big city, told her husband she would no longer tolerate living in Lowell. She gave him two choices,

Boston or New York, in both of which he had offices. After spending a week exploring these places, husband and wife came back with the problem solved. Renting a pair of horses in each city, they discovered that it took two hours to drive out to the country from New York, while it took twenty minutes from Boston. Accordingly, in 1905, Frederick Ayer bought an estate at Prides Crossing. A year later he tore down the old house and built Avalon, an Italian Renaissance mansion named for the village on Catalina where the Pattons and Bannings spent the summers.[91]

Despite this activity within the Ayer family, Patton saw Bea several times during the year. "I certainly think that Beatrice likes me," he told his father in May, "for she answers all my letters and in her last asked if I would mind if she stayed after graduation of course I hastened to tell her nothing would be finer."[92]

But as his plebe year at West Point closed, Patton sensed doom. He was doing poorly in both mathematics and French, "and so you see," he wrote his father, "I am nearly hopeless. I don't know what is the matter for I certainly work. Sometimes I think it would be a good thing to get conditioned and turned back a year for then I would almost certainly get a corp and probably a very high stand what do you think of the idea."[93]

Like many other cadets, Patton, without knowing it, was squeezed in the squabble between the academy's administration and the mathematics department. Angered because of plans to deemphasize his subject, the new professor of mathematics declared 40 percent of the third class, the one above Patton's, deficient in June 1905. Patton, who despite his complaints had stood fiftieth in his class in mathematics in February and sixtieth in March, was declared deficient that June and turned back to repeat his plebe year. In his other subjects Patton finished creditably. In French he ranked 109th, in English 69th, in conduct 19th, and in drill regulations second. As it was, he did better than Hodges, also destined to lead an army in France and Germany. Found deficient in both mathematics and French, Hodges was dismissed from the academy.[94]

Adding to his woes, Georgie, a crack hurdler, tripped during a race. An understanding George Patton consoled his son with a reference to mythology. Once, reading Rudyard Kipling's poem "The Destroyers," father and son had come across the phrase "the choosers of the slain," which neither understood. In an essay George Patton had just read, Thomas Carlyle explained its meaning.

> It seems that in the Norse mythology—that of our ancestors the Vikings—the warriors who died in battle were accounted the real heroes—above those who survived—and before every battle the Valkyrie—or Valkyrs *chose* those who were adjudged worthy of death—and entrance into Valhalla—and these Valkyrs were thus called the "choosers of the slain," as the slain were called and esteemed "The Chosen."
>
> So in Life's battles you can find the real heroes among the *apparently* defeated. The honors which are bestowed upon the *apparently* successful ones—are most often the prizes of accident and circumstance—and at least are mere baubles—but again and again in some sequestered walk of Life—unknown and unnoticed by the multitude we meet and instinctively recognize the "Heroes of the Strife"—and the *wise* and *true* know these when they meet them.
>
> This is a long homily on a disappointment which you will no doubt have forgotten before you can read it—but it is to urge you not to allow yourself to give way to bitterness at apparent failure. . . . Take it with a smile—and keep on trying—your reward will come.[95]

IX

Returning to the West, Georgie followed his father's wise advice and did not waste too much time pining over his misfortunes. He spent much of the summer at Avalon, where he sailed, fished, hunted wild goats, and flirted with a girl named Debora. Leaving this paradise in mid-August, Patton first visited Bea in Massachusetts. "While in Beverly I had absolutely a perfect time," he informed his father. "The Ayers did every thing in the world that they could for me. . . . That Beat is certainly the best thing in her line in the world and I swallowed her hook to the swivle (as one says of a fish) I guess that I am a fool to have such a case at such an early age but? what would you. I will never see an other such and damn that God forsaken Debora."[96]

The class of 1909 that Patton now entered ranked among the most distinguished to come out of West Point. Among his classmates were Jacob L. Devers of Pennsylvania and Robert L. Eichelberger of Ohio, both of whom, like Patton, would become full generals. Also destined to wear four stars was William Hood Simpson of Texas, who, despite standing third from the bottom in the class, joined Patton and Hodges in leading armies across Europe.

Starting a plebe year for the third time—the first had been at VMI— Patton found the work easier. His report for September was encouraging. In a class of 155, Patton stood sixtieth in English, seventeenth in mathematics, and second in drill regulations. The only disappointment came when Patton dislocated his right arm trying to make the football team and was out for the season.[97]

Realizing his limitations, Patton concentrated his ambitions not in academics but in military matters. To his classmates Patton became known as "Quill," literally a demerit but also a cadet unduly interested in achieving rank. In his notebook, which he kept from August 1905 on, Patton recorded his seven "Essentials of Quill." Among these were bracing "at all times"; "when you get any new clothes let everyone know it"; and "never stop quilling." Simpson recalled that in those days cadets pressed their trousers by placing them between two boards and sleeping on them at night. Patton bought an iron and pressed his pants every day.[98]

That June, Patton finally completed his plebe year, doing much better than he had the first time around. He ended the year fifty-second in his class in French, thirty-first in mathematics, thirtieth in English, tenth in conduct, and first in drill regulations. Overall, he finished twenty-fifth in his class. In contrast, Jake Devers finished fifty-second, Eichelberger fifty-seventh, and Simpson, who had trouble with everything but drill regulations, 116th.[99]

Rewarded for his good work on June 13, 1906, by being appointed the second corporal of his class, Patton was assigned to summer camp to supervise the incoming plebes. In a position of authority for the first time, he proved to be a terror. "The Plebes are here at last," he informed Bea on July 9, 1906, "but sad to say they do not afford as much amusement as I had hoped. At first I hated to get after them and felt like a bruit when ever I 'crawled' (got after) them but soon I began to feel angry when ever I saw a Plebe and have been mad for a bout three days and that is not a very pleasing condition of mind."[100]

As second corporal, Patton always carried his "skin," or demerit, book with him. As the camp ended, he remarked to Bea "that I reported more men than any other officer of the Day this summer." Robert Sears described his strictness. "Cadet Officer of the Day had a much greater responsibility for reporting breaches of military discipline and dereliction than the Officer of the Guard. I well remember one occasion when I was Officer of the Day and George Patton was Officer of the Guard. I turned in 4 skins and George turned in two sheets of skins. You can well imagine that George would never have succeeded in politics."[101]

Equally unfortunate, Patton was tempted to use his position as a vehicle for revenge. "If possible skin Beere for sacrelidge during devine service," he jotted down in his notebook. "If possible skin Wright for at least 5 & 10." Years later, rereading these comments, Patton was shocked. "Such sentiments are unworthy of a man and a soldier," he noted. "I never acted on them or similar ones they are left in this book to show what a fool a boy of twenty is."[102]

On August 27 Patton reaped as he had sown. He was reduced to sixth corporal. "A lot of cadets have told me that I dropped from 2 to 6 because I was too military," he lamented to his father, "and the cadet officers thought I was sort of reflecting on them. However that may be, I am certain that I am the best officer of my class. . . . I have not given up being adjutant yet, though at first I felt pretty bad." To Bea, Georgie complained about the reduction: "Why I don't know unless I was too d— military."[103]

X

As Georgie struggled with his new classes, his family experienced excitement of its own. On Monday, November 12, 1906, Nita made her "formal debut" at, as one newspaper described it, "one of the most brilliant of the fall season's functions among the socially elect." The debutante was "a tall, graceful girl, with much beauty of face and form." Her family lived at Lake Vineyard, one of the few older California houses still remaining. "In the Spanish patio still hangs the old iron bell that used to call the workmen home, from over the vast estates in early days. . . . This home was in the early days one of the centers of the social life of Southern California, and here the young belles danced and were wooed by some of the men whose names are known to all here." Selena Ingram noted of Nita and of the occasion: "She looked prettier than I ever saw her—& every body looked well—& there were many handsome toilettes."[104]

During the fall of 1906 Patton busied himself with football. A substitute end on the academy's second team, he had his biggest moment not during a game but during a practice against the varsity before the Yale contest. When Patton's block against the starting right tackle enabled the scrubs to gain fifteen yards, he drew compliments. But generally he played so poorly that he was not even in the practice games.[105]

Struggling during the first semester of his second year with French and during the second semester with Spanish, Patton continued his quest for cadet advancement. In mid-February he admitted to Bea that he reported one of his best friends for an infraction, "but I only did it because I thought it was my duty and not because I wanted to." Asking Aunt Nannie to send him white trousers, he explained: "You see I must get a high ranking corp and to do it I must have lots of white trousers. The Commandant is such a fool that he will only let me have ten pair so I must get at least five more pair. Be sure that you make the tailor copy those trousers in every particular of cut and material."[106]

By the end of his year as a third classman, Patton had slipped. Among the 112 members of his class, he stood 108th in French, 102nd in Spanish, fifty-ninth in mathematics, fifty-third in English, forty-fourth in drawing, sixteenth in conduct, and eighth in military engineering. In class standing he slipped from twenty-fifth the previous year to seventieth. Devers, on the other hand, finished his first year ranking fifty-second and his second standing forty-fifth.[107]

In 1907, for the first time in two years, Georgie was able to spend the summer in Catalina. There he sailed his new boat, built in the San Pedro shipyard, played golf, and attended dances. But the summer flew by, and in mid-August Georgie prepared to leave. "It is awfully hard on them to have to let Georgie go," Selena Ingram wrote of the Pattons. "It will be for two years this time. They all expect to go East next summer & locate for the summer some where near West Point so they can be together as much as possible. . . . We shall miss them as they are such fine people."[108]

XI

Going east, Patton spent the last days of his furlough visiting the Ayers at their summer home, Avalon, at Prides Crossing. "Their place here is lovely," he reported to his father, "more beautiful than it is possible to imagine. It is right on the shore. B is here and I have no doubt at all which is the only girl I ever *loved* she is a *peach* and I am a fool but in earnest."[109]

Although he was now the cadet sergeant major, Patton found little about which to crow during the first semester of his third year. He was so unimpressive in football that the coach left him home when the team traveled to Philadelphia to play Navy. During the first two months of school, moreover, he hobbled along academically. Of the 108 members of his class, he ranked ninety-sixth in chemistry, seventy-fifth in philosophy, and sixty-sixth in drawing.[110]

During the winter of 1907–1908, Patton's most noteworthy achievement came during the Washington's Birthday Ride, a competition held on the morning of February 22, 1908. Atop Harrison, named for former President Benjamin Harrison, he joined three others in clearing four feet eight inches. He "could have gone higher," he told Bea, "but they made us stop." Patton also reported that the class with which he had entered was preparing to graduate, his friend George Goethals placing fourth. With the disappearance of the class of 1908, Patton received his long-desired appointment. He was named adjutant of the corps of cadets, a position his father had held at VMI.[111]

The transition was anything but smooth. Everett Hughes, the outgoing adjutant, objected to Patton's appointment. "Patton was once a West Point classmate of mine," Hughes later observed in his "Notes on Patton." At the academy each adjutant signed a board that inscribed his name and indicated his approval of the cadet named to follow him. "When I graduated I refused to sign the Adjutants Board because he was to be my successor," Hughes related of himself and Patton. Later one of Patton's greatest supporters, Hughes discussed the matter with a Mrs. Kutz, who lived near the academy and whom he frequently visited. She "persuaded me that I was a damned fool so I signed while I was back at West Point for duty shortly after graduation."[112]

That spring Patton spent much time with fencing, riding, and track. He also devoted some of his energy to girls. In March he confessed to

Bea that he had taken a Miss Cunningham to the hop. But he found distasteful most of the young ladies who hovered about West Point. "I had no idea girls were so nasty," he observed, "but then they were not true girls only the college sort and they are a pretty sad lot."[113]

Despite such professions, Georgie came close to falling in love with a college girl. But Kate Grosvenor Fowler came from no ordinary family. As a young man her father, Elderidge M. Fowler, had amassed a fortune when iron was found on timberland he owned in Minnesota. He accumulated even greater wealth helping to run the International Harvester Company, controlled by his sister, the widow of Cyrus Hall McCormick, the inventor of the reaper. From 1900 to his death in 1904 Fowler lived in Pasadena, near the Pattons and the Huntingtons. All three families were benefactors of what later became the California Institute of Technology.[114]

By the time she came East to attend Vassar College, Kate Fowler was immensely wealthy. From her father she had reportedly inherited $40 million. In October 1907 Georgie took her to the Yale football game. By April 1908 Patton could not decide. Was it to be Bea or Kate? "From all this you can see that your devoted brother is in the devil of a fix," Georgie confided to Nita, "and the only thing I can do to help the 'Gods annihilate both space and time and etc' is to invite Miss Fowler up here and fall in love with her or try to for she is a very pretty girl indeed."[115]

Not that Bea lived in poverty. When Selena Ingram, accompanied by Ellen Banning Ayer's mother and sisters, visited the Ayers in mid-March 1908, she hardly believed her eyes. She found the Boston home at 398 Commonwealth Avenue "most sumptuous in its appointments—with every luxury & comfort. We have the 4th floor to ourselves—& an elevator carries us up & down. There are magnificent flowers everywhere—roses, roses, roses—& roaming plants—& longewilts—violets—&c."[116]

Two days later the party "traveled out by luxury automobile" to Prides Crossing "on the seashore—where Mrs. Ayer's elegant seashore home is located." The group "passed through Revere first, where the 'Coney Island' of Boston is located," then through Lynn, Marblehead, Salem, and Beverly, "& finally into the woodland on the shore—where so many magnificent houses are situated. . . . The home at Pride's is simply magnificent! The location—overlooking Massachusetts Bay—is superb—& the exterior of the house is like an Italian villa. The beautiful circular stairway leading to the 3rd floor & dome facing the marble rotunda is lovely & very handsome. The living room—over sixty ft long—is grand—& the library & reception room, dining room & breakfast room downstairs are lovely." The upper two floors contained suites of apartments. "I remember seeing as many as 8 bathrooms on the second floor & think there were the same on the third."[117]

As grand as these homes were, George Patton had, according to Bea, convinced Henry Huntington to build a home and garden like no other. Spending most of his time in New York, Huntington had hired a remarkable German horticulturist, William Hertrich, to fix up and landscape the old Shorb place. When Patton, who supervised Huntington's affairs in Southern California, heard the cost, he was "somewhat dismayed." But after speaking to Hertrich, who was bringing in rare plants from all over the world, Patton was convinced that Huntington "was making what will be the most magnificent and stately private estate in the United States. I think you were extremely fortunate in finding Hertrich. I am more and more impressed with the idea that he is a very extraordinary man, and that you and he together make a team of landscape architects far and away ahead of any who hold that title that I know of." Rather than a splendid home, Huntington's treasure was destined to become, at Patton's suggestion, an incomparably beautiful repository of history and literature.[118]

Back at West Point, Georgie was finishing his third year. Unsuccessful as a football player, he displayed enormous skill in track. At his last West Point Field Day in June 1908, he won the 120-yard and 220-yard hurdles, setting an academy record in the latter event, and came in second in the 220-yard dash. Academically, he did better in his third year than he had in his second. In a class of 108, he ranked seventy-second in chemistry, seventieth in philosophy, fifty-eighth in drawing, twenty-second in drill regulations, sixteenth in conduct, and eighth in hygiene. In class ranking he pulled himself up from seventieth the previous year to sixty-first.[119]

XII

Going into his last summer at West Point, Patton found himself in love with—or almost in love with—two very attractive young women. The first was Kate, "she of the yellow hair and . . . blue eyes." The second was Bea, "she of the raven locks and . . . dark eyes." "It is very sad to realize it is over for me," he lamented to Bea on July 8, "that never again will I dance with you at a summer hop as a cadet. But I have had lots of happy evenings during the short visits which you have paied us and I want to thank you for that pleasure."[120]

That fall Patton was involved in two sports, romance with Bea and Kate, and football. Still a substitute on Army's second team, he hoped, he told Bea in early September, "to play every day some where. I don't care but deliver me from side lines this Fall it is too hard on ones pride. Realy it is awful to see men worse than you think your self put in a head of you." As Patton wrote his mother: "I am more foot ball crazy on the game this year than ever."[121]

By mid-September, Patton saw his last year of football going the way of his first three. "We are in one H—— of a fix for foot ball men," he told Bea,

> we have no tackle and not a single scrub. . . . I am about as heavy as any body on the scrub and I can only just get 160 in undress it is awful. . . .
>
> When the Navy got us last year I swore a great swear that come what would I would do anything in my power to beat them this year and if the destined way is to be a center a center I will be. If only we can win.
>
> This perhaps sounds silly but my thoughts are far from light on this subject. I have never placed any thing higher than a foot ball A except the beating of the Navy. We have less than four hundred and seven men and they have nine hundred so as Nelson said, "West Point expects every man to do his duty."[122]

At the end of September, Patton sent Bea the terrible news.

> We had a very hard practice Monday and I did my self proud until the last down when I broke the small bone of my left arm. I am

rather put out over it (so is the bone) as I was going in the game Saturday also it has kept me awake and bids fair to continue to do so. Still the doctor says I will be out in five weeks and that would give me four weeks more of this my last season; I have already devised a brace so hope to get in again. . . .

I would rather that you say nothing to any body about this little accident to my flipper realy it can't be helped and it might worry them.

You are tuffened so I can tell you.[123]

At the very time Patton courted Bea, urging her week after week to attend football games and dances, he did the same with Kate Fowler. "Perhaps my letter arrived too late about the game and hop," he wrote Kate in mid-October of 1908 while recovering from his injury,

but as I told you, I had but just learned that I could dance. If it did (the letter) there is another hop and game on the fourteenth to which I might persuade you to come; or perhaps you will honor me with both, please do.

Well, I suppose I must say it, though I hate to think that my coming words may prevent my seeing you for two whole weeks.[124]

After Army beat Navy, Patton sent Kate a glowing letter.

You must have had a glorious time Thanksgiving, but I am still selfish enough to wish that you had been in Philadelphia to see a little of our glory there. Oh! But it was wonderful, such a game, such cheering, and such a scene as there was in the dressing room afterwards. I got so carried away that I kissed all the team, though naturally they were not as clean as a ladies hand—the only other thing I ever so honored! Half the team got carried to the hotel and the rest would have been, but they hid and the men hunting for them, to the number of almost two hundred missed the train.

Do you know it seems that I never will be able to go to Vassar for no sooner is Frat Ball over than some poor fool decides to have a New Year's Ride and some other poor fools, among these, your most obedient servant, decide to enter it; so instead of being able to look forward to a very pleasant afternoon talking to a very charming person—should she permit me such a pleasure—I have only visions of tan bricks and horses.

For fear of being a bother, I will not beg this lady of my dreams to come to a hop, but [should] she find that she has nothing particular to do on the twelfth, there is a hop on that date and there is a cadet still in hopes of the happiness of again dancing with her. His name is George Patton.[125]

Kate or Bea, Bea or Kate. Patton's letters to each reflected his feelings. To Kate he sent notes filled with awe and worship—of her beauty and of her intelligence, if not of her wealth. To Bea, however, he confided his innermost yearnings. Just before the Army-Navy game, he told her how he had called on Captain Charles P. Summerall, who advised him to join the cavalry rather than the infantry, even though promotion was slower there. In peacetime, Summerall said, rank meant nothing, and in wartime "they begin to look for any body no matter what his rank so long as he could win. . . . I don't want pleasure I want success. I would rather work a hundred years to win one battle than play a thousand and be put away a chunk of mud that had never done any thing but laugh."[126]

That Christmas the Ayers invited Patton to Boston, and on December 30 Georgie revealed to Bea his love for her. Still, "at about 4:12 P.M." on that day, Patton entered into his notebook a poem that echoed his confusion:

Two maids uprose in the shimmering light
Of the battle main
And one was tressed like the bird at night
And one like ripning corn.

Then out spoke she of the raven locks
And her dark eyes glowed like wine
If he slay the foe the knight I know
He shall win this heart of mine.

But subtlier she of the yellow hair
And her blue eyes 'gan to fill
Though he gain or loose the knight I choose
He shall be my true-love still.[127]

To his father Patton reflected his uncertainty. "Undoubtedly I am in the hell of a fix yet this did not prevent me from going up to Vassar with Kate and falling in love with her for the entire afternoon. Yet if you put the $40000000 against the B. I fear that I would take the B. ass that I am when with the money I could be a general in no time. . . . *Never forget that you know nothing of my heart.*"[128]

A week later Patton explained to his parents his dilemma.

When however I proposed to Beatrice I did something from instinct and against reason at least it seems unlogical because she does not like war because she is not as rich as another girl "Kate" who would I think have married me and because a soldier should not marry. This because money seems an excellent tool, not for my own use, but to buy success and if I were unmarried I could get more things by paying attention to daughters of prominent people if necessary marrying one of them. Now these things are not nice but they are logical and I had carefully planned to climb the ladder and I had a pretty clear field. But when I see B. all my logic goes to hell! It was so clear at Xmas that she loved me that I played the fool and would do it again.[129]

To his enormous credit, Patton never hid from Bea his brief flirtation with Kate Fowler. Over the years Georgie and Bea frequently saw, and enjoyed the friendship of, Kate and her husband, Van S. Merle-Smith, Sr. Ever faithful to friends, Patton, just after the end of the Second World War, appointed their son, Major Van S. Merle-Smith, Jr., as his aide. Major Merle-Smith was still Patton's aide when the general died.[130]

As the cadet adjutant, Patton fulfilled a dream. During parades, the adjutant was the star, barking out the commands of the first captain and strutting about in his white trousers. In the yearbook under Patton's picture, his classmates described an earthquake during which the cadets "came tumbling out . . . in all stages of dishabille." Suddenly Patton appeared, "faultlessly attired as usual." After executing flawless movements, he barked out the orders: "Cadets will refrain from being unduly shaken up. There will be no yelling in the area. The earthquake will cease immediately. By order-r-r-r of Lieutenant Colonel Howze!"[131]

The Furlough Book of the Class of 1909 contained, as it did for all grad-

uates, Patton's signature and two humorous entries about him. It listed
his desire: "To get back, so as to be near that dear skin book." Next
came a description of him: "He stands erect, right martial in his air, His
form and movements."[132]

Two seemingly innocent statements made during his last days as a
cadet reveal much about Patton. In late April, still in a quandary over
where he wished to be stationed, he wrote his father that he should like
to visit the Ayers. Three years before, President William Howard Taft
had vacationed at Beverly Point, just two hundred yards from the estate
at Prides Crossing. Perhaps if he met the president, Patton might be
assigned to Washington.

The second statement questions Patton's supposed belief in previous
lives. Visiting the battlefield at Gettysburg, where his great uncle, Colonel Waller Tazewell Patton, had died during Pickett's charge, the
young man commented: "There is to me strange fascination in looking
at the scenes of the awful struggles which raged over this country—fascination and a regret. I would like to have been there too."[133] In later
years Patton might have said that in a previous life he had been there.

For the class of 1909 commencement took place on June 11. Of the
103 graduates, Jake Devers finished thirty-ninth; Patton, who in his
senior year was near the bottom in French and Spanish but first in his
class in Military Efficiency and Soldierly Deportment, ended up forty-
sixth; Eichelberger, who bore the nickname Ike, came out sixty-eighth;
and Simpson finished 101st.[134]

Generally Patton behaved impeccably at West Point. But two delinquencies he received perhaps epitomized him as he left West Point for
duty at Fort Sheridan, Illinois. On May 2, 1907, he received two demer-
its for "Submitting illegibly written explanation and endorsement containing misspelled words." And on August 10, 1908, he committed one
of his two five-demerit offenses for using "Profanity at 10:10 P.M."[135]

Fulfilling a dream, Patton had graduated from the academy, but, as
Colonel Roger H. Nye has ably pointed out, his military education
never ended.

A DAY AS A LION

I

Assigned to K Troop of the 15th Regiment of Cavalry, Second Lieutenant George S. Patton, Jr., arrived at Fort Sheridan, Illinois, on the evening of September 12. At the train station he bumped into his West Point classmate Stanley M. Rumbough. "We were a little scared," he informed Bea, "but things went on well. The first thing he did was to congratulate me on my supposed marriage to the most divine of humans—guess who?" At the fort Robert E. O'Brien of the class of 1908 did the same. The condition of his quarters, however, soured the young officer. "Just at present my only strong impression is the in adequacy of the words two rooms and a bath to express my quarters they are awful but don't tell any one. They will be better when I have been in them a little longer. . . . The post is beautiful and very large I will have to get a bicycle."[1]

The socially conscious Patton found most of the families at the fort "nice not very nice." The "best of the bunch" was the commander of Patton's troop, Captain Francis C. Marshall, and his family. Another "bunch" of eight or ten officers was "not even decent they belong to what is called the sin of 1898 to the crowd that got in from the militia" during the Spanish-American War.[2]

One of Patton's first duties was supervising the camp prisoners, "drunks and absentees" and others who had committed offenses. "I have been through the cages twice," he lamented to Bea, "once by my self and once with a sergeant for I would hated to have any of them get away from me. In their sleep they look like the people in Hell in a book of Dante I used to read and I bet they smell worse most of them are or seem under twenty-five. Think of it a hundred and twenty ruined souls it is to me a very sad sight."[3]

For Patton life at Sheridan proved uneventful. Accordingly, he filled his letters to Bea with chitchat about routine army duties, routine social events, and routine hopes. "God but I wish there would be a war," he pleaded on the first day of October. "Until there is I see no hope of my ever needing to buy any more furnature for you cant fill an empty heart with chairs." Even as a second lieutenant, he envisioned the time when he would be a general. "Some day I will have a big tent too and a refrigerator and a stove and a trunk and a lot of men cussing me for having so much baggage."[4]

By December Patton, even though he went to dances and dinners with socially prominent girls from the Chicago suburbs, yearned for his beloved. "I sent Beatrice a quotation from the Bible about Abraham being engaged 107 years," he wrote his father, "and told her that not having the longevity of her family I feared that I would be unable to break such a record in spite of her efforts but it did not bother her a bit, it does me."[5]

Even at this age and at this rank, Patton possessed a temper that sometimes caused him pain. In mid-December he told Beatrice that he had spied an untied horse in the stable. Finding the man responsible, "I cussed him and then told him to run down and tie the horse and then run back," an "excellent punishment," for it "makes the other men laugh at him." When the offender disobeyed orders and walked, "I got mad and yelled 'Run dam you Run' he did but then I got to thinking that it was an insult." Assembling "the men who had heard me swear," Patton apologized for his behavior. "It sounds easy to write about," he explained, "but was one of the hardest things I ever did. I think though I am glad I did it now that it is done."[6]

In early 1910 Patton wrote to Bea constantly. He confessed to her that he considered West Point "a holy place" about which he could "never think with out reverence and affection." This was partly because his first letter from there, "written four o'clock in the morning was to you the second to your mother and during the five years I was there you were my last thought on going to sleep my first thought on waking. I never did a thing with out calculating its effect on you. I even skinned less than I wanted to because I thought that if I got too unpopular you would not have so nice a time" during visits there.[7]

Although Bea consented to a May 26 wedding, she still doubted whether she could adjust to army life. Six weeks before the wedding, Bea visited Fort Sheridan, finding it charming. Much of their time, she related, was spent at parties given by army wives "trying to get me primed on army etiquette." After the third night there, she "offered to give my true love his freedom." "Quite upset," Patton asked the reason. "You're ambitious," Bea explained. "Why don't you marry some nice Army girl who knows all the ropes? I'll never make a success of it." Patton refused to listen to her.[8]

Informing his father, who was in California delving into politics, of the date of the wedding and of his honeymoon plans, Patton made one of his few risqué references to his betrothed. "Thirty five days, the length of the leave is not over much time in which to visit Europe but we can at least get there and back and I suppose the privacy of a cabin is as good a place as any other in which to make love to Beatrice at least that is what she thinks."[9]

Two weeks before their marriage, Patton wrote Bea about their prospective home at Fort Sheridan, which he considered nicer and more convenient than a second lieutenant had a right to expect. "It will be such a cute little house with such a cute little girl in it," he gushed. "I am quite anxious to be in it. . . . I think it is much better to get married young than to wait until we are older for things are so much more real to us and so splendid. Beaty we must amount to some thing."[10]

As the invitation announced, the gala wedding took place "at half after 3 o'clock" on May 26 in St. John's Church at Beverly Farms. A special railroad car transported guests from Boston to the church. Four of Patton's classmates and two of his cousins served as ushers, while Bea's brother, Frederick Ayer, Jr., was best man. After a reception at Avalon, during which the bride cut the wedding cake with the groom's sword, the happy couple spent the night in Boston. At dawn the next morning they were met by Mrs. Ayer, carrying a perfect white rose in a crystal vase, and Bea's siblings. They had taken the early train so as to be in Boston when "the children awoke." Bea considered the gesture "thoughtful," but Georgie did not.[11]

II

By the time Georgie and Bea returned to the United States, much was going on. Until the wedding, George Patton continued to run Henry Huntington's affairs in California. "I have been up quite frequently to your house," he told his friend and neighbor that February, "and think that it is progressing rapidly and satisfactorily. The final result is really indescribably beautiful, and I do not think that there is another house anywhere that will be a more dignified and tasteful monument than this." At the end of April, finding his personal business overwhelming, George Patton resigned as vice president of the Huntington companies, although the two neighbors always remained warm friends.[12]

One of these personal matters was the construction of a new house. Since their marriage Ruth and George had lived at Benjamin Wilson's Lake Vineyard Rancho. Now, in the year of Georgie's marriage, they completed their new home. Three stories high, the house possessed thick walls; a slate roof with broad eaves; a heavy teak front door with a carved design of olive leaves; seven bedrooms, each with its own bath; seven fireplaces; a marble patio; and exquisite floor-to-ceiling walnut paneling in the living room. It also had a gun room. One architect called the design of the house "early California with an English accent." Throughout his life General Patton maintained special quarters on the second floor for his family and for visiting friends, among them Generals John J. Pershing and James Doolittle. In 1911, when the Ingrams stayed in Georgie's rooms, they were overwhelmed. "It is all so perfect," observed Selena Ingram, "and so luxurious—and they are such lovely people."

While building their new home, the Pattons did not knock down their old. Using the walls of Wilson's rancho, they constructed a guest cottage west of the main house. They also kept the original fireplace, about four feet high with bookshelves above it. Here George Patton kept an office, and here Henry Huntington often came to chat. Also west of the main house was the caretaker's cottage, occupied for decades by Georgie's companion Nacho Callahan.[13]

In 1913 the new house became the focal point of an unusual political maneuver. In a basement room George Patton, Huntington, and their fellow conspirators, disgusted when neighboring towns threatened to take over their prosperous farms, plotted to incorporate the community of San Marino. Later in the year San Marino's first city council meeting was held in the house, and Patton became the town's first mayor.[14]

After their honeymoon, Bea and Georgie began housekeeping at Fort Sheridan. On her first morning there Bea heard footsteps on the porch and found a long paper sticking out of the mailbox. Headed "Order of the Day," it read: "The sun will rise at 5:05 A.M. and will set at 6:30 P.M. By order of W. S. Pickett, Col Nth Inf. Commanding." Bea thought: "This army must amount to something. Even the sun conforms."[15]

Bea found the wives at Fort Sheridan a dedicated group. Most skimped to pay the insurance and commissary bills or to throw a party. Almost all related stories of loyalty and devotion. One woman told how she sat for two days on the stern of a tugboat in the Yalu River watching corpses float by, praying her husband's was not among them. Another had cared for a neighbor's children during a cholera epidemic in the Philippines. As a bride, a major's wife had nursed an entire garrison afflicted with dengue fever. "Gradually," Bea observed, "I came to realize what they were doing. These wives of the Old Army were inculcating me little by little with the store of courage which is the legacy of every army woman and which we hand from one generation to the next."[16]

Generally, during her first months at Fort Sheridan, Bea kept to herself. "Remember," her mother had advised her, "you are going among strangers. Be friends with everyone, but confide in no one." On her honeymoon Bea had become pregnant, and one day she answered the bell wearing a dress from her trousseau that no longer fit around the waist. The caller, the oldest woman on the post, said to her: "My dear, the ladies of Fort Sheridan have asked me to call on you, as they are very much concerned about you. We have decided you are going to have a baby, and, since you have not confided in anyone, we wonder if you know it."[17]

During his first few months back at Fort Sheridan, Patton, skilled at so many things, tried to revive interest in something at which he hardly excelled. "At last I have made a football team," he informed Nita that September. "Made it in many senses too. I constructed it made the grounds and the team. Last Saturday we had a practice game with The Lake Forest University team and did well though I have navigated with difficulty since owing to a bruised muscle in the leg. Tonight I was showing them the way to put out a block and got a black eye for my trouble."[18]

Unlike some of the generals who later served under him in Europe, such as John S. Wood, a star end, and Geoffrey Keyes, an outstanding halfback, Patton made as slight a dent in camp football as he had in West Point football. In October, after losing to the team from the Chicago Veterinarian College, he could not even "move a pen," Bea told her father-in-law. "He's not hurt—only stiff. . . . The post is at last beginning to take an interest in the team; and it really is a splendid thing for the soldiers."[19]

On March 19, 1911, the baby girl, named Beatrice Smith Patton, arrived. For at least two years Georgie referred to her as Smith, even naming a room in the new Patton house "Smith's room." Later the new parents renamed the baby Beatrice Ayer Patton, Jr., and in letters usually referred to her as Bee, Jr.[20]

When Ruth Patton, accompanied by Nannie and Nita, visited her son's family just after the birth of the child, she was upset for two reasons. First, what developed into the Mexican Revolution began in 1911, and Georgie yearned for American intervention and war. "It does frighten me terribly when I think that Georgie may be sent to Mexico," she informed her husband, "but he would be delighted and of course should be, as it would give him a chance to show what he could do— but it does seem so useless." The second scary thing was the way Patton handled his new car.

> I do not enjoy automobiling in this country, but don't tell Georgie so, as he took us for a forty mile ride on Sunday, and it should have been fine, as the day was lovely, and so was the country, but we always went thirty miles an hour, and sometimes faster, and the roads are so narrow, and crammed up so, that passing other machines is too exciting for my taste. And G's machine is so powerful that it seems to skid all the time—I will be very glad to get back to the Cadillac.[21]

While at Fort Sheridan, Ruth and Nita attended church at nearby Highland Park. During his sermon the minister mentioned that a wealthy man had recently paid $50,000 for a Gutenberg Bible. "It seemed strange," Ruth reported, "to think that our neighbor was the man."[22]

Back in California George Patton, who had fought Collis Huntington and the Southern Pacific for years, was now accused of turning tail and becoming a tool of the Huntingtons. Judge Henry C. Dillon, who twenty years earlier had campaigned with Patton against the Southern Pacific, charged him with selling out to Henry Huntington, who in reality could not be compared with his late uncle. Said Dillon of the elder Patton:

> He was younger than now, more chivalric, a veritable knight errant whose keen blade was turned against oppression of all kinds. . . . Now, for many years, that eloquent voice has been silent. He left the rostrum and was found in the Pacific Electric building, among the trusted leaders of the Southern Pacific. George has been taken into partnership, his cannon had been spiked, his sword had fallen from his nerveless grasp, and he had ceased to be an advocate of equal rights.

Dillon pointed especially to Patton's opposition to the women's suffrage amendment then being proposed for the California state constitution.[23]

III

Aware of his father's political influence, Georgie wanted him to use it. George Patton was going to Washington during the winter of 1911–1912. Perhaps, through his friend General Fred C. Ainsworth, the adjutant of the army, he could arrange his son's transfer to the capital. "I should like to be there a winter for it has ever seemed to me nearer God than else where and the place where all people with aspirations should attempt to dwell."[24]

That December Georgie received a transfer to Fort Myer, Virginia, just west of Washington, where he was to join Troop A of the 15th Regiment of Cavalry. Patton, however, owed his good fortune as much to his godfather, Captain Arthur J. Hutchinson, who first taught him to ride, as to his father. The home of the army's chief of staff, Fort Myer was the nation's cavalry center, but its polo team hardly reflected that fact. For years the engineers at Washington Barracks had trounced the Fort Myer team. Finally, remembered Captain Frank McCoy of the office of the chief of staff, someone said: "Let's get George brought to

Washington. He'll turn the scales against the Engineers." Young, strong, and energetic, Patton helped do just that. "You know," McCoy recalled, "when George came he looked to me like a young Greek demigod and he was."[25]

Coming east before his wife to arrange things, Patton reported what today must be viewed as an unusual coincidence. In mid-December of 1911 he dined in Washington with several of Bea's relatives, including William M. Wood, who was married to Bea's half sister, Ellen Wheaton Ayer, and ran the family's American Woolen Company. A month later a strike broke out in the firm's Ayer, Wood, and Washington Mills.

One of the bitterest disputes in American history, the Lawrence, Massachusetts, strike influenced the outlook of the family of Frederick Ayer, the largest stockholder in the $75 million firm, and sent George Patton down the road that eventually led to his losing the Third Army in 1945. A monstrosity of a city, Lawrence contained eighty-six thousand people, 86 percent of whom were immigrants or the children of immigrants. Nearly a third of its population worked in the woolen mills. Their families lived in three-decker wooden tenements that investigators described as "vile beyond description" and filled with "vermin, filthy alleys, voracious rats and evil smells."

Seventy years after the strike, Wood's biographer described him— and in effect the Ayer family—as uncaring.

> The real world in which his 25,000 mill operatives toiled and sickened was beyond his knowledge or imagination. The vile smells and filth of the tenement district had never reached his Arden estate in Andover. It is doubtful that Wood had ever driven, let alone walked, along the pitiful streets and alleys that were home to most of his employees.[26]

The strike among the mainly Italian laborers began after a state law cut the work week from fifty-six to fifty-four hours. The American Woolen Company's answer was to reduce the weekly pay, averaging $8.76, by thirty cents. When the radical International Workers of the World took over the strike, Wood, the second highest paid executive in the United States, frequently condemned labor leaders, socialists, and communists.

Jews, too, were involved. Representative Victor S. Berger, one of the founders of the Socialist Party of America, sponsored the congressional hearings on the strike, and Samuel Gompers of the American Federation of Labor actively supported the workers. Given this background, the Ayer family's hatred of Jews becomes understandable.

The Red Scare of 1919 heightened the family's fear of radicals. Along with Supreme Court Justice Oliver Wendell Holmes, Jr., the banker J. P. Morgan, and the oil magnate John D. Rockefeller, Wood was one of thirty-six prominent men to whom the IWW mailed bombs, intercepted by post office officials. After that, according to his biographer, Wood, who committed suicide in 1926, frequently denounced Bolsheviki.[27]

At the very time the strike broke out, Patton and Bea were settling at Fort Myer, which, compared with Sheridan, was heaven. Here they mixed with the elite of the army and the government—high-ranking officers, congressmen, and cabinet members. Having been brought east partly because of his riding skills, Patton began searching for horses. "You see," he informed his father, "though I had the best horses at Sheridan, I did not here so have been hunting them."

Try as he might, Patton lost many of the army races held at local tracks. In these the engineers, led by Patton's West Point classmate Albert K. B. "Queen" Lyman, a Hawaiian, provided the chief opposition. "Queen Lyman had an Army remount named Kryatt that was champion in Army races," observed Bradford G. Chynoweth, Patton's longtime friend. "George Patton paid huge sums trying to get a horse to beat Kryatt." The engineers hired a professional to manage their stable, while the cavalry trained its own horses. "But horse racing is a profession," Chynoweth reflected, "and you can't beat a professional. Kryatt remained champ."[28]

Other things soon occupied Patton's attention. He had settled down to his duties as quartermaster when, on May 10, 1912, he learned he was to represent the army in the Modern Pentathlon at the Olympic games in Stockholm. An updated version of the event held at the ancient Hellenic games, it consisted of pistol shooting at twenty-five meters, a swimming race of three hundred meters, fencing with the dueling sword, a cross-country steeplechase of five thousand meters (about three miles), and a cross-country run of four thousand meters (about two and a half miles). The competition, Patton noted, tested "the fitness of a perfect man-at-arms of the present day." It represented the obstacles a courier faced delivering a message in battle.

Having just over a month before sailing for Europe, Patton began training. He was "in excellent physical condition," but he had not run for two years or swum for three. Making what he later considered a mistake, he began running immediately rather than beginning with long walks. He also started swimming the required distance, instead of building up to it. He practiced shooting daily, and considered it his best event. He also fenced three times a week and "was in pretty good form." He saw no need for practicing riding. While training for the Olympics, Patton limited his diet to "hardy food," reasoning that anything that did not give him indigestion promoted health.[29]

Accompanied by Bea, Nita, and his parents, Patton sailed for Stockholm aboard the SS *Finland*. During the two-week trip he continued practicing. At six in the morning he ran on deck with the cross-country team; he shot from ten to twelve; and he fenced with the fencing team from three to five. Later in the afternoon Patton practiced with the swimming team in a contraption he called "ingenious." Placed in a canvas tank only twenty feet long with a belt attached to a rope fastened about him, the swimmer worked against the rope, requiring all his effort to stay in one place.[30]

On July 7, 1912, the Modern Pentathlon began in the worst possible way for Patton. The lone American among the forty-two competitors, Patton, using a .38 Colt Special, came in twenty-first in the pistol shooting. Lieutenant Colonel Frederick Foltz, who supervised the army athletes at the game, attributed the poor results "to the misfortune of nervousness." That night Patton, a crack shot, said: "I don't know whether I lost my nerve or my ammunition was defective, but I did nothing like my best."

Having largely overcome his nervousness, Patton did much better in the remaining four events. In the swimming competition, on the morning of July 8, he finished seventh. In the next event, fencing with the épée, which took place at the Royal Tennis Club, Patton bested twenty-three of twenty-nine opponents. In a bitterly fought match he inflicted the only defeat on the French army champion, Lieutenant J. de Mas Latrie. One of the world's best fencers, the Frenchman took the first two points of the match. Patton recovered and won the next two, and then took the fiercely contested fifth point.

For Patton the remaining two events added to the excitement and glory. In the steeplechase he was to have ridden a horse from Fort Riley, Kansas, but the animal developed "a slight lameness" and Patton was given a Swedish troop horse, "a most excellent animal." Riding a strange horse over an unfamiliar course, Patton did remarkably well. He navigated the course perfectly, but on the basis of time was placed third, behind two Swedish riders familiar with the terrain.

The cross-country run provided a fitting climax to the story of Patton and the Olympics. As with many of today's longer Olympic runs, the contestants started inside the stadium in front of the royal box, followed a set course outside it, and then reentered the stadium to finish. In this case the course was rugged, "being largely over sheer rock hills and again through heavy forests and in swamps six inches deep in mud. I do not believe," Patton reported, "such a course could be found anywhere else, certainly none of the foreign competitors had seen anything so difficult." Starting with a burst of speed, Patton left the stadium amid a mighty cheer. When he reentered the stadium, he had a lead of twenty yards over the Swedish officer, K. G. Äsbrink. But during the last fifty yards of the race Patton lost ground and ended third, being the only non-Swede to finish in the top thirteen. After crossing the finish line, he fell, almost fainting, on the grass. Several men rushed to him, rubbed his arms and legs, and after a few minutes he was able to walk, holding the arm of a friend. One newspaper marveled at his "fine performance" in the event.

Patton's overall skill—he finished fifth—was indeed remarkable. With a minimum of preparation he had traveled halfway across the world and was forced to mount strange horses and to cover strange courses. Unfortunately he did poorest in something in which he should have done best, pistol shooting. The only non-Swede to finish the competition in the top seven, he was a credit to himself and to the army.[31]

On his way to Stockholm, Patton had decided to spend the time from July 17, the end of the games, to his departure for home perfecting his fencing. Asking the other fencers, he was told that the finest master in Europe was Monsieur l'Adjutant Cléry, the senior instructor at the French Cavalry School at Saumur. For about two weeks Patton took daily lessons from Cléry, the professional European champion, in the dueling sword and the saber, especially the latter.[32] His interest in the subject piqued, Patton would soon write articles on the subject.

After the Pattons returned home, Georgie received a letter containing the only recorded instance of his father's attitude toward Jews. The elder Patton began by justly praising his son.

> It is too bad you are not able to be here just now. It would give you a graphic idea of that elusive thing called "fame." I can hardly walk a block in town without meeting some enthusiast who rings my hand and says "that son of yours is surely a wonder," or some similar expression. I have been trying to find out what they think they know—but find it difficult. As nearly as I can make out—it seems to be the general understanding that you constituted nearly the "whole show" at Stockholm—That you were an "easy first" in swimming—and riding—in the latter event after your horse fell and rolled over you—you got him on his feet without leaving the saddle and forced him to jump a seven foot wall and dyke and came in riding easy. In the cross country run—you only lost by a nose—the victor being a jew—and having the advantage of you in that feature.
>
> In shooting it is universally conceded you must have been doped—or your cartridges tampered with—But it is the fencing which fills the popular imagination. By all it is understood this spectacular event took place in the Stadium before the Royal box in the presence of 20,000 breathless spectators. Some believe it was on horseback—with sharp sabres—others that it was with "dueling swords" which are conceived to be wonderful and sanguinary weapons—But all agree that you defeated every one of 42 contestants—Your defeat of the unhappy De Mas Latrie is regarded as the crowning event of the whole show, and you are greatly praised for having spared his life after disarming him. He is understood to have been a huge "Napoleonic Sabreur" with mustachios—and a terrifying frown which had hitherto terrified all combatants and gained for him the undisputed championship of the world. . . .
>
> Great is fame—Few enjoy it while alive. You ought to come

home before it is forgotten. Capt. Banning . . . thinks that climb-
ing the Catalina hills is what gave you your marvelous strength.

The elder Patton had returned home in time to share the excitement
over the three-cornered race for the presidency in 1912. Counting out
the Republican, William Howard Taft, he believed either Theodore
Roosevelt, the Progressive, or Woodrow Wilson, the Democrat, would
carry California. "I heard 'Teddy' make a speech. It was disappointing—
lacked fire—& he seemed dead tired." The next day William Jennings
Bryan, thrice the Democratic nominee for President, was to speak on
Wilson's behalf, and Patton was on the welcoming committee. "Things
are 'booming' here more than ever—and this Winter I hope I can sell
enough [oranges] to nearly make us all very easy."[33]

IV

If George Patton took part in one kind of politics, his son took part in
another. A celebrity because of his performance in Stockholm, he was
invited to dinner by General Leonard Wood, the army chief of staff, and
Secretary of War Henry L. Stimson. The next morning Patton, who frequently went horseback riding with Stimson, rode with Wood.[34]

From his return to Fort Myer in August until December 1912, Patton engaged in varied activities. With Captains Dickey Graham and
Gordon Johnston he constituted the heart of the post polo team, and at
the request of Colonel Joseph Garrard, the commander of the 15th Cavalry, he began expanding the section of his Olympic report on the saber
into an article for the *Journal of the United States Cavalry Association*.[35]

Charming and accomplished, Patton, even as a second lieutenant,
made the right acquaintances. In mid-December he received orders
temporarily transferring him to the office of the chief of staff, where at
times he acted as an aide to both Wood and Stimson.[36] Wood always
remained to Patton a distant and unfathomable figure, but Patton
cemented his relationship with the man he and Bea always called
Henry. Over the years Stimson proved to be a valuable and devoted
friend.

While at the War Department, Patton's most notable accomplishment was the design and production of the double-edged cavalry saber. Immediately after returning from the Olympics, Patton experimented with a design that made the cavalry saber a thrusting weapon, or, as its detractors said, a sword instead of a saber. Its blade, tapered to a sharp point, was almost completely straight, making the saber an extension of the cavalryman's arm. Its guard, resembling that of English and French sabers, was more open than the old bell guard. The *Army and Navy Journal* called the saber "a remarkably well balanced weapon" and referred to Patton as a "recognized authority on such subjects."

Some army officers objected to the new design, citing the difficulty in instructing men in the use of a straight sword suitable for thrusting. Against this, Patton, identified only as "an officer at the War Department who has given the subject a great deal of earnest thought," argued vehemently. In the *Army and Navy Journal* for January 11, 1913, he noted that the curved saber then in use stemmed from the Orient, where this kind of blade cut through an enemy's wool-padded protective clothing. At the dawn of the modern age, after gunpowder rendered suits of armor useless, Europeans, following the example of the Moors, who had invaded Spain, gave their unarmored cavalry—renamed light cavalry—curved swords. Citing the ineffectiveness of such weapons, Patton argued that the Highlanders of Scotland and the Moros of the Philippines possessed two of the deadliest weapons ever known, both straight and with sharp points.

The advantages of the point were, Patton insisted, many. First, to get the best results from a curved blade the object attacked must be struck with the portion of the blade a foot from the point. In a thrust with a pointed saber the object to be struck was thus a foot closer. Second, the charging cavalryman preparing to use the point leaned as low as possible over his horse, presenting a smaller target. A cavalryman about to use the edge, on the other hand, sat erect. Finally, the point, far more difficult to parry than the edge, was "vastly more deadly."

In his article in the *Journal of the United States Cavalry Association,* published in March 1913, Patton expanded his arguments with pictures and with numerous other historical illustrations, including Napoleon's admonition to his light cavalry at Wagram to avoid cutting and to instead use "the point! the point!" All this obviously impressed his superiors. After Patton modified the new weapon, making it slightly lighter and easier to handle, the War Department adopted it.[37] With his

Olympic prowess and his knowledge of swords and sabers, Patton was obviously an officer to watch.

Amid these activities Patton, returning to Fort Myer, still desired war. "I hope by the time this reaches you," he informed his father in a letter dotted with misspellings, "that we will have declared war with Japan, but I suppose with our natural ambition to apoligize for living we will have let them dictate to us what we should do." He called Bryan, now President Wilson's pacifistic secretary of state, "truly fit . . . for a country whose ambition is to be the punching bag of the world. His trouble is that he missed his calling he should have been the greasy irish preast he looks and have forced the last cent out of his ignorant followers on the pretense of saving them from a hell he invented for the purpose."[38]

During the spring of 1913 Patton spent much of his time with polo and racing. In flat races he labored under a handicap, for his horse Roman Wing, who in 1912 had won the Army and Navy Flat Race, had a bad leg. Consequently Patton was forced to ride Gilbert, who was not as well bred as Roman Wing. He did better in steeplechase races. Aboard mounts owned by his colleague in the 15th Cavalry, Lieutenant Karl S. Bradford, he won on May 22 the Henry of Navarre Steeplechase at the Washington Riding and Hunt Club in the District of Columbia and on June 9 a race at the Piping Rock Club on Long Island. "There is a belief in some quarters that Army officers who race amass large fortunes by the purses or by betting," Patton explained in a magazine article. "I regret deeply that this is not the case. Within my knowledge, no officer owning his horses has ever come out even. What he does has been for sport, not gain."[39]

In late June Patton received new orders. That October he was to report to the cavalry center of Fort Riley, Kansas. Meantime, at his own expense, he was free to go back to France to study swordsmanship, preliminary, he hoped, to establishing a course in swordsmanship somewhere in the United States.

Before leaving with Bea, Patton had one last duty to perform. Commemorating the fiftieth anniversary of the greatest of all Civil War battles, veterans were gathering at Gettysburg. Patton was sent, Bea later explained,

to patrol the battlefield, act as a sort of guide and do anything he could for the veterans who came in. They came in uniform, blue and grey, and were so old even then that 200 coffins had been sent ahead in case they should be needed.

The veterans were still assembling when he heard the most awful row up the road and hurried to where a big crowd were milling and yelling over what he thought must be an accident. When he finally got to the center, he found that it was a fight. Two veterans were belaboring each other with umbrellas, each claiming that he had fired the first shot at Gettysburg. Thats veterans for you. The older they get the worse they fight.[40]

V

——

A year after the Olympics, Patton and Bea were back in Europe. On July 14, Bastille Day, they reached Paris, "just too late for the review." Remaining there a couple of days to handle military matters, the Pattons then went on to Cherbourg, to which their car had been shipped. Illustrating his daring on the roads, Patton drove the fifty-two miles to Saint-Lô in an hour and ten minutes. After Bea bought some antique furniture, they drove on to Saumur, where as in the previous year they stayed at the Hotel Budon, the more expensive of the town's two establishments. This time, however, their room had a bathtub.[41]

The Cavalry School of Application at Saumur was indeed unique. Its students were primarily French soldiers, but warriors also came from every great power except Germany and Austria, which for four decades had been allied against France. In addition to giving advanced training in riding, the school contained schools for saddlers, horseshoers, cavalry telegraphists, and veterinarians. Among its least important schools, according to Captain Guy V. Henry of the 13th Cavalry, was the School of Fencing. Here thirty students who were already masters of arms received further instruction in the art.[42]

For five weeks Patton was reunited with Cléry. Except for some trips through the countryside, fencing constituted his existence. But the time passed, and at August's end the Pattons left for a final trip through the country. Then it was on to Paris for a few days before sailing for home from Cherbourg on the tenth of September.[43]

By late September Patton was at Fort Riley preparing what passed for a house—it was built in 1881 and Patton swore it had never been cleaned—for his wife and daughter. "I am sorry," he wrote Bea, "you are so sorry about the house but you can't imagine it worse than it is." It was small and uncomfortable. The fort was three miles from Junction City and about a dozen miles from the once bustling rail town of Abilene, where a current West Point cadet, Dwight D. Eisenhower, had grown up. Like Abilene, Junction City was isolated. Patton's friend Lieutenant Robert F. Tate, who had served with him in the 15th Cavalry at Myer and had competed against him in numerous horse races, joshed "that fort Riley must have been selected by a hermit who thought he was quite alone when he got here." Patton warned Bea that "to survive this place at all you will have to ride horse back as there is not another thing to do there is not even a place to go in an automobile."[44]

Patton found Fort Riley "the most strictly army place I have ever been in and also the most strictly business." Riding began at eight in the morning and continued until Patton began his fencing instruction at one in the afternoon. From then to three-thirty he conducted three classes. Those in the two largest, numbering thirteen and fourteen, were, like Patton, students in the first year of the two-year program at the Mounted Service School. The third group, only five in number, consisted of second-year men and assistant instructors. After observing Patton almost daily, Colonel Joseph A. Gaston, the school commandant, ordered all field officers to take fencing instruction. Beginning November 1 Second Lieutenant Patton, the Master of the Sword, would be teaching majors and lieutenant colonels.[45]

Luckily, Georgie's friend, Lieutenant Adna R. Chaffee, was leaving Riley, and Patton was able to get his house. It "is nice and large," he told his father in mid-October, "and has a guest room of sorts so we are in luck. B gets here the 25."[46]

When Nita, accompanied by her mother and Aunt Nannie, visited Riley just after Bea's arrival, she found things in a turmoil. "When we first got there," she wrote her father, "Bee was disciplining Smith & Ma failed to appreciate the screams but Bee finally gave in & all was serene when we left. I went riding one day with G & Bee and made a goat of myself on an English saddle & trotting nag. I prefer Rex & your saddle."[47]

Patton's life at Riley can best be described as routine. He studied, taught, put together a manual for the War Department on the use of the new cavalry sword, and wrote articles for *The Rasp,* the magazine of the Mounted Service School. By far the most significant of Patton's literary efforts at this time was his illustrated article "Mounted Swordsmanship," which appeared in the journal in 1914. Still battling those who railed against the new sword, Patton traced what he believed to be its evolution. In his pursuit of "food and female," ancient man developed the club and then the sharpened pole tipped first with flint and later with stone or bronze. Like these "hairy half human men," the conquerers of the ancient world, the Greeks, the Romans, and others, triumphed using the tips of their weapons, whether they were spears or short swords. In medieval and modern times, Patton went on, "the point and its winged brother the bullet have ever won."

Wherever the straight weapon has met the curved one, it has triumphed. He called his new sword "an ideal thrusting weapon" and "one which can give a cutting blow at least one third harder than our former saber." Its sharpened back edge, moreover, made it "easier to withdraw from a body than would be the case if it were single edged." By lying almost prone, the cavalryman using the point presented an almost impossible target. The same trooper, charging to cut, sat erect, almost entirely exposed. "Will the point always be successful?" Patton asked. "No," he answered, "but in all circumstances it gives the largest chance of success."[48]

In July 1914, completing his first year at the Mounted School, Patton was notified he had been accepted for the second. About that time he became involved in some sort of accident, either on horseback or in a car, while visiting the Ayers at Prides Crossing. Believing Georgie to be seriously injured, George Patton rushed to Massachusetts to be with him. In mid-September he accompanied his son back to Riley, while Bea and the baby, now called young Bee, stayed in the East. "Georgie is fine," he assured Bea on arriving at Riley. "He had a fine welcome from every body." His superiors, Major Charles D. Rhodes and Captain Henry R. Richmond, "both seemed emotionally glad to see him. . . . And this morning it is ideally beautiful. Geo. is off riding Sylvia Green—and I am sitting at your desk up stairs—writing to the dearest little daughter a man has ever had—and the finest and truest son's wife. . . . I feel sure G. is all right, and I will stay as long as I can."[49]

Although in the middle of Kansas, Patton associated his life at Riley with his youth at Lake Vineyard. On November 12, 1914, the day after his birthday, he recalled to his father that as a child he "used to have wars with the ice plants on the grass. I fixed twenty seven as the age when I should be a brigadier and now I am twenty nine and not a first Lt. yet things are going on well here and I am doing well both in the 2d year and as an instructor but I will be glad to leave as it is very tedious work." The previous week he had gone duck hunting, "the first I have killed since I used to hunt on the lake with Ed Cal[l]ahan when I was twelve."[50]

At Lake Vineyard itself, the family of Ruth and Nannie's half sister, Sue Wilson Shorb, whose husband had once owned what was now the Huntington estate, was making things unpleasant. Sue's son Norbert was the cause of much of the trouble. Norbert, "living with one of the most notorious women" in San Francisco, had depleted what little money Sue had by signing her name to checks and cashing them at "saloons and cigar stores." Supposedly addicted to morphine, he had already tried to kill himself. "I am glad dear Ruth that you have been blessed with such children. Dear Nita I think one of the finest girls I have ever known. When you meet people and so very few like Nita you certainly appreciate Nita. You deserve to be so blest."[51]

With the outbreak of the First World War in August, Patton toyed with the idea of getting a year's leave so that he could go to France. He wrote Wood, now in charge of the army's Eastern Department, but the general discouraged him. "We don't want to waste youngsters of your sort in the service of foreign nations," Wood answered, "unless they need you more than appears to be the case now. Stick to the present job and go ahead."[52]

During the first quarter of 1915 a death and a birth occupied Patton's thoughts. The death was that of George Hugh Smith. "He did not have the military mind in its highest development," Patton observed to his father, "because he was swayed by ideas of right or wrong rather than those of policy. Still he was probably more noble for his fault. Also the education of law hampered him."[53]

The birth was that of Bea and Georgie's second child. Busy with his military career, Patton did not especially desire more children, but his wife wished to give him a son. With Bea expecting in February 1915, Ruth and Nita came to Fort Riley and escorted her to San Marino. With the elder Patton, they would be with her when the time arrived. Bee, Jr., stayed in Kansas with her father.

To her father's delight, Bee seemed to be turning into a real Patton.

The past November he had taken her to the old riding hall at Riley, where with an air gun he began shooting at pigeons. Killing one, he yanked off its head. Bee retrieved it and, covered with blood, announced that if Patton had let her she could have pulled off the head. She then tiptoed around the hall looking for more birds to behead.

Bea had had a difficult first birth, and the second promised to be no easier. "You must tell the doctor," Georgie told his father, "that if there is the least question between her life and that of the child the child must go. This is probably an unnecessary caution but I insist on it. If he will not subscribe to it get another doctor who will."

Throughout February 28, the day of delivery, George Patton paced the hall. When Bea found out that the child was another girl, she remarked to Ruth Patton: "Better luck next time." "Please don't mention next time," her mother-in-law answered. "My husband has had a very hard day."[54]

What should the baby be named? "You had better have it named out there," Patton advised Bea the day after the birth, "where you can get more advice." He disliked both Ruth and Ellen, the names of the child's grandmothers. "You might call it Beatrice Second like a race horse. I certainly like the sound of that name the best of any." Ignoring her husband, Bea called the child Ruth Ellen.[55]

During the remainder of Patton's stay at Fort Riley, little of significance occurred. The sinking of the British-owned liner *Lusitania* by a German submarine in May heightened the differences between father and son over President Woodrow Wilson. Being a lawyer, George Patton would never understand the soldier's position, his son believed, for law was designed to protect the weak against the strong. To argue that the submarine should have stopped and warned the *Lusitania* was "utter folly," for "one shot from one of her hundred parts would have sent the submarine down. . . . There is but one International Law—the best army."

Itching for battle, Patton resented Wilson's peaceful ways. Three days after the torpedoing, the president spoke of being "too proud to fight." Answering this comment and the "utterances" of "such scum" as Henry Ford, who had gone to Europe to urge an end to the war, Patton wrote his poem "Valor." On Judgment Day, he prophesied:

Then shall we know what once we knew
Before wealth dimmed our sight
That of all the sins, the blackest is
The pride which will not fight.[56]

In June, as Patton finished his course at Riley, he heard horrible news. The 15th Regiment of Cavalry was heading for the Philippines. With two small girls Bea was horrified. Given a special leave, Georgie headed for Washington. Perhaps he could get his orders changed. The next month came the fruits of his lobbying. The 15th was indeed going to the Pacific, but on August 15, 1915, Patton was transferred to the 8th Regiment of Cavalry, then commanded by Colonel Charles W. Taylor at Fort Bliss. Located just outside El Paso, Bliss was a few miles from Mexico, which since 1911 had been locked in revolution. But at the very time Patton was using influence to get his orders changed, he wrote another poem decrying the "Rulers from the corn belt" who used political influence to get what they wanted. They saw not the real enemy: "That tide of 'Yellow Hell'" from Japan. Needed was "a single man" who with iron hand would rule.[57] Did Patton envision himself as the American Napoleon?

VI

Patton now faced the problem of moving to Bliss. Leaving the children at Prides Crossing, he and Bea returned to Riley, packed their belongings, and drove to San Marino to visit his parents. They then took the train to El Paso. Georgie got off, but Bea continued on and returned to Massachusetts.[58]

Patton's stay at Bliss began routinely, but it was not destined to end that way. During his first month at the post, he hunted with local residents, played polo, studied for the examination that would make him eligible for promotion to first lieutenant, instructed the troops in cavalry techniques and in the care of horses, and mixed with the other officers, most of whom he liked immensely.[59]

Exactly when he met Brigadier General John J. Pershing, soon to command Fort Bliss, is uncertain, but it must have been early in the fall of 1915. Like the careers of so many American generals, Pershing's was an example of ability pushed to the fore by political influence. For years after graduating from West Point, Black Jack seemed to be going nowhere. Then in 1905 he married Frances Warren, whose father, a United States senator from Wyoming, was a member of the Senate Military Affairs Committee. Suddenly, in September 1906, a dormant career blossomed. Over the heads of 862 other officers, Pershing was promoted from captain to brigadier general.[60]

At the very time Georgie and Bea, their children secure at Prides Crossing, were resting in San Marino, Pershing was living through a nightmare. In January 1914, returning from the Philippines, Pershing was stationed at the Presidio in San Francisco. Then, in April, rumors flew about that Francisco "Pancho" Villa, the Mexican revolutionary, was about to attack El Paso. Pershing and his men were rushed to the Mexican border, where Pershing took command of Fort Bliss.

Uncertain of his plans, Pershing left Frances and their four children at the Presidio. In the summer of 1915, realizing he was to be at Bliss permanently, he decided to move his family there. But on the morning of August 27, 1915, a fire broke out in the Pershing home. Frances and the three girls suffocated to death. Only a son survived. Not realizing that he was soon to become the hated enemy, Villa was among those who sent letters of condolence.[61]

During October 1915 events moved swiftly, both in Mexico and at Bliss. On the nineteenth the United States and six Latin American countries infuriated Villa by recognizing his rival, Venustiano Carranza, as the de facto head of Mexico. And on the twenty-eighth, hours after passing examinations in cavalry drill regulations, applied field service, and applied tactics, making him eligible for promotion, Patton was drawn into the mess. He received a telegram ordering him to guard the railroad at Hot Wells, Texas, twenty-three miles east of Sierra Blanca, Texas, while some of Carranza's troops moved over it. With only ten men Patton was to protect thirty miles of railroad. "But really," he wrote Bea on the twenty-ninth, "I think that there will be nothing to guard on this part of the line. Any way I will soon know as the first train comes past at 5 and it is now two."[62]

Supervising trains, Patton got little sleep. "It may be fine to die with ones boots on," he informed Bea on November 1, "but it is very hard on the feet to sleep with them on which is what I have been doing up to last night." Patton described those who came through on the trains as "the greatest side show you ever saw." At least a quarter of the passengers were women, those accompanying the Mexican officers being attractive. "One very dirty and fairly pretty girl on the last train told me that she would come and live with me if I would feed her as the mexicans gave her no food. I had to refuse." The women and children were not the only ones hungry. Patton observed to Aunt Nannie that "their horses were the thinest thing you ever saw."[63]

At Thanksgiving time of 1915 Patton learned that if armies moved on their stomachs, they also marched to the beat of rumors. At 6 P.M. on the twenty-fourth, with all the officers except Second Lieutenant William A. Raborg away at El Paso, Patton, then at Sierra Blanca, received a telegram. Chico Caño, the Mexican bandit, "was on his way to raid this town. I did not believe it," Patton wrote his father, but he called Raborg "and the two 1st Sgts and told them to have the men sleep with their rifles beside them." In case of danger each cavalry troop was to assemble at the tent of its first sergeant. "I hoped that Mr. Cano would come for he would have never gotten back."

At eleven o'clock, as Patton was about to retire, he got three more telegrams. One was from Pershing, repeating the warning about Caño. The other two warned that Villa had driven eighty Carranza men to the American side of the Rio Grande near Calduan. Patton was either to capture them or drive them back into Mexico. He immediately sent out patrols, which heard from various people that Villa, leading two hundred troops, had indeed forced Carranza's men across the river. Raborg, however, found no sign of the men.

The next night, about eleven o'clock, Patton received a telegram from Colonel William C. Rivers, the commander of the West Texas Cavalry Patrol, repeating the story about the eighty Carranza soldiers. Patton was to "act with vigor." He immediately told the first sergeant of Troop D that the men would leave at 4 A.M. That would get them to Fort Quitman, near where the Mexicans were supposed to have crossed, by daylight.

Even though he had only a few hours to rest, Patton tossed in his bed. Interpreting to "act with vigor" as meaning "to attack first and ask questions next," he decided to make a saber charge into the Mexican camp. Surely, Patton thought, this glorious exploit would win for him the Medal of Honor. But in the midst of these dreams two of Patton's superiors, Captain James C. Rhea and First Lieutenant Daniel D. Tompkins, returned and took command. Though suffering from dysentery, Tompkins "decided to go and being a d——[amned] f——[ool] he decided to leave the sabers." When the expedition set off, "the men were in great spirits. They were tickled to death at the chance of a fight. . . . We met nothing," Patton complained. "There was nothing to meet. It was just another false rumor." But to Patton the events added up to "a most exciting thanksgiving."[64]

In late January, after being in the post hospital with the grippe, Patton reported a happy event. "I moved into the house Saturday," he told Bea, who had stayed with him for much of December and January but had now gone back to Massachusetts, "and am about unpacked now. It proved impossible to get a chink so I wired your mother to get Julia and I expect her shortly." Meantime, he was hiring the wife of a soldier for seventeen dollars a month. "Washing of course will be extra."[65]

In late February, after Bea's return, Nita came out to visit. "I am afraid Nita has had a very poor visit," Patton wrote his father in early March, "it has blown every day but one since she has been here and as Mrs. Raborg left the day she got here she has not had a very good time."[66]

At Fort Bliss, Nita met Pershing. She was then twenty-eight, and at five feet nine inches was just three or four inches shorter than Pershing. Only six months before he had lost his wife and daughters. The hurt never went away. A perfect daughter, Nita was kind, considerate, and devoted to her family. If she and Georgie ever fought, they left no trace of it. Pershing was drawn to her, but one impediment to the relationship always existed. The general owed his career to Senator Warren, who had plucked him out of the military multitude and thrust him forward. What would Senator and Mrs. Warren, leaders in Washington politics and society, think of the romance?

In that same letter Patton passed along to his father news that the Cavalry Equipment Board was thinking of returning to the curved saber. "I am much excited and will probably have to go to Rock Island Arsenal to convince them what D. F.s they are. Still I shall enjoy the trip as any absence from this place is welcome."[67]

VII

On the night of March 8, 1916, Villa provided the reason for Patton to get out of "this place." Swooping down on Columbus, New Mexico, the home of the 13th Cavalry, he killed seventeen Americans, nine of them civilians. Two days later Wilson authorized an incursion into Mexico with the sole purpose of capturing Villa and stopping the raids. Pershing was chosen to lead this Punitive Expedition.[68]

Hearing the news, Patton moped about, afraid that the 8th Cavalry would not go and that he would miss the only war then available. Consequently he began pestering people: Major John L. Hines, already selected as Pershing's adjutant; Lieutenant Martin C. Shallenberger, one of Pershing's aides; and the general himself. Under such persistent nagging, Pershing gave in and agreed to take Patton along as an aide until the return of Lieutenant James L. Collins, who had fought under Pershing against the Moros in the Philippines. Three years later Patton learned why Pershing had relented. In 1898, when the Spanish-American War broke out, Pershing had been stationed at West Point. In vain he tried to circumvent the policy that no instructors be sent off to war. In desperation Pershing finally went absent without leave and, like Patton, pestered superiors until he was allowed to go to Cuba.[69]

On March 16 Patton crossed over into Mexico from Columbus. At first he exuded hopefulness. After all, the soldiers took along the most modern equipment—a Telefunken or radio set, an aero squadron, a Buick, a Dodge, and two Fords. "All the Mexicans are very friendly," he wrote Bea from Casas Grandes, about sixty miles inside Mexico, on the twentieth, "and inspite of what the papers say *not* a shot has been fired at us. We met no Mexicans at all until we got here. I fear that in my position I will see no active fighting. . . . The Chicago Tribune has the only accurate stuff in it by a man named Gibon [Floyd Gibbons]. The A.P. stuff is accurate also the rest is mostly made up at the offices."[70]

A week later, after roaming about much of northern Mexico, Patton already entertained doubts about the success of the mission. *"This is personal and pvt,"* he told Bea. "If we don't get Villa in a week or so we wont get him for a long time. It will be a slow chase with no fighting. In that event I think you had better go to Boston as you would have a much better time than at Bliss. You will do no good at Bliss as I am safe as if I were there safer in fact as I can't play polo. . . . Make Pa run for the Senate. Write Lucy if he can use a hundred or two in the campaign now and if yes send it."[71]

During this period Pershing frequently traveled lightly and swiftly. He often drove about in a single car, accompanied only by Patton, of whom he was growing fonder; his driver; and his black cook. On April 12, 1916, such casualness changed. About noon, leaving the supposedly friendly town of Parral, deep in the province of Chihuahua, Major Frank Tompkins and two troops of the 13th Cavalry were fired upon. Harassed all the way, the Americans retreated eighteen miles to another village, where they dug in and waited, they hoped, to be rescued. The incident convinced the Americans that no Mexicans could be trusted.[72]

Villa, meanwhile, was hiding. At Guerrero, halfway between Casas Grandes and Parral, on March 28 he had been hit in the right leg by a stray bullet fired by Mexican federals. The wounded general took refuge in a cave passed frequently by Americans and Carranzistas.[73]

Amid all this, Pershing and his staff became celebrities. As early as April 7 the *New Orleans Times-Picayune* splashed across its front page a huge picture of the general and the seven members of his staff. In the Mexican heat Colonel DeRosey C. Cabell, the chief of staff, sported a heavy coat. The three youngest men were aides: Patton, Collins, and Shallenberger. Given the conditions, all appeared neatly dressed. Patton alone wore a tie.[74]

By mid-April, with Villa hiding out, Patton was disgusted with the Mexicans. "They are much lower than the Indians," he apprised Bea on the thirteenth.

> They have absolutely no morals and there have been no marriages for five years. Imagine that any woman would sell what else where would be called her virtue for a peso or less and a girl could be bought for about 20 pesos. When Villa was in power he used to take a girl from every town he passed through and had a car full of girls on his train with a general who was also his barber to look after them. The country's full of young Villas. But old Villa is damned hard to find as we are finding.[75]

In early May Patton finally got into action. Pershing gave him permission to hunt for Julio Cárdenas, Villa's bodyguard, and the captain

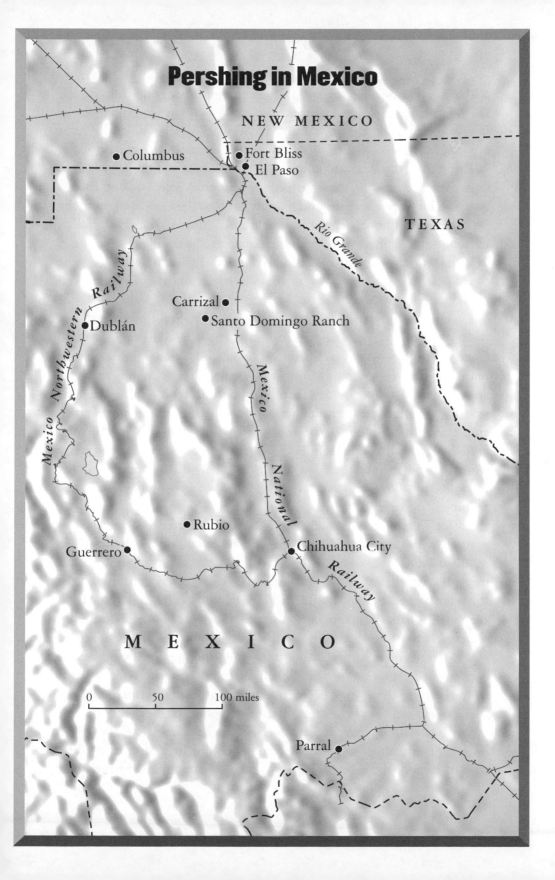

Pershing in Mexico

NEW MEXICO

● Columbus

● Fort Bliss
● El Paso

TEXAS

Rio Grande

● Carrizal
● Santo Domingo Ranch

Mexico Northwestern Railway

● Dublán

Mexico National Railway

● Rubio

● Guerrero

● Chihuahua City

M E X I C O

0   50   100 miles

● Parral

of the group known as the Dorados. Accompanied by Lemuel Spilsbury, the Mormon guide, and Lieutenant Innis P. Swift, who during World War II commanded the 1st Cavalry Division, plus Troop C of the 13th Cavalry, he rode out to Cárdenas's ranch house at San Miguelito, ten miles north of the Villa stronghold of Rubio. Warned of the approach of horsemen by the dust they stirred up, Cárdenas escaped, but Patton captured his uncle, his wife, and his baby. Patton then behaved savagely. "Spillbury and I hung Cardeneses uncle three times to make him talk," Patton related, "finally he did, though he fainted a couple of times first. I think I wrote you about it," he informed Bea. To his father Patton conceded that "the uncle was a very brave man and nearly died before he would tell me anything."

Even below the border Patton stood out. "The most engaging personality of my Mexican service was my tent-mate, Georgie Patton," General Hugh S. Johnson, then a lieutenant but later the head of the National Recovery Administration, observed in 1935, when Patton was an obscure lieutenant colonel. Patton "used to sit in his tent by the hour practicing 'trigger-pull' with either hand on a pistol fitted with a spring and a rod which would dart out at a swinging pith ball at which he aimed. We used to call Georgie a Sears-Roebuck cowboy, because he wore a pistol cartridge belt low about his hips with two pearl handled forty-five revolvers in holsters, one on each groin—he never used an automatic pistol."[76]

Patton's great day came on May 14, 1916. Before trucks began supplying the Punitive Expedition, the soldiers lived on the country. This required a different officer to go out with cars every day to buy corn and hay from friendly ranchers. The fourteenth of May was Patton's day. In three autos the party sped off, Patton in the lead car. Deciding to check the ranch at San Miguelito, Patton stopped the autos in the road immediately below the ranch house. As he and Heaton Lunt, an unarmed scout, ran to the east toward the front gate, the men in the other two cars covered the western side. When Patton was about twenty yards from the gate, three armed Mexicans emerged riding horses. Thinking they might be Carranza men, Patton—then carrying but one six-shooter, which, as was the cavalry custom, held only five shots, the hammer being on the empty chamber—held his fire. After first riding toward Patton, the three turned and tried to escape around the other side of the building. Seeing the Americans there, they headed back toward Patton and Lunt, "all firing at me at about 20 yards or less," Patton informed his father. "I fired back five times with my new pistol and one of them ducked back into the house. I found out later that this was Cardenes and that I had hit both he and his horse." As Patton reloaded his pistol, a Mexican dashed by on horseback, not ten yards away. Remembering what "old Dave Allison," the marshal at Sierra Blanca, had told him—"it was always best to kill the horse of a running man," for a wounded man still might ride away—Patton fired at the animal, breaking its stifle joint with his first shot. As the Mexican got up, four Americans "shot him and he crumpled up." He turned out to be Juan Gaza, a Villista private. At that point the second man of the trio was about 150 yards off. The Americans shot at him and killed him. He was Captain Isador Lopez. "Two men ran down to search him," Patton continued, "and called back that there was another man escaping down a stone wall." The fleeing Mexican was Cárdenas, whose right arm Patton had broken with his previous shots. Hit twice more in the right lung while trying to escape, he "still ran about five hundred yards and shot 30 times." When E. L. Holmdahl, another American scout, approached him, Cárdenas held up his left arm to indicate surrender. But with Holmdahl about twenty feet away, Cárdenas dropped the arm and opened fire. The scout then shot him through the head.

Searching about after the incident, Patton was surprised. He saw in front of the house four Mexicans who during the fight had hardly looked up. Amid the shooting, they had continued skinning a cow. He also found Cárdenas's mother, wife, and daughter. They had witnessed the entire fight, the first ever fought by American soldiers springing from automobiles.

Patton responded to all this nonchalantly. Strapping the bodies across the steaming hoods of the cars, the Americans continued searching for corn and hay. That evening Patton returned to camp and reported to Pershing that he knew the whereabouts of about two thousand bushels of corn and a hundred tons of hay. He added that he also "had three Mexican bandits." When Pershing asked what he meant by "had three Mexican bandits," Patton answered: "That is correct, sir. I have them back of your tent on my automobile, if you want to see them." Viewing the bodies, Pershing suggested that Patton dispose of them at once. The sun and engine heat had made them "very puffy," Patton later told his friend, General Kenyon A. Joyce.

Patton also related to Joyce that his attachment to two ivory-handled revolvers stemmed from the incident. During the fray, he had had to stop and reload his six-shooter. While he did, three shots just missed his head. Henceforth, in times of danger, he preferred to wear two Colt Frontier-model 45-caliber revolvers. Newspapers often described them as pearl-handled because it sounded more colorful.[77]

While Patton learned in Mexico the value of being properly armed, he disregarded another essential. "When we enter the Army," Pershing told him, "we do so with full knowledge that our first duty is toward the government, entirely regardless of our own views." A soldier's personal views must never "govern our actions." At least once in Mexico, Patton countermanded an order, but he did so only after much consideration. One day when Pershing was at El Cobre, he sent Major James A. Ryan out with a squadron of cavalry to hunt for Villistas. After a few days, Pershing wished to change his orders. He told Patton to find Ryan and tell him to go to the Providencia Rancho and "search the mountains to the west." As Pershing spoke, he glanced at the mountains in that direction. Starting off in an old Ford, Patton drove as far as he could and then got a horse and began riding. All night he rode through a storm that began as rain and in the mountains turned into snow and sleet. But he noticed that he had gone west. He was sure the mountains at which Pershing glanced were now to his east, not to the west. Told by Patton to go east, Ryan objected. By doing so he would be violating written orders. Patton said he would take responsibility for the change in direction, so Ryan went east. Finding nothing, he told Pershing about the incident. After Patton explained what had happened, Pershing said to the lieutenant: "You were perfectly right!"[78] Unfortunately, after the Second World War, a more blatant disregard of orders would lead to Patton losing command of his Third Army.

From Pershing, Patton learned other things. Scrupulously clean and neat, the general shaved daily no matter what the conditions. And, like everyone else, he slept on the ground without a tent for three months, usually doubling up with one of his aides for warmth. Patton was always a stickler for cleanliness, but Pershing was even worse. On the hottest days he would make a soldier open his shirt to make sure he was

wearing an undershirt. One thing was surprising about Pershing, however. He permitted football games, but he also allowed cockfights at the
encampment at El Valle.[79]

Pershing did not hide his fondness for Patton. Lieutenant Joseph W.
Viner told of an incident during a dress parade. Viner was riding a stal-
lion that made an amorous advance toward Pershing's mare, which
belonged to Patton. Pershing was so angry that he threatened to send
Viner back to the United States, but Patton talked him out of it. Recalling the incident years later, Viner noted that in Mexico he recognized
Patton's military genius. "He always said," Viner related, "he'd rather
live a day as a lion than 100 years as a lamb."[80]

After the affair of May 14, described in a long article by Frank Elser
of the *New York Times* on May 23, Patton became to Pershing even more
of a pet. "The general has been very complimentary," he informed Bea,
"telling some of the officers that I did more in half a day than the whole
13th Cav did in a week. He calls me the Bandit. There is another bandit near here and I asked him to let me take a try at him but he would
not. It is just as well because my luck might change and I might miss
this one."[81]

Back at Fort Bliss, Bea, hearing of her husband's exploits while park-
ing, almost wrecked their car. "I was coming home from town," she
informed her father-in-law, "& had bought a paper but hadn't read it.
Mrs. Duncan, my next door neighbor, stuck her head out of the kitchen
& called: 'Your husband's a medal of honor man now, Mrs. Patton!'
Everything went black & I ran the car sping into the side of the garage.
I didn't hurt either of them, however, and its not likely to happen
again." Nita, who was visiting Bea, was "still having a good time in
spite of the loss of her beau. She is rapidly getting several more in place
of the dear departed [Pershing]. She is out at the club playing tennis
now. Of course I know how you miss her but I don't know how I would
possibly get along without her!"[82]

By June, Patton was bored. Being promoted to first lieutenant—the
army bill recently passed by Congress eliminated the rank of second
lieutenant—helped, but not much. "It is almost three months since this
darned war started," he lamented to Bea on the first,

> and for the last month it has amounted to nothing but a sitting
> match most destructive to ones trousers. The worst part of it is

that there seems no probability of its ever getting any better at least people here have lost hope though I still think my luck will hold and that I will see you soon at least to do that is the height of my ambition. I hold with Capt Crain that "a married man is a poor officer" at least if he is married to such a charmer as you are because he wants to see her all the time.

Still, Patton presented some cheery news. His friends predicted he would be a captain by the middle of next year. "Perhaps they are right at least it will be soon. I found the 1st Lt. bars in the canteen today and sewed them on so feel quite an old soldier though the power will be short lived as there will be no 2nd Lts. after July 1st."[83]

Patton's last exciting adventure came in mid-June. On the twelfth he and eight other cavalrymen searched for Pedro Lujan, "the last living chief of the Villa forces." Riding seventy miles in thirty-two hours, they surrounded Lujan's hacienda and galloped up to the door. The Mexican immediately surrendered. "They would not shoot," Patton told his father, "if they had we would have murdered them."[84]

From home Patton heard that his father was the Democratic candidate for the United States Senate, opposing the Republican, Governor Hiram Johnson. "Pa has decided to run for the Senate," he informed Bea. "I don't see how he can win but he must at least hope to and if he does not and Wilson gets in he might get a job." To aid the campaign Patton intended to sell his Pacific Light and Power bonds and give his father the money. "It will be about $7000.00 and may do some good. I hope it does."[85]

Completely bored, Patton spent much of his time writing what he called "disgusting poems." He also sent Bea a copy of a Mexican ditty, "a sort of 'Dixie'" sung to the tune of "La Cucaracha." He described it as "the vilest thing ever written. Don't ask any one any of the words in it and don't get some friend to translate it."

The poem began by ridiculing Carranza:

> *With the beard of Carranza*
> *I am going to make a toquilla*
> *To put on the hat*
> *Of the valiant Pancho Villa.*

Villa fared even worse:

> *Pancho Villa is a fool,*
> *A disgraced, disgusting fool,*
> *Who doesn't know enough to clean himself*
> *After sitting on the stool.*

And again:

> *With his thieves and cutthroats,*
> *Pancho Villa did no good.*
> *He lost his reputation as a warrior,*
> *Along with the symbol of his manhood.*[86]

Even the poetry failed to soothe the pain. "To day has been the worst I have had," Patton wrote Bea in mid-July. "I was out of reading matter and my horses were being shod so I had nothing to do. . . . But if we dont get out of here soon we will all go crazy."[87]

Hoping to get to El Paso to see Bea and the children, Patton concocted a scheme. He would tell Pershing he had to go to California for a short time to help his father's senatorial campaign. "I thought that this would move the General as it would give him a lean on Pa if he were elected. I took all one night and part of a day to get up my courage to ask him. I even had to resort to the candy eating start I used proposing to you." Pershing "was very nice and believed me and said he would think it over." Eventually, however, he asked Patton to try to arrange matters some other way. "In view of this," Patton admitted, "I could not consider carrying the lie further. That is the trouble with a really great man. You have to treat them as fairly as they treat you. . . . The result is that I think more of General P and less of my self than I did."[88]

During his boredom, Patton revived his correspondence with Kate Fowler. "This was G—— D—— country," he advised her. "As we do not expect to stay here, we have only one tent in which we all exist; it is very intimate, at least. Fortunately, the intelligence officer, who is Champion Snorer, is not here." That June, Kate had married the New York lawyer and banker Van S. Merle-Smith. Just after the wedding Merle-Smith, an officer in the 69th Regiment of the New York National

Guard, had been sent to the Mexican border. "I am delighted that Mr. Merle-Smith is in the Cavalry," Patton flattered the new bride, "for besides the fact that you selected him, the fact of his choice of a Gem proves him very superior. Just fancy had he been a doughboy or a wagon soldier?" Happily, Patton had been able to steal off to El Paso on August 4th to see Bea and the girls for a day. "I certainly was glad as I had been away for five months and feared she might have fallen in love with someone else. She had not."[89]

In early October Patton reported an accident to Bea. "You are indeed fortunate in not being able to kiss me right now." Returning from the movies on the second, Patton decided to do some work. He lit his lamp. When it failed to work, he pumped the gasoline again. When he stopped, lit gas squirted over him, burning his face and hair. Running outside, he "put my self out" and then returned to extinguish the fire in the tent. Going first to General Pershing, he rushed over to the hospital, where he found only a dentist. A physician finally arrived, "but every thing he tried to get for my face was 'just out' like a cheap hash house so at last he put vasaline on it. It was hurting like hell by then." Patton's ears were red and his hair, eyebrows, and eyelashes were singed, but the physician assured him that the burns resembled a bad sunburn and that he would recover fully. Pershing, his entire staff, and all of the important officers came to visit, and on the ninth Pershing gave Patton a fifteen-day leave.[90]

VIII

Transported by truck, Patton reached Columbus, New Mexico, on the tenth. With Bea he boarded a train that took him to Los Angeles. In San Marino he found his father immersed in the political campaign. Going sometimes by train and sometimes in his big Pierce-Arrow, George Patton, accompanied by his manager, the Los Angeles Democratic leader John T. Gaffey, traveled four thousand miles and visited eighty-three cities and towns in a month. To those who, like himself, grew oranges—he had "a grove of about 6,000 trees"—he offered a tariff on foreign fruit. "I have never seen the citrus men given a square deal in Washington," he said, borrowing one of Teddy Roosevelt's favorite phrases. ". . . But now it will be different." To Progressives he recalled his bitter struggle two decades before with that "live lion," the Southern Pacific, now "a dead jackass" that was "out of politics, and has been for a number of years." Everywhere he spoke of a noble Wilson, who had kept the peace while Europe wallowed in blood. "On the other side of the Atlantic seven million men have gone to unmarked graves," he reported, "and seven million mothers' hearts are torn and bleeding. Here the mother clasps her boy to her breast, the wife welcomes her husband home from his daily toils, and brother and sister are together at the fireside."

George Patton's greatest burden proved to be his earlier opposition to California's women's suffrage amendment. Republican papers reminded readers that in October 1911 George Patton had said: "Women, I believe, are incapable of balloting discreetly and wisely, because the ballot is a new and dangerous weapon in their hands." A half million women, many seeking revenge, now voted in California.[91]

Back in Lake Vineyard, Nita, Pershing's constant companion when he and Georgie visited Columbus in early September, noted the "great excitement in the Patton household" on October 11. "I had been gone all day, attending my lecture, and later working at Fathers headquarters, where we are busy getting out the precinct lists. Well," she told Pershing, recently promoted to major general, "when I returned home what should I find, but Beatrice and George back here. I certainly gasped with surprise. Poor George, surely did get in a 'mix up' with that lamp. But he was very lucky not to hurt his eyes. We are so happy to have him home again. He was pretty weary when he got here."[92]

Head bandaged, young Patton began accompanying his father on campaign trips. The odd-looking lieutenant became an immediate celebrity, predicting in newspaper interviews the success of the Americans in Mexico and of his father in the current canvass. Winfield Hogaboom, George Patton's publicity manager, noted the son's steadying influence on his father. On one trip George, Sr., was scheduled to speak at Imperial Valley. He was not informed of it, and at six the next morning the Pattons had to drag themselves off the train practically undressed to make connections for the engagement. The father was furious until his son, showing his skill as a diplomat, calmed him down. They had to get dressed in the lee of the freighthouse and had to get breakfast in a Japanese restaurant, the only establishment open. Within an hour, in sweltering heat, a jovial George Patton was shaking hands with voters, as if nothing had happened. At San Bernadino the next night Georgie showed Hogaboom a poem he had written in Mexico, where "we had lots of time on our hands." Entitled "Might-Right," the piece, the direct opposite of what his father preached about Wilson, had all the elements of Patton's poetry: simplicity and directness of theme, four-line stanzas with the second and fourth lines rhyming, and a glorification of war and a denigration of the "craven souls" who preached peace.

When the cave man sat in his stinking lair,
With his low browed mate hard by;
Gibbering the while he sank his teeth
In a new killed reindeer's thigh.

Thus he learned that to fight was noble;
Thus he learned that to shirk was base;
Thus he conquered the creatures one and all,
And founded a warrior race.

What would he have thought, could his foggy brain,
Have pictured our hapless day,
When craven souls of dreaming fools
Should habit our human clay.

When cowards born of Fear and Greed
Should preach to kindred slaves;
That Right may stand by its self alone,
And needs not Might to save.

They speak but lies these sexless souls,
Lies born of fear of strife
And nurtured in soft indulgence
They see not War is Life.

They dare not admit the truth,
Though writ in letters red,
That man shall triumph now as then
By blood, which man has shed.[93]

As election day approached, the Pattons sensed defeat. "Only one week more!" Nita lamented to Pershing. "I am working like a dog, but the average voter—well I should hate to tell you what I think of the average voter's intelligence. So we cannot look into the future, it is only a guess." That Friday night she heard Governor Johnson speak. "He is a forceful speaker, but he was trying a little too hard to secure votes for himself from all parties, and so weakened his own cause. It is hard to carry water on both shoulders." Pershing had promised to tell Nita when he would next be in Columbus if, in return, she promised to be there. "Tell anyway," she teased, "and I'll come if I can, because I do not make promises, I am not sure I can keep. I had fun last time and I'd have fun again, especially as Columbus now boasts a bran, span new hotel, also suspecting is interesting. . . . Georgie's ears are still sights, and you certainly filled the family with joy when you extended his leave. . . . He certainly was lucky to get off so well, it was a very narrow escape. George can do more awful things to himself than anyone I ever saw."[94]

Just after the election Nita transmitted to Pershing the mixed news. The popular Johnson had easily defeated her father, but Wilson, after trailing all night, had taken California at the last minute and defeated the Republican candidate for President, Charles Evans Hughes.

> Never in all my life was I ever so excited over anything. Election night I was in Los Angeles until two, and Hughes seemed elected as well as Johnson and the state appeared to have gone dry and I was perfectly furious!!! Of course that was silly, but I felt that all was lost if Hughes won, I hated the Republicans, the poor innocents, fortunately (?) they did not know of my wrath or the G.O.P would have trembled, I am sure!! However I have now recovered, and while I am terribly disappointed that father did not get in, still I realize that he was against an almost impossible proposition in fighting a machine and a governor. So I wiped my eyes, bought a new hat, ordered a new dress and felt better. It was very interesting at the campaign headquarters, where one met such different types of women, from ones usual friends, but still I am unconverted. I am *not* a suffragette.[95]

As George Patton and numerous other Californians saw it, the defeated senatorial candidate, more than anyone else in the country, was responsible for Wilson's reelection. To Wilson's adviser, Colonel Edward M. House, Patton stressed that he had had no desire to run. Afraid that Johnson would get both the Republican and Democratic nominations, he waited until August 12, the last possible moment, and then, when no one else appeared, he consented to run. If no one had challenged Johnson, Wilson would have stood no chance in California, for an unopposed governor would have dragged to Hughes numerous Democratic votes. Senator James D. Phelan, the state's leading Democrat, was among those who urged George Patton to oppose Johnson. With help from neither the California nor the national Democratic committee, Patton, facing "hopeless odds," used his own money. Beginning on September 1, he traveled over six thousand miles by car and train, campaigning "from the Oregon line to Mexico," urging all Progressives to vote for Wilson. As a result, Johnson never mentioned or attacked Wilson. "I forced Johnson to silence against the President," Patton told House.[96]

An episode during the campaign led to George Patton's resignation from the board of trustees of Throop College of Technology, later the California Institute of Technology. When Johnson came to Pasadena to speak, he was introduced by J. A. B. Scherer, the college's president. Insulted, Patton severed all connection with the school. Scherer argued that "this is a free country" and any college professor had the right "to say what he pleases," but even Dr. Norman Bridge, the head of the board, sided with Patton. To introduce the opponent of someone who had done so much for the college was in poor taste. "I feel also bound to say to you," Bridge wrote Scherer, "that had I been in your place I do not think I could have been induced to do what you did in the matter referred to."[97]

IX

Reporting back to duty on November 13, Georgie Patton found himself mired in army routine. "There is no news here as to when we will come out," he reported to Bea. "No one expects to before Christmas though this morning there is a report that Carranza is hopeful of an immediate settlement." Also on Patton's mind was his father's future. George Patton, Sr., had saved Wilson and deserved a cabinet position, but he was reluctant to seek a reward.[98]

By this time Pershing had lost all hope of capturing Villa. In the middle of September, while the American forces were stuck north of Colonia Dublán, the Mexican fugitive twice took Chihùahua City, far to the south. Pershing sought permission to send his men south, but in November the secretary of war refused the request. Feeling secure, Villa gloated. On December 11, 1916, the *New York World* published an interview in which he denounced the invaders and vowed to "drive them out, or make them fight, and after they are I will make a gap between the two countries so wide and deep that no *americans* will ever be able to steal Mexican land, gold or oil."[99]

All that was left for Pershing—and for Patton—were maneuvers and papers about the use of cavalry during the Mexican adventure. During one maneuever Patton and Pershing, standing atop "a big hill," watched as the whole 7th Cavalry circled the rear of the infantry. "Just before the seventh came in sight," Patton exulted to Bea, "two big deer, a buck and a doe, rushed by with in twenty five yards of where Gen. P. and I stood . . . and jumped over a skirmish line laying down. It was the prettiest thing I ever saw in Mexico."[100]

With nothing else to do, Patton devoted time to military writing. At Pershing's urging he composed a paper on the use of advance guard by cavalry. In it Patton argued that, like the rest of the army, the advance guard must be aggressive. It must go forward until it spotted the enemy and then must quickly transmit information back to the main force. "We frequently see patrol leaders who never send reports," he argued, "and at times others who erring on the other side send negative ones." The cavalry must use its mobility to assume the offensive "and not poke along like Infantry must until it bumps its nose."[101]

Patton's most important literary effort at this time was an article entitled "Cavalry Work of the Punitive Expedition," published in the January 1917 issue of the *Journal of the United States Cavalry Association*. After describing the rigorous training program set up by Pershing for his four regiments of cavalry and his single regiment of infantry, "camped together" after July 1916 in the vast expanse about Dublán, Patton urged the same audacious tactics for cavalry as he had in his brief paper on the advance guard. The worst mistake a cavalry unit, even one ambushed by an enemy, could make was to abandon its horses. "No," Patton argued, ". . . the thing to do would be to charge mounted if no obstacle prevented it. If the charge was impossible they should gallop off to where a proper attack, either mounted or on foot, could be inaugurated." Mounted or dismounted, the cavalryman must have perfect control of three things: his horse, his pistol, and his saber. As Pershing preached, every cavalryman must fight on foot like the best infantry and mounted better than any other cavalry in the world.[102]

At the end of January 1917 the Americans began pulling out of Mexico. On the twenty-eighth Patton accompanied Pershing on a visit to the refugee camps that had sprung up around Dublán and Palomas in northern Mexico. Chinese immigrants, Mormons, and Mexicans who feared Villa were piling all their possessions onto animals or into rickety wagons and heading north, "leaving," Patton told Bea, "a country where neither life or virtue is respected. . . . One old man limped after the thinnest cow and calf you ever saw. All he had. It was very cold and they were shaking. Then in the midst two wagons full of painted whores under a guard. . . . I expect that all the Carranzistas will follow us out." Patton sent home one photo, which he titled "A Good Load," showing ten adults, three children, and their goods shoved into one wagon. Another, "All Their Worldly Possessions," showed a line of refugees fleeing with loaded donkeys.

Patton spent the twenty-ninth "busting up houses all day. We do it a funny way simply pull the roof off and then back a truck against the wall. It pushes them over as nice as you please."[103]

After leaving Mexico, Patton continued to see Pershing. In late February, after Major General Frederick Funston died suddenly, Pershing was placed in charge of all the troops on the Mexican border and stationed at Fort Sam Houston, Texas. The following month, visiting Los Angeles to speak before the local chapter of the American Red Cross, he spent several days with the Pattons in San Marino. As newspapers buzzed about Pershing's pending engagement, the general drove about with Georgie, discussed worldly matters with Georgie's father, and spent evenings with Nita.[104]

Strangely enough, although Patton for years yearned for battle, the American declaration of war against Germany on April 6, 1917, failed to excite him. At that very time Bea's father had developed pneumonia, and Patton thought of little else. He wrote Pershing that he would go east with Bea and seek an assignment there so he could be near Frederick Ayer. "In view of illness in your family," Pershing telegraphed in answer, "have no objection to your detail training camp east but suggest you consider possibly more important service elsewhere. . . . Hope Beatrice's father is better."[105]

As Pershing realized, America now needed its trained soldiers.

Three

THE SUICIDE CLUB

I

Patton believed that he had learned much from his experiences with the Punitive Expedition, but Pershing felt just the opposite. "When the true history of the Expedition, especially the diplomatic side of it, is written," he confided to his father-in-law, Senator Warren, "it will not be a very inspiring chapter for school children or even grown-ups to contemplate. Having dashed into Mexico with the intention of eating the Mexicans raw, we turn back at the very first repulse and are now sneaking home under cover like a whipped cur with his tail between his legs. I would not dare to write this to anybody but you nor repeat it before anybody but a confidential stenographer."[1]

Despite the failure of the venture, Pershing returned to the United States a hero. Following a week with the Patton family in California, the general left for Fort Sam Houston after giving Ruth Wilson Patton the impression that something serious was going on between Nita and him. From Fort Sam Houston, Pershing wrote Ruth and again hinted at the romance. "As you said in your letter to me," Ruth answered the general on April 12,

> there were so many things you wanted to say, you can sympathize with me. I seemed to be struck dumb, and said nothing to you that I wanted to. Every thing seemed so sudden, but I do feel that I know you much better than the short time warrants, and you know that Georgie was with you for eleven months in Mexico, and of course I heard of you through him, then my family all tell me that my judgment of any one is generally quite good on first

acquaintance and I certainly liked you very much the first time I met you. My little girl I know too would not care, or I should say love any one who was not worthy of her, and it makes me so happy to know that you appreciate her. It was such a pleasure to have you in our home, but entirely too short a visit, and I am more than glad if the rest did you good. When you showed me the picture of your little family that morning I wanted to tell you how much I had always sympathized with you in your terrible loss, but it is difficult for me to express my feelings, but I do think that you deserve great happiness in the future, and I hope and pray you will have it. With much love for my new son, and thanking you for your lovely letter.[2]

Late in April, George Patton, Sr., hoping to get some reward for his part in Wilson's reelection, traveled to Washington. There he found disappointment, being offered, he told his son, "some second class job at Washington—which is all there is likely to be for some time." With the coming of war the capital was all talk and preparation. "If I were younger I would wish above all things to go," the senior Patton lamented, "first because of duty—but also to enjoy the thrill of fighting the German menace to civilization." Like the ancient Romans, the Germans wished to conquer the world. "It is now—as it is developing another struggle between the Teuton & the Celt—it is only another outburst from the North—and as in the past, it will be broken only to rear again in another generation or two."[3]

Promoted to captain on May 15, Patton began another campaign to see action. He "ducked" one job as the mess officer for twenty-five hundred reserve officers. "I would be a Mess at it," he joked to Bea. Hearing from Captain Malin Craig that "J.J.P. wanted me," he telegraphed Shallenberger to find out if it were so.[4]

Happily Pershing, the commander of the small division of about twelve thousand men that was to be the first American unit sent to France, saved Patton from a fate that to him would have constituted cruel and unusual punishment. When the adjutant general ordered Patton to Front Royal, Virginia, where he was to buy horses for the army, Pershing arranged to have these instructions changed. Patton would sail from New York on May 28 with the other members of the headquarters of this American Expeditionary Force.

Receiving the new orders while at Prides Crossing on May 18, Patton, accompanied by Bea, went at once to Washington. There, on Saturday the nineteenth, they were joined by Patton's parents and sister, who stayed until Patton left for Europe. As the days whisked by, Patton occupied himself with such tasks as getting uniforms—he had one made at Keen's and borrowed another from his old West Point rival, Captain Everett S. Hughes, who during their Mexican days became his friend. The big event of the stay in Washington was dinner with Secretary of the Interior Franklin K. Lane, a San Franciscan. George, Sr., beamed, Georgie remembered, when Lane said to him: "That boy of yours is all wool and a yard wide or I am no judge."

Amid "much tears" and a pouring rain, Patton bid farewell to his family early on the morning of the twenty-eighth. Late that afternoon he and the other 187 members of Pershing's party, who had come to New York by train, sailed out of Gravesend Bay, at the southern tip of Brooklyn, aboard the White Star liner HMS *Baltic,* bound for Liverpool. On board Patton drilled the enlisted men and gave French classes for the Americans. To his delight, he discovered that one sergeant was able to help, for he had taught French at the City College of New York. Pershing himself regularly attended these classes.

Pershing also had bigger things on his mind. After conferences with his staff and with the British officers on board, he concluded that defeating the Germans would take one million Americans. A second concern was the submarine menace. "Every one jokes about the U-Boats," Patton recorded in his diary on June 3, "but we would all like to see a convoy show up. Some are quite nervous and sleep in their clothes. The temperature of the sea which has been 52 F is now 60 which will be a comfort if we have to get in it."[5]

For Pershing, Patton, and the others, the submarine menace lessened considerably on June 6, when, waking up in the morning, they found a British destroyer on either side of the *Baltic.* Two days later, amid much hoopla, the ship pulled into Liverpool. At three-thirty that afternoon the special train carrying them reached London. While Pershing was busy receiving welcomes from all the British and American officials who could spare the time to meet him, Patton rounded up his men and, accompanied by Captain Collins of the Honorable Artillery Corps and Captain Richard B. Paddock of the American army, took them "by buss" to the Tower of London, where they were to be lodged. "When we got to the gate," Patton informed Bea, "the band met us and we marched under the middle gate & the Byward gate around the 'white tower' to the Waterloo Barracks where the men are to stay." The reception from the HAC men, lined up on both sides, and later from the British colonel at the officers' mess, "was most thrilling. That night we saw the ceremony of the 'Keys' a most interesting affair. . . . That evening we sat around and had a fine time with the officers they are a very good lot. Most of them have been wounded and are here resting up."

Patton spent much of the next day, Saturday the ninth, running official errands. In Pershing's name he called on the American ambassador, Walter Hines Page; on the Duke of Connaught; and at Buckingham Palace. That night Brigadier-General Lord Guy Brooke, the British liaison officer who had accompanied Patton throughout the day, took him to White's, "the oldest club in the world," for dinner and then to the theater.

Until June 13, when Pershing and his staff left London for Paris, the social activities continued. "Things here are very little affected by the war," Patton told Bea just before leaving, "and we would hardly know it was going on but for the many uniforms. Food is plentiful and good, though there is not much sugar. Quite a lot of busses and taxies are operated by women as well as the 'Lifts.' There are also some women porters."[6]

Landing in France, Patton saw his "first signs of war," several train-loads of British soldiers, wounded and looking very unhappy. During the train ride from the coast to Paris, he observed several British camps. "The discipline did not appear good." In Paris people who "threw flowers on us and raised Hell generally" thronged the streets from the station to the hotels. "I was in a machine with some majors and the girls kept calling to me 'vive le jeune.' "[7]

After getting settled at the Hotel Continental, Patton wandered about. He went over to the airport "to see the flying machines," four hundred of them that he believed approached "perfection." That night he returned to the theater at which he and Bea had "caught such colds" when they were last in Paris. "The show was much as usual so were the women but we got a box and kept out of their way. They are nothing however to London. There I was spoken to twenty times in two blocks."[8]

Patton filled his first letters to Bea with sharp observations. He was apartment hunting with Lieutenant André de Coppet, an interpreter whom he described as "a very nice chap," not at all like "my other prospective room mate," his friend from the Punitive Expedition, Captain William A. Reed, who spent his evenings "chasing girls, with success. . . . Things cost a lot here," he related to Bea "and I have spent lots of money as one has to entertain. Men at the front get leave of seven days every four months and as they usually expect to be killed on going back they spend as much money as they can." Patton was "just as safe here as you are at Avalon. It is hard to think that war is going on so near, about sixty miles."[9]

Although busy during his first days in France, Pershing too devoted time to personal matters. In New York before sailing to Europe, he had seen Nita, and one of his earliest letters from Paris was to her. "The papers at home have no doubt been filled up with accounts of our arrival," he wrote her on June 23,

> and it is hardly worth while for me to try to express to you the very sincere atttitude of the French people, but I will say that it is a very weepy sort of feeling when people run alongside your carriage and scream "Vive l'Amerique," with tears streaming down their cheeks. I do not know just how to describe the situation. It is, however, more or less touchy. The French are holding on like grim death and I expect them to continue to do so until we are able to take our place in the line. . . . I was pleased to have Beatrice say that you are such a brave girl and that you are cut out for the army. I always knew that though without her saying it.[10]

Hardly as busy as Pershing—"if a sergeant could not do all I have to do, I would bust him"—Patton had several desires at this time. The first was to assure the marriage of Nita, now thirty, and Pershing. Twice in two days Patton spoke to Pershing about the romance, finally concluding that with the pressures upon the commander it was wrong to press the matter now. As for Bea, Georgie hoped she would do everything she could to come to France. Pershing was against wives coming to Europe, so Bea should send "Nita's suitor" a "very sweet" and "juicy" letter saying she wished to visit Saumur and the French Cavalry School. Bea must be careful not to mention Georgie. Patton also reported that he had become friends with Colonel Billy Mitchell, the flyer. Mitchell had arranged for him to go up in a plane, and the two later had a long talk.[11]

Being a member of Pershing's staff did not guarantee success as an officer, as Patton soon found out. Almost daily he ran across interesting people. On July 13, for example, he met a young captain on the staff of General William L. Sibert, George C. Marshall. But his job, mainly taking care of and allotting automobiles, was, he confided to Bea, "a rotter. . . . The work is very confining. I am a sort of 'Pooh-Bah' and do everything no one else does." Sitting around much of the time, Patton kept in shape by fencing for an hour each morning. "I enjoy it hugely . . . and it is about the only thing I like doing much."[12]

Patton's most interesting episode that July occurred when, with Pershing and some other members of the staff, he visited the headquarters of Field Marshal Sir Douglas Haig, the British commander on the Western front. Patton "had a great trip" and at one point sat next to Haig, an enthusiastic supporter of Patton's ideas on cavalry charges and on using the point of the saber. Another time Patton walked around "for some time" with the hand of a British soldier on his shoulder. When he turned and saw its owner was General Hubert Gough, the distinguished leader of the British Fifth Army, he "nearly fainted." Getting his first taste of the World War on the trip, Patton twice saw German Fokkers drop bombs on the headquarters and the accompanying antiaircraft and machine-gun fire. In one town Patton heard the fifteen-inch shells propelled twenty-two miles by German guns. The shells made craters ten feet deep and twenty wide. Haig himself was unimpressed with the members of Pershing's staff. In his diary he noted the lone exception of Patton, whom he described as "a fire-eater who longed for the fray."[13]

But generally the summer of 1917 saw Patton as much concerned with Bea as with war. In letter after letter he schemed to get her to France. Even though Pershing was behind the recent order barring wives from coming overseas, Bea could do it if she used her political and social connections. "It is perfectly clear that you should not be here and be tied down to a nursing job," Patton advised his wife on July 16. "It is very hard work. I could not see you and there are too many now. You could find plenty to do in Paris or else where by your self."

For Bea's brother-in-law, Keith Merrill, whose wife, Bea's sister Katharine, was with him in London, where he worked for the State

Department, Georgie had only scorn. "I certainly can't give Keith much for his evident desire not to be killed. He is what the French call 'un embusqué' [a shirker] which is not a nice thing to be. Still use him for all he is worth with Mr. Carr."[14]

The next day Patton offered his wife some new plans. He had just talked with another member of Pershing's staff, Major Robert Bacon, who had served briefly as secretary of state under Theodore Roosevelt and had later been ambassador to France. Like Bea, Bacon's wife was trying to get to Paris. "He assured me that by the use of influence any thing can be gotten out of the State Dept. He also agrees with the other information I have had that you should not come as a nurse. . . . Of course," Patton reasoned, "if the head of some ambulance unit from Boston would bring you as a secretary with the agreement that you would be released on getting here it would be fine; you might agree to hire a substitute for your self on arrival in France. The only objection to this scheme is that you could not bring Baby B. If Pa gets a diplomatic job you could come either as his secretary or as his interpreter and he could leave you when he went home." But, Patton advised, Bea might not have to employ such a subterfuge. By using such family friends as Senators Henry Cabot Lodge of Massachusetts and James D. Phelan of California and Colonel House, "you can swing a regular passport and that is what you ought to try to do."[15]

Throughout the rest of the summer Bea and Patton fought not against the Germans but against the State Department's dictum, put in effect at Pershing's suggestion, that wives of soldiers be barred from coming to France. Clutching at anything, Patton reported on August 5 Kay and Keith Merrill's plan for getting Bea and the children to Spain, from which she could visit George in France. "If you come alone," he added, "from what Kay says you had best come by England as the other way is too messy." Three days later Patton sent along terrible news. The wife of Colonel William D. Connor had tried so persistently to come over, even getting a job with the YMCA in Paris, that the War Department had warned him that it "would recall him if he did it again. Of course they would not but it shows that they are foolish. . . . You remember her in Washington," George reported. "Her husband is an engineer and she is chiefly noted for having worn dinner dresses which would have permitted her to nurse a baby at any time with out unbuttoning any thing. . . . B. you don't know how terribly I feel at not having told you to come right after I did but at the time no one could have foreseen the present situation and it seemed much better to be sure of conditions here before telling you to come."[16]

Bea's efforts led to the same warning the Connors received. "Also heard that Mrs. Patton—wife of one of your aides—has been making every effort to join [her] husband," Pershing's mother-in-law, Mrs. Clara Warren, informed the general, "and that she had been told that if she insisted—that her husband would be sent home!!!"[17]

Bitterly Patton blamed it all on Pershing and Secretary of War Newton D. Baker. "I wish Sec. B. was in hell," he wrote Bea, "and his wife was not allowed to join him. . . . I have a sneaky suspicion that it is for fear Nita would come that all these laws were made. Though that is hardly just either as there is nothing against the sisters of officers. The only thing left to do is to get divorced so far as I can see so you had better go to Reno."[18]

II

On the first day of September 1917, Patton left with Colonel Fox Conner for Chaumont, on the Marne River 130 miles southeast of Paris, Pershing's new headquarters. "We got in at 4:30. Things were in great confusion. Hundreds of clearks rushing about and officers shouting for a place to stay. We could do nothing so let them yell." Located "on a high hill with rivers on each side and a pretty canal," Chaumont was twice as far as Paris from the battlefront and was, Patton assured Bea, "quite safe."

Through it all Georgie yearned for his beloved. "I dreamed that I had a letter from you saying you had sailed and I put it in my mouth to keep some one from seeing it and it got stuck in my teeth and choked me. I tried so hard to get it out that I woke up."[19]

If Patton longed for Bea, Pershing, busy as he was, missed Nita. "The country round about is perfectly lovely," he informed her on the tenth,

> as is the whole of France, to my notion—I love it all. The only sad part of it is that you cannot be here with me. There are many bridle paths and country roads for horseback riding and motoring.
>
> We have a very agreeable mess in rather a pretentious house in

town. . . . There are eight of us in the mess. With Collins, Patton
and Shallenberger, we have part of the same crowd that we had in
Mexico. Collins is now doing duty with the general staff and Shallenberger is provost marshal, while George commands the headquarters guard and drills clerks.[20]

Discontented with his role at headquarters, Patton considered himself "nothing but [a] hired flunky. I shall be glad to get back to the line
again and will try to do so in the spring. . . . These d——— French are
bothering us with a lot of fool details which have nothing to do with
any thing. I have a hard time keeping my patience."[21]

Almost from his first days at Chaumont, Patton felt the limitations of
his position. Petty and boring, it seemed to lead nowhere. In mid-
September six of his fellow staff members were promoted to major, lieutenant colonel, and colonel, but he remained a captain. His West Point
classmates in the Field Artillery were already majors. Looking about for
other things, he heard a lot of talk about something called "Tanks." He
advised Bea not to worry, for although the casualty rates in that new
branch were high, "it will be a long time yet before we have any."

By month's end, however, he propelled forth another idea. After the
leading British bayonet expert lectured to his men, Patton thought that
perhaps he could do better as a bayonet instructor than at anything else.
"The trouble is that there is no promotion in it and it is the same old
physical over the mental game I have been at so long."[22]

By October Patton was disgusted enough to transfer anywhere.
"There is very little news," he informed Bea on the second, "except that
I am darned sick of my job. . . . I would trade jobs with almost any one
for any thing." The next day Patton wrote a letter to Pershing outlining
his qualifications for command of the tank service.[23]

Amid Patton's unhappiness, Pershing seemed to have recovered from
the disaster that had struck him two years before. In October 1917 he
received another promotion. That same month newspapers throughout
the West repeated rumors of the famous general's impending marriage
to Anne Patton. A San Francisco paper described her as a "beautiful
blonde" and speculated on how the romance had blossomed, for Pershing had made few trips to Los Angeles.[24]

On Sunday, October 14, Anne took time out from war work—wrap-
ping bandages and the like—to write to Pershing her tenderest letter.

It is just at the hour of dusk, when all the world seems to bow its head in prayer. If you were only here we would go onto the porch and watch daylight fade, but because you are not, because you are so far away, I do not go alone, it would make me sad and the hurt of our parting would be too severe. It was a Sunday evening when we kissed good bye. So many weeks have gone since then. All kinds of things have happened. For you very wonderful things, experiences that have marked epochs in the worlds history. For me much lesser things some jolly some otherwise. But in it all our love has lain warm in our hearts. Just think if you had gone away before you asked if I loved you. Unspoken love is such a feeble thing a prey to so many doubts and fears. Our letters would have been one long list of things we could not say. Would our love have survived I wonder. I thank God, that he let you, my darling, come to California. That later he let us have those three unforgettable weeks. That the night before you sailed we could see each other and kissed each others tears away before we parted. God has been kind to us, therefore we must be patient now when the skies are overcast.

My precious, I do seem to be full of rather serious thoughts to-night do I not. I suppose it is the effect of Sunday and going to church. Still if one were not serious sometimes one would degener-ate into a buffoon, and lose some of the very sweetest moments of life. Sunday plays an important part with you and me. You left here on a Sunday too. Our day, and we could not have a better. John, I hate to stop. I feel near you now. I wonder if away over there you are thinking just a wee speck of me, right now. You should be asleep, maybe you are dreaming. Anyway I love you with my whole heart. God bless you.[25]

Pershing's answer, centering on a theme that caused him some irrita-tion, was pointed and passionless. "I had a nice letter from Beatrice the other day," Pershing informed Nita, "which I think is about the second one I have received since we left. Confidentially, I learn from Mrs. War-ren that Beatrice has made serious efforts to get over to France, but that the War Department has turned her down. She did not say anything about it in her letter and I hope you will not mention it to her. Army officers' wives over here would be a great nuisance," Pershing believed, "and I am glad I had the forethought to forestall it. The few who are here are talking their heads off, especially of things they know nothing about." He concluded with a pointed remark: "Women, as a rule, are a nuisance unless they are in their proper places—isn't that so?"[26]

On the day after Pershing wrote this letter, Bea addressed one to "John." "When I get to thinking of you as the greatest man in America," she flattered him from Thomasville, Georgia, where her family was spending the winter, "the fact that you are almost my Brother gets dim, and I become very modest; and then a lovely letter from you, like the one I have just received, tips the scale the other way and I remember only that you are my affectionate J.J.P. and that you have my little girls' picture on your desk." Because he was so close to the Pattons, Bea was "going to call you just John—not General any more."

Bea then got onto the subject at hand.

Of course I don't feel hard towards you about the order against army wives going to France. Naturally, I am sorry I didn't get over before the general order came out; but that was nobody's fault. And I wouldn't for the world do anything against your wishes in the matter. As you know, my sister is in London, and I planned to go there, when I found France was barred, so that I might be nearer Georgie and perhaps be able to see him in England on his regular leaves. Then I heard in a roundabout way that, if I went, it might hurt him, so I gave it up until I could find out for sure. I have not yet found out.

Christmas seems almost impossible this year, but I am trying to look on it as a milestone on the way to peace. I hope, however, that we shall not have peace until Germany is crushed and divided, and until our men have had a chance to fight, no matter what the personal sacrifice. This war is going to make a true America out of our old United States.[27]

In his letter to Nita, Pershing mentioned that he had just seen her brother, who had left the hospital after a two-week stay. Patton was "rather thin" and would be unable to "do any hard work for some time." On October 16 he had contracted jaundice and was, fittingly, "a fine cavalry yellow all over. It is not at all a painful disease," Patton wrote his father, "one just feels tired all the time and low in ones mind." In the hospital Patton had roomed with Fox Conner, who had been operated on for an intestinal disorder. Conner advised Patton that if he wished to advance in rank, he must leave Pershing. He recommended the infantry. But Patton's old troop commander, Colonel LeRoy Eltinge, now a member of the general staff, brought news that the Americans wanted to start a tank school at Langres, just south of Chaumont. He suggested Patton for the job.[28]

Undecided, Patton roamed in his mind from one branch to another. One day it was the infantry. The next the tanks. Then back to the infantry. Again to the tanks. The "sporting side of it," Patton told his father, was that there would be a hundred majors of infantry but only one of light tanks. If the armored vehicles did work and Patton ran the school and commanded the tanks, he might eventually be in charge of a brigade and be made a brigadier general. Also influencing Patton was his friend from Fort Sheridan days, Colonel Paul B. Malone, who now headed the training section in Europe. Responsible for setting up the tank school, Malone urged Patton to apply for the new post.[29]

Most of Patton's superiors at Pershing's headquarters joined Eltinge and Malone in advising Patton to head the tanks. These included Shallenberger, Colonel Hugh A. Drum, Colonel Frank McCoy, and Colonel Robert C. Davis. Against the move were Conner and General James G. Harbord, both of whom considered the infantry less of a gamble. Everyone agreed, however, that Patton possessed no future at headquarters and must get out.

In November Patton made his choice. "I will have a most interesting time learning this Tank game," Patton informed Bea on the tenth, "as I will go to a French School near Paris for two weeks and then to the [Renault] Factory in Paris for a week. . . . We will only have one tank till some time next summer so don't picture me dashing to battle in them there will be none in which to dash."[30]

At eleven on the morning of November 18, 1917, Patton left Pershing's headquarters at Chaumont to attend the French Light Tank Training Center for two weeks. Located in the Forest of Compiègne at Chamlieu, northeast of Paris, the school was near a chateau that Georgie and Bea had visited in 1913. Patton found the place very cold, but his two weeks there shaped much of the rest of his career. Assigned "a very nice room in a Temporary barracks" and given a French orderly, he went right to work. On the twentieth, the day after his arrival, he drove a Renault tank. "It is easy to do after an auto and quite comfortable though you can see nothing at all. . . . They go about as fast as one can run and turn like lightning. It is funny to hit small trees and see them go down. They are noisy but easy riding. They rear up like a horse or stand on their head with perfect immunity."[31]

During his first days at Chamlieu Patton especially enjoyed the mess, at which he ate with fourteen French officers. All were decorated heroes, and arguments raged over whose regiment was bravest. "Yes," a captain of the Fourth Zouaves said to Patton, "all are brave. At the Marne my regiment lost 1700 men out of 3000; many brave men are dead." Practically every French officer, differing sharply from the English, who depicted the Germans as cowards, praised the enemy army.[32]

The British success at the battle of Cambrai on November 20, 1917, the very day Patton first drove a tank, turned the world's attention to those mysterious, crawling creatures. On that day the British sent 378 Mark IV tanks, immune to German armor-piercing ammunition, against a six-mile stretch of the seemingly impenetrable Hindenburg Line, called by the Germans the Siegfried Line. By noon the odd-looking devices had advanced four miles, as deep as a previous infantry assault had penetrated in four months. But the British lost 179 tanks on the first day, sixty-five as a result of direct hits, seventy-one from mechanical failures, and forty-three for other reasons. After this initial success, however, Patton heard "lots of people" suddenly praise tanks. They "now express a desire to accept command of them," he informed Bea on November 26, "but fortunately I beat them to it by about four days." That afternoon he went to a maneuver where the tanks crawled about "in a sort of impersonal way among the ranks of the infantry," resembling, he supposed, the Martians in H. G. Wells's novel *War of the Worlds*.[33]

After being joined during his last week at Chamlieu by his assistant, Lieutenant Elgin Braine of the 6th Field Artillery, Patton finished his stay as a German counterattack reversed the gains made during the first day at Cambrai. Leaving Chamlieu on December 1 with Colonel Frank Parker, the American liaison to the French forces in the area, Patton stopped to see Major J. F. C. Fuller, the British theorist behind the attack at Cambrai and the chief of staff to Brigadier-General Hugh J. Elles, who led the assault there. Continuing through "destroyed villages and cut down orchards," Patton could see clearly "the flash of the guns and the trench rockets going up." Between Amies and Paris, he had "my usual yearly car accident." His machine slammed into a closed railroad gate. Patton's head smashed through the front window, cutting an artery on his left temple. The impact also cut a hole on the right side of his jaw. "It missed the carroted artery and jugular and facial nerve about an eighth of an inch," Patton reported to Bea. "If it had gotten them I would probably have cashed in but it did not bleed much."[34]

On December 3 Patton and Braine visited the Renault factory at Boulogne-Billancourt in Paris, where French light tanks were made. While there, they suggested four adjustments in the light tank, each of which the French eventually adopted. These included a self-starter, improvements in the fuel tank so as to prevent leaks if hit by enemy fire, an interchangeable mount that permitted the vehicle to carry either a 37-millimeter cannon or a machine gun, and finally a bulkhead that separated the crew's compartment from the engine so as to protect the crew in case of fire.[35]

By today's standards the Renault was a pygmy. So, too, was Patton's Tank Corps. Weighing six and a half tons, the Renault possessed a crew of two, the gunner (a sergeant) and the driver (a corporal). As for the corps, a platoon eventually consisted of five tanks, three possessing a 37-millimeter cannon and two a French-designed Hotchkiss machine gun, each on a revolving turret mounted on top of the forward part of the chassis. A second lieutenant, who acted as gunner in one of the five tanks, commanded each platoon, three of which, in turn, constituted a company. The company commander, a captain, ran his own tank. Each company also included a signal tank and seven reserve tanks, making twenty-four tanks in all. Capable of traveling six miles an hour, the Renault was, according to Patton's associate, Captain Sereno E. Brett, "exceedingly adaptable and crosses the ordinary Infantry trench without difficulty." Fuller, on the other hand, dismissed the Renaults as "nothing more than cleverly made mountings for machine guns."[36]

Seeing in tanks "the chance I have always been looking for," Patton spent the fifth to the twelfth of December at Chaumont working on his report on light tanks. When finished it consisted of four sections and covered fifty-eight pages. In the first segment Patton delved into the mechanics of the Renault, describing its tracks, its weapons, its engine. Undoubtedly with the aide of Braine, an engineer, he devoted a large portion of this section to specifications and mathematics, ending with a list of changes that would improve the tank's performance. The second segment embodied Patton's ideas about the makeup of tank battalions. In it he described problems of organization, of repairs, and of equipment. Next came Patton's favorite subject, the history of tanks and the lessons to be learned from the British and French experience with these machines. In these pages Patton saw the light tank as the ally of the infantry. Its function was to shatter the enemy's initial position. The tank would then "assume the role of pursuit cavalry and 'ride the enemy to death.'" He then pointed to what analysts later believed to be the reason for the failure to hold ground at Cambrai. Disregarding the advice of Fuller to hold back at least two of the nine tank battalions, the high command kept in reserve only fifty-four of the 378 tanks, thereby enabling the Germans to catch their breath. Finally Patton talked about the training of personnel. He recommended the creation of separate schools for those operating light and heavy tanks. Men recruited for these schools should have experience driving automobiles or riding motorcycles. If possible, they should possess appropriate mechanical skills. He proposed a four-week training program, with graduates of the first class instructing the class that followed. By the end of two months these two classes could train four more, thus providing six companies or two battalions of tankers within three months.[37]

On the day that Patton finished his report he learned that the irascible, quarrelsome, but admirable Colonel Samuel D. Rockenbach, "who was at Riley in the Field Officer Class of 1913," was to be chief of tanks. Unlike some of his successors, infantrymen who believed the sole function of the tank should be to help the foot soldier, Rockenbach proved to be, in the words of Brigadier General Bradford G. Chynoweth, "wholly devoted to tanks." Patton was to remain "chief of the light ones." Three days later, about to leave Chaumont for Langres, Patton recorded his thoughts: "This is last day as staff officer. Now I rise or fall on my own. 'God judge the right.'"[38]

III

From his first glimpses of Langres and Chamlieu, Patton felt an unusual attachment to each. "It is a very pretty town," he informed Bea when visiting Langres, twenty-two miles south of Chaumont, in mid-

November. The Roman emperor Marcus Aurelius had founded it, "and there is still a roman gate in the wall. It . . . has draw bridges that work. The streets are very narrow but clean."[39]

The stay at Langres profoundly affected Patton. It gave him his first practical experience with tanks. Almost as important, his reflections there helped him tie together some loose strands of his childhood and of his later life. At Langres, without men for weeks and tanks for months, hemmed into the house he lived in by heavy snows and cold, Patton began to reinforce his belief that he had lived previously.[40]

To his family Patton later described his first experience with reincarnation, but the incident itself raises questions. As a small boy in California he was playing war with his five first cousins, the Browns, the children of his father's sister. Seating them in a wagon, he instructed them to use barrelheads as shields and told them to hurl sticks, the equivalent of arrows, at the enemy. He then shoved the wagon down a hill and into a turkey shed at the bottom, mangling some of the birds. Asked where he got the idea for the maneuver, young George explained that during the Middle Ages, John the Blind of Bohemia had defeated the Turks—signified by the turkeys—with such a vehicle, called by Patton the first modern armored vehicle. John the Blind was led into battle, Patton related, by his squire, who complained that they would both be killed. "That is my duty and that is your privilege," John answered. Indeed, both died in the battle, but the Bohemians won. Patton knew of the incident because, he said, "I was there."[41]

In 1990 when Colonel Roger Nye, the accomplished former head of the West Point history department and close friend of the Patton family, investigated the details, he found several inaccuracies in the story. "Following your lead, I put one of my best sleuths on John-the-Blind," he wrote Patton's daughter, Ruth Ellen Patton Totten. The detective, General Sumner Willard, who taught foreign languages at West Point, "reported back that our John was born in 1296 and died at the battle of Crècy in 1346 as the 'Blind King of Bohemia,' fighting on the side of the French because of the intertwining of royal families (he was also John of Luxemburg)." Possibly, Nye speculated, Patton picked up the story of the squire and his "privilege" of dying from reading about Crècy, where English longbowmen defeated a huge French force. "Since the Turks were not into Europe that early," Nye, then working on his book *The Patton Mind,* continued, "John probably used the wagons against the Lithuanians. So I dropped the Turks from my text, but kept the turkeys and wagons, and transferred the squire to Crècy. I suggest we go with that story, which should keep the deconstructionist historians at bay."[42]

Yet Colonel Nye's book, and subsequent books on Patton, repeat the tale as Ruth Ellen told it. John the Blind won a great victory over the Turks, symbolized by the turkeys. The place was Bohemia. General Patton insisted he was there.[43]

Surrounded by Roman ruins, Patton, who probably had read *Caesar's Commentaries* by this time, for he owned an 1852 edition of the work,[44] saw himself as a Roman soldier returned to life. At Langres he told Captain Harry H. Semmes of two incidents that seemed to prove it. When coming to Langres, Patton followed all kinds of intricate train directions before being met by a soldier driving a staff car. Approaching the top of a hill, Patton leaned forward and asked if the camp was over the hill and to the right. "No, sir," the driver answered, "our camp where we are going is further ahead, but there is an old Roman camp over there to the right. I have seen it myself."

After reporting to headquarters, Patton was about to leave when he said to an officer: "Your theater is over here straight ahead, isn't it?" "We have no theater here," the officer replied, "but I do know that there is an old Roman theater only about three hundred yards away."[45] These incidents convinced Patton that he had lived in Roman days.

Approaching the time when he would be in battle, Patton used reincarnation as a device for controlling fear. Years before his father had told him about Valhalla, the home of the immortals who died in battle. Valhalla symbolized "death but not oblivion," for it remained the resting place of the seemingly defeated who returned to fight again.[46]

The lesson was among the most important George Patton, Sr., transmitted to his son. In June 1905, after Georgie tripped over a hurdle and finished last instead of a sure second in a race, the father wrote:

Your letter of the 3rd came to-day and I can't tell you how my soul sympathized with you in your defeat in the hurdle race— but it was only because I knew how much you had set your heart on success. It is a good thing to be ambitious and to strive mightily to win in every contest in which you engage; but you

must school yourself to meet defeat and failure without bitterness—and to take your comfort in having striven worthily and
done your best.

The elder Patton then discussed the "sort of glory that crowns
defeat." In Norse mythology the Valkyries rode over the battlefield and
"chose those who were acknowledged worthy of death—& entrance
into Valhalla." There these "chosen" prepared for their next life and
their next battle for the god Odin.[47] For a soldier no philosophy could
be more comforting, for death in battle constituted a step in the unending process of reincarnation.

Forever influenced by his father's words, Patton dwelt on conquering
fear in his poem "The Attack," composed in Mexico in September 1916.
Attempting to show that fear was natural in a soldier, he explained that
pride and tradition overcame it.

> *It is not courage holds him,*
> *But fear in its mightiest form*
> *Born of a race of soldiers,*
> *He dares not face their scorn.*
>
> *His eyes can see Valhalla,*
> *Where, staring from the skies,*
> *The men who fought for England*
> *Watch how their offspring dies.*[48]

Inspired by the Roman ruins about him, Patton gave further form to
such thoughts on November 23, 1917. At Chamlieu he saw what the
French called the *char d'assaut,* the chariot of assault, in a setting punctuated by Roman walls and a Roman theater. The result was his poem
"A Dream," suggesting that in a previous life the driver of the modern
armored vehicle had guided a Roman chariot.

> *We sat in the throbbing Char d'Assaut*
> *My Gallic friend and I,*
> *In the shade of a Roman theater,*
> *Which lives, though ages die.*

And as we waited in the rear
For the hour of "H" to come
The scales were lifted and I knew
That the ruined walls were home.

Instead of the men in muddied blue,
A brass clad host stood there.
The plumed crests rose where the marmites {big shells} burst,
And the eagles of Rome shone clear.

I looked at the Frenchman by my side,
And a skin clad Gaul I saw;
The gasping motor ceased to throb,
For the war was Roman war.

The foe no longer lurked below,
His hosts rushed over the plain,
But the cry that rose as the legions closed,
Was the guttural Boche {Germans} again.[49]

With utmost sophistication and brilliance Patton thus came upon a way of conquering fear in battle.

IV

Hampered by the heavy snows—by the end of the month a foot covered the ground—Patton and Braine accomplished but one thing during the last ten days of 1917. They selected for the tank training an area called the Bois d'Amour, the Wood of Love. They chose it because it was near two good roads—one an old Roman road—and a railroad. The spot picked was a piece of rising ground crowned by woods. Patton hoped to build there temporary barracks "and get going to some extent at least by the end of the month."[50]

In early January 1918, as part of a tour to introduce Rockenbach, a cavalryman who had been detailed to the Quartermaster Corps, to tanks, Patton accompanied him to Bernecourt, where they spoke to the officers who engineered the Cambrai assault. General Hugh J. Elles, "a very fine looking man," was, Patton told Bea, "not much older than I am." A "real major," he was a "temporary Brigadier." As tough as a soldier could be, Elles insisted on leading the attack, even though Fuller argued against it. Just as brave was Elles's aide, Captain I. M. Stewart, who "looked like a inocent girl" but turned out to be "quite a man." He described how, during one battle, a German knocked him down with a grenade. Another then threw a second grenade on top of him. As a result, his nose was split in two, his jaw and both legs were broken, and he had a hole in his head. "Dirty beggars put me in the Hospital a year," he lamented to Patton. In the midst of the Battle of Cambrai he and Elles had walked about, looking over the German lines, completely oblivious to enemy fire.[51]

Meantime, Bea exhibited a different kind of valor. She and the girls were spending the winter with her parents at Thomasville, Georgia, when, early in 1918, she received a telegram from her brother-in-law reading: "George killed in action. Deepest sympathy." Stunned, Bea handed the telegram to her mother, who told her: "Do you suppose you are married to the only George S. Patton in the U.S. Army?" Mrs. Ayer advised Bea to call the Boston paper and get a list of the recent casualties from Massachusetts. The call went from Atlanta to Louisville and then to a half dozen other cities before reaching Boston. Late that night the telephone rang, and a voice said: "This is Atlanta speaking. I have a message for you, relayed from the Boston Transcript. There are seven George S. Patton Jrs. commissioned in the U.S. Army and fighting overseas. The one killed in action was in the Medical Corps."[52]

Back in Langres in mid-January, Patton lost patience with the French. On the eighth and ninth two doughboys and twenty-one second lieutenants, transferred from the Coast Artillery, reported to the Tank Corps. The French, however, refused to give Patton the land he needed for his center. "You would think they were doing us a great favor to let us fight in their d—— country." He was, he assured Bea, safer in a tank than in the infantry. Since the enemy had no idea which tank held "the Chief," he was in no more danger than anyone else. Patton also transmitted some personal news. "Kate Fowlers husband is around here some where and I believe that she has just had a son. All the world is getting married or doing some thing foolish."[53] This son, Van S. Merle-Smith, Jr., would one day serve as Patton's aide.

At the end of January, with no tanks and only two doughboys, Patton was disgusted. Braine was off for the United States, where he was to supervise the construction of tanks, but Rockenbach, "the most contrary old cuss I ever worked with," was giving Patton trouble. Though thoroughly committed to tanks, Rockenbach opposed anything anyone suggested, but after a vigorous argument he came around and proposed the original idea as his own. "It is good discipline however for me," Patton told his wife, "for I have to keep my temper. At the end of each argument I feel completely done up. I guess he does too. Still he is trying to have me made a lieutenant colonel so I ought not to be too hard on him."[54]

During the first week in February, Rockenbach sent Patton to Paris in the hope of persuading the French to give the Americans a few tanks. Patton was able to extract from French officials a promise that he would get some armored vehicles by mid-March.

Since American officers were forbidden to go to Paris except on business, Patton and Pershing's aide, Colonel James L. Collins, took advantage of their visit to see what Georgie called "A Review." He described it to Bea.

One of the things was a statue of a naked woman of "Parts," one of which was covered with a huge fig leaf bright green. The leading woman took a pointer and described the statue. Finally she got to the fig leaf and said, "This is a historic spot on the Western front. There is a long hill called the Chemin de Dame [Path of the Woman]. Here we have a short valley named the Chemin des Hommes [Path of the Man]." This was a great joke. The last thing was a Tableau called "Chaste nudity" a lot of girls were behind a black curtain with their heads sticking through holes at a signal all of them thrust their breasts through other holes. When every one was getting ready to be shocked they let the apparent breasts fall and they turned out to be paper forms. This was an even greater joke.[55]

For much of mid-February Patton occupied himself with odd jobs. On the tenth he hurried over to Pershing's headquarters to console his friend from the Punitive Expedition, Bill Reed, who was being cashiered off the general staff because of drunkenness. "We feared he might kill himself he had not slept a wink for five days so I gave him some nock out drops which I got from the surgeon and put him to sleep. He certainly is a fool." A better piece of news involved Stimson, now a lieutenant colonel. In Langres to attend the American Staff College, he had moved into Patton's house and joined the mess attended by Patton and his friend from West Point and Sheridan days, Major Stanley Rumbough.[56]

Finally, in mid-February, things began to take shape, both for Patton and for the Tank Corps. On February 16 Patton bumped into a West Point classmate who conveyed the welcome news that on December 15 Patton had been promoted to major. Although he heard nothing official, Patton immediately pinned on the gold maple leaves appropriate to the rank. The next day 195 volunteers arrived and formed the first two companies of the 1st Battalion of the Tank Corps. Patton found these first recruits, all draftees, to be "really a very fine bunch of men much above ordinary." The sergeant major, Fred Murphy, was part owner of the Mark Cross utensil stores and a graduate of Yale. Twenty others were graduates of noted colleges, and about forty owned their own cars, several of them Pierce-Arrows.[57]

These first recruits trained every day but Sunday, which was reserved for inspections. They engaged in signaling, tank foot drill, machine gunnery, and pistol practice. Using the only vehicle available, a broken-down Atlas truck, two of Patton's lieutenants taught the recruits about gas motors. "To hell with difficulties!" Patton later said of the recruits. "It was their job to learn."[58]

Patton's skill with tanks and engines surprised even Bea. "I think I am more or less of a mechanical genius," he joked, "for I simply know by looking at an engine all about it." After the first few days of training, he was more convinced than ever "that we can not punch a hole without tanks. There are too many instruments of death in the way, but I believe that tanks well worked up will do the job. I hope the war lasts long enough for us to try our hand. The tanks have attracted a lot of good men and I get requests from them to transfer nearly daily."[59]

Though Patton temporarily lived at Langres, his men and officers moved on the twenty-second to Bourg, five miles to the southeast. In sole command for the first time in his career, Patton found himself "the absolute boss." He set himself to cleaning up Bourg, which, unlike Langres, was a town of "manure and smells." Here also Patton developed at least one of the rules of discipline for which he became noted during the Second World War. "I make the chauffeurs wash their machines after the last trip each night no matter what the hour," he told Bea. "This I got from the English." Twenty-five years later clean vehicles would be one of the distinguishing characteristics of his Third Army. And, copying something for which he admired Pershing in Mexico, he ordered all officers to shave daily, even though, he conceded, "they all did anyway."[60]

In early March, when Patton spent two days accompanying Pershing on an inspection tour, two topics dominated the conversation: war and Nita. On the trip Patton saw the French premier, Georges Clemenceau, whom he described as "quite an active little chap and nice to meet." Strangely, Nita presented a more pressing problem than war. Amid reports in papers like the *New York Times* that Pershing and Nita would soon marry, Pershing acted less than gallant. His answer to Nita's passionate letter of the previous October was to suggest to Patton that she might benefit from spending six months with Bea, learning about domesticity and motherhood, a suggestion both women considered condescending. "J. was most contrite over Nita," Patton reported after speaking to him; "neither of us imagined that she would be hurt and we are both sorry. There are no doubts that he feels the same as ever only more so and he said he wished they had married. Of course don't tell him I said so."[61]

After spending a week in England with Rockenbach arranging tanks matters, Patton returned to France "pretty tired and dirty." He was also disgusted. "We have a stupendous job and little time and none of the officers are worth a damn. I have to instruct all of them in every thing under heaven except infantry drill and I have to check them up at that." He was hoping that his friend from Mexico days, Captain Joseph W. Viner, a Virginian, would soon be assigned to him, "and that will be a help."[62]

As for Nita, he pleaded that he meant well, but without Bea's guidance he was "apt to make mistakes of judgment. All of which shows that I did a good thing by marrying you even if I don't treat you with 'respect' as you say or rather infer I don't in one of your letters. In which you say that a girl needs respect before she is married even if she fails to get it afterwards. Well I am sorry I have treated you that way for you are one of the few people man or woman for whom I have any." When

Bea read this letter, she marked across the top: "Nonsense! I didn't mean it that way at all."[63]

Patton's talks to his men resembled Knute Rockne's to the Notre Dame football team. In a "Lecture on Discipline," delivered to the members of the 304th Brigade of the Tank Corps on March 18, he spoke of the days "When I used to play football," not mentioning that at West Point he never appeared in a varsity game. A soldier must instinctively follow an officer's orders. "We are the quarterbacks who give the signal," he explained, "you are at attention, on your toes, waiting for the orders for the ball to be snapped." Only at the end did Patton contrast the importance of football and combat: "The prize for a game is nothing. The prize for war is the greatest of all prizes—Freedom." Even though he was not to be promoted again for three weeks, Patton signed his address: "Lt. Col. Tank Corps."[64]

Four days later, on March 22, Patton got tragic news. On the fourteenth Bea's father, Frederick Ayer, had died at the age of ninety-five. "Our commander has gone," Ellen Banning Ayer telegraphed Patton, "his love for you shown in every word and deed." Writing to "My darling Little Beatrice," Patton knew "what the death of your father must mean to you," but Bea should "take great very great comfort" in her "beautiful and unselfish love for him." Bea hardly held a higher opinion of her father than did her husband. In November 1917, "Somewhere in France," Patton had written a poem titled "F. A." and dedicated to "the finest gentleman I ever knew." It concluded:

> *For greatness shines about him as does light;*
> *And all who see him know that in his face,*
> *They see a force of perfect love and might.*[65]

Oblivious to Frederick Ayer's role in creating the horrible slums of Lawrence, his descendants would forever point to his statement: "I have never earned a dollar of which I was ashamed."[66]

Patton hardly had time for grieving when, on March 23, 1918, he received word from two of his subordinates, Lieutenant Baker and Sergeant Murphy, that they were returning that day with ten Renault tanks. To maintain secrecy the tanks arrived at night by railroad. Up to that time only Patton had seen one of the machines. But by nine on "a beautiful moonlight night . . . ideal for the purpose," his men were at the railroad siding with gas and water. They built an unloading ramp and gassed and watered the monsters. The soldiers were so ignorant that by mistake one poured a bucket of gas into a radiator. Patton drove all the tanks down the ramp and lined them up. In the dark the nine most experienced Atlas drivers were shown the gearshift. The tanks were cranked up and off the procession started for the Bois, a mile away. By 12:30 A.M. on March 24, 1918, the last tank was safely hidden in the bushes. Patton later called this "The Spirit of the Tank Corps." "They certainly are saucy looking little fellows," Patton wrote Bea of the tanks the following day, "and very active just like insects from under a wooden log in the forest. . . . I took one through some heavy woods this morning and it just ate up the brush like nothing."[67]

Finally possessing tanks, Patton was able to train his men properly. Lieutenant Julian K. Morrison later described what it was like.

> Looking back now over the months spent in training at the old Tank School at Bourg, France, the writer can recall many pleasant ones interspersed with long days of tedious study. It's a working organization, this Tank Corps, and were it not for the indominable spirit of its members and the ability not only to make the best of things, but to find pleasure in their work there might have been a number of A.W.O.L.'s not only among the enlisted men but of officers as well. Every day, some Sundays excepted, a fixed schedule was carried out from daylight to dark and then for the officers school at night. The writer always got a great deal of encouragement from these lectures, usually given by Colonel Patton. He was made to understand by the Colonel that a tank officer was meant to die. His favorite message to his officers was "Go forward, go forward. If your tank breaks down go forward with the Infantry. There will be no excuse for your failure in this, and if I find any tank officer behind the Infantry I will ——." All tank officers know the rest.

Patton was so fierce that those at Bourg labeled the corps the "Suicide Club."[68]

Patton even devised a "test of suitability" for his officers. Lieutenant Newell P. Weed, who transferred to the Tank Corps with Semmes, described it as "an examination on gas engines and with the help of a small book on engines, issued by some oil company, we passed on the test, neither knowing a magneto from a carburetor." Calling "a Tank Corps without tanks quite as exciting as a dance without girls," Weed saw a welcome change once the vehicles began arriving. "Augmented by others, great fleets of tanks were tearing up wheat fields and forests to the delight of the French."[69]

By the first week of April several other noteworthy things happened. First, enough men arrived for Patton to form a third company. And Patton visited Pershing. When he entered Pershing's house, General James G. Harbord, the chief of staff, called out: "Hello, Colonel." Patton, who just a week before had been notified that he had been promoted to major, was now a lieutenant colonel. "I feel more or less like a fool being a colonel," Patton observed, for he had just pinned on his major's leaves.

Even more important was Patton's growing attachment to the new machines. "This morning," he told Bea, "I was under a Tank looking at its bottom and about a pint of fine black oil got in my face. What I don't know about a tank is 'torn out' as Maj. Tate would say."[70]

Then, on April 3, a second tragedy struck the Ayer family. Just twenty days after losing her husband, Ellen Banning Ayer died. "Beaty you have a dreadful time," Patton consoled his grieving wife,

> and I was not there to help you. Not that I could have done much good but I could have tried. I have always known you would lose your parents and I had always fancied that I would be there to help but it could not be. What has happened has quite reconciled me to your not having come to France. You would have felt so terribly to have been away.
>
> It seems a heartless thing to say but I think that Ellen is happier than she would have been to have continued on with out your father. They were as nearly one as is possible to be—as nearly one as we are.[71]

In mid-April Patton renewed his correspondence with Kate Fowler, whose husband, a captain, was now in France with the 42nd Infantry, the famed Rainbow Division. "There is I know," he explained to Kate,

> a general idea that tanks are dangerous but the fact of my being in them disproves that to anyone who knows me. They really are fine

and very interesting and with luck one might be able to get quite close to the Bosch. I have always thought I should prefer to see the man who gets me. And my brief experience in Mexico, when I had to kill Col. Cardenas and his friend increased the notion. For once I was shot at a long way off and it was unpleasant, but when I was only twenty feet from Cardenas, I was too frightened to notice it.

Patton "heartily" endorsed Kate's "views on the ordnance and the non-flying aviators and such trash. May God cause them to die in misery and poverty."[72]

During the second half of April Patton supervised a series of combat exercises to introduce tank warfare both to his men and to high-ranking officers. On the twenty-second, during a demonstration in heavy rain for the officers of the Army General Staff College in Langres, one tank got stuck in a shell hole, but this proved to be the only mishap during an otherwise flawless performance. Six days later, having sufficient troops, Patton organized the 1st Light Battalion, which he commanded. A captain led each of the three companies, Company A being commanded by Patton's trusted friend Viner.

As for the troops, Patton enforced at Bourg the discipline for which he became noted. "Why you God damned sons of bitches," he screamed at one group of men, "do you think the Marines are tough? Well you just wait until I get through with you. Being tough will save lives." The young colonel was especially strict about salutes, a perfect one becoming known at Bourg as a George Patton.[73]

V

Training troops and designing equipment was not fighting. Yearning for battle, Patton expressed his displeasure to Bea on May 7. Just about a year before he was in Mexico, but as one of his officers said: "We are just beginning to think about getting ready to start fighting." At times he felt he had done his job. At other times he feared he was "lazy. It is hard to say. I guess the point of view depends on the food and the weather as much as on any thing else."[74]

On May 21 Patton got part of his wish. Accompanying some French tanks, he left for a two-week tour of the front. "I'm hoping that the

Bosch will start something," he told his father before his departure, "but the prospects are not good and besides I have too much rank to see any thing as the French colonels do not go in with their tanks as ours do. Still there is a great deal of gas in that sector and they may get me."[75]

Preparing for the worst, Patton told Viner where to send his uniforms and other things should "they get me." He also gave Viner a neatly typed paper. "I remember that day in France," Viner said years later. "The Germans had driven us back and things looked bad. Patton told me it looked like we might not both get out and wanted to give me a will." He asked Viner to give his mare to Pershing, his military saddle to Shallenberger, and his other saddles to Tate and Rockenbach. Viner would get Patton's polo pony "and the flat saddle that fits him." He was to send Patton's sword to Bea and was to burn an envelope full of papers left on the top of Patton's trunk.[76]

Having dropped off this gloomy missive, Patton and five of his officers left for the front. By May 25 he was "in the funniest village," just six miles from the battle zone. "At night the sky is quite bright where the guns are," he reported to Bea. "It is funny every once in a while you can hear a machine gun above all the other noise for though it is much less loud it has a more penetrating voice."[77]

On the next day Patton complained that he "nearly died of nothing to do since I have been here." Unlike the British, who believed all Americans to be "d—— fools," the French were friendly, but they were reluctant to give out information. By accident Patton had met the major who commanded the French tanks at Moulin-la-Faux, and he hoped "to get some valuable information but it may turn out to be a joy ride and nothing more. . . . A Company of French niggers came yesterday they are full of lice and religion and are all at church now."[78]

For the next several days Patton and the French major, La Fevre, toured battle sites and mapped out battle formations. On May 30 the two walked to within two hundred yards of the German lines. At one point La Fevre, showing his contempt for the Germans, who he was sure were watching them, stopped to fix his leggings, "exposing his bottom" to enemy sharpshooters. Not to be outdone, Patton, curious as to why the Germans did not fire at a major and a colonel who were visible to them, took off his helmet and lit a cigarette.

Speaking with La Fevre and a French colonel who lived thirty feet

underground because of enemy artillery fire, Patton heard for the first
time an argument that would be reprised by advocates of tanks during
the Second World War. Both French officers longed for the return of
1914, the war of mobility, when armies tried to outmaneuver and out-
fox one another. They spoke with disgust of wars with bogged-down
armies in trenches, with constant artillery bombardments, and with
generals willing to sacrifice a hundred thousand lives in frontal attacks
that gained a few miles of territory.[79] In 1944, shortly before the Normandy invasion, the British tank advocate Captain Basil H. Liddell
Hart and Major General John S. Wood, the most skillful American tank
commander in Europe, would discuss with horror the views of Field
Marshal Sir Alan Brooke, the chief of the Imperial General Staff, that
tanks were useless and that the Allies must return to "1918 methods."

Back in Bourg in early June, Patton reorganized his tank units. Creating a second battalion, now called the 327th, he placed Viner, who, he
told Bea, "did well while I was gone so that every thing is in fine shape,"
in charge of the first, renumbered the 326th, and Captain Sereno E.
Brett in charge of the second. Viner also became the chief instructor at
the tank school, which was expanded to a nine-week program. The last
week consisted of "battle practice," during which the students lived and
operated their tanks "under battle conditions."

The tactics worked out by Patton and his officers were simple
enough. Heavy tanks would lead the assault, with each platoon and
each tank being assigned a specific objective. Light tanks would follow
about a hundred meters behind the heavy tanks, and lines of infantry
would come next. After the experience at Cambrai, Patton made sure a
sufficient number of light tanks would be held in reserve to exploit a
breakout and to brace against counterattacks.

Patton stressed that, "like a polo team," tanks must always retain
their formation. Tanks scattered about were useless. "It must be so
indelibly stamped on your brain that gassed and scared and tired and
wounded as you will be it never for one instant escapes you. Your last
conscientious effort must be to regain your formation and push on and
ever on until there are no more Huns before you and the smiling vine-
yards of the Rhine [are] open to your eyes."[80]

With Viner taking over so many of the responsibilities at the tank
school, Patton found time to enage in his usual shenanigans. Viner, who
testified that "Patton didn't cuss that much in my presence," remem-

bered when the brilliant but impulsive colonel used a tank to hunt boars, cutting a path through a forest and enraging French officials. The French blamed Viner, the commander of the tank school, for the damage, but Patton came forward and took responsibility. On another occasion Viner and Patton were supposed to escort a French official who was so heavy that he could not fit into their two-door Packard. Patton received permission to borrow Pershing's car, which had rear doors. "I remember Patton and I riding all over France driving Pershing's car," Viner remarked.

In yet another episode Viner and Patton faced the job of fixing cracks in several onyx fireplaces they had damaged in a château in Bourg. "I suggested to Patton that we call in a dentist to fill the cracks," Viner related, "and Patton laughed. That's what we did, and the fireplaces were as good as new." Late in 1945 Patton told Viner he intended to return to Bourg to see how the fireplaces had stood up, but he never made it back there.[81]

VI

On June 12 Patton told Bea about one piece of good luck. Along with Viner and a couple of others, he was to attend the next class, beginning on the seventeenth, at the Army General Staff College in Langres. "I will be glad when the staff school starts on Sunday," he confided to her the next day, "as I have not got enough to do right now and am in consequence a great bore to my self as well as to others." Meantime, "our tanks" continued to amaze Patton. They were "awful and wonderful to behold close up," and after "a camouflage man" painted them they could not be seen from a distance. "It is very funny how the bright crazy colors blend with the most ordinary colors." One day, after Patton placed one under a net, he told some officers that a tank was within a hundred yards of them. They thought he was joking, for "they could not see it at all." Even in night maneuvers, the tank churned "through thick woods and gullies." It recognized neither light nor dark.[82]

On June 19 this third course at the Army College began. Supervised by Brigadier General Harry A. Smith, the school sought to train staff officers as rapidly as possible. Among the instructors were Patton's friend Major Adna R. Chaffee and Lieutenant Colonel George C. Mar-

shall, later the army chief of staff. Patton's class included Major Harold
R. Bull, who would serve as Dwight D. Eisenhower's operations officer
in Europe in 1944 and 1945; Major William H. Simpson, who later led
the Ninth Army in France and Germany; Captain Joseph Stilwell, who
commanded in China and Burma; and Wood, whose 4th Armored Division
engineered the breakout from the hedgerows in late July 1944.[83]

Like most others, Patton found the course taxing. On the first day he
worked at his desk from 8 A.M. to 4:40 P.M. At the end of the day several
officers, although talented, "said they had not gotten a thing on
paper."

Even while attending the course, Patton paid attention to his tanks.
During one maneuver a tank crew tried unsuccessfully to get over a
hole thirty feet wide and ten feet deep. Showing the machine's versatility,
another tank crew came along and pulled the first one out "in a
minute." Borrowing an idea from the English and the French, Patton
had one company of tankers drill each night from 8 P.M. to midnight.
"It is remarkable," he informed Bea, "how soon they improve with a little
night work."[84]

Still, Patton yearned for battle. He had, he lamented to Bea, "no
medals or decorations. A friend of mine got five one day last week and
also two wounds and gas still he is getting well and will be some person
later on." Patton was too young to become a general in this war, and in
the next he would be too old. "Still one can never tell and having a
young and charming wife may keep me from aging too fast."[85]

Amid his tank duties and attending classes, Patton gave several lectures
on tanks to officers at the Staff College. "I have undoubtedly
inherited Pa's 'gift of gab,' " he rejoiced to Bea after one successful talk.
"All war is simple," he concluded after devising a new maneuver for
tanks, "and we all err by allowing its complexities to divert our minds
from the few basic truths which fill it. As Gen R[ockenbach] would say
'we are all poor weak mortals after all.' "[86]

During the fighting in the midsummer of 1918, Patton's innovations
proved far-reaching. Three months before, when he had submitted a
memorandum on tanks to Colonel Eltinge, "even he thought I was
crazy." Now everyone was using his suggestions. He had advocated
night raids by small units of tanks, and three weeks later the British
successfully "pulled one." Patton had also recommended that "the sec-

ond line" of tanks be half the size of the first, instead of the other way around, as some tankers had done in battle. The British had seconded this notion, too. "I advocated using cavalry & tanks in raids. People said I was clearly crazy. In the present battle the British are doing just that." Finally, Patton thought tanks should replace the creeping artillery barrage. Guns should be used only for "counter battery. Today we had a lecture by a British artillery general advocating my idea in toto. Hence," Patton joked to Bea, "I have a swelled head for which I ask no pardon. But I still love you more everyday."[87]

What Patton yearned for came on August 20. He had just received word, he informed his father, that, preliminary to engaging his tanks in battle, he was "to go some where for some time. Of course," he added, "there is always danger of remaining longer than one wishes on such trips perhaps for ever."[88]

Again placing Viner in charge of the center, Patton, Rockenbach, and Lieutenant Maurice K. Knowles left for the headquarters of the First Army, commanded by Pershing. That day Patton learned of preparations for an attack against the Saint-Mihiel salient, a bulge twenty-five miles wide and fifteen miles deep in the Allied line that left exposed Verdun to the west and Nancy to the east. The plan called for using tanks in the assault. To ascertain whether the ground, which the French considered marshy, was suitable for the new machines, Patton and Knowles joined a patrol into no-man's-land, the interval between the French and German trenches.

Patton found the experience "interesting" but "not up to expectations." Even when relatively close to each other, the enemies did no more than whistle at one another. "Both sides were anxious not to disturb the other." As a result of the excursion, Patton deemed the land, hard from dry weather, satisfactory for tanks, for now at least.[89]

Returning to Bourg late in August, Patton showed his relief. "In your last letter," he wrote Bea, "you said it was so hot that you were sitting around naked. I wish I had been with you but it would have to be at home for we have had only two days a year hot enough for such a procedure."[90]

For the next week and a half Patton prepared for the coming struggle to eliminate the salient. For the assault Patton's 304th Tank Brigade, consisting of the 326th and 327th Battalions, possessed 144 Renaults.

Attached to Patton's force were two groups of French tankers, commanded by Major Charles M. Chanoine. They drove Schneider tanks.

If Fuller disliked the Renault tank, he must have detested the Schneider, so-called because it was made at the Schneider Creusot works. Heavier than the Renault, it was an armored box mounted on a copy of the British Holt caterpillar tractor. The tank possessed a 75-millimeter Schneider gun, but limited rotation hindered the gun's effectiveness. Hot inside with poor ventilation and a poor view of its field, the Schneider caught fire easily, and its tracks were too narrow for soft going.[91]

Given the mission of supporting the American IV Corps with his tanks, Patton worked out his plan. With the 326th Battalion, Brett would lead the doughboys of the 1st Division, holding the left, or west, of the line. Since the 1st Division had operated with tanks at Cantigny late that May, Patton foresaw no problems in this area. In the center, where Chanoine's Schneider tanks and the 327th, now commanded by Captain Ranulf Compton, were to aid the famed Rainbow Division, Patton had more worries, for the division had never worked with tanks.

Appearing at Rainbow headquarters, Patton promptly irritated everyone by urging that his officers be allowed to instruct the officers of the division. "No other means of training is available," he argued. "This will be better than nothing." Lieutenant Colonel Grayson M. P. Murphy, the operations officer of the 42d, ignored the suggestion.

Other things also worried Patton. He knew less about Compton's abilities than he did about Brett's. The Schneider tanks, moreover, would have trouble crossing streams and other obstacles. Accordingly, Patton instructed Chanoine to follow, rather than lead, the infantry. To Chanoine's right Compton was to first follow the 167th Regiment and then to pass through it and lead the way to Essey and Pannes, in the eastern portion of the salient.[92]

By September 9 Patton had received all his tanks and ten thousand gallons of gas, but to his disgust "no oil or 600 W of grease." Before putting his tanks on trains, he had his men mark each vehicle on its turret. The key marking was a playing card suit, which identified the platoon, one of four in each company, to which the tank belonged. These card markings were stenciled in black on white backgrounds, the shape of the latter indicating the company to which the tank belonged. Stenciled next to the card suit was a number, ranging from one to five, designating which tank it was in the platoon. The Five of Hearts, which proved to be one of the most famous tanks in the 326th, had a black heart painted on a white diamond. Completing its markings was a "5."[93]

Just before leaving for battle, Patton issued a message to his troops. It contained sentiments similar to those he would always preach.

No tank is to be surrendered or abandoned to the enemy. If you are left alone in the midst of the enemy keep shooting. If your gun is disabled use your pistols and squash the enemy with your tracks. . . . You must establish the fact that AMERICAN TANKS DO NOT SURRENDER. . . . This is our BIG CHANCE; WHAT WE HAVE WORKED FOR. . . . MAKE IT WORTH WHILE.[94]

For the tankers of Brett's 326th Battalion, getting into battle formation during the night of September 11 proved a problem. On that evening the worst fears of Rockenbach and Patton came true. "The rain was pouring down," Brett recorded. "The night was intensely dark and the mud knee deep when the battalion squirmed out of its hiding place at 9:00 P.M. and its long column began rolling forward to its battle position." The quiet of the night soon ended, as unit after unit moved toward the front. "Long lines of Infantry and Engineers appeared suddenly out of nothing, slid by and disappeared into the blackness of the night. Artillery and machine gun outfits packed the roads, the drivers cursing their animals and the cannoneers heaving on the wheels. Every animate and mechanical thing seemed to be moving forward. It was an impressive sight."[95]

In the early hours of September 12, events accelerated. At one o'clock, when the first shells from the American batteries "whined overhead," Brett and his men realized "that the show had really commenced." An hour later the 326th reached its battle position near Xivray-Narvoisin. Then began, noted Brett, "the hardest period of the entire fight, the three hours wait before they went over."[96]

The attack started at five. Everything went well until the tanks reached the first trenches, which for some of the vehicles proved impassable. By eight-fifteen Brett, his tanks leading the 1st Division, sent back a message by pigeon: "Twenty tanks now in action over first Boche

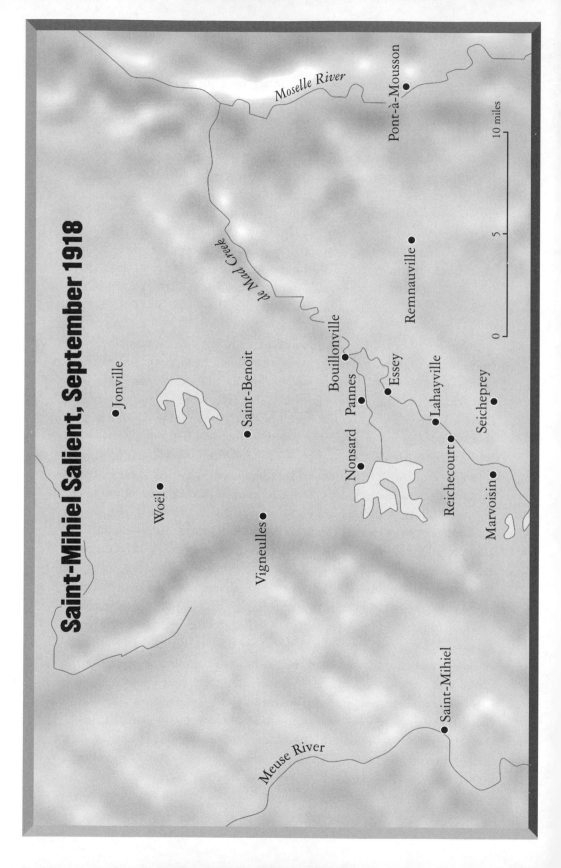

Saint-Mihiel Salient, September 1918

Moselle River

Pont-à-Mousson

10 miles

5

0

de Nap Creek

Remnauville

Jonville

Saint-Benoit

Bouillonville

Essey

Lahayville

Seicheprey

Pannes

Nonsard

Reichecourt

Woël

Marvoisin

Vigneulles

Meuse River

Saint-Mihiel

trenches. Trenches in horrible shape for tanks. . . . Doing all possible to get tanks unditched and sent forward."

For Brett's men the enemy proved to be both the Germans and the "sticky, soggy, awful mud in which the tanks," as First Lieutenant Don C. Wilson of Patton's Repair and Salvage Company described it, "wallowed belly deep." In many areas the fighting boiled down to individual skirmishes. "It looked," reported one American, "as if there were at least six different wars going on instead of one."

Brett himself was forced to abandon three vehicles. His first two tanks got stuck in ditches, his third entangled in rubble. Finally, violating Patton's orders to stay a thousand meters behind his lead tanks, he began directing the attack on foot. Three of his company commanders, Semmes, Weed, and Captain Matthew L. English, went through similar experiences.[97]

Amid the chaos, Patton vented his anger. Four days before the Saint-Mihiel offensive began, he had requested that Murphy employ smoke shells to shield his tanks. Murphy refused, arguing that the stencils containing the orders for the assault had already been typed. Patton's request would require new orders for the entire 42d Division.

Patton fumed. Murphy, he wrote in his diary, was an "S.O.B." The comment was "the biggest fool remark I ever heard." Patton protested to the division chief of staff, saying that "if tanks fail in 42 Div it will be his Murphy's fault."

At 9:30 A.M. on the morning of the attack Patton got a small measure of revenge. His tanks scattered over the battlefield, he telegraphed Murphy with obvious sarcasm: "Smoke screen excellent."[98]

Assigned to aid Brigadier General Douglas MacArthur's 84th Brigade of the Rainbow Division, Compton's 327th also ran into difficulties. At 9 A.M. only twenty-five of the 327th's tanks were chasing the Germans. Ten had been disabled, ten more were still at or near the jumping-off point, and three were about to go into action. Others were scattered about, performing various functions.[99]

Having lost track of Compton's battalion, Patton, accompanied by a lieutenant and four runners, went forward to find it. Passing through several towns, Patton admitted that he ducked on hearing shell fire, but then decided that he could not dodge fate. "Besides," he told his father, "I was the only officer around who had left on his shoulder straps and I had to live up to them."

At Essey, Patton came across the 84th Brigade. Once the assault had begun MacArthur's men quickly overran the enemy positions, even though, as MacArthur put it, Patton's tanks "soon bogged down in . . . mud." Walking along the firing line, Patton noticed all the men hiding in shell holes. MacArthur, however, stood on a little hill. "I joined him," Patton related to his father, "and the creeping barrage came along toward us, but it was very thin and not dangerous." Each man probably wanted to leave, "but each hated to say so." MacArthur remembered Patton flinching as one shell came over, whereupon he said: "Don't worry, major; you never hear the one that gets you."[100]

At Essey, Patton received permission from MacArthur to move his tanks across the Rupt de Mad Creek, provided the bridge had not been mined. "We walked over the bridge in a cat-like manner," Patton related, "expecting to be blown to heaven any moment, but to our great relief we found that the bridge had not been tampered with." Guiding the only three available tanks over the structure, Patton directed the vehicles toward Pannes, just west of Essey, the foot soldiers following. But when the infantry, fearing that Germans still held Pannes, refused to enter it, Patton, Knowles, and a runner got atop one of the tanks and rode it into town. At the north end of Pannes, Knowles and the runner saw a German soldier. Getting off the tank, they found twenty-nine more, all of whom they captured by simply brandishing their pistols.[101]

Patton's adventures continued. Leaving Pannes, he was still atop the tank, riding with his legs hanging down on the left side, as the machine rumbled north toward Béney. All of a sudden he noticed that paint was starting to chip off the left side just six inches below his hand. It was from machine-gun fire. Jumping off the tank, Patton landed in a shell hole. Every time he tried to look up "the boshe shot at me. . . . All the time," he reported to his father, "the infernal tank was going on alone as the men had not noticed my hurried departure." Running "like h———" obliquely across an open field, Patton managed to make it to safety. Finally finding the tank about four hundred yards into another field, he ordered it to await reinforcements before entering Béney. Rummaging together five of his mechanical monsters, Patton decided to attack that town. With infantry support the tankers captured four field guns and sixteen machine guns.[102]

His tanks running out of fuel, Patton tried about 3 P.M. to find Brett and the 326th Battalion, then aiding the 1st Division on the left. Not having slept for four nights or eaten all day—he had "lost my sack chasing a boshe"—he took some crackers off the body of a dead German and proceeded on foot. Coming upon the 326th at Nonsard, four miles from Béney, he found Brett, who had been grazed in the nose, crying because he had run out of fuel. Patton consoled Brett and then started off to get gas. "It was most interesting," he observed, "quite like the books but much less dramatic. The dead were about mostly hit in the head. There were a lot of our men stripping off buttons and other things but they always covered the face of the dead in a nice way."[103]

For much of the next day, September 13, the 304th Brigade halted. The reasons for this were twofold: the Germans were offering little resistance, and the gas trucks had difficulty getting through the jammed roads. The shortage demonstrated to Patton the need for having caterpillar tractors loaded with gas accompany each battalion, for it took thirty-two hours to move gas trucks fourteen kilometers.[104]

On the fourteenth Patton sent Brett to find the enemy. Early that morning Brett headed north with fifty-one tanks, but he found neither Germans nor Americans. The first sign of the enemy came about 2 P.M., when a German battalion, reinforced by eight machine guns and a battery of 77-millimeter cannons, attacked Lieutenant Edwin A. McClure's patrol of three tanks and five dismounted soldiers. Informed by a runner of the skirmish, Patton sent five tanks, commanded by Second Lieutenant Gordon M. Grant, to aid McClure. The eight American tanks drove the enemy back almost four miles to Jonville, on the Hindenburg Line at the eastern tip of the salient, capturing four cannons and twelve machine guns. While attempting to attach the cannons to the backs of their tanks, McClure, Grant, and four of their men were hit by shrapnel. McClure then removed the breechblocks and left the guns.[105] Fighting by themselves, American tankers had for the first time defeated German ground forces.

During the fighting, Patton had been all over the battlefield, violating Rockenbach's dictum that brigade and battalion commanders should remain in command posts. But what Rockenbach considered a weakness, Viner considered a strength. "George Patton was always there on the front lines, never in the rear with the Red Cross. That was one of the secrets to his greatness."[106]

VII

At 9 P.M. on September 14 Patton received orders to take his brigade to the Bois de la Hazelle, near the rear of the Saint-Mihiel battlefield. There the tankers remained until the nineteenth, repairing their vehicles and preparing for the coming campaign in the Meuse-Argonne against the Hindenburg Line. On the fourteenth the brigade contained 131 operational tanks. During the recent fighting, three had been hit by artillery fire and forty more were either stuck in the mud or disabled by mechanical problems. The casualties in Patton's brigade were low: five enlisted men killed, and four officers and fifteen men wounded.[107]

The scope of the preparations for the new offensive enthralled Patton. "This country here is like a haunted forest," he informed Bea on the twentieth. "It is nearly deserted but from dark to dawn it is alive with men and horses & guns you never dreamed of much less saw such numbers of guns. It is wonderful. Still one looses respect for guns as they shoot eternally and never hit one. When they do then it is quelque chose [something]. I saw a man hit the other day nearly square with a shell 6". All that was needed was a basket, to collect what was left."[108]

From September 15, when Rockenbach first told him of the new operation, to the jumping-off date of September 26, Patton spent all his time preparing for it. After a three-hour artillery bombardment, the American First Army, divided into three corps, was to attack at 5:30 A.M. on the twenty-sixth from south to north. The area to be attacked was relatively compact, twenty miles wide and thirteen miles long. But here its virtues ended. Its eastern border consisted of the unfordable Meuse River, its western the dense Argonne Forest. General Hunter Liggett, who commanded the First Army, called the region "a natural fortress beside which the Virginia Wilderness in which Grant and Lee fought was a park." The Germans had intensified the problem with trenches, concrete dugouts, and numerous other obstacles.

In the battle Patton's brigade was to support the 28th and 35th Divisions of the I Corps in the western segment of the First Army zone. Dressed in a French uniform, Patton went over some of the territory from which his men would start, noticing that the trenches were narrower and the ground firmer than had been the case at Saint-Mihiel.[109]

Patton tried to profit from the lessons of the previous battle. As would be the case in World War II, fuel shortages presented a problem.

Hoping to avoid what happened at Saint-Mihiel, Patton stockpiled twenty thousand gallons of gas for use after the first day's action. Each of his light tanks, now numbering 141, was to carry two twenty-liter gas cans on its tail, even though enemy fire penetrating a can would turn the tank into a furnace.[110]

The most important innovation came from a suggestion by a private in the Tank Corps. The soldier noticed that at Saint-Mihiel many tanks that broke down needed minor repairs, such as a new fan belt. Since repairs took place well behind the lines, these vehicles remained out of service for a long time. The soldier suggested that a repair tank follow the first line of tanks by about a mile and a half and make minor repairs on the field. In the battle the 321st Repair and Salvage Company tried the idea, used extensively during the Second World War.[111]

Patton's plan for the offensive called for Brett's battalion, renumbered the 344th, to lead and Compton's, now the 345th, to be in support a mile back. Chanoine's Schneider tanks, less mobile than the Renaults, would occupy the rear. After the first day's fighting, Compton's battalion would pass through Brett's and assume the lead. For the tanks the front would be a mile and a half, the area west of Cheppy and Varennes between the Aire River and the eastern edge of the Argonne Forest.

On the day before the attack Patton confided to Bea that he was as nervous as if he were waiting for a polo match or a football game to start. "We go up a stinking river valley which will not be at all a comfortable place in a few hours but we are better off than last time. The bosch has been trying to hit this place all afternoon but so far has not done so so we will probably leave on time."[112]

For Patton the Meuse-Argonne campaign started and ended the first day. At five-thirty in the morning the infantry assault began. "It was terribly foggy," Patton informed his wife, "and in addition they were shooting lots of smoke shells so we could not see ten feet." About six-thirty Patton grew impatient and, accompanied by Knowles, six runners, and everyone else he could find, left to see what was going on. Three hours later the party approached Cheppy. As the weather cleared, Patton spied a chilling sight. "Twice the infantry started to run but we followed at them and called them all sorts of names so they staid. But they were scared some and acted badly. . . . None did a damn thing to kill Bosch."

While resting on the reverse slope of a small hill, Patton noticed five of Compton's tanks just sitting there. They were unable, he subsequently found out, to traverse two wide, deep German trenches because a Schneider had stalled at the only decent crossing. Storming down the hill, Patton directed the dismantling of the trench. When, during the operation, Patton and the commander of Company C of Brett's battalion, Captain Matthew L. English, stood exposed to heavy enemy fire, Patton answered shouts by soldiers that they take cover in the trenches: "To Hell with them—they can't hit me." Joined by Patton's striker, Private First Class Joseph T. Angelo, the two officers chained together several tanks, giving them better traction, and directed the movement over the trenches. "It was exciting for they shot at us all the time," Patton assured Bea, "but I got mad and walked on the parapet."

Free at last, the five tanks lumbered up the hill and out of sight. Inspired by the incident, Patton waved his walking stick and yelled "come on." About 150 men followed him up the hill, but at its crest "the fire got fierce right along the ground." Refusing to fall back, Patton yelled: "Who's with me?" Only five others, Angelo and four doughboys, started forward. One by one the enemy machine gunners picked off the Yankee chargers, until only Patton and Angelo were left. Still advancing, Patton suddenly "felt a blow in the leg," but he was able to advance another forty feet. Then his leg gave way. "Oh God," Angelo shouted, "the colonels hit and there aint no one left." Helping Patton into a shell hole, Angelo waited with him for about an hour until the tanks cleared out twenty-five or so German machine-gun nests. The orderly carried two pigeons with him, "and it was funny," Patton observed, "when you think of it to be sending 'Doves of Peace' from a hole right under the nose of the Bosch." Hit about 11:15 A.M., Patton reached an evacuation center at three-thirty. There he learned that the bullet had entered his left leg and come out "just at the crack of my bottom about two inches to the left of my rectum." Emerging, it had made a hole about the size of a silver dollar.[113]

After three days at the evacuation hospital just back of the line, Patton was shipped in a boxcar to Base Hospital No. 49, "missing half of my bottom but other wise all right." While recuperating, Patton closely followed the activities of his brigade, now commanded by Brett. By October 10 six of his seven captains had been hit. English had been killed. Captain E. A. Higgins and his driver, both blinded, had continued to run their tank until they drove into a large shell crater. In addition, two of Patton's lieutenants had been killed and fifteen wounded. "But the tank corps established its reputation for not giving ground," Patton confided to Bea. "They only went forward. And they are the only troops in the attack of whom that can be said."[114]

On the seventeenth, his "d—— wound still full of bugs so they can't sew me up," Patton received news that he had been promoted to full colonel. Elated, he addressed Bea as "Mrs. Colonel G. S. Patton Jr." Still, Patton was worried because the doctors guessed his age as forty-five, not almost thirty-three. Responding to Patton's inquiries about Bea, Braine, who had just returned from the United States, told him that she had dyed her gray hair. "I hope you will also [fix] your chin. I always think of you as Undine," he wrote, recalling the play about the water nymph they had put on the summer they met at Catalina, "so I don't want you to look 33, even if I do."[115]

At noon on October 18 Patton left the hospital. "Back in my own room sitting by a fire" at Bourg, he informed Bea that he had two boils on his back and two on his chest, "which hurt like hell but are getting better."[116]

Peace came on November 11, Patton's thirty-third birthday. The colonel was justifiably proud of his achievements and those of his men. The 304th Brigade had fought at Saint-Mihiel and then in the Argonne from September 26 to November 1. By the Armistice the Tank Corps in Europe consisted of 752 officers and 11,277 enlisted men. In the United States the corps contained 483 officers and 7,700 enlisted men, almost equally divided between Camp Polk, Louisiana, and Camp Colt, Pennsylvania, the latter commanded by Lieutenant Colonel Dwight D. Eisenhower.

At war's end even Patton had reservations about the future of the Tank Corps. "Tanks are not motorized cavalry," he explained, "or armored infantry accompanying guns; *they are tanks, a new auxiliary arm* whose purpose is ever and always to facilitate the advance of the master arm, the Infantry, on the field of battle."[117] The next twenty-five years would constitute a battleground between tank advocates and defenders of the infantry who detested and feared the power of this new arm.

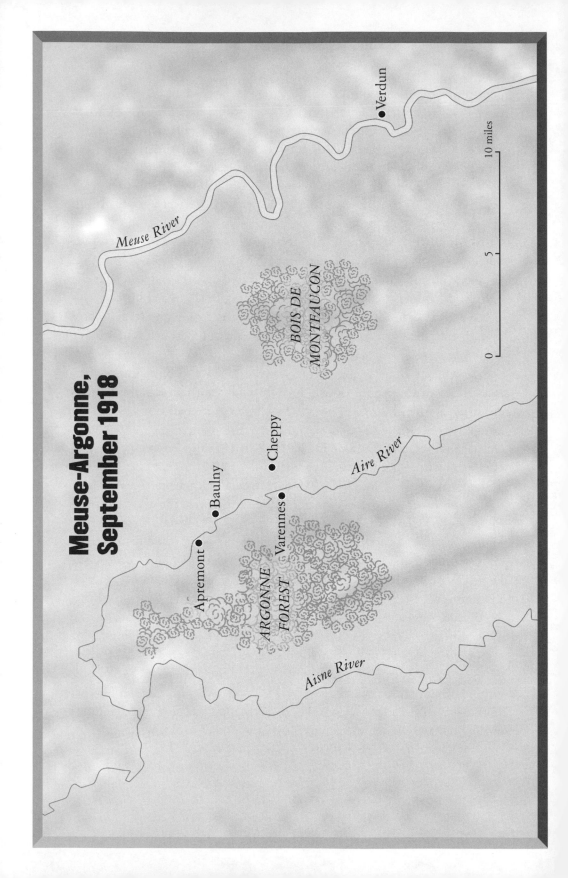

Meuse-Argonne, September 1918

Verdun

Meuse River

BOIS DE MONTFAUCON

Apremont

Baulny

Cheppy

Varennes

ARGONNE FOREST

Aire River

Aisne River

0 5 10 miles

LEAVENWORTH AND ALL THAT

I

Wartime is a career soldier's golden age. In peacetime promotions come slowly, and glory often comes from seeing that your branch of service survives, often at the expense of another branch. With the army small and almost everyone knowing everyone else, the social game often becomes as important as the talent game, and at the first of these Beatrice and George Patton excelled. Like competent people in other fields, however, a great soldier never stops learning his craft. Being one, Patton never ceased reading and writing.

One of the great misfortunes of war is that it separates sweethearts, even when one of them happens to be the commanding general. From Bourg two weeks before the Armistice, Patton still expressed hope that Nita and Pershing would marry. The immediate task was to get his sister overseas so the courtship could continue. "I will call and tell your friend about you," Patton wrote Nita on October 26, 1918, referring to Pershing. "You are right not to be a Red Crosser they are rotten. All the Red Cross women who come over get 'bad.' "[1]

With peace Patton became especially concerned with his career. At a dinner he saw Lieutenant Colonel Clarence Liniger wearing the Distinguished Service Medal he had won for service in Mexico. "He had just gotten it," Patton informed Bea, "and it is a very pretty ribbon. I wish I had one for killing Cardenes."[2]

The next day Patton asked Pershing for two favors. The 304th Brigade of the Tank Corps had, he pointed out, fought in the Battle of Saint-Mihiel and then, with no rest and moving at night, had fought almost continuously from September 26 to November 1 in the Meuse-

Argonne struggle. On the first day of the latter battle Patton himself
had been wounded. Of Patton's fifty-five officers, three had been killed
and eighteen wounded. Of his 757 men sixteen had been killed and 118
wounded. In view of their bravery Patton urged Pershing to issue a
statement praising the tankers. He would make sure that each soldier
received a copy of the cherished document.

Patton then moved on to something personal. Liniger, formerly a
first lieutenant with the 13th Cavalry, had recently received the Distinguished Service Medal, which he was now wearing at parties and dinners, for his exploits in Mexico. Patton's encounter with Julio Cárdenas
at San Miguel "might equally be considered as a service to the Government," for he had done "in one morning with nine men what a whole
regiment of cavalry the 13th had failed to do in one week. I would not
dare bother you with this were it not that it is only you and Gen. Cabel
who know any thing about it."[3]

This letter ushered in Patton's campaign to get the DSM. "I wish I
had one for killing Cardenes," he lamented to Bea on the seventeenth.
"Perhaps I will get one." It was "one degree lower than the D.S.C.,"
which Patton believed he also merited.[4]

The next day Patton heard rumors that he would not get the Distinguished Service Cross because Rockenbach, "in too big a hurry," had
submitted the recommendation "with out sufficient data. . . . It was the
whole war to me," he noted of his desire for a medal. What else could
compensate him for being away from Bea for two years? "But I will be
G. D. if I am beat yet." He might "resign and join the French army as a
Captain or something. Gen. R. thinks my colonelcy is a compensation
but it is nothing. I would rather be a second Lt. with the D.S.C. than a
general with out it. It means more than an 'A' and it would be of vast
value in future."[5]

The campaign continued. A few minutes before consulting General
Eltinge about a medal, Patton hoped "I get something out of it besides
giggles. But I am like Bill Reed and am loosing faith in men. Bill says
that every one is your friend until you want something and then you
have only your self for friend."[6]

Awaiting further word, Patton busied himself with odds and ends.
He tested American Renault tanks, which he found faster and better
built than the French Renault light tanks. "If we could only have had a
few hundred of them during the war," he mused to Bea, "it would have

been something." With nothing better to do, he helped form a football team, of which he was captain. "We have a Yale half and a Princeton Guard besides a lot of lesser lights it ought to be good fun and some exercise."

Sitting around, Georgie allowed himself to stew about something else. Bea's sister, Kay, had invited Bea and Nita to visit her and her husband, Keith Merrill, in London. "I think that Keith's sudden desire for battle is the most absurd thing I ever heard of," Patton advised his wife. "He was in the militia and got out. Had he not produced an infant I should not have believed him a man at all. As it is I think his manhood does not reach above his belt. . . . Well this is a hellish stupid world now and life has lost its zest. . . . I think I will get fat and lazy," Patton warned Bea, "but I hope not. Don't you dare do to."[7]

That December 4 Patton heard the good news. He had been awarded the D.S.C. Celebrating, he bought Bea a gold folding cigarette holder. "It is very chick and pretty," he wrote, "so when you smoke you can use it." Rewarding himself, he spent $200 for a pedigreed police dog. "Since marrying you," Patton teased, "I have never been satisfied with any thing but the best even in dogs."[8]

II

Writing to Nita, Pershing described Yuletide in France.

I hope you got my Christmas telegram, and I, in return, must acknowledge the one from your father. George had dinner with us and was the cutup of the evening. He had an abundance of new stories, which kept everybody killing themselves with laughter. Being a Colonel has not changed him. He and the old crowd—Collins, Boyd and others whom you do not know, and including myself, Colonel Boyd's wife and little girl—had a very delightful Christmas evening.

During the day the President and Mrs. Wilson visited head-quarters and reviewed the troops, and afterwards came to tea and left at 6 o'clock in the evening. The day was miserable—cold and damp, but everything went off in very good shape and the guests were very well satisfied.[9]

As 1919 dawned, Patton, like most American soldiers, yearned to return home. "We are still here and even likely to remain until 1920," he informed his father, "for Wilson will never make up his mind before then, being handicapped by the fact that he has no mind to make."

The homesick doughboys sang a song, one verse of which expressed their sentiments accurately:

> *And when at last we all are dead*
> *Our friends will truly tell,*
> *They all have gone to Heaven*
> *For they done their Hitch in Hell.*[10]

Not that Patton thought he would be home very long. Late in 1918 the Communists took over Russia. Patton was sure that "in six months we will have to go to Russia for a war." He hoped to come home "for a while any way." Then he would be off to the new war, "so as to get the Medal of Honor which I missed getting this time on account of all the witnesses getting killed or being Bosch."[11]

On January 17, finally getting something to do, Patton and Lieutenant Colonel Henry E. Mitchell, Rockenbach's chief of staff, left to lecture the troops of the Second Army on tanks. Covering ground over which he would lead an army during the next war, Patton drove through, among others, Thionville, "the cleanest town I have seen," and Diekirch, "a very nice town." "Right now I am in the north end of Luxembourg," he wrote Bea on January 28. "It is a very rich country and has also many mines. The people speak German and look it. You know my feelings towards the Germans before the war. Well they are more so now." Patton billeted with an old woman whose son-in-law, a major, commanded the Luxembourg army. Right then, however, the son-in-law had few men to command. After going out on strike, his troopers had been discharged, leaving him with only a handful of policemen acting as soldiers. "This is the first country in the world to have no army. It is a horrible example of what not to do."[12]

Back once more in his quarters at Bourg, just outside of Langres, Patton heard bad news. After his tank brigade was ordered home, he was to be sent to Germany for occupation duty. "God-Dam," he recorded in his diary. To make matters worse, Bea was ill. "You poor thing," he comforted her on February 7, "you surely have a hell of a time. Please die your hair I am going to."

In his letter Patton hinted at something that turned out to be true. "As to J. and Nita," he observed. "It is possible that the game is up. You see he could get any one in the world and they are after him. Ambition is a great thing and with out soul. I have no reason for knowing this but??? 'C'est possible.' "[13]

That Georgie still idolized and emulated the general he made clear in his next letter to Bea. "I have seen JJP make people cry," he asserted, "but to day is the first time I ever did it. I surely gave one of my captains hell and he howled but it did him good. It is a great accomplishment and I set out to do it."[14]

On the tenth Patton had what he considered "a most interesting day." Going to Pershing's house with some shell cases made into tobacco and cigar boxes as a gift for Wilson, he found there a reception for Medal of Honor winners. In a tribute to the recipients, generals served them. "I wish I had gotten a M.H.," Patton commented enviously, "but one can't have you and every other good thing too at least not all at once. I will get a M.H. in the next war. I hope."

The bulk of Patton's conversation with Pershing concerned Nita. The general said that army wives were still barred from coming to Europe and that he would be stationed in Europe until late next fall. Then he blurted out: "Why can't Anne come over in the Y.M.C.A.? I want her and I could arrange her coming so that no one would know I had." "General," Patton answered, "she can't come unless it is known. She belongs to a distinguished family in her state and it would cause remark. That is why she has not come. Out of consideration for you." When Pershing said he thought all those rumors of romance were dead and that Nita could probably leave from Washington without being noticed, Georgie answered: "You are wrong but I don't think any thing can hurt you. Shall I write?" "Yes do," Pershing responded.

After the conversation, Patton analyzed the situation for Bea.

Nita loves him and he her (or she) it might be unpleasant for her to come but it would be more unpleasant for her to loose him. He is great and much sought after. One more year of separation might ruin two lives and loves. It is better for her pride to suffer a little

than for her to loose such a Great man. Therefore I say tell her to
come. One word from her and he can fix it. This is my best judgment in the matter. If she comes they will be married here I am
sure or nearly so. If she does not who can say what may happen. . . . Consider what I have said from your *head* not from your
sentiment.[15]

Anxious to get home, Patton addressed an impassioned letter to
Major General James W. McAndrew, Pershing's chief of staff. Happily,
McAndrew agreed to the request. But Patton's joy was soon interrupted, for on February 13 he learned that Colonel Boyd, with whom
the staff had celebrated Christmas, had died of pneumonia the day
before. Traveling with Pershing and about two dozen others on a special
train, Patton visited Mrs. Boyd and her young daughter, Ann. "I told
them stories for 3 hours," Patton informed Nita, "and got them to
laugh."

At Chaumont that Sunday Patton met the Prince of Wales, later
King Edward VIII, and his aide, Captain Claude Hamilton of the Cold-
stream Guards. With one of Pershing's aides, Lieutenant Colonel
Edward Bowditch, Jr., Patton joined the two Britons on a tour of General Henry T. Allen's VIII Corps. On the way back the prince, as loqua-
cious as Patton, told "a lot of stories supposed to be bad some were."
Loving a good time, the prince complained: "Being a dashed prince
rather cramps ones style what?" After dinner, he wanted to play poker,
but no one else knew how, so, sitting on the floor, they settled for dice.
Patton lost 150 francs. Years later the story somehow circulated that
Patton had taught the prince how to gamble.

The next day, joined by Pershing and other officers, the party went to
Commercy to inspect the twenty thousand men of the 35th Division.
Walking about seven miles during the day, Pershing and the prince
stopped to talk to every soldier who wore a wound stripe. "It was most
interesting," Patton told Nita. "On the way back I rode in the Machine
with J. and we talked for about three hours. He told me all sorts of
secret history and was most interesting."

Patton later recalled what the prince said when they separated. "Patton," the prince asked, "you are a vulgar and licentious mercenary, are
you not?" When Patton went along with the statement, the prince
added: "Well, then, perhaps after the war, you will again be billeted on

the border, and if that should occur, how would it be if I should visit you, quite incognito, of course, and you could get me a few senoritas, what?"

Patton ended his report by again advising Nita to come to Europe. While visiting Allen's corps, he had run into Caroline Trask, who was with the YMCA. She believed Nita should come over at once, for with the war over the Red Cross and the YMCA had little to do. If Patton returned home, that would "make it easier for you to leave Pa and Ma," for he would be there to comfort them.[16]

At this point Patton's father gave him advice that, if followed, might have spared him much grief. At one time or another several of Patton's associates noted his desire to dominate a conversation. In describing the activities of the previous Christmas, Pershing had called him "the cutup of the evening." Patton's friend, Major Bradford G. Chynoweth, once stopped off to see Patton's father, and the two ended up discussing ways of getting Georgie to stop cursing. And General and Mrs. George C. Marshall both observed that Patton often said something shocking and then looked about to see the response. Patton had, moreover, developed the habit of composing poems for effect. One of these, "The Song of the Turds of Langres," written in 1918, contained numerous distasteful words and images. With horror Patton's father witnessed his son's conduct. Among other things, he wrote the younger Patton from Washington, where he was being considered by Wilson for an ambassadorship,

I have been worrying for fear that the "gift of gab" you have developed may get you in trouble. Unless restrained such a gift is always dangerous. The temptation to say smart or striking things is hard to resist—and it is only next day that cold reason condemns. You are now 34—and a Col. and the dignity going with your rank invests what you say with more importance so I hope in your speeches you will be very careful and self restrained—for your own good & for your future—Another gift you have developed I really regret and that is the ability to write verse upon vulgar & smutty subjects—That is very dangerous. The very men to whom you read & recite such stuff as your last one will laugh—and apparently enjoy it—but you have really lowered yourself in their eyes—above all it lacks *dignity*—and you need to cultivate that especially in view of your rank.

All my life I have known such instances—and never has it failed
in my experience—that the Club wit—who indulges in smutty
stuff hurts himself. You may some day want to enter public life—
but you must couple with your talent in these two respects great
self restraint & sense of dignity—most men have no real sense of
humor—& fail to distinguish other matters of this sort from reali-
ties & judge one accordingly. All the really big men I have
known—abstained from repeating vulgar stories—and all who
were facile in speech—cultivate great reserve—or if they sometimes forgot themselves—always suffered for the lapse. I don't
want to preach and will say no more but I am sure your own judgment—upon reflection will agree with mine.[17]

What most bothered the elder Patton was that he considered his son
a talented poet. Answering a local historian who requested information
on Colonel Patton, the father sent along the poem "Memories of a
Roman Ruin in France," later polished up and called "Memories Roused
by a Roman Theater." It "is certainly quite a poetic conceit," he wrote,
"the idea being the third reincarnation of warriors fighting for the third
time at this spot." Sitting in his "throbbing Char d'Assault," the modern warrior—Patton—recalled his two previous existences:

> First it was in the brass of Rome
> With the white dust on my brow;
> And the second time 'neath the flag of a Duke
> Whose name is legend now. . . .
> And now again I am here for war
> Where as Roman and knight I have been;
> Again I practice to fight the Hun
> And attack him by machine.[18]

At tank headquarters on February 23 Patton heard news that cheered
him and obviously cheered his father. For the past two weeks he had
campaigned for permission to accompany the tank brigade when it
returned to New York. He had been away from home almost continuously for the past two and a half years, he told Pershing. He also argued
that Bea was sick and needed him, even though, in the letter warning
his son about his behavior, Patton's father had reported that "B is much

improved." "I have attempted in a small way to model my self on you," Georgie flattered Pershing, "and what ever success I have had has been due to you as an inspiration."[19]

For whatever reason Pershing agreed to let Georgie go home, and at eleven o'clock on the morning of February 26, Patton began loading his men on the train. After a ride of two days they reached Marseilles. From there, on the second of March, they sailed for home on the French steamship *Patria*.[20]

The highlight, if it may be called that, of the voyage to the United States took place, as Patton told Pershing, in Gibraltar. Arriving there on the fourth of March, the *Patria* stayed until the seventh, stocking up on coal. In small boats Spaniards approached the French vessel, supposedly peddling baskets of oranges. In the baskets, however, they hid bottles of brandy. The next day, when the Spaniards came again, Patton fired at the water near them and scared them away.

On the ship, and later in the United States, Georgie heard much anti-Pershing talk. One reporter aboard the *Patria* scoffed to Patton that any man could have done as well as Pershing. "I told him that that depended on his definition of 'man' but that so far no other man in the sense you were a man had yet been born." The journalist "also made remarks" about the filth of the American camp at Brest on the Brittany peninsula in France, a deathtrap for the Americans during the Second World War. "I told him that I had been there and that it was much better than any camp we ever had in Mexico or any other place before the war." Similarly, a returning officer described Pershing to Bea as a "vague personality who no one saw." Patton warned Pershing to be aware of such comments.[21]

At noon on March 17, the *Patria,* delayed several hours by fog, chugged into a berth at the foot of Thirty-first Street in South Brooklyn. Along with 2,109 other Americans, Patton was home. An unfortunate incident at the pier greatly disturbed the colonel. Greeted by a police boat containing members of a welcoming committee appointed by the mayor of New York, the soldiers leaned over the ship's rail and yelled: "Is William Randolph Hearst aboard?" With that one soldier threw down a packet tied with string and said: "Give that to the Mayor." The packet contained a petition signed by a hundred soldiers protesting the mayor's selection of Hearst, the owner of a string of newspapers that included the *New York Journal,* as a member of the welcoming committee. The soldiers accused Hearst, long friendly with German officials, of being "un-American, pro-German, and inhumanitarian."

Reporting the arrival of the 304th Brigade, New York newspapers played up the unit's achievements. The eight hundred tankers had received two French medals and twenty Distinguished Service Crosses. Focusing on Patton, newspapers like the *New York Times* and the *New York Herald* vividly depicted the battle in which he was wounded. In a statement he was later to regret, Patton told the *Times* "that when he was shot he fell down on the field and would have been killed if it had not been for the bravery of Private Joseph Angelo, of Camden, N.J., who risked his life to drag him to a shell hole. For his bravery Angelo received the D.S.C." The papers reported that Patton had also received that medal. Knowing nothing about Patton's campaign to get the D.S.C., the papers depicted the award of the medal as a spontaneous action by superiors to honor the brave and deserving soldier.[22]

III

At the dock Patton found a just reward, Bea, still fresh and lovely and in the prime of womanhood. During the two weeks before Georgie's arrival, Bea had campaigned for her father-in-law's appointment as ambassador to Italy. The current ambassador, the author Thomas Nelson Page, was sick of the job, and the elder Patton would make an ideal replacement. She had already spoken to Senator David I. Walsh of Massachusetts and to her neighbor John Hay Hammond, who had influence with the Wilson administration. Hammond had estimated that as ambassador George Patton's expenses each year would exceed his salary by $30,000. To Bea the sum was inconsequential, but would it be so for the Pattons?

To her father-in-law Bea described a side benefit of the ambassadorship. The appointment "would make *some* impression on John," for whom Nita still pined. Forwarding to her father-in-law Georgie's recent letters, in which he told of Pershing's desire to have Nita come over to Europe, Bea urged: "As for Nita—you can see by these letters what it would mean to her: a dignified, suitable way of seeing John again, or a great diversion if she doesn't marry. Uncle George, you *couldn't* turn it down? & it would make us all so happy."[23]

For a week after landing Patton was stationed at Camp Mills on Long Island. Then he and the men of his brigade, along with the tanks, were transferred to Camp Meade, Maryland, halfway between Baltimore and Washington. For Bea and Patton the move meant setting up house again, after an interlude of almost three years. Bea later described the quarters assigned to the family as "the queerest house I ever had. It was an old Officers' Barracks," she recalled,

> made of tar paper and stripping with a big recreation room and eighteen sleeping cubicles, with some prints and original drawings all over the walls. We took out some of the partitions and painted the walls, but it had no kitchen and I heard that the Commanding Officer had ruled that we must eat at the Officers' Mess. This, I had privately determined not to do on account of the children. For when children go to an Officers' Mess, everyone makes a fuss over them, ruins their manners, and then turns around and says how sweet they used to be, but that now they have become completely spoiled.
>
> We moved out to Camp on our Tin Wedding Anniversary, and had a nice box lunch in our new quarters. My husband was feeling a bit stormy. "You might as well go to the Mess and get it over-with," he said. I took a long breath. "I am not going to the Mess," I said. "You will have to fix it some other way."

Patton put on his cap and went out. Bea waited for him all afternoon. As darkness approached, Bea and the girls heard "an awful clanking and roaring outside." Patton appeared, leading a tank that was dragging a little house. "Here is your God-damned kitchen," Patton announced. "I found it in a field." The soldiers placed it against the house, and from parts of eight stoves they had found in a salvage dump they made a workable stove. "It was," Bea related, "a fine kitchen."

Bea remembered Meade as "a funny Post—no grass there just sand. But we had horses, and we planted oats to keep the dust down."[24]

With Camp Meade only an hour and a quarter from Washington by car, Patton decided to indulge himself. He bought a Pierce-Arrow automobile because, he informed his father on April 1, he might be detailed in Washington to write drill regulations for tankers. Besides, "I can afford it and believe in enjoying myself between wars." Having "been away from the 'flesh pots' so long," he yearned "for a bath tub and warm water to shave." For now he planned to stay with the tanks, "as I will thus probably keep my rank and besides I owe it to the Corps." Still hoping for a match between his sister, who with her mother was visiting him, and Pershing, Georgie hoped she might yet go to England, "as that will finally settle the matter one way or another."[25]

Two days later Patton wrote to Pershing himself. "Last week," he began,

> there was enacted here and at the other camps in the U.S. a most weak kneed performance. Namely a recruit drive conducted on the same lines as a "Liberty Loan" drive. There were a lot of flannel mouthed officers here who lectured the soldiers on the virtue of reenlisting. They painted in glowing terms the pleasures of the soldiers life—in peace, the chances for travel, and the different forms of schools for vocational training with which they intend to take the soldiers mind off his work. The whole thing was peculiarly nauseating to me as I believe in compulsory service as a national duty. . . . After these foolish lectures officers in the audience are detailed to go and buttonhole the soldiers and try to sign them up on the spot like the old "Press gangs" in England in the last century.

Patton had been back in the United States only two weeks, but he already yearned for a return to the experiences of the past three years. "I forgot to say that a lot of the officers and quite a proportion of the men are already talking of the next war with great hopes. Of course those are my sentiments. I went to a war Play last night and the noise of the shell and the machine guns made me feel very homesick. War is the only place where a man really lives."[26]

IV

At Camp Meade Patton met Dwight David Eisenhower, also a champion of tanks. Ike Eisenhower and George Patton also shared something else: a disdain for the antiwar sentiment then sweeping the United States. Congress already talked about tightening purse strings.

The Tank Corps led the casualties. And why not? Unlike infantry-men, armored vehicles tended to break down or to run out of gas, usu-ally when needed most. When working fine, they often outran the infantry.[27]

Like Patton, Eisenhower was caught in the postwar disdain for tanks or for anything military. A member of the West Point class of 1915, he was engaged in the prosaic task of training officers at Fort Oglethorpe, Georgia, when Colonel Ira C. Welborn was notified that he was to organize a tank battalion at Camp Colt in Gettysburg, Pennsylvania. Given the option of taking one of his lieutenants with him, he chose Ike Eisenhower. "We were all a little bit disgusted," remembered Lieu-tenant John W. Leonard, Ike's classmate at West Point. "We thought we were pretty damned good too, you know," related Leonard, later a lieutenant general. At Gettysburg, Eisenhower found he was to train tankers without the benefit of tanks, but he was so successful that by October 14, 1918, just three days before Patton was promoted to the temporary rank of colonel, Eisenhower reached the temporary rank of lieutenant colonel. A week before Ike was scheduled to go overseas, the war ended.[28]

Fate soon drove Ike and Georgie together. Ordered to report to Camp Meade on March 15, 1919, Eisenhower was soon drawn to Pat-ton, whom he described as "tall" (six feet one), "straight" (he carried his 170 pounds with ramrod posture), and "soldierly looking." Patton's most "noticeable characteristic," perhaps the one that led him to curse so frequently to draw attention from it, was his

> high, squeaking voice, quite out of keeping with his bearing. He had two passions, the military service and polo. Side issues for George Patton were pleasure riding—he had a fine stable of good horses—and pistol shooting. From the beginning he and I got along famously. I did not play polo (neither my background nor my knee was much help) but I was devoted to riding and shoot-ing. Both of us were students of current military doctrine. Part of our passion was a belief in tanks—a belief derided at the time by others.[29]

In mid-April, when Patton, Viner, Lieutenant Colonel James E. Ware, and Major Ralph I. Sasse reported to Welborn in Washington and

were assigned to write tank regulations and a drill manual, Eisenhower
was placed in temporary command of the tankers at Meade. After
working on the project for a month, the members of the Tank Board,
accompanied by Colonel Henry Mitchell, journeyed to the Rock Island
Arsenal in Illinois and the Springfield Armory in Massachusetts to
inspect tank production. Patton found particularly impressive the
thirty-five-ton Mark VIII tank, which, he wrote his father from the
Mississippi River in early June, "works much better than we thought."
Georgie transmitted other news. Deciding to bring matters with Pershing to a head, Nita had vowed to go to England. "Nita must be over
by this time," he advised, "and things always come out for the best.
Even the Pox," which he had recently contracted, "is giving me a good
rest."[30]

Returning to Washington, Patton, on edge over Nita's prospects,
wrote Pershing his usual flattering letter. Traveling halfway across the
continent, he had been astounded by the presidential boom of Pershing's rival, General Leonard Wood.

There is no strong civilian candidate. The wall street interests
want a strong man. One of my fathers cousins who is in the J. P.
Morgan company told my father that he (Wood) could get all the
money backing he wanted. In other words the strong man can get
all the money necessary the question is who is the strongest?????

W. is laying great stress on the fact that you are a simple soldier
while he is a soldier in part but above all a great organizer. You
should tell some of the things you have organized, like the Moro
Islands, Mexico, and the Great A. E. F. Really there is a popular
belief that you are some hard fighting man dripping blood while
he is the great organizer. You have organized more things than any
man now living.

I respectfully call your attention to another point which to me
seems important. If he is elected what will happen to you? You will
command the Island of Guam.[31]

In his letter to Pershing, Patton was especially concerned with the
cuts Congress was about to make in the army. "Unless a military man is
elected it will be the end of the army," he predicted. "People like the late
Maj. Le Gardia [Fiorello H. LaGuardia] now congressman are trying to

dictate what shall become of the army." Unfortunately some of Patton's fears came true, for on July 11, 1919, Congress reduced the strength of the Tank Corps to 154 officers and 2,508 enlisted men. Rockenbach was to command the force, which would remain at Camp Meade.[32]

From Chaumont in July, Pershing answered Patton evasively about two subjects: politics and Nita. "My own theory is that all the booms so far started have been sprung a little too early," he wrote of politics. On the subject of Nita, he gave no details but said he had seen her at the London home of the Keith Merrills. He found the visit pleasant, but he had no plans to see her again.[33]

Having gone to England as a Red Cross worker to be closer to the general, Nita was heading for heartbreak. In England in mid-June she received a letter that Pershing had sent to her in California explaining his three reasons for slowing down the romance. The first was the twenty-seven-year difference in their ages. The second was his strong feelings for his late wife. The third was the cruelest. He feared that Nita would abuse his only surviving child, his son, Warren. After reading the letter, Nita wrote to her mother: "If John sat up nights thinking he could not further miss the mark with me. . . . Who in H—— gave him this morbid poison I would bet he never thought of those things alone. It would take the female of the species."[34]

Learning that Nita was staying in Berkshire, England, Pershing wrote her again in late June. He explained his neglect of her on the grounds that he was terribly busy. He had just received an honorary degree from Oxford and would soon be similarly honored by Cambridge. After urging Georgie to tell Nita to come to Europe, Pershing now discouraged her from coming to Paris for a weekend. He had no idea, he told her, what would be required if she desired to make the trip from England to the continent, but he knew it would not be easy. Pershing concluded on an impersonal note: "The signing of the Peace last Saturday was very interesting."[35]

In July, Nita heard that Pershing was coming to London to take part in an International Peace Parade. Emerging one day from her Red Cross office, she saw a military convoy. Standing in one vehicle waving to the crowd were Pershing and two British generals. Waving back, Nita was sure Pershing saw her, but he gave no indication of it. Two days later Nita decided to phone him. The call led nowhere, for Pershing said he was too busy to see her. But on July 20, the day after the Peace Parade,

Pershing phoned her. They met and had "one hell of an evening" discussing the "bugaboos" tormenting him. The upshot of the meeting was that the two decided to marry before Pershing went home. The next day Pershing sent her flowers.

Nita never saw him again. A final time he wrote her saying his doubts had returned. Deciding to go back home, Nita vowed to spend her life with her parents. She asked them never to speak again of her romance. When her brother hinted that things might yet be patched up, Nita retorted: "Anything is better than the H—— of wishing, longing and futile hoping that I have been through."[36]

Was Pershing, as Nita suspected, involved with another woman? In Paris he was courting Louise Cromwell Brooks. A prominent debutante—her stepfather was a partner of the banker J. P. Morgan, and her brother later married the tobacco heiress Doris Duke—she was divorcing her husband when Pershing became infatuated with her, short skirts, bobbed hair, and all. As the Washington lawyer and government official Thurman Arnold, who served as an artillery officer in France, swore, she hoped to marry Pershing, and after the Armistice hinted that she would leave him if he did not marry her. According to Arnold, he replied: "Marrying you would be like buying a book for someone else to read." Then, on Valentine's Day of 1922, Louise became the wife of Douglas MacArthur. Pershing, then chief of staff, sent MacArthur a portrait of Louise painted by a Hungarian artist along with a card that said: "With my compliments." MacArthur later unsuccessfully sued the columnist Drew Pearson, whose daughter was married to Arnold's son, for printing what Louise had told him: her stepfather had lobbied with the secretary of war to get MacArthur promoted to major general.[37]

With Nita's love affair and his own career not going well, Patton wished to escape from it all. Informing Aunt Nannie on the very day Congress was cutting the Tank Corps that by September 30, 1919, he would revert back to his old rank, he yearned for the restful summers of his youth. He would soon go on leave and planned to return to California and Catalina. "How is the fishing at the island?" he asked. "I hope that the Japs have left a fiew fish."[38]

Actually changes had taken place on the island since Patton and Bea had last been there. A mysterious fire had destroyed the old Metropole Hotel, a three-story wooden structure. George Patton, Sr., had helped replace it with the Catalina Hotel, constructed of Catalina serpentine marble that salt water could not corrode.

The greatest change took place in this very year. The Banning Company had owned Catalina since 1892. Throughout the years the Bannings revered the place as deeply as the Pattons did. Hancock Banning, Sr., the husband of George Patton's half sister, Anne Ophelia Smith, often piloted vessels to the island. In 1919, however, the Bannings sold Catalina to William Wrigley, Jr., the gum manufacturer and owner of the Chicago Cubs baseball team. The sale closed a chapter in the history of the Pattons, of the Bannings, and of the island.[39]

In July Georgie, Bea, and their two daughters visited California. "Papa and I had long talks about the war," Patton remembered. "He had followed it carefully and was a delight to talk with. . . . He was so proud of me that he embarrassed me. When he presented me to his friends he always said: 'Mr. so and so you remember my son Colonel Patton.'" True to his word, Georgie spent time fishing off Catalina.[40]

V

Returning to Camp Meade, Patton found Rockenbach, back in the United States, in charge of the Tank Corps. Welborn became his deputy. Occupying his time with minor assignments, Patton dreamed of the glories so close in time but so removed from what he was now doing. "One year ago to day we were in the battle of St. Mihiel and having a fine time," he exaggerated to his father. "Now I am in the dust and have hay fever and a hell of a time. Where will we be next year???" Despite the recent cuts, Patton planned to stay with the tanks at least until July. "So we are trying to get a house near here and have as good a time as possible." Rocky had given Patton command of all the Renault light tanks, "which means," Patton explained, "that if we fight I do it as the heavy tanks are not yet built." He commanded four battalions, broken down into twelve companies with about three hundred Renaults, but had enough men to fill only one company. "The rest are simple skeletons. Also I was directed to formulate a method of street fighting in latin-american cities. Which I did and it is a beauty. This last item is confidential."[41]

Unlike many other would-be generals, such as Omar N. Bradley, who graduated from West Point in the same class as Eisenhower, Georgie knew how to play the social game. Having the money to do so, the Pattons entertained constantly. One night it was Kate Fowler and her husband, Van S. Merle-Smith, Sr., who after serving in France was now the third assistant secretary of state. Then it was Colonel Charles L. Scott, later Patton's commander in the 2nd Armored Division in Georgia, who with his wife stayed with the Pattons for three days. Next came the party given by Bea and Georgie at the Chevy Chase Club for Bea's cousin, Beatrice Banning, "a very nice girl and quite pretty. Gen. R. is going to the party," Patton informed Aunt Nannie, "and will stay all night with us." They also attended a dinner given for them by Senator Phelan. Present were Secretary of War Newton Baker, two assistant secretaries of state, and two other senators. "It was very nice of him," Patton told his father, "but we did not know till next day that we were the guests of honor." Most important of all, the Pattons renewed acquaintances with their old friend Henry L. Stimson. Through Stimson, who spent much of his time in Washington, Bea and Patton met Senator James Wadsworth of New York, a member of the committee handling military affairs. In the coming years both of these important men would steadfastly support Patton.[42]

Aware of the value of political allies, Patton relished the stories in the papers that his father was one of three men being considered by Wilson for the post of secretary of commerce. "I do hope that they are true," he wrote his father of the reports, "and that you will accept the job if it is offered. It would be of such short duration as to in no way injure your health while on the other hand it would give you a new interest and insure your meeting many interesting people. If you get the offer accept!!!!"[43]

As 1919 drew on, Patton spent more and more time with Eisenhower discussing tanks. In the First World War tanks functioned to support the infantry, the Queen of Battles. Everything seemed to be based on linear tactics and the straightforward movement of masses of troops. Preceding the first line of infantry by about fifty yards, the new monsters destroyed the machine gun nests that prevented infantry from moving effectively. Unfortunately those who saw the tank solely as an infantry support had no interest in further developing the machines. They were content to leave the speed of the tank at three miles an hour, roughly as fast as an infantryman could walk. Along with some of the other young officers at Meade, Ike and Patton criticized such narrow thinking. They believed that tanks should be speedy and that, used in mass, they could envelop the enemy and strike behind enemy lines.[44]

Patton's friend Bradford G. Chynoweth saw the struggle between Tank Corps and infantry in historical perspective. He "thought of the conflict in terms of the comparison between the Grecian Phalanx," which attacked straight ahead, "and the Roman Legion, with the modification as introduced by Hannibal, whose elephants and heavy cavalry I thought of as forerunners of the modern tank and armored forces. Hannibal's classic battle of Cannae—the tactics of envelopment was a keynote."[45]

Even now the Mark VIII constituted a vast improvement over the Renault. The Renault possessed a speed of about five miles an hour, the Mark VIII eight miles an hour. The Mark VIII, moreover, had great firepower: two mounted cannons, one on either side, and five machine guns. It could crawl up wide, steep ditches and cross trenches.[46]

Desiring to learn even more about tanks, Eisenhower and Patton decided to rip one apart, nuts, bolts, and all. "Now if a clock that has been disassembled can frighten the amateur," Eisenhower recalled, "a tank, even a small one, is infinitely worse. I had doubts that we would ever restore the vehicle to running order." During their afternoon hours the two officers began reassembling the tank, "and so carefully had we done the work, that no pieces were left over and the machine operated when we were finished."[47]

During the fall of 1919 events occurred that excited Patton. "We have had great luck in tanks lately," Patton advised his mother in early November. "A man who is an inventor came here and after he got our ideas as to what was necessary from a fighting viewpoint he designed what I think will be the greatest machine in the world. It is as far ahead of the old tanks as day is from night. And for a wonder there is lots of room in it."[48]

The man was John Walter Christie and his machine was, reported a board that included Patton and Brett, the first tank "designed and constructed solely from the military standpoint." It featured "a radically new idea of track-suspension with potential achievement of much greater cross country speed than had been thought of in the early tank history." Set across the entire length of the machine, the power plant saved space and avoided the loss of power so noticeable in earlier tanks. The motor and transmission were also far simpler than in other tanks, saving space and granting easy access to both units when repairs were needed. The Infantry and the Ordnance Departments, however, considered the new design too revolutionary, and the United States Army never fully supported Christie.[49]

Meantime, Ike and Georgie spent much of their time testing by trial and error changes in tactics and strategy they were sure the tank would bring about. "Every mistake we made," Eisenhower related, "every correction, every scrap of information about the exploitation of terrain was added to World War I's lessons." With "the enthusiasm of zealots," the two analyzed the tactical problems used at Fort Leavenworth, Kansas, in the courses at the Command and General Staff School. Solving the problems first in the accepted manner, the tankers then added tanks to the equation and solved them again. In every case the troops supported by tanks won.[50]

Two incidents, Ike recalled, took the adventure out of both officers. The Renaults, small and light, often bogged down, and Patton and Eisenhower began using the heavier Mark VIII to tow the Renaults over rough spots. One day, in the midst of one such operation, they heard a ripping sound. A towing cable had snapped. "As it broke," Ike remembered, "the front half whirled around like a striking black snake." At the speed of a bullet fired from a machine gun, the cable whisked past the faces of the two officers, "cutting off brush and saplings as if the ground had been shaved with a sharp razor." The two experimenters had escaped sudden death by five or six inches. The second narrow escape came when a water-cooled machine gun, hot from constant use, fired at the two. Patton was able to stop it by twisting the belt feeding the rounds into the chamber. After the breaking cable and self-feeding gun, Patton and Eisenhower decided to slow down a bit. They had used up their allotment of luck, which, Eisenhower observed, in Patton's case was "little enough."[51]

Amid this self-inflicted danger, Patton continued to study the lives of great commanders, not just the famous ones like Napoleon and Wellington but those lesser known. Especially influential on the young soldier were the ideas of British Lieutenant-General Sir Stanley Maude. In almost every respect Patton's ideas paralleled Maude's. To Maude's observation that continued staff service stultified an officer's ability to lead, Patton wrote: "Truly." War, Maude believed, involved taking risks. Orders must be short, clear, and given promptly. Victory could only be achieved by inflicting "sledge-hammer blows against the enemy's field army." Despite his unending concern for the well-being of his troops, Maude "never shrank from losing men when there was a definite strategical or tactical object to be gained by doing so." After the battle, no matter how small the success, troops must be praised and given confidence. Maude visited hospitals daily, and whenever possible attended the funerals of commissioned and noncommissioned officers. Above all, Maude preached, "there should be no half-measures—it only means further sacrifices in blood and money, which are heavy enough." Studying the life of Maude, who died of cholera after capturing Baghdad during the war, Patton found someone to emulate. "Except for his adiction to Paper Work," he noted with his usual misspellings, "a very grate soldier."[52]

VI

Back in the real world, Bea and Georgie Patton continued their social whirl. Late in November 1919 they left Camp Meade for the Army-Navy football game in New York, where Bea's brother, Frederick Ayer, Jr., and his wife, Hilda, joined them. "We will stay at the Pennsylvania Hotel and have Captain Banning to dinner," Patton told Aunt Nannie. "That was the only place we could get rooms." That Monday, after they returned, they entertained General and Mrs. Harbord, General and Mrs. Conner, and Bea's Massachusetts neighbor, Mrs. John Hay Hammond, at dinner.[53]

Always close to his sister, Fred handled her finances. Frederick Ayer, Sr., had left an estate then valued at $19,207,719, and, as events showed, he passed almost all of it on to his children without taxes. How much Bea inherited probably even she did not know. "Her accounts are very complicated," Fred told George Patton, Sr., in early 1920, "and it requires considerable work to get the reports in shape."[54]

Patton possessed far less money than Bea, and he never understood finances. During his adult life people devoted to him handled such matters for him. While George Patton lived he took care of some of his son's business. Then the task fell to Bea's brother and to Georgie's cousin, the attorney Arvin H. "Jerry" Brown, the son of George Patton's sister Nellie Patton Brown. At first Georgie seemed to distrust his cousin, whom he nicknamed "the Jew." In April 1920 he warned his father: "I see in an announcement that Jerry is in a new business and that you are a director. Be careful that this modern Shylock does not get more than a pound of your flesh."[55]

Patton, however, soon learned that Jerry possessed a keen business and legal sense and a devotion to the Pattons and Wilsons. He, and later his son, worked for them, advised them, and negotiated for them, accepting payments only when they were practically forced on him. By the time he was a general, Patton trusted few people as completely as he trusted Jerry Brown.

On the day in 1920 that Fred Ayer wrote to George Patton about Bea's finances, Patton wrote his father about his own. To Patton income tax always presented a puzzle. His salary in 1919 amounted to $6,313.93, and his father handled the California tax.[56]

Busy with his career, Patton invariably ignored his finances. Again in 1923, when he earned $5,769 in salary, $506 from partnerships, and $19,290 from stock dividends, Patton neglected to pay his California tax. "*You* evidently have no business instinct and in an age of speculation, perhaps it is just as well," his father wrote him. "Let Big Business continue on its predestined course and eventually it will be looking about for a Man on Horseback and you may be the man."[57]

Strangely enough, Patton's dividends indicated an influence at work on him far more conservative than that of his father, a Wilsonian Democrat who hated corporations and the extremely wealthy. On November 26, 1921, Bea established for her husband a trust, from which he received the dividends. In charge of the trust was Fred and Bea's half brother, Charles Fanning Ayer. Thus was Patton drawn closer to Charles Ayer, a director, along with William Wood, of the family's woolen factories, the scene of the bitter strike of 1912.[58] From Charles Ayer and Wood, not from his father, Patton absorbed much of his distrust of labor and of radicals, many of them Jews and Italians.

In 1920 Georgie worried a good deal about his parents. He urged his father, who was not feeling well, to play golf five times a week.

If you go and die on me, the only man friend or companion I ever had will be gone and half my incentive to do things will be gone with it. Why cant you persuade Ma to do the same thing. I feel sure that if she wore heavy clothing so as to sweat she would have much fiewer attacks of rheumatism. Now dont put off doing what I ask and think about it. I am so much like you that I know unless you do a thing at once you will not do it at all. Get busy!!!![59]

As for politics, Patton took his usual gloomy view. "Universal training has been beaten and things for the future of the U.S. are very black," he wrote his father in February 1920. "We will surely have a revolution and there are no troops to hold. Unless they change the Army bill the Cav. will be reduced to about eleven regiments all always on the Border. The infantry will almost certainly gobble the Tanks and there will be general hell to pay."[60]

By April Patton was indeed bored. Eight tank companies had been disbanded, "so I shall have very few men left here." His superiors had urged him to participate in the fencing matches in the coming Olympics in Holland, but Patton believed himself so out of practice that he hesitated to compete in meets. "Who will you vote for BRYAN?" he asked his father about the coming election. "You had best change over to the republican side. The other is too maloderous. . . . B. Jr. is getting quite grown up and is a good rider. She and Gen. Rhodes have been riding several times and she refers to Gen. Mitchell as 'My friend Billy Mitchell.' "[61]

With his polo ponies, his riding horses, and his show horses, Patton hardly resembled the typical peacetime officer who had to live on his salary. In late May and early June, taking a vacation without his family, he traveled to Florida in the private railroad car of the Virginia financier and banker, Frederic William Scott. On a huge yacht called the *Lady Fish,* which had four launches, each with its own navigator, cook, waiter, and deckhand, the party sailed to several fishing spots off the Florida Keys. At one place Patton caught three tarpon, "one of which," he reported to his father, "was the record for the last two seasons being 187 pounds. I had him mounted so you had better look for a place to put him." He also landed a 150-pound jew fish and five or six Mexican pompanes, each weighing about twenty pounds. "I have not seen so many fish since you and I and Jim Gardner went fishing that time I caught the big yellow tale years ago." Hanging over the trip, however, was Georgie's realization that on June 30 he would revert to his permanent rank of captain, but he hoped to be promoted to major soon thereafter.[62]

While Patton fished, Congress transferred the Tank Corps, making it part of the infantry. Ike and Georgie were two of the few officers who believed the corps should be independent. In separate articles published in 1920 in the *Infantry Journal,* they lamented the inevitable. Patton's piece, "Tanks in Future Wars," published in May, decried the lack of interest in the big machines, which even now "were far superior to the slow, lumbering babies of 1918. Several nations already had tanks capable of speeds of from twelve to fifteen miles an hour across country and of up to twenty miles an hour on roads." Impervious to small arms fire, these monsters could advance two hundred miles without being resupplied. With deadlier weapons, future wars in Asia, Africa, and the Americas, "the vast continents of the A's," would not be conflicts "with endless entrenchments and flankless armies." They would be wars in which tanks would guard rears and flanks, defend positions, and be used as offensive weapons. "The tank is new," Patton argued, "and, for the fulfillment of its destiny, it must remain independent. . . . The tank corps grafted on infantry, cavalry, artillery, or engineers, will be like the third leg to a duck—worthless for control, for combat impotent."[63]

Six months later Eisenhower's piece appeared in the same journal. Exceptionally well reasoned, the article acknowledged the tank's limitations in battle—it could not, for example, cross unbridged bodies of water—and then took up one by one the three arguments commonly used against tanks. First, Eisenhower pointed out that far from being of value only in trench warfare, tanks could be used, as they were in the past war, any time to overcome obstacles such as barbed wire and machine guns. Against the second argument, that "We will probably never again be engaged in truly 'trench warfare,'" Eisenhower noted that in the last stages of any war between great powers "the Infantry must invariably expect to have to penetrate belts of wire and difficult systems of trenches. . . . Under such conditions, what infantry commander is not going to thank his stars that he has on hand a number of tanks to lead and to support his unit through this stage of the attack?" Finally, against those who stressed "the mechanical inefficiency of the tank," Eisenhower argued that the wartime machine had to be thrown together hastily. With more time factories now were producing tanks of ideal size and speed. Having justified the use of the tank, Eisenhower recommended a change in the makeup of each infantry division. He suggested that a tank company with fifteen tanks replace the motorized machine gun battalion of fifty-seven vehicles. This would give the division a unit of swift movement and great firepower, a unit capable of rapid advances and of protecting flanks.[64]

Eisenhower later recalled that he was severely chastised for his article. Called before the chief of infantry, he was told his ideas were wrong and dangerous. He should keep them to himself. If he persisted in publishing such articles, he would be subject to court-martial.[65]

By this time Eisenhower and Patton had gained an ally in their fight for tanks. He was Bradford G. Chynoweth, and he had known both since their cadet days. "When I was a plebe," he wrote of Patton, "we had a first class cadet adjutant who was a sight to see. A perfect type of soldier. He came there determined to be cadet adjutant and he made the grade. . . . Now of course it was caste, because he never looked at us plebes; unless a man violated an order when he would give him the works; or unless a man did something good, like football, when he would pat him on the back." Eisenhower, on the other hand, was "my rear rank file while he was a plebe at West Point, and I tried to start him out correctly then."[66]

Like Ike, Chynoweth never made it overseas during the war. After serving as a major of engineers, he left the service for a year, returning as an infantry major. Reporting to the "portly Chief of Infantry," General Charles S. Farnsworth, with whom Patton had served in Mexico, Chynoweth heard that he was being sent to the Tank School at Meade. There he studied tank tactics and learned to drive the six-ton Renault and the larger Mark VIII.[67]

At Meade, Patton gave his friend lessons in handling Rockenbach's fiery temper.

> I remember going to one big Christie demonstration in 1920, with General Rockenbach, in Rock Creek Park, D.C. Old Rocky was fuming with rage against the Ordnance Dept. during that show. But I cannot say how much justice he had on his side. He was a famous Old Army martinet and was always fuming against somebody. I had several fuming matches with him, myself. The only man I knew who could handle Rocky was George Patton. Georgie told me his method. When he wanted to put over something, he

wrote it up in a letter which he left on Rocky's desk. Then he would stay away from him for a week. Finally, he would go into the Old Man's office and argue heatedly against his own ideas. Rocky would rise up in arms and defend Georgie's original idea; whereupon Georgie would gracefully concede.[68]

One of the army's best marksmen, Chynoweth described another encounter with Rockenbach.

The day I left, Rocky said: "What do you infantry people know about shooting? George Patton with pistol could hold off your whole Infantry team." I replied: "That's nonsense, General!" WHAM. UP he went again.

At such times Rocky would yell: "Get out of my office or I'll throw you out!!"[69]

One of the army's finest writers—he served as Rockenbach's intelligence officer in charge of publicity—Chynoweth could hardly be expected to remain silent on the subject of tanks. In an article appropriately titled "Cavalry Tanks," published in the *Cavalry Journal,* he argued that the Tank Corps should not be independent, for tanks constituted "a natural and normal auxiliary to the horse. From the cavalry viewpoint, the tank is truly no more than a great iron horse. It should be welcomed in support of horses of flesh and blood." Asked by Chynoweth to comment on the piece, Patton argued that the horse cavalry worked well at certain times. Cavalrymen and their mounts could live off the land and therefore, unlike tanks, required no supplies. Patton could not picture tanks "operating in the mountains of Mexico, the rice paddies of the Philippines, the forests of Canada, or, in the face of competent artillery, on the sandy and gully-infested plains of Texas." The tank, he insisted, was "a special, technical, and vastly powerful weapon. It certainly is neither a cavalryman nor an infantryman." But given "half a chance" and the proper time, "it will mean the difference between defeat and victory to the infantry or cavalry with which it is co-operating." Patton urged the creation of a separate Tank Corps, "neither infantry tanks nor cavalry tanks," but a "special mobile general headquarters reserve" that could be used "as circumstances demand."[70]

Facing the demise of their beloved corps, the tankers went different

ways. Viner, who had reached the rank of lieutenant colonel, resigned
from the army and went into the printing business. Welborn returned
to the infantry. Patton, now a major, realized that he had no future in a
unit commanded by the infantry. He requested a transfer to the cavalry.
Accordingly, on September 30, 1920, his three years with the tanks
would end. He was to be transferred to Fort Myer and the 3rd Cavalry,
commanded by Colonel William C. Rivers.[71]

Two days before he left the 304th Brigade, the parting ceremony
took place. Bea described it to Aunt Nannie:

> G. assembled all his men—700—and made a very touching
> farewell speech. . . . Then the headquarters Sgt. Maj. & 2 others
> advanced and presented me with a beautiful cup. About a foot
> high, solid & very heavy. On one side was etched a light tank. On
> the other was "To Colonel & Mrs. George S. Patton, Jr. from the
> enlisted personnel of the 304th Brigade." I made a little speech &
> we all cried some, especially G & me & the Sgt. Major. . . . It was
> very touching.[72]

VII

During the fall of 1920, Patton was more interested in his horses, horse
shows, and games than in anything else, the highlight of the season
being the New York Horse Show in Madison Square Garden in mid-
November. Accompanied by Bea, Patton, the captain of both the cavalry horse show and polo teams, spent three days in the city with Fred
and Hilda Ayer. At the show Patton pulled a muscle in his leg, and his
big horse got sick and could not perform. Still, Fred told the elder Patton, Georgie won three blue ribbons, "which is a record not to be
sneezed at at Madison Square. He and B. both seemed in good form."[73]

The peacetime army usually occupies itself with training, maintenance of equipment, and social events, and Patton excelled at each of
these. "We are having all sorts of funerals," he complained to his father
after two months at Fort Myer, "and it is raising hell with our training.
The army is gone to hell."

All the while Georgie and Bea lived a social life that few other army
officers could afford. Late in November they went to New York for the

Army-Navy football game. While there, they went to the theater, then to the Astor Hotel, "where we saw a lot of army people," and finally, with his classmate Philip S. Gage and his wife, to a dance.[74]

Recalling that Patton possessed a "bubbling sense of humor and a love for childish pranks," Chynoweth described a stag party his friend gave at Fort Myer when Bea visited her family.

> He arranged his dining room to reflect the decor and fragrance of the stables. Bales of hay were the seats. Straw and manure littered the floor. The punch bowl was champagne afloat with doughnuts. A horse was gotten in to the pantry. With a bait of oats, they induced Dobbin to stick his head through the pantry cubbyhole into the salon. The party was a wild success until, suddenly, a telegram arrived. Bea was returning unexpectedly that very evening. Georgie called for troopers to clean up that mess. It proved more difficult to get Dobbin out of the pantry than it had been to get him in. Dobbin ran amok and made a wreck of the dining room. He kicked to pieces Bea's favorite tea table. On her arrival, Bea also ran amok. George was in the doghouse for a week.[75]

Into 1921 the social whirl continued. In late February, a week before the inauguration of Warren G. Harding, a Republican, as president and the installation of John W. Weeks as the secretary of war, the Pattons went into action. "Beatrice and I let the grass NOT grow under our feet," Georgie wrote his father, "but went and called on the new sec. of War to day. We are having him and his wife to dinner on the first army dance after inauguration."[76]

Surprisingly, Patton's social activities helped Eisenhower. In the United States, Patton remained close to Brigadier General Fox Conner, who had been Pershing's operations officer in France. In mid-June the two were going to Florida but were coming back by way of Havana, where, Patton wrote his mother, "Gen. Conner and I expect confidently to remain drunk continuously."

One Sunday, while still at Meade, the Conners accepted a dinner invitation from the Pattons. Also guests were Ike and Mamie Eisenhower. After an early afternoon dinner, Conner, Ike, and Patton walked down to the tank shops, where Conner hurled at Ike a barrage of questions about the machines, finishing as evening approached. A few months later Conner asked Eisenhower if he would like to accompany him to Panama as the executive officer of an infantry brigade. At first Rockenbach declined to forward Eisenhower's application to the War Department. When he finally sent the application on, the War Department rejected it. Conner then appealed directly to Pershing, now chief of staff, and, Eisenhower remembered, "the red tape was torn to pieces."[77]

Patton spent much of the fall of 1921 preparing for the dedication of the Tomb of the Unknown Soldier in Arlington National Cemetery, where his men assisted Brigadier General Harry H. Bandholtz, the army commander in Washington. "We are all putting much effort to five the unknown stiff-probably a shirker," he joshed to his father. ". . . As Col. Rivers says: 'We play safe on his religious beliefs as the Ampitheater where he is to be stored is completely heathen.' Any how we got extra men to do it with so have no kick coming."[78]

The day of the dedication, November 11, 1921, dawned "nasty . . . wet and cold but," Georgie wrote home, "quite a lot of people turned out the same." After picking up the coffin at the Capitol, Patton and his men accompanied it to the cemetery. "There was a dense crowd all the way," he reported, "but naturally no cheering."

Reaching the amphitheater, Patton saw an impressive sight. Seated with Harding were the military elite of the Allied powers, including Field Marshal Ferdinand Foch of France, British Vice Admiral David Beatty, and Pershing and Harbord of the United States. But, Patton believed, Harding's speech ruined the occasion.

As the Presidents speech progressed and became more and more political and **PACIFIC** it was most interesting to watch the faces of these great soldiers. At the beginning they were open and smiling then the eyes began to pucker up not with tears but with the mean look I try so hard to emulate and the smiling lips began to assume hard lines, while the chins protruded. They could not listen with out emotion to an arraignment of war and their eyes lit with the "Passionless passion of slaughter," though they knew it not, or at least could not admit it afterwards—the ones I asked. The speech its self had no pep in the delivery and to me at least carried no message or conviction. He described to men who had seen the real thing a scene in mimic war which he had recently seen at the infantry school, and which had naturally impressed his civilian mind.

Depressingly for Patton, the ceremony ushered in the beginning of the Washington Conference to reduce armaments. Inheriting his father's "happy facility for gloom," he noted that, having just turned thirty-six, "Half my allotted span is out." A new war seemed a distant prospect.[79]

Still, Georgie observed to his father, war constituted part of man's nature. "I think there was some reason why you read me such bloody books when I was young. Though God knows it looks pacific enough right now to discourage Mars him self."[80]

In late 1921 and early 1922 Patton busied himself writing papers, the most important of which was a seven-page opus he first titled "Tactical Tendencies." When published in April 1922 in the *Cavalry Journal,* the piece became "What the World War Did for Cavalry." Patton admitted that many of the ideas in these articles came from a recently published volume by a British colonel, R. M. P. Preston, entitled *The Desert Mounted Corps: An Account of the Cavalry Operations in Palestine and Syria, 1917–1918.* Proving, Patton argued, the worth of the cavalry and the saber in an age of growing mechanization, the book described in detail and with maps the thirty-two successful and two unsuccessful cavalry charges in Palestine during the recent war. Calling the volume "the finest military book I have ever read," Patton sent copies to his father and to Pershing.

In his articles Patton, agreeing with Sir Isaac Newton's observation about action and reaction, pointed out that every military innovation inspired a countermove. The machine gun brought on trench warfare, which then led to the tank, which, in turn, led to more elastic defenses.

Patton's conclusions were those of the major of cavalry, not those of the colonel of tanks. The Great War had fostered the birth of "men who would either bomb, gas or squash the enemy into oblivion." Yet, in many ways, the men on horseback, wielding sabers, attained the victory. The cavalry still retained two advantages over the foot soldiers: mobility and surprise. For years the cavalry operated in "open unfenced pasture land." Now, because of "the ever growing menace of air bombardment," it must shift to "closed country, preferably wooded." Patton still believed that the bayonet charge of the infantry and the saber charge of the cavalry were the high points of war. But whereas the infantry charge often failed because the enemy retreated "before the Bayonets ever reach him," the saber charge was usually successful. "Remember," he concluded, "that there is nothing too good for the man who brings off a successful saber charge."[81]

VIII

The late Colonel Roger H. Nye has pointed to the connection between Patton's continued reading and writing and his belief in an everlasting soul, reincarnated through the ages. In an unpublished memorandum he noted that Patton learned in childhood that education continued after formal schooling ended. This led him to accumulate a vast military library, and his reading inspired "a torrent of writing. Both activities," Nye commented, "closely wove together his beliefs about his everlasting soul and fated destiny with his fixed star of the battle hero and military gentleman."[82]

In accord with Colonel Nye's observations, Patton continued to develop the idea that he had lived previous lives. In the poem "The Soul of Battle," he returned to a theme he and his father often discussed, Norse mythology. He had, he observed, "seen the curtain parted" and "glimpsed the flinty trail" that "the spirits have all trod."

His most ambitious work was a direct descendant of his father's favorite, "Memories of a Roman Ruin in France." Written on May 27, 1922, "Through a Glass, Darkly" depicted a soldier repeatedly reborn. In it Patton saw his previous existences: a Greek opposing the Persian king Cyrus; a soldier in a Roman Legion; an Englishman fighting the French at Crécy in 1346; a cavalryman with Napoleon's marshal, Joachim Murat; and finally a tanker in the Great War. Each life, excluding the last, ended in horrible death: by "arrows in my neck," by lance "through my entrails . . . on Crecy's field," by "a rope around my neck," by "doom" at Waterloo. The pattern would go on:

> *So for ever in the future*
> *Shall I battle as of yore*
> *Dying to be born a fighter*
> *But to die again once more.*[83]

What might have been interpreted as visions inspired by his vast military reading and writing, Patton and his daughter Ruth Ellen Patton Totten considered evidence of previous existences. In another of these he saw himself as a slingshot soldier with the great Carthaginian general Hannibal in the second century B.C. The Romans had destroyed the aqueduct supplying fresh water, and he was forced to drink urine out of his helmet. In 1937, awakening in a hospital from a kick in the leg by one of Bea's horses, Patton told of another episode. He had seen himself bloody and lying on a round Viking shield made of animal hide. At first the Vikings believed he was dead, but when they realized he was not they placed him among the living. Patton interpreted this as a sign that he yet had military work to do. A third instance occurred in Virginia one wintry morning in 1934 while Patton and Bea awaited the start of a fox hunt. Since he had burned his face in Mexico, Patton's ears and cheeks turned a deep red in the cold. In pain he closed his eyes. When he opened them, he said to his wife: "The dead were in carts. We carried the dead in carts so the Russians wouldn't know how many of us they'd killed. It was so cold the blood was brown on the snow." The scene was Napoleon's retreat from Moscow. Patton had lost an arm, and the other, which he kept inside his coat, ached with pain from the cold, just as his face did now. "I saw a small man on a horse riding ahead," he said of Napoleon. "He didn't care what happened to us."[84]

Amid his writings and visions, Patton experienced a touch of activity at the end of January 1922. One Saturday night he was sent to the Knickerbocker theater in Washington after its roof collapsed during a heavy snowfall. Ninety-seven people were killed. With a hundred men Patton helped get out "about a dozen corpses. . . . They were pretty well squashed," he informed his father. "Many of the heads being only three or four inches thick this made it rather hard to identify people as they were a sort of purple color."[85]

Such serious duty being rare, Patton busied himself with other things. In mid-March he and two other officers from Fort Myer went to Annapolis to fence the navy team. "We beat them ten to six," he informed his father. "It is the first time that they have been licked this year. I beat the Intercoligate Dueling Sword Champion. It was the first time he had lost this year. Last year he beat me."[86]

During the spring and summer of 1922, while Bea was in England visiting her sister Kay, who was sick, Patton continued such activities.

Around Easter he took part in his first polo match of the season, he informed Bea, "and Javalin went very fine almost too good to be true." At the match Mrs. Charles Dawes, the wife of the famous financier, invited Bea to lunch, which, because she was away, she could not attend. "The children went to the egg roll at the White House but there was such a crowd that they came away at once."[87]

Early in the summer, while training with an army team on Long Island, Patton hobnobbed with the polo-playing elite, "the greatest players in the world. . . . I have been dining and lunching with Belmonts, Harrimans, Penn Smiths, Stoddard, Brice Wings, etc. to a great extent," he informed Bea. "These are the nicest very rich people I have ever seen. Their houses are very simple and they drive Fords and Dodges with out chauffeurs. All the women do something to their hair to keep it from getting gray. Other wise they don't make up except their lips."[88]

Bea's return in August only seemed to heighten her husband's interest in polo. "The more I see of soldiering," he wrote his father in September, "the more I think of Polo. It certainly is a bore to teach a lot of men to shoot well only to loose them and get a bunch next season who have to be taught all over again." But by the time Patton wrote this letter he knew that he would soon leave the comfort of Fort Myer for the isolation of Kansas. He was to attend the Advanced Cavalry School at Fort Riley in lonely Junction City. "The thought of moving to Riley . . . is far from pleasant but I suppose that it is the best thing to do and any way we shall have little to say in the matter."[89]

Patton grew even more morose about leaving the comforts of Washington when his old tanker friend, Ralph I. Sasse, described Kansas as a "pretty hard" place. According to Sasse, Patton's impending move was the talk of Riley and Fort Leavenworth. "One of my horse friends hearing that I was to go there went to several men at a dinner begging them in drunken fervor to write 'Old Weeks not to send Patton to any more riding schools as he wins all the prizes now.' "[90]

That December, Georgie, Bea, young Bea, and Ruth Ellen left Washington by train and headed for Lake Vineyard and Christmas with the Pattons. The first leg of the seven-day journey took them to Chicago, where they rested at the Blackstone Hotel before again heading for the West Coast. On Christmas Eve the festivities began. Following a California tradition, the family enjoyed a Mexican-Spanish fiesta. An old, blind Indian woman came up, as she had for many years, from the Mission in San Gabriel to grind the cornmeal for tortillas and enchiladas with a stone pestle in a stone metate. "Our father adored Mexican food," Ruth Ellen remembered, "and our grandmother saw to it that the best was there for Georgie, who came home so infrequently." By dark the families of those who had worked for Benjamin D. Wilson and then for George Patton, Sr., had arrived: the Verdugos; the Picos (Wilson, serving under the two Pico brothers, had once led a company of militia against the Mojave Indians); the D'Orsos; and the Callahans. Ruth Ellen hinted that they had all intermarried with Mexicans, for, in contrast with the two blue-eyed Patton girls, the dozen other children present were black-haired and black-eyed.

The highlight of the stay was Christmas dinner. Among the guests, numbering at least twenty-four, were Bea's relatives, the Bannings. Although George Patton, Sr., always considered himself a Southerner, Bea's family did not share this feeling. Her mother had come from Minnesota, her father from Massachusetts. The Bannings were Westerners, having started a coach line that ran from Wilmington, Delaware, to Wilmington, California, the port for Los Angeles. The coach house at the Banning home in Los Angeles still contained six-horse coaches in mint condition, and Georgie himself, after taking lessons from that mustachioed throwback to the Old West, Captain William Banning, was able to drive a four-horse coach.

Dinner was Georgie's time to shine. Ruth Wilson Patton's mother, Margaret Hereford, had been a superb cook, even publishing in 1873 a cookbook, *Fifty Years in a Maryland Kitchen*. At West Point, Georgie had learned to carve, but, knowing his skill at it could not match that of his father, "he made carving an adventure." Attacking a roast as if he were leading a cavalry charge, Georgie waved the knife as if it were a saber. "Sometimes he would sneak up on the meat, from the pantry." On Christmas he would test every knife, sharpen the one he had chosen, tell the story of Saladin's sword that was so sharp it could cut a floating feather in half, leap into the air, and, uttering his version of the rebel yell, plunge the carving fork into the poor turkey's breast. "Then," Ruth Ellen remembered, "he would carefully withdraw the fork, put his ear to the turkey's breast, nod in a sad, wise way, and say, 'She's gone, alright,' and then start carving." During the meal Georgie often told stories, such as the one about how one year his grandmother's olives were unusually tasty. When the Pattons reached the bottom of the barrel, they found, marinating in the brine, a huge skunk. One of the desserts was a homemade plum pudding, sent all the way from Virginia. As it was being brought into the room blazing with warmed brandy, Georgie yelled at the top of his lungs: "Fire! Fire! Get the women and children out of here!" The cook then rushed in with chilled brandy, which would not burn, and put out the fire. "It smelled wonderful!" recalled Ruth Ellen.

In the evening Patton tradition took over. George Patton went down to the wine cellar and returned with a dusty bottle of port. He also brought to the drawing room a japanned tin box, the key to which he carried on his watch chain. He wiped the bottle clean, looked at its label, and said to his son: "Yes, this is the '85 vintage. I laid this port the year you were born, boy." Then came the box, which contained remnants of Patton family history. Ruth Ellen was entrusted with a daguerreotype of Colonel Waller Tazewell Patton, who died in Pickett's charge at Gettysburg, and with the five-dollar gold piece that stopped the bullet that would have killed Colonel George S. Patton in the first battle of Winchester. Young Bea received the shell fragment, wrapped in a portion of a blood-stained shirttail, that killed George Patton's father at Cedar Creek. Georgie was handed his grandfather's sword. "And the stories went on."[91]

IX

"We are gradually shaking down in our new house, and expect to be quite happy & comfortable here," Bea wrote her father-in-law on January 18, 1923, from 303 North Jefferson Street in Junction City.

> Georgie is getting into his stride at the School; he is home more than we expected he would be—gets here for lunch Wed. & Sat. & does not have to go back again; but so far, he studies every minute that he is at home. However—he can do far better work here than if he had to stay in the quarters assigned to him, in a shack, with shouting men & pounding typewriters going noon & night. Here,

he has a big quiet study to work in. He has no time at all, even to write a letter, but I plan to do all the odd jobs & will typewrite his notes for him daily. He is required to ride two hours daily, so should keep in good shape.[92]

The previous evening, when the Pattons had dined with Brigadier General Malin Craig, the commandant of the school, and his wife, "he gave me *quite* a talk about Georgie." The conversation "turned" on the second highest school, the Command and General Staff School at Fort Leavenworth. Bea informed General Craig that "Georgie wanted to go there, but that we would not count on going until we were ordered. He informed me that, out of G's class of 39 officers, 20 or 25 would be selected by him to go & that G. was selected already 'barring accidents.' He says that G. has the professional reputation of a student & that they want him at Leavenworth. Now we are going to show him that G. is even better than his reputation!"[93]

Patton took to the course at Fort Riley, standing second in his class at the end of March. But a trip to Leavenworth, where he attended a West Point dinner, soured his view of those there. He wrote his father the details:

It was interesting to see so many men whom I had not seen for years. I talked to a man for over half an hour at my table before I found that he was a class mate: I last saw him on graduation he has since gained a hundred pounds. Harding Polk weighs 219 and is still gaining. He was drunk most of the time and gave me an impassioned appeal not to come to Leavenworth as it will sap my youth as it has his, or if I must come not to do so until I have waited a year and let him coach me. As he is suppose to stand near the bottom of his class the offer was not alluring.

I dont think much of the place. All the men have a haunted look and all lie heavily about 75% claiming to have good marks and having bad and 25% claiming to be getting zeros and are realy at the top. To add to the joys of the prospect there are three large penetentiaries in view at all times also a lunatic assilum. Still as one must go and as many fools have survived it I suppose I will. Most of the men are fat and dress badly all of them play golf??? a hell of a game for heros???[94]

Graduating from the course at Riley in early June, Patton received a leave of three months. He then was to report to Leavenworth. Two months pregnant with their third child, Bea had already left for Prides Crossing, where she would remain until the child's birth. Accompanying her, Patton apprised his father, were the children's governess, "two servants, two dogs and two extra children that she is taking east for indigent friends. I had a wire from her at Chicago saying things were all right that far."

Much to his father's disappointment, Patton expected to spend all his leave in Massachusetts. "I certainly could not have passed a summer in California drinking Port, and done any thing at Leavenworth next year."[95]

Not that Patton did not drink at Prides Crossing. In this day of prohibition he and Bea turned to a common source of supply, "an 'Honest and High-Minded Bootlager.'" In mid-June he told his father that "you would have a nice time if you and Mama come. . . . This life of complete worthlessness is funny to me. This morning little B and I rode about fifteen miles and then I got some fresh horses and rode an hour more."[96]

After a summer of inactivity, Patton enrolled at the Command and General Staff School at Leavenworth on September 10, 1923. "The C & GS School was where they separated the sheep from the goats," observed Chynoweth, who attended the course four years after Patton. "In previous years, there were suicides of officers who failed to make the grade. My class made a joint resolve that if anyone contemplated suicide, he would first kill an instructor."[97]

Many of those who attended the course in the 1920s, including Patton and Chynoweth, believed it to be based on a faulty premise. Army authorities believed that during the World War American commanders lacked initiative and could not think clearly during the fog of battle. The school presented its remedy for this deficiency. Students were given a series of problems, each requiring a decision. The first problem presented to Patton's class required the students to focus on the surrender of Fort Henry, the Confederate installation on the Tennessee River captured by Ulysses S. Grant in February 1862. Did the Confederate commander, Brigadier General Lloyd Tilghman, as he argued in his report, find it impossible to defend the fort? Using documents provided in a sourcebook, each officer had to answer the question. On this and every other problem, students were graded on the basis of an approved solution, which the students labeled school doctrine. "They were not teaching War," Chynoweth complained. "They were teaching Dogma. . . . In that school, doctrine was the Gospel." The institution's commandant, Brigadier General Harry A. Smith, who had directed the Army General Staff College in Langres when Patton was there, justified this system to Patton's class by comparing it to the case method then used at Harvard and other law schools.[98]

Chynoweth, who was captured by the Japanese on Cebú and spent most of World War II in a prison camp, deemed the " 'approved solution' a nightmare to me, at Leavenworth—because it was so often absurd, yet if you departed from it, you were marked down." He related its consequences.

> I thought of the influence of Leavenworth, during the fiasco in the Philippines in 1941–2. The approved solution to resist enemy landings was to "DEFEAT THEM AT THE BEACH." So that was the plan in Doug's Philippine Army. It was utterly absurd, as demonstrated promptly by successive disasters.
>
> My immediate commander, General [William F.] Sharp, was a graduate of Leavenworth who had obviously given little thought to actual war. When ordered to organize for guerrilla warfare, Lo and Behold he dug deep dugouts and bottled up his command on a main road where all he could do was to surrender.[99]

Chynoweth often "Compared notes with George Patton," who "agreed with my view of The School." While a student, each wrote a skit satirizing the place, much to the chagrin of the instructors. "But Eisenhower, by contrast, stood first in his class. School doctrine was his religion."[100]

A decade later Patton described to his friend Floyd L. Parks, who was about to enter the school, his formula for success there.

> When at the school study hard but not excessively. . . . Personally I studied every evening except Saturday and Friday from SEVEN TO ELEVEN. If I was not through at that time I went to bed. If I finished earlier I also went to bed and did not devil my self with extra work. On Friday after the map problem I went home and took several big drinks to relax my mind. I did not touch alcohol at any other time.

High marks at LEAVENWORTH depend more on technique than on INTELLIGENCE. While I was there I copied in long hand one order every night. The purpose of this practice is to make the correct writing of orders automatic.

Never fight the problem or look for "Niggers in the Wood Pile" there aint any.

Never read an approved solution or talk about it to any one else until you get your mark back. Never try to dope out what the next problem will be about.

On problem days lectures stop at 11:00 A.M. Do not study between then and 1:00 P.M. when the problem starts. Take some vigorous exercise and dont eat much for lunch. A glass of milk and some soup is all you need. Dont smoke during the year it wastes time at the problems.

I will send you a bunch of notes that I made which may be of help.[101]

At Leavenworth Patton met a young infantry major from Mississippi who shared his ambitions. He and Troy H. Middleton took long walks together, and one snowy day, after the two had known each other for a while, Patton swore he would graduate from the school with honors, meaning he would be in the top 25 percent of the class. Middleton remembered his new friend as a wealthy man married to a very wealthy woman. Patton brought to the fort enough ponies for a polo team. Then, desiring competition, he shipped in enough ponies for a rival team. "George played polo with great confidence," Middleton related, "just as he had confidently predicted a high rank for himself in the school at Leavenworth."[102]

A break from school came in December. Georgie, Nita, and their mother, Ruth Wilson Patton, gathered for the birth of the baby. From the home at Prides Crossing, which she deemed as "rather a mess" because "there are so many servants they are falling over each other," Ruth Patton wrote her husband the story on Christmas Eve:

I had the most strenuous day of my life yesterday. Beatrice and I went to meet Georgie at half past ten, and his train was several hours late. When he arrived, B, Nita & I started for Prides with Keiths chauffeur who did not know the roads in a pouring rain and were nearly killed on the way by skidding—We got Kay, and Keith, went to Freddies to lunch—where Nita and I were supposed to spend the night. . . . After lunch I concluded I would go back to Prides, as I felt sure something would happen that night and I did not want to arouse Frederick's family in the middle of the night—Sure enough at half past eleven Georgie came flying down my hall calling to me to get up—so B, Kay, Keith, Georgie, and I started for Boston, in the pouring rain, Keith driving fifty miles an hour, but he drove well and we arrived at the "Phillips House" safe and sound, and waited all night for the baby to be born. We all had breakfast at the Hospital, and soon afterwards we were rewarded by the arrival of the fine baby boy—Georgie came back here to lunch with me, and went down to Prides this afternoon—We are all going to the Charles Ayers to dinner tomorrow.

The baby weighed ten and a half pounds "and has fine lungs."[103]

Three days later Ruth sent more happy news. "The baby is the talk of the hospital. He is so big, and does not look like a new born baby. He has huge hands and feet, but beautifully formed—I think Georgie is very much delighted."[104]

At the end of December, as Patton returned to Leavenworth, Bea informed his father that they had decided to give the baby the elder Patton's original name, George William. "I rather favor the '3rd' as it shows that the race at least knows its own grandfather. If he doesn't like it (the Baby not the grandfather) he can leave it out later—but he's going to be a real blonde like Georgie."[105]

Back at Leavenworth, Patton began worrying about his future. He especially sought advice from the commandant of the Army War College, Colonel George S. Simonds, whose wife was a friend of the Pattons and Wilsons. Praised by Chynoweth as "the finest commander I ever served under," Simonds suggested, in order of preference, instructorships at Leavenworth, Fort Riley, and West Point. Such positions would enable Patton to influence the careers of young men and to gain a knowledge of the characters of the men he would later command. "Grant, Lee, Stonewall Jackson, Sherman and other great leaders of the Civil War were often able to utilize their knowledge of the characters of their subordinates and opponents gained while cadets, and they have testified to it. I have heard General Pershing say the same thing."[106]

As the course at Leavenworth neared its end, Patton worried more and more about his next assignment. He toyed with the notion of staying at Leavenworth as an instructor, but hearing from General Smith of a vacancy on the staff of the 1st Cavalry Division at Fort Bliss, he "decided to go after it with all I have" as "a direct step on the ladder to the silver stars. You see there are 30 instructors," he reasoned to his father, "and only one Assistant Chief of Staff to the cavalry division also there is but one cavalry division."[107]

On the last day of April, returning from a visit to his parents, Patton learned that he was to get neither of these posts. General Smith told Beatrice that Patton was headed for the headquarters of the 1st Corps in Boston. "B is delighted," Georgie informed his father. "Personally I fear that it will be too easy for me and that I will become soft. I hope not."[108]

True to his vow, Patton graduated that June with honors. In a class of 248, he ranked twenty-fifth. Middleton stood eighth in the class and was asked to stay on as an instructor. The distinguished graduates, the next twenty-five percent of the class, included Chynoweth's roommate at West Point, Major John S. Wood of the field artillery, destined to serve under Patton and Middleton and to become one of the outstanding American soldiers of the Second World War.[109]

At a dance just after the class standings were posted, Patton spoke to Colonel Robert H. Allen, the assistant commandant of the school. "Patton," said Allen, later the chief of infantry, "it is a real pleasure to me to see a 'He' soldier graduate in the honors."[110] In this peacetime army what would fate hold for such an officer?

Five

THE WARRIOR SOUL

I

Patton had hardly settled in Boston, where, as the G-1, he was in charge of personnel, when a minor tragedy struck. Barney, his police dog, crawled under the car of the British ambassador, who was calling on the Ayer family at Prides, and was run over when the car started. "It is the first time I have cried in years," Georgie confessed to his father, "and realy I have seldom felt worse over any thing." Patton had raised Barney from a puppy, and the dog had been his sole companion when Patton lived alone for six months. "He was the best nature and smartest dog I ever saw still it cant be helped." Patton made a coffin for Barney, buried him at Prides, and vowed to put up a monument to him.

At the end of July, Patton had "found nothing interesting or instructive in this job but still hope for the best. If there is nothing to it I shall at least have plenty of time in which to read and work problems."[1]

Patton found solace in the outdoor activities available in New England. In the summer he, Bea, and the two girls "had a fine sail coming clear down to the mouth of Boston Harbor." During the winter, he at first abhorred the cold and snow. "I find in it a reason for the New England character as we know it," he reported to his father. "No one but a mean nature could survive such a climate." Patton, however, soon found something to do in the harsh weather. "I have been learning to skee and cut my face all up on Sunday in the learning but it is quite exciting when it goes well. . . . Most of us have colds but they dont amount to much and seem to be the vogue around here."[2]

Late in January 1925 Patton received a surprise. "Certainly there is plenty of change in the Army," he apprised his father.

We are ordered to Hawaii—I sail from N.Y. on the 4th of March. It was a complete surprise to us as on the cavalry foreign service list I was away down. However they have a different one on the General staff at the top of which I stand. Since foreign service is a law not a regulation there is no way of evading it.

It is terribly hard on B as she likes hunting more than any thing she has ever done and of course there is no hunting in Hawaii. However she is a good sport and does not complain.

Professionally it is possibly better for me as there are lots of soldiers out there and there is a real war problem always to be faced. Also if I stayed here I might get fat and lazy which would be bad for me. Also the climate will be fine for the children and it will be easy for us to visit you or you visit us.

Patton expected to go to Hawaii alone. He would get a house and uncrate the furniture. Bea and the children would follow in April or May. "So far in my life every thing has been for the best," he told his father, "so I think that though at present I dont see it this will also work out that way; I hope so."[3]

Patton's letter reached his father during a period of mourning. The Virginia branch of the Patton family seemed to be crumbling. In January 1925 J. Mercer Patton, who taught at Virginia Military Institute, climaxed a series of family tragedies by shooting himself. "It is a strange thing, George," Sadie Patton Hutchinson, the wife of Georgie's godfather and first riding instructor, Captain Arthur Hutchinson, wrote her cousin, George Patton, Sr., "but every death in our family seems to have been under peculiarly sad circumstances—Mercer—Alex—Lindsay—Willy." Brilliant and accomplished, the Pattons were also high-strung.[4]

Amid the grief, the younger George completed his travel plans. He expected to leave New York on the transport *Chateau-Thierry* on March 4, sail through the Panama Canal, and reach California about the twenty-first of the month. If he could get off the ship, he hoped to visit his parents before sailing on the twenty-fifth for Hawaii. "Having become reconciled to the move I am rather looking forward to it," he confided to his father. "I think I must be a natural wanderer." He and Bea had already sold their sailboat for a slight loss. They planned to sell three of their horses, to give two away, and to take seven with them.[5]

Writing again the next week, Patton was in good spirits. Always

proud of his father, he was now doubly delighted, for George Patton
had been elected vice president of the boards of the California Institute
of Technology and the Huntington Library. Imbued with his father's
spirit, he saw in his transfer to Hawaii a hidden reason.

> I agree with you that though the move be a bore while it is in
> progress it will probably work out for the best. As you have so
> often told me there is a destiny which guides our ends. I may flat-
> ter my self but it often seems to me that I have had a hidden hand
> in my goings and comings. I only hope that the event for which I
> seem to have been trained will come out before I am too old to do
> my self justice. However I am very young for my age and still keep
> the vision before me which is most necessary. It is only when one
> loses the dream that one becomes old.[6]

Sailing on the *Chateau-Thierry,* Patton found the trip "pretty hard,"
but, he wrote Bea after two weeks at sea, "I have gotten used to it and
am not impatient." The ship was now opposite Lower California, but it
was "so far out that there is little to see except turtles and whales and
dolphins." On board the vessel one woman complained to the general in
charge that Patton was "vicious and brutal" because he disciplined her
screaming son, "but otherwise I have gotten on all right."[7]

Landing at San Francisco, Patton made a hasty visit to his family.
Then he boarded the army transport *Grant.*

Fortunately Patton had a companion for both legs of the voyage to
Hawaii. Also making the trip was Major Bradford G. Chynoweth, Patton's friend from Fort Meade days, who was being sent to the islands as
press officer to cover a maneuver. On the *Grant* Chynoweth served as
the commander of the enlisted men aboard. As such, he was given "a
palatial stateroom with private bath," which he invited Patton to share
with him. The *Grant* was a rickety old tub, and as it left San Francisco
someone yelled from the pier: "I hope you make it!" Outside the
Golden Gate, the steering gear broke and for a while the ship circled
aimlessly.[8]

Something worse occurred on the third day out. Patton awoke to find
the ship had stopped. Going on deck, he saw smoke pouring out of the
afterhatch. As Patton learned, the fire had a peculiar origin. A loading
hook had made a hole in some containers of sulphuric acid. The acid

had saturated a case of khaki breeches, which began burning. Inspecting the damage after breakfast, Patton and the others found eight feet of water in the hold. "Floating happily around" were two automobiles and Bea's piano. Luckily, Bea and Georgie's Packard was so big that it had to be stored on deck. It escaped damage. But Patton lost one of his great treasures, a large box of books that "was burned all to pieces." He was reading a "fine book called Beau Gest," which his father had given him in California. "You ought to get it," he advised Bea. "I gave my copy to the Ship library." Sounding a more ominous note, Patton reported that eight albatrosses, a sign of tragedy at sea, had followed the ship all the way.[9]

During the voyage Patton and Chynoweth sat at the captain's table. Also there were some congressmen, whom Patton shocked "with his best profanity." In sight of Diamond Head, the steering gear again went awry. The ship circled about.[10]

Shortly after noon on March 31, Patton and his shipmates sighted Hawaii. "It looks very much like Catalina," he informed Bea, "but the surf was heavier. Even I could smell the islands as much as six miles off shore." Reaching Schofield Barracks, the home of the Hawaiian Division, Patton moved in with Lieutenant Colonel John B. Murphy, whose daughter Bea had entertained in Junction City. Schofield was on a flat piece of land with mountains on each side. Like Sheridan, the post formed loops, "only each loop is as big as all sheridan."

To Patton, Hawaii resembled southern California with rain. "The Island does not look foreign or Tropical in any way and is rather disappointing in that respect." Honolulu, twenty-one miles from Schofield Barracks via a concrete road, "was not quite as good as El Paso when we were there." It was "sort of a cross between Leavenworth and Kansas City. . . . The climate while seeming cool is very sweaty if you walk seven or eight blocks you are very wet like a melon in an ice box."

After just two days in Hawaii Patton was sure that "some inside politics of the island" had led to his assignment there. The man he was replacing was being transferred to the Hawaiian Department at Fort Shafter, which exercised command over much of the Pacific area, as G-4, in charge of supplies, "the place I was to have had." He was "supposed to be the meanest man in the Army. I think it was a scheme to get rid of him." At first glance Patton believed the "official family here seems to me to be much too large and in a sort of cat fight. . . . All of them except me are ex Coast Artillery men." Even though he was "not supposed to come here I think it was the luckiest thing in the world that we did as it is cooler and in all ways nicer" than Washington, "except as to houses."[11]

Even this early the Hawaiian Division possessed one principal function. Japan had emerged from the First World War as a military power, receiving several groups of islands in the Pacific. Fearing further Japanese expansion, United States officials devised Plan Orange—Patton was among those who talked about Orange, rather than Yellow, people—to counter the Rising Sun. In this plan Pearl Harbor was a key, the staging ground for a counterattack against the Japanese. The division's chief function was to protect Pearl and to prevent a Japanese invasion of the island of Oahu. Swept up by the Orange menace, "George Patton and I tried hard to cook up a war while together in Honolulu," Chynoweth wrote Ike Eisenhower, his friend from West Point days. "We thought we had one well started with Japan, but it seemed to fizzle out."[12]

On the first Sunday ashore Georgie "drove around half the island," finding it "beautiful and most interesting. Being in scenery as sort of combination between Mexico and Florida." Patton had been "riding twice and it is fine with some of the best scenery you can imagine. The trails in the hills are wonderful in their tropical beauty though you can all but walk on it before you can see any of it. Not one person in a hundred seems to ever do any thing. The first day or so I was here I did not like it much and was disappointed but now it seems to me like a swell place and I am sure we shall have a good time."[13]

Eclipsing the good news about Hawaii was the bad news in Patton's next letter to Bea. Uncrating their household possessions, he found almost everything ruined: linens and blankets still waterlogged, a big mahogany table "busted to pieces," mildew and rust on numerous things, gold frame mirrors broken, the typewriter "junk." The backs were off three-quarters of Patton's books, which had swelled, bursting the boxes in which they had been packed.

Still, Patton did not seem discouraged. Schofield Barracks was a large post, he told Bea, with eight bands and thirteen thousand men in ranks for parades. "The busiest lady on the Post Mrs (Col) Merron lives opposite and is very nice. I think you will like it. . . . It certainly is not too hot here and the beauty of the place grows on one."[14]

While awaiting Bea and the children, Patton invited Chynoweth to spend a few days with him in his new quarters. The two rode horses around the island and, while Patton wiped and varnished every book in his military library, discussed warfare. Attending a huge ball in the Moana Hotel for Douglas MacArthur, Chynoweth watched as MacArthur and Brigadier General George Van Horn Moseley, Pershing's supply officer during the World War, got drunk on champagne and leapfrogged up the hotel's marble staircase.

The maneuver in Hawaii strengthened Chynoweth's distrust of the doctrines taught at Leavenworth. The instructors there insisted that invasions of islands must be stopped on the beaches, but during a night exercise three-fourths of the machine guns jammed "at the end of five minutes," rendering them useless.

After the maneuver Patton invited Chynoweth to visit his father in San Marino. There the elder Patton showed Chynoweth Georgie's war trophies. Asked his opinion of Mr. Patton's "boy," Chynoweth answered that "George was my favorite combat soldier but that he ought to moderate his profanity. Mr. Patton said that he had worked hard on George but couldn't reform him."[15]

II

Even though he found Hawaii beautiful, Patton yearned for the true glory. Using force, the British had recently put down demonstrations in various segments of their empire. "Personally," Patton reported to his father, "I am in hope that the Russians and the Chinees combined may start a war and that I can get in it. I have been to the two generals on this Island who would be sent and asked each of them to promise to Take me they have promised. However," he lamented, "I would not get excited over it yet as China is difficult to arouse and we are hard to insult. Too damned hard."[16]

On July 2, 1925, Bea and the children arrived in Hawaii. "We've been here 4 days now & its just too heavenly," she wrote her mother-in-law. "Georgie has been in bed by 9(!!!) every night & takes a *long* nap every afternoon!!! We have a lot of horses which the kids catch and ride around & I lead the small fry on a pony with the cutest little stock saddle you ever saw. This is much nicer than we expected in every way. We don't dress up," and the "Dillingham crowd," led by Georgie's polo-

playing companion Walter F. Dillingham, the railroad and land recla-
mation magnate, "is just near enough for society—about 3 miles. This
place is a sort of paradise for children—everything to play with & nothing to hurt them."[17]

As part of the "Dillingham crowd," Patton, during this first tour of
duty in Hawaii, became a dashing figure in society. One day he came
into the office of Ralph Scott, who ran a large insurance agency, reached
into his pocket, pulled out some jewelry, scattered it on Scott's desk,
and said he wanted to insure it. The jewelry had not been appraised, so
Scott said he would give it to his appraiser. It turned out to be worth
$150,000. Learning its value, Scott called Patton and told him to pick
it up from the appraiser, for he did not wish to be responsible for such
an amount.[18]

In late 1925 and early 1926 Georgie worried most about his father's
health. During the fall of 1925 George Patton had his teeth extracted.
"I have seen some wonderful results from loss of teeth," his son encouraged him. General William Wallace Wotherspoon, the former army
chief of staff, looked twenty years younger after he had his taken out.
Colonel Barney, who was serving with Patton in Hawaii, was "a different man," and Aunt Nannie "has certainly improved since she had hers
fixed." At this very time Pershing, "his system poisoned," was having all
of his teeth extracted.[19]

When Georgie and his family spent Christmas of 1925 in California, they were shocked by George Patton's appearance. Georgie diag-
nosed the ailment as "Auto-Intoxication due to lack of exercise. Beatrice
was the same way in Washington in 1919. It is a vicious circle. Lack of
exercise and consequently elimination makes you feel lazy. Feeling lazy
you don't feel like exercising and sleep all the time. Aside from the fact
that this is killing you it is doing it in a very unpleasant way." Patton
recommended that his father play nine holes of golf every day, even if he
did not want to. "I have the same sensations about using dental floss at
night," confided the appearance-conscious major. "Still I use it."[20]

In late February 1926 Patton experienced a memorable episode.
Hearing that one of his heroes, Field Marshal Edmund H. H. Allenby,
whose cavalry victories in Palestine during the World War still thrilled
him, was to visit Hawaii, Patton volunteered to serve as his aide. Drawing Allenby out on war whenever he had the opportunity, he used the
information to reinforce his belief that the horse cavalry still retained a

future. Patton had on "my big sabre" and at one point Allenby reached over, took it out, twirled it about, and said: "A lovely tool major I should like vastly to stick some one with it. You know I am a great sticker. When I had the Cavalry in France I told my fellows, When ever you ride about keep your swords in your hands and when you meet any huns ride at 'em and holler. They did and would you believe it those Huns were so alarmed that they would wheel about and fling away their big lances and skdaddle so fast that my fellows could not even stick 'em in the posterior."

Throughout the day Allenby regaled Patton with stories of cavalry triumphs. He told of some Indian horsemen who came upon a long line of Turkish machine guns across a causeway about a thousand yards from them. "They were commanded by a jolly old sport (the Marharaja of something I think) so he spread out and galloped at them. Jolly stout fellow that old heathen. He rode through 'em and fell off his horse dead about a mile back of the lines. It was a sporting finish. Takes stout fellows to gallop at these things when they are popping at you but a horse can carry a surprising amount of lead and still gallop."

Still, Patton came away unimpressed. "He is SIMPLE," he wrote Chynoweth of Allenby, "which is possibly the secret of his ability. People who make war complex do so to exalt them selves and to counteract lacks which they feel but fear to admit."[21]

During the latter part of 1925 and the first three quarters of 1926, Patton was on detached service at Fort Shafter. While Bea, ever Undine, participated in acting groups, Patton handled personnel problems. Questioned by two War Department inspectors who were "over here asking a lot of fool questions" as to how he would employ twenty thousand men in case of war, Patton answered that he was able only "to squeeze 7000 infantry out of the ruck of air service, quartermasters, doctors, and other useless apendages we think we need." The present garrison of thirteen thousand men contained only forty-four hundred infantry. "Every one thinks he can keep the enemy from landing by shooting at him in the water. As a matter of fact I could land here any time I wanted to and then beat hell out of the skeleton battalions sent to counter attack me. As a result of the last war we glorify machines and discount men where as it is men who win wars."[22]

Patton reflected his reliance on infantry and cavalry, rather than on new weapons, in a book review in 1926. Writing in the *Cavalry Journal* on British Captain Basil H. Liddell Hart's work *The Remaking of Modern Armies,* Patton scoffed: "We are informed that 'Sudden and overwhelming blows from the air—could destroy Essen or Berlin in a matter of hours.' Having learned by experience and by reading, the difficulty of destroying anything and the obstacles incident to the production of overwhelming instruments, one is tempted to suggest that . . . a steam roller . . . would be as useful and as attainable."[23]

Early in July Patton heard good news about a kindred spirit. Ike Eisenhower had completed the course at the Command and General Staff School at Fort Leavenworth and with the help of Patton's notes had finished first in his class. "It shows that Leavenworth is a good school," Patton praised his friend, "if a HE man can come out one."[24]

In reality, to Patton and to Chynoweth, who completed the course a year after Ike and graduated with an "excellent," Eisenhower's success at Leavenworth indicated a rigidity of mind that led Patton to criticize him constantly. Patton and Chynoweth frequently discussed the course, which as students each had ridiculed in skits. The assumption governing the school was that the World War had shown that American officers rarely thought clearly in battle. Employing a system that those who ran the school compared to case studies in law school, the course presented a variety of military problems, each with an approved solution that became part of School Doctrine. To get an "excellent," the student had to hit upon the approved solution. Otherwise he was in danger of receiving a "satisfactory" or an "unsatisfactory." The result, Patton and Chynoweth concluded, was to discourage initiative and thinking. "Of course," Chynoweth chided, "Ike had been 100 percent conformist, never deviated, and stood first in his class."[25]

Around this time Patton met someone who would prove to be as important in his life as Ike. Living across the street from the Pattons was a young major who had been Eisenhower's classmate at West Point. At the academy Omar N. Bradley had been an outstanding baseball player, probably good enough to make the major leagues. In Hawaii he had little to do with the Pattons. "We were not inclined," he noted, "toward the heavy social life they led." Patton, moreover, always seemed to be busy playing polo or teaching a ladies' riding class. But the most important reason was more subtle. Earlier Bradley was stationed with Patton's classmate, Edwin Forrest Harding. Possessing all of Patton's professional intellectualism but little of his push, Harding had organized weekly discussions at his home, from which Bradley came away with an immense desire to learn. Even Chynoweth conceded that but for his outspokenness Harding would have risen far higher than just commanding the 32d Infantry Division in the Pacific for eleven months. Bradley always seemed to contrast Patton and Harding, to the former's disadvantage.

Bradley's only association with Patton came when Georgie organized a trapshooting team. Hearing that Bradley was a fine marksman, Patton invited him to try out for the squad. Bradley missed with the first two shots, then hit with the next twenty-three. "You'll do," Patton told him. Bradley was not sure he wanted to be on the team, but he "signed on for the sport of it."[26]

Bradley undoubtedly resented Patton's capacity for making headlines with his athletic ability. Of the generals who played prominent roles in the European fighting in World War II, many had been fine athletes at West Point. Bradley, a superb left fielder on the baseball team, possessed a throwing arm opposing runners dared not test and batted .383 in his senior year. Jake Devers had been a forward on the basketball team and the shortstop of the baseball team. Ike Eisenhower had been touted as a star halfback before breaking his knee in a game against Tufts in his sophomore year. Geoff Keyes, a halfback, and John S. Wood, a lineman, had been mentioned as All-American football players. All this was now hidden.

Yet Patton's polo playing continued to thrust him into the spotlight. In late August 1926 his army squad beat opponents from Maui and Oahu and captured the Hawaiian championship. "This is the first time that we have ever won it," Patton wrote his father of the army group, "and we did it with a rather weak team but a lot of hard riding. Both the generals were there and they were delighted with the results."[27]

That August a legal case that had dragged on for years threatened to force Bea to return to Massachusetts. In 1910, at the wedding of Bea and Georgie, the elder Frederick Ayer had confided to George Patton, Sr., that he was worried about inheritance taxes gobbling up his estate. He was conferring with Richard Olney, the Boston lawyer who had been secretary of state under President Grover Cleveland and was a leading authority on estates and wills. Four years later, just after the outbreak of the First World War, while the two pored over maps studying events in Europe, Ayer told Patton "that this had been partially accomplished and was in the course of further accomplishments." In the second half of 1917 alone, Ayer transferred to his children assets worth close to $7 million.[28]

After Frederick Ayer's death, the children set the taxable estate at $4,888,174. The government, arguing that the elder Ayer had deliberately given away his property to avoid taxes, set the value of the estate at $19,207,719. Seeking $5,705,357 in additional taxes and interest, the government sued the Ayers, who had paid only $660,000 thus far. The United States attorney for Massachusetts pursued the case half-heartedly until April 1926, when the United States Circuit Court of Appeals in Boston ruled that the government possessed the right to seek the additional money. "Beatrice, of course, will be affected by the outcome of all this," her brother Frederick Ayer wrote George Patton, Sr., asking for his aid and that of the Bannings.[29]

In August 1926, with the case scheduled for trial, Bea prepared to leave her husband, back at the headquarters of the Hawaiian Division, and return to Massachusetts. "About noon yesterday," Patton told his father on the last day of the month, "B got a wire from Fred that the trial was postponed so we cancelled her reservation for to day."

Try as they might, the federal lawyers in Boston could find no evidence that the elder Ayer had transferred assets to evade taxes. With no alternative the government filed to dismiss the case on April 13, 1927. Frederick Ayer, Sr., had successfully passed on to his children the bulk of his estate.[30]

In December 1926, at the very time the elder Patton was giving a deposition in the case, Bea and Georgie went to southern California for Christmas. While there, George Patton, Sr., confided to his son that he was seriously ill, having developed tuberculosis in his left kidney. He asked Georgie not to tell the other members of the family, whom he did not wish to alarm.

During this visit, George Patton also discussed his son's career. He had often said that an invisible hand guided his son and that Georgie was being prepared for something special. He was convinced that civilization as they had known it was ending, to be followed by the event for which his son yearned, the greatest war in history. "He was most convincing," Georgie observed, "and I believed him, particularly as I have always felt the same thing concerning my self."[31]

Patton returned to Hawaii feeling uneasy. "Awfully worried," he urged his father in early February of 1927 to lay aside business matters and to take care of himself. "Please do not postpone doing something right away. Even if you don't care about living the rest of us want you to continue in this universe and not start on a premature exploration of the uncharted nebulae. . . . The distinction which I hope to gain in war would be but dust if you and Mama were not around to be pleased at it."[32]

After Georgie and his family returned to Hawaii, his father took a turn for the worse. In February Nita telegraphed her brother to come back to California. George Patton did the same thing, but getting second thoughts he believed he was inconveniencing his son and urged him to stay put. Georgie came anyway. In California he found that four physicians had examined his father and recommended an operation. "They found the left kidney practically useless," Georgie reported to Bea, "while the right one was functioning normally." When the physicians "took some bugs out of the left kidney and inoculated a guinea pig at the proper time the pig developed T. B. . . . I am certainly glad I came as it seems to have done them all good."[33]

George Patton came through the operation, performed on the morning of February 28, "in fine shape. . . . The kidney was covered with sort of pimples said to be tubercular," Georgie wrote Bea, "and there were two abcesses in it. Of course Pa is not well yet but I feel that his chances of recovery are vastly better than they were when we left him in January."[34]

After staying with his father until the thirteenth of March, Patton started for Hawaii. At San Francisco he boarded the SS *President Polk,* which was carrying passengers—almost all of them elderly, for they alone could afford the expensive trip—around the world. "All the crew seem to be boot legers," he told his father, "so that one can get 'Scotch' cheap and fairly good."

During Georgie's visit home, his father's courage had impressed him.

I never saw one go out to die with as much calmness and assurance as you did. When they wheeled you out of the room you waved

your hand to me and said "Aurey War" with a smile and in a perfectly natural voice. . . . I feel sure that you have no reason for
being ill. Try to think you are getting better and at the same time
take care of your self so that in 1936 we can talk over the last war
down in the old office over a couple of pipes and a bottle of port.[35]

But on June 10, 1927, the dreaded event occurred. Never recovering
his strength, George Patton died. Leaving little George and Ruth Ellen
with Captain Floyd L. Parks, who had known Georgie and Nita in California and had served with Patton in the Tank Corps, Georgie and Bea
took off for San Marino, arriving after the funeral. "You don't know
what a comfort your radios are," Bea thanked Parks. "To know, hot off
the wire, that things are all right at home—especially George . . . well,
it's the greatest comfort one could have. . . . It was wonderful of you to
arrange that airplane. Poor Georgie, he is broken-hearted. But he is
being a great help to the family and particularly taking a lot off Nita's
shoulders." To rest, Nita and Ruth had taken a cottage in Carmel for
two months beginning in the middle of July. Bea and Georgie hoped to
stay at Lake Vineyard until then, "and all leave at once so as to keep the
house full of family till the last hour. Kiss George for me, will you?"[36]

To settle their father's estate, Georgie and Nita turned to their wise
and generous cousin, Arvin H. "Jerry" Brown, who over the years
would do them favor after favor, never expecting anything in return.
Childhood playmates—Georgie had shoved Arvin and his brother
Eltinge over the crest of the hill and into the turkeys—Arvin and
George always had special names for one another. To Jerry alone
Georgie was "Pat," and to Georgie his cousin was "the Jew" or "the
Israelite," possibly because of, as George hinted in one letter, the shape
of Jerry's nose, but more likely because Jerry fit the stereotype of the
Jew as being shrewd.

George Patton left a sizable estate, but his assets were small compared with Frederic Ayer's $19,207,719. After expenses, they totaled
$394,414.98, all of it going to his widow. In his will he appointed Nita
his executrix.[37]

A minor matter illustrated how much the Pattons began to rely on
Arvin. While in San Marino the previous Christmas, Bea had given her
father-in-law $10,000 to be used for a storm drain on the Patton house.

After his father's death, Patton asked Jerry to see if he could get someone to complete the work for that price. To Patton's delight Eltinge, an engineer and contractor, agreed to do it.[38]

Told by Jerry that Eltinge was to do the job, Patton, now serving with the G-2, or intelligence, unit of the Hawaiian Division, answered with a letter that hardly indicated a deep-seated hatred of Jews. Rather, like his father's comment about Jewish noses in the Olympics, his views at this time fit more the stereotype than anything else.

Due to the press of work which does not exist I forgot to answer your letter of July 29 and only found it today when searching for bills I had not paid.

I am glad that Elt found it possible to build the drain for if I must pay the Jews I prefer them to be in the family also. I think he will do the best job.

As to the family property Nita wrote me that the arch hebrew Jack Dotten had offered $100,000.00 for all the Pasadena lots and that you had advised against selling. I feel sure you were correct as I have the highest opinion of your business acumen.

However what the asking price should be you are the best judge. $100,000 seems to me pretty low and at five percent would only give them $7500.

The whole thing is to get Mama fixed so that for the rest of her life she will be as comfortable as possible and that when she dies Nita will have no worries. I dont want to inherit any thing as I have much more than will satisfy a retired colonel of cavalry.

With you on the job and your affection reinforced by those high Sematic qualities so nobly predestined by your nose I have the utmost confidence in the result.

. . . With lots of love to Frida and the children of Isriel.[39]

With the help of his parents, Patton had amassed a good deal of real estate. Jerry advised him to sell some of it, but "not at a sacrifice." Patton's property in southern California included orange groves—his father had been one of the founders of Sunkist—and orchards. With Nita he also owned land in Wilmington, which the Bannings had founded, and in Pasadena.[40]

III

In November 1926, approaching his forty-first birthday, Patton uttered his usual moans to Beatrice, then in Massachusetts. He had "always hoped that as a result of a great war" he, like Napoleon, would "secure supreme command" and that after the war he would "become President or dictator by the ballot or by force." Time, however, brought no great war, no "marble palace at the flag pole at Fort Myer," nothing but the prospect of retiring "a useless soldier."[41]

In the islands Patton's brusqueness backfired on him. Appointed the Hawaiian Division's G-3, or operations officer, in charge of planning, in the fall of 1926, he engaged in something that he should not have: stepping on the toes of superiors. First Major Patton criticized a brigadier general. Then, at the end of May 1927, he alienated senior officers with a scathing report about a demonstration on ground defenses against air attacks. The upshot was that Major General William R. Smith, the division commander, removed Patton as G-3 and transferred him to G-2, or intelligence. "Gen. S. must think he was wrong," Georgie consoled Bea, "as he had both Floyd and Capt. Coffey tell me that it was only dire necessity which made him relieve me as G-3. Of course he is either a fool or a liar probably both."[42]

Luckily for Patton, an old friend soon took over command of the Hawaiian Division. "I am having a lot of fun since the New General, Fox Conner, arrived," Georgie joked to Jerry Brown,

> since for the first time over here my superlative abilities are receiving their due recognition.
>
> Last week I commanded a Jap army euphoniously called the BLACKS in an attack on the north coast in the course of which despite 30% losses we captured the Island. Next week I again lead my paper cohorts in a violent assault on the south coast. BHANZI THE MECADO [MIKADO].
>
> Beatrice joins me in love to Frida and the young jews.[43]

In these maneuvers of October and November 1927 Patton presented a strange picture. As the leader of the Imperial Forces of Japan, he set Pearl Harbor as his objective and notified his troops: "The Emperor expects the most dauntless courage and vigorous leadership from all his officers. We shall not disappoint. G. S. Patton, Jr., Viscount and Lieut. General, Commanding [the] Corps."[44]

Late in 1927 Patton asked to stay in Hawaii, with its swimming, polo, yachting, and hiking, for another year. The War Department refused his request. He was to leave the islands in 1928 and report to the chief of cavalry in Washington.[45]

Bea and Ruth Ellen were as sad as Patton about leaving. Both expressed their attachment to Hawaii in poems published in the magazine *Paradise of the Pacific*. Describing how "a god molded the islands," Bea's poem concluded:

> *He has made you all fair,*
> *You in purple and gold,*
> *You in silver and green,*
> *Till no eye that's seen*
> *Without love can behold.*
>
> *I have left you behind*
> *In the path of the past,*
> *With the white breath of flowers,*
> *With the best of life's hours,*
> *I have you at last.*[46]

In January 1928, preparing to leave Hawaii, Patton revealed his state of mind in notes written in a book he was reading. Studying Field Marshal William Robertson's account of the First World War, he constantly compared events then with events now: the constant interference by politicians with war offices; the short-sightedness of pacificists like Senator William Borah of Idaho; the lack of preparedness for war and its resulting sacrifice of lives. Patton also endorsed Robertson's belief that the plans of a General Staff were "guides not systems," subject to change by those in the field. His most telling observation came when Robertson discussed the disastrous Gallipoli campaign, which brought the British only death, not glory. One day Lord Kitchener reported that he would never sanction a British evacuation, for it would be admitting failure. The next day he recommended "getting the troops off the Peninsula." To this Patton commented: "Change of mind like Mexico in 1916. . . . That war must have been 'Hell.' "[47]

IV

On April 3, 1928, four days before he left Hawaii, Patton read and made notes on a paper that paralleled his views on the innovations of the twentieth century. Entitled "The Armies of Today," the paper was written by Colonel General Hans von Seeckt, who, as the head of the German armed force called the Reichswehr after the First World War, was instrumental in rearming his country in violation of the Versailles Treaty. Like Patton, Seeckt argued that a mere machine could never defeat "the immortal human brain." A new weapon might give momentary advantage to one side, but eventually the foe would find a way to counter it. "Science works for both sides," Seeckt reasoned. "It is, therefore, misleading to talk of the triumph of the machine over man." The airplane, for example, might expand the battlefield, but it did not change "the principles of war," for technicians would find a way of countering it. The next war might begin with air battles, but it would degenerate into a stalemate and become a struggle between professional armies, supplemented by civilian recruits. The peacetime army, therefore, must be of the highest quality. It must possess three essentials: the best possible armaments; a steady stream of men and equipment; and great mobility, attainable through a large and efficient cavalry. Reading these words, Patton, forsaking his tank background, noted: "Mechanization is a catch word against which the trained soldier must beware."[48]

Such pro-cavalry ideas implanted in his mind, Patton, accompanied by his family, left Hawaii for the mainland. After reporting to Major General Herbert B. Croly, the chief of cavalry in Washington, he was sent to Mitchel Field on Long Island, where he spent the season playing polo. "I am glad to think that my highly intellectual summer is almost over," he wrote Jerry Brown in early August. "I have had so far two hard falls in one of which I broke nine bones in my shoulder which are now well. However the detail here has enabled me to go to Boston oftener than would have been the case had I been in Washington." Nor did the Long Island weather appeal to Patton. "It is hotter than Hell here," he complained. "I have on nothing but a pair of glasses and am dripping as I write. I wish I was back in the tropics."[49]

Returning to Washington, the Pattons moved into a house at 3117

Woodland Drive Northeast. At the Woodley, a club at 3000 Cathedral Avenue, they stabled their horses.

Late in the summer of 1928, a seemingly unimportant figure entered their lives. Then finishing his plebe year at West Point, Cadet John K. Waters received a call from Floyd Parks, now an aide to the academy superintendent, and Clovis E. Byers, a cavalryman and master of the sword serving as a plebe football coach. The Pattons were at West Point showing the academy to young Bea. Would Waters be available to have dinner with them and then take Bea to the hop as his "blind drag?" At the academy Waters had participated in fencing, football, soccer, lacrosse, and hockey, so he had little time for dances. Nevertheless, he agreed to go to this one.

Leaving his barracks early that evening, the young cadet walked down to the Hotel Thayer, at the entrance to the academy, for dinner with the Pattons. He and young Bea then walked back to Cullum Hall for the dance. Years later, asked his first impression of the family, the observant Waters, who was destined to become a four-star general, remembered Patton mentioning that he was then in the chief of cavalry's office in one of those small buildings near the Lincoln Memorial. The cadet then mused about Patton:

> What manner of man do we have there? Yes, really. This man is unusual. You wanted to listen to him. His interests and knowledge were limitless. That's just the way he was all his life. One could sense he was a man with fantastic heart and of course, as you know, of great background and fund of knowledge. He was warm within but gruff on the exterior. He was an interesting host and soon put me at ease. I might at this time, add too, how lovely, charming, gracious and natural Mrs. Patton was—throughout her whole life she was always that way—as great and famous in her way as was General Patton in his.

Young Bea and Waters liked each other immediately, and a friendship developed. Waters spent his first leave visiting the Pattons in their new home, Green Meadows, in South Hamilton, Massachusetts.[50]

Life, however, was not all dances and leaves. That October brought more heartache. On the fifth Ruth Wilson Patton suffered a heart attack. She died the next day. Georgie and Bea immediately made plans to go west. "So glad you are coming," Nita telegraphed her brother on the eighth. "Awaiting your arrival Thursday morning. Funeral at church Thursday at Two P.M."[51]

Having inherited property from her parents, Ruth Wilson Patton left an estate much larger than that of her husband. Before taxes, it totaled $922,191.67. Under the terms of her will, Nita inherited the house at Lake Vineyard, in which she lived until her death in 1971; stocks and bonds; and one half of the remaining real estate. After state taxes, her inheritance totaled $691,583.53. Never making a move without seeking Jerry Brown's wise guidance, Nita remained financially independent even through the trying times of the Great Depression. Georgie, who had generously said that he desired nothing from his parents, inherited the remaining half of the real estate, worth $191,770.08.[52]

Following the distribution of her mother's estate, Nita brought up the subject of paying a fee to Jerry, who handled her finances and those of Aunt Nannie. Estimating their "combined wealth" to be "in the neighborhood of $1,500,000," Jerry consulted specialists on the subject. He then cut their suggestions by a quarter and proposed charging Nita $600 a month and Aunt Nannie $300. He refused, however, to accept anything without Patton's approval.

After talking to Fred Ayer, Patton reported that the arrangement was fine. He wanted to pay his cousin for handling his affairs in California, but Jerry would not take money from him.[53]

For whatever reason Patton continued joking about Jerry's purportedly Jewish traits. Hoping Jerry would use his influence to get a West Point appointment for the grandson of his friend, Major Adna R. Chaffee, Patton explained:

> I have written to Mr. Graves, Mr. Jack Miller, Mr. O'Melveny, and Mr. Robinson, the idea being that Graves and Robinson can fix [Congressman] Crail through his bank account, that Miller can shut off his electricity, and that O'Melveny can put him in jail. If you can use your Jewish instincts to pawn his watch, or can have O'Melveny beat him up, it might be possible to exert even more influence in behalf of young Chaffee. I have never heard or seen

this man Crail, but from the way he spells his name I believe that he must belong to your own tribe.[54]

After the funeral, Nita, Bea, and Patton took the Sunset Limited out of Los Angeles for the East. "Nearly all the Army boarded the train at El Paso and went to San Antonio," Nita reported to Jerry. "So Georgie had a wild day, planning wars. We are apparently about to fight anyone at anytime. However they got off at San Antonio so we may have peace to-day. . . . We reach New Orleans to-night and Bee and I are planning a Fish dinner. I don't know what Geo. will eat. He hates fish!!"[55]

Reaching Washington, Nita prepared for a tour of Europe with Bea, young Bea, Aunt Nannie, and Aunt Sadie Patton Hutchinson, whose husband had been best man at the wedding of Ruth and George and had taught Georgie how to ride a horse. Meantime, Nita wrote Jerry on November 21, "Bee & Pat are off to-day seeing a new model Tank, which claims to go 70 miles an hour. If that is true I surely would not stand up against a bunch of them, would you?"

The machine in question was the "convertible tank." J. Walter Christie's most famous innovation, it could speed along at forty-five miles an hour on its tracks and seventy on its wheels. Weighing only 8.6 tons, it was powered by a 338-horsepower Liberty aircraft engine. Its speed was deceiving, for it was not a complete tank. It had no armament and no turret. Still, Christie called it "Model 1940," for he believed it to be years ahead of its time.[56]

The Christie tank pointed up Patton's dilemma. Tied to tanks by his World War experience, Patton belonged to the cavalry. Federal law limited tanks to the infantry, leading Patton to deny the power of new weapons in coming wars. In book reviews that appeared in the *Cavalry Journal* in early 1929 he again sounded like Seeckt. Reviewing books by two Britons, Liddell Hart and Major Basil C. Dening, he repeated a wrestling maxim: "There is a block for every hold." Of those who, like Liddell Hart, stressed modern weapons in fighting the next war, Patton observed: "In the passion of their new thought they forget the ages it has taken to evolve the system just anterior to their own with the result that they attempt to revolutionize evolution with the inevitable congestive results." Patton viewed Dening's *The Future of the British Army* similarly: "He fails to consider the historical fact that the initial appearance of every new weapon has invariably marked the zenith of its influence despite the fact that usually the weapon itself has become thereafter increasingly deadly."[57]

Caught between two loves, Patton reflected his unhappiness by attacking those who saw tanks playing a vital role in coming wars. "Surely the remarks of Colonel J. F. C. Fuller (British Army) who during the course of four years' war replete with opportunities attained only the rank of Lieutenant-Colonel, or the opinions of such a hack-writer as Captain Lyle Hart seem puerile when compared with the forceful statements of the elite of the military world," he wrote in 1929 in a paper titled "The Value of Cavalry." "Despite this fact the effects of often repeated misstatements and halftruths are so far reaching and so readily swallowed by a gullible and motor minded public that a critical examination of the value of cavalry as compared with or modified by the so-called scientific arms is necessary in order to reach a definite conclusion."[58]

V

Patton's home life at this time reflected the tensions in his professional life. To Jerry Brown, Nita hinted that things in the Patton house were in constant turmoil. Asking Jerry to take care of her affairs while she was away, she commented: "This wild household certainly is careless with mail, which just gets piled up on Bees desk."[59]   ·

Patton, too, conceded that he and Bea were arguing. After spending much of the winter in Europe, Bea had left Nita, Bea, Jr., Aunt Nannie, and Aunt Sadie in Rome and returned home. "Beatrice got back from Vatican City last evening," George told Jerry on March 28, "and immediately gave me indigestion to a marked degree. Salts for mine."[60]

Nor was Patton's professional life happy. While in the office of the chief of cavalry, he continued to justify the branch's existence. In doing so, to Chynoweth's surprise, he slammed armor.

I am as strong for mechanization as any one and know more about it than any one I have met. I don't refer to past experience but to present research. However I find that the greatest enthusiasts are found among the timid or the lazy. When I say enthusiasts I mean the all or nothing type. The timid are attracted to it because their feet hurt and because due to congenital hook worm they have no idea what the term cross country implies. . . . If these people who talk so glibly of **CROSS COUNTRY** machines would ever stray far enough from concrete or asphalt . . . they would find that country is not so easy to traverse. I have flown ridden and walked over every part of every place that I have been stationed ever since mechanization came up and I have seldom found places where any machines could operate with out the assistance of infantry to fight for it and cavalry to see for it.

The future of mechanization—in our military lifetime, and who cares for any other—lies in the creation with it of a small powerful striking force capable of operating for a specific purpose for a fixed time.

In other words an offensive reserve used to give the nock out punch after normal troops have fought the enemy sufficiently—several days probably—to determine his weak spot. The great benefit of this theory lies in the fact that it is so sane cheap and simple that no one will stoop to consider it so in the next war you and I can beat the hell out of our friends.[61]

A confirmed believer in tanks, along with his and Patton's friend Gilbert R. "Doc" Cook, Chynoweth countered Patton's arguments one by one. Timidity and laziness "have done as much to create material progress as any other characteristics on earth. I know—because I have sensed in my own make-up, strong dashes of both. . . . I believe that properly harnessed, they are potent influences." Over was the day of "the animal drawn gun and transport," both "too vulnerable to air attacks. Infantry can hold its own against low attacks. So can cavalry. But mules and horses, without mobility, and without massed rifle fire, seem like cat meat to me." Moreover, Chynoweth pointed out, only "mechanized elements" possessed "a real punch against machine guns in the open." Not desiring to prolong the discussion, Chynoweth concluded: "I will not bother you with further argumentation because I am not arguing."[62]

In a welcome change from the drudgery of Washington, Patton spent October 1929 in Fort Bliss observing the maneuvers of the First Cavalry Division. "I saw our old house the other day," he informed Bea, recalling his days on the border with Pershing. "It is still the only two story house in its part of town." In an article in the *Cavalry Journal,* Patton summarized the lessons learned. Used with cavalry, armored cars proved hard to detect. This did not mean that cavalry was useless, for when cavalry movements were rapid infantry patrols could not keep track of them. Finally, airplanes with radios provided vast amounts of information on changing situations. To Bea, Patton called the exercises "most interesting. The value of the commander is most evident. When he is active the maneuvers are fine. When he is slow like Col [Henry R.] Smalley of the 1st Cav they are a wash out."[63]

The year 1930 saw Patton still struggling with the problem of the decade. Would the tank replace the horse? In an article entitled "Mechanization and Cavalry," published in the April issue of the *Cavalry Journal,* Patton and Major Clarence C. Benson argued the case for equinines. The tank possessed three limitations that did not plague horses. First, "Unlike men and horses, machines must have full rations." When tanks ran out of gas, they stopped. Second, the British maneuvers of 1929 showed that tanks were hard to control. They broke formation, and, amid the dust and smoke of battle, it became impossible to distinguish friend from foe. Finally, terrain limited where mechanized vehicles could go. Patton and Benson had witnessed the recent test of the Christie tank. Having served with Pershing in Mexico, they knew that Christie's vehicle would have been useless there.

Going one step further than before, Patton and Benson recommended a union of tanks and cavalry. "Fighting machines" could warn cavalry of the approach of enemy aircraft and could protect the cavalry's flanks. "In short," Patton and Benson reasoned, "wherever the terrain is suitable and particularly in open country, fighting machines will be to the Cavalry what Cavalry is to Infantry."[64]

In the July issue of the *Journal,* Patton repeated these arguments. He began by quoting Pershing: "Future wars may begin in the air but they will end in the mud." To describe the function of cavalry in war, Patton used his favorite saying: "Grab the enemy by the nose and kick him in the pants."

> Cavalry tries to do just this. It grabs the hostile nose and tries to hold it by a violent and noisy head-on attack, using its automatic weapons and some dismounted troopers; while with most of its

force mounted, it moves rapidly to a place from which the pant attack can be made with vigor and by surprise. We have dismounted part of our force to hold the enemy and have sent the rest off mounted to gain a position in the rear from which they may attack.

If the enemy learns what is going on in time to deploy an effective unshaken firing line against the turning movement the attacker has the choice of either repeating the nose and pant attack by dismounting a portion of his own force to grab the new nose and again turning with the rest, or to risk the fire and charge home.

In two ways armored vehicles could aid such operations. "First, to add to the fire power of the nose attack by joining in the fire fight from a defiladed position. Second, by facilitating the march of the pant group."[65]

Patton devised the "nose and pants" strategy to justify the role of cavalry in an age of growing mechanization. Later, when horsemen proved impotent against tanks and the *Cavalry Journal* changed its name to *Armor,* he would apply the term to the role of mechanized weapons in war.

Becoming a literary lion, Patton agreed in July 1930 to write for the *North American Review* an article exploring his belief that every new weapon reached its highest effectiveness when first introduced. Rejected by the *Review,* the paper appeared instead in the *Infantry Journal* that November. From the time "Samson took the fresh jawbone of an ass and slew a thousand men therewith," Patton argued, new weapons have been "heralded as . . . the key to victory." In past times the chariot, the elephant, armor, the longbow, and gunpowder were so acclaimed. Then came "the dynamite gun and the submarine. . . . Today the tank, gas, and the airplane are aspirants for a place on the list." But, Patton warned, few, if any, victories were "traceable to weapons." Caesar defeated the poorly armed Gauls and the well-armed legions of Pompeii. Similarly, the Prussians defeated the poorly armed Austrians in 1866 and the well-armed French in 1871. "Wars are fought with men, not weapons. It is the spirit of the men who fight, and of the man who leads which gains the victory." The spirit of the Lord—courage—made Samson victorious. "Not the jawbone of an ass."[66]

VI

Living in Washington enabled the Pattons to engage in two of their favorite activities: entertaining and being entertained. The Pattons' close friends included General Sherman Miles, the son of General Nelson A. Miles and the grand-nephew of William Tecumseh Sherman, who was stationed in Washington but lived in Beverly. Another Massachusetts neighbor was Henry Cabot Lodge, the grandson of the senator who had opposed Wilson and the Treaty of Versailles. Lodge found Patton odd but interesting. He remembered that as they were leaving the dinner table at the Patton house one night Georgie grabbed a decanter from a sideboard and said to Lodge's wife: "Did you know that a decanter, if properly used, can be a lethal weapon? My grandfather killed the governor of the Bahamas with one."[67]

The most important relationship was with Henry L. Stimson, now Hoover's secretary of state. The Stimsons and Pattons rode horseback together, frequently dined together, and went to social events together. Through Stimson, Patton possessed a pipeline into the heart of the Hoover administration, just as, through Stimson, he would, to the disgust of his West Point classmate, Jacob L. Devers, later have one into the heart of the Franklin D. Roosevelt administration.[68]

For the Pattons the highlight of the social season took place on Saturday, December 13, 1930. At the Patton house young Bea had her dual graduation and coming-out celebration. "The party was a howling success," Nita, who came East with Aunt Nannie and the Wilsons' and Pattons' lifelong friend and servant, Mary A. Crowley, reported to Arvin Brown. After spending the day at the State Department, Stimson went over to the Pattons, where his wife, Mabel, was pouring tea, "so to bring her home. It was a very pleasant party. I am very fond of the Pattons. Beatrice Patton, the debutante, was very attractive and looked very well, and I was glad I had gone."[69]

Mary Crowley found the event exhilarating. "Mary, the party at Major Patton's was very beautiful," she informed Georgie and Nita's childhood nurse, Mary Scally, who still lived with Nita.

Mrs. P. & Beatrice also Miss Patton were the loveliest of all there. All their dresses were elegant and all looked beautiful. I never saw the whole Patton family look more handsome.

The Major is getting more handsome every day & looking more like his Father. His expressions are like Mr. P. Thousands of people were there and every body exclaimed how beautiful they all were and how grand it was.

I'll say I never saw anything so swell. They had an orchestra playing in the ball room & every body was gay & dancing. Miss Nita's dress was beautiful and she looked so young in it. I never saw her looking lovelier.[70]

While young Bea took part in the social whirl, Ruth Ellen, attending finishing school in New York, became immersed in Patton history. At a family reunion her cousin, French Patton Howie, showed her the letters, discovered among her father's papers, from Susan Glassell Patton to Colonel John Mercer Patton's wife, Sally Taylor Patton. In them, Susan described the journey with her four children to California and her hardships there. Ruth Ellen found particularly captivating the references to her grandfather, whom she affectionately called Bamps, and to his sisters, Nellie Brown, Arvin's mother, and Susan LeMoyne. Ruth Ellen described some of the letters to Aunt Nannie.

The first one was written on the Steamship Arizona off the coast of Cuba and she is telling all about their trip and the people on the boat. How the wife of a Yankee wanted to kiss Bamps and how he said he'd never kiss a Yank. The letters are a picture of her life and the children. I know Aunt Nelly and Aunt Susy and Bamps and even poor Glassell better than many of those who surround me. As for Mrs. Patton she was an extraordinary person, wasn't she? In all the letters there is not one word of complaint or abuse and yet there is an undertone of tragedy and longing that made both Mother and I cry. She tells of how good [her brother] Andrew was to her and yet you sense thro' a few careless words how she couldn't get on at all with Mrs. Andrew. She certainly loved my great grandfather. She seemed to cling to his memory as a tangible link between herself and her beloved Virginia. In spite of her sad life, she had a certain lightness of touch, a sense of humor that is perfectly charming. She had great comfort from her religion, too. I would have loved to know her.

As for Bamps, "His letters are full of 'Yanks' and 'Uncle Andrew says's.' He must have been a very fiery little boy."[71] Captivated by history, Ruth Ellen was becoming the Clio of the Patton family.

Disturbed as he was about the cavalry's prospects, Patton turned, about the time of his daughter's coming-out party, to a far greater problem. The result was his most revealing and most brilliantly argued and written article, "Success in War," published in the January 1931 issue of the *Cavalry Journal*. Conceding that war could not be explained "by fixed formulas," Patton explored the role of history's great warriors and great armies looking for a key. His conclusions explain his outward behavior for the rest of his life: his dress, his speeches to large audiences of troops, and his belief that despite horrible deaths in previous existences his soul rested in Valhalla until a warrior was again needed.

In his search for military success Patton threw out soldierly mechanics.

> Beyond question no soldier ever sought more diligently than the Germans for prewar perfection. They builded and tested and adjusted their mighty machine and became so engrossed in its visible perfection, in the accuracy of its bearings and the compression of its cylinders, that they neglected the battery. When the moment came, their masterpiece proved inefficient through lack of the divine afflatus, the soul of the leader.[72]

"An impalpable something," not drilling, brought victory in war. Knowledge did not ensure success, for many a losing general knew as much about fighting as the victor. Nor did planning ensure victory. "Hooker's plan at Chancellorville was masterly, its execution cost him the battle. The converse was true at Marengo."

What then guaranteed military triumph? "Above and beyond staff systems and mechanical communications . . . must be the commander; not as a disembodied brain linked to his men by lines of fire and waves of ether, but as a living presence, an all-pervading, visible personality. The unleavened bread of knowledge will sustain life," Patton argued, "but it is dull unless seasoned by the yeast of personality."

Conceding that self-confidence, courage, and enthusiasm were important, Patton believed that something else was needed.

But as with the Biblical candle, these traits are of no military value if concealed. A man of diffident manner will never inspire confidence. A cold reserve cannot beget enthusiasm, and so with the others there must be an outward and visible sign of the inward and spiritual grace.

It then appears that the leader must be an actor, and such is the fact. But with him, as with his bewigged compeer, he is unconvincing unless he lives his part.

Can men then acquire and demonstrate these characteristics? The answer is they have—they can. For "As a man thinketh so is he." The fixed determination to acquire the warrior soul and having acquired it, to conquer or perish with honor, is the secret of success in war.[73]

VII

In September 1931 Patton was among those chosen to study for a year at the Army War College, the service's premier school. Strangely enough, Patton's selection for the course indicated his slow progress in the army. Many of his classmates were friends, but most had graduated from West Point several years after Patton. They included Chynoweth; Gilbert R. "Doc" Cook, a talented infantryman who, like Chynoweth, recognized the value of tanks and later led a corps under Patton; and Alexander "Sandy" Patch, who subsequently commanded an army in Europe. Years younger than Patton, Ike Eisenhower had attended the school in 1927–1928.

Located in the beautiful War College building from which Chynoweth's father had graduated in 1909, the school was run by three acquaintances of Patton. Commandant was Major General William D. Connor of the engineers, whom Patton had known in France. Chief instructor was Colonel Leon B. Kromer, with whom Patton also served in France. The secretary was Simon Bolivar Buckner, who later commanded the Tenth Army in the Pacific and was killed on Okinawa.

Chynoweth, a confirmed and imaginative supporter of tanks, called Connor "a brainy hard worker." But the general was "preeminently unsuited for his job. Like many of those who had won distinction in

World War I, he believed that military history ended in 1918." In one exercise a student who was a major in the air force drew up plans for an envelopment by parachute troops. Connor immediately suspended the game, assembled the entire class in the lecture hall, and warned that he would not tolerate such daydreams.

Known as a "gentleman's course," the college gave no grades. Committees performed most of the work, encouraging some members of the class to do little. "Committee output," Chynoweth remembered, "was the work of the few who enjoyed working on military problems. Doc Cook was an indefatigible worker. The outstanding worker in the class was George Patton. George had a reputation as a playboy. He played hard, when he played. But he was a lifelong worker, dedicated to learning everything that he could about War—a tireless student of military history. In every War College assignment, whether as chairman or subordinate, he went all-out. During discussion meetings, he was a ruthless critic of outworn traditions."[74]

Chynoweth recalled one clash. During a session on wartime publicity, Patton insisted that Major Clesen H. Tenney, who gave the report, had ignored the importance of keeping girls back home informed of what their men were doing. When Tenney replied that such things were inconsequential, Patton said: "I fear that you are speaking from the viewpoint of great age!" Insulted, Tenney, who was seven years younger than Patton, fired back: "I resent the implication that I am overage!" Such exchanges, Chynoweth observed, typified the "bickering in our discussions. It was fun!"[75]

While at the War College, Patton did not give up polo. He dressed for the sport each noon and left to play as soon as class ended. With him on the Army Polo Club were such distinguished soldiers as Major Joseph M. Swing, later the commander of the 11th Airborne Division, Captain Lucian K. Truscott, Jr., who served under Patton in Sicily, and Major Jacob L. Devers, who commanded an army group in Europe.

Chynoweth described the one time he dared to play with these enthusiasts.

Georgie crowded my heels, screaming in his high tenor, "Ride! Ride! RIDE!" It made me so angry that I couldn't think. Coming off the field, I turned on him. "Georgie, if you will play your position and let me play mine, we will be a better team!" He said nothing. Jakey Devers smiled, superciliously. The cold fact was that I was a bushleaguer. They were pros. I played for fun. They played to win. So I returned to the second string where I really enjoyed it.[76]

On November 26, 1931, in the midst of Patton's stay at the War College, Aunt Nannie died. Given her attachment to Nita and Georgie, and their love for her, her will was predictable. She made minor bequests to Bea, to the Patton children, and to Mary Scally. To Ethel Shorb, the only child of her half sister with whom she remained friendly, she left $10,000. And, taking care of her lifelong servant and companion, Aunt Nannie set up a trust fund that yielded Mary Crowley an income of $275 a month.

The rest of her estate went to her beloved niece and nephew. Each inherited sixteen parcels of land in and around San Marino and Pasadena, bonds worth $54,305, and blocks of stock in such companies as Standard Oil of California, now Chevron; Tidewater Oil, now Getty Oil; Caterpillar Tractor; General Motors; and Standard Brands. Like that of her sister, Aunt Nannie's estate was worth close to a million dollars, but its exact value is hard to determine, for in appraising it Jerry Brown undervalued these assets. To illustrate, Nita and Georgie each inherited 250 shares of Tidewater. Jerry valued each parcel at $875, but on January 22, 1934, he sold 167 shares of the stock for more than $70 a share, making each parcel of 250 shares worth more than $17,500. Similarly, he valued each share of Standard Brands, which produced Chase and Sanborn coffee, at $10, even though it was worth $23, and each share of Caterpillar Tractor, worth $28, at $14.[77]

In 1931 Georgie commented to Arvin Brown about his "fortuitous choice of a wife." While not as well off as Nita, Patton owned a great deal of property. In addition to the bequests from his parents and from Aunt Nannie, he owned a parcel of land given to him, probably by his parents, on August 26, 1919, and appraised then at $54,885. Another tract in Pasadena and San Marino, given to him on the same day, was worth $19,260. Counting his inheritances, Patton's assets, while nothing like Bea's, probably totaled over a half million dollars.[78]

Nannie's will brought trouble. The remaining Shorb children, all of whom Nita and Georgie detested, sued to break it. Aunt Nannie's lawyer, Henry William O'Melveny of Los Angeles, believed they stood no chance of succeeding, but a lawsuit could tie up the estate for years. Because of this and because a suit would bring unfavorable publicity to Georgie and Nita, O'Melveny asked their permission to settle the matter.

Arvin Brown offered another reason for settling. "As you may know," he confided to Patton, "some years ago Aunt Nannie was struggling with a weakness regarding drink, which weakness she entirely overcame in a most heroic and glorious manner. Mr. O'Melveny believes that any contest would naturally operate to accentuate this little temporary weakness to a degree that would give Aunt Nannie's lovely name a great deal of prolonged publicity. The very fact that she was a member of a famous pioneer family would be an additional reason for the press to seize upon the situation with avidity." Brown's final argument revolved about the considerable amount of real estate Aunt Nannie had left. Should the Shorbs break the will, they would "become partners with you and Nita" in every piece of property left to them under the will, an intolerable condition.

The final settlement gave the Shorbs $30,000. Each of the four living children excluded from the will received $5,000. This included Norbert Shorb, who, after an adult life filled with widely publicized affairs with women, was in an insane asylum. The remaining $10,000 went to the children of Ramona and Bernardo, both now dead. "It seems to me that we got out of the mess fine," Patton wrote Nita. Ever devoted, he insisted on paying his half of the $30,000.[79]

During the trouble with the Shorbs, Nita thought of adopting children, eventually selecting two sons. "I think the adopting idea might be fine," her brother advised her. "Be sure that the children are not illegitimate stinkers. That would be a joke and there are probably lots of them about."[80]

Meantime, on February 29, 1932, Patton submitted his War College paper on "The Probable Characteristics of the Next War and the Organization, Tactics and Equipment Necessary to Meet Them." Using his knowledge of history, Patton compared mass armies, which went back to 2500 B.C., with professional armies, which he traced to 722 B.C. Alexander the Great used a professional army to conquer the known world and in every battle defeated mass armies greatly outnumbering his own. "For wars of conquest and distant campaigns," Patton observed, "professional armies are necessary." From his study Patton drew other lessons: quality was superior to quantity; when armies employed similar organization, tactics, and equipment, long, indecisive conflicts like the Thirty Years' War and the the American Civil War developed; highly efficient and superlatively trained armies, like that of Frederick the Great, overcame their numerical inferiority in battle.

In every instance Patton found the professional army superior to the mass army. The professional soldier was able to master complicated, costly equipment. He was mobile and capable of distant military operations. He fought because of discipline rather than because of emotion.

Using as his example the World War, which had degenerated into a conflict of mass armies unable to move because of the new weapons, Patton predicted that the next conflict would be different. "Historical analogy and enlightened opinion both point to the probability that this remedy will take the form of a war of movement conducted with small mobile armies." Composed of "self-contained units," such armies offer a solution "for the restoring of mobility and, hence, for shorter and more decisive wars."[81]

From the perspective of the greater part of a century, Patton's essay reflects both his brilliance and his immaturity. Thrusting aside its conclusions—the next war was fought by massive armies, one of which Patton commanded—it is brilliant because it tried to make sense out of all of military history. This very quality, however, was its weakness. No individual was capable of mastering all the world's military history. As shown by the books in his collection now at the West Point library, Patton's study of military history was episodic and haphazard. Reading several books on, say, Frederick the Great or the Civil War did not make him an authority on these subjects. While Patton's observations were interesting, they were merely educated guesses that a knowing faculty might well have challenged.

After graduating from the War College on the morning of June 25, 1932, Patton cruised with Bea for two days and then reported on July 1 to the 3d Cavalry Regiment at Fort Myer. The Pattons moved into a comfortable house in nearby Rosslyn. Two years old, it had a gas stove and furnace, five bedrooms, four rooms for servants, two guest rooms, and a flower garden. Bea loved it.[82]

At Fort Myer Patton saw old friends. In command of the 3d Cavalry and of the fort itself was Colonel Harry N. Cootes, a courtly Virginian whom Patton first met in 1920. Among those at the post were Truscott, who was with the 3d Cavalry, and Devers, with whom Patton would later have running battles.[83]

With the economy still spinning downward and a presidential election looming, Bea found Washington hectic. "This town is a madhouse right now," she reported to Jerry Brown, "Congress trying to make itself solid for the next election by voting for every appropriation and hoping the Senate will hold them back; and everybody waiting to beat the other fellow's tax—There is very little patriotism shown here." Unfortunately Bea exemplified the spirit she condemned, for at this time she, Patton, and Nita telegraphed their congressmen and senators opposing a bill to raise income and inheritance taxes. Instead, they proposed a sales tax, the most regressive tax imaginable.[84]

Almost as soon as he joined the 3d Cavalry, where he served as the regimental executive officer, Patton began stewing. Late in May the Bonus Expeditionary Force, an estimated seventeen thousand needy veterans who wanted Congress to redeem their bonus certificates in cash, had descended on Washington. On July 8, after only one week at Fort Myer, Patton denounced these veterans as "revolutionists," pampered by Hoover and the Democratic nominees for president and vice president, Governor Franklin D. Roosevelt of New York and Speaker of the House John Nance Garner. To Nita, Patton wrote:

> It seems nice to be back in the Army, in spite of the fact that we can none of us leave the post for the present on account of having to remain prepared to bust the B. E. F. if they start any thing. Yesterday the rough element to the number of about 300 though the papers called them 3000 tried to form up to demonstrate in the capitol. The rest of the revolutionists surrounded them armed with bricks and said they would bash them if they moved so they did not move. It is funny and rather pathetic.
>
> . . . I am completely disgusted with both political parties. I can not imagine two more spineless candidates, and at a time when the country needs back bone far more than brains. I am glad I dont vote as I certainly would not dishonor my self by casting one for either of the straw men we have to choose from.

Patton concluded with a tidbit that indicated why he did not understand the plight of the veterans.

I have been elected master of the Hounds of the Cobler Fox Hounds. It is an honor that will cost me about two thousand dollars but on the other hand normal hunting costs me about some 1200 so the glory and the convenience of riding in front is worth the trouble and the cost. Also some one has to keep up these ancient things during periods of depression because the *nouveau riches* who are so sporty in good times run for cover when they lose a nickle.[85]

The son of a Wilsonian Democrat who had opposed the domination of California by railroads and corporations and had supported Wilson's income tax and child labor laws, Patton now reflected not the views of his father but those of the Ayer family.

Writing to Nita a week later, Patton yearned for action against "the mob."

This B. E. F. is a disgrace. This morning a number of them rushed into the capitol and forced their way into the west wing. In which instead of breaking their damned heads that heroic standard bearer of the Democrats—Mr. Garner had a conference with them and said that if they would stop he would do his best to see that congress did not ajurn. With Mr. Roosevelt an invalid and Mr. Garner the VP we are headed for ruin if the democrats win. Just recall how every successful revolution has started by temporising the mob.

We have been under arms all day right now my war belt and my saber are on the desk as I write but due to the cowardly act of Garner's we have been released from the alert.

Really I think we are at the end of an era, and that the RED dawn of some terrible catastrophy is just around the corner. The worst thing about it is that I don't know what to do or what to advise others. I expect Prayer is as good as any thing but it has yet to stop its first mob.[86]

The key day in the history of the Bonus March turned out to be July 28. During a scuffle with veterans who occupied some buildings on Pennsylvania Avenue at Third Street, a policeman killed an ex-soldier. Without consulting the Washington police chief, General Pelham D.

Glassford, Hoover authorized MacArthur to quell the disturbance—a mistake, for MacArthur vastly exceeded his authority. At two that afternoon Patton sent Major Alexander D. Surles and the cavalry into Washington. Through Arlington National Cemetery, over the newly finished Memorial Bridge, to the Ellipse south of the White House the troops moved. Joined by infantry with the pygmy World War tanks, the column proceeded down Pennsylvania Avenue toward the Capitol. At Pennsylvania and Third soldiers moved into the disputed buildings and forced the veterans out.

Raymond P. Brandt, the chief of the *St. Louis Post-Dispatch*'s Washington bureau, told a story of horror. He remembered being "tear gassed three times that day and I know I went over a fence about seven feet high to get away from it." Infantrymen with bayonets prodded the veterans across the Navy Yard bridge and into Anacostia Flats, where they burned the shacks being used by the veterans. Contradicting Truscott's claim that "not one drop of veterans' blood was shed," Brandt saw a black veteran "stabbed in the back." The *New York Times* reported one dead and fifty-five injured.[87]

Patton never questioned the morality of MacArthur's actions. "After all," he told the author Matthew Josephson, "these veterans were only four blocks from the Capitol. It might have been a bad thing if they had got in there. I myself was hit on the head and had to be taken to the rear."[88]

Truscott remembered sitting with some officers the next morning on bales of hay that had been brought from Fort Myer to feed the horses when a tall sergeant approached with a small civilian and asked for Patton. The man claimed to be a friend of Patton. He was Joe Angelo, one of the attractions of the Bonus Army. He had been one of those who took part in the "buried-veteran act," during which a veteran was interred, supposedly until Congress paid the bonus. Peering through an aperture in the coffin, spectators paid a fee to see the man. Spying Angelo, Patton said: "Sergeant, I do not know this man. Take him away, and under no circumstances permit him to return!" Patton then turned to his fellow officers and explained how Angelo had "dragged me from a shell hole under fire" after he had been wounded. "I got him a decoration for it. Since the war, my mother and I have more than supported him. We have given him money. We have set him up in business several times. Can you imagine the headlines if the papers got word of our meeting here this morning!" Patton then added: "Of course, we'll take care of him anyway!"[89]

Unfortunately for Patton, the *New York Times* did "get wind" of the episode. "Cavalry Major Evicts Veteran Who Saved His Life in Battle," read its headline. The accompanying article told how Patton "chased out of the camp Joe Angelo . . . who wears four military decorations." Alongside the story, the *Times* published numerous quotes from other newspapers, which were "practically unanimous in expressing the opinion that President Hoover was justified in his course."[90]

In contrast to Patton and Truscott, Eisenhower commiserated with the veterans. Then serving on MacArthur's staff, he pleaded with the general not to take personal command of the exercise. The veterans, he recalled, "were ragged, ill-fed, and felt themselves badly abused. To suddenly see the whole encampment going up in flames just added to the pity one had to feel for them."[91]

Given his wealth and his slight study of social and political problems, Patton's attitude toward the Bonus Marchers is understandable. By this time, however, even he and Bea were feeling the economic pinch. "Just had a letter from Georgie," Nita told Jerry Brown that spring. "In it he says he has just learned of the Depression, and hopes I am not wiped out, some of their dividends must have stopped."[92]

VIII

That November Jerry sent Patton good financial news. The Huntington Land Company had bought a parcel of land from Nita and Georgie for $20,000, wiping out all but a thousand dollars of the debt they had owed the company. "You now owe $20,000 less than before," Jerry wrote his cousin.[93]

Barely hit by the Great Depression up to this point, the Pattons continued in the Washington social whirl. Stimson recorded seeing them frequently. Just nine days before he and Hoover left office, Stimson and his wife attended "a very pleasant dinner at the Keith Merrills." Patton and young Bea were there, along with some friends of the Merrills. In his diary Stimson left an intriguing note: "The only trouble was that Merrill gave me some bad news which filled me with anxiety and foreboding, and I came home very much depressed." A guess—and it is only that—might be that despite the rapid disintegration of the nation's banking system, Roosevelt, in whose cabinet Stimson was destined to serve for five years, was "coming in without any definite plan . . . to meet the financial crisis." This bothered Stimson and his associate Herbert Feis.[94]

Nita felt the brunt of the Depression far earlier than did her brother. Jerry's suggestion that they dispose of the old Patton house to help her saddened Georgie. "Due both to my own feelings and in consideration of your own," he informed Nita on March 2, 1933, "I would hate to sell the old place." He and Bea suggested that Nita might pull through by disposing of the land around it. Always generous with his sister, Patton assured her that she was welcome to use any of his income from Aunt Nannie's estate. "I do not believe that it would be ethical for me to use B's money to maintain the place in Cal.," he informed Nita. "Further the time is fast approaching when there wont be any income available for such a purpose. It is not impossible that I with my army pay of about $600.00 a month will be the richest member of the connection."

Writing two days before Roosevelt's inauguration, Patton foresaw trouble. "As I have often told you the chances of a general revolution are becoming more and more of a probability. Personally," he told his sister, "I see no other solution. The trouble is that I fear this revolt will come from the bottom rather than from the top down by way of the dictator route. This Roosevelt is apparently just a very pleasant individual with not one but both ears to the ground. I fear he is not the stuff of which dictators are made."[95]

In early 1933 a new commander took over both Fort Myer and the 3d Cavalry. Colonel Kenyon A. Joyce was a quiet man who took part in hunts and horse shows. At first Patton found him trying. "If you hear that I have killed my self," he complained to Bea, "it will be due to Col. Joyce. He is the most perfect Spinster I have ever met. No wonder they have no children."[96]

Joyce, for his part, liked Patton but considered him odd. He remembered the hot summer day when Patton, then his executive officer, approached Joyce and some others and announced that he had just finished the first chapter of what promised to be a best-seller. Asked why it was going to be a best-seller, "George came forth with one of his classic replies, saying 'How the Hell could it help being? It has two rapes, a murder and a crucifixion in the first chapter and if that doesn't make it a best seller, the American public has changed and lost its reading taste.' "[97]

Meantime, Bea Jr.'s romance with Waters was blossoming. Waters had wanted to get married six months after graduating from West Point, but Patton had different thoughts. "Waters," he told the future four-star general, "I don't know who you are, you haven't proven yourself. You've been a cadet and dressed up in that uniform. They all have good reports on you up there, but they also have good reports on a lot of cadets. But, I don't know you."

Waters's first assignment after graduation was at Fort Myer. While there, he and Patton became better acquainted, and Patton, true to his word, consented to the marriage, which was to take place in Beverly Farms, Massachusetts, on June 27, 1934.[98]

As with so many things, Georgie, promoted to lieutenant colonel on March 1, 1934, was away when much of the serious planning for the wedding took place. In late April he was sent to Fort Riley to observe the cavalry maneuvers that used both mechanized equipment and horse cavalry. "This is really a wonderful trip," Patton wrote Bea. "Just to be around with a bunch of rather selected lot of officers who talk and think nothing but war."[99]

Spending a weekend at Leavenworth, Patton attended a horse show and race meeting. He saw "a lot of our friends especially Floyd Parks who sent love. . . . General Henry went up with me and is as changed as possible he actually laughed several times we got stuck in the mud and had a hell of a time and bent one fender by slipping into a post—nothing serious."[100]

Returning to the East, Patton let his wife and daughter handle the wedding. "From my view point as 'wedding guest,'" he told Bea, still exceedingly attractive, "I want to say again what a realy great organizer I think you are. No show could have been better and it was a very large show too. Also no mother of a bride ever looked better or cried less."[101]

The wedding over, Patton entertained that fall an unusual visitor, the historian Matthew Josephson. Investigating stories that General Hugh Johnson, now one of Roosevelt's key administrators, was somehow involved in a scheme to set up a fascist government in America, Josephson was directed to Patton, who had shared a tent with Johnson in Mexico. Patton treated him with the utmost kindness speaking freely of "Tuffy" Johnson, so nicknamed because of his loud voice and gruff man-

ner. Patton made it clear he did not think much of Tuffy's abilities. Like
Patton, however, Johnson considered himself a literary figure, writing
Westerns and dime novels. Turning to politics, Patton thought it peculiar that he once had to protect the conservative Hoover and now had to
do the same for Roosevelt and his "socialist schemes." Patton broke out
a bottle of "excellent whiskey" and after a few drinks showed Josephson, the friend of artists and writers, some of his poems. Josephson dismissed them as "poor doggerel." They "had something of the Boy Scout
spirit that imbued Hugh Johnson's youthful literature." When Josephson, who had just returned home after a long stay in Europe, predicted
a general war within five years, "Colonel Patton's face brightened visibly." He "was absolutely radiant with hope."[102]

An incident in 1934 indicated that Patton had not completely forsaken tanks. Lieutenant Colonel James Archer Dorst filled an old Ford
with inflated inner tubes of tires. He then drove the car into the
Potomac River, where it floated. General Simonds, now the deputy chief
of staff, thought highly of the possibility of amphibious vehicles, including tanks, but the Ordnance Department argued against it. "Archie
tells me," observed Chynoweth, who saw the demonstration, "that he
first got the idea in a discussion with George Patton."[103]

At Leavenworth, General Henry had suggested that Patton's next
assignment might be there. Such, however, was not to be the case. In
March 1935, after seven years around Washington, Patton learned that
he was going to Hawaii. He was returning to Paradise.[104]

Six

"1918 MINDS, ALL"

I

When ordered to Hawaii for the second time, Patton was six months shy of fifty. The year before he had been promoted to the regular grade of lieutenant colonel, the rank he had held during the First World War. But what would the future bring? If Patton were to attain some kind of glory in war, he would have to do it within the next five years. Matthew Josephson had predicted a European conflagration, but he was a man of letters, not a political analyst. In 1935 Patton's dreams seemed unattainable.

Ever adventurous, the Pattons decided to go to Hawaii a different way. They bought the *Arcturus,* a sturdy fifty-two-foot New England schooner, moved it to the West Coast by steamer, and made plans to sail from San Pedro, California, to Hawaii. The crew was to consist of Bea, Mr. and Mrs. Gordon Prince of Boston, and Joe Ekeland, who had sailed in international competitions. Patton was to be his own navigator, having studied the art with J. E. Lawton, a Washington lumberman and lecturer on navigation.[1]

Leaving San Pedro on May 7, 1935, the Pattons reached Honolulu a month and a day later. At the dock the Dillingham family welcomed them back. Assigned by the Hawaiian Department commander, Major General Hugh A. Drum, to be the G-2, or intelligence officer, Patton arrived in time to observe the June maneuvers, which he criticized as being unimaginative. He also arrived in time to play in August with the army polo squad against teams led by his two wealthy friends, Walter Dillingham and Frank Baldwin, the latter the descendant of a missionary-doctor and the owner of a palatial ranch.[2]

Known as a player "with a reckless abandon," Patton almost got into serious trouble before a match between the army and Oahu teams in 1936. Sitting in the front row of the stadium, Drum heard Patton yell to Dillingham: "God damn it, Walter, you old son of a bitch. I'll run you right down front street." Furious, Drum called Patton over, told him he was relieving him from the captaincy of the team for using offensive language before ladies, and ordered him off the field. Only the intervention of Dillingham and Baldwin, who denied Patton had said anything insulting, saved their friend.[3]

General James H. Polk later elucidated on Patton, polo, and profanity. "I never heard George Patton tell a dirty story or even utter an off-color remark," he related, "but his profanity was, to say the least, quite effective." In a game at Fort Riley, Polk cursed after missing an easy shot that Patton had set up in front of the goal. Riding up, Patton said to him: "Lt. Polk, you will not use profanity on this polo field, but it's a goddamned shame you can't hit the ball."[4]

Hobnobbing with the nabobs of Hawaiian society, Patton sometimes acted foolishly. On Independence Day of 1936 his team lost a match. That evening at a party at Baldwin's beautiful ranch, according to Baldwin's nephews, Richard and Harold Rice, both members of the Maui team, Patton filled a glass with scotch, gin, and bourbon. He then stood on his head, braced his feet against the sides of a doorway, and defied gravity by drinking the concoction.[5]

In addition to polo and parties, Patton shared with Dillingham anti-Japanese sentiments. Dillingham argued that the children of the Japanese in Hawaii, immersed in their native culture rather than in Americanism, could never be loyal citizens. He favored immigration restrictions and, in times of trouble, martial law in the islands.

Patton approached race, as the writer and publisher John D. Holt, who had numerous conversations with him, put it, as a livestock breeder viewed animals. He believed that each ethnic group possessed established characteristics that might only be slightly modified by environment. Patton distinguished between two kinds of Japanese. He admired the samurai, the warriors, whom he saw as energetic and intelligent. He deplored the tendency of Americans to underrate these Japanese as militarists. Patton saw Hawaii's Japanese differently. For the most part they were agricultural laborers who knew nothing of the glorious ways of the warrior. In wartime they would function as spies.[6]

Drum, too, feared the Japanese. In 1935, about the time Patton returned to the islands, he warned the War Department of a surprise attack upon Hawaii. If such were the case, certain residents—he did not specify the Japanese, but his meaning was clear—would institute "local uprisings . . . on all the islands of the territory."[7]

Holding such beliefs, Drum asked his new G-2 to devise a plan to deal with Hawaii's Japanese community, numbering 151,000 people, in time of war. Using the word "Orange" rather than "Japanese," Patton came up with a Draconian scheme. He recommended the internment of dangerous Oranges and the seizure of Orange ships in port, of Orange-owned banks and travel companies, and of Orange-owned automobiles and taxicabs. Most frightening of all, Patton recommended that martial law be declared and that military commissions try persons accused of military offenses. The writ of habeas corpus was to be suspended.

Assuming that during a war all the Japanese on the islands would be disloyal, Patton submitted a list of 128 persons to be arrested and held as hostages. Of these ninety-five were aliens and thirty-three were American citizens. Swinging wildly, Patton included on the list Wilfred Tsukiyama, a World War veteran who later became the chief justice of the Hawaii State Supreme Court; Masaji Marumoto, who became an associate justice of that court; two Japanese Americans who later became circuit court judges; and two future members of the state legislature. The hostages were to be rounded up and held in the Schofield Barracks hospital.[8]

After studying the plan, the historian Michael Slackman, who in 1983 found it in the National Records Center at Suitland, Maryland, concluded that it displayed Patton "as something more than a bloody-minded simpleton." It showed Patton's conviction that he "was the individual best qualified to control the course of events." Under his scheme the Hawaiian Department's G-2 would be supreme. The G-2, in this case Patton, would activate the plan by issuing orders to the Hawaiian Division and to other units. The G-2 would also direct the 64th Coast Artillery to begin arresting the hostages. "One is left with the impression," Slackman concluded, "that Patton considered the Department commanding general a cipher whose sole function was to invest the G-2's actions with authority."[9] All this, even though Patton, as events in Europe proved in 1945, possessed meager political skill.

Patton followed his report on the Orange Race with a memorandum on "Surprise." Addressed to the Hawaiian Department's chief of staff, it pointed out that during the last four years Japanese armies had invaded three Asian countries without warning. "Since becoming modernized," Patton wrote, "Japan has never declared war." Japanese troops might now be on their way toward Hawaii from one of the many isolated islands "only 2,500 miles distant, seven days' steaming over the loneliest sea lanes in the world." Having recently completed a paper on amphibious operations, Patton now applied his conclusions to a Japanese attack on Pearl Harbor. "During a period of profound peace," a Japanese force, shielded by darkness and preceded by submarines, could easily get within two hundred miles of Pearl Harbor. While saboteurs assassinated high-ranking American officers, disrupted utilities, and started fires, Japanese naval aircraft would bomb American air stations and the submarine base. In the midst of a surprise attack, American retaliation would be slow, if not impossible. To prevent such a scenario from occurring, Patton recommended that troops be given at least half a day's ammunition, that lamps and candles be kept in supply rooms, and that alarm systems be established on all military bases. "It is the duty of the military," he concluded, "to foresee and prepare against the worst possible eventuality."[10]

Hancock Banning, Jr., testified to Patton's preoccupation with the subject while in Hawaii. "My cousin Georgie Patton was over there as G-2, for quite a while," he recalled. "He sailed over there in his schooner and he used to be at the waterfront around the sampans and fishboats. He was perfectly sure they had admirals running around in the fish boats. . . . I never met an admiral in a fish boat. I don't think he did either." Perhaps Japan had minor naval officers at the docks masquerading as fishermen, but, Banning speculated, no admirals.[11]

II

Amid his polo playing, his drinking, and his report on the Orange Race, Patton's relations with Bea fell to a low point. In a remarkable book that describes the family's bitterness toward Patton, his grandson has recorded how Patton deeply hurt his loyal wife of a quarter of a century. While in Hawaii, Bea spent much of her time writing a novel, *Blood of the Shark,* the story of a romance between a naval officer and an island princess. Eventually the clash of cultures divides the two lovers, and the hero bleeds to death from wounds received while knifing a shark, the symbol of his wife's descent.

During the period when his wife should have been basking in the sunlight of successful authorship, Patton deprived her of that privilege. Both Bea and Ruth Ellen were sure he was having an affair. The girl was twenty-one-year-old Jean Gordon, the daughter of Bea's half sister, Louise Raynor Ayer. On her way to the Far East, Jean stopped in Hawaii. Patton, the story went, was soon captivated by her. Bea and the Patton family believed that the two were intimate during a trip to buy horses. As Georgie waved frantically at Jean's ship, leaving to continue the tour, Bea told Ruth Ellen that luckily she had no mother, for if she had she would pack "and go to her now."[12]

His career seeming to evaporate into old age, Patton tried several times to become commandant of cadets at West Point. When the appointment went instead to Colonel Charles W. Ryder, who led the 34th Division during the Second World War, Patton told Pershing: "I have gained the impression that possibly the fact that I am very outspoken is held against me in some quarters but as I never noticed you doing very much pussy-footing, I do not take this criticism to heart much as I should. Possibly the candor of a fighting soldier is not too well received in peace." In writing to Pershing about the appointment, Patton used for one of the first times an expression he made famous. Since the World War, none of the commandants at the academy had war service. "True," he told Pershing, "it was not their fault but their misfortune but none the less I think that a little blood and gutts would be good for cadets."[13]

Instead of getting the West Point job, Patton was ordered back to Fort Riley. The departure of the *Arcturus* for home on June 13, 1937, resembled more the sailing of a crowded ocean liner than of a schooner carrying only Georgie, Bea, young George, Joe Ekeland, Francis "Doc" Graves, and a cook. "We left on the dot yesterday at nine a.m.," Bea recorded, ". . . over two hundred people on the dock to wave us good-bye." Presents included 180 leis, liquor, cakes, and Life Savers. "Joe said we had more flowers than a gangster's funeral." Near Diamond Head, seven airplanes "swooped out of nowhere and sailed right over us, all changing their positions directly overhead—an Aloha!"[14]

Arriving in Los Angeles on July 12, the Pattons briefly visited San Marino and then went on to South Hamilton. There, on July 25, while the Pattons were out riding with Johnny Waters, Bea's horse kicked, striking Patton in the right leg and breaking both the front and back bones. Learning of the accident from General Leon B. Kromer, who had served with Patton in Mexico and was now the chief of cavalry, Joyce tried to cheer Patton. "In discussing your misfortune with General Kromer I could not refrain from wishing for a dictaphone report of your remarks on doctors, nurses, the leg and life in a hospital in general. I wanted it for educational purposes—Sunday School classes especially."[15]

Patton spent the next six and a half months recovering from the leg injury. For three and a half months he was in the hospital in Beverly and for three he recuperated at Green Meadows. While at home he wrote General Pershing pushing the candidacy of Drum to replace General Malin Craig, the retiring army chief of staff. Patton thought that the choice lay between Drum and General John L. DeWitt, who had spent most of his career in supply and would later supervise the relocation of Japanese Americans from the West Coast. Would Pershing support Drum? "My loyalty to Gen. Drum makes it incumbent on me to ask you this question but since you are the center of all my loyalty I do not wish to place you in a position which might prove inconvenient to you."[16]

In Hawaii, Patton had been away from the cavalry and infantry versus mechanization argument. Reporting for duty at Fort Riley in February 1938, he was thrust back into the controversy. Stationed at Riley were some of those who, unlike Patton at this time, believed wholeheartedly in tanks. One of them, Colonel Clarence Lininger, who had known Patton in Mexico, was the assistant commandant of the Cavalry School, to which Georgie was assigned as a faculty and staff member. Scattered about the country were others who argued for mechanization. Brigadier General Daniel Van Voorhis commanded the 7th Cavalry Brigade (Mechanized) at Fort Knox. That September Patton's friend, Adna R. Chaffee, now a brigadier general, replaced Van Voorhis. Writing about the struggle for mechanization in this period, Robert W. Grow, then on Kromer's staff and later the commander of the 6th Armored Division in Europe, remarked: "In my mind, Chaffee was the finest tactician that I ever knew. George Patton was the next."[17]

During the two years he served under Kromer, Grow sensed "the development of an ever-growing feeling that the problem of mechanization was too big for the Cavalry arm." But Kromer retired on March 25,

1938, and his successor, General John K. Herr, opposed mechanization if it meant losing horse units. To Grow, Herr vowed that the War Department "would take a single horse soldier over his dead body." As Grow remembered, "He wanted a mechanized cavalry unit at Fort Riley, but I did not see how he could get it without giving up a horse unit."[18]

In a minor way the squabble played into the hands of Patton, still an advocate of horsemen brandishing swords. Spurred on by Patton, who designed three sabers especially for him, Herr proposed to reopen the question of cavalrymen carrying such weapons, the practice having been abolished in 1934. Greatly impressed with Patton, Herr appointed him to command the 5th Cavalry Regiment at Fort Clark, Texas. Relaxing the rule that prohibited an officer from being transferred before he had served two years in his current post, Herr had Patton promoted to full colonel on July 1, 1938. At Fort Clark Patton would rejoin his friend Joyce, the post commander.[19]

Just after receiving his new orders, Patton asked Joyce about a racial problem. "The colored couple who work for me here are anxious to accompany me to Clark. What would be your reaction to this? Will they get on all right in Texas?"[20]

Joyce's answer reflected the common attitude toward race in a segregated army. "In reply to your note of yesterday, by all means bring your colored servants. No really competent servants are obtainable here. There is quite a colored colony hereabouts, but they call themselves seminoles. However, it's the breed."[21] Encouraged by Joyce's letter, Patton brought with him from Fort Riley his new orderly, Sergeant William George Meeks of Junction City, who remained with him until his death.

On July 24 Patton arrived at Fort Clark, two and a half hours from San Antonio. On the way down he stopped at Fort Sam Houston, where he visited Lieutenant Daniel S. Campbell of the West Point class of 1932, whom Ruth Ellen had been seeing. But the romance was now over. "He was most 'filial,'" Patton reported to "Darling B," "and said he had several letters from R-E. It seems to me a poor way of ending it all." Patton found Clark "very compact and about all the houses were built 90 years ago by Col. R. E. Lee." The fort was "the last frontier post and it is quite frontier; if it were not for the hard road it might be 90 years ago but I think I will like it. . . . Gen J. runs the post and I run the regiment which makes it very nice. The Joyces were delighted to see me and are more human than at Myer."[22]

By early August Patton was settling into his job as commander of the 5th Cavalry and second in command, under Joyce, of the post. "One of us has to be here," he told Bea, who was in Europe, on the fourth, "as Tillson the next ranking officer is not considered suitable to command the post. However he is doing all right for me."

At Clark the weather slowed everything. A march to San Antonio, 138 miles due east, took five days. "You never saw heat like this," Patton informed Bea as the march began. "It makes your blooming eyeballs crawl and by night one is realy tired out just from sweating and the intense light. However by October it will be cool and nice since it never freezes here." Patton was using soldiers to fix up his house, but he avoided any impropriety by having them work on their own time and by paying them.[23]

In Joyce, Patton found a kindred cavalry soul who put his faith in horses and sabers. "He certainly seems to have taken a shine to me," Patton reported to Bea, "and I have developed into the greatest YES MAN unhung but it is the best way to get along with him. As a matter of fact he is very nice but I am making mental notes what I will do to two members of his staff if he ever leaves them in my clutches." Joyce believed that he would replace General Ben Lear in command of the 1st Cavalry Division. If he did, Patton would take over Fort Clark and be there "for a long time."[24]

Just three weeks to the day after arriving at his new post, Patton led the 5th Cavalry in a mock war. On the first day he "marched" his men "35 miles in the worst heat I have ever seen and secured our objective with out a fight." But "the infantry wont get up for another 18 hours and as the enemy who is 4 miles north of us wont fight I guess we will just sit." Following his own advice, noted in a half dozen books he had read and kept in his library, now at West Point, Patton was planning a night march, almost always a success. "It will be a very long trip over slippery roads," he told Bea, "still at night it is cool."[25]

During the maneuver, a nonmilitary matter encroached on Patton's thoughts. Upon returning from Hawaii, he and Bea had sold the *Arcturus* and hired John G. Alden of Boston, who had designed that vessel and was known for his speedy fisherman-style schooners, to design for them a yacht capable of sailing the world's oceans. Built by F. F. Pendleton at Wiscasset, Maine, the vessel was to be called the *When and If,* the expression the Pattons used to describe the time they hoped to circumnavigate the globe. Although on maneuvers, Georgie urged Bea to take the children and check on the construction of the boat. "As if you wait too long she will be all planked and you wont know how well she is built. Tell Pendleton how to spell the name. Make Boston the home port."[26]

Even with horses, Patton demonstrated on the last day of the maneuver what a daring and imaginative officer could do against unimaginative opponents. After three days of seeking permission from his superiors, Patton on the fourth day of the exercises finally made his flank march. Moving "about ten miles mostly as a gallop," the cavalrymen got into the enemy's rear, capturing artillery, kitchens, a command post, and the colonel of the 69th Artillery. "The colonel of the 69th was very mad and refused to surrender to Capt Doyle till I came up and stuck my white pistol in his face then he was very quiet especially as I paroled him as I had no men to guard prisoners."[27]

Patton enjoyed the maneuvers and the hunting and riding at Fort Clark, but two things bothered him. One was the afternoon heat, which often reached 130 degrees in the sun. Even more on his mind was Ruth Ellen, now twenty-three and still single. Fort Clark contained no marriage prospects. "I think," Patton advised Bea, "that you had best make arrangements for R-E to visit B or some of the rest of the family quite a lot while we are here. All the lieutenants are just out of WP and so far are not a very choice lot. The captains are all married there are no first lieutenants."[28]

Once more performing what he considered real army duty, Patton thought much about his future. He hoped to become a brigadier general within two years. Happily the petroleum fields Patton and Nita had leased in 1937 to the Raleigh Oil Company were starting to pay royalties. Why not put some of the money where it could do political good? Patton suggested that Arvin Brown give up to $500 to some California Democrat who might help the cause. He would make a like contribution to a Massachusetts Republican, thus ensuring he would have friends on both sides of the political aisle. Politically wiser than his cousin, Arvin vetoed the suggestion.[29]

Bea and Ruth Ellen arrived in September to find Patton in a blissfulness that did not last. Unhappily the family was not destined to stay long in the house Patton had redone. That November Georgie received a call from the chief of cavalry. He was to be transferred to Fort Myer to command the post and the 3d Cavalry Regiment, both largely ceremonial offices. General Jonathan Wainwright had gone into debt fullfilling the social functions connected with the positions. Bea and Patton had always given the world the impression that they ranked financially with the Belmonts, the Harrimans, and the Dillinghams. Now it had backfired. "You and your money have ruined my career," Patton, ignoring his taste for fancy uniforms, for yachts, and for horses, yelled at his wife. After arguing, Bea threw up her hands and went to bed.[30] She had been attacked by the financial monster she had created.

III

As the 1930s drew to a close, the challenge of mechanization created anguish among cavalrymen and infantrymen. Responding to events in Europe, where war loomed because of Nazi aggression, Generals Adna R. Chaffee and Daniel Van Voorhis pushed for the creation of a mechanized division, even if the soldiers had to come from horse units. In 1939 the chief of cavalry, John K. Herr, who had vowed never to transfer a single horse soldier, relented and reluctantly accepted the idea.[31]

But even after Herr's change of heart, Joyce and Patton were among the unrelenting. "Three cheers and a tiger for your action in putting the SABERS back on," Joyce wrote slightly more than a month after Patton had returned to Fort Myer. Joyce still retained notions of cavalrymen engaging "in hand to hand combat" with doughboys and cutting barbed wire "with one slash" of the saber. "By all means show the Cavalry as a *fighting branch* in all exhibitions you give," Joyce urged. "Our theme of supreme battlefield mobility, coupled with great fire power, is one that cannot be controverted, and if we can only bring this forcibly to the attention of Congress and the public, our return to a real place in the sun is assured."[32]

For Joyce and Patton the selection of a new army chief of staff to replace General Craig, a cavalryman, was of utmost importance. The two favored General Drum, but the appointment went instead to an infantryman, General George C. Marshall. "By the way, how is Marshall in the matter of the horse and horse cavalry?" an apprehensive Joyce asked his friend just after the appointment was announced. "While I know him very pleasantly I know him but slightly in an official way."[33]

From experience Joyce knew that the chief of staff lived at Fort Myer. This afforded Patton, the post commander, a chance to work on the new army head. Even before Marshall moved to Fort Myer, Joyce sent advice: "Don't fail to indoctrinate George Marshall with the potency of the horse in war. We must have a more liberal attitude toward this thesis during the next four years."[34]

Engineering what he called "a pretty snappy move," Patton, who was living alone at the time, arranged to have Marshall stay with him while the chief of staff's house was being readied. "I think that once I can get my natural charm working," Patton wrote Bea on July 27, "I wont need any letters from John J. P. or any one else."[35]

Two days later Patton reported to Bea on the progress of his relationship with the new chief. "Gen M. is just like an old shoe last night he was dining out and instead of having a chauffeur he drove himself." That day Patton was taking Marshall out in the newly finished *When and If*. "He does not seem to have many friends. I called up Capt Benson of the navy who is Morris Jones' brother-in-law so when we get to Annapolis they are sending a boat out to take us ashore."[36]

If Patton expected to foster a warm relationship with Marshall, he was mistaken. Marshall never grew fond of him, even though, as Omar Bradley pointed out, Patton was the only one Marshall ever called by his first name. To his biographer, Forrest C. Pogue, Marshall related some incidents that shaped his view of Patton. At a party at Fort Myer, Colonel Patton made one of his off-color remarks in the presence of Marshall's wife, Katherine Tupper Marshall. Mrs. Marshall then said to him: "George, you mustn't talk like that. You say these outrageous things and then you look at me to see if I'm going to smile. Now you could do that as a captain or a major, but you aspire to be a general, and a general cannot talk in any such way." Patton "just laughed at her and that was the end of it. But she hit the nail on the head."[37]

Marshall also mentioned a conversation he had with General "Vinegar Joe" Stilwell about Patton. "I asked him if he and Patton were alike," Marshall recalled. "Said no. Patton was a braggart. Liked to make a show." Mrs. Patton, Marshall believed, "made him worse. She adored him to the point of making him worse. Once, when someone at a party made a slighting remark about the way Patton was dressed and acting, Beatrice went after the man's face with her long nails and tore up his face. She had to be taken out forcibly."[38] If Bea pined over her husband's treatment of her in Hawaii, she did not show it in public.

In August 1939 Patton left Marshall at Fort Myer and took part in the 3d Corps maneuvers at Manassas, the site of two Civil War battles. Patton's 3d Horse Cavalry constituted the Red force. The newsmen loved Patton, remembered Major Edwin H. Randle, then with the Blue team, and every morning one of them would say: "'Let's go over and see what Georgie is going to do today.' And off would troop the whole pack to observe 'the enemy,' especially 'Georgie.'"

Even then Patton insisted that all officers be forward with their troops, not safely behind the lines, something that some other generals, including Lloyd R. Fredendall, might well have learned. "It used to be said—in World War I—that second lieutenants were expendable," Randle observed. Patton's version of the saying included colonels and generals, "and you never found his dawdling where it was safe."[39]

Polk, then commanding G Troop, remembered Patton's enthusiasm during the Manassas exercises. At Fort Belvoir, Virginia, after Polk proudly led his men into perfect position, Patton approached and barked: "What the hell is going on here?" Why, he asked, had Polk not opened fire with live ammunition immediately upon seeing the enemy target? When Polk answered that it was against peacetime regulations to issue ammunition or open fire earlier than permitted, Patton responded: "I helped write those very same stupid regulations for damn fools like you. Now let's have a real exercise." The result, Polk remembered, was "a realistic, exciting, hell-roaring battle that violated every regulation in the book. . . . It was obvious to all of us that our colonel was preparing us for the real thing."[40]

Reporting to Joyce, now his warmest confidant, on the exercises, Patton roared with glee. "We had a swell time at maneuvers," he exuded, "and succeeded in capturing a General, two batteries of Artillery, and in harassing and demoralized a brigade of motorized infantry." Patton then joked about something that would later drive him wild in Europe. "Incidentally, we had the pleasure of seeing this brigade stalled due to lack of gasoline."[41]

Just before the maneuver, Joyce had made a quick visit to Washington, aimed, it seems, at selling the horse cavalry to top government officials. He now thanked Patton "for that delightful party you gave. It was

fine of you to do it, and I appreciated the evening a lot." Ever the politician, Joyce set his eyes on Brigadier General Edwin Watson, President
Roosevelt's friend and military adviser. *"Do not fail to get Pa Watson on
your side,"* he advised. "This is confidential, *but most important.* As things
are now you are nicely fixed I know."[42]

On September 1, a week after Joyce wrote this letter, the invasion of
Poland by Germany and the Soviet Union brought on the European war
for which Patton craved. On the twenty-ninth General Chaffee,
addressing the Army War College, called for the creation of four mechanized divisions, all to be led by regular cavalry officers. "He didn't
mince any words as to what he thought of mechanized versus horse,"
Grow recorded in his diary. Chaffee suggested that horse units be relegated to the National Guard.[43]

A Texas maneuver late in October should have given Joyce additional
warning that the end was near for the horse cavalry, but it did not. From
General Herr and General Frank Andrews, Patton heard "quite amusing rumors" about a motorized brigade of infantry outflanking and capturing a brigade of Joyce's 1st Cavalry Division. Joyce responded that
by making a wide turning movement of one hundred miles a battalion
and a battery of the motorized infantry had reached the cavalrymen,
but "when they arrived they were stopped and separated from their
main command," technically wiping out the invaders. "There are many
pros and cons in regard to the venture," the conservative Joyce commented. "Personally I think it was too risky a tactical movement on
their part. However, General [Herbert J.] Brees does not agree with me.
In any event it could not have happened had there been proper distant
night reconnaissance on the part of the cavalry. Naturally I do not wish
to be quoted on the subject."[44]

IV

Joyce may not have learned the lesson of the Texas maneuver, but Patton did. It revived Patton's interest, never dormant, in tanks. While
Patton was dabbling with Joyce and cavalry, his friend Chynoweth had
also stumbled back into mechanization. Trained at Patton's tank school
at Fort Meade, rather than at the Infantry School Tank Section at Fort
Benning, Chynoweth faced the problem of an infantryman who differed

sharply with his branch's view of tanks. While serving on the Infantry Board in 1929 and 1930, Chynoweth, along with such progressives as Charles W. "Doc" Ryder and Doc Cook, "collided head-on" with the army chief of staff, General Charles P. Summerall. The infantry school taught that the tank was a weapon of support, a spearhead for dismounted infantry attack. "As such," Chynoweth wrote, "it must always remain within supporting distance of the foot troops." Chynoweth saw infantry attacks as "essentially linear," whereas tanks constituted a weapon of envelopment. He envisioned "the conflict in terms of the comparison between Grecian Phalanx and the Roman Legion with the modification as introduced by Hannibal, whose elephants and heavy cavalry I thought of as a forerunner of the modern tank and armored forces. Hannibal's classic battle of Cannae—the tactics of envelopment, was a keynote." Boldly Chynoweth drew up and presented to the Infantry Board at Fort Benning a proposal for a new kind of division, one with more tanks and fewer infantrymen. Summerall responded with a plan for a huge division "suitable for powerful frontal attack against intrenched lines," such as those in the First World War. He also shipped Chynoweth off to a remote post in Texas. George C. Marshall, then stationed at Benning, told Chynoweth that he approved of his proposal, but he believed Chynoweth erred in making an issue of it.[45]

Returning from duty in England a month after the Second World War broke out, Chynoweth was put in charge of an infantry tank battalion at Fort Meade. There he shared the same frustration that plagued Chaffee and the others who saw tanks as the wave of the future. Assigned to Chynoweth's unit were Captain Fernand G. "Dinny" Dumont as executive officer and Captain Charles F. Colson as operations officer. Both were products of Benning's Infantry School Tank Course, Colson in 1935 and Dumont in 1937. Both kept in touch with the chief of infantry, General George Lynch. "Later," Chynoweth noted, "I came to suspect that they were planted in this battalion to protect Infantry Tank Doctrines. More and more, they looked upon me as a subversive influence."

On Chynoweth's first day at Meade his battalion took part in a maneuver conducted by the post commander. Always interested in tanks, Patton came up from Fort Myer to watch. From a tent that he never left, Dinny Dumont ran the show. Moving pins around on his operations map, he proclaimed to Patton and Chynoweth: "This is the way we handle tanks, today." With that Patton turned to Chynoweth "with a big wink. He and I had discussed tanks," Chynoweth related, "and we both believed that they should be commanded from a tank—a mobile command post, especially now that tanks had radio sets for Intercom. But Dumont and Colson never questioned the 'School Dogma.' "[46]

After German tanks rolled through the Polish cavalry, newspapermen asked Marshall, the new chief of staff, if the United States had an armored force. America's few tanks were scattered all about, but Marshall told reporters that if they came to Fort Benning on a specified date in December, they could see the tanks in a maneuver. He then ordered every tank unit in the country to entrain for Benning at once.

At a party at his sister's home just before leaving for Benning, Chynoweth learned something depressing to advocates of tanks. Lynch told him that he was reorganizing the tank brigade. He had already inserted Dumont and Colson into the tank battalion to watch over Chynoweth. He now put Colonel Alvan C. Gillem, Jr., in command of the infantry tank regiment and Brigadier General Bruce Magruder in charge of the infantry tank brigade. Both had served for long periods at the infantry school. When Gillem arrived, Chynoweth offered to teach him how to drive a tank. Gillem contemptuously answered that he had no desire to learn the art. He had, in fact, never ridden in a tank and hoped never to. In a kinder way Magruder conveyed the same message. "The only one to whom I could turn at that time was George Patton," Chynoweth lamented, "and he, of course, was not infantry."[47]

Arriving at Benning in bitter cold, Chynoweth's men moved into tents far out in the woods. Happily, Patton came down for a few days. Sharing a tent, the two smoked cigars—Patton had sworn off smoking, but he never refused a cigar when offered—and spent their time discussing tank tactics.

Throughout the maneuver Patton, at his own request, rode in Chynoweth's tank "to observe my method of control. There wasn't any control," Chynoweth observed, "just, 'Rainbow—Forward—Go!' "

Kept on roads behind the infantry, tanks were stifled during the maneuver. "In 1939–40 we had a tank that would travel 45 to 50 mph on roads, and 25 to 30 mph across country," Chynoweth related. "Yet the Infantry still tried to tie it down to the role of close support, which I considered ridiculous." Under the thumb of the infantry, the umpires "made decisions in terms of 'moving a line' forward or back. This was a fatal handicap to anybody who attempted to maneuver in depth."[48]

In 1939 a close friend of Patton who had been Chynoweth's roommate at West Point was experiencing a similar frustration. As the chief of staff of the Third Army, Lieutenant Colonel John S. Wood ran the first large maneuver in Louisiana. Wood always believed that Lieutenant General Lesley J. McNair, who was in charge of building the army, rigged the umpiring to show the superiority of infantry over armor and artillery. Wood later described the experience.

> One of the objectives set for the maneuvers in '39 was to determine whether the 75 or the 105 should become the supporting artillery as if it could be determined in that way. Our report, written by me prior to the exercise, stated that the maneuvers have definitely proved the superiority of the 105 howitzer as the division artillery weapon. Selah!
>
> . . . The Louisiana maneuvers showed nothing of the possibilities of armored warfare to people steeped in the Infantry School doctrines like Eisenhower and Bradley and Marshall. They, like McNair, never did learn; and they had no conception of the proper use of armor, from first to last.[49]

V

The war in Europe inspired plans for another maneuver, to be held in April and May 1940. To study the comparative value of horse and tank, Marshall asked Major General Stanley D. Embick, the Third Army commander, to draw up plans for the exercises. The maneuver would pit the infantry, augmented by Joyce's 1st Cavalry, against tank units commanded by Chaffee and Colonel John Millikin.

As the maneuver approached, Patton, moving back and forth between cavalry and tanks, passed on to Joyce confidential information told him by Wood, Embick's chief of staff. In late January Wood visited Patton in Washington and hinted that Joyce's division would be used to protect the concentration of infantry troops. Wood revealed that the opposing concentration points would be a hundred miles apart, "and seemed to hint that the mission of covering these points would begin prior to the arrival at the point of concentration. If I get any further information from him I shall inform you at once."

Digesting what Wood had told him, Patton offered two suggestions. He advised Joyce to jam the radio frequencies used by tanks. "I think it would be a great joke if our friendly enemy on wheels and tracks could be totally deafened." Patton's second recommendation came from Wood's revelation that a river so deep that horses could cross only by swimming ran through the maneuver area. "Perhaps you could find some place near Bliss where you could practice this and so steal another march on Chaffee, Millikin and Company." Patton ended his letter with a handwritten P.S.: "Please keep the dope I get from Col. Wood SECRET so I can get more. Copy of my letter to Col. Wood attached."[50]

Learning that Patton was to be an umpire "in the big spring maneuver," Joyce revealed his uncertainty about the coming games. "No matter where you are I am sure you will bump into the Cavalry Division as from what I can gather we are going to have to be everywhere. I am looking forward to a red hot campaign."[51]

The advance information failed to help Joyce. In the main phase of the 1940 maneuvers, taking place near Alexandria, Louisiana, from May 5 to May 25, the tankers, thanks largely to Chaffee's 7th Mechanized Cavalry Brigade from Fort Knox, outmaneuvered and crushed the horse cavalry. But Chynoweth, who participated as part of Magruder's Provisional Tank Brigade, lamented that his tanks were not allowed to perform properly. "The area had been ravaged by clear lumbering," he observed. "It was a badlands of tree stumps, swamps, and gullies. But it was ideal for tank maneuver—if tanks had been unleashed."[52]

At one point Chynoweth's battalion was attached to that of his friend, Colonel James R. N. Weaver, who graduated from the Infantry School Tank Course in 1938. Their front contained only a regiment of enemy artillery, about a mile away. Chynoweth wanted to send his tanks into the gap between the two armies and then onto the artillery's flank, but Weaver, "a disciple of the Infantry School Tank Doctrine," would not hear of it. He got out of his tank and ordered his staff officers to report on the situation. When Chynoweth said, "Jim, for God's sake, we ought to be moving," Weaver replied: "All right, Chen. *You* can go if you want to." Chynoweth immediately led his tanks towards the enemy, but every hundred yards or so the umpires stopped him with the news that imaginary fire had knocked out another half dozen tanks. With only a handful of vehicles left, Chynoweth rejoined Weaver, who had not moved. "Tank Brigade Headquarters said nothing about this exploit," Chynoweth remembered. "But Gen. Magruder, Gillem, Dumont and Colson . . . met me after the Maneuver with cold hostility. I now had undisputed occupancy of the Dog House." That June, General Lynch told Chynoweth that he was again reorganizing the Infantry tank force. Magruder was to be in charge, Gillem received the tank brigade, and Weaver was to command the regiment. Chynoweth was shipped off to an Infantry regiment at Fort Ord, California.

In the Louisiana maneuver, Chynoweth argued, Infantry tanks "had accomplished nothing." The following year George Patton, who had been an umpire during the 1940 Louisiana games, was similarly stymied. "It was simply not a tank era in the U.S. Army. I attributed this to the Tank Doctrines of the Infantry School. In Europe, George Patton made pungent remarks about certain Tank commanders who had been indoctrinated by the Infantry School." Patton especially criticized Major General Lindsey McD. Silvester, the commander of the 7th Armored Division and a product of the Infantry School Advanced Course. He considered Silvester so incompetent that in September 1944, in the midst of the attempt to capture Metz, he transferred the 7th Armored from his Third Army to General Courtney H. Hodges's First Army.[53]

As a result of the maneuver, Patton finally joined those who considered tanks the wave of the future. Meeting in the basement of the Alexandria High School with Chaffee, Embick, and others, he endorsed the "Alexandria Recommendations." These called for combining the existing cavalry and infantry tank units and for the establishment of four armored divisions, one for each field army. The signers sent the recommendations to Marshall, who the next month wrote Embick that the Louisiana maneuvers had shown the need for what they requested.[54]

Events in Europe unquestionably influenced Marshall. After a period called the Phony War, during which little action took place on the French-German front, German tank units, led by General Heinz Guderian, broke through the French lines between Sedan and Namur, territory familiar to Patton, and on the thirteenth of May crossed the Meuse River.

The German advance shocked many but not Liddell Hart, the British military thinker and writer. In 1937 and 1938, as the personal adviser to the secretary of state for war, Liddell Hart had urged the creation of three armored divisions for the British army in case the Germans should advance past the French frontier defenses. The proposal was, he recalled in a memorandum he sent to Wood, "hotly" resisted "by the military chiefs." In May 1940, when the Germans concentrated their tanks and broke through the French front, the British had thirteen divisions in France, not one of them armored. The Germans, on the other hand, possessed ten armored divisions. The best the British did was a counterattack at Arras, just before Dunkirk and the English Channel, by the Royal Tank Regiment.[55] The lesson was clear. By torpedoing the formation of armored divisions, the British generals had defeated themselves.

After the Louisiana maneuvers, Patton tried to let Joyce down easily. Preparing a critique of the exercises, he sent it to his friend, who still retained his faith in horse cavalry. "What you say in paragraph 'M' relative to saddle bags and cantle rolls is just 100% wrong," Joyce responded, completely unmoved.

> The individual mounted soldier should not be dependent on a truck in any way for periods up to 48 hours. He should have his cantle roll and a feed of grain on his horse and an emergency ration in his saddle pockets. This belief that the cavalry soldier must have a truck with him all the time is as bad as the infantry soldier having to ride with him all the time in a truck. *We must get away from such stuff.* Save the horse—YES, but in any active service have the individual fighting man self-supporting in every way and ready to go.
>
> What you say in paragraph "N" is also totally at variance with my belief. I could write much on this one, but shall spare you.[56]

Perhaps the saddest part of it all was that Joyce did not realize that his day, and that of the horse cavalry, had come and gone. At this very time Marshall was congratulating General Embick on his management of the maneuvers, noting that the army must create armored divisions. Accordingly, on July 10, 1940, over the objection of General Herr, Chaffee became the commander of the Armored Force and of the First Armored Corps.[57] By this time France had fallen and England seemed to be next.

VI

On July 6, 1940, just four days before the creation of the Armored Force, the Pattons were in Massachusetts attending Ruth Ellen's wedding. The groom was Lieutenant James Willoughby Totten, a White House aide and a West Point graduate in the class of 1935. Jim Totten was a Catholic, but the wedding took place at St. John's Church (Episcopal) in Beverly Farms. The reception was at Green Meadows.[58]

Nine days after the wedding, Patton opened his morning paper and read that he was being sent to Benning to command one of the newly created units, the 2d Brigade of the 2d Armored Division. The division itself was to be led by General Charles L. Scott, a fifty-seven-year-old cavalryman who was as superb an equestrian as Patton. "This will thwart my ambition of again having the pleasure of serving under you," Patton flattered Joyce, who was being left behind in the army's way of thinking. "However, I fear that there is nothing that can be done about it."[59]

Suddenly converted to the tank philosophy of Chaffee, Patton began training his brigade. But just as Patton's career looked up, his relationship with Bea deteriorated. Bea accompanied her husband to Columbus, Georgia, a mill town noted for its Ku Klux Klan activity, where they settled into Benning's round of horseback rides, parties, and courtesy calls.

By the end of August, however, while the division was in the midst of its first exercise, Bea left Patton and returned to Green Meadows. "Had things been otherwise you might perhaps have been there to see the largest command I have as yet had," Patton told her in late August.

> I missed you a lot but did not blame any one but my self because you were not there.
>
> I am writing this not with the thought that you will ever read it but simply because for so long when I have done any thing worth while you have always been the gallery. It is hard to have no gallery any more and I feel quite sorry for my self but more sorry for you because I have shattered all your ideals.
>
> I am shipping your books and things to Boston tomorrow. . . . In order to keep up the pretense that you may come here I am

keeping some things which will not be useful to any one any more.[60]

Writing to Bea four days later, Patton left no doubt about the cause of the breakup.

I just heard that [Walter J.] Kilner who was with me in Mexico gassed himself on account of a disgrace he got into with another woman. I am inclined to think that he had more guts than I have or perhaps not, it is pretty hard to go on living and wishing one was dead when I realise that I have made it so hard for you who are inocent it makes me feel even worse. . . . I hope some day you may forgive me but I will be damned if I see why you should. I love you anyhow.[61]

Even an offer from General Herr to take over the cavalry division when Joyce was relieved failed to console Patton. "I wish I had you to discuss the question with," he told his wife. He would "rather command" the cavalry unit "than any thing," but, he believed, promotion would be faster in the tanks, and he would unquestionably stay there. "It makes little difference any how," he wrote. "I am not kicking I have only my self to blame and you are the one I have hurt. I suppose the most charitable thing to think is that I was crazy. But I cant see how you or any other self respecting person could ever forgive me. . . . You are the only person I have ever loved."[62]

Obeying this impulse, Patton turned down Herr's offer. "Of course it is the dream of every cavalry man who is worth a damn to command that outfit," he answered, "and I think I could do a job of it." But since he "was selected to come here to help make this Brigade I should in loyalty finish the job. You are probably the only person who can realize how hard it was for me to write the above—I think in my case you would have done the same thing. . . . These Armored Divisions are pure cavalry in their functions and tactics," Patton flattered Herr, "and all the foreign writers so state. We are having a lot of delay on equipment but are nearly full up on men and *aledged* officers. I am doing my humble best to make something out of these R[eserve] O[fficers] but it is uphill work." Just the other day Patton had found a reserve officer who had been a bus driver in civilian life. "I have directed the colonels to be very hard on them and keep a book so that when we get enough dope we can can them."[63]

Even while in the cavalry, Patton never stopped reading about tanks, but with his transfer to the 2d Armored he stepped up his studies. About this time he was greatly influenced by Austrian General Ludwig Ritter von Eimannsberger's *Mechanized Warfare,* published in Munich in 1934 and translated into English the next year. While Eimannsberger believed some tanks should be available to support infantry, he urged that tanks be assembled into mechanized divisions consisting of three brigades of tanks supported by motorized artillery, antitank units, and artillery units. Such highly mobile divisions would, he believed, be capable of flank and rear attacks.[64]

Patton expressed some of this thinking in a speech titled "Armored Operations in Poland," given on September 3, 1940, to the officers of his division. "It took me a week to write," Patton told Bea, "and then I memorized it and then I talked with out notes and was the first one to get clapped so it must have been good." In his address Patton described how the Germans had used the newest weapons—tanks and airplanes—and the oldest known tactic, the double envelopment, "invented by the cavemen when they surrounded the mammoth to destroy him" and perfected by Hannibal against the Romans at Cannae. Borrowing, as Colonel Roger Nye has pointed out, from an idea he first jotted down in 1931, Patton noted that "to win a great victory, you must have a dumb enemy commander," and that was what Hannibal faced in 216 B.C. and what the Germans faced in Poland in 1939.[65]

VII

Almost as soon as he returned to tanks, Patton invited an old friend to join him. "It would be great to be in the tanks once more," Ike Eisenhower answered from Fort Lewis, Washington, "and even better to be associated with you again." If he joined Patton, he preferred leading a regiment to desk duty. Such a command, however, called for a colonel, and Ike was "still almost three years away from my colonelcy. But I *think* I could do a damn good job of commanding a regiment and I hear that Douglas Greene, who won't get his colonelcy for some time yet, has one of the armored regiments. Explain that one to me!!"[66]

Patton answered that he hoped to get one of the two armored divisions to be created in early 1941. He would then ask for Ike, preferably as chief of staff but if not as a regimental commander. Patton hoped "we are together in a long and BLOODY War."[67]

For Patton events moved swiftly in the fall of 1940. In late September Bea returned. Then, on October 1, in the midst of training his brigade, Patton was promoted to brigadier general, and Scott, the division commander, to major general. At a ceremony two days later Scott supposedly turned to Patton and said: "Well, George, they just promoted the two most profane men in the Army." Exactly a month later Scott left Benning for Knox, where he took over some of the duties of the ailing armor commander, General Chaffee. Patton then assumed command of the entire 2d Division. Starting on July 15, 1940, with ninety-nine officers and 2,202 men, the division grew rapidly. By March 1941 it contained 776 officers and 10,121 men.[68]

On November 16, 1940, the very day he took over the division, Patton greeted a guest. That July, aiming at bipartisanship, President Roosevelt had appointed Henry L. Stimson, a Republican, to the post he had held under William Howard Taft, secretary of war. Arriving at Benning with his aide, Major George Harrison, Stimson went right to the Patton house for lunch. He spent the afternoon driving around the post with Patton and the post commander, General Lloyd R. Fredendall. Viewing the Tank Division, which, he reflected, had been in existence only since July, he was greatly impressed. "The progress which has been made in that time is astounding," he commented in his diary, "and reflects great credit upon the two men who have had charge at one time or another during the last three or four months, one of them being General Scott who is now commanding the other mechanized Division at Fort Knox and the other one is General Patton—George Patton."[69]

That Monday, the eighteenth, Stimson flew to Louisiana, but he was back in time to accompany Patton to the infantry school at Benning, where Patton was to be one of two speakers. Unlike Dwight Eisenhower, who liked to mingle with the troops rather than to address large gatherings, Patton preferred the opposite, a practice that would lead to chaos during the early days of the Sicilian campaign. Each Monday evening Patton assembled his officers and in his fiery tone spoke on whatever popped into his head. On this occasion he addressed "some 500 officers . . . collected in a big room. . . . For myself," Stimson observed,

"I was pretty sleepy and I imagine that most of the auditors there after their hard day in the open air were sleepy also. The first lecturer, of whom I don't remember the name of, made rather a dry dull lecture on German airworks. General Patton followed with one of his characteristic snappy speeches full of cuss words and sharp remarks and that waked them up again and they seemed to understand that."[70]

The next day Patton's mechanized division put on for the secretary a demonstration that showed some precision but little originality. "They followed substantially the method used by the Germans in last May and June," Stimson recorded, "with such improvements as they could think of." First came a probe by a reconnaissance force aimed at locating the enemy's position. Next came a simulated attack by dive bombers, followed by an artillery bombardment. Patton's tanks then plunged through fortifications, up hills, over roads, and through ditches, making a hole in the enemy line large enough for infantry to push through.

Stimson found "the synchronization . . . astonishing." Particularly impressive was the way Patton kept his artillery "right up almost with the front line." As soon as the tanks had passed, the artillery came up, taking positions where, with the aid of the engineers, it guided the tanks across a river.[71]

At Benning Patton searched for new ideas. Lieutenant General Raymond S. McLain, then a National Guard officer, remembered first meeting Patton, under whom he later served in Sicily and France, in December 1940. Emerging from a car, McLain saw a strange figure leaning against a tree not ten feet away. Patton was dressed in tight-fitting trousers and a tight pea-green jacket with brass buttons running from the waist to the right shoulder. His pistol was under his left arm, and his helmet had around it a raised gold band. Asked by Patton what he thought of the uniform, McLain replied: "I don't quite understand it." Patton explained that he was trying to devise an outfit, called the Flash Gordon by his troops, that would permit his men to get in and out of tanks quickly and safely. Making McLain get into a nearby tank, he pointed out that a pistol worn around the waist would be hung up in the turret. Even the slightest delay might bring tragedy to the tanker. "I am trying to find a way to save his life," Patton explained.[72]

Training his division arduously, Patton marched his men 170 miles to Panama City, Florida, on the Gulf of Mexico. On the twelfth of December 392 officers and 6,079 men, driving 1,126 vehicles, including 231 tanks, left Benning in two columns for Florida. Checking the columns numerous times, Patton was highly pleased with their appearance. The return trip included a night march ending with a simulated attack on Benning. Patton's stress on maintenance paid dividends, for by the end of the march only one tank had broken down and had to be towed into the fort.[73]

On New Year's Day the Pattons demonstrated that they had reconciled. Following an army custom they invited the division's officers to their quarters at noon for military punch. The guests also included Fredendall and his staff. Patton wore army full dress blues with the gold sash of a general officer around his waist. His subordinates wore dark green uniforms. Colonel August E. Schanze, who served on Fredendall's staff, remembered the Pattons as the perfect hosts.[74]

Patton was becoming a national figure. On February 14, 1941, *Time* magazine covered, from the perspective of Company D of the 68th Armored Regiment, the division's first mounted review, an exercise involving ten thousand officers and men and twelve hundred vehicles (tanks, scout cars, trucks, motorcycles, and the like). Patton, erroneously promoted in the story to a major general, was The Old Man, a role he relished. "His rank kept him remote from the men of Company D," *Time* reported.

> Yet to all of them, The Old Man was as near and real as the pine bark on the outer walls of their makeshift mess hall. Like God (they said) he had the damndest way of showing up when things went wrong. Unlike God, he had been known to dash leg-long into a creek, get a stalled tank and its wretched crew out of the water and back into the line of march, practically by the power of his curses. Last week Company D prayed that none of its tanks, on this, of all days, should lay an egg before The Old Man.

Like most of the outfits in the division, Company D had undergone a massive personnel change. Originally its men were all Regular Army soldiers, many having completed three and four enlistments. But the 2d Armored now had few veterans, most having been shipped off to the 1st Armored at Fort Knox or to the newly organized 3d and 4th Armored Divisions.

For those who operated each of the nine light tanks in Company D, dressing was an experience. Over khaki uniforms, the tanker yanked dungarees and a warm canvas jacket. On his head the tanker wore the standard headgear, a heavy, padded leather helmet. Around his neck he reluctantly carried a much-hated device, the recently designed dust mask. Issued to prevent silicosis, it was, in Company D parlance, "a goddam nuisance after hours of heavy nose-pinching."

Painted dark brown, the light tanks were squat, twenty-seven-thousand-pound monstrosities. They contained one-inch armor, five guns, and a single turret. Each tank carried enough gas for about seventy miles of combat operations at speeds under thirty-five miles an hour. A tank leader and a three-man crew operated each of the demons.

The parade began with Patton's tank, the turret ringed with red, white, and blue stripes, roaring around the field. Standing in the turret of his tank, The Old Man was barely visible. After whirling about the field, Patton's tank ended up at the reviewing stand.

Responding to the order "Turn 'em over," the tank crews started their vehicles and prepared to pass in review. When a tank buttoned up, with the turret top and port closed, the tank commander, peering through the main gun port, guided the tank with foot signals to the driver. A light kick in the back meant start, a steady pressure on the head meant stop. Today, however, the tank commanders scorned the foot signals, driving the tanks solely with the limited vision available through the armor slits. At twenty miles an hour in lines of five tanks each, the monsters progressed, finally reaching and passing the reviewing stand. Safely past Patton's eye, the tankers stopped and relaxed.

The came the hardest part of all: the wait. Returning to the company area, the men of D fidgeted. Finally the word came down. "The Old Man liked the tanks!" Happily the men of Company D congregated in the mess hall. The day had been a success.[75]

VIII

By spring 1941 Patton's ability and his social contacts again began paying off. In late March, Stimson, given a promotions list by General Marshall, especially urged the advancement of Patton and of Colonel Julius Ochs Adler, whose family owned the *New York Times*. Stimson had known both "for many years, including the Great War," in which both served honorably. Stimson "had heard that there was some prejudice against these two men" in the White House, especially on the part of Pa Watson, who had graduated from West Point in Patton's original class. "Watson had reported that as coming from the President," Stimson noted in his diary, "but I wasn't sure of that. At any rate I thought it was a piece of injustice if for any political reason they failed to obtain a promotion which they had so eminently deserved. So I took the responsibility on my shoulders."[76]

The secretary got his way. Two days after entering this notation, he made public Patton's pending promotion. "I see by Secretary Stimson's announcement that he has evaluated you perfectly as a potential menace to all living things," Joyce congratulated his friend. "I always did think our Secretary knew his menaces."[77]

Caught up in military events, Patton found a personal matter a distraction. In the early months of 1941 word spread around San Marino that Father Divine, who led a black church in Newark, was negotiating to buy property adjoining Patton's. Petrified, the residents of San Marino formed the Civic Betterment Association to block the move and urged Georgie and Nita to sign the covenant restricting the sale of property to non-Caucasians.[78]

Forwarding the agreement to Georgie, Arvin Brown urged him to sign it. "I think it is the thing to do," he advised. But Patton saw things differently. "Referring to the efforts of the San Marino Civic Betterment Association," he answered his cousin, "they have my hearty moral support, but owing to the tenuous nature of the position I hold, it is not expedient that I express myself on the subject in writing. Probably the best thing to do is to tell them that you couldn't locate me. You as my administrator can make any verbal promises you wish, but they must be verbal, and if anything comes up I will call you a liar."[79]

In describing the makeup of his armored division to Pershing the previous September, Patton wrote in thinly veiled terms of prejudice, both educational and sectional. He pointed out that less than 25 percent of his officers came from reserve officers training programs. "Still we are working hell out of them and may get results. I should prefer all college men but we have to take what we can get."

In commenting more favorably upon the enlisted personnel, Patton displayed his belief in Southern supremacy. "The men we have in this Division are all southern boys and it seems to me that over seventy percent of them have light hair and eyes—the old fighting breed; not subway soldiers as one gets in northern recruits especially from New York and Penn."[80]

One of Patton's drinking companions later disagreed with his assessment of soldiers from the East. In May 1942, a year and a half after Patton made his statement, John S. Wood took over the 4th Armored Division, then at Pine Camp, New York. "You must know that this division was recruited with men in that vicinity," Wood's wife told Liddell Hart after her husband's death, "Pennsylvania, New Jersey, but mostly New York and the large proportion were Jewish; for Gen. John said his best fighters were his Jews! Aggressive with enormous *Drive*."[81] Destiny was already planning for the 4th Armored a remarkable career in France and Germany.

Amid all this, Patton bought a plane. "If you see a small yellow airplane with a black band on its tail arriving at your Headquarters, that will be me," he warned Joyce, "and I think, should I get that far, a salute will be in order, although I leave this to your invariably excellent judgment." Joyce promised that if he saw Patton's plane "coming over the horizon I shall make ready to give you a salute with cannon and turn out the choicest dancing girls."[82]

IX

Knowing that war must come soon, army officials deemed 1941 the year of maneuvers, and in several of these the 2d Armored played a prominent role. With the first one scheduled to take place in Tennessee in June, Patton made a long speech to his men emphasizing what he expected of them. He also explained the two principles in which he believed. The first was by now almost part of his soul. "Years ago I wrote, and I see no reason to change it now, that the whole art of war consisted in catching the enemy by the nose and kicking him in the pants. Try to do that in the maneuvers, and in the war, if it comes. . . . Make it a fixed principle, to find out where the enemy is, hold him in front by fire, and get around him." The second maxim was also something to which Patton always adhered. "Remember, that one of the greatest qualities which we have, is the ability to produce in our enemy the fear of the unknown." Patton urged his men to "keep on, see what else you can do to raise the devil with the enemy." He recalled that when he tried to play football at West Point, the coach came up to him and said: "Mr. Patton. If you can't do anything else, throw a fit!" Patton urged his men to do "the same thing. . . . If you can't think of anything else to do, throw a fit, burn a town, do something!"[83]

Consisting of four problems, the Second Army games in south-central Tennessee showed that at this stage of his tank career Patton made mistakes. In the first exercise Patton's command, the Red force, was pitted against Major General Frederick H. Smith's Seventh Army Corps, which contained four times the infantry strength of the Red force. "The empirical formula worked," observed Patton's supply officer, Lieutenant Colonel Oscar W. Koch. "Hold the enemy by the nose while you kick him in the pants. The Fifth Division did the nasal operation and the Second Armored did the rest." But the exercise was hardly a glorious achievement, for Patton lost approximately 135 tanks, numerous other vehicles, and many men. Both sides claimed victory.

In the second and third exercises Patton's troops became part of the Blue force. During the second they captured Brigadier General Cortlandt Parker, the commander of the 5th Infantry Division, and his staff. As a reward, Patton gave the tankers who corralled Parker $25 each. Remaining part of the Blue force, the 2d Armored Division showed its might during the third exercise. Again using the nose-and-pants technique, Patton's men roared through the enemy in three hours. Observers noted the speed with which tanks and half-tracks pushed through forests and fields, knocking down fences and other obstacles.[84]

Stimson deemed the final problem in the Tennessee maneuvers so important that he flew out to observe it. Meeting with the commanders of the opposing forces on June 25, 1941, the day before the exercise was to begin, he was struck by the differences between the two men. General Smith was to defend the area between two rivers, the Elk on the west and the Duck on the east. With the 2d Armored and 5th Infantry divisions, Patton was to attack. "Even at this preliminary presentation of the plans of the respective commanders," Stimson commented, "I was impressed by the vigor and dash of Patton's plan as compared with the ultra caution and even timidity of the passive defense contemplated by Smith." Smith believed that it would take Patton an entire day to get into position to cross one of the two rivers bordering on the Blue force and that a crossing could not be made until the morning of the second day. Patton, on the other hand, planned to move forward at the zero hour. Feinting with a small force across the Elk, he was set to make an enveloping movement across the Duck. "I foresaw," Stimson observed, "that Smith was in for a surprise, and events bore out my prognosis."

At 5 A.M. the next morning Patton began his assault. Arriving at the Blue command post shortly after that, Stimson found that Smith was receiving accurate reports of Patton's movements, but he made no attempt to stop Patton at the river crossings. "He was planning on a purely passive defense afterwards," the secretary lamented.

From the Blue headquarters Stimson and his aide, Major Harrison, went on to Shelbyville, where they met Patton, his head sticking out of the top of the lead tank. Unfortunately Patton's crossing of the Duck River just west of Shelbyville was anything but a work of art. His men wasted considerable time ferrying motorcycles across the river in small boats and pulling small cars across the ford, which was too deep for a fast crossing. Stimson then visited a second crossing point. Here a column of Patton's division was making better progress, for the river was shallow enough to permit the engineers to lay wire tracks, over which Patton's units could quickly pass.

Once his forces were over the river, Patton moved rapidly. By noon of the twenty-sixth, Stimson believed, "the fate of the maneuvers was settled, Patton having accomplished his aim and having placed himself in a position to dominate the position of the Blue forces." At one-thirty the maneuver ended, Patton being declared the victor in less than half the time it was expected to take.[85]

Patton's quick victory meant only that he had taken advantage of his superior fire power and mobility, rather than that he was ready for war. Observers criticized his handling of his troops. While praising the "morale and spirit" of the division, Major Harrison commented: "Had the Red commander been faced with a more aggressive and energetic enemy, the wide dispersal of his troops in a double envelopment, separated by two formidable obstacles, the Duck and Elk Rivers, might have subjected him to defeat in detail." Harrison also criticized Patton's failure to hide his movements. The Blue G-2 knew exactly where the enemy was at all times, but Smith failed to act on his intelligence reports.[86]

Observing the maneuvers for Lieutenant General Ben Lear, the commander of the Second Army, Lieutenant Colonel Robert W. Grow was equally severe on the tankers. Like Harrison, Grow recounted the troubles the tanks had in crossing the Duck River. Instead of dashing across it, the division had advanced piecemeal, scrambling its units and leaving them susceptible to an aggressive enemy. Grow blamed this on a division headquarters racked by personality differences, surprising considering that Patton had made the skillful Lieutenant Colonel Geoffrey Keyes his chief of staff.[87]

Such comments deeply wounded Patton. Writing to Floyd Parks, now on McNair's staff, he answered these criticisms and those of the umpires during the Tennessee maneuvers. His first comment dealt with his lack of coordination. "This is a fine old military word and can be used with equal facility to describe the operations of Alexander the Great, of Napoleon, or of Allenby." With sabers and bayonets a soldier could coordinate a lunge. But tanks could not, and should not, be coordinated in that fashion.

Patton thought the same of concentrated or mass attacks, the desire for which, he told Parks, "results from undigested memories of teachings at Leavenworth or the War College or of reading about Cambrai. But it should be noted that the teachings of that period and the action at Cambrai were based on the invulnerability of tanks. That invulnerability no longer exists, and hence the use of tanks in mass is futile and suicidal." Tanks should attack only "to attain a position astride the enemy's lines of communication."

Patton also answered criticism that he should have been in his command post, rather then riding around in the lead tank. An infantry commander might receive messages two or three hours late, he reasoned, but in three hours tanks "might well be 15 to 20 miles from the point indicated on the map. We have many Generals capable of keeping G-2—G-3 maps, and very few capable of leading anything. . . . It is my convinced opinion that General Scott and I are the only general officers who participated in the maneuvers who knew by personal observations how our troops behaved. If there were no other reason for going forward, the one I have just mentioned is of paramount importance."[88]

Returning to Benning with his division, Patton found himself involved in camp shenanigans. Schanze, then serving as Fredendall's adjutant, remembered two of these. The first took place on a hot day in

August 1941, when the 2d Armored was to put on a demonstration for the adjutant generals of the state militias, all major generals. At two o'clock, with the adjutants broiling in the Georgia sun, a tank arrived. The door opened and Patton jumped to the ground wearing his Flash Gordon outfit. "It closed on the right side," Schanze remembered, "buttons ran up to the shoulder, along the shoulder to the neck, then up the standing collar. . . . One of the visiting generals brought down the house when he said, 'My God, a man from Mars.' "[89]

Nor was Patton through. One day a sergeant in the military police came to Schanze's office and reported that he had followed a car that was speeding in the thirty-mile-per-hour zone. The car stopped at the headquarters of the 2d Armored Division, and out of it came Patton. The sergeant saluted and told Patton he had clocked the vehicle at sixty miles an hour. The sergeant quoted Patton as saying: "All right Sergeant, you have done your duty. Now get out." Hearing the story, Fredendall told Schanze to have Patton there at ten the next morning. Patton arrived on time, and with Fredendall's permission Schanze left the door ajar to hear. "Lloyd," Patton, a perpetual speeder, began, "I think I know what you asked me here for. I don't know what in the hell made me tell the driver to go that fast. I know what the speed limit was, and I did not use good judgment. I won't do it again." The two generals shook hands and Patton left.[90]

Actually Patton's stay at Benning was dotted with speeding infractions. His personal driver, Master Sergeant J. L. Mims of Abbeville, Alabama, remembered how, in episode after episode, Patton would egg him on to greater speeds. Among Patton's more notable gems to Mims, who loved him, were: "Where the hell do you think you're going, I want to go over there, (as if I didn't know) don't drive all over the field like a God dam Chicken with his head chopped off," and "if you're afraid to drive this God Dam thing, just stop and get the hell out and I'll drive myself." To a military policeman who told him he could not go the wrong way up a one-way street, Patton shouted: "The hell I can't." He hated the military police so much that when he later assumed command of the 1st Armored Corps he ordered that all MPs were to be relieved from traffic duties and reassigned to guarding camp prisoners. Issuing the order, Patton said to Mims: "that will hold them for a while."[91]

X

During the summer of 1941 tragedy befell the Armored Force. Chaffee, the key spirit of mechanization, died of cancer. Appointed to replace him was not Scott but Patton's West Point classmate Jacob L. Devers. Like Wood, Devers was an artilleryman, concerned not only with the speed and mobility of vehicles but with their firepower. "I was very much impressed with Devers," Patton informed Bea in early August. "He had developed a lot and is a fine leader. It is easy to see how any one comparing him to Scotty would be inclined toward Devers unless he knew how realy smart Scotty is inspite of his chipmunk expression. So far as I am concerned I think the change will not be to my disadvantage."[92]

During the next four years Patton and Devers would see their lives often intertwine, but neither seemed to like or to trust the other. Patton was sure Devers was appointed because, he told Bea, who was back in Massachusetts participating in horse shows, "he has a drag with the President and Pa Watson." For his part Devers complained because Patton ignored the chain of command when he wanted something and instead went directly to Stimson. Almost twenty years after Patton's death, Devers recalled this with some bitterness.

> Well, George Patton wasn't telling me anything, but he was writing little notes to Secretary Stimson. . . . There was talk about replacing the steel on the tracks of the tanks with rubber. Mr. Stimson called me in to talk about it. He was great. Mr. Stimson was one of the finest men I ever dealt with. I used to have a lot of fun because when I went in to see him I was always prepared. If I didn't know an answer I'd say, "Mr. Stimson, I don't know; I'm going to Detroit, and on the way home I'll get the answer; I'll be in here day after tomorrow and I'll tell you." And I was able to do this. Well, frankly, I went down to Ft. Benning and I told George I was coming down to inspect his command. He had a house, he lived out in the woods with his wife—and I knew the children; we'd been together at Ft. Myer—I'd commanded the 16th Field Artillery at Myer—and he was the executive officer to the Commanding General, Kenyon Joyce. He was also Master of the

Hounds at Warrenton. I played polo. I played a lot of polo with George. So I knew him well. I had known him as a cadet. He was the highest ranking, not the senior officer, but the one that got in the parade most because he was the adjutant at West Point, and of course very much senior to me for I was a buck private in the rear ranks. I didn't have much to do with him then because he was a bit taller and in one of the taller companies—I was in the medium. But after we graduated I kept moving around. And suddenly it comes out in the paper that I'm commanding the Armored Force. I laughed when I read it, and I said to myself, "I'll bet George will have a hard time about this."

Going down to Benning, Devers had dinner with the Pattons and another man,

an old cavalryman. When he left and George's wife started to leave, I asked her to stay. I said, "I need a judge in here. George and I are going to settle some things right here, and you know George, and I know him." They had a big open fire. And so I said, "Now, George, I have your recommendations and we've given them all careful consideration." Then I went on, "I don't give a damn who commands, but I'm the commanding officer right now, and I'm going to command, and I'm going to make the decisions, and here they are." Now I said, "You went this way; we want to go a little differently than you do. You're too much of a horse cavalry-man. I'm a little more on fire power." I gave him all the facts. I said, "Are you going to play ball or aren't you?" And he stood up and said, "Yes, boss." And that was the end of it. . . . He was a good soldier—always was.[93]

By August 1941 Patton was concentrating on the next maneuver. "We are leaving in exactly one week for Louisiana," he informed Arvin Brown on the second. Patton expected his division to be there until October, "unless prior to that time we are fighting with the Japs, the Russians, the Germans, the Italians, or any other nation except the British."[94]

The Louisiana maneuvers were meant to correct some of the deficien-cies of the Tennessee exercise. In theory, it was to be another testing ground for tanks. Covering more than thirteen million acres, the maneuver area contained rice fields, swamps, dense forests, and the like. It was hardly tank country. In the main exercise, to be held in September, the two opposing armies were the Red, a supposedly invaded nation consisting of the Second Army, commanded by Lieutenant General Ben Lear, and the Blue, the aggressor nation, consisting of the Third Army, commanded by the German-born Lieutenant General Walter Krueger. Krueger's newly appointed chief of staff was Lieutenant Colonel Dwight D. Eisenhower. As the exercises began, Patton's neighbor, Senator Henry Cabot Lodge, a reserve officer, heard Patton say to a group of soldiers: "I will give anyone a $50 prize who will take prisoner a certain so-and-so named Colonel Eisenhower." Lodge added: "Needless to say, Patton never had to part with his $50.00."[95]

Even before the Louisiana games began, Wood questioned their purpose. During the summer of 1941 two events encouraged the opponents of armor. In one battle in North Africa the Germans destroyed over two hundred British machines, indicating that tanks could be stopped. The Second Army maneuvers in Tennessee, moreover, had shown that large enemy tank units could be tracked, permitting anti-tank units to counter them. These two things led to the calling in July of an antitank conference, resulting in the creation of a Tank Destroyer Center, headed by an infantryman, Lieutenant Colonel Andrew D. Bruce. With the aid of McNair, the commander of the Army Ground Forces and the director of the maneuvers, Bruce developed for the Louisiana games the so-called Tank Destroyer, which Wood renamed the "Tank Annoyer," and, he wrote, it "did not even live up to that sobriquet." Consisting "of a jeep on which scantlings were mounted to represent guns, its only effect on tanks was to delay our own tank program." Just before the Louisiana exercises, McNair told Patton and Wood, now Patton's artillery chief, that despite the successes of the German tanks in Poland and France, "the real value of armor in the face of tank destroyers" had to be determined "in our maneuver." McNair questioned "the nature of the resistance" put forth by Germany's enemies. "The maneuvers," Wood concluded, "were designed and staged to limit the possibility of proper armored action."[96]

The preliminary exercises in Louisiana involved only Krueger's army, which was split into Red and Blue teams. In the first of these the Reds were to land at Lake Charles in southern Louisiana, move north, and capture the oil fields. The Blues, which included Patton's division, were to try to drive the Reds into the Gulf of Mexico. For the push southward Patton divided his force into three columns, each containing light and medium tanks, artillery, infantry and engineers. Beginning the march in rain on August 17, the 2d Armored Division soon bogged down. In Tennessee it had specialized in wide enveloping movements and in long marches. Here the tanks were forced into narrow corridors between bogs. The Reds placed simulated antitank guns at spots perpendicular to the route of attack. Even Major I. D. White's 82d Reconnaissance Battalion was slowed down by antitank guns and had to proceed on foot. After losing between forty and fifty tanks in frontal attacks, Patton's 66th Armored Regiment circled the enemy, its lead elements ending up thirty miles ahead of the rest of the division, where it remained like the famed Lost Battalion of the First World War. For two more days the exercise continued. Even though his side won, Patton was far from pleased with his and his division's performance.[97]

During the second preliminary exercise Patton made a mistake that he never repeated in Europe. Following a plan mapped out by Grow, the 2d Armored Division, this time part of the Red team, was to cross the Sabine River near its southernmost segment, make a wide envelopment into Texas, advance to the north, and attack the rear of the Blue force. Following the plan, the 2d Armored crossed into Texas on August 24. The next morning the division proceeded northward in three columns on a march of 186 miles. At Carthage, Texas, one column turned east and captured a bridge that could be used to recross the Sabine. Grow, who accompanied the column, sent word to Patton to dispatch an armored regiment across the bridge at once, thereby securing it, but for some reason Patton decided not to listen. Getting back across the Sabine then required repairing a damaged bridge at Logansport, Louisiana, and the construction of a pontoon bridge.

In his critique of this exercise Major General George V. Strong, the commander of VIII Corps, found fault with the umpires, with Patton, and with the 1st Cavalry Division, commanded by Major General Innis P. Swift. The bridge at Logansport had been severely damaged, he argued, requiring more than the hundred man-hours Patton was penalized to repair it. "Some engineering," he scoffed. By theoretically repairing the bridge so quickly, Patton was able to cross before Strong had time to position his antitank units. Strong also suggested that Patton must have possessed kangaroo tanks, for they traveled undamaged over mines placed and properly marked by Strong's engineers. After commenting on similar violations of the rules by Swift, Strong observed that "hell will have an awful stench of the burning of hair and flesh when these two divisions are called to their final reward."[98]

In the final Third Army exercise Patton did much better, displaying a speed that to Leon Kay of the United Press "looked like a flashback from a Nazi advance of the European war." While enemy dive bombers swooped over them, Patton's engineers ferried his tanks across the 150-foot-wide Red River at Montgomery, Louisiana. High on the river bank stood Patton, his white hair waving in the breeze and his tanned face creased with a smile. "Look at that, will you?" he said to Kay. "We left Kurthwood at 7 last night and traveled over 40 miles of rough roads and countryside to reach the banks of the Red River at 12:30 this afternoon. I guess Krueger will be pleased this time."[99]

Beginning on September 15, the main phase of the maneuver pitted Krueger against Lear, Patton's division occasionally moving to Lear's side. In one problem Krueger's Blues, outnumbering the Reds almost two to one, was to attack up the Mississippi Valley, cutting the United States in two. Countering the move, Lear sent Patton's division south across the Red River. The 2d Armored captured Mount Carmel, where five roads intersected, but Krueger, who had no armored divisions but had mastered the art of moving troops by truck, soon retook the town. The fighting then turned into a race for the town of Hornbeck, just south of the Red River. Winning, Krueger's Blue Army threatened to encircle the 2d Armored. Meantime, the 1st Cavalry Division, now part of the Blue team, attacked Patton's gasoline dumps and supply lines. Without fuel the tanks were useless. Lear's entire army found itself pinned against the Red River. "Had it been a real war," Hanson Baldwin, the *New York Times*'s military analyst, reported, "Lear's forces would have been annihilated."[100]

For an obvious reason the final exercise, in which Patton's division joined Krueger's Blues, became part of the Patton legend. Held from September 24 to 28, it was designed by McNair to be a test of tanks against antitank weapons. The Blues were to advance to the north, capturing Shreveport. Moving in heavy rain, the Blue force found that the Reds had destroyed over nine hundred bridges, the struggle becoming, in McNair's words, "the Battle of the Bridges. If there is any one lesson which stands out above all others," he observed, "it is the decisive influence of destroyed bridges."[101]

Again Patton turned to envelopment. Following a plan developed by Eisenhower, Patton was to lead the regiment-size outer, or western, column of a two-pronged force that would envelop Shreveport. Finding the bridge over the Sabine at Bon Weir destroyed, he took his men sixty-five miles farther south to Orange, near the Gulf of Mexico, where the tanks crossed over. Racing directly west, and out of the maneuver area, to Beaumont, the tankers then turned north and by noon of the twenty-sixth approached Woodville, fifty miles north of Beaumont. At the rain-swollen Angelina River, sixty miles farther north, Patton got a huge break. An umpire ruled that a bridge, supposedly destroyed by the Reds, was still standing, for water covered the charges. By midnight Patton's men were at Henderson, having raced nearly two hundred miles from the bridge at Orange in twenty-four hours.[102]

Advancing farther north, Patton ran into antitank guns. His orders called for him to turn east at Marshall, Texas, almost directly west of Shreveport, which he would then attack from that direction. But, hearing that the Red force at Greenwood, just inside Louisiana and along the route, had been reinforced by an antitank battalion, he decided to drive on to Caddo Lake, north of Shreveport. He would then attack Shreveport from the north, or rear. About noon on the twenty-seventh a Red plane spotted Patton's column. Lear rushed antitank units to the scene. At day's end on the twenty-seventh Patton's tanks and the Red units faced one another along a line fifteen miles north of Shreveport.[103]

The next day the battle for Shreveport ended. Advancing north between the Sabine and Red rivers, the bulk of Krueger's force caught up with the main body of Red troops, which had been retreating from position to position while avoiding battle. On the morning of the twenty-eighth the Blues opened a gap in the Red line. Late that afternoon the exercise ended.[104]

Patton's dash through Texas, including buying gas from local dealers, captured the attention of reporters but contributed little to the final result. Perhaps Colonel Harry B. Crea provided the best analysis of Patton's conduct during the maneuvers. "I went through West Point with him," Crea informed his friend, General Omar Bradley, of Patton, "and later through the War College. When he took his 2d Div. into its first maneuvers I was his Chief Umpire. The fact that Ben Lear couldn't curb him didn't bother me any, but I found that no one could handle an army officer who felt secure due to his friendship with Stimson."[105]

Patton himself was dissatisfied with his division's performance. "We still fail to use every weapon every time," he told his officers. "Each time we fight with only one weapon when we could use several weapons, we are not winning a battle, we are making fools of ourselves." Agreeing, Devers cited the lack of cooperation among the division's tank, infantry, and reconnaissance units. Each had acted independently.[106]

The War Department, moreover, complained about something that was out of character for Patton. After observing the British care for equipment during the First World War, Patton developed a fetish for keeping trucks and tanks clean. During the Second World War, he made his men wash vehicles daily. But at the end of the Shreveport exercise he turned in for shipment to Fort Knox fifty-four filthy tanks. Informing Patton that "You will receive under separate cover an official communication giving you hell," General Scott said that he had tried to block the censure, for Patton had been told "to turn in these tanks regardless of condition." Devers's intelligence and operations officers had agreed with Scott, but Devers himself approved of the censure and sent the letter of criticism forward.[107]

XI

In October Patton was able to relax and to think of personal matters. Young George was uppermost in his father's mind. Now approaching the age when he would be eligible for appointment to West Point, he was attending the Hill School. Even though George was having difficulties there, Patton, young Bea, and Johnny Waters thought he should remain at the school. "If his work does improve," Patton wrote Bea, "he will demonstrate that he is in earnest and not just a flash in the pan."[108]

In late October Patton took a short leave to sail his schooner, the *When and If,* from the harbor at Manchester-by-the-Sea, near Prides Crossing, south toward Georgia. Struggling through "a half gale right on the nose all the way," the ship took six days to reach Cape May in southern New Jersey. There Patton left Bea with the boat and took the train back to Fort Benning. "That is the last time I go Cruising with a time clock," Patton told Joyce. "There is nothing to it."

Patton complained to Joyce about another matter. In July his picture had appeared on the cover of *Life* magazine, which had a huge circulation. Recognized almost everywhere he went, Patton believed "my style is cramped—you get the idea."[109]

That November the final maneuvers of 1941 took place in the Carolinas. Like the Tennessee and Louisiana areas, this region, between Columbia, South Carolina, on the southwest and Salisbury-Sanford, North Carolina, on the northeast, contained numerous rivers. The maneuver promised to be another battle for the bridges.

The Carolina exercises involved roughly 400,000 troops. Lieutenant General Hugh A. Drum, Patton's commander in Hawaii, led the First Army, the Blues. To test the ability of tanks to move against enemy fire, Drum's force possessed 764 mobile antitank guns. Major General Oscar W. Griswold commanded the opposition Red Army, which had 765 tanks. General Headquarters thinking dictated that a proper test of tanks and antitank guns required an equal number of each. "We want tanks for offensive purposes," McNair reasoned, "not to throw them against enemy tanks, which is like butting our heads against a stone wall & reduces their offensive power."[110]

The initial two exercises turned out predictably. In the first, held in South Carolina, Patton's force, part of the Red team, moved directly south from Chester toward Columbia, its objective, which it reached in three days, thus ending this phase. In the second phase Scott's I Armored Corps, consisting of Magruder's 1st Armored Division and Patton's 2d, was part of the Blue force. The movement took place in virtually the same territory as the first, but this time the tankers moved north, rather than south. Starting on the morning of November 10, the Armored Corps rolled steadily forward, capturing its objective at noon of the next day, a day ahead of schedule.[111]

In the third exercise Scott's corps returned to the Red side. In this problem the Wateree River, east of Chester and Columbia, became the boundary separating two nations. Having established a beachhead on the west bank, the Blues were to push inland and conquer the enemy. Scott's corps was to cross the Wateree, get behind the Blue force, and cut its communications, going as far as the Pee Dee, the next river to the east.

Crossing the Wateree in the early hours of November 16, Patton's 82d Reconnaissance Battalion opened the affair with a highly publicized move. Once over the Wateree, Captain John H. Huckins, the commander of D Company, set up roadblocks. At one of these his men stopped and captured Drum, then returning to his headquarters. Within a few minutes umpires ordered that he be released, but the incident appeared in papers like the *New York Times*.[112]

Despite this widely noted achievement, Drum's First Army walked away the victor. Time after time the antitank units were deemed to have knocked out Patton's and Magruder's tanks. At the conclusion of the problem McNair praised the antitank forces, noting their improvement since the Louisiana exercises.[113]

For Patton's division the final problem, taking place from the twenty-fifth to the twenty-eighth, resembled its predecessor. Moving north from Ruby, South Carolina, the 2d Armored ran into Fredendall's Blue II Corps. His men overwhelmed at several points, Patton had no choice but to withdraw during the night. By the next night he was back at Ruby, having suffered heavy losses. Sent to rescue the 1st Battalion of the 41st Armored Infantry Regiment, the 3d Battalion of the 67th Armored Regiment lost all its tanks.

During the night of November 26, Patton tried to regroup his force. Combining two of his three columns under Brigadier General Willis D. Crittenberger, he sent it to outflank the Blue force. But by noon of the 27th Patton was again forced to retreat. This final exercise ended the next day with Patton continuing to withdraw in the face of heavy enemy forces.[114]

Even though his troops did not shine in the last problem, Patton came out of the Carolina maneuvers as a man to watch. On the twenty-seventh General Marshall flew to North Carolina to view the conclusion of the exercises. Questioned by Senator Homer Ferguson about leaving Washington when relations with Japan were so strained, Marshall talked about the outstanding performance of Patton, whom he had earmarked for high command.[115]

In an interview with his biographer, Forrest C. Pogue, Marshall revealed what impressed him most during the maneuver. While in Carolina, Marshall observed the way Magruder and Patton handled their divisions. The enemy captured Magruder, a product of the Infantry School Tank Section, every day, but it never got near Patton. Marshall decided then and there that Patton was his man.[116]

Devers was less pleased than Marshall with the performance of the

Armored Force. "There were many things about the maneuver which were well below our standards," he wrote Patton, "and these things must be corrected by urgent work and night schools if necessary. . . . My staff is fast rounding into shape and if we can get GHQ and the War Department to speed up their work and give us a task but not tell us how to do it we will go places."[117]

An army officer destined to become far more prominent than Devers looked at Patton's performance and gasped. In February 1941 Marshall had plucked Omar N. Bradley, then a lieutenant colonel, out of routine army work and appointed him to head the infantry school at Fort Benning. Accepting the appointment and promotion—he was jumped to the rank of brigadier general—Bradley was elated and sad, for he was replacing Brigadier General Courtney H. Hodges, who had flunked out of Patton's original West Point class of 1908. Bradley remembered Hodges, his classmate at the Army War College, as "an august figure like Marshall and a man I admired almost equally." Later, in Europe, "he was on a par with George Patton, but owing to his modesty and low profile, he has been all but forgotten."[118]

As the commandant of Fort Benning, Bradley spent a year in close association with Patton, calling him

> the most fiercely ambitious man and the strangest duck I have ever known. He seemed to be motivated by some deep, inexplicable martial spirit. . . . He dressed as though he had just stepped out of a custom military tailor shop and had his own private bootblack. He was unmercifully hard on his men, demanding the utmost in military efficiency and bearing. Most of them respected but despised him. Although he could be the epitome of grace and charm at social or official functions, he was at the same time the most earthly profane man I ever knew. I sometimes wondered if this macho profanity was unconscious overcompensation for his most serious personal flaw: a voice that was almost comically squeaky and high-pitched, altogether lacking in command authority.[119]

Bradley found Patton anything but the self-deprecating individual depicted by those who insist that Patton suffered from dyslexia. "He wrote obsessively candid self-congratulatory (or self-abnegating) letters and diaries," a bitter Bradley observed in 1983, "which have recently been edited and published in two volumes. Reading these volumes was one of the most astonishing literary experiences of my life."[120]

Bradley saw Patton as the daredevil of the 1941 maneuvers, breaking "all the old-fashioned rules, smashing his mechanized forces ever onward with dazzling speed and surprise." The umpires criticized Patton for leaving his command post and for riding roughshod through the supposed enemy. But, Bradley admitted, Patton showed himself to be "one of the most extraordinary fighting generals the Army has ever produced." He was neither a planner nor a deep thinker—"logistics were and would remain a mystery to him, and he improvised war plans as he went along—but if you wanted an objective or a favorable headline, Patton was clearly the man for it."[121]

Wood looked at the maneuvers differently. "Our top people—Marshall, McNair, Krueger, etc.—all did their utmost to retard & delay & cast doubt on the development of our armor," he told Liddell Hart, "even when the lesson of armored war was written in blood all over France and Poland. 1918 minds, all!"[122]

In his letter summarizing the maneuvers, Devers spoke of changes in the armored command. Scott was going to Africa as an adviser to the British and probably would not return to armor. Despite their differences, Devers had recommended that Patton succeed Scott and that armored headquarters be moved from Fort Knox to Fort Benning. Crittenberger would succeed Patton as commander of the 2d Armored Division.[123]

By this time the Japanese had attacked Pearl Harbor. The United States was at war with Japan, Germany, and Italy. As "the world blew up," Joyce sent Patton a message: "Would be delighted if you and I could team up at some later date and engage effectively in the one mission we have now which is killing slant-eyed rats."[124]

Seven

FIELD OF HONOR

I

By 1942 Patton had demonstrated the way tanks should be used, shocking McNair, Magruder, and the others who believed that tanks could go only a half dozen miles an hour and that they should be used for support, advancing side by side with the infantry. "But, that's not the Armor concept at all," explained John Waters, who served under Patton at Fort Benning.

> The Armor concept is that striking forces move rapidly, go through, destroy as you go and then allow the following troops to mop up. What you want to do is get behind the enemy—well, you know the tactics of armor—get behind into their rear areas, and then the front will collapse. That was General Patton's theory. He would hold them by the nose and then kick them in the ass. . . . He was fire and brimstone about it. He was always pushing, pushing, pushing and pushing to do it, so they should have expected that. But you had some of these old-time generals who had fought in World War I, I guess, or seemed like they had, to whom everything was four miles an hour, or maybe three and a half.

The soldiers knew war was coming. They grumbled, as soldiers do, but they realized that training saved lives. As Patton always said, "Hard in maneuvers, easy in war." In training and in maneuvers he forced his tankers to move at night, one tank behind another. "The poor drivers were inhaling the fumes from that tank in front of him and the dust was dense. They were going along and all of a sudden they'd have to slam their brakes on to keep from running into the vehicle in front of them. And, it was bitter. It was the most bitter, roughest training I've ever had, those Louisiana and Carolina maneuvers." Waters considered the Louisiana games the more important, for they changed army thinking. The Carolina maneuver, however, was the more difficult. The weather was so cold that water froze in the canteens.[1]

While at Benning as commander of the I Armored Corps, Patton took care of two important but different details. First, he equipped each tank with a powerful radio. Second, he chose a new chief of staff. Major Hobart R. Gay was helping train the troops when Patton's adjutant came to see him. "I have something for you, stand up, please," he ordered. Putting on Gay the staff insignia, he said: "You are now General Patton's Chief of Staff." Gay was destined to serve in this post, with brief interruptions, until the general died.[2]

In early 1942 Patton again became concerned with the future of his son, George, now eighteen. Never a brilliant student, George had received an appointment to West Point for June 1942 from Senator Henry Cabot Lodge of Massachusetts, a reserve captain then serving at Benning under Brigadier General Willis D. Crittenberger. But George was not prepared for the academic rigors of the academy and had to relinquish the appointment. With standards lowered because of the need for officers in wartime, West Point was easier academically than before, leading Patton to believe his son would be able to stay if he were reappointed. It was now too late for June, he told his longtime friend, Republican Congressman James W. Wadsworth of New York, so the next thing was an appointment for 1943. "It is highly probable—and this is confidential—that I may not be in this country much longer, and as you know, the chances of ever coming back vertical are not good. Therefore I should like to settle the appointment business before I depart." Patton explained that he was a native Californian, but he spent little time there and now lived in Massachusetts.[3]

Wadsworth answered immediately. "If I were you I would fish in two ponds—California and Massachusetts," he advised. "Perhaps I'd fish a little deeper in Massachusetts, as you are actually an official resident there." Not knowing that Patton's father had run against Hiram Johnson for the Senate seat from California in 1916, Wadsworth suggested he try Johnson, still a senator. "Undoubtedly he knows of you and would not be offended. He might be pleased." Patton should also try

Lodge, as well as David Walsh, the other senator from Massachusetts, and the congressman representing San Marino. "And let me add this: the story would be different if you had ever lived in the thirty-ninth congressional district of New York." Wadsworth reported that his son, commissioned a second lieutenant in the cavalry on December 23, was now on guard duty at the White House. "Never did I suspect that a son of mine would be guarding Franklin Delano Roosevelt. War is hell."[4]

During the early months of 1942, the Armored Force expanded rapidly. By mid-February the army had "activated"—"Army for 'hatched,' " *Time* explained—six armored divisions, which now constituted two corps. Showing that antitank sentiment still lived in the United States Army, Alvan C. Gillem took over the newly formed II Corps. Gillem, who "with cool contempt" had "assured" Chynoweth "he never wanted to drive, and wouldn't even ride in a tank—ever," now ruled over half the army's tanks.

Chief of I Corps, *Time* reported, was "tough, profane, gimlet-eyed" George Patton, "variously known to his men as 'Flash Gordon,' 'Old Blood and Guts,' 'the Green Hornet.' " Patton had replaced the "gnarled, toothy" Scott, "who looked too brittle to ride the Armored Corps's mechanical monsters." Patton enjoyed "bouncing around" in tanks, and during the Carolina maneuvers he usually led his division. "His bellows to his men on maneuvers were always succinct," *Time* continued. He once asked a private what he was shooting at. "A concealed machine gun," the soldier said. "Goddammit," Patton corrected him. "That's not a machine gun. It's a dirty Nazi bastard."[5]

About the time this article appeared Stimson and his assistant secretary of war, John J. McCloy, "cooked up and initiated" another project, which Marshall and his staff immediately pushed. Since the fighting between England and Germany now centered in North Africa, the War Department decided to create a desert warfare training center. Marshall agreed that Patton, not Gillem or Magruder, both of whom knew little about tanks, should head it.[6]

Ordered to reconnoiter southeastern California and western Arizona for a training site, Patton selected an area of ten thousand square miles, ninety miles by 180 miles, much of which was controlled by the Interior Department. It ran from the Colorado River in the east to near Desert Center, California, in the west, from Searchlight, Nevada, in the north, to Yuma, Arizona, in the south. Patton called it "probably the largest and best training ground in the United States."[7]

The armored units soon began leaving the East for the West. On March 21, three days after selecting the site, Patton dispatched some of his officers to the desert. That April 1 troops began leaving Fort Benning by train and convoy. Major Isaac D. White, who later commanded the 2d Armored Division, remembered Patton's departure. The staff and the unit commanders assembled at Patton's elaborate log cabin in the pine woods. Patton toasted the division with a glass of champagne. Then his officers toasted him. Patton started to make a speech, but tears rolled down his cheeks. He abruptly left to enter his waiting car.[8]

That same month Bea rented the Whittier ranch house in Indio, California, twenty-nine feet below sea level. Patton established Camp Young, named for Lieutenant General S. B. M. Young, the Indian fighter who was the first army chief of staff, and usually stayed there, but from late Saturday to late Sunday and for an occasional supper during the week, he joined Bea at the ranch.[9]

Known as "the place that God forgot," Camp Young became the last word in training horror. At Faid Pass, a trail through the Tunisian mountains, Patton is said to have threatened some armored forces: "You men get in there and fight, or by God I'll send you back to Camp Young."

Colonel Nye described the atmosphere. "They were basically indentured civilians," he said of the twenty thousand men Patton commanded.

> To develop their warrior spirit he [Patton] designated 100 buglers to play taps at 2200 each night. This was to remind them of the rich 2000-year heritage of soldiering that they had just joined. But as the bugling echoed through the valley, through encampments that stretched for 200 miles, the coyotes in the hills chimed in with their howls. Soon everyone was waiting up breathlessly for the 10 o'clock symphony.

In the desert, where the temperature reached 130 degrees in the sun, water conservation was essential. Patton limited each man to a gallon a day, each vehicle to one to three gallons a day. "However," Patton noted

in an article in the *Cavalry Journal,* "there have been strangely few occasions necessitating the addition of water to the radiators of the vehicles."

The general especially pushed maneuvers. On paper an exercise
seemed simple. A force consisting of tanks, tank destroyers, troop carriers, and other vehicles shoved off from the tank parks at 1 A.M. The
machines traveled by highway for twenty miles and then swung to the
left and charged in several columns into the Colorado Desert. By 4 P.M.
the columns had merged and the search began for a camping spot for
the night. The dust-covered men dropped to the ground. Some opened
cans of C rations, surprisingly tasty concoctions of beef or chicken with
vegetables. These they heated over fires made in tin cans filled up to an
inch from the top with sand and then doused with gasoline and lit. Others dug slit trenches six feet long, a couple of feet wide, and two feet
deep. Should an enemy tank unit charge through the tank park, men
lying in these slits would be able to survive unless a tank tread traversed
the trench lengthwise.

The next morning, after shaving, washing, and brushing their teeth,
all with the daily ration of water, the men consumed their breakfast
and, neat enough to stand inspection, reentered the tanks and took off.
Both the tankers and Patton were pleased with the performance of these
vehicles. "Our stuff is rugged and dependable," Patton said. "We've got
some of the latest equipment." During the maneuvers the previous
year, his tanks logged ten million vehicular miles, he related. "And on
the last day only 1.3 per cent of them weren't functioning." Much of
the credit belonged to the maintenance battalions, which seldom took
more than three hours to repair any tank.

Patton termed the "general health" of his command "remarkably
good." Working hard, most of the men had replaced fat with muscle.
The famous wrestler "Man Mountain" Dean, now a sergeant in Patton's
unit, had lost sixty pounds, "but is still quite a figure of a man!"[10]

Patton kept discipline strict. At a reunion at Camp Young forty years
after the end of World War II, Porter B. Williamson, then a young lieutenant and later the author of *The Patton Principles,* which tried to apply
these doctrines to business success, commented that if Patton saw him
standing in the shade, as he was then doing, "he'd have my hide for sure.
We all stood in the sun then." Patton, he said, "looked like a general,
but talked like a top kick," his curses matching those of any sergeant.

Williamson recalled that Patton often made surprise inspections of the night guards. One evening he asked Williamson to question a guard about his orders, while Patton stayed out of sight. "From which direction do you expect trouble?" Williamson asked the guard. When the guard pointed to the center of the camp, Williamson, knowing Patton was listening, began dressing him down. "That's the center of our camp," Williamson answered. "The enemy would be in the opposite direction." The guard stared back at him and said: "You didn't ask me anything about the enemy, sir. I know where the enemy is. You asked me where I expected trouble, and I expect trouble from right back there. That's Patton's headquarters, and that's where I expect trouble." Patton, who heard the conversation, roared. "Come on back, Williamson," he called out. "That man understands his mission."

At the Desert Training Center, Patton loved to tease his officers. Walter Hennessey, who spent four years overseas as a tank driver, remembered a day his unit was practicing decontaminating the tanks in case of a gas attack. "Out of nowhere pops the general," Hennessey related. Jumping onto a tank, he began talking to a Sergeant Rucker, while officers, including the battalion colonel, gathered at the foot of the vehicle. At the conclusion of the conversation Patton shook hands with the sergeant, whispered something in his ear, and jumped off. Without saying a word, he got into his car and left. As soon as the sergeant got off his tank, the officers wanted to know what Patton had said. Rucker then let them in on the secret: "What General Patton whispered in my ear was: 'The minute you get off the tank, sergeant, those dizzy bastards will want to know what I whispered into your ear.'"[11]

Almost a half century later the men still remembered the heat. In June 1942 Hennessey wrote to his mother that he had recorded 185 degrees within his tank. Tools and equipment laid out in the sun burned the hands of those not wearing gloves. Water in the Lister bags used to purify each company's supply reached ninety degrees, but it seemed cool compared with the heat inside the tanks.[12]

Patton was also hard on the entertainers who came out to Indio to entertain his troops. During the stay in the desert, he asked John Maschio, the agent for such movie stars as Fred Astaire, Ginger Rogers, James Stewart, Henry Fonda, and Gene Kelly, to help allieviate the isolation. Once a week Maschio came out to Indio and put on a show for the troops. "Then," the agent remembered, "that son of a gun would make us do what his soldiers had to do, even the girls." He had the men put on Army fatigues and crawl under barbed wire while bullets blasted over them. Patton forced the women to don fatigues and take long jeep rides over bumpy roads and through the dusty desert. All this was to show the entertainers, who had put on the show without pay, what his men were going through.[13]

Among those who congratulated Patton on his new assignment was Eisenhower. Having yearned in 1941 and in early 1942 to serve with Patton in the revived Tank Corps, Ike, in the midst of a meteoric rise resembling that of Pershing before the First World War, predicted on April 4 that his old friend would be "the 'Black Jack' of the damn war." In a strange twist Eisenhower would become what he predicted for Patton. Brought to Washington in December 1941 as assistant chief of the War Plans Division, he was appointed its head the following February, thus ending all chance of his returning to tanks. Patton realized this when he wrote to his friend on April 13: "While I appreciate your natural desires, owing to the fact that you were red-headed before you became bald, to quit your present job, I personally believe that for you to abandon it now would be little short of a national calamity. However, being selfish, there is nothing I would like more than to be the 'Black Jack' of this war with you as assistant 'B. J.' or even the other way around."[14]

Later in the month Patton invited Ike to visit Indio "sometime in the next two months to see what we are doing." He relished Eisenhower's "candid opinion on tactics," for with the "possible exception" of Brigadier General Geoffrey Keyes, Patton respected Ike's opinions more than any others. "We are entering a wholly uninvestigated field of tactics," he informed his friend.

In his letter to Ike, Patton seemed to contradict his assertions about reincarnation. "Sometimes I think your life and mine are under the protection of some supreme being or fate, because after many years of parallel thought, we find ourselves in the situations which we now occupy. But remember that my fate largely depends on you, because in this distant locality, one can very easily be forgotten, despite the fact in my case I have spent more time in command of troops in the field than any other officer in the army."[15]

In selecting heroes and villains, God's will was indeed strange. Like William Tecumseh Sherman, who always revered the Army of the Tennessee as his own, Patton loved the 2d Armored. But no armored division eventually accomplished more than the 4th, under Chynoweth's roommate at West Point, John Shirley Wood. Bluff and short-tempered, Wood was one of the few army officers who roared back when Patton roared at him, leading some officers to dub him "Tiger Jack." Like Patton, he was a stickler for discipline. Creighton W. Abrams, later the army chief of staff but a captain when Wood took over the division at Pine Camp, New York, in May 1942, remembered that in the heat of the Desert Training Center, Wood ordered that the sleeves of fatigues be rolled down and that collars be buttoned.[16]

In one way, however, Wood differed sharply from Patton. Wood avoided moving tanks at night. During a night exercise at Lebanon, Tennessee, held shortly after Wood took over the division, some tanks ran off a pontoon bridge and fell into the Cumberland River. Several soldiers drowned. At a critique of the exercise held in a large school auditorium, General Ben Lear excoriated the division commanders, several of whom were eventually removed. Wood got up and, knowing he had much to lose, said the dead soldiers had given their lives for their country, just as if they died in battle. He saluted their memory and sat down.[17]

Despite his enormous talents, Wood got no publicity and today remains unknown to the general public. Such was not the case with Patton, who was fast becoming a celebrity. The *Saturday Evening Post* sent a reporter to the California desert, but after seeing the curses in the completed article Devers refused to let the magazine publish it. When Patton asked why, Devers replied: "Well, George, I'm not interested in what you think about this. I'm just interested in this command, and I'll be doggoned if I'm going to have the mothers of these kids thinking that we have a commanding officer who uses such profane language." That, Devers reported, "straightened that out. . . . He was colorful, you know, and when he was on the defensive he really swore, and he had a squeaky voice when he did it, and that was when he was at his worst."[18]

While Patton was in the desert, another issue again came up. In May, Arvin Brown wrote Patton about the racial covenant sponsored by the San Marino Civic Betterment Association. All of Patton's neighbors had signed it. They were wondering why Patton, who owned four parcels of land in San Marino, had not.

Using what today seems like peculiar logic, Brown urged him to do so.

It isn't as though it were a new movement of discrimination against any one race, such as the Ethiopians, but for the most part it is more in the nature of a re-imposition and standardization of similar restrictions which were formerly in force in various forms for the purpose of excluding from this area all races excepting the Caucasians. These old restrictions in many cases have expired. Therefore, as I see it, if you should join with the other property owners in this endeavor, there would be little likelihood of any just criticism being directed against you by those belonging to the excluded races; on the other hand, if you fail to join with them I am confident that, at least as far as some of the property owners are concerned, the present wonderment at your not signing, will grow to resentment.

Brown believed that Patton should let Nita, who held his power of attorney, "sign the necessary agreements in your stead." In her own and in her brother's name, Nita had already approved, on April 28, 1942, of the Race Restriction Agreements covering the sixteen parcels of land they owned in South Pasadena. She should do the same for their other parcels of land. Patton obviously followed his cousin's advice, for on June 1, 1942, Nita signed for her brother the restrictive agreements covering the property in San Marino.[19] Looked at from the perspective of over half a century, Arvin Brown's advice on the matter was probably the worst he ever gave any of the Pattons.

II

For the Allies the month of June 1942 brought disaster. On the twenty-first German forces in Libya, commanded by Erwin Rommel, inflicted a stunning defeat on the British at Tobruk. Rommel's army then swept eastward into Egypt, stopping at El Alamein, just seventy miles from Alexandria. In Washington at the time Tobruk fell, the British prime minister, Winston Churchill, urged the Americans to send two armored divisions to Alexandria or Cairo. To Pogue, General Marshall told the rest of the story.

Well, I brought Patton on and sent him down to the War College to make plans for moving a division into this thing, hoping against hope that I wouldn't have to do it, but feeling I should be prepared to do it in case the president ordered the move. I told Patton when he came that we were opposed to this, but I thought it was necessary to make the plans. I said there had been a big discussion about it, particularly as to what we would send and the decision is final that it would be a division, a total of eighteen thousand troops (a division then was about twelve thousand). That's all the special troops we could send. But there would be no question of sending another division—making it a corps. I didn't want to hear from him on that. That was settled.

So he'd get down to the War College and get to work on the thing. He went down to the War College, and to my surprise, early the next morning, I got a letter from Patton vigorously proposing sending an additional division. So I sent one of the secretaries of the General Staff to get General Patton and put him on a plane and send him back to California that morning, which they did. Scared him half to death.[20]

Shortly before the fall of Tobruk, Marshall again showed his faith in Eisenhower, designating him commanding general of the European Theater of Operations. Accompanied by several aides, Ike left the United States on June 23 and arrived in London the following evening. "George Marshall was a genius," Devers explained, discussing Ike's rapid rise. ". . . He took the best man he knew—Eisenhower—and sent him to London." Also sent to Europe was Ike's friend, General Mark Wayne Clark, under whose father Patton served at Fort Sheridan. "He believed in Clark," Devers said of Marshall, "because he thought Clark was the only man who knew anything about amphibious landings. I know that because he talked to me about amphibious landings." Clark had supposedly become an expert on the subject while stationed with Ike at Fort Lewis, Washington.[21]

In early July Ike was promoted to lieutenant general. "We know each other so well," Patton congratulated his friend, "that I guess you know with out my saying it how truly delighted I am at your success and how earnestly I wish you all good fortune for the future."[22]

Returning to Indio from Washington, Patton learned that his son had again been appointed to West Point. But the big news was that the scare Marshall had put into Patton was just that: a scare. Patton was indeed heading for overseas. On the morning of July 30 he received a phone call to come to Washington. Patton came in from the Training Center at 1 P.M., and Bea immediately drove him to Palm Springs airport, where a plane was waiting. Continuing on, Bea drove to Nita's house in San Marino, where she left her car. She then took a plane from Los Angeles to Washington, joining her husband on the first of August at the home of the Merrills. By that time Patton had already learned his mission. At the direction of Roosevelt and Churchill, he was to go to London and help Ike plan the invasion of North Africa by a great task force, a segment of which he would command.[23]

Taking off from Gander Air Field in Nova Scotia, Patton arrived in London on August 6, encountering a situation he immediately disliked. From his first days in London, Ike had found himself involved in a squabble. Agreeing with the Soviets, then battling the Germans at Stalingrad, he favored the creation of a second front in France. Bitterly opposed to this was Churchill, whom Patton in the diary he now began to keep derisively dubbed "the Former Naval Person." "All seemed scared to death of 'the Former Naval Person,' who thinks himself a strategist," Patton observed, "though why, with his record of consistent failure, I don't know." Flattered by the British, Ike seemed to do just as they wanted. As for Clark, his deputy commander, he was "working for himself."[24]

Immediately upon conferring with Ike, Patton found there was to be no second European front. Instead, he and his friend and fellow Californian, Brigadier General James H. Doolittle, who had engineered the bombing of Tokyo that April, would help plan Operation Torch, aimed at capturing French Morocco and Algeria, segments of the African empire of the Hitler-puppet Vichy France regime. Colonel Everett S. Hughes, who as the cadet commander of Patton's original class at West Point so detested his ambitious fellow cadet that he initially refused to sign the appointment board designating Patton adjutant of the class of 1909, has left a vivid description of the way the specifics hit Patton. Coming to London from his station at Cheltenham, Hughes entered the American headquarters at 20 Grovesnor Square, near the present site of the American embassy, and "was told that Geo was in the building. I went to his room and opened the door. Behind a desk sat P with his head in his hands. Without taking his head out of one hand he tossed me a document and said, 'Read that.' I did. It was the order to P to return to the US and organize the Western Task Force for the NA campaign." That afternoon Hughes lunched with Ike, Patton, and the secretary of the British chiefs of staff, Major-General Hastings L. "Pug" Ismay, who became and remained Eisenhower's devoted friend. "Ike overworked and irritable," Hughes recorded in his diary. "Talk about gas & rations."[25]

The next night, at dinner at Eisenhower's apartment, Georgie and Ike talked over various aspects of Torch. Patton was worried because his intelligence officer reported that the enemy would have eight thousand more troops than he at the landing places on the west coast of Africa. He also worried about the heavy swells in the Atlantic, which ran to fifty feet and made landing precarious, and about the lack of suitable landing sites. Patton reported that someone had told him to have a good second in command—it turned out to be Geoff Keyes—for chances were he would be drowned during the landing. He admitted his ignorance "in many particulars," but boasted of his ability to inspire troops. "Interesting to hear Ike and Patton talk army personalities," Ike's naval aide, Lieutenant Commander Harry C. Butcher, noted in an unpublished portion of his diary. "Although friendship had a place, this is cast aside for merit and ability to get things done."[26]

Leaving the apartment at 1 A.M., Patton had difficulty getting back to his plush suite at Claridge's Hotel. "London looks like a dead city," he wrote Bea, "in that there are no motor cars except military and a *very* few taxis on the street and very few people." Patton "would have been walking yet" had a policeman not stopped and taken him home. "All of us think that if there ever were any pretty women in England they must have died. They are hideous with fat ankles."[27]

On the morning of the eleventh Patton attended what he described as a "big US Navy parley" to discuss the coming invasion. "They are certainly not on their toes," he observed after hearing the admirals complain about the size of the operation. "It is very noticeable that most of the American officers here are pro-British, even Ike." Colonel Ray W. Barker, Ike's assistant chief of staff for plans, was "terrible. I am not, repeat not, pro-British."[28]

Meeting with Doolittle and Clark on the fifteenth, Patton and Ike feared failure. All four concurred with the sentiments in a telegram sent to Washington that, as Patton put it, "it was better than even money we could land, but a poor bet that we could get Tunis ahead of the Boches." Called in to give his opinion, Lieutenant-General Kenneth Arthur Noel

Anderson, the Scotsman who commanded the British First Army, veterans of Flanders and Dunkirk, agreed that Patton's mission to establish beachheads at Casablanca and two other spots stood a slightly greater chance of defeat than of victory, 52 to 48 against. Patton's chief concern was that the railroad from Casablanca east, on which Anderson must rely if he hoped to push into Tunisia, "was only good now to sustain 5000 men at Oran." This meant that to ensure the flow of supplies the invaders had to capture airfields almost immediately. The big question was what the French, now allied with the Germans and possessing in Africa five hundred planes, would do. If they resisted, the Germans could rush reinforcements to Western Africa before the Allies could push inland.[29]

Back home, Stimson strongly objected to the plan. He had, his wife, Mabel, told Bea, done everything he could to stop it, short of threatening to resign. When told of Patton's pessimism, Roosevelt purportedly said of the invasion: "It must go on. I have promised Churchill that we would fight in Africa."[30]

On August 17 Ike and Patton threw their cares aside. That morning Ike's adjutant general, Colonel Thomas Jefferson Davis, who had served with Patton and Eisenhower under MacArthur in the early 1930s, called to say he was arranging a special dinner that evening for old times' sake. It was to commemorate a similar affair they had attended nine years before in J. Walter Christie's factory near the Pennsylvania Railroad track in Linden, New Jersey. Christie possessed a mild insanity on the subject of army officers, believing they deceived and cheated him whenever possible. Knowing this, the Japanese government had used civilians to negotiate with him in 1925, when they bought the idea for his pioneer amphibious tank. But Christie felt differently about Patton and Eisenhower, two of the few American officers interested in the development of the tank. When asked by Butcher about having dinner to celebrate the 1933 warehouse meeting, Ike responded with an emphatic "Yes."

During the dinner at the apartment Butcher shared with Ike, the conversation ranged over numerous topics. Though he still entertained doubts about Torch, Patton had already composed his victory paean, a demand to the French that they surrender Casablanca. His ultimatum described how painful it was for him to attack a former ally, but warned that if the French did not yield within ten minutes he would order the

Navy to "shoot the hell out of 'em. . . . No wonder Ike is so pleased to have him," Butcher observed.

Much of the evening was spent talking about playing and coaching sports. As a plebe and a second-year cadet, Ike had been a promising left halfback, and even the roly-poly Davis had been a coach, "although admittedly of poor teams." Not much in football, Patton was a track star. At the dinner Patton repeated his assertion that he could mesmerize troops into performing great deeds, and as he left he said reassuringly: "I just want you to know, Ike, that after studying my job in Africa my mind is at ease."[31]

Leaving Brigadier General Lucian K. Truscott in London to handle the details relative to amphibious training, Patton, "keyed," as Butcher put it, "to a pitch as high as his falsetto voice," left for home. "He was in London 2 weeks," Bea told Arvin Brown, "and had an exciting trip back, as the head winds took so much gas that the pilot left it to him whether to turn back or go ahead & possibly down. He said 'go ahead' & they landed with one hour of gas left. However, all's well that ends well, and that is what we hope & pray for now. . . . Your cousin Georgie's a big man & I hope he gets a free enough hand to show it."[32]

After landing in Washington on the evening of Friday, August 21, Patton made the rounds of friends and government officials. "As soon as I had arrived, I called on Mamie [Eisenhower] and found that she and Mrs. Butcher were very nicely installed and seemed to be in excellent spirits," he informed Ike on the twenty-fifth. "They were both glad of my first hand account of you and 'Butch.'" The next morning Patton talked to Marshall, who "seemed highly satisfied with the progress made." In Washington Patton met Rear Admiral Henry Kent Hewitt, who was to command the American naval forces in the North African campaign. "He did not strike me as 'a ball of fire,'" Patton told Ike, "but I believe he is thoroughly competent. However up to now nobody has been able to pin the Navy down as to how many ships they can provide."[33]

On the twenty-sixth Patton and Stimson had "a very intimate and thrilling talk. . . . He has no illusions," the secretary of war commented in his diary, "but he thinks with luck he can do it, and I gave him my best wishes and blessing. He had been extremely loyal and grateful to me throughout his career in the Armored Corps and this is now the culmination of it. I feel rather somber but was very much bucked up by the actual advent of the crisis and my talk with him over the whole situation. He has just the right spirit and I believe will do everything that humanly can be done to make the matter a success."[34]

On the following day the Pattons attended a dinner party given by Stimson and his wife, Mabel. "The Pattons are a wonderful couple," Stimson observed after the affair. "He is full of courage, vigor and push in the preparation of his new great task and his wife is the true soldier's wife with even greater courage than the husband has to show. The spirit of the dinner could not have been better."[35]

Ordered to leave Indio and bring his troops East, Patton delivered a fiery farewell to California. Speaking, as his friend Doolittle remembered it, "in a high-pitched almost feminine-sounding voice," he tried to fulfill his boast, given twice to Ike in London, that he could inspire troops into doing great things.

> Well, they've given us a job to do. A tough job, a mansize job. We can go down on our bended knees, every one of us, and thank God the chance has been given to us to serve our country. I can't tell you where we're going, but it will be where we can do the most good. And where we can do the most good is where we can fight those damn Germans or the yellow-bellied Eyetalians. And when we do, by God, we're going to go right in and kill the dirty bastards. We won't just shoot the sonsabitches. We're going to cut out their living guts—and use them to grease the treads of our tanks. We're going to murder those lousy Hun bastards by the bushel.[36]

To the tankers in the Southeast, Patton talked similarly. Lindsey Nelson, who later broadcast the New York Mets and San Francisco Giants baseball games on television and radio, remembered the hot late-summer afternoon when the 9th Infantry Division, commanded by Brigadier General Manton S. Eddy, assembled on the parade ground at Fort Bragg, North Carolina. After broiling for an hour in the sun, the soldiers heard the wail of sirens. An army sedan pulled up, and out stepped the speaker. Introduced as "the man who will be in command of our Task Force, an officer who has never asked anyone to do anything he wouldn't do himself," the speaker was wearing cavalry boots and riding breeches. In his hand he carried a riding crop. On his chest he wore numerous decorations. In the hot sun he looked cool, having come from the direction of the air-conditioned officers' club. In a high, squeaky voice he told the troops what they were going to do. "We'll rape their women and pillage their towns and run the pusillanimous sons of bitches into the sea." His allusions to rape and his continued use of the phrase "those pusillanimous sons of bitches," among others, induced the nurses from the nearby dental clinic who had come out to hear him to scamper back inside. This, Nelson observed, was his introduction to Major General George S. Patton, Jr.[37]

Patton spent the next two months in Washington planning the invasion. "We are all fine and still together," Bea informed Jerry Brown from her sister Kay's house on Belmont Road in Washington on October 3. "I am trying to remember all the time how awful my life would be (this is K's idea!) if Georgie *didn't* get to go. . . . there's something in this, but it's hard any way you look at it."[38]

As finally adopted, Torch consisted of three distinct operations, stretching from mid-Mediterranean to the Atlantic coast of Africa. The Eastern Task Force, consisting of twenty-three thousand British and ten thousand American troops, was to be commanded by the British General Anderson. It was to land at Algiers, a city of 252,000 people, and advance east along the coast to Tunisia, capturing Bizerte and Tunis. Anderson was to be accompanied by an American, Major General Charles W. Ryder, extolled to the American public as a crack infantryman with a deep understanding of the French people. The Center Task Force contained thirty-nine thousand soldiers. Its commander was Fredendall, who, according to *Newsweek,* also had "the reputation of being a top infantryman," an opinion with which John Waters would soon disagree. Its objective was Oran, on the Mediterranean side of Africa. These task forces were to sail from the Mersey and Clyde rivers in the United Kingdom in late October and land on November 8.

Patton was to lead the Western Task Force, thirty-five thousand men and 250 tanks. Leaving from Hampton Roads, Virginia, it consisted of three segments. Truscott would command the nine thousand soldiers of the Northern Landing Group, which was to debark at the beach resort of Mehedia and proceed fifteen miles inland to Port Lyautey and its airport. The Center Landing Group, nineteen thousand men led by Major General Jonathan W. Anderson, an Annapolis graduate, was to land at the small fishing town of Fedhala and proceed south about fifteen miles to Casablanca. Patton would accompany this force. Finally, Major General Ernest N. Harmon would land with the 2d Armored and 9th Infantry Divisions, about sixty-five hundred troops and 108 tanks, at Safi, 140 miles south of Casablanca. He was to advance up an excellent highway toward Casablanca, at the same time moving inland toward the Moroccan army base at Marrakech, a hundred miles from the sea in the Atlas Mountains. Harmon was to prevent the Moroccan army from reinforcing the French at Casablanca. Patton's invasion, like the others, was set for November 8.[39]

As Lieutenant Colonel Benjamin A. "Monk" Dickson, the intelligence officer, noted, "Operation Torch was planned in an atmosphere of unparalleled intrigue." Numerous Frenchmen claimed to represent their country. After the failure in September 1940 of an attempt by the British navy and the Free French, under General Charles de Gaulle, to capture Dakar in French West Africa, the British disliked de Gaulle and excluded him from Torch. Completely subservient to the Germans, the French Vichy government, led by General Henri Pétain, was similarly excluded. The Allies also distrusted Admiral Jean Darlan, already designated Pétain's successor. Stirring the pot of intrigue was Robert Murphy, the American consul general at Algiers. Flying to London under the nom de guerre of "Lieutenant Colonel McGowan," he briefed intelligence officers on the political situation, favoring the claims to power of General Henri Giraud, who was anti-Vichy. Finally, Brigadier Eric E. Mockler-Ferryman, the head of Allied intelligence, considered General Auguste Paul Noguès, the French commander of the Moroccan Theater of Operations, a tool of Vichy, but Mockler-Ferryman believed Noguès would come over if the invasion succeeded. Dickson appropriately summarized the situation: "The air was filled with false whiskers, double agents and whispered passwords."[40]

A practice landing on the sixth of October was discouraging. The day before, going down to the Washington shipyard where the *When and If* was anchored, Patton displayed unbridled emotion. "She was O.K.," Bea recorded, "and G kissed her good bye on the mainmast in the after-cabin." Patton spent the night aboard the *U.S.S. Augusta,* the cruiser that served as Hewitt's flagship. Having nothing else to do, he stayed "in bed and read." Bea, meantime, passed the night in an empty house on Chesapeake Bay with Patton's aide, Captain Dick Jenson of

Pasadena, the son of Echo Jenson, whose family had come to California with Benjamin Davis Wilson.

The trial landing at Solomon's Island in Chesapeake Bay began at four-thirty the next morning, when Bea "saw flashlights like fireflies on the beach." Then came several waves of naval personnel and vessels: scouts in dark blue jeans, with knives and flashlights, who swam ashore from rubber boats a mile and a half from shore; assault boats, two at first and then more; landing craft with let-down fronts carrying vehicles, towed howitzers, a road mender, ammunition, a Red Cross dressing station, and a radio with amplifiers, to be used when offering the French surrender terms. By the end of the maneuver about five thousand men had landed from the eighteen transports out in the bay.[41]

None of this impressed Patton. "The timing of the landing by the Navy was very bad," he recorded in his diary, "over 40 minutes late to start with, but all we can hope is that they do better next time." Patton considered most of the naval officers, as Bea put it, "not only indifferent but unhelpful up to almost the very last. They do not seem to realize that their reputation depends on this too, because they are in command till G gets ashore, after which he takes command." Patton greatly admired Captain John L. Hall, Jr., the capable chief of staff of the crossing fleet, but he had no use for anyone else. "All the others, especially Hewitt, expect the worst and are without fire," he observed. Captain Robert R. M. Emmet, the commander of the transports, "is the worst."[42]

Hall's zeal matched that of Patton. Responsible for clearing the ports and landing supplies, he asked Hewitt and Patton for room in the assault convoy for several hundred—it turned out to be eight hundred—men and about eight hundred tons of equipment to clear the captured Moroccan ports of rubble. Neither would give him anything. Then came the big Washington meeting on the operation. Present were Clark, representing Eisenhower, Admiral Sir Andrew B. Cunningham, the naval commander of the North African Expeditionary Force, Hewitt, Patton, and other officers. They started talking about running a convoy into Casablanca on the fifth day after the invasion. Hall, then only a captain, interrupted and said: "Gentlemen, there can't possibly be any D plus 5 day convoy at Casablanca." With "sneers on their lips," the officers asked why. "Because I'm supposed to have naval command, and I can't even get anybody to let me take the men and equipment necessary to have those ports ready to operate. They act as if they're sailing into peacetime well-equipped ports, with all the operations going normally. They don't seem to realize that there's going to be fighting going on, that the French probably have these ports fixed so that we can't possibly use them."

The next day Hall was appointed Hewitt's temporary chief of staff. He now got all the room he needed. "And it's a mighty good thing I did," he later explained. "Casablanca was a shambles, and that was the principal port. You couldn't possibly land stores over the beaches on the northwest coast of Morocco, at any time. I never saw coasts where the seas are higher, 99% of the time, than they are on that coast. It's a tough coast. Casablanca is not a natural harbor; it's a man made harbor. The French constructed a great concrete pouring plant that could pour 150-ton concrete blocks, with big cranes and rails to take them out and replace them. The sea throws them around like pebbles in the breakwaters to Casablanca harbor."[43]

Hewitt had a different complaint. Early in the preparations, he met Patton in Washington, but Patton had so many details to work out with the War Department that the staffs did not confer until the week before the sailing. The generals were at Washington, the admirals at Ocean View, Virginia, off Norfolk. "We tried to convince them that daily personal contact between opposite numbers of the staff and the commanders was very important," Hewitt explained, "but we couldn't convince them. . . . The last week or so we managed to get General {Jonathan} Anderson of the 3rd division and Captain [Robert R. M.] Emmet, who was to have command of the details of the landing, together; Admiral {Lyal A.} Davidson and General Harmon—we gave them rooms in the hotel; and Admiral [Monroe] Kelly and General Truscott and their staffs. They were able to work together just a short time before they left. They didn't have a long enough time."

Equally troubling was the lack of training. Anderson's men had engaged in some amphibious maneuvers, but hardly enough. Harmon's 2d Division also needed more practice. None of the invading units was prepared for landing in the surf.[44]

On October 14 Patton did something that he long believed a successful commander must do. Bea recalled the incident.

> G called in Anderson, Harmon and Truscott to say good by and said: "If you don't succeed, I don't want to see you alive." (He

himself had already written to General Marshall saying that he would leave the beaches of Africa either a conqueror or a corpse.)

These three men were all friends of his and when he came home to lunch alone with me, he was more shaken than I could believe. He had a strong drink, a glass of beer, two cups of coffee, and then told me about it. He had asked General Marshall in to shake hands with them, but the General "had to go to the Senate" and excused himself. I think G was very much hurt.[45]

Patton spent the twenty-first, three days before his force was to leave, visiting people. At 8:15 A.M. he saw Marshall, who was friendly and encouraging. "Don't scare the Navy, they know you have sailed in more danger," Marshall said, referring to the storm through which the *Arcturus* came in 1937, "and can navigate better than any of them." Hewitt seemed especially frightened of Georgie. Just the opposite was Hall, who vowed he would get the troops ashore even if the French blew up the docks and he had to run his ships onto land.

Patton then went over to Walter Reed Hospital to see Pershing. "He did not recognize me when I went in," Patton observed, "but the minute I spoke, he did." When Patton said that his success as a warrior began when Pershing took him to Mexico, the old general remarked: "I've always been good at picking a fighting man and there are damn few of them." Pershing looked "very old, pale and sunk at the temples." He noted that he was just Patton's age when he was sent to France. "A good age and a good omen," he remarked. Patton knelt and asked for his blessing, "which he gave me with great emotion. I kissed his hand; then I put on my cap and gave him the salute. Twenty years dropped from him."[46]

That afternoon Patton and Hewitt had an appointment with the president. Taken to the White House by Marshall's liaison officer, Major Frank McCarthy, who later produced the movie *Patton,* the general wore his slick helmet with two oversize stars on the front and his two ivory-handled pistols. Roosevelt loved it, and later said to McCarthy: "What a fine figure of a man General Patton is."

So that no one would connect him with Patton, Hewitt had entered the White House through a different door. He knew Roosevelt, having taken him to South America aboard the *Indianapolis* in 1936. "Consequently," Hewitt related, "I greeted the President first, said I was very glad to see him again, and presented General Patton."[47]

To Patton the half-hour meeting proved a disappointment. Roosevelt filled it with small talk, such as telling of his experiences maneuvering his yacht by the stern. "I had fixed up the meeting with the hope that he would put some heat on Hewitt about the necessity of landing," Patton recorded in his diary. He told Roosevelt "that we must get ashore regardless of cost as the fate of the war hinges on our success." The president simply commented: "Certainly you must." Roosevelt concluded with a statement typical of a smiling politician: "Well, fellows, everything's grand." The news from Stalingrad, where the Soviets had stopped the Germans and would soon begin a massive offensive, was "much better and improving every minute. Everything is grand."[48]

The following day, October 22, was for Bea and Georgie the day of parting. Patton was to leave Washington, where he had been staying with the Merrills, for Hampton Roads, the port of embarkation. Getting up early, Bea trimmed her black hat with a red bird, which seemed to please her husband, but he said nothing. "My eyes," Bea recalled, "were as red as the bird. The waiting has been terrible. He went to Mexico on one and a half hour's notice, and on five days' notice to France in 1917. But after all, eleven weeks is a short time to organize the greatest expeditionary force ever to sail at one time from the U.S."

Georgie, too, felt the nervousness, for he asked Bea to accompany him to the airport at Bolling Field. There they found Patton's staff, including Geoff Keyes, Patton's deputy commander; Hap Gay, now a lieutenant colonel; Kent Lambert, Patton's operations officer (G-3); and Lieutenant Colonel Paul D. Harkins, who was then Lambert's assistant but who was destined to become a four-star general. General George Stratemeyer of the air force, who was flying the party to Norfolk, invited Bea to go along, and she readily accepted. "We flew down the Potomac, across the bay where we have sailed so much, and over the submarine net, which was open with a destroyer on guard at the opening, right over the convoy. When G landed, he was so excited that he jumped right out of the plane and I had to call him back to say good bye, but I was glad, for the great strain was over for him at last. Proud to tell, I did not cry."

The next day Patton called to tell Bea he was leaving. He felt better and better about the chances for success and believed that his entire life had been preparation for this expedition: his command of tanks during the First World War; his study of the operations of Allenby and other desert commanders in that conflict; his preoccupation with landing operations in their outboard in Oahu during their last stay there; and finally all of their blue water sailing and navigating.[49]

That same day, the twenty-third, Patton and the other expedition leaders addressed an assembly of about 150 of his senior officers, telling them for the first time where they were going. "Captain Emmet talked for three hours and said nothing," Patton noted. "He is a fool. I talked blood and guts for five minutes and got an ovation." Hoping to stir up the officers, he displayed far more pessimism in his talk than he did in his phone conversation with Bea. He chided the navy and said that he did not expect to land anywhere near where they were supposed to and nowhere near the right time. He said, however, that his men would fight wherever and whenever the ships landed them. "Knowing General Patton as I do know him," Hewitt later observed, "I know that was just said for effect."[50]

That afternoon at two forty-five Patton came aboard Hewitt's flagship, the *Augusta*. In a conversation with Hewitt and Captain John J. Ballantine, who commanded the navy's air units during the invasion, Patton said something that appalled both of them: he did not care if he lost three-quarters of his men as long as he gained the victory.[51]

III

Loading onto the transport *Harris* with his troops, Colonel Edwin H. Randle, who commanded the 47th Infantry Regiment of the 9th Infantry Division, met Patton for the first time. Patton was on deck talking to Harmon. "This is Col. Randle," Harmon said. "He commands the Safi assault force." As the two strangers shook hands, Patton remarked: "Well, Randle, when you get on the beaches over there don't get messed up in any feline fecal matter." Years later, Randle commented that Patton did not "use those fancy words, but the short vulgar ones which meant the same thing."[52]

The plan for crossing the Atlantic was ingenious. To avoid having a long convoy, the troops left Hampton Roads in two stages. The Southern Landing Group, headed for Safi, departed on the twenty-third, sailed south as if bound for maneuvers in Haiti, and then turned northeast. To cover this movement the United States had asked Haiti for permission to hold exercises in the area. The remainder of the expedition left the next day. When the Safi force joined up with it, along its south, this second group fanned out, the northern force, heading for Mehedia, taking the left flank, and the group aiming for Fedhala in the middle. Off the Moroccan coast each of the three units would be in position to peel off and without confusion head toward its objective.

As the convoy traversed the Atlantic, it continually shifted course, trying to deceive the enemy. After the units converged, the convoy moved in the direction of Halifax and Newfoundland, as if bound for the British Isles. South of Newfoundland, it turned southeast in the general direction of Dakar. South of the Azores, the convoy, well over a hundred ships, changed course to the northeast to make it seem as if it was heading for the Mediterranean. The final shift set the ships on a course for French Morocco.[53]

During the trip Patton had little to do, for Hewitt made all the decisions. "Of course," Hewitt later said, "I informed General Patton, kept him in touch with what was going on. But I was the seaman. I was the one who was supposed to be able to determine whether the troops could be landed in the surf. It was my responsibility."

Hewitt recalled that Patton "was a great reader and on the way over he amused himself as he could. One of the things he did was to read the *Koran*. He wanted to get some insight into the character of the native Moroccan population." Reading the Koran, Patton became especially concerned, because he feared that some of the invading troops would have to pass through and desecrate a burial ground. This act might arouse the native population, something Patton wished to avoid.[54]

Having not much to do, Patton entertained himself as best he could. The officers' mess aboard the *Augusta* was the finest at which he had ever eaten, and he found himself exercising to avoid putting on weight. He borrowed a rowing machine from Captain Gordon Hutchins, who commanded the *Augusta,* and used it whenever he could. He also ran in place for what was a quarter of a mile in his cabin. Less strenuous was shooting practice on the fantail one afternoon using the new army carbine, which Patton described as "a lovely thing and very accurate."[55]

Randle remembered another form of Patton entertainment. One morning in the middle of the Atlantic, he and Harmon were on the deck of the *Harris* when they suddenly saw the *Augusta* leave the formation and make a complete circle around the other ships. Harmon, an ex-cavalryman, laughed and said to Randle: "There goes George getting in a little horse exercise."[56]

Less laughable was something that occurred on the *Augusta*. Patton was getting a haircut when the ship lurched and the barber clipped a chunk out of Patton's hair. Patton cursed him and warned him "never to do that again."[57]

On the trip across one strategic complication bothered Patton—as it did Ike and the invasion planners. The attack on the Vichy French, puppets of Hitler, might bring another Fascist country, Spain, whose portion of Morocco was just north of the French, into the war. The Spanish might even try to close the Straits of Gibraltar, both sides of which bordered their territory.

"But," Dickson pointed out, "the paramount problem was weather." In the days before the invasion a gale south of Iceland created waves eighteen feet high. Flying to the command post at Gibraltar several days before the invasion, Eisenhower and Clark learned that the weather forecast from Washington predicted impossible landing conditions for Patton's Western Task Force.

Fortunately, however, one of the first lieutenants attached to Mockler-Ferryman's G-2 section was a meteorologist. "Each day," Dickson recorded, "he flew from Gibraltar to Horta in the Azores on what he called a Base Line, making observations. When he returned he consulted a notebook full of cabalistic symbols and then produced his predictions. Two days before D-Day he stuck his neck out, 'There is a new phenomenon, a strong current is flowing out of the Mediterranean and breaking up the ground swell. The breakers on the Moroccan shore are subsiding.'" Photos showed the waves at Fedhala and Safi down to eight feet.

The next day, after studying his base line to Horta, the young lieutenant predicted that the surf would be down to three or four feet. "Mockler-Ferryman took the lieutenant into Ike's office after I could not shake his conviction," Dickson explained, "and further stereophotos showed further amelioration of the waves. Eisenhower made the fateful decision that Patton would land on schedule and he was right. When the Western Task Force were safe ashore I recommended the weather wizard for a Legion of Merit which was awarded."[58]

As the young meteorologist predicted, the sea went down, and, Patton noted, November 7 dawned "very quiet and cool, almost too good to be true. . . . Thank God. I hope He stays on our side!" At six that morning the ships heading for Safi peeled off, and at three that afternoon those bound for Mehedia and Port Lyautey left. "In 15 hours," Patton wrote at two-thirty, "I should be ashore."[59]

To the end of the voyage Patton teased Hewitt. "He was always insisting that the Navy would never get the Army in the right place at the right time," Hewitt remembered, "or words to that effect, but that wherever we put him, he was going to go ashore and fight. Well, we did land him exactly at the right place, the bulk of his forces—a couple of boats went adrift—at the time specified. That went off all right."[60]

Patton and Hewitt especially feared the French navy, which, remembering the defeat at Trafalgar in 1805 by Horatio Nelson and the recent debacle at Dakar, hated everything British. In port were the thirty-five-thousand-ton French battleship *Jean Bart,* a French light cruiser, several large destroyers, numerous merchant ships, and submarines. But, Hewitt related, the Navy "air people did their job well. When hostilities started some of the French submarines were sunk at the docks before they could sortie."[61]

At midnight of the seventh, as Truscott readied his group for the assault on Mehedia and Port Lyautey and Harmon did the same to the south at Safi, Hewitt guided the ships of the Center Group off the shores of Fedhala. In preparation for the attack the landing craft were lowered and moved to the troop transports to which they had been assigned. To the southwest the lights of Fedhala and Casablanca burned brightly, indicative of the poor quality of French intelligence. A few days after the invasion, Admiral François Michelier, the French naval commander in Morocco, told Gay that at 11:30 P.M. on the night of the seventh he had received a report that no American transports were on the Atlantic Ocean.

At five-thirty on the morning of the eighth, the fighting began. A French spotlight picked up one of the American landing craft. "This was the signal," Gay recorded, "for hell to break loose." The cruiser *Brooklyn* immediately answered back, destroying the spotlights and the French batteries near them. At that hour the first Americans landed and rapidly proceeded inland, capturing the Hotel Miramar, where the members of the German Armistice Commission, the economic czars of French Morocco, stayed.

Patton's first attempt to go ashore, at 8 A.M., ended swiftly. His staff loaded all of his and their belongings into a Higgins boat, a thirty-two-foot vessel made of heavy plywood and run by a diesel engine. At that very time three French destroyers, guns blazing, steamed out of Casablanca. In the ensuing fight the muzzle blast from the *Augusta's* rear turret tore the Higgins boat apart. Patton was able to salvage only his pistols. Gay even lost his rifle.

The *Jean Bart* was able to fire its huge shells, all containing brilliant yellow dye (to make the target ship more visible in the water). One of them landed near the *Augusta,* sending a column of water over two hundred feet high over the starboard side of the ship. Dye covered Patton's leather jacket. When his aides and bodyguard rushed with towels to clean it, Patton ordered: "Leave it there. This will stay on the [curse] jacket as long as I am able to wear it."[62]

About one o'clock on Sunday, the eighth, Patton, accompanied by Hall, Gay, George Meeks, and his two aides, Captains Dick Jenson and Alexander Stiller, finally went ashore in a landing craft. By then Harmon, completely surprising the French Foreign Legion, had taken Safi, but the French were still fighting around Casablanca. On shore a friendly French colonel suggested that Patton send a delegation to Admiral Michelier to demand the surrender of Casablanca, for the French did not wish to battle the Americans. Patton thereupon sent Gay, Colonel William H. Wilbur, and the French colonel on the mission. "The Admiral refused to see us," Gay recorded, "in fact his representative told us to be on our way." Gay "did not blame him much," for at that moment American dive bombers were pounding the port. "I politely remarked to the Admiral's representative to tell the Admiral that the next time we came to see him he would be damn glad to see us."[63]

During the mission through French lines, Gay and Wilbur learned from a high-ranking French officer, also friendly to the Americans, that Casablanca was susceptible to an attack from the rear. Accordingly, late on Monday, November 9, Patton drew up plans for an assault on the city beginning at seven o'clock that Wednesday morning. As Patton devised it, airplanes would start bombing enemy positions. Fifteen minutes later the heavy navy guns would open up. The ground troops would start at seven-thirty, with Jonathan Anderson's 3d Infantry Division attacking from the north and northwest. With a battalion of tanks—the M-3 (Grant), soon to be replaced by the M-4 (Sherman)—Harmon would come up from the south and southwest at ten-thirty.

Patton's orders specified that, if necessary, Casablanca was to be destroyed and its defenders captured or killed.[64]

A catastrophe on Tuesday, November 10, signaled the end of French resistance. Taking off from Ballantine's flagship, *Ranger,* Navy dive bombers hit the *Jean Bart* with two one-thousand-pound bombs, sinking the battleship and silencing its four fifteen-inch guns.[65]

The day of the planned attacks proved eventful. At three o'clock in the morning a mission from the headquarters of General Noguès, long suspected of being pro-Nazi, reached Patton's headquarters. They had come, its members said, to arrange an armistice. Gay, who despite his gruffness—or maybe because of it—had Patton's complete confidence and was empowered, as the extraordinarily capable air force General Otto P. Weyland would later be in Europe, to act in the general's name, immediately rejected the proposal. The Allies would accept nothing less than complete surrender. The French must decide by seven o'clock, Gay warned, for an all-out attack would begin soon after that. The navy airplanes were in the air and ready to bomb Casablanca when Ballantine got word, at ten to seven, that the French had surrendered. From the *Ranger* he managed to inform the pilots of all the planes before they dropped their bombs.[66]

At two o'clock that afternoon the preliminary armistice meeting took place at Patton's headquarters. The French were represented by Admiral Michelier, Noguès, and two other generals. Present for the Americans were Patton, Keyes, Hewitt, Hall, and Gay. Hewitt recalled the tension as the meeting opened:

> When I first arrived and met Admiral Michelier we shook hands a little gravely, perhaps. Then I said, "Admiral, we are very sorry to have had to fire on the French flag in order to carry out our operation. We always considered the French our friends and we still want them as our friends." He looked at me and smiled and said, "Admiral, you carried out your orders, I carried out mine. Now I'm ready to cooperate with you in every possible way." And that is what he did. He leaned over backward to cooperate with us.

Patton, calling the surrender "a nice birthday present," offered the French generous terms. Not wishing to discredit them in the eyes of the Arabs, he allowed them to keep their arms with the promise that they would no longer fight. As the conference concluded, Patton said he had one more serious duty to perform. "You should have seen the look of consternation upon their faces," Gay recorded; "but when he told them that duty was to ask them to have a drink of champagne with him, there was a sudden change in their expressions. They appeared very happy that the conference had reached such a successful conclusion."[67]

An important element in the success at Casablanca was the work of the London Controlling Section, the British unit whose purpose was to deceive the enemy. Among other things, the Controlling Section convinced the Germans that the Allies were determined to invade Western Europe. To help with the deception the unit arranged a commando raid on Dieppe, France, in mid-August of 1942. To cover preparations for Torch, the Allies concocted two interrelated plans. As noted, Patton's men were told they were heading for tropical training in Haiti, preparatory to going to Syria, where they would relieve the British forces. Patton and his staff did a masterful job in implementing this plan, called Sweater. The second scheme was Solo II. The British and American troops in England were informed they were going to the tropics. Several incidents, however, threatened Solo II. Two British officers were court-martialed for "serious indiscretions" concerning the plan, and, as a result of a plane crash, the Fascist government of Spain picked up documents that revealed the original date for the invasion, November 4. Ignoring the hints, the enemy in North Africa was unprepared for the American landings. The Allies captured the Italian Armistice Commission in Algiers, and the German Commission in Casablanca barely got away.[68]

Patton had fulfilled his promise to end the hostilities by the third day after the invasion, but, Hewitt believed, he made a serious mistake that cost lives. After Casablanca fell, Hewitt sent Patton several messages trying to get the lights turned off at night, all to no avail. Guided by the illumination from the city, enemy submarines penetrated the screen around Casablanca and Fedhala Bay and sank five American transports. None contained troops, but the captain of the *Hughes* died during the explosion on his ship.[69]

Under the surrender terms Hall became empowered to do two

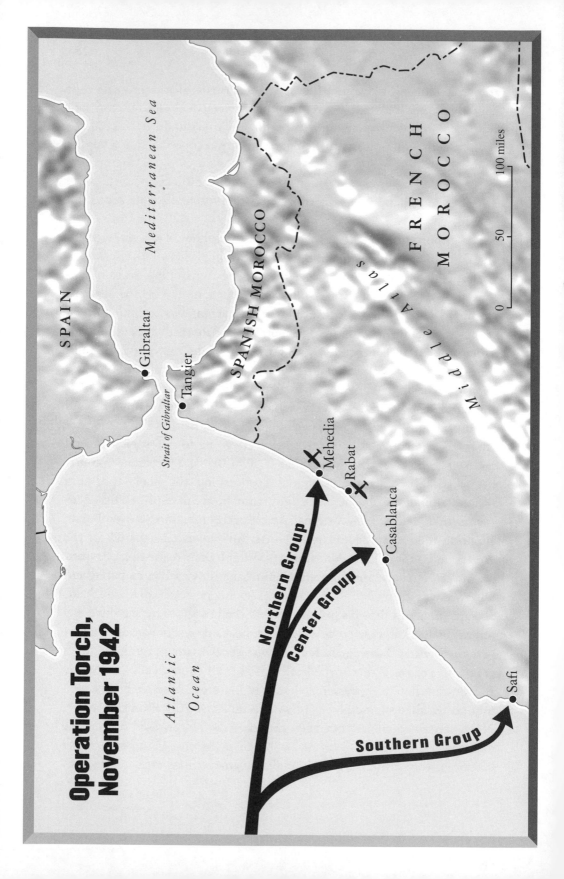

Operation Torch, November 1942

SPAIN

Mediterranean Sea

Gibraltar

Tangier

Strait of Gibraltar

SPANISH MOROCCO

F R E N C H
M O R O C C O

Middle Atlas

Mehedia

Rabat

Casablanca

*Atlantic
Ocean*

Northern Group

Center Group

Safi

Southern Group

0   50   100 miles

things. Following what he believed to be instructions from the president, he began paying the French forces. He also began refitting the *Jean Bart* and a few of the French destroyers, making them capable of again going to sea. A couple of the French ships were taken to the United States for repairs.[70]

In the fighting the Western Task Force lost eight hundred men. The French lost more, Patton estimating that nine hundred died at Port Lyautey alone. After the two sides became friendlier, they held a service for those killed. "General Patton, and his deputy, General Keyes, and I were sitting together," Hall related. "It was a Catholic church, of course, and there were not many Catholics. I knew Jeff Keyes was, and I thought General Patton was, because he knew more about the protocol than I did. So I watched him to see what I was supposed to do. I'm an Episcopalian. I didn't want to stand when I should be kneeling. But I found out that George Patton was an Episcopalian, too, and I should have been watching Jeff Keyes."[71]

Patton's visit to the American cemetery at Port Lyautey developed into an unusual episode. During the fighting there, Second Lieutenant Stephen W. Sprindis, using what Patton called "the new rocket gun," the bazooka, deceived the French into thinking his platoon was a battalion with a battery of 75-millimeter guns. On November 18 Sprindis was told by his regimental commander to meet Patton and escort him around the cemetery. When Patton arrived, Sprindis saluted and said: "Second Lieutenant Stephen W. Sprindis reporting as directed, sir." Patton saluted, put his right arm around Sprindis's shoulder and responded: "Come, let us pay our respects to our fallen comrades and tell me of your personal exploits that I partly heard about." When Sprindis was through talking, Patton took one step back and said: "Lieutenant, you're a god-damn liar . . . about being a Second Lieutenant I mean, from now on you're a First Lieutenant." As they continued their walk through the cemetery, Patton stopped, pointed to a grave, and said: "You know, Lieutenant, it's a helluva lot better, and a privilege, to die this way than by sugar diabetes or some other confounded disease." Sprindis, who rose to the rank of lieutenant colonel, insisted that this conversation always inspired him.[72]

With peace Patton's greatest problem became handling two people: Noguès, with a reputation for being a fascist, and the sultan of

Morocco. On the sixteenth, accompanied by some members of his staff and by Hall and several naval officers, Patton went to Rabat to pay the sultan a formal visit. Greeted, Gay remembered, in the palace courtyard by "a magnificently turned out guard of Moroccan colored troops" dressed in red, the Americans were escorted to a large room on the third floor, at the end of which the sultan sat on a slightly raised platform. To his right were his advisers, the "twelve old men." The conversation between the general and the sultan turned out to be more comical than serious. Knowing the sultan spoke French, Patton tried to communicate with him in what he could remember of that language, which was not much. Tradition called for the sultan, an Oxford graduate, to speak Arabic, and so all his remarks had to pass through interpreters, eventually reaching Patton in French. "The General wouldn't know what the devil he was talking about because his French was almost as bad as mine," Hall explained, "though he had gone to the École Militaire de Guerre in Paris for a while."

During all this, Gay's thoughts were "almost heathenish." His first was that "this is some place for a farmer boy" from the cornfields of Illinois. His second was that after having viewed the magnificent Oriental rugs in the palace he could forever brag to carpet experts at home that he "had seen some real ones." On the way out Harmon's aide, "a rather big-footed country boy," tripped over the rugs and fell down.

After the visit to the palace, Patton and his associates went to Noguès's home for lunch. Hall always considered Patton's courtship of Noguès, which would later bring upon the general newspaper criticism, odd. "General Noguès was a five-star general, General Patton was a two-star general," he observed. "General Patton would inspect the troops, either Moroccan or French, with General Noguès. Patton would be standing up there in full uniform, with his pearl-handled revolvers, and little Noguès there by his side and you could tell who had the respect of the troops. It was the two-star general."[73]

Actually Patton displayed great skill in handling matters in Casablanca. Flying in from Algiers, his friends Generals Doolittle and Alfred M. Gruenther gave him the latest news. Ike had recognized Admiral Darlan as the civil head of French North Africa. General Giraud was to be in charge of the military, and Noguès was to remain commander of Morocco. "The first and last are crooks," Patton noted in his diary. Noguès had arrested General Émile Béthouart and several other French army officers who had wanted to receive the Americans peacefully. Patton sent Wilbur and another colonel to see Noguès "and tell him if he doesn't come across it will be too bad." Responding, Noguès postponed Béthouart's trial indefinitely. "It was evident at the initial meeting," Patton wrote Eisenhower of the French,

> that they feared above all else to lose face with the Arabs. Had we forced a disarmament that certainly would have been the case, and an Arab uprising might, and in fact would certainly, I believe, have resulted. As it is now, they have not lost face, and by main-taining their prestige will, I think, remove from us the necessity of using possibly 60,000 men to control this country. I have repeat-edly told them that our whole interest here is the securing of a door and a corridor, and that so far as their control of the country is concerned, we prefer it to remain in their hands.[74]

Disturbing to the Americans was Noguès's tirades against Jews. Repeating the Nazi line, he insisted that the country "was completely calm except for a stirring of the Jewish population." Noguès said that "the Jews in Morocco are of the lowest order." They were plotting to take over the government, he insisted, and were "agitating against French authorities," neglecting to point out that their agitation con-sisted of opposing the anti-Jewish laws promulgated by the pro-Nazi Vichy government. Noguès promised, however, to keep things quiet in Morocco.[75]

On November 17 a strange statement about Jews came from an unexpected source. On that day Patton made the trip to Gibraltar—fly-ing time one hour, fifteen minutes, and two seconds—in a light bomber to visit Ike, then "living in a cave in the middle of the rock—in great danger." There Eisenhower had surrounded himself with Britons. His chief of staff, G-2, and G-4 were British. Ike, Patton told Bea, even used British words: lunch was "tiffin," gas "petrol," and antiaircraft fire "flak. I truly fear that London has conquered Abaline [sic]."

During their conversation, Eisenhower touched on Mark Clark, per-haps his closest friend in the army. "He asked me if Clark was a Jew," Patton recorded. "I said at least one quarter, probably one half."[76]

The problems of early November continued to dominate Patton's thoughts during late November. One was the Jewish question. The

Vichy government had placed restrictions on Morocco's three hundred thousand Jews, who lived among eleven million Arabs. Spurred on by Vichy, some Arab leaders spread stories that the Allies intended to place Jews over the Arabs. After all, as Berlin radio preached, were not Roosevelt and Eisenhower Jews? Echoing these sentiments, Colonel Guillame, Noguès's assistant for native affairs, told Patton that American Jews were behind this Jewish plot to control Morocco. "They will try to take a lead here," Guillame warned of the Jews, "and when they do the Arabs will murder them." Patton answered that the colonel and the sultan would have to handle the matter, "as we could not touch it."[77]

Also troubling was Clark. With Morocco captured and Rommel being pushed across Libya and toward Tunisia by British General Bernard Law Montgomery, the Americans began planning their next move. Clark, "who has never commanded a battalion," was almost sure to get the Fifth Army, to be formed in North Africa. The "lost his pants" episode helped Clark. Returning from a daring meeting with Darlan in Algiers before the Allied invasion, Clark, wearing only his overseas cap, lost all his clothes, which he did not want to get wet, when a wave overturned the small canvas boat that was taking him out to a submarine. Swimming back to shore, he was able to find a new outfit, a fancy French silk tablecloth and a pair of pants. The escapade made Clark famous, but General Marshall disliked having his generals appear to the public as buffoons.[78]

Early in December the issue was settled. Flying to Ike's new headquarters at Algiers, Patton had dinner with Clark and Eisenhower, "the sacred family," when about nine-thirty Ike got a phone call from Gibraltar. He then said to Clark: "Well, Wayne, you get the Fifth Army." Patton assumed that he and Fredendall, who commanded the Center Task Force, would get the two corps under Clark. "I am sorry for Geoff and the rest who came along with me in the opinion that I would get an army," Patton confided to Bea. "But c'est la Guerre."[79]

Bitterly disappointed, Patton consoled himself in a letter to Bea three days later. "It makes me mad but there is nothing that can be done about it. Ike and Wayne have the inside track. Their Hq. certainly is a mess and gets out contradictory orders almost daily. Some day they will be found out." Ike was "not well and is very quarrelsome and keeps saying how hard it is to be so high and never to have heard a hostile shot. He could correct that very easily if he wanted to. I almost think he is timid. When he goes out a peep of armed men precede and follow his armored limousine. . . . I don't think that he or Clark have any idea of what they are going to do next."

The intrigue, both Moroccan and military, bored Patton. Yearning for another fight, he hoped the Spanish would attack from their segment of Morocco, north of French Morocco. Discussing the situation with Patton on December 9, Butcher observed that "General Patton was figuratively racing through Spanish Morocco like a gay *caballero* on the back of a tank."[80]

While Patton dreamed of more war, Eisenhower purportedly used some of his spare time another way. One day in December, Everett Hughes, now a brigadier general handling supplies, asked Ike about his relationship with his chauffeur, Kay Summersby. "I don't know whether Ike is alibing or not," the catty Hughes recorded. "Says he likes her. Wants to hold her hand. Doesn't sleep with her. He doth protest too much especially in view of the gal's reputation in London."[81]

IV

During the first half of December 1942, Patton's activities varied greatly. On the sixth he and nine members of his staff hunted wild boar in the Middle Atlas Mountains. During the hunt, they used the twelve-gauge Belgian shotgun, very light and beautifully made. The right barrel contained a hollow slug that had an explosive effect, the left buckshot, the logic being that if the hollow slug merely wounded the pig and it charged, the hunter could stop it with the buckshot at close range. Patton and Colonel Albert W. Kenner, the chief surgeon of the Western Task Force, turned out to be the stars of the hunt. The physician killed three boars, the general two. Patton hit the first at a distance of about ninety-five yards with a hollow slug in the middle of the forehead. He killed the second at about fifty yards with a shot through the heart. He also stopped an African jackal with buckshot from a distance of fifty yards.

The sultan's lunch after the hunt startled the Westerners. Served in two conical tents painted red, green, and blue, it was a feast to end all feasts. The first course consisted of a whole barbecued sheep for each table of six persons. Using three fingers of the right hand, a guest pulled meat from the sheep and ate it without a plate. With the left hand the guest swatted flies. Next came six chickens per table, one for each person. This was followed by barley with meat and turnips. Patton tried to make a ball of it and throw it into his mouth. Mint tea ended the luncheon. The slaughtered pigs and jackal were then brought in and offered to the Americans, who refused them. Thereupon the French accepted four of the boars.[82]

At a lunch with Noguès two days later Patton, Keyes, and eight other officers met the grand vizier, the sultan's chief adviser. Speaking in French, the ninety-two-year-old official explained to the Americans the sultan's desire for peace. "I assured him that I was a profound student of history," Patton observed, "and that since my earliest infancy my whole idea had been to maintain peace." The grand vizier then talked about "race antipathies," repeating stories about Jews being the sultan's enemies. "I told him," Patton answered, employing a peculiar logic, "that I fully understood those things because as a child I had been raised on a large ranch, and it had the governance of 20,000 sheep—which was not quite true but had a good effect on the Arabs—and as a result of my acquaintance with sheep, I understood perfectly about race antipathies, and therefore I would do nothing about it because I felt that since the Sultan's ancestors had handled such questions for 1300 years, they were better fitted than I was to continue their management."

Patton then discussed the control of his army. Despite his strict discipline, he told the grand vizier, some men would commit rape. He intended to hang the offenders. The grand vizier answered that such punishment would bring joy to Moroccans. His conversation with Patton constituted the happiest fifteen minutes of his life, "to which I replied that if I had afforded happiness for fifteen minutes, I felt that I had not lived in vain. He ended by saying that it was necessary to converse with a great man to fully realize his greatness, and that there was an Arabic saying to the effect that those who said all men were equal were either fools or liars—and that he and the Sultan were neither."[83]

The next day Patton was off to survey the faltering campaign of the Eastern Task Force. Led by Lieutenant-General Kenneth Arthur Noel Anderson, the British First Army, reinforced by American troops under

Major General Charles W. Ryder, had landed near Algiers and made its way along the coast to Tunisia, where, in the oak groves and citrus valleys, it suffered heavy losses. "Anderson is just good enough not to get relieved," Patton informed Bea on the fifth of December, "but I think his health will get him. He has lost ten pounds and is skin and bones. . . . I should not be surprised to see the Brit 1st Army get driven back. The supply problem for them is most difficult and is not being well run." Anderson's headquarters was, Patton mused, a hundred miles behind the front, "Too Far by 95 miles."[84] With an American army Fredendall would soon repeat this blunder.

Leaving Casablanca at eleven in the morning on December 9, Patton reached British First Army headquarters at eleven forty-five the next morning. Patton's longest stay was with Brigadier General Lunsford E. Oliver, who led Combat Command B of the American 1st Armored Division, now at Souk el Khémis, in northern Tunisia about twenty-five miles from the Mediterranean Sea. With Oliver, Patton drove for a hundred miles along mountaintops, then into a tremendous valley that extended to Bizerte. "The Arabs here are lower—if this is possible—than the Arabs in Morocco," he observed. "Most of the dwellings look like manure piles, and I believe they are, they have no chimneys and the smoke oozes out through the straw. In these dwellings they take their cattle, donkeys, sheep and goats, and apparently spend a happy night together." The men had "fierce mustaches," not beards. "The women are not veiled which is unfortunate because it certainly destroys all illusions as to the beauty of Arabian women."

From Oliver, Patton learned that the Americans with the British were at Medjez el Bab, to which Anderson had withdrawn after failing to conquer Tunisia. Going there, Patton ran into Johnny Waters, who was with a battalion of tanks on the road. "I am very worried about John," Patton confided to Bea, "as I fear he will be cut off and captured but I told him my ideas of how to get clear if he had to. I was very proud of him. He has done the best of any officer so far. He looks very well." The men told Patton that he "was the only General Officer they had seen in their 24 days at the front. I think this is true and is a sad commentary on our idea of leadership."[85]

Back home, Bea, digesting everything her husband sent her, spent much of her time keeping up the spirits of others, as well as her own.

Her brother-in-law Keith Merrill was about to go into the navy, and Bea and her sister Kay "have a song about it which we do with a little dance." Living with Kay in Washington, she had no plans to return to Green Meadows. Everywhere Bea went Patton was the topic of conversation. At lunch at the home of General McNair, his wife rushed up to Bea and, holding the latest issue of *Life,* showed her a photo of Patton. "I said something insulting about it," Bea told Patton on December 3, "and a perfectly strange woman jumped up from her chair and cried, 'Don't you run down our hero. Do you know him?'"

With the daughter of Harry Semmes, who was a lieutenant colonel with Patton in Morocco, Bea drove to Walter Reed Hospital to visit the 103 wounded veterans of Torch recuperating there. "I'll tell you something you didn't know," a soldier with a broken leg told her, ". . . the password. You'd never guess it. Well, they wanted to give us a word we couldn't forget, so what did they do? Our officers told us to yell 'George' at the first man we seed, and if he didn't yell 'Patton' right now, to shoot hell out of him. There was one man in my outfit forgot to yell 'Patton,' he was that excited, and boy, they ruined *him*."[86]

On the eighth Bea reflected her great pride in her husband's achievements. "This is Pa's birthday," she began her letter to him. "Were he alive he would be a hundred and twenty, yet he seems always the same as the last time I saw him." That was in March 1918, when she was about to leave for Washington, where she hoped to meet Lieutenant Elgin Braine, who had just returned from Europe with news of her husband. When Bea went into her father's room the night before she left to say good-bye, he asked how Georgie's "finances were fixed." Bea answered that since her husband had not mentioned money in his letters, she presumed he must be all right. "My little daughter," Frederick Ayer said. "You must be sure he has what he needs. George is bringing in much glory to our family and we must always see that he is as comfortable as we can make him." Bea commented: "That was the last thing he ever said to me. Pa always loved you and trusted you."

Bea's activities were varied. With Mamie Eisenhower she went to tea at the White House. Mrs. Roosevelt talked about her recent trip to Europe, but Bea found it "hardly comparable to your visit with the Sultan of Morocco." A couple of days later General Marshall told her "that he was more off old men than ever." When Bea asked why, he answered that he had just seen fifteen soldiers over forty-five in the same hospital ward, all with hernias. "I naturally made no comment," Bea related, "but thought to myself that that is to be expected of a former white collar draftee, while an older officer who has kept in good shape would be a horse of another color."[87]

Tormented by his inactivity, Patton spent the rest of December performing ceremonial functions and worrying about his future. On the twentieth he reported that he was receiving ovations—people cheering, clapping, and taking off their hats—everywhere he went. "I really think I have their number," he said to Bea of the Arabs. "I am certain that when and if Wayne tries to run this country it will be different. . . . I have a feeling that he had no idea of ever assuming command. I cant quite fathom his game, he is very clever and very indirect." From Clark, Patton learned that on Christmas Eve the Allies planned an all-out assault to capture Tunisia. "I feel that this is most unwise," Patton informed Bea's brother Fred, "as, unless things have changed at the front, there is not enough force on our side to make a go of it."[88]

Patton's analysis proved correct. In an act he later described to Hanson W. Baldwin, the military analyst of the *New York Times,* as his low point in the war, Eisenhower called off the attack on the day it was supposed to begin. He then realized that to control Tunisia the Allies would have to conduct a winter campaign. "The battle line at that time was in a hell of a mess," Eisenhower told Baldwin. "It was the most messed up thing imaginable. We had gambled everything sending small bits and pieces from many outfits to the front to try to take Tunis and Bizerte quickly and all the outfits were mixed up together strung out over hundreds of miles of hills and muddy country."[89]

Another matter added to the woes of Eisenhower and his chief of staff since September, Major General Walter Bedell Smith. On the day Ike called off the Tunisian offensive, an assassin in Algiers killed Admiral Darlan, whom Eisenhower had appointed the chief of state in French Africa. Ignoring de Gaulle, Ike selected Giraud to succeed Darlan. Darlan's assassin, a young man of twenty, was tried and executed so hastily—within thirty-six hours of the murder—that a thorough investigation of his motives and of others involved became impossible. Was

he a monarchist who wished to see the count of Paris, the pretender to
the French throne, rise to power? Was he a discontented de Gaullist?
Was he a British agent, for he had been trained in a camp set up in
Algeria by the English?[90]

Coming to Patton's office on December 31, 1942, Noguès capped
an exciting series of events by presenting his answers to these questions. For Patton the day opened at 3:50 A.M. with a German air raid
on Casablanca. Sending Dick Jenson and Brigadier General Hugh
Gaffey to town to report on the damage, he watched the raid, which
continued until after six, from the roof of his headquarters. At one
point two four-engine bombers crossed over the house at two thousand feet. In all, eleven American soldiers were injured, none seriously. Ninety-two Arabs, however, were killed or wounded, creating,
Patton told Ike, a great deal of pro-American and anti-German feeling. By giving the pasha at Casablanca 100,000 francs from his general funds for the families of those killed by the German bombs,
Patton pushed the Arabs even closer to the Allies. Calling on Patton
to thank him, the pasha promised to publish the general's letter
offering the money in Arab and French newspapers so that all would
know about it.

At nine that morning Noguès arrived with his version of the assassination. Darlan was killed by a de Gaullist, he told Patton. According
to his informants, he, Giraud, and two others were also to have been
murdered. The plot involved fourteen men. Darlan had suspected and
arrested them, but Eisenhower had released them. Thirteen had been
arrested again. After the assassination de Gaulle had supposedly written Giraud of his willingness to replace Darlan. De Gaulle would then
allow Giraud to remain as head of the French military. Giraud
answered that "he did not have time to talk nonsense." The count of
Paris had also come to Algiers, hoping to be selected, but he got
"nothing."

Noguès saved his most distressing news for the end. He did not
believe the British could attack in Tunisia before March or April. Patton
commented: "I fear he is right." Receiving her husband's letter detailing
these events, Bea considered it so important that she immediately went
over to the Stimsons and read it aloud to them.[91]

As 1942, the year that saw Patton's emergence as a national figure, ended, an advertisement appeared in *Trade-a-Plane Service,* a paper for those buying and selling aircraft. It offered buyers a 1941 Stinson 10A Voyager with 290 hours of flying time. The advertisement concluded: "Price $5,000 cash. Communicate with . . . attorney for Maj. Gen. George S. Patton, Jr., now spending the winter on the African Riviera."[92]

Eight

"NOT MUCH OF A WAR"

I

Separated from her husband by an ocean, Bea opened 1943 with a series of gossipy letters intended to cheer him. Happily she reported that young George, a plebe at West Point, had struggled through, and passed, his written examinations. "He doesn't stand well," Bea observed, "and probably never will, but I don't care a bit about that and neither will you as long as he gets through." At a recent dance his "blind drag" turned out to be a "girl well known to the corps." She wore "a dress so low that he wouldn't even take her through the receiving line." *Time* had recently published a photo of the sons of Clark, Eisenhower, Patton, and Doolittle, all cadets at West Point, posing "trim and scrubbed" before a map of Africa. Bea suspected that the girl "made a deal with her first classman to get a date with one of the boys in that picture," and young George turned out to be the unsuspecting victim. He "had sense enough to drop her and I fancy will be less innocent next time."

Bea recalled her visit, with her parents, her brother Fred, and her sister Kay, to Algiers at the age of ten. At "a sort of tourist luau" similar to the one Patton had attended after the wild boar hunt, she tired of sitting and wandered into the harem. "I had a wonderful time sitting on a sort of bunk in the wall and being fed rose petal jelly with a spoon in a tumbler of water, while the women played with my pigtail and from time to time fingered the gold band on my crooked teeth, exclaiming over it." The episode ended with her mother bursting in and yelling: "Beatrice Ayer, I'm going to have you boiled and sterilized."[1]

Bea's letters also displayed her darker side. In mid-January she attended a lecture on the North African landings given by Commander Samuel Eliot Morison, the Harvard historian whose biography of Christopher Columbus, *Admiral of the Ocean Seas,* had just won the Pulitzer Prize. "It was entirely from the Navy point of view," Bea reported of the talk. With the exception of Colonel Wilbur, whose mission to the French helped bring about the armistice, Morison was forbidden by the War Department to mention army officers involved in the landings. Giving Bea a copy of his book, he introduced her to Adolf A. Berle, Jr., the Harvard-educated assistant secretary of state. Berle's father, a rabbi who taught at Tufts, had criticized the Ayer family in 1912 because of the living conditions in Lawrence, Massachusetts. "He is an objectionable little Jew, with a strong accent," Bea observed of the younger Berle. She then mimicked Berle's comment on the assassination of Darlan and the ensuing political mess in French Africa: "Mrs. Patton, your husband is doing a fine job over dere in spite of de newspapers." Bea answered sharply: "Mr. Berle, the papers have not mentioned General Patton at all in connection with the African political situation. He is in Morocco, and I understand that the situation there is a most happy one."[2]

In Morocco Patton was doing his own belittling. A visit on the sixth of January by Jake Devers and General Sir Alan Francis Brooke, the chief of the British Imperial General Staff, gave Patton the opportunity to deride his polo-playing rival. "Jake, who has at last heard a gun go off in anger, talked in a big way till 1201 the 7th. He now has become a great strategical expert, but he believes everything he is told until someone tells him different."[3]

If anything, Brooke thought of Patton what Patton thought of Devers. "My meeting with Patton has been of great interest," Brooke commented several days later. "I had already heard of him, but must confess that his swash-buckling personality exceeded my expectation. I did not form any high opinion of him, nor had I any reason to alter this view at any later date. A dashing, courageous, wild and unbalanced leader, good for operations requiring thrust and push but at a loss in any operation requiring skill and judgment."[4]

Meantime, Roosevelt and Churchill decided to meet at Casablanca in mid-January to discuss future operations. Informed that the president and the prime minister were to stay in the suburb called Anfa, the center of which was the Anfa Hotel, Patton and Keyes inspected the area to make sure it was safe. Irritating to them was the absence of arrangements for the French. "The French have been told nothing," Patton lamented, "and when they find out, as they will, it is going to take a hell of a lot of talk to restore their confidence. This is too bad and so terribly foolish."[5]

Patton was to take no part in the discussions at the Casablanca conference, but as the commander in the area he was responsible for the safety of the president and the prime minister. Learning of the conference, he asked Captain William A. Sullivan, who was directing naval salvage in Casablanca, for a piece of armor plate at least four inches thick. Not knowing why Patton wanted it, Sullivan recalled seeing on the *Jean Bart* steel plates of various shapes. But before he stole anything, he insisted on being told what Patton intended to do with the metal. Patton revealed that he wanted to build an air raid shelter for Churchill and Roosevelt and thought a piece of armor plate on top would provide added protection. Sullivan talked him into using steel, which he could get from the wrecks in the harbor. With steel and with concrete and sandbags the army engineers built a fine shelter.[6]

Concerned as he was with protecting the two distinguished visitors, Patton objected to Clark's plan to install American troops at El Hank, just south of Casablanca, "to see that guns there manned by the French did not fire on Anpha [sic]. I went to see him," Patton related, "and argued him out of the idea. I had to state that if it were done I would request to be relieved. It would have been the crowning insult to the French and would have given the Nazis a wonderful propaganda weapon and roused the Arabs."[7]

By the fourteenth the Allied political leaders had arrived. Roosevelt moved into a villa fifty yards from that occupied by Churchill. That evening Patton invited General Marshall to his Casablanca home, the Villa Maas, a four-and-a-half-million-dollar mansion shaped like a violin. "Never asked a question and talked steadily about South Pacific," Patton wrote of the chief of staff. Just as the dinner began, Marshall got a message "to dine same night with A number 1," Patton's code for Roosevelt, "so left at 8:10."[8]

The next morning Eisenhower and Butcher flew in. Patton met them at the airport and drove them to Anfa. At Marshall's request Patton that night entertained Admiral Ernest J. King, the commander in chief of the United States Fleet, who, Patton commented, "when off duty is

most affable." Also there were Field Marshal Sir John Dill of the British
Mission to Washington; Vice Admiral Lord Louis Mountbatten; Lieutenant General Brehon B. Somervell, the chief of the army's services of
supply; and Patton's friend Major General Albert C. Wedemeyer. Marshall, who suggested the dinner, failed to show up. Nor did Ike, who
dined with Roosevelt. After discussing combined army and navy operations with Mountbatten, Patton observed: "He is charming but not
impressive. I think he got more from us than we got from him." Driving Mountbatten back to the hotel, Patton picked up Ike, who stayed
with him until 1:30 A.M. discussing things. Ike seemed ready to fire
Clark, as hungry for publicity as he was ambitious. "Ike was his old self
and listened," Patton wrote. Responding to Patton's comment that to
know what was going on in Tunisia he must go "to the front," Ike complained that he could not because of politics. He had suggested to
higher-ups that Patton be made his deputy commanding general to run
the war. Ike would then handle politics.[9]

The next day, pinning a second Distinguished Service Medal on
Georgie, Eisenhower repeated his idea about making Patton his second
in command. That night Patton entertained Marshall; Marshall's aide,
Lieutenant Colonel Frank McCarthy; Brooke; and Admiral Sir Dudley
Pound, the chief of Britain's naval staff, at dinner. "Brook is nothing but
a clerk," Patton retaliated. "Pound slept most of the time."

Walking back to the hotel with Patton and McCarthy, Marshall suggested a shortcut. As they progressed, they came upon a guard, who
stopped them. Patton asked the guard if he recognized him. The guard
said yes. Patton then asked if the guard knew who was with him. The
guard said no. Patton answered that it was the army chief of staff. The
guard responded that it did not matter who they were. His orders were
to let no one through. Patton then congratulated the enlisted man, saying if he had let them pass he would have gigged the guard, possibly
even sent him to the stockade. To McCarthy this showed that Patton
never expected special treatment. "Another general would have said,
'Oh, you know me, I'm rescinding the order.' But not Patton."[10]

During the Casablanca gathering, the conferees, Patton not being
one of them, met in the Great Room of the Anfa Hotel. During one session, Marshall came to the door and asked if McCarthy could get
Churchill some cigars. At first McCarthy and his friends were perplexed, but Dick Jenson said: "I can solve the problem. A friend of mine

just came in from the States and my wife sent me a box of cigars by him and you can have these." The cigars were White Owls, which sold for five cents each. Inking out the price, Jenson gave the cigars to Marshall. That night Marshall commented to McCarthy that the prime minister must be giving up smoking. He usually smoked three or four cigars at a session, but that day he took one or two puffs on a cigar and put it out.[11]

At dinner on the eighteenth Patton had a chance to speak to Churchill and to Roosevelt's adviser and friend Harry Hopkins. Patton found Churchill "cunning rather than brilliant" and "easily flattered." Patton, on the other hand, admired Hopkins, who was "very clever and intuitive—like a Pilot Fish for a shark. He did not drink excessively and smoked my last three good cigars." Hopkins praised Patton's diplomatic ability and asked him if he would like to be an ambassador. Patton answered that he would resign and go fishing rather than take such a job.[12]

On the twenty-first Patton got to know Hopkins and the president much better. Joined by Patton's polo-playing companion from Long Island days, W. Averell Harriman, soon to become the ambassador to the Soviet Union, the group rode eighty-five miles in jeeps to visit Clark's Fifth Army at Rabat. There, while a band played, they lunched in the field "alfresco," as Patton called it, on troop rations—boiled ham, spinach, sweet potatoes, green beans, fruit salad, coffee, bread, and peanut butter, the president keeping his mess kit as a souvenir. Patton found Hopkins "extremely intelligent and well informed. To my surprise he is quite war-like and is in favor of discipline." When Hopkins saw the wounded and decorated men, he called attention to something Patton had noticed when viewing the heroes of the First World War: the determined set of mouth. "I had known this for years," Patton recorded, "but was surprised that he did." Hopkins's remark at a cemetery fed a belief that Patton inherited from his father: "The Pilot fish noted to me that nearly all the men killed were Anglo-Saxon." Two days later Patton observed: "Hopkins is quite a man."[13]

At twelve-thirty the next afternoon Roosevelt, still recovering from the jeep ride, honored Colonel Wilbur for his role in bringing peace to Morocco. In the garden of his villa he presented to Wilbur the first Congressional Medal of Honor awarded in the Second World War. Standing next to Patton during the ceremony, Pug Ismay congratulated him for the honor given to one of his officers. Tears in his eyes, Patton answered: "I'd love to get that medal posthumously." Ismay believed that Patton meant what he said, but he had no idea that Patton's statement reflected the lesson his father had taught him in 1905:

> It seems that in Norse mythology—that of our ancestors the Vikings—the warriors who died in battle were accounted the real heroes—above those who survived—and before every battle the Valkyrie—or Valkyrs *chose* those who were adjudged worthy of death—and entrance into Valhalla—and these Valkyrs were thus called the "choosers of the slain," as the slain were called and esteemed "The Chosen."
>
> So in all Life's battles you can find the real heroes among the *apparently* defeated.[14]

A visit to Roosevelt, whom Patton dubbed A-1 in contrast to Churchill's B-1, as the conference neared its conclusion increased Patton's distrust of the British. Accompanied by General Noguès and Admiral Michelier, he waited "some time" until the president finished a press conference. When Patton's party went in to see Roosevelt, the British minister to Algeria "hung around the door" until Captain John L. McCrea, Roosevelt's naval aide, "pushed him out. A-1 started to talk about de Gaulle and was very frank when B-1 came in without being asked and hung around, started to leave, and then came back. The whole thing was so patent a fear on the part of the British to have the French and Americans alone together, that it was laughable. The two French saw and commented on it. I hope A-1 did too."[15]

Patton's next-to-last dinner during the Casablanca conference proved to be the most enjoyable. After dinner King; Keyes; Hall; Rear Admiral Charles M. Cooke, the navy's chief planner; and Patton were drinking coffee when Patton suddenly said: "Admiral King, if I ever have to go on another of these joint operations, which God forbid, I want Admiral Hall there to be my naval commander." Hall remembered that he "was very much embarrassed because it was entirely unsolicited, and I didn't know how Admiral King was going to react." Neither Hall nor Patton had attended any of the Casablanca discussions, and neither knew what was being planned. "We weren't invited," Hall observed. "We were simply the housekeepers. . . . I don't think he [King] liked it very much," Hall

added, "and I don't blame him." Both Hall and Patton assumed that Rear
Admiral Andrew C. Bennett would supervise amphibious operations for
any coming invasion, just as he had for Torch. The next day King asked
Hall how long it would take to turn his command over to the British or to
his chief of staff. "He knew, and I didn't, that Patton was going to command the Seventh Army going into Sicily. I doubt that Patton knew it.
But from then on I was very closely associated with planning for the landings in Sicily—after I relieved Admiral Bennett, that is. Maybe I should
thank General Patton for getting me into amphibious command."[16]

II

As the Casablanca conference broke up, Eisenhower's Allied Forces in
North Africa, facing eastward, had barely crossed the borders of Tunisia.
Attacking from El Alamein, Lieutenant-General Bernard Law Montgomery's Eighth British Army, equipped with three hundred new Sherman tanks, had pushed German General Erwin Rommel's Army Group
Africa steadily west. On January 23, 1943, the British took Tripoli,
Rommel's main supply base, ending what *Time* called "the longest chase
in military history—1,300 miles in 13 weeks." By week's end Rommel
withdrew to the Mareth Line, dubbed the "little Maginot." Running
east-west, this position, aimed at keeping invaders from Tripolitania out
of Tunisia, consisted of a thirty-mile chain of concrete fortifications. Its
eastern flank rested on the Gulf of Gabès, its western on the rugged
escarpment of Djebel Matmata. With the British clearly the dominant
Allied force in Africa, Patton's friend, Brigadier General Everett S.
Hughes, observed: "Soon it will be a British war and Montgomery will
be in command."[17]

In the face of this good news about the German retreat, Stimson was
shocked by the way Churchill, opposed to an invasion of Europe, had
outmaneuvered Roosevelt. On a day that Bea visited the Stimsons, the
secretary appraised the decisions made at Casablanca much as Patton
did: ". . . it seems clear that the British are getting away with their own
theories and that the President must be yielding to their views as
against those of our own General Staff and the Chief of Staff." Rather
than push for an invasion of France, Roosevelt had agreed to "further

entanglements in the Mediterranean, and this seemed to me a pretty serious situation unless the Germans are very much less strong than I think we should assume."[18]

A growing distrust of Clark also emerged from the Casablanca meetings. On the twenty-eighth Ike told Butcher that though he had known Clark for twenty-five years he was worried about Clark's "weakness of self-promotion and over-zealous ambition." Clark repeatedly issued publicity releases glorifying himself. Eisenhower had promoted him to lieutenant general over older and more senior officers, including Patton, so that he would be in a position to assume command should something happen to Ike. Now Clark's ambitiousness perplexed Eisenhower and Marshall. "They don't like cheap publicity," Butcher recorded. Nor should "thinking" parents "be made to feel their boys are being led by buffoons."[19]

On the very day that Butcher made these notations in his diary, Patton flew in his B-25 to Clark's headquarters. "Wayne had just gotten in from seeing Dwight," Patton commented. "He was too friendly and I feared a stab in the back at any moment but none came." The plan for attacking Tunisia from the west, while Montgomery shoved the Germans from the east, upset Patton. The western force, to be called the British First Army, included the American II Corps and was to be commanded by Anderson, the dour Scot who had proven to be no Napoleon the previous fall.

Dickson, the intelligence officer of II Corps, described why the Americans detested Anderson. At Constantine in northeast Algeria

> we attended a conference with General Eisenhower and General Anderson, under whose command we were. The latter was a tall, soldierly figure but brusque and arrogant to the point of rudeness. . . . While General Eisenhower expressed his views and desires for the II Corps' campaign, General Anderson kept his eyes on the ceiling or the floor, the picture of inattention and boredom. . . . We came away from that meeting appalled by the patronizing patience displayed by Anderson.

Putting American troops under the British "shocked and distressed" Patton. "The set up is so absurd," he observed, "that I doubt if it ever comes off. There are 67,000 Boches in Tunisia now with Rommel yet to come in. I don't think they can evict that many men by May 1st as hopefully planned."[20]

On the first of February Patton forgot his troubles. With ten of his officers he flew to Marrakech to go hunting with the pasha. Patton estimated the cost of the guest house that he shared with Wilbur, now a brigadier general, to be at least a million dollars. The museum on the first floor contained a Crusader's sword and a suit of chain mail in the most perfect condition he had ever seen. "It was impossible to admire any of these," he lamented, "because had I done so, they would have immediately been presented to me."

At seven on the morning of February 2 the hunters were off. Riding for two hundred miles with Patton in his Rolls-Royce, the pasha related his history. A Berber, he was a member of a family that had ruled "as absolute chiefs" for three hundred years, fighting Arabs much of the time. In many of the battles, the Arabs hid inside buildings. If they stayed outside, the pasha's forces shot them. If they remained inside, the Berbers blew holes in the walls and killed them with swords. The Pasha showed Patton an olive grove where, he said, so many Arabs were killed that the jackals got sick eating the bodies.

Patton enjoyed the hunt immensely. At one point "the largest and blackest boar I have ever seen" charged at him. "I hit him in the left eye with a slug, at about fifteen feet," Patton recorded, "and his momentum carried him so that he hit close enough to splash blood on me. It was really quite exciting, because had I failed to stop him, he would probably have hit me, and he had very fine teeth."[21]

Returning to his army duties on February 3, Patton accompanied Clark to Algiers, where Ike wanted to see them both. Talking "in glittering generalities," Eisenhower warned: "George, you are my oldest friend, but if you or anyone else criticizes the British by God I will reduce him to his permanent grade and send him home." He had not promoted Patton to lieutenant general, he explained, because he intended to promote at the same time two others, one of whom was Fredendall. In charge of II Corps, Fredendall was "reported to have talked against the British. If he has," Ike fumed, "by God I'll bust him. In any case you will get promoted in less than a month." Clark later assured Patton that Ike had talked to him the same way on orders from

Marshall. To Patton this subservience to the British proved that Marshall, like Oliver Cromwell in the seventeenth century, entertained ambitions higher than those of a mere general.[22]

Patton saw all this as "the old story about criticism. Just like Jake gave us in the Armored Force but this time it is about allies." Nevertheless, the day after Ike delivered his lecture, Patton called in or wrote Gaffey, Harmon, Eddy, and other subordinates "and told them that in order for the Allies to work together there must be no criticisms of Russians, British, French or any others."[23]

During the next few days Eisenhower occupied the minds of both Patton and Hughes, now back in Algiers. In a "secret letter" Ike urged Patton "to be more circumspect and less flip in my conversation on military matters." In one instance, however, Eisenhower acted foolishly. Patton and Hughes both noted that he had brought to Algiers Kay Summersby, his driver in the United Kingdom. "I see no use in women drivers—simply as drivers—at the front," Patton commented, "as they have to have a soldier guard with them." Knowing that Patton's writings contained references to Kay, Ike would one day dread their publication.[24]

During the next two weeks Patton's sole excitement came on February 14, when he flew to Montgomery's headquarters at Tripoli, where, he told Bea, "there were three full generals, 9 Lt. Gens and me." Attending lectures by Montgomery, he sat with General Sir Bernard Paget, the head of the Home Forces, who was visiting North Africa. His evaluation of the others he met was severe. He viewed as unspectacular most of Montgomery's subordinates, including the two lieutenant generals who would lead Monty's armies in France and Germany, Henry D. G. Crerar, who commanded the Canadian forces, and Miles C. Dempsey, who led the XIII Corps of the British Eighth Army. Patton mentioned especially General Raymond Briggs, "whom I liked a lot." Twice wounded in the First World War, Briggs commanded the 1st Armored Division of the Royal Tank Corps. Except for height, Patton's description of Monty might have fit himself: "He is small, very alert, wonderfully conceited and the best soldier . . . I have met in this war. My friend, General Briggs, says he is the best soldier and most disagreeable man he knows." Patton also met Lieutenant-General Sir Harold Alexander, the commander in chief of the Middle East forces. "He is very quiet and not impressive looking. The British say that

Montgomery commands and Alexander supplies—this may be so." On the third day of the visit Patton, who had learned Sicily would be his next objective, told Alexander that he expected to be under him in the next operation. "Yes," Alexander replied, "unless the Boches put troops in there in which case it is off."[25]

Montgomery recalled but one thing about Patton at Tripoli: his presence. "From the party from Tunisia . . . not one British general had come," he wrote; "no infantry brigade commanders; only one American general . . . an old man of 60."[26] Patton's presence, nonetheless, was a testament to his desire to learn about war.

On the fifteenth Monty, using a sand model, described the victory at Alamein. General Brian Horrocks, who later commanded the British XXX Corps, considered it

> a brilliant performance. When it was over I found myself walking back with Patton to his billet, so I seized the opportunity to ask what he thought of it. With a twinkle in his eye, he answered in his Southern drawl, "I may be old, I may be slow, I may be stoopid, but it just don't mean a thing to me!" From that moment he developed an almost pathological dislike of Montgomery, who, I must admit, did little to heal the breach.

British General Oliver Leese, whose beautiful wife, Lady Margaret Leese, later became Patton's friend, remembered that Patton chewed gum—the British called him "Chewing Gum"—and yawned throughout the presentation.[27]

Leaving Tripoli on the eighteenth, Patton flew directly to Algiers, where, after landing in bad weather, he learned more about the planned invasion of Sicily. "I will have a very important job in what seems to me a desperate operation," Patton concluded, "especially as at least two of my divisions will not have had battle experience. Shores are mined and wired. If Germans are present it will not work but I shall do my best." When Brigadier C. S. Sudgen, Ike's chief planner, asked what he thought of the design to capture Sicily, Patton replied: "I have always been lucky and I am going to need all I have." Patton, however, questioned the value of Sicily, if captured, to the Allies.[28]

III

By late January Rommel had retreated to the Mareth Line, which he began strengthening for the stand against Montgomery. The British, to Rommel's east, were following very slowly, American intelligence estimating that Montgomery would reach the Mareth Line about the seventh of March. This freed Rommel to turn to the west and the American II Corps.

All this was not lost on Dickson. His G-2 Estimate of January 25 predicted an attack. "Rommel can be expected to act offensively in southern Tunisia," it read, "as soon as rested and rearmed and prior to arrival of the 8th Army before the Mareth line in threatening strength and state of supply. Note his superiority in Infantry over II Corps." Dickson believed that the Germans needed 32,500 men to garrison the Mareth Line, leaving free two of Rommel's Panzer divisions from about January 29 to the British arrival. During the first week of February, he concluded that the German buildup, "behind a screen of Italian forces," was so strong that an attack could come momentarily.[29]

Fredendall, in command of II Corps, was reluctant to accept these reports. Most of his staff members were in their thirties and early forties, leading him to declare: "By God. I am going to war surrounded by children." This, however, was essentially the staff that later served, in order, Generals Patton, Omar Bradley, and Courtney Hodges.[30]

Patton's son-in-law, Lieutenant Colonel John Waters, then the executive officer of Major General Orlando Ward's 1st Armored Division, later described Fredendall's shortcomings. "First of all," he said, "General Fredendall, God bless him. He's dead and gone, but it's unfortunate that he ever went over because people had reacted unfavorably to him, even down to the ranks, to his inability to even command in maneuvers, effectively and efficiently. But, he went over as a corps commander." Patton always believed in placing his command posts near the front lines, but Fredendall established his thirty miles behind the front. Consequently, he had no idea what was going on.

Waters recalled receiving a message about eight or nine o'clock one evening to come to Fredendall's headquarters, a hole drilled under the rimrock. Fredendall wanted to know what was happening. "It was a pure waste of time," Waters, stationed at Sidi Bou Zid, just west of the

Eastern Dorsal mountains, said. "There's no reason in the world he couldn't have been only 5 or 10 miles behind us, instead of 30 miles— or come forward for his information. He wanted just a first-hand report of the situation." Waters got back to his men at three that morning and had to get up at five.[31]

Fredendall insisted on positioning the men and equipment himself, and he did it poorly. "Never have I seen anything like this before," Ward complained to Waters. "Here I'm a Division Commander, my division has been taken away from me, all I have left is a medical battalion. I have no command. I can't tell you what to do. I'm delivering this message from General Fredendall, telling you where to put your troops on this hill. I've never seen anything like that in my life. I'm desperate. I don't know what to do. My division is taken away from me completely and I'm not commanding it."[32]

According to Waters, the incompetence stretched to Brigadier General Raymond E. McQuillin, who led one of the 1st Armored's self-sufficient units, Combat Command A. McQuillin insisted that any German attack would come at Fondouk and Pinchon, roughly forty miles north of Faid Pass and Sidi Bou Zid. "Well, then, General McQuillin," Waters asked, "suppose tomorrow morning I wake up and find a division out here coming through here, facing me and coming through Faid Pass, what do I do about it?" "Oh, Waters," McQuillin answered, "don't suggest that." Years later Waters called McQuillin "dead wood."[33]

McQuillin erred grossly. On the fourteenth the 10th Panzer Division, veterans of the fighting in France and Russia, attacked through Faid Pass. While the 10th Panzer advanced through the pass and assaulted Sidi Bou Zid from the front, the 21st Panzer attacked the town from the south. Capturing it, the Germans moved west through Kasserine Pass, conquering four thousand square miles of Tunisia. Waters became a casualty of the German pincer, being captured on February 16.[34]

Explaining the disaster, Dickson cited the superiority of German weapons. The enemy possessed the "new Mark IV and Mark VI tank. Their dual purpose 88's were far superior to anything we had in the way of artillery. Our 37 mm. anti-tank gun was so hopeless against German armor that General Fredendall declared, 'The only way to hurt a Kraut with a 37 mm. is to catch him and give him an enema with it.' "[35]

After a week, the German advance fizzled. "Time and gasoline were running out for Rommel," Dickson observed, "and he was stopped in his tracks. On the night of the 22nd to 23rd of February he did one of the greatest Arabian tent-folding acts of all time and dawn found the Kasserine Valley empty of German troops except for a rearguard at the entrance to the Pass; Rommel had vanished in the night. He had a big date with Montgomery in early March at the Mareth Line."[36]

IV

Unaware of his son-in-law's capture, Patton continued planning for the invasion of Sicily. On the nineteenth, along with Rear Admiral Alan Goodrich Kirk, the commander of Amphibious Forces for the Atlantic Fleet, he took off in a specially fitted B-17 from Algiers for Clark's headquarters in Morocco. Sitting alongside Patton in the belly of the plane, Kirk noticed Patton's pistols, which the general had taken off and placed alongside him as they started down the coast. In the face of heavy rain and poor visibility, the pilot doubted whether he could take the usual route across Africa. "Well, Georgie," asked Kirk, who had known Patton from meetings in Washington and other places, "don't you think we'd better go through the straits and come around?" The suggestion that the plane go through Gibraltar, adjacent on the African side to Spanish Morocco, petrified Patton. "Oh no, no, no, we can't do that," he answered. "Can't do that. They might shoot at us. They'd shoot at us." When Kirk said that the Spanish artillerymen never hit anything, Patton jumped in: "This'd be just the time they would hit us, so we won't do that. We'll go up." Accordingly, the pilot headed west along the north coast of Africa. Just at the point when it seemed he might have to go through the straits, the sun popped out. The pilot turned south and through a valley, barely avoiding the tops of several mountains. When heavy rain suddenly developed, Patton grabbed his two revolvers and said: "I have these handy." Asked by a member of his staff why he needed them, Patton answered in his high, squeaky voice: "Well, you know how it is. We might bump into one of these hills, and some of those damned A-rabs might come around, and these would come in mighty handy!"[37]

As Kirk saw it, Patton "was always putting on a big show. Well, the fact of the matter was, we go up to this airfield. It had been raining, and the mud was a foot thick. Al Gruenther was Chief of Staff to Mark Clark. He was out there in a 6 by 4 and hip boots. They had the fire department out, and they had everybody out there, to haul us out of the wreckage and so on. And the pilot set us down in this sea of mud like a butterfly on a flower!"

The visit to Clark proved pleasant. Over a turkey dinner and a bottle of whiskey Kirk had brought, Clark hinted at the magnitude of the American rout at Sidi Bou Zid and Kasserine Pass. Ike had heard that Johnny Waters was "in a big fight on the 17th but got out all right many were not so fortunate." Clark added another piece of gossip. Rumor had it that the gravel-voiced, profane Ernest Harmon would be sent to the 1st Armored, replacing Ward.[38]

By the twentieth, the day Patton and Kirk returned to their headquarters, Eisenhower learned the extent of the defeat in Tunisia. At a morning news conference Ike revealed some of the details and assumed blame for the setback. He also said that Alexander was being sent to the front. Among the reports that had come in, Butcher found one especially disturbing: "A couple of days ago Fredendall communicated that he was issuing orders to an isolated and surrounded American infantry battalion to surrender as it was out of food and ammunition. It did not sound like the spirit of Bataan."[39]

On the twenty-third, just after Rommel, not wishing to extend his lines farther west, retreated back to the Mareth Line, Patton told Bea of his fears. "Johns battalion was practically wiped out but he is thought to be safe. Harmon went up to take command of the 1st A.D. and will let me know. The show was very bad—very bad indeed."[40]

The debacle at Kasserine Pass threw Eisenhower's headquarters into turmoil. "We sent out some 120 tanks," Butcher observed in an unpublished portion of his diary, "and 112 didn't come back." Truscott, since January Ike's deputy chief of staff at Constantine, Algeria, the advance command post, reported that "Fredendall is all right, but his G-2, G-3, and G-4 are inefficient and totally incapable of carrying out the important job of II Corps headquarters. Says they definitely should be removed. . . . The outstanding fact to me," Butcher lamented, "is that the proud and cocky Americans today stand humiliated by one of the greatest defeats in our history. This is particularly embarrassing to us with the British, who are courteous and understanding."[41]

Although realizing that Fredendall had botched things, Eisenhower was reluctant to remove him. The report of Colonel Don E. Carleton, Truscott's chief of staff, explained what had happened. Carleton had visited Kasserine Pass after Fredendall had placed there two battalions of infantry, "one on each side of the two-mile cut through the mountains." The soldiers had been poorly placed, allowing the German infantry, under cover of darkness, to get around them and onto the higher ground behind them. With the American infantry neutralized, the Germans poured seventy tanks through the pass. Carleton believed that "Fredendall has failed to inspire his men or get his staff officers out to actually look at troop positions. If you ask me," Butcher recorded, "it should have been Patton in the first place, and if it weren't for Ike not wanting to let a commander down when he is drooping, Fredendall would be out, but Ike isn't the kind to let his commander down. Ike told me a week ago he wished he had sent Patton instead, but Patton had to be held in Morocco to cover possible Spanish moves, and also for the American attack in HUSKY [Sicily]."[42]

Learning more about John on March 2, Patton fell into deep depression. Returning from Tunisia, Harmon related that Waters had been missing since February 16, when his battalion had been surrounded near Sidi Bou Zid by eighty German tanks that came in from the northeast and destroyed thirty-six of the forty American tanks. "John told his battalion and the infantry with it to cut their way out," Patton related in his diary. "He stayed on the hill with 150 men to cover the retreat. Later Fredendall radioed him to surrender as he could not be rescued. This was a mistake but I hope John complied. According to Harmon Fredendall is a physical and moral coward."[43]

Writing to his distraught daughter, Bea, Jr., Patton intentionally omitted one detail of the capture. "The saddest part of it is," he confided to his wife, "and this I did not tell B. is that Ward knew John was to be ordered home and so sent him to the rear to do a job which he thought would take five days and so keep J. out of the fight. J. did the job in three days and got back for the fight." Had their son, George, "been in John's place I could not feel worse."[44]

Busying himself with preparations for Husky, Patton returned from a horseback ride on the afternoon of March 4 to find that Ike had phoned. Patton was to pack and be ready to leave the next day "for extended field service." Patton immediately called Bedell Smith and asked what the message meant. Bedell answered that Patton might relieve Fredendall. "Well, it is taking over rather a mess," Patton noted in his diary, "but I will make a go of it. I think I will have more trouble with the British than with the Boches. 'God favors the brave, victory is to the audacious.' "[45]

For several reasons Ike decided to remove Fredendall. In his manuscript diary Butcher noted that most important of all Fredendall had permitted a bitter anti-British feeling to permeate his corps. The Americans had since regained the territory lost around Kasserine, but the story circulated among the Americans that Anderson had sat back and offered no assistance in stopping Rommel's advance. Nor had Montgomery, the story went, properly pressed the retreating Rommel, permitting the Germans to turn about and maul the Americans. Besides allowing anti-British feeling, Fredendall had not instilled fighting spirit in his troops and in some of his commanders. Ward, for example, openly criticized Fredendall. But, according to the military historian and analyst Brigadier General S. L. A. Marshall, neither of these constituted the ultimate reason for Fredendall's relief. "It had nothing to do with Kasserine Pass," Marshall later insisted, relating an odd story, "except that the shadow of Kasserine Pass was still over Fredendall. What happened was that Ike had given Fredendall a direct order that he should not organize cat-houses for his troops. He knew the papers would get hold of that and it would cause a scandal back in the United States. Fredendall violated the order. Ike said, 'That was just one too many to take and I decided to relieve him. I just couldn't go along with it.' "[46]

At Algiers on the fifth Eisenhower and Smith met Patton at the airport and told him he was to replace Fredendall. The campaign "was primarily a tank show," they argued, and Patton knew "more about tanks" than Fredendall. Ike stressed that criticism of the British had to end. "I fear he has sold his soul to the devil on 'Cooperation,' " Patton observed, "which I think means we are pulling the chestnuts for our noble allies."

Flying to Constantine, Patton met with Alexander, who told him that on the eighth an American sector would be created in southern Tunisia with Patton as its head. The commander of the newly created 18th Army Group, Alexander would be Patton's immediate superior. "He was very friendly," Patton commented, "and complimentary in his remarks, stating he wanted the best Corps Commander he could get and had been informed I was the man."[47]

Privately, Alexander downgraded the Americans. In a letter to

Brooke, written after he inspected the front, he complained that "Unless we can do something about it, the American Army in the European theatre of operations will be quite useless and play no useful part whatsoever." The Americans were "ignorant ill-trained and rather at a loss, consequently not too happy." Nor did he think much of Eisenhower, Smith, and Patton, writing: "they are not professional soldiers, not as we understand that term."[48]

At best Patton and Alexander tolerated one another. When Patton first heard of the defeat at Kasserine, he lashed out at the British, telling Butcher that "those mealy-mouthed Limeys couldn't have pushed me around." Alexander, on the other hand, saw Patton as "a dashing steed" and a mass of contradictions: ambitious yet inspirational, ruthless yet sentimental, irreverent yet moral. Probably irked by Ike's relationship with Kay Summersby, Patton once told Alexander that in wartime no soldier of high rank should associate with women, a remark Alexander admired.

Patton put up with Alexander more than he did with any other British general. He did not object when Alexander suggested the creation of a II Corps school, manned mainly by British officers, to instruct the Americans and to improve their morale. Alexander, moreover, pleased Patton when he separated the British, French, and American units, giving each its own sector. Holding the extreme south of Tunisia, Patton's chief task was to help Monty penetrate the Mareth Line. He was to tie up as much of Rommel's army as he could and secure Gafsa, about fifty miles southwest of Sidi Bou Zid, as a supply base for the British army. The impossibility of Rommel's position was emphasized on March 6, when he sent his armor against the British east of the Mareth Line at Médenine. The Germans lost fifty-two tanks, leaving them but 109, and gained nothing. "For the Army Group to remain longer in Africa was now plain suicide," Rommel later commented. Unconvinced, Hitler recalled Rommel, who was ill, as of March 9, but ordered the army to fight to the end.[49]

Accompanied by six special scout cars and an entourage of about twenty-five subordinates, Patton reached II Corps headquarters at Djebel Kouif, a small phosphate mining town about fifteen miles northeast of Tébessa, at ten on the morning of the sixth. He found Fredendall, who was being promoted to lieutenant general and sent home to take over the Second Army, then training at Memphis, pleasant but understandably upset. In effect questioning Truscott's harsh appraisal of the II Corps staff, Patton replaced only two of its important members. Brigadier General Hugh G. Gaffey became his chief of staff, and Colonel Kent C. Lambert became the G-3, or operations officer. Colonel Oscar Koch, Patton's intelligence officer, was brought in to work for two weeks with Dickson. After that, Patton left Dickson alone.[50]

Anderson had mutilated the American corps, separating the units of each division and requiring his approval before a division commander could commit any of his troops to battle. To his credit Alexander reassembled the pieces of II Corps. "After being parceled out like free samples and scattered for three months," Dickson explained, the 1st Infantry Division, commanded by Terry de la Mesa Allen and Theodore Roosevelt, Jr., was reunited. So, too, were Manton Eddy's 9th Infantry Division, most of which was off watching the border of Spanish Morocco, the 1st Armored Division, led until April by Ward, and Charles W. "Doc" Ryder's 34th Infantry Division. With one hundred thousand men "II Corps was at last a real corps with three Infantry and one Armored Divisions."[51]

Immediately after taking over the corps, Patton strengthened discipline. He fined anyone caught without his steel helmet or his leggings $50. "He was quick as a hair trigger to inflict this penalty," Dickson pointed out, "and no explanations were heard. One cold afternoon I watched a Signal Corps Lieutenant doff his tin hat and pull on his knitted head cover. As he lifted his helmet to his head he was spotted by Georgie and fined $50." Patton seemed a "little quick on the draw. If your head itched you could save money by scratching it through your tin lid."[52]

Time told of a messenger who ran up to a lieutenant at an advanced observation post during a skirmish. Expecting a compliment on the way he was handling his troops, the lieutenant asked: "What is the message?" The runner answered: "The General said for you to put your leggings on."[53]

Patton's acquaintance from Hawaii, Major General Omar N. Bradley, thought he knew why Patton stressed proper dress. Then "up in the II Corps area" as Ike's special observer, Bradley believed Patton wanted to impress upon the men

that something new had happened. He would cuss a man out for the least infraction. He immediately ordered everyone to wear

steel helmets all the time; they had got into the habit of wearing
stocking caps, which normally would go on under your helmet to
keep your ears warm, but they would just leave off the helmet. . . .
But he immediately stopped that. And made everybody keep their
shirtsleeves down and their shirt-collar buttoned and wear a tie.
All this, I feel certain, although he never said so, was primarily
designed to impress upon the members of that Corps, and there
were about . . . a hundred thousand men in the Corps—to impress
them that something new was taking place, and that they had a
different commander.[54]

Under Fredendall the II Corps staff went to breakfast about nine
o'clock in the morning. Patton changed that, closing the mess halls at 6
A.M. "Therefore," observed Bradley's aide, Major Chester B. Hansen, "it
was necessary for us to stumble out of bed at about 5, hurry down and
grab a breakfast. It was quite cold at that time in the morning. Patton
also insisted that the aides stand a watch, which we did all night long
and for that reason we were always delighted to see those big generals
come with aides because it simply meant another man and a shorter
watch."[55]

Dickson disliked Patton's tendency to deliver "speeches in a
Napoleonic vein." He called them "off pitch to American ears although
the Old Guard would have cheered them to the sky." On the morning
of the attack to retake Gafsa, Patton told his staff essentially what he
had told his tankers in 1918: "Gentlemen, if we are not victorious, let
no officer come back alive."[56] Later, in Sicily, Patton's fiery speeches led
to tragedy.

In Tunisia, Patton seemed incapable of getting along with aviators.
Colonel Paul I. Williams commanded the XII Air Support Group,
whose fighter-bombers and reconnaissance planes supported II Corps.
While Fredendall was in command, Williams and his staff lived with
the corps and maintained cordial relations with its officers. Patton, however, was a different story. The winter rains made the airfields morasses
and prevented planes from taking off. At other times, Dickson noted,
Patton's requests for air support went unfulfilled because bombers
needed fighter escorts for their missions. Patton and Gaffey would have
none of it and frequently argued with Williams. Patton and Williams
soon stopped speaking to each other. "I became II Corps' Ambassador

to XII Air Support Command," Dickson lamented. "General Patton's oft-repeated conclusion was, 'You can't get the Air Force to do a God-dam thing.'"[57] Not until Western Europe and the advent of two tactical air geniuses, Generals Otto P. Weyland and Elwood P. Quesada, did Patton change his mind.

Disliking the notion of a general just roaming about and reporting to Ike what he saw, Patton asked Bedell Smith, Ike's chief of staff, to appoint Bradley his deputy. "As he expressed it," Bradley remembered, "he didn't want a 'goddam spy' up there. But anyhow, I became his deputy and it was a very fine association. During the fighting, we would alternate days—I would stay at headquarters where I would be available to make decisions, in an emergency, and he would go to the front. The next day I would go out and visit the front-line troops, and he would stay at the Corps headquarters. So it was a very fine association."[58]

In Allen and Roosevelt, Patton inherited two odd souls. The military writer S. L. A. Marshall noted how both loved liquor. When together, the two reinforced each other's habit and were often drunk.[59]

As Bradley and Hansen saw it, Patton went out of his way to degrade Allen. Hansen related one story:

> Down in Africa there, out near El Guettar, Terry Allen had his CP in a little oasis, and these are the only palm and fig trees around the place, and it was a perfectly obvious target for the enemy air, and there was a good deal of German air, and so Terry Allen and his whole staff, they lived in little tents there, but they also had very carefully dug an awful lot of slit trenches around that they could jump in when the enemy air came over strafing. And Patton went down there to visit Terry Allen and he walked into this little oasis, and he saw these slit trenches around the place, and he said, "What are all these things for?" And someone said, "Well, you know, there is a lot of enemy air here." And Patton was rather offended by the idea of his senior officers jumping into a slit trench when they were being hit by German air, so he went over to Terry Allen and he said, "Terry, which one is yours?" Terry said, "That one over there, General." Whereupon Patton went over, urinated into it, and said, "Now use it."

The incident appalled Bradley. "With this earthy gesture," he later observed, "Patton had virtually labeled Allen a coward in front of his own men. I was no less shocked than Terry, and I had to wonder if this was indeed good leadership."[60]

Patton handled Eddy, who commanded the 9th Infantry Division, almost as roughly. Lindsey Nelson, later famous as a sportscaster, remembered seeing Patton three times. The first was when Patton, speaking under the hot Carolina sun, told the troops what they were going to do to the Germans: "We'll rape their women and pillage their towns and run the pusillanimous sons of bitches into the sea." Then, in North Africa, Patton took over II Corps. "So there we were," related Nelson, who because of his newspaper experience was handling public relations for Eddy's division, "under Old Blood 'n' Guts, ready to 'rape their women and pillage their towns.' A surprising order came down saying that we would wear neckties at all times. I thought this was a strange touch." Other instructions called for shoes to be shined and sleeves to be kept at arm's length and buttoned, even in battle. Most surprisingly, Patton, who had spoken about raping enemy women, warned that molesting civilians would bring forth the death penalty.

In North Africa, Nelson ran across Patton twice. The first encounter took place late one afternoon when, after riding in a jeep from Tébessa to the 9th's headquarters at Bou Chebka, on the Algeria-Tunisia border, Nelson had an uncontrollable urge to go to the bathroom. Dashing to the officer's latrine, he found Patton, holding a helmet adorned with three large stars, which he was not yet entitled to wear, sitting there. The second meeting revolved about an incident much like Patton's with Allen. Sharing a tent with the division's G-1, who handled daily reports, recommendations for promotion, and other personnel matters, Nelson heard Patton pull up to headquarters one day. In a voice loud enough for everyone to hear, Patton said to Eddy: "Manton, I want you to get these staff officers out of those holes and out here where they can be shot at." The division's G-1 so feared Patton that he had a nervous breakdown. Nelson replaced him.[61]

Bradley remembered when some soldiers got Patton nervous. Rangers captured an eight-wheeled German vehicle with a 75-millimeter gun. To show it off, they brought it to Fériana, about twenty miles southwest of Kasserine, and parked it almost under

Patton's window. Someone noticed the lanyard and pulled it. The gun boomed, and a shell went flaming across the town. "Patton," Bradley related, "had a fit."[62]

Brigadier General Paul M. Robinett, who led Combat Command B of the 1st Armored, also had unpleasant memories of Patton. The two had known each other since 1923, when Patton, then a major, attended the Advanced Course at Fort Riley's cavalry school. Robinett taught Patton machine gunnery, and in return Patton gave some of the instructors fencing lessons every Sunday. Shortly after the Allies lost the race for Tunisia in late December 1942, Patton pulled up at CCB headquarters, jumped from his car, and shouted in his squeaky, shrill voice: "Where are the damned Germans, I want to get shot at!" Patton then regaled Robinett with stories, both old and new, expressing the most concern about the possible entry of Spain and Spanish Morocco into the fight. At bedtime Patton came into Robinett's little room and sat on the end of Robinett's bedding. As both men took a drink from Patton's flask, Patton said: "A night cap for old times between two cavalrymen." Patton had changed little, Robinett noted. "Ambition, self confidence, enthusiasm, and cheerfulness still marked him. He still figuratively carried a bucket of blood with him wherever he went."[63]

When Patton took over II Corps, Robinett was alternately dismayed and admiring. To his dismay, Patton raced around the countryside in a scout car bearing a metallic flag indicating his rank, a far cry from the usual cloth flag that needed a wind to unfurl it. Bedecked with stars, Patton "came with a Martian speech and a song of hate; gross, vulgar, and profane, although touchingly beautiful and spiritual at times. His high-pitched voice belied his warlike mien, but he thirsted for glory and battle in which it could be found."

Patton made "some caustic remarks about his new command," insisting that "three of the four divisions had an inferiority complex and the other but the valor of ignorance." He also said that in six days he had restored discipline to the command. "While admiring Patton very much," Robinett related, "I consider these but the exaggerations of a man of unlimited ambition who had just come into a combat zone from a training area." Robinett saw "no change in myself or in those under me. Everyone continued on the job exactly as before." Patton made no speeches to the battalions under Robinett, but he did address an assembly of officers. "It was so fantastic that the best of us could not give a good report of just what was said," Robinett wrote. "In any case, it would be unprintable. . . . Intemperate and vile language, vanity, lack of judgment, and excessive ambition are not commendable in anyone."[64]

As Robinett saw it, Patton possessed one outstanding attribute. Of all the prominent Allied generals in World War II, he best understood the dictum "of one of the very greatest American soldiers, Gen. William T. Sherman," who in the next to last paragraph of his *Memoirs* observed that a leader must be at the front with his troops. "Some men think that modern armies may be so regulated that a general can sit in an office and play on his several columns as on the keys of a piano; this is a fearful mistake." The directing mind must, Sherman believed, be constantly seen, his energy felt by all. "Every attempt to make war easy and safe will result in humiliation and disaster." Much of Patton's success came from following this principle. Maintaining a close relationship with his troops, he established a "bond of mutual respect and affection with them."[65] If anything, this, rather than the wearing of ties, is what Patton brought to II Corps.

V

Writing about the 1st Armored Division ten years after the North African camapign, George F. Howe agreed with Robinett's assessment of Patton and II Corps. "There was little he needed to do about the plans," Howe wrote, "but he went to work on the problem of morale with almost theatrical energy. But it is hard today to find anyone who was then in the 1st Armored Division who remembers any substantial boost in spirit as a result of Patton's short exercise of the Corps command."[66]

Whether true or not, Patton believed he was shaking up the troops, notably Doc Ryder's division. "As you know I only got here 6 March," he told Eisenhower in a handwritten letter the following week. "There was and still is a slightly defensive attitude of mind here especially in the 34th but Doct R. is correcting that. . . . The uniform regulations were unknown here also there was no discipline—none. There is very little yet but I will have it O.K. in a while. Just soaked two officers $25.00 each for not wearing Tin Hats as we have ordered. I guess I am a S.O.B. but Discipline will win the war."[67]

During his early days at II Corps, Patton tried to find out what had happened to his son-in-law. While visiting some troops on March 10, he spoke with the men of the Graves Registration Unit. They had searched the Sidi Bou Zid area but had not found a grave for John. This meant, they assured Patton, that his son-in-law was alive. "I feel much better about John," Patton wrote Bea. "I will capture the place soon and have a look myself."[68]

In London in August 1942 Patton had told Butcher and Ike that he knew the key to stirring up an army. "In a week's time," he said, "I can spur any outfit to a high state of morale." He was convinced that his predecessor knew nothing of the art. "Fredendall just existed—he did not command," Patton recorded, "and with few exceptions, his staff was worthless due to youth and lack of leadership." Near the end of his first week at II Corps, not knowing Rommel had been recalled to Germany, Patton feared "Rommel will take the initiative, but I will not assume the defensive. Sent General Bradley to 34th Division to preach bloody war. Thirty-fourth is too defensive. Ninth Division had 'Valor of Ignorance.' First Division is good. First Armored Division is timid."[69]

Good news came on the twelfth. At nine that night Eddy called. He had heard on the radio that Patton had been promoted to lieutenant general. Celebrating, Dick Jenson brought Patton a flag with three stars that he had been carrying about for a year. "I am sleeping under three stars," Patton noted. "When I was a little boy at home I used to wear a wooden sword and say to myself 'George S. Patton, Jr., Lieutenant General.' At that time I did not know there were full generals. Now I want and will get four stars."[70]

Waiting for the seventeenth, the day the Allied push was to begin, Patton hoped to inspect his troops, but heavy rains made the roads impassable. He was "so plastered with mud" that his orderly, George Meeks, "had to wash all my outer clothes," Patton recorded. "Kasserine Pass is fierce and a sea of mud." As Patton envisioned it, the coming battle constituted a repeat of the Civil War's Second Battle of Manassas, fought in late August 1862. Like Stonewall Jackson's army in the earlier battle, Patton's was to fight in the west so that in the east Montgomery's Eighth Army, like James Longstreet's in 1862, "can make a breakthrough. This being so it makes no difference where we fight provided we take and hold Gafsa."[71]

After all the waiting, the beginning of the battle for Gafsa seemed anticlimactic. The air attack began at nine-thirty on the morning of the seventeenth, and a half hour later Terry Allen and the 1st Infantry headed for Gafsa. Sitting atop a hill with Jenson, Patton saw the division literally push the enemy out onto the road to Gabès. Near the end of the battle the Americans had what Patton called "a little scare." After Patton had ordered Allen to place his tank destroyers northeast of Gafsa to cover any threat from that direction, the Americans received a report that forty tanks were approaching from the south. They turned out to be twenty friendly French tanks.[72]

From Gafsa Patton planned a two-pronged assault. The 1st Armored, augmented by Regimental Combat Team 60 from Eddy's 9th Division, would constitute the northern force and would drive to Sened Station and then on to Maknassy. Simultaneously, the 1st and 9th Infantry Divisions would push on to El Guettar, ten miles southeast of Gafsa, and then dash the seventy-five miles to Gabès and the rear of the German forces confronting Montgomery at the Mareth Line.[73]

As dramatic as all this appeared, Robinett considered the plan unimaginative. The proper approach, he believed, should have been to launch attacks at several of the passes through the Eastern Dorsal Mountains. Surprising the enemy, the Americans would quickly penetrate one of the passes, removing the mountain barrier and allowing a mass of troops and equipment to flow onto the plains behind the Eastern Dorsal. The Americans could then race toward Tunis and Bizerte, the Axis supply bases.[74]

Not surprisingly, when Patton visited the 1st Armored on March 19, he found fault with Robinett's "mental attitude." Robinett was "defensive and lacks confidence," he complained. "I talked attack." For his part Robinett remembered Patton listening silently as he explained the situation. At the conclusion of Robinett's talk, Patton said: "We will kick the bastards out of Africa!" As Patton left, Robinett told him how honored his troops were to have the corps commander visit them. Slapping Robinett on the back, Patton answered: "By God, it will not be the last time you see me!"[75]

Continuing his visits, Patton found Ward's division "in a sea of mud, really awful." The command post was immersed in water, and the men of McQuillin's Combat Command A bivouacked in water up to their waists. With Ward, Patton went over the plans to capture Sened Station, twice taken by the 1st Armored and twice retaken by the Germans. Ward's plan called for attacking two hills, Djebel Goussa and Djebel Madjoura, overlooking Sened Station. By capturing either hill and the road intersection north of Sened Station, the Americans would force the enemy to abandon the town. Ward, however, feared that because of the mud he could not use tanks in the operation. Patton then told him to do it with infantry. "I want to hit Rommel before he hits us," Patton said, "also to help Eighth Army which attacks tomorrow night."[76]

Returning to his headquarters in Fériana, Patton found Major General Sir Richard L. McCreery, Alexander's chief of staff, with new orders. The Americans were to seize the high ground east of Maknassy and to raid Mezzouna airfield and destroy enemy positions there. They were then prohibited from going past a line just beyond the Eastern Dorsal. "In other words," Patton fumed, "we continue to threaten the enemy's right flank, but we do not participate in cutting him off. . . . The more I think about the plan of pinching us out the madder I get, but no one knows that except me." Just as upset was Bradley, who was scheduled to take over II Corps when Patton left.[77]

The twentieth brought both good news and bad. About midnight Bradley awakened Patton and read him a radio message that indicated that Johnny Waters was a prisoner but safe. On the other hand, Ward's units, particularly Combat Team 60, performed "O.K. but not brilliantly," capturing the two hills overlooking Sened Station. That day Montgomery's Eighth Army also pushed off. "I think if Rommel reacts," Patton observed, not knowing Rommel was back in Germany, "he will do it tomorrow. I feel that we will lick him so long as the Lord stays with me."[78]

The following day Patton, accompanied by Keyes, viewed his troops. Allen's 1st Division had performed admirably, having marched all night "over extremely rough terrain." By a "clever maneuver" the 1st Division had circled the enemy's flank and captured the hills east of El Guettar, taking several hundred prisoners. But the 1st Armored was "going too slow." Dashing off a message to Ward, Patton urged him "to use more drive and keep his Command Post at the front."[79]

On the twenty-second Patton faced two old problems. At Bradley's urging he allowed him to fly "to Algiers to tell Ike the situation, and that is apparently the British aim to steal the show." Ward, however, still displayed great caution. At seven-fifteen that morning the 1st

Armored had moved into Maknassy, which the enemy had evacuated. Instead of pushing to the pass east of Maknassy, Ward halted. Even Gaffey, whom Patton sent over to try to spur Ward on, failed to budge him. "It is very apparent that the enemy is building up to the northeast," Patton feared. Dickson's reports indicated that German General Fritz Freiherr von Broich's 10th Panzer Division, the unit that had smashed the Americans at Faid Pass, was moving south by night. The German attack would come at either Maknassy or El Guettar that night or the next morning.[80]

When Robinett visited Ward's command post, in an olive grove southwest of Maknassy, he was shocked. It was an open target for German hit-and-run bombing and strafing, but Robinett noticed something even worse. "General Ward was always surrounded by visitors, observers, high powered liaison officers, deputy commanders, correspondents, and the like. I sometimes wondered how he could think with so much interference. It was like commanding a division in a goldfish bowl with a bunch of sharp eyed cats outside ready to scoop you up."[81]

Attacking with tanks and infantry at 6:30 A.M. on the twenty-third, the 10th Panzer penetrated three miles before being shoved back with the loss of over thirty tanks. Warned by an intercepted message of a second assault, the Americans repulsed it in late afternoon. "This has been a great day for the American army," Patton exulted to Bea that day. "The 1st Div stopped the famous 10th Panzer cold in two attacks."[82]

Bradley, an infantryman, clearly remembered the attacks of March 23, the first in which a purely American force repulsed the 10th Panzer. Even though Patton was a cavalryman, he was, Bradley recalled,

a great admirer of good infantry, and I remember when the Germans attacked Gafsa on March 23rd, 1943, they threw a very strong attack against us, and George happened to be out with the First Division, and he described it to me afterwards. He said, "These German infantrymen came on and came on, and we put down 16 battalions of artillery on the counter-attack, and they kept on coming." And then our artillery shifted to what is known as time-fire, where the shells burst up in the air, instead of just sitting on the ground and causing a small area to be dangerous. When they burst up in the air, they rain shell fragments right down on top of everybody, and our artillery shifted to time-fire, and George said you could just see these fine infantrymen melting away. He just hated to see such good infantrymen murdered that way. But they were Germans, you see, but I mean, he could appreciate well-trained infantrymen although he had been a cavalryman all his life.[83]

Allen had done well, but Ward continued to flounder. The hills east of Maknassy were just twenty-five miles from the Gulf of Gabès, and Patton envisioned a drive from there north to the Mediterranean, thereby blocking the retreat of the Germans being pushed out of the Mareth Line by Montgomery's army. But even though Rommel had left Africa in secret, the British had troubles. The Wadi Zigzaou, a wide, moatlike gulley that shielded the Axis forces along the end of the Mareth Line, proved an enormous obstacle. By the early hours of March 23 the first British bridgehead over the Wadi had been thrown back. "This is not pleasant at any time," Montgomery informed Brooke, "but it is particularly unpleasant at 0200 hrs in the early morning!!!"[84]

In these circumstances Patton showed impatience. On the twenty-fourth, examining the site of the previous day's battles with Terry Allen, he concluded that the Americans had taken unnecessary losses. They lost twenty-four out of their thirty-four primitive tank destroyers, half tracks with a 75-millimeter gun, and seven of their twelve M-10 tank destroyers, three-inch guns mounted on M-4 tank chassis. Neither Allen nor Roosevelt understood how to use these weapons. Patton had warned that tank destroyers did not possess enough differential speed and enough armor to fight tanks. Tank destroyers must occupy a position, preferably on a flank, set their firing sites, and then withdraw to a camouflaged position a few hundred yards to the rear, leaving one man near, but not at, the firing position to signal the approach of the enemy. When the enemy tanks appeared, the tank destroyers should move back to their original positions and begin firing. Unfortunately, during the heat of battle, the Americans had ignored Patton's instructions and reverted to what they had been taught at the Tank Destroyer School. Chasing enemy tanks, they became vulnerable to the superior weapons and armor of the German vehicles.[85]

That same day, frustrated by the failure to take the hills east of Maknassy, Patton called Ward on the phone and ordered him to lead an attack himself. "He did with the same results," Robinett recalled. "I happened to be at division headquarters the night following the attack. It was only a miracle that Ward survived. Lines made by machine gun bullets were traced on his combat jacket, as if he had been swiped with a red hot poker. One of his eyes was bloodshot from a shell fragment."[86]

An encouraging aspect of the attack was that Americans used tank destroyers properly. Stopped east of Maknassy by enemy fortifications at the end of a long valley, one of Ward's M-10 tank destroyers moved into a position overlooking the enemy's rear. With a three-inch gun, it shelled German supply dumps and destroyed forty-eight enemy vehicles in an area well beyond the range of regular artillery pieces.[87]

Though unsuccessful, Ward's attack helped the Allies another way. On March 23, as Patton egged Ward on and Montgomery licked his wounds at the Mareth Line, the London Controlling Section, the British unit handling deception, came up with Plan Hostage. Its object was to guarantee that the Germans did not transfer infantry and tanks from the American front to the British front. To relieve the pressure on Montgomery, Patton was to give the impression that he was redeploying part of his corps in the vicinity of Gafsa. From there he would supposedly send the 9th Infantry and the 1st Armored eastward to Gabès, blocking the German escape route from the Mareth Line north to Tunis and Bizerte. At the same time Patton was to help retain the German force around Maknassy. The story was to be circulated that Patton would push the remainder of his corps from Maknassy to Mahares, just north of Gabès, thus blocking the Germans at two points.

On the twenty-sixth of March Lieutenant Colonel David I. Strangeways, who handled tactical field deception for Alexander's 18th Army Group, visited II Corps headquarters and explained the details of the plan to Patton and his staff. Greatly impressed, Patton immediately placed at Strangeways' disposal a reconnaissance unit of Eddy's division. With its aid Strangeways started on the morning of the twenty-seventh a wireless deception scheme, sending forth streams of messages saying that Patton was heading for the coast. Strangeways then went to Sened Station and with the aid of the camouflage staff of the British First Army arranged a display of dummy tanks, aimed at convincing the Germans that Patton was massing for some undefined push north to the Mediterranean Sea.[88]

Meantime, Montgomery planned a new offensive, scheduled for March 27 or 28. As in the London Controlling Section's scheme, Patton's movements were to prevent German troops from reinforcing those at the Mareth Line. The 1st and 9th Divisions would continue to draw off the 10th Panzer, and Ryder's 34th would attack Fondouk and seem to aim for the holy city of Kairouan, 120 miles north of Gabès, blocking German withdrawal from Tunisia.[89]

The American push began at dawn of March 28, when Allen's 1st Division and Eddy's 9th jumped off. Patton described the fighting in the "high rugged hills," too steep for men to bring in mortars, as "nasty. . . . We could use a pack train to great advantage." Opposing the Americans, the 10th Panzer and the Italian Centauro Division occupied concrete positions, some of them blasted out of solid rock. Minefields were everywhere.[90]

As the Americans attacked, Montgomery was elated, for his men had penetrated the German defenses. "The Battle of Mareth was the toughest fight I have had since Alamein in October last," he observed in his diary on March 28. He attacked on the right, then when the enemy reinforced that side, he outflanked them on the left. In boxing parlance he described the battle as a "right thrust" followed by a "left hook." Montgomery depicted the German fortifications as "very, very strong; when I walked over it after the battle, and examined it, one saw that to have turned the enemy out of the position in a space of one week was a truly amazing performance." After capturing the Mareth Line from the French, the Germans had strengthened it greatly. "I think the real reason for the victory," Montgomery added, "was that we never lost the initiative, and we made the enemy dance to our tune the whole time."[91]

Under continuing pressure to draw away the Germans, who had withdrawn to the Wadi Akarit, a gulch north of Gabès, Alexander ordered Patton to send units of the 1st Armored on a move to break out of the Eastern Dorsal along the road from Gafsa to Gabès. At eleven in the evening of March 29, Brigadier L. C. Holmes, Alexander's operations officer, arrived at Patton's headquarters with details of the movement. Distrusting Patton's impulsiveness, Holmes specified which units were to be used and where they were to be placed. Patton, in turn, found the plan useless. All of his infantry was in action, and none could be deployed where the British suggested. If, moreover, he followed Holmes's orders and left one battalion of medium tanks at Gafsa, he would have but one to use elsewhere. Holmes responded that he would have to call McCreery, which he later did, to authorize the change. The British had assumed Patton had three medium tank battalions available.

All this upset Patton greatly. "I feel," he wrote that night, "I must call General Alexander's attention to the fact that in the United States Army we tell officers what to do, not how to do it; that to do otherwise suggests lack of confidence in the officer and reduces him to the status of Adjutant General. I doubt if General Alexander himself issued any such order. I feel that for the honor and prestige of the U.S. Army I must protest."[92]

To lead the force attempting to break through the hills beyond El Guettar, Patton selected his World War I comrade, Colonel Clarence C. Benson, the commander of the 13th Armored Regiment of the 1st Armored. The attacking force contained two medium tank battalions, a tank destroyer battalion, two field artillery battalions, a company of engineers, and an infantry and an armored infantry battalion. The force took with it enough gas for between 120 and 160 miles. "I am sending Gaffey along to keep an eye on the show," Patton noted on the night of the twenty-ninth. "If the enemy has plenty of artillery Benson may not get through. The worst danger is that the hole may close behind him. I feel confident that with God's help it will work."[93]

Pushing off at noon of the thirtieth, Benson immediately stalled. Allied infantry and artillery had cleared the Germans from the north-east side of the Gabès road, but enemy artillery and antitank guns still occupied the other side. Between these and a minefield, the Germans knocked out three tanks and two tank destroyers.

The next morning Patton observed that "things look pretty bad. We seem to be stuck everywhere." He sent Lambert, his G-3, to Benson "to stir things up." At first Patton told Benson "to expend a whole tank company if necessary to break through." After thinking it over, he ordered a coordinated attack, using air, infantry, and artillery, to begin at 4 P.M. All this proved unnecessary, for at twelve-thirty Benson began his own attempt at a breakout. His tanks and infantry pushed forward and then halted. In all, he lost thirteen tanks and two tank destroyers.[94]

The next morning brought Patton personal and military tragedy. Throughout his career Patton displayed great concern for the children of his friends. In Europe in 1945 he would add to his staff Van S. Merle-Smith, Jr., the son of his former sweetheart and lifelong friend, Kate

Fowler, with whom, since his West Point days and Kate's Vassar days, he and Bea never lost touch. At this very moment Kate's husband, Colonel Van S. Merle-Smith, Sr., was serving on the staff of General Douglas MacArthur in the Pacific, where he would contract an illness from which he would die in 1943.

Like Kate Fowler, Dick Jenson came from a Pasadena family close to the Pattons, the Bannings, and the Browns. His father, a retired naval officer, was now dead. His mother, Echo, came from a family that had migrated to California with Patton's maternal grandfather. Growing up with Echo, Patton, just as he had with Kate Fowler, courted her briefly in his youth.[95]

On the morning of April 1, Dick Jenson, who had turned twenty-seven the week before, was among those who went up to Benson's lines to view operations. The party included Bradley, Major General Harold R. "Pink" Bull, the War Department G-3, and Brigadier Charles A. L. Dunphie, who led a British armored brigade. Suddenly a dozen twin-engine Junker 88s, armed with five-hundred-pound bombs, appeared. The Allied officers dove into the slit trenches around the command post. A bomb hit right at the edge of Jenson's trench, shattering his bones and killing him instantly. His watch stopped at 10:12 A.M.[96]

Patton's letter to Echo, written that day, reflected his grief. "Had Dick been my own son I could hardly feel worse," he comforted her. "You should not so much feel regret that he died as give thanks that you are the mother of such a gallant Christian soldier. Truly God's doings are beyond our understanding. He seems to take the bravest and best." Enclosing some of Dick's hair, Patton explained: "I cut the enclosed lock from his right temple. I kissed him on the forehead as a proxy for you." Just the day before, while they were standing around waiting for Benson to "jump off," Patton insisted on taking a picture of his officers.

> Dick said I hope this is not a final picture. I reminded him that just before we landed at Casablanca I took pictures of all the staff. Just then it was time to go and he waved to me. He was in fine spirits and thirsting for battle. I can never tell you how near and dear he was to me nor how loyal and gallant he was. He looked after me as if I was an invalid.
>
> Truly Echo it is just awful. I can't realize it.

Words fail me when I try to express to you my sorrow and sympathy.[97]

Patton could not hide his sorrow. Accompanied by Colonel Charles E. Hart, the II Corps Artillery Officer, Lieutenant Colonel Barksdale Hamlett of Harmon's staff visited Patton at this time. He recalled Patton "as a man who felt things very deeply. I remember being with him right after his aide was killed in North Africa. . . . General Patton was really broken up. He was weeping, weeping, and we tried to comfort him, Ed Hart & I in his office."[98]

Through Eisenhower, Patton radioed Bea word of the tragedy. "Dick Jenson's death is a dreadful loss," Bea informed Arvin Brown on the third. "The telegram came to me yesterday and I had to call his family. Then I called Nita and she went right over to their house. There is probably no one in the world who can soothe a heart any better."[99]

VI

For Patton, Dick Jenson's death brought to a head one squabble. Early in the Tunisian campaign Patton had a run-in with thirty-six-year-old Brigadier General Laurence S. Kuter. Considering that in France and Germany Patton's relations with Weyland and Bradley's with Quesada can only be described as superb, Kuter probably projected a superior attitude to the ground generals. In Tunisia Kuter failed to persuade Patton that the air corps should be allowed to act independently. Patton clung, in Kuter's words, to the idea of the "sanctity of area command," believing that as the American commander he should tell the airmen what to do. Montgomery yielded and accepted the idea of an independent air command, but Patton and Bradley only became more stubborn.[100]

Jenson's death worsened things. Benson's command post had three radios and Patton was sure the post had remained in one spot too long, allowing the Germans to fix in on the position. On the morning Jenson died Patton complained about the lack of air cover. Instead of protecting Benson, Allied airmen employed a thousand planes trying to destroy "the Hun air force." Without air protection, "we had the hell bombed out of us all day." Between 8:30 A.M. and 12:30 P.M. the Americans lost fifteen men killed and fifty-five wounded. Over his signature Patton issued a situation report criticizing the British: "Total lack of air cover for our Units has allowed German air forces to operate almost at will." The next day Patton twice called Alexander, asking that the air force bomb enemy tanks. Both times he was told that the planes were engaged in other missions.[101]

For Patton April 3 opened innocently enough. Visiting his troops, he found that Allen's division "was going well and taking prisoners and guns." In the mountain fighting, however, Eddy's division had lost—either wounded or killed—all six of its battalion commanders. To succeed in this kind of fighting, Patton advised, Allied patrols must advance at night, secure the mountain ridges and observation posts, and then work along the ridges down into the valleys.[102]

Returning to his headquarters, Patton found "the most outrageous telegram I have ever seen." The response of British Air Marshal Sir Arthur Coningham, the commander of the Northwest African Tactical Air Force, to Patton's situation report, it defended the airmen and "assumed" that Patton had "no intention" of adopting the "discredited action of using Air Force as an alibi for lack of success on ground. If Sitrep is in earnest and balanced against above facts it can only be assumed Two Corps personnel concerned are not battleworthy in terms of present operation. . . . 12 Air Support Command have been instructed not to allow their brilliant and conscientious air support of Two Corps to be affected by this false cry of wolf."[103]

Reading the exchange between Patton and Coningham, Lieutenant General Carl Spaatz, the commander of the Northwest African Air Forces, and Air Chief Marshal Sir Arthur W. Tedder, the commander in chief of the Mediterranean Allied Air Forces, envisioned the collapse of the British-American alliance. Flying to the air base at Thélepte, they conferred with Williams, who, to get away from Patton, had moved to Sbeitla, sixty miles north of Gafsa. So far removed from Patton that he could not possibly know what was going on, Williams nonetheless insisted that his XII Air Support Group was doing its job.[104]

Patton's description of his meeting on the third with the air chiefs remains a classic of sarcasm. At noon Tedder, Spaatz, "and some other boy wonder by the name of Kuter" arrived at his headquarters at Gafsa. Tedder said they had come not to discuss Coningham's message but because they wanted to see Patton. "They were clearly uncomfortable," Patton observed, "and talked a lot about air superiority." During the meeting, "4 German planes flew right down the street not 50 feet from the window, firing machine guns and dropping small bombs. No one was hurt except a camel, who moved so fast he dislocated his leg. An Arab ran out and put it back and the camel then bolted pursued by all available Arabs. The raid had a good effect. We were raided twice more last night."[105]

Considering Patton's constant complaints about air support in North Africa and his complete satisfaction with Weyland later, Kuter's account of the meeting verged on daydreaming. He, Williams, Spaatz, and Tedder drove to Gafsa, where Patton supposedly said that Williams was giving him "good air support." A sole plane then bombed Gafsa, and Patton went wild, "wearing his fiercest scowl" throughout the rest of the meeting. "Patton appeared to me," Kuter continued, "to act like a small boy who had done wrong, but thought he would get away with it."[106]

On the next day the matter came to a head. That morning Coningham called and asked if he could see Patton around noon. Gaffey, whom Patton asked to be present, left no account of the meeting, but Patton and Coningham each insisted that he shouted, stared, and scowled down the other. The meeting ended, however, with smiles, handshakes, and lunch.[107]

Eisenhower took the incident harder than even Coningham or Patton. Trying to smooth things over, Tedder had telephoned Ike with word that he had ordered Coningham to visit Patton and apologize to him. But Ike was so upset that he prepared a message for Washington saying he could not control the Allied commanders and asking to be relieved. According to Tedder, Bedell Smith "talked him out of sending it."[108]

VII

Already bearing the burdens of Dick Jenson's death, of the bog down of Benson's force, and of the squabble with Coningham, Patton received more bad news. While he was at supper on April 3, Brigadier Holmes, "a bird of ill omen," arrived with Alexander's revised plan for the next phase of the operation. Under it, Ryder's 34th Division, now near Fon-douk, thirty-five miles north of Faid, would be taken from him and given to Lieutenant-General Sir John T. Crocker, the commander of the British IX Corps. Sending the 34th toward the Fondouk Gap, a key to the German and Italian effort to retreat up the Mediterranean coast to Tunis and Bizerte, Patton had ordered Ryder to act as if he were threatening the prospective Axis withdrawal, but not to run risks merely to gain ground. A German counterattack against Ryder proved so effective that a German inspector wrote on April 2: "The American gives up the fight as soon as he is attacked. Our men feel superior to the enemy in every respect."

Under Alexander's revised plan, Patton would lose yet another division. As the Germans passed north of Maknassy, Eddy's 9th would also fall under British control. "In this way," Patton complained, "the U.S. Troops get wholly separated, and all chance of being in at the kill and getting some natural credit, is lost. Bradley and I explained this to Ike and he said he would stop it. He has done nothing."[109]

Amid the prospect of his corps being dismembered, Patton asked Bradley to go to Maknassy and inform Ward he was being relieved. Harmon was to take over the 1st Armored. Bradley recalled Patton's reluctance to tell Ward himself:

> Patton was a very kindhearted man underneath. He just couldn't get himself into the state of going down and relieving this guy, so he sends me, and this guy was one of my closest friends. He had been in my cadet company at West Point, and I had served with him any number of times, and I didn't think Patton was completely right in relieving him, because I thought Patton had expected too much of him under the circumstances. But anyhow, he relieved him and the guy came back—he wasn't reduced—he went back to the States, and came over later with another Armored Division.[110]

Arriving at Gafsa, Harmon received a reception similar to that Patton probably would have given Rommel. Patton had just awakened from a midday nap on April 5 when Harmon walked in. He was seated on the edge of his bed, lacing up his boots, his dog Jimmy, who sported a black patch over one eye, panting and scratching nearby. Muttering a greeting, Patton told Harmon to go immediately to Maknassy, forty miles to the east, where he was replacing Ward. When Harmon asked whether Patton wanted him to attack or defend, Patton, his "always short fuse even shorter that day," yelled: "What have you come here for, asking me a lot of goddamned stupid questions? . . . Get the hell out of here and get on with what I told you to do, or I'll send you back to Morocco." Gaffey, still acting as Patton's chief of staff, later apologized for such behavior, explaining that Ward's caution had frustrated Patton. Bogged down, Ward had withdrawn a few thousand feet each morning and attacked each evening trying to regain the lost ground.[111]

Patton and Harmon quarreled, but Bradley pointed to one characteristic they shared. Harmon "had a pretty good vocabulary of his own, but it didn't equal George's. And they used to call him the poor man's George Patton. And during the northern Tunisia campaign, when men would be on the radio and they didn't have any messages to take or send, if they had free moments, they would tune in on his wave length to pick up, to hear what he was saying. But anyhow, as you know, George was noted for his vocabulary and the way he used it. He thought it was a way to impress himself upon a new command."[112]

Similar though they might be, Harmon criticized one of Patton's moves as needlessly harsh. As the Germans slowly moved northward, the 1st Armored found itself just south of Faid Pass, near where it had been mauled during the fighting preceding Kasserine Pass. Patton ordered Harmon to send a combat brigade through a pass leading to the spot of the 1st Armored's defeat. Harmon gave the job to McQuillin's Combat Command A, which, because of mine fields, advanced too slowly for Patton, who had come up in his scout car to see the movement. Despite Harmon's protests that the pass contained mines capable of blowing off the legs of a man who stepped on one, Patton expressed displeasure. He replaced McQuillin with Lambert and sent McQuillin to the rear.[113]

A gentler view of Patton came from Randle, the commander of the 47th Regiment of the 9th Division. Because of the terrain Randle kept his command post "pretty far back," but he spent most of his time at an observation post that enabled him to view the front lines. On the morning of April 7 Randle was about to leave for the observation post when Patton's car, top down and flags flying, pulled up. Patton hopped out of the vehicle and asked: "Randle, have you got some place where I can see what's going on?" In two jeeps they crossed wadis, went down a valley, and finally climbed a ridge to the observation post, all within view of the enemy. Obviously pleased because Randle stayed so close to his men, Patton blurted out: "Gee! I had no idea it looked like this up here!" Patton stayed for about an hour, at one point calling Bradley and telling him to do something with some tanks. Returning to the command post after noon, Randle said: "General, will you stay for lunch? I'm sorry, but all I can offer is cold C rations." Grinning, Patton answered: "Sure!" The two men then sat down on a bench. Each opened a can and ate with a spoon.[114]

On the way to Randle's command post Patton, accompanied by Geoff Keyes, who was visiting him, stopped at Benson's CP and "told him that he must succeed or else." Going back that afternoon, he found Benson eating lunch, "so I told him to stop eating and get out in front and he moved out." Shortly after Patton left, Benson's advance guard met a patrol from Montgomery's Eighth Army.

About eight that evening Holmes, that "bird of ill omen," called. Patton told him he "had broken through and that Benson was going to the sea." In the morning Patton had been ordered "to push on regardless of losses." Holmes now instructed him to pull back. "Actually," Patton observed, "were we allowed to continue we could cut in beyond the Grand Dorsal Mountains and head off the Germans in front of the Eighth Army, because, by moving north, we could clear Maknassy and permit the rest of the First Armored Division to come through. We could then head for Faid. In place of this, we were told to immediately withdraw the 9th Division and to complete the move to the assembly area at Bou Chebka not later than April 10."[115]

In Tunisia the British stopped Patton, but at home he was becoming a celebrity. On April 12 his face, carrying a stern expression but with a hint of a smile, graced the cover of *Time*. Inside a three-page story depicted his strengths and weaknesses—and his "Fight Against the Champ," as *Time* labeled Rommel. It began with the oft-repeated anecdote about how Patton, like the medieval knight he was, would prefer to joust to the death with Rommel in a tank. On the battlefield Patton's thrust toward Gabès and the Gulf of Gabès had failed. Driven out of the Mareth Line, Rommel had swiftly moved his armor past the Gabès bottleneck. He was now at Wadi Akarit, a gulch about sixteen miles north of Gabès. Patton, meanwhile, was bogged down in the hills.

"These hills are the toughest sort of going," he told the *Time* reporter in his high-pitched voice. "A few men holding good positions are the hardest to lick. We can't kill many of them. They must have gotten their mortars in there with mules. I'd give anything for one good pack." When they did advance, Patton's men progressed slowly. "A man in a track suit could make only half a mile an hour in those hills," Patton lamented.[116]

Anxious to return to Morocco and the planning for Sicily, Patton prepared to turn the II Corps over to Bradley at midnight of April 15. Analyzing this phase of the Tunisian campaign, Robinett, an armor officer, and Bradley, an infantryman, agreed that it lacked imagination and vigor. Never facing a large enemy force, Patton had made his thrust, Robinett noted, "frontally at the farthest point from the twin strategic objectives of Tunis and Bizerte." The final triumph came, Robinett believed, not because of superior generalship but because of "superiority of numbers, tonnage, equipment, and fire power."[117]

Years later Barksdale Hamlett, then a four-star general, also gave lukewarm approval to Patton's performance. "I don't think he was very sound logistically in Africa," Hamlett said. "He pushed beyond the logistic capability, but this is something that all people who've been involved in logistics and logistics planning feel about the commander who operates along these lines. . . . Patton was a soldier's soldier. He was a fighter and a good tactician, and that's about as far as I could go."[118]

VIII

On April 16, when Patton was back at Eisenhower's headquarters in Algiers, the two reflected different emotions. Patton was as angry as ever at the British, while Ike, in Patton's favorite words, had sunk as low as "whale tracks on the bottom of the sea," both because of the same incident. To American reporters Crocker had blasted Ryder's division.

But a report to Ike by Bull, overheard by Butcher, blamed Crocker as much as Ryder. Launching an attack toward the holy city of Kairouan, northeast of Fondouk, Crocker's IX Corps came upon a valley, at the end of which stood a cliff heavily protected by German artillery. On the left a high hill, "likewise heavily embedded and protected by dug-in fortifications," overlooked and commanded the valley. As Bull found out, Crocker's initial plan called for Ryder to lead elements of his division into the valley and straight ahead to the cliff. Crocker's corps, meantime, would take the hill on the left. Crocker, however, changed his plan without telling Ryder. He delayed the British attack until the hill could be overrun from the rear.

Not informed of the change, the Americans in the valley found themselves caught in a devastating crossfire from artillery and small arms. The American troops "dug in and practically refused to leave their foxholes." Ryder and one of his colonels attempted to lead the troops toward the cliff and made some progress. Even with the aid of tanks, the attack stalled.

Furious, Crocker publicly denounced the 34th as having caused unnecessary British casualties. The division was not battleworthy. Summoning Patton to his headquarters, Alexander told him of the criticism. In the final campaign in Tunisia, he told Patton and Bradley on April 11, he intended to use only the 1st and 9th Divisions and perhaps a combat command of the 1st Armored. The rest of the 1st Armored and the entire 34th were not ready for the new assignment. Justifiably fuming because Crocker had gone directly to American reporters, Patton castigated Crocker as an "s.o.b."[119]

During the meeting with Alexander, another comment bothered Patton. When Patton asked whether, in the final push, II Corps would become part of Anderson's First British Army, then inching toward Bizerte and Tunis in horrible weather, Alexander became "uncomfortable and said that the question of communication made it necessary. He said," Patton recorded, "that if any time I did not get on with General Anderson I was to call him direct." Since this meant ignoring the chain of command, jumping over Anderson, and going directly to Alexander, Patton considered this "A very improper procedure." Alexander then said: "if by chance we (the British) are about to enter Tunis I will send for an American and a French Combat Team to march in with us." Patton considered such a condescending suggestion "an insult, but I failed to see it, on purpose. God Damn all British and all so called Americans who have their legs pulled by them."[120]

Protesting in a letter to Alexander the treatment of the 34th, Patton pointed out that the division "was a National Guard unit from a section of the country where Pacifism was rampant." Removing it "on the say so of a British General . . . would have a very far reaching political repercussion" in the United States. Presenting the letter, Bradley argued the case for the division so persuasively that Alexander laughed and said to him: "Take them, they're yours."[121]

Patton was sure Ike would do nothing about Crocker's insults, but, as he learned in Algiers, he was wrong. "This bad news, coming on top of the American retreat in Kasserine Gap in February," Butcher wrote, "tended to make Ike's face red in dealing with the British." By plane and car Ike went to Alexander's headquarters at Haidra, where, with Patton and Bradley present, he conferred with the British leader. In his diary Patton related that "Ike talked a lot and let Alex do just what he wanted to. Ike said that he 'did not come as an American but as an ally.' And he told the truth. What an ass and how tragic for us."

Butcher, however, saw a masterful Ike. Eisenhower made the trip to extract from Alexander a promise that American divisions would no longer be split up. Henceforth each must fight as a unit. Eisenhower also insisted that this unified American force be given a chance to capture Bizerte. He argued that the British possessed much American equipment, including ammunition and Sherman tanks. If the American public felt that its troops were being slighted, it might well call for stronger prosecution of the war against Japan, rather than adhere to the strategy of defeating Hitler first. As Butcher saw it, Alexander had no choice but to agree to each of Ike's suggestions.

After the conference Ike sat around and discussed things with Bradley, Patton, and Brigadier General Ray E. Porter, who later commanded the 75th Infantry Division. Unaware of Patton's comments on his subservience, he, in effect, turned Patton and Bradley on their heads, calling them too subservient to the British. As Butcher wrote in an unpublished portion of his diary:

> Ike felt that his orders to the American commanders, particularly to Patton, to get along with the British, had been taken so literally that they had been too meek in acquiescing without argument to orders from above which they possibly felt involved use of poor tactics or that the same result could be accomplished by slightly different procedure. They hesitated, even refrained from interposing their own views. Ike had purposely brought Patton and Bradley into the conference with Alexander so that they could be

parties to a frank and open discussion and to see how frankly Ike deals with the British. Both Patton and Bradley expressed themselves as delighted and satisfied with the conference.

Yet so frequently when the commanders meet for discussion of a given problem and reach an agreement to be carried out by the staff officers, the individuals under the commanders, whose job it is to give force and effect to the intentions of the top level authorities, fail properly to interpret them. From General Patton's standpoint, his contact with General Alexander when personally made was harmonious and understanding, but when the Liaison Officer from General Alexander's Headquarters [Brigadier Holmes] sought to deal with General Patton's staff, his attitude was described as "sneering and supercilious."[122]

In a more public way Ike displayed regard for his old friend. While in Tunisia, he dictated, as Butcher described it, "a brief letter to Patton, its contents to be made known to his corps because Ike was fearful that the change from Fredendall to Patton and now Patton to Bradley would give rise to a feeling amongst the troops that they had done badly and consequently their commander is paying the penalty. In addition, he and Patton were somewhat apprehensive that the public would feel that Patton had failed." Actually, Ike believed that II Corps had not only carried out the mission assigned to it by Alexander but had broken through and reached a point twenty miles beyond its objective. Alexander had then ordered the Americans back.

Unfortunately the public was not aware that Patton had such limited objective—one that was probably dictated by Montgomery's desire to have a clear path for the Eighth Army after it had broken through the Mareth line and the Wadi Akarit. Amateur strategists have looked at the map and determined that Patton should push to the sea and cut off Rommel. However, this was corrected in part by an "on the record" press conference by Ike on Saturday, April 17, in which he made clear the missions of the II Corps. . . . I told Ike after the press conference I thought the main question had not been asked by the press—"why didn't Patton go through to the sea."[123]

On the evening of the press conference Ike and Butcher welcomed Patton to the home they shared. Almost immediately Patton began talking about Dick Jenson, whom he missed terribly. He described how a five-hundred-pound bomb hit so close to Dick's slit trench "that every bone in his body was broken, and the skin wasn't scratched." In nearby trenches Bull and Bradley remained unharmed. "Jenson was the son of one of Patton's boyhood sweethearts, and the lad's grandfather had pioneered to California with Patton's grandfather. He had developed a deep affection for the Captain."

Eisenhower and Patton then talked about the need for toughness when building and running an army. They agreed that a commander must be ruthless, even when dealing with friends. Butcher "could not help but comment that both gave every exterior indication of toughness but actually were chicken-hearted underneath. Scarcely had I made this comment when Patton said he had taken some time before leaving the II Corps Headquarters to pick some wild flowers to place them on the grave of his aide. As he recalled the incident, he said: 'I guess I really am a Goddam old fool.' His voice quivered, tears ran down his cheeks."

The next morning General Marshall sent a message congratulating Patton on the fine job he had done. "When I relayed this to General Patton," Butcher wrote, "again tears welled in his eyes and he said: 'I owe this to you, Ike.'" "The hell you do," Ike responded.[124]

SICILY ON MY MIND

I

Now at Mostaganem, a cool city on the northern coast of Algeria about fifty miles east of Oran, preparing his Western Task Force for Husky, Patton was not alone in believing that the Americans had sold out to the British. "Geoff Keyes writes 'Why not more publicity for the US troops?'" Everett Hughes, since February Ike's deputy theater commander at Allied Forces Headquarters in Algiers, recorded in his diary on the sixteenth of April. "'Why all British?'" Keyes asked.[1]

The next day a series of such complaints came to Hughes. "Geo. Patton to lunch. Says Ike is crazy. Too pro British in combat zone. So now we have the whole field covered, he in front and I find something in the rear. Geo. is back at planning. I wonder if the British got him out." After Patton left, Colonel Clarence L. Adcock, who helped plan the North African invasion, "came in and talked about how difficult it is to get along with the British." Topping things off, that evening at a party Brigadier General Lowell W. Rooks of Ike's staff "talked on same subject. Must be getting bad. Geo. says he told Ike that some day a reporter would send home as fact the story of American capitulation to British terms."[2]

Preparing for Husky, which was to involve 160,000 Allied troops, half of them American, along with fourteen thousand vehicles, six hundred tanks, and eighteen hundred guns, Patton faced the task of choosing subordinates and units. Of the six American divisions to be involved, Major General Ernest J. Dawley, a field artilleryman with World War I experience, was to command two, constituted as the VI Corps. But on May 10 Patton decided to pull strings and, after the fighting ended in Tunisia, replaced VI Corps with Bradley's II Corps, consisting of two divisions, Allen's 1st and Troy H. Middleton's 45th, the Oklahoma National Guard. Of the other divisions Truscott's 3d and Matthew B. Ridgway's 82d Airborne would also be under Patton. Gaffey's 2d Armored and Eddy's 9th Infantry would be held in reserve, the 2d off the beaches and the 9th in North Africa.[3]

Patton and Bradley argued about the 1st Division. Patton liked Allen, but Bradley considered Allen and Ted Roosevelt, Jr., woefully inadequate. Both were brave soldiers. Roosevelt was fearless and would just walk in leading men in invasions. The division, however, lacked discipline, something Bradley persuaded Patton to note in an appraisal of Allen.[4]

Middleton's 45th Division presented a different problem. Convinced, as he twice told Butcher and Ike in London, that he could instill the warrior spirit into any group of soldiers, Patton in the early fall of 1942 gave the officers and senior noncommissioned officers of the 45th the same medicine he had previously given Eddy's men in North Carolina and his own men in Indio. Middleton's chief of staff, Colonel George E. Martin, recalled how the speech, delivered in a theater at Fort Devens, Massachusetts, shook the faith of the division's officers in Patton.

He had much to say, all interlarded with shockingly coarse and profane language. . . . He was telling of occurrences when British infantry moving forward to attack would bypass enemy pockets, only to find themselves engaged by this enemy to their rear. Then when the British turned to mop-up, the German soldiers would fling down their weapons and raise their hands in surrender. If this should happen to us, said General Patton, we should not accept their surrender; instead, we should kill every last one of the bastardly "S.O.B.s."

We were then told that our division probably would see more combat than any other American division, and he wanted us to be known to the Germans as the "Killer Division." In line with this, we would never remove our shoulder patches before entering combat in a new area.

We were making our exit from the theater when a young officer turned to me and said, "Colonel, after listening to him, one is almost ashamed to be an American!"[5]

Unfortunately, at Mostaganem Patton continued such talk. On April 23 his staff held for some officers a session on Husky. "I gave a talk on valor and killing," Patton noted, "and cited a few lessons."[6]

At April's end Patton found more reason to resent Monty and the British. Late in the evening of the twenty-seventh Alexander called and told him to be in Algiers for a meeting of Allied leaders at noon the next day. Arriving at one-thirty the following afternoon after being delayed by fog, Patton found the talks postponed for a day. Montgomery was sick. His replacement, Lieutenant-General Oliver Leese, who led the British XXX Corps, had been grounded. That night Patton had dinner with Ike's chief of staff, Walter Bedell Smith, and conferred with Hughes about army politics. "Patton picture on cover of Life," Hughes recorded. "He looks heroic and yet he comes to me for advice."[7]

The original design for Sicily called for two widely separated invasions. Monty would take Catania on the east coast, Patton Palermo on the north coast. Both armies would then advance to Messina, just across the straits from Italy, driving the Axis forces from the island. Studying the plan, Monty found fault with it.

At the conference, which took place on the twenty-ninth, Patton found himself surrounded by Britons, including the officers with whom he had just quarreled. Present were Alexander, known by the number 141, who was to command the land forces in Sicily; Tedder; Tedder's deputy, Air Vice-Marshal H. E. P. Wigglesworth; Admiral Sir Andrew Cunningham, the commander of the Allied naval forces; Admiral Sir Bertram H. Ramsay, the British naval commander in the Mediterranean; and Patton's nemesis, Coningham. The only other American there was Brigadier General Arthur S. Nevins of Alexander's staff.

Opening the session, Leese read a paper embodying Montgomery's ideas. In a statement that infuriated Patton, whose II Corps had been split up in Tunisia, Monty refused to separate his forces. He would use his entire army to attack near Siracusa, below Catania on the east coast of Sicily. Montgomery further argued that Leese's corps, consisting of two divisions and a brigade, was too weak to attack Licata and Gela, along the southeastern coast of the island, and to take the three nearby airfields, Biscari, Comiso, and Ponte Olivio, considered essential for Allied success. The implication was that the Americans would have to land on the southern shore and capture these heavily defended airfields. "The whole change was predicated on the possibility that the Germans could move the 10th, 18th, 21st Panzers and 90th Light to the Island," Patton observed. "And further, in my opinion to make a sure thing attack for the Eighth Army and its 'ever victorious General,' and to hell with the rest of the war."

Even British officers criticized the plan. "Really, Gentlemen," Tedder commented, "I don't want to be difficult but I am profoundly moved. Without the capture of these airports the operation is impossible." Cunningham also objected, pointing out that to assemble so many ships near Siracusa was "to invite disaster and besides, the chief merit of an amphibious attack is to do so on a broad front and disperse enemy effort. I am definitely opposed to the plan." When Alexander argued that if the army required the plan, "we must do it," Tedder responded: "We are all in it, it is not an army show but three arms are in it. Besides we can't support Patton unless we get those fields." To this Patton added: "I would like to stress that point because I am sure that without the airfields, while I may get ashore, I won't live long."

The debate continued for two and three quarter hours. To Cunningham's suggestion that he might be able to transport another British division "if Montgomery adhered to the original plan," Leese reiterated that Montgomery would never agree to separating his army. "To me," Patton recorded, "this is a small minded attitude and very selfish. I whispered to Tedder that my force was split by more than forty-five miles. He said, 'Say it out loud.' I did." After Alexander bumbled "that the man on the ground must decide" whether or not to split his army, Patton diplomatically retracted his remark but added "that I felt sure that if I refused to attack because my force was split I would be relieved." To that Leese responded: "I am sure of it in your case and there would be a file of aspirants." The conferees then argued about to whom to refer the matter: Alexander suggested Churchill, while Cunningham thought it should be Eisenhower. Someone suggested that Alexander, Tedder, and Cunningham talk the matter over with Montgomery, but Cunningham, who resented Monty almost as much as Patton did, vetoed the proposal. At one point he declared: "Well, if the Army can't agree, let them do the show alone. I wish to God they would."

The conversation after the meeting was as informative as that during it. As the gathering broke up, Patton asked Cunningham if he had been too frank. Assuring Patton he had not been, Cunningham said: "You were the only one that said anything and in spite of your tasteful retraction what you said had a profound effect." Overhearing this comment, Tedder agreed and invited Patton to lunch. Talking afterward, Tedder confided to Patton: "It is bad form for officers to critcize each other so I shall. The other day Alexander, who is very selfish, said of General Anderson, 'As a soldier he is a good plain military cook.' This remark applies absolutely—to Montgomery. He is a little FELLOW of average ability who has had such a build up that he thinks of himself as Napoleon—he is not."

After mulling things over, Patton attributed the "impasse" to "lack of force on the part of Alexander, who cut a sorry figure at all times. He is a fence walker." Patton also believed Eisenhower's indecisiveness encouraged such squabbling. Calling the meeting "of momentous importance," he was "sure" it would lead to "a complete change in the high command."[8]

That evening Patton again consulted Ev Hughes. "Patton calls," Hughes observed in his diary. "Geo likes to run things by me. I feed him what he needs." Describing to Hughes Tedder's "plain military cook" comment, Patton added: "The description fits him well—Monty."[9]

Compounding the gloom, things were not going well in Tunisia. At 10:25 A.M on April 30 General Alfred M. Gruenther, Bedell Smith's deputy, called with word that Truscott's 3d Division was being sent to the battle zone. Receiving the order, Patton called Ike and asked if he could attach an artillery battalion to Truscott's division. "I also asked to go back to the front. Ike had not heard that the Third was moving— what a General!!!"

Late that afternoon, Patton's friend, Major General Clarence R. Huebner, Alexander's American deputy chief of staff, arrived with word that things were bad in Tunisia. German radio boasted that the Axis forces had won a great victory, stopping the British and the Americans. For four months Patton had requested two more infantry divisions for Tunisia. "This war is not won," he believed. Ike thought of nothing but Services of Supply troops. "I hear there are 120,000 of them here now. It is horrible to have a spineless desk soldier in command." The war in Tunisia, he estimated, could not end before July 1.[10]

Bea was sure that Ike avoided anyone who might threaten him. In mid-April General Lesley J. McNair went abroad to talk to Ike about the training of troops that were being sent overseas. In Africa he saw

Eisenhower but once, at a large luncheon that offered no opportunity for private conversation. While overseas, McNair was grazed by an exploding shell. "I was only slightly wounded and did not want to be sent home," he told Bea back in the United States, "but they shipped me out fast in spite of myself, just as if they wanted to get rid of me."[11]

Meantime, the quarrel over Husky continued. On the night of May 2 Bedell Smith called, summoning Patton to Algiers. Monty had just been there, and Ike wished to discuss with Georgie the new plan. After driving in a pouring rain, Patton, along with his aide Captain Alexander C. Stiller and his supply officer, Colonel Walter J. Muller, got caught in the 3d Division convoys. Reporting to Ike, Patton explained: "I am sorry I am late for the meeting but I did the best I could." "Oh, that's alright," Ike replied. "I knew you would do what you were ordered without question and told them so." In a conference room Alexander then explained the new plan to Georgie. Carrying the main thrust of the invasion, Monty's Eighth Army was to land along the east coast of Sicily at Siracusa and other small ports and head to Messina. Patton was to protect Monty's left flank. His Western Task Force would land along the southeastern coast at Licata, Gela, and Scoglitti, capture the three airfields, and then proceed north. Under the new plan, the Allied forces would be relatively close and would be in a better position to support one another. Disliking the plan, Patton pointed out that the ports along the east coast were too small to support Monty's army. While stressing his willingness to obey orders, he termed Monty's plan "logistically impossible." The change also meant that the Germans and Italians would continue to hold the airfields in the western portion of the island, thereby retaining the capacity to threaten the invasion force. "Well," Patton concluded, "we will do it anyway."[12]

That night Ike offered a concession to Georgie. The two sat up until 1:20 A.M. talking. "I was quite frank with him about the British," Patton noted, "and he took it." Suddenly Ike suggested that "perhaps the Western Task Force should be an Army." Thinking Ike planned to make the Western Task Force part of the Fifth Army, Patton answered: "I should hate to serve under Clark." To that Ike responded: "I don't mean that."[13] Thus were planted the seeds of the creation of the Seventh Army.

Along with Keyes, Muller, Colonel Paul D. Harkins, and Bedell Smith, Patton met on May 7 with Monty and Alexander's chief of staff for Sicily, Major-General Charles M. Gairdner. "Monty had very definite ideas and avoided being pinned down as to what he would or would not do," Patton observed. "I tried to get him to define a boundary and a phase line {between Monty's and Patton's armies} but could not. Smith talked a lot and made nasty remarks about Nevins and 141 but really said nothing."

Moving on to the headquarters of 141, Patton "found all my staff confused on details and full of reasons why things cannot be done." Showing confidence in the new plan, Patton "straightened them out. . . . I again brought up the subject of more troops with Bedell but got no where." General Thomas T. Hardy, who had formerly led an artillery unit under Patton but was now on Marshall's staff, overheard the request and "said Ike could have them any time he asked but he wont."[14]

That night and the next Patton stayed at Hughes's villa. While Patton had struggled with the problem of Husky, Hughes, a font of gossip, spent much of his time following Ike's relationship with his chauffeur, Kay Summersby. "Butch came to lunch today," Hughes observed on May 6 in a special paper he had prepared on Kay. "We talked about Kay whose coming marriage on June 22 has us stumped."[15] The wedding never took place, for the prospective groom was killed in battle.

Patton's two nights at Hughes's villa resembled a prolonged therapy session. "Patton stays with me," Hughes noted on the seventh. "He is low and needs bolstering. He doesn't like either Alex or Monty. I wish we could forget our egos for a while." Hughes's entry the next day reflected like sentiments: "Patton spends another night with me. How he hates the British."[16]

II

Writing to his famous cousin on April 3, 1943, Arvin "Jerry" Brown was struck by

the similarity between your career and accomplishments and those of some of the old Roman warriors of about 2000 years ago, notably Scipio Africanus and Gaius Julius Caesar. Who can doubt but that "Africanus" would have been one of your appellations had you lived at that time and had carried on as you are doing at present? Your resemblance to Julius Caesar lies not only in the military sphere but in the literary as well. Perhaps in the ages to come, when English will be—or may be—a dead language, the little oriental school children of that future time will struggle with Patton's Commentaries on World War II and wish—as you and I doubtless did in our youth when studying Caesar's Commentaries—that there never had been a war to develop a Patton or a Patton to develop a war.[17]

Georgie relished the comparison to Caesar. "As a matter of fact," he answered Jerry on May 5, "I have written an expurgated edition of my diary covering the period of active operations which some poor student yet unknown may have to study. Reading it over just now it is a little like Caesar's monumental work." Georgie then hinted to his cousin that Sicily would be the next target: "Speaking of C. reminds me that I may be playing the part of Hannibal some day too. Make a mental note of that. It may be of interest."[18]

Meantime, Patton was adjusting his staff for the coming campaign. On April 1 he selected as his G-2, or intelligence officer, Colonel Oscar W. Koch, who had served with him in various posts since the days at Indio. "He seems solid, sensible & capable," Major Bernard S. Carter, the new assistant, wrote of Koch to his wife.[19]

A New York banker and socialite who had a home in France, Carter had graduated from Groton and then from Harvard, where he knew Bea's brother Fred Ayer. At both schools Carter roomed with Charles Codman. Because they spoke perfect French, Carter and Codman, also a major, had served as interpreters at the Casablanca conference. Now, replacing Dick Jenson, Patton selected Codman as his new aide, partly because of Fred Ayer and partly because Codman, a buyer for the S. S. Pierce fine foods company in Boston, knew as much about wines and liquors as any American then in Europe and North Africa. For the next two years he would serve as Patton's confidant and, as Codman later complained to another Harvard classmate, the distinguished novelist, essayist, and playwright John P. Marquand, Patton's wine and liquor procurer.[20]

From the beginning Codman found the experience exhausting. "Charley and I have decided that G[eorgie]. is much like the Rector at Groton when we were small boys," Carter told his wife.

Poor C. is being run off his feet. The other day he had accompanied his boss all day jumping in & out of tanks etc & finally they whirled back tired & dusty to the general's villa. Charley was grey with fatigue & was looking forward to a nap & tub before dinner when G. said "Now then Codman we really *must* get a little exercise to keep fit" & off they went on a long 5 mile tramp at top speed! Charley's so funny telling me about it.[21]

Koch, Carter, and Codman ranked among Patton's better appointments. Among his poorest was his former operations officer, Colonel Kent C. Lambert, now the leader of Combat Command A of the 1st Armored Division. Lambert proved incapable of keeping a secret. In a letter to his wife, dated November 16, 1942, he divulged the details of the Moroccan landings down to the number of troops in the Western Task Force. As Harmon later noted, Lambert compounded his poor judgment by trying to sneak the letter through the State Department mail pouch in Tangier. The censors got hold of it and sent a copy to Patton marked "For Action," but, Lambert told his brother, "my friend Patton said, 'Nuts, file it,' so I escaped. It is a shame because it gave all the details of our attack."[22]

Strangely enough, the sudden end of the fighting in Tunisia brought Lambert's fine combat record and his indiscretions to the attention of Hughes, now in Algiers with Ike. On May 7 British tanks broke through the enemy lines and surprised German soldiers dining in sidewalk cafes in Tunis. The next day Americans entered Bizerte. On May 13 Axis resistance ended. "Well," Bradley remembered years later,

I think . . . by far the greatest thrill of the whole war was in Tunisia when we suddenly ended the campaign by two days of whirlwind action, and found ourselves receiving 40,000 German prisoners. I mean it came very suddenly and because of the very effective action of our troops, and to start down the road and suddenly see . . . a string of Germans as far as you could see coming down the road in German trucks, walking, Arab wagons and horses, anything they could get, they were riding down the road toward our headquarters at Mateur in northern Tunisia, and you could just see they had been fighting hard for a considerable time, and if you could capture a dozen German prisoners in one day, that was quite an accomplishment, and to suddenly see 40,000 of them![23]

When, after the victory at Bizerte, both Harmon and Ike recommended Lambert for promotion, the colonel's indiscretion came to the fore. "Patton violates censorship regulations," Hughes observed in his diary on May 10. "So does Lambert P's G-3. May have to bust L."[24]

Hughes consulted Patton, whose response, marked "Secret," indicated that Hughes, as a favor to Patton, had destroyed one document relating to Lambert.

Thanks for destroying Exhibit "A." As to Lambert, I in no way condone his offense in sending a letter by friend—I do the same myself whenever I can.

Lambert has commanded Combat Command "A" of the 1st Armored Division since April 15. It is my belief that his Combat Command made the break through and later entered Bizerte. This was the first successful offensive action of American armor in this war and required great nerve and the acceptance of risks.

The II Corps is credited with having taken 34,000 prisoners. It would seem to me only just that Lambert should get the credit for about a third of them.

As compared between such actions and the violation of a sumptuary regulation of dubious intelligence, the balance so far as I can see, is very much tipped in Lambert's direction. Knowing you as I do, I believe that you have the same idea. I have written Lambert a letter cursing him out of which I enclose a copy.

My advice, which you asked for, is to tear up Exhibit "B" also. Men like Lambert will not survive this war, and it is too bad to lose them for trivial reasons.[25]

Writing to Lambert, Patton urged him to "stop being a goddam fool! . . . In the present case, your letter to Mrs. Lambert, examined March 8, in which you start out by cursing the censors and end up by

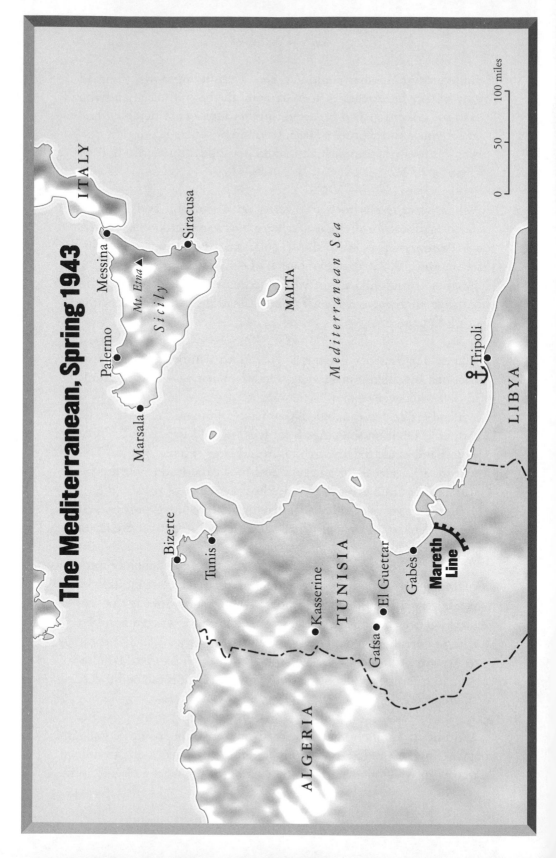

The Mediterranean, Spring 1943

ITALY

Messina

Mt. Etna ▲

Palermo

Siracusa

S i c i l y

Marsala

MALTA

M e d i t e r r a n e a n   S e a

Tripoli

LIBYA

Bizerte

Tunis

Kasserine

TUNISIA

El Guettar

Gafsa

Gabès

Mareth
Line

ALGERIA

0   50   100 miles

stating that you sent the letter by friend, might very well cause your relief and trial." Were it not for Hughes, "the most broad-minded and fair thinking man in the U.S. Army," Patton believed such would be the case. "Had it not been for your stupid act, I would congratulate you for your magnificent performance, but I repeat, no magnificent performance as a soldier can get by in the face of stupidity." Patton hoped this would end the episode, but he was to be disappointed.[26]

The Lambert incident, completely unknown to the American public, took place at the time Patton emerged as a celebrity. But the story accompanying his portrait on the cover of *Time* on April 12, 1943, stirred discontent among his officers. "That damned article in Time has just raised hell," the general told Bea on May 7. "Terry accused me of criticizing our troops and I hear Doc [Ryder] feels the same way. Of course I never said any of the things against Americans. I am their great advocate but I cant help it." Three days later Patton reported that the objectionable article had been rewritten in New York and that the *Time* correspondent in Algiers sent home a long protest. In a lighter vein Patton noted that he had "moved into a new Villa very pretentious with a horse shoe stair and occasional hot water. It has statues of nude ladies painted at appropriate places—bad Greek art?"[27]

Preparing his soldiers for Husky, Patton, ever innovative, carried on experiments. On the afternoon of the thirteenth he and the equally two-fisted infantryman, Brigadier General John W. "Iron Mike" O'Daniel, fired a 50-caliber machine gun, a rocket, antitank grenades, two kinds of armor-piercing shells, and high-explosive shells from a howitzer at pillboxes, sure to be all over Sicily. They found the high-explosive shells most effective, two rounds busting a hole in a pillbox. A flamethrower was found to suffocate the troops in a pillbox, while Bangalore torpedoes, fired within long segments of pipe, cut barbed wire the best. "The tests were very encouraging," Patton observed.[28]

Happily, Bradley, who had left Tunisia on May 13, joined Patton at Mostaganem on the sixteenth. "I met him at the air port to congratulate him in person," Patton noted. That afternoon Patton gave a lunch, highlighted by a toast from two bottles of champagne, to honor the conqueror of Bizerte and his staff. Among those present was Terry Allen, who unknown to Patton had irritated Bradley in Tunisia by conducting an unauthorized attack, suffering heavy casualties in the process. Had victory not come, Bradley would have relieved Allen and Ted Roosevelt.[29]

Two days later Eisenhower invited Bradley and Patton to a victory parade in Tunis on the twentieth, setting Patton off on a recurrent theme. "If we don't go there will be only British there," he lamented, "so we are going." The "British element" at Allied Forces Headquarters was "setting up the rehearsals" for the Sicilian invasion to "suit the British and bother us, and no one is doing anything about it. AFHQ is really a British Headquarters with a neuter General if he is not pro-British. It is a hell of a note. Some day some one at home will tumble to what is going on. I have a hope that owing to the loss of over 150,000 Germans in Tunis, the Germans may not be too keen to put Germans in Husky. If they don't we should not have too much trouble. If they do, it will be bad."[30]

Strangely, Montgomery joined Patton in disliking Ike's headquarters, calling it "a most curious place. The atmosphere there is international," he observed,

> cum War Office, cum Washington, cum Downing Street. The great thing is to reach an agreement, or find a formula, and little or no attention is paid to the fact that the agreement or formula is NOT one that will win the battle. There is little knowledge there as to what is wanted to win battles.
>
> Eisenhower is a grand chap; so too is Bedell-Smith, the Chief of Staff; both of these two are first-class. The remainder live in an atmosphere of their own, and one far removed from the realities of battle.[31]

For Patton the day of the Grand Victory parade reinforced his fears. Leaving the airport at Nouvion in a B-25, he and Bradley flew over the Tunisian battlefields and the site where Carthage, home of Hannibal, once existed. Passing over the wrecks of numerous planes, they landed in Tunis at 9:45 A.M. In the presence of such British notables as Cunningham, Tedder, Alexander, and Coningham, Ike virtually ignored the two Americans. British officers surrounded Ike on the reviewing stand, while Patton and Bradley were relegated to an adjacent stand. "Omar and I were very mad and chagrined," Georgie informed Bea, "for reasons you can guess, and they were not selfish ones either." During the parade countless British and French units passed, the United States being represented only by a regiment from Doc Ryder's 34th Infantry Division. The French "marched well but their weapons were 1914— one had to respect them for fighting so well with such junk. . . . The show took two hours and the U.S. came out a poor third."[32]

Training his troops, Patton searched for ways of making them as proud and as warlike as the British and French. "Here is a serious question," he asked Bea. "We are fighting fanatics. Cromwell was faced with the same thing, and in answer to it produced the 'New Model Army.' He used religious intolerance. That wont work now. I have thought of 'War of America for America by America.' It wont work for two reasons one of which you can guess the other is that it is too weak. Read up on Cromwell and send me some ideas."[33]

Patton hoped fiery speeches would help. Unlike Ike and Bradley, who preferred to mingle with the troops, talking to groups of soldiers, Georgie enjoyed giving formal speeches to captive audiences, his officers and men. Colonel James M. Gavin, whose 505th Parachute Infantry Regiment of the 82d Airborne was to jump beyond the beach at Gela during the invasion, remembered Patton speaking to the men about the tactics to be used against the Germans and Italians. The paratroopers must avoid a direct assault on the enemy, enveloping instead the enemy flanks.

> However, in doing so, the general used terms applicable to sexual relations. He did so in a very clever manner, emphasizing the point that when one arrived in the rear of one of their positions, the Italians would invariably quickly try to switch to a new position to protect themselves, and at that moment would become vulnerable to an attack from the rear. It was not so much what he said as how he said it that caused us to remember the point he wanted to make—though I did feel somewhat embarrassed at times, and I sensed that some of his troops felt a bit embarrassed too.[34]

Rear Admiral Richard L. Conolly, who handled the training for the navy and was responsible for landing Truscott's 3d Division, observed that the initial amphibious assault on Sicily was the biggest of the war. The landing force consisted of six reinforced American divisions, plus the seven divisions of Monty's Eighth Army. At Normandy the initial

American contingent was only five divisions, but, Conolly explained, the "follow-up was tremendous." The air drop at Normandy was several divisions. At Sicily it was two, one British and one American, and because of a shortage of planes only two regiments of the 82d Airborne jumped. The remainder of the division came in by sea.[35]

Of the four principal American naval officers involved in Husky, only Conolly remained on the scene from February to July 1943. Hewitt, the commander of the Western Naval Task Force, was sick in the United States for a time. Hall, whose Naval Task Force 81 was to deposit Allen's men at Gela, designated the Dime beaches, outranked Conolly, but despite Patton's earlier endorsement of him he had not been involved with the planning in Washington. Kirk's Task Force 85 was at Hampton Roads, Virginia, training Middleton's division, the Cent force, for its landing at the fishing village of Scoglitti. That left Conolly, whose Task Force 86 was training Truscott's division for the landing at Licata, designated the Joss beaches. Conolly alone was present for all of the naval preparations in North Africa.[36]

For Koch and Dickson the planning proved arduous. "Our map situation," Dickson observed, "left much to be desired." After discarding several British and American maps because they were unreadable, the intelligence officers settled on an American road map at a scale of 1:200,000. The beaches presented another problem. Many, especially those facing Bradley's II Corps, were narrow stretches of sand between low, rocky land, with only cattle paths leading to the coastal road. The coast itself contained false beaches, bars of land out in the water on which landing craft would get stuck and troops might drown.

The enemy forces on the island varied in skill and desire to fight. Italian infantrymen and artillerymen, many bored and tired of the war, guarded the coast. Far more dangerous were the three German divisions on the island: the Herman Goering Panzer Division, the 15th Infantry Division, and the 29th Infantry Division. With a large number of airfields the Luftwaffe was also strong. For the Allies capturing the airfields became an imperative.[37]

For the training Eisenhower set up an amphibious center on the Gulf of Arzew, northeast of Oran. O'Daniel, the fiery commander of the center, came up with a novel notion. He wanted to use rubber boats and surprise the enemy by invading Sicily at night. "How ridiculous that is!" Conolly responded. "We were all pioneers. Nobody knew anything about what we had or what we were going to get. The thing came to a head at a conference at Port-aux-Poules, in the Gulf of Arzew, which was presided over by Patton and Admiral Hewitt." After Hewitt said that Conolly and Hall opposed using rubber boats, some army officers demanded the floor, prepared to engage in a debate. At that point Patton yelled: "Sit down! I'll settle this. Once and for all, the Navy is responsible for getting you ashore and they can put you ashore in any damned thing they want to."

Still not satisfied, O'Daniel ordered Conolly to see him the next morning. Despite Patton's remark he asked if the navy intended to go ahead with the rubber boats. "They're completely out," Conolly answered. From then on the training was in LCVPs, landing craft that could transport either vehicles or personnel.[38]

Landing craft was only one of the problems perplexing the trainers. Throughout the planning Patton could not get the air force to send a representative over to discuss the invasion with Hewitt and himself. If Patton wanted air support, he had to go through the involved process of requesting it from Tunis, and the air commanders there could refuse the request if they wished. This procedure took from twelve to twenty-four hours, far too long. A frustrated Patton urged Hewitt to ask for air support from carriers, but the admiral could not logically do so, for with the air force so close the navy would have turned down any request for use of its carriers.[39]

During the training Truscott kept harping on one theme. "This is something that always worries me, the navigation," he repeatedly told Conolly. "General," Conolly responded,

> don't let that worry you. That's my problem. That's my worry. Now, set your mind at rest. I'm qualified for this job. There's no guarantee that you'll hit everything right on the button, but if anybody can do it, I think I can, because I served for fifteen months as navigator of a battleship. I know my vessels. Furthermore, I've had a lot of experience in navigating yachts and small craft, and I know how to do that. I know that and all the factors that enter into that, which is of the essence in dealing with landing craft . . . I know my vessels.

Even though the 3d Division rehearsed the landing again and again, Truscott never felt completely relaxed. "It was lucky we did," Conolly commented about the frequent rehearsals, for on the way to the landing beaches Conolly's convoy encountered gales and high seas.[40]

Concerned with the training, General Marshall, accompanied by Generals Bull and Thomas T. Handy, Lieutenant Colonel Frank McCarthy, and Ike, arrived on June 2 to see what was going on. Thoughtfully Patton called Bradley, whose corps had been banished to the filthy, fly-infested town of Relizane, about thirty-two miles south of Mostaganem, to join them. In his diary Patton called Marshall "well pleased" with the exercises, but Bradley recalled a practice landing of the 1st Infantry during which the soldiers forgot to fix bayonets. Running to the troops, Patton cursed and raged. "Ike stood by in embarrassed silence," Bradley related. Nodding toward Marshall, Bull turned to Bradley and whispered: "Well, there goes George's chance for a crack at high command. That temper of his is going to finish him yet."[41]

McCarthy remembered another incident during a demonstration of demolitions for Marshall. A lieutenant who had set a Bangalore torpedo pulled the plunger but nothing went off. "As we turned and walked away," McCarthy recorded, "suddenly the torpedo went off in a delayed action. General Patton didn't even look around. He turned to General Marshall and said, simply, 'I hope it killed that God-damned Lieutenant of Engineers.'"[42]

A completely unrelated series of events sent Marshall home angry. Discussing Patton's generals, Marshall admitted that he had been wrong in originally doubting the ability of Harmon, whom he seemed to be considering for command of the II Corps when Bradley moved on to higher things. "I talked up Keyes to him," Patton recorded, "but when I tried to do something for Colonel Lambert he got mad." Despite Hughes's attempt to cover up the incident, Marshall had found out about it.

Unfortunately all this worked against Harmon. At Marshall's request Harmon and Eddy joined the visitors at dinner that night, and Marshall, Harmon noted, "questioned me closely about the Tunisian campaign." That very day, June 2, Bradley's promotion to lieutenant general became effective, and Harmon realized that command of II Corps would bring someone a third star. That night Marshall told Patton that Harmon had greatly impressed him.

All this evaporated the next morning. As Marshall was leaving, Harmon, who did not know about Lambert's attempt to sneak a letter to his wife, asked about Lambert, whom he had recommended for promotion. Over a quarter of a century later, Harmon remembered how Marshall had attacked him and said that anyone who had recommended Lambert was unfit for high command. He then left the room and drove off. Telling Patton the story later that morning, Harmon called Lambert an able commander. If Harmon had it to do all over again, he would still recommend him for promotion.[43]

The following week Patton flew to Algiers to speak to Ike. "I could see that he had something on his mind," Patton recorded. "Pretty soon he said, 'I have got to give you Hell about Lambert.'" Marshall had raged about the incident, particularly Lambert's comment in a second letter that Patton had said, "Oh, nuts, forget it." Denying he had made the statement, Patton insisted "that 'nuts' is about the only expletive I do not use." Hughes, to whom Patton spoke after the meeting, believed Ike was merely trying to save face at Patton's expense. As for Marshall being angry at Patton, Butcher had already written Patton that Marshall had "been greatly impressed with what I was doing."[44]

The aftermath of the incident occurred in November 1943, while the 1st Armored was fighting in Italy as part of Clark's Fifth Army. Undaunted by what had taken place the previous spring, Harmon wrote to Hughes saying that Clark intended to promote Lambert "after we have been in battle for a short time here." For eight months Lambert had filled the position vacated by Brigadier General Robert I. Stack, who had back trouble. "I therefore voice the desire of General Clark, which he expressed to me yesterday, that Stack be sent somewhere other than to the First Armored Division, as we expect Lambert to be eventually promoted and have the rank of the job that he has now filled so efficiently."[45]

Hughes answered curtly. "If I were to write you in full all that the Theater Commander directed me to write when we discussed the matter of the absorption of Stack, I would require a volume." Ike agreed to let Lambert stay with Harmon, but he said nothing about Lambert's promotion, which never came through. Unfortunately neither did that of Harmon.[46]

III

On June 7, when Patton's old friend Major General John P. Lucas, sent by Marshall to be one of Eisenhower's deputies, inspected the training for Husky, he was disappointed. "The situation at AFHQ is not satisfactory," Marshall had warned Lucas before he left Washington, "or I should say it is very dangerous." Ike was a staff officer, Lucas agreed, not a combat soldier.

Viewing the training of the 1st Division with Patton, Lucas found things a mess. "They were working on the beach with landing craft," he noted in his diary. "Also some bayonet work and attack of a village. The beach work amounted to little. The boats were late, the Navy's fault I was told (by the Army), and the men sat around most of the morning doing nothing. They were not a very clean-looking lot, few had shaved or even washed their faces. The bayonet work was poor, it usually is, but the attack of the village was well put on and very dangerous."

One deficiency bothered both Lucas and Patton. After the exercise Lucas complained about the lack of air support in the coming invasion. "Our air force is the poorest set of people we have," Patton agreed, "and is wholly uninterested in ground support."[47]

Brigadier General Albert C. Wedemeyer, who joined Patton as an observer for Marshall in mid-June of 1943, also listed this deficiency. Admiring Wedemeyer greatly, Patton asked him to analyze the plan for Husky and to suggest improvements. Wedemeyer found two things wrong with Monty's scheme. First, it contained no diversionary movement, something that the British rectified with a brilliant movement aimed at Tripani, on the western tip of the island. Second, it contained no provision for air support. Since the Germans and Italians were numerically superior to the Allies and possessed manned fortified positions, Wedemeyer considered such support essential. At Patton's urging he sent a memorandum to Alexander expressing these views, but even Alexander failed to budge the air chiefs.[48]

The final high-level conference for Husky took place in Algiers on June 21. Of the top officers only Montgomery, then entertaining the king, failed to attend it. The speeches, Patton believed, ranged from poor to excellent. Eisenhower talked for "about ten minutes, rather badly I thought. He acted as an associate, not as a commander." Called on before he expected, Hewitt spoke without a map for half of his talk.

"He just giggled and rambled." The British air marshal, whom Patton liked, behaved even worse. "Tedder went to sleep about this time and stayed so for the duration. We all noted it."

Patton's team "came on just after tea and so got all our maps up. We stole the show," he bragged, "by using the War College method at Keyes' suggestion." Patton opened with a six-minute summary of the operation. Then Koch, his intelligence officer; Muller, his supply officer; Colonel Halley G. Maddox, his operations officer; and Colonel Elton F. Hammond, his signal officer, spoke briefly. "Total time 22 minutes 30 seconds. Even Ike was pleased and for a change said so."[49]

Although engaged in the latter stages of planning for Husky, Patton attended to a family matter. In mid-June he learned that his son George and Hap Gay's son had both failed one subject and had been dismissed from West Point in late May. Now studying at Dr. Jacob R. Silverman's Prep School in New York City, young George was to be reexamined in the deficient subject on August 19 and 20. If he passed, he would be allowed to reenter the academy with the new plebe class.

To his friend, Congressman James W. Wadsworth of New York, Patton called this system "utterly stupid." At a time when the army needed qualified officers, young George was being forced to repeat his plebe year at a cost to the government of $10,000 because of one subject. Such cadets should either be discharged or "conditioned and carried on at the foot of their class until the condition was passed. . . . It might further interest you to note that as a turn back I at present rank every man in the class with which I originally entered." Although busy with Husky, Patton considered this letter so important that he sent a copy to General Marshall.[50]

Patton faced other problems in the final weeks before the invasion of Sicily. One was the establishment of civil government. To be the Allied governor for Sicily and Italy, Secretary of War Stimson selected a prominent fellow New Yorker. Lieutenant Colonel Charles Poletti had been a judge, the state's lieutenant governor, and for a month in December 1942 the state's governor. From January to March 1943 he served as a special assistant to Stimson, who then sent him overseas to be Patton's G-5, or head of the Seventh Army's civil section.

Setting up a small office in Mostaganem, Poletti tried to report to Patton. The general, however, refused to see him. Every day for four days the lieutenant colonel went to his little office and, despite Patton's indifference, began planning what he would do when he got to Sicily. Finally he got a message from Hap Gay saying that Patton wanted to see him. Reporting at seven o'clock in the morning, Poletti entered a big room, at the end of which Patton sat at a desk between two flags. "I walked down," Poletti remembered,

> and when I got in front of him I saluted and I started sitting down in a chair, and I hadn't quite gotten settled in the chair when he jumped out of his chair and he pointed his hand at me, and he said, "DO YOU KILL?" Well, I recognized that as a technique too, to see what my reaction would be and whether I had presence of mind, and I said, "General, if necessary I'll kill. I am armed with a carbine and with a revolver, but that's not really my work. I am supposed to be handling civil affairs."

Satisfied with the answer, Patton began talking seriously, showing, Poletti noted, he was up on the rules of the Geneva Convention pertaining to occupied territory. He knew all about the currency that was to be used in Sicily and about other civil problems. After that Patton accepted Poletti as a member of his staff.[51]

One thing that disturbed Poletti did not bother Patton at all. Just before the invasion Poletti asked if the general was concerned about having so many American troops of Italian extraction. "Hell, no man!" Patton responded. "They are as good soldiers as anybody else. They are not going to pay any attention, and if they are asked to bombard the village of their father or grandfather they are going to bombard it and fight to capture it." Poletti later conceded that Patton "was absolutely right."[52]

When he got to know Patton better, Poletti asked about something that troubled him and numerous others who heard Patton's talks. "In North Africa," Poletti said of the training for Husky, "you made us run and you made us go out to the beach and swim and you put us through all these things, and then you gave us speeches about KILL! KILL! KILL! What was all this for?" Looking at Poletti, Patton answered: "Well, the more I can excite my own people to be alert and kill, the fewer men I am going to lose."[53]

While preparing his troops for a bloody campaign, Patton hoped for the opposite. "This is the advantage of the offense against the defense," he argued to Conolly. "Imagine yourself sitting there on those defenses on the island of Sicily. . . . They've been there four years. They can't keep alert all the time. We're going to land there and all of a sudden we'll be on their necks. That's the advantage. They don't know when we're coming."[54]

Captain Sullivan, who became friends with Patton in Morocco, remembered his determination to win. Just before the Allies were scheduled to leave North Africa and move across the Mediterranean, Sullivan, the navy's repair and salvage expert, got from the United States two large shipments of jeeps and trucks and a couple of station wagons, which his men kept inside a compound at Bizerte. A week or so before D-Day, Sullivan's transportation officer told him that a lieutenant colonel had come to him with orders to deliver all the trucks and jeeps to Patton by the next morning. Knowing Patton's tricks, Sullivan instructed his officer to ignore the order. If the lieutenant colonel returned, Sullivan's subordinate was to throw him out.

That night Sullivan bumped into Patton. "I told him," Sullivan recalled,

> I had just ordered my officer to kick the tail of one of his lieutenant colonels if he showed up in the morning, and tried to squeeze us out of our trucks. Patton laughed. He said he himself was responsible for sending the officer around. He had seen our trucks in driving around Bizerte. He said a certain son of a b— was trying to slow him up in Sicily, but when he hit Sicily he was going to go through that place like a dose of salts. He needed every truck he could get, steal or hijack. He knew I had no need of trucks until we took Palermo. He would have to take Palermo before we could start working there. How about it? I had his word that I could have all the trucks I needed once we hit Palermo. I said OK.[55]

Preparing to leave for Sicily, Patton followed one of his key dictums. He made himself visible to his troops. As Poletti was going up the gangplank of a ship, he heard the command: "Push away, the General is coming down." Sure enough, down came an immaculately dressed Patton, his pistols visible. Poletti heard one soldier say to his buddies: "GEEZ! HE LOOKS LIKE A GENERAL!!" Patton exuded confidence and passed it on to his troops.[56]

In early July the Allied convoys moved out of the ports in Morocco and Tunisia and in the Middle East. On Independence Day Bradley came aboard Kirk's flagship, the *Ancon*. On that day Truscott boarded Conolly's flagship, the *Biscayne,* one of 276 vessels of the Joss convoy. Two days later Patton, Ridgway, and Lucas climbed the gangplank of Hewitt's flagship, the *Monrovia*.[57]

As Conolly remembered, the ships of the different forces seemed to be going every which way. "After we sailed we had to detour to the south, and then at various times pass through certain points and all come together on the night of the landing."[58]

Hewitt, in turn, recalled his and Patton's preoccupation with the lack of air support. "When we went into Sicily, we strove to get the air to join with us in making plans," he noted. "They never did, and so we put to sea without knowing what the Air Force plan was." Coming to Hewitt, Patton told him: "Admiral, I wish you'd get one of your Navy carriers to back us up on this landing. I can't get that blankety blankety blank air force to do anything!" The air force was, Hewitt recollected, "interested in long distance bombing of enemy air fields and things of that sort, and anything like the supporting of a landing or supporting the troops on the shore seemed to be a sideshow for them. They were not interested in that primarily which was most unfortunate."[59]

As Hewitt suspected, this lack of coordination between ground and air forces would lead to one mishap in a campaign marked by swift successes and numerous atrocities.

Beatrice Ayer's parents.

Patton, age two years, four months.

Nita in 1905.

Cadet Patton at West Point, 1908.

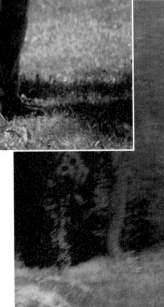

Patton running
cross-country, 1912.

Patton with parents at the Olympics, 1912.

Patton with little Bea,
summer of 1914.

George Patton, Sr., and little Bea,
summer of 1914.

Bea (*second from left*) and Nita (*center*) visit General Pershing,
left of Nita, in Columbus, New Mexico, 1916.

Tank crews receive instruction near Langres, France, July 15, 1918.
Captain Ranulf Compton is to Patton's left.

Patton at Camp Meade, 1919, after returning home.

Beatrice Ayer Patton sailing in Hawaii in 1927.

The Pattons and crew of *Arcturus* about to sail from San Diego to Hawaii, 1935.

Stimson visits Patton during 1941 maneuvers. Crittenberger is
behind civilian next to Stimson. Chaffee is fourth from left.

McNair and Patton plan strategy, 1941.

Patton and prewar troops. (Note old-style helmets.)

The armored generals. *Left to right:* Silvester, Devers, Patton, Gillem, Crittenberger, Walker, and Wood.

The Pattons with Mrs. Keyes at Fort Benning, April 1942. At left is Walter J. Muller, Patton's supply officer.

Wood, Patton, and probably, Ben Lear at Fort Benning, about June 1942.

Patton in the desert, 1942.

Patton as commander of the 7th Army in Sicily.

Alan Brooke, Bradley, and Montgomery greet Patton on arrival in France, July 7, 1944.

Bradley, Weyland, Patton, and a sleeping Willy in
France, September 28, 1944.

Patton, Marshall, Bradley, and an indifferent Willy in
Nancy, France, October 1944.

Patton threatened to court-martial Bing Crosby, shown here with Bradley, for wearing soft hat. October 1944.

Generals Leonard, Middleton, Bradley, and a thirsty Eisenhower, November 8, 1944.

Patton and Bradley in Bradley's Map Room at Verdun. (Note new-style helmets.)

Bradley, Ike, and Patton in battered Bastogne, February 4, 1945.

Generals Simpson, John B. Anderson, Bradley, and
Alan Brooke with Montgomery, March 1945.

Manton Eddy with bags of gold in salt mine in
Merkers, Germany, April 8, 1945.

Patton, Walker, and Gay at ceremony for a
Soviet general, May 12, 1945.

Patton, Hodges, Bradley, Simpson, and Gerow
wearing Soviet decorations, May 15, 1945.

Patton with Count and Countess Bernadotte in
Sweden, November 1945.

Eisenhower and Bradley in 1965 at the fiftieth reunion of their West Point class.

ATROCITIES AMID THE TRIUMPHS

I

In other works dealing with the Allies in Sicily, Patton's slapping of two soldiers is looked upon as the campaign's great misfortune. Actually the slappings were minor events in a campaign that began with five atrocities, capped by the shootings at Canicatti. If Eisenhower and Marshall had known of these, they unquestionably would have relieved Patton, thereby altering the course of the European war. Even more to be censured in the worst of these episodes was Major General Lucian K. Truscott, Jr., and his chief of staff, Colonel Don E. Carleton, who transmitted over the phone what became interpreted as an order to slaughter civilians.

Accompanying Hall's Dime force, headed for the beaches at Gela, Hewitt's flagship *Monrovia,* carrying Patton and his staff, left Algiers at 5:10 P.M. on the afternoon of July 6. "I hope God and the Navy do their stuff," Patton recorded. "To be stopped now would have the most adverse effect on the future of the world. We will not be stopped."[1]

When, in a short ceremony after the sailing, Hewitt presented to Patton the first Seventh Army flag, Hal Boyle of the Associated Press noticed the "fire of pride" in Patton's eyes. "It was not to him a ship's deck he stood upon, but a peak of glory." Patton kept the flag with him as long as he lived.[2]

By daylight of the eighth the armada carrying the Allied forces began to merge. The British convoy, Hall's Dime ships, transporting Allen's division and elements of the 2d Armored, and Kirk's Cent convoy, with Middleton's division, came together. "I have the usual shortness of breath I always have before a polo game," Patton observed as the ships approached Malta. The men, however, seemed relaxed, laughing and singing.[3]

On the afternoon of July 9, the day before the invasion, the weather seemed to turn against the Allies. A wind of about twenty miles an hour blew in a little west of north. "This will delay Truscott and his light craft, I fear," Patton wrote, "and will certainly make the men seasick." Patton remained calm and read a detective story until eleven that night.[4]

Three hours later, when Patton went on deck, he saw a coastline that was a mass of flame from Allied air and naval bombardments. He found the deck of the *Monrovia* so bright that he could read a newspaper, but refraction and the haze of the fires prevented those on shore from seeing anything. When enemy searchlights clicked on, tracer bullets from destroyers and patrol boats immediately darkened them. Aflame were the wheat fields near the coast. The wheat had been harvested, but the stubble remained.[5]

On board the *Monrovia* Poletti saw one enemy bomb land so close that the vessel shook terribly. Another missile hit a nearby ammunition ship, setting off a great explosion and fire.[6]

During the initial landings the British Eighth Army, holding the right, or east, of the Allied position, met little resistance. So, too, did Truscott's 3d Infantry, on the extreme left of the American line. It seized the port of Licata. Truscott then positioned his men for a move west to the walled port of Agrigento and northwest to the town of Canicatti. On the right Middleton's 45th Infantry also moved rapidly, linking up with the Canadians holding the center of the invasion front.[7]

The early trouble came at Gela and its beaches. With two battalions of Rangers, Lieutenant Colonel William O. Darby led the first wave of Americans into Gela. When some Italian tanks moved to retake the town, Darby tried to stop one of them with the machine gun from his peep. Finding these bullets could not penetrate the tank's armor, he hurried back to the beach, got hold of a 37-millimeter. gun that had just been unloaded, split open a box of ammunition with an ax, and hurried back up the hill. Firing at a tank less than a hundred yards away, he failed to stop it with his first shot, but he succeeded with his second. The enemy crew stayed in the tank until Darby placed a thermite grenade atop it and roasted them out. A few days later Darby refused a promotion and command of a regiment because he wanted to stay with his men. That same day General Wedemeyer requested a demotion to the rank of colonel so he could command a combat regiment. "I consider these two acts outstanding," Patton observed.[8]

At the time of the invasion Italian troops bore the brunt of Sicily's defense. The island contained but two German divisions, the Herman Goering Division and the Fifteenth Panzergrenadier Division, both rebuilt from units that had escaped from Tunisia. Even so, the Americans found things difficult. After interviewing two experts on landings, Guy Cameron Pollock of the British Navy League and Lieutenant-Colonel R. B. Bethell of the Royal Artillery, who served as the official British observer, or narrator, of the assault, Basil H. Liddell Hart recorded their views:

> Our forces were lucky to get ashore in Sicily. They would hardly have done so if the two German divisions on the island had manned the beaches. The Italians had laid comparatively few mines, their defences as a whole were rather worse than those the Home Guard constructed in England in 1940, and there were no demolitions in rear.
>
> Our intelligence estimated before the landing that there were 320,000 enemy troops to oppose us. Fortunately, it boiled down, in reality, to the 2 under-strength German divisions. The Germans had no more than 30 tanks, and with these nearly threw the Americans into the sea at Gela. The experience showed that the tricky time of a landing is above all the first day.
>
> . . . Before our landing we had a 10 to 1 air superiority that we could use to dominate the German air forces and drive them out of the sky—we had 24 squadrons operating from Malta alone.[9]

Patton's force at Gela ran into difficulty even though the Allies employed a deception scheme that kept the German forces on the western side of Sicily there until the third day of the invasion. Known as Derrick, it contained two phases. The first was a display of dummy equipment at Bizerte from July 9 to July 12, seemingly pointing to an assault near Marsala, on the western tip of Sicily. The second consisted of naval and air operations against Marsala and Tripani, also on Sicily's western tip, that again seemed to indicate an invasion. Because of bad weather and the poor handling of the equipment, the dummy display in

Bizerte failed completely. The naval and air diversion, on the other hand, proved to be a great success. On the afternoon of July 11 convoys and their naval escorts destined for Patton's men at Gela diverted to make it seem that they were headed for Marsala. After dark these ships returned to their true course. From 11 P.M. to 2:30 A.M. the air force bombed Marsala, Tripani, and the neighboring island of Marittino, and the navy demonstrated off the beaches with smoke and sonic apparatus, making it seem as if a landing were imminent. Allied planes also dropped thirty-eight dummy parachutists. So successful was this phase of the operation that on July 12 German radio announced the annihilation of an Allied invasion force near Marsala.[10]

Admiral Conolly described another way the navy helped the army. At Licata, on the left of the invasion force, Truscott called for help to subdue enemy artillery that was holding up his troops. "Show me on the map where these batteries are," Conolly said to Truscott. The admiral then ordered the *Brooklyn,* a cruiser with fifteen six-inch guns, to fire at the batteries for five minutes. Then, for good measure, he decided to shoot for another five minutes. "My God, Admiral," Conolly's chief of staff said to him, "do you know how many rounds of ammunition those guns will fire in five minutes?" With the ammunition for the gun stored right underneath it, each could fire about ten rounds a minute. And that from fifteen guns. "That's more ammunition than the Third Infantry Division would use for their artillery for probably two days or a week," Conolly estimated. A standard army artillery piece was 105 millimeters and was a four-inch gun. "We think a six-inch gun is a small gun in the Navy," the admiral explained. "In the Army that's a big gun." Navy intelligence reported to Conolly that dust and smoke engulfed the entire valley.

Conolly recalled a similar episode at the beach to his right. "I heard Admiral Hall tell about an incident at Gela where they knocked out the enemy tanks. The Germans didn't understand what the hell hit them."[11]

The cooperation among the services was not always this good. On July 10 Patton noted in his diary that he asked for dive bombers at 9:25 A.M. They did not arrive until one in the afternoon, "too late." Patton also observed another dangerous omen: "The Navy anti-air fired often and badly at our own planes." Conolly suspected that the lack of coordination might lead to tragedy. Neither Patton nor Hewitt saw the

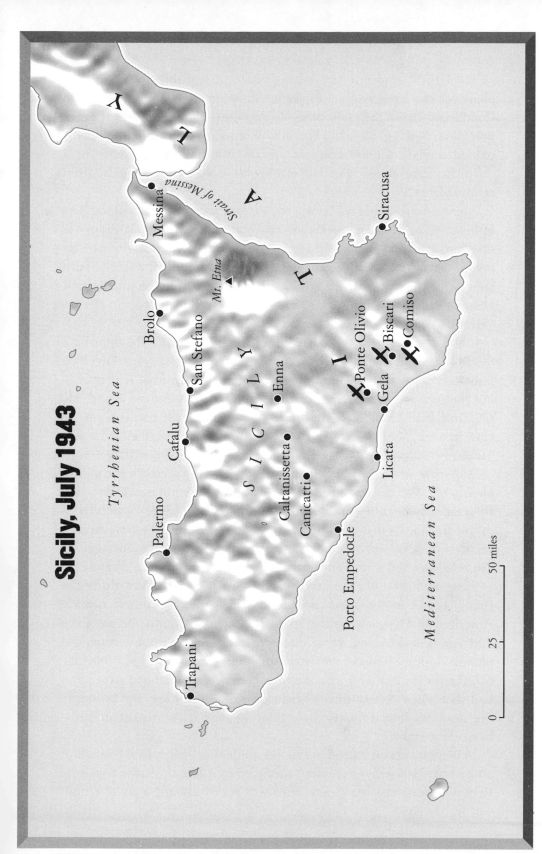

Sicily, July 1943

Tyrrhenian Sea

Palermo

Trapani

Cafalù

San Stefano

Brolo

Messina

Strait of Messina

Mt. Etna

▲

I T A L Y

Enna

Caltanissetta

Canicatti

S I C I L Y

Porto Empedocle

Licata

Ponte Olivio

Gela

Biscari

Comiso

Siracusa

Mediterranean Sea

0   25   50 miles

plans for the proposed air drops in Sicily until the last minute. To Conolly's surprise the plans brought the returning planes over the seaports where each of the main landings was made. This, he believed, portended tragedy, for the army ashore and the navy afloat sent up "a terrific concentration" of antiaircraft fire to protect the beachhead from enemy planes.[12]

Anxious to see what was going on, Patton, accompanied by members of his staff, went ashore on the morning of Sunday, July 11. Riding in the launch of his friend, Admiral Lord Louis Mountbatten, directly behind Patton's, Noel Monks of the *London Daily Mail* watched with awe as the general, oblivious to danger, stood up throughout the trip. Leaping into water up to his waist, Patton waved his pistols in the air. "Here's a general for you," Monks thought.

Once ashore, Patton acted the role of the lion. During the fight for a foothold on the island, the beachheads of the 1st and 45th Divisions remained unconnected. Without telling Bradley, Patton, instead of closing the gap, ordered Terry Allen to send his 16th Regiment inland. He then informed Eisenhower that Bradley was not aggressive enough. To close the gap and protect the 1st Division's flank, Bradley, who was furious, was forced to borrow units of the 2d Armored Division.[13]

Almost from the time of the first landings, Gay feared some sort of air tragedy. On the afternoon of the eleventh he reminded Darby and the commander of a tank detachment that planes were scheduled to drop parachutists in a zone north of Gela. They were "to warn everyone *not* to fire upon them." The tank officer conveyed the message to Truscott, and Ted Roosevelt, who was at the meeting, told Allen.[14]

That night brought the long feared air tragedy. At eleven-thirty the enemy began its strongest airplane attack of the day. Simultaneously American C-47s, carrying the 504th Regimental Combat Team of the 82d Airborne Division, came into sight. The German and American planes "appeared to be all mixed together," Gay observed. "No one could tell who was who." By the time the shooting stopped Americans had shot down twenty-three of their own planes. Of the 318 casualties the dead numbered eighty-three. Hap termed it "a strange and disheartening sight."[15]

When he radioed Patton asking for a meeting either on the beach or aboard the *Monrovia,* Eisenhower was in an ugly mood. Patton chose the ship. Coming in at 6:30 A.M. on the twelfth aboard a light cruiser escorted by a destroyer, Eisenhower brought with him a party of eleven officers, including Major General Clarence R. Huebner, the only American attached to Alexander's staff, and British Major-General John F. M. Whiteley, Ike's deputy chief of staff. In his manuscript diary Butcher left a picture of an Eisenhower so disgusted that he contemplated replacing Patton with Bradley.

After Ike and his party boarded the *Monrovia,* Patton took them to his "war room," which was also his cabin. Using a map, he indicated to the visitors that the American invasion was ahead of schedule. Truscott, occupying the left flank, had captured Licata and was fine. So, too, was Middleton, on the right flank. But, as Bethell and Pollack later indicated to Liddell Hart, Terry Allen's men were meeting stiff opposition around Gela.

Eisenhower remained unimpressed. Butcher described the confrontation.

Ike spoke vigorously to Patton about the inadequacy of his reports reaching headquarters at Malta. Because of our inability to know at headquarters of even his impressions of progress, we were unable to determine just what assistance, particularly in the air, he needed. It had been obvious after a few hours that the Axis had expected any landings in Sicily to come on the western side and thus were better prepared to meet the Americans than the British on the east. In addition the enemy apparently was concentrating its air attack on the west.

Most dishearteningly, Eisenhower and Butcher considered Patton's staff ill-prepared. Butcher continued his narrative:

Colonel Abraham, the British quartermaster, had hoped to discuss supply problems with Patton's G-4. I was requested to find him and after having him "paged" over the louspeaker system, found he had gone ashore. In connection with the study of progress in Patton's war room, he had asked his chief of staff, Brigadier General Gay, to have the G-2 and G-3 available, but these too, were not found. Gay seemed in a fog. I took a rather "poor view" of his management ability and reluctantly took a similar view on General Patton's bumptious but rather disorganized executive management. Perhaps it was caused by inadequate facilities around the *Monrovia* for both Army and Navy command. Communications from the ship likewise were heavily burdened. I was told even operational messages were running seven hours behind. . . .

When we left General Patton I thought was angry. Ike had stepped on him hard. There was an air of tenseness. I had a feeling Ike was disappointed. He had said previously that he would be happy if after about five days from D-Day General Bradley were to take over because of his calm and matter-of-fact direction.[16]

Eisenhower may have been disappointed with Patton, but Patton found nothing wrong with his performance thus far. "I think he means well," Patton commented about Ike after the meeting, "but it is most upsetting to get only piddling criticism when one knows one had done a good job. Ike is now wearing suede shoes a la British."[17]

Patton took Ike's complaints about the air tragedy as a personal affront. The men of the 82d Airborne did not, he argued, come in along the prescribed route. "I am having a full report made," he wrote, "but will not try anyone. If they want a goat, I am it." Luckily, Generals Wedemeyer, Lucas, and Joseph M. Swing, who led an airborne division that was still in the United States, were with Patton

and know the facts. It is rather trying to have more trouble from the rear than from the enemy. There were 160 planes over us the day of the 11th, and many more during the night. Men who have been bombed all day get itchy fingers. Ike has never been subjected to air attacks or any other form of death. However he is such a straw man that his future is secure. The British will never let him go.[18]

Swing's report, dated July 16, placed much of the responsibility for the tragedy on navy gunners, who were determined to shoot at any planes that approached at night. British historians, however, continue to blame Patton. "He flatly refused," noted Coningham's biographer, Vincent Orange, "to accept that Coningham—or even an American airman—could exercise a legitimate independent authority on the battlefield; aircraft, in his view, were flying tanks, subject to the orders of the senior soldier." Consequently, Orange argued, American gunners fired at all planes during the Sicilian campaign, inflicting numerous casualties on Allied airmen.[19]

To his credit, Patton continued to study battlefields, hoping to learn more about the use of armor. Visiting the site of a July 12th battle between the German 15th Division and the Italian 4th Light (Liverno) Division, on the one hand, and the American 1st Division and 2d Armored Division, on the other, he was, he wrote John S. Wood, "very much impressed with the fact that the majority of tanks put out first had their tracks shot off. I believe that we cannot too strongly emphasize shooting low. The German track is not so good, and a hit with almost anything will go through it." Lighter but more maneuverable than the German tanks, the American tanks must shoot first, preferably "at ranges up to 1500 or 2000 yards. Most of the fights between tank and tank or between tank and anti-tank gun are decided like a barroom engagement—the quick draw, the accurate shot."

Patton believed that tanks should, if possible, avoid battles with other armored vehicles. But if such combat was unavoidable, American tanks should have ready a shell of smoke-producing white phosphorus, to be used if the first round missed the enemy. "This gives the tank a chance to maneuver and get in a second telling shot."[20]

Patton was at lunch on July 13 when Alexander arrived with several British officers, including Coningham and Major-General Frederick A. M. Browning, a British paratrooper assigned to Ike's staff. They informed Patton of Montgomery's latest concoction. Blocked by the Germans at Catania, halfway up the east coast of Sicily, Montgomery desired to send Leese's XXX Corps along the west side of Mount Etna, just north of Catania, and then on to Messina, the closest point in Sicily to the Italian mainland. On this mission Leese would use Route 124, the only good road that passed west of Mount Etna. Without consulting anyone, even Alexander, Monty went ahead with the plan on the morning of the thirteenth, dispatching Leese onto the road and cutting off Bradley's II Corps, which was but a thousand yards from Route 124. Only then did Montgomery present his proposal to Alexander. Under it, the Americans were to be moved west, acting as Monty's rear and flank guard while he dashed to Messina. Informed of the plan, Patton offered no opposition.

That afternoon, when Patton told them the news, Bradley and his staff were dumbfounded. The entire American Seventh Army, much of which had to fight its way ashore, was to be shunted aside. The plan meant giving up Route 124, which had been won after hard fighting, the repositioning of Middleton's 45th Division to the west of the 1st Division, the reassignment of all of Bradley's artillery and engineers, and the slowing down of a drive by the Americans just as it was beginning to move rapidly. "My God," Bradley remembered saying to Patton, "you can't allow him to do that!" Patton's response was that it was too late to change things. Reviewing the episode Monk Dickson later observed: "General Bradley executed this preposterous order silently and skillfully, but inwardly he was as hot as Mount Etna."[21]

Although Patton said nothing to Alexander opposing the plan, he, too, soon raged. "It is noteworthy," he said of Alexander, "that the Allied Commander of a British and an American Army had no Americans with him. What fools we are." Patton did squeeze from Alexander one concession, permission to take Agrigento and Porto Empedocle, about twenty-five miles west of Licata and halfway across the southern boundary of Sicily.

What should have been a high point in Patton's life thus turned into the opposite. Even though the Allies had established a foothold in Sicily, Patton had been criticized by Eisenhower, outmaneuvered by Monty, and challenged by Bradley. But his request, approved by Alexander, allowing him to send Truscott's 3d Division to Agrigento, indicated that he was planning some sort of redemption. "If we take Agrigento," he reasoned, "we can supply the 3rd Division through it and also the 2nd Armored Division; the 1st Division through Licata; and the 45th, 82d, and 39th RCT through Gela and adjacent Dime beaches. This will permit the abandonment of the Cent beaches, which are difficult and distant."[22]

II

Early in the Sicilian campaign two of the characteristics that made Patton an outstanding officer might have led to his relief and that of Truscott and his chief of staff, Colonel Don E. Carleton. Patton's fiery disposition and his unquenchable desire for victory led to events that, had they been known, probably would have ended his military career.

Ironically Patton, who of all American generals stressed discipline, lost control of his army between July 12 and July 14.

Attempting to inspire his soldiers, Patton repeatedly invited atrocities with his talk. At Indio he told his officers: "I cannot see any reason for taking any prisoner alive." In London in August 1942 he twice told Ike and Butcher that, in Butcher's words, "he can mesmerize troops into a high state of morale." Lindsey Nelson and Colonel Martin left accounts of what Patton meant: speeches about devastating the enemy, about "raping their women," about "pillaging their towns," and about "Killer Divisions."[23]

Just before the invasion of Sicily, Patton delivered four such talks to segments of his army. The first came on June 16, when he addressed the officers of the 9th Infantry. "I told them," Patton observed, "that I had come to tell them how to fight but that after seeing them I knew I had nothing to tell them—they knew it. I then stressed shooting and killing and the fact that Americans are the pick of the more adventurous people of all races."[24]

Colonel Homer W. Jones, the judge advocate of the Seventh Army, left a record of a second speech, delivered sometime during the second half of June 1943 at Patton's headquarters at Mostaganem in Algeria. Patton spoke to the members of his staff, to his division leaders, and to Bradley, the commander of II Corps. "The 45th Division had not yet arrived," Jones noted,

> but the advanced group had. In his talk, General Patton, as I recall, told of some of the experiences he had had in Tunisia, or that he had known of where Germans had indicated they were offering to surrender and when our troops arrived, the Germans immediately shot them down. He did indicate in a situation of this sort, if the enemy waited until our troops were about to capture them, and then immediately offered to surrender, that the American soldiers could not afford to take the chance—that it was too late, and they should kill them.

Disturbed, Jones suggested to Gay that Patton clarify his comments, "otherwise we might have his remarks misinterpreted, and have violations of international law."[25]

On June 27 Patton made two speeches to the officers of the newly arrived 45th. "General Patton made it very plain over there that we were to kill the enemy wherever we found him," said Captain Howard Cry of the division's 180th Regimental Combat Team. "He said to kill and to continue to kill and that the more we killed then the less we'd have to kill later and the better off the Division would be in the long run." While some witnesses testified that Patton talked about killing those who surrendered within two hundred yards, Cry said: "It didn't make any difference. He just said 'Kill him.' . . . He did say that the more prisoners we took the more men we'd have to feed and not to fool around with prisoners. He said that there was only one good German and that was a dead one."[26]

Between the day of the invasion and July 14, when the Americans captured the airfields at Biscari, Comiso, and Ponte Olivio, these comments bore bitter fruit. In his diary Patton conveyed the impression that he first learned of an atrocity on the fifteenth, when

> Bradley—a most loyal man—arrived in great excitement about 0900 to report that a Captain in the 180 RCT, 45th Division, had taken my injunction to kill men who kept on shooting until we got within 200 yards, seriously, and had shot some 50 prisoners in cold blood and also in ranks, which was an even greater error. I told him that it was probably an exaggeration, but in any case to tell the officer to certify that the dead men were snipers or had attempted to escape or something, as it would make a stink in the press and also would make the civilians mad.[27]

In this entry Patton referred to one of two shootings at Biscari, where the fighting on the night of July 13–14 had been fierce. "We walked right into a sheer wall of machine gun fire there that was coming down from the crest of the ridge," one captain of the 180th asserted. "I remember they were up there on the top of it yelling that they were the Master Race and to come and get them. They said that in good American english." Ten minutes after the surrender of some forty snipers, most of them dressed in Italian uniforms and a few of them in civilian clothes, Captain John C. Compton, who commanded Company C of the 180th, ordered a firing squad of about two dozen men to shoot the prisoners.

Informed of the massacre by Lieutenant Colonel William E. King, the chaplain of the 45th Division, Colonel Martin drove to Biscari. There he saw "three mounds of bodies, stacked like cordwood. . . . There was no doubt in my mind but that they had been prisoners of war slaughtered while being moved to the rear." Martin told Middleton what he had seen, "and he said he would take care of the matter," but Martin "heard nothing further" about it. "It was an occurrence so revolting as to remain indelibly stamped in my memory since that day," he wrote in 1986, "and I include it reluctantly at this time only to set the record straight."[28]

Sergeant Horace T. West of Company A committed the second Biscari atrocity. Tried for killing thirty-six prisoners, thirty-four of them Italians and two of them Germans, West offered several defenses. First, he had been in combat for four days, from the landing on July 10 to the day of the massacre, and had seen three German soldiers take two captured Americans into a blockhouse, where they butchered them. "I know they killed them after taking them prisoners," West testified. ". . . It was the damdest feeling I ever had in my life. The worst feeling."[29]

At the trial West and his defenders also argued, as Compton had, that Patton's speeches inspired the killings. On the night before the invasion Lieutenant Colonel William H. Schaefer, the commander of the regiment's 1st Battalion, repeated over the ship's loudspeaker Patton's words. He "said that we would not take any prisoners," swore Second Lieutenant David T. Duncan of West's company. ". . . The impression I got was that no prisoners were to be taken." Other officers testified to the same thing.[30]

At West's trial Captain Robert C. Dean, the commander of Company D of the 180th, described the effects of these talks.

> My impression goes back to the speech General Patton made to us while in Africa, in which he said he did not want any prisoners taken. I told my company that there was a fine line there and I wanted nobody killed after they had been taken. After Lt. Col. Schaefer's speech I had no time to talk to the company. A lot of men had the impression within my unit that nobody was to be taken. Lt. Col. Schaefer had the same thing to say that General Patton did. One day I picked up a couple of pieces of shrapnel and went back to the rear to get fixed up. On the way back some aid men stopped me. They had two wounded Italians there. The aid men requested that I send men over to shoot them. I went over and

looked at them. They were pretty bad shot and I told them to fix them up. That actually happened on my way back to the front.[31]

What worked as a defense for one man failed for the other. A military court acquitted Compton, but another sentenced West to life in prison. In November 1943 Compton was shot and killed in Italy, "going forward alone," Colonel Martin heard, "to investigate a white flag raised by the Germans." Exactly one year later West was freed and returned to duty as a private.[32]

The massacres did not end here. Alexander Clifford of the *London Daily Mail* witnessed two others. Clifford, whose reports on the fighting in Sicily appeared in such American newspapers as the *New York Times* and the *Washington Post,* later described these to Liddell Hart, who entitled his memorandum on their conversation "The American Commanders (and American Mass Killing)." Liddell Hart left no doubt about whom Clifford blamed for the series of atrocities.

> Patton's bloodthirsty way of talking, and wording of his instructions, before the landing in Sicily was taken too literally by the American troops of the 45th Division particularly. On or about the third day after the landing, Clifford visited the Comiso Airfield along with an American War Correspondent. There they saw a lorry-load of German prisoners brought in who, when they started to debus, were shot down by a heavy machine-gun turned on them. All were killed except two or three, who were merely wounded. Clifford also saw a batch of about 60 Italian prisoners shot in the same way, after they had been brought in. Clifford and the American War Correspondent went off to Patton and protested. Patton then sent off orders to the Division to stop such killing.

While in Sicily Clifford discussed the Comiso murders with Clark Lee, the reporter for William Randolph Hearst's International News Service. Lee "told Clifford of several even worse American atrocities." These presumably were the shootings at Biscari.[33]

Differing from the West and Compton cases in location, in the way the executions were carried out, in the weapons used, and in the number and nationalities of those killed, the Comiso incidents were unquestionably separate events. Clifford's comment about rushing off to tell Patton, moreover, casts doubt on Patton's diary entry that he first learned about such things from an excited Bradley on the morning of July 15.

Clifford had more to tell. "Much worse still," Liddell Hart recorded, "was the behaviour of the French native troops. A battalion (Tabor) of Goums was sent to Sicily as a French contribution to the Allied invasion. They left a swathe of looted and burnt villages along their path, raping and killing as they went. The Sicilians blamed this on the Americans."[34]

Long after the war's end and Patton's death, Liddell Hart sought permission to make public the details of the Comiso shootings. Opposing the trial of Gert von Rundstedt and two other German field marshals for war crimes, he wrote Clifford:

> In this connection I have mentioned in various discussions about the trial the account you gave me of the way you saw Patton's troops (of the U.S. 45th Division) shooting down the lorry-loads of German and Italian prisoners on the Comiso airfield in Sicily. While I made a note of what you told me at the time, I have not felt at liberty to mention your name as a witness of the affair, but it would be a great help if I could do so—in view of your high standing and reputation for reliability. Have you any objections?[35]

Clifford had no sympathy for war trials, but he refused the request. He sent Liddell Hart an elaborate explanation:

> I am very sorry—I fear I can't give you permission to use my name or call me as a witness in the Comiso shootings. The main reason is that I promised General Patton I never would make use of the incident in public. The shootings took place from ignorance and stupidity rather than brutality, and Patton felt himself partly responsible. He put it right instantly, and I, rightly or wrongly, promised I would never publish it.
>
> In addition to that I feel it is no defence of any German or other soldiers to try and prove that our own Allies were just as bad.[36]

Liddell Hart answered with a long plea plus an analysis of Patton.

> I am sorry to hear what you say about the difficulty of citing you in substantiation of what you told me about the Comiso shootings.

When you told me about them you didn't mention that there was any objection to speaking about them. While I can well understand Patton's natural desire not to have the episode published, and the difficulty in which that placed you at the time, I do not quite see why such a check on historical truth should apply after the war, especially as Patton is dead, and it can have no detrimental effect on his position. If such conditions about keeping matters confidential were to be observed in perpetuity after the men concerned are dead, there would be no chance of ever getting at the truth of history.

Moreover, the very fact that other generals are now on trial for their lives because their troops did similar things to what happened at Comiso might well be regarded by Patton himself, if he were still alive, as justifying release from such a promise as you gave him. It is notable that a number of the other American military and naval chiefs have given evidence of what they did themselves as an aid to the defense in other trials. . . . It would weigh with any fair-minded court if it can be shown that similar things were done on the Allied side. There have been several cases, to my knowledge, where sentences have been cancelled by British Review Boards in the light of such evidence on behalf of the defense.[37]

While Patton learned from Bradley, from Clifford, and from Clifford's American correspondent friend of the episodes at Biscari and Comiso, he probably never knew of the worst tragedy, one involving civilians. During the Compton trial, Captain Jean Reed was asked what Patton said about civilians. "He said something about if the people living in the cities persisted in staying in the vicinity of the battle and were enemy," Reed answered, "we were to ruthlessly kill them and get them out of the way."[38]

This last incident took place in the town of Canicatti, almost in the center of Sicily, which Truscott's troops took at 3 P.M. on July 12. Entering the town, the lieutenant colonel in charge of American Military Government for the division found what he called a "shortage of food," which "resulted in a riot." The lieutenant colonel "reported the situation" to Carleton, who then issued an order that should never have been issued over the phone. Knowing, as he observed in his book *Command Missions,* Patton's emotionalism, Truscott, through Carleton, nevertheless authorized the lieutenant colonel "to shoot looters in the act, if necessary, to reestablish order." Carleton also sent the lieutenant colonel a platoon of infantry from Colonel Charles R. Johnson, Jr.'s 15th Infantry Regiment.[39]

The phone call led to the shooting of unarmed civilians. A brief report in the National Archives presents the lieutenant colonel's version of the story.

> At another point in the town, Lt. Col. ——— caught a number of looters in the act of carrying away soap. He arrested them. He saw others with similar bundles moving down the streets in carts. He ordered them to stop and when the drivers continued, he fired over their heads. The drivers fled. In following the fleeing carts, he came upon a soap factory outside of which there was a large crowd obviously looting the place. Lt. Col. ——— and the infantry platoon endeavored to stop the looting and round up the looters. Their orders were disobeyed. Lt. Col. ——— then shot at some of the men in the crowd and the infantry rounded up others. Six men were killed. Some of those who escaped may have been wounded.[40]

But according to one American eyewitness, the lieutenant colonel fired twenty-one shots from his 45-caliber pistol point-blank into the crowd, whose members had entered the grounds through a hole in the factory wall and were guilty only of filling buckets with liquid soap from pits. After killing an unknown number of civilians, perhaps twenty-one, without provocation, the lieutenant colonel drove off.

Instead of investigating the incident, perhaps the only one of its kind involving American troops in the European fighting, the American Military Government suppressed word of it. In May 1944, when Lieutenant Colonel B. E. Prescott arrived from the Command and General Staff School at Leavenworth to study government in Sicily, he was not shown anything about the affair, as "it comes from a report made by an individual and not from official Headquarters."[41] For almost sixty years the episode has been hushed up.

III

Sitting in his office in Algiers on July 15, Everett Hughes read a message handed to him by Patton's aide, presumably Codman. "Patton wants 2300 replacements for the 82nd Airborne," Hughes wrote in his diary. "They must have taken a licking. Ben says that they lost 33 out of 40 transports. Patton's emissary wants some cigars and decorations for Geo who can't be badly off. With the liquor I sent he should be well off."[42]

On the night of July 16 a radio message from Alexander fed Patton's anti-Anglicanism. Alexander decreed that Montgomery's Eighth Army was to drive northward to the Messina Peninsula in three columns. Patton's Seventh was relegated to protecting Monty's rear and flank. Flying to Alexander's headquarters in Tunis with Wedemeyer, who was about to return to Washington, Patton for once showed his fury. On a map he demonstrated how he wished to push north and northwest with Bradley's corps and cut the coast road, while Keyes would lead a provisional corps "on a long end run to West and North to capture Palermo." As John Lucas told Hughes, Wedemeyer, General Marshall's emissary in Sicily, spoke firmly to Alexander, saying that the "American people would not stand" for Alexander's order. Yielding, Alexander gave Patton permission to head first to Palermo, along the northern coast of Sicily, and then east to Messina. The next afternoon Patton ordered Truscott, whose Third Division had already taken Porto Empedocle and Agrigento, to head north toward Palermo. As the meeting in Tunis ended, Ike suddenly appeared at Alexander's headquarters and, Patton noted, "failed to criticize me for the first time since I have served under him, in fact he was most complimentary and said, 'You ought to see the radio I am going to send Marshall about you tonight. If I keep picking Army Commanders like you they may think I am a Napoleon.' "[43]

The Americans emerged from the confrontation with Alexander exuding confidence. "Fire out," Keyes telegraphed Hughes. "Total damage $10. God & British willing we are still a Republic." Patton shared the elation. "Geo P says it is a good war," Hughes wrote on July 20, "best he was ever in—thinks he is doing OK. Got the liquor & had lots of takers. Sicily is ½ taken. Geo says our cousins got a bloody nose!"[44]

As Monty's men stalled around Catania—on the eighteenth he sent an entire division against the city, advancing, Patton observed, only four hundred yards—Patton put into operation the plan he had presented to Alexander. Keyes took over the Provisional Corps, consisting of the 3d Infantry, the 82d Airborne, and the 2d Armored Divisions, with Palermo as its objective. By capturing that city the Americans would split the island in two.

For an army the first hundred miles from Agrigento north to Palermo presented problems. The roads traversed mountains as high as four thousand feet and contained steep grades and hairpin turns. At Prizzi the mountains led into the central plateau that ended at the range of hills encircling Palermo.

At 5 A.M. on the nineteenth Truscott's 3d Division began its drive north. A week earlier Patton bet British Air Vice-Marshal Horace E. P. Wigglesworth a bottle of whiskey against a bottle of gin that he would be in Palermo by midnight of July 23. Keyes's corps progressed so satisfactorily that Patton now believed he would win his bet.[45]

Amid this push, a clarifying message from Alexander to Patton, received at 11:30 P.M. on the night of the eighteenth, worsened relations between the two American lieutenant generals. Bradley disliked the idea of a push to Palermo, dismissing it as another of Georgie's schemes to grab headlines. As he saw it, Messina, not Palermo, constituted the logical target in Sicily. Patton's plan, moreover, relegated Bradley's II Corps to the task against which Patton himself had rebelled, guarding Monty's army.

Alexander's message directed Patton to establish, before pushing to Messina, a line, running from Campofelice on the north to Agrigento on the south, splitting Sicily in two. Considering it too late to change Truscott's orders, Gay instead sent Bradley a message to secure this north-south line. Objecting to being relegated to such duty, Bradley later contended that Gay withheld the order from Patton for four days, a questionable assertion considering that Patton and Chynoweth's prewar tormentor, Major General Alvan C. Gillem, Jr., visited Bradley on the morning of the nineteenth.[46]

Bradley, in fact, took calmly the news that he was to be a watchdog. After writing Patton that the change of plans and directions might "open a dangerous gap between the 7th and 8th Armies which may prove serious," he scribbled in longhand: "General Patton: Please don't worry too much about this I propose to turn the 1st Div against Enna [in central Sicily] probably tomorrow night."[47]

Meantime, in the drive toward Palermo, Truscott's men made remarkable progress. With the Tabor of Goums, Robinson's regiment held the left of Truscott's line. Led by Lieutenant Colonel Edgar C. Doleman, its 3d Battalion marched over mountain trails, covering fifty-four miles in thirty-three hours. It then attacked San Stefano, taking the town just before dark on the twentieth. Truscott next decided to send a portion of his division on a night move that he described as a "wide envelopment." This would enable him to attack Prizzi from the west as well as the south. The maneuver, made over more than fifty miles of bad roads covered with enemy demolitions and obstructions, would, Truscott believed, have gotten a "U" at Fort Leavenworth, but by six on the morning of the twenty-first his men were in position to attack Prizzi from the two directions. Amid "blistering heat and stifling dust," the 3d took the town and moved on to Corleone. By noon of the twenty-second Truscott's division was poised at the Blue Line, an imaginary crescent along the range of hills encircling Palermo. To prevent the 3d Division from becoming entangled with Gaffey's 2d Armored Division, which was also to attack the city, Patton had ordered Truscott to halt at this line.

From the Blue Line, Truscott observed explosions in Palermo. Just as the Confederates in the Civil War blew up much of Atlanta before leaving it, the Germans were now destroying everything of military value in Palermo, the ancient capital of Sicily. Keyes rejected Truscott's repeated requests to occupy Palermo, whose population was 390,000 people, to stop the destruction. But about six o'clock that evening some civilians came out of the city and offered to surrender it to Brigadier General William W. Eagles, Truscott's assistant division commander. Finally Keyes yielded. To protect the port he allowed reconnaissance units to enter the city. When Patton rode into Palermo at ten-thirty that night at the head of a tank column, Truscott's soldiers were already patrolling its streets. According to Michael Chinigo of the International News Service, who accompanied Truscott, the honor of first entering Palermo went to Lieutenant Colonel Harry Sherman, whose outfit was also the first to enter Agrigento.[48]

Reviewing this phase of the campaign, Patton praised the American use of tanks.

I feel that future students of the Command and General Staff School will study the campaign of Palermo as a classic example of the use of tanks. I held them back far enough so that the enemy could not tell where they were to be used; then when the infantry had found the hole, the tanks went through and in large numbers as FAST. Such methods assure victory and reduce losses, but it takes fine leadership to insure the execution. General Keyes provided perfect leadership and great drive. The praise should be his.[49]

IV

During the Palermo campaign, the feisty General Clarence R. Huebner, the only American on Alexander's staff, frequently visited Patton's headquarters. On July 21, the day Seventh Army headquarters moved from Gela to Agrigento, Huebner, finding Patton out, discussed with Hap Gay his observations about the British, requesting that Gay divulge his remarks only to Patton. Irritated because Bradley, in the eastern portion of the island, had been ordered off vital highways that were being reserved for Montgomery's army, Huebner believed that Patton

must insist and demand the road CALTANISSETTA-NICOSIA, road junction 520, which is north and west of FRANCAVILLA, and furthermore, that the Commanding General of the 7th Army must realize and must enforce the principle that he as an Army Commander did not receive orders, but an Army Commander received letters of direction outlining missions, and that he, the Army Commander, is the sole judge as to how these missions are accomplished.

He emphasized the fact that our Allies were not cognizant of this procedure, but that this time-worn custom of the American Army must be maintained.

In handwriting in his diary Gay added Huebner's most important observation. "General Huebner was convinced that a determined effort was being made at Force 141 (15th Army Group) to place Gen Patton in a secondary role. I am sure Gen Huebner is acting on his own initiative—and not by direction."[50]

Three days later, on the twenty-fourth, Huebner; Major General Alfred M. Gruenther, Clark's chief of staff; and Brigadier General Archeleus L. Hamblen arrived at Patton's headquarters at Agrigento with shocking news. Telling Huebner, as Ev Hughes found out, that "he is too strong for British Staff" and that his was a "British not Allied Staff," Alexander had relieved Huebner, replacing him with what he hoped would be a more agreeable American, Brigadier General Lyman L. Lemnitzer. Hughes uncovered another tidbit: "Huebner says Patton wanted to turn in his command as a protest against H's relief."

Huebner showed Patton proof of his assertion, told to Gay on the twenty-first, that Alexander seemed determined "to place Gen Patton in a secondary role." In a dispatch to Alexander labeled "Most Secret—Most Immediate," Monty argued that two Allied armies could not operate on Sicily's roads. He suggested that his army move northward toward Messina and that the Americans be relegated to defensive movements along a line running down the southern half of the island from Caltanissetta to Canicatti and then to Licata. In effect, Patton observed after reading the dispatch, Monty "was trying to command both armies and getting away with it," for Alexander's orders of July 13 and July 17 followed Monty's advice.

Musing over the incident, Patton believed he had won out anyway. Had the order of the thirteenth given him Route 117, leading from Gela north to Enna and Nicosia, he could have easily taken Enna and then moved northeast to Messina. "The Canadians never took Enna," he observed, "and lost 700 men trying; then they took three days to take Leonforte. The rest of the 8th Army has not gained a foot and the 7th Army has taken most of the island." On the sixteenth the British Colonel Robert Henriques had passed on to Patton a remark by Monty's chief of staff, Major-General Francis W. "Freddie" de Guingand, that Alexander's orders should be ignored. "Whether this is in good faith," Patton wondered, "or as a bait I did not and do not know. Nice people."[51]

With his deputy chief of staff, Colonel Paul Harkins, and the ever-present Charley Codman, Patton flew on the twenty-fifth to Siracusa to confer with Montgomery. "When we arrived," Patton noted, "no one

paid any attention to us until I finally spotted General Montgomery."
Spreading a map across the hood of his car, Monty began to iron out a
territorial agreement with the Americans. Humbled by the difficulties
his army had faced, Monty proposed giving Patton both roads from
Palermo to Messina: Route 113, which ran along the coast; and Route
120, which ran between twenty and twenty-five miles below the northern coast of Sicily from Termini, just east of Palermo, to Taormina,
which Montgomery hoped to capture. If Patton approached Taormina
from the west and Monty from the south, the British Eighth Army and
the American Seventh Army might trap the two German divisions facing Monty before Catania. With this gesture Monty acknowledged that
he needed Patton's help. He nevertheless predicted the fall of Sicily by
August's end. Patton did not answer, but he later told his staff the campaign would end by mid-August.[52]

At the meeting of July 25 Patton unveiled a new wrinkle. He asked
Alexander, who came by, for enough small craft to land a reinforced
battalion behind the enemy. "Alex did not think much of this," Patton
recorded, "but agreed to try." Patton also asked for cruisers, and General Robert Richardson of the British army generously responded that
he would get them for the Americans. "I doubt if he does," a distrustful
Patton wrote. These requests, Gay believed, constituted the "1st plan"
for Patton's "famous end run made by the 7th Army" along the northern coast of Sicily east to Messina.[53]

The British failure in Sicily threw Churchill into his customary panic.
When Stimson visited the prime minister in London on July 22,
Churchill again attacked the idea of a cross-channel invasion. "The
check received by the British attack at Catania, Sicily, during the past
few days evidently alarmed him," Stimson observed in his diary. "He
referred to it and praised the superlative fighting ability of the Germans."[54]

Visiting Ike's headquarters, Stimson was jubilant. "He chatted about
his ex-aide Geo P jr who is doing right well," Hughes recorded. "Conversation started by my saying that Geo had written that 'Our cousins
had got a bloody nose.' S knew all about 'our cousins' apparently."[55]

V

Returning to Palermo, Patton moved into the palace formerly occupied by the king of Italy. "I am in the King's room," Patton exulted, "and there are, by count, seven Anti-rooms between my room and the State dining room." Although it contained three mattresses, his bed was "very uncomfortable," but his suite contained a bathroom, electric lights, paintings on the walls, and gold furniture. Stiller, his aide and World War I companion, chided him about finding "a nice place in some good boarding house," but Patton reveled in the glory of sleeping in a royal bed, uncomfortable though it was, and of rinsing his teeth, which always contained a cavity or two because of his love of candy, using "a glass etched with the Arms of Savoy."[56]

Into these regal surroundings Montgomery came with his staff on July 28. While de Guingand and Harkins discussed some of the problems incident to the coming campaign, Montgomery wrote in his diary observations far different from those of Patton: "We had a great reception. The Americans are most delightful people and are very easy to work with." Monty, however, noted two weaknesses within the United States Army. First, the American generals did not understand "administration in the field," Monty's diplomatic way of calling Patton's staff inefficient. Equally important, the ground and air forces seemed incapable of cooperating with one another.[57] In Patton's case this latter deficiency would soon be corrected, for within six months Brigadier General Otto P. Weyland would arrive in Europe and provide Patton with the kind of air support of which he dreamed.

After Patton established his headquarters in Palermo, correspondents poured in, among them Quentin Reynolds, covering the war for *Collier's* magazine. At press headquarters in the Sole Hotel, Reynolds bumped into another newcomer, Demaree Bess of the *Saturday Evening Post,* and Sammy Schulman, the International News photographer who had covered the North African invasion and the Casablanca conference. Since newsmen, out of courtesy, paid their respects to the commanding general when entering a theater of operations, Sammy volunteered to introduce the new arrivals to Patton.

At Seventh Army headquarters Patton jumped up from his chair to greet Schulman. His famous revolvers and lacquered helmet lying side by side on his desk, Patton agreed to let Bess and Reynolds cover the drive to Messina, even offering them a jeep. At Sammy's suggestion Patton walked over to his wall map, picked up a pointer, and brought the two reporters up to date. He first pointed to Gela, where Terry Allen had landed. "Surely you recall what happened at Gela, gentlemen?" Patton asked. "It was there that the Greek playwright Aeschylus met his death when an eagle, mistaking his bald dome for a rock, dropped a tortoise on it and fractured his skull."

After displaying what Reynolds called "this flash of erudition," Patton talked about his campaign. "Terry Allen had worse than the onshore wind to contend with at Gela; he had the whole goddam Hermann Goering Division, tough sons-of-bitches loaded with tanks." At the mention of tanks, Patton's eyes sparkled. "Two of our cruisers, the *Savannah* and the *Boise,* opened up on them and added something new to military history—the first engagement between tanks and cruisers."

Patton then discussed the historical background of Agrigento, first conquered in 406 B.C. by the Carthaginian general Hannibal. Eleven hundred years later the Saracens took the city. "Before our 3rd Division got through with the goddam place," Patton went on, "I'll bet the Nazis wished they'd never heard of it. And," he said, tapping Riberia with the pointer, "now look at this. Palermo to Riberia is seventy-two miles. The 3rd Division made it there in two days. They'll be studying that one in the goddam textbooks when we're all dead." Sammy Schulman ended the briefing by jumping to his feet and saying he had to take Reynolds and Bess back to the hotel for a cold lemonade.

Outside, Reynolds wondered what power Schulman possessed to receive such favors from Patton. "You boys don't understand," the photographer confided. "He just loves to have his picture taken."

Several times after that Reynolds ran across Patton. Each time the general roared by in a car or a jeep escorted by a dozen military policemen on motorcycles and wearing white helmets. His victories, the reporter noted, instilled pride in his troops. But many of them resented the "Patton discipline," which required even those on patrol to wear neckties. Above all, Patton's contradictions intrigued Reynolds. "Just when I thought I had him figured as a naughty boy who never quite grew up, I heard that he wrote religious poetry in his off hours, and that really set me back."[58]

On the final day of July, Patton inadvertently took the steam out of a magazine whose accuracy he had questioned since his arrival overseas.

In May, after visiting the 1st Division in Tunisia, Eisenhower had concluded that Allen needed a rest. Bradley, too, had run-ins with Allen, especially after Allen conducted an unauthorized attack. Visiting Palermo on the last day of July, Ike gave Patton "permission to relieve both Allen and Roosevelt on the same terms on the theory of the rotation of command. There will be a kick over Teddy," Patton observed of the son of the former president, "but he has to go: brave but otherwise no soldier." Huebner, Patton's friend since the chase after Pancho Villa, and Colonel Willard G. Lyman were "to go up in the morning."[59]

The appointment of Huebner, who in a Washington newspaper in the spring of 1969 labeled Churchill "arrogant" and "supercilious" and Montgomery "an obnoxious bastard," hardly pleased the British. It also frustrated *Time* magazine, which on August 9 carried Allen's picture on its cover. Inside, a six-page article depicted Allen, not Bradley or Patton, as the G.I.'s general. "He is a gentle man," the story revealed. "He does not like the fact that men will be killed carrying out his orders, but he has accepted the inevitability of it. He will spare or spend his men as military necessity demands; while they live he will see that they get every comfort and consideration. That is one reason why the spirit of the 1st Division is second to none in the U.S. Army."[60] A reader would never guess that Ike and Patton had just relieved Allen.

Patton had chosen Truscott to lead the dash from Palermo to Messina. Accordingly, during the daylight hours of August 1, the 3d Division concentrated around San Stefano di Camastra, about fifty miles east of Palermo. Via Route 113, the coastal road, Messina lay just 105 miles east of San Stefano, but for much of that distance the highway ran parallel to the Nebrodi Mountains, called by Patton "the worst I have ever seen." Averaging between four and five thousand feet in height, the Nebrodi Mountains contain sharp slopes, deep gorges, and numerous cliffs. They left Truscott little room for operating. In the rush toward Palermo much of the terrain allowed the Americans to swing wide and attack enemy positions from the rear or the flank. But between San Stefano, slightly less than halfway to Messina, and Messina itself, every move became difficult and men progressed slowly. "Our effort," Truscott remembered, "was always to encircle the enemy and prevent his escape, but in such terrain the advantage was all with the Boche. Our maneuver required days of laborious struggling under the blistering Sicilian sun and enemy fire, to reach positions from which we

could strike. The enemy could hold to the last minute and then withdraw by motor while we could only follow up on foot."[61]

Patton realized the severity of the operation, but for two reasons he
urged speed. "It is a miracle that our men can get through them," he
wrote of the mountains on the first of August, "but we must keep up
our steady pressure. The enemy simply can't stand it. Beside we must
beat the 8th Army to Messina."[62]

This desire to beat Monty irritated Bradley, now being touted by the
war correspondent Ernie Pyle, who spent five days interviewing him, as
the wonder of the campaign. "In Sicily there were a lot of things in
which I thought he was not too much of an Army commander," Bradley
later said of Patton. Bradley was sure that Keyes "did most of the direction of the planning instead of George." He especially resented Patton's
"attitude towards thinking it more important to get into Messina ahead
of the men than it was to do it in the way which would save lives."[63]

On the third of August Patton, accompanied by Lucas and Stiller,
was about to visit Bradley's headquarters in eastern Sicily when he
made an innocent enough decision. In his diary Patton left a detailed
account of what happened:

> On the way I stopped at an evacuation hospital and talked to 350
> newly wounded. One poor fellow who had lost his right arm cried;
> another had lost a leg. All were brave and cheerful. The 1st
> Sergeant of "C" Company, 39th Infantry, was in for his second
> wound. He laughed and said that after he got his third wound he
> was going to ask to go home. I had told General Marshall some
> months ago that an enlisted man hit 3 times should be sent home.
> In the hospital was one louse. He was unhurt but told me that he
> was unable to take it—just a coward. I gave him hell and slapped
> his face with my gloves. Companies should deal with such men
> and if they shirk, try them for cowardice.

Patton vowed to "issue an order on the subject tomorrow."[64]

Arriving at II Corps headquarters, Patton told Bradley of the incident. "He was bragging about how he treated the man," Bradley recollected, "to try to snap him out of being a coward. His idea was that if
you could make a man mad you could maybe make him mad enough to
fight and mad enough to go up on the front lines and fight. He thought

these men were just showing a yellow streak." Patton was "rather pleased" with what he had done. He "bragged about it."[65]

Not giving much thought to the episode, Patton planned an amphibious end run behind German lines. He discussed the matter with Bradley, who argued that the maneuver must be coordinated with attacks on land, in this case the assault on the village of San Fratello, one of the series of naturally strong positions held by the Germans. Accordingly, before daylight on August 8, Lieutenant Colonel Lyle W. Bernard's reinforced battalion landed not east of the Rosmarine River as planned but west of it, nearer Sant' Agata di Militello. While achieving surprise, the amphibious operation failed to cut off the German 29th Infantry Division. At best, noted the official army historians of the campaign, it "probably did encourage the Germans to give up San Fratello ridge a few hours earlier than they had intended. Even a landing on the beaches east of the Rosmarine River would have done little better."[66]

Citing the capture of sixteen hundred prisoners, Patton deemed the landing a great success. Visiting Patton on the ninth, Bradley had other things on his mind. Patton, who later bragged that he had West and Compton court-martialed, had done nothing about the Biscari massacres. Bradley insisted that West and Compton be arrested, something Patton did not do for another fifteen days. Instead Patton busied himself with a second amphibious landing, scheduled for August 11 at Brolo, almost thirty miles closer to Messina.

Recent remarks heard in Sicily over the British Broadcasting Company spurred Patton on. The broadcast had asserted that while Montgomery faced the bulk of the enemy forces, Patton's troops, finding things easy, were sitting around eating grapes and swimming. After receiving protests from American officers who heard the broadcast, Ike complained to Churchill and Alexander, suggesting "that a representative of the British Chiefs of Staff should scrutinize every script dealing with Allied operations here before it was put on the air."[67]

On the morning of the tenth Keyes came to Patton with the good news. "Everything was set" for the second invasion by Bernard. But later in the day Truscott, concluding that he could not get his artillery and troops in position to support Bernard, decided to postpone the operation for twenty-four hours. Keyes, who had just arrived at Truscott's headquarters, warned that Patton would not agree to any delay. Reached by telephone, Bradley, Truscott's immediate superior, concurred that the landing must not go on "unless it was properly timed with the operation of the remainder of the Division." At 7:45 P.M. Keyes phoned Patton, Truscott remembered, "saying that I did not want to carry out the landing operation." Truscott got on the phone and tried to give his reasons, but Patton would not listen. "Dammit," he interrupted, "that operation will go on." With that he hung up. Having no choice, Truscott ordered Bernard to prepare for the landing.

Exercised by the turmoil, Patton decided to visit Truscott. Arriving at Truscott's command post at 8:45 P.M., he bumped into navy Captain Davis, the chief of staff of Rear Admiral Lyal A. Davidson, who was to handle the ships involved in the landing. Because Bernard had started an hour late and could not land before 4 A.M., Davis, too, urged Patton to call off the project. Patton answered that it must go on even if the landing did not take place until 6 A.M.[68]

In their versions of their meeting Truscott and Patton agreed on several things. Both conceded that Patton arrived angry and threatened to remove Truscott. When Truscott replied just as firmly, Patton cooled down. At that moment Bradley called and asked if the attack would go on. Patton said it would. If it failed, he would take the blame. If it succeeded, Bradley and Truscott could have the credit. "I then told Truscott I had complete confidence in him," Patton recorded, "and, to show it, was going home to bed, and left. On the way back alone I worried a little, but feel it was right. I thought of Grant and Nelson and feel O.K. That is the value of history."[69]

This second landing, consisting of Bernard's 650 men reinforced by a company of medium tanks and a battery of self-propelled guns, proved disastrous. The battalion landed in the rear of the Germans and seized a steep hill. Unable to get up the hill, the tanks and self-propelled guns remained at the bottom near the main road. In severe fighting the Germans knocked them all out. Because of Patton's insistence on a rapid movement, the rest of the division "could not adhere to the usual method of outflanking from the high ground. It attacked straight ahead. . . . It was some 24 hours later that we were able to fight along the coast road to relieve them," Bradley bitterly observed. "This involved incurring much heavier casualties than we had expected, because the frontal assault met very stiff resistance and, of course, the casualties among the amphibious forces were very heavy. It was difficult to estimate additional casualties caused by launching this attack one day before it could be coordinated."[70]

On the morning after this second operation, an incident occurred that permanently soured Bradley. On the coast road Bradley bumped into Patton, who was accompanied by Senator Henry Cabot Lodge of Massachusetts. Patton was planning a third amphibious operation at Falcone, just ten miles west of Messina. "General Patton told me," Bradley wrote in 1947 in a memoir he marked "Secret," "that he wanted me to get to Messina as quickly as possible, that he was determined to get there ahead of the British. He told me that if I could get there one day earlier by losing additional men, I was to lose them. He said he had a bet with 'Monty' and wanted to win it."[71]

Bradley was shocked. "I tried to talk Patton out of this because I considered it unnecessary," he recalled, "as I expected my advance to reach this beach before the amphibious force could be landed."[72] This third landing force, not Bernard's but the 157th Regimental Combat Team of the 45th Division, might be detected by enemy submarines, now on the alert. "I told Patton that if he insisted on landing it," Bradley later said, "that the landing force should watch for our guides who would be on the beach with lanterns to meet them. Actually, this did happen. Units of the column going along the road met them on the beaches with lanterns. The whole effort accomplished nothing. Fortunately, they did not receive any attack by hostile vessels."[73]

VI

During the afternoon of the tenth, the day of the disagreement between Patton and Truscott, Georgie decided to stop at the 93d Evacuation Hospital, commanded by a neighbor of the Ayer family from Wenham, Massachusetts, Colonel Donald E. Currier. "Saw another alleged nervous patient—really a coward," he noted in his diary. "I told the doctor to return him to his company and he began to cry so I cursed him well and he shut up." Patton then made a strange statement: "I may have saved his soul if he had one." Continuing his inspection of the hospital, Patton considered himself well received. "All seemed glad to see me except one man with a head wound who kept shouting 'How about chow?' They said he would die."[74]

Within army medical circles the incident of August 3 had soon become known. Following a verbal request, the commander of the 15th Evacuation Hospital, the site of the incident, sent the details to his superior the next day. Visiting patients in the receiving tent, Patton had praised each one "by shaking his hand or patting his head and telling him what a fine job he had done in the war effort." When Patton asked one patient, "who was not visibly wounded," why he was being admitted, the man, Private Charles H. Kuhl of the First Division, answered that he just "couldn't take it" any longer. Patton then called the patient "a coward" and with "many profane adjectives ordered him out of the hospital. General Patton slapped his face with a glove, raised him to his feet by the collar of his shirt, and pushed him out of the Receiving Tent with a final 'kick in the rear.' " When leaving the hospital, Patton said that most of the patients who "just couldn't take it" were nothing but cowards.[75]

News of this first incident did not leak to the press. Patton was hardly as fortunate with the second. Noel Monks remembered how he and his American friend and colleague, H. R. Knickerbocker of the International News Service, inadvertently stumbled onto this second scene. He and Knickerbocker were driving in a jeep along the ocean highway toward the front lines, happy, as Monks put it, "to be able to breathe sea air instead of the volcanic dust we had been inhaling for weeks past." After passing several batteries of American Long Toms, 155-millimeter guns, blasting away at the enemy, they noticed a group of tents that served as a hospital. In front of them stood Patton's jeep and the vehicles of several reporters.

Monks had no interest in the visit of an American general to a hospital, but Knickerbocker insisted on stopping. "We were walking towards the main hospital tent," Monks related, "when General Patton emerged. He was shouting and gesticulating to a worried-looking Army doctor and several nurses. We distinctly heard him shout: 'There's no such thing as shell shock. It's an invention of the Jews.' General Patton, with a scowl at us, climbed into his jeep and drove off in a cloud of dust."

Being a British correspondent, Monks decided not to go into the hospital tent, but Knickerbocker did. "What he related to me," Monks observed, "could never have happened in the British Army, which made it seem all the more incredible to me that it had happened in America's more democratic Army. 'We are all going back to camp to have a meeting,' Nick said gravely when he had finished. 'No war for us to-day.'"

At the correspondents' camp, near an olive grove, about twenty newspapermen, "most of them big and famous names in American journalism," gathered to discuss the slapping. Being the only non-American, Monks offered to leave, but the others would not have it, so he stayed. At the outset the reporters decided that no one would send the story. One by one they spoke. All believed the soldier "cruelly wronged." The dean of reporters, Ernie Pyle, was almost in tears, Monks remembered, "as he said his piece." Finally the newspapermen decided to send Demaree Bess of the *Saturday Evening Post* to see Ike in Algiers. "He was to take with him a letter signed by us all, asking that General Patton be made to apologize to the soldier he had struck." If he did not, the letter went on, the reporters intended to "ask our offices to recall us, and give them our reason for doing so."[76]

Doing his homework for the proposed meeting with Ike, Bess drove over on the eleventh to the 93d Evacuation Hospital, then located near the north coast of Sicily about ten miles behind Truscott's front. Interviewing the main characters, he pieced together a story that was hardly pretty. At 1:30 P.M. on the tenth Patton had unexpectedly arrived at the hospital. Greeted by Major Charles H. Etter, the receiving officer, he was taken to the tent housing fifteen newly arrived patients. Patton went down the line, inquiring about each patient and commending each. When asked the routine question, Private Paul G. Bennett, the fourth patient, replied: "It's my nerves. I can hear the shells come over, but I can't hear them burst." Turning impatiently to Etter, Patton asked: "What's this man talking about? What's wrong with him, if anything?" Without waiting for a response from Etter, who was reaching for Bennett's chart, Patton screamed at the soldier: "You dirty no-good son-of-a-bitch! You cowardly bastard! You're a disgrace to the army and you're going right back to the front to fight, although that's too good for you. You ought to be lined up against a wall and shot, although that's too good for you. In fact, I ought to shoot you myself right now, God damn you!" Saying that, Patton reached for his pistol, pulled it out of its holster, and waved it in Bennett's face. Striking Bennett sharply across the face, Patton ordered Currier, who had heard the commotion and entered the tent: "I want you to get that man out of here right away. I won't have these other brave boys seeing such a bastard babied."

Patton was about to leave when he noticed Bennett sitting on his cot crying. Rushing back, he hit Bennett "with such force that his helmet was knocked off and rolled outside the tent." By this time nurses and orderlies from other tents, hearing the uproar, had come in to see what was going on. They witnessed "this second blow."

Continuing his inspection with Colonel Currier, Patton saw several patients in another tent. "I can't help it," he told Currier, "but it breaks me down to see you brave boys." Visiting a third tent, he screamed: "it makes my blood boil to think of a yellow bastard being babied." Leaving the hospital, Patton said to Currier: "I meant what I said about getting that coward out of here. I won't have these cowardly bastards hanging around our hospitals. We'll probably have to shoot them sometime any day, or we'll raise a breed of morons."

Unlike Patton, Bess looked into Bennett's record. The slapped man had enlisted, not been drafted, into the army and had served for four years, participating in the Tunisian and Sicilian campaigns. The hospital psychiatrist had determined that he was unfit for duty in his current state. Bess referred anyone who doubted the accuracy of his report to three other correspondents who had investigated the incident: Merrill "Red" Mueller of the National Broadcasting Company; John Daly of the Columbia Broadcasting System; and Al Newman of *Newsweek*.[77]

In Algiers, Ike learned of the Kuhl and Bennett slappings on or about August 13. To ascertain what had happened, he sent to Sicily one of his staff physicians, Lieutenant Colonel Perrin H. Long, who in his report of August 16 substantiated what Bess subsequently submitted to Ike. Long also learned that Kuhl had twice before been admitted to the hospital and that this third time physicians found him to be suffering from dysentery and malaria. Long similarly sympathized with Bennett, who had served four years in the Regular Army. Suffering from insomnia since his best friend had been wounded, Bennett had begged his medical officer to allow him to remain with his unit, but the physician had ordered him hospitalized. Long concluded with a condemnation of

Patton: "The deleterious effects of such incidents upon the wellbeing of patients, upon the professional morale of hospital staffs and upon the relationship of patient to physician are incalculable."[78]

With his troops approaching Messina, Patton forgot the slappings, ignoring them in his diary entries. At ten o'clock on the night of the sixteenth, lead elements of Truscott's division entered Messina. Truscott's field artillery placed a Long Tom on the heights overlooking the city, and at 11:33 P.M. lobbed the first of one hundred shells across the Straits of Messina and onto the European mainland.

Keyes had ordered Truscott, occupying the heights, to await Patton before entering Messina. At about 10 A.M. on the seventeenth Patton arrived with what Truscott called "his characteristic flurry," greeting Truscott with the words: "What in hell are you all standing around for?" About a half hour later Patton, Gay, Lucas, and Truscott—Bradley was absent—started downhill on the road toward Messina, badly battered by American artillery. Gay remembered that as the caravan moved forward an Italian woman dressed in a Red Cross uniform ran out onto the road and tried to stop Patton's car. "He did not stop—but immediately thereafter enemy shells hit the road. I wonder how she knew this was going to happen. I am sure she was trying to protect us."[79]

In Messina, Patton found three tanks and a few men from the British 4th Armoured Division. Sent by Montgomery on his own end run to get into the city before the Americans arrived, they had landed from an LCT, a landing craft for tanks, about fifteen miles south of Messina, and dashed northward, only to find that the Americans had beaten them by ten hours. In his diary Patton related that in Messina he had Truscott "do the honors," but Truscott disagreed, saying that Patton stayed only long enough "to receive the formal surrender from the civil and military officials in the square and for a few photographs."[80]

Eisenhower's emissaries, Bedell Smith and Brigadier General Lyman Lemnitzer, arrived too late to witness the ceremony. Gay, however, recorded in longhand what happened when Patton's entourage met Smith, Lemnitzer, and Gay's aide, George Murnane.

On the way back from Messina—just a short way beyond the crest of the hill was a C & R car parked along the side of the road. In front of the car stood Lieut George Murnane—looking utterly disgusted, in the car sat a Brig General now a 4 star general [Lemnitzer]—down the embankment crouched a high ranking staff officer—from Gen Eisenhower's HQ's—hiding or seeking protection from Artillery fire—actually our own not enemy. I have never seen Patton so completely abashed, ashamed of an American.[81]

Such behavior as that of Smith led combat officers like Patton and Wood to rail against those who commanded but had never been under fire.

Amid the congratulations over pushing the Axis forces out of Sicily, the Germans successfully withdrew their troops and equipment across the Straits of Messina and onto the Italian mainland. In view of the Allied air supremacy, Lieutenant-General John T. Crocker, who had commanded the British IX Corps in Tunisia and had publicly criticized Ryder and his division, called the German performance "most remarkable."[82]

German reports, however, indicated that Allied bumbling made possible the escape. During the night of August 11–12, noted Field Marshal Albert Kesselring, who commanded the German army in Italy, Allied planes attacked the Messina Straits in such force that they "practically paralyzed the ferry traffic." The Germans, who attempted to cross from such Sicilian stations as Faro, Villa San Giovanni, and Gazirri, were heavily strafed, and several German generals reported the suspension of the ferrying across the river. But for some unknown reason Allied air action ceased during daylight. Traffic proceeded briskly after the night's suspension, and huge numbers of men and much equipment crossed. The vessels consisted of six ferry barges, fourteen landing craft, and eleven Siebel ferries—ten-ton, flat-bottomed troop and supply carriers. That day the Germans brought out of Sicily 950 vehicles, 103 tons of ammunition, and 1,370 tons of equipment. The following nights and days brought forth the same scenario: heavy night attacks followed by daytime lulls. On the thirteenth of August alone the Germans evacuated 14,916 men, twenty-one tanks, and twenty-two assault guns. In all, using four routes in an operation that worked smoothly, the Germans ferried across the straits approximately fifty-three thousand troops.[83]

During the campaign the Seventh Army captured numerous prisoners. The official historians of the campaign put the figure at 122,204, of whom 118,700 were Italians. About seventy-five thousand were taken to North Africa, and about thirty-four thousand were Sicilians who were granted paroles on the island.[84]

Patton can hardly be blamed for the vast numbers of Germans who escaped, but Bradley held him responsible for some of them. By ordering Truscott to remain in the hills outside Messina until he arrived, Patton had allowed the last of the Germans to cross the straits. "I was so angry at Patton's megalomania," Bradley wrote, "that I was half tempted to enter the city myself and greet him on a street corner when he arrived."

Even though Allied casualties totaled 22,811, of whom 5,532 were killed, Bradley considered the campaign immeasurably valuable. Four divisions, the 3d, 45th, 82d Airborne, and 2d Armored, had become hardened to combat. So, too, had the Ranger battalions. And Patton, Bradley, Truscott, Middleton, Eddy, Gaffey, Huebner, Keyes, and others "had gained invaluable experience in battlefield management."[85]

The day after entering Messina, Patton summarized things for Bea. Ignoring the five massacres, the three semi-botched end runs, and the two slappings, about all of which Bea knew nothing, he considered Sicily "a perfect campaign. . . . Few people especially generals have no regrets but in this case I have none. Had I to do it over again I would not change a thing."[86] Patton hardly realized it, but the known mistakes of this "perfect campaign" would haunt him for the next year.

VII

At the very time Messina fell Quentin Reynolds "found Palermo buzzing" about the slappings. When his friend Terry Allen received orders to report to Eisenhower in Algiers, Reynolds hitched a ride with him and invited Demaree Bess and Red Mueller to come along.

In Algiers Reynolds telephoned Butcher for an appointment with Ike. "I know what you're coming to see him about," Butcher replied. "The general hasn't slept for two nights worrying about it." At the meeting Ike listened to Mueller and Bess, then said: "You men have got yourselves good stories, and as you know, there's no question of censorship involved." Bess answered that the three were Americans first and journalists second. They did not wish to break the story. "Every mother would figure her son's next," he explained. Mueller then said they "were not only going to kill the story but deny it if any of the correspondents broke it." Only then did Ike reveal that British newsmen also knew of the slappings and had decided against revealing the story. If it were printed, Ike said, "Georgie, the best armor man we've got, would be destroyed." Without pressure from Ike and his press attaché, Brigadier General Robert A. McClure, the sixty American and British newsmen in Algiers and Sicily kept the story secret.[87]

Eisenhower, however, was determined to discipline Patton. For several days he tried to figure out what to do. Citing history, he told Butcher that great generals, in their zeal to win battles, often went crazy on the battlefield. Patton was probably the most successful Allied commander. Striking a soldier was a high offense. If Ike decided on a court-martial, Patton would have to be reduced to his permanent rank, for the North African Theater of Operations did not contain enough high-ranking officers to make up the board. If tried and convicted, Patton would be sent home in disgrace, something Ike wished to avoid.[88]

Rather than a court-martial, Ike decided on disciplinary measures. On the seventeenth he sent Brigadier General Frederick A. Blessé, the chief surgeon of the Allied Forces Headquarters, to Sicily with a letter ordering Patton to apologize to the individuals and units involved in the slappings. Patton had probably forgotten the episodes when, after lunch on August 20, General Blessé "brought me a very nasty letter from Ike. Evidently I acted precipitantly and on insignificant knowledge," he wrote in longhand in his diary. Patton then repeated his reason for doing what he had done: "My motive was correct, as I was trying to restore the men's souls by making them mad with me. I shall make what amends I can. . . . I regret the incident as I hate to make Ike mad when it is my earnest study to please him. . . . I feel very low."[89]

That evening Lucas, also sent by Ike, arrived in Sicily. "Ike wants Lucas to tell Geo Patton he must stop wearing his guns and acting like a mad man," Ev Hughes recorded, "or he is doomed. Ike says that correspondents have some stories about Geo they are dying to tell."[90]

By now Patton was desperate. Three days after the fall of Messina, the comedian Bob Hope arrived in Sicily with three other performers and drove to Palermo for a show before sixteen thousand soldiers in the soccer field. While Frances Langford sang, Patton's aide, presumably Codman, came to invite them to dinner at the king's palace in Palermo.

"Look," the aide said, "General Patton wants you for dinner and if you don't go it's my ass and yours too."

Hope and his company obeyed the decree. After dinner, which the four entertainers ate at a little table, they put on a brief show for Patton. They then took pictures with the general. Hope later recorded what happened when he said they had better leave.

> And he said, "I want to speak to you," and he took me over in the corner and put his arm around me and said, "You know you can do a lot for me when you get back home."
>
> And here was our hero saying this to me and I looked up at him and said, "What do you mean?"
>
> And he said, "I want you to tell the people that I love my men. See."
>
> I looked at this guy and I thought he was suffering from some kind of battle fatigue. And I said, "You're the biggest general in our country. You're in the headlines all the time . . . You don't have to worry about anything."
>
> He said, "No, I want you to go on radio when you get back. I want the people to know that I love my men."

When Hope and his fellow entertainers returned to the Excelsior Hotel in Palermo, Ernie Pyle awaited them. Hope told him they had just come from the king's palace, and Pyle answered: "How did you like that son of a bitch." Hope did not know what he meant. "And he said, 'Didn't you hear about it?' and he told us all about Patton slapping a kid in the hospital."[91]

Patton's version of his apology, on August 21, to Private Paul G. Bennett showed that he still believed he had acted correctly. Georgie "explained to him that I had cussed him out in the hope of restoring his manhood, that I was sorry, and that if he cared, I would like to shake hands with him. We shook." General John A. Crane, who commanded Bennett's regiment, "told me later that this Bennett was a skulker and had got to the hospital by falsely representing his condition."[92]

But Lieutenant Colonel Joseph R. Couch, who commanded the 1st Battalion of the 17th Field Artillery and knew Bennett as "a brave and dedicated man," saw things differently. Told by the unit chaplain that Patton had slapped Bennett, a Regular Army soldier who had contracted malaria in Sicily, without asking physicians why he was in the hospital, Couch wanted to do something about it. But his superior, a full colonel, advised him not to, for Patton was a lieutenant general capable of ruining his career.

Couch remembered vividly the morning of Patton's conference with Bennett. A full colonel in the well-pressed uniform of a staff officer pulled up to battalion headquarters and "barked" that Patton wanted to see Bennett. "Bennett was hustled off with scarcely time to button his shirt," Couch related. "On his face was the look of a man en route to the gallows." Returning that evening, Bennett reported that Patton had apologized to him.[93]

On that same day Ike, shielding his old friend, decided to handle the Patton matter himself, rather than send the papers to Marshall in Washington. In his diary Hughes noted: "Ike seals and files the Patton report against my advice to send it to the War Department."[94]

The next day Patton "had in all the doctors and nurses and enlisted men who witnessed the affair with the skulkers. I told them about my friend in the last war who shirked, was let get by with it, and eventually killed himself. I told them that I had taken the action I had, to correct such a future tragedy."[95]

Currier for one remained unimpressed. He had, he informed Eisenhower, known the Pattons before the war, having lived in Wenham, two miles from the Patton house in South Hamilton. He used to shop in the same stores as Patton and knew most of the Ayer family, also residents of Wenham.

With so many witnesses, Currier went on, word of the second slapping, that involving Bennett, spread rapidly. The morning after the episode Bess, Newman, and Mueller arrived looking for details. "They already knew enough to make it silly for me to be coy about it," Currier told Ike, "so after extracting a promise from them to keep my name out of any publicity, they got the story."

Currier scoffed at the meeting of August 22. "I would particularly enjoy telling you about the so-called apology," he wrote. "It really wasn't an apology at all, just an abortive attempt to justify what he had done. Anyway it was pure, unadulterated ham, and it was terribly funny. At one point the temptation to laugh was almost too much for us. Fortunately we managed to keep a straight face."[96]

For the next nine days Patton continued to spend much of his time supposedly complying with Ike's instructions. On the twenty-third he called in Kuhl and ended up shaking hands with him. And between August 24 and August 30 he visited each of his divisions, delivering to the officers, noncommissioned officers, and as many enlisted men as could be assembled a speech that followed a set pattern. First, he spoke of the successes in Sicily, attributing them "to continued offensive—day and night, relentless and unceasing—and to the fact that we used maneuver. We held the enemy by the nose and kicked him in the pants. We never, except in the initial landing, attacked head on."

Toward the end of his talk Patton referred obtusely to some unspecified misdeed. He had, he conceded, been "guilty" of criticizing too much and of talking too loudly. "For every man I have criticized in this Army, I have probably stopped, talked to, and complimented a thousand, but people are more prone to remember ill usage than to recall compliments; therefore, I want you officers and men who are here to explain to the other soldiers, who think perhaps that I am too hard, my motives and to express to them my sincere regrets."[97] In none of his appearances did he directly refer to the controversial acts.

The response to Patton's talks varied with each storyteller. Years later General Theodore J. Conway, then a major, described how the men of his unit, the 60th Infantry of the 9th Division, cheered so loudly that Patton could not address them. "He was our hero," Conway related. "We were on his side. We knew the problem. We knew what he had done and why he had done it."[98]

Monks, however, disagreed sharply with those who said the soldiers supported Patton. Word of the second slapping, and of Patton's gratuitous remark about Jews, had spread throughout the American army. "It threw the troops into a grave state of bewilderment," Monks observed. "Blood-and-Guts Patton was their hero, yet here he was hitting a sick G.I. and shouting anti-Jewish slogans in the best Hitler tradition. 'What are we fighting this god-damned war for anyhow?' they asked."[99]

Monks, who covered all the great wars of the 1930s, 1940s, and 1950s, never understood why Patton did what he did. The campaign was winding down. Patton encountered no shortage of troops at the front. "A British general would have been court-martialled and probably dismissed from the service. . . . In the intervening years," Monks wrote in 1955,

I have discussed the Patton incident with many American generals, some of whom were fellow West Pointers, but I have never been offered a reasonable explanation as to his conduct that hot August day in Sicily. . . .

Anyhow, the incident put a blight on our coverage of the last days of the Sicily campaign. We weren't popular with the generals, who thought we'd acted in a high-handed manner, and we weren't popular with the G.I.s for not writing the story. They thought we were protecting the "brass."[100]

Visiting Patton in Palermo, Hughes tried to assist him, but like Monks he found Patton's explanation ridiculous. "Helped Geo write his reply to letter Ike sent him cussing Geo out for maltreating EM," Hughes observed on August 27, the day he arrived. "I insisted that Geo quit saying that he had done no wrong and that he had saved the immortal souls of the EM."[101]

To Bea, Patton called Hughes "a swell friend," but he disregarded his advice. In his letter to Eisenhower, dated August 29, he explained in full his oft-repeated "saving souls" statement:

In World War I, I had a dear friend and former schoolmate who lost his nerve in an exactly analogous manner, and who, after years of mental anguish, committed suicide. Both my friend and the medical men with whom I discussed his case assured me that had he been roundly checked at the time of his first behavior, he would have been restored to a normal state.

Naturally, this memory activated me when I very aptly tried to apply the remedies suggested. After each incident I stated to officers with me that I felt I had probably saved an immortal soul.[102]

On the surface Eisenhower seemed to care little about the slappings and about Patton's response to his letter. On the twenty-ninth Patton, Bradley, Hughes, Keyes, Truscott, and Gay went to Montgomery's headquarters at Taormina, on the east coast of Sicily. There Ike decorated Montgomery "with the Big cross of the Legion of Merit." Friendly and "most effusive," Ike told the assembled generals that the Seventh Army would probably remain in Sicily for two or three more weeks.

After that, preparing for the invasion of France, seven divisions, four American and three British, would be transferred to Great Britain. Eisenhower praised the feeling of cooperation that existed between the Americans and British and hoped it would continue.

When Patton handed Eisenhower the letter explaining the slappings, Ike, seemingly indifferent to it all, "just put it in his pocket. I had a letter from Lucas," Patton recorded, "saying that Ike had written General Marshall a glowing account of me. Well, that was a near thing but I feel much better."[103]

Engulfed in self-deception, Patton soon faced a furious Eisenhower. At lunch on the second of September a morose Patton got "tight" and spilled out to Hughes the details of the verbal thrashing Ike had given him. "Ike has ordered him to apologize to Montgomery for losing his temper," Hughes recorded in his diary. "Ike says that Geo. has ruined Monty's career by getting to Messina first; that Ike is going to send an IG to Sicily to ask soldiers what they think about their Army commander." As Eisenhower's deputy, Hughes, friend of Patton that he was, had no choice but "to investigate the Patton incident." Accordingly, he was sending to Sicily Herbert Slayden "Bertie" Clarkson, the naval academy graduate who was now Ike's inspector general.[104]

On the very day Patton was telling his troubles to Hughes, Allied headquarters in North Africa buzzed with stories about Patton. Returning from America, Edward Kennedy, the Associated Press bureau chief in Algiers, reported hearing about Patton's misdeeds in Marrakech while changing planes. Still hoping to handle things quietly, Eisenhower "was amazed to learn how the stories are snowballing towards home." He thought that Patton might ease things by holding a press conference to explain what had happened and how he had apologized, an idea Butcher thought too precipitous. To Butcher, Ike reiterated his determination to have his inspector general get the real story of Patton in Sicily.

Unfortunately the scandals detracted from the important business at hand. At four-thirty on the morning of the third, Montgomery was scheduled to land British and Canadian troops on the Italian mainland. At their recent meeting he had taken Eisenhower and Butcher to Messina, where, looking across the straits, he described how, with the entire British army, he had been pushed off the continent at Dunkirk.

Now, on the fourth anniversary of the British declaration of war against Germany, he was returning to the European mainland.[105]

An entry in the diary of Bradley's aide, Chester B. Hansen, indicated what Patton's army thought of him. On September 4 he wrote:

> Saw the Time article that spoke of the entry into Palermo as "the greatest blitz in history." Patton gets palm on DSC for work on roads. Stiller gets silver star for some reason he can't explain. Later citation explains that he shot down an airplane with 50 caliber. Keyes gets DSM for work in campaign and silver star for flying about in cub. Talk of Army is now smoldering and vicious. Even the nurses in for dinner are swapping stories on Patton—all of them bad. Klotz from 1st tells us [of] Patton's visit to that Division and the stoney silence that greeted him. Profanity and vulgarity. Men don't like it. Officers detest it. Hospital story resulted in rumor that General Patton would be courts martialed. Officers ask us. Glad above everything else to get out from under [Patton's] Army as is everyone else. They all ask why aren't people wise to the green hornet—newspaper men are. They roundly dislike him.[106]

VIII

For the Allies the Sicilian campaign had enormous pluses. It gave them control of the Mediterranean and brought about the downfall of the Italian dictator Benito Mussolini. The Sicilian operation also gave the American combat forces needed experience. And, as Admiral Conolly pointed out, the Allies learned much about amphibious invasions and the use of naval artillery against ground forces.

Sharing the military glory and the learning experience, Patton stumbled regrettably. His speeches and orders, meant to inspire soldiers, inspired instead a series of atrocities. In the irony of the campaign, Patton ran into trouble not because of the killings but because of two slappings that dwarf when compared with the atrocities. If known by Marshall and Eisenhower, the Canicatti affair alone probably would have led to the relief of Patton, Truscott, and Carleton.

Of what earthly value is uncovering and writing about such events sixty years after they occurred? The twentieth century might well be labeled the century of bold talk leading to holocausts and ethnic cleansings. The more such tragedies are discussed, perhaps the rarer they will become.

Eleven

"LOWER THAN WHALE TRACKS"

I

On April 23, 1944, eight months after the capture of Sicily, John P. Marquand, the Pulitzer Prize–winning novelist, essayist, and playwright, opened his copies of New York and Washington newspapers and faced a picture of George Patton, then training troops in England. In his most creative prose he described what he saw.

There he was, in a uniform which was certainly not regulation. There he was, looking more like a polo player than a General. He was wearing an army steel helmet. On the front of the helmet were three stars denoting his rank—an invention, I believe, which was the General's own. He was wearing something which looked like a monkey or a mess-jacket. He was wearing circular, elaborate riding britches that only the best Bond Street tailor could possibly have created, and high riding boots that fitted his symmetrical calves to absolute perfection, and, even in that dingy photograph, it was obvious that his orderly had sat up all night to give those boots the hand-polished lustre of a Steinway piano.

It was certainly General George Patton, Jr., back in London, fresh from the military dog-house, and you could see, by God, that the General was raring to go, and that he was going to show Ike Eisenhower and Omar Bradley, and every British so-and-so (and General Montgomery in particular) that he knew how to crack the German wall. You could almost hear him admitting in his high, raucous voice, that God damn it he was the best God-damned fighting General in the whole U.S. Army, and U.S. troops were the best God-damned troops in the world.[1]

The photograph inspired Marquand to record the details of his meetings with Patton just after Sicily's fall. During the summer of 1943 the War Department sent Marquand, who had been an artillery officer during the First World War, and Brigadier General James S. Simmons, the former dean of the Harvard School of Public Health, on a tour of battle areas to study biological warfare. Arriving in Algiers on September 1, Marquand was moping around when, on the fourth, he bumped into his Harvard classmate, Lieutenant Colonel Charles Codman, in the lobby of the Hotel Aletti. Codman, who had been a wine buyer for the S. S. Pierce company in Boston, proudly wore the ribbon of the French Legion of Honor, but he "looked somewhat drawn and tired." Told that Marquand was traveling with a brigadier general from the Medical Corps, Codman responded: "I know everything about generals, all my life is spent bringing them drinks and pocket handkerchiefs. It's a very funny thing to see a lot of generals in a room all together. Two-star generals laugh at three-star generals' jokes and if a four-star general says anything amusing everyone rolls on the floor. You have to learn how to do it."

Codman's mission had nothing to do with battles and constituted a prime example of why he hated being an aide. Patton had sent Codman, an aviator in World War I, to Algiers to get a hundred cases of whiskey, Patton's reward for the victorious officers of the Seventh Army. Facing a deadline—Patton had ordered that the liquor had to be aboard his plane by four the next morning—Codman had no idea where to look for it. Luckily General Simmons had gone to Casablanca for three days, leaving his car for Marquand, who spent the afternoon driving his friend about searching not for an enemy but for whiskey.

During the drive Codman told of his early experiences with Patton. He first met the famous general during the siege of Casablanca and was added to his staff because of his familiarity with the French army, the French language, and liquor. Codman conceded that Patton had handled the French surrender in Morocco brilliantly. If the surrender was not signed by eleven in the evening, the Americans were to attack Casablanca by land, sea, and air. "Tell these French officers we are all gentlemen here," Patton had notified his subordinates. "Just tell them I want their troops to stay in quarters and let it go at that." By not demanding anything specific, Patton settled matters. The terms were signed at 10:55 P.M.[2]

"The General is really very good," Codman conceded, "but it's very hard working for three and four-star generals, because they want everything done in a hurry—whether it is impossible or not. For example, the General doesn't realize how much whiskey weighs. He doesn't know that his plane won't carry a hundred cases, but he would be very angry if I were to tell him. The only thing is to get another plane from somewhere or possibly two planes and God knows how I'm going to do it."

Codman warned his friend to "call me first when you get to Palermo." Hap Gay, Patton's chief of staff, was "very disagreeable." A Midwesterner, he distrusted "the morals of anyone who speaks with a broad 'A.'" Codman had no use either for Patton's other aide, Captain Alex Stiller, a rough-hewn First World War sergeant from Texas. "He is simpleminded and carries two guns in shoulder holsters. The General keeps him in case he wants a trigger-man." With that Codman disappeared.[3]

Two days later, on the sixth, Marquand and Simmons flew from Algiers to Palermo. Driving in from the airport, Marquand observed the condition of the city, which he had visited in 1921. Except for the waterfront, which was "a shambles of sunken ships and rubble," Palermo was much as he remembered it, "ornate, baroque buildings simmering in the sun." Patton's soldiers bore his disciplinary trademarks. Despite the oppressive heat they "were very neat—all in woolen with sleeves rolled down."[4]

Arriving with Codman at the palace where the king used to stay when visiting Sicily, the visitors received no greeting. Gruff, unfriendly, and anything but happy, Gay made them sit about for half an hour. Finally he announced that Patton was ready. Codman tapped on the white folding doors that separated the chief of staff from the main room. "What the hell is it now?" someone inside barked. The door was opened and the visitors were ushered into the state apartment, a long room with crystal chandeliers, damask-covered gold chairs, and a rosewood desk, on which rested Patton's revolvers and steel helmet. As Simmons and Marquand entered, Patton rose and shook hands with them. His appearance struck Marquand: the neatness of the clothes; the once-sandy hair now white and closely cropped; the lean, freckled face; the

slate-colored blue eyes that rested under sandy eyelashes; and the thin
lips. "Hell," Patton greeted them,

> sit down. You know what's happened to me now? I've just had my
> ears pinned back. All they do is pin my ears back. You know what
> they've pinned them back for? It seems I haven't given the Italian
> prisoners enough latrines. God damn it, they didn't know what a
> latrine was until I built one for them. Will you join me at dinner
> tonight? Half past seven. Have them called for, Colonel and see
> that they have decent rooms and a bath at the hotel.

Patton then walked the visitors to the door. Having seen the way
Patton treated them, Gay was beaming. "Well, well," he said gently,
"did you have a comfortable trip? Just let me know if you're not comfortable at the hotel. And, Colonel," he said to Codman, "see that they
have a car. Let them have my car."[5]

That evening before dinner Patton and his guests gathered in the
king's intimate reception room, "a highly over-decorated red plush
apartment with a sofa and not enough chairs. There were a great many
officers," Marquand related, "and the sight of them made me feel as one
does in those dreams where one discovers oneself walking naked in the
street." Marquand had bought officer's khaki pants and shirt, but he
had forgotten to buy a tie. A grease-spotted gray felt hat and tennis
shoes completed his outfit. "My appearance had already disturbed the
military police in Palermo," Marquand observed, "and I could see it also
disturbed the great brains of the Seventh Army. There were a great
many generals, one-star and two-stars, with several colonels behind
them." Each general had brought aides. "These all stood in a timid
flock." Ill-dressed as Marquand was, Patton, knowing his importance,
paid special attention to him. "Do you like Irish whiskey?" he asked.
After Marquand said he did, Patton added: "Well, I don't. The damn
stuff makes me sick, but I won two cases of it from the British. They bet
we wouldn't get into San Stefano ahead of them. Drink all the damn
stuff you can."[6]

Set up to accommodate the army's caste system, the king's dining
room contained two tables, a large one for the generals and a side one
for the colonels. Marquand moved toward the side table, but Gay
stopped him and directed him to Patton's table. "At dinner the generals

talked very carefully according to rank and laughed at jokes according to rank," Marquand related. "We ate off the King's china and used the King's silver. We had clear soup, steak, salad and ice cream. When General Patton pushed back his chair, we left the room according to rank. I lingered behind to try to stay with the aides, but the Chief of Staff pushed me gently."[7]

Back in the king's intimate apartment, the generals took all the available chairs. Codman passed out cigars, and Stiller, "the Texas gunman," came around with liqueurs. The colonels "stood stiffly against the wall," Marquand recorded. "I stood with them until General Patton saw me. 'No, No,' he said, 'God damn it, come over here. Get him a chair. I want to talk to you about the war.'" Patton then asked what the American newspapers had said about the Sicilian campaign, just ended, and Marquand answered that he gathered that the British had faced the "real opposition around Catania," while the Americans had engaged disaffected Italian troops. "God damn it," Patton responded. "What the hell is the matter with them in the States? Don't they know we've got the best God-damned army in the world? Don't they know we licked the pants off the Herman Goering Division? Italians, hell! I'll tell you who we had in front of us." His voice filled with emotion, Patton began ticking off the German units on his fingers. "And most of them have been sent to hell. We've got the best God-damned army in the world, and the people at home don't know it. . . . God-damn it," Patton went on, "you can see what we were up against on the way to Messina. Codman. Where's Codman? Get four cub planes tomorrow morning and take this party up the line towards Messina. Have them met and take them inland. I'll tell you why we moved and the British didn't," Patton advised. "We fought them day and night and hit them on the flank. All the British know is artillery preparation and frontal attack and that's why they stopped at Catania. This is a war of movement. This is a damn fine war." His voice again choked as he added: "I hope to God I get killed up front somewhere. This is a damn fine war."[8]

Patton then discoursed on leadership. "Every officer has got to inspire hero-worship. God-damn it," he said of the troops, "they've got to love their officers." Calling out, he asked: "Codman, do you remember when I got emotional in front of Troina? . . . Sometimes, I get God-damned emotional. I get choked up inside and by God I want to cry. They said the road was mined in front of Troina and they were hanging around

there. I got so damned emotional that I drove the car right over it."
Codman attested to the fact. "I don't give a damn," the General said,
"who the man is. He can be a nigger or a Jew, but if he has the stuff and
does his duty, he can have anything I've got. By God! I love him. You've
got to love them. You've got to be proud of them. You've got to give
them loyalty when they give you loyalty." With that the evening
ended.[9]

On September 9, just after the Allies signed an armistice with the
Italian government but not with the Germans, Marquand and Simmons visited Patton again. Sitting behind his rosewood desk, a pile of
letters in front of him, Patton reflected his anxiety about the slapping
incidents, about which Marquand knew nothing. "It's a funny thing
that loyalty is the cheapest thing in the world," he said. "It's a part of
duty when it comes from the bottom up, but loyalty is the rarest thing
in the world coming from the top down." He had written numerous
notes thanking the men under him. "But," he added, "have I ever got a
letter of thanks? Not a God-damned letter. I only get my ears pinned
back by some little squirt from the Inspector General's office." Patton
paused and smiled. "I just had my ears pinned back again yesterday. It
seems that I'm ever-critical of the British. If I said anything last night
forget it."

Assessing Patton, Marquand was hardly flattering. "I believe I have
given a fairly accurate transcription of General Patton's speech and
General Patton's language. I hope it combines to give an impression of
what he was like—a tactless, high-strung, profane officer with a one-
cell, juvenile mind."[10]

The author saw the general once more in Palermo, but the two did
not speak. Marquand spotted Patton's car, a huge red flag with three
stars attached to its radiator, rolling down a street. "In fact," Marquand
commented, "you had an impression that the whole automobile was
made of flags." On this stifling day two orderlies dressed in wool and
wearing steel helmets sat on the front seat next to the driver. Each carried a Garand rifle at the ready. In the Seventh Army every man wore
wool, the battle uniform, no matter what the temperature. Each member of Patton's army wore his steel helmet and carried a full canteen of
water, because, Marquand observed, "those were the General's orders
and those orders set the Seventh apart from other troops." In the rear
seat of the car Patton "sat staring straight ahead of him like Washington

crossing the Delaware. . . . The General sat looking straight ahead," Marquand surmised, "but undoubtedly loved it. He had a sentimental streak. He wanted his men to admire him as much as he admired himself. And furthermore, God damn it, he wanted to be loved!"

Not wishing to injure Codman, Marquand always refused to publish his essay on Patton, which he called "The General." For Codman's book on Patton, entitled *Drive,* published posthumously in 1957, he wrote a saccharine introduction that hid his true feelings. Marquand omitted "one of Charley's main reasons for coming to Algiers, namely to buy liquor for General Patton to present to the officers of the Seventh Army." He also left out "the paragraph about general officers laughing according to rank at other officers' jokes." To his editor at Little, Brown, who wanted to publish the essay, he wrote: "I do not want to print it under any circumstances. It is too personal and too careless and makes my friend Charlie Codman say a lot of things he would not want to say in print."[11]

At the very moment Marquand left Sicily, Carter revealed another way Patton seemed to torment Codman, who had complained to his wife about Sicily's strong sun. "Charley told me yesterday that Theo had sent him a sun-helmet for his threatened sun-stroke," Carter wrote home. "The day it arrived Georgie announced at dinner about some officer, 'He's an S.O.B. in every way, but the worst thing he does is to wear an Elephant Hat!' Charley quickly packed his away in his trunk!"[12]

II

On September 6, the day Marquand and Simmons arrived at Palermo, Patton received two discouraging radio messages. The first indicated that he was to receive no additional men or spare parts, for his army was to be withdrawn from Sicily. "The second one ruined me," Patton lamented. Bradley was to be pushed over him and would, after returning home to meet the president, go to the United Kingdom to activate the First Army. Bolero, the buildup of men and materials in preparation for the invasion of France, would involve "green troops trained in the US and UK," rather than Patton's veterans of North Africa and Sicily. "It is heartbreaking. The only time I have felt worse was the night of

December 9th when Clark got the 5th Army for losing his pants. I feel like death but will survive—I always have." Calling in the heads of his staff sections, Patton read the telegrams to them and offered to help them find other jobs, if they so wished. But the members of the staff adored Patton, who told Bea: "They stuck like limpets."[13]

Patton had reason to question the handling of the Italian invasion. Informing the troops that the Italian government had signed an armistice was, Patton believed, an enormous mistake. "Should they get resistance instead of friendship" while at Salerno, "it would have a very bad effect."[14]

Now covering the American landing at Salerno for the *London Daily Mail,* Monks went even further in denouncing Eisenhower and Clark. In 1955 he wrote:

> I can run a temperature even now, twelve years after, when I think of the crass stupidity of announcing Italy's surrender to our troops a few hours before they hit the beaches. I call it the greatest psychological blunder of the war, a cruel, heartless thing to do to the troops who'd resigned themselves to a battle to the death to establish a bridgehead. I know there were many Texans—and British— who died that September day in 1943 thinking they'd been told a lie. What else could the poor chaps think when, a few days after hearing General Eisenhower's voice say: "Italy has surrendered," they ran slap into the reception the Germans had prepared for them on Salerno's bloody beaches?

Consisting of four divisions and seventy-five thousand men, the Fifth Army, "scantily equipped," faced in Italy a German force of nineteen divisions and three hundred thousand men. By the third day of the invasion empty transports, instead of returning to Algiers for more men and equipment, stood by to evacuate the Allied troops.[15]

On the fourteenth, when Patton and Keyes went to the docks to see off Truscott, who was taking his division to Italy, Patton considered the situation grave. "I told him to see whether it is possible to shorten the front," he wrote, "use the 10th Corps to hold and attack with the Americans. We must attack or it will become a second Gallipoli. Two marines who were here yesterday told me that on D-Day the LST they were in was under machine gun fire while beached to unload. They also said that a British Brigade were in bivouac on the beach at dusk at D-Day. Will they never learn——?"[16]

Reflecting on the reason the Salerno operation immediately bogged down, Liddell Hart came to the same conclusion as Patton. Even though, at this point, he had never met Patton, he reasoned that too few Allied generals resembled the American tank expert.

> The root of the trouble is that all our higher leaders, even the best of them, were not only brought up on the slow-motion methods of 1914–1918, but had to go on practising them for the next twenty years. The few men who were emancipated from these habits of deliberation, by serving with our experimental mechanized forces, have never been allowed a chance to command in the field. That is an ironical aspect of this mechanized war.

In his own army Liddell Hart found but one tank commander who possessed Patton's imagination and boldness, Brigadier John Alan Lyde Caunter, and his story showed the narrow view held by the British Imperial Staff. Put in charge of the 7th Armoured Division, the famous "Desert Rats," during the Egyptian campaign because its commander had developed an abscess on the tongue, Caunter engineered in February 1941 a brilliant tank victory at Beda Fomm in Libya, for which his absent superior was knighted. To rid themselves of Caunter, the British commanders shipped him to India. "The subsequent campaigns have seen no such dashing exploits in the handling of armoured forces," Liddell Hart lamented, "despite the superiority of means that we have increasingly enjoyed."[17]

III

Visitors to Patton's headquarters found him depressed and aged. Illustrating that Patton's anti-Jewish outbursts came and went, Al Jolson, whose singing often reflected his heritage, entertained Patton in mid-September and momentarily cheered him, promising to call Bea as soon as he got home. But Jack Benny, the radio comedian, found Patton to be "a very emotional character."[18]

That month British General Sir Charles Richardson, Clark's deputy chief of staff, also stopped at Palermo, at the suggestion of Clark's chief of staff, General Alfred M. Gruenther. Having previously seen Patton at Monty's teach-in in Tripoli just before the Tunisian campaign, he now found Patton "very old and desicated . . . still keeping a low profile after his public disgrace." His famous revolver "strapped to his hip," Patton "greeted me in a movietone accent. Was I at war, or was I in Hollywood, I wondered?"[19]

With Lucas, who had replaced Bradley as the commander of II Corps, and Geoff Keyes both about to join Clark in Italy, Patton felt more alone than ever. When Eisenhower, on his way to view the Fifth Army, visited Sicily on the seventeenth, Patton pleaded with him. "I told Ike I was willing to fight a Corps under Clark," he commented. "I would serve under the Devil to get in a fight. He said Clark and I were not soul mates so he could not do it. When I first heard that Ike was coming I thought it might be to relieve Clark but no such luck. . . . Destiny had better get busy."[20]

The next day Major General Arthur Wilson, the head of the military police for the Mediterranean Base Section, "came to supper full of life and lies, but very amusing. He swears that Clark got his job due to the efforts of Jews in the U.S. and that Clark's mother made speeches in favor of it. I think I will run on the colored ticket." That same day Lucas felt "quite blue about going. I am certainly sorry to see him go. He is a fine soldier and a good friend."[21]

Poletti found a distraught Patton living in the royal palace with a few officers. "He was doing absolutely nothing," Poletti remembered, "but he was a gentleman throughout. One time I was so impressed, I asked him, I said, 'What do you do all day?' He said, 'Well, at the present time I am studying the history of the Punic Wars.' And that just flabbergasted me. Here we were in the middle of a war and this fellow is just so steeped in war that he is studying the history of the Punic Wars, there in the Royal Palace at Palermo." Poletti's appraisal of Patton differed sharply from that of Marquand: "He was as I told you a very cultured fellow and I liked him."[22]

During the Salerno troubles, Ike, by punishing Patton, also punished himself. To Butcher he wondered aloud on the sixteenth if he had made a mistake sending Clark, rather than Patton. Patton, he knew, would never have planned an evacuation of his own headquarters, as Clark had done. "In the case of evacuation," Butcher noted of Patton in an unpublished portion of his diary, "it would have suited his personality and philosophy as a fighter to have been the last off the beach, if indeed he came off at all as he would prefer to die fighting."

Sitting around with Butcher that evening, Bedell Smith stated what Ike wondered. He and Butcher agreed that Patton or Bradley would have been wiser choices than Clark, who lacked confidence and battlefield experience. For the same reasons Bedell questioned the decision to send to Salerno the 36th Division, which the Germans had badly mauled.[23]

Patton's behavior indeed created a problem for Ike, who yearned to use his friend but found it impossible to do so. Bertie Clarkson, who investigated the slappings, exacerbated the problem. "Spent the day with Clarkson working on his Patton report," Everett Hughes recorded in his diary on September 19. "Bertie thinks Patton is through and recommends his relief. I get him to agree that Geo is a bum but a good army commander."[24]

In his report Clarkson dismissed Patton's rationalizations as unsatisfactory. Georgie first told Bertie that he had "put on an act" to cure the men of their nervous condition "by administering a counter shock." He later said that the sight of those with cases of nerves mingling with the wounded "made him see red." Wrote Clarkson: "The inherent contradiction of these two statements is worthy of note." Clarkson also found that many soldiers had lost their respect for Patton. The men of such units as the 2d Armored Division, who had served under Patton a long time, still considered him a great leader. But those who had been with Patton only a short time, such as the troops of the 1st and 9th Divisions, gobbled up the unfavorable stories. Clarkson urged that Ike inform General Marshall of the incidents, ensuring that Patton would be disciplined, probably relieved.[25]

Even though Bertie Clarkson recommended that he be disciplined, Patton still saw nothing wrong with what he had done. The slappings and the American massacres, both reported and unreported, occupied his thoughts not because he considered them wrong but because of their possible consequences. "I wrote Hughes a personal letter to see if he could find out what is going on," Patton noted on September 21. "I did not mention that I have gotten nothing for Sicily except a reprimand for doing my plain duty to a couple of cowards. Of course I realize I did my duty in a very tactless way, but so long as my method pleased the God of Battles I am content."[26]

Having nothing better to do, Patton began reliving the Sicilian campaign. Visiting Gela, where the Germans tried to drive the Americans into the sea on the morning of July 11, he was struck by

> the utter stupidity of the German attack. They sent 40 tanks down the Gela valley at about 40 miles an hour without artillery support and with no infantry present. They must have been very ignorant of the strength of our landing. At that they nearly won— we had great luck in stopping them, in fact, they turned back with a loss of only 14 out of between 40 and 50. Had they waited behind some little hills just north of the Gela-Ragusa Road till their infantry had captured our observation post, nothing could have stopped them. My ancient contention that the way to beat tanks is to destroy their tracks was clearly borne out—every Mark IV I saw had first been stopped with a hit in the tracks.[27]

After examing the site of British operations, Patton came away with less respect than ever for Monty. "The British certainly made fools of themselves in the attack on Catania. They came right down the road although it is fine tank country all around. When the history of the war is written 50 years hence, Monty will catch hell for being so timid and stupid."[28]

On October 16 Patton flew to Algiers to see Ike. After lunch with his old friend General Kenyon A. Joyce, who was visiting, Georgie had dinner with Ike, Hughes, and Kay Summersby. In a foul mood because rumors had it that he was returning to the United States to become chief of staff while Marshall would come to Europe to plan the invasion of France, Ike, after dinner, "gave a long monologue on himself and his early training. He then said," Georgie recorded, "I was always acting a part, that it was probably due to my having an inferiority complex. This amused me a lot but I agreed. The truth is that I have too little of such a complex—in fact I look down my nose at the world and too often let them know it." Hughes later told Patton: "Ike's trouble is that he is not humble." Eisenhower dared not "cuss out or criticize the British," so, Hughes believed, he took it out on his American friends, such as Patton.

Joyce, too, comforted Patton. Eisenhower, he said, was merely acting, for before such visitors as Secretary of the Treasury Henry Morgenthau, Ambassador W. Averell Harriman, and a "lot of British," he had spoken highly of Patton.[29]

Having no particular mission, Patton kept his staff functioning by drawing up a series of plans for amphibious operations. The first was for an assault near Leghorn in northwestern Italy. A second outlined an invasion near Genoa, far to the north, and a third an invasion in southern France, where the Americans eventually landed. According to Harkins, Patton, when studying the Genoa plan, said: "Let us go in there. There are more Germans; we can kill more Germans."[30]

By this time Eisenhower and Alexander, the Allied chieftain in Italy, had developed their own plan of deception. Labeled Fairlands, it aimed to keep German troops in northern Italy and prevent reinforcements from being sent south to counter the Allied invasion. Approved by Eisenhower on September 23, 1943, it called for movements that seemed to indicate that twelve Allied divisions—Patton's Seventh Army reinforced by a French corps from the island of Corsica, which the Germans had abandoned after Sicily fell, and an Anglo-French force of four divisions from North Africa—would land near Leghorn and Pisa in northwest Italy. This would prevent Rommel, who commanded the Axis forces in Rome and the area north of it, from sending men south to Field Marshal Albert Kesselring, whose troops faced Clark. In reality Patton's Seventh Army had been reduced by this time to a skeleton. Truscott, Keyes, and Lucas were either in Italy or about to leave for it. Bradley, selected by Eisenhower and Marshall to command the American ground forces in the invasion of France, was in Washington, hoping to convince President Roosevelt, whom he had never met, that he was the right choice. But the American authorities took pains to preserve the appearance that the Seventh Army remained at full strength.[31]

Marshall added one wrinkle to the plan. At his suggestion Ike called Patton and several members of his staff to Algiers. There, on October 27, Bedell Smith told Patton "that the operation on which I was to embark was a cover plan for the purpose of using the prestige of the 7th Army to draw attention to Corsica and that in order to do the thing right we would have to pass through Tunis because it was felt that there was a German there who would inform his people of our proposed trip. This is the end of my hopes for war."

Leaving Algiers on the twenty-ninth, Patton and his party flew to Tunis, where he picked up General Alphonse Juin, who had directed the French army in Africa. The party then flew to Corsica, almost directly west of Leghorn, where Patton and Juin spent two days inspecting military installations and troops. During the visit Patton and his staff prominently displayed the patch of the Seventh Army, conveying the impression that the unit was still a viable force. Patton then returned to Tunis, where General Juin left the party, and from there went back to Palermo.

As much as anything, this inspection of Corsica focused German attention on the Leghorn-Pisa coast. "We discovered later," observed one of the British architects of the plan, "that it was in fact the threat of action by the Seventh Army which perplexed the enemy during the whole period of operation of 'Fairlands.'" Evidence of its success came when German and Swedish radio broadcasts talked about the likelihood of Patton's Seventh Army invading northern Italy and pushing east toward the Balkans.[32]

During much of the last week of October Kenyon Joyce stayed with his former subordinate. In Algiers ten days before, Joyce had assured Patton that Ike, no matter how much he grumbled during their meetings, had praised him to Harriman, Morgenthau, and the British. Ever the horse soldier, Joyce asked if the old 1st Cavalry Division might have been used in the mountains during the push from Palermo to Messina. To that Patton replied: "Not a ———— German would have got off the Island."[33]

Patton conceded to Joyce that he had made a terrible mistake slapping the two soldiers. He explained the first incident by saying that it occurred in the midst of the campaign, and he was nervous and under stress. According to Patton the man he slapped "looked like a cowardly rat and whined like one." Patton ordered him to his feet and asked if the example of the brave men in the ward did not stir him. "Oh, no," he supposedly answered, "those guys don't mean nothin'. I just can't take it." With that Patton exploded. "It was inexcusable on my part," Patton told Joyce. "I was a damned fool but the contrast between those men of valor and this creeping thing did something to me."[34]

During his stay in Palermo, Joyce took long walks with Patton. Before each walk Patton would place a short-barreled 38-caliber Colt revolver in his right breeches pocket. Asked why, Georgie explained: "It is for social purposes only." Joyce said a Remington automatic pistol would be better and later sent him one.[35]

While with Patton at the palace Joyce saw a frail cleric enter its chapel. "George," he said to Patton that evening, "why on earth don't you do something for that poor little Cardinal whom I saw entering the chapel today? He was the most emaciated, forlorn individual I have ever laid eyes on. Why the devil don't you give him some American rations and put some flesh on him?"

Patton replied that "the little Cardinal" was "his friend." The cleric, in fact, had celebrated a Mass for Patton in the chapel the previous Saturday. He was "positively fat now. You should have seen him a month ago. You see, I am building him up and getting him strong as I intend to run for Pope and I want his vote."[36]

IV

Having mentioned to Bedell Smith on October 27 that he would like to see the fighting in Italy, Patton saw his wish come true. On November 3 Bedell's plane stopped at Palermo, picked up Patton, and, along with Butcher and Major-General J. S. Nichols of the British Army, took him to Naples. The next day he drove to the headquarters of the VI Corps, where he saw Lucas, who said that his troops were tired and shy, relying too much on artillery support. "I fear he is right," Patton wisely observed. "If troops are kept at it too long they lose their dash and simply claw up after the guns. When we will have finer guns they won't move."

On the way back to Naples, Patton saw Clark, who was cordial but complained about the British. "Their men are braver than ours," Patton noted, "but their officers have no push."

Three things about Clark bothered Patton. First, Clark and his chief of staff, Al Gruenther, displayed on their maps the position of every battalion in their command. "This," Patton reasoned, "is bad as it tempts people to deal in battalions instead of army corps."

Patton coupled the other two criticisms. Believing that "a very narrow margin" separated a successful from an unsuccessful general, Clark had declared: "I was almost pushed into the sea." Patton insisted that "no general in a landing operation must be pushed into the sea. He must either die or stay there." And, like Fredendall at Kasserine Pass,

Clark's headquarters, "in the garden of a palace after which Versailles was copied," was too far back from his forward positions, being a two-and-a-half hour drive away. "He might just as well, and it would be more comfortable, be in Naples."[37]

On November 7, back in his headquarters, Patton contemplated the meaning of the past year. Exactly one year ago Patton had first seen action, but, he complained to Bea, during the past 365 days he had been in battle only seventy-two. His biggest mistake had been obeying British orders, especially that of April 7, 1943, instructing him to pull back after breaking through at El Guettar. He should, he mused, have told Brigadier L. C. Holmes, Alexander's operations officer, "to go to hell when he phoned me the order. . . . As a result of that experience, I refused to stay put on July 17th and made Alex let me start to take Palermo, though he was very much opposed to my doing it. Live and Learn."[38]

In the Mediterranean Base Section and the North African Theater of Operations rapes and killings created a problem. Patton, who had to be pushed by Bradley into doing anything about the West and Compton massacres, vigorously prosecuted such cases, seeing in them issues of race. On July 20, 1943, he had written Bea cryptically: "Some of George Meeks cousins did a little of their usual stunt and will wear rope ties." Now, on November 8, he made a more direct observation in his diary:

> In the first five rape cases we had one was white and 4 were negroes. Through a miscarriage of justice the white man only got life and the niggers were hung. When three more negroes from the same battalion were arrested for rape I put two negro officers on the court. Although the men were guilty as hell the colored officers would not vote death . . . a useless race.[39]

Not that Patton limited such remarks to blacks. The very next day he told about an episode involving the British that he saw when he went down to the docks to see off Eddy, who was on his way to Italy. A brigadier who had gotten on at Naples "for a joy ride" had taken Eddy's stateroom. "Of course Eddy moved him," Patton observed, "but the act is typical of the race. They have no shame nor modesty and will take all they can get."[40]

Feeling, as he told Bea, "lower than whale tracks," Patton interested himself in a subject with which he was not ordinarily concerned. In mid-November he became "quite disturbed" about the ability of the Allied Military Government of Occupied Territory to deal with Sicily's food shortages. "I think that if one or two hoarders and black market men were hanged," he observed, "that there would be plenty of grain." Patton pointed to one resident, who told him: "All Sicilians are crooks. The trouble with you Americans is that you think we are not and treat us as if we are not." When Patton asked his friend the cardinal about hanging a few cheaters, the prelate replied: "My friend, I am a priest of God and one of the Chief Assistants of his Vicar on earth, therefore I cannot approve of the methods which you advocate. However, if I were not what I am, I would approve."[41]

Four days later Patton believed the food situation would only get worse. "Amgot has neither the capacity nor the ability to administer a captured country. The only answer is ruthless enforcement of law by the death penalty. Especially is this true among a bastard race like the Sicilians. . . . Poletti is a very brilliant man, but does not understand how to govern a conquered people."[42]

V

Having once commanded 240,000 men, Patton had but five thousand left. Then, on November 22, things got worse. Codman picked up a message from Allied Forces Headquarters that indicated Drew Pearson, the Washington columnist, had said something about the slappings during his weekly radio program.[43]

The next day Bedell telegraphed the details to Patton. On November 21 Pearson had broadcast "a very vicious and exaggerated version of the Sicilian hospital incident. . . . It resulted immediately in a flood of messages from the press associations to their representatives here demanding confirmation or denial." Since Eisenhower was busy preparing for the upcoming Cairo and Teheran conferences of Allied leaders and had a cold to boot, Bedell took it upon himself to answer the press associations, making the mistake of admitting that Patton had escaped reprimand. At a press conference Bedell represented Ike and said Patton had made amends "by apologizing personally to the individuals concerned and by speaking to the divisions of your army."

Even Butcher, in an unpublished segment of his diary, criticized Bedell's clumsiness in admitting that Patton had escaped punishment,

> and this without Ike's knowledge. Beetle was furious to know that I had been contacted by the press and wished to withdraw from any consideration in the handling of the matter. I told Ike I thought he would need to have a press conference and talk frankly of the situation off-the-record, but to day he is resting, trying to cure a bad head cold in anticipation of hard sessions at Cairo. Beetle is an efficient Chief of Staff, but he is also a bit bumbling when dealing with the press, if not bungling, and also I might say, too touchy about his prerogatives as Chief of Staff.[44]

In telling the world about the slapping incidents Pearson had broadcast what dozens of American reporters in Sicily had pledged to keep secret. His motive was simple and selfish. Blaming Secretary of State Cordell Hull for the delay in establishing a second front in Europe, Pearson asserted in his newspaper column that Hull wanted to see "Russia bled white." Furious, President Roosevelt held a press conference and called Pearson "a chronic liar." To take the pressure off himself, Pearson broke the slapping story, which had been leaked to him by his friend Ernest Cuneo, an official of the Office of Strategic Services.[45]

Spurred on by Pearson's revelation, Seymour Korman of the Mutual Broadcasting System jumped in on November 23 with other details supposedly illustrating Patton's instability. On August 21 Patton had told Korman about a hospital episode, saying only that he had been hasty in cursing—he did not say striking—an enlisted man. Patton said he had since learned that the man was ill. He intended to apologize to him and to as many of his soldiers as he could assemble.

Korman then described other incidents that had been hushed up in Sicily. Early in the campaign Patton had come upon a peasant crossing a bridge with his heavily laden mule. Fuming "that the bridge was only for military traffic," Patton "ordered one of his aides to shoot the mule. The aide had no alternative but to obey." Another time Patton called in a reporter for *Stars and Stripes,* the service newspaper, and accused him of printing lies when he said American soldiers stuck to their foxholes under fire. "It happened," Korman commented, "that the reporter's knee was still hurting him. He had jumped into a foxhole when the Germans viciously strafed Gela. His knee was injured when an American major general leaped into the foxhole on top of him."[46]

On the twenty-third, after learning "that Drew Pearson has publicized George P's action in hospitals," Ike discussed the matter with his staff. Colonel Arthur J. McChrystal, his chief of Information and Censorship, "says Geo is through," Hughes noted in his diary. Lieutenant Colonel Joseph B. Phillips, formerly the editor of *Newsweek* and now Ike's public relations officer, agreed with this appraisal.[47]

Luckily for Patton, Codman was visiting Hughes in Algiers when General Joseph T. McNarney of the War Department, whom General Marshall himself considered "a merciless man, a true hatchetman," demanded an explanation from Ike. With Ike busy, Bedell wrote "the answering cable." He had the good sense, however, to let Codman and Hughes revise it, "and which Bedell apparently accepts. It doesn't tear Geo down so much."[48]

Throughout the crisis Codman and Hughes proved invaluable to Patton. "Codman got back from Algiers today," Patton observed on the twenty-eighth, "with a very complete appreciation of my sad state. I seem to be the means by which McNarney is trying to hurt Ike so as to become Chief of Staff in the event that General Marshall leaves. Ike and Bedell are not at all interested in me but simply in saving their own faces. I might act the same if the case were reversed, but I doubt it."[49]

Not knowing what else to do, Patton wrote a long explanation of the slappings. Fortunately for him, he sent the letter, a rehash of his previous explanations, to Hughes for his opinion. More of a diplomat than Georgie would ever be, Ev saw no point to it. "Stopped Patton from sending a letter on his case to Sec. War," he noted on the next to last day of November.[50]

Back home, Patton's family and friends rallied to his defense. "I think I am almost as mad as you are," General Sherman Miles wrote Bea. "Drew Pearson is a loathsome varmint, & the rest of the yapping gang now on Georgie's trail are not much better. *I* would like to command a firing squad, and choose my clients!" An anguished Bea answered Miles, the family's friend and neighbor: "I do not know anything about this trouble except what is in the news; but there seems to be so much foul play in it that I am willing to have Georgie resign if he has to do it to tell the truth."[51]

Amid the crisis Nita did her best to comfort Bea. "I arrived here last night," she wrote Arvin Brown on December 4 from South Hamilton,

> after a very good trip across the country. Bee Sr. is here, she had come up from Washington when she knew I was to be here first. She looks very badly poor thing, and really knows nothing more about Georgie than we do. She told me Mrs. Marshall called her up and said: "I'm sorry the general is out of the country otherwise he would speak up for George." Also ten of his former sergeants sent her red roses and orchids. She has had hundreds of wonderful letters and only about five mean ones and four of them were unsigned which is the usual way with meaness!![52]

If Patton thought Pearson was through with him, he was sadly mistaken. On December 8, Stimson was shocked to read a Pearson article on Patton, "a very dangerous one," he commented in his diary. "That scoundrel may succeed in killing Patton's usefulness if he keeps on." Not knowing that Cuneo had been feeding information to Pearson from the Office of Strategic Services, Stimson asked McNarney "to put an inspector on the War Department to see who has been leaking out information. Pearson's articles are about three-quarters false but there's just a germ of truth in them that somebody must have given him."[53]

Published in papers throughout the country, the article of the eighth covered Patton's entire career. Ever since his West Point days, Patton had been, Pearson asserted, "one of the stormiest and most discussed officers. . . . Incidents about Patton were reported to members of the Senate Military Affairs Committee, including the polo days, when he is reported to have shot a horse which didn't come through. The Committee is beseiged by Patton friends and foes."

Pearson devoted much of his column to Patton's supposed fascination with "pro-Vichy society." Even though General Noguès had fired on American troops and imprisoned pro-American French officers, Patton, saying he was a soldier and not a politician, found nothing wrong with hobnobbing with him. "Noguès," Pearson related, "had even sought to persuade the Sultan of Morocco to declare a holy war against us. . . . This and reports of how the General ordered an Italian peasant's mule shot when it went over a military bridge, and his manner of firing his pearl-handled revolvers into the air when dressing down a fellow officer, are under Senate probe."[54]

Three days after the Pearson column appeared, Hughes noted its failure to stir up the American public. A poll taken by George Gallup indicated that by four to one Americans favored not relieving Patton. Destiny had again favored the general.[55]

VI

On December 5 Patton began to get some inkling of what was being decided at the summit conferences. His classmate General John C. H. Lee, who headed Ike's Services of Supply, reported that Joseph Stalin "had the whip hand and used it." Once, when discussing something, Churchill said: "We can leave that to our military advisors." To that Stalin asked whether Churchill needed the chief of the Imperial General Staff, General Alan Francis Brooke, to "make up your mind for you."[56]

On the seventh, the second anniversary of the bombing of Pearl Harbor, John J. McCloy, the assistant secretary of war, arrived with Brigadier General Julius Holmes, the head of Ike's Liaison Section, and confirmed Lee's reports. Opposing an invasion of France, Churchill still maneuvered for some attack in the Aegean Sea. Churchill began talking about this operation, but Stalin dismissed it with the comment: "That is nothing. This is the last round of a prize fight and it is not the time to dance around the ring but to go in and slug." He had "whittled the enemy down to your size" and advocated invasions in both the north and south of France. When Churchill suggested that a committee discuss the next move, Stalin countered: "If we three can't decide, who can? I don't have to ask my generals to make up my mind for me. I have no time for discussion by juniors. I have to get back to Moscow and win a war and win it fast so I can reconstruct my country."

McCloy brought other news. Marshall would remain in Washington as chief of staff and Ike would move to England, where he would command the Allied forces in the invasion. Praising Patton, McCloy said that when he asked what was to become of the tormented general Marshall answered: "He will have an Army."[57]

After the Teheran conference Roosevelt came to Sicily. On December

8 at Castelvetrano he conferred with the senior army officers. "I met him with Hap Arnold, and Marshall was there and Ike was there and Georgie Patton, very much downhearted because he'd been relieved of his command," Mark Clark remembered. ". . . The President was very gracious. After decorating several of my men for valor at Salerno, he took us into his confidence and told us about Overlord and Ike told Georgie Patton, 'You will have an army in that command,' which pleased Georgie no end."[58]

Meantime, Ike kept Georgie busy with an elaborate deception plan called Oakfield, again designed to stop the Germans from reinforcing their troops in southern Italy with forces from the north. Approved by Ike on November 19, the plan would aid Clark and Montgomery by supposedly threatening the Axis lines of communication north of Florence. As revised after consultations with General Alexander, commanding the Fifteenth Army Group in Italy, Oakfield called for fictional landings on the eastern and western coasts of northern Italy during January 1944. The Allied forces would purportedly push inland and join at Bologna, just above Florence, thus cutting the Italian peninsula into two segments and isolating the German army facing Alexander in the south. With a total of eleven divisions Patton, then doing nothing in Palermo, would supposedly supervise both landings. Truscott's 3d Infantry and one British division from Naples, supported by two French divisions from Corsica and Algeria, would land in the west at Pisa. The eastern assault would take place at Rimini. There the initial landing force would consist of the two divisions of General Wladyslaw Anders's II Polish Corps, then in Egypt, two airborne divisions, the 82d American and the 1st British, and the 88th American Infantry Division. Support would come from the fictitious British XIV Corps, supposedly being formed in North Africa.

Patton's staff contributed immeasurably to the plan. Although his command had been reduced "to the barest skeleton," Patton had his headquarters send numerous radio messages announcing that the Seventh Army was ready for battle. To convince the enemy that the two airborne divisions, then in southern Italy, were in Sicily, Patton's staff staged parachute training for the troops still in Sicily and concentrated all available gliders on the island.

At the same time the British sent out reports from Algiers describing the creation of the XIV Corps. For the fake corps the British even devised a shoulder patch, a wolf's head with a lolling red tongue. Along the roads in Tunis and Algeria, they posted signs pointing to the XIV's camps. A corps headquarters sent out specially printed Christmas cards and invitations to a staff Christmas party. Some of these cards and invitations found their way to places as distant as Spain and Turkey.[59]

Patton himself helped establish the relationship between the Seventh Army in Sicily and the Polish corps in Egypt. On December 12 he flew to Egypt with eight staff officers and for a week appeared prominently before residents of the country and newspapermen. He lectured British officers on amphibious operations and visited pyramids and mosques.

The high point of the tour came on December 17, when Patton and Major-General Beaumont Nesbitt, the British liaison officer in Egypt, met with General Anders at the Polish camp near Faqus, on the eastern side of the delta. "He struck me as very much of a man," Patton wrote of Anders. "He was a Chief of Staff of a Russian division in World War One. He has been hit seven times and won the Polish decoration for valor twice. His troops are the best looking troops, including British and American, that I have ever seen." Anders hated the Russians, who, he said, referring to the Katyn Forest massacres, murdered fifteen hundred Polish officers. Laughing, he told Patton that if his troops got between the Germans and Russians, "they would have difficulty in deciding which they wanted to fight the most."

By exchanging soldier patches and insignia Patton and Anders fostered the deception. Photographs of Anders wearing a Seventh Army patch appeared in several publications, including an illustrated weekly magazine published in Istanbul. Patton returned to Sicily on December 20, leaving a host of journalists to speculate about the purpose of his visit. Most of them connected it to possible operations in the Adriatic Sea, although the widely followed American military analyst Major George Fielding Eliot predicted a new invasion would take place along the Balkan coast, rather than in eastern Italy.[60]

The Germans, however, feared the worst. They bolstered their forces along the Riviera coast and issued stories describing the strong defenses along the Adriatic to discourage landings by the Allies there. In January an article in the Budapest journal *Pester Lloyd* presented an account of German preparations to repeal an invasion.

Proof of Oakfield's success came in January with Operation Shingle. Hoping to relieve the pressure at Salerno, the Allies planned to duplicate Patton's end-runs in Sicily by landing above Salerno at Anzio. The operation, which turned into a nightmare, at first met little opposition from the Germans, who were busy elsewhere. As a leading British intelligence officer put it: "Had the later developments of 'Shingle' met with the same success as on its opening day, then Oakfield might have gone down as the most successful Deception Plan of the whole Mediterranean War."[61]

VII

Returning to Palermo on December 21, Patton found thirty-eight letters on the slappings. Of these only six were unfavorable. The next day he received twenty-nine more, all but four or five favorable. "They are from all sorts of people," Patton told Bea. "Doctors, lawyers, a State Supreme Court judge, parents, soldiers, nuns, Jews, welfare workers, English soldiers etc also whole classes from high schools quite a cross section." Codman, who was leaving for Algiers "to buy some Christmas food and drink and to get the latest reaction," was taking a sample of the letters to show Hughes.[62]

Just before Christmas Jimmy Doolittle arrived bearing rumors of future assignments. Ike and Marshall had spent much of December quarreling about who was to command what during the coming invasions of France, Overlord in the west and Anvil in the south. Among other things Ike wanted Patton to lead an army during Overlord. When the long-expected confirmation came from Washington, Ike went to the United Kingdom to plan Overlord. Jake Devers was to plan Anvil.[63]

On Christmas Day Patton, still unsure what would happen to him, "inspected all that is left of the 7th Army and they were all glad to see me. My men are crazy about me," he bragged in his diary, "and that is what makes me most angry with Drew Pearson. I will live to see him die. As a matter of fact, the ability to survive this has had a good effect on America and on me. My destiny is sure and I am a fool and a coward ever to doubt it."[64]

Apprehensive about the future, Patton awoke in the middle of the night of the twenty-sixth from a dream that depicted endless miles of beaches with soldiers training on them. As rumors had it, he was to train for Overlord nine divisions: five French infantry, two French armored, and two American infantry. To help with the armored units he hoped to get General Isaac D. White, who later commanded the 2d Armored Division, for the infantry possibly Troy Middleton or Terry Allen. He was sure Hughes would help him, but Ike and Bedell were a different story. "I wish to God Ike would leave and take Bettle Smith with him. They cramp my style."[65]

New Year's Day of 1944 brought news, but the message Patton received from the headquarters of the North African Theater of Operations hardly cleared up the uncertainty. At some future time Patton was to be relieved from the Seventh Army and ordered to Algiers. His staff, loyal to him throughout his ordeal, was to remain and help Devers plan Anvil, which Clark would lead. "I feel terribly," Patton mused, "not so much for myself as for my staff who have stuck with me all the time in good weather and bad. I suppose I am going to England but if they use me simply for training and not for command I will resign. It is, I think, unpardonable to keep a man of my rank and attainment waiting."[66]

The next day, a Sunday, Patton attended church and then flew to Algiers, where he visited a skeptical Hughes. "Patton has lost his Army and is coming at 1:15 to cry on my shoulder," Hughes noted in his diary. During their discussions Patton and Hughes both viewed Anvil as "totally impractical and crazy. . . . I cannot see how any normally intelligent person could inspire this fool change of staff," Patton fumed. "It is unfair and insulting to me, but is heartbreaking for the staff of 7th Army who have been utterly loyal and now find that their efforts get them nowhere. It is damnable. I hope I find out who did it and then get to a position so that I can really hurt him."[67]

Unknown to Patton, Devers devised the scheme to combine the staffs of the Fifth and Seventh armies. Years later, Devers described how he and Eisenhower, like boys picking members of their baseball teams, split up their generals. Ike agreed to give Clark the Fifth and Seventh armies, but he wanted to take Patton with him to England. "I was glad to let him go," Devers said of Patton, but Devers insisted on keeping members of Patton's staff, including Patton's chief engineer, Colonel Garrison H. Davidson, whom he needed to "carry on the planning. . . . The first man to come in my office was Gar Davidson from over in Sicily. He said, 'I know what went on here. My brother-in-law had something to do with this.' That was Al Gruenther, who was the chief of staff of the Fifth Army." Davidson wanted to stay with Patton. "I said, 'Gar, you were head football coach at West Point when I was graduate manager of athletics and *I've* selected you, and you're not going to go. You're going to stay here and tie this plan in and after we get it going and I know what's going on, if you think you wanted to go, you can go.' "[68]

Conferring with Hughes on January 2, 1944, the day after Patton accepted an invitation from Field Marshal Lord John Gort, the governor of Malta, to tour that island, Devers, who resented Patton since their West Point days, seemed to relish Patton's misfortunes. "He says Geo done for," Hughes observed. "Jake says Patton through."[69]

On the fourth Patton was off for Malta. Even more thrilling than the stay on the island was the trip there. "Looking over the country where we fought during the battle of El Guettar," he informed his cousins, the Bannings,

> gives me a definite idea of the greatness of the American soldier. The mountains are impossibly difficult. I am glad that at that time when I fought this battle I did not know how hard the country was, since we could not get an airplane from which to look at it and we had to make our decision from the map. Had I known how difficult it was, I might have been less bold—but it is always well to remember, that the country is just as hard on the enemy as it is on you.[70]

Still awaiting orders, Patton decided to view things in Italy. He found Clark and Gruenther at Caserta on the grounds of the Bourbon palace. Living "some three hours hard driving from the nearest front line," they, like Fredendall at Kasserine Pass, had no idea what was going on at the front. "Both Gruenther and Clark were most condescending and treated me as an undertaker treats the family of the deceased."

Accompanied by Codman, Patton spent two days with the American army in Italy, visiting Keyes, Lucas, and Truscott. Ever Patton's disciple, Keyes had his command post "well up," near the front line. Lucas was nervous about the entire Italian campaign. Truscott, however, "was as usual, and we had a long talk on river crossings. He has done one."

Patton came away convinced that both Shingle and Anvil were ill-fated. Believing that any cross-channel operation would fail, Churchill was monopolizing boats and men for Shingle, but, Patton noted, everything exemplified confusion. Between them Clark and the British had switched the date of Shingle three times and planned no rehearsals of the invasion. Clark, moreover, changed the proposed date for Anvil, months off, three times during Patton's visit, moving "it backward and forward. The left hand corner of Clark's mouth is slightly drawn as if he had been paralyzed. He is quite jumpy and so is Gruenther."[71]

While Patton stewed about his future, Devers, unknown to him, held things up. Planning for Anvil, he decided that Clark had best remain in Italy with the Fifth Army. To lead the Americans assigned to Anvil, he asked for either of two of Patton's West Point classmates, Courtney B. Hodges, who had been chief of infantry in Washington, or William H. Simpson, a tall, thin, bald infantryman. To this request Marshall answered: "You have to have a commander for the Seventh Army who has been bloodied in war, who's had experience in combat, and there are only two of them: Patton and Clark." Devers wanted neither. From their cadet days he and Patton merely tolerated each other. And his relations with Clark had soured. "He is his own worst enemy," Devers said of Clark in 1976, "and he still is, I guess. Anyhow—his problem was just his personality; Clark criticized the British and did little things to irriate them." Devers finally asked for and got another polo player, Major General Alexander M. "Sandy" Patch, who had seen combat on Guadalcanal in the Pacific. "And Sandy proved to be a great army commander," Devers observed, "if not the best."[72]

On January 22 Patton's luck began to change. He received orders to proceed to Algiers, from which he was to go to the United Kingdom. With Codman he arrived in Algiers on the twenty-fourth. On the next morning, accompanied by Hughes, he went to the Ecole Normale "to say Au Revoir to his staff." That noon he and Codman left in a C-54 for England.[73]

At nine forty-five the next morning, after a "perfect trip," Patton and Codman arrived at Prestwick, where Butcher and John C. H. Lee met them. "Lee put Codman and myself up at his flat," Patton recorded. Calling on Ike, Patton learned he was to put together and command the Third Army. "All novices and in support of Bradley's First Army—not such a good job but better than nothing."

Dinner at Ike's that evening evolved into an adventure. Present were Kay Summersby, Butcher, a British aide-de-camp, and a Women's

Army Corps captain. "Ike very nasty and show-offish," Patton lamented, "—he always is when Kay is present—and criticized Lee for his flamboyance which he—Ike—would give a million to possess. Well, I have an Army and it is up to me. 'God show me the right.'"

Butcher viewed the evening differently. That afternoon Ike had scolded Patton for failing to count ten before acting. At dinner that night Patton seemed "most contrite." A "master of flattery," he turned every disagreement with Ike into a vehicle for praising the supreme commander. At one point he said it would be foolish for anyone to disagree with Ike, whom Patton called "the most powerful person in the world."[74]

As Patton began the task of picking subordinates and training his army, he talked not of reincarnation and of his previous lives but of an amorphous spirit he labeled Destiny. "Geo P. says, 'Destiny I am sure has you in his divine keeping,'" Hughes recorded, "and is also much put out with Jake. What it means I don't know."[75]

Twelve

WHITHER DESTINY?

I

Settling down to business late in January, Patton studied Bradley's first invasion plan, "which I consider bad; the landings are so close that an attack against one affects the whole thing." Bradley's First Army, six infantry and two armored divisions, would land on a front big enough for two divisions. To his left the British would land on a three-division front. Patton's Third Army would come ashore after the British had taken a port. "We take Normandy and Brittany, then countermarch and come right up on the right of the First Army. While all this is going on two other U.S. Armies land. A hell of a lot of things can happen before that time." On a brighter note Patton got Bedell Smith's approval to recover fifteen of his Seventh Army officers, partially nullifying the order transferring his staff to Devers.[1]

On the twenty-ninth Patton reached Third Army facilities near Knutsford, just southwest of Manchester. There he visited Toft Hall, the site of his headquarters, and Peover Hall, a half Tudor, half Georgian mansion that served as his command post. Still supposed to be in Sicily, Patton told the first group of officers and men to arrive "that I was not to be mentioned." Similarly, to some of Lee's services of supply men in Cheltenham, a hundred miles south of Knutsford, he made a speech that was "good and alive but warned them that I was a myth."[2]

On February 1 Patton began inspecting his units. Driving directly south of Cheltenham to Chippenham, he passed the dolmen, supposedly set up by the seer Merlin, covering sixteen acres. King Charles II was said to have climbed the structure, which was several hundred feet high. Finally Patton reached the camp of the 4th Armored Division,

trained by Major General John Shirley Wood, nicknamed "P." for professor, for in his West Point days he gladly tutored failing classmates. "P.
was delighted to see me," Patton observed. Patton rated the division
"superior" and to Bea wrote: "P. is much less gloomy than usual and has
a fine outfit."[3]

Presenting "the then-under-wraps Army Commander" to the officers
of his division, Wood, according to Colonel DeWitt Smith, Jr., displayed his affection for Georgie. "Patton was in poor public repute
then—the slapping incident—but General Wood took a clear stand in
his introduction of him. General Patton, he said, was a good and old
friend of his, and the greatest combat commander in the U.S. Army."[4]

On the third Patton had a long talk with Lieutenant General Carl
Spaatz, who commanded the United States Strategic Air Forces in
Europe. Patton "told him that he and I might have to pull the chestnuts
out of the fire if the attack of the First Army bitches." Strangely
enough, he and Spaatz were of "one mind on going shorter water route
and blasting a hole," meaning that the two believed heavy bombers
should pulverize the Pas de Calais, directly across the English Channel,
where German fortifications were the strongest but closest. "He is fed
up with the British," Patton noted, "and said 'we have paid a hell of a
price for the Supreme Command.' We have. . . . We both feel that
instead of 'Overlord' we should have shot the works in Italy and
Toulon." Patton was "sure" that if he had commanded in Italy "we
would have had Rome by now, and would have been towards the Alps.
However, I did not command, so there is no use arguing." At dinner
that evening Patton met Lady Cavendish, the former actress-dancer
Adele Astaire, the sister of the movie star Fred Astaire. Patton charac-
terized her as "the most profane person I have ever seen or heard, otherwise not attractive."[5]

To Patton's joy some of his staff members began to arrive. Keeping
his word, Bedell sent along Colonel Robert E. Cummings, Patton's
adjutant; Hap Gay; Gay's aide, Captain Murnane; and Colonel Charles
B. Odom, the Third Army's medical officer. Patton momentarily
expected Koch, Muller, Maddox, and Hammond.[6]

The next day, February 11, brought a series of conferences. That
morning Bradley and Patton went to Montgomery's headquarters,
where, with de Guingard, Monty presented his invasion ideas. "In some
things," Patton revealed, "I think him too optimistic, in others too cau-

tious." One of Patton's four corps, plus possibly two armored divisions, would join Bradley, starting about D-Day plus ten. Patton's other three corps would be in France on D-Day plus twenty-five. "It is not a very critical job for me," Patton observed, for he would not be in the invasion, "but things can develop almost any way at any time. One can make his own job." In Sicily he was supposed to cover Monty's left and rear, but he broke away and won the race to Messina. During this visit Patton learned that late in the Sicilian operation the British Brigadier C. S. Sugden, who was one of Ike's chief planners, had complimented Patton by saying: "He's got the Eighth Army bloody well surrounded."[7]

After this meeting Patton stopped at Eisenhower's house for a talk. Ike began by saying he was bringing up something reluctantly. Devers, who was taking over the North African Theater of Operations, did not want Hughes as his deputy. Would Patton be willing to take Hughes as his chief of staff? Ike insisted that he made the request not because of any lack of confidence in Gay, but the inference was there. "I said I would take Hughes and felt sure that Gay would understand," Patton observed. "I had already guessed the move and had spoken to Gay. It will not be too easy on any of us but I doubt if it lasts." During the visit Patton dispensed his usual dose of flattery, telling Butcher that Ike was on the verge of becoming "the greatest general of all time—including Napoleon."[8]

Mid-February brought depressing news from Italy. The Anzio invasion, launched in late January with two divisions aimed at Rome, had bogged down. At their meeting Montgomery had told Patton that the Allies had already evacuated four thousand vehicles. "If we lost that beach it will be bad," Patton believed, "but so much sloth or timidity was shown at the start that the thing was doomed. Only 8 miles in 12 days."[9]

The early morning of February 16 brought an important message. At 1:30 A.M. Butcher phoned that Ike again wished to see Patton. When Patton and Codman arrived at Allied headquarters at 20 Grosvenor Square in London, down the block from where John Adams, the first American minister to England, lived in the 1780s, Ike announced to Patton: "I am afraid you will have to eat crow for a while." "What have I done now?" Patton asked. Patton, Eisenhower explained, might have to take over at Anzio. He then read a message from Alexander criticizing Lucas, who commanded the VI Corps, then on the beachhead. To

Alex's comment that as of now the British had sustained most of the losses, Patton mused: "I doubt that." Alex requested "a thruster like George Patton." If not Patton, he recommended "putting a British officer in command," something to which Ike said he would never consent. Ike and Churchill had sent a telegram to Alex and the other commanders offering Patton for a month. Two airplanes were already waiting at the airport to fly Patton to Italy. Patton consented to go, but, he told Eisenhower, "I must be backed up by him, as otherwise, I would have my throat cut. . . . I suppose I am the only person in the world who would be elated at a chance to commit physical and official suicide, but I am tickled to death and will make a go of it."[10]

Patton's joy lasted one day. While he was at the hospital having a spot on his lip treated with x-ray, Lieutenant Colonel Ernest Lee, Ike's aide, "phoned to say that Ike said I could return to Knutsford. Nothing more. He did not even think it worthwhile to tell me what had happened." Having already enlisted Hugh Gaffey as his chief of staff and General Isaac D. White as his operations officer, Patton now canceled the arrangements.[11]

Before returning to his headquarters, Patton went over to see Bradley. There he suggested that if the planned invasion of Normandy "got boxed up as was highly possible," he and the Third Army "should be prepared to land" at Calais, the point on the French coast closest to England. "I feel," Patton observed, "that there is much merit in the plan as it would disperse the German reserves and give room for maneuver." At the moment the Germans had fifty-two divisions in Holland, Belgium, and France, forty of which could oppose the Allied invasion. "I hope the strength of the opposition does not bluff us out at the last minute. I still feel the British do not have their heart in it." Just the day before, Butcher had told Patton that quarrels over postwar objectives were already creating problems between the Americans and British and "coloring military operations." Truscott had replaced Lucas at Anzio, and Alexander was still blaming the Americans for the failure there. A talk with Brigadier General John E. Hull, who had come from Washington to help plan the invasion, elated Patton. "He told me that General Marshall said, 'I wish Patton was commanding at the Beachhead.' He also said that Middleton and an unnamed Colonel (probably Rooks) told him that I had captured Sicily in spite of Monty, and while I had driven them further than they thought men could endure they would love to fight under me anytime."[12]

II

For Patton England constituted almost as much of a classroom as the battlefields of North Africa and Sicily. He was constantly learning and thinking about war. Before reaching England Patton knew nothing about air support for ground troops. His experiences with aviators were invariably unpleasant.

All that changed beginning in late January 1944 with the arrival in England of two imaginative tactical airmen, Major General Elwood P. Quesada and Brigadier General Otto P. "Opie" Weyland. A few days after Weyland's arrival the major American tactical unit in England, the 9th Fighter Command, was divided in two. Quesada assumed command of the fighter planes and fighter-bombers of the 9th Tactical Air Command, assigned to support the American units in northern France, and Weyland took control of the 19th Tactical Air Command, which was to support Patton's Third Army, to the south. During the invasion, Quesada later said of the two tactical air units and of Weyland, "I commanded both, and as the forces moved over—he took over one and I took the other. Which worked out very, very well."[13]

A career officer since his graduation from Texas A&M in 1923, the tall, blond, handsome Weyland squirmed when he found out he was to work with Patton.

This was not a particularly thrilling proposition at that time, because George Patton had somehow or other gotten a rather crusty reputation and that he didn't get along worth a damn with aviators. This was derived from his experience in North Africa, where the British did most of the air work. At least in connection with his work. And, in that regard, you must realize that we were just getting a foothold in Europe, we were just in the initial stages of fighting back at the Germans, and the Germans really had considerable ascendancy. So his experiences, perhaps, in North Africa were not too happy.[14]

From February on Patton received basic training in tactical aviation from Weyland, who displayed patience, understanding, and an enormous desire to work with ground forces. Visiting Weyland's headquarters, Patton was, the aviator observed, "quite impressed; though he had more years of service than I, and as a ground soldier rather prided himself on military precision, he learned a new order of military precision which he had never before experienced." Weyland at his side, Patton sat in on the briefings given to combat wings preparing to fly into Germany. "In some cases they would escort Eighth Air Force bombers and in other cases would be striking ground targets, bridges, or something of that sort, in preparation for the invasion. In any event, there was a great deal of meticulous planning that went into this." In the briefings "we'd say, 'Well we will start engines at 04:27 (shall we say), first elements take off at 4:29¼, set course at 31½, coast out at such-and-such time, coast in on the French coast such-and-such time, first units on targets such-and-such time.' Or, 'Rendezvous with the bombers 25 miles short of Berlin at 05:49½.' Well, old Uncle George'd sit there, and he would say, 'What's all this stuff about fractions of a second? Are you trying to pull my leg or what?' " Unperturbed, Weyland would then ask Patton how fast a tank could go. Patton answered that in combat it could go perhaps thirty miles an hour for one or two hours. The tankers, moreover, used road markers and maps to guide themselves. Even when coordinating with artillery fire, Patton said, a minute or two did not matter.

Weyland explained the difference.

Well, that's very reasonable. Now, let's back off and apply some of the same logic to air action. Your tanks move at 30 mph. These fighter aircraft which I'm flying move at about 400 mph—350—400—well over ten times as fast. These boys are going out to rendezvous with bombers at around 25–28,000 feet; they are above the clouds, by the way, in most cases at this time of the year over Europe. There are winds aloft sometimes up to 100 knots. The fighter pilot is his own navigator, he's his own pilot, he's his own radio operator. So these things must be pre-planned as much as possible. To rendezvous with these bombers close to Berlin, it's just a point in space, they're thousands of feet above the clouds, there are no road markers or signs to see how they're coming along, they perhaps have a cross-wind of 50–75 knots—sometimes as much as 100 knots—they must plan as far as possible on these contingencies, they must take all these things into consideration. Now, when you're up there about as far as you can see will be a mile or two—just a few miles. You're traveling at some 400 mph. You travel the distance of your visual sight in just a very few moments. So they have to arrive at a point in space darn close to where they should be at that time. And the other fellow has to be there, if they're going to rendezvous. They then have to find their way back, don't you see, or else they may wind up in a neutral country or in an enemy country. They're operating under maximum conditions; they barely have enough gas to get back to the base. So they must come out very, very precisely indeed.

To this explanation Patton responded: "I'll be damned." Going out with Weyland, he watched the fighter planes take off and was amazed at the precision. "Now they've disappeared into the mists of U.K. skies," Weyland pointed out,

and it's generally foggy, and whatnot. They've just disappeared, by pairs usually. Now they're going around in a pattern, which they've memorized through practice. They will be assembled as a group and will be in the last stages of assembly when they pass over, and when you see them, you will probably see the leader roll over a little bit and straighten out. That will be when he sets course right directly over this field. Then out of the mist you'll see them coming and then probably the last element of planes are just falling into place.

Things happened just as Weyland described them. "So he learned about military precision and began to appreciate it at an early stage," the aviator said of Patton. Then, when the planes returned—some of the men wounded, two or three out of the forty-eight or so planes lost—Patton would sit in on the debriefing and hear about the accuracy of the German antiaircraft fire, about the encounters with enemy fighter planes, and about the weather. There, in England, Patton gained "a respect and an understanding of aviation, which later on was quite valuable."[15] He eventually authorized Weyland to speak for him in any situation and to commit his Third Army to any operation, which Weyland later did.

III

From February 22 on an even more noted military thinker than Patton began visiting American installations, meeting important generals. Captain Basil H. Liddell Hart never attained high rank. Rather, his fame came from his writings, which, like those of his fellow proponents of mechanization, Colonel J. F. C. Fuller and Colonel Giffard Le Q. Martel, both of whom served on the staff of Hugh Elles in the First World War, Patton gobbled up.[16]

In 1937 Liddell Hart had been at the center of the controversy over armor. As the personal adviser to the new secretary of state for war, Leslie Hore-Belisha, he had urged the formation of armored divisions for the British army in case, during a war, the Germans should break through the French frontier defenses. The proposal, Liddell Hart recalled, was "hotly resisted by the military chiefs." The struggle culminated with the appointment that November of Gort, a highly decorated infantryman, as the chief of the Imperial General Staff and of Brooke, an artilleryman, as the commander of the new Mobile Division. As his biographer has noted, Brooke had recently spoken "dubiously of the tank, as possibly favouring the defence." Like the Americans Wood and Chynoweth, Liddell Hart thereafter railed against infantry control of tanks as the return to "1918 methods."[17]

Liddell Hart believed that the French defeat in 1940 corroborated his views. That May, when the German General Heinz Guderian, who had studied the writings of Fuller, Martel, and Liddell Hart, engineered the breakthrough of the French front, the British had thirteen divisions in France, not one of them armored. Germany, in contrast, had ten armored divisions. When the French prime minister telephoned Churchill to tell him of the German penetration at Sedan, the Briton, referring to the Great German March Offensive in the First World War, reassuringly predicted the end of the German drive. "I remember the 21st of March, 1918," he said. "After five or six days they will have to wait for supplies."[18]

In early 1944, as the Allies prepared for the invasion of France, such ideas dominated the thinking of the planners. That February Churchill, showing he had changed little, said: "We have too much armour—tanks are finished." Brooke, now a field marshal and the chief of the Imperial General Staff, agreed. At a conference of British and American generals that included Wood, he urged the officers to go "back to 1918." The lightning drives of 1940 were no longer possible. And Montgomery told a group of American commanders that he was opposed to the creation of an armored corps. He especially disliked the organization of American mechanized divisions, in which all infantry was armored, transported in vehicles with tracks. Montgomery made his comments even though his late wife's brother, Major-General Sir Percy Hobart, equaled Martel, Fuller, and Liddell Hart in his advocacy of mechanization.[19]

The dispute heightened when, in 1944, Martel, now a lieutenant general, visited Brooke. Liddell Hart recorded what Martel told him:

> When he saw Brooke on his return from Russia early in the year, Brooke had taken the line that tanks were virtually "finished" as an important factor, in the war, and that they would never have scope again in exploiting a break-through—merely as a supporting arm. Martel had been shocked at Brooke's outlook, and had remarked to Brooke that it reminded him of what G. H. Q., particularly [General Sir Kenneth] "Kitten" Wigiam, had said about the prospects of the tank in 1916. Their argument became heated, though in the end Brooke cooled down and asked Martel to stay on for tea with him.

After that clash, Liddell Hart noted, Martel never again received an important army assignment.[20]

Against this background, Liddell Hart began visiting American generals then in England. His first trip, on February 22, brought him to Taunton and the headquarters of Patton's old acquaintance, Major General Leonard T. Gerow, who in the invasion was to command the V Corps of Bradley's First Army and land at Omaha Beach. Thoroughly impressed, Liddell Hart called Gerow "a vigorous and live-minded soldier. Found that we had many ideas in common about tactics, organization and training. He also shared my doubts about whether the importance of the unexpected was sufficiently considered in our planning. Gave him various memoranda. He wanted me to stay for the evening, but I could find no accommodation for the night in or near Taunton, though his aide telephoned everywhere possible."[21]

Two weeks passed before Liddell Hart spoke to his second American general, but this visit brought him a lifelong friend. On Tuesday, March 7, Liddell Hart drove to Chippenham, where he met Wood, whose 4th Armored had recently entertained Patton. After Wood's death, his wife, Abigail, described to Liddell Hart the makeup of the division, which Wood took over in May 1942. "You must know that this division was recruited with men in that vicinity—Pennsylvania, New Jersey but mostly from New York and the large proportion were Jewish for General John said his best fighters were his Jews! Aggressive with enormous *Drive.*"[22]

Brigadier General Albin F. Irzyk, who served with the division, remembered that during the Tennessee maneuvers of late 1942, Wood seemed years ahead of anyone else in his use of tanks. "While there, General Wood was reprimanded, ridiculed, and rebuked during weekend critiques of those maneuvers. His superiors told him that he had moved too fast, too far. They informed him that he just could not do it in combat with the enemy shooting, fighting and attacking, so why was he doing it in Tennessee? He stood his ground and quietly told them 'We can do it, and we will do it.' (And he did!)." Later, Patton also restrained Wood. As Chynoweth pointed out, Patton never let Wood go as far and as fast as he wished.[23]

Wood's division produced a number of great soldiers, but Abigail Wood recalled that her husband's favorite was a Methodist captain from an old New England family with a Jewish-sounding last name. Devers later described the captain, Creighton W. Abrams, as "the greatest tanker of all time." Abigail Wood remembered that in England her husband "promoted 'Abe' over and over" and kept him "by his side." Probably believing, like everyone else, that Abrams was Jewish, she called his wife Julie "charming and an ardent Catholic."[24]

In Chippenham, Liddell Hart encountered a Wood dejected by the recent conference at which Brooke had spoken "about the impossibility of repeating blitzkrieg tactics, and far-reaching thrusts and how armour would have to go back to methods similar to those of 1918." Spending a Tuesday evening with Wood, Liddell Hart "found him a great enthusiast for armoured forces. While not a big intellect, he was obviously dynamic, and much better-read than one would have expected from a man of his bluff type."

Wood confirmed what Liddell Hart feared: "that the U.S. Army is tending to repeat our lamentable habit of shelving those who are experts in armoured warfare, in order to bring the armoured forces more into line with orthodox methods." The original American armored corps had 390 tanks. Its infantry was armored, conveyed in vehicles with tracks, and its artillery was self-propelled. At one time Scott commanded the corps, and Wood served as its chief of staff.[25]

Wood pointed out that only five American generals possessed "mechanised experience." Scott, Patton's commander in 1940 and 1941, was once considered the darling of the force. In December 1941, however, he had been transferred from the armored corps and sent to Egypt to assist the British commander, General Claude Auchinleck. Returning home, Scott "has been shelved, being merely given command of the Armoured Replacement Center." Devers, who later bragged that "I knew more about armor than either Patton or Eisenhower," had been chief of the Armored Forces at Fort Knox from April 1941 to May 1943, but he was now involved with the campaign in Italy, "where armour has little scope now." Crittenberger, who had succeeded Patton as commander of the 2d Armored Division, "has just been moved from command of the XIXth Corps, and sent out to the Mediterranean somewhere. So Wood is the only one left apart from Patton. I asked about Hodges," Liddell Hart noted of his conversation with Wood, "who I heard was taking over the 1st Army. He is a rather conservative infantryman."

A rundown of the American armored division commanders illustrated Wood's point. Gaffey, who had led the 2d Armored since May 1943, was a field artillerist; Leroy H. Watson of the 3rd was an infantryman; Wood himself had drifted from artillery to armor; and Lunsford E. Oliver of the 5th was an engineer. Robert W. Grow, the commander of the 6th Armored, had long been a proponent of tanks, but for years he had served on staffs. A classic illustration was Lindsey McD. Silvester of the 7th Armored. A product of the Infantry School Tank Course, he proved so unacceptable that Patton transferred him to Hodges's army.

Wood concluded this first meeting on another unhappy note. "He felt that in tactics we were all going back to 1917," Liddell Hart recorded, "and at Anzio to 1915," meaning Gallipoli. Wood regularly read Liddell Hart's Monday column in the *London Daily Mail* "with a keen eye for any suggestions. He is a friend of Patton and feels that Patton will not let chances slip in the way that so many of the infantry-artillery school of commanders do. He was anxious for me to see Patton, and emphasize the problem."[26]

Liddell Hart was so taken with Wood that he returned to Chippenham the next morning. During the night Wood had studied several papers that Liddell Hart had left, "sketching out at the bottom of one of them a proposed new organisation which he spoke of putting up to Patton." Wood's armored division would contain four battalions of tanks, four of armored infantry, and four of artillery, the last consisting of three of self-propelled 105-millimeter and one of 155-millimeter howitzers. Wood also believed that each division should contain an armored reconnaissance regiment, which would have at its disposal, for rapid movements on land and in the sky, cross-country tractors and air transports. His current division, a far cry from this organization, had only three battalions of tanks.

Wood shared Patton's distrust of Monty, but for a different reason. Like Brooke, Monty considered armor insignificant, favoring a corps that consisted of two infantry divisions and one armored division. "This means," Liddell Hart surmised, "dependence on infantry, with the armour merely as support to them." Wood preferred a corps of one armored and one infantry divisions, and two armored divisions to one infantry division would be even better.

Displaying the depth of his study of battle, Wood questioned, as Patton had in both North Africa and Sicily, the difficulty in getting air support for ground operations. A Soviet general who recently visited him "related how divisions in the Red Army could call up air support within ten minutes. He was astonished at our slow methods, and the need for reference back to Army Headquarters before such support could be provided."

To Liddell Hart's delight, Wood endorsed several of his ideas on the way the war should be fought. Wood spoke "at length of the need for disposition in depth with armoured divisions, of operation on several different lines of approach, and of threatening alternative objectives. He agreed emphatically with my ideas about the invasion problem." Liddell

Hart argued that the invasion should take place at an area of "least expectation," such as near the Loire River along the western coast of France, rather than at a place offering "direct approach," such as Calais, opposite the White Cliffs of Dover.[27]

Wood again urged Liddell Hart to see Patton, who, in his current desperate state, might be "got at" and induced to accept Alan Brooke's dictum that tank drives could no longer be successful. Flatteringly Wood added that Patton read everything Liddell Hart wrote.

Accordingly, on Tuesday, March 14, 1944, Liddell Hart drove to Peover Hall. At first sight Patton's appearance shocked Liddell Hart, an immaculate dresser whose trousers always had a razor-sharp crease, for Patton dressed "like a W.P. cadet." Jumping from theme to theme, Patton began by calling for greater cooperation between the American and British armies. He next asked to see everything Liddell Hart had written on tanks, for, he praised the Briton, "You have imagination." Patton then said that he preferred "light tanks in quantity, against a few large ones" such as the Germans possessed in "close in" fighting. "Given suitable ground & skill," tanks like the American Sherman were invincible.

The bulk of the conversation, however, proved what Wood had feared. Beaten down by the furor over the slappings, Patton was yielding to infantry doctrine. He expressed his views while discussing Liddell Hart's book, published in 1929, on General William Tecumseh Sherman and the tactics of the Atlanta campaign. The Briton summarized the conversation.

> We had a very good talk, and found ourselves in the closest agreement about tank tactics. But I was rather disconcerted to find him saying he did not think, when the Allied armies got to France, they would be able to repeat the kind of armoured drives the Germans had achieved in 1940. He felt that we should have to go back to 1918 methods. While questioning this, I felt it best to put the contrary argument in the form of an "indirect approach." He told me that before the war he had spent a long vacation studying Sherman's campaigns on the ground in Georgia and the Carolinas, with the aid of my book. So I talked of the possibilities of applying "Sherman methods" in modern warfare—moving stripped of impediments to quicken the pace, cutting loose from communications, if necessary, and swerving past opposition, instead of getting

hung up in trying to overcome it by direct attack. It seemed to me that by the development and exploitation of such Sherman methods, on a greater scale, it would be possible to reach the enemy's rear and unhinge his position—as the Germans had already done in 1940.[28]

Patton left no account of the meeting, but he sent Bea a comment on it. "Liddell Hart has developed a great love for me," he wrote. "He is very well read but badly balanced and has no personal knowledge of the facts of life so far as war is concerned—in that he is not alone." He described Liddell Hart as "a funny looking man, tall and skinny."[29]

Five years after Patton's death, Liddell Hart asked Wood about something that still puzzled him. Why at this point had Patton wavered on the value of tanks? Wood answered succinctly.

Regarding my urging you to see George Patton in 1944, I did not think he had really changed his conceptions, which I knew to be the same as mine, but I feared he might feel forced to agree to other ideas brought forth by some of the people in high authority. As you know, he was under a bit of pressure at the time and was anxious to do nothing that would prejudice his chances of command. Fortunately, we were able to demonstrate our own ideas in rapid fashion. This, however, did not prevent some very stupid employment of armor.[30]

On March 21 Liddell Hart concluded this first round of meetings with American generals by visiting Bradley in London. Of all the conversations this one, if Liddell Hart's notes are any indication, was the pleasantest but the least profitable. Saying that he had read most of Liddell Hart's books—he was now reading Douglas Southall Freeman's *Lee's Lieutenants*—Bradley talked about the nature of war and about what he had learned in Tunisia. Referring to current conditions in the United Kingdom, Liddell Hart responded that despite the problems the British and American armies were "getting on better than any two Allied armies in history." He considered this all the "more reasonable because of 2 big handicapping conditions—difference of pay & crowded island."[31]

After completing his tour, Liddell Hart wrote notes to those he had visited. Sending Patton a copy of his recently expanded book, *British Way in Warfare,* the Briton told the general

> how very much I enjoyed meeting you and how stimulating I found it. The forbidding photographs (in a steel helmet) that have appeared in the newspapers, and the rather lurid stories that have been published, certainly don't do you justice.
>
> In that connection, I was amused to pass an inn, shortly before I reached your headquarters, bearing the curious sign "Legs of Man"—a cannibalistic note that was heightened by the words underneath "steaks and gulls." I was still more "tickled" when, at the very entrance to your drive, I saw another inn called "The Whipping Stocks Inn." It made me wonder whether some practical joker had been responsible for choosing the location of your headquarters.
>
> But these anticipations were soon revised after we had been talking for a bit. It was really good to come into contact with a soldier so full of ideas, progressive ideas, and so markedly dynamic. I shall look forward greatly to extending that contact.[32]

Despite this letter, Patton and Liddell Hart remained casual acquaintances, meeting just one more time. Liddell Hart's meeting with Wood, however, blossomed into a lifelong friendship, during which they frequently discussed Eisenhower, Marshall, Bradley, and especially Patton. "I immensely enjoyed our meetings," Liddell Hart complimented Wood.

> It was very refreshing to find someone who had such a clear grasp of the value and use of armoured forces, at a time when all too many people are swinging back to the conceptions of 1917. While it is clear that they have their limitations, it should also be clear that one of the outstanding lessons of this war is that it is only where armoured forces have scope and are used adequately, that there can be any decisiveness in operations. Otherwise, we are always dragged back to 1917 conditions. Perhaps the prominent part played by armoured forces in the latest Russian drives may help to bring home this lesson to people in our countries who have been so ready to write off armoured warfare as a passing phase.[33]

Reading Liddell Hart's book, *The Strategy of Indirect Approach,* Wood found himself

about 99% in agreement. Hope its three great lessons: surprise, alternate objectives, and sustained but flexible power are being duly considered by our planners. If not, 1915 will reappear like a gory ghost to damn us. The Russian operations & our Pacific moves are most encouraging in their recognition of the great fundamentals of indirect approach & least expectation. Maybe we shall see it here—at least I pray for it.[34]

IV

During his stay in England, Patton, friendly and sociable, sought out those, or the families of those, who had played important roles in his life. On the first of March he called on the sister-in-law of his godfather and first riding instructor, Captain Arthur John Lindsey Hutchinson, who, having married Aunt Sadie Patton, was also Georgie's uncle. The Hutchinsons were obviously athletic, for Horace Hutchinson, Arthur's brother, had been the English amateur golf champion around 1890. In England Patton also visited Sir Hugh Elles, who commanded the British tank force at Cambrai during the First World War. Despite his earlier espousal of armor, Elles would have fit Liddell Hart's and Wood's definition of a 1918 mind, for by 1935 he had concluded that "tanks were useless owing to anti-tank guns, rifles and mines." By the next year he conceded that heavily armored tanks might be used to support infantry. But Elles could not visualize, as such Americans as Patton and Wood and such Britons as Liddell Hart, Hobart, and Martel could, the use of light tanks for deep penetration and lightning thrusts behind the enemy.[35]

Too often during Patton's early months in England, strategy and tactics gave way to petty matters. On March 1 Ike advised Patton to replace Gay, who "did not," as Patton recorded it, have "the personality or background to represent me at other headquarters or to take over should I get hit. . . . I will try to get Gaffey," Patton noted. "Of course if something should happen to make Keyes available I will take him like a shot. Ike and I dined alone and had a very pleasant time. He is drinking too much and is terribly lonely. I really feel sorry for him—I think that in his heart he knows he is not really commanding anything."[36]

On the sixth Patton talked the matter over with Cummings, his adjutant, who advised telling Gay about the change. "It was most distasteful," Patton recorded of his meeting with Gay. "Gay was fine—could not have been better. I told him the exact truth that Ike ordered me to do it."[37]

The next day Patton settled the matter. "The two men I had in mind had been Middleton and Gaffey," he wrote. "Since Middleton was sent over by General Marshall to command a corps, he is out. Gaffey said that while he did not wish to give up the 2d Armored Division, he felt that since he owed me so much he would do it, if I can get Bradley to turn him loose, and I think I can. That will be a good solution because when Gaffey quit being chief of staff in the Desert he recommended Gay, and they are therefore good friends." Bradley readily consented to the change. Gaffey would be Patton's chief of staff, and Middleton would command Patton's VIII Corps.[38]

As Patton began inspecting and training his troops, a companion joined him. In mid-February Lady Margaret Leese, the extremely attractive wife of the British Lieutenant-General Oliver Leese, and Kay Summersby began searching for a pet for Patton. In early March a bulldog, whose name Patton changed from Punch to Willie, arrived. "He is 15 months old," Patton told Bea, "and pure white except for a little lemon on his tail which to a cursory glance would seem to indicate that he had used toilet paper." His previous owner, a Royal Air Force pilot, had failed to return from a mission. Leading a life almost as adventurous as that of his new master, Willie was run over by a truck the first week Patton had him. "He was pretty well skinned up and was very sorry for him self but otherwise is all right."[39]

Visiting Oliver's 5th Armored, Patton came away displeased. The men wore "bad and dirty" uniforms, with "no attempt to have all the men dress alike." Quarters, kitchens, and latrines were filthy. In marked contrast Patton found Bob Grow's 6th Armored "in superior shape." He planned to have General Walton Walker, the infantryman who commanded Patton's XX Corps, take Oliver with him on an inspection of the 6th and "note as painlessly as possible the difference."[40]

Studying the preliminary invasion plan of Bradley's First Army, Patton showed that he still adhered to some of Liddell Hart's beliefs. "It says," he observed, "that the object of Overlord is 'to secure a lodgment on the Continent from which further offensive operations can be developed.' The words 'further offensive operations' indicate to me the intention of halting on a phase line,—this is clearly wrong. We must land and keep on going. After we land we must keep driving as we did in Sicily. I am very much afraid this operation is going to be conducted in a timid manner. If so, it will not succeed."[41]

Flying on March 26 to London to see Hughes, fired by Devers in North Africa and subsequently appointed Ike's personal representative, Patton found him with Lucas, who had been replaced in Italy by Truscott. Patton came away from the meeting believing timidity had led to chaos at Anzio.

> As a result of my talk with Lucas, I think that he was timid on the beachhead. He said he did not feel justified in expending a corps. He did not expend it because he did not try. Had he taken the high ground he might have been cut off, but again he might not have been. Without the high ground in his possession, the landing was useless. Our losses to date in the beachhead are in excess of 18,000 which is more than a division and a half, so he made the expenditure without any justifiable gain.

On D-Day both Alexander and Clark were on the Anzio beach and, Lucas told Patton, "Kept breathing down his neck." Neither, however, "had the guts to order Lucas forward. I feel very sorry for Lucas," Patton commiserated, "as I think he knows he did wrong, yet thinks he did his duty. . . . I learned from Lucas that in the initial landing the British as usual failed to land until evening—14 hours late."[42]

On March 27 Patton visited Supreme Allied Headquarters, where he and Eddy were to be decorated with the British Companion of the Order of the Bath. Representing the king, Brooke, pinning on the ribbon, remarked: "Don't wince, Patton, I shan't kiss you." He said Georgie deserved the honor more than any other American, a compliment, Patton believed, he uttered to each person he decorated. Admiral Andrew B. Cunningham, now the First Sea Lord, "was there, and very nice as usual."[43]

By the end of the month Patton, who had taken formal command of the Third Army on the twenty-sixth, was again inspecting his units, this time Wade Haislip's XV Corps in northern Ireland. Accompanied by Hughes, Patton visited the 5th and 8th Infantry Divisions, the former commanded by Major General Stafford L. Irwin, who had served as an artillery officer in Tunisia. In a speech he himself considered "a little too long," Patton praised the members of the division for their two years of tedious service in Iceland. But in his diary Hughes noted something else about the address: "Geo talk to 5th (Irwin)—vile foul talk."[44]

If the address to Irwin's men was "vile foul talk," that to the other division showed Patton had not changed. Edward O. Williamson, a young officer who heard it, likened the speech to one by a Latin American dictator or a Southern demagogue. "He thought Patton's talk was mostly bombast interloaded with profanity," Patton's biographer Martin Blumenson has related, "and he had the distinct feeling that Patton came close to advocating the killing of prisoners."[45]

V

Returning to Peover early on the morning of April 4, Patton found that the killing of prisoners in Sicily had popped up again. Gaffey informed him that a War Department inspector general, who turned out to be Lieutenant Colonel Curtis L. Williams, was in London investigating the West and Compton episodes, matters Patton thought closed. Even though Patton had promised Alexander Clifford and the American correspondent who saw the Comiso shootings that he would right things immediately, he had to be pushed by Bradley on August 9 into arresting West and Compton. And, by continuing his fiery talks, he showed that he believed he bore no responsibility for the numerous incidents. "When the question of trying these two men for what was clearly barefaced murder came up, some of my friends advised me not to do it," Patton explained in his diary, "as they said that what has happened would happen because that would be the natural line that the defense counsel would take. However, I did not believe then and do not believe now that I can condone murder for my own benefit."[46]

Writing to Bea on the fourth of April, Patton absolved himself of responsibility in the shootings of the American paratroopers at Gela and in the known massacres. General Swing "has all the dope on the Parashoot business which was investigated by my inspectors and found perfectly OK also. They got lost, came over the wrong beaches during a German attack and damned few of them were hit except by the huns. Now some fair haired boys are trying to say that I killed too many prisoners. Yet the same people cheer at the far greater killing of Japs. Well the more I killed the fewer men I lost but they dont think of that."[47]

Unknown to Patton, the investigation of the Biscari episodes had begun that February in Washington. There Colonel Jones, the judge advocate of Patton's Seventh Army, described Patton's speech at Mostaganem during the preparations for the invasion of Sicily. Patton's comments so disturbed Jones that he spoke to Gay about them and suggested that Patton clarify his statements, "otherwise we might have his remarks misinterpreted and have violations of international law."[48]

The testimony of Colonel Forrest E. Cookson, also taken that February at the office of the inspector general, further damaged Patton. The commander of the regiment in which West and Compton served, Cookson said that Bradley knew of the West incident because he "came up one morning while we were in the field and talked to us about it, but I don't remember exactly what he said." He was sure that Bradley made no written report on either Biscari incident.

Cookson offered his interpretation of Patton's speech to the officers of the division.

> He said, in effect: "If the enemy, and you are advancing, and the enemy fires on you, and you see your comrades fall, you would continue to advance, and unless he attempts to surrender, he shall not live—or, advance to within one hundred yards, he shall not live." The remark was also made to the effect that snipers should not live. All this seems to me to be an effort, or a desire to kill on the part of the men, which is right, but in so doing, it is difficult to allow for the mentality of a man who cannot differentiate between what is right and what is wrong.

Taking notes on the talk, Cookson was sure that he had accurately transmitted Patton's comments to the men of his regiment. He thought West "of such a mentality that he did not differentiate between taking a prisoner in the heat of battle, i. e., taking as a prisoner one who fights to the last and then attempts to surrender and the killing of a man who has the status of a prisoner."

Cookson made it clear that he opposed Patton's policy of making rash statements. He testified "that it had worked out badly, and he, a regimental commander, took steps after the two incidents to inculcate in his men a different feeling towards prisoners."[49]

Not knowing the extent to which he had been implicated in the West and Compton episodes, Patton tried to cover his trail. On April 5 he spoke to Middleton about the two addresses he had made to the 45th Division, then

> camped in two different spots. . . . His memory of what I said was the same as my own and was also corroborated by Stiller and Codman who were present. . . . What I had said, or as nearly as I can remember was "In a close fight when you get within one or two hundred yards of the enemy and he shows signs of wishing to surrender, don't cease fighting and go in to get him, but keep on shooting until he comes to you with his hands up." Concerning snipers I said, "When you are sniped, especially from the rear, the snipers must be destroyed." Of course in neither case did I contemplate murder of men who had surrendered. The fact that Johnnie Waters is a prisoner would, aside from anything else, have made me the last one to do a thing to retaliate on him.[50]

Good friend that he was, Hughes helped out. He sent an endorsement of Patton to his West Point classmate, Major General Virgil L. Peterson, the United States Army's inspector general. "I have been with Patton probably more than any other officer in this theater except members of his immediate staff," Hughes explained. "I am firmly convinced that Patton never at any moment advocated the destruction of prisoners of war under any circumstances. I am convinced that Patton is a fighter for he looks at war realistically and does what few men in our army have yet dared to do—talk openly about killing. George believes that the best way of shortening the war is to kill as many Germans as possible and as quickly as possible." Patton was "too good a soldier and sportsman to advocate anything contrary to the strict rules." Hughes was writing to Peterson "as an old friend and also the Inspector General to tell you what I must tell someone."[51]

The top secret report of the investigation condemned Patton but did not recommend that any action be taken against him. Written by Lieutenant Colonel William R. Cook, it left no doubt that Patton's speeches had inspired the Biscari episodes. Even Middleton had testified that, in Cook's words, "both General Bradley and General Patton knew of the incidents and quoted General Patton as saying: 'If a son-of-a-bitch shoots at you, and keeps on shooting at you up to 200 or 300 yards, kill the bastard;' but that he did not interpret that as meaning you should shoot a prisoner. General Patton made at least two talks to the assembled officers of the Division, and after these talks, the officers, in one way or another, transmitted the remarks to their commands."[52]

Unfortunately, the story of Patton and the Sicilian massacres was far more complicated than even the inspector general's office realized. Clark Lee, who had witnessed and told Alexander Clifford about what must have been the Biscari murders, wrote nothing about them, perhaps adhering to the same promise Clifford and his American war correspondent friend had made to Patton after the Comiso incidents. Long after Patton's death, Clifford refused to let Liddell Hart reveal what he had seen. Even if Patton had not known of the worst of the incidents, the killing of civilians at Canicatti, he unquestionably realized from speaking to Bradley, to Clifford, to the unidentified American correspondent, and to Lee that the early days of the Sicilian invasion had brought forth a pattern of atrocities. He had promised Clifford to set things right. Yet by the early spring of 1944 Patton had convinced himself that he bore no responsibility for the incidents and, judging by his address to the 8th Infantry Division, continued to make fiery speeches.

VI

On April 7, 1944, accompanied by Maddox, Muller, and Gaffey, Patton attended the briefing of the American and British army commanders at St. Paul's School in London. In the morning Montgomery talked for two hours. Then came Air Chief Marshal Sir Trafford Leigh-Mallory, who commanded the tactical air forces supporting the invasion, and Admiral Sir Bertram H. Ramsay, the commander of the Allied ships in the invasion. This indicated to Patton that cooperation between the services was better than it had been before the invasion of Sicily, a tribute to Eisenhower. The navy, however, offered "lots of reasons why the thing would fail."

After lunch the Americans had their turn. Bradley, in charge of the First Army, spoke. He was followed by his corps commanders, Gerow and J. Lawton Collins. The Americans "did well," Patton believed. "The British were much too prolix and vague at the same time. . . . They have not got the training in such conferences which we have received from the War College and it always shows up."

Churchill delivered the final, and to Patton the most satisfying, address. "Remember," he said, "that this is an invasion, not a creation of a fortified beachhead." Agreeing with Patton, he called for a continuous push against the enemy.

That night Patton had dinner with a group that included Eisenhower, Assistant Secretary of War John J. McCloy, McNarney, Bradley, and Bedell. "McNarney jumped on Ike about the mishandling of replacements in Africa which is correct," Patton observed, "and they are doing a worse job here. I can't get anyone to realize that even without fighting, a unit is always about 8% below strength due to sickness etc., and that a unit 15% low in manpower is at least 30% low in efficiency. That is because none of our topflight generals have ever fought."

At dinner Ike brought up the inspector general's investigation. "You talk too much," he told Patton, who responded that if Ike ordered him not to talk he would stop. "Otherwise," he said, "I will continue to influence men the only way I know." To that Eisenhower answered: "Go ahead but watch yourself." The conversation led Patton to conclude: "All of them but me are scared to death."[53]

When McCloy and McNarney visited Peover, both warned Patton to stay out of trouble. "I was called on a number of times to try to calm down or cool off George Patton," McCloy remembered long after the war ended. McCloy, who had been the operations officer of a division during the First World War, was, like Stimson, a prominent lawyer and banker. Since becoming the assistant secretary of war in 1940, he had learned the story of Stimson's fondness for the Pattons. In 1911, after becoming secretary of war under President William Howard Taft, Stimson selected Patton as an aide. "From time to time Patton as we now know would get into difficulties," McCloy related, "because of his aggressive character." Stimson would bail him out. One instance came when, on maneuvers, Patton captured General Drum and spent more of his own money on gas for his tanks than even the government allotment. "So now and then when Patton would get in trouble Stimson would ask me to go out and calm him down or patch up the difficulty."

This time, however, Ike, whom McCloy was visiting, induced him to speak to Patton. As McCloy told the story:

> I recall one time before the landings, Patton wasn't scheduled to take part in the original landings and he was making all sorts of noises about it. He was quite clear that he was the one most competent to lead the armies against the Germans and he felt he ought to have been put in the first wave. Eisenhower got hold of me one time and said, "I know you've helped save Patton's skin, thanks to the Secretary of War, two or three times. . . . You go down and tell Georgie, I'm trying to get him, I'm going to get him in where he's going to have all the fighting he wants, but in the meantime you go down there and tell him to keep his God damned mouth shut!"

Taking "this mission seriously," McCloy went to Patton's headquarters, where, after lunch, he maneuvered Patton into "a little room by himself." There McCloy told the general that he was "getting to be quite a nuisance, that he was causing Eisenhower a lot of trouble and doing himself no good." McCloy said he had come to deliver a message straight from the commanding general: "Keep your God damned mouth shut, George, and you'll get all the fighting you want."

Patton's response was hardly what McCloy expected.

> He took me back a little by drawing himself up to his full height, which was rather impressive, particularly when he had that General's belt on and with his ivory handled pistols. (You musn't refer to them as pearl handled pistols because he was very sensitive about that). And he said, "You're taking a great deal of responsibility on yourself, Mr. Secretary, to come here on eve of battle," he didn't say "eve of the battle," he said "eve of battle, and to destroy a man's confidence in himself who is about to face the enemy." This took me back. This wasn't the way I thought the conversation would go. I thought he'd be rather humble over the fact that I had just given him this directive from the commanding general. But I recovered myself sufficiently to say, "Listen, George, if we thought

your confidence was as easily destroyed as that you wouldn't be where you are today." Immediately Patton replied—"Well, you'll never hear another word out of me." That wasn't true because we did, throughout the war, keep hearing from him. Every now and then when I'd see Eisenhower he'd say, "Maybe you'd better go down and see Patton again." But he was very partial to Patton. Eisenhower saw his virtues and his qualities, and but for his rather tenacious confidence in Patton, and also the fact that the Secretary of War several times intervened with Marshall, who I think was on the verge from time to time of at least considering whether Patton wasn't more of a nuisance than he was worth—though Marshall was also aware of Patton's qualities. But it was primarily Eisenhower's confidence in Patton that kept him at the front and as I say I think the Secretary of War had a good bit to do with it.

McCloy referred to the incident to show Eisenhower's wisdom and skill.

I had the feeling that Eisenhower did see clearer, more clearly than the British commanders did, the Montgomeries and Alan Brookes, the significance of air, the significance of modern warfare, and he had a concept that I think they lacked, and I think it's rather presumptuous of some of those people who were critical of Eisenhower in indicating that he was something of a—you know, good chairman of the board not a real commander. He was a real commander, and he was prepared to make prompt and difficult decisions. . . . He was in my judgment a real commander and a good cut above some of his postwar critical subordinates.[54]

Just after the meeting with McCloy, Patton innocently stumbled into more trouble. Accompanied by the ever-present Stiller, now a major; his old friend, Colonel Nicholas Campanole, who had served with Patton in Mexico; and several others, he drove on the twenty-fifth to Knutsford, where, almost against his will, he was asked to speak to the fifty or sixty guests at the opening of a Welcome Club. Patton, whose presence in England had been announced, over Ike's objection, just the week before by Bedell Smith, had no inkling a reporter was in the audience. Consequently he made a few charming, offhand remarks that, viewed today, should not have attracted the slightest attention. "I feel," he said, "that such clubs as this are a very real value, because I believe with Mr. Bernard Shaw, I think it was he, that the British and Americans are two people separated by a common language, and since it is the evident destiny of the British and Americans, and, of course, the Russians to rule the world, the better we know each other, the better job we will do."[55]

The next day, April 26, Marshall read in American newspapers "glaring reports of General Patton's statements." They could not, he telegraphed Ike, come at a worse time, for Congress was then considering a promotion list that would have elevated the permanent rank of both Patton and Bedell. Hoping to create a campaign issue for the coming election, the Republicans had latched on to Patton's innocent statement as an intrusion of the military into political matters.[56]

With Ike, Air Chief Marshal Tedder, Bradley, and Butcher away observing an amphibious landing exercise by the 4th Infantry Division, Bedell answered Marshall's telegram. He and Colonel Justus "Jock" Lawrence, the chief public relations officer in the European Theater, had persuaded a reluctant Ike to reveal Patton's presence in England. "His reluctance was due," Bedell wrote,

> to his belief that some incident like the present one would occur as soon as Patton could be quoted in the press. We argued that if Patton's name was not released, it would provide ammunition for some unscrupulous columnist to write that General Eisenhower and the War Department were keeping Patton's presence here concealed because of unwillingness to let the American people know that he was to exercise a command in the invasion forces. British press carried nothing that I have seen regarding any statement of the nature that Britain and America would rule the world. Coverage here was limited to rather innocuous quotes of the blood and guts type.[57]

On April 29 Marshall left the decision about Patton to Ike. But he made it clear he favored retaining Patton, the only American general with experience against Rommel, now in charge of German coastal defenses, and in landing operations followed by rapid inland movements. An editorial in the *Washington Post* of that day greatly troubled Marshall. The paper jibed that Patton had "progressed from simple assault on individuals to collective assault on entire nationalities." It quoted Congressman Karl Mundt, the South Dakota Republican, who said Patton "succeeded in slapping the face of every one of the United Nations except Great Britain." In his brief speech Patton had purportedly bragged about welcoming 170,000 German and Italian soldiers "to the Infernal Regions." He had also referred to English women as "ladies" and American women as "dames." The *Post* commented caustically:

> This was intended no doubt as gallantry and perhaps as a rough sort of military humor. The truth is however that it is neither gracious nor amusing. We do not mean to be prissy about the matter but we think that Lieutenant Generals even temporary ones ought to talk with rather more dignity than this. When they do not they run the danger of losing the respect of the men they command and the confidence of the public they serve. We think this has happened to General Patton. Whatever his merits as a strategist or tactician he has revealed glaring defects as a leader of men. It is more than fortunate that these have become apparent before the Senate takes action to pass upon his recommended promotion in permanent rank from colonel to major general. All thought of such promotion should now be abandoned.[58]

The editorial also horrified Stimson, who followed the "interchange between Eisenhower and Marshall" closely. The *Post,* he recorded in his diary, had "always been bitterly hostile to Patton" and to the War Department and

> therefore does not represent public opinion fairly. . . . But Patton's fate is hanging in the balance. It is all up to Eisenhower and the responsibility has been put on him, while at the same time General Marshall points out that Eisenhower must not be influenced by the fear that Patton's indiscretion is making it harder for us here. We can put up with it, Marshall says, perfectly well and the papers here, while they criticize his indiscretion have not gone so far as to seek his relief—that is, all except this one editorial in the Post.[59]

Patton could not have found a better friend than Eisenhower, but even Ike feared the worst. On May 2, just before Butcher left for four days of sea duty with Admiral Hall, Ike told him "he was afraid Patton's goose was cooked. Patton had violated Ike's order, i.e. no public speeches and interviews for the press." In the latest incident Patton did not know any reporters were present. "The furor raised by the Press and in Congress," Butcher observed, "simply emphasized Patton's instability and Ike was fearful he would be unable to save him this time. In fact Ike said Patton's chance of retaining his command was only one in a thousand."[60]

The accounts of what happened next are so contradictory that they seem to be describing different events. According to Patton, he received a call from Bedell on April 30 to report to Ike the next day. "In spite of possible execution I slept well," Patton noted on May 1, "and trust to my destiny. God has never let me or my country down yet." When Patton reported at eleven o'clock, Ike greeted him cordially, asking him to sit down, something that reassured Patton. "George, you have gotten yourself into a very serious fix," Ike began. Patton answered that Ike's job was far more important than his. He did not want Eisenhower, in trying to save Patton, to hurt himself. "I have now got all that the army can give me," Eisenhower responded; "it is not a question of hurting me but of hurting yourself and depriving me of a fighting army commander." At this point Patton clearly got confused, for in his diary he wrote that Marshall had telegraphed Eisenhower "that my repeated mistakes have shaken the confidence of the country and the War Department. General Marshall even harked back to the Kent Lambert incident in November 1942,—certainly a forgiving s.o.b." Actually, in a letter to Marshall on April 30, Ike had brought up Lambert's violation of censorship and Patton's "lifelong habit of posing and of self-dramatization which causes him to break out in these extraordinary ways."

During the conversation, as Patton recorded it, Ike admitted that he needed his old friend. "I am not threatening," Patton remembered answering, "but I want to tell you that this attack is badly planned and on too narrow a front and may well result in an Anzio, especially if I am not there." Ike replied: "Don't I know it, but what can I do?" Believing the front as planned was "too short," Patton recommended "three separate attacks on at least a 90 mile front." Ike did transmit one bit of good news. When he had spoken to the prime minister about Patton, Churchill said that "Patton had simply told the truth."

Patton's account of his emergence from the meeting with Ike is especially revealing. "When I came out," he wrote, "I don't think anyone could tell that I had just been killed. I have lost of competitions in the sporting way but I never did better. I feel like death, but I am not out yet. . . . All the way home, 5 hours, I recited poetry to myself."[61]

As Patton told it, his ordeal ended on May 3. Returning from an army hospital, where he had his teeth cleaned, Patton read a telegram from Eisenhower that said, in effect: "Since the War Department has placed the decision of relieving you on me, I have decided to keep you. . . . Go ahead and train your army." Ike later called Patton "and was very nice. Sometimes I am very fond of him and this is one of the times. When I read the wire, I called to Gay, 'The war is over,' which I always say when I mean that trouble is over. Captain Murnane heard me and thought I meant that the war was over for me. So when Hugh, Gay, Codman, Stiller and I all took a drink to celebrate, he thought we were very callous."[62]

In April 1951, over five years after Patton's death, Eisenhower told Jock Lawrence, the former publicity director for the movie producer Samuel Goldwyn; Brigadier General Anthony Drexel Biddle, Jr.; and an unnamed French officer a far different version of what happened. From the beginning of the planning for the invasion of France, Patton's flamboyance bothered Ike. Such staid but capable generals as Hodges, Simpson, Patch, and J. Lawton Collins always seemed overshadowed by Patton. Following the Knutsford speech, Ike said he had received a dispatch from Marshall directing him to relieve Patton and to ship him home. Eisenhower answered that he would quit if forced to relieve Patton. "If I am not considered capable in wartime of handling problems of my own officers and troops," Ike said he responded, "I can no longer properly continue to command in these posts. I therefore propose to accompany General Patton to the United States." Within a few hours Marshall instructed Ike to disregard the message about firing Patton.

While this portion of the story runs counter to the existing letters and telegrams exchanged between Marshall and Eisenhower, the rest of Ike's version probably contains some truth. In response to Ike's orders, Patton showed up at Supreme Headquarters Allied Expeditionary Force "resplendent as always in his get-up. He wore very shiny, highly-polished cavalry boots; his riding trousers were perfectly creased and immaculate; those two ivory-handled pistols were hanging in holsters at his waist; the left chest of his tunic was laden with ribbons; his shiny steel combat helmet bore three stars in front." Stepping forward, Patton "saluted smartly, stood at attention—and remained silent."

Patton held "the position of strict attention" as Ike handed him, one by one, three cables. The first called for Patton's relief, the second Ike's threat to resign. Patton read them, "showing no visible emotion." Ike next gave Patton the third cable, authorizing the Supreme Commander to do as he pleased. Ike then related the remainder of the story:

> Patton read this cable carefully as he had the others. Then he started to sob. It was horrible to see this tough old officer begin to blubber. Since he was much taller than I, he put his head on my right shoulder and continued to sob. Then his helmet fell off and bounced on the floor. He immediately stopped crying, stooped over, picked up his helmet, replaced it carefully on his head—and started to cry all over again.

Even when Eisenhower told the story, he showed amusement.

> I could no longer stand it. This was too much for me! I stretched out on the couch in my office and burst into laughter. George *couldn't even cry without his helmet!* Imagine that! All through my laughter, which I now regret for it was, in retrospect, cruel, General Patton stood at strict attention, not even looking at me lying on the couch, laughing. To look at me he would have had to change his position of rigid attention!
>
> That is how I informed George Patton that he was *not* to be returned to the U.S. But, I added, "I expect, George, from now on that you will please keep your goddamned mouth shut. When it is time for you to speak, *I will tell you!* I intend to use you to the fullest—you will have every opportunity to get into all the combat you ever dreamed of. That is all for the moment!"

Patton then saluted smartly, dried his eyes with a handkerchief, executed a perfect about-face, and briskly walked out of Ike's office. "I had to tell someone," Eisenhower related. "So I called in Beetle and told him what had happened. It is probably the only time in all the years of my long experience with Smith that I saw Beetle really lose himself in laughter!"[63]

Added up, these stories and correspondence indicate that Patton owed much to Ike. "Patton's skin has been saved again," Butcher observed on May 11th in an unpublished entry in his diary. "Ike told me last night he had written a blistering letter to Patton and although he told him it would be placed in his official record, actually it had not been." In a note to Bea, Georgie wrote that "the Lord came through again."[64] He might well have substituted "Ike" for "the Lord."

Thirteen

INVASION BLUES

I

"Every thing is O.K.," a happy George Patton wrote his wife on May 3, "because divine destiny came through in a big way. I am sorry that in some of my recent letters I sounded whiny I don't often indulge. I guess my trouble is that I dont realize that I am always news but you can bet I know it now. Well the Lord came through again but I was really badly frightened. . . . I have youthed thirty years since my last letter."[1]

His fear of being sent home eased—Marshall and Eisenhower would certainly have recalled Patton, Truscott, and Carleton had they known of the Canicatti massacre of civilians—Patton turned his thoughts to other things, including the coming presidential election at home. Since Patton's "divine destiny," as he loved to put it, received help from Stimson, he shuddered at the thought of a victory for the Republican candidate for president, Thomas E. Dewey, who, rumor had it, would replace Stimson with Patton's enemy, General Hugh A. Drum. "I hope he dont," Patton wrote Bea of Dewey. "But if he did . . . I guess I would be in the sawdust basket along with the rest. . . . After this war I am going to retire and call myself Mister Patton and cruise and fox hunt. For a few days I thought I was going to have to do it sooner than I wanted to but now all is rosy. Nock on wood."[2]

Continuing the training of his troops, Patton discussed with P. Wood on the eighth of May the tank and infantry demonstrations put on by his army over the past month. In a paper finished on that day Patton concluded that to be effective tanks must stay within three hundred yards of the infantry they supported. Like Wood, who would later argue that machine guns gave armored vehicles their potency, Patton called tanks "armored killing weapons of great fire power. . . . This fire power is useless," Patton brilliantly observed, "unless it can be applied 'on the spot' and rapidly. . . . Not *firing*," tanks were "junk." From experience he knew that the Germans always attempted to counter American infantry assaults with small groups of tanks. The lighter American tanks, operating at a range of four hundred yards or less, could best disrupt these counterattacks. They must begin firing immediately and keep firing. "They are 'in' on every possible target. Need no orders."

Supported by heavy artillery, the Germans usually delivered much of their firepower to the front, which Patton called the "top." If American troops massed "on top of objectives," they would "be blasted off." American antitank weapons must always be used on flanks and in depth. "*Never* on top. Rarely near top. . . . *Never* where *they* can be seen beyond their best range."[3]

Viewing from a half-track the rehearsal of an exercise to be held on May 10, a coordinated attack by infantry and tanks, Patton, accompanied by one of Wood's talented pets, Brigadier General Holmes E. Dager, later the commander of the 11th Armored Division, found much to criticize. "The support and reserves were so far back as to be wholly useless," he noted. The infantry officers and noncommissioned officers "just went along as members of the chorus, and gave no orders. It was very sad." During a second rehearsal the ground troops and the antitank units deployed poorly. That evening, when Patton assembled his leading armor officers and read his paper to them, he got slight response. "Hardly any officer even projects what he does in training into battle," he observed. "That is why they do so badly."[4]

Happily the exercise itself went off well. "I was delighted, and feel that I have at last illustrated the use of marching fire and of tanks and infantry."[5]

Two days later Patton attended a lunch at Eisenhower's headquarters at Widewing to commemorate the success of the African campaign. Present were thirty-two high-ranking British and American officers, to whom a relaxed Ike delivered one of his finest speeches. Eisenhower suggested they all stand and drink a silent toast to those who had been killed during the African fighting. At that Patton turned and "made the suggestion to Air Marshal Conyngham that I hoped neither he nor I would shortly be the object of a similar toast."[6]

On the fifteenth of May Patton saw many of these men again. The event was a briefing on the invasion given to 111 Allied leaders at Montgomery's headquarters at St. Paul's School in London. After Ike greeted the guests, his subordinates took over. "The beaches were outlined," commented Lieutenant General William H. Simpson, the future commander of the Ninth Army. "Oh, it was a grand terrain job they did there. It showed the obstacles out there in front and all that. Montgomery as the ground commander got up, you see, and talked about the thing." Monty then introduced Bradley, the commander of the American First Army and his subordinate during the invasion, and the British Lieutenant-General Miles C. Dempsey. "And then the Navy got in on the thing," Simpson continued, "and the rest of it. It was really a very historic thing."

After these talks the political leaders occupied the stage. Prime Minister Jan Christian Smuts of South Africa, King George VI of England, and Churchill spoke. "I don't remember General Eisenhower's speech very well," related Patton's close friend from North Africa and Sicily days, Admiral Hall, "but I remember Mr. Smuts very well because he told us that we were attempting something that had never succeeded in history and he doubted whether we would succeed. I often wondered why they let him talk to us." If Hall resented Smuts, he admired King George. "I remember so well his standing up before us and with a slight quivering of his chin, which indicated the stammer he had been afflicted with earlier but had overcome so well, telling us in a very sincere and earnest way that he had great confidence because God was on our side." Churchill, too, made an inspiring speech that Hall "enjoyed."

Patton played no role in the proceedings, but, Hall related, he made his presence known.

> I can remember sitting right behind me was George Patton, commanding the Third Army, which wasn't to become active until the breakthrough at Normandy, and his Chief-of-Staff, General Gaffey. And I remember that when one of the Canadian Generals got up and went into much more detail than any other General or Admiral had gone in presenting his plan, George Patton got quite bored and whispered in a loud enough voice so I could hear, "If that So-and-So doesn't shut up, I'm going to do so-and-so," both terms very vulgar, and I started snickering, and General Montgomery's Chief-of-Staff in the front row heard him and got up and

whispered in the ear of the Canadian General and he shut up right away.[7]

Years later, while visiting Admiral Hall in Honolulu, Lieutenant-General Henry D. G. Crerar, the commander of the Canadian forces in the invasion, recalled the episode. Even though Patton had insulted one of his subordinates, Crerar, who had been sitting next to Hall at St. Paul's, practically rolled on the floor laughing as he repeated Patton's words.[8]

II

In England Patton's staff labored endlessly. "Our work days are long," Lieutenant Colonel Bernard S. Carter, the assistant to Patton's G-2, Colonel Oscar Koch, wrote his wife. ". . . The camp has calls at 7:02—a lunch takes about 10 minutes to swallow." Amid the training and the planning, the officers sought relaxation during off-hours at the dinners and dances attended, as Carter freely admitted to his wife and to his father-in-law, by American and British women.[9]

Carter, now like Codman a lieutenant colonel, gave some indication of the hardworking yet relaxed atmosphere at Patton's headquarters. "I can quite understand your wanting to know more about Oscar," he answered his wife several weeks after joining the Third Army, "as he forms such an important part of my life over here. He really is a wonderful person—he's just good—very thoughtful & kind & unselfish & modest—perhaps not quite self-assertive enough, very naive in worldly things & shy of women. . . . He's an excellent G-2 & grand to work for as he's such a good organizer & you know what he wants."[10]

A short time later Carter sent more details about Koch. "He's a fine boss to work for in every way," Carter observed, "& all his subordinates are devoted to him. He suffers terribly when he feels compelled to get rid of an inefficient man. He adores anything sweet, so if you can scrape together some chocolate in any form, *please send a little*."[11]

With Codman, his roommate at both Groton and Harvard, Koch, Hammond, Harkins, and other staff members, Carter made the rounds of social events given by wealthy Britons for the Americans. Patton himself loved visiting the thousand-acre estate of Major Cuthbert

Leicester-Warren and his wife. Attending a dance at the estate—Patton, Codman, and Koch were also there—at the end of March, Carter described their home as "early Georgian & huge—with Reynolds, Romneys etc." and the Leicester-Warrens as "a charming, refined frail old couple" served by "a very old butler creeping around with claret, port & brandy. . . . There were some U.S. nurses there," Carter informed his wife of the dance, "looking rather grim in their thick uniforms. Poor dears they had a hard time competing with the English girls—most of whom were surprisingly pretty." The hit of the occasion was the Leicester-Warrens' lovely daughter, Lady Margaret Leese. The wife of Lieutenant-General Oliver Leese, who had commanded the British XXX Corps in Sicily and who now, with Montgomery in England, led the British Eighth Army in Italy, Lady Leese ran a nearby Red Cross club for officers. "She's really pretty," Carter commented, "though Oscar did not think so—not enough oomph!"[12]

Agreeing with Carter's assessment of Lady Leese, Patton found her captivating—in a purely Platonic way, for she loved her husband deeply. At their first meeting in February she had promised to join Kay Summersby in the search for a dog for Patton. A couple of days later Patton

> went to a big city near here to see Lady Leese open a red cross officers club. There were several Lord Mayors there all dressed up with huge chains and medals over their shoulders . . . but the greatest thing in the show was Lord Darby. He came right out of a book. He is very old and wears the strangest collar I have ever seen but is full of fire and demanded that two men lift him to his feet so he could meet me "Properly and like a soldier that I was once by God." We got on fine and talked horses. He asked me to stay with him if I ever came to Liverpool.[13]

That May Codman, Carter, and Patton went over to the Leicester-Warrens to arrange the details of another dance. "Lady Leese was there," Carter told his wife, "looking very pretty but a bit vapid." She seemed to come just for Patton, who paid her great attention and "walked her home. Apparently she made a big hit with him. As Charlie says he's invited up here to stay for the dance—isn't that amusing.

She'll be moving in such high circles that a mere Lt. Col. won't see much of her, but 'tant pis.' "[14]

Meantime, Bea was passing on to her husband, whose father had long ago warned him he had no understanding of business and economics,[15] the Ayer family's disdain for labor and its fear of postwar domination by America's current allies. In January, after workers struck and the army began running the railroads, General Marshall blasted the Railway Brotherhoods for prolonging the war. Along with her thoughts on internationalism, Bea wrote her husband the details. "I agree with you about the strikes and about Post War," he answered her. "The first shows weakness the second is bad as already there are family squabbles which are beginning to be reflected in the forces."[16]

Without realizing it Patton's wife was planting in her husband's mind the ideas that would end with him losing what he had struggled so hard to get—the Third Army.

III

For a good reason Patton's Third Army was not to participate in the Normandy invasion. Sir Ronald Wingate of the London Controlling Section, which devised and handled plans of deception against Germany and Italy, later summarized the deception problem facing the Allies. They could not deny that they intended to invade the continent and that they were building up men and supplies in the United Kingdom. The London Controlling Section, therefore, tried to make the date and place of the invasion confusing. "To sum up," Sir Ronald observed, "where a campaign is in progress in a theatre, no security can prevent the enemy assuming that you are going to launch operations somewhere and at some *particular* time. In the opposite case, perfect security can keep him uncertain as to if, to say nothing of when or where, you are going to launch an operation."[17]

British ingenuity led to the creation of an elaborate scheme. During the war British intelligence broke the supposedly unbreakable German ciphers, from which the Allies got vast amounts of information. In late 1943 one of these Ultra messages revealed that Field Marshal Gert von Rundstedt, the German Commander in Chief West, believed that an

Allied invasion force would come across what the French called the Pas de Calais and the English called the Straits of Dover. At its narrowest point the Pas de Calais separated the White Cliffs of Dover and France by only twenty miles. Armed with this information, the British Lieutenant-General Frederick E. Morgan, who was in charge of planning the invasion, thought of deceiving the Germans into believing the Allies were assembling an army for such an assault. Thus was created Fortitude South, approved by General Eisenhower on February 21.[18]

A seemingly discredited Patton fit perfectly into the plan. "All the Germans thought that Patton was a Sherman and Sheridan combined in one," Admiral Kirk commented. Fortitude South capitalized on this fear of Patton. It created a paper First United States Army Group, or FUSAG, containing over one million men. Formed to carry out the invasion, FUSAG supposedly consisted of Patton's Third Army, located in Cheshire, north of the Thames River, and the First Canadian Army, then south of the Thames. Patton was to be the group commander.[19]

An actor as well as a soldier, Patton relished his role. Fortitude South became his stage. Movie-set designers from the Shepperton Studios supplied Patton's dummy force with tanks, trucks, cannons, and other military equipment, all of inflatable rubber. Landing craft, made of canvas and wood and floating on oil drums, crowded the harbor. The movie men also constructed near Dover a phony dock and large numbers of oil tanks, supposedly the gas supply for Patton's tanks. Adding credence to the deception, King George and Ike visited the facility, and Ike attended a dinner at the White Cliffs Hotel in Dover, honoring the construction crews.

Patton played his role to the hilt. General James Gavin, who had led the parachute jump at Gela in Sicily, later told the historian William B. Breuer of an episode that took place in Claridge's Hotel in London in mid-May 1944. In the hotel lobby Gavin bumped into Patton, who greeted him warmly. After a brief conversation, Georgie shouted in a voice loud enough for everyone in the lobby to hear: "See you in the Pas de Calais, Gavin!"

Further fostering the deception, the Allies used German General Hans Cramer, the last commander of the vaunted Africa Corps. Captured when Tunisia fell, Cramer grew ill in an Allied prisoner of war camp in Wales. The British decided to send him home via Sweden, which was neutral. Taken to London, he met Patton, who was introduced as the commander of FUSAG. In a gesture reminiscent of the prewar French movie *Grand Illusion,* Patton gave a dinner honoring his onetime opponent, during which he and his corps and division commanders several times referred to the Pas de Calais invasion. Reaching Germany, Cramer reported to the German leaders and to Hitler personally what he had learned in England. The invasion, led by the feared General Patton, would come at the Pas de Calais.[20]

During May the Allies received several indications that the Germans had fallen for the ruse. A captured map, dated May 15, indicated that the Germans had fifty-eight divisions in France and the Low Countries. The Germans, however, credited the Allies with fifty-six infantry divisions, seven airborne divisions, fifteen armored divisions, five independent infantry brigades, fourteen tank regiments, and six parachute battalions, all ready for the invasion. The captured map indicated that the Germans included in these figures Patton's notional FUSAG force, then supposedly preparing for the assault at the Pas de Calais. Another map, captured on May 20, showed that the Germans still inflated the number of Allied troops. As D-Day approached, the massing of Nazi formations near the Pas de Calais became more and more evident. Concentrated in this sector, the German Fifteenth Army contained nineteen divisions, in contrast to the ten German divisions in Normandy and the eight in Brittany.[21]

Patton's staff contributed greatly to the deception. It issued orders, freely spread about, covering training and personnel for FUSAG. One fictitious military exercise followed another. These bore such colorful names as "Haircut," "Vanity," "Jitterbug," "Filmstar," and "Honeysuckle."[22]

IV

A self-admitted "goddamed natural-born ham" who enjoyed "playing Sarah Bernhardt,"[23] George Patton displayed his theatrical talents during the FUSAG deception. He also showed his acting ability while repeatedly giving, in May and June 1944, what some historians have termed "the speech," a cleansed version of which opened the movie *Patton.* Patton gave the carefully rehearsed and orchestrated address at least four times, and possibly more, to segments of his Third Army. On May

29, according to Colonel Theodore J. Krokus of the 514th Quartermaster Truck Group, he delivered the address to a meeting of the Third Army's Group and Higher Commands. Two days later, after being introduced by his and Chynoweth's friend and Army War College classmate Major General Gilbert R. Cook and by Simpson, Patton gave the talk to the officers and the noncommissioned officers of the top three grades stationed around Camp Bewdley, near Stourport, England. Patton spoke a third time on June 5, 1944, to an audience composed largely of enlisted men.[24]

The fourth instance seems to have been just before the Third Army left England for France. "I remember vaguely a big amphitheater," observed Lieutenant Joshua Miner of the 696th Armored Field Artillery Battalion. "It must have been an old soccer stadium of some sort, and it was filled with officers. Very few G.I.s. But there were nurses as well as male officers. And Patton made a speech. . . . He was very profane."[25]

In every case "the speech," as taken down or recalled by those who heard it, was substantially the same. The introduction of Patton, however, varied from camp to camp. "We are here," Simpson, the commander of the XII Corps, began, "to listen to the words of a great man. A man who will lead you into whatever you may face, with heroism, ability, and foresight. A man who has proved himself amid shot and shell. My greatest hope is that someday soon, I will have my own great army fighting with him, side by side."

Striding to the microphone, Patton, on each occasion, ordered his troops, then standing, to be seated. He began by speaking of the desire of Americans to win, whether it be in athletics or war. "The Americans love a winner," he said, "and cannot tolerate a loser. Americans despise cowards. Americans play to win—all the time. I wouldn't give a hoot for a man who lost and laughed. That's why Americans have never lost and will never lose a war, for the very thought of losing is hateful to an American." Counseling his men to overcome their fears, Patton explained: "The real man never lets the fear of death overpower his honor, his duty to his country and his innate manhood." An army was a team. "It lives, sleeps, eats, fights as a team. This individual heroic stuff is a lot of crap. The bilious bastards who wrote that kind of stuff for the Saturday Evening Post don't know any more about real battle than they do about fucking."

One observer related what came next:

"We have the finest food, the finest equipment, the finest spirited men in the world," Patton bellowed. He lowered his head, shook it pensively. Suddenly he slapped his hand and facing the men belligerently, said, "Why, by God, I actually pity these sons of bitches we are going up against—by God, I do." The men clapped and howled delightedly. There would be many a barracks tale about the old man's choice phrases. This would become a part of a parcel of Third Army history.

Everyone, Patton pointed out, had an important job to do. He told of the soldier in Tunis who sat atop a telegraph pole repairing the wire amid ferocious enemy fire. When Patton stopped and asked him if it was not "a little unhealthy right now," the soldier replied: "Yes sir, but this goddam wire has got to be fixed." Patton also told of the truck drivers on the road to Gabès. "All the day they drove along those son-of-a-bitching roads, never stopping, never diverting from their course, with shells bursting all around them. We got through on good American guts. Many of the men drove over 40 consecutive hours."

Patton then turned to a personal note.

Don't forget. You don't know I'm here at all. No word of the facts is to be mentioned in any letter. The world is not supposed to know what the hell they did to me. I'm not supposed to be commanding this army—I'm not supposed to be in England. Let the first bastards to find out be the goddamn Germans. Some day I want them to raise up on their hind legs and howl, "Jesus Christ! It's the goddam Third Army and that son-of-a-bitch Patton again!!"

We want to get the hell over there! We want to get over there and clean the goddam thing up. Then we'll have to take just a little jaunt against the purple-pissing Japanese and clean their nest out before the Marines get all the credit. . . .

Sure, we all want to go home—we want to get this thing over with—but you don't win a war lying down. The quickest way to get it over is to go get the bastards. The quicker they are whipped the quicker we go home. The shortest way home is through Berlin. . . .

There is one thing you all will be able to say when you go home. You may all thank God for it. Thank God that at least thirty years from now, when you are sitting around the fireside with your brat on your knee, and he asks you what you did in the great World War II, you won't have to say that you shoveled shit in Louisiana![26]

Interspersed between deliveries of this speech, Patton made other addresses to his troops. Harry M. Kemp, later a colonel, remembered Patton's talk, in a large theater, to the officers and NCOs of the 28th Infantry Division. Mounting the stage, Patton, wearing riding boots and holding a riding crop, which he snapped about crisply, seemed, with his white hair and aristocratic air, to be what his speech belied. Instead of a high-minded address, the soldiers got a barracks talk filled with curses and vulgarities. In a high-pitched, almost falsetto voice, Patton resorted to his pre-Sicily address. The troops were urged to "kill, kill, kill—or be killed." The Germans, well trained and fully equipped, were prepared to die for their country. His message over, Patton, with the troops at attention, left the stage. Kemp, a great admirer of Bradley, the former commander of the division, noted one difference in Patton's appearance. Since the slapping incidents, Bradley had refused to let Patton wear his twin revolvers. During the speech, Patton carried only a revolver in a holster under his left armpit.[27]

V

Late May and early June became for Patton a time for speeches and meetings. On May 29 he met with his four corps commanders—Major Generals Walton Walker, who commanded the XX Corps; Wade Haislip of the XV Corps; Cook of the XII Corps; and Middleton of the VIII Corps. Also present was Weyland of the XIX Tactical Air Command.[28]

That June 1 Patton drove to Bristol in what Chester Hansen described as "a huge, black Packard automobile, eloquently outfitted with silver flag staffs, a plethora of stars, . . . and a giant Greyhound bus horn" to see Bradley. The two then flew to Portsmouth to visit Monty, who lived nearby. After the taste of Patton he had gotten in Sicily, Monty was especially interested in the Third Army's role in the French operation. Having "rehearsed the whole thing for General Simpson" two days before, Patton boasted that "I was very fluent." Twice Monty said to Bradley: "Patton should take over for the Brittany campaign, and possibly for the Rennes Operation."

Dempsey and Crerar later joined the group. "General Dempsey had the Corps in Sicily which failed to take Catania," Patton commented. "He is not very impressive looking, and I take him to be a yes-man." Crerar was "better but not impressive." Patton considered Monty's chief of staff, Francis W. de Guingand, "very clever but he was extremely nervous and continuously twists his long black oily hair into little pigtails about the size of a match."

When Patton returned to Bristol that evening, Bradley's staff met him "with a great convoy of chattering motorcycles, knowing of his fondness for noisy escorts. Dick Dudley," Hansen related, "assigned him a room at the Holmes and after dinner we quickly turned him to a movie, 'The Bridge of San Luis Rey' which he viewed with a glass of port delicately balanced on one knee."

At ten the following morning "a gleaming ship" with the insignia of the 9th Air Force arrived to pick Patton up. "Bradley and Patton said goodbye," Hansen recorded. "Patton clenched Bradley's hand, hitched up his trousers under the custom tailored British tunic to say, 'Brad, the best of luck to you. We'll be meeting again—soon, I hope.'"

That evening Patton was the topic of conversation among the senior members of Bradley's staff. Again Hansen recorded the gist of the discussion.

General Patton, of course, is extremely unpopular in this Headquarters. Most of our officers have carried with them the punctured legend from Sicily. When I told the Captain of the MPs to provide a motorcycle escort for Patton's arrival, he grinned and asked, "Shall we have them wear boxing gloves?" He was referring, of course, to the slapping incident. We have a picture of Patton, a belligerent one, with the wrestling belt, the silver handled revolver, the chin back, staring at the sun. [Monk] Dixon snorts and says it looks like the photos of Mussolini we saw in Sicily. Patton's uniform consists of a tight battle dress of his own design, with brass studs around the waist mark, and shiny brass buttons in place of the dark ones.[29]

When the fifth, the scheduled date of the invasion, arrived, Patton, not being a featured player, was unsure whether it went off. A report from Ike seemed to indicate that bad weather had forced him to shove it back a day. "Bradley hoped this would be the case," Patton recorded, "because the tide situation on the 6th is better than that of this morning, and gives more time for daylight naval bombardment." In longhand he added: "I still believe in night attacks."[30]

For Patton the invasion brought hope of American success and fear that he would be left out of it. He felt

> sure that all the so-called information we get over the radio is imaginary, as, from my previous experiences in landings, I know that were I on the beach I would not know a damn thing at this time of the operation, so how can the commentators know anything? . . . I have horrible feelings that the fighting will be over before I get in but I know this is not so, as destiny means me to be in. . . . I started to pack up my clothes a little bit, always hoping, I suppose, that someone will get killed and I will have to go.[31]

Patton was unquestionably the most famous American left behind. On the fifteenth of June, he told Bea, he went to the theater in Manchester with Lady Leese. At the curtain call Leslie Henson, the leading man,

> said that he had played in Africa before the 8th Army and that the wife of its general was in the audience. Every one clapped then he said that with her was the most famous American general a man noted for blood and I will not say guts in front of ladies. Then every one cheered and yelled for a long time. After the show we went back stage and when we came out there was a huge crowd around the car and we had quite an ovation. I had a hell of a time keeping it out of the papers. As a matter of fact it would have been a good thing except that some people would have said I staged it which of course I did not.[32]

Although still in England, Patton continued to play a key role in the Normandy campaign. When General Brian Horrocks, after spending fourteen months recovering from wounds he received in North Africa, took command of the British XXX Corps that August, he asked Montgomery why the D-Day landings had succeeded. Monty's first reason was Patton and Fortitude. The Germans, whom Montgomery denigrated as possessing "card-index minds" that, once fixed, remained obstinate, held onto the notion that the real invasion would come at the city of Calais, the location of most of the German unmanned V-bomb launching sites. Playing their roles to the hilt, the Allies assembled dummy landing craft in the Thames River and dummy gliders on the airfields in Kent. Monty especially praised the role of the Allied Air Forces in the deception. Preparing for the invasion of Western Europe, the Germans had fifty-eight divisions strung out along the coast from Holland to Normandy. To prevent the Germans from moving troops from the Calais area to Normandy, Allied planes ceaselessly attacked railway yards, rail junctions, and bridges. Patton added great force to the deception simply by appearing to lead the new invasion force. "Montgomery then added," Horrocks wrote, "that he had dealt with the main points of 'Fortitude' in considerable detail because this was, in his opinion, the most carefully prepared and completely successful cover plan in the history of war."[33]

The enemy diplomatic communiques decoded by the Americans, known as Magic intercepts, indicated that from Hitler on down the Germans fell for the deception. On the twenty-seventh of May the Japanese Ambassador to Germany, General Ōshima Hiroshi, met with Hitler, who said:

> Well, judging from relatively clear portents I think that diversion-ary actions will take place in a number of places—against Norway, Denmark, and the southern part of western France, and the French Mediterranean coast. After that—when they have estab-lished bridgeheads in Normandy and Brittany and have sized up their prospects—they will come forward with an all-out second front along the Straits of Dover. We ourselves would like nothing better than to strike one great blow as soon as possible. But that would not be feasible if the enemy does what I anticipate; their men will be dispersed. In that event, we intend to finish off the enemy's troops at the several bridgeheads. The number of German troops in the west still amounts to about 60 divisions.[34]

The Normandy invasion on June 6 failed to change German minds. On the nineteenth Ōshima spoke to Undersecretary Adolf von Steen-gracht of the German Foreign Ministry, who confessed that because

Normandy was being defended "by a relatively small number of German troops, we are afraid that it may soon fall." Steengracht revealed why the Germans declined to reinforce their forces there.

> Information obtained from prisoners, captured documents, etc., indicates that twenty-three divisions commanded by General Patton are being held in readiness to make new landings. This threat is one reason why Germany has avoided pouring in a great number of men into the Normandy area. . . . The forces under General Patton's command are in addition to the total of thirty-six divisions assigned to Montgomery. As originally planned, Montgomery was to capture both Cherbourg and Le Havre with seventeen divisions and then advance with his main forces southeast along the Seine River; simultaneously, Patton's force was to land in the area east of Dieppe. However, Montgomery has already employed twenty-five divisions—of which two have been annihilated and others have suffered considerable losses—and is still fighting his way forward west of Caen. Nevertheless, we still consider Patton's forces will probably land between Dieppe and Boulogne, and preparations have been made accordingly.[35]

On June 27, three weeks after the landings, Steengracht indicated to Ōshima that his government's thinking remained the same. He admitted that the fall of Normandy would "have a bad effect from a psychological and political point of view rather than a military one." German leaders believed that "the forces under Patton are still assembled east of Southampton and are preparing a fleet of more than three hundred and fifty vessels of various sizes in order to stage another invasion in the near future." Neither Ōshima nor the Nazis were sure exactly where Patton would land, but the best guess was east of the present invasion site, somewhere near Le Havre. "Germany hopes to surprise this invasion force," Steengracht said, "and, after destroying it, to proceed to make short work of the Anglo-American forces in Normandy."[36]

Digesting such messages, Allied leaders desired to continue Fortitude South as long as possible. For the good of the invasion forces, Patton must remain in England.

VI

On June 19, while the cover plan was in full bloom, Liddell Hart again visited Patton. This time their discussion, held as before at Peover Hall, ranged over the entire scope of warfare. Patton began by revealing to Liddell Hart that his Third Army now contained thirteen divisions. Calling the results of air force bombings "much overrated," he remarked "that he could put down more explosives in a day than the whole Allied bombing force." To illustrate his point, Patton showed Liddell Hart an aerial photograph of some bridges over the Seine River that the air force, despite the weight of its bombs, failed to damage. His army could, he believed, easily destroy the bridge. "He went on to quote an officer," Liddell Hart remembered, "who had recently said that bombers in the next war would be like gas in this war—merely a suspended threat." Patton agreed and predicted that "the experience of this war would lead nations to realize the futility of the mutual devastation that bombing produces, compared with its limited military effect."

Patton had just returned from London. There, on the eighteenth, a member of his staff was killed by the flying bombs that destroyed the Guards' Chapel at Wellington Barracks. His thoughts about aviation spilling over onto one another, Patton said that he always flew to London, the trip, including the drives to and from the airport, taking an hour and a half each way. Although he denigrated the air force, he himself got a pilot's license in 1928. He then bought a three-seater plane and with Bea used to fly around the country. Testing himself, he once flew across the United States alone. Because of troubles getting gas, the trip took longer than it would have by car. His plane held enough fuel for only 360 miles, which meant that Patton frequently had to stop at a military post to get gas for the next leg of the trip. Officers at every camp refused to sell him fuel, for he was not traveling on military assignment, but in each case the post commander ended up giving him free gas, "on the quiet."[37]

Turning to the battle now taking place in Normandy, Patton freely exhibited his dislike of the British. Summarizing Patton's views, Liddell Hart found them odd.

He remarked that the American forces had penetrated much deeper than the British, at every stage, and that round Caen the

British had failed to gain any of their objectives, while the Americans were overrunning the Cherbourg peninsula. I queried this statement, pointing out that the British forces had, surely, absorbed the enemy's strength at the critical time, and thus provided the shield under cover of which the American advance across the Cherbourg peninsula had become possible. He did not agree, and went on to remark that the British had more men ashore than the Americans. I queried this, citing the number of divisions respectively. He replied that the actual number of troops was greater in the British forces, but they had landed too large a proportion of "condiment-troops." He also said that there were more German divisions facing the Americans than facing the British. I queried this, remarking that I understood that 4 Panzer divisions were engaged on the British front at present, and only 1 on the American front. He disagreed, saying that the proportion of German armour on each front was about equal—2½ Panzer divisions apiece—while there were more infantry divisions on the American front. (This was quite contrary to the facts. It struck me as curious that he should express such slighting comparisons between the American and British effort to anyone with whom he had quite a short acquaintance.)

Not done, Patton argued that the Americans landed on worse beaches than the British. Liddell Hart found it "difficult to reconcile this assertion with the fact that a North-Westerly wind was blowing, from which the Cherbourg peninsula should have sheltered the American beaches rather more than it did the British beaches."[38]

The two men went on to discuss the bungling of "the stroke to cut across the Cherbourg peninsula." Patton and Liddell Hart both blamed the overcautiousness of Major General Raymond O. Barton, whom Liddell Hart mistakenly believed had been removed from command of the 4th Infantry Division.

P. believed that one should never penalize a commander for making mistakes that were due to audacity, even where it was carried to the point of rashness, but only for failing to take risks—so often in war the apparently rash move came off. In further discussions of this subject, P. remarked that if he himself were to make another mistake, there was always one remedy he could take—to go and get killed. "No one criticizes a dead general,"—that is if he dies on the battlefield. (P. is evidently very sensitive still about the trouble into which he got by striking a soldier in the hospital during the Sicilian campaign, and the outcry it produced. This doubtless accounted for his frequent reiteration in conversation of such phrases as "You musn't quote me"; "This is off the record"; "You haven't seen me"; etc—which became rather wearisome.)[39]

To Liddell Hart, Patton's next statement seemed curious. Obviously unaware of the Magic intercepts that indicated the Germans expected him to land at Calais, he argued that the invasion should have taken place there, rather than at Normandy, "as it was nearer to the objective." To support this dubious contention, he cited the belief of the sixteenth-century English sailor Sir Francis Drake that Calais was the logical place for a British invasion of France. While Patton's comment indicated the depth of his historical reading, it did not, Liddell Hart thought, "show an adequate appreciation of the difference in the conditions of warfare, and the difference in the problems involved in deploying large modern forces so that they should have ample room for maneuver." When Liddell Hart argued that the high cliffs near Calais presented a more severe obstacle than the flatter Normandy coast, Patton answered that the concrete wall Gerow's V Corps had faced in Normandy proved more troublesome than any cliff, "and that in any case the defenders are unable to shoot down on the beaches effectively from high cliffs. I said that while this might be true, troops who landed on beaches beneath high cliffs had still got to scale the cliffs before they could deploy properly, and it was particularly difficult to use tanks effectively under such conditions."

This led to a discussion of tanks and infantry that shocked Liddell Hart, for Patton spoke as he had the previous March. Like his countrymen Fuller, Martel, and Hobart, Liddell Hart had long maintained that tanks, properly used, could outmaneuver and defeat infantry. He heard Patton's words with distress.

He argued that it was necessary for us now to go back to 1918 tactics, with the Infantry moving ahead of the Tanks. The British 7th Armoured Division had forfeited the fruits of its thrust to Villers-

Bocage last week because the Infantry were not on hand to complete the task. He had changed his mind about the relative importance of infantry and tanks, and now had come round to the view, which he used to deny, that it was the infantry who decided the issue. I qualified this, arguing that it would be truer to say that the infantry action was indispensable in completing the issue, rather than that it was their action that decided the issue. He agreed that this was a better way of putting it.[40]

Downgrading armor, Patton emphasized the foolhardiness of tanks battling antitank weapons. Before tanks could operate successfully, these weapons must be knocked out by fire from guns of superior caliber, shooting from longer range. The British seventeen-pounder, designed for desert conditions, could not accomplish this in Normandy, where the field of fire was shorter than in the desert. The American 76-millimeter bore a like handicap. As for tanks themselves, Patton praised the American Mark IV, "which you call the Sherman," as "the best tank in the Allied armies." He disliked the two popular British models, the Cromwell and the Churchill.

Patton said that in his operations he had learned to trust no one. The intelligence branch always overestimated "the enemy's strength and the difficulties of a problem." If he believed what intelligence had told him, he never would have attempted his advance from Palermo to Messina. "He related with relish how at a recent conference at his Army headquarters, he had first said that the 'G-2 of the Third Army is the best in the whole U. S. Army,'—but then added 'It is always 50% wrong.'" The Quartermaster Corps, too, was consistently conservative. In Africa, Patton found

that it was possible to do three times better than they reckoned—in the amount of troops that could be moved and maintained.

Similarly, in landings from the sea, it pays to take chances. The day when he landed on the West coast of Morocco was the only one in five months that would have been suitable. Even as it was, many boats were swamped on the second day, and he was forced to stop the process of disembarkation on the beaches—but he found a way round the difficulty by sending all the boats into a tiny harbour that had been captured in the first day's coup. Even a petty port is better than the best of beaches. He admitted, however, that our development of a "synthetic" harbour, for use on the Normandy beaches, had been a great success. He also expressed a high opinion of the staff organization of the 21st Army Group.[41]

Patton then attempted to answer a question that had puzzled Liddell Hart for a year. Why, in Sicily, had so many Germans escaped? In Patton's view, Liddell Hart wrote, "if our forces had included a horsed cavalry division—the 'Germans would not have got a man away from Sicily.'" Cavalry, Patton believed, moved through difficult country faster than infantry and could outflank tanks. In Sicily Patton had pieced together a cavalry regiment using horses, mules, and even cows, which he had rounded up locally. Liddell Hart suggested

> that the value of the horse in moving across rough country was apt to be offset by its high vulnerability, and that where any large number of horsemen were moving they could be too easily stopped by a concentration of fire. He replied that he valued the horse mainly as a means of movement from point to point. (While there was something in his argument he left me with a feeling that he was inclined to build too much on the particular experience of Sicily, where the bulk of the opposing forces were composed of Italians, who surrendered easily, and thus left the nucleus of German troops too small to cover the ground effectively.)
>
> He remarked that, in Sicily, his Army knocked out 13.6 enemy soldiers for every American casualty. (This, in itself, was indirect testimony to the feebleness of the opposition.)[42]

Near the end of the discussion Liddell Hart brought up the subject of the American armored divisions and their commanders. Only the 2d, now led by Major General Edward H. Brooks, a cavalryman from Vermont, was in France. The 3rd, 4th, and 5th were already in England when Liddell Hart last saw Patton. The 6th, commanded by Grow, long an advocate of armor, and the 7th, led by Silvester, an infantryman, had since arrived, and the 9th, commanded by Major General John W. Leonard, another infantryman, was on its way. The inclination to put those not associated with cavalry and tanks in charge of American armored units distressed Liddell Hart, a witness to Churchill's and Alan Brooke's attempts to downplay the value of tanks.

Of the American armored division and corps leaders then in France or about to go there, only Gerow, Brooks, and Wood had experience with cavalry or tanks. If Liddell Hart had known, he might have pointed to the absurdity of having Bruce Magruder and Alvan Gillem, infantrymen who detested tanks and tankers, command them. As distressed by this kind of thing as Liddell Hart and Wood, Patton indicated that all three corps commanders in Italy were cavalrymen: Truscott, who had replaced Lucas at Anzio; Keyes, who Patton considered the best of all his generals; and the capable Crittenberger, who years before had succeeded Patton as commander of the 2d Armored. "That more of the armoured divisions are not commanded by cavalrymen," Liddell Hart noted, "is due to the former Chief of Cavalry, who objected to them leaving their own arm to serve with armoured troops. P. himself defied this ban, and the General in question [John K. Herr] would not speak to him afterward as a result."[43]

The talk concluded with a discussion of security measures, which Patton considered extreme. He mentioned that his own security officer had once stopped him from sending home some snapshots of an armored division. Patton called the ban absurd, for he had taken the photos as long ago as last summer.

Liddell Hart, on the other hand, considered American security too lax.

> When I mentioned that I had discovered the arrival of the 6th Armoured Division through seeing a lot of the troops in the Banbury area, wearing the usual armoured division shoulder badge, with the numeral "6" he said that he, himself, had designed the shoulder badge, when commanding the 2nd Armoured Division. Likewise, his Headquarters troops here were wearing the 3rd Army badge, which he had introduced,—it fostered esprit de corps. (I forebore to tell him that I had cited the way that the troops of the various American armoured divisions revealed the identity of the formation to which they belonged by this obvious sign, as an example of faults in security at my recent conferences on the subject!)[44]

VII

During the final days of June and the first of July events changed things for both Patton and the enemy. On June 30 Patton left his headquarters at Peover Hall and moved south to Breamore House in Hampshire, nineteen miles west of Southampton, from which he prepared to leave for France. In Germany in early July Hitler made his own moves. On the second he relieved Rundstedt and replaced him with Field Marshal Guenther von Kluge, who had served on the Eastern front.[45]

As late as July 1 intercepted messages indicated that the Germans still awaited Patton's invasion at Calais. To his government late in June Ōshima wrote of Patton's movement: "the expected landing may come (1) relatively soon and in conjunction with the operation in Normandy—the Germans consider this very likely—or (2) only after the enemy has taken Cherbourg, brought up reserves and heavy equipment, and extended their bridgehead to include Le Havre. In the latter event, Germany may have to attack the present bridgehead with all available force without waiting for a new landing."[46]

British intelligence verified the continuing effectiveness of Fortitude South. Before the invasion the British believed that by June 14 six enemy divisions would reach the Allied bridgehead from north of the Seine River. By that date, however, the Germans had transferred only one to Normandy.

But Patton's impending departure for France seemed to threaten the continuance of the deception. He would soon have to be revealed as the commander of the Third Army, not of the First United States Army Group, thereby ending the ruse. "If we were to keep the threat alive in July," Sir Ronald Wingate observed, "it would be necessary to find some explanation for the transfer of FUSAG forces to 21st Army Group, and for the disposition of General Patton from the command of an army group to that of an army." To explain the change the London Controlling Section devised an intricate tale. Montgomery, the story went, had met fierce opposition in Normandy and had asked Eisenhower for reinforcements. FUSAG constituted the only manpower source available. Patton so objected to being stripped to help the British that he quarreled with Ike, who consequently demoted him from a group commander to an army commander. Although those involved in the deception approved the cover story before the end of June, Montgomery asked for a delay in its execution for as long as possible. Since the story talked about the Allied intention to send heavy reinforcements to Normandy, it might induce the Germans to send additional forces there, too.[47]

Even as Patton prepared to head for France, the Germans believed the cover plan. On July 3, 1944, Hitler's Chief Operations Officer, Colonel General Alfred Jodl, told a conference that Montgomery's Army Group, the Allied invading force in France, possessed in England reserves of not more than four or five infantry divisions and two armored divisions. Patton's Army Group, on the other hand, supposedly contained eighteen infantry divisions, six armored divisions, and five airborne divisions. It was training, around London and in southern England, for another invasion. "It is also evident," Jodl reasoned, "from the operational sectors of the two enemy groups, and the state of preparations, and from the fact that it would be difficult for the port of Cherbourg alone to supply two army groups, that the landing will be in the channel region facing the German 15th Army. We conclude that the enemy will plan operations with both army groups on both sides of the Seine, heading towards Paris." Compounding his miscalculation, Jodl dismissed hints that the Allies would soon land on the Mediterranean coast of Southern France, an expedition that Jake Devers would command, as "largely deliberate propaganda reports by the enemy."

Jodl convinced himself that both Allied invasions would fail. Nearly all of the enemy's seasoned troops, those with experience in North Africa and Sicily, had been wasted in the Normandy fighting. Patton's Army Group, which was to carry out the next landing, contained only two battle-tested divisions. Facing "strong German defences" and "the extremely strong" German Fifteenth Army, Patton would be pushed into the sea.[48]

In their stories the Germans used the transfer of the First Canadian and Third American armies to Normandy as a theme. By the nineteenth of July they knew that these two units were arriving in France. Nazi propaganda depicted their coming as evidence that strong German resistance in Normandy had led to the postponement of the invasion further east by FUSAG.[49]

After Patton's release from his fictitious command, a replacement was found in Lieutenant General Lesley J. McNair, the sixty-one-year-old chief of Army Ground Forces. Sent to England from Washington at Eisenhower's request, he met with Ike on July 15, only to be told he was to command a paper army. "He was white with fury," noted one observer. "I had never seen a man looking quite so angry or disappointed." Two weeks later, in a tragic accident, McNair died instantly when a bomb from errant American planes landed in his slit trench. A few days later Marshall sent General Calvin De Witt, Jr., to replace him.[50]

Even with these changes, the cover scheme worked beyond the expectations of its planners. At the beginning of July the German forces in the Pas de Calais actually exceeded those there on D-Day, and for the remainder of the month the Germans kept these troops there. Not until the end of July, when the battle of Normandy was lost, did the enemy drain the Fifteenth Army to save the remnants of the smashed Seventh and Fifth German Armies.[51]

An unfortunate footnote to the Allied plan of deception occurred on September 1, 1944, when the military analyst Hanson W. Baldwin published the details of the cover operation in the *New York Times*. Noticing the article, Brigadier A. T. Cornwall-Jones of the British military mission in Washington immediately complained to General Andrew J. McFarland, the secretary of the American Joint Chiefs of Staff. "Even after the finish of the European War it will be undesirable to publish details of the deception practised on the Germans by the Allies," Cornwall-Jones pointed out, "but is especially unfortunate at a time when the same channels which conveyed the false information to the Germans about General Patton may be still in use in connection with current operations."[52]

VIII

Even while in England, Patton was the talk of the Allied forces in France. On July 2 Ike marveled at the success of the British plan of deception that had Patton leading the real invasion. The Americans, he informed Bradley and Chester Hansen, were far behind their ally in concocting and implementing such schemes. The story on the beaches soon after the landings, Ike had learned, was that Patton had taken his army to Norway, which he had conquered in a day or two. The "impulsive Patton" had, Ike further revealed, offered him a thousand dollars for each week he pushed up Patton's arrival in France.

"Took off for France at 1025 almost a year to the time we left Algiers for Sicily," Patton noted on July 6, 1944. "Our first glimpse of 'The Mother of Swords' was when through the haze, we could just see Cherbourg, where Beatrice and I landed in 1913." From the airport Patton and his party drove along the shoreline. "The whole beach" contained the wrecks of ships destroyed not by enemy fire but by the storm that had raged for several days after the landings.

Hansen described the arrival at Bradley's headquarters.

> Shortly before noon Patton came in with Codman and a medico. Jaunty and well dressed in green jacket with the bright buttons and in ice cream pants with the fancy leather belt though I did not notice the pearl handled revolver which has been put under bans it was so highly publicized. Chastened as a result of this experience with the newspapers but he is still basically the same showman.[53]

At the briefing at St. Paul's School on the fifteenth of May Monty had spoken hopefully. His Army Group would, he estimated, capture Caen and move toward Falaise within the first few days of the invasion. When Patton landed in France, Montgomery still had not taken Caen.

The Americans, too, were bogged down. From the beaches the troops moved into the hedgerows that divided the Cotentin, or Cherbourg, peninsula into innumerable enclosures. Three to six feet high and sometimes almost as thick, the hedgerows seemed to be even higher to vehicles that tried to cross the region along the ancient sunken lanes. Tanks found it impossible to traverse such terrain. "They would run up on this thing," Bradley explained, "and their nose would come up over the top of the hedgerow, then the Germans on the other side just had to shoot through the bottom of them. There was no armor underneath. And they couldn't get over."

A different problem faced those on the right of the American line. At the base of the Cotentin peninsula, the hedgerows gave way to lowlands that could be easily flooded by the Germans, trapping almost all traffic.[54]

Arriving in France during an American attempt, begun on July 3, to break out of this box, Patton drove over to Bradley's headquarters south of Isigny, east of Cherbourg and near Saint-Lô. Wandering about while awaiting Bradley, Patton bumped into Group Captain Fred W. Winterbotham, the British Intelligence Officer who had helped break the German code and had fed Patton information in Sicily. With Willie, his bull terrier, at his side, Patton, a broad grin on his face, told Winterbotham that he could no longer stand the inactivity and had just flown in from England. After spying Patton, Monk Dickson, now Bradley's intelligence officer, called together the American reporters. "Gentlemen," he said, "I don't know whether any of you have seen what you took to be General Patton around here with his dog. You were mistaken." Bidding the reporters "Good morning," he then left.[55]

That afternoon Patton conferred with Bradley, Middleton, and General J. Lawton Collins, who commanded the VII Corps. In the evening Hodges came in for supper with Bradley and Patton and explained how the Germans were fighting, information he got by observing the enemy with a "32-power telescope at a distance of 1000 yards in their flank." The enemy opened up with machine guns, which invariably stopped the American infantrymen. They followed this in five or ten minutes with mortar fire directed by an observer in a tree. At this point the Americans usually called for artillery fire, suffering additional casualties while awaiting it. "When things get too hot," Patton explained, "the Germans move down to the next hedgerow at the cross hedge and repeat. They move one at a time at a full run and well spread out. A violent tank attack, covered by air bursts, would certainly break up this form of defense."[56]

On the next day, July 7, Patton and Gaffey went searching for Montgomery, whom they found decorating soldiers of Bradley's First Army. Filming the event was the noted Hollywood director Lieutenant Colonel George Stevens, whose movies included *Gunga Din*. "There were at least twenty-five camera men of various types," Patton observed, "also a loudspeaker on a pole was held over Montgomery's head so his priceless words would not be lost." Stevens wanted to film Patton, "but I told him I was still a secret as the Germans expect me to land at Calais. Actually they don't."

After lunch Bradley, Montgomery, and Patton went to "the war tent," where Montgomery "went to great length" explaining why he had not yet taken Caen. He tried, Patton thought, to get Bradley to promise not to make the Third Army operational until Middleton's VIII Corps took Avranches, at the base of the peninsula, but Bradley "refused to bite because he is using me as a means of getting out from under the 21st Army Group. I hope he succeeds."[57]

Traveling about, Patton found that each American commander had his pet scheme for breaking through the hedgerows. Middleton advocated "an artillery concentration on each hedge, followed by a rush." Patton dismissed this as "a slow, costly method." Eddy, who commanded the 9th Infantry Division, "puts machine gun and mortar fire on the corners of the hedges, then advances using marching fire." Huebner, still leading the 1st Infantry Division, advocated an attack by a team consisting of a battalion of infantry, a platoon of tanks, a platoon of self-propelled tank destroyers, and some engineers. By the time the team reached the third row of hedges, the German defensive detachments would, Huebner reasoned, be wiped out.[58]

Doubting whether such involved procedures would ever work, Patton had his own solution.

> Brad and Hodges are such nothings. Their one virtue is that they get along by doing nothing. I could break through in three days if I commanded. They try to push all along the front and have no power anywhere. . . . All that is necessary now is to take chances by leading with armored divisions and covering their advance with air bursts. Such an attack would have to be made on a narrow sector, whereas at present we are trying to attack all along the line.[59]

Discussing with Bradley the American breakout attempt that was launched on July 3, Montgomery unknowingly agreed with Patton. Coming to Monty's caravan on the tenth, Bradley admitted that his troops had made "small and slow progress." Montgomery urged Bradley not to worry and to "take all the time you need." The British, on the left or east of the line, would "go on hitting, drawing the German strength" from the Americans, on the right or west. Politely Montgomery offered Bradley advice: "If I were you I think I should concentrate my forces a little more." So saying, he put his two fingers together on the map in his characteristic way.[60]

After Bradley left, Dempsey, now commanding the British Second Army, suggested to Montgomery what became Operation Goodwood.

As Dempsey conceived it, Goodwood was to be a concentrated movement by his three armored divisions to the south of Caen. Its two objectives, Dempsey later told interviewers, were to give the British "a trifle
more elbow room east of the River Orne" and to attract the enemy's
armor to the British front, thereby weakening the German capacity to
resist a renewed breakout attempt by the Americans. But, Dempsey
explained, to get air support for a tank thrust against the Germans,
"Monty felt it necessary to overstate the aims of the operation. In doing
this he did not take Eisenhower into his confidence. Such reticence was
a habit of his—he often used to say: 'There's no need to tell Ike.'" To
protect himself Montgomery, for the only time in his career, wrote a
memorandum, "Notes on Second Army Operation." As he spelled them
out, Dempsey's aims were to "gain a good bridgehead over the River
Orne through Caen" and seize all the crossings over the river from Caen
south to Falaise, thus isolating the enemy troops in the pocket.

Montgomery's overstatement to get bomber support backfired.
When the tanks bogged down, the attack turned into something
Dempsey desired to avoid, an infantry battle. The press viewed the
operation as a breakout thrust that had failed. So, too, did the Royal Air
Force and SHAEF, Ike's headquarters. At a press conference Monty
spoke of Dempsey's failure. An embittered Dempsey, believing Montgomery had brought him undeserved criticism, consoled himself with
the thought that the Germans, fearing what they thought might be
another assault near Caen, would keep their troops there, thus aiding
Bradley's attempts elsewhere.[61]

IX

Ever the student of the past, Patton had brought with him to France the
six volumes of the British historian Edward Freeman's *History of the Norman Conquest,* from which he hoped to learn about the roads in western
France. The volumes, however, gave him no better hint than anyone
else had about how to break out of the hedgerows. By mid-July Bradley
had come up with another plan, Cobra. Scheduled to begin on July 21,
but postponed by bad weather until the twenty-fifth, Cobra was to be
preceded by an air bombardment heavier than even the seven thousand
tons of bombs dropped on the German lines before Goodwood. The

first wave of Cobra would consist of three infantry divisions, to be followed by three more divisions, two of them armored. Knowingly or unknowingly, Bradley adopted the advice of Monty and of Georgie: the attack would be concentrated within a four-mile front and hit General Fritz Bayerlein's Panzer Lehr Division along the Saint-Lô-Périers road.[62]

About two weeks before the campaign began, the Americans finally solved one problem. Bradley got word that Sergeant Curtis G. Culin, Jr., of the 2d Division had designed a device that enabled tanks to pass through the hedgerows. Bradley related what happened.

> So, early the next morning I took my Ordnance Officer and two or three other members of my staff and went down to see this out-fit—they were down toward the front—and I found this man had put two iron prongs on the front of the tanks, the prongs being about two feet long, they stuck out that far in front of the tank. When the tank would run up to this wall of dirt, instead of bellying up and trying to climb over it, the two prongs would stick up into the dirt and that would prevent the thing from going up. The prongs wouldn't let the front of the tank come up, so the tank had enough power to just push right on through, and . . . it would carry trees and everything else with it. He had one pair fixed on a light tank and another one on a medium tank, and the medium tank particularly would just go right on through and when you got through, you had a road through the hedge, as well as going right on through. Well, after taking a good look at these two tanks, I went back, and on the way back I told my Ordnance Officer to put every Ordnance company in the beach-head busy making these things, to fly a couple of them back to England, and get as many Ordnance companies as possible working on them in England. We had a ready supply of steel because the angle irons the Germans had put on the beaches as underwater obstacles were perfect for it. They were angle irons, each flange being about three or four inches wide, and all you had to do was cut them up and sharpen them, . . . fit them so they could go on the tank, be bolted onto the tank. And so, when we broke out, a couple of weeks later, about 50% of our tanks were equipped with these prongs, and they took the Germans completely by surprise, because they had been expecting these tanks to belly up and be able to let them

knock them out. But instead of that, the tanks just broke right on through, shooting right and left. And a lot of these detachments would surrender right there because they had no way to compete with the tank when it got through there.[63]

Told of Cobra by Bradley, Patton informed his staff of the plan, repeatedly warning them that they were to tell no one. But on July 17 Bradley called Patton and said that Colonel Charles C. Blakeney, Patton's psychological warfare and public relations officer, had told the newspaper reporters assigned to the Third Army about Cobra. These correspondents, in turn, had bragged to colleagues covering Bradley's First Army that they knew of this forthcoming operation. "He was quite upset," Patton wrote of Bradley, "and so was I as this is a very dangerous breach of security." Calling the reporters together, Patton "told them how dangerous this slip was and that they had violated my trust in them. . . . You must understand," Patton informed them, "that both Colonel Blakeney and myself can be tried for what has happened. I am sure that none of you want to have us tried."

For Blakeney the error in judgment was the beginning of the end. "Apparently he did it from dumbness," Patton observed after speaking to him, "and from a misplaced sense of loyalty to me. I think he is honest but stupid. . . . But I will have to relieve him—I will not do it until Cobra is over as it might cause a leak if I did it now."[64]

Amid these doings two more of Patton's friends died. In mid-July Teddy Roosevelt, who had made three landings on D-Day with the leadings waves and had survived, died in his sleep. "He was one of the bravest men I ever knew," Patton told Bea. Two weeks later a German rifleman killed the equally fearless Colonel Paddy Flint. "Stiller just got an eye witness account of the fight," Patton reported to his wife after the tragedy. Patton hoped his old friend would be posthumously awarded either the Medal of Honor or the Distinguished Service Cross. "I hope he gets one. He was a dauntless soul. The Sgt with him got the Bosch who shot P. if that is any comfort."[65]

Paddy Flint's funeral contained one unusual aspect. Believing that with a name like Paddy Flint the deceased hero must have been a Catholic, Hap Gay arranged a Catholic funeral. Too late to change things, Major General Wade H. Haislip, who led Patton's XV Corps and had been Paddy's roommate at West Point, informed Gay that

Paddy was a Protestant. Later, when Paddy's body was interred at Arlington National Cemetery, he received a Protestant service.[66]

If anything, Patton's activities during his first three weeks in France indicated the further deterioration of the German intelligence system. Patton had roamed about the Allied beachheads, had conferred with the leading generals and with Wood and Grow, who led his 4th and 6th Armored Divisions, had served as a pallbearer at funerals, and had addressed reporters. Yet the Germans still believed that he was in England training his troops for the projected invasion opposite Dover. On July 5 a member of Ambassador Ōshima's staff discussed the European situation with the Japanese embassy's "usual contact man" in Berlin. "Germany is still waiting for the forces under Patton to engage in a second landing operation across the Channel," the informant told the Japanese. "I do not feel that there is any very great danger in the Normandy area as long as we are facing only Montgomery's forces; there will be time for the Germans to work out counter-measures after it becomes clear what Patton's forces intend to do."

The next day, in a conversation with Ōshima, Steengracht revealed that Kluge had replaced Rundstedt as the commander of German forces in the West. Kluge, Steengracht went on, "did not want to commit his forces until the intentions of the enemy troops still in England were apparent. Germany is still expecting further enemy landing operations across the Channel."[67]

Exactly a week later Steengracht's remarks to Ōshima indicated Fortitude South continued to dominate German thinking. "According to intelligence in our possession," Steengracht now said, "it appears that virtually all the forces assigned to Montgomery are already in the Normandy area, but that no part of Patton's army has yet been landed." The Germans believed "that Patton's forces will land in the neighborhood of Dieppe," almost halfway between Cherbourg and Calais, for each day the Allies had made large-scale air raids "on coastal positions in that area. This seems to indicate that the enemy is going to use the very same technique he employed in bombing the Normandy area before the landings there. We have not," Steengracht revealed, "changed our original plan of making a surprise attack upon the newly landed forces and then launching a general counter-offensive upon the enemy forces in Normandy."[68]

Meeting with the German foreign minister, Joachim von Ribbentrop, on July 23, at the very time Bradley was preparing Cobra, Ōshima learned that the Nazis still thought Patton would land in France, but not within the next few weeks. German intelligence, as confused as could be, indicated that Patton, still in England, had recently sent three divisions to the London area to help stem the chaos created by the German V-1 rockets. "For that reason," Ribbentrop said, "it would be difficult for those forces to begin landing operations at once." A German War Ministry official who had been present at the conference later told Ōshima: "We have information that about five of Patton's divisions have been transferred to Montgomery. In addition, three divisions have been sent to the London area. Accordingly, it would now be difficult for Patton's army group to undertake a landing at an early date."[69] The Nazis remained completely fooled.

X

Even with Patton supposedly in England, the Germans knew that the Allies possessed an advantage in manpower. On July 27 they estimated that the British and Americans had forty-two or forty-three divisions in Normandy, while they had the equivalent of only seventeen or eighteen full divisions.[70]

The American advantage seemed overwhelming. On the eve of the new attack they possessed twenty-one divisions, all part of Bradley's First Army. While the Germans had placed seven Panzer divisions and seven infantry divisions opposite Dempsey's fourteen divisions, they faced Bradley with two battered Panzer divisions, possessing barely one hundred tanks, a Panzer Grenadier division with no tanks, and six infantry divisions that had been weakened considerably by combat.[71]

Cobra opened tragically. Scheduled to begin on July 24, the operation had to be postponed because of bad weather. On both the twenty-fourth and twenty-fifth some American planes mistakenly attacked American targets, killing McNair in one of the short bombings. After the bombings the three infantry divisions of Major General J. Lawton Collins's VII Corps were to attack along a relatively concentrated front of four miles. Three more divisions, Huebner's 1st Infantry plus the 2d and 3d Armored, constituted the second line.

Patton, who had nothing to do with the operation, derided it as "a

Patton and the Normandy Breakout, July – August 1944

FRANCE

Argentan

Alençon

Falaise

Le Mans

Loire River

COTENTIN

Cherbourg

Avranches

XV CORPS

XX CORPS

Chateaubriant

Angers

U.S. 3rd ARMY

Saint-Malo

Rennes

Saint-Nazaire

BRITTANY

VIII CORPS

Vannes

Atlantic Ocean

Brest

Lorient

0   20   40   60 miles

timid affair but Brad thinks he is a devil to risk it. He also has a nebulous idea of sending the XIX Corps further southwest. If he does it should be under the Third Army as it is two of our divisions, the 5th and 35th, but he wants to hold on."[72]

The Allied explosives created chaos within Bayerlein's Panzer Lehr Division. The bombings knocked out two-thirds of Bayerlein's troops, and by the night of the twenty-fifth he possessed only fourteen tanks. Nevertheless, Collins's men progressed slowly through the crater-filled territory, advancing less than two miles on the twenty-fifth and only three miles on the twenty-sixth. But during the night of the twenty-sixth the 2d Armored pushed through the gap and covered four miles, opening the way for a swifter advance on the twenty-seventh.[73]

The breakout came along the right flank of the American line. There on the twenty-eighth Troy Middleton, commanding the VIII Corps, ordered his two armored divisions, Wood's 4th and Grow's 6th, down the west coast routes of the peninsula. During the movement his two armored divisions presented studies in contrast. On the twenty-eighth Wood's tanks reached the outskirts of Countances, halfway down the peninsula. Entering the northern edge of the town, Colonel DeWitt C. Smith, Jr., whose rifle company constituted one of the lead elements in the division, found Wood by the side of the road. The small arms fire was intense, having knocked out a jeep and a tank. Walking down the road with Smith, with whom he played tennis in England, Wood said: "Smith, it doesn't look like we'll get in much tennis today."[74]

In contrast to Wood, who raced in three columns toward Avranches, at the base of the peninsula, Grow stalled. On the twenty-ninth Patton, whose Third Army would not be activated until noon of August 1, drove with Stiller southwest of Countances and found Grow's division held up by enemy fire at a river. Patton related what happened.

General Grow was sitting on the side of the road and General Taylor had a large group of officers studying a map. I asked Grow what he was doing and he said that Taylor was in charge of the advanced guard and that he personally was doing nothing. I asked him whether he had been down to look at the river, and he said, "No," so I told him that unless he did do something, he would be out of a job. I then went down and looked at the river and was not fired at, although you could see a few Germans on a hill to the left where there was a churchtower or a windmill. So I directed the 6th Armored Division to advance across the river, because the fact that the bridge was out didn't matter as the river was not over a foot deep.[75]

Wood's lightning dash to Avranches, which he took on July 31, to Rennes, which fell on August 4, and beyond constitutes one of the most misinterpreted episodes of Patton's military life. In his 1961 book, *Breakout and Pursuit,* a volume in the army's official history of the war, the noted historian Martin Blumenson argued that Patton, conferring with Bradley on July 27, shaped the advance, a totally unwarranted assumption against which Wood complained for years. "Though Patton remained in the background of command to the best of his ability," Blumenson wrote, "his presence was unmistakable, and his imprint on the operation that developed was as visible as his shadow on the wall of the operation tent."[76]

A couple of things contradict this assumption. In a "Confidential & Personal Memoir" written in 1947, Bradley made it clear that Patton was at this time inactive.

Many people give Patton and his Third Army credit for the breakout. He had nothing to do with its planning or execution except that I told him to follow the action on the right flank so that he could take over command of his divisions sort of "on the fly." I did not want any pause to take place in the change of the command set-up. He followed the 4th and 6th Armored Divisions and helped them coordinate their movements in the vicinity of Countances.[77]

Wood also left abundant evidence that Patton was not involved in military operations. In December 1948, thirteen years before the appearance of Blumenson's book, he explained to Liddell Hart what happened:

Patton, of course, had no part in the Avranches break-through. I was part of the First Army at that time and my advance on Avranches had to be made by cutting through elements of our own 1st and 2nd Armored Divisions which had been directed toward Granville *across my front* instead of on Mayenne and Le

Mans, as they should have been. . . . There was no conception of far-reaching directions for armor in the minds of our people— Eisenhower or Bradley—nor of supplying such thrusts. Patton did not come along until after I had taken Rennes. My movements to that time had not been on Army orders, but simply by consultation with Middleton, VIII Corps Commander, and a fine soldier, as to where I would go next.

Wood took Avranches on July 31, only to find scattered German battalions in the ninety-mile-wide corridor between that point and the Loire River. Allied spearheads might have driven eastward without opposition. But Bradley and Eisenhower threw away this opportunity by sticking, Wood argued, to the outdated preinvasion plan drawn up by the British Lieutenant-General Frederick E. Morgan. It ordered a westward movement by Patton's armored divisions to capture the Brittany ports of Brest, Lorient, and Saint-Nazaire, needed, according to Morgan, to supply the Allied troops in France.[78]

By the time Blumenson's *Breakout and Pursuit* came out, Patton had been dead for sixteen years, and Wood and many others who had performed such great services had been forgotten by the public. "His chapters on our operations in Brittany are quite imaginative," Wood wrote Liddell Hart of Blumenson. "Troy Middleton and I had a good deal to do with the performance, all prior to George Patton's arrival and all on our own."[79]

Over the years Liddell Hart frequently recalled what had originally drawn him to Wood. Visiting Wood at Chippenham in March 1944, he "found your outlook on the use of armour such a refreshing contrast to those of the other Armoured Division Commanders I had met before. You told me how dismayed you were by the way Alan Brooke and others had talked at a recent conference about the impossibility of repeating blitzkrieg tactics, and far-reaching thrusts and how armour would have to go back to methods similar to those of 1918." This first meeting convinced Liddell Hart "that here, at last, I had met someone on the Allied side who had really grasped the essentials of armoured mobility, and was capable of fulfilling them."[80]

Fourteen

HURRY UP AND WAIT

I

At a conference in an apple orchard a few days before the activation of his Third Army at noon on August 1, Patton told his officers what he expected. Unaware that on July 31 Wood, racing down the Cotentin peninsula, would take Avranches, whose high ground commanded the area, he circled the place in red on a huge map. He vowed to push hard and strike fast. The more rapidly his men moved, the more Germans they would kill. Some of his staff members later quoted him to William Randolph Hearst, Jr., who was covering the war for his father's International News Service: "Some goddamn fool once said that flanks have got to be secure. Since then sonofabitches all over the globe have been guarding their flanks. I don't agree with that. My flanks are something for the enemy to worry about, not me. Before he finds out where my flanks are, I'll be cutting the bastard's throat."[1]

At last the great day arrived. "I was very nervous all morning," Patton observed on the first, "because it seemed impossible to get any definite news and the clock seemed to have stopped." At noon Patton and Colonel Paul Harkins, "the only ones at headquarters," celebrated by taking "a drink of horrible brandy" given to Harkins by Patton's friend from the Mexican expedition days, Colonel Nicholas Campanole.[2]

Middleton, whom Patton immediately visited, found the change of command trying. In seven days his VIII Corps, occupying the western flank of the American line, had advanced nearly fifty miles, past Avranches to the bridge at Pentaubault leading into Brittany. "In such a situation," Middleton noted, you'd always run a chance of getting an order from one man to do this and shortly thereafter an order from another to do something else. This happened to me. I'd get an order from Bradley to do something and Patton would come along and say, "No, let's do this." The confusion lasted for several days. For instance, Bradley told me, "When you get out through Avranches to the south, be sure to guard the south flank very heavily because it's wide open not only to the south but in the direction of Paris." There was a town named Feugères; I was ready to send the Seventy-ninth Division there to block when Patton came along. "Hell, no," George said, "we're going to Brest."[3]

Bradley had also told Middleton that, after the breakout, he was to capture the port of Saint-Malo, the first large town on the north coast of Brittany, about thirty-five miles west of Avranches. But when Patton took over he instructed Middleton to bypass Saint-Malo. "There is nothing there anyway," Patton said, "there aren't 500 troops in there." As it turned out, the Germans in Saint-Malo held out until August 17. They fired so heavily on the passing Americans that, Middleton recalled, "I had to turn the Eighty-third Division loose on the town. It was quite an undertaking. The Eighty-third captured 14,000 Germans in St. Malo. I don't know how many they killed. There was a little island in the St. Malo harbor which we didn't capture for a couple of weeks. The Germans stayed out there; we would bomb them and they'd shoot back."[4]

Middleton found Patton's figures on enemy troops wildly inaccurate. Told by Patton that the Germans had only about one thousand troops between Saint-Malo and Brest, on the tip of Brittany, Middleton ordered Grow to "just get in the middle of the road and barrel on out to Brest, 150 miles or so from St. Malo, and capture the fortified port before the Germans can get ready. . . . I never thought any armored outfit could capture Brest," Middleton later related, "because it was an important port city which housed the pens for the German submarines that operated in the Atlantic. I knew from the maps and aerial photographs that it was heavily organized not only to shoot toward the sea and into the air but to shoot to the rear. The Germans weren't going to let the city go by forfeit. They had 90-millimeter guns dug into the ground and set in concrete pillboxes."[5]

If, early in the campaign, Middleton found fault with Patton, Patton, in turn, criticized Middleton for sending Wood south to Rennes without infantry support. At Rennes, Middleton defended himself, "we had decided at the planning tables back in England, the greatest battle of World War II would take place." Patton disagreed. "I cannot make out why Middleton was so apathetic or dumb," he complained of the rush to Rennes. "I don't know what was the matter with him. Of course it is a little nerve wracking to send troops straight into the middle of the enemy with front, flanks, and rear open. I had to keep repeating to myself, 'Do not take counsel of your fears.' "[6]

At three in the afternoon on August 1 Bradley, now commanding the Twelfth Army Group, which by the end of August consisted of Hodges's First Army, Patton's Third Army, and William H. Simpson's Ninth Army, arrived at Patton's headquarters. Concerned because Patton depended for reinforcements and supplies on a single bridge that crossed the Sée River at Avranches, Bradley suspected that the Germans might be planning to retake the town from Mortain, twenty miles to the east. Patton "did not give much credence to this," but to cover his exposed eastern flank he started forward by truck the 90th Infantry Division, which Major General Raymond McLain had just taken over. But truck movements of infantry, especially over one bridge, were so dangerous that Patton ordered Haislip to be there "to see that the 90th Division gets through without a jam."[7]

It did not take Bradley long to find fault with another way Patton had deployed Middleton's corps. Driving to Middleton's headquarters on the second—he ate a K ration on the way because he did not wish "to run in on people at noontime"—Bradley found that Middleton was right about reinforcing the troops at Fougères, at the entrance to the Brittany peninsula. "I'm wide open here," Middleton complained, "nothing to fend with if he [the enemy] hits me when my stuff is turned the other way. Hate to attack with enemy at my rear and with my rear exposed the way it is. If he cuts through the hinge, I'd be stuck." Sending the 79th Infantry Division to bolster the position, Bradley answered:

Some people are more concerned with the headlines and the news they'll make than the soundness of their tactics. I don't care if we get Brest tomorrow or ten days later. If we cut the peninsula, we'll

get it anyhow. But we can't risk a loose hinge. I want the 79th
Division near Fougères and I want a buildup there. Germans could
hit us with three divisions there and it'll make us look very foolish.
It would be embarrassing to George. George is used to attacks
from a single division. He's buttoned up well enough for that. But
he's not used to having three or four divisions hit him. He doesn't
know what it means yet.

Patton took the rebuff "in good form." When Stiller and Codman
learned of it, they spoke roughly to Hansen. Neither, however, excelled
as a tactician. "For Christ sake, George," Bradley explained to Patton,
"what are you going to do about this open flank you have; I've sent the
79th down there and I hate to have to bypass a commander, it's your
army." Patton laughed, put his arm around Bradley, and told him he
had done the right thing.[8]

The first two days of activity in France produced a pleasant surprise.
On the first, believing Wood was being threatened by an enemy column
southwest of Rennes, Patton asked Weyland for air support. Weyland
immediately dispatched three groups of fighter-bombers. "It was," Patton said, "the best cooperation between air and ground so far achieved
in this war." The next day Patton passed "many dead Germans, horses
and guns." He also saw a German ambulance unit that, he was sure, the
pilots had hit by mistake.[9]

From the moment the XIX TAC became operational on the first,
Weyland provided Patton and his division commanders with unmatched
support. On the second he received a request to protect the fifteen-mile-
wide corridor that the troops used to get out of the Cotentin. Weyland
sent five daytime missions over the area and kept planes on constant
patrol at night.[10]

Weyland recalled how he did his best to isolate the battlefield so German reserves could not be moved in to meet the breakout

at the decisive point. . . . And in the first two or three days General Patton was highly elated. When he came back he was practically screaming; he had a rather high squeaky voice when he was
excited. "Opie," he said, "Goddam (his language was rather colorful too), my goodness, the roads are just littered with German
tanks and artillery and whatnot. What in the hell happened? I

think it was your airplanes." I said, "Yeh, that's right. When they try to move in there, we would precede your people and try to knock out the opposition before they get there."

After that Patton and Weyland kept their headquarters close together, usually in a woods, not a city, so they would be mobile. Near Avranches "we were moving the Third Army across a single bridge. The Third Army was just moving, and he [Patton] was highly elated, and practically all they had to do was just to get out and roll. So one evening Patton called up and said, 'Opie, come on over.'" At Patton's headquarters the two stayed up until 2 A.M. finishing a quart of bourbon. "Whereas prior to that time," Weyland explained, "we had sort of cautious mutual respect, in the course of the evening, we became very close friends, and we vowed that he would keep no secrets from me, and we would play purely as a team, and we would really go to town. From there out, we had a very close relationship, which was based not only on respect and confidence but a very strong friendship along with it."[11]

Colonel Anthony V. Grossetta, who commanded Weyland's 406th Fighter Group, later described the way Patton and Weyland worked.

I don't believe there was ever a closer or more friendly cooperative effort between air and ground than there was between the 19th TAC and the 3rd Army, and it was primarily due to the close relationship, I believe, between General Patton who appreciated air support and General Weyland who would jump through a hoop to do anything he could to keep the 3rd Army moving. On a number of occasions I sat in on the combined briefings the night before the operation of the next day, and General Patton and General Weyland were sitting in the front row with their arms around each other, and it was "Opie this"—stands for his name—and "George this," you know. The 3rd Army operations officer would say, "Now we want the 19th TAC to do such-and-such," and General [James] Ferguson who was the operations officer for 19th TAC would say, "Well, we only have so many planes," or "We don't have this," or "We can't do that," and then Patton would say, "Can't you do that, Opie?" "No, sorry, George!" "Okay."

This is the kind of relationship that they had, and they were together at these operations briefings at least 90% of the time.[12]

Grossetta attributed much of the success of the relationship to Weyland's personality.

Well, he was one of the easiest men to work for that I've ever known. He was extremely cooperative as I've said with the Army. He'd do anything. He realized what his mission was and he would do anything to advance that Army across Europe. He was kind of a happy-go-lucky sort of a fellow. I guess he got mad once in a while—I never saw him mad—but he had the capability of getting the most out of the people who worked for him. They just loved him, and he would somehow or other manage to build up a tremendous esprit de corps in his whole 19th TAC, his staff officers and the combat units.[13]

A couple of days after the drinking episode, Patton showed his faith in Weyland. As part of his army drove east, its southern flank lengthened and stood exposed. On August 6 Patton asked the XIX to protect that flank. His force increased to nine groups, Weyland happily took care of the problem.[14]

II

While Patton was establishing a close friendship with Weyland, an associate of both fumed. Wood, who later observed that he and Weyland had "developed a murderous combination of air-armored action in France,"[15] had his own ideas about the way the war should proceed. By August 1 Wood's 4th Armored was spotted less than ten miles from Rennes, the highway center fifty miles south of Avranches. But in true Liddell Hart fashion Wood desired to let Brigadier General Donald A. Stroh's 8th Infantry Division, which Patton had sent to protect the 4th's flanks and rear, capture Rennes. He would skirt around the city and head for Châteaubriant, about twenty miles farther south. Then he would drive another forty-five miles to Angers, which Patton, in his diary entry for August 1, had designated a primary target. Finally, as he recalled to a friend of Captain Blumenson in 1954, he proposed to strike east "toward Chartres before the Germans were able to regroup. I am convinced that we could have moved on Chartres and cut deeply into the German vitals."

On the night of the third Wood, who without orders had put his plan into motion, called Middleton on the radio, told him he was "just outside of Rennes," and urged him to "get in your Jeep and come on down here." Middleton described what happened next.

> Well, it wasn't like driving out to pay a call on a neighbor. It was enemy country, and there were Germans everywhere. So I get a couple of halftracks, a couple of Jeeps and a few soldiers. We got to Wood's headquarters about daylight. Wood was stripped to the waist, near a little trailer with his maps all out on the ground. He came over and threw his arms around me. I said, "What's the matter, John, you lost your division?" He said, "Heck, no, we're winning this war the wrong way; we ought to be going toward Paris."
>
> I said, "Where is your division?" He said, "I've got one combat command south of Rennes and another in Châteaubriant (about twenty miles in the direction of Paris)." He had no orders at all to go in that direction. So I had to get him back on the track and get him started toward Lorient—much to his disgust. Maybe he was right—I am inclined to believe that he was—but those weren't the orders we had had from Bradley.[16]

Unfortunately for Wood, Patton agreed with Ike and Bradley. Just after noon on the first of August, when his Third Army and Weyland's XIX Tactical Air Command became operational, Patton listed Brest as one of his objectives. In his diary on the fourth he showed no sympathy for Wood. " 'P' Wood, 4th Armored, got bull headed and turned east after Rennes and had to be turned back to his objective, Vannes and Lorient. He wasted a day."

On the fourth Patton sent Gay to speak to Wood. Gay told Wood "that he fully appreciated the wishes of the Commanding General, 4th Armored Division, but that he, General Wood, would have to comply with the orders issued reference his movement on Vannes and Lorient, and that he could not advance further to the southeast unless other orders were issued him by the Corps and by the Army."

Just after the war ended, Gay sympathized with Wood's anger at being halted. "Everyone in the Third Army from the Army commander down to include Willie, the white bulldog, remembered your remarkable advance across France," he praised Wood. "Coutances, Avranches, Rennes, Vannes, Orleans, Chalons, Commercy, Luneville, and the Saar are all bywords of the Third Army . . . coupled with your name and the name of the 4th Armored Division. I have also remembered the time when I came up to see you in Rennes and you were convinced you were headed in the wrong direction. History proved that you were correct, but, Alas! as you know, wars are not fought on history."[17]

For his part Wood forever resented what he considered Patton's abandonment of him. His 1954 letter reflected his bitterness.

> In my opinion, the decision of the High Command to move the two armored divisions away from the pursuit of a disorganized enemy for the purpose of driving toward the fortresses of Lorient and Brest was one of the great mistakes of the war. A rapid move toward Chartres at this time would have been of immense value and I believe it would have greatly shortened the time it took us to arrive on the Rhine. I stated these opinions as forcefully as I could to General Patton through his Chief of Staff, General Gay, but no change of orders could be obtained. . . . This was the place for an Armored Corps, but the wise acres of the War Dept. had disbanded our Armored Corps.[18]

In a memoir, moreover, Middleton cast doubt on Patton's judgment at this time. Having just taken his Third Army into battle, Patton had no idea what kind of resistance his armored divisions would face in Brittany.

> I had asked Patton for his estimate of the German force in Brest at the time he was hell-bent on sending a single armored division to take the city. He told me "I don't know exactly how many there are in Brest, but there aren't more than 10,000 Krauts in the

entire peninsula." Whether he was just guessing or whether his G-2 had estimated for him, I don't know. In the final capture of Brest, we took something like 38,000 prisoners. There were 20,000 down in Lorient. I don't know how many escaped to the south. Around Rennes, where the biggest battle of the war was supposed to take place, there were very few troops. We captured 400 or 500 prisoners and killed a few there.

As it turned out, the movement to Brittany proved questionable. When the Allies finally captured Brest on September 19, the city was so horribly destroyed by the fighting that General James Van Fleet compared it to Stalingrad. And Saint-Nazaire and Lorient remained in enemy hands until the end of the war. "I do know this," Middleton wrote Wood in 1962, "and it is: Ike and Brad could have left a corporals guard at Rennes and followed you to Paris, Belgium, etc., and the Battle of the Bulge would never have happened. I presume, however, they felt it was imperative to secure Brest as a Port."[19]

III

While his troops fanned out to the west, the southwest, and the south, Patton became a player in a controversial episode. In his diary he noted on August 7: "We got a rumor last night from a secret source that several Panzer Divisions will attack west from the line of Mortain-Barenton on Avranches. Personally, I think it is a German bluff to cover a withdrawal, but I stopped the 80th, French 2nd Armored, and 35th in the vicinity of St. Hilaire just in case something might happen."[20]

The "rumor" was an intercept of a German communication and the "secret source" was Major Melvin C. Helfers, the Third Army's special intelligence officer. Using a large map onto which he drew the contents of the decoded Ultra messages he had received, Helfers warned Koch that Hitler hoped to retake Mortain, which the Americans had captured on August 3. From there five Panzer divisions were to roll westward and attempt to close the corridor, bounded by the German army on one side and the ocean on the other, through which Patton's men and supplies squeezed. When Koch, who brought Helfers to Patton, said that he believed the report to be accurate, Patton went to the phone and ordered General Walton Walker, who commanded the XX Corps, to prepare General Paul W. Baade's 35th Infantry Division for the coming assault.[21]

Just after midnight on August 7, the Germans attacked Major General Leland S. Hobbs's 30th Infantry Division at Mortain. Aided by the two nearby infantry divisions and by fighter-bombers firing rockets, the 30th stopped the German advance sixteen miles from Avranches. As a result of Hitler's miscalculation, large numbers of German soldiers were now concentrated in the southwestern segment of the Cotentin peninsula. With part of Patton's army moving to the southeast and the British and Canadians coming down from the north, these Germans faced the prospect of being surrounded and annihilated.[22]

Finding Helfers's information accurate, Patton had him present every morning whatever news he had gathered. Each day at 9 A.M. Patton held a briefing for about forty of his staff officers. At its conclusion Patton, Gaffey, Gay, Harkins, Maddox, Koch, one of Koch's assistants, Lieutenant Colonel Robert S. Allen, and Weyland, when he was available, stayed for a briefing by Helfers, who likened these sessions to a college seminar, "with the exception of a bit of hazing now and then." Spreading out his map, Helfers, sometimes having spent all night in preparation, presented the data sent to him. Gaffey later cited the Avranches episode as one of the instances in which Helfers's information proved invaluable.[23]

IV

Although the fighting around Mortain continued into the eighth, Allied generals realized on the first day of fighting that Major General J. Lawton Collins's VII Corps and the air force possessed the capacity to stop the Germans. By ordering their troops toward Avranches, Hitler and his new Commander in Chief West, Field Marshal Guenther von Kluge, had concentrated large numbers of Germans in the western portion of the Cotentin. This offered the Allies the opportunity of surrounding the enemy forces. "It was one of those almost unbelievable occasions," observed the British military historian Eversley Belfield, "which military commanders may dream of, but which very rarely materialize."[24]

At first Bradley failed to sense the opportunity. Driving over to Patton's command post on the seventh, he described his plan for a deep envelopment around Paris and then north to Dieppe, directly across from Brighton, England. Worried because the 83rd Infantry Division was taking heavy casualties trying to capture Saint-Malo, the Brittany port west of Avranches, Patton seemed to favor the idea, but he hoped for a greater role in the movement than Bradley assigned to Hodges.[25]

That night Bradley realized the enormity of Hitler's mistake. "Greatest tactical blunder I've ever heard of," he told his aide, Major Chester Hansen. "Probably won't happen again in a thousand years." That day a Canadian corps, supported by the Polish 1st Armored Division, had begun an offensive that, the Allies hoped, would take them to Falaise, twenty-one miles southeast of Caen. If the Canadians could reach Falaise and Argentan, just below it, from the north and Wade Haislip's XV Corps could come up from the south, the Germans would be encircled and trapped.[26]

Ignoring those who argued that Patton should continue on to Paris, Bradley ordered Patton on the morning of the eighth "to turn north and keep it going." He was returning to Patton the three divisions, the 35th Infantry, the 80th Infantry, and the 2d French Armored, that he had taken the day before and dispatched toward Mortain, where they were no longer needed. Patton was to send the 5th Armored and the 79th and 90th Infantry Divisions, all part of Haislip's corps, to Le Mans. The force would then drive thirty miles north to Alençon and finally eleven more to Sée, south of Argentan. "This is, in my opinion, too close in," Patton, who continued to favor a grand encircling movement around Paris, observed. "The one we should use is either on Chartres or Dreux, but Bradley will not permit us to go that far afield."[27]

Still, Patton described August 8 as "a big day. We took St. Malo, Le Mans, and Angers," he told Bea, "and in addition launched an attack of four divs which will be in the papers before you get this." Deceived because his troops faced light German opposition, Patton added: "I am the only one who realizes how little the enemy can do—he is finished we may end this in ten days."[28]

As described by Brigadier General William G. Weaver, the assistant commander of the 90th Infantry, the American thrust "through enemy infested country" to Le Mans might have ended tragically. "We were too green at that time to know that we were supposed to have been preceded by an Armored Division, so dumb, doughboy-like, we just went ahead and did the job by ourselves. The going had been so rugged and the speed so great that General George Patton came up to congratulate us right away. Enthusiastically he grabbed Ray McLain in one big, powerful arm and me in his other, slammed us together and said, 'I knew you two so-and-so's would do it.' "[29]

With his Canadian units attacking toward Falaise, Montgomery, in charge of all the Allied ground forces, still favored the wide envelopment that would send Patton toward Orleans and then north toward Paris. Only the urging of his chief of staff, Major General Francis de Guingand, and of his chief of intelligence, Brigadier Edgar T. "Bill" Williams, convinced him. "[Monty] Did not change this," one British brigadier later said, "till *after* Mortain began—and then only on urging of Freddie, Bradley and Bill."[30]

Bradley presented his plan so enticingly that it became hard to resist. As the Falaise battle evolved, he told two British officers who had helped break the German code, Alan Pryce-Jones and Peter Calvo-coressi, "that the German army was no longer a factor with which we need reckon, and the only brake on our advance was our supply problem. He explicitly said that the Allied armies would clear France within 3 weeks, and be in Berlin within 6 weeks."[31]

Visiting Patton's front lines, British Wing Commander E. J. B. "Jim" Rose, who also decoded Ultra messages, was struck by the speed with which the Americans moved supplies. Three days after the Third Army took Le Mans, the first train arrived with supplies from Cherbourg.[32]

Patton, Middleton, and the other generals often mentioned that some of their bold actions, such as moving two armored divisions down one highway at night so that German planes would not spot them, would have received a failing grade at Fort Leavenworth. An instructor looking at the Third Army, its three corps separated by about five hundred miles on August 9, would probably have flunked Patton and Bradley. Weyland later talked about the German threat to the troops heading toward Argentan from Le Mans. "They attempted from time to time to strike the Third Army flanks, which were very open and very, very vulnerable, particularly the supply lines; they were completely unprotected except for the air. When they approached the Loire River, somewhere like that, then I'd throw in some fighter bombers and we'd chew them up and they'd change their mind."[33]

The XV Corps's initial push northeast from Le Mans on August 9 troubled Patton. The corps advanced with the 2d French Armored and the 90th Infantry on the left and the 5th Armored and the 79th Infantry on the right. But two gaps developed in the line of advance. When Haislip reached Carrouges, forty miles north of Le Mans, his left flank stood roughly twenty-five miles from the right flank of Collins's VII Corps at Mayenne. Similarly, Haislip's right flank stood exposed southwest of Alençon.[34]

Trying to cover these gaps, Patton, in effect, conceded he had made two mistakes. First, he could not do what he bragged to his staff he would do, ignore his flanks, counting on swiftness and Weyland's planes to avoid tragedy. Second, he erred when he supported Bradley and agreed to send Wood to Lorient and Brest. Dispatching the 7th Armored to cover Haislip's left, he decided on the eleventh to replace the 4th Armored "on the Brest Peninsula" with two combat commands of Grow's 6th Armored. The 4th Armored would then be transferred from Middleton's VIII Corps to Major General Gilbert R. Cook's XII Corps. It was to arrive by August 14 and guard Haislip's right.

But in this case Patton became trapped in his own error. On the eleventh, returning to his headquarters after visiting Haislip, he noted: "Get home to find that Gaffey had not yet got the VIII Corps going so we can release the 4th Armored. I was quite angry." Wood's division, now before Lorient, could not possibly reach Haislip in time to help. The diversion to Brittany, so bitterly opposed by Wood, had deprived Patton of a crack armored unit when he most needed it.[35]

Visiting Patton in his new command post five miles northwest of Laval, Bradley late on Saturday, August 12, showed confusion. According to the account in Gay's diary, he approved Patton's plan to protect Haislip's left with Walton Walker's XX Corps and Haislip's right with Cook's XII Corps, augmented by Wood's 4th Armored and the 5th Infantry. But, Bradley warned, still adhering to British Lieutenant-General Frederick E. Morgan's original invasion plan, "It is necessary that the Brittany Peninsula be reduced by 1 September." If the entire peninsula was not captured by August 20—as it turned out, Brest fell on September 19 and Lorient and Saint-Nazaire, both on the southern coast of Brittany, held out until the end of the war—Bradley promised to try to transfer to Patton "one or more infantry divisions from the First Army for this purpose. Presently," Bradley went on, "I think our first priority should be the destruction of the German Army now thought to be generally north, northwest and northeast of Alençon."[36]

Thinking how best to trap the Germans, Patton and Bradley disagreed on August 13. During the previous night Haislip approached Argentan. He advanced north of the city, but he was still about eighteen miles from the Canadians, who were stopped six miles north of Falaise. Without consulting Bradley, Patton authorized Haislip to continue on cautiously until he met the Canadians. General Weaver remembered Patton saying that if he could get permission to attack the rear of Colonel General Paul Hausser's Seventh German Army, which Haislip approached, he would trample Hausser and push on so rapidly that he would "drive the British into the sea if they got into his way."

Weaver considered Patton's reasoning impeccable. Having won the battle of Mortain, Hodges's First Army was moving east to join Patton's army. "It was true enough," Weaver commented, "that this German Seventh Army would come pouring east in a desperate and determined effort to free itself. . . . It was further true there were an awful lot of Nazis in the pocket." But to prevent the pocket from collapsing, the Germans would have to keep troops around the perimeter. Therefore, Patton reasoned, he would not be forced to face more of the enemy than his men could handle. "But more than all of this," Weaver added, "German units were depleted, disintegrated and mingled with the full normal unity of command gone with the wind. George was so firmly convinced that the odds were in his favor that it would not even be a gamble."[37]

All of this turned out to be speculation, for Bradley, learning of Patton's order to Haislip to move farther north, countermanded it. In a "Memorandum for the Record" on the "Gap Operation," he offered two reasons for stopping the Third Army. The first was that Haislip, if allowed to continue, would advance into an area, between Argentan and Falaise, saturated with time bombs. "It would have taken several hours to change the bombing area," Bradley argued, "because many of the planes were coming from England and this involved a long line of communications." Bradley's second argument was that Patton's advance would have made an already thin American line thinner.

Trapped within the Allied net were "some 17 German divisions," containing about 100,000 men, a force strong enough to break through a weakened Allied line.[38]

Correctly or incorrectly, Bradley believed the bomb story and most likely believed the thin line argument as well. In his diary entry for August 13, Patton noted that the XV Corps had already moved north of Argentan. "This Corps could easily advance to Falaise and completely close the gap," he believed, "but we have been ordered to halt because the British sewed the area between with a large number of time bombs. I am sure that this halt is a great mistake, as I am certain that the British will not close on Falaise. As a matter of fact, we had reconnaissance parties within a few miles of it when we were ordered back."[39]

In halting Patton, Bradley undid an agreement he had entered into with the British. Just after noon on the thirteenth General Miles C. Dempsey, in charge of the Second British Army, met with Bradley and Montgomery at Montgomery's headquarters. "We discussed future operations—," Dempsey recorded in his diary, "particularly as regards Army Group and Army boundaries; and the bringing up of Corps. . . . So long as the Northward move of Third Army meets little opposition the two leading Corps will disregard inter-Army boundaries. The whole aim is to establish forces across the enemy's lines of communication so as to impede—if not prevent entirely—his withdrawal."[40]

When Ike joined the conferees, Monty explained that four Canadian divisions would attack on the fourteenth in a fresh attempt to reach Falaise. Supporting this assault, Dempsey's army was to drive toward Falaise from the northwest. But rather than closing the pocket, Dempsey's move would push the Germans east and out of it before the Canadians had closed it. Weaver, then at Argentan with the 90th Infantry Division, was sure he knew the British motive: "This was for the purpose of whittling the foe down to what Monty deemed proper size for digestion before sinking his teeth into the most palatable morsel."[41]

On the fourteenth faulty intelligence contributed to the failure to close the Argentan-Falaise gap. Informed by intelligence that numerous German divisions had already escaped, Bradley decided to divide Haislip's corps, giving Haislip the 5th Armored and the 79th Infantry and General Leonard T. Gerow of Hodges's army the 2d French Armored and the 80th and 90th Infantry. Haislip would then join Patton's other corps in a drive not to close the gap but to Dreux, about seventy miles directly east of Argentan and forty west of Paris.[42]

Patton, meantime, had concocted other ideas for a deep envelopment. On the fourteenth Patton conferred with Bradley, who, in light of his own plan for an envelopment, agreed to let Patton move Walker on Chartres, Haislip on Dreux, and Cook on Orleans. "It is really a great plan, wholly my own," Patton beamed, "and I made Bradley think he thought of it. 'Oh what a tangled web we weave when first we practice to deceive.'" A "happy and elated" Patton, seeing visions of his army advancing to Chartres and Orleans and then on to Metz and Espinal, just west of the German border, and finally to the West Wall, "got all the Corps moving by 2030 so that if Monty tries to be careful, it will be too late."[43]

An intelligence report on the fifteenth dismayed Bradley. The Germans, the report said, had not yet withdrawn from the pocket. Just the previous day, believing the bulk of the enemy force had escaped, Bradley had weakened what he called the Argentan shoulder of the pocket by sending Haislip to the northeast. Rushing over to Patton's headquarters, Bradley tried to revise the order. "Bradley came to see me, suffering from nerves," Patton scoffed. "There is a rumor, which I doubt, that there are five Panzer Divisions at Argentan, so Bradley wants me to halt my move to the east. . . . His motto seems to be, 'In case of doubt, halt.' I am complying with the order, and by tomorrow I can probably persuade him to let me advance. I wish I was Supreme Commander."[44]

At Patton's headquarters the news on the fifteenth that Lieutenant General Alexander M. Patch's Seventh Army had landed just east of Toulon on the Mediterranean coast of France perked up the staff. Patton had commanded the Seventh in Sicily, and many of his current staff members had served with him there.

Coupled with this was the public announcement that Patton was in France. Gay noted that this first mention of the Third Army came after it had "over-run a very large portion of France, had captured upwards of 35,000 prisoners, and destroyed many German installations and much German equipment."[45]

The days of comparative inactivity ended on August 16. Walker captured Chartres, which twelve days before Wood argued he could take without opposition. Haislip, meanwhile, reached the outskirts of

Dreux. Most important of all, Bradley called Patton on the phone at eight-thirty that evening and, in effect, reversed his stand of three days before. He told Patton that the Canadians, still bogged down, were being ordered to push southward to Trun, thereby closing about half the gap between Falaise and Argentan. Following the suggestion of Montgomery, Bradley wanted Patton to organize a temporary corps, consisting of the 2d French Armored and the 80th and 90th Infantry Divisions, for a movement north to Trun and to Chambois, four miles southeast of Trun, where the Americans would meet the Canadians. Since Gerow, whom Patton later called "one of the leading mediocre corps commanders in Europe," had not yet arrived, Patton put Gaffey in temporary charge of the makeshift corps.[46]

Late that night Gaffey ran into a short-lived mutiny. With Colonel Paul Harkins, his acting chief of staff, Gaffey began describing the assault, slated for the next day, to McLain, the commander of the 90th Infantry, and to Brigadier General Jacques-Philippe Leclerc, who led the 2d French Armored. McLain's main force was to attack Trun on the right, and the French were to follow when the 90th Division had seized a bridgehead over the Dives River, which ran just below Trun and through Chambois. Objecting because the plan, as outlined, called for splitting his division, Leclerc said he would not carry it out, for he would be defeated piecemeal. He wanted Patton to be so informed. Gaffey answered that he had been ordered to attack and that he expected his division commanders to carry out his orders. He then asked whether Leclerc, instructed to begin the assault the next morning, would refuse to obey the order. "This was taken down by a stenographer," Gay related, "and General Leclerc edged out by saying he would attack, but the attack was impossible; his Division would be ruined. After a further discussion, General Gaffey told General Leclerc the attack would go on as planned, and General Leclerc conceded."[47]

The conclusion of the Falaise struggle took place from the seventeenth to the twenty-first around Trun and Chambois. By the evening of the seventeenth the Canadians were just outside Trun. On that day the temporary corps, with Gerow now in command, attacked from the south, shrinking the pocket to an area roughly six miles deep and seven miles wide.

Along the pocket the fighting was some of the fiercest of the war. "Body after body of the Nazis threw themselves against our battalions,"

Weaver commented, "only to be mowed down; reforming and trying a new direction of escape they would receive the same mauling by another of our units. We literally bounced them from one of our organizations to another as they frantically but hopelessly sought one avenue of escape after another until they were all killed or captured." The 90th Infantry alone took thirteen thousand prisoners and killed or wounded eight thousand Germans.

Amid the ferocious fighting Field Marshal Walter Model, the ardent Nazi whom Hitler appointed to replace Kluge as Commander in Chief West on August 17, used a technique developed by the retreating Germans in the Soviet Union. Those Panzers who successfully broke out of the pocket turned about and kept open a gap that permitted the escape of their best-trained comrades, such as tank crews. This maneuver forced the Allies to face Germans from the west trying to break out and from the east trying to keep open the pocket.[48]

The artillery and air force played significant roles in the fighting. By the evening of August 19 the Allies had over three thousand guns firing into the German forces. General Quesada, who in France lived in a tent next to that of Bradley, described the damage inflicted by the IX and XIX Tactical Air Commands: "In the Falaise Gap, the aircraft just slaughtered the German army. The German army was attempting to escape, and small units on the perimeter were in actual combat with ours, and these vast units in the center, all trying to get out. Our air units would just slaughter them."[49]

German losses between August 17 and August 21 were high. In his official history Blumenson estimated that the Americans captured twenty-five thousand Germans and the British and Canadians another twenty-five thousand. About ten thousand Germans lay dead on the field.[50]

But General Brian Horrocks, who led the British XXX Corps in France, lamented the results. At least one-third of the Seventh Army and segments of the Fifth Panzer Army escaped. "This should not have happened," he observed in 1977; "many reasons have been put forward but to my mind few Germans would have escaped if Bradley had not halted Patton's northerly advance."

Bradley, on the other hand, blamed Montgomery, whom he hated. "General Eisenhower, Patton, and I were all disgusted with the way Montgomery made his attack," he lamented. Instead of moving south from Falaise, as he had promised, "Montgomery attacked the right end and hit the depth of the German penetration. . . . We had held our conference a few days before at a common meeting place where we placed a map on the back of the jeep and reached complete agreement as to what each was to do."[51]

V

While three of his divisions fought the battle of the gap, Patton spent his time checking on the movement to the Seine. By the nineteenth he was able to drive through Dreux to Mantes-Gassicourt, on the Seine just above Paris. That same day Patton received "reluctant permission" from Bradley to send the 79th Infantry Division across the river at Mantes-Gassicourt and establish a bridgehead on the eastern bank. Patton then asked authorization to take Melun, Fontainebleau, and Sens, below Paris. With Haislip's half corps blocking German escape routes north of Paris, Patton wished also to seize the escape routes south of the city. "Bradley said it was too risky," Patton complained. But Bradley agreed to let Patton try on Monday the twenty-first, "if I do not receive a stop order by midnight the 20th."[52]

Returning from the trip, Patton indulged in a highly publicized escapade. He told reporters, as General Weaver diplomatically put it, "about having used the Seine as a latrine during which bodily relief nothing occurred to disturb his virility and manhood." Still angry because he believed Montgomery was responsible for halting the XV Corps at Argentan at a time when he could have easily closed the gap, Patton, Weaver surmised, made his remark about the Seine to irritate Monty. The story that got back to the Americans was that, hearing of Patton's boldness, "Monty was shocked beyond measure."[53]

By now Patton stories filled American newspapers. According to one he had vowed, the day he sent Grow to Brittany, to "have tea in Brest Sunday," a promise that remained unfulfilled. Another report had him waving a thousand-dollar bill as he came ashore at Normandy and betting that he would beat Bradley and Montgomery to Paris. A third had him poring over his maps during a big operation wearing, of all things, a pince-nez and looking more like a businessman than a general. In addition to his revolvers, Patton supposedly carried a needle-pointed

French hand sword. For emphasis when speaking he often whacked the sword against a table or against the side of his breeches.

According to the *New York Times* Patton seemed to be everywhere. He "bounces over the countryside in a jeep or fast six-wheel cavalry reconnaissance car. At the end of a hot, dusty day his face is covered with black French dust and his eyelids look like the pollen-covered legs of a honey bee." Patton was "usually found somewhere up front, fanning himself with his helmet shell and swapping yarns with GIs and brass."[54]

The most interesting story about Patton did not appear in the newspapers. During the North African landings, Patton began keeping a diary. Sometimes it consisted of jottings on little slips of paper that he would stuff into his pockets and then give to his personal secretary, Sergeant Joseph D. Rosevich, to type. Often Patton dictated statements to Rosevich. Somehow William Randolph Hearst, Sr., learned of the diary. So, too, did William Randolph Hearst, Jr., who first met Patton in mid-August 1944 at Vire, twenty-one miles south of Saint-Lô, near the base of the Cotentin peninsula. "It was one of the most memorable moments of my life," the younger Hearst recalled. "We simply shook hands, but I felt instinctively that this was a great man." Patton, the only person the younger Hearst ever met who reminded him of his father, possessed "an aura about him, a quiet poise, a self-confidence that radiated from his face and body. Yet we were very different men. I prized gentility—and that was a luxury Patton could not afford."

Learning of the diary, the elder Hearst tried to buy it. Larry Newman, who covered the Third Army for Hearst's International News Service, carried with him a check for $250,000 made out to Patton. But Patton, the younger Hearst wrote, "proved remarkably humble. He had no plans to write about himself and the war, so he turned us down."[55] Unfortunately, however, the Hearsts would later get hold of a portion of the diary and, because of their hatred of Eisenhower, would hurt Bea and the Patton family in a way that matched Drew Pearson with his exposure of the slappings.

While in France, Patton remembered his old friends. On the day he first saw the Seine he sent Codman to Vannes, on the southern coast of Brittany, to bring to him the old French general J. L. Koechlin-Schwarz, Patton's instructor at the college at Langres during the First World War. In October 1918, visiting the wounded Patton, the Frenchman had said: "My dear Patton, I am so glad you were wounded. For when you left I said to my wife that is the end of Patton. He is one of those gallant fellows who always get killed."

The French general had unreserved praise for his American pupil. "Had I taught 25 years ago what you are doing," he told Patton, "I should have been put in a mad house, but when I heard that an armored division was headed for Brest I knew it was you." Koechlin-Schwarz said that the Germans had defeated the French army in 1940 because for ten years the French "had taught, thought and practiced defense, never attack." Patton, in turn, reminded him that at Langres he had observed: "The poorer the infantry, the more artillery it needs; the American infantry needs all it can get." Patton believed his friend was correct in 1918 "and still is."[56]

Weyland remembered having lunch with Patton and an old French general from World War I, undoubtedly Koechlin-Schwarz. At the lunch Patton served some very good wine, about which he boasted. He said that one of his divisions had overrun a warehouse filled with fine wines carefully labeled: "Verboten for sale, Reserved for Wehrmacht [Armed Forces]." Weyland suggested that it would buoy the spirits of his men if Patton sent them some of the wine. Pounding the table, Patton vowed to do it. Under the procedure worked out, Weyland dispatched twenty or thirty cases of wine to each of his groups and to each of his supply and service units with a note saying that "so-and-so Division, or the Eighth Corps or the Twentieth Corps, sent this back with their compliments in appreciation of the help that the boys had given them." Every unit in his command, Weyland said, "loved this association with the Third Army." The Germans had warehouses all over France, and the supply of goods sent back to the aviators became constant. "The same applied to captured German pistols and stuff like that." The airmen grew so close to the Third Army that the members of the 29th Tactical Air Group insisted before being transferred that "they wanted to fly one last mission for the old Third Army. Which they did, and it brought tears to old George Patton's eyes, when he heard about it."[57]

In eleven days during August Patton's forces pushed up to 160 miles into France. The month of September also saw some advances. During such periods, Weyland became innovative.

We'd sort of thrown away the book, and we were making up new rules of engagement as we went along. I had what we called armored-column cover, for example. All during the daylight hours when the ground forces were fighting or advancing, Gen. Patton advanced in parallel columns normally, and always spearheaded by armor. I had liaison officers up in the lead tanks in every one of these columns—an Air Force officer guiding the leading tank with a radio, so that he could talk with the aircraft. Then I had fighter bombers, which preceded the columns, knowing where they were supposed to go. They would locate enemy opposition, tanks, troops, guns, or obstacles, or tank barriers, or what have you; let them know, and in most cases knock out the opposition before the American tanks got there. . . .

Here's the reason I say we threw the book out the window: We used to say at service schools that anything within reach of artillery, it was a waste to use an airplane to knock out a target that artillery could strike. But we dropped that one because of the time element. We tried to knock the target out before our ground forces ever arrived on the scene, if possible. Sometimes we missed them. If the tanks actually arrived, then they would be slowed down. . . . Yes, the artillery could have done it, but it would stop the entire column. . . . It would take hours to do it. . . . The secret was to keep the Germans off balance, just to keep the show on the road.[58]

On August 20 Patton showed how deeply he relied on Weyland. During the advance toward the Seine, Cook, commanding the XII Corps, developed circulatory problems. Losing feeling in his arms and legs, he found it impossible to walk a hundred yards. Both he and Patton realized he could not go on.

If Patton had selected Cook's successor on the basis of talent, he would have chosen Wood, Cook's temporary replacement. Chynoweth, Wood, and Cook had been classmates at West Point and lifelong friends. Though Cook, like Chynoweth, spent his career in the infantry, he, like Chynoweth, always pushed for army modernization. But Patton, perhaps fearing the outspoken Wood, went a different way. Walton H. Walker, an infantryman, already led Patton's XX Corps.

Also a member of the class of 1912 at West Point, Walker knew nothing about tanks, which he often used as artillery. To replace Cook, Patton turned to another unimaginative infantryman, Manton Eddy.

On the twentieth Patton told Walker and Eddy to prepare to attack the next morning. "Eddy asked me how much he should worry about his right flank," Patton recorded, "and I told him that depended on how nervous he was. If you worry about flanks you could never fight this sort of war. Our air can spot any group of enemy large enough to hurt us and I can always pull something out of the hat." When Eddy said that he would be happy to advance a mile a day, Patton "told him to go fifty and he turned pale."[59]

Another matter came up that day. Brigadier General Benjamin O. Davis, the army's first black general, visited Patton. "We are having too much raping murder by the colored troops," Patton observed, "at least 15 rape cases, 2 murders, and a riot. Davis is a very sensible man."[60]

Because the European Theater of Operations contained no black infantry units and only a few black artillery, tank, and tank destroyer units, almost all African Americans served in the quartermaster and other services of supply organizations. After viewing the unattractive and filthy women in North Africa and Sicily, the American soldiers found French women clean and pretty. Racing across France, Patton's units near the Seine had little time for thoughts of women. But, as the court-martial records reveal, the troops in Brittany, bogged down before Lorient and the other cities, committed numerous rapes. On August 17, for example, four soldiers, unquestionably black, serving with the Brittany Base Section, were arrested for rape. In Sicily under Patton such an offense would have probably ended with a sentence of hanging, but all four received life in prison.[61]

Patton found the French women the most attractive he had yet seen. "After nearly two years of being accustomed to the inarticulate shapes of the Arab women, the over-stuffed profiles of the Italians, and to the boyish figures of the British women," he commented, "the obtrusive and meticulously displayed figures of the Norman and Brittan women is quite striking. In a way they remind me of a British engine with two bumpers in front and powerful driving wheels behind."[62]

Despite the excesses of a few soldiers, Patton found much to admire in his black units. "A colored detachment" of his Quartermaster Corps had, he observed, "the unusual, and as far as I know the only opportunity of capturing a German Lieutenant General," General Hahn, the commander of the 82d German Corps, who surrendered along with a colonel, a major, a lieutenant, and seven privates. "They were apparently fed up with fighting and simply waited until the troops passed. I have never seen more elated troops than those negroes who had captured them."[63]

The greatest day of the drive to Paris came on August 21, when, Patton told Bea, "we jumped seventy miles today." Moving so fast that the Germans did not have time to destroy the bridges south of the city, Eddy took Sens on the Vanne River and Walker captured Melun and Montereau on the Seine. From there Patton hoped to drive with three corps, "two up and one back," directly east. If allowed to make the dash, "we can be in Germany in ten days. . . . It can be done with three armored and six infantry divisions. . . . It is such a sure thing that I fear these blind moles don't see it." Tomorrow he intended to present his case to Bradley. "I will now read the Bible to get some support for my argument in the morning."[64]

The speed with which Patton was able to move from Argentan to the outskirts of Paris indicated two things. First, he had enough gas for the movement. Second, he was meeting but scattered resistance from the Germans. And, according to the *New York Times*, when he did encounter opposition, he often went around it.[65]

Patton's new proposal would extend his lines to Metz, Nancy, and Epinal, each along the Moselle River and over three hundred miles from Paris. With Harkins he flew to Bradley's headquarters on the twenty-second to explain it. Finding that Bradley had gone to see Eisenhower and Montgomery, Patton spoke to Bradley's chief of staff, Major General Leven C. Allen, who was not sure whether the Twelfth Army Group would go north after passing Paris or whether it would be allowed to continue east. Entertaining views similar to those of Patton, Bradley desired to continue east, but Monty was pushing for something different. Disliking the "two-thrust" strategy of the British in the north and the Americans in the south, Montgomery proposed a "single thrust" by four Allied armies that he would command. With this force, he would destroy the remainder of the German Fifteenth Army at the Pas de Calais, then march through Belgium and Holland to the Ruhr and Berlin.[66]

Montgomery's plan infuriated the Americans. Gay considered it an attempt to "slow down the Third Army so [the] British can go ahead." Even more incensed, it turned out, was Bradley. Having only four divisions with which to move east, Patton on the twenty-third visited Bradley at Laval, west of Le Mans, "to try to steal or borrow all or part" of Collins's VII Corps, then supposedly closing on Chartres. "I rather hate to go east with only four divisions," Patton observed, "especially if I have to leave one north of Orleans." Arriving at Laval with Muller, his supply officer, Patton found a Bradley anxious to talk to him before going to see Ike and Monty. "He was quite worried," Patton noted, "as he feels that Ike wont go against Monty and that the American armies will have to turn north in whole or in part." Air Chief Marshal Trafford Leigh-Mallory

> had been with him all day, trying to sell the idea to Bradley. He was madder than I have ever seen him and wondered aloud "what the Supreme Commander amounted to" . . . I cannot understand why Monty keeps on asking for all four armies in the Calais area and then through Belgium, where the tanks are practically useless now, and will be wholly useless this winter. Unfortunately, he has some way of talking General Eisenhower into his way of thinking.

Patton suggested that he, Bradley, and Hodges "offer to resign unless we went east. Ike would have to yield, but Bradley would not agree and said we owed it to the troops to hold on. . . . I feel that in such a showdown we would win, as Ike would not dare to relieve us."[67]

To Allen later that day, Patton suggested two possible courses of action for the American troops after reaching Paris. Under Plan A, Patton's forces would turn north from Melun, Montereau, and Sens. Heading toward Beauvais, directly north of Paris, the Third Army would pick up the 4th and 79th Infantry divisions and block the rear of the Germans defending the east bank of the Seine. Patton estimated that by opening the Seine to the British and Canadians and having supplies cross the river at Mantes-Gassicourt, just above Paris, this plan would cut the present supply routes in half. "This is the best strategical idea I have ever had," Patton commented. Plan B was much simpler, being Patton's original scheme to move directly east toward Metz and Nancy.[68]

On the twenty-fifth Patton received his answer. Called with Hodges to Bradley's headquarters, now at Chartres, Patton heard the new orders. Hodges, with nine divisions, would cross the Seine at Melun and Mantes-Gassicourt and would more or less follow Plan A, driving northeast of Paris, which the Allies had taken that very day, toward Lille and Belgium. Patton's Third Army, on the other hand, would follow Plan B. With seven divisions—the 4th Armored and the 35th and 80th Infantry from Eddy's Corps; the 2d French Armored, given the honor of being the first division to enter Paris, and the 90th Infantry from Haislip's Corps, and the 7th Armored and 5th Infantry from Walker's Corps—Patton would go east. He would first seize Troyes and Nogent-sur-Seine, next move to Reims and Vitry-le-François, then attack the great fortress of Metz, and finally assault Strasbourg, on the German border.[69]

Racing across France the Americans skillfully used their superiority in the number, if not in the quality, of their weapons. On August 26 Brigadier General John M. Devine, who commanded the artillery of the 90th Division and would soon command the 8th Armored Division, told Patton and Gay that during the recent action near Chambois, about eight miles northeast of Argentan, "the death and destruction caused by his artillery on the German army was something beyond the wildest dreams of man; that he felt that over 3,000 vehicles, including 500 tanks, were destroyed; over 1000 horses were killed; and well over 2000 Germans were killed; that the stench in the area was insufferable."[70]

Wood, too, talked of the destruction his men inflicted fighting "more German tanks than anyone else." The 4th Armored often faced the Mark V or Panther, with its high-velocity 75-millimeter gun, and the Mark VI or Tiger, possessing an 88-millimeter gun, both capable of knocking out the lighter American Sherman at twenty-five hundred yards. "I have never been satisfied unless we could get something like 4 to 1," Wood told Brigadier General William A. Borden. "I don't like to trade with them, but if it's a matter of standing off and fighting at 2,000 or 3,000 yards they've got it on us, but we don't do that. Our people close in with them, and we were able at 300 or 400 yards to get in a couple of hits on them, and we have knocked out many Bosch tanks, a great number of them."

As he frequently told Liddell Hart, Wood abhorred frontal attacks. "We try to get into the rear of the enemy," he related, "and the great weapon that we used to such a large extent in the month of August where we were cutting through the Bosch on all sides is the machine gun. . . . Our 50-caliber machine gun is especially potent. . . . That is the tank weapon. When the tanks are really being used to their full extent to cut into the enemy's vitals, we use these machine guns to just rip to pieces him and his personnel."[71]

The scoresheet of losses as of August 26 showed the potency of the American attack. As Patton recorded, American casualties totaled 18,239, compared with 136,506 for the Germans. Just as significant were the tank figures, the known German losses totaling 558, the American 269. Since the Germans possessed only about four hundred Panthers and Tigers in France, the bulk of their losses seemed to be lighter tanks.[72]

On the twenty-eighth Patton received news that Gay called "historic." "Bradley came in at 1030," Patton related, "and I had to beg like a beggar for permission to keep on to the line of the Meuse. What a life." Bradley authorized the advance to the Meuse, but he insisted that upon approaching the river Patton keep an armored division on the right rear as a reserve unit.

More importantly, Bradley revealed that he had been ordered to furnish three thousand tons of supplies daily to Paris, liberated on the twenty-fifth, and its surrounding area. These were to come from Patton's army, whose supplies were to be cut to two thousand tons a day. To the north Hodges's First Army, which was supporting Mongtomery, would continue to receive five thousand tons daily.[73]

As Bradley pointed out, fuel provided "our greatest logistical problem." Patton and Hodges each consumed 400,000 gallons of gas a day. In mid-August the cross-channel gasoline pipeline became operational and began funneling to the continent sufficient fuel. But the Red Ball Express, the trucking system inaugurated to supply the American armies, could not deliver the gas fast enough. Indeed, the Red Ball itself devoured three hundred thousand gallons a day.[74]

The shortage first hit Patton on August 29. Driving to the headquarters of the XII Corps, just outside Troyes, on the Seine about seventy-five miles southeast of Paris, Patton found Eddy and Wood, whose Combat Command A had taken the city. There Patton instructed Eddy to advance eighty miles east to Commercy, a World War I battleground on the Meuse. Walker was to move to another World War site on the Meuse, Verdun. Then it would be on to Metz and Nancy, both on the

Moselle. The Rhine River would be but a hundred miles farther east. "While at XII Corps," Patton observed, "I found that for unknown reasons we had not been given our share of gas—140,000 gallons short. This may be an attempt to stop me in a backhanded manner, but I doubt it. I will go and kick to Bradley in the morning."[75]

The next day, finding he could not fly to Bradley's headquarters at Chartres in the bad weather, Patton drove there in a new Cadillac given to him by the 5th Division. There Bradley and Leven Allen were with Ike's G-3, Major General Harold R. Bull. Patton presented "my case for an immediate advance to the east and a rupture of the Siegfried Line before it can be manned. Bradley was sympathetic but General Bull— and I gather the rest of Eisenhower's staff—do not concur, and are letting General Montgomery over-persuade General Eisenhower to go north."

Returning to his new command post ten kilometers north of Sens, Patton found that his tanks were running dry. The Third Army had received that day only thirty-two thousand gallons of gas and would not get more until the third of September. During Patton's absence, when Eddy doubted whether he had enough gas to make it to Commercy and the Meuse River, Gaffey had told him to halt at Saint-Dizier, just below Vitry-le-François on the Marne River, thirty-two miles west of Commercy. "I will get up to see you tomorrow," Gaffey informed Eddy over the phone, "because there is a lot behind this, Mant." Countermanding the order, Patton "told Gaffey to have Eddy run till his engines stop and then go on foot. We must and will get a crossing on the Meuse. In the last war I drained three quarters of my tanks to keep the other quarter going. Eddy can do the same."[76]

For Patton the issue involved not just gas but a philosophy of war. The faster the Americans crossed the Rhine, the fewer "lives and munitions" it would take. "No one realizes the terrible value of the 'unforgiving minute' except me. Someway I will get on yet."[77]

With much justification Patton especially resented noncombatants who bossed combat soldiers. In his eyes one of the chief culprits was his West Point classmate Lieutenant General John C. H. Lee, Ike's deputy theater commander and the head of the Communications Zone, which controlled supplies. Once, Bradley noted, Lee insisted that he needed infantry troops to guard his supply dumps. "I remember Patton hit the ceiling when I told him about that. It was one hell of a job for him to go back and guard supplies. He said, 'He's got enough men back there. All he's got to do is take a few extra truck drivers and give them a rifle.' So he wasn't too popular with the fighting troops."[78]

Patton reflected his dislike after Lee, Everett Hughes, and Brigadier General Ewart G. Plank of the Services of Supply visited him on August 7. "As usual," Patton wrote, "Lee was in a great hurry to do nothing and covered with smiles. I have seldom seen a man less suited for his job. Someone described him very aptly the other day, 'He is a pompous little son-of-a-bitch only interested in self-advertisement.' "[79]

In the midst of the gasoline shortage Lee decided to move his headquarters, with its numerous detachments, from Valognes on the Cherbourg peninsula to Paris. "There is no need of denying it," General Weaver commented, "the expedition did use up quite a number of trucks and a sizeable amount of gasoline. When rumors of this event got noised around, emotions bubbled over in the fighting zone, since all were crying for the S.O.S. means with which to charge forward." Patton, Weaver remembered, led the complainers. When Ike found out about the move to Paris, he tried to stop it, but it had already gone too far.[80]

Bradley disapproved of something else Lee did. "One thing was when he went into a hospital, he inspected the hospitals quite a bit. . . . He'd go into a hospital and he expected everybody in there to get up and stand at attention, regardless of how sick they were. And sometimes you don't feel like standing at attention when you are in the hospital, but he expected that."[81]

Telling reporters of the capture by Eddy's XII Corps of Troyes on August 25 and of Commercy six days later, Patton rejoiced not just because his troops had taken these cities but because of the American success in fighting German tanks. "There is a fellow named Clarke in the 4th Armored Division who is really a great soldier," he said of Colonel Bruce C. Clarke, who was destined to become a four-star general but who now led Wood's Combat Command A. "He attacked Troyes the other day with 17 tanks in a line, followed by two companies of armored infantry and their carriers. He advanced 5,000 meters over a perfectly level field, killed 600 Germans, and didn't have a man or vehicle hit." At Commercy Clarke, leading a company of tanks, crossed the bridge over the Meuse and attacked and destroyed four German 88-

millimeter guns. "Went in there just like a Western movie with all guns blazing, like we have been trying to teach them for a number of years. He went in there about 40 miles an hour." Patton then said about Clarke what Koechlin-Schwarz remarked about him in 1918: "He is a good boy, he is a great fighter. I don't think he will live very long; sooner or later, one will hit him."[82]

At a news conference that September Patton further explained his philosophy of armored battle.

> You know, a tank fight is just like a barroom fight—the fellow who gets the hit wins. Our men, especially in the 4th Armored, are magnificent shots. The 4th, 2nd and 3rd Armored are old divisions and have plenty of practice. I used to train them to get on a target of 30 degrees off target in three seconds. They did not do it, but they got awfully fast.
>
> . . . The whole thing in tank fighting is to train crews not as individuals but as crews. We have on our tank turrets a special sight for the tank gunner. . . . I don't think the Germans have it. We devised that in the desert.[83]

Even with the gasoline shortage, Patton and his men ended August and began September on a high note. Taking Reims and Epernay, the troops discovered champagne caves and warehouses. They then passed through the Argonne Forest with only scattered resistance. Located between the cathedral town of Reims and Verdun, the forest had proved a bloody obstacle for the Americans in 1918. Moving on, Major General Lindsey McD. Silvester's 7th Armored Division entered Verdun and on the first of September crossed the bridge over the Meuse. The advances provided the Americans with another bonus. At Châlons-sur-Marne on August 29 and at Reims on August 30, they captured excellent Luftwaffe airfields that Weyland immediately used. From close in, Weyland's fighter-bombers on September 1 destroyed or damaged a record 833 enemy vehicles.[84]

Along with the gas shortage, the sourest note for Patton at August's close was Middleton's attack with three full divisions against Brest. Begun on the twenty-fifth, the assault made little progress. "Middleton is not too sanguine about the capture of Brest," Patton observed on the

last day of the month after visiting VIII Corps headquarters. "He is full
of alibies and complaints, about the fact that his infantry does not fight
very well."[85]

Spending the night at Bradley's headquarters at Chartres, Patton discussed Brest and other matters. Both generals conceded that Brest was
now of little value. But, as Bradley put it, they also agreed that Brest
must be taken to "maintain the illusion . . . that the U.S. Army cannot
be beaten." Simpson was also at Bradley's headquarters, and the three
generals arranged for his Ninth Army, soon to be activated, to take over
the Brest campaign, thereby enabling Grow's 6th Armored Division to
rejoin Patton at Troyes.[86] Neither Patton nor Bradley would concede it,
but Wood had been right about the diversion to Brittany all along.

Moping about his command post on the first of the new month, Patton heard on the radio that Ike had called Montgomery, whose army
was moving toward Brussels and the deepwater port of Antwerp, the
greatest living soldier. This comment inspired Patton to send a friendly
note to General Marshall. Patton began by decrying the wild stories
that had appeared in the *New York Times* about him. One was that he
had arrived in France waving a thousand-dollar bill and offering to bet
that he would beat Bradley and Montgomery to Paris. "There is not a
word of truth to the statement," Patton asserted. "I have never seen a
$1000 bill. I arrived in Normandy incognito, and, as the result of previ-
ous experiences, I have said nothing to any correspondent at any time
which can be quoted." Having just spoken to Bradley, Patton transmitted a request: "I should like to add my request to the one Bradley has
made for himself, that when this war is over, which it will shortly be, he
and I get a chance to go to the Pacific. I am perfectly willing to go in
any capacity so long as I can fight that particular race."[87]

Meantime, a change in the command structure irritated Monty, who
later discussed the matter with the British newspaperman and historian
Chester Wilmot.

When Ike came to see me in Normandy on Aug. 23, he said first
that he intended to take over command of the battle himself at the
end of the month, and second that his policy was to advance to the
Rhine on a broad front. I told him it couldn't be done. We couldn't
win that way. I said, "Administratively we haven't got the stuff to
maintain both Army Groups at full pressure. The only policy is to

halt the left and strike with the right or halt the right and strike with the left. We must decide on one thrust, and put all the maintenance to support that. If we split the maintenance and advance on a broad front it will mean that we are so weak everywhere that we will have no chance of success." He did not agree. He said 21 Army Group should go for the Saar-Frankfurt area. The root of the trouble was that politically he did not dare to stop George Patton. Patton was the most public hero of the moment. If he had grounded Patton's Army, as he should have done, there would have been a tremendous outcry in America. He wasn't big enough to face it. He was so convinced that "public opinion wins wars" and that he could not fly in the face of public opinion.

Ike's decision to take over command was a disaster. He had not the experience nor the organisation. He had never really directed any battle himself. He did not know the technique of command and he had no firm principles of strategy and no firm strategic policy. Because he had no ideas of his own he used to go round from one Commander to another getting their ideas and then he would try to rationalize a plan which was essentially compromise between the demands and suggestions of his Junior Commanders. A Supreme Commander must have strong principles and a clear plan and must issue his orders to his Commanders on the basis of these. It is hopeless if he tries to work the other way round and evolve a compromise plan from the various suggestions of his subordinates. In Ike's case it was particularly unfortunate because he was extremely susceptible to the personality of the last Commander he saw before he made his decisions. In modern war the Supreme Command must have a firm, consistent and continuous control over the battle. Modern war moves so fast that the battle can go off the rails in 12 hours. The Supreme Commander must be in such a position that he always has firm control. Otherwise some headstrong Commander like Patton will muck up your battle plan before you know where you are.

On September 1 Ike moved his headquarters from London to Granville on the western coast of the Cherbourg peninsula. There, Monty pointed out, he was three to four hundred miles from the battle area, farther than he had been in London. "He had no communications, . . . no telephone not even radiophone—it took 24 hours for information to reach him from the front, and another 24 hours for his orders to get back. This meant a 48 hour delay and no modern battle can be run in those circumstances."[88]

A telling meeting took place on September 2, when Ike conferred with Patton, Bradley, Hodges, and Major General Hoyt Vandenberg, the new commander of the Ninth Air Force. Ike insisted that Monty be allowed to clean up the Calais area before Patton and Hodges moved forward. "Until this is done," Patton noted in his diary, "we will not be able to get gas or ammunition for a further advance." Trying to dissuade Eisenhower, Patton exaggerated his own progress, which was to the Meuse. Unmindful of what the Moselle would hold for him, he had, he told Ike, patrols near Metz and Nancy, forty miles farther on. "Ike was very pontifical and quoted Clausewitz to us, who have commanded larger forces than C ever heard of. . . . He kept talking about the future great battle of Germany, while we assured him that the Germans had nothing to fight with if we pushed on now. If we wait, there will be a great battle of Germany."[89]

Interviewed thirty years later, S. L. A. Marshall considered Patton's statements exaggerated.

> As for his being . . . his having any chance to get to Berlin at the time he was stopped by a shortage of gasoline, absolute nonsense. That army was spread out from the Moselle to the Brest Peninsula. It was in no shape to attack. It was not just short of fuel; it was short of everything. It was short of concentration for one thing, and the Germans were in strength across the Moselle. So, that's one of the myths that came up in the Patton film. And General Bradley helped perpetuate it. But it isn't true. My deputy [Hugh M. Cole] was historian of the Third Army at that time and when they stopped he made a total survey of the situation in the Army. His conclusion was there wasn't a chance for the Third Army to get even across the Moselle.[90]

As Marshall, with the advantage of being able to look back, indicated, Patton was in for a shock at the river.

In his diary entry for September 3, Patton noted that Red Cross girls, serving coffee and doughnuts from a truck, had followed his soldiers right up to the front lines. Among them, noted Alein Gersten, one of the minor staff officers at his headquarters, was Patton's niece, Jean Gordon. The daughter of Bea's half sister, Jean had arrived in France in mid-August. Whether true or not, Bea believed she had had an affair with Patton in Hawaii.

Gersten made it clear that the staff officers considered Patton's relationship with his niece to be casual. Such, however, was not the case with two famous singers who came to France to entertain the troops. No matter what happened, Patton expected his officers to be immaculate and ready for combat. If not, they were subject to a fine of $25 for each offense. The same was true of visitors. Near Paris, Patton almost court-martialed Bing Crosby for wearing a soft cap instead of his helmet.

Without realizing it, Gersten attacked the Jean Gordon story. He believed that Patton, the son of a believer in Anglo-Saxon supremacy, and Dinah Shore, who came from a well-to-do Jewish family in Tennessee, were attracted to each other. Then in the flower of young womanhood, Dinah, a movie star and the most popular woman vocalist in America, met Patton when she came to entertain the troops below Paris. Instead of moving about, she stayed close to Patton during the entire gasoline shortage. The staff officers were sure that the two saw each other frequently. That, perhaps, was why Patton never mentioned Dinah in his diary.[91]

STUMBLING INTO THE BULGE

I

For the Third Army the gas shortage eased almost as suddenly as it had developed. To Patton's "delight" Eddy captured one hundred thousand gallons of gas on September 3 and began moving forward. The next day Patton's army, which consumed between 350,000 and 400,000 gallons daily, received 240,265 gallons, and during the following three days almost 1.4 million gallons, more than it usually used.[1]

The gasoline shortage came amid a squabble between Eisenhower and Montgomery. On August 23 Ike decided to separate again Monty's Twenty-first Army Group and Bradley's Twelfth Army Group, then both under Montgomery's command. Disagreeing, Montgomery argued that the ground forces should remain one unit. Ike persisted, and on September 1, the day Montgomery became a field marshal and Eisenhower came to France and took command of the Allied ground forces, the two army groups were split and put under the direct command of the Supreme Headquarters Allied Expeditionary Force.

The key date in the debate turned out to be September 4, when Monty cabled Eisenhower reiterating his views. Pointing to the two possible paths the Allies might follow to advance to Berlin, the northern route through the Ruhr Valley and the southern through the Saar Basin, Montgomery pushed for "one thrust," the northern, under his command. This cable crossed one from Ike saying that the armies north of the Ardennes would break the West Wall, or Siegfried Line, and seize the Ruhr, while those south of the Ardennes would penetrate the Wall in the Saar and then proceed seventy-five miles farther east to Frankfurt-am-Main. Both thrusts were to begin as soon as possible.[2]

The issue remained unresolved until a week later. On the tenth Eisenhower conferred in Brussels with Montgomery, where, despite Montgomery's strong language, he held firm to the two-thrust strategy. The next day Bedell Smith visited Montgomery and agreed to give priority in supplies to the Ruhr campaign, at the expense of Patton and the Saar campaign.[3]

In 1946, in an interview with the military analyst Hanson Baldwin of the *New York Times,* Eisenhower explained why he gave greater emphasis to Montgomery's thrust. Ike

> stressed the fact—and said that Beedle Smith had maps to prove it—that before France had been invaded a schedule of operations had been drawn up, in which British and American planners concurred and which envisioned what actually occurred, on the continent. The advance to the Rhine, the crossing of the Rhine, the double envelopment of the Ruhr, etc. He said that people never understood that the left wing naturally would advance more rapidly than the right and was in better shape than the right because it captured ports as it went along. The invasion of Germany could not have been supplied from Cherbourg alone. It was foolish to assert that the right wing (the Third Army) could have pushed ahead into Germany; supplies alone would have stopped this. After crossing the Rhine and the double envelopment of the Ruhr it was intended to use the strategic reserves to support whatever prong of the offensive had advanced fastest. Original weight was given to Montgomery's armies but no more than 36 divisions could be supplied up there. In all we had calculated about 80 divisions to defeat Germany which was about what we had. These preliminary plans, which proved to be remarkably correct in retrospect, were made in March–April 1944.[4]

A meeting in Berlin on the day that Montgomery's and Eisenhower's messages crisscrossed showed that many Allied generals, Patton included, underestimated the strength and determination of the Germans. On the fourth of September Hitler assured Baron Ōshima that his army still intended to fight and win. Once Patton's tanks had breached the German lines in France, Hitler explained, the Germans had no choice but to fall back to new positions along the West Wall, leaving garrisons only "in the most important coastal fortifications such as Bordeaux, Le Havre and the Brittany ports." German troops were now massing southeast of Nancy, to which Patton's 80th Infantry and 4th Armored Divisions were heading, in order to strike the flank of the American forces, "which have been pursuing us in five or six columns, each composed of three to four divisions." The German attack, Hitler revealed, would be led by Army Group G, commanded by Colonel General Johannes Blaskowitz, and by troops moved up from Germany itself. Blaskowitz's Army Group was already "falling back to a planned line without suffering serious losses."

Far from feeling defeated, Hitler explained to the Japanese ambassador his plan for a massive offensive against the Allies. The Luftwaffe was going through what Hitler called a "current replenishment," and a million additional men, many having previously been deferred from military service, were being trained for the ground army. Combining "the new units with the units to be withdrawn from all possible areas," Hitler hoped to open "a large-scale offensive in the West" after the beginning of November. "We will be aided in holding off the enemy in Sept. & Oct.," he predicted, "by the comparatively rainy weather which will restrict the enemy's employment of their superior air power."[5] Thus came an early hint of what became the Ardennes offensive.

On September 5 both Ike and Bradley gave the Third Army permission to advance into the French region known as Lorraine and then into Germany. Visiting Patton and his three corps commanders at the new Third Army headquarters southeast of Châlons, Bradley outlined the plans for the advance. Hodges's First Army, in the north, and Patton's Third, in the south, would both move east. The Third Army would head toward Metz and Nancy on the Moselle River and then to the Rhine River and a line connecting, from left to right, Frankfurt-am-Main, Mannheim, and Karlsruhe. In a memorandum on the advance, Eisenhower epitomized the American view of what his troops, pushing toward the Fatherland, might expect: "The defeat of the German armies is complete, and the only thing now needed to realize the whole conception is speed."[6]

That same day an anxious Patton sent into action the bulk of two corps. The four divisions of Walker's XX Corps would advance to Metz, while the 35th and 80th Infantry and the 4th Armored Divisions of

Eddy's XII Corps were to establish and secure a beachhead across the Moselle at Nancy. "I was present for the jump-off," Bradley remembered. "Patton was confident that he could smash right through to the Rhine. But he was in for a rude shock."[7]

When visiting Eddy on September 3, Patton had talked of dashing across the Moselle and of breaching the West Wall. Advancing, Horace McBride's 80th Division ran into immediate trouble at Pont-à-Mousson, where, after traversing the Moselle, two companies of the 317th Regiment were shoved back across it with a loss of 294 men. "All this comes from the fatal decision of the Supreme Commander to halt the Third Army until the Pas-de-Calais was cleaned up," Patton lamented. "A fateful blunder." Oddly, the Brittany campaign contributed to the repulse, for Weyland, using his entire force against the enemy-held ports, was unable to send planes to the Moselle.[8]

During early September, Patton entertained a variety of visitors. One was Mrs. Samuel Rosenman, the wife of Roosevelt's adviser, "who is in Europe ostensibly making a study of how the soldiers react to the so-called G.I. Bill of Rights, but who is really I believe on a sightseeing tour." Patton found her "an interesting and attractive woman and we have a very pleasant hour's conversation together." To this Patton added in longhand: "She is just sightseeing and a very Jewy Jewess."[9]

Having nothing much better to do, Patton spoke on September 7 to the reporters covering his army. From the press conference two salient points emerged. First, despite the "bloody nose" at Pont-à-Mousson, Patton still considered the Germans disorganized. "You can't have men retreating for 300 or 400 miles and then hold anything," he reasoned. Unknowingly, moreover, Patton disagreed with Hitler, who predicted to Ōshima that the American advance would bog down in the autumn rains. "The American Army destroyed the Indian by fighting in bad weather," he said. With their superior equipment and clothing, Americans had always been able to fight in weather that stopped other armies.[10]

The day after Patton expressed these views, the Germans contradicted his first point. Enemy Mark VI tanks stumbled onto the command post of the 90th Division, forcing McLain to move his headquarters three or four miles to the rear. Using 57-millimeter anti-tank guns and a new ammunition that pierced the Tigers any place it hit, the Americans destroyed forty German tanks and forty armored vehicles, but the incident indicated that the Germans were not about to give up.[11]

A conference between Bradley and Patton on the ninth centered on an old topic: Brest. Repeating almost word for word what he had said on the last day of August, Bradley confided: "I would not say this to anyone but you, and have given different excuses to my staff and higher echelons, but we must take Brest in order to maintain the illusion of the fact that the U.S. Army cannot be beaten." In his diary Patton commented: "More emotion than I thought he had. I fully concur in this view. Anytime we put our hand to a job we must finish it."[12] Such thinking, reminiscent of that of the First World War generals who sacrificed lives freely to gain a few thousand yards of territory, would soon draw Patton into a misguided assault.

A historic episode on the eleventh of September reinforced the Allied illusion that the Germans were preparing to surrender. Activated on the fifth, Simpson's Ninth Army began taking over operations in Brittany and on Bradley's southern flank. Facing Simpson as well as the Americans and the French Forces of the Interior who, as part of Devers's Sixth Army Group, were pushing north after invading southern France, German troops tried to get out of the region. By skip-bombing the railroad lines Weyland's fighter-bombers prevented their troop trains from moving. Joining in, French Resistance forces dynamited roads and bridges. If the Germans tried to move during the day, Weyland remembered, his planes "would rake them and chew them all up. Whereupon, they decided to heck with it." The Germans sent word to Simpson that they wanted to give up. Simpson could not understand why until Weyland showed him pictures of the damage done to their convoys. At the Beaugency Bridge, which crossed the Loire River southwest of Orléans, twenty thousand Germans capitulated. For the first time in history airplanes, unaided by ground troops, had forced the surrender of a large enemy force.[13]

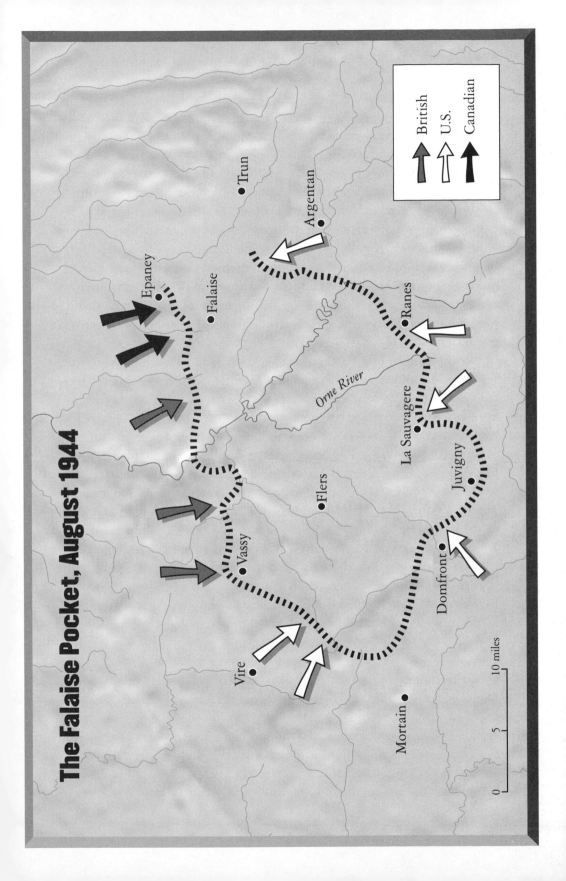

The Falaise Pocket, August 1944

British
U.S.
Canadian

Trun

Argentan

Epaney
Falaise

Ranes

Orne River

La Sauvagere

Juvigny

Flers

Vassy

Domfront

Vire

Mortain

0   5   10 miles

II

By this time Eisenhower had approved Montgomery's plan for a massive ground-airborne attack designed to capture bridgeheads leading to Arnhem on the Lower Rhine River in Holland and to open a corridor to the Ruhr. Denounced by Bradley as a "full-blooded thrust to Berlin," the operation, named Market-Garden, was Montgomery's original plan camouflaged to appear as if it were not. "The fourteen divisions he would command," Bradley observed, "equaled the combined strength of my First and Third armies—sixteen divisions—then poised at the German border. If Market-Garden was successful—if it captured a bridgehead across the Rhine—there was little doubt that Monty would keep right on going across the north German plains in an attempt to reach Berlin."[14]

On the twelfth at a conference of his commanders, Bradley briefed Patton and Hodges on developments. Hodges, with his supply officer, the "canny Bob Wilson," arrived first, Hansen noted, "neat and trim in his battle jacket and cigarette holder." Patton, "towering and slick in his brass buttoned jacket," came next, accompanied by Muller, his supply officer. At the meeting Patton persuaded Bradley to allow him to continue the attempt to cross the Moselle until the night of the fourteenth. If not successful by then, he agreed to move north to help Hodges and Monty.

Even more important was the discussion on supplies, led by Generals Ewart G. Plank and Raymond G. Moses of Ike's staff. Ever believing that he was being shortchanged, Patton walked over to Muller to tell him he was leaving. When Muller, who was conferring with Moses, Plank, and Wilson, said he would be ready in a moment, Patton replied: "Goddamit I don't want you to leave a moment before Bob Wilson does."[15]

As the generals talked, Eddy's units poured across the Moselle below Metz. By noon of the twelfth, eight infantry companies of the 35th Division, accompanied by Brigadier General Holmes E. Dager's Combat Command B of the 4th Armored Division, were across south of Nancy. By the next day the 80th Division had five battalions on the east side of the river south of Pont-à-Mousson, about halfway between Metz and Nancy. But a German counterattack pushed these units to the bridge they had used to cross. "Fortunately," Patton noted, "Colonel

[Bruce C.] Clarke's 4th Armored arrived in the nick of time and drove the enemy back and took a lot of prisoners." That day Patton, accompanied by Ev Hughes, crossed the Moselle, visited an observation post, and viewed "a nice tank fight, about 1500 yards away."[16]

In the middle of September, Eisenhower, Bradley, and Patton exuded optimism. On the fifteenth Ike envisioned a rapid advance through the Ruhr and the Saar and then on to Frankfurt. Especially encouraging was the daring drive into the German rear near Nancy by Clarke's Combat Command A of Wood's 4th Armored. Standing on the west bank of the Moselle in the early hours of the thirteenth, Eddy, referring to the east bank beachhead, drastically reduced by the Germans, asked Clarke whether he considered it safe to cross his entire CCA. Clarke turned and requested the opinion of Lieutenant Colonel Creighton W. Abrams, who commanded the 37th Tank Battalion. Pointing across the river, Abrams answered: "That is the shortest way home." With Eddy's approval Clarke gave the order: "Get going." In a move Eddy compared to Confederate General Jeb Stuart's daring cavalry rides around the Union Army, Abrams crossed the river and by night had penetrated twenty miles into the German rear. To Bradley, Patton, and Ike, Abrams's move indicated that beyond the crust of Germans along the east bank of the Moselle, enemy defenses were sparse.[17]

Montgomery's grand scheme egged Patton on. Facing the prospect of being stopped so that Monty could, as Bradley scoffed to Patton, "Make a dagger-thrust with the 21st Army Group at the heart of Germany," Patton vowed to push ahead. "To hell with Monty," he observed. "I must get so involved that they can't stop me. I told Bradley not to call me until after dark on the 19th. He agreed."

The plan that emerged from Patton's pen on the sixteenth narrowed the Third Army's front. Haislip's XV Corps, now occupying Patton's right rear, would remain there but must be prepared, on Patton's order, either to capture Mannheim, south of Frankfurt, or to cross the Rhine over bridgeheads established by Patton's other corps. Meantime, Eddy's XII Corps, consisting of the 4th and 6th Armored and the 35th Infantry, would continue northeast, pierce the German West Wall, and advance to and cross the Rhine.

As difficult as these assignments were, that given to Walker's XX Corps, holding the Third Army's left, or north, verged on the impossible. Already tied up at Metz, Walker was to capture it and then push on and take Frankfurt.[18]

As Patton, a student of history, should have realized but did not, Metz, unlike Nancy, which fell on the fifteenth, constituted an invader's nightmare. It had last been captured by the Huns in A.D. 451. Thereafter those who dreamed of conquering it met disaster. After the modification of its fortifications in 1552, the Holy Roman Emperor, Charles V, unsuccessfully bombarded the city for two and a half months. Strengthened again in the late 1600s by the great French military engineer Vauban, the city contained layers of fortifications that, Vauban told King Louis XIV, defended not a province but all of France.

Ceded in 1871 by a defeated France to a victorious Prussia as part of Alsace and Lorraine, Metz underwent further strengthening. Eventually nine forts circled the city. As if cognizant of the kind of warfare to be fought in 1914, the Germans built around each fort tunnels, railroads to bring in men and supplies, trenches, bunkers capable of withstanding artillery attacks, and barbed-wire fortifications.[19] Against such a mélange, frontal attacks were at once foolhardy and suicidal.

The American campaign against Metz constituted one of Patton's worst moments. He preferred to forget it. In a 1953 analysis the American armor expert Colonel Robert J. Icks, whose book *The Fighting Tanks Since 1916* Patton had read and admired, depicted it as a product of faulty intelligence and blind leadership. He was especially critical of Walker, an intractable advocate of infantry methods. In his posthumously published work *War As I Knew It,* based largely on his diaries, Patton practically avoided mentioning Metz. "Nowhere," Icks observed of Patton, "does he criticize the 20th Corps Commander, General Walker, and yet it was Walker who, once committed, became the 'Bulldog' he was nicknamed regardless of the sense of what he was doing."[20]

In early September Patton thought the Germans to be fleeing, but such was not the case. Rather, the enemy retreated strategically, shortening its interior lines. Resupplied, Walker's corps resumed its eastward push on the sixth of September as part of the general advance. Hoping the Germans would not defend the Moselle very strongly, the Americans planned to bypass Metz should the Germans defend it. They would advance instead through Thionville, about twenty miles north of Metz, and from there push on and cross the Saar River, thirty miles east of the Moselle. Lindsey Silvester's 7th Armored Division was to spearhead the attack, while Major General Stafford L. "Red" Irwin's 5th Infantry Division was to approach Metz and the 90th Infantry, protecting the left flank of Patton's army, would go on to Thionville.

Oblivious of the history of Metz, which indicated that the city could not be stormed, Walker, in the words of Lieutenant Colonel Hugh M. Cole, the official historian of the Lorraine campaign, "was not too impressed with the strength of the fortified works around Metz." Preparing to attack Fort Driant, whose batteries commanded "not only the southwestern approaches to Metz but the Moselle valley as well," Walker assigned the task to only one battalion of the 5th Division's 11th Infantry Regiment.[21]

When the Americans began to move, they were hit hard by the Germans. Knowing nothing about the detailed construction of Fort Driant or of the field fortifications surrounding it, elements of the 5th Division attacked unsuccessfully on the twenty-seventh of September. Two and a half miles to the north of Fort Driant, McLain's 90th Division ran into the 106th Panzer Brigade, equipped with Mark V Panther tanks, and was equally unsuccessful.[22]

Meeting with Irwin on the twenty-eighth to discuss the failure of the previous day, Patton and Walker presented contrasting views. Sympathizing with Irwin's plight, Patton urged him to use the pause in operations to rest and to rotate his tired men. Walker, on the other hand, attempted to overwhelm Irwin, insisting that more forceful leadership by the regimental and battalion commanders who led the attack would have brought success. Countering Walker's argument, Irwin pointed out that his men had met unexpected obstacles, for aerial photos had not shown the involved wire entanglements and the large number of pillboxes that surrounded and protected Fort Driant.[23]

What happened next seemed contrary to everything Patton had taught during the war. "By now," Icks observed, "the original missions and instructions to bypass Metz were completely forgotten. The mobility of the 7th Armored was not being used to locate a soft spot. Instead its fire power was being used as artillery and the Americans were committed to a frontal assault on a fortified city that had withstood siege for hundreds of years." A meeting between Patton and Eisenhower on the twenty-ninth compounded the error. Instead of coming up with ways of avoiding Metz, the two pored over maps and devised a plan to encircle the city.[24]

Shortly after the war, when Liddell Hart interviewed important German officers, two generals pointed to the direct attack on Metz as a great Allied mistake. Günther Blumentritt, at one time the chief of staff of the Western front, and Siegfried Westphal, Field Marshal Albert Kesselring's chief of staff, both noted that if Patton had avoided Metz and swerved northward to Luxembourg, he would have reached the long and thinly defended stretch of the Ardennes country between Metz and Aachen. Patton would then have been able to advance to Coblenz, where the Rhine and Moselle met, cutting off the German Seventh Army before it could retreat behind the Rhine.[25]

In 1953 Liddell Hart and Wood exchanged letters on Metz—and on Patton's role in the September campaign. "Recently," Liddell Hart informed Wood in June, "Colonel Robert J. Icks sent me a very interesting and illuminating analysis he had made of the operations in Lorraine in September 1944, showing how the chance of continued exploitation of successes had been forfeited by the way that Patton let himself become entangled in a too direct attack on Metz. Icks, in his accompanying letter, said of Patton, 'He was far from the stature of Wood, Grow, Chaffee, or even Devers.'" Since Wood's 4th Armored took part in the Lorraine campaign, Liddell Hart invited his comments on the subject.[26]

Wood answered with typical bluntness.

I would like very much also to see the analysis of our Lorraine operations made by Colonel Icks. His remark about Patton is most interesting. I do not believe that George would have become involved in a direct attack on a fortress like Metz if he had not been pushed into it by higher authority. There was also the factor which always governed his actions—the desire for such renown as the early capture of Metz might have brought him. As to Bob Grow, he was a most earnest, hard-working, routine soldier with very little imagination as to the employment of armor or otherwise. This is for your private information.[27]

III

On the afternoon of October 7 Patton was studying plans for an attack by three divisions of the XII Corps to gain certain high ground and to straighten out the lines, scheduled to push off the next day, when Bradley arrived. With him was General Marshall, who went over the plans and, according to Patton, "asked very incisive questions, but we could answer them. He was more pleasant than usual and regretted that he had to go and see General Montgomery in the morning and so miss the battle."[28]

That evening Marshall, Patton, and some members of their staffs, including Frank McCarthy, went into an officers' mess for dinner. Seated next to Patton, McCarthy recalled, was the young aide to the general in command of the headquarters they were visiting. Each place setting contained two cups, one for red wine, the other for coffee. Patton was telling a story and without realizing what he was doing poured sugar and cream into his red wine. As he lifted the cup to drink from it, the young aide touched him on the arm and said: "I beg your pardon, sir. You put sugar and cream in your wine." Patton answered, "I like it that way," and drank it down.[29]

Metz, however, still remained a problem. A second assault on Fort Driant, begun on October 3, was going the way of the first. On the third overcast skies prevented the XIX Tactical Air Command from sending fighter-bombers over the area, and mud hampered the infantrymen. Attacking just north of the fort, the men of Company E, 2d Battalion, of the 5th Division's 11th Regiment, encountered heavy small arms and artillery fire. Withdrawing after four days without having set foot in the fort, the company lost 55 of its 140 men.[30]

By the ninth of the month Patton again realized something must be done. "The Fort Driant show is going sour," he noted. "We will have to pull out." On that day he sent Gay to talk things over with Walker, Irwin, and Brigadier General A. D. Warnock, Irwin's assistant division commander. Arguing that the surface attacks had proven too costly and that it would take four more infantry battalions to seize the fort and capture its defenders, Warnock convinced Gay to use the authority granted him by Patton to end the assault. During this second unsuccessful operation, the 5th Infantry Division had suffered huge casualties: 64 men killed, 547 wounded, and 187 missing, approximately half of the attacking force. In his diary Gay made it clear that he agreed with Warnock's assessment: "It is the opinion of General Gay that this attack, when initially made, was made with too small a force; that had it been started with a force of four battalions—three in the attack and one in reserve—the fort could have been taken with but little difficulty."[31]

On October 12 Patton, his army headquarters being transferred from Etain, between Verdun and Metz, south to Nancy, found himself idle, so he welcomed an invitation to visit Bradley at Verdun. There Patton met an admirer, Supreme Court Justice James F. Byrnes. Taking an immediate shine to Byrnes, Patton asked him "if he would like to go over my old [World War] battlefields. He was," Patton recorded, "quite enthusiastic about it." Accompanying them were Byrnes's military aide, Major Donald Russell, and an aide whom Patton called "Shorty" and identified as a former Texas Ranger and a former sergeant in Patton's outfit in 1918. The mystery man was Stiller. Having been wounded in the same engagement, Patton and Stiller were anxious to find the site.

The trip stirred up memories. At Clermont Patton "stopped at the railway station where my tanks detrained in 1918, and where the train was actually hit by shell fire without waking up some 20 men sleeping in a box car." Taking the road south toward Neuville, the convoy of jeeps passed "the little woods where Brett's battalion spent the first night after detraining." Luckily, Brett moved his men out the next morning, for that second night enemy shells practically destroyed the woods. Patton remembered Neuville as the place where German fire stopped his tanks from crossing a bridge. Timing the interval between enemy rounds with his stopwatch, Patton was able to direct the tanks over the bridge "without a hit."

Byrnes told the rest of the story.

As our jeep cavalcade neared Montfaucon, Patton ordered his driver to stop, and when Shorty's jeep had caught up, jumped out. "Shorty," he said, "the whole place is changed, but I remember this tree. I'm sure this is where we camped the night prior to the fight." When Shorty expressed his doubts, Patton said: "If we did not camp here, we should have." He offered to wager that when we had driven a half mile farther down the road we would find a side road, and off that road would be a creek.

To my surprise, after we had gone that distance, we found both road and creek, and within sight of a monument erected by the State of Pennsylvania in memory of those in the Pennsylvania National Guard who had fallen there. In a few moments Shorty had found the spot where he had received his wound, but Patton could not locate the place where he had been when wounded. Unfortunately, what had once been a wooded area was now cultivated land, and after some thirty minutes the General gave up in disgust.[32]

Returning to Bradley's headquarters, Byrnes spent the rest of the day with Patton. At Byrnes's request Patton used a huge wall map to describe the breakout, criticizing Montgomery's slowness, which, he argued, enabled the Germans to bring up reinforcements, as he went along. At one point Patton turned away from the map and bragged to Byrnes: "You know this advance was planned by Bradley; but I was the only man who could have executed it."

At lunch Byrnes watched as "some thirty officers" listened to Patton with awe. Perhaps daydreaming, Patton expected his Third Army to end the war soon and hoped Byrnes would help get the entire army transferred to the Pacific. Throughout the conversation, Patton "complained repeatedly and bitterly about cuts in supplies of gasoline and ammunition which had stopped his drive into Germany. . . . I am no military expert," Byrnes concluded, "but I think my military friends are right in regarding him as one of the most brilliant field commanders ever to wear our country's uniform."[33]

The following day Patton, responding to a request from Eisenhower, flew to Hodges's residence in Belgium, where, on the fourteenth, the king of England was to honor Bradley. Hodges had his headquarters staked out somewhere else, but he lived and had his mess in a chateau three stories high. That evening Bradley, Eisenhower, Patton, Hodges, and Simpson had dinner together, "very informal," Simpson remembered,

very nice, very pleasant. And later on we said, "Well, let's go to bed. We got to get up with the King tomorrow." And I went up on the third floor where my room was and went in there, and I hadn't any more gotten there when in walked George Patton who was just across the hall from me.

. . . We were pretty good friends and had been at West Point. He said, "Let's have a visit." I think maybe we had a drink of cognac or something. I'm not sure.

And he said, "You know, it's a funny thing. You and I here now. We were at West Point together. Here we are commanding armies." And he said, "You know, you and Hodges and I are older than either Eisenhower or Bradley, but we're going to do an awful lot of fighting for them."

He had no bitterness about it. He talked to me either that time or another similar time like that about the slapping incident, too, you know. . . . No bitterness at all. The only remark was, "Well, we older foxes are carrying the ball here as army commanders for them."[34]

Even with the Metz debacle, Patton retained his taste for the good life. Using Charley Codman in a way that probably would have appalled Bradley and Eisenhower had they known of it, he sent his aide to Burgundy to buy wines for his table. "That is certainly right up his alley," Bernard Carter noted of Codman, his Groton and Harvard class-mate and the wine buyer for the Boston purveyor of fine groceries, S.S. Pierce, "& I can picture him with envy being entertained by all his many & hospitable wine friends!"

On the evening of the twenty-first Codman, in Patton's stead, enter-tained at a dinner party "in a restaurant we used to frequent 26 years ago. I must say it was delicious," Carter told his wife, "especially the wines." The guests included "Freddy Ayer's son (the boss's nephew)" and the actress Marlene Dietrich, who, quite unfairly, was sometimes linked romantically with Patton. "It was a rather incongruous mixture but went off very well. I was amazed at Marlene's excellent French. She was a bit disappointing in looks—a bit ty-ty, but made herself very agreeable—unaffected."[35]

Amid these activities Patton searched for a way out of the Metz mess. Meeting on the seventeenth with Gaffey, Gay, Harkins, and the other leading members of his staff, he worked out a new plan. The operation would begin with a push south of Metz by three infantry divisions of the

XII Corps. The 4th and 6th Armored divisions would then move through the infantry, the 6th to get the high ground east of Metz and the 4th to advance across the Saar River and, if possible, proceed to the Rhine. Meantime, the 90th Division of the XX Corps, now commanded by Brigadier General James A. Van Fleet, would cross the Moselle north of Metz and Thionville, "the idea being," Patton observed, "a double envelopment of Metz without getting mixed up with the forts. The sooner we can start this the better, as the enemy continues to dig and mine ahead of us." That afternoon Ike and Devers happened to come to Third Army headquarters. Patton "showed them the plans with which they found no fault."[36]

Perhaps the saddest thing was that the astute Hap Gay had recommended a similar plan a month before. Visiting XX Corps headquarters on September 19, he went to the forward observation post just above Thionville. Gay immediately noticed that the area "lends itself to a crossing," for the high ground sat on the west side of the Moselle. On the east side of the river the terrain sloped back for at least several miles. Learning of this, Patton appealed to Bradley for Major General Robert C. Macon's 83d Infantry Division, which he wanted to send across the Moselle near Thionville "and thence," Gay noted, "to encircle Metz from the north and northeast." Macon was set to make the move when, on the twenty-third, Eisenhower, through Bradley, informed Patton that Third Army supplies would be cut to thirty-five hundred tons a day, insufficient to support the northern thrust. Even though Market-Garden was collapsing, Montgomery was still getting the bulk of the Allied resources, something Eisenhower admitted to Patton and his leading officers at a meeting on September 29. "Again and again," a bitter Gay wrote in his diary, "Higher HQ resorts to every subterfuge to stop the 3rd Army."[37]

Ike saw nothing wrong with the double envelopment plan worked out on October 17, but Bradley still had to be convinced. Accordingly, on the nineteenth, Patton sent Colonel Harkins to Bradley's headquarters with the completed plan. "I also gave Harkins some additional reasons which he could advance should Bradley prove balky," Patton recorded. "I called Bradley on the phone and asked that he talk to Harkins personally."

In a letter Harkins carried with him, Patton advanced his reasons. The Germans along the Moselle had, he argued, concentrated their forces near the front line. Once Patton broke through this shell, he could, he assured Bradley, reach the West Wall "in not to exceed D plus 2 days." From there Patton could drive rapidly to the Rhine. But to be successful the Third Army needed sufficient supplies.[38]

While exuding optimism to Bradley, Patton on the same day displayed his anxiety about Metz. In a letter to his friend Lieutenant General Jimmy Doolittle, he wrote:

> This is to inform you that those low bastards, the Germans, gave me my first bloody nose when they compelled us to abandon our attack on Fort Driant in the Metz area. I have requested a revenge bombardment from the air to teach those sons-of-bitches that they cannot fool with Americans. I believe that this request will eventually get to you, and I am therefore asking that you see that the Patton-Doolittle combination is not shamed in the eyes of the world, and that you provide large bombs of the nastiest type, and as many as you can spare, to blow up this damn fort so that it becomes nothing but a hole.[39]

Bradley answered Patton on October 22, when he and his chief of staff, Leven Allen, visited Third Army headquarters. Bradley pointed out what Patton already suspected: the scarcity of supplies would not permit Patton to attack immediately. He thought, however, that an offensive could start on or about the tenth of November. Expanding Patton's plan, Bradley hoped to put all three of his armies—Hodges's First, Patton's Third, and Simpson's Ninth—on the offensive by then. Bradley also promised to request the impossible: he would ask Montgomery, who would never agree, to use but two armies in the November attack. He would ask the same of Devers. The Germans, Bradley insisted, could not possibly resist seven Allied armies launched at them simultaneously. Arguing that he could be prepared to move forward in two days, Patton countered that the date set should not be a calendar date, like the tenth, but a date determined by the prospect of three or four days of good weather. "Bradley is too conservative," Patton observed after the talk, "—he wants to wait until we can all jump together by which time half of our men will have flu or trench foot."[40]

With this plan Bradley hoped to break through the West Wall before the onset of winter. His three armies consisted of twenty-two divisions and about a half million men. Since September 28, when Eisenhower transferred to Devers Haislip's XV Corps, Patton possessed but two corps, Eddy's XII and Walker's XX, but these contained the equivalent of seven infantry and three armored divisions, about 220,000 men. In Bradley's movement the Third Army would generally follow the outline devised by Patton's staff. South of Metz the infantry divisions of XII Corps would attack, followed the next day by Wood's and Grow's armored divisions. North and west of Metz, the 95th Infantry Division of Walker's corps would engage the Germans, and the next day the 90th Infantry would cross the Moselle near Thionville. Without the seizure or investiture of the Metz forts, the city would be surrounded and, hopefully, reduced.[41]

As the big day approached, Patton found trouble developing within the 4th Armored. On October 30 Bradley, as dissatisfied as Patton with Silvester, relieved him from command of the 7th Armored Division. He was sending Clarke, who led Wood's Combat Command A, there to help reshape the division. "This is a blow," Patton moaned, "as he was the sparkplug of all our attack across France, but he may get a promotion out of it." At lunch with several officers Patton, moreover, noticed a change in Wood. "P. is getting morose because he is not a Corps Commander," Patton observed. As Patton sensed, Wood deeply resented taking orders from Eddy, an infantryman. Patton had already written Bradley asking that Wood, "who is the best Division Commander I know," replace Major General John Millikin, newly arrived in Normandy, as commander of the recently formed III Corps, assigned to Patton but containing few troops. "It is a blunder," Patton noted, "to send untried Corps Commanders to command veteran divisions."

In fairness to Patton it must be noted that he did his best to get a corps for Wood. On the second of November Bradley and his staff spent the day at Patton's house in Nancy, described by Hansen as "a grotesque place owned by a coal mine operator and filled with the most impossible bricabrac including gilded angels three feet high and cherubs hanging from the ceilings, cheap and showy statuary lining the halls along with the dull green brown and purple tapestries you find covering the walls of such houses." Just the night before three enemy shells had landed within fifty feet of the "mournful" and "depressing" place, almost destroying it and Patton with it. "Goddamit," Patton said, "that was once when I was really scared."

All day Patton pushed "hard" for Wood's elevation to corps commander. But Bradley, a lifelong infantryman who was naturally drawn to other infantrymen, resisted the move, remarking that a good division commander did not necessarily make a good corps commander. As Wood himself frequently and bitterly wrote, Bradley never did or could understand Wood and Patton and their imaginative use of tanks.[42]

In November the weather turned against the Americans. The first three days of the month brought a deluge that converted roads into mud and caused rivers to overflow. Amid the downpours, air support became impossible.

Occupying himself by speaking to his divisions, Patton took "long nasty" drives in chilling downpours. He addressed all but his two favorites, Wood's and Grow's. "But they both demanded that I talk to them," Patton told Bea, "so I did. I simply said it would be a presumption on my part to tell them how to fight as they had shown the world. I thought of one good line when I was talking to P's bunch. I said that to quote the Bible 'The first will be last and the fourth will be first.' "[43]

Just before the attack, scheduled for November 8, Patton exhibited his usual signs of anxiety: shortness of breath and vomiting. Far from resorting to talk of predestination and other glamorous beliefs often associated with him, Patton turned to his usual source of comfort: prayer and a faith in the Lord. The show put on by the German-born Dietrich made Patton even sicker: "very low comedy, almost an insult to human intelligence."[44]

Writing to Bea late on the day of the attack, Georgie exulted that "The Lord came across again. It rained like the Devil all day yesterday," he related, and at 7 P.M. on the seventh Eddy and Grow arrived and asked Patton to call off the offensive. "I declined but it took some doing as the ground is a bog."[45]

Awakening at three on the morning of the offensive, Patton found it "raining worse than ever. I had to repeat to my self, Don't take council of your fears. Demand the impossible." Unable to sleep, he went into Willie's room and began reading Rommel's *Infantry Attacks*. In September 1914 the young Rommel had successfully assaulted the enemy despite heavy rains. Buoyed by the account, Patton "went to sleep with out taking a drink or a green pill."

At five-fifteen the sound of four hundred blasting guns awakened the general. "The whole eastern sky flickered and twinkled with heat lightning. The sound is like the constant slamming of heavy doors in a large empty house."

A half hour later on this second anniversary of the landings in Morocco, Eddy's infantry began the attack south of Metz. The 26th Division held the right, or south, the 35th the center, and the 80th the left. North of Metz, the 95th Division, which with the 5th and 90th constituted Walker's infantry, pushed off at 3 P.M.

At 10 A.M. God "came across." With the day "as clear as a bell," Weyland's fighter-bombers attacked the enemy's command posts. "I hope," Patton wrote Bea, "they killed a lot of generals."[46]

Although the ninth was also clear, Patton on that day found Walker's drive stalled by the high waters of the Moselle. "It is said by the local inhabitants," he observed, "that this is the biggest flood in the history of the Moselle Valley." Numerous trucks, planes, and even a hospital platoon were stuck in the water. "Our chief trouble in this war is the inefficiency and lack of sense of responsibility on the part of company officers."[47]

Inspecting the 90th Infantry Division on November 11, Patton's fifty-ninth birthday, Gay found a condition probably never dreamed of at the Army War College. Three of the division's regiments had crossed the Moselle north of Thionville, but the floodwaters prevented the transfer of heavy equipment across the river. The regiments successfully transported five 57-millimeter antitank guns to the east bank, but they had practically no ammunition for them. On the west bank units of the division and corps artillery were in position to fire across the river and protect the three isolated regiments, but no telephone communication linked the Americans on both sides. Accordingly, ground observers and pilots of Cub planes used radios to direct the artillery fire. Gay found the nearby bridge intact, but for three-quarters of a mile water fifty-six inches deep blocked the approaches to the bridge. "The current was so swift," Gay recorded, "that the cumbersome Engineer boats without power were useless."

On the east bank the infantrymen ran short of medical supplies, blood plasma, and food. They possessed no blankets and no clothing other than what they were wearing when the assault began three days before. Some stood in water up to their shoulders pulling cables attached to powerless boats.

Crossing the river, Gay came away with enormous respect for Van Fleet. Ignoring his own safety, Van Fleet at one point drove past his front-line infantry in a truck. He instructed the 359th Infantry Regiment to take a hill from which the Germans could fire on the Americans and ordered food, clothing, and antitank weapons. By radio Gay called Patton's headquarters and requested that the Third Army's DUKW company, which possessed two-and-a-half-ton amphibious trucks, be sent to the 90th Division. Two platoons of the DUKW company arrived the next day, and by nighttime on November 12 the 90th had one tank company and one company of tank destroyers on the east bank of the Moselle.[48]

As the XX Corps crossed the river in the north and inched toward Metz and the XII Corps in the south advanced north and northwest, reaching a point five miles from the center of Metz, Eisenhower visited Patton on November 15. Ike "seemed well pleased," Patton reported to Bea, "and got copiously photographed standing in the mud talking to soldiers."

The next day Eisenhower sat in on the Third Army briefing and then addressed Patton's staff. "In substance," Gay recorded,

> he emphasized the fact that the enemy was now being attacked from all sides and that in desperation he was throwing his last reserves, consisting of old men and young boys, in the line; that while the weather conditions were terrible for us, it probably was worse for the Germans because they had nothing but certain defeat in front of them. He further emphasized the fact that every effort should be made to keep our troops as comfortable as possible, because in the long run the man in the front lines who feels he is better clothed and better equipped than the enemy is the man who will win.[49]

The main movement of the November offensive began on the sixteenth, the day Ike delivered his talk. With four corps, containing twelve divisions, of the First and Ninth Armies, Bradley hoped to advance, north of the Ardennes, to the Roer River and then on to Cologne and Bonn. The result was the battle of the Huertgen Forest, the unworthy successor to the Civil War and First World War battles fought in woods. As in all such struggles, the defender's hidden guns pinned down the attacker. Even Bradley, whose writings, like those of Patton and Eisenhower, tended to justify his every decision, described the three-week engagement as "sheer butchery on both sides. . . . In this November drive to the Roer, the First and Ninth Armies suffered a total of 35,000 casualties."[50]

Meantime, with the XX Corps continuing its encirclement of Metz, Patton hoped for a quicker thrust by the XII Corps, holding his southern flank. On the eighteenth he sent the 26th and 35th Divisions toward Saarbrücken, along the east bank of the Saar River. After the infantry divisions had penetrated four miles, the 4th Armored and one combat command of the 6th Armored were to advance through the infantry and hopefully break through to the Saar.[51]

Oddly enough, this scenario set Wood on the road to dismissal. Since the offensive began on the eighth of November, Eddy's two armored divisions had, in Wood's eyes, been misused, forced to slug it out with the German 11th Panzer Division in the mud and in the minefields. The 4th sustained 1,063 casualties during the operation, which Wood later condemned as "a classic example of the manner in which armored divisions should *never* be employed, if avoidable."[52]

On the eighteenth Eddy ordered Wood to assist the 26th Division in taking Dieuze, twenty-five miles east of Nancy. Considering the town a mass of rubble unsuitable for tanks, Wood disregarded Eddy's instructions. Because of floods he also ignored an order to send tanks south of the city. Visiting XII Corps headquarters late in the day, Gay heard Eddy repeat the orders to Wood.[53]

Coming to Patton's headquarters at Nancy at nine-thirty on the morning of the nineteenth, Eddy complained about Wood's failure to obey him. Calling Gaffey and Gay to his office as witnesses, Patton thereupon dictated a letter warning that Wood's "actions" toward Eddy "verged on insubordination." Patton was sending Gaffey with the letter. If Wood could not assure Gaffey "that you will carry out your instructions, both in the letter and in the spirit, I will be forced to relieve you."[54]

The key day in the controversy was Monday, the twentieth of

November. Even though Wood apologized to Eddy, Patton drove over to XII Corps headquarters to discuss the matter with Eddy. That evening, according to Gay, he called Major General Robert M. Littlejohn, Ike's chief of Quartermaster Service, about Wood. "I am trying to find some nice way of easing him out," Patton wrote of his good friend.[55]

Even though four forts, including Driant and Jeanne d'Arc, still held out, Patton declared Metz cleared of the enemy as of 2:35 P.M. on November 22. But, Gay lamented, "Progress along the front of the entire Third Army was quite slow." Ever optimistic, Patton nonetheless drew up a plan for crossing the Saar River and proceeding to the Rhine. Assuming the return of Haislip's XV Corps from Devers, the design called for each corps to establish a beachhead across the Saar. The remainder of each corps would then probably cross at that spot. Visiting Patton with Bradley on the twenty-fourth, Ike promised to study the plan and give a decision later.[56]

Generally, however, Eisenhower's self-imposed isolation from things puzzled observers. Late in November W. Averell Harriman, the American ambassador to the Soviet Union, visited France. He saw "no reason in the world" that Eisenhower and his aides, despite the protests of Bedell Smith and British Major-General John F. M. Whiteley, the deputy operations officer of SHAEF, lived in a house and trailer next to a golf course seven miles northwest of Reims when his headquarters was dozens of miles away at Versailles.

In one of his few diary passages praising Patton, Alan Brooke protested about the same thing. Eisenhower, he wrote, was

> by himself with his Lady chauffeur in the golf links at Reims— entirely detached from the war. Matters got so bad lately that a deputation of Whiteley, Bedell Smith and a few others went up to tell him that he must get down to it and RUN the war, which he said he would. Personally I think he is incapable of running the war even if he tries.
>
> We discussed the advisability of getting Marshall to come out to discuss the matter, but we are doubtful if he would appreciate the situation. Finally decided that I am to see the P.M. to discuss the situation with him. It is one of the most difficult problems I have had to tackle. I know the only solution, but doubt whether we can

bring it off. Bradley should be made Commander of the Land Forces with Tedder as the Air Commander, working closely with him. The front should then be divided into two groups of armies, one north of the Ardennes under Monty, and one south under Patton, whilst Ike returns to the line duties of Supreme Commander.[57]

Nonetheless, the Allied halt greatly disturbed Ike. Patton, Weyland remembered, had come to a stop against the West Wall. "This was winter-time. George Patton and I got out of the woods and established our headquarters in the city of Nancy; we took over some houses, which were a little more comfortable than our field headquarters."[58]

During the Third Army's November offensive, the weather often made flying impossible. Weyland's men encountered only eleven days good for flying. In contrast, five days proved partially suitable and fourteen completely unsuitable. Three times during November bad weather grounded Weyland's entire force for three-day periods.

When able to send his planes up, Weyland switched tactics. With the lines static, American artillery assumed the task of bombarding enemy positions. Using five-hundred-pound bombs and napalm, Weyland went after rear echelon supply yards, railroad facilities, bridges, and troop concentrations. With the longer trips he lost sixty-two planes in November, as opposed to half that number in October.[59]

Then, one day in November, Weyland, a mere brigadier general, received a call to attend a meeting at the headquarters, near Paris, of General Carl "Tooey" Spaatz, the commander of the United States Strategic Air Forces in Europe. All of the leading British and American aviators were there, including the head of the Royal Air Force Bomber Command, Air Chief Marshal Arthur T. "Bomber" Harris, and Doolittle, who headed the American Eighth Air Force. Weyland described what took place.

The gist of this conversation was: the strategic air had about cleaned up their strategic targets; they'd done about everything they could, and unless the ground armies got moving—get off their behinds and get moving—through the Siegfried Line and so forth, they were very much afraid that the war would be prolonged unacceptably, and we might not even win it. The Germans just might be able to dig in and hold. So the burden of the thing was: did the tactical air commanders feel that the strategic air could be used tactically to get the ground forces rolling?

Ike went around the room asking for suggestions. Answering first, the British airmen thought that the entire idea constituted an improper use of strategic air. Pete Quesada, whose IX TAC supported Hodges, next related the problem presented by the Roer River dams. "He thought he would sure like to get hold of these airplanes," Weyland said, but much of the First Army was near "a great big lake and they had to advance across some lowlands, and if they started to go across there, the Germans could simply cut the water loose, and drown them all out, and they'd been trying to knock out that dam but hadn't been able to do it. There was just no bomb up there big enough to knock that thing out. He said that until they solved that problem, there was no use."

Weyland spoke far differently.

I said, "Well, I've got an Army that will fight." And, incidentally, a rather interesting commentary, Gen. Patton some time or another, fortunately, had said, "Opie, you can commit the Third Army in my name any time you want to." He had implicit confidence in me. He offered me the command of a corps division, for example, than which there is no greater compliment from a ground soldier. He said, "Any time, in any meeting, you can commit my army, the Third Army, just as though you were me, and I will accept it." Well, here was the occasion. So I said, "I've got an army that will fight. If I can get the assistance of all the strategic air,—British, American, and some additional help—I will guarantee to cut the American Third Army right through the Siegfried Line and up to the Rhine River, and then I would suggest that the thing to do would be that they cross the Rhine River and slice up there and surround the main part of the German forces. And I think the war will be over." Gen. Eisenhower was the only ground soldier there. Well, he laughed. He said, "O.K." And then he said to Spaatz, "What about it?" Spaatz said, "It sounds fine to me." So that was it. The decision was made.

Right after the meeting, Weyland called Patton. "Uncle Georgie," he told his friend, "I just committed the American Third Army to a helluva big operation just prior to Christmas." Patton answered calmly: "What are we going to do?" Weyland then explained the operation: "We're going to go through the Siegfried Line, we're going to head toward Berlin, and win the war. Now before you get excited about this, we will have every airplane in the European theater to help pave the way for you. And we can do it." Patton responded typically: "Hot dam."

Weyland continued the story.

> So Spaatz, Doolittle came on up to my headquarters with me and we got [together] with Georgie Patton that night. I already had a plan, fortunately. We'd tried it on a small basis with [Brigadier General] Sammy Anderson's Ninth Bomber Command, and we had actually established a foothold across the little river, whose name I've forgotten. I knew we could do it. We laid these plans and things were rocking along beautifully. This was to be called Operation Tink: that happens to be my wife's nickname. This operation was to take place I think it was the 21st of December.[60]

IV

With his army hardly progressing, Patton had time in November for social activities. On Thanksgiving Day, the twenty-third, he attended the buffet supper, "with five turkeys, a band, champagne, 12 nurses, & 8 Red Cross girls," given in their "fine house" by Koch's staff officers. "He stayed quite late & danced," Carter related to his wife, "which was considered a great compliment. What a bore it must be to have to maintain that semi-royalty status. I'm sure he would like to relax, but can't very well in his position. The nurses especially seemed to have a good time—there were about 12 of them—poor darlings—it was the first party they had had in 4 months."[61]

Then, on the twenty-sixth, Ike called with news that Harriman would arrive the following day. Eisenhower wanted Patton to take Harriman on a tour of about three hours to the front-line troops, then knee-deep in mud and water from the flooded Saar River. He hoped that upon returning to the Soviet Union, Harriman might explain the slow movement to Josef Stalin.

Visiting the 4th Armored, experiencing "the worst flood conditions"; the 26th Infantry; and some other divisions, Harriman spent "a very interesting day" with Patton. "At one divisional headquarters," surely not Wood's, Patton "gave the commanding general and his staff unshirted hell for not driving ahead faster. Patton was in one of his toughest moods." At another he "applied his talent for leadership to a commander whose exhausted troops, having suffered heavy casualties, were expected to be relieved. 'If you can make it to the top of that hill,' Patton said, 'it will make a hell of a difference to the unit that takes over from you. I know you've had a tough time, and I know it's a lot to ask of your men, but, if you can do it, it'll make a lot of difference.' It was an amazing experience, seeing how he put the fighting spirit back into those men, knowing exactly when to give them hell and when to encourage them instead."

Before leaving, Harriman told Patton that Stalin had praised the Third Army in the highest terms. In front of the chief of staff of the Red Army, Stalin said that the Soviets could not have "conceived" and "executed the advance of the Third Army across France." Harriman, however, feared Stalin, whom he called, in Patton's words, "a strong, ruthless revolutionist and therefore a very potential threat to future world conditions. He says that discipline in the Red Army is the most rigid and ruthless he has ever seen, and that the officer caste is a new nobility. This is a strange result of communism."[62]

The end of Wood's European experience came on the first of December with another argument with Eddy. On November 24 Eisenhower had visited Sarrebourg, east of Nancy, and had ordered Patch's Seventh Army to go north into the zone occupied by the 4th Armored. A week later, to the chagrin of Haislip, whose XV Corps was to take over the area, Wood was still there. Visiting Wood about noon on the first, Eddy made the mistake of saying that the 4th, which had a remarkable record, was not fighting hard enough. Wood was still blocking the roads. Haislip was complaining to Eddy every day. Wood answered defiantly. "God Damn it Matt," he told Eddy, "my boys have bought every foot of this ground with their blood, they have done everything humanly possible and I will not ask any more of them. We will get out as fast as we can but no faster." He then stormed out. Eddy immediately called Patton's headquarters, saying he thought Wood was too nervous to retain command of the 4th Armored. The next day Patton relieved his old friend and replaced him with Gaffey.[63]

Patton's diary entry on the episode was needlessly cruel. "Wood came to say goodbye," he wrote on December 3. "I had gotten Eisenhower's permission to send Wood home on a sixty-day Detached Service. I doubt that he was really sorry to go."[64]

Always opinionated and high-strung, Wood unquestionably was worn out. "P Wood—," the military historian S. L. A. Marshall later said, "I was with him right after he was relieved. He was a very likeable guy. I thought the world of General Wood. But he was as batty as a bed bug. Really he would walk around my room saying, 'Why have they relieved me? I can kill Germans. I can kill them by the thousands,' . . . that kind of thing. I could see he was no longer in possession of his senses."[65]

Flying in Patton's plane to Versailles and SHAEF headquarters at the Trianon Palace Hotel, Wood conferred with both Bedell Smith and Eisenhower. Smith told Wood that he would later return to the 4th, while Ike hoped Wood would either return to the 4th or be given a corps. Instead, after a month's rest, Wood was sent to Fort Knox to train armor replacements.[66]

These meetings reinforced Wood's contempt for Eisenhower. "You write of Eisenhower 'trudging in the snow,'" he later chided his friend and biographer Hanson Baldwin. "What snow? His butler at the Trianon Palace must have been remiss that day—not to have the walks cleaned off. I came out of the snow and slime and mud and blood of the Saar at that time; and the sight of the luxury of Eisenhower's Versailles court was a nauseating experience for a soldier."[67]

Despite the episode, Wood never lost his respect for Patton, or his love for the Patton family. "Upon arrival in N.Y.," Patton's son, later a major general, noted, "he called my mother (BAP) and reported everything with absolutely no animosity. He was one of GSP jr's best friends."[68]

Ike and Bradley may never have appreciated Wood and the division he led, but one Army Group commander did. Interviewed thirty years after Wood's relief, Jake Devers said: "Patton was a good soldier, but if I was giving credit to anybody I'd give it to the 4th Armored Division that led the Third Army into battle. . . . The 4th Armored Division was the spear point of the Third Army. They were the ones that got things done." Devers considered Wood "one of the greatest leaders in the Army."[69]

His great services to his country ending thus, Wood remained "embittered. . . . I think it was intensified by the tangle in his matrimonial affairs," Chynoweth told General Sidney R. Hinds, who in 1945 led a combat command of the 2d Armored Division. "The more I see of the way history is written, the more I believe that one should fight shy of bitterness. I used to tell P to forget his troubles, get a dog, and go fishing or something. P's invariable reply was: 'Dogs belong under the house with pigs!' Dear old P!!!!"[70]

V

———

By December 5 Patton had four distinct crossings over the Saar River, but progress beyond that was often nonexistent. "The fight we are now having is less spectacular than the fight across France," he wrote his friend Gilbert R. Cook, "but it is a damn sight harder. Forty per cent of our losses since August 1 have accrued since the last thirty days. However, I believe we are breaking through—at least we are doing our damdest."[71]

The sixth of December was a day of visitors. First came a delegation from Congress that included Representative Clare Boothe Luce, whose admirers loved to depict her as the paragon of conservative virtue. According to this version, she and Patton got along famously. While the other congressmen attended military briefings, Luce, in "a heart-wringing experience which took more courage than facing bombs or artillery fire," visited "the forward hospitals" in the "frozen mud of the Saar Valley." Luce supposedly capped this performance by pulling the lanyard of a large howitzer, "and the crash of the great gun woke echoes of savage satisfaction in her heart."[72]

Actually, Luce's behavior appalled both Gay and Patton. "Congress woman Luce was definitely under the influence of Alcohol," recorded Gay, who, with Gaffey gone, again became Patton's chief of staff. Patton was forced to call in his personal physician, Colonel Charles B. Odom, to treat the drunken congresswoman.[73]

Then, at six forty-five that evening, Patton learned that Luce and Congressman Matthew J. Merritt of New York "had pulled the lanyards on two of our guns firing on Fort Driant. I remember a similar incident in the last war which caused a great deal of unpleasant notoriety, so I called the Public Relations Officer to cut the story, only to find that this idiocy had been passed by the SHAEF censor and sent out at 5:40. I am very angry."[74] Justifiably, Patton soon relieved his PRO.

For Patton that evening proved more productive. Spaatz, Doolittle, and Major General Hoyt S. Vandenberg, Weyland's commander and the head of the Ninth Air Force, came and spent the night planning Operation Tink. They "arranged," Patton wrote, "for a future heavy bombing attack" past the West Wall along a line in southern Germany running from Kaiserslautern, forty miles inside Germany, southwest to Zweibrücken, east of Saarbrücken.

The three guests next planned to visit Devers, whose army group was south of the intended target. Conferring with Patton on the fifth, Devers had "promised complete cooperation, and so far has given it. I am not sure that as the lesser of two evils it might not be better to be in his Army Group. He interferes less and is not as timid as Bradley. It would perhaps be a mercy if the latter were gathered—a fine man but not great."[75]

Meantime, around Metz, Patton and Walker engaged in psychological warfare. Hoping to secure the surrender of the resisting forts, Walker sent an officer to talk to the German commanding each of them. The American began by praising the Germans as gallant soldiers who had fought honorably in a losing cause. Now, however, the Third Army was moving toward the Saar River. It was turning the Metz campaign over to the men of the Communications Zone. Each of the forts would soon be starved out, and the Germans would capitulate not to combat troops but to troops handling communications, "in all probability to colored troops." If the Germans wished to surrender to fighting units, they must do so now. "The result of this talk," Gay confided, "was that three of the main forts surrendered." Fort Driant fell on the eighth and the last of the strongholds, Jeanne d'Arc, on the thirteenth.[76]

At the same time in two conferences, one on December 10 and the other on December 13, those involved ironed out the procedure for the grand operation proposed by Weyland. Attending one or both meetings were Patton, whose XII Corps would assault the southern area of the West Wall; Sandy Patch; Brigadier General Gordon P. Saville, whose XII TAC supported Patch's infantry; Weyland; and the operations officers of the major units involved. Gay, Harkins, and Maddox, the last just promoted to brigadier general, sat in on both conferences.

The massive air attacks, so informally suggested by Weyland to Ike and Spaatz at the meeting of aviators, were to begin on the nineteenth. The Americans would open the bombardment with five hundred to six hundred medium bombers and twelve hundred to fifteen hundred heavy bombers, all supported by fighter-bombers. Following this, the RAF would send six hundred to one thousand bombers farther into Germany. The air bombardment was to continue for three to four days before a single infantryman attacked. After the meeting of the thirteenth, Gay summarized his view of the operation.

> As envisioned at this time, this is the largest single air offensive incident to this war, and it is my belief that this meeting, if its plans are carried out, might well turn out to be one of the most important meetings held during the entire war. From a personal viewpoint, I add that it is my belief that if this air attack is carried out as planned, and if the ground attack is carried out as planned, it will breach the Siegfried Line, which means the advance of American troops to the Rhine and might well terminate the war.[77]

Preparing for the attack, Weyland did his best to confuse the enemy. Learning from German prisoners and from American intelligence that Rundstedt, since September again the commander of German ground forces in the West, maintained his headquarters in an old castle near Frankfurt, Weyland sent fifty to sixty aircraft against it. "It was quite successful," he later said of the raid. The bombardment began with thousand-pound bombs. Then came squadrons with napalm and jellied gasoline. "There was quite an inferno," recalled Weyland, who later spoke with Rundstedt. During the attack Rundstedt "happened to be down in the underground headquarters, it turned out, but a chandelier shook loose and hit him on the head. He thought that was a helluva way to fight a war; he didn't like it a bit."[78]

Other preparations also went on. After Gaffey took over for Wood, the 4th Armored had engaged in one battle after another, sometimes operating in conjunction with McBride's 80th Infantry. Now, Colonel Harkins remembered, both were "pulled out" of the line "to refurbish and retrain and get them ready for the breakthrough. We had 1500 airplanes that were going to bomb for three days. Then we were going to breakthrough. We had been practicing how close they could bomb to the leading tanks."[79]

By now the problem of replacements had become acute. During November, a month marred by trench foot and heavy losses, the 26th Infantry had a casualty rate of 40 percent. As early as the twelfth of November, Patton had complained to Eisenhower about the manpower shortage. Then he lost to Hodges the 83rd Infantry Division, deemed by Bradley essential to the campaign in the Huertgen Forest.[80]

The losses in the forest exacerbated an already difficult manpower situation. The engagement chewed up four American divisions, the 4th, 8th, and 28th Infantry and the 5th Armored. Years later, studying the carnage, Wood saw it "as an example and an indictment of the infantry mind in action—feed 'em in frontally, one after another; keep 'em coming; exhort commanders to drive 'em in or be relieved when their tired minds and weary bodies sicken of the senseless slaughter. Yes, but we won didn't we? True, but at what useless cost of young lives? It is too bad," Wood informed Liddell Hart, "that your writings and those of Fuller were not required reading at our Infantry School before the war, for our part in it was dominated by its graduates, from Marshall, Eisenhower, and Bradley on down to army and corps commanders in Europe, and by their infantry-minded conceptions. Luckily, we had MacArthur in the Pacific."[81]

Wood, Gaffey, and Patton agreed on one thing: armies must remain active. The Germans would cleverly exploit inactivity. An incident just before Thanksgiving brought this to the fore. Devers's and Patch's operations officers came to Third Army headquarters with a scheme that Gaffey, in Patton's absence, rejected. Readjusting the boundaries between Patch's and Patton's armies, the plan, Patton complained, "would pinch the Third Army out." Devers had already taken away Haislip's corps. Now he had come up with a "stupid" plan that was "almost impossible tactically."

Although Devers withdrew his proposal, Patton called Bradley and presented arguments for more troops. Occupying narrower fronts than his army, the First and Ninth Armies needed fewer divisions. Hodges was not even using the troops he had. Instead of probing and attacking, Middleton's VIII Corps, which covered the Third Army's left flank and faced the Ardennes, stood motionless. Patton rightly feared that "the 1st Army is making a terrible mistake in leaving the VIII Corps static, as it is highly probable that the Germans are building up east of them."[82]

At least two important officers, Monk Dickson, now Hodges's G-2, and Oscar Koch, saw signs that Patton was correct. In Dickson's case, however, historians have debated how specific the reports were.

With some proof Dickson always said that he foresaw what was to come. After reporting on November 20 that the Germans possessed "no offensive capability," he confessed in early December that he "was now utterly wrong." According to his unpublished memoirs, he first became aware of the German concentration on the seventh, when Colonel Clarence M. Mendenhall, Jr., who ran the Target Section of Hodges's G-2, drew a map he labeled "Study of Enemy Reserves." The next day Mendenhall revised it and posted it in the army's War Room with the "recommendation that these targets be bombed at once." Both Hodges and Quesada approved the recommendation and asked Spaatz to send medium and heavy bombers to destroy the enemy sites. "The target areas lay so close to our front line that exposure to flak was minimal," Dickson pointed out, "since we could reach the first ten miles of German anti-aircraft with our counter-battery fire. An air umbrella of this kind along our wide, weak VIII Corps front would protect the vulnerable line. . . . But General Spaatz never showed up; the only word that came was that the targets were unremunerative."[83]

On the tenth a disappointed Dickson issued his Estimate No. 37, long the subject of controversy. In his memoirs he cited its strongest sentence: "The enemy is capable of a concentrated counterattack with air, armor, infantry and secret weapons at a selected focal point at a time of his own choosing." The report included a list of twenty-two divisions available to Rundstedt.[84]

As the historian Forrest C. Pogue has pointed out, Estimate No. 37 gave no indication where the enemy attack would come. It merely predicted renewed enemy action somewhere north of the Ardennes, where it actually took place. To Dickson the most important factor was the Roer River dams, still unbreached by Allied bombers, for it gave the enemy the capacity "of flooding the Roer in conjunction with his counterattack."[85]

Despite its generalities, Estimate No. 37 disturbed Hodges. After reading it and discussing it with Dickson on the tenth, he called Bradley and "asked for two divisions for VIII Corps. He was turned down."[86]

Intelligence information assembled on the eleventh indicated to Dickson that the target would be the Ardennes. In his Periodic Report he noted the heightened German rail and road traffic. The Panzer Lehr Division was moving north away from Patton's front, and the German 85th Infantry Division was moving south from Holland. The report placed the headquarters of the Sixth SS Panzer Army, which later mauled Hodges's troops, near Zülpich, in Germany opposite Belgium. The army's 2d Panzer Division and the German 352d Division were between Bitburg and Wittlich, bordering the southeast edge of the Ardennes.

Dickson related a confirming event that took place two days later.

> On the 13th a German woman came into VIII Corps' lines and rang the fire gong. From the 10th of December she had observed many horse-drawn vehicles carrying pontoons, small boats and bridging equipment moving west from Bitburg. . . . She described the engineers' uniforms. Her information was evaluated as "reliable" but both aerial photography and prisoners gave confirmation. No military force not bent on forward, offensive movement would bring bridging equipment into its front lines.[87]

Dickson cited another incident that, he insisted, confirmed the accuracy of his reports. After the campaign, First Army headquarters received a cable from the War Department ordering Hodges to send home the officer responsible for the surprise. Hodges's chief of staff, General William B. Kean, told Dickson, who handed him his Estimate No. 37 and the Periodic Reports. "It's all there, Monk," Kean said to Dickson, who had gone to Paris the day before the Germans attacked.

"And I remember that before you left for Paris you said it was the Ardennes." When Kean added, "I wish you could have made it more emphatic," Dickson responded: "How could I?" Headquarters informed the War Department that the officer responsible for the surprise was not in Hodges's army.[88]

Like Dickson, Koch suspected trouble. From November 20 on he, too, reported the growing strength of the Sixth Panzer Army and warned of a German counteroffensive. By December 12 Patton was alarmed enough to ask Gay and Maddox to report on "what the Third Army would do if called upon through . . . a breakthrough" along Middleton's front. German radio silence on the night of December 15–16 further upset Patton, who asked Koch its significance. "I don't know what it means when the *Germans* go on radio silence," Koch answered. "But when we place one of our units in radio silence, it means they're going to move. In this particular case, sir, I believe the Germans are launching an attack, probably at Luxembourg." Certain that the movement would be to his north against Middleton, whose VIII Corps "had been sitting still—a sure invitation to trouble," Patton asked Gay and Maddox to draw up plans for altering the Third Army's course. Instead of continuing east toward the West Wall, the Third Army might be forced to turn ninety degrees and move toward Luxembourg.[89]

Patton heard of the first German strike innocently enough. Early on December 16, 1944, he visited Eddy, whom he found "in a very depressed and nervous state," similar to Wood's condition earlier in the month. Because of this and because of the prevalence of trench foot, Patton feared "we cannot be ready for the blitz before the 22nd of December. I hope we don't lose it to dirt." Next visiting Haislip, Patton found him "not over-enthusiastic" about the coming offensive.

Returning to his headquarters, Patton learned that General Leven C. Allen had called with word that the Germans had attacked Middleton's corps. For Weyland's blitz Bradley had attached Major General William Morris, Jr.'s 10th Armored Division to Walker's XX Corps. Middleton needed the 10th, so Bradley was transferring it to his corps. Telephoning Bradley, Patton "called his attention to the fact that the Third Army had paid a very heavy price in blood in the hope of a break-through at Saarlautern and Saarbrücken and that when it came we would need the 10th Armored." When Bradley insisted on the transfer, Patton conceded: "He probably knows more of the situation than he can say over the telephone."[90]

By the next day Patton realized that the "German attack is on a wide front and moving fast." During the night the Germans had advanced "into my area. This may be a feint," Patton shrewdly commented, "or the attack on the front of the VIII Corps may be, although at the moment it looks like the real thing." But Patton was confident. "If the Germans are feinting in front of the VIII Corps and are intending to attack me, we will stop them as we are very well placed."

Patton, however, remained convinced that the planned offensive should go on. "As an afterthought," he ordered Eddy "to move the 4th Armored into action so that no one can withdraw it, because I still feel that if we put on the blitz and break through, as it will, we will halt the German attack." Had Middleton and General Gerow's Vth Corps "been more aggressive, the Germans could not have prepared this attack—one must never sit still."[91]

Patton's subordinates agreed with him about the American assault. That morning, responding to a question from Patton, Maddox pointed out that the Germans, pushing ahead in the Ardennes, would be unable to repulse an attack in the south by Patton and Patch. Within a week the Third and Seventh Armies could be in the rear of the Germans, who would be trapped west of the Rhine.[92]

Weyland was especially eager to go ahead with the operation named for his wife.

Everything was set up, and it was about to roll, when the Battle of the Bulge started. The Germans took the initiative. I wanted to go on with our plan. It would have worked slick as a whistle, in my estimation. The British and the American First Army would have been temporarily embarrassed, shall we say, because they would have had the world's biggest pinwheel. Yes, the Germans probably would have gone down to, and got through, the British, and probably would have reached Antwerp, which would have had some bad aspects, but in the meantime, the American Third Army would have been right back to cut right up behind them, and I think the war would have been over. But, of course, we had Allies in this, and the Allies would not have looked too good.[93]

All thoughts of the American offensive ceased at ten-thirty the next morning. Bradley called and asked Patton to come to Luxembourg, along with his G-2, G-3, and G-4, for an important meeting. Within ten minutes of receiving the call, Patton, accompanied by Koch, Maddox, and Muller, left.[94] The blitz had ended before it had begun.

Sixteen

HITS AND ERRORS

I

When Patton, with some members of his staff, arrived at Bradley's headquarters, he learned that the situation was serious. "The German penetration is much greater than I had thought," he commented. Asked by Bradley "what I could do," Patton said he would send the 4th Armored to Longwy, just below the French border with Luxembourg, that midnight and start Horace McBride's 80th Division toward Luxembourg the next morning. He would also alert Major General Willard S. Paul's 26th Division to move within twenty-four hours.[1]

On December 18 Gay demonstrated his administrative talents. At the conclusion of his conference with Bradley, Patton called Gay with instructions to stop Gaffey and McBride, both going east, and alert them for a movement to the north. Gaffey's 4th Armored could move on its own, but Gay had to provide transportation for the 80th. Finally, Gay was to tell Weyland that for the present the operation they hoped would end the war with Germany was off.

Later that day Bradley phoned Gay with a more specific request. Bradley, Gay related, "wanted to know if General Gay thought one combat command of the 4th Armored Division could be moved tonight. General Gay replied that he knew it could; furthermore that the 80th Division and remainder of the 4th Armored could be moved early tomorrow morning."

Calling Bradley at eight that evening Patton discovered that, in Bradley's words, "The situation up there is much worse than it was when I talked to you." Bradley was transferring the 4th Armored and the 80th Infantry from Eddy to Millikin's III Corps. He wanted Millikin to report to Leven Allen at eleven the next day at Bradley's command post. With a staff officer Patton was to meet at that hour with Bradley and Ike at Verdun. "I understand from General Eisenhower," Bradley informed Patton, "that you are to take over the VIII Corps as well as the offensive to be launched by the new troops coming in the area."

In the flurry of activity, Patton's staff performed admirably. Fifteen minutes after the conversation between Bradley and Patton, Millikin and his section chiefs met with Patton and his section chiefs. Explaining the plan to move north, Gay described the routes Gaffey's and McBride's divisions would take. At thirty minutes after midnight Dager led Combat Command B of the 4th Armored toward Longwy.[2]

Convinced that a primary purpose of the German attack was to divert the First and Third Armies from the Siegfried Line, Gay still believed that the American offensive should go on. "It is thought that if we had the nerve and would let this German attack penetrate into our lines for some forty to fifty miles," he argued, "it would be possible by a bold move to cut them off from the rear and destroy their entire thrust, which in my opinion would end the war." He called the attack the "last desperate effort on the part of the Germans. It bears all the earmarks of their thrust in March, 1918, and it is my opinion that if this thrust is not only stopped, but destroyed, it will end the war for Germany."[3]

At eight the next morning Patton presided over a meeting attended by numerous officers, including Weyland, Eddy, and Millikin. With the bulk of his army poised behind Eddy's corps preparing to attack the West Wall, Patton discussed the problems relative to moving troops and supplies in another direction. To help Bradley had sent along his chief combat liaison officer, Colonel Karl R. Bendetsen, who arrived as the briefing began. Bendetsen remembered Patton's mastery of the situation.

> He welcomed me and said, "Sit down and listen in, maybe you can help." He was required to undertake a military maneuver of great complexity. His Third Army was a very large and powerful force of three corps of three divisions each. These were based upon Army supply areas that were on the axis of the attack which the Third Army had been following. Patton faced the task of turning 90

degrees and attacking at right angles to the axis of attack his forces had been pursuing. This is complex and difficult at best and in battle conditions it is vastly more so with only a limited road net available. He wanted to be sure of his supplies of P.O.L. (petroleum, oil and lubricants), ammunition, ordnance, transport, replacements, rations, etc. He then said, "Bendetsen, there's something you can do for me and I believe you can do it if you really want to."

I said, "Sir, anything you request is an order. I will give it all I've got."

He said, "I need a freight train. I'm not going to be satisfied unless the Third Army can have its own freight train for this temporary period." He said, "You know where more supplies and equipment and transportation gear are located in France than anybody else I know. In the past you've always seemed to be able to come up with something that didn't seem to be available." He added, "I do not know whether there are any freight trains immediately available; nevertheless I want one and I call upon you to provide it by all means, fair or foul."

To make a long story short, I managed to steal a freight train for him and survived the operation. It probably made some contribution toward providing the vital supply and support required for the critically important success of the Third Army in turning back the last major lunge of Nazi ground forces.[4]

After this meeting on the morning of the nineteenth Patton, Harkins, and Codman left for Verdun. Arriving at 10:45 A.M., they found a large gathering that included Eisenhower, Bradley, Tedder, and Devers. There Ike's intelligence officer, British Major-General Kenneth W. D. Strong, revealed that the Germans had reached Bastogne, a highway center in southern Belgium, just north of Luxembourg. Trapped in Bastogne were one combat command from both the 9th and 10th Armored divisions and the entire 101st Airborne Division, temporarily led by Brigadier General Anthony C. McAuliffe. Following some talk about Devers taking over the American line south of Saarlautern on the Saar River, Eisenhower asked how soon Patton could attack toward Bastogne. Harkins, Patton's deputy chief of staff for operations, recalled the conversation.

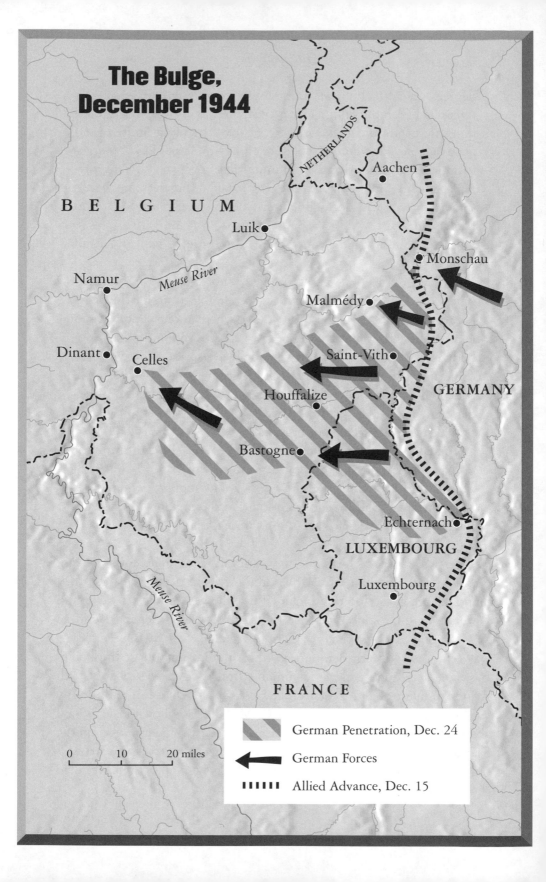

The Bulge,
December 1944

NETHERLANDS

Aachen

BELGIUM

Luik

Monschau

Namur

Meuse River

Malmédy

Dinant

Celles

Saint-Vith

GERMANY

Houffalize

Bastogne

Echternach

LUXEMBOURG

Meuse River

Luxembourg

FRANCE

German Penetration, Dec. 24

German Forces

IIIIII Allied Advance, Dec. 15

0   10   20 miles

Patton said: "I'll make a meeting engagement in three days and I'll give you a six division coordinated attack in six days." Well, that brought a bit of a chuckle. Ike's staff didn't think that was possible. General Patton turned to me and said, "We can do that," and I said "Yes, sir." There wasn't much else I could say. We had it pretty well figured out. So, he went to Luxembourg from Verdun and I went back to Nancy, to brief the Third Army staff. I told them what we had to do and got things moving.[5]

Before leaving Verdun for Walker's headquarters, Patton phoned Gay and told him that Harkins would be back by five-thirty with the plan worked out by Supreme Headquarters Allied Expeditionary Force. Patton was to lead a force that would hit the enemy's rear and left. He was to take three corps: Millikin's III; Middleton's VIII, whose inactivity, Patton and Koch believed, had led to the German buildup; and Eddy's XII. Walker's corps, minus Red Irwin's 5th Infantry Division, would stay east and south of the Moselle River, protecting the hard-won gains.

Thanks to the efficiency of Patton, Gay, Harkins, and the rest of the staff, the 4th Armored and 80th Infantry Divisions were already on their way north. Paul's 26th Infantry and one combat command of Irwin's 5th Infantry would start on December 20, and the following day Eddy's headquarters was to move to Luxembourg.[6]

Harkins himself exemplified the skill and energy of the staff. Right after the five-thirty meeting of the twentieth, he left to rejoin Patton, arriving at Walker's headquarters after supper. Harkins wanted to go out again that night, but Patton, warning that the American units were scattered about and the Germans were all around, refused to let him leave.

The next day, while Gay and the staff remained in Nancy coordinating the movement of Third Army troops, Patton moved to Luxembourg, where he and Harkins began reorganizing units for the push north. Because of the power of the German attack, the troops, Harkins remembered, were badly jumbled, antiaircraft units, for example, being scrambled with the infantry. Patton first created task forces, small, aggressive units named after their commanders, such as Task Force Jones or Task Force Gregory. Years later Harkins lavishly praised Patton's creativity.

I don't think if you sat down in Fort Leavenworth and tried to figure out how you could save that thing, you could have done better
than he did. He just had a knack of what should go together and
what they should do. In the first place, he just turned them all
around and sent them north. It was absolutely fantastic, and when
we got all straightened out, in two or three days, and the divisions
started coming up and taking over and absorbing these little Task
Forces. They, the Task Forces, really held the enemy off while the
divisions moved up. As I say, it was fantastic, quite a job.[7]

While Patton was at Bradley's headquarters in Luxembourg Ike
called and confirmed something Bedell Smith had said to Bradley the
previous day. "He told Brad he was putting Monty in operational control of the 1st and 9th Armies," Patton recorded. Patton would thus
control the forces south of the Bulge and Monty those north of it. "I
don't know why, except that in this way he may be able to induce
Monty to put in some British troops. He certainly can't or won't command Monty."[8] Stripped of his command, Bradley would forever hate
Monty.

Patton spent the rest of December 20 evaluating things. "The VIII
Corps is fighting very well," he noted, "but is being destroyed at the
moment consisting of nothing but remnants, except in the case of the
101st Airborne which is holding Bastogne." Also at Bastogne, in addition to the single combat commands from the 9th and 10th Armored
Divisions, were two companies of tank destroyers "and some colored
artillery." Facing overwhelming odds, Patton suggested that the Americans withdraw from the town. But at the urging of Bradley, Middleton,
and Koch "we decided to hang on to Bastogne, because it is a very
important road net, and I do not believe the enemy dare pass it without
reducing it."[9]

On the very day Patton regrouped his forces, an unusual incident
took place in Bastogne itself. Led by the 8th Tank Battalion, Dager's
Combat Command B had set out for Longwy just after midnight on the
morning of December 19. Possessing the only map, Dager directed the
tanks as best he could: he radioed instructions from his jeep, shouted
directions to Major Albin F. Irzyk in the lead tank, and stood at inter-
sections pointing the way.[10]

Having no idea where they were going, the tankers rolled into Belgium and then turned northeast. At 2300 hours the caravan stopped just below Bastogne, having traveled 161 miles in twenty-two hours. The following morning Dager, a slightly built officer from New Jersey, called Irzyk and ordered him to send a task force into the beleaguered town. When Irzyk protested that CCB should wait for the rest of the division before venturing forward, Dager said he had argued with Middleton, who, with Bradley's permission, wanted to send the entire CCB into Bastogne. They compromised on a task force. In Bastogne the task force was to report to McAuliffe, commanding the 101st Airborne in the absence of General Maxwell Taylor. Irzyk thereupon formed Task Force Ezell. Consisting of a tank company, an armored infantry company, and a battery of field artillery, it was commanded by Irzyk's executive officer, Captain Bert P. Ezell.

Storming down the road to Bastogne, Task Force Ezell entered the town without opposition. Just after noon on December 20, while reporting for instructions to Colonel William Roberts, the head of Combat Command B of the 10th Armored Division, Ezell received a call from Irzyk. Gaffey had ordered Task Force Ezell to return immediately. Again encountering no enemy, Ezell's men hauled back with them numerous abandoned artillery pieces.[11]

Years later, in a vivid article, Irzyk speculated on the meaning of the episode. During the conference with Bradley in Luxembourg on the twentieth, Patton learned that, without consulting him, Bradley had sent CCB of the 4th Armored to a position just southwest of Bastogne. Driving next to Arlon, Belgium, just north of Longwy, Patton found Middleton and Millikin, along with Gaffey and Paul, whose 26th Division had just been transferred to Millikin. There, Irzyk believed, Millikin and Gaffey surely argued for the return of CCB, essential to the attack planned for December 22. "In retrospect," Irzyk observed, "General Dager's resistance to committing CCB into Bastogne may have saved the unit. If he had not protested, CCB would have probably been in Bastogne before General Patton was aware that it had been given away by General Bradley." It probably would have been trapped there.[12]

On the eve of battle both Eisenhower and the British feared that Patton would fail. Describing Ike's morning staff conference of December 21, British Air Marshal James M. Robb, the chief of the air staff, noted in his diary: "The Supreme Commander mentioned that what he was afraid of was that the impetuous Patton would talk Bradley round into allowing him to attack at once with the object of going right through and not waiting for a fully coordinated counter-offensive."

Patton, who alone volunteered to do something about Bastogne, saw things differently. Ike and his operations officer, General Bull, "are getting jittery about my attacking too soon and too weak," he commented as his forces neared their destination. "I have all I can get. If I wait I will lose surprise." To the north the First Army, now under Montgomery, "could in my opinion, attack on the 23rd if they were pushed to, but they seem to have no ambition in that line."[13]

The attack by Millikin's revamped III Corps against the enemy's left flank, aimed at Bastogne from Arlon, began at six on the morning of December 22. True to his word at Verdun, Patton used three divisions. On the left the 4th Armored, denounced by German radio as "Roosevelt's Butchers," ran into craters and road blocks but made, according to Patton, "reasonable progress." In the center Paul's 26th Infantry did "well against delaying action," and on the right McBride's 80th Infantry began pushing ahead after crossing a river. Despite the obstacles, the American advance averaged seven miles.

While Patton engaged in what was perhaps his greatest military achievement, Bradley presented a picture of a despondent general stripped of his army. During the crisis, Patton stayed with Bradley at Luxembourg City, hurrying each morning to the battle sites in his jeep, elaborately equipped with Plexiglas doors and a 30-caliber machine gun. "He and Brad get along famously with their 'Brad' and 'George' adlibbing," Hansen observed. " 'Don't come in George, if you're not bringing good news,' and Brad would laugh."[14]

Driving about on the twentieth Patton had found the troops of Major General John W. Leonard's 9th Armored and Major General William Morris's 10th Armored, both of which had a combat command in Bastogne, "very badly scrambled." To straighten out the mess Patton reorganized each division, transferring a combat command from one to the other. He then attached the 9th to Middleton's corps and the 10th to Eddy's.

That afternoon Patton drove over to Leonard's command post at Mersch, Luxembourg, ten miles north of Luxembourg City. Jumping from his jeep he told Leonard: "I want you to get out of here and go over to Middleton." Unfortunately Morris, who was to relieve Leonard, did not arrive until the twenty-second. On that day Leonard received an urgent phone call to report to Lucky Six, Patton's code name, at Luxembourg City. Patton, Leonard remembered, was "in this deep room. And, Jesus, you have to walk down that last mile, you know." At first Patton spoke gruffly: "I thought I told you to get the hell over to Middleton three days ago!" "Well," Leonard answered, "you did. But Morris didn't get up till just now." Again Patton spoke gruffly: "Well, get the hell over there right now." He then softened and said: "Well, I guess this turned out better the way it was. What do you think?" "I don't know, but I hope it has," Leonard responded.[15]

After a series of very bad days the weather cleared on the twenty-third. To be closer to Patton Weyland, who was given responsibility for the Bulge area, had also moved his headquarters to Luxembourg City. During the crisis Quesada transferred three fighter groups from the IX to the XIX TAC, and the Eighth Air Force sent along a P-51 fighter-bomber group. The striking power of the Ninth Air Force, also assigned to Patton, was augmented by the transfer of the 2d Bombardment Division from the Eighth Air Force.

But until the twenty-third the planes could not fly. "The weather was so terrible," Weyland recalled. "It was white when you looked down, white when you looked up, white when you looked out that way. Tanks and trucks were painted white. It was a most difficult situation."[16]

On the twenty-third things changed for the better. Weyland sent up seven groups of fighter-bombers, the Ninth Air Force eleven groups of medium bombers plus the borrowed 2d Bombardment Division. Some Royal Air Force planes also helped out. The Allied planes destroyed the bridges in the vicinity of Saarburg, just over the German border, hopefully trapping the German soldiers in the Bulge. "If any enemy are in the pocket," Patton observed, "they will be very well scared."

Not that the air attacks were completely successful. "Unfortunately," Weyland observed, "our planes occasionally hit some of our own troops. Conversely, some of our own troops shot down my planes. It was quite mixed up."[17]

On a depressing Christmas Eve—the day before a German counterattack had crippled ten of Dager's tanks and forced his Combat Command B, acting on the left flank of III Corps, to pull back—Montgomery predicted defeat for the Third Army. Convinced that the German Fifth and Sixth Panzer armies were bypassing Bastogne and heading straight for him, he cabled Brooke that he feared nothing, for he "had tidied up the mess and have got the two American armies properly organised." Respecting Patton about as much as Patton respected him, he wrote of the American push toward Bastogne: "This attack was launched through a front which had not been properly stabilized; as a result it went off half-cock, and it was soon clear that the enemy would be able to hold it, at any rate for a time."[18]

On Christmas Day Bradley visited Montgomery, whose idea of tidying up the mess had been to order American withdrawal from the Saint-Vith area, northeast of Bastogne, and to place J. Lawton Collins's VII Corps on the defensive. In his notes on the campaign Monty described how he told Bradley that the Allies had suffered a "bloody nose" and were too weak to resist the Germans. "The defeat," Montgomery argued, "was the result of trying to develop two thrusts at the same time, neither of which had been strong enough to gain decisive results. The Allies were now in a proper muddle, and sufficient troops for a further offensive could be collected only by pulling back in one sector and going over to the defensive there." Patton, on the southern front, must stop his offensive at once and send his excess divisions to Monty in the north. Considering that Bradley detested Montgomery for taking away his army group, Monty's next sentence verged on self-deception: "General Bradley agreed with this summary of the situation and agreed also that it was his own plan which had produced these unpleasant results."[19]

Patton learned of the meeting between Bradley and Montgomery late on Christmas Day. Early that morning, as was his custom, he set off to greet all the divisions in combat with the enemy. Visiting the 4th Armored, he saw Gaffey, Dager, and Brigadier General Herbert L. Earnest, the last recently put in charge of Combat Command A. From there he visited Paul of the 26th Infantry, McBride of the 80th, and Irwin of the 5th. "All were very cheerful," Patton noted, but he was not, since for the past two days his lead divisions had gained but two miles a day.

That night, after "a quiet dinner at Bradley's mess," Patton heard of the conversation earlier in the day. His diary entry reflected his opinion of Monty's defensive strategy.

Monty says that the 1st Army cannot attack for three months and that the only attack that can be made is by me, but that I am too weak; hence we should fall back to the Saar-Vesges Line or even to the Moselle to gain more divisions. I feel that this is disgusting and might remove the valor of our army and the confidence of our people. It will have tremendous political implications and probably condemn to death or slavery all the inhabitants of Alsace and Lorraine, if we abandon them to the Germans. If ordered to fall back, I think I will ask to be relieved.

In his postwar interviews with Chester Wilmot, especially those conducted after the publication of Patton's *War As I Knew It,* which discussed Monty's reluctance to aid the Americans, Montgomery denied having told Bradley that he could not attack for three months. For two reasons, however, Wilmot remained unconvinced by the denials. First of all, on December 26, when the Ardennes battle was still at its height and Horrocks's XXX British Corps seemed about to become involved, Montgomery sent Horrocks back to England. In 1949 Monty explained that Horrocks had supposedly come up with a plan to let the Germans cross the Meuse and advance toward Brussels, so that Monty could finish the war on the battlefield of Waterloo, where the Duke of Wellington had defeated Napoleon. "M says," Wilmot wrote, "that when he discovered this he immediately ordered Horrocks to go home on leave." Second of all, throughout the Ardennes battle Monty spent as much time as possible planning Veritable-Grenade, his February operation aimed at driving into Germany.

Additional evidence that Monty had warned the Americans to hold "on a defensive line for three months through the winter" came from Bradley's aide, Chester Hansen. "Bradley hotly contested this view," Hansen recorded in his diary on April 12, 1945, "called it tommyrot and announced that he would initiate an offensive on the southern front immediately to close the gap. Patton, supporting Bradley's view, is supposed to have spoken dramatically, 'The American army has never had a single American soldier incapable of offensive action at any time.' The implications of Monty's recommendation are enormous. It becomes all the more damning when you recall that the British press colored him as the hero of the campaign."[20]

In Bastogne the members of the 101st Airborne Division experienced a different kind of Christmas. For dinner many of the soldiers had K rations. The Americans inside the city possessed plenty of flour and liquor, so, McAuliffe remembered, some of the troops had pancakes with cognac. In constant touch with Middleton, McAuliffe knew of the approach of Patton's lead elements.[21]

During the eight days his division was bottled up in Bastogne, McAuliffe, as Patton subsequently observed, complained and said things that were better unsaid. But twenty years after the battle he expressed great admiration for Patton. "I knew Patton well," he remarked. "I'd played polo with him. I'd known him for years. And most of us thought he never had a very good staff but he certainly accomplished miracles with it." He considered Patton's drive north to relieve him "remarkable. Well, I mean the success of moving an unwieldy mass like that; to change your lines of supply, and everything, to turn that cumbersome, heavy-going outfit in the snow, in the fog and the rain, and turn them around as quickly as he did to get them going to the north, was really a remarkable task to accomplish."[22]

As McAuliffe and numerous others indicated, the movement to Bastogne was enormously complicated. On the first two days about 100,000 troops, "accompanied by thousands of tons of supplies and equipment," turned north. Tens of thousands of jeeps, tanks, trucks, and howitzers sped toward Bastogne, 125 miles away, over roads that were sheets of mud, ice, and snow. At night the drivers ignored the blackout rules and traveled at full speed with their lights on. The traffic, one student of the move has written, "was congested and sometimes snarled." Spending much of his time in his jeep in frigid weather, Patton rode "herd on the convoys that were suddenly turned toward Luxembourg." His communications teams did their part, laying more than 19,500 miles of wire and establishing an entirely new communications network.[23]

On Christmas Day Gay sensed the turn of the tide. He received word of the success of the air drop of supplies to the trapped division. Not one plane was lost. Christmas, a Monday, brought with it the third consecutive day of suitable flying weather; a reward, Gay speculated, for the much-publicized prayer for good weather written by the Third Army's chaplain at Patton's order. "A few more clear days," Gay observed, "and it is my opinion that the German advance will be completely wrecked and that the highways again will resemble those in the vicinity of Le Mans incident to the advance of the Third Army during August of this year." The Allies estimated that they had destroyed five hundred vehicles the day before. Planes intercepted and set on fire a German convoy of seventy-odd trucks carrying gasoline. Every truck burned.[24]

The big day turned out to be the twenty-sixth. Colonel Wendell Blanchard's Combat Command R of the 4th Armored Division approached the outskirts of Bastogne. Led by two lieutenant colonels, Creighton W. Abrams of the 37th Tank Battalion and George L. Jaques of the 53d Armored Infantry Battalion, the command had bypassed the fortified towns while approaching Bastogne. At 2 P.M. Gaffey phoned to say that if Patton authorized it Blanchard thought he could break through to Bastogne. "I told him to try it," Patton commented. Led by Captain William Dwight, who was Abrams's operations officer, American tanks reached the perimeter of the city at 6:45 P.M. Emerging from a nearby command post, McAuliffe returned Dwight's salute and remembered saying: "I sure am glad to see you." Abrams then came up and accompanied McAuliffe into the town. "It was a dramatic moment," McAuliffe later said. "All of our people knew about it at once, but no more dramatic a moment, I guess, than in daylight when the airplanes dropped the supplies to us. That was really exciting business. Everyone knew we were short of ammunition and were hungry."[25]

The much-publicized rescue opened a narrow corridor into Bastogne. That night forty trucks filled with supplies roared into the city, and that night and the next morning ambulances evacuated 652 wounded Americans. The relief of Bastogne took seven days. In addition to the 4th Armored, Patton assigned special credit to the 318th Infantry Regiment of the 80th Division and to Combat Command A of the 9th Armored Division.[26]

Despite the rescue Patton soon became "a little fed up" with the 101st. "On Christmas Day," he told his friend Lieutenant General Thomas T. Handy of Marshall's staff, "McAuliffe called the VIII Corps (Middleton) and said that the finest present they could receive would be to be rescued on Christmas Day." When they were not, McAuliffe phoned Middleton about midnight and said that the division "had been let down." While Patton did not "deprecate their valor," he assigned "a good deal more credit" to the 4th Armored, to Paul's 26th Infantry, which advanced along a front of ten kilometers, and to McBride's 80th Infantry, attacking along a front of twenty kilometers. "However," Patton observed, "there is no use getting into a pissing match with a skunk; so, unless they get too vituperative, I will leave it at that."[27]

The relief of Bastogne and the ensuing Allied victories brought to the fore the dispute about what to do next. Thankfully on Christmas Day the 2d Armored Division caught the 2d Panzer Division of the Fifth Panzer Army out of gas at Celles, about thirty-five miles northwest of Bastogne, and mauled it. Subsequently British tankers stopped the Germans, who had reached the Meuse River at three places, near Givet in France and Dinant in Belgium. Monty now favored the most conservative course, a slow eastward push by his forces alone. Under his plan, Hodges would hold the northern flank of the corridor and Patton the southern, allowing Horrocks's XXX Corps to advance in the center.

Ike, Bradley, and Hodges advocated a different course. This envisioned Patton moving north from Bastogne and Hodges moving south along a line traversing the Belgian towns of Hotton to the west and Trois-Ponts to the east. The two would meet at Houffalize, roughly fifteen miles from each starting point. This maneuver would reduce the Bulge and cut off the Germans west of Houffalize.

Patton, Collins, and Horrocks himself advocated the most aggressive policy. Along with Gay, Weyland, and Bedell Smith, they favored a rapid movement across the base of the Bulge, trapping all the German troops west of it. To Patton speed constituted the central ingredient in such a maneuver. "The speed of our movements is amazing even to me," he observed on the twenty-sixth, "and must be a constant source of surprise to the Germans. . . . Why in hell the SHAEF thinkers hold the 11th Armored Division, 17th Airborne and 87th Infantry Divisions at Reims is beyond me. They should be attacking."[28]

Now, Patton believed, was the time to strike. On the twenty-eighth he began planning a campaign that would carry his army from Luxembourg City northeast along what his staff called "The Honeymoon Trail" to Bitburg and Prüm and then to the Rhine River crossings at Bonn, about thirty-five miles inside Germany. "If I could get three more divisions I could win this war now," he lamented. "If Ike will put Bradley back in command of the 1st and 9th Armies, we can bag the whole German army. . . . Monty is a tired little fart. War requires the taking of risks and he wont take them. Of course Bradley made a bad mistake in being passive on the front of the VIII Corps."[29]

The plan that Eisenhower and Bradley approved was not the campaign to Bonn and the Rhine crossings. Instead Ike decided on a thrust from Bastogne northeast to Houffalize and then on to Saint-Vith. For use during the movement, he assigned to Patton on the twenty-eighth two untested divisions, Brigadier General Frank L. Culin's 87th Infantry and Brigadier General Charles S. Kilburn's 11th Armored. Meeting with his corps commanders that night, Patton worked out the details. Middleton's VIII Corps would leave Bastogne on December 30 and advance until it seized the high ground and the road center just south of Houffalize. After Middleton had taken these positions, Millikin's III Corps would join in and attempt to capture Saint-Vith, northeast of Houffalize.[30]

S. L. A. Marshall, then the chief of military history in the European theater and later the author of the first full-scale study of the Bastogne operation, considered the plan among Patton's worst. "With respect to his operation out of the Bastogne salient," he said of Patton,

at the time I was there and I thought he was hopelessly mistaken, that what he was attempting was a tactical monstrosity. He was trying what could not be done. When you're attacking out of a narrow salient, you must be aware that men, as they move into fire, converge toward one another so the formation will be, you know, like a triangle. If they are opposed by an enemy that is fixed in high ground, well fixed with artillery and tank gunfire, that means that all around that salient you've got a series of exposed flanks. So, the operation will be killed off very quickly. Well, this happened, not just to the 17th Airborne [Division], but it also happened to the 506th [Parachute Infantry Regiment] of the 101st; those operations were an unnecessary sacrifice of troops. We were in no shape to move at that time. All we could get out of it would be a complete rebuff, at terrific loss. And so, I could not understand either Patton's issuing the order or General Taylor accepting the order because it was bound to work out to no good end. I felt this about Patton: He was as a fighting operator perhaps the most effective commander we've ever had in a fluid situation. But when he got up against solid works and an entrenched enemy he was . . . he had no more rabbits in his hat than any other general.[31]

In his diary Gay, too, found fault with the movement. Exhibiting "a complete misunderstanding of the problem involved," Middleton launched the 87th Infantry and the 11th Armored "along an east-west line some five miles south of Bastogne." From this angle Middleton "would drive the enemy back on this high ground rather than take it away from him."[32]

Both analyses proved right. In four days of bitter fighting the 11th Armored advanced but six miles. The human toll was 220 killed and missing and 441 wounded. The division also lost forty-two medium tanks and twelve light tanks.[33]

The destruction around Houffalize astounded visitors. On February 10 Charles Sawyer, the American ambassador to Belgium and Luxembourg, visited Patton and found the signs of battle far greater at Houffalize than at Bastogne. "Tanks, trucks, wrecked planes, dead horses and cows were everywhere," he observed. "Although people had smiled in every town through which we had passed no one smiled in Houffalize."[34]

II

In 1974 S. L. A. Marshall commented that "one of the interesting things" about Patton "was the enormous prejudices that he had. Prejudices against the high command became almost a hatred of the high command—prejudices against the First Army, prejudices against the British, prejudices against the Jews. And these prejudices were reflected in most of the members of his staff. There may have been one or two exceptions; the others went right along with the way the old man felt."[35]

In his autobiography Marshall amplified his statement about two of these prejudices, those against Jews and the British. At the time of the Battle of the Bulge Marshall, who had just been appointed chief historian of the European Theater of Operations, began planning a multivolume account of the campaigns there. As his deputy, Marshall wanted Major Hugh M. Cole, who was assigned to the Third Army. Traveling to Luxembourg City, to which the entire Third Army staff had moved on December 27, Marshall "put the question to the immortal Georgie and his chief of staff, General Hap Gay, an old friend." Marshall also requested the transfer of Cole's executive officer, also a major, and of a sergeant who was "a topflight writer." In partial payment for the three Marshall promised Patton that the volume on the Lorraine campaign would be the first published in the series. When Marshall said he would also replace the three men he took, Gay snapped: "Don't send me any Jewish officers as replacements."

Since Cole would be in charge of lieutenant colonels, Marshall asked Gay to promote him. Two days later Gay transferred Cole in the grade of major. When Marshall called Gay to protest, Patton got on the phone and admitted: "Slam, it wasn't Hap's fault."

"Patton had done it," Marshall later observed, "and I thought I knew why. Patton was a large hater, and the apple-polishers on his staff went along with his hates. He hated the Supreme Command, the First Army, the Jews, and above all the British." Cole had applied to Patton for permission to marry a British girl. That was enough to damn him. "I thought Patton's smallness nauseating."

Refusing to let the matter rest, Marshall took it to Bradley, who called Patton. Bradley told him to rescind the old order, to promote Cole, and then to transfer him to Marshall. Seeking revenge, Marshall sent Gay "the three ablest Jewish officers on my staff. Each was a whiz kid." When Gay called to complain, Marshall told him: "Okay, Hap, send me a memo saying Patton doesn't like them because they're Jewish, and I'll pull them back."[36]

Such accounts, however, hardly reflect the complexity of Patton's thinking. Everything Patton and Bea ever said or wrote about Oscar Koch indicated how greatly they respected him. Yet in appearance Koch resembled the stereotype of the Jew, something Patton undoubtedly noticed. Carter, like Codman the incarnation of the aristocrat, sent his wife a description of Koch: "He is a very sweet & sensitive person—poor darling, very conscious of his looks—much too much so. He says he hates to look so Jewish & to have such a chunky figure—neither of which can be denied—but his innate kindness and generosity radiate from him."[37]

The relationship with Koch demonstrated that Patton was not about to let race or religion interfere with the efficiency of his organization. No evidence exists that he ever treated Koch with anything but respect. His prejudices were only for junior officers who could easily be replaced.

On the last day of December 1944 Patton became involved in an episode more serious than that with Slam Marshall. In one of those incidents that occurred too often, American planes strafed and bombed Patton's troops. Among the targets mistakenly hit was the headquarters of the 4th Armored Division. Patton immediately called Tooey Spaatz, who in turn phoned Doolittle, in charge of the Eighth Air Force, and Vandenberg, who led the Ninth Air Force. "We both checked," Doolittle related, "and we couldn't find where one of our aircraft had strafed Georgie Patton's troops." Finally Spaatz said to Doolittle: "All right, you and Van come over and we'll go over to see Georgie." At Patton's headquarters the three air force generals apologized and discussed ways of avoiding mishaps such as that of the previous day, when American gunners, believing that Germans were flying captured American P-47 Thunderbolt fighter-bombers, shot one down near Luxembourg.

Having apologized, the airmen left. "I was flying a C-45, and Tooey was my passenger," Doolittle recalled, "and Vandenberg was in another C-45, the old black twintail plane, and as we started back we didn't know yet that the Germans had just come over and strafed our troops pretty badly, and had also attacked one of our flying fields. We got that in the air, after we got in the air, but hadn't received the word before taking off from Georgie Patton's quarters. So immediately we flew over our own troops, they started shooting at us." Furious, Spaatz wanted to turn back "to talk to Georgie." Doolittle continued the story:

> I said, "Now wait, let's give a little thought to this. We are through this fire, and we are beyond. Do you want to go back through it to report to Georgie?" He said, "No, go ahead." But he was so anxious to go back and get Georgie's apologies for shooting us up.

The next day Spaatz, fire in his voice, called Patton and complained that both planes had been hit by Third Army antiaircraft fire as they were returning home. Checking with Vandenberg, Patton found out that "they may have thought they were hit but they were not." On that same day three P-47s attacked Eddy on the road and, Patton noted, "chased" him "into a ditch."[38]

III

The year 1944 had begun disastrously for Patton. On New Year's Day he had received a telegram relieving him from command of the Seventh Army. Now the Allies were calling on Patton to stop the German offensive. "Headquarters of the Seventh Army one year ago today was in disgrace," Gay commented. "Headquarters of the Third Army, which is practically the same staff, today is being acclaimed by the world."[39]

If Patton continually battled the Allied high command, he was also forced to fight some of his subordinates. At seven o'clock on the evening of January 3, Middleton called to tell Patton of an enemy buildup near Bastogne. He urged the postponement of an attack scheduled for the next morning. With Hodges finally having sent Collins's corps southeast toward Houffalize that day, Patton, hoping for a quick victory, rejected Middleton's request. "During the last two years," Gay observed, "this 'scene' has repeated itself many times and in each and every case the Army commander has been correct. He has continuously held that once an attack is set to be launched, it should be launched; that our main mission is to destroy the German Army, and we can do it better by attacking them than we can by waiting for them."[40]

The campaign, with the 17th Airborne Division replacing the battered 11th Armored, proved, as Slam Marshall commented, ill-conceived. On January 4, the day of the assault, German units ranging in size from a platoon to a regiment launched seventeen counterattacks. Perhaps the strongest came against the 194th Glider Infantry Regiment of the 17th Airborne. One battalion was, Gay conceded, "to a large extent destroyed" and the entire regiment "was badly handled by the Germans."[41]

Visiting Middleton the next day Gay found him "quite depressed." Middleton could not continue the attack. Indeed, he "questioned if he could hold against the enemy's attacks." Feeling that in such a mood Middleton could never defeat an opponent, Gay, using his own authority, called off the operation.

When Gay got to the headquarters of Colonel James R. Pierce, the commander of the 194th Glider Infantry, he got a more hopeful picture. "God," Pierce told Gay, "how green we are, but we are learning fast and the next time we will beat them." Pierce explained the mauling. The

87th Infantry Division, protecting his regiment's left flank, did not advance as rapidly as the 194th, leaving that flank exposed. The Americans, however, did well and repulsed an attack on the left. Almost simultaneously, German tanks assaulted the regiment's right, left unprotected when the American artillery shifted to another target. "The infantry, having nothing to fight with but their rifles, had a rough time. This is told here," Gay wrote in his diary, "for the purpose of showing how close supervision must be given to new divisions."[42]

Reviewing the setbacks, Patton added a note that recalled the American atrocities in Sicily in July 1943. The 11th Armored was now engaged in its first operation. On January 2 its Combat Command B, attacking the town of Mande-Saint-Etienne, four miles west of Bastogne, found itself in street-to-street and cellar-to-cellar combat, suffering heavy casualties. Calling the division "very green," Patton believed it "took unnecessary losses to no effect. There were also some unfortunate incidents in the shooting of prisoners (I hope we can conceal this)."[43]

Unlike the atrocities in Sicily, these shootings were undoubtedly sparked not by fiery speeches but by the killings by the Germans, especially the murders of American prisoners and Belgian civilians by Waffen-SS Lieutenant Colonel Joachim Peiper's combat group, a unit of the 1st SS Panzer Division. At a dozen different places between December 17 and 20, Peiper's troops slaughtered about 350 Americans and one hundred Belgians. The most famous incident took place at Malmédy, where on the seventeenth at least eighty-six Americans were butchered. Among American troops, word of the massacres spread quickly, probably causing retaliation.[44]

Bea's brother, Fred Ayer, provided a final note to the question of who did what and why. After the war, when General Patton was dying, Fred flew to Europe to be with and comfort his sister. There he spoke with a high-ranking American officer, with whom he spent a good deal of time, about the treatment of prisoners by both sides. He wrote of the conversation:

I was cautioned by . . . that we were really not in a position to say very much and that our own boys were not so lily-white and had killed plenty of POWs. This was from a fighting officer who had been in the thick of it. In answer to my question as to how he thought the honors lay, after thinking a bit he said that his guess would be that the Americans shot four or five prisoners for every prisoner killed by a German, but he said of course our boys were pretty angry about what had been done to some of us first.

Ayer then told of an ex-airman who had driven him in England. After being wounded in the arm and shot down over Bremen, the aviator was sent to a prison camp, where the Germans interrogated him. After these grueling sessions, however, he received decent treatment. When a guard grabbed his wounded arm, he slapped the German, "who," Ayer explained, "then really started after him. The guard was knocked down by a German officer who said, 'If I catch you treating a prisoner of war like that again I will kill you.' "[45]

IV

Gay's diary for the early days of January 1945 indicated the confusion within Bradley's army group. After two unsuccessful attacks aimed at joining with the First Army at Houffalize, thereby cutting off the Bastogne pocket and annihilating the enemy troops caught within it, Patton began planning another assault on January 6. But on that very day Bradley came to Patton's headquarters and announced that the Germans were pulling out of the Bastogne pocket. Enemy resistance seemed to be weakening. To determine the truth of this observation, Patton directed Middleton to make one or two thrusts forward to see what his men would encounter.

The next evening Bradley called Patton with the same message. The Germans, he insisted, had withdrawn their armor from the Bastogne area and were pulling out their troops. Checking with the intelligence officers of Patton's divisions and corps, Koch found the report unfounded. At that very moment Grow's 6th Armored Division was battling the strongest German counterattack, by an infantry regiment supported by tanks and self-propelled guns, it had faced in the Ardennes. During a three-hour battle, the 6th Armored fell back almost a mile, but the division was able to retake the lost ground and surround a sizable force of Germans in a woods.[46]

On Monday, January 8, the day before the new attack, the errors

compounded. German infantry and armor cut off a battalion of the
17th Airborne Division's 513th Parachute Regiment. While the Germans inflicted heavy casualties on the Americans, two combat commands of the 11th Armored Division stood idly by just to the rear of the
battle. "This was a bad tactical error," complained Gay, who blamed
Middleton, not the inexperienced Kilburn. Middleton's headquarters
was a "battle-trained Corps Headquarters—experienced both in the use
of infantry and armor—and it must have been known to them that
armor and tank destroyers must be up close with the infantry." Gay, in
fact, had personally warned both Middleton and Major General
William M. Miley of the 17th Airborne of this a few days before.

Learning of the failure to use the 11th Armored Division to support
the 17th Airborne, Patton immediately called Middleton. "He stated,"
Gay recorded, "that this would not be allowed to happen again; that
the 11th Armored Division was in rear of the 17th Airborne and it
would be used and used vigorously and promptly; that this was a *must*
order and failure to do so would not be tolerated."[47] As for Kilburn, he
would soon be replaced by General Dager, one of Wood's most accomplished disciples.

In bitter cold and heavy snow that prevented air support, Patton's
latest assault, still aimed at Houffalize, jumped off at ten on the morning of Tuesday, January 9. By mid-afternoon the 101st Airborne, supported by the 4th Armored, had advanced halfway toward its initial
objective, Noville, five miles south of Houffalize.

The 4th Armored had just begun to move on the morning of the
tenth when Bradley phoned. Ike's headquarters had ordered that the
Third Army halt. SHAEF's intelligence reports indicated that the Germans intended to attack along the Moselle River, southeast of Luxembourg, where the line of the XX Corps was thin. Patton objected
strongly, arguing that the Germans were trying to stop the Third
Army's move toward Houffalize by forcing it to shift divisions to the
south. SHAEF was playing into German hands. But having no choice,
Patton at one o'clock that afternoon ordered a halt to the drive. The 4th
Armored was to be pulled out of the line and sent south.

Gay saw in the command to stop "a very grievous error in strategy on
the part of higher command." Just the day before Gay had received permission to move a combat command of the 94th Division south to reinforce the XX Corps. Ike had recently directed that as soon as the First

and Third armies met at Houffalize, control of the First Army would pass from Montgomery back to Bradley. Obviously the British were trying to delay the transfer.[48]

Tracing the origins of the story that the Germans intended to attack southeast of Luxembourg, Koch found it to be the product of the same intelligence officer who, unlike himself, had been caught unaware by the Ardennes offensive. Someone at SHAEF heard a message broadcast by an unknown radio station. He told it to a colonel at SHAEF, who then conveyed it to higher authorities. Neither Weyland's reconnaissance planes nor the Third Army's cub planes could find any evidence of the supposed German movement. Eisenhower and Bradley conceded as much on the twelfth, when they approved a resumption of Patton's thrust to capture the high ground around Houffalize.[49]

At 9:05 A.M. on January 16, Patton's 11th Armored Division finally met troops from Hodges's 2d Armored, ending the Third Army's Bastogne operation. "This restores Bradley to command of the First Army . . . and terminates the German offensive," Patton wrote. But in one way at least the meeting constituted, as the official Army historian has noted, "an empty accomplishment; so measured had been the advance, such delays had the Germans imposed, that most of the troops in what might have been a sizable pocket had escaped."[50] Houffalize joined Metz as Patton's worst moments on the continent.

V

On January 18, as the Third Army continued its operations to wipe out the German advance, Ev Hughes visited Patton with news. From Lieutenant General Ben Lear, whom Ike had just brought in to handle the manpower problems, he had learned that he might become chief of staff of the European Theater of Operations. "I certainly hope he does," Patton commented. "He has had a very raw deal and is a very able officer. In my opinion he should have Lee's job." Hughes also brought a good word. During their last meeting, Ike had said to him: "Do you know, Everett, George is really a very great soldier and I must get Marshall to do something for him before the war is over."[51]

An incident that day illustrated what Washington officials thought of Patton. Wearing a huge fur coat, Leon Henderson, who supervised the government agency that controlled wartime prices, showed up at Third Army headquarters, only to learn from Gay that Patton was out among the troops. Told that Patton would regret missing him, Henderson replied: "I feel much better in knowing that the Army Commander is out in the attacking line than I would if he were back here waiting to see me."[52]

By the twenty-third, despite snow, sleet, ice, and wind, Patton had the III and XII Corps moving forward. Walker's XX Corps, meanwhile, attacked in an attempt to clear out the "Saar-Moselle Triangle," a region extending from the meeting of the Saar and Moselle rivers just below Trier, Germany, to a base east of Luxembourg's southern border. Beginning the movement, the 94th Infantry Division "got into quite a fight with part of the 11th Panzer but is handling the situation. They caught a cub bear by the tail but are pushing on."[53]

Fortunately the day became perfect for Weyland's aviators. Pushed by the American ground attacks, the Germans broke ranks and tried to retreat along the highway. In what Gay called "the biggest day in the history of the XIX Tactical Air Command," Weyland's pilots flew approximately eight hundred missions and caused damage greater than they had in the Falaise Gap. Catching miles of German vehicles bumper to bumper, Weyland's planes destroyed about a thousand. American pilots also wrecked two bridges over the Our River, thereby trapping the retreating enemy soldiers. Viewing the destruction, Gay commented: "At this time it is safe to state that the Bastogne salient is no longer a salient. It might be termed a slight bulge."[54]

As Bradley, once more in charge of the First Army, planned, with Patton and Hodges, to break through the West Wall, a hitch developed. The enemy still controlled the segment of Alsace that the Allied soldiers labeled "the Colmar pocket." At first Devers promised that his Sixth Army Group would wipe out the pocket if SHAEF sent him one of Patton's divisions. But by January 22 Supreme Headquarters found it necessary to send Devers three of Patton's divisions: the 10th Armored, the 28th Infantry, and the 101st Airborne. Now, on the twenty-second, with Strasbourg, thirty-seven miles north of Colmar, threatened, SHAEF ordered that Patton transfer to Devers the 35th Infantry.[55]

On the twenty-third Bradley unveiled to Patton his plan for breaking through the West Wall. On the left of the American line, Hodges's army would attack on Sunday, January 28, east and north of Saint-Vith, twenty-five miles above Houffalize. On Hodges's right Middleton's VIII Corps, consisting of four infantry divisions and an armored division, supported by Weyland's planes, would also move forward, but on a concentrated front. All of Middleton's divisions would be at full strength, giving him a powerful force. After breeching the West Wall, Hodges's army would fan out to the north, Middleton's corps to the south.[56]

The next day, however, Bradley and his plan ran head-on into Devers and the Colmar pocket problem. Meeting at Third Army headquarters, Bradley, Patton, and Hodges had just worked out the details of the Sunday drive when the phone rang. It was Whiteley, the deputy G-3 of SHAEF, who ordered Bradley to send Devers an additional division and a corps headquarters. Gay, who was at the meeting, vividly described the American response.

> The Army Group Commander [Bradley] stated, "I want you to understand that there is more at stake than the mere moving of divisions and corps, and of a certain tactical plan. The reputation and the good will of the American soldiers and the American Army and its commanders are at stake. If you feel that way about it, then as far as I am concerned, you can take any goddam divisions and/or corps in the Twelfth Army Group, do with them as you see fit, and those of us that you leave back will set on our ass until hell freezes over. I trust you do not think I am angry, but I want to impress upon you that I am goddam well incensed." At this time, practically every officer in the room stood up and clapped and the Army Commander [Patton] stated in a voice that could well be heard over the telephone, "Tell them to go to hell and all three of us will resign. I will lead the procession." As to what was said over the telephone I do not know, but evidently it was something, to say the least, that slightly irritated General Bradley.

When Bull, the G-3 of SHAEF, got on the phone, Bradley repeated his comments.

Behind the SHAEF request Patton saw his old nemesis. Saying that he could not attack before February 8, Montgomery had fourteen divisions that were currently doing nothing. He hoped the Americans would fail, so that he could again ask for command of their armies. "Why isn't Ike a man?" an angry Patton wrote. "We will attack and win in spite of Ike and Monty."[57]

The story of this first offensive after the Battle of the Bulge can, as the official army historian of this phase of the European war has observed, be summarized by the word "weather." The campaign began hopefully, and on the twenty-seventh Gay observed: "I believe that final defeat of the German army is now within the offing." But more than a month of heavy snowfalls and low temperatures everywhere left a layer of the white stuff from one to two feet deep. In numerous spots drifts were waist-high.[58]

Behind the scenes Montgomery and Alan Brooke did as much as the weather and the Germans to torpedo the new drive. On the night of the twenty-seventh, seated around the fire at SHAEF headquarters, Bedell Smith told Roosevelt's adviser Harry Hopkins, Harry Butcher, and others that Montgomery, whom he despised, had come to SHAEF and made sniping remarks. "Monty had made representations to the Supreme Commander that Bradley's attack was bound to fail," Butcher noted in an unpublished portion of his diary, "and quite apparently had gone on record with this view." Montgomery argued that the divisions in the Ardennes were tired. The country was, moreover, better suited to defense than offense. At the meeting of the Combined Chiefs of Staff, to take place at Malta about January 29, Brooke was going to push this argument. He also planned to revive the one-thrust idea, under which Montgomery would command American troops during his drive on what Ike would later denounce as a pencil-thin line to the Ruhr Valley.[59]

The bad news began on the twenty-ninth, the day the Malta conference opened. Patton received orders to transfer the 35th Division to Simpson's Ninth Army. When Patton complained, Bradley, realizing what was happening, told Patton he had done everything he could to stop the transfer, but he had failed. "The 35th Division is one of the oldest Divisions in the Third Army," Gay lamented, "and it is with deep regret that we learn of its separation from our Army."[60]

On Thursday, February 1, Patton received another jolt. Eddy presented to Patton a plan for a movement through Echternach, in southern Luxembourg, to Bitburg and the West Wall. After setting the fifth as the date for the attack, Patton called Bradley, only to be told that it could not take place. Higher authority—it turned out to be the Combined Chiefs—had decided to make the main thrust in the north. For this assault Montgomery would retain command of Simpson's Ninth Army, which would be further reinforced by the 95th Division and a half dozen artillery battalions from the Third Army.[61]

Confirmation of the bad news came on the next day at a meeting of the American generals held at Hodges's headquarters at Spa, Belgium. The chiefs had decided that Monty would move northeast from his present position and cross the Rhine. Built up at the expense of the First and Third armies, the American Ninth Army would join Monty's Twenty-first Army Group in the drive east, scheduled to begin after February 10. Hodges's First Army would help Monty in two ways. First, it must protect Simpson's right flank. Second, as soon as possible Hodges must destroy the two dams on the Roer River, directly in front of his present position. Relegated to a minor spot, Patton and Hodges could continue their present drive forward until Montgomery moved. After that, these two armies might continue on if they had sufficient replacements and ammunition. Clearly, Patton and Bradley believed, Montgomery, whose fourteen British divisions "have been sitting in northern Belgium for the last two months without fighting," had won out. "We are all very gloomy," Patton recorded. "It is a mistake. Monty is so slow and timid that he will find a German build-up in front of him and will stall."[62]

Conferring with Bradley and Eisenhower on February 5, Patton withheld his secret from them. He still planned to have Eddy move forward at 1 A.M. on the morning of February 7. "If things work out," he wrote Bea on the sixth, "I may be able to cut Hugh and Bob loose and repeat the Driant show. If I lose I will be where I am now. As usual I am short of men owing to the need of supporting Big Simp." In addition to the previous transfers, the Third Army was to lose the 17th Airborne Division and an Armored Group Headquarters to Simpson's Ninth.[63]

Eddy's corps pushed off into a different problem. Ending the bitter winter, the weather turned unseasonably mild, melting the snows. Water engulfed motor pools and supply areas. By February 4 the Moselle River had risen over a dozen feet, dislodging the floating bridges uniting Eddy's XII Corps and Walker's XX Corps. The Sauer River, which Eddy's corps faced, became a mass of rushing water.[64]

Given these conditions, the attempt of Irwin's 5th Division to cross the Sauer immediately north of Echternach turned sour. The river, whose current raged downstream at twelve miles an hour, was now double its normal width of ninety feet. Using inflatable rubber boats, holding six to eight men, that had been found in a Luftwaffe storehouse, the 5th Division lost about sixty men by drowning.[65]

By the tenth Eddy's XII Corps had about two and a half battalions of infantry across the Sauer, but the raging river, coupled with enemy small arms fire, still prevented the construction of a bridge. In the flooded river the corps had lost over 150 rubber boats. Monty, moreover, was still taking away Patton's troops. On the tenth, protesting the transfer of three of his engineer battalions to Monty, Patton exploded. The Germans had blown up the Roer River dams, stalling Simpson indefinitely. Having only his Second British Army and the First Canadian Army, Montgomery could not possibly succeed. Agreeing, Bradley speculated that Eisenhower might yet revert to the original plan of sending the First and Third Armies towards Coblenz and Cologne. "He referred to the plan for Monty to attack using the 9th Army as the biggest mistake SHAEF had yet made," Patton wrote of Bradley. "The biggest mistake," Patton disagreed, "was when Eisenhower decided to turn the 1st Army north to help Monty at the end of August and cut off my gas. But for that we would have beat the Russians to Berlin."

One of Bradley's comments infuriated Patton. "He also asked me how soon I can go on the defensive. I said that I was the oldest leader both in age and in combat experience in the Army, and that if I had to go on the defensive I would ask to be relieved. He said I owed it to the troops to stay. I said that there was a lot owed to me too. I was very mad."[66]

By the thirteenth the 5th Division had completed what Patton called "a magnificent feat of arms performed . . . under terribly bad conditions of weather and water." Crossing the Sauer into Germany that day, Patton drove along its eastern bank. "The Siegfried line runs right along the river," he told Bea, "with hundreds of pill boxes and submerged barbed wire." Patton saw one pillbox, with an 88-millimeter cannon and a two-meter-thick concrete wall, camouflaged as a wooden barn; another, with three machine guns, lay inside a house. And yet the 5th Division, "veteran troops magnificently led," took these and similar entrenchments. Patton was indeed joyous, observing: "I will be the first over the Rhine yet."[67]

With nothing planned until the seventeenth, Patton decided that both he and some members of his staff needed a rest. With Codman, he left for Paris, where Hughes had gotten rooms for him at the George V Hotel. It was his first leave since October 1942. Ever thoughtful, he sent Gay, who "looks badly," to Cannes for a week's rest.[68]

VI

To Bea, Patton displayed his mastery of the past by calling the American crossing of the Sauer and Our rivers "an Homeric feat." Years later Harkins offered two other examples of Patton's use of history. During the fighting around Avranches, Grow's 6th Armored Division came to a river. "He bivouaced on our side," Harkins related.

> General Patton and I went down and Patton said, "You get your division across there tonight." General Grow was going to let them rest. General Patton said, "Well, if you study history," he said, "I can give you five examples where people stopped on this side of the river and the bridge wasn't there in the morning. Now, I'm going to get two or three divisions across there tonight and then we can take a rest." I asked him why he made Grow do that and he said, "You don't study history just to know the dates." He said, "That's probably the way you did it." I had to agree that that was most of the way I did it. He said, "No, you got to find out what happened. What made the success and what made the failure." He carried that through and I've sort of tried to carry it through ever since.[69]

Patton also used the past to denounce fortifications like that French monstrosity the Maginot Line. Just after the Bulge campaign, Harkins and Patton visited some headquarters. On the way back they stopped to look at the Maginot Line. "They had quite a set-up there," Harkins remembered. ". . . The turrets would come up and the gun would shoot and the turrets would go down. There were underground quarters." Looking over things, Patton commented to Harkins: "This is man's monument to stupidity. The enemy knows where you are and they'll just leave you there."

The prime example of using history also came in France, where Patton carried Julius Caesar's *Commentaries* in his pocket. "You know," Patton later told J. P. McEvoy of the *New York Journal-American,* "that old baldheaded Roman was one of the greatest students of terrain this world has ever seen. Well, all the rivers and hills in France are in just the same spot as they were in Caesar's day. So all I had to do when I was chasing those Krauts across France and we came to a river or a ridge of hills was say, 'Where did that old Roman so-and-so cross or get through?' And then I'd say, 'If it was good enough for Julius it's good enough for George,' and over we'd go."[70]

Now in Paris for a few days, Patton would next have to face the West Wall, the German version of the Maginot Line. On the afternoon of the sixteenth, his first full day in Paris, he went over to Versailles to discuss things with Bedell Smith. Unusually friendly, Bedell told Patton that "my northern effort cannot logistically support more than 35 divisions." Since Smith now had eighty-three divisions at his disposal, he suggested that Patton "be prepared to resume the old offensive through Saarlautern and Sarreguemines," below Luxembourg. When Patton said he could make the attack with five divisions, Smith offered him twelve. "I had never known how great he really was," Patton sarcastically commented.[71]

Returning to his army, Patton fumed over the inactivity of the American forces. On the nineteenth he wrote Bradley, "saying that all U.S. troops except the Third Army were doing nothing" and asking for from one to three additional divisions.

Then, at eleven-thirty, Walker called with a request. Though relatively inexperienced, Major General Harry J. Malony's 94th Infantry Division was prepared, with the aid of an armored division, to penetrate the Saar-Moselle Triangle. Could Walker get General Morris's 10th Armored to help? Patton thereupon phoned Bradley, who was out. He then called Bull at Ike's headquarters and requested the 10th Armored. In a display of military procedure Bull phoned Colonel Edgar H. Kibler, Jr., of Bradley's staff, who in turn called Harkins—Gay was still away. The upshot was that Walker got the 10th Armored for three or four days and specifically to clear out the triangle. That very night the 10th Armored moved up behind Malony's division and got into position for an attack at seven the next morning.[72]

Walker's judgment proved better here than at Metz. On the twentieth the 10th Armored passed through the positions of the 94th Infantry and reached a point three miles from the junction of the Saar and Moselle rivers. By the next day the division was at the Saar, only to find the two bridges over the river blown up. Using the armored division until instructed not to, Walker in midafternoon of the twenty-first told Morris to begin crossing that night. In two days of fighting the Germans lost an estimated three thousand dead and wounded and a like number of captured.[73]

On the afternoon of the twenty-first Bradley visited Third Army headquarters and revealed to Patton and a group of his officers what he knew about coming operations. Reinforced by Simpson's Ninth Army, which would occupy the right of the attacking force, Montgomery's Twenty-first Army Group would finally make its push into the Ruhr on February 23. Arriving at the Rhine, Monty would try to get a bridgehead across it. All the while Hodges would protect Simpson's right, while Patton, in theory at least, would remain still. When the Twenty-first Army Group and the Ninth Army were over the river, Hodges would send his left corps toward Cologne. Reduced to a tertiary role, Patton would advance to Prüm, ten miles inside Germany, and to Coblenz only after Montgomery had crossed the Rhine. "I asked definitely if there were any objection to my making a run for Coblenz ahead of time, or of taking Cologne if opportunity suddenly developed," Patton recorded. "He said there was no objection."

Having returned that day from a week's rest, Gay found Bradley's presentation vague. "There appeared to be no definite plans, as there were many 'ifs' and 'ands,' so to the Staff of the Third Army, it was not clear that higher command had any definite plans. However, this might well be due to the fact that General Bradley did not see fit to divulge everything to the assembled group."[74]

Something Patton called "a new toy," the SHAEF Reserve, added to the annoyance. On the twenty-second Bradley phoned and asked Gay if the Third Army could place two green divisions in the line. Gay assured Bradley that it could. In return, however, Patton must send to the SHAEF Reserve two seasoned divisions. If Patton kept Morris's 10th Armored, he must send back to Ike another armored division, even though, Patton lamented, "all these divisions are properly placed to attack. I just hope something will turn up to prevent my having to do this."[75]

Ever the social lion, Patton tried to gain by wile what he could not get any other way. On Sunday, February 25, he invited Middleton; Walker; Gaffey, who had temporarily replaced the tired Eddy as commander of the XII Corps; and Weyland, who had just been promoted to major general, in for lunch. Bradley happened to call and asked if he and Leven Allen could join the party. "We were delighted," wrote Patton, who immediately began coaching the others on what to say to "sell the idea" of allowing Walker to keep the 10th Armored until, in collaboration with the 65th and 94th Infantry divisions, he took Trier, ten miles inside Germany. Weyland presented the strongest argument. The capture of the airfields near Trier would shorten considerably the distance from his bases to his targets, giving him the equivalent of two additional air groups.

At Patton's headquarters Bradley explained that the Combined Chiefs of Staff had ordered Eisenhower to keep certain divisions in reserve. Montgomery was to make the main thrust into Germany. Bradley agreed, however, to ask permission for Patton to keep the 10th Armored for two more days, starting Monday. Bradley also urged Patton to push east with the VIII and XII Corps to the Kyll River, two miles northeast of Bitburg. Bridgeheads over the Kyll might then be used as departure points for operations against Coblenz and the Rhine. As the conference ended, Patton said to Bradley: "It is my understanding that I have authority to push the attack of the Third Army east to secure the line of the Kyll River . . . and furthermore, if opportunity presents itself for a quick breakthrough by armor supported by motorized infantry to the Rhine River, that I have authority to take advantage of the situation." Bradley replied: "You have that authority." That very day the 4th Armored crossed the Prüm River, seizing two bridges intact, and advanced to within two miles of the Kyll.

Gay aptly summarized the conference.

This meeting was one of the most interesting meetings that the writer of this Diary has ever attended. The writer could not help but think, as he sat there listening to an Army commander and his three Corps commanders pleading for the right to fight and destroy the German Army, what would be the comments in the future by those historians in America who might know that this was the fact.

Koch had estimated that fewer than twenty thousand German troops opposed the Third Army, meaning that the enemy could not stop the advance to the Rhine River. "In fact," Gay observed, "they could not stop the Third Army if they had three times as many troops, providing weather conditions would permit the use of armor."[76]

On the twenty-seventh, as the XII Corps surrounded Bitburg and the XX Corps positioned itself for an attack on Trier, Patton finally praised Bradley. "I called Bradley because we were supposed to stop at dark today if we had not taken Trier. He said to keep on going with the 10th Armored until higher authority steps in. He also said he would not listen for the telephone."[77]

VII

The events of the past two months had heightened interest in Patton, already a celebrity. But at the time Patton was involved with the relief of Bastogne, the newspaper correspondents assigned to the Third Army sent both Gay and Bedell Smith a petition calling for the removal of the Third Army's unpopular public relations officer, Lieutenant Colonel Kent Hunter. At year's end Major James T. Quirk replaced Hunter.[78]

A month after assuming his new post, Quirk finally met Patton. On January 25 he described Patton as

> more than interesting. He is quite tall, baldish, with white bushy eye brows over penetrating eyes, a chin like a rock and a small thin lipped mouth which relaxes into a sort of a grin when he is pleased. The Chief of Staff, General Gay, told me that the general just wanted to "chat" with me and that's just about what he did. He didn't make any long inquiries about my background or qualifications or experience and he did more of the talking . . . He is quite interesting with a very fine historical knowledge, a real consciousness of the fact that he has his place in history. He talks well and easily and is really quite charming. He seems to be very frank and open (he insists that his staff always be fully informed) and he radiated an incurable optimism. He wound up by telling me that I am to come to see him whenever I want anything.[79]

Part of Quirk's job consisted of educating the newspapermen assigned to Patton's army. Some of them, Quirk complained to Chester

Hansen, knew nothing about war. "Many of them," Hansen observed, "have the notion that an Army Commander such as Patton or Hodges simply awakens on a sunny morning infected with the thought of an attack and immediately hurries off to consult with his staff and make it." One reporter even asked Quirk "the function" of Bradley's Twelfth Army Group, "and seemed surprised to hear that it coordinated the activities of the Armies."[80]

Quirk also sorted out and brought to Patton visiting celebrities. On February 27, as an example, they ranged from Butcher to President Roosevelt's press secretary Stephen Early to the journalist Vincent Sheean and finally to the cartoonist Staff Sergeant Bill Mauldin. "The general is going to get a little tired of me," Quirk wrote to his wife.

> This morning he had Jimmy (Vincent) Sheean in for almost an hour giving him a lot of stuff on a piece he is doing on generalship and what it takes to make a leader. He is always interesting and they had quite a chat. Not too long afterward I took over Mauldin, the Stars and Stripes cartoonist, for a little session that didn't take too long but which did tie him up a little. Now he will have another session tomorrow. A general in the field has a tough time because all the floating visitors want to see him just so that they can tell people about it back home. It makes a wonderful thing to stick into a conversation . . . "Now when I was talking to General Patton, he told me etc." I try to steer them away but it is rather hard to do and he doesn't seem to mind. He handles them all very well and they all come to scoff and remain to pray. He is a most impressive guy. I think that they expect some sort of circus performance and are always a little surprised to find out that he knows more about more things than they do. He is the complete soldier and I am sure that he is one of the happiest people in the world right where he is. I am sure that he has no post war ambitions and for that reason he has none of the hokum that marks MacArthur.[81]

Patton's confrontation with Mauldin, whose scruffy, unsoldierly characters Willie and Joe seemed to Patton to undermine cleanliness and morale, had long been brewing. Patton had earlier complained to *Stars and Stripes* about Mauldin, who, stationed in Italy, was beyond his reach.

Then in mid-February Mauldin arrived in France. Hoping to patch things up, Butcher called Gay about a possible meeting between the sergeant and the general, only to learn that Patton was in Paris. When Butcher finally located Patton, in Hughes's office, the general told him: "That fellow's a bad influence on the Army and if he comes into Third Army area I'll throw him in jail for thirty days."[82]

Still, Butcher and Gay arranged a meeting. Following Butcher's advice, Mauldin showed up at Patton's office on February 27 immaculately dressed. "Undoubtedly Sgt. Mauldin is a great cartoonist," Gay observed in his diary, "and much to the surprise of the Author, he is merely a boy." But, as Mauldin reported to his friends when he returned to Rome, he did not change Patton and Patton did not change him.[83]

A *Time* magazine article reopened the wound. Altering the account of the meeting transmitted from Europe, an editor in New York added that Butcher, a navy captain, had "ordered" Patton, a three-star general, and Mauldin to meet and resolve their differences. Patton seemed unconcerned until Butcher read to him the last paragraph of the story, relating Mauldin's belief that neither he nor Patton had budged. "Why, if that little s.o.b. ever comes in the Third Army area again," Patton told Butcher, "I'll throw him in jail." He then described how the anti-war cartoons of Bruce Bairnsfather had hurt British morale during the First World War. Bairnsfather's predecessors of Willie and Joe were Old Bill, a middle-aged Cockney with a bulbous nose and a walrus mustache, and Bert, a blank-faced young man with a cigarette perpetually dangling from his lips. His most famous cartoon—the basis of a Broadway play in the 1920s—showed the two seeking refuge in a shallow shell crater during an artillery barrage. The caption read: "Well, if you knows a better 'ole, go to it."

In April Ike settled the matter. He forbade any general from interfering with or criticizing anything in *Stars and Stripes*. As Butcher put it, Patton lost "the battle of Mauldin."[84]

Such defeats hardly dented Patton's belief that cleanliness and discipline won battles. In 1973, when the Third Army was being phased out, Paul R. Allerup, who served in it for two years during World War II, described what Patton's strictness meant to him and his fellow soldiers. During the winter of 1944–1945, one of the bitterest in Europe in a century, Patton insisted that his men change their socks every day. The soldiers washed them in their helmets. Feet problems crippled other units, but the Third Army had the lowest incidence of trench foot in the European Theater of Operations.

Allerup, who rose from private to technical sergeant, recalled accompanying a group of visiting congressmen, one of whom was Clare Boothe Luce. Spying an approaching convoy of trucks, jeeps, and tanks, the captain in charge of the detail commented: "3rd Army." Asked by a congressman how he knew, the captain answered: "Easy. Look at the trim of those jeeps and trucks. They've all been recently washed. There's only one army looks like that—Patton's 3rd."

Allerup remembered what happened after the Third Army took Erlangen, a tank center deep in Germany. Patton and Bradley came up to inspect the troops. "In my own company alone," Allerup wrote, "incredible as it sounds now, three men were put in the stockade for 24 hours because their pants weren't creased."

Concluding, Allerup displayed pride in having served where he did. "The 3rd under Patton was probably the cleanest, neatest army that ever fought a war. Patton saw to that. And I've always believed that was one of the reasons it was such a damn fine army. We hated the rules. But we never lost a battle."[85]

VIII

On the last day of February Patton revived an echo of the past. He visited the road center of Saarburg, just inside Germany on the west bank of the Saar River. Currently the headquarters of Malony's 94th Division, Saarburg contained the castle of John the Blind, the king of Bohemia who died fighting with the French against the English in 1346. "I was there," Patton had insisted when telling his daughter Ruth Ellen of John the Blind's death. Viewing what was left of the castle, Patton took pictures of it.[86]

The first of March brought good news. At 2:15 P.M. Walker called to tell Patton that the 10th Armored had taken Trier, on the Moselle in western Germany, along with a bridge there over the river. Walker's move had been superb. Crossing into Germany at Saarburg, a dozen miles south of Trier, he had feigned a movement farther south. The Germans sent "all they could scrape together" to stop him. Walker then made a "quick turn to the north," completely surprising the enemy. "In spite of being fat," Patton told Bea, "Walker is good."

Elated, Patton called Bedell Smith with the news. Both Bradley and Smith "were very much pleased," Patton noted about the capture. "Eisenhower was in the room, as I heard Bradley talking to him, but he did not make any statement over the phone, congratulatory or other wise."[87]

On March 3, as Patton planned his next move, Gay, accompanied by Patton's nephew, Fred Ayer, Jr., who was in Europe on assignment with the Federal Bureau of Investigation, visited the battlefronts of the three American armies. Viewing Trier, which still contained German snipers, Ayer observed: "There is not going to be much left of Germany after this kind of thing is over." Of the operation at the Roer River, which Simpson's Ninth Army and Collins's VII Corps of the First Army had just crossed, Ayer wrote: "It did not seem to me that there was enough human courage in the world to try a thing like that." Concrete and steel pillboxes dominated the east bank. A steel dome fourteen inches thick protected the key fort. Still, the Americans captured the forts, proving to Ayer what Patton said all along: "The thing that seemed to stick on the most from all of this was the absolute futility of defense in wartime . . . The strongest defense belt the world has ever known was completely smashed in three days after the attack was launched."[88]

On March 4 Gay noticed what he called the "disintegration of the German forces west of the Rhine and in front of the American armies." Against collapsing resistance, the First and Ninth armies had reached the west bank of the river, and the Germans had moved most of their heavy equipment to positions east of the river.

Abandoning all thought of turning southeast and enveloping the Saar industrial region, Patton urged his troops toward the Rhine. He ordered both the VIII and the XII Corps to establish bridgeheads over the Kyll River, from which an armored division of each corps was to drive northeast over good roads and, he hoped, quickly cover the fifty or so miles from the Kyll to the Rhine. By the fourth of March the 5th Infantry Division of the XII Corps had already established a bridgehead six miles long and three miles wide across the Kyll, and the 4th Armored began to move through the bridgehead.[89]

Over the next week Middleton's VIII and Walker's XX Corps made little progress, but the 4th Armored pushed ahead. On March 5 it drove ten miles, capturing bridges over rivers intact. On that day Bradley, not knowing of the division's rapid advance, called Patton's headquarters and told Harkins he hoped the Third Army would soon be at the Rhine. Harkins kept to himself the information that the XII Corps was almost there.[90]

For the American armies the sixth and seventh of March became notable days. On the sixth the 4th Armored captured General of Cavalry Edwin Graf Rothkirch und Trach, the commander of the LIII Corps. During a five-minute interview, Patton exhibited kindness to the German, asking about his treatment and telling of his own experience in the 8th Cavalry Regiment years before. When Patton asked why the Germans, who were surrendering to the Third Army at the rate of a thousand a day, continued to fight, Rothkirch answered that as soldiers he and his men followed the orders given them.

The seventh proved to be even more noteworthy. At five that afternoon the 4th Armored reached the west bank of the Rhine north of Coblenz. In what Patton called "a very remarkable performance," the division had covered nearly sixty miles in a day and a half. Even more exciting was the news that Hodges's 9th Armored Division that evening had captured the bridge over the Rhine at Remagen. Hitler used the loss of the bridge as an excuse to replace Rundstedt, the Commander in Chief West, with the German commander in Italy, Field Marshal Albert Kesselring.

Hap Gay once told Colonel Martin, Middleton's chief of staff, about a phone call from Sandy Patch after Patton's armor got to the river. " 'Georgie,' " the conversation began. "This is 'Sandy.' Let me be the *first* to congratulate you on being the *last* to reach the Rhine!" Patton's answer was just as sharp. " 'Sandy,' let me be the *last* to congratulate you on being the *first* to be driven from Germany!"[91]

A few days later Henry J. Taylor of the Scripps-Howard newspapers, visiting Patton, added a footnote to the advance to the river. "He was with Tedder the day the 4th Armored broke through to the Rhine," Patton recorded, "and when Tedder saw it on the map he said, 'There goes Patton with another of his Phallic symbols.' Taylor did not know what the word meant, and asked me."[92]

Having arrived at the Rhine, two of Patton's armored divisions began pushing toward Hodges's army. Capturing numerous towns, the 4th Armored and the 11th Armored moved north from Coblenz. In doing so, the 11th took approximately seven thousand prisoners, including a major general and his staff.[93]

But SHAEF quashed Patton's hope for a quick thrust east of the Rhine. Bradley told Patton of the plan being developed for the northern offensive. After clearing out the northern area west of the Rhine, approximately sixty Allied divisions would attack to the east and southeast. Bradley did not reveal who would command this vast army, but the assumption was that it would be Montgomery. "It was further stated that the Supreme Commander was not in favor of this," Gay noted, "but was afraid it would have to be done." Why, Gay asked himself, did Ike not look "back into history when another commander," in this case Pershing, facing the demands of French Marshal Ferdinand Foch to control everything, "pounded on his desk and said, 'No, goddamit, no!', and thereby made history?"[94]

Despite the news, Patton began mapping out his new offensive. Beginning at 3 A.M. on March 13, the XII and XX Corps would wipe out the pockets of enemy resistance south of the Moselle River and west of the Rhine. Then, aided by an attack by Patch's Seventh Army, the two corps would cross the Rhine around Mainz and Worms and dash eastward.[95]

On the night before the attack, Patton thought not about glory but about his men. Lying on his bed in his trailer in Luxembourg City, he told Taylor: "Who do you suppose knows what it means to order an attack and know that in a few hours thousands of our boys are going to be killed or hurt? War is my work and I know I sound sometimes as though I liked it; perhaps I do—how can I tell?—but this war hurts everybody, and at times like this I wish I could just fight single-handed, alone."[96]

Patton considered this the final push of the war. The Germans faced frantic manpower problems. Men sixteen and sixty had been thrust into something called the Volksturm, or Home Guard. Old sailors and crews from the grounded Luftwaffe were now in the ground forces. In Patton's sector only the First German Army, for some reason Hitler's pet, remained intact.[97]

At the meeting Taylor had his own news. The New York office of the United Press had asked him to verify the rumor that Patton had been killed and that the government was hiding word of the tragedy. "You can print that I am not dead," Patton assured Taylor, "and that I do not propose to die at the convenience of Dr. Goebbels." This, he said, was the second such rumor. During the news blackout accompanying the Bastogne operation, a similar story spread to England and to the United States. In the middle of the night one of the local papers shocked Bea, at the farm in South Hamilton, and one of Patton's daughters in Washington, asking if that report was true. The family passed "a bad night and day" until Major General Alexander D. Surles of the War Department "squashed the rumor to them privately." After the fighting in Europe ended, Patton desired only "to go on a Jap hunt out east and help set those overstuffed monkeys on their heads in front of the Imperial Palace. Meanwhile, the report that I am dead, like the report about Mark Twain, is exaggerated."[98]

On the morning of the thirteenth three divisions of Walker's XX Corps launched the new campaign. During the first day and a half the 80th Infantry Division advanced only three miles and the 26th Division but one mile. Calling on the fourteenth to apologize for the slow progress, Walker promised Gay that things would improve within the next twenty-four hours. In his diary on March 11 Gay had prophesied that "initially it will be slow," for the enemy had concentrated its troops in front of both divisions. Ever observant, Gay reassured Walker by repeating his prediction that after three days the attacking corps "would break out and rapidly move towards the northeast."

As it was, Gay looked back at the campaign just ended, running from January 29 to March 12, with pride. Aimed at capturing and destroying the enemy forces west of the Rhine and south of the Moselle, not at advancing beyond the Rhine, the campaign limited the Third Army by establishing a boundary between it and the First Army. Despite the limitation, Gay called the endeavor "highly successful," resulting in the capture of over sixty thousand prisoners and in the burial by the Third Army of over sixty-five hundred German dead.[99]

In the history of Patton and his Third Army in Europe, two pivotal days turned out to be Friday, March 16, and Saturday, March 17, when Eisenhower and Bradley directly and indirectly praised the army. To supplement the 4th Armored, Patton had assigned to Eddy's corps the 11th Armored, now commanded by Holmes Dager. While the 4th was to search for a bridge across the Rhine near Worms or Mainz, the 11th was to drive south beyond the rear of the West Wall.

Arriving unexpectedly with Bedell Smith at eleven-thirty on the morning of the sixteenth, Eisenhower became, in Gay's words, "very highly pleased" at the prospect of "striking the Germans back of the Siegfried Line." Such a move, Ike said, "would save many thousand lives." After Patton described his plan as "the best conceived campaign yet by the Third Army," Ike directed Devers to send Patton an additional armored division, the 12th. For the first time in months Patton, instead of being stripped, welcomed reinforcements.

Emboldened, Gay called Leven Allen with a request. Perhaps like no other army, Patton's had perfected the art of passing an armored division through an infantry division to exploit a bridgehead. "One should note," observed Patton's son, Major General George S. Patton IV, "that the passing thru of an armored Div through an inf. Division is no easy task!" Yet General Patton's armor repeatedly accomplished this feat. Soon, Gay told Allen, the 11th Armored would pass through the bridgehead created by the VIII Corps. Could Bradley spare another infantry division? Allen said he would try to send at least one, probably the 28th Infantry, which had served under Middleton and knew him well. An hour and a half later Allen called back. Bradley had approved the transfer of the 28th. These additions brought Patton's strength to ten infantry and four armored divisions, exactly what it was before the transfer of the 6th Armored and the 4th Infantry to Devers's Sixth Army Group.[100]

On the morning of the next day, the seventeenth, Patton received another pleasant surprise. Attending the Third Army briefing, "Ike paid me the first compliment he has ever vouchsafed." The Third Army did not appreciate its own greatness, Ike said. It "should be more cocky and boastful, because otherwise people will not realize how good the American soldiers are." Newspapers had reported that the German force in front of the 4th Armored was "very weak, but did not mention the fact that it was weak on account of the phenomenal speed with which the 4th Armored has advanced." Eisenhower called Patton not only "a good general but also a lucky general, and Napoleon preferred luck to greatness. I told him this was the first time he had ever complimented me in the 2½ years we served together."[101]

On the eighteenth Patton remained cautious, but Gay foresaw a great victory. Almost along the entire front the Third Army had penetrated beyond the German First Army and had entered the area held by the German Seventh Army, which, down to four divisions, would soon

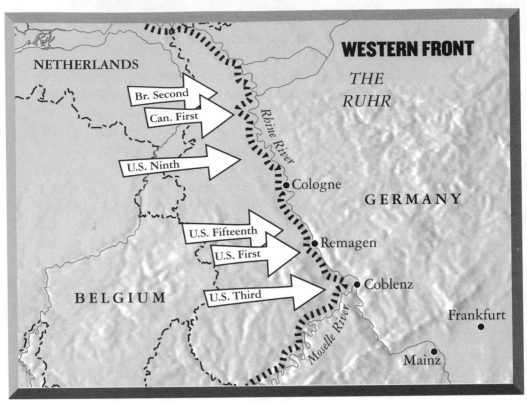

Nearing The End, March 1945

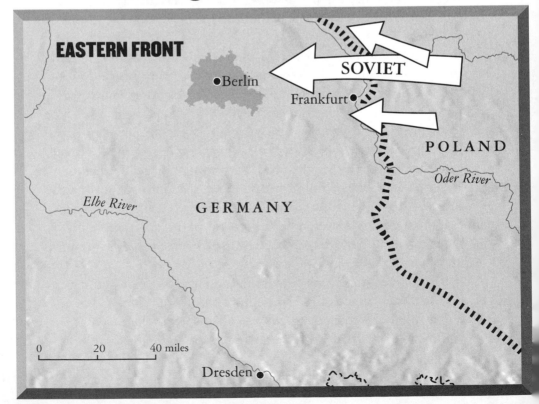

be withdrawn across the Rhine. Spearheading the drive east, Patton's four armored divisions were advancing toward that river. Along the northern boundary of the Third Army the 4th Armored was driving toward Mainz, the 11th toward Worms. The 12th Armored approached Mannheim, twenty miles south of Worms, while the 10th aimed for Kaiserslautern, fifty miles west of Mannheim. These drives would, Gay observed, put "the Third Army behind the Siegfried Line generally across the entire front of the Seventh Army." Gay deduced "that the Germans intend to stick in the Siegfried Line and fight, even though they are being attacked from the front and the rear. This is perhaps due to the fact that they have received orders to fight to the finish in this line, and also probably due to the fact that they do not know the situation, their lines of communication having been disrupted to such an extent that they are practically non-existent." Patton agreed that "If these operations succeed and I think they will, we should bag most of the 1st and 7th German Armies—it will be a great operation."[102]

The next two days brought triumphs. On the nineteenth Middleton called Gay to announce that his VIII Corps had taken Coblenz, an "historic event," Gay enthused, because the city had been the Third Army's headquarters in 1918. On that day the 10th Armored reached Kaiserslautern and the 12th Armored, moving to a point three miles east and six miles north of Kaiserslautern, destroyed a huge number of enemy vehicles and horse-drawn artillery pieces.

On the twentieth the 90th Division of the XII Corps reached the Rhine near Mainz, and the 4th Armored took Worms. In seven days the corps had advanced sixty miles. "On the part of the Third Army," Gay observed,

> the Campaign south of the Moselle and west of the Rhine is now completed with the exception of mopping up. In this Diary several days ago, it was predicted that this attack, which was then being launched, might be the greatest Campaign of the Third Army to date. On this day it can safely be said that it is and has been the greatest Campaign of the Third Army. The entire First German Army has been entrapped, the Siegfried Line has been encircled and taken from the rear, and the amount of German equipment captured and destroyed is stupendous. Students of military history will study this Campaign for many years to come.[103]

Returning from a meeting with Bradley, Patch, and Devers, Patton related that Patch had wanted to bet him a case of whiskey that his Seventh Army would reach Kaiserslautern before the Third. Patton refused the bet, for he knew that the 10th Armored had passed through the town and was already beyond it.[104]

Seventeen

"HAVEN'T YOU LEARNED NOT TO TAKE THIS MAN SERIOUSLY?"

I

Having penetrated to the Rhine River, Patton faced the task of crossing infantry to the east bank. The Germans, he believed, expected the crossing to be made from Mainz, which the 90th Division had reached. Instead, at 10 P.M. on the night of March 22, Stafford Irwin's 5th Division launched an attack at Oppenheim, fifteen miles south of Mainz. By eight the next morning Irwin, his men using assault boats, had six infantry battalions on the east bank of the Rhine. At ten-thirty that morning Devers's chief of staff called to ask about the rumor that Patton's infantry had crossed the river. Since Patton had kept his activities quiet, Gay replied that he could not answer the question and begged to be excused. After the conversation, he went to Patton and suggested that Patton tell Bradley that seven battalions were now over the Rhine.[1]

Not surprisingly, Patton's staff used the momentous event to embarrass Churchill and Montgomery. Extremely pleased by Patton's news, Bradley went on the radio just before midnight of the twenty-third to announce that American forces could now cross the Rhine at almost any point. And they could do this, as Patton's troops had, without the aid of air bombardments, paratroopers, and heavy artillery. The crossing had, moreover, been made with a minimum of casualties, the 5th Division suffering only twenty-eight killed and wounded.

The announcement came just four hours before the broadcast of a recorded speech in which Churchill bragged to the world that Monty and the British had begun to traverse the Rhine. This, Churchill boasted, constituted the first assault crossing of the Rhine in history. Montgomery's move had come only after an artillery bombardment of seventy thousand rounds, an aerial bombardment, smokescreens, and landings by airborne troops. "I think perhaps the credit, or discredit, of this duplicity should go to Colonel Harkins," Gay observed, "as he is the one who first suggested that we announce it late on the night of the 23rd in order to beat the British announcement."[2]

On Saturday, March 24, Patton celebrated the occasion as he had previously done when crossing the Seine. With Eddy, Codman, and Stiller, he "drove to the river and went across on the pontoon bridge, stopping in the middle to take a piss in the Rhine, and then pick up some dirt on the far side as a Seizin in emulation of William the Conqueror."[3]

Amid the Third Army's triumphs, newspapers assigned their top reporters to Patton and his troops. These included Larry Newman of the International News Service, who still carried in his wallet Hearst's check for $250,000 for permission to publish the general's wartime diary, and Cornelius Ryan of the *London Telegraph*. Ryan later wrote two of the most popular books on the Western European campaign, *The Longest Day* on the invasion and *A Bridge Too Far* on Market-Garden. When the columnist Ernest K. Lindley visited the Third Army, he had, Jim Quirk reported, "the common American desire to meet General Patton. They all want to see Patton but I have to sort them out very carefully and only bother with the cream of the crop." At the meeting "the General was his usual brilliant self. Ernie was enthralled, as is everyone."[4]

During the last week in March, two especially important press representatives came to Patton's camp. On the twenty-fifth Margaret Bourke-White, the *Life* photographer, received permission to photograph Patton and Weyland, partners in the advance across Western Europe. Later that week Sid Olsen of *Time* arrived seeking material for a story about Patton, whose picture was soon to appear on the cover of the magazine. Quirk described Olsen's visit:

> I gave him a lot of material, gave him hell about some of the previous articles in Time long ago, and took him over to see the general this morning. The general was as interesting as usual and Olsen was duly impressed. The session had a couple of interesting

things purely from my stand point. We were chatting about one thing or another when Olsen said, "The Major said this morning that the Germans will probably quit when they have lost the last piece of high ground." The general looked at me with a somewhat surprised expression and said, "That's a very intelligent remark. Very intelligent . . . and quite true." He seemed surprised that such a statement should come from a P[ublic] R[elations] O[ffi-cer] and then went on to enlarge on that thesis. A little later when he was talking about Alexander he said, "Now when Alexander crossed . . . not the Euphrates . . . that river in India . . ." I picked him up and said, "The Indus." He peered at me again and said, "yes, the Indus." I better shut my big mouth or he will decide that I am too smart and put me in an infantry platoon where they need brains . . . and blood. It was an interesting session and I hope that the piece will be a good one.[5]

Moving into Germany, Patton received orders to warn the troops about fraternization. Consequently, at the end of March, Quirk delivered his first lecture on the subject. Again Quirk summarized things for his wife.

I spoke very briefly and very much to the point in my best military manner but have no idea of how successful the pep talk will be. Soldiers always look completely blank on such occasions and you don't know whether they are thrilled, interested, bored or completely disapproving. The major factor in their minds is that I pointed out that it costs them $65 per violation and that the best woman in Germany isn't worth that much. That's probably a cold and immoral approach but it is one that the men understand. I think that it was a pretty good talk.[6]

II

As March ended, Patton's armored divisions sliced rapidly into the German interior. On March 25 the 4th Armored captured three bridges across the Main River, one two miles south of Hanau, just east of Frankfurt-am-Main, and two farther south opposite Aschaffenburg.

Moving through portions of the 5th and 90th Infantry Divisions, Grow's 6th Armored advanced that day to within five miles of Frankfurt. "I told Grow that if he did not get into Frankfurt tonight," a jubilant Patton joked on the twenty-sixth, "I would relieve him."[7]

For the British, Patton had only scorn. "The war looks over to me," he wrote Bea on March 29. "We seem to be able to go anywhere though: 'The enemy is still resisting fiercely in front of the British 2d Army.'" That day Patton's units went twenty-nine miles and took another eight thousand prisoners. "They," he said of the British, "went two miles."[8]

But by this time Patton had Johnny Waters on his mind. Captured in Tunisia in February 1943, Patton's son-in-law had been moved from camp to camp, eventually reaching one near Szubin, in central Poland. Then, on February 9, 1945, Captain Ruth M. Briggs, Bedell Smith's secretary, called from SHAEF headquarters and told Gay that with the Soviets advancing toward Szubin, the Germans had shipped Waters westward. The Soviet commander in the area knew Colonel Waters was Patton's son-in-law and would inform Patton of any new developments.[9]

From the Tunisian campaign on, Johnny Waters remained in Patton's thoughts. Butcher told of a brief meeting between Ike and Patton and their staffs in March 1943 during which Patton made his feelings clear. "Patton, who normally hates the Hun—as Ike says, like the devil hates holy water—and who now is all the more embittered because his son-in-law, Johnnie Waters, is reported missing in action—damned the Germans so violently and emotionally that tears came to his eyes three times during the short conference." Two years later Patton told Bea that "I dreamed I was talking to John and that he was wounded in the hand."[10]

As his troops stormed through the triangle formed by the cities of Mainz, Frankfurt, and Darmstadt, and across the beachheads established over the Main River near Hanau and Aschaffenburg, Patton thought more about finding and freeing Waters. Hammelburg, less than forty miles east of Aschaffenburg, housed a prisoner of war camp holding Allied officers. Perhaps Waters had been moved there.

Broaching the subject of a lightning raid to Hammelburg, Patton encountered opposition from Eddy and from Brigadier General William M. Hoge, the new commander of the 4th Armored. As adventurous as

Patton—he had led the unit that captured the bridge at Remagen intact—Hoge joined Eddy in opposing the thrust as Patton envisioned it: about three thousand men and fifty tanks, along with artillery and other supporting units. Because they insisted on a small force, Patton shaved the size down to two companies.[11]

To head the expedition Abrams, who now led the 4th Division's Combat Command B, originally selected Lieutenant Harold Cohen. But Cohen was suffering from piles. Observing Cohen firsthand, Patton remembered that because of piles Napoleon had directed his army at Waterloo from his tent instead of from his horse and had lost the battle. Command of the expedition then went to Captain Abraham Baum, the operations officer of a battalion in Abrams's combat command. Task Force Baum consisted of fifteen tanks, three self-propelled guns, and trucks and jeeps. In all, it contained fifty-three vehicles and 294 men. At Patton's request Stiller went along supposedly as an observer. Asked before the expedition left why he was included, Stiller replied: "Because I'll recognize Johnny Waters, his son-in-law."

In addition to the distance to Hammelburg, Task Force Baum faced several other obstacles. No one knew the route, and Baum had to rely on ordinary road maps. The vehicles, moreover, did not have enough gas for the return trip. They might get to Hammelburg, but how would they get back?[12]

To the Israeli military hero Moshe Dayan, Baum later described his tactics. Ordered by his superiors to push ahead as rapidly as possible, Baum kept moving all the time. "If we see a German," he instructed his subordinates, "we open up with everything we have in all directions. . . . It worked," Baum explained. "I don't know what you're doing in Israel, but I suggest that the moment you come to an obstacle, you open fire in all directions with whatever you have, machine guns, mortars. You shoot and drive, shoot and drive."[13]

As Baum started out, just before midnight on Sunday, March 25, Gay estimated the number of Americans incarcerated at Hammelburg to be between eight hundred and nine hundred. The true number turned out to be twelve hundred officers. After several battles, Baum's men reached the outskirts of Hammelburg on the twenty-seventh. According to two prisoners who were lucky enough to escape and who, on April 4, brought Patton the first news of the expedition and of

Johnny Waters, the German general commanding the camp came to the ranking American officer at 4:10 P.M. on the twenty-seventh and told him an enemy armored column was approaching. The prisoners were free to do as they wished.

The two escapees called treatment at the camp extremely harsh. Each had been captured near Bastogne and had since lost thirty pounds. At the camp breakfast consisted of substitute coffee with no milk or sugar, lunch a gruel of water and potatoes, and supper a gruel of potatoes, carrots, or beets. The guards had been cruel. While the escapees were imprisoned, two American officers had been killed. One had been at the latrine when the air raid signal went off. At the siren the prisoners were given two minutes to get to their barracks. This officer was running toward the barracks when the two minutes expired. The guards shot him. After this, prisoners were permitted to go to the latrine when given permission during air raids, which often lasted several hours. The second American was shot on the way to the latrine because the German lieutenant who had given him permission neglected to inform the sentinels.

The escapees brought word of Waters. He had been one of a group of about a thousand prisoners who had started out from the Polish prison camp on January 19. Marched to Hammelburg, about 325 miles away, the group lost about 40 percent of its members by the time it arrived, on March 5. The two officers knew that Waters had been recently wounded, but they were not sure where and how. As it turned out, he had volunteered to help the German commandant surrender the camp. Marching with his hands up in front of the commandant, Waters was shot by a German sniper hiding in a hedge. The bullet crossed his buttocks, tearing off the lower segment of his spinal column. "I felt very gloomy over the fact that I may have caused Waters' death," Patton lamented after talking to the escapees, "but I believe that I did the right thing, and I certainly could never have lived with myself had I known that I was within 40 miles of 900 Americans and not made any attempt to rescue them."[14]

Baum remained bitter about the whole episode. He hoped to take back with him three hundred of the prisoners, all he could fit onto his vehicles, but as the caravan began moving out of the camp, the Germans unleashed a devastating fire. Within three minutes every vehicle in the task force lay immobile. Wounded, Baum finally met Waters in the POW hospital. During the heavy fire, an unknown number of American prisoners lost their lives.

On April 6 Combat Command B of Major General Albert C. Smith's 14th Armored Division liberated the camp. Sent by Patton to take care of his son-in-law, Colonel Odom accompanied the force. Baum watched from a window as Waters was placed into one Piper Cub airplane. Odom took off in another. He never even bothered to ask about Baum.

Baum's task force had started out with fifty-three vehicles and 294 men. All the vehicles were either captured or destroyed. Nine men were killed and thirty-two were wounded. Sixteen were never accounted for and were presumably killed. No record was kept of the number of American prisoners who died trying to escape.[15]

One student of the Hammelburg raid has emphasized its accomplishments. General of Infantry Hans von Obstfelder later testified that he believed the entire 4th Armored would follow Task Force Baum. The Germans diverted portions of three divisions to the area to meet such an attack. Baum's force, moreover, destroyed German trucks, tanks, and trains. The raid deep into German territory also struck at enemy morale, creating panic among soldiers and civilians.[16]

But these gains could not counterbalance the most unfortunate result of the raid. When the 14th Armored entered Hammelburg, it found only about seventy-five Americans, most of them wounded. The rest had been marched east after the raid.[17]

Resentful, Bradley believed he had been deceived. Asked about the raid, he later said:

> I didn't find out about that until they had been gone two days. And then some newspapermen told me about it and I asked George and he sheepishly admitted he had sent them. He knew damn well if he asked me for permission I would have vetoed it. Because it was a foolhardy thing to do. He lost the whole force. And he swore that he didn't know that his son-in-law was in there but I have good reason to believe he did know it. And it was just a spectacular stunt. If he could have rescued his son-in-law and gotten a lot of headlines about this raid and so forth. But I think it was doomed from the start and it was a foolhardy operation to do.[18]

III

In early April 1945 Robert Reid of the British Broadcasting Company found it impossible to keep up with Patton's tank columns, then racing across Germany. "This is surely the fastest advance in the history of war," he observed, "an advance where divisional command posts make big jumps forward two or three times a day which is some indication of the way things are going out here."[19]

Sid Olsen's *Time* article began with an anecdote reporters covering SHAEF had concocted about the "unpredictable" and rapidly advancing Patton. An Allied officer asked Ike where in Germany Patton was. "Hell, I don't know," Eisenhower answered. "I haven't heard from him for three hours."[20]

During the push Gay painted contrasting pictures of Patton's three corps commanders. He depicted Walker as "always the most willing and cooperative. He apparently will fight at any time, any place, with anything that the Army Commander desired to give him." Gay found Middleton "the most methodical" and "probably the best tactician" of the three. Finally, Gay considered Eddy "very nervous, very much inclined to be grasping, and always worried that some other Corps Commander is getting a better deal than he is, but when the decision is made, he always does as he is told."[21] Worn out, Eddy would soon go the way of John S. Wood.

As the Third Army advanced, German prisoners, surrendering at the rate of over a thousand a day since Patton arrived in France, and displaced persons aggravated things. "It would appear that ample plans for these two things have not been prepared by higher headquarters," Gay, just promoted to major general, observed on April 5, "and it is thought that these problems, as they are worked out, will probably leave a bad taste for years to come. . . . Starvation for a great many German civilians seems to be in the offing."[22]

Although his armies, pending the establishment by politicians of a line of demarcation separating the Americans and British coming east from the Soviets driving west, were supposed to halt from April 5 to April 9, Patton urged his corps commanders "to keep pushing along so as to prevent the enemy from getting set." On the fourth Gay noticed something especially troubling. "What would happen when the Third

Army reached the Czechoslovakian border, which was some sixty miles away?"[23] This early Gay sensed the making of a tragedy.

On the sixth an unusual complication arose. Eddy's chief of staff informed Gay that the XII Corps had discovered a great quantity of German gold in a chemical salt mine in Merkers. To handle the gold and treasure, Ike sent to Germany Colonel Bernard Bernstein, his financial adviser for civil affairs and military government. Bernstein had arranged money matters for Patton during the Sicilian invasion, helping to set up as the currency there the Allied Military Lire.

Bernstein's first problem was finding a storehouse for the treasure. General Lucius D. Clay, Eisenhower's deputy military governor for Germany, told him that during the First World War the Americans had used Cologne as a big depot, but Bernstein thought that Frankfurt-am-Main would be better. There the branch of the Reichsbank sat less than a mile from Ike's projected new headquarters in the luxurious seven-story I. G. Farbenindustrie building.[24]

On April 9, after viewing the salt mine, Bernstein drove over to see Patton. When Bernstein said he considered the branch of the Reichsbank in Frankfurt an ideal depository, Patton answered that it was safe to leave the gold, whose estimated value was about $43 million, where it was. He assured Bernstein there was no danger of the Germans recapturing the area.

> I said to General Patton that I didn't for a minute question the correctness of his statement that the Germans were not going to push him out of this area, but that under the Big Three arrangements this part of Germany would be taken over by the Russians for military government control after the fighting ends and we certainly wanted to get all of this out of here before the Russians get here.
>
> General Patton looked astounded at what I had told him. He said he didn't know that at all, but he would do everything possible to facilitate me in my mission, which he very much did. I felt it was a great honor and privilege to work with General Patton and his senior staff officers on this matter.[25]

The gold matter and the Third Army's proposed advance eastward to the Elbe River thus intertwined, Patton's headquarters issued orders for the resumption of the offensive on April 11. Preparing for the move, which Bradley approved over the phone, each corps commander moved his armor up and placed infantry behind it.[26]

Affirmation of Bernstein's warning came on the day of the attack. When Patton conferred with Bradley and Eisenhower at Bradley's headquarters at Wiesbaden, he learned that his troops were to stop at the west bank of the Mulde River, along a line roughly fifty miles west of Dresden and the Elbe.

Pushing off on the eleventh, Patton's three corps advanced rapidly. To Gay, Walker summarized the movement:

> This is the first time that I, as a Corps Commander, have been completely pleased with the actions of the Divisions within the Corps. I stood on a hill looking down in the valley and saw twenty-five towns burning; I could see the armor of two Divisions moving forward rapidly, and I think the coordination between the 4th Armored Division and the 80th Infantry Division was probably the best in history. Our one difficulty was that we simply bogged down with prisoners.[27]

The next morning at nine Bernstein, obeying orders from Patton, was at the entrance of the salt mine when a jeep, the front of which held a plaque with five stars in a circle, pulled up. Out of the vehicle came Ike, Patton, and Bradley. For well over an hour the four men toured the mine. "I had some bad moments which I didn't reveal to them," Bernstein later related. "We were going down a long elevator shaft on what was essentially a wooden platform that was operated by a German. There were an awful lot of stars there at risk, but we managed to go down to the mine and get back up safely with the German-operated elevator."

Once in the mine Bernstein described to the generals its contents. He pointed to the gold bars, to the gold coins, to the boxes containing almost three billion reichsmarks, and to the valises bulging with loot confiscated by the Germans from the victims in their concentration camps, the first of which, at Ohrdruf, Patton's men had just come across. Bernstein also described the art treasures, which he later estimated to be almost a quarter of the contents of the Berlin Art Museum, and the plates used for printing German currency. "I told General

Eisenhower how I was planning to proceed," Bernstein recalled, "to take an inventory of everything that was there, so that we would know just what we had, and to begin our studies on certain matters, especially with respect to the gold and art treasures, and that I was arranging to move the treasures as promptly as possible to the branch of the Reichsbank in Frankfurt. General Eisenhower approved the entire program."[28]

At one point when they were walking around the mine, Ike noticed some writing on the wall. He asked if Bernstein knew what it meant. Bernstein did not know German, but from his knowledge of Yiddish he was able to make it out: "The State is everything and the individual is nothing." Eisenhower called it "an appalling doctrine."[29]

Anxious to get the treasures out before the Soviets arrived, Patton provided trucks, tanks, air cover, and a battalion of Rangers. Since each truck contained only a driver and a Ranger, who sat up front, Bernstein feared that Germans might try to steal some of the gold as it was being transported. He asked a Ranger colonel if an additional soldier might be placed in the back of each truck. The colonel looked at him and said he thought the Americans could take "our chances with the Germans. These are very tough soldiers," he said of his Rangers.[30]

After visiting the mine, the generals drove to the concentration camp at Ohrdruf. Ike described what he saw as "beyond the American mind to comprehend." Walker, Gay noted, "brought as many soldiers as he could possibly spare to see this, using it as evidence of what they might expect should they be captured by the Germans, and also as an inkling, perhaps, of what treatment should be afforded to people of such sadistic temperaments. Among these soldiers were a group of the 80th Division, which later that day attacked and took the city of Erfurt. The city of Erfurt was badly damaged in the attack by the 80th Division."[31]

That evening, at Third Army headquarters, Eisenhower, Bradley, and Patton discussed the stop line set by politicians. Simpson's and Hodges's armies were to halt near the Saale River, just west of Leipzig. That very day Patton's army, to the south, had reached that river. The Third Army itself would stop going east and turn south. During the conversation, Ike said that he hoped the politicians would not force him to go on to Berlin, for he believed the city had no military value. Moving that far east would force the Americans to care for thousands and thousands of displaced Germans, displaced persons of other nationalities, and recaptured Allied war prisoners. Ever fearful of the Soviets,

Patton replied: "Ike, I don't see how you figure that one. We had better take Berlin and quick and move on to the Oder."[32]

The eventful day ended with another shock. Just after midnight Patton, whose watch had stopped, turned on the radio to get the right time. He immediately heard of President Roosevelt's death. Patton told Ike and Bradley, and "we had quite a discussion as to what might happen." The conversation centered on Harry S. Truman, whom neither the party politicians nor the Lord had ever intended to be president.[33]

Meantime, Patton's men uncovered, four miles north of Weimar, the concentration camp at Buchenwald. On Saturday, April 14, after walking through the place with Codman, Walker, and Lieutenant Colonel George R. Pfann of Patton's staff, Gay observed:

> The sight of dead men does not affect the writer of this article, as during the last two and a half years he has seen many—in fact, too many. But the sight and the stench of these living dead (because this is exactly what they were) was entirely too much for his stomach to stand. . . . No race and no people other than those which are strictly sadists could commit crimes like these.

The few instances where Americans had shot prisoners were, Gay believed, "kind" compared with the atrocities at Buchenwald.[34]

Following Patton's suggestion, Ike sent as many newspaper reporters and radio commentators as possible to view the horrors. "The big junketers are here," Quirk, a former broadcaster, told his wife on April 18. Lowell Thomas and John W. Vandercook of the National Broadcasting Company, Howard Barnes of the Columbia Broadcasting System, "and a couple of others that you probably never heard of," were already at Patton's headquarters.

> They visited Buchenwald today and found it so bad that they stayed about three minutes and got right out again. I'll admit that it is the most horrible spectacle ever seen by men but they are supposed to be reporters and should be able to take it without turning pale and gasping like gold fish. I can't imagine what would happen if they ever heard a shot fired or saw a guy that had just stepped on a mine. They will go back home without ever having seen the war but their broadcasts will probably be something.

Radio commentators are oracular enough without having the additional feeling that they know all because they were in some rear area in Germany.[35]

After the bitter winter, through which the men suffered terribly, Quirk found spring in Germany haunting. "It could be lovely except that in some of those green woods are places like Ohrdruf and Buchenwald to mar all the beauty of it."[36]

IV

His army stationary, Patton flew to Paris on the seventeenth with a group that included Codman and Odom. With Odom he twice visited Johnny Waters, who had been taken to a hospital there, where he was improving rapidly.[37]

But even as the war was ending, all was not well. Everett Hughes met Patton at the airport and played tennis with him. The two then talked into the night. "Geo sore because Ike had cursed him out for taking a gold mine in Russian territory," Hughes related in his diary. Patton also spoke about Jean Gordon, with whom, Hughes assumed, Patton was carrying on. Hughes's own writings, however, indicated that Patton, who had last seen Jean in Paris that February when they had dinner with Codman and Hughes, had no idea where she was. "Sore at Jean," Hughes noted of Patton, "because she promised to be there [in Luxembourg]. She is here! Bea heard it before Geo did and wrote him. Hell to pay."

His wife's letter no longer exists, but Patton's answer to it does. "Don't worry about Jean," he reassured Bea as March ended. "I wrote you months ago that she was in this army. . . . I have seen her in the company of other Red Cross several times but I am not a fool so quit worrying."[38]

At breakfast the next day Hughes noticed a front-page article in the army newspaper on a different subject. Three times he had to tell a disinterested Patton to look for it. "Geo gets promoted," he observed, "and I have a hard time getting him to read the news in Stars & Stripes. He is soon to be promoted as an after thought. I don't blame him [for being upset]."[39]

If any of this bothered Patton, he did not show it. After his return from Paris, Carter found him "very genial." As usual, Carter reported, Codman bore the burden of the promotion. "He was terribly busy getting the general his fourth star sewn on—wasn't that good news!"[40]

With the war ending, Patton asked General Marshall to use him against the Japanese. "I also am of such an age that this is my last war," he argued, "and I would therefore like to see it through to the end."[41]

That April Patton turned to Gilbert R. Cook, now assigned to the headquarters of the Army Ground Forces in Washington, to "work it to get me to China." Cook, however, was discouraging. "Just after receiving your letters," he answered, "I began working on it." He had spoken to General Joseph Stilwell, now in Washington, and to Major General John E. Hull, the chief of Marshall's Operations Division.

> The major point raised adversely is that your type of fighting is suited for operations against the Germans but not necessaruly against the Jap. It was pointed out that the tempo of combat against the Jap is much slower, because he holes up in caves and dugouts, fighting to the bitter end. The operations against him, consequently, must be conducted more methodically and carefully; otherwise the cost in casualties will be prohibitive.

Cook suggested that his friend have his staff work out a plan of operations against the Japanese. "You personally wrote three or four very fine letters in England on your conception of staff and tactical operations prior to 'D' day. I suggest that you sit down now and write personally a new one on your tactical conceptions. Send me a copy. I might be able to put it to some use. The War in the Pacific, if conducted slowly, may last just long enough for you to be called upon to end it."[42]

In his letters Patton passed on to Cook unfortunate news. Eddy, who had been with Patton since the Tunisian campaign and had succeeded Cook as commander of XII Corps the previous August, "has cracked up, and we will have to send him home." To replace Eddy, Patton picked Red Irwin, who had been with him since serving in Africa as the artillery commander of Eddy's 9th Infantry Division.[43]

Those who had served in the 4th Armored Division thought Patton might have replaced Eddy with another great soldier. On the day before

Irwin took over the XII Corps, John S. Wood, exiled to Fort Knox, where he was training tankers, begged Patton for a post. "No one regrets more than I that you are where you are," Patton answered his friend, "but you should take tremendous pride in the fact that through your efforts the 4th Armored Division is certainly the outstanding armored outfit in the American Army." Patton concluded with a comment that he must have known would never be realized: "We may yet get together in China."[44]

Dager, who in March had replaced Kilburn as commander of the 11th Armored, saw no reason that Wood should not be in Europe. "ONE THING not another Major Gen. in the U.S. Army can point to as HIS contribution to the War, what you can—that's the 4th Armored Division," he wrote Wood. "YOU built it, trained it, and fought it. No one can ever take THAT from you." With the war ending Dager, whom Wood called "one of my generals & one of the best ever," lamented the "flatfoot pace with a restraining line every 5 kms. . . . If I survive this 'creeping paralysis advance' we hope to settle in our final 'area' soon."[45]

Perhaps Abrams best described what Wood meant to the 4th Armored and to Patton's army.

> Whatever facility we have handling our equipment you taught us, the fighting heart you instilled in us, the unwavering belief that any task could be done if we just copied from yourself. I have heard it said that you left the Division—you never left and never will. You are so indelibly a part that even persistent "time" could not take you away. The other night there was a noisy party—in the midst of the music, laughter & talk {Lieutenant Colonel George L.} Jaques arose and wanted to make a toast. Those who could hear him requesting silence booed him and the noise went on. Jaques spoke again. "I propose a toast to Maj. General John S. Wood." There was silence, every officer rose and joined the toast.[46]

Wood, however, would never again see combat. As brilliant and opinionated as ever, he continued, for the next twenty years, to serve in government posts and to comment on wars and the people who fought them, especially to his friend Liddell Hart.

V

On April 18, the day Patton returned from Paris, troops of the 90th Infantry Division crossed the border of Czechoslovakia, still under German domination. "This is a new country for the Third Army to enter," Gay observed. Told not to mix with the Germans, some members of the division carried on their jeeps the slogan: "On to Czechoslovakia and Fraternization."[47]

On the next day Ike, at a meeting at Bradley's headquarters, told Patton he was not to advance to meet the Soviets, marching northwest from Vienna. "This is a definite restraining order," Gay noted, "and probably has a political background." Patton's corps commanders had already indicated that they faced slight opposition and that their armored units could penetrate fifteen miles a day. On that day Dager's division had, in fact, moved forward twenty miles.[48]

Czechoslovakia and the restraining line were on Patton's mind when, on April 25, Lewis W. Douglas, the economic adviser to General Clay, arrived at Third Army headquarters. He had already visited Simpson, who spoke with regret about the order from SHAEF to pull back after his men had crossed the Elbe. Patton was even franker. His troops were now engaged in what he called "a phony war," having advanced as much as 107 miles in four days. Walker's corps was now at the Danube. His army, Patton told Douglas, should advance into Czechoslovakia, capture Prague, and then continue on to Moscow. Douglas countered by recalling Napoleon's disastrous Russian campaign, but the talks with Patton and Simpson induced him to recommend that the Americans be allowed to enter Czechoslovakia and that the British be permitted to move into the Baltic countries. According to Douglas, *"dear Lucius got livid with anger and made the observation that the Soviets were our companions in the postwar period, that they would behave as we expected them to behave."*[49]

Not until May 4 did Patton receive orders to proceed northeast into Czechoslovakia. Even then the movement was to be limited, for Bradley authorized Patton to advance only to a restraining line through Karlsbad, Pilsen, and Ceské Budejovic, each between fifty-five and seventy-five miles west of Prague. Bradley wondered if it were possible to begin the attack on the sixth, and Patton answered that he could start on the fifth "without fail." Gay immediately called the XII Corps and asked when the 5th Infantry, the 90th Infantry, and the 4th Armored could advance toward the restraining line. Irwin's chief of staff responded: "Before 0700 tomorrow morning." Asked by Gay if he needed any further instructions, the chief of staff replied: "Hell, no! We are practically on our way." Instructing the chief of staff of the V Corps, just assigned to Patton, to move the next morning toward Pilsen, Gay received a similar response. Gay recorded these conversations because he wanted future historians to see

> how easy it is to throw into action trained and battle scarred units. For instance, the three divisions in the XII Corps, namely, the 5th Division, 90th Division and 4th Armored Division, are probably three of the best divisions in the world today—all full strength, all seasoned by months of combat, all well led and all have been successful. I cannot help but think if in Tunisia in 1943 we had had divisions like these, what would have happened to the German army at that time. Also it is my belief that this is probably the last time in this war against Germany when the Third Army will put its troops into action on short notice. During the past months, in fact, since 1 August 1944, this has been repeated on many occasions, but as the Army Commander said last night, "We will probably never do this—again—at least, not in Germany."[50]

On the fifth Patton's men pushed into Czechoslovakia, but the restraining line led to tragedy. Hearing a British Broadcasting Company announcement that American troops were approaching from the south and west, the Czechs in Prague revolted. Not knowing of the stop order, Prague radio broadcast appeals from the Czechs for the Americans to come to their rescue and saying that they could hold out against the SS until the Americans arrived. "I felt a little badly," Quirk told his wife, "because I knew that our 4th Armored had a phase line that would stop them far short of Prague. That was a little tough on the Czechs." German tanks answered by patrolling the streets and wantonly firing into homes, killing fifteen thousand Czechs. On May 6, with his reconnaissance units near Prague, Patton asked Bradley for permission to push into the city, but he was again told not to advance beyond Pilsen. "I was very much chagrined," Patton wrote, "because I felt, and still feel, that we should have gone on to the Moldau River, and, if the Russians didn't like it, let them go to hell." As it was, the Soviets, taking two and a half days to travel from Berlin, did not reach Prague until Wednesday, May 9. Despite the slaughter of Czechs, the Soviets now portrayed themselves as the liberators of Prague.[51]

Like almost everyone else on Patton's staff, Quirk spent Monday, May 7, tracking down stories of peace. Hearing a rumor that Germany had surrendered, he rushed over to Patton's morning briefing, which was also attended by Undersecretary of War Robert Patterson, an ardent admirer of the general. After the briefing Quirk and Harkins went to see Gay, who confided to them that the Germans had surrendered, effective one minute after midnight on the morning of May 9. Pending announcements by the Allied leaders, no one was to say anything. As of eight o'clock on the morning of the seventh, Patton's Third Army had been ordered to "cease fire and stand fast." The last of Patton's units to advance was supposed to have been General Horace McBride's 80th Infantry Division. Weyland's fighter-bombers were already in the air, preparing to attack at 8:45 A.M. enemy positions in front of the 80th when they were called back. While Quirk was in Gay's office, Major General Harold Blakeley, the commander of the 4th Infantry Division, came in. "He is a fine looking soldier and a very pleasant person," Quirk informed his wife. "He said, 'This is very embarrassing. Here we are with a big army and no war. I suspect that in the next couple of months we may wish that we were back in a nice, clean fight again.' On that note I left."[52]

Going to the press camp, Quirk called together the reporters covering the Third Army and, under the veil of secrecy, told them what he knew. About two that afternoon, listening to radio programs from the United States on three or four stations, he heard an Associated Press report giving the details of the German surrender. Four hours later Ike's headquarters called and informed Quirk that no Associated Press correspondents in Europe were to be allowed to file "any copy at all." That midnight Quirk learned that only Ed Kennedy of the Associated Press was barred. "I knew then that he had broken the embargo."[53]

Patton's briefing early the next morning was, Quirk reported, "a rather sad affair. It followed the normal formula but there was not much to say." After the session, an emotional Patton got up and gave his farewell speech to his staff, saying in essence: "This is our last briefing in Europe. The war is over for us here. I think that I have had to do less work than any army commander in history, because each one of you on the staff has performed so well. I thank you very much and I congratulate you on what you have accomplished." He then put on his helmet and, while "we all stood stiffly at attention and were for a moment very proud," left the room.[54]

At eleven-thirty that morning Patton met for the final time with the reporters covering his army. "He was in very good form," Quirk wrote home, "very witty and very good and they all enjoyed their last meeting with him. He had little to add to what I had already told them but they always enjoy listening to him. After that was over we made the class picture with the general on the steps and he was very patient." As a sign that the Third Army was no longer news, some of the newspapermen left on the afternoon plane for Paris. "The whole army is downcast and dispirited," Quirk noted. "So am I. *I can only wonder what I shall get up for tomorrow.*"[55]

Halfway across the globe another bitter note for Patton occurred on May 8, the day John Hersey won the Pulitzer Prize for his novel *A Bell for Adano*. Basing, as he admitted in 1987, the character General Marvin on Patton, Hersey, who covered the Sicilian campaign for *Life,* always viewed both the fictional and real-life generals as the incarnation of military evil. Hersey's opinion of Patton, who among other things in Sicily ordered shot and thrown into a ditch—or was it off a bridge?—a mule that blocked a road, ranged even lower than that held by John P. Marquand. "But I can tell you perfectly calmly," one character in the novel says, "that General Marvin showed himself during the invasion to be a bad man, something worse than what our troops were trying to throw out."[56]

To one observer Patton seemed more concerned with saving horses than with saving human beings. On May 7 Patton and Judge Patterson attended a performance by the Spanish Riding School, which had been located in Vienna for four centuries before the troupe fled 250 miles that March. As the performance ended, Colonel Alois Podhajsky, the troupe's leader, rode up to the general's box, doffed his two-cornered hat, and asked Patton to place the school under military protection. After conferring with Patterson, Patton agreed to the request. He flew Podhajsky to Hostoun, Czechoslovakia, where the colonel retrieved the school's Lipizzaner brood mares, foals, and breeding stallions, all driven north by the Nazis early in the war.

Even though he consented to help the riding school, Patton considered the episode "rather peculiar." With "a world tearing itself apart in war, about twenty middle-aged men in perfect physical condition, and about an equal number of grooms, had spent their time teaching horses tricks. As much as I like horses, it seems to me there is a place for everything." This did not stop a member of the family of Secretary of the Treasury Henry Morgenthau, Jr., from commenting, most unfairly, that Patton "became more interested in corralling and repatriating strayed Lipizzaner horses . . . than in the plight of the DPs."[57]

VI

With the war over, General McAuliffe, now in command of the 103d Infantry Division, occupying Innsbruck, found fraternization a problem. "These Austrian girls are perfectly beautiful," he commented, "blond and sunburned and gay. Oh, they were most cordial and gave us a very hearty welcome. . . . Initially, I permitted the Austrians to go to the same shows with the American soldiers, the feeling was so cordial, but when General Patton heard about it, he raised hell about it because Eisenhower still had this silly idea about not fraternizing with the enemy. So, we'd give the show on two nights, and the Austrians would attend on one night and the Americans the other."[58]

Like Patton, McAuliffe entertained dreams of being sent to the Pacific. Patton, however, discouraged him. "He told me I was a damned fool to take on any such thing," McAuliffe recalled, "that I'd get a bad deal from MacArthur, and I said, 'Never mind, I'd like to do it anyway.'" Patton then said he would help, but the war in the Pacific ended before anything happened.[59]

Even though he discouraged McAuliffe, Patton continued to push for an assignment against the Japanese. In a long letter to Cook he explained why he and his staff were well suited for the Pacific war. Good friend that he was, Cook then summarized Patton's arguments and sent them to his West Point classmate, Major General Stephen J. Chamberlin, MacArthur's assistant chief of operations.[60]

Cook did not trust his letter to the mails. Instead, he gave it to Major James Gerard, who carried it across the Pacific to another of Cook's classmates, Colonel Henry C. McLean. "It does not take great penetration to observe that MacArthur does not want Patton to come to the

Pacific," McLean noted in his diary. "He does not want anyone who will steal the limelight or any of the glory from him. It would be very easy to do, as Patton has plenty of color and appeal which MacArthur lacks." The United States had a million and a half men in the Pacific. Yet MacArthur treated the theater as his "private preserve." He had just accepted Hodges for assignment in the Pacific, but, McLean observed of Hodges, "He had no color and no dash and very modest ability. No competition was in prospect."

Even Quirk conceded that MacArthur possessed good reason for not wanting Patton and his staff nearby. He explained why to his wife:

> The Pacific situation could be very interesting. MacArthur has been in control and has very successfully played down all his subordinate commanders who have done all the fighting. Patton would be rather hard to play down. We have learned a few things here and I think that we could give MacArthur a run for his money. We have never built up Patton at the expense of anyone and our divisions have gotten more credit for what they have done than those of any other army. That's the Old Man's policy and we have fought for it and won with higher Headquarters. He is a great man for passing the credit around and he always has been. I have no special yen for the Pacific, but I know that we could keep MacArthur's PRO awake a few nights worrying about us. We have learned what we can get away with and I have always been willing to take chances and haven't tripped too hard yet. Higher headquarters frequently disapproves of us but we are usually within our rights, at least technically. The passing around of the credit is one of the reasons for the high morale of our troops.[61]

After reading Cook's arguments, Chamberlin answered as both Quirk and McLean suspected. "Unfortunately the Army Commanders had all been selected prior to receipt of your letter and there was no opportunity to push Patton forward," Chamberlin told Cook. MacArthur had fought his campaigns with General Walter Krueger in charge of the Sixth Army and Patton's classmate, General Robert Eichelberger, leading the Eighth. He had recently agreed to give his old friend Stilwell command of the Tenth Army "for special reasons over which we had little control." This left no room for Patton.[62]

Meantime, Patton, like so many officers in Europe, indulged in well-deserved luxury. On the second of May he moved into the palace of Prince Albert, on the southern edge of Regensburg in Bavaria. Ten days later Carter and Codman visited him. "I've never seen such a conglomeration of furniture, bibelots, silver, paintings, etc.," Carter informed his wife from Paris. "The Patron [Patton] was in grand form & arranged for me to fly back here—he took me part of the way himself & flew the plane some of the time which was rather terrifying as he circled bombed out cities very low to show me the ruins." With Stiller back in the United States after being rescued from a German prisoner of war camp, Codman, now Patton's sole aide, "still doesn't know how to get out of his present job."[63]

Codman was among those who attended the banquet given for Patton on May 14 by Soviet Marshal F. I. Tolbukhin at an Austrian palace. To his friend James Wadsworth, Patton described the scene.

> I took my smartest outfit along as an honor guard. We looked pretty good, but those Russians had gone us two or three better! They had swept the whole twelve miles of road clean and strewn it with *rose petals*. There was a sentry at present arms every hundred feet. They flew the whole Moscow ballet down to entertain us. The party that night was pretty tough. But I drank some olive oil to coat my stomach for the drinking bout I knew would happen. At the end the Russian marshal was lying under the table, and I walked out on my own two feet. . . . We shouldn't have stopped. We should have gone on and taken those Russians. They're out to conquer the world![64]

After speaking to General Keyes, Bea's brother Fred left another account of the affair.

> The palace, General Keyes said, was one of the handsomest and most beautifully furnished buildings he saw abroad; the dining room to seat about 100, oriental rugs, beautiful tapestries and everything to go with it. However, he said, at the banquet, which was a sit-down affair, they used neither plates, knives nor forks. They grabbed the food in their fists out of platters arranged in the center of the table. If they got a mouthful of bones or anything

else they didn't like, they just spat it right out on the table, and since some general next to him did not particularly like some tart or other sticky item, he just slapped it over his shoulder against the tapestry behind him. After they arose from the table, General Tolbukhin, then very tight, wished to drink a special toast with George, which was done by locking arms and drinking, so to speak, over the other fellow's elbow. Tolbukhin was just able to swallow his drink and slid to the floor unconscious. George turned on his heels, said, "We must hurry to catch that plane," and walked out.

None of these accounts mentioned the most intriguing part of the story. Patton supposedly took with him to the banquet Doris Duke, the tobacco heiress often referred to as the richest girl in the world. Having known Patton from his second stay in Hawaii, where she had given him a gift of polo ponies, Doris was now one of Hearst's correspondents. Bumping into the heiress at the Linz, Austria, airport, Patton invited her to come along. "Patton would go for someone like her in a minute," Coy Eldund, an officer at Patton's headquarters, informed Stephanie Mansfield, Duke's biographer. "He was socially conscious. He had a lot of well-to-do friends. He liked the celebrities. And Doris was somebody." At the banquet Tolbukhin supposedly pinned a medal on Doris and kissed her on both cheeks. After that, according to Tex McCrary, then an air force public relations officer and later a radio personality, Patton and Doris spent four days together, an intriguing observation considering that Patton and his entourage left on the sixteenth for Paris and London. Ironically, Doris Duke's first husband, James Cromwell, was the brother of Louise Cromwell, the Jazz Age symbol for whom General Pershing abandoned Nita Patton.[65]

While Patton lived in the palace in Regensburg, Quirk, Koch, Codman, Carter, and other important members of his staff stayed in "a very attractive Bavarian chalet with a gorgeous view of the Alps." Shortly after moving in, Codman and Carter, at the invitation of Prince Felix of Luxembourg, drove to the castle of the grand duchess for a visit. "It's a huge grim place in the mountains," Carter observed, "& we were enthusiastically greeted by the old Luxembourg agent & his daughter, who told us the Nazi supervisor was still living in a wing. So Charley had him arrested." Looking over the wing occupied by the Nazi, the Amer-

icans found "all the contents of all the Munich museums! It was unbelievable—pictures piled to the ceiling—you'd turn one over & it would
be a Rembrandt or a Rubens, there was even a huge room full of cases—
it was a complete dinosaur!"[66]

On the sixteenth Patton, accompanied by Hughes, Codman, and
George Meeks, left for Paris and then London. In London a telephone
call to his friends Alfred Lunt and Lynn Fontanne produced two tickets
to their latest play, which Patton described as "most amusing." Emerging from the theater, Patton found the street for about three blocks "a
solid mass of people waiting to see me, and there was much yelling,
handshaking, etc."[67]

The next day Patton received a phone call from General Bull. Eisenhower wanted to see him. At Reims Ike told him that the Yugoslav
Communist, Marshal Tito, "is raising hell at the north end of the Adriatic." General Marshall wanted Patton, with at least five armored divisions, "to bluff him." Ever suspicious, Patton hoped that the Soviets
were not using Tito "as a red herring to pull us to the south so that the
Russians may resume an offensive in Central Germany."[68]

As important as this was, the War Department had other plans for its
top European names. Teaming an airman with a ground general, it
scheduled for each pair a tour of the United States: Eisenhower with
Spaatz, Bradley with Vandenberg, and Patton with his fellow Californian, Doolittle. Despite Quirk's pleas that he be allowed to go along,
Patton took home with him only Codman and Meeks. Quirk, who thoroughly understood Patton, thought this a great mistake, for, Quirk told
his wife, the general was already skirting trouble.

The Old Man made a trip to London and then came back here to
make faces at Marshal Tito on the Jugo-Slav border. Tito went
back home and that worked out very well. Now he [Patton] is on
his way to Los Angeles for an appearance and many of us, especially I, are scared to death. He will be all right on the set speeches
but I am just frightened that he will come up with one or two of
his Pattonisms and they won't be understood by people who don't
know him. Here we had a lot of safeguards and controls and he
got to know that we were always backstopping and that he could
speak freely and he did. All he has to do in the States is come up

with a crack like, "The SS are just like the Democrats in America" or "We shouldn't worry too much about the guards of the concentration camps. We could find enough bastards in America to run places like that." OR "For God's sake don't say that I said the war will be over soon or every son of a bitch in America will quit work." I hope that he doesn't say anything like that but he has and he might. I am not sure that my being there would help matters but it might.[69]

When Patton reached Paris Hughes found him "scared to death about going home." The newspapers were full of stories about Patton bringing Doris Duke to Tolbukhin's palace. Even Bedell Smith needled Patton about the incident. An embarrassed Patton told Hughes he "doesn't know how she got there." Tolbukhin, in turn, said he thought Duke was an army officer on a diplomatic mission.[70]

On Thursday, June 7, Patton and Doolittle landed in Boston. "New England had rarely seen anything like it," reported *Time,* as 750,000 people jammed the twenty-mile route from the airport to downtown Boston. Patton was, the magazine observed, the "24-star general," sporting four stars on his shiny steel helmet, four on each shoulder and each collar, and four on the black handle of his pistol. That night Patton spoke to a dinner gathering that included his wife, his two daughters, and his son. After talking about the heroic dead he left in Europe, he sat down and cried. Recovering his composure, he lit a big cigar.

Two days later 130,000 people crowded into the Los Angeles Coliseum to honor Patton and Doolittle. In a show put together by the Hollywood producer Mervyn Le Roy, Edward G. Robinson spoke as Patton would have on the eve of battle, and Humphrey Bogart portrayed Doolittle briefing his famous Tokyo raiders.[71]

Doolittle remembered one episode involving Patton at the coliseum.

Georgie had said something a little out of order on the radio, and on the podium they had a little guy sitting under the podium with a switch to turn Georgie off if Georgie said anything he shouldn't. There were just thousands and thousands of people out there, and Georgie started out by saying, "If I were to say what I think about the Japanese, I would be taken off the air, but I do want to tell you that these . . ." and then he went into "little dirty So-and-sos" and this guy was busily engaged in shutting him off, but he was too late. Georgie had it out.[72]

Another incident took place the next day. At the Episcopal Church of Our Saviour at San Gabriel, where he had been baptized and confirmed, Patton sang "Onward Christian Soldiers" with the Sunday school children and then told them: "In my opinion there will be another war because there have always been wars. . . . You are the soldiers, sailors and nurses of the next war if we don't stop wars."[73]

Reading the Los Angeles papers, Frank McCarthy was shocked. According to the press, McCarthy told General Marshall, Patton's coliseum speech had been full of "bombast and profanity." He had been quoted as saying "that men were frequently fools when they got killed in battle and that it is quite safe to go into modern battle." Patton was now on his way to Washington. "It seems extremely important to me, therefore, that you see General Patton at the earliest possible opportunity and reiterate very forcibly the comments you made in the letter which you sent to him upon his arrival in the U.S."[74]

At the War Department on the morning of Wednesday, June 13, Secretary Stimson was at his desk working on a speech when Marshall stuck his head in and asked if the secretary "had a moment to see him. I said 'Yes,'" Stimson recorded, "and went on writing. When about two minutes later I looked up, there was a tall figure standing in front of my desk who had come in silently and was standing there at attention waiting for me to look up. It was General George Patton." The two "had a short little talk," during which Stimson invited Patton and his daughter Bea to dinner. He later "got hold" of another former aide now back in the United States, General Eugene A. Regnier, who had led Combat Command A of the 5th Armored Division, and invited him to dinner.

Although he had a "long day," Stimson enjoyed the evening. "It was Mabel's birthday," he noted of his wife, "so I proposed a toast of champagne to the two Generals and Mabel. Then there was great excitement. They hadn't realized that it was her birthday and we interchanged more toasts and we had a very cheerful evening together. Mabel looked very pretty in her light dress, and both Gene Regnier and George Patton were very open in their admiration."[75]

Stimson awakened on Thursday, June 14, apprehensive because Patton was to join him at his news conference. He "knew that there would be a good deal of care and deliberation and earnest attention necessary to keep him from shooting off with something that the press would seize upon and make a row." Stimson had "talked it over with him a little the night before," and as soon as he got to the War Department he conferred with Patton, Regnier, and several of his advisers, including Harvey H. Bundy, his special assistant, and Major General Alexander D. Surles, the army's chief public relations officer and an old friend of the Pattons. Stimson described the rest of the episode.

> I went over with Patton pretty carefully what he was to say and the subjects he was to take up; also the subjects that he was not to allow himself to be drawn into. So as a result the press conference went off admirably. I cut down my weekly review to pretty short range and then answered some questions and then gave my chair to Patton and asked him to give a talk on tank tactics and several other subjects which I had selected. He did it very well. Instead of being the roaring swashbuckler, he turned into the careful and thoughtful general officer, and I think he made a very good impression on the pressmen who were there. Regnier also came into the press conference and I introduced him, but there was no time for any talk by him and I don't think he particularly wanted to. On the whole, the thing was a great success.[76]

Oblivious to his own weaknesses and to Stimson's desire to protect him, as he had done many times over the years, Patton interpreted the secretary's guidance as censorship. Years later Bea's brother Fred recalled that Patton, before going to Washington, had asked for an appointment with Archbishop Richard J. Cushing of Boston, presumably to discuss the Communist threat in Europe. "The next morning before I had time to do it," Ayer related to Hanson Baldwin, "he phoned me from Washington and told me to call the engagement off as he had been muzzled and would be unable to express his views to the then Archbishop."[77]

Despite his complaint about being muzzled, Patton received an indication of Marshall's high regard for him. In Washington the chief of staff confided to him the greatest secret of the war. The United States had developed, and would soon use against Japan, an atomic bomb.[78]

Patton spent the remainder of his stay in the United States at his home in Massachusetts, but even that did not end the controversies. The *Stars and Stripes* revived things with a fantasy letter from "Private X, one of 30,000 who died under Patton's command." "It is no fun to die," Private X wrote, "particularly when the general you followed turns to the homefolks and tells them you died in vain." Calling cuts in the military budget "stupid," Patton answered that "it's terribly foolish not to be prepared, and I think young people who may have to carry on in another war, should know that many men were wounded or killed, due to lack of preparedness in this war."[79]

Bill Mauldin joined the assault. Now a civilian, he accused Patton of trying to control the thoughts of his men. Recalling his meeting with the general in Luxembourg the past March, Mauldin, whose "Willie" graced the cover of the issue of *Time* that carried the story of Patton's reception in Boston and Los Angeles, announced: "He said my cartoons were undermining the morale of the Army, were destroying confidence in the command, were making soldiers unsoldierly." Wisely, Patton responded to Mauldin: "It is just one of those mosquito bites you are bound to get and I won't make any comment."[80]

Battered by the press, Patton yearned to return to Europe. Of all those close to Patton, Quirk unquestionably understood him the best. Unlike Patton's wife and the Ayer family, all of whom tended to defend the great soldier's every move, no matter how senseless, Quirk separated Patton the Soldier from Patton the Everything Else. From the beginning he considered it a mistake for Patton to take with him only Codman and Meeks. "I just couldn't chisel in on the trip although I tried very hard," Quirk informed his wife from Paris on June 22. Quirk had just seen a cable from Patton

saying that he was in trouble and was coming back here. I don't know how much of what has happened could have been prevented but I am sure that I could have helped had he taken me along. I do know him and understand him and feel that a lot of it could have been headed off. He promised not to make any statements without writing them out and having Charley Codman check them but he and Codman never could seem to understand that his slightest reference would make print. It is really too bad that it worked out as it did but I suspected it and other people did too.

Patton's trouble, Quirk insisted, stemmed from his inability to "be quiet." In Paris "officers and correspondents" accused Quirk of misrepresenting Patton to the public,

> and there is a lot of truth in that. The general is the ideal soldier. . . . Militarily he is incomparable. He has never made a mistake and has never made a bad decision. He has won every fight that he ever had and he can inspire troops to great heights of combat. . . . He has said that he feels that he will be killed in battle and I think that the wish is father to the thought. He is a medieval knight in O{live} D{rab} armor and could probably sign the code of Bushido with no mental reservations. . . . He is pure soldier. He thinks like a soldier, he acts like a soldier, and his reactions are those of a soldier.

Patton, however, was hardly a scholar. Stories that depicted him as one had, Quirk insisted, neglected to mention that his learning covered only

> things military. . . . We can't accept in America the simple fact that greatness may have only one dimension. General Patton is only a soldier but a very great one. His opinions on anything military are invaluable and probably right. His opinions on anything else are valueless and shouldn't be given the slightest credence. In America we have always insisted on asking Henry Ford for his opinions on education and Thomas Edison for his opinions on the hoop skirt or smoking cigarettes. We can't believe that any genius has a peculiar talent. We have to think that he is the fully rounded man, an oracle, an authority on every subject.

Quirk saw Patton as "neither philosopher, politician or saint." In Boston the general had wept at the mention of those who had died, but, Quirk commented, "that is only a surface emotion, and there are no tears in his heart. We made much of the fact that our losses in the Third Army were the lowest of any army." Quirk attributed Patton's regard for life to his belief that he needed men to win, just as he needed tanks and trucks. "There is no room for sentimentality and he knew that. He was a soldier . . . he wanted to win, to kill the enemy . . . and he always did. . . . We must learn," Quirk added, "to appreciate our great men for what they are and know that they are great none the less." Patton's odd "political and moral opinions" no more detracted from his military greatness than the late actress Jeanne Eagels's cocaine addiction "detracted from her art on the stage." In Europe Quirk had stopped reporters from quoting Patton's staements, such as those on labor and on Americans willing to serve as guards at the concentration camps. "They are not good statements and their publication would have produced a terrible storm." Unprotected by Quirk, Patton created a furor by repeating these sentiments while in America.[81]

As Quirk said in his letter to his wife, Patton, reflecting the thinking of William Wood and Charles Fanning Ayer, made anti-union remarks. Labor leaders, in turn, detested him. While the fighting was still going on in France, Judge Patterson sent a delegation of labor officials to Europe to talk to the troops about wartime strikes. An eminently fair person, Patterson feared that management organizations, such as the United States Chamber of Commerce, were feeding the soldiers propaganda about the number and intensity of the strikes back home.

For at least one member of the delegation, Rolland Jay Thomas, the president of the United Auto Workers, the meeting with Patton boiled down to a series of disputes. When Thomas mentioned one of the soldiers the general had slapped, Patton called the man a coward.

> I asked him if he didn't think there was a possibility that the man might have been battle shocked or neurotic. But General Patton said that he didn't believe in neurosis. I said that in my opinion that proved to me that he was a neurotic himself. He raised about six feet off his chair when I said that. He was very proud of carrying his pearl-handled gun and he acted as though he was going to try to intimidate me, but I had credentials from the War Department myself and I just wouldn't permit him to intimidate me.

Another argument developed after some of Patton's subordinates came in and told him where the Germans were.

> I never heard a man use viler language in my life expressing that he was happy that here was where the sons of bitches would be killed. After he went through all this brutal talk I said to him, "In

my opinion, General Patton, I suppose that's what war is but did you ever stop to realize that when you say those things our boys are getting killed too? It seems to me you have no sympathy at all. You're completely brutalized." Of course he claimed that that was the only way a war could be won but yet I didn't think he had to make such a rough approach to it as he was making.

These conversations convinced Thomas "that General Patton, if he had the opportunity, would be violently anti-labor and I told this to the other members of the committee. It was proven to be true because shortly after the peace was signed he came back to the United States and the first job he did was to make a speech in Los Angeles blasting the labor movement."[82]

VII

On Independence Day a relieved Patton arrived back in Paris. "Says he is not going to Pacific while Mac in command there," Hughes recorded in his diary. ". . . Sgt Meeks says family life aint so good." Undoubtedly annoyed at her husband because Jean Gordon was still in France, "B gave him hell—glad to be in Europe."[83]

His wife ill, Codman remained at home. In replacing him Patton did a friend a favor. Over the years the Pattons had kept in touch with Georgie's old flame Kate Fowler and her husband, Van S. Merle-Smith, a World War I veteran and corporation lawyer. Returning to service in 1941, Merle-Smith joined MacArthur's staff as an intelligence officer. In July 1943, however, he broke down physically and, sent home, died that November. Loyal to his friends, Patton had appointed Dick Jenson, the son of one former sweetheart, an aide early in the war. Now, after its conclusion in Europe, he selected as his aide Major Van S. Merle-Smith, Jr., the son of another former sweetheart and of her hero husband.[84]

For Patton the most interesting events of July involved Stimson. On Friday the twentieth Patton came up from his headquarters near Munich and with General Floyd L. Parks, now commanding the Berlin district, dropped in to see Stimson, then attending the summit conference at Potsdam. After reviewing the 2d Armored Division, the members of the party, which included Bundy, McCloy, and Stimson's military aide Colonel William H. Kyle, hastily ate lunch and then drove to the Little White House, the name given to President Truman's temporary residence. Led by the car carrying the president, the party went on to Berlin and the headquarters of the American Group Control Council, which governed the American zone in Germany. "This is a day I shall not forget," Colonel David "Mickey" Marcus, the assistant deputy military governor in Germany, told his wife. With Stimson, Eisenhower, Bradley, and Patton looking on, Truman raised over the headquarters the flag that had flown over the United States Capitol when the Japanese bombed Pearl Harbor. The previous year Stimson had seen this flag raised in Rome. "Next time it will be Tokyo," he vowed. "From the first note of 'Hail to the Chief' until the last note of our Anthem," Marcus commented, "my heart was standing at attention. . . . I felt proud to be one of the Guard of Honor."[85]

On the next morning Patton dropped in to say good-bye to Stimson. During the conversation Bundy pointed to a decoration, the Order of Kutusov, presented to Patton by Marshal Tolbukhin on May 14. He asked why the general wore it, since he hated the Russians. "General Patton's reply," Stimson wrote, "was that when you get a ribbon at a horse show, the best thing to do is to accept it regardless of whether or not you like the judge that made the award."[86]

The following Wednesday, July 25, was for Stimson an exciting day. In the morning he learned that he had been invited to confer with Stalin. The only others present were interpreters. Following that, the secretary and his aides boarded a C-54 and headed for Munich and a visit with Patton. After a parade, during which he awarded the Distinguished Service Medal to Major General Louis Craig, now commanding the XX Corps, Stimson drove around Munich, finding much of it "totally destroyed but the population of Munich, however, were going about their business in a quiet manner." The city's "historical section . . . including the art buildings, was in almost complete ruins."

From Munich, Stimson and his party, accompanied by Patton and Gay, drove thirty miles to Bad Tölz. There Patton had his headquarters in a structure that formed a huge quadrangle. A former school for SS troops, the building contained a riding stable, an ordnance shop, a twenty-five-meter swimming pool, and a mess hall. "The officers' mess and cocktail lounge was comparable," Stimson observed, "to the same facilities in a first rate hotel." Built for the Nazis in 1936, the building passed into American hands two days after the Nazis fled. During those two days displaced persons, "their habits being absolutely filthy," occupied it and did "a lot of damage."[87]

From Third Army headquarters the group drove to Tegernsee, in an area completely untouched by war. There Patton occupied a hillside villa about a hundred feet above the lake that formed "the bottom of a saucer at the base of the foothills of the Bavarian Alps." Max Amann, Hitler's first sergeant in World War I and the publisher of his book *Mein Kampf,* formerly owned the estate, which contained modern furniture and a bowling alley. When the Nazis came to power Hitler had sold Amann a newspaper taken from Jews and worth a billion marks for a hundred thousand marks. Around Tegernsee, Rundstedt, Heinrich Himmler, "and many other notorious Nazis had their summer homes."[88]

During their two-day stay the last evening provided the most controversy. At nine o'clock Stimson, Patton, and the others heard that in the British elections Clement Attlee, the Laborite, had defeated Churchill and would become the prime minister. "The conversation during the evening," Stimson recorded, "was much on the initiative of General Patton who, in his customary way, was outspoken and profane."

Years later Bundy left a more complete picture of what happened.

Patton was throwing his weight around and indulged in a lot of flamboyant talk. Patton and I disagreed one evening. Stimson had gone to bed and Patton and I disagreed all evening about something and started the battle again at breakfast the next morning when the Secretary was there. And the Secretary put his hand on my shoulder and said, "Haven't you learned not to take this man seriously?" I don't remember what it was about. The general's theory was, "Just give me the order and I'll drive these Russians beyond the Vistula." That sort of thing.[89]

If anything, the summit conference depressed Patton. At Potsdam he was, he informed Bea on August 8, "just a visitor." It had, however, enabled him to have "long talks" with Marshall and several other generals. "Hap Arnold is the only one who understands the Mongols except me. But the rest are waking up."[90]

On that same day Patton elaborated on his view of the Soviets.

The difficulty in understanding the Russians is that we do not take cognizance of the fact that he is not a European, but an Asiatic, and therefore thinks deviously. We can no more understand a Russian than we can understand a Chinaman or a Japanese and, from what I have seen of them, I have no particular desire to understand them, except to ascertain how much lead or iron it takes to kill them. In addition to his other Asiatic characteristics, the Russian has no regard for human life and is an all out son of a bitch, barbarian, and chronic drunk.[91]

The end of the war in the Pacific reinforced Patton's fear that the world had passed him by. "Now the horrors of peace, pacifism and union will have unlimited sway," he lamented to Bea. "I wish I were young enough to fight in the next one. It would be real fun killing Mongols. . . . Last time a war stopped I wrote a poem 'Then Pass in peace blood glutted Bosch etc.' Now I feel too low. It is hell to be old and passé and know it."[92]

Even more ominous for Patton was an incident that had taken place a couple of months before. With the other American army commanders, Patton saw a fifteen-minute film, *Your Job in Germany,* on fraternization made by the noted moviemakers Frank Capra and Anatole Litvak. The other army commanders praised the film, but Patton emerged from the screening with a terse review: "Bullshit."[93] His failure to remove Nazis, and not his hatred of the Soviets, would lead to Patton's downfall.

Eighteen

HEADLONG TOWARD DISASTER

I

After the defeat of Germany, the Allied governments handed their generals, trained as soldiers and engineers, not as politicians and governors, the impossible task of ruling over and denazifying the battered country. On May 21, 1945, Joint Chiefs of Staff Directive 1067, calling for the removal from government positions of members of the Nazi Party plus trials for war criminals, became known to the American planning staff at Versailles and created an immediate furor. Lieutenant General Lucius D. Clay, Ike's deputy military governor for Germany, considered the directive too broad and hoped it would be modified. Lewis Douglas, his economic adviser, agreed, and after a tour of the American zone, during which he spoke to Bradley, Patton, and other leading generals, he became convinced it could not work. At Clay's request Douglas flew to Washington in early July to lobby for its revision. Failing, he resigned.[1]

Of the important generals Patton, whose Third Army controlled Bavaria, probably least desired to govern. His first postwar choice was to head the Army War College. Answering a letter from Bea telling him that Gerow had gotten that post, Patton lamented on August 18: "This is too bad, as he was one of the leading mediocre corps commanders in Europe and only got the Fifteenth Army because he was General Eisenhower's friend. With the War College gone, there is nothing open to me, so far as now seems plausible."[2]

Patton and his brother-in-law, Keith Merrill, both noted that Patton arrested "many notorious characters" in Bavaria. These included Julius Streicher, the "notorious Jew persecutor"; Angela Hamnitzsch, Hitler's sister; Gertrude Melchior, who broadcast Nazi propaganda as "Dirty

Gertie from Bizerte"; and the commandant of Buchenwald. Merrill noted that by October 1945 over sixty-one thousand Bavarians had been classified as Nazis and denied employment.[3] Unfortunately, however, all this tells but a minor portion of the story.

As Bruce Clarke, now commanding the 4th Armored Division in eastern Bavaria, observed, the American army faced vast problems in Germany. "We tried to get the water supply going again, the sewage straightened out, the light plants running. We were building bridges and we were fixing roads and we were trying to get the place operating again."[4]

In fulfilling his mission in Bavaria, Patton laid himself open to criticism. He gave a free hand to the first minister president of the province, Fritz Schaeffer, the leader of the most popular party, the conservative Christian Social Union. At best Schaeffer possessed a spotty record. The former chairman of the Bavarian People's Party, he had gained the favor of Patton's subordinates because, Professor Walter L. Dorn later wrote in a report to Eisenhower's headquarters, he had been

> both dismissed and persecuted by National Socialists. . . . What apparently was not fully appreciated at the time, was that Schaeffer belonged to the right wing of the Bavarian People's Party, which had many things in common with National Socialists and the militarist elements of Germany.
>
> It would be absurd to recall a speech which Schaeffer made as far back as 1922, if it did not throw some light on his subsequent behavior. At this time he publicly defended the National Socialists as the "saviors of our Fatherland in 1919" when he opposed a motion introduced in the Bavarian Parliament by the Social Democrats for state action against their early activities. He later became an enemy of National Socialism, but his hostility even now lacks a clear line and resolute determination. He is no doubt sincere in desiring the elimination of the most notorious Nazis from the Bavarian administrative apparatus, but on repeated occasions he has criticized publicly and privately the de-Nazification directives of Military Government as being excessively severe. He has made every effort to retain in office not only those key officials who have been marked for discretionary removal but those who fall into the mandatory removal category.[5]

As early as May 31 stories appeared in the left wing New York daily *PM* about Patton's failure in Bavaria. Written by Victor M. Bernstein, the articles accused Schaeffer of retaining those who had profited from Nazi rule. His minister of economics, Karl Arthur Lange, had become the general manager of the Lowenbrau brewery after the former manager, Herman Schulein, a Jew, was forced out. Schulein, who had come to the United States, now served as a director of the Rheingold brewery in New York. Schaeffer's assistant, August Fischer, had also profited from Hitler's rule, directing during the war a German school in Prague.[6]

To Patton such accusations meant nothing. On August 11 he complained to Ike that in Germany, as in other countries, civilian officials had to join the ruling political party. "It is no more possible for a man to be a civil servant in Germany and not have paid lip service to Nazism," he argued, "than it is possible for a man to be a postmaster in America and not have paid at least lip service to the Democratic Party, or the Republican Party when it is in power." By "throwing out too many what you might call middle class civil servants in our so-called de-Nazification program . . . we are getting a great many inexperienced or inefficient people in their place. It would seem to me that a word to the people directly responsible for civil government, along these lines, might be beneficial."

Eisenhower disagreed with this view. Reiterating that JCS 1067 made mandatory the removal from office of all Nazi Party members, he answered that the policy "laid down for us by the Joint Chiefs of Staff" must be obeyed. The German government could be run as efficiently without Nazis as with them. Intoned in Eisenhower's reply, which he wrote after consulting the assistant chief of staff for military government, Brigadier General Clarence L. Adcock, was the fundamental military dictum: the sanctity of orders from above.[7]

Unfortunately Patton, an amateur when it came to political matters, disregarded Ike's letter. Attending a meeting of the military government on August 27 he proposed freeing the interned Nazis, many of whom were, he argued, "either aged or pregnant." In his diary he denigrated the speeches of Ike, Clay, and the others as "unrealistic, and in every case the chief interest of the speaker was to say nothing which could be used against him. It is very patent that what the Military Government is trying to do is undemocratic and follows practically Gestapo methods." Eisenhower and the rest were advocating the plan of former Secretary of the Treasury Henry Morganthau, denounced by both Stimson and the secretary of state, to prevent future wars by dismantling German industry and reducing Germany to an agricultural nation. Such a scheme, Patton informed Bea, constituted an attempt "by Jews to get revenge. Actually the Germans are the only decent race left in Europe. It's a choice between them and the Russians. I prefer the Germans."[8]

Disturbed, Patton wrote a letter to Stimson "on the question of the pro-Jewish influence in the Military Government of Germany." He brought up the subject, he told the secretary, only because in Washington Stimson had read to Patton "the minutes of some of the meetings you and the former Secretary of the Treasury had had in which the future of Germany was discussed." Patton feared that "in our treatment of the Germans" Morganthau's ideas were holding sway. "This is particularly evident in the activities of a certain Colonel Bernstein who, as you probably know, was one of Mr. M's most valued allies. In any event, we appear to be leaning over backwards to be nice to the descendants of Ghengis Khan. Personally, I dislike them very much; in fact, that is a pale expression for my feelings." Patton thought that Stimson might profit from talking to Father Bernard Hubbard of the Society of Jesus, who had just spent the night at Third Army headquarters. Patton observed of Hubbard: "He is very anti-Russian and anti-Semite, and talks very well when he forgets to advertise himself."[9]

Amid this debate on Germany's future, Patton, relying on his diary, spent much of his time working on an autobiography that he had begun late in the war. In May he had given the first four chapters to Stimson's undersecretary, the kindly Judge Patterson, who found Patton's frankness startling. "I know that you will keep close control of this story," Patterson diplomatically commented to Patton.

> Some of the material, if given general circulation, would cause a lot of futile controversy. At the same time I hope that you will give consideration to preparing another text for general publication. The story would be of interest to all soldiers, particularly to the hundreds of thousands of men who served in the Third Army. If you do this, you will, I am sure, get the help of a competent and experienced adviser who will have some ideas of what to expand and what to omit.[10]

Thanking Patterson, who replaced Stimson as secretary of war that September, for reading the chapters, Patton answered that he did not wish to publish anything, "as it has been my observation that soldiers who write autobiographies usually utterly condemn themselves." Patton then launched into his favorite theme:

It is a great source of grief to us here to see the avidity with which politicians and others jump on the Army as soon as the Army has done its job. They seem utterly oblivious to the fact that we are probably facing the greatest peril in the history of the world in that the somewhat diluted descendants of Ghengis Kahn have, in my opinion, no possible idea of quitting, and I can envision the time when the last American troops will move out of Europe with a rear guard formation.[11]

II

Having little aptitude for the administration of government, Patton found himself plunging headlong toward disaster. As the military governor of the Eastern District of Bavaria, he had already been quoted as saying that "more than half of the German people are Nazis and you would be in a hell of a fix if you tried to remove all Party members." He saw a need to "compromise with the devil a little."

Patton's waywardness reflected the general tendency within his army not to take military government seriously. In the Third Army area reports abounded of the interference of tactical commanders in government. Local mayors and other officials came and went according to the whims and prejudices of army officers, and the army itself had no overall policy. "In the main," complained Professor Dorn, who was to play a great role in the events of the next month, "it was impossible to persuade the tactical commanders to use Military Government in dealing with the Germans."

As one-sided in one direction as Patton was in the other, Dorn analyzed the general:

Patton saw his problem in the following terms: either apply the purge with a relentless consistency and thus impair or temporarily cripple essential administrative services, especially those of the Ministry of Food, which was under obligation to supply from the German economy the crowded displaced persons and expellee camps, or to relax and postpone the purge in the interests of maintaining the efficiency of these supply services.[12]

Unfortunately Patton's behavior did not help. According to Dorn, Patton deviated so from established policy that at an August meeting the officials of the military government voted to reprimand him. Then on September 5 Patton visited prison Camp Number 8 in Garmisch Partenkirchen. The camp housed the worst of the interned Germans, the SS troops that had run the Buchenwald and Dachau concentration camps, for instance. There, after speaking to Karl Vogel, the Austrian publisher who had been a member of the SS since 1933 and now represented the prisoners as their camp commandant, and a half dozen others, Patton said that it was madness to imprison such people. "Did General Patton know," his earlier biographer Ladislas Farago asked, "that 238 of the inmates were former bloodhounds of the Gestapo with a frightful record of torture and murder?" Did he know that twenty-three of them were being held for killing American flyers unfortunate enough to have parachuted from their planes while over Germany? Did he know that one "inconspicuous little brunette" had condemned four thousand people to their deaths?[13]

That September 12 Eisenhower, in a letter to Patton and to Jeff Keyes, who governed Bavaria's Western District from Bad Homburg, made his policy absolutely clear. "I know that certain field commanders have felt some modification of this policy should be made," he wrote his subordinates. "This question has long since been decided. We will not compromise with Nazism in any way. I wish to make particularly sure that all your individual commanders realize that the discussion stage of this question is long past and any expressed opposition to the faithful execution of the order cannot be regarded leniently by me."[14]

Into this scene came Professor Dorn, who became on September 2 Adcock's adviser on denazification. "He is a very slick individual," Patton wrote of Dorn after their first meeting. "I think a pure German, and very probably a Communist in disguise. I had great difficulty in not losing my temper with him but knew if I did, I would simply get more adverse reports than I already had."[15]

Viewed by Patton in the most simplistic terms, Dorn already stood among the outstanding American scholars of German history. In 1940 he published a book that is still read today on the eighteenth-century power rivalries, *Competition for Empire.* Unfortunately Patton failed to see Dorn, a lifelong student of enlightened despotism, as an advocate of democracy. He saw him, instead, as he saw all those who disagreed with him, as a stooge of the Communists.

Alarmed by what he knew of the situation in Bavaria, Adcock sent Dorn there in mid-September to check on Schaeffer. Arriving in Munich, Dorn got his first shock. Colonel Roy L. Dalferes, who had replaced the inefficient Bronx politico Colonel Charles Keegan as Patton's G-5, or director of the Third Army's government section, cared nothing about denazification and had stopped checking on Schaeffer. Investigating, Dorn found things as he and Adcock suspected. "Schaeffer will smile skeptically when you charge him with close association with militarist elements," Dorn commented in his report to Ike and Bedell Smith, now hidden in the National Archives. The evidence, however, confirmed the truth of the suspicion. During the five weeks before August 28, 1945, Schaeffer employed Dr. Otto Gessler, who had served as minister of war during the Weimar Republic, as his unofficial adviser, participating in all Bavarian cabinet meetings. Schaeffer had done this without the approval of the American military government and had relented only after the Military Government prohibited Gessler from entering the government offices. Together with General Hans von Seeckt, Gessler had engineered the secret rearmament of Germany in the 1920s and had helped create the Reichswehr, the supposedly defensive unit that in 1933 became the kernel of Hitler's army. The Reichswehr contained the nucleus of a German army of thirty-five divisions.

As revealed in his report, Dorn found much more that disturbed him. The list of Schaeffer's Nazi appointees seemed endless. Schaeffer had put in charge of the Regional Economic Office a Dr. Schwink, "who was a former member of the German General Staff and occupied important positions in the administration of occupied Poland, France, and Italy." Schaeffer's minister of education, Dr. Otto Hipp, refused to denazify Bavarian schools, and his minister of the interior, Karl August Fischer, had been a Nazi official in Czechoslovakia. Another appointee, "Ritter von Lex, was not acceptable because in 1933 he had denounced the

Republic and insisted on the similarity in program of the Bavarian People's Party and the National Socialist Party." Schaeffer's minister of economics was Dr. Karl Lange, who had been Hitler's general manager for the machine industry. Lange had "increased his business through close association with notorious Nazis such as Christian Weber, the close friend of Hitler, and Dr. Thierfelder of the Munich office of the 'Abwehrstelle,'" the so-called Nazi defense force.

Dorn believed that "more serious still was Schaeffer's continued employment of key officials for weeks after their removal had been ordered." In the Ministry of Finance, which Schaeffer ran himself,

> there were four officials . . . all of them in the mandatory removal category and ordered removed early in August, who were still working in their offices on September 26, 1945. Schaeffer's tactics on such occasions were to urge indispensability and then ask for a reconsideration of the cases and in the interim continue to employ the civil servants in question. At one time there were no less than nine officials in the mandatory removal category who continued to be employed in the Ministry of Finance.

Still at their desks in late September were numerous officials whose removal had been ordered in early August: two at the Ministry of Economics, four at the Ministry of the Interior, six at the Regional Economic Office, and sixteen at the Ministry of Food and Agriculture. In the last bureau an army officer had illegally approved the retention of those ordered dismissed. When the chief of the agency, Ernest Rattenhuber, argued that he could not supply food to the displaced persons camps unless he kept sixteen of the twenty-five mandatory removals in his office, a Lieutenant Colonel Durus agreed on his own to keep them.

Compounding things, Schaeffer had encouraged employees in writing to ignore their questionnaires on Nazism, called Fragebogen. While saying that no one should lie, he told his workers to cross out questions they disliked. On August 27, 1945, the Special Branch of the Regional Military Government found that in the Ministry of Food and Agriculture only fourteen out of thirty-nine key officials had submitted Fragebogen, due in early June. In the Ministry of the Interior only five of fifty-one had been turned in, and in the Ministry of Economics only nine of twenty-two. Within a week after being put on the job the special branch collected the missing questionnaires.[16] All in all, Dorn told a story of complete indifference to established policy.

Coupled with Dorn's revelations came damaging reports in newspapers about army officers and denazification. In the *New York Times* on the twentieth of September, Raymond Daniell cited Patton's answer when he was told a businessman, a member of Hitler's elite guard, had ignored his Fragebogen. "Fragebogen?" Patton asked. "What the hell's a Fragebogen? Listen, if you need these men, keep them and forget about anything else." Daniell believed that Bavarian industrial and commercial companies were "still managed and controlled by the same old gang that helped Adolf Hitler to build a war machine." Of nineteen industrial firms in Munich, Nazis operated six. Despite a directive from Eisenhower that July ordering an investigation of firms worth more than a million marks, Nazis retained control of five breweries in Munich. Of the six construction companies in the city, "only one had been denazified."[17]

Meantime, in mid-September, two reports brought Eisenhower deeper into the Bavarian situation. One from Adcock spoke of Patton's failures in Bavaria, even relating the story of Patton's visit to Camp Number 8 and of his conversation with Vogel. The second, from Earl G. Harrison, the former commissioner of the Immigration and Naturalization Service, who was sent by Truman to investigate the condition of displaced persons, stressed Patton's disdain for Jews.

Eisenhower immediately decided to fly from the Riviera, where he was vacationing, to Munich to see Patton. Bad weather delayed his plane, but at the Munich airport his G-5, Brigadier General Stanley R. Mickelson, showed Patton a letter from Truman to Ike and the Harrison report. The letter, Patton commented, "was in much less considerate language than I would have used in cussing out a 2d Lieutenant." The Harrison report objected to DPs, "particularly Jews," being kept in unsanitary camps, fenced in by barbed wire and forced to wear either concentration camp clothes or discarded German uniforms. "As matters now stand," Harrison reported, "we appear to be treating the Jews as the Nazis treated them, except that we do not exterminate them."

If the camps were not enclosed, Patton responded, the DPs would "spread over the country like locusts and would eventually have to be rounded up after quite a few of them had been shot and quite a few Germans murdered and pillaged." As for sanitary conditions, Patton argued that "we frequently have to use force" to prevent Germans, Jews, and others from going to the bathroom on the floor. Harrison also suggested housing displaced persons in the homes of known Nazis. "It is against my Anglo-Saxon conscience to remove a person from a house, which is a punishment," Patton argued, "without due process of law. In the second place, Harrison and his ilk believe that a displaced person is a human being, which he is not, and this applies particularly to the Jews, who are lower than animals."[18]

At eight on the evening of the sixteenth Ike finally arrived. He and Patton stayed up until three discussing not conditions in Germany but their futures. Eisenhower was sure that he was to be the new chief of staff and that McNarney would take over in Europe. Declining to serve under McNarney, who had no combat experience, Patton said he preferred the Army War College, which had gone to Gerow, or command of the Army Ground Forces, which had gone to Devers. Ike expressed a willingness to replace Devers, but if the proposed separation of the air force from the army took place, "he could see no reason for having an Army Ground Force." Patton "agreed with him. Therefore," he noted, "at the present writing it would seem the only thing I can do is go home and retire."[19]

The next day Ike and Patton began inspecting displaced persons camps. The first was a facility housing those from the Baltic countries. Patton found the camp "extremely clean in all respects." Next came the Jews, celebrating what Patton called "the feast of Yom Kippur," in reality the only day of fasting in the Jewish calendar. He found that "these Jewish DPs, or at least a majority of them, have no sense of human relationships." In the wooden building they used as a synagogue, Eisenhower addressed these former death camp inmates, but Patton dismissed them as "the greatest stinking bunch of humanity I have ever seen. . . . The smell was so terrible that I almost fainted, and actually about three hours later, lost my lunch as the result of remembering it."

Returning to Bad Tölz, Patton and Ike went fishing on the lake. "While not successful," Patton noted of the fishing expedition, "at least it removed from our minds the nauseous odors and aspects of the camps we had inspected. We then took as long and as hot a bath as we could stand, to remove from our persons the germs which must have accumulated during the day."[20]

The next day Patton was off for a hunting trip with his gravel-voiced, profane other self, Ernest Harmon. Like Patton in Bavaria, Harmon was doing his best to undermine government policy in Bohemia. He, too, tolerated Nazis and preached hatred of the Soviets. And what better place to do it than from the huge chateau, complete with museum and zoo, of the descendants of Prince Schwartzenburg, whom Patton admired as "the only General who actually ever defeated Napoleon on the field of battle, before Waterloo."[21]

III

The rapid demobilization of the American army hurt Patton enormously. Suddenly gone were such steadying influences as Quirk, Codman, and Carter. Both Carter and Codman were as aristocratic as their Harvard friend, Bea's brother Fred Ayer, but they possessed none of the prejudices endemic to the Ayer family, particularly to the late William Wood, who had attributed his labor troubles to radical foreigners, and to Charles F. Ayer, who believed Jews were plotting to take over the world.[22]

Quirk, however, constituted the greatest loss. From January to May 1945 Patton had stayed out of trouble, and much of the credit had to go to Quirk, who controlled both Patton and the reporters. With Quirk gone, Patton fell into the hands of his press officer, Major Ernest C. Deane, who possessed none of Quirk's skill at protecting the general.

Understanding Patton's weaknesses and strengths, Quirk would never have allowed to happen what next happened. Reading in the *New York Times* Daniell's critical account of his handling of denazification, Patton agreed to do what Quirk would have urged him not to do: allow reporters to attend the staff meeting of the twenty-second, a Saturday, and then to ask questions. As Martin Blumenson had noted, only eleven reporters showed up for the conference at Bad Tölz. Among those present were Daniell; Edward P. Morgan, later a radio commentator for the AFL-CIO but then of the *Chicago Daily News;* Carl Levin of the *New York Herald-Tribune;* and Daniell's wife, Tania Long, also of the *New York*

Times. By all accounts, the staff meeting went well. Then, as Patton started to leave, the newspapermen began asking pointed questions. Unshielded from their aggressiveness, Patton uttered words that allowed Daniell's paper to insist, in a headline, that the general had equated Nazis and non-Nazis with Democrats and Republicans in the United States, something he had come close to doing in his letter to Ike of August 11, 1945. Eisenhower was so concerned that on the twenty-fifth he had Bedell Smith suggest that Patton hold another news conference to clarify what he had said three days before. "I did this and wrote out a statement," Patton noted in his diary. He also made sure that a stenographer took down all the comments made during this second press conference, something he had failed to do at the first conference.[23]

In his diary entry for the twenty-fifth, Patton also noted that "a Mr. Mason," formerly of the Scripps-Howard and Hearst newspapers, "came in with a long story about the attempt on the part of Jewish and Communist elements to put the bug on people like myself. While his story sounded plausible, I have developed such a low opinion of all newspaper people that I think he is probably a liar."[24]

Pieced together from his letters, Frank E. Mason's account of how he thrust himself into this latest Patton affair was unusual. Mason happened to be in Germany studying the availability of food for former President Herbert Hoover, who later showed how much he really respected Bea and the Patton family by joining the plot to get hold of Patton's diary so it could be used against General Eisenhower in the 1952 Republican presidential primaries. Having run into bad flying weather, Mason called Patton's office to pay his respects to the general. After all, he said, he had had lunch with Patton when both were stationed in Germany in 1919. Supposedly overjoyed, Patton invited Mason, the former head of Hearst's International News Service, to visit him. At their meeting Mason, an ardent Catholic, spewed out his tale of a conspiracy, led by Jews such as Morganthau, Levin, and Colonel Bernstein, to topple the pro-Catholic, anti-Communist government of Schaeffer. Patton seemed so bored by the story that he did not even mention the first press conference. Coming out of Patton's office, Mason ran into Deane, an old friend. Groping for allies, the battered Deane "took me back into Patton's office for the second press conference."[25]

From Deane and Pierre J. Huss, an INS reporter, Mason learned the details of the first press conference, which Mason and Huss saw as an attempt to get rid of Patton, Schaeffer, and Schaeffer's chief sponsor, Cardinal Michael Ritter von Faulhaber, the seventy-six-year-old archbishop of Munich and Freysing. Going to Deane's room at Bad Wiessee, the three men drafted a letter on the episode. Although written by all three men, the final draft contained only the signature of Mason, who sent copies to Patton's old commander, General Harbord, to Hoover, and through Patton's West Point classmate, Colonel Robert Fletcher, to General Marshall. After finishing the letter, Mason "rode all night" to Frankfurt, where he delivered the most important copy to Colonel Francis V. Fitzgerald, formerly Bradley's director of public relations and now Ike's, with instructions to make sure Eisenhower read it.

As Mason, Huss, and Deane saw it, the rowdy press conference constituted an attempt to defame Cardinal von Faulhaber and the Catholic Church, which alone stood in the way of Soviet domination of Germany. "Victor Bernstein of PM, came to Bavaria to eliminate Faulhaber," Mason's letter read. "He devoted himself to a smear campaign on the cardinal. He tried to assassinate Faulhaber's reputation." Patton, the cardinal's ally and defender, also had to be eliminated. In accord with this plot "the Big Three," Morgan, Daniell, and Levin, "came down to take General Patton apart, and hold him up as a terrible example to any other general who might feel that the opinions of a small handful of radical journalists are not to be respected in the formation of the local German government."[26] The letter said nothing about the failure to denazify Bavaria, a subject which did not interest its authors.

In arguing the conspiracy theory Mason and Deane contradicted each other. In a letter to Marshall, his Leesburg, Virginia, neighbor, in November 1945, Mason wrote, "A newspaperman who used to work for me, told me at Patton's headquarters, that he overheard the three men and one woman who came down to stage the Patton attack discussing how to get the General to blow up." This ex-employee, Huss, sat at the next table during breakfast and purportedly heard the discussion "as to how they could entangle George Patton in his talk."[27]

Painting his picture of radicals openly conspiring, Deane contradicted Mason and himself. In 1950 he said that Charlie Haacker, the photographer for the Acme Photo Service, had sat next to the three plotters at breakfast that fateful morning and had heard them planning "to make the Old Man angry and to blow his top." By 1972, however, the witness had become "a Canadian, Marshall Yarrow, who told me later he'd always regret he didn't tip me off, but he didn't."[28]

Somehow, too, Nora Waln, who covered the first press conference for the *Atlantic Monthly,* had a role in cornering Patton. "Nora Waln never would tell which of the trio it was who put her up to asking the general the question about the Nazis which opened up the fireworks," Deane wrote Mason in 1950. "She did it innocently, she swore to me, but refused to go into details because she is a Quaker and avoids controversy."[29]

Unconcerned by Patton's refusal to denazify Bavaria, Mason saw the opposition to Patton as a radical, pro-Jewish, anti-Catholic plot. Events would place him among the conspirators, plotting with the conservative publisher Henry Regnery and President Hoover to get hold of the general's diary so it could be rushed into print and used against Eisenhower. To her great credit Beatrice Ayer Patton recognized and refused to go along with the scheme.

IV

On the evening of Tuesday the twenty-fifth, the day Mason visited Patton, the great general received a telegram from Eisenhower asking him to fly to Frankfurt to discuss denazification in Bavaria. "It may well be," Patton observed in his diary, "that the Philistines have at last got me. On the other hand, every time I have been in serious trouble, or thought I was, it has turned out to my advantage. At least, this time I do not have to go on the defensive."[30]

Unmindful of his failure, Patton seemed so unconcerned about the meeting that on the next day, the weather preventing his flying to Frankfurt, he accepted the invitation of French General Béthouart to go hunting. While Patton was relaxing Dorn was telling Third Army officials of his findings, later submitted in writing to his superiors. A Colonel Reese, the executive officer of the Bavarian Military Government, refused to believe him. So, too, did a Mr. Schweitzer, the chief civil affairs officer. Meantime, Major Goodwin Ordway of the Special Branch of the Regional Military Government tested the accuracy of Dorn's statements by sending Germans unknown to Schaeffer to the ministry buildings, where they saw ex-Nazis at work. Dorn was discussing his findings with Dalferes when Patton called on the phone. "While I sat there," Dorn remembered, "Col. Dalferes communicated to General Patton the substance of my report."[31]

Returning to Frankfurt, Dorn submitted his findings to Adcock, who immediately told Bedell Smith. At a press conference on the twenty-sixth Bedell himself came under heavy fire. "We will not compromise with Nazism in any way," he announced. ". . . Now that is the thing in a nutshell." Questions and comments, uttered by the same reporters who were at the Saturday press conference, centered on Patton. Could American policies "be carried out by people who are temperamentally and emotionally in disagreement with it?" Patton, another correspondent pointed out, had said Schaeffer could "run the Province any way he sees fit." Patton did not "know what reactionaries were, but he did ask, 'What do you want—a lot of communists?'" Finally, Patton had forced American soldiers to live in railway cars and tents because he refused to dispossess Nazis. In Bad Wiessee the daughter of the Nazi governor of Poland, Dr. Hans Frank, who was tried at Nuremberg and hanged as a war criminal, was working as the secretary to an American military organization and living in a large house filled with treasures her father had stolen. Presented with all this, Bedell spoke of Patton the way professional soldiers never publicly speak of each other: "His mouth does not always carry out the functions of his brain. George acts on the theory that it is better to be damned than say nothing—that some publicity is better than none."[32]

The eventful meeting took place on Friday, the twenty-eighth. That morning, finding the weather still bad for flying, Patton took off by vehicle for Ike's headquarters in Frankfurt, accompanied only by his aide, the younger Van S. Merle-Smith. Driving through Munich, Augsburg, and Mannheim, he entertained himself by visualizing how he would attack or defend positions along the route. Then he realized he had fought his last battle. Others would now have to figure out these things.

The ride reminded Patton of the one he and Codman had taken from Knutsford to London after he had delivered his controversial speech. He believed then he would be relieved and sent home, "if not tried." This time he thought he would not be tried, "but I thought I might be relieved of command."[33]

The meeting took place in Eisenhower's headquarters, the largest room in the I. G. Farbenindustrie building. Ike was seated at a table with a large flag behind him and Patton was seated in front of Ike when, at 4:30 P.M., Adcock and Dorn entered. Only these four men were present. No one took notes, and nothing was published about the conference. Years later, Dorn revealed the details.

Eisenhower opened the meeting by asking Dorn to tell briefly what he had found. As Dorn spoke, Patton frequently interjected: "That's true. That is quite correct. So I have myself learned," for in Dorn's presence Colonel Dalferes had transmitted the essence of the report to Patton over the phone. Eisenhower then asked Dorn, whom he had never met, why he had not delivered his report to Patton personally. Dorn responded that he felt obligated to report to Dalferes and was in the room when Dalferes, answering a call from Patton, told Patton the findings. Skeptically Ike then asked how Dorn found out these things when the army could not. In a display of great consideration, Dorn hesitated to tell Eisenhower that Dalferes and Reese had stopped investigating the Schaeffer government because, Dorn believed, they refused "to be stampeded by the newspaper reporters." Instead of revealing this damaging fact, Dorn began to fumble out some explanation when Adcock interrupted "and said that was precisely the function for which Dr. Dorn was appointed."

At that point Eisenhower decided to test Dorn. He got up, stopped in front of Dorn, and asked what Dorn's profession was. Dorn, who taught European history at Ohio State, said that he was a university professor. Rattenhuber had contended that removing sixteen or seventeen Nazis from his Ministry of Food and Agriculture would cripple the agency and prevent it from supplying the DP camps with food. Ike asked if a university president "could dismiss 16 or 17 of his professors and still have a functioning university. My reply was, 'Of course the university could function, not as efficiently as before, but it could function. There is no human being who is ever irreplaceable for a long time.' " Ike next wanted to know if the Ministry of Food could function with seventeen of its "key men suddenly thrown out of office." Dorn answered that no seventeen men had a monopoly on the distribution of food. As it turned out, Dorn later observed, once the Nazis were removed this ministry operated even more efficiently than it had before.[34]

The issue was denazification, and at no time did Patton's hatred of the Russians come up. Dorn clearly remembered Ike's response to all this.

> Suddenly Gen. Eisenhower was seized by a holy rage of anger and he asked in vigorous and colorful language "what the hell" the American army was doing in Germany if not to purify the German government and the administration of notorious and conspicuous Nazis. He said the Russians were killing off the leading Nazis and we were keeping some of them in office. Then he launched out on a discussion that lasted for some 10 or 15 minutes of the thousands of soldiers he had sent to their certain death in order to destroy this foul and inhuman thing called National Socialism. I might say at this point that Eisenhower's sincerity about denazification had previously repeatedly been questioned by newspaper reporters, but there can be no doubt in my own mind that such a speech as he now delivered could come only from an officer who felt the full weight of the responsibility of the mission which he had been asked to perform.

Several times during his speech Eisenhower stepped in front of Dorn and asked for the names of those responsible for this scandal, "a question which," Dorn wrote,

> I usually tried to evade. Finally, he stopped in front of me and asked me to indicate who had the full responsibility for this. I said certainly the executive officer of the Bavarian government and the G-5 of the Third Army. To my knowledge I did not say these two individuals had been responsible for the stoppage of any further investigation of the Schaeffer government, because I did not feel it my duty to indicate that unless I was forced to do so. Then Gen. Eisenhower indicated his firm resolution to have Dr. Schaeffer removed from office, indicated that he should really be thrown in prison for having so flagrantly evaded and attempted to defeat by delaying tactics the real purpose of denazification, and having proved his unwillingness to carry out military government instructions.

Ike was not through. He ordered the removal of those who had collaborated with Schaeffer in delaying denazification and then asked Dorn to name someone "who would be reliable enough to carry out military government instructions." Dorn mentioned Dr. Wilhelm Hoegner, an anti-Nazi who during the war had been connected with the underground in Switzerland. In Bavaria, which was 90 percent Catholic, Schaeffer led the conservative Christian Social Union. Hoegner, on the other hand, was a Social Democrat. Dorn mentioned that the CSU had a majority in Bavaria, and Ike responded: "I don't care what kind of a political majority there is in Bavaria so long as our military government instructions will be faithfully carried out." When Eisenhower indicated that Patton take down the name, a subdued Patton promptly moved to a nearby table and asked Dorn to spell Dr. Hoegner's name. He then asked Dorn to suggest other candidates for important positions, "but at that," Dorn recorded,

> Gen. Adcock tugged at my sleeve and led me to believe that I should give no further names, and I ceased to give further names, indicating that it was the general responsibility of Dr. Hoegner to choose his own cabinet. I firmly believe that Gen. Eisenhower had already made up his mind to remove Gen. Patton from his command of the Third Army and that he used this conference simply to convince Gen. Patton of the necessity of a change, not that at any time during this moment Gen. Eisenhower said anything to Gen. Patton that might be construed as a breach of their firm and time-tested friendship. Quite to the contrary, when the conference was over and Gen. Adcock and myself walked out of the office, Gen. Eisenhower led Patton by the arm and said to the whole crowd of reporters who had gathered to wait for the upshot of the conference that "Gen. Patton and myself remain the best of friends." On Monday October 1st it was announced that Gen. Patton was relieved of his post as commander of the Third Army and appointed commander of the 15th Army. In conclusion I merely wish to add that this is an instance of Gen. Patton's assumption of full responsibility for the behavior of his G-5, whom he himself had appointed and for the executive officer of the Bavarian military government, Col. Reese. No harm came to either of these individuals, because Col. Dalferes continued on as

G-5 and later became one of Brigadier General Walter J. Muller's deputies after Muller was appointed the Military Governor of Bavaria . . . and Gen. Truscott was appointed in Gen. Patton's place.[35]

Ike was so insistent on the immediate removal of Schaeffer that he sent Patton back to Bad Tölz that evening to make the change. That midnight the military police arrived at Hoegner's house in Munich to summon him to army headquarters, where to his surprise he was told he had just been appointed the minister president of Bavaria. Hoegner later confided that he thought he was being arrested in one of those misunderstandings common to Germany at that time. The military police had no idea why they were ordered to pick Hoegner up.[36]

Dorn always viewed Patton's removal as a turning point in the denazification of Bavaria. In an unpublished manuscript on the episode he concluded:

> The impact of the Patton affair upon the administration of the U.S. zone can scarcely be exaggerated. Henceforth, a new atmosphere prevailed and the Americans began to acquire a reputation for pursuing the purges with a ruthlessness that had no counterpart in other zones. The Russians dealt more quickly and ruthlessly with the top echelon Nazis, but the scale of the purges was much smaller than the American. . . . Both General Eisenhower and his Deputy, General Clay, left no doubt that henceforth the purge was the first and foremost immediate purpose of American zonal policy. Hitherto local Military Government detachments had been left largely to their own devices. This was now to be a thing of the past.[37]

General James M. Gavin was convinced that on his way out of the conference Patton learned of his relief from Bedell Smith. In Smith's office that day, Gavin, who "liked George very much," saw Smith talking at length to Patton. Gavin believed that Patton there heard he was to be transferred to the Fifteenth Army, a paper organization devoted to studying the lessons of the war just ended.[38]

Patton himself thought he saw one lesson in the episode. Robert D. Murphy, who had helped plan the postwar occupation of Germany, remembered Patton saying on the day he lost his army: "Ike wants to be President so much you can taste it."[39]

Like her husband, Beatrice Ayer Patton learned nothing from the episode. Instead of blaming her brothers and half brothers, who instilled in Patton, the son of a Wilsonian Democrat, antilabor, anti-Semitic, ultra-conservative doctrines that pulled him down the road to dismissal, she saw in his removal a plot most foul. Shortly after Patton's death, she sent a telling letter to Floyd Parks: "When Georgie was kicked out of the Third Army, I wrote him that he ought to demand an official investigation. He answered that not only would it be impossible for him to get justice under the present set-up, but that the smear against him would eventually include the entire army and navy, and was inspired by subversive elements to destory the confidence of the return-ing soldiers in the men who had led them in battle; and the army must therefore stick together."[40]

V

"I feel just like an undertaker arranging his own funeral but no one else can guess it," Patton informed Bea about his transfer, scheduled for October 8. To spare Patton prolonged embarrassment, Eisenhower had intended to announce the move at the last moment, but on the second he told Patton that someone had leaked the news in Berlin. Conse-quently, he would make the announcement at noon on Wednesday, the third. Harkins, who listened in on the conversation, thought Murphy "had let it spill in Berlin," but Patton attributed the leak to Bedell Smith, his enemy since the remark to reporters that Patton's mouth did not "always carry out the functions of his brain," or to Ike, who was worrying about the response to the transfer at home.[41]

Not surprisingly, much of the American press sympathized with Pat-ton. In the *New York Daily Mirror* and other papers, Drew Pearson blamed the entire episode on Murphy, who in August had assured Eisenhower that the denazification program was completed, even though it had scarcely begun. Pearson further charged that members of Ike's staff knew of, and winked at, Patton's disregard of orders. The newspaper criticism then got so severe that it forced a crackdown.[42]

The most forceful defense of Patton appeared in John O'Donnell's

"Capital Stuff" column in the *New York Daily News*. Reading like one of Patton's diary entries, O'Donnell's column of the third of October blamed Jews for Patton's ouster. It read in part:

> Behind the successful drive to disgrace and remove Gen. George S. Patton from his army command in occupied Germany is the secret and astoundingly effective might of this republic's foreign-born political leaders—such as Justice of the Supreme Court Felix Frankfurter, of Vienna, White House administrative assistant Dave (Devious Dave) Niles alias Neyhus and the Latvian ex-rabbinical student now known as Sidney Hillman.

What did "these boys and their pals" have against Patton? On November 21, 1943, Drew Pearson had reported that Patton "had ordered a 'battle-fatigued' soldier out of his cot and boxed his ears and told him to snap out of it and get back in the lines. The neurologist in the medical corps on the scene told us later this was the proper treatment. . . . What was not reported at the time was that the soldier who got slapped was of Jewish descent."

After this incident, O'Donnell informed his readers, the Jews were out to get Patton. "Secretary of the Treasury Morganthau and Associate Justice Frankfurter bellowed in the White House that the important issue was that Patton used the word 'Jew' in reprimanding the reluctant warrior ('after all, what are we fighting this war for anyway, Mr. President') and the various breast-beaters, world-savers and payroll patriots, safe in their Washington foxholes, howled for the dismissal of old Blood and Guts." When Patton committed "errors of administration in Germany," they succeeded.[43]

Word that O'Donnell's article was filled with errors—neither of the men Patton slapped and kicked out of the hospital tents was Jewish or suffered from neurosis, and the physicians present thought Patton's actions ghastly—did not stop the *Daily News* from depicting Patton's relief in an imaginative way. Owned in part by Patton's World War I acquaintance, the conservative Colonel Robert R. McCormick, the paper saw Patton's dismissal as a step in the "liberal" plot to get rid of MacArthur in the Pacific. Harking back to MacArthur's destruction of the Bonus Army in 1932, the "liberal" hatred of him had intensified ever since he had left the Philippines early in the recent war. "Looking over the 'liberal' campaigns against MacArthur and Patton, with their technique of trying to label these great war leaders Fascists, we think our 'liberals' are out to overturn the American system of government—just as are the American Communists from whom our 'liberals' get so many of their ideas and so much of their strategy."[44]

The sanest approach to the incident came not from a political columnist or an editorial writer but from Ed Sullivan, whose "Little Old New York" column appeared in the *Daily News*. Wherever he went in New York, Sullivan found Patton's dismissal the main topic of conversation. In one restaurant a group of movie stars was discussing miscasting, exactly what happened to Patton when he moved from the "innards" of a tank to a desk. Patton himself liked to tell the story of a fish mounted on a friend's wall under the inscription: "If I hadn't opened my big mouth, I wouldn't be here." Sullivan concluded with sage advice: "Patton was a great general and he deserves well of his country, cheers rather than a mongrel chorus of abuse from the unthinking."[45]

The transfer of the Third Army from Patton to Truscott at noon on October 7 presented a strange picture. Because of rain, the ceremony took place in the gymnasium. Truscott and Patton marched in shoulder to shoulder, followed by Truscott's longtime chief of staff, Brigadier General Don E. Carleton, and Harkins. "He was very much perturbed at taking over command," Patton observed of Truscott. In a note to her husband's diary Mrs. Patton agreed that somehow Truscott felt guilty. When she met him on her husband's funeral train that December 24, he gave her the impression that he feared she would ignore him. After Bea graciously offered him her hands, he embraced her and began crying.[46]

Truscott's record, however, contained a blemish. More than Patton, who probably never knew of it, Truscott and Carleton had been responsible for the Canicattì massacre of July 1943, during which perhaps twenty-one civilians were killed. In his statement justifying what he had done, the lieutenant colonel who fired the shots said that the chief of staff of the 3rd Division had authorized him over the phone to kill looters, a word he applied to the unthinking civilians scooping up buckets of liquid soap. Busy as they were, Carelton and Truscott unquestionably read the account submitted by the lieutenant colonel and did nothing to investigate the shootings.[47]

Reaching Bad Nauheim, a small resort town north of Frankfurt, the next morning, Patton had breakfast and then met with Leven Allen, who explained to him the duties of the Fifteenth Army. He was to study and to write about the strategy used in the European theater during the war. Jumping right into the work, Patton, the author of numerous articles on tanks and warfare in general, seemed to enjoy it. In two days he finished and sent to Bea his first paper, which he described as "rather coarse for the purpose for which it is realy useful. This is very much like duty in the old Historical Section in Wash. We are writing a lot of stuff which no one will ever read."[48]

Meantime, back in San Marino, Patton somehow emerged as a candidate for the Republican nomination for Congress. Asked about the suggestion, Nita said that she did not know whether her brother was a Democrat or Republican. "I doubt that he is a member of either party," she revealed. "He has been a soldier all his life and never took part in politics."[49]

Dining together on the evening of the twelfth, Eisenhower encouraged Patton to run for Congress. "I presume," Patton suspiciously commented, "in the belief that I might help him." During the discussion, Eisenhower said that his son John, a lieutenant in the Fifteenth Army, had told him that since Patton had taken over people within the army had begun to work. Patton, in turn, "stated to him that I could not hereafter eat at the same table with General Beedle Smith," a remark that must have cut Ike deeply.[50]

Not that Patton thought more of Eisenhower than he did of Bedell. "There is some thing in physics about 'Action equals reaction,'" he wrote Bea on October 19. "My reaction fan mail has just started also telegrams. I think things will come out for the best and may result in my getting lined up with the Anti-Communists because it is they [the Communists] and the Jews who are back of it and succeeded due to the lack of spine of D. D."

The conservative press, Patton noted, had rallied around his flag. His friend McCormick, whose chief journal was the *Chicago Tribune,* "wired a nice message so his paper will be telling the truth." So, too, had Bill Cunningham of the *Boston Herald.* And William Randolph Hearst, Sr., having failed to buy Patton's diary for $250,000, "offered $150,000 for a statement and wants to send a man to see me."[51]

For Patton the highlight of late October came on the twenty-fifth. Accompanied by Allen, Merle-Smith, and General Raymond G. Moses, he went to Paris for a special luncheon given in his honor at the Ministry of War by General Charles de Gaulle. At the end of the meal General de Gaulle made a long speech "in which he compared me to everybody from Napoleon up and down." Patton responded by saying that France's great generals had always inspired American soldiers. Busts of two French heroes of the Thirty Years' War, Turenne and Condé, decorated the room, while two other inspirational leaders, de Gaulle and General Alphonse Juin, were at the lunch. At dinner that night "Juin got on the question of the Russians, whom he distrusts and fears as much as I do."[52]

The most unfortunate part of the story was that Patton seemed incapable of understanding what he had done in Bavaria. After completing the tour of France, during which "I collected ten Citizen of Honor certificates, two plaques and a tremendous case of indigestion," Patton returned to his headquarters intent upon showing the world that he had been wronged. He continued to seek advice from Bea's half brother, Charles F. Ayer, whose depiction of Jews and Communists had swayed him during his visit home. "I will shortly send you a set of facts," Patton told Bea on October 31, "which after consulting Charley you might spoon feed to Bill Cunningham who seems to be a man. Destiny [Eisenhower] relieved me simply in a state of funk and because he has no moral courage. Perhaps Bill could say that some day but not until he has been spoon fed."[53]

Writing to his friend Gilbert R. Cook on the first of November, Patton commented on his own work and on the state of Europe. Even those who had been in Europe in 1919 and remembered "the chaotic conditions" then could not appreciate "the utter anarchical conditions now prevailing in a Europe which is filled to repletion with 'envy, hatred, malice and all uncharitableness' and which is dominated by a semi-heathen group of international bandits of Mongolian ancestry." On a brighter side Patton liked the work assigned to him. He had already written three papers on the reorganization of the army. "If I ever get time and if my eyes hold out I shall complete an analytical study on casualties, their cause and cure, which I think will further point my opinion on tactical organization."[54]

Patton hoped to finish his work and come home for good just after the first of the year. Before that, however, he became caught up in a strange twist of fate. Just after Patton's sixtieth birthday on November 11, Eisenhower intended to return to the United States for a brief time.

Patton would then become the acting commander of the United States Forces European Theater, which had replaced SHAEF that July 1. With glee Patton painted the picture for Bea. "Beedle and I will have some fun any how. He has never apologized but sent word he had been misquoted. I have never seen him in any case he will be investigated by Congress on P[earl] H[arbor] in December and they will have negligence on him if they want to prove it."[55]

Patton's sixtieth birthday party, held in the ballroom of the Grand Hotel in Bad Nauheim, was a bittersweet affair. On the surface it could not have been happier: old friends, waiters in tails, a distinguished Hungarian chef who had been found in a DP camp. Underneath, however, were the gnawing political issues, the loss of the Third Army, the end of a forty-year army career this way.[56] Here indeed was the Viking warrior grown old and discarded.

Taking Ike's place, Patton maintained strained relations with Bedell. "Of course we don't get on," he commented to Bea on the fifteenth. "It is not very pleasant. But since Ike will be back—so it is said—on the 23rd I am not being much more than a rubber stamp. If I had the job permanently—which God forbid—I would certainly change things."[57]

Bedell was not the only one who felt uncomfortable with Patton around. Adcock, who had been promoted to major general, now had to deal with Patton the Theater Commander. At a meeting of the USFET on the twenty-third, Bedell told of some Polish DPs who the previous night had attacked a German farmhouse, murdered eight people, and wounded two others. After Smith outlined the steps he wished to take to prevent a repetition of such atrocities, he asked Patton's permission. Patton, in turn, requested the opinions of the members of the staff. Everyone spoke but Adcock. "I specifically asked him if he concurred," Patton observed, "to which he replied, 'Yes, certainly I concur.' This is important, as I believe Adcock is a double-crossing s.o.b."[58]

On the twenty-seventh Patton, accompanied by Merle-Smith, now a lieutenant colonel; Sergeant Meeks; and another sergeant, left on what proved to be the last trip he would ever take. Arriving, after a stop in Copenhagen, at Stockholm the next morning at eight, Patton was met by the heads of the Swedish army and by eight of his competitors in the 1912 Pentathlon. Patrick de Laval, the winner of the Pentathlon, failed to arrive in time to greet Patton. In Stockholm the four Americans received royal treatment. They stayed in a suite at the Grand Hotel, where Patton had stayed in 1912, had breakfast and lunch with Count Folke Bernadotte, who a few years later attempted to mediate the Arab-Israeli War and was assassinated for his trouble, and met the king and the crown prince. Later, in a replica of the 1912 pistol competition, de Laval again won the event, scoring 192 out of 200 points. Patton came in second with a score of 187, which, he believed, "is 13 points better than I made in 1912."[59]

After a speech before the Swedish-American Society, "the ostensible reason for my going to Stockholm," and a brief return to Copenhagen, where he visited the Danish king, Patton arrived home in time for a luncheon given by Bedell Smith on December 3 for McNarney, the new theater commander. "With the exception of General Keyes, Truscott, Allen, Gay and myself and a limited number of others," Patton commented, "I have rarely seen assembled a greater bunch of sons-of-bitches. . . . The whole luncheon party reminded me of a meeting of the Rotary Club in Hawaii where everyone slaps everyone else's back while looking for an appropriate place to thrust the knife. I admit I was guilty of this practice, although at the moment I have no appropriate weapon."[60]

VI

Ordered on December 7 to proceed to Paris on or about the fourteenth for air travel home, Patton decided, on the morning of Sunday the ninth, to go pheasant hunting with Hap Gay. About 11:45 A.M. on the Autobahn just outside Mannheim, T/5 Robert L. Thompson, driving a quarter-ton Signal Corps truck, made a sudden move to the left just as the Cadillac carrying Patton, Gay, and Patton's dog Willie began moving after waiting for a train to pass. The impact, while not great, shoved the Cadillac down an embankment, throwing Patton and Gay to the floor. The collision smashed the Cadillac's radiator and shoved back its motor. Gay suffered minor injuries, Patton major. Summoned to the scene by a Red Cross girl who had seen the accident from the nearby dugout from which she served doughnuts, Captain Ned Snyder, the medical officer of C Battalion, 290th Engineers, examined Patton, motionless on the backseat of the Cadillac, and told Major Charles Tucker, who commanded the battalion: "He broke his neck. He needs the very best we've got." The general would be taken to the big hospital at Heidelberg, twenty miles away.[61]

Arriving at the hospital, Patton was conscious but in severe traumatic shock. His blood pressure was extremely low, his hands and feet cold, his pulse weak, and his face pallid. "He complained," remembered Dr. Warren A. Lapp, one of the physicians at the hospital, "of pain in his neck and inability to move his arms or legs." To help relieve the shock Patton's stretcher was placed on wooden horses, his feet well above his head. With Patton's permission his clothes were cut away. The building housing the hospital had no elevator, and so an X-ray machine had to be carried and dragged downstairs to the admitting ward, where Patton was. The x-rays "revealed a fracture of the third cervical vertebra, with a posterior dislocation of the fourth cervical vertebra on the fifth," Dr. Lapp recalled. "Whether or not the spinal cord had been transected or merely traumatized by the fracture-dislocation was a matter for conjecture, but the injury was considered to be of the utmost seriousness."[62]

Learning of the accident, Patton's friends and associates rushed to the hospital. These included Keyes and Major General Albert W. Kenner, formerly the Third Army's chief medical officer and now the head surgeon of the European forces. When Kenner saw the seriousness of Patton's condition, he called Washington. The surgeon general advised him to get in touch with Brigadier Hugh Cairns, professor of neurosurgery at Oxford University, and Lieutenant Colonel Gilbert Phillips, a British specialist in head injuries. When they agreed to come to Heidelberg, Kenner sent a plane for them.

Bea, too, immediately decided to fly to Heidelberg. Joined by Colonel Roy G. Spurling, the army's senior consultant in neurosurgery, and Lieutenant Colonel Walter T. Kerwin, Jr., an aide of General Marshall, she left the Military Air Transport Command terminal in Washington at 10 P.M. on the tenth, arriving, after an arduous trip, in her husband's room at 3:30 P.M. on the eleventh.

Examining the patient, the two Britons—Cairns and Phillips—and the American—Spurling—concurred with the diagnosis and with the treatment Patton had received. Because Patton's bladder was paralyzed and had to be emptied via a catheter, Spurling suggested that the general be given daily doses of the newly discovered antibiotic streptomycin, not yet available in Europe. Accordingly, a supply of the drug was flown in from Washington.[63]

Numerous steps were taken to comfort and cheer Patton, who had been transferred the first day to a private room, number thirteen, on the first floor of the hospital. Bea was given a room on the hospital grounds. The prettiest nurses in the hospital were assigned to Patton. And Captain William Duane, a Philadelphia neurosurgeon, slept across the hall from Patton. On duty the entire day Captain Duane, remembered Bea's brother Fred Ayer, who arrived on Saturday the fifteenth, "did a marvelous job of professional care and nursing."[64]

Monday, the seventeenth, brought hope and discouragement. "This morning George demonstrated very slight muscular function in thighs," Ayer noted, "and doctors seemed excited. It did not last."[65]

The general spent his waking hours dictating chapters of his memoirs to Bea, who took down each word in longhand. This routine ended when an ultimatum came from the White House. Patton must not be allowed to die in Germany. He was to be sent home immediately. Although the neurosurgeons at the hospital believed he should not be disturbed for another six weeks, Patton, bravely joking during the procedure, was fully encased on the morning of the twentieth in a coating of plaster of Paris. He was ready for the trip home.[66]

The eventful day came on Friday, the twenty-first. That morning the general whispered to his wife, "It's too dark . . . I mean, too late." Bea cheered him with word that he would soon be back in the United States. Fred Ayer spent the forenoon with his brother-in-law and waited as General Kenner and Lieutenant Colonel Herbert J. Pollock, the chief internist in the European theater, both examined Patton. Fred went hunting for a few hours that afternoon. Returning to the hospital at 5:55 P.M., he learned that Patton had died, "presumably," he wrote, "because his heart could not carry the load." Dr. Lapp assumed death came from "a blood clot to a vital area of the brain."

To his friend and fellow physician, Colonal Robert B. Hill, a grieving Kenner described what had happened.

Poor Georgie passed out on me, as you know by this time, but he certainly received everything in the way of medical care. Two days before his demise, he had a shower emboli that hit his right chest and he started to fill up with his own sputum. We managed to get that pretty well under control, only to see him die very suddenly as a result of another shower of emboli. As a matter of fact, he went out like a light and certainly suffered no pain. The service lost its best field commander and I lost a damn good friend.[67]

Burial brought forth an immediate problem. War Department policy prohibited bringing home those who had died overseas. Beatrice believed that once buried her husband's body should not be moved, so if he were to be brought home now would be the time. Patton's associates agreed that he desired to be buried at West Point, that magnificent center of military education that had nurtured him. Neither Bea nor Fred wished for any special favors. Keyes, with whom they had spent much of the past week, therefore suggested that General Bull send a telegram, in General McNarney's name, to Eisenhower, now chief of staff, about bringing home General Patton's body. Fred and Bea never heard anything more about the matter. Asked by Fred whether the message had been sent, Keyes replied that he assumed it had. The War Department had ignored it.

Amid her grief on the twenty-second, Bea was forced to make a decision. Gay, Harkins, Hughes, and the others believed that if Patton were not taken to West Point, he would want to rest among his troops in Luxembourg. Fred told of the agony of deciding:

> That evening at Bad Nauheim General E. S. Hughes blurted out without anyone asking that if he had been Chief of Staff without hesitation he would have ordered George's body brought home— that he thought that was the obvious and only proper thing to do. . . . It seems strange to me that when these suggestions were received by General Eisenhower, as they must have been, he should reply only by gushing cables to Beatrice offering to do anything for her, the "anything" being underlined by text in the cable. Perhaps I expect too much, but it seemed to be an occasion to offer to do whatever had been suggested without being asked for it.[68]

After spending the evening of the twenty-second at Bad Nauheim, Bea, Fred, Gay, Harkins, and their party drove back to Heidelberg the next morning. Fred went over to the villa where General Patton's body rested and found that the arrangements, "largely made by Captain Moran" of the Women's Army Corps, "could not have been in better taste or more beautifully carried out." Potted plants, trees, and greenery lined the vestibule and doorway of the villa, "so that one entered through a green arch directly facing the feet of the casket, which was open." At the head of the casket rested the colors of the three armies Patton had commanded: the Third, the Seventh, and the Fifteenth. Sconces, with three or four candles in each, lined the walls. Two aisles led to either side of the casket, each aisle containing a border of three tall candles backed first by flowers, "mostly white lilies and white lilacs," and then by other flowers and greenery. A reception room on the right contained a guest book signed by the "steady stream" of visitors passing through the villa. "Bea did not wish to see George again," an appreciative Fred recorded, "so I have made this memo of the setting, which was beautifully done."

After lunch with General Keyes, Bea, Fred, and the rest of the party went to the church. Following the service the mourners drove past sidewalks packed with Germans to the railroad depot. "Only a rare Hitler Youth," Fred observed, "failed to remove his hat." Driving right into the station, Bea and Fred boarded the long train, composed of the private cars of Nazi officials, supplied by McNarney.

Shortly after dark, the train reached the French border. At six different French stations guards of honor and bands mourned with the family. "In their tributes," Fred noted, "they referred without exception to the 'General who won the war,' and the demonstrations were very touching and a clear proof of where he stood in the affection and esteem of the French."[69]

The next morning in a rain Patton's body was interred in the cemetery at Hamm in Luxembourg. Bea and Fred, accompanied by Harkins and Captain Duane, then started for home. At 6:20 A.M. on Christmas morning they arrived at Bedford, Massachusetts, "after a fine smooth trip."[70] General Patton was sleeping forever in the Europe his military genius had helped free.

Nineteen

A DIARY AND A MOVIE

I

In a real sense General Patton lived after he died. The quarter of a century after his death was largely the story of friends and supposed friends who desired to use the general's words and renown for monetary and political gain. It is also the story of a family that stood together and warded off the demands of others.

In the dismal days just after Patton's death, Robert Patterson proved as thoughtful to the general's family as Stimson, his predecessor as secretary of war, had been to the general himself. Like many others, Patterson sent the family a touching letter, but he and his wife did more. "When I read your lovely letter," Bea wrote Patterson on December 29, "my only wish was that Georgie might be looking over my shoulder. I wish you could know how deeply touched my girls were by your and Mrs. Patterson's call on them. So was I, when I heard about it; they said of your call 'they must have loved Daddy because they wanted to help us.' Please tell this to your dear wife."[1]

Early in 1946, when Patterson went to Europe, he stopped to see Patton's grave. "He is buried in a military cemetery," he told Field Marshal Archibald P. Wavell, with whom he had discussed Patton several weeks before, "along with 9,000 of his former soldiers. His grave is marked by a plain cross precisely like the others, and is in one of the long rows, not set apart in any way. That is the way he would have wished it."[2]

From the summer of 1945 on, Patton had sent Patterson chapters of the memoir he was writing, with the request that he show the work only to those closest to him. The day after Patton died, Patterson sent the chapters to President Truman, a keen student of military history, with a warning about its contents.

> You will see why it cannot be published. Patton has plenty of criticism about others, particularly about some British generals. He steps on other people's toes pretty freely. He was that way,— impulsive, explosive, far from impartial. He did not take a balanced view of things, but he was a great fighter and a great American. He once said to me, when I urged him not to make speeches, "I have strong opinions and I like to express them." Then he added after a pause, "Quite often I found they were wrong, and then I changed them."

After reading the manuscript, Truman returned it with a nondescript comment: "It certainly is interesting."[3]

The end of the war saw a mad dash to exploit its heroes. Among the first volumes to appear was Butcher's *My Three Years with Eisenhower,* a compilation of anecdotes and observations about Ike, Bradley, Patton, Bedell, the British, and everyone else who had anything to do with Eisenhower.

Published in both the United States and England, the book embarrassed Eisenhower. Writing to his beloved associate, Lieutenant-General Sir Hastings L. Ismay, Ike apologized to his British friends.

> In the first place, the view presented is that of the newsman looking for daily items of "human interest." By some strange quirk of fate these always center around points of momentary disagreement; record of constructive cooperation is apparently not "news." The result is that every little point of disagreement is unfailingly dwelt upon. Momentary exhibitions of temper (such as the time the Prime Minister, to show his disgust with all of us present at the table, including the British Chiefs of Staff, practically overturned his soup to show his displeasure) and every difference of strategic or tactical conception are all played up. On the other hand, there is not running through the book that continuous thread, repeated over and over again, of the miracle of international and inter-service cooperation which was soul and source of the victory. Oh well.[4]

Like Ike, Bea found herself and her husband's memory exploited by journalists. The Butcher in this instance was Drew Pearson's former partner, Lieutenant Colonel Robert S. Allen, who had served on Koch's staff and had lost an arm late in the war. In 1947, after Bea and Georgie's friend and neighbor, General Sherman Miles, reviewed Patton's *War As I Knew It* and Allen's paean to the Third Army, *Lucky Forward,* for the *Atlantic Monthly,* Bea told him the story of the two books. When in Europe during the war, Judge Patterson had received from Patton a copy of what became *War As I Knew It,*

> all but the last chapter, which he had not yet written. He told me several times how much he thought of it; then in April '46, he asked me to go to his office to discuss its publication (he knew I contemplated it) and discouraged the idea in no uncertain terms, saying that it might not do justice to Georgie and emphasizing the fact that it was confidential and that I should treat it as so. He then said—"I myself have treated it as absolutely confidential—except that I gave it to Allen to read. Allen's all right." I said: "Did you know he is writing a book?" He said: "Oh, is he?" and that was all. Allen wrote a lot of the Judge's speeches for him at that time. Later he wrote me a letter in 3 sealed envelopes marked "confidential" urging me not to publish. I did not answer it till the book was well under way and then very nicely, of course.

About that time Allen sent Mrs. Patton the manuscript of *Lucky Forward.* "I think he was nervous," Bea informed Miles. Comparing it with Patton's *War As I Knew It,* Bea "decided it was practically plagiarized and took it to a lawyer. He said that nothing could be done about it as Allen might have been original, but none of us thought so. Allen came down to see me & was very suave & said he would prefer to have the book follow Georgie's & would persuade the publisher to that effect. The publisher declined, and Allen has never let out a peep." Bea especially resented the way Allen advertised himself as the Third Army's G-2. "This was Col. Oscar Koch," she pointed out. "Allen was the assistant of the assistant ad nauseam ad infinitum. However, Georgie thought well of him and considered him able and loyal."[5]

Even in death Patton stirred emotions. One instance came on August

19, 1950, with the unveiling of the huge statue of Patton in war gear opposite the library at West Point. In the principal address Douglas Southall Freeman, the biographer of Robert E. Lee, called for a return to the leadership of the days of old: "Oh, for an hour of Webster in the halls of Congress; for a day of Stimson and Patterson in the Department of the Army. Oh, for a day of Patton at the front of his army, crying, 'Onward, onward. Take no counsel of your fears.' "[6]

Admiral Hall, who worked with Patton in the early invasions, later told a story about the speech that reflected as much on Freeman's fickleness as on Patton's ability. Shortly before the unveiling of the statue, Hall, then serving as commandant of the Armed Forces Staff College at Norfolk, invited Freeman to come down to the school to deliver his famous lecture on leadership. After the talk, a colonel got up and asked Freeman how long after a war a true history of that conflict could be written. Freeman speculated anywhere from forty to a hundred years and then said that the wife of a famous soldier, obviously Bea Patton, had been after him to write a biography of her husband. "But I had lived for 20 years with a great man," Freeman added, referring to Lee. "How could I waste my time on a scrub?"

Hall knew immediately that Freeman was talking about Patton.

So, much to my surprise, I went up to West Point for the unveiling of the statue, and the orator of the occasion was Douglas Southall Freeman, and when the time came to unveil the statue and Mrs. Patton pulled the cord, Douglas Freeman turned to him and described him as the "personification of leadership." Well, I knew that he didn't think that General Patton was the personification of leadership, and neither did I, because General Patton was 10 years old in some ways, but I think he was the greatest master of quick tactical movement that World War II developed. . . . I think one reason for it was that either before or during or after his short time as a student at VMI, he became the greatest admirer of Stonewall Jackson that I ever saw. He's walked over every battlefield that Stonewall ever fought on and he knows every thought that Stonewall Jackson ever had, and he had intense admiration for Stonewall Jackson. And I think that probably often he thought, "Well, what would Rommel do? What would Stonewall Jackson do?" and he'd just try to do one better, and perhaps he did at times.[7]

In 1972 the statue also conjured up thoughts of Patton for Chynoweth, who disclosed them to George F. Hofmann, then studying the development of American tanks.

The inter-relationship between Eisenhower, Patton, and Wood are a closed book, since they are all deceased. I have never forgiven Ike for one remark he made at a West Point reunion. Passing the statue of Patton (in his war finery) a reporter remarked: "General Patton was quite a legend." Ike replied: "Yes, mostly a legend!" This appeared in the Press.

When Ike was President of Columbia, I went to talk to him about Education, which was my chief interest after retirement. He brushed off the question of Education and walked up and down his office fulminating about George Patton and Douglas MacArthur, whom he called "megalomaniacs." I was astounded! Too much so to strike back in defense of Georgie, as I wanted to *after* getting out of the office. Discussing this incident that night, with another old friend in New York, he remarked that Ike had dearly wanted to be the Democratic nominee for President (this was 1948) and that he was in a vile humor because he had been thwarted. Please do not quote this paragraph. Ike is gone, and I do not wish to detract from his glory.[8]

II

Those who posed as friends of General Patton and his family often were not. This was especially true during the Republican primaries and convention of 1952, when Eisenhower vied with Senator Robert Taft of Ohio for the party's presidential nomination.

Strangely, Patton's diary played an important role in the campaign. Until masterfully edited and published in the early 1970s by Martin Blumenson as part of *The Patton Papers,* the diary took on a life of its own. During the war Patton had written entries on slips of paper that he often stuffed into his pockets. He then gave them to his stenographer, Sergeant Joseph D. Rosevich. Unknown to the Patton family, Rosevich purportedly kept a copy of the entries, which he later sold to one of Patton's earliest biographers, Ladislas Farago, in Paris. In 1955 Farago confirmed these facts during a visit to Drew Pearson.[9]

In December 1951 Eisenhower admitted to John Bennett of Pearson's staff that he feared that Mrs. Patton would publish segments of her husband's diary and letters. Ike asked Bennett what the public response might be if Mrs. Patton released material saying that Ike desired to divorce his wife, Mamie, and marry Kay Summersby. Even at this late date, Mamie knew little—if anything—about Ike's relationship with his wartime chauffeur.[10]

In 1952 rumors spread through conservative Republican circles that Patton's diary contained material damaging to Eisenhower. William Loeb of the *Manchester* (New Hampshire) *Union-Leader* suspected as much and told Patton's First World War friend Colonel Robert R. McCormick of the *Chicago Tribune*. Sure that the diary told of Eisenhower's desire to divorce Mamie—it did not—McCormick sent his London correspondent to interview Summersby, but the reporter found out nothing.[11]

Into this scene came other supposed friends of Patton and the Patton family: ex-President Herbert Hoover, the publisher Henry Regnery, and General Patton's former defender Frank E. Mason. In April 1952 Mason, after a lapse of seven years, suddenly wrote to Mrs. Patton. Feeding on the Ayer family's misapprehension that Ike had relieved Patton from command of the Third Army not because of his refusal to denazify Bavaria but because he opposed Communism, Mason reaffirmed his devotion to the memory of the great soldier. He vowed to "do anything that ever lies within my power to right the wrong against the reputation of General Patton."[12]

The next step came on April 22, 1952, when Regnery, the ultraconservative Chicago book publisher, warned Mrs. Patton of the political threat posed by Eisenhower, whom he denounced as "a 'yes' man, an opportunist." In battling Ike and pushing forward Taft, Patton's diary "may be of critical importance." Having briefly glanced at Farago's copy of the diary, Regnery was convinced "it would have an enormous impact" and "would clarify a number of things which are very much in need of being clarified. I remember you remarked, when Truman Smith and I were in your house, that General Eisenhower's record is available, and anybody can find out about him who will take the trouble, so that you couldn't see why anything your husband wrote six or seven years ago should make any difference." General Patton, Regnery argued, was "the one man in the world, probably, with the prestige and acknowledged integrity to speak about the military record of General Eisenhower, and what General Patton wrote in his Diary was written at the time the decisions were made, not long afterward."

Regnery saw the diary solely as a weapon in a political fight. With Bea's permission he hoped to have Colonel Smith, Hoover's military adviser, and Hugh Gibson, the former minister to Poland who had collaborated with Hoover on two books, edit it. He hoped MacArthur would write an introduction. Instead of taking years, as when Blumenson scrupulously edited Patton's papers, the preparation of the manuscript would require just two weeks. The printer would need only three weeks or so, and the book would be out in the middle of June, "several weeks before the Republican Convention. . . . I am sure that the only decisive factor in your mind is the public interest; I intrude myself in this way only because I feel that you may agree with me, that the Diary ought to be published, and before the Republican Convention."

In his letter, written three years before Farago told Drew Pearson how he got hold of the diary, Regnery related the same story. "I might add, by the way," he went on, "that I was able to get a rather full report on Mr. Farago, whose reputation is not the best. I am trying to get more information about Rosevich—I am curious to find out, if I can, why he never returned to this country, and how he happened to turn his material over to Farago. I would also be glad to know how it happened to come into his hands."[13]

Deeply involved in this scheme to rush out Patton's diary to hurt Ike was Hoover. At Mason's suggestion Regnery sent the former president a copy of his letter to Mrs. Patton. "If anything further develops," Regnery told Hoover, "I will keep you informed either directly or through Mr. Mason."[14]

On a limited scale William Randolph Hearst, Jr., succeeded where Regnery failed. Farago later conceded that he had made the mistake of lending his copy of the diary to the younger Hearst, who, as the Republican convention met in Chicago, proceeded to publish excerpts, all unfavorable to Eisenhower. On the first of July Bea was in Newark,

New Jersey, helping to launch the Army's new M-48, or Patton 48, fifty-ton tank. The front-page story in the next day's *New York Journal-American*, Hearst's leading newspaper, shocked her and her daughters. Written by Frank Conniff of Hearst's staff, the article left no doubt about its intent. "Patton Diary Tells Views on Eisenhower," the headline announced. Not being able to admit that he got the diary without the Patton family's consent, Conniff commented: "I am not at liberty to disclose how I came into possession of the Patton diary, except to say that its authenticity cannot be doubted."

Attacking both Eisenhower, Taft's rival for the Republican nomination, and Bradley, who as chief of staff was instrumental in relieving MacArthur from command of the United Nations forces in Korea, Conniff presented Patton at his most opinionated. He began by quoting Patton's entry for March 8, 1944, when Ike, threatening to resign, complained to Air Chief Marshal Sir Arthur W. Tedder that he was "tired of dealing with a lot of prima donnas." Then came the entry for May 10, 1945, when Ike, according to Patton, displayed "symptoms of political aspirations" by asking his generals to cooperate with the British and the other Allies.

If Conniff and Hearst disliked Ike, they detested Bradley. Conniff quoted in full the most anti-Bradley passage in the entire diary, written on February 3, 1944.

> Bradley is a man of great mediocrity, yet he is a loyal friend and a fine subordinate. At Benning when he was there, he failed to enforce discipline and on several occasions he had displayed timidity, notably at Gafsa on April 5–6, when he wanted to withdraw the CP when our right was threatened, and I had to intervene. Also when we first started East on the north coast of Sicily, he halted the 45th Division short of Cefalu, because he was afraid the Germans might land on the beach at Termini. It was necessary for me to order the Division forward.
>
> On the other hand, Bradley has many of the attributes which are considered desirable in a General. He wears glasses, has a strong jaw, and says little. I consider him among our better generals.

Carefully picking his quotes, Conniff even cited Patton's unfavorable impression of Clare Booth Luce. Visiting Patton in December 1944 with thirteen other Congressmen, Luce somehow was allowed to pull the lanyard of a cannon. "I am very angry," Patton noted on the sixth. Conniff never bothered to mention that Luce's husband, Henry Luce, owned *Time, Life,* and *Fortune,* which supported Ike for the Republican nomination, which he eventually got.[15]

On October 24, 1952, much more shocking news than the publication of segments of the diary stunned the Patton family. Beatrice Patton Waters, only forty-two, died of a heart attack at Highland Falls, the village adjacent to West Point. Her mother, sailing toward Norfolk on the *When and If,* learned of the tragedy only after a widespread radio search. John K. Waters, now a brigadier general, flew home from Korea for the funeral. "Beatrice Waters apparently was a victim of complete exhaustion," Nita Patton, who attended her niece's funeral, told Arvin Brown, "too long a strain I guess. She too is a war casualty."[16]

The terrible news continued in September 1953. Riding with about thirty friends in a drag hunt, Beatrice Ayer Patton was thrown from a horse. At a checkpoint her companions noticed she was missing. Riding back over the course they found her body on the ground. She apparently died instantly of head injuries.[17]

As if the diaries and the deaths were not enough, a new problem soon arose for Ruth Ellen Totten and her brother, Captain George S. Patton IV. Hollywood had discovered General Patton. Early in 1954 Ruth Ellen had read and been told that Warner Bros. desired to make a movie about her father. Raoul Walsh, who a few years before had made *White Heat* with James Cagney, was to direct it. "The whole business makes me so mad," Ruth Ellen told George Clark Lyon, a senior partner in the Los Angeles law firm of her cousins, Arvin M. Brown, Sr., and Arvin M. Brown, Jr.

The movies cheapen everything they touch, with, of course, a few notable exceptions such as "Henry V," "Hamlet" & "Julius Caesar" and it does seem that Daddy could be spared the claptrap, as they would never either realize it or put it across that he was a well-bred & considerable gentleman with a remarkable memory, who could recite reams of poetry, the Bible, the Book of Common Prayer & volumes of military history by heart, & who was adored by small children, dogs & old ladies. I kept the scrapbooks for my Mother & I used to sometimes think to myself "Who *is* this

George S. Patton Jr.? I've never met him & hope I never will." The newspapers never "got him right" & the movies most certainly wouldn't.[18]

Still mourning the deaths of her sister and her mother, Ruth Ellen found herself pestered by those who either wanted to make a movie about her father or to get hold of his diary. To Arvin Brown, Jr., she even proposed suing Warner Bros. in all forty-eight states. "I suppose it was most unreasonable of me," she answered Arvin's letter calming her down, "to suggest threatening Warner Bros. to sue 'in every state in the union,' I just get to feeling pushed sometimes! We are always involved with *some* kind of deal about Daddy." After her brother served in Korea, for example, he, along with his wife, visited the cemetery at Hamm. There they "found Daddy's grave was the *only one* in the cemetery without a marble cross." On inquiry they learned that for the third time the Battle Monuments Commission planned to move the grave. "No Rest in Peace for GSP Jr, apparently!"

Most disheartening was something Ruth Ellen confided to Arvin Brown, Jr., only because "you're ¼ Patton." Brigadier General Harry Semmes, "a very dear friend of Ma & Daddy's," began working on a book that he intended to call *Portrait of Patton*. A successful patent attorney in Washington, he had been in both World Wars and had two Distinguished Service Crosses.

Ma was all for it & loaned him a copy of Daddy's diary. While she was alive it was OK, his book was no good but she was helping him to write it & it was shaping up. Well, Ma died & "someone got to" Harry & the next thing you know, he approaches me with an offer from the Sat Eve Post to him, to get $45,000, for letting 8 articles be written by a ghost writer, under Harry's name, to be called "The Patton Diaries" & purporting to skim the cream of the diary. He was so bemused by the money it never occurred to him he was selling something that didn't belong to him! The diary was left to George, Bee—in this case, her boys—& me in Daddy's will so there is no question, according to our lawyer, that it is our property & cannot be used without permission. . . . We had an awful time last year getting back the version of the diary Daddy's soldier secretary stole & sold to Hearst.

The proposed movie presented another problem. "Right now" Ruth Ellen's brother was living in the Bachelor Officers Quarters "at West Point waiting for quarters & James Warner Bellah is up there *stalking* him literally. . . . Ma was *dead set* against a movie, so are we." The Patton "the world saw frequently *was* pretty crude. He did it on purpose. We don't want our kids growing up with that mental picture & remembrance of their grandfather, who was in reality a great & good & gentle man. So even if they make the movie, we want to be able to disavow it." The War Department had already asked George to go on leave with pay

& sort of help direct it, & he turned it down with our approval. Another small detail—we found out that Harry Semmes had practically made a deal with the movies to sell his damn book & we discouraged him on that too. I guess it's pretty thwarting for him, but it is to the interests of *everyone* in the family that Daddy's diary is *not* made public for many years. Ma didn't realize that he would do this, nor did we. He is a fine friend to do what he is contemplating doing.[19]

Refusing to respect the Patton family's desire for privacy, other World War II generals began pestering the children. In September 1955 Mark Clark approached Ruth Ellen, George Patton IV, Bea's brother Fred, and General Maxwell Taylor about a movie for which he would be the adviser. "He was not, in our opinion, sufficiently close to my father," George wrote General Williston B. Palmer, the former commander of the 82d Airborne Division, "nor did my father have a particularly high opinion of him; as certain paragraphs of the unpublished diary will indicate." The Patton family was convinced that Clark's concern was financial. "We think he is vitally interested in it for this reason, perhaps more than any other."[20]

The next July General Ira Eaker, who at one time commanded the Eighth Air Force, tried to sway the family. Now a vice president of the Hughes Aircraft Company, Eaker called Arvin Brown, Jr., said he was an old friend of General Patton, and talked about a proposed movie to be made by Twentieth Century–Fox. A few days later Bert E. Friedlob of Fox called Arvin. He promised to give the family the right to edit any movie and to avoid all controversies, such as Patton's "difficulties with General Eisenhower."[21]

Ruth Ellen thought little of this project, too. She immediately answered her cousin's letter telling her of it.

I don't know why Gen. Eaker thinks he is such a pal of Daddy's. He wired Johnnie Walker pages about it all. I suppose eventually someone will pirate a movie, but it's bound to be in poor taste & lousy & so long as the family isn't connected with it in any way, we are still in the clear. I don't trust 20th Century Fox any more than I do Warner Bros. I have been to a couple of so-called "good" movies lately & they really didn't seem so earth-shaking. So tell the gentleman the answer is still NO & thanks a million for keeping us posted.[22]

In September 1956 Columbia Pictures jumped into the fray. The company wanted to make a movie based on William Bancroft Mellor's book *Patton: Fighting Man*. "The family feels very strongly," Arvin Brown, Jr., wrote Mellor, "that a motion picture on the life of General George S. Patton, to be of financial interest to the maker, would necessarily be based upon current misapprehension of his character and outlook, and such a picture would be most repugnant to his family."[23]

A television depiction of General Patton in January 1957 reinforced the family's distrust of moviemakers. Answering George's letter objecting to the program, Arvin told him that he could not win a lawsuit. In 1951 the California Appellate Court had settled the issue. In the case of *Stryker v. Republic Pictures Corporation,* the court had declared members of the armed forces public figures who could not be defamed.[24]

The Patton family might have taken solace in the complaints of other generals objecting to the way they were depicted. Late in the decade an exasperated President Eisenhower sent to his friend Pug Ismay a letter marked "PERSONAL AND CONFIDENTIAL" on every page. In it Ike gave his opinion of Montgomery and his memoirs. Montgomery, he argued, "would scarcely stand much chance of going down in history as one of the great British captains." Eisenhower agreed with Patton on almost every phase of Monty's career.

I recall the impatience with which we waited for any northern movement of Montgomery's out of the Catania Plains and the long and unnecessary wait before he stepped across the Messina Strait. Do you remember the great promises that he made during the planning for OVERLORD about moving quickly to the southward beyond Caen and Bayeux to get ground fit for airfields, and his post-war assertions that such a movement was never included in the plan? Next consider his preposterous proposal to drive on a single pencil-line thrust on to Berlin and later his failure even to make good his effort for a lodgment across the Rhine, and this after I had promised and given to him everything he requested until that particular operation was completed.

I cannot forget his readiness to belittle his associates in those critical moments when the cooperation of all was needed. So, I personally believe that, on his record, historians could never be tempted to gild his status too heavily, even if his memoirs had not reflected traits far from admirable. . . .

P.S.: Because I have never before, to my knowledge, put on paper or spoken publicly in a disparaging fashion about any other public figure . . . I hope you will understand why I am marking this letter personal and confidential.[25]

III

Despite the resistance of the general's family, movie producers continued to push for a Patton movie. By 1961 the Hollywood figure most capable of producing the film had entered the scene. As a member of General Marshall's staff, Frank McCarthy had met all the leading figures in the Second World War. After graduating from the Virginia Military Institute, he had served as the publicist for several films, including *Brother Rat,* a comedy about the college. Now a producer at Twentieth Century–Fox, he told John S. Wood about the project. Bob Allen was collecting material on which the movie would be based.[26]

Wood, meanwhile, continued until his death in 1966 at the age of seventy-eight to push forward the lessons he had learned during the campaigns in Europe. "Armor has not yet been used as armor in Korea, in my judgment," he reported to Liddell Hart during the war there. "O. P. Weyland, the Far East Air Force commander, with whom I developed a murderous combination of air-armored action in France, says all that hard-bought experience has been lost. No such combination has ever been used out there, although it could have been."[27]

A full-page interview with Eisenhower that appeared in the *New York Herald-Tribune* and the *San Francisco Examiner* on June 10, 1964, twenty years after the invasion of France, angered Wood, who had no love for Ike. Sending a copy of the interview, conducted by the television commentator Walter Cronkite, to Liddell Hart, Wood ridiculed everything Eisenhower said about Patton. Where Ike remarked that Patton "was always talking about wanting to serve as my lieutenant in active operations," Wood observed: "Tommyrot! George used flattery freely whenever he felt it might help him!" Where Ike talked of his thirty-year friendship with Patton and said "I was always devoted to him very closely and deeply," Wood countered: "His real feelings about Eisenhower, as often expressed to me, couldn't be printed."

Wood was at his bitterest answering Eisenhower's statement that "Patton had an instinct for pursuit, and that was his great capacity." His comment to Liddell Hart indicated that he still considered the diversion to the Brittany ports a mistake.

> "Pursuit," indeed! A fair measure of Eisenhower's military genius—this evaluation of George Patton. A pity neither he nor Bradley nor even Montgomery knew so little about *exploitation*. Montgomery is right about Eisenhower being in a fog after the landings, but he was not much better. None of them had any true conception of the possibilities of exploitation at that critical moment. Even George Patton was indulging in puerile bets with Montgomery as to when *he would* take Brest & Lorient.[28]

The publication in 1964 of Farago's biography of Patton, based largely on notes he had taken while possessing Patton's diary, brought from Wood another burst of recollections. "Well written, a bit exhausting, but subject seems inexhaustible," he informed Hanson Baldwin. "Book includes many minor errors & is filled with sweeping assumptions, but nevertheless, gives a fair picture of the complexities of George's nature & actions. Before Geoff Keyes, Hap Gay, & yours truly pass on (Eisenhower & Bradley wouldn't be frank) *you* should use our judgment of George & write a definitive George."

Wood then touched on something unusual. Patton's children had supposedly gotten an order prohibiting Farago from citing Patton's diary, but Ivan Obolensky, the publisher, "must have got around the court injunction on the Patton book. I wrote Ruth Ellen and young George my impressions of it on November 11th—a day when George and I used to get a bit tight to celebrate the date of his birth and to commiserate the ending of World War I before we really got at the Hun."[29]

Wood's final blast at the leading Allied generals came when Baldwin sent him three articles he had published in the *New York Times* on the European war. In response, Wood made his remarks about their overindulgence during wartime.

> I agree with you that the Bulge was a case history of the operation of military intelligence—and a dismal one. The intelligence that was lacking in the mental equipment of the top commanders— actually a mediocre lot in that respect, with no quick perceptions or immediate reactions. In discussing the G-2 machinery and its conflicting personalities, I think you have let off the three top commanders too easily. The situation you describe was the direct result of defects in the character of the top command: Eisenhower the compromiser and conciliator with no deep convictions or loyalties; Montgomery the vainglorious with his manifest and egregious egotism; Bradley the plodder, hidebound and dull, mutely vain and resentful. Not one of them had ever rightly grasped the realities of combat at the front. In the ease and relative comfort and quiet and luxury of their headquarters, they sat and acted on plans that were already outmoded by the events of combat—not an inspiring character among the lot of them.[30]

Bea's brother Fred, meantime, made Baldwin the latest object in the campaign to convince the world that Patton had lost the Third Army not because he kept Nazis in office but because he saw "the Russian menace. . . . All this hullabaloo about the Army in politics makes me feel ill," Fred told Baldwin. "General Patton never voted because he felt he should not even remotely become involved in politics, but nobody was going to muzzle him on the national foreign policy, even though he had to give up his career."[31] Sadly, the campaign has been largely successful.

IV

Amid discussions of the war, the slappings were never far from the fore. In 1957, when Patton's friend William Cunningham of the *Boston Herald* referred to Private Paul G. Bennett, whom Patton slapped on August 10, 1943, as a "sniveling soldier," Dr. Donald E. Currier, who commanded the 93rd Evacuation Hospital, where the incident took place, objected. He informed Cunningham that the

> soldier was abused both verbally and physically by a nasty bully. It all happened in the hospital I commanded in World War II and it all happened in my presence. As considerably more took place then has ever appeared in print, I am the only person now living who could tell it all to you.
>
> In the first place, the soldier was not sniveling. In the second place, the attack was completely unjustified and out of order. The General's obscenities and blasphemies in the presence of professional personnel, both male and female, were beneath contempt. If you had seen and heard what I did, you would feel as I do, that what happened to Patton was very much less than he deserved.[32]

The publication by Bea's nephew, Fred Ayer, Jr., of *Before the Colors Fade,* a laudatory study of Patton, further infuriated Dr. Currier, who called the account of the Bennett slapping grossly inaccurate. "He was not hysterical," Currier wrote Ayer, "until General Patton had finished his vicious verbal and physical abuse. Your uncle by his inexcusable and asinine conduct converted an ordinary case of dehydration and exhaustion, which could have been straightened out in forty-eight hours—as many others were, into a neuro-psychiatric problem which took weeks to resolve." Ayer, moreover, quoted someone named Currier who praised Patton.[33]

Ayer's answer worsened things. In his book, he said, he quoted not Dr. Currier but a Daniel Currier, a medical corpsman serving in the evacuation hospital. He happened to meet this second Currier in nearby Beverly, Massachusetts. "Having been brought up in the company of physicians," he responded, "and in the shadow of Beverly Hospital where father was president for thirty-five years, I do know the difference."[34]

After consulting his lawyer, Daniel Needham, Currier realized that he had no legal case against Ayer. He did, however, investigate Ayer's explanation and found it baseless. Neither the Massachusetts nor the federal army records indicated the existence of a Daniel Currier. "If you think for one moment that I believe that you accepted such a statement from a total stranger without making any effort to verify what he was saying, then you think I am a monumental damn fool. Of course, I don't believe a word of it and think what you have done is beneath contempt." Currier demanded a public admission that the statement was a hoax. If Ayer refused, Currier threatened to make public all the documents he had on the slapping.[35]

Having no choice, Patton's nephew acceded to the request. His apology appeared in the *Boston Herald* on December 4, 1964, and in the *Boston Globe* the following day. "I fully accept the fact that there was no Daniel Currier on duty at your hospital in Sicily," he conceded to Currier. "Therefore, it is clear, as I wrote Dan Needham, I must have had a lapse of memory or been mistaken in my understanding of the man's name." Still, Ayer did not consider himself guilty of spreading a falsehood. "I have made mistakes before and I shall certainly make them again. But I do not lie."[36] The matter hardly did credit to Ayer.

V

The publication of Farago's biography spurred Twentieth Century–Fox on. The studio bought the rights to it, to Bradley's *A Soldier's Story,* to Jack Pearl's *Blood and Guts Patton,* and to Bob Allen's history of the Third Army, *Lucky Forward.*[37]

As word spread of Fox's plan to go ahead with the project, Frank McCarthy received numerous letters about it. One of the most novel came from William M. Riddle of Oshkosh, Wisconsin, who offered the studio his 16-millimeter color film of General Patton in his famous Flash Gordon uniform directing combat exercises at Fort Benning in the presence of Secretary Stimson. The uniform consisted of a gold 1930s-version football helmet, green tight-fitting trousers, and a high-necked jacket with brass buttons. Patton wore his two pistols in shoulder holsters.[38]

On the Barry Gray radio program just after the film came out,

Franklin Schaffner, its director, told how George C. Scott happened to be picked to play Patton. The studio's first choice was Burt Lancaster. One day Schaffner and McCarthy met with Lancaster and described the proposed film, which would open with Patton's famous speech. The narrative would start just after the American defeat at Kasserine Pass and end with Patton's removal from command of the Third Army, erroneously depicted as the result of his hatred of the Soviets. In deference to the Patton children, the family would not be characters in the movie. For an hour the Fox people tried to make the role of Patton as appealing as possible. After saying nothing, Lancaster got up, said only, "I am not impressed," and left the room. Following refusals from several other actors the role went to Scott, who gave a masterful performance.

Inexplicable was Frank McCarthy's selection of Harkins, now a retired but discredited four-star general, as one of his two military advisers, General Bradley being the other. An unimaginative, vain staff officer who had never fought a battle, Harkins had demonstrated, during a tour of duty in Vietnam in 1962 and 1963, that none of Patton's brilliance had rubbed off on him. David Halberstam of the *New York Times* described Harkins, who exaggerated enemy casualties so as to deceive Washington officials and never dirtied his uniform by visiting a battle site, as "a man of compelling mediocrity" and "a lying sonofabitch." Hoping to entice the army into sending more Americans to Vietnam, Harkins ran "the great Saigon lying machine." Similarly, Neil Sheehan, who covered Harkins for the United Press International, found laughable the comparison between Patton, a great and imaginative leader who almost sacrificed his career because of his honesty with reporters, and the deceitful Harkins.[39]

The picture, among the best film biographies ever made, drew some interesting comments. Monty's chief of staff, Major General Sir Francis de Guingard, wrote Bradley about a newsreel depicting the American and British forces coming together in Africa. "You are entirely right about the two armies meeting in the middle of Tripoli being dramatic license," Bradley conceded. "The need for this was dictated by the availability of newsreel footage. In fact, as you well know, the two armies met after the Eighth Army broke through the Mareth line and came north toward Tunis, and the Americans advanced east from Gafsa. The footage shown was the closest we could get to this."[40]

Colonel John Eisenhower, now the American ambassador to Belgium, offered two comments. First, he believed that the unflattering depiction of Montgomery probably stemmed from Bradley's "hatred" of him. He also questioned leaving his father out of the movie. "As a result," he told McCarthy, "the meeting of 19 December 1944 lost the impact of the exchange between Patton and DDE. I shouldn't be so sensitive about this, but I think that the Verdun meeting was one of my Dad's finest hours."[41]

A different omission struck Colonel Thomas S. Bigland, who had served under Bradley. "It must have been difficult to decide what to include in the film," he related to Bradley, "but I was surprised that the amazing drive across the Palatinate and the Rhine crossing were omitted. I well remember your 8:00 A.M. briefing, at which I reported Monty's plan for the Rhine crossing, and then Richard Stillman reported the U.S. 3rd army's crossing without fuss! I was grateful to you for your reference to Patton's long-laid plans, and that my leg was not to be pulled too much!"[42]

The Frank McCarthy Papers at the Virginia Military Institute contain a copy of Patton's diary, indicating that the filmmakers had access to it. Rejecting Henry Regnery as a publisher of Patton's writings in 1958, his son and daughter turned instead to Houghton Mifflin, which had issued *Before the Colors Fade*. To edit Patton's writing, they selected Martin Blumenson, whose magnificent two-volume *The Patton Papers* has been cited in dozens of books.[43]

Thus ended the twenty-five-year quest for the rights to the diary and the movie. The results of the family's resistance to those who would exploit General Patton's words and deeds were a movie that won seven Academy Awards and a two-volume collection of superbly edited papers.

Twenty

PATTON: A BRIEF ASSESSMENT

In evaluating Patton one fact stands out. By any standards he was an extraordinary tactical commander, perhaps, as Admiral Hall suggested, "the greatest master of quick tactical movement that World War II developed." Among his great assets were his imagination and his ability to visualize the entire battlefield. His achievements are all the more remarkable because, Colonel Nye has pointed out, "Patton spent only 391 days in combat in his whole life—just 13 months, between Meuse-Argonne, Casablanca, Tunisia, Sicily, and the cruise from Avranches to Bavaria. It took a decade for Alexander the Great and Napoleon to earn their reputations as military geniuses, and Grant and Lee at least four years."[1]

Among the military leaders of his time, Patton seemed unique in another way. "No American officer," Nye continued, "ever did more to advance his career—letters of petition; dinner parties in honor of the Secretary of War, Vice-President and visiting generals; telephone calls; publicity releases; even keeping a string of horses in central Washington for Mr. Stimson and others to ride. But no one cared more for his soldiers than George Patton—always out in the cold and rain with them, seeing that they had the best food and medical attention; listening, listening, listening, talking their language."[2]

Patton's ambition and fame often created resentment. "Another phase of WWII history which might well be put into proper perspective is the 'Only Patton Armor' myth," Brigadier General Sidney R. Hinds, who led Combat Command B of the 2d Armored in 1945, complained to Donald E. Houston, the author of a history of that division. "General

Simpson's Ninth Army probably had more tanks most of the time than did Patton and was at least as aggressive in making deep thrusts and wide sweeps, but with much less publicity—then and now! General McLain's XIX Corps was especially heavy with armored mobile Infantry in trucks to follow up, particularly the 30th Division under Leland Hobbs. The History of the XIX Corps should give a pretty good picture of the use of armor on the north flank German plains between Würm and Elbe rivers."[3]

Happily for Patton, he commanded some extraordinary soldiers. Wood and Weyland, both largely forgotten, were innovative and brilliant. For twenty-five years those who served under Patton contributed to the greatness of the American army: Matthew B. Ridgway, Creighton W. Abrams, Bruce C. Clarke, James M. Gavin, Maxwell D. Taylor, and numerous others.

And yet, despite the presence of Harkins, Gay, Koch, and Gaffey, both S. L. A. Marshall and Bradley downgraded Patton's staff—and the notion that the Third Army got the best of everything. In 1966 Bradley explained why.

> I had three armies in the same line—Patton's Third Army, Hodges' First Army, and Simpson's Ninth Army. But Simpson was another very thorough and a well-trained Infantryman. He had probably one of the best staffs over there. They worked beautifully together. And you can pick this up by listening to divisions that are transferred from one Army to another Army, or one Corps that is transferred from one Army to the other one—how much better they are taken care of and supplied, for example, in one Army than they would be in another. For example, Patton's staff was not as efficient a staff as the First or Ninth Armies, and divisions would notice this when they would be transferred from Patton's Army, say, to the First Army—they would get better supplies, and quicker replacements, and so forth.[4]

Clearly, Patton was a better tactician than strategist. Officers who took part in or later studied his campaigns have questioned several of his broad movements. Bradley and Truscott found fault with his attempted landings, some complete failures, behind German lines from Palermo to Messina. Wood criticized the diversion of Patton's armored divisions from the east to Brest and Lorient in Brittany. Colonel Icks questioned his frontal attacks on Metz. And S. L. A. Marshall disagreed with his bungled moves toward Houffalize from Bastogne.

But perhaps the saddest aspect of Patton's record, and indeed of his life, was the effect of his warlike speeches on his troops in Sicily. On July 13 and 14 Patton's soldiers committed as many as five atrocities, including the murder of civilians at the Canicatti soap factory. Almost sixty years after it took place, this last incident has been documented by a memorandum in a rarely cited record group in the National Archives.[5]

Preoccupied with disputes among the various services, historians have tended to slight another kind of rivalry. From the 1920s to D-Day in Normandy politicians and generals who downgraded tanks controlled the American and British armies. Even after the fall of Poland and France, those who believed that infantry alone would win the war ran roughshod over such American tank advocates as Chaffee, Chynoweth, Wood, Grow, and Cook and such British proponents of tanks as Martel, Hobart, and Liddell Hart. In the United States men who bragged that they had never ridden in a tank and never would commanded armored units. The story told by Chynoweth was symptomatic. During a 1939 maneuver at Fort Meade, a captain who had attended the infantry tank course at Fort Benning moved pins around on a board and announced: "This is the way we handle tanks today." With that Patton turned to Chynoweth "with a big wink."[6]

Regretfully, much that historians have written about Patton is questionable. Psychoanalyzing someone from his letters and diary is risky, but those who argue that Patton was dyslexic have done just that. In reality, Patton displayed few of the signs of dyslexia. His poor spelling probably stemmed from his father's ideas on education. Constantly read to, Patton never saw a printed page until he began school at the age of twelve. Despite doing well in spelling at school, he never made up the lost ground, Nor is dyslexia as common as some people argue, affecting, according to the National Association of School Psychologists, perhaps 3 percent of school-age children, hardly the 20 percent cited by one historian.

Equally intriguing is the oft-repeated story of Patton's love affair with Jean Gordon. Much of the information about this relationship came from Ruth Ellen Patton Totten. But in a letter to Arvin H. Brown, Jr., in 1954, in which she opposed the making of a movie about her father by Warner Bros., Ruth Ellen seemingly contradicted the story.

> It would seem to me that Daddy's military life would make too technical a movie without some of his personal life (altho' how Hollywood would handle the theme of rich-boy-with-normal-parents-and-happy-normal-childhood-makes-good-at-West-Point-married-childhood-sweetheart-also-rich-and-normal-has-three-normal-kids-who-manage-to-make-happy-normal-marriages-and-never-has-a-love-affair-or-gets-maladjusted is a thing to make one ponder).[7]

Perhaps nothing has captivated the public more than Patton's ideas on reincarnation. In 1991 Colonel Nye summarized them.

> Patton wrote that he may have initiated his many lives as a cave-man hunting for meat, and he may have been a soldier who stabbed Christ on the cross. He fought alongside the Greeks, Alexander at Tyre, and the Roman legionnaires. He was once a pirate, a cavalryman with Napoleon, and finally a tanker in the Great War. He always suffered horrible deaths. God determined when he should return and fight again. All of this, then, is the heart of the warrior soul or warrior spirit that Patton referred to in so many of his speeches and writings. Few in his audience may have realized how much these simple terms were bound to concepts of eternity and reincarnation in his complex mind. But these ideas were undoubtedly the means by which he controlled his fear in battle.[8]

Did Patton really believe in reincarnation? Writing to his friend Colonel Nye, Colonel Arthur H. Blair, who once taught English at West Point and was a combat veteran of the Korean and Vietnam wars, answered that he did not.

> No, Patton never lived any life other than the one we know of in this century. . . . On the other hand, like so many geniuses, he

lived in his peculiar reality. If you couple a remarkable memory, a great curiosity, a showman's personality, a tremendous ego, and a strain of lack of self-confidence, you get a person who has no difficulty mixing his intellectual world with his physical world to the point that the difference (to an ordinary person) between fact and fiction doesn't exist. In effect, it didn't matter to Patton if it were literally impossible for him to have been one of Napoleon's marshals. As far as he was concerned, he had been one.[9]

Nye disagreed, pointing out that "the Patton family's references to reincarnation were casual and familiar." Mrs. Patton joined her husband in believing in it. At the end of the television movie *The Last Days of Patton,* Eva Marie Saint, who played Mrs. Patton, said of her dying husband: " 'It's time we let him go. He will return when a soldier is needed again.' Even today when I am sailing with George '46, and a porpoise races by, he says, 'Hi, ma,' because she wanted to be a porpoise in her next life. (I say, 'Hello, Mrs. Patton,' and we both smile.)"

With enormous insight Nye analyzed Patton's thinking.

So, "I was there" was much more than just a metaphor for saying "I could have been there." Reincarnation was the core of Patton's battle to control his fear in combat—a subject about which he continuously lectured officer groups. (He thought the main purpose of West Point was to instill in young men a conscience so great that they would not run away on the battlefield.) In his poem ["Through a Glass, Darkly"] he always dies a valorous but terrible death. In a high percentage of reincarnation cases that have been studied, the life that is passed on to another has often had a violent end. It is much easier to be brave if one knows there is a Valhalla and another life waiting.[10]

As Chester Hansen noted, Patton never wavered from the Viking doctrine that an afterlife existed for the brave. "Patton earnestly believes in a warrior's Valhalla," Hansen observed in December 1944. "He honestly thinks it is to the glory of a man to die in the service of his country. Admittedly, there is no better way to die if die one must. But the solution lies in averting the need for dying."

This faith may explain two of the most publicized incidents of Patton's life, the slappings in Sicily. With H. R. Knickerbocker of the International News Service, Noel Monks of the *London Daily Mail* stumbled upon Patton after one of the slappings and heard him say: "There is no such thing as shell shock. It's an invention of the Jews." In 1955, still puzzled, Monks commented: "In the intervening years I have discussed the Patton Incident with many American generals, some of whom were fellow West Pointers, but I have never been offered a reasonable explanation for his conduct that hot August day in Sicily."[11]

Everett Hughes perhaps provided the answer. "Helped Geo write his reply to the letter Ike sent him cussing Geo out for maltreating E[nlisted] M[en]," Hughes noted on August 27, 1943. "I insisted that Geo quit saying that he had done no wrong and that he had saved the immortal souls of the EM."[12]

If Patton was convinced that death in battle led to reincarnation and immortality, he was also sure that neglect of duty brought damnation. Officers must face death with their troops. That explains why Patton urinated into Terry Allen's foxhole, something Bradley could not comprehend, and why, as Lindsey Nelson recorded, he told Manton Eddy to get his staff officers up front and out in the open, where the enemy might shoot at them. As Patton saw it, the slappings indeed "saved the immortal souls of the EM."

Usually viewed solely as a soldier, Patton presents a political puzzle. How did the son of a Wilsonian Democrat end up a right-wing conservative? In a letter to Hanson Baldwin in 1962, Bea's brother, Fred Ayer, repeated the argument that Patton lost command of the Third Army because he alone saw and opposed the Soviet menace in Europe. He added that "General Patton never voted because he felt he should not even remotely be involved in politics."[13] In reality, Patton surely voted in 1916, when his father ran for the Senate.

But Patton's conversion raises questions. Why should someone whose father detested and fought that California octopus, the Southern Pacific, become enamored of big business? Why should someone who never held a civilian job become antilabor? Why did Patton detest Jews and Italians? What compelled him to suspect that anyone who disagreed with him, such as Professor Dorn, was a Communist? Rather

than from his parents and from his California and Virginia relatives—
the Pattons, the Browns, the Wilsons, the Bannings—Patton, especially
after his father's death, seemed drawn to the ideas of his wife's family.

The Ayer family engaged in practices that must have appalled
George S. Patton, Sr., who, as his letters and those of his workers now in
his papers at the Huntington Library show, treated his employees with
dignity and fairness. In January 1912 the employees at the Ayer family's American Woolen Company, protesting wage cuts and unbearable
filth in the company-owned tenements, went on strike. The dispute
provided the background for the family's hatred of unions and for its
notions about radicals. Leading the strike was the International Workers of the World. The strikers were mainly Italian, and many of the
nation's labor leaders were Jews.[14] What better proof could there be
that these people were Socialists and Communists?

The Ayer family, especially Charles Fanning Ayer, whom Patton
mentions in some of his last letters as being his adviser, pushed the general down the road that ended with his loss of the Third Army. In his
report on Patton's failure in Bavaria, buried in the National Archives,
Dorn never mentioned Patton's hatred of the Soviets. During the fateful meeting in Ike's office, the subject never even came up. The sole
issue was Patton's refusal, in the face of orders, to remove Nazis from
office. Those who, basing their writings on those of the Ayer family,
argue differently do Eisenhower and Bedell Smith a great injustice.

There have, in effect, been two General Pattons. One is the Patton of
public renown: poet, intellectual, reincarnationist, and farsighted
leader. The other is the Patton of reality: devoted son, materialist,
inspiring but often cold leader, a man of narrow social and political
vision. As a soldier, his rescue of the trapped forces in Bastogne ranks
with Ulysses S. Grant's running the Confederate batteries at Vicksburg
and George Washington's crossing of the Delaware at Trenton in daring
and ingenuity. But Colonel Nye described it aptly when he wrote of
Patton's "complex mind," at once broad and narrow, genteel and vulgar,
receptive to new military ideas but in other ways stagnant and even
regressive.

More than any other prominent general, Patton encompassed America and its regions. On his father's side his forebears came from the
South. He grew up in the Far West and was educated in the East. And

he eventually settled in New England. British generals saw him as a totally American product, epitomizing his country's contradictions, and referring to him in 1943 as "Chewing Gum" and "Cowboy." Always believing, as his father first taught him in 1905, in Valhalla, Patton indeed personified the American version of his ideal, "the warrior soul."

Endnotes

PRELUDE

1. Testimony of Colonel Homer W. Jones, p. 30, Washington, D.C., Feb. 17, 1944, File 333.9, Box 67, Records of the Office of the Inspector General, Record Group 159, National Archives II, College Park, Md. Jones was testifying at the investigation of two American atrocities committed in Sicily.

2. Testimony of Captain Howard Cry, p. 48, Record of the Trial of Captain John T. Compton by General Court-Martial, October 23, 1943, Judge Advocate General's Files, Falls Church, Va.

3. James J. Weingartner, "Massacre at Biscari: Patton and an American War Crime," *Historian* 52 (November 1989); 27–39. Quoted on Compton's death is George E. Martin, *Blow, Bugle, Blow* (Bradenton, Fla.: Opuscula, 1986), p. 97. Martin, then a colonel but later a major general, was the division's chief of staff.

4. Basil H. Liddell Hart, "Notes for History: Talk with Alexander Clifford, 4th April 1944," LM 11/1944/29, Basil H. Liddell Hart Papers, Liddell Hart Centre for Military Archives, King's College, London; Frank James Price, *Troy H. Middleton: A Biography* (Baton Rouge: Louisiana State University Press, 1974), pp. 146, 148, 161. Comiso fell to Middleton's division on the afternoon of July 12, the third day of fighting, Biscari on July 14, the fifth. See Carlo D'Este, *Bitter Victory: The Battle for Sicily, 1943* (New York: E. P. Dutton, 1988), p. 307. In his diary Patton never mentioned Clifford.

5. "Sicily: The First Phase of Occupation," File 319.1, Box 72, Records of the War Department General and Special Staffs, Civil Affairs Division, Record Group 165, National Archives II, College Park, Md. I am most grateful to Professor Joseph Salemi of New York University and Brooklyn College for telling me of the incident. Professor Salemi's father, an army corporal serving as an interpreter, was one of from fifteen to eighteen American soldiers who saw the incident, which has haunted him ever since. In deference to Professor Salemi and his father, who do not wish to hurt the lieutenant colonel's family, I have not revealed the officer's name.

6. John P. Marquand, "The General," Draft A, p. 19, Folder 676, John P. Marquand Papers, Beinicke Rare Book and Manuscript Library, Yale University, New Haven, Ct.; Reminiscences of Charles Poletti, pp. 434–436, May 1978, Oral History Research Office, Columbia University Library, New York City.

7. Roger H. Nye, "Patton's Deja Vu: A Talk to Phi Alpha Theta Honor Society, 25 February 1992," p. 5, Box 1, Roger H. Nye Papers, Special Collections, United States Military Academy Library, West Point, N.Y.

CHAPTER ONE   GLASSELLS AND HEREFORDS, WILSONS AND PATTONS

1. Lesley J. McNair, "Memorandum for General Marshall," Oct. 7, 1941, George S. Patton, Jr., Papers, Special Collections, United States Military Academy Library, West Point, N.Y.; George S. Patton IV to Roger H. Nye, South Hamilton, Mass., Sept. 18, 1989, Patton Papers. (After the initial reference to the Patton Papers at West Point in each chapter, each additional reference to "Patton Papers" refers to the West Point collection. Other Patton collections are identified every time they are cited.)

2. Charles Richardson, *Flashback: A Soldier's Story* (London: William Kimber, 1985), pp. 158–159. As has often been pointed out, Patton's guns were ivory-handled.

3. Speech of Douglas Southall Freeman at West Point, Aug. 19, 1950, p. 2, Box 8, Patton Papers; William C. Pendleton, *History of Tazewell County and Southwest Virginia, 1748–1921* (Richmond, Va.: W. C. Mill, 1920), pp. 164–165, 207, 217.

4. John T. Goolrick, *The Life of General Hugh Mercer* (New York and Washington, D.C.: Neale Publishing, 1906), pp. 103–112; George Smith Patton Genealogy, Addendum II, Box 33, Benjamin D. Wilson Papers, Henry E. Huntington Library, San Marino, Cal.; Philip Slaughter, *A History of St. Mark's Parish, Culpeper County, Virginia* (Baltimore: Innes, 1877), pp. 158, 170; Horace Edwin Hayden, *Virginia Genealogies: A Genealogy of the Glassell Family of Scotland and Virginia* (Wilkes-Barre, Pa.: n.p., 1891), pp. 32–34.

5. John McFarnham to George S. Patton, Sr., Pling, W.V., Oct. 23, 1923, Box 7, George S. Patton, Sr., Papers, Henry E. Huntington Library, San Marino, Cal.; Hayden, *Virginia Genealogies,* p. 32.

6. Susan Thornton Glassell [Patton] to Virginia Ring, Richmond, Va., Nov. 24, 1854, Addendum, Box 9, Banning Company Papers, Henry E. Huntington Library, San Marino, Cal.

7. Andrew Glassell, Sr., to Susan Thompson Thornton Glassell, Near Smiths, Ala., Jan. 3, 1835, Addendum, Box 9, Banning Company Papers.

8. Andrew Glassell, Sr., to Susan Thompson Thornton Glassell, Greensboro, Ala., Jan. 19, 1836, Addendum, Box 9, Banning Company Papers.

9. Ellen B. Thornton's Sister to Ellen B. Thornton, Baltimore, Dec. 5, 1836, Addendum, Box 10, Banning Company Papers; Andrew Glassell, Sr., to William T. Glassell, Mobile, Ala. June 28, 1854, Addendum, Box 9, Banning Company Papers; John Steven McGroarty, *California of the South: A History* (Chicago: S. J. Clarke, 1935), V, pp. 355–358.

10. Andrew Glassell, Jr., to Andrew Glassell, Sr., San Francisco, June 4, 1857, Addendum, Box 9, Banning Company Papers.

11. Eleanor B. Thornton to Andrew Glassell, Sr., Charleston, Va., Nov. 11, 1856, Addendum, Box 10, Banning Company Papers.

12. Susan Glassell Patton to Ring, Charleston, Va., Nov. 22, 1857, Addendum, Box 9, Banning Company Papers.

13. Susan Patton to George Smith Patton, Richmond, Va., Feb. 27, 1861, Addendum, Box 9, Banning Company Papers.

14. Susan Patton to George Smith Patton, Richmond, Va., April 14, 1861, Addendum, Box 9, Banning Company Papers.

15. George S. Patton, Sr., "A Child's Memory of the Civil War," pp. 1–3, Box 5, George S. Patton, Jr., Papers, Manuscript Division, Library of Congress; Slaughter, *History of St. Mark's Parish,* pp. 136–139.

16. Patton, "Child's Memory of the Civil War," p. 4.

17. Ibid., pp. 5–6.

18. Ibid., p. 9.

19. Ibid., pp. 8–11; Goolrick, *Life of General Hugh Mercer,* pp. 109–110.

20. Patton, "Child's Memory of the Civil War," pp. 11–12.

21. McGroarty, *California of the South,* V, pp. 355–358; Andrew Glassell, Jr., to William T. Glassell, Los Angeles, June 24, 1866, Addendum, Box 9, Banning Company Papers.

22. Susan Patton to Sally Taylor Patton, Steamer *Arizona* off Cuba, Nov. 15, 1866, Addendum II, Box 25, Wilson Papers.

23. Susan Patton to Ring, Los Angeles, Feb. 24, 1867, Addendum, Box 9, Banning Company Papers; Susan Patton to Sally Patton, Los Angeles, Dec. 19, 1866, Addendum II, Box 25, Wilson Papers.

24. Susan Patton to Sally Patton, Los Angeles, May 30, 1867, Addendum II, Box 25, Wilson Papers.

25. Susan Patton to Elisa Patton Gilmer, Los Angeles, Aug. 18, 1867, Addendum II, Box 25, Wilson Papers.

26. Susan Patton to Sally Patton, Los Angeles, Sept. 21, 1867, Addendum II, Box 25, Wilson Papers; Susan Patton to Margaret French Patton, n.p., Oct. 20, 1867, Addendum II, Box 25, Wilson Papers; Susan Patton to Ring, Los Angeles, Oct. 5, 1867, Addendum, Box 9, Banning Company Papers.

27. Susan Patton to Sally Patton, Los Angeles, Sept. 21, 1867, and March 22, 1868, Addendum II, Box 25, Wilson Papers; McGroarty, *California of the South,* V, p. 357.

28. Susan Patton to Sally Patton, Los Angeles, May 6, 1868, Addendum II, Box 25, Wilson Papers.

29. Susan Patton to Sally Patton, Los Angeles, Dec. 7, 1868, Addendum II, Box 25, Wilson Papers; Ruth Ellen Patton Totten to J. C. Broderick, n.p., Oct. 3, 1964, Box 5, Patton Papers, Library of Congress; George Norbury Mackenzie, *Colonial Families of the United States of America* (Baltimore: Genealogical Publishing Company, 1914), IV, pp. 569, 570.

30. Susan Patton to Sally Patton, Los Angeles, Dec. 7, 1868, Addendum II, Box 25, Wilson Papers; Joseph Mesmer to Hallock Wright, Huntington Park, Cal., March 18, 1943, Miscellaneous Box, Patton Papers; *Los Angeles Star,* Dec. 19, 1868, clipping in Addendum II, Box 25, Wilson Papers.

31. McGroarty, *California of the South,* V, pp. 245–249; Hayden, *Virginia Genealogies,* p. 34.

32. Joseph R. Anderson to George Patton, Sr., Goochland County, Va., March 3, 1905, Box 2, George Patton, Sr., Papers; George Patton, Sr., to John Mercer Patton, Los Angeles, Jan. 10, 1879, Addendum II, Box 25, Wilson Papers.

33. Anne Wilson Diary, Oct. 6, 1883, and Nov. 16, 1883, Addendum IV, Box 2, Wilson Papers.

34. Benjamin D. Wilson Autobiography, pp. 16–17, Wilson Papers; *San Francisco Call,* Dec. 19, 1897, clipping in Addendum IV, Box 1, Wilson Papers; *New York Evening Post,* July ?, 1866, clipping in Addendum II, Box 19, Wilson Papers; Harris Newmark, *Sixty Years in Southern California, 1853–1913* (New York: Knickerbocker Press, 1916), p. 169.

35. *San Francisco Call,* Dec. 19, 1897, clipping in Addendum IV, Box 1, Wilson Papers; *Los Angeles Times,* Oct. 4, 1993; *New York Evening Post,* July, 1866, clipping in Addendum II, Box 19, Wilson Papers.

36. Thomas A. Hereford to Margaret S. Hereford, Santa Fe, July 4, 1847, and July 26, 1847, Box 1, Wilson Papers; Margaret S. Hereford to Esther Sale Hereford, Chihuahua, Mexico, March 9, 1850, and San Francisco, June 1, 1850, Box 1, Wilson Papers; Thomas A. Hereford Will, copy, Box 2, Wilson Papers; Biographical Sketch of Benjamin D. Wilson, Addendum II, Box 19, Wilson Papers; Thomas A. Hereford to Thomas S. Hereford, Durango, Mexico, April 15, 1850, Box 1, Wilson Papers.

37. Anne Wilson Diary, April 28, 1873, July 6, 1874, and Aug. 19, 1876; unidentified clipping, Feb. 19, 1868, Addendum II, Box 19, Wilson Papers; Margaret Hereford Wilson Diary, Jan. 7, 1866, Addendum II, Box 1, Wilson Papers; *Los Angeles Times,* June 11, 1927.

38. Anne Wilson Diary, Sept. 8, 1882, Dec. 9, 1883, and Jan. 13, 1884. Although the date of Wilson's death is often given as March 11, 1878, Nannie recorded the sad event in her diary on March 9, 1878.

39. Ibid., Sept. 7, 1882.

40. Wedding Invitation, Box 5, Patton Papers, Library of Congress.

41. Eulogy of George S. Patton, Sr., June 18, 1927, Addendum II, Box 33, Wilson Papers; Wilson Genealogy, Addendum II, Box 19, Wilson Papers; Margaret Hereford Wilson Diary, Nov. 11, 1891, and Aug. 24, 1893.

42. George Patton, Sr., to Anne Wilson, Los Angeles, Jan. 10, 1888, Addendum IV, Box 25, Wilson Papers.

43. Ellen B. Ayer to George Patton, Sr., Boston, Dec. 21, 1915, Box 2, George Patton, Sr., Papers; Ruth Wilson Patton to Anne Wilson, n.p., Dec. 6, 1887, Box 28, Wilson Papers; Ruth Wilson Patton to Anne Wilson, San Gabriel, May 17, 1889, Box 29, Wilson Papers; *Boston Advertiser,* Aug. 11, 1943.

44. Margaret Hereford Wilson Diary, Aug. 27, 1891; *Los Angeles Times,* Oct. 4, 1993.

45. *Los Angeles Times,* Nov. 9, 1967, and Oct. 4, 1993; Photo Album 282, Numbers 9 and 31, Henry E. Huntington Library, San Marino, Cal.; George Patton, Jr., to George Patton, Sr., Fort Riley, Nov. 12, 1914, Patton Papers; Speech of Douglas Southall Freeman at West Point, August 19, 1950, pp. 1–2, Box 8, Patton Papers.

46. Written comments of George S. Patton, Jr., on undated clipping, *Los Angeles Examiner,* Addendum II, Box 29, Wilson Papers.

47. See the Wedding Invitation, Box 54, George Patton, Sr., Papers; *Catalina Islander,* Aug. 12, 1925, in Box 13, Banning Company Papers.

48. Unidentified Los Angeles newspaper clipping, Aug. 10, 1894, Addendum II, Box 26, Wilson Papers; George Patton, Sr., to James de Barth Shorb, Atlantic City, June 27, 1894, Box 91, James de Barth Shorb Papers, Henry E. Huntington Library, San Marino, Cal.

49. George S. Patton, Sr., *Address to the Voters of the 6th Congressional District of California* (Los Angeles: Kinsell and Doan, 1894), pp. 1–23, in Addendum II, Box 33, Wilson Papers.

50. *Los Angeles Examiner,* July 26, 1916, clipping in George Patton, Sr., Scrapbook V, George Patton, Sr., Papers; *Los Angeles Times,* Aug. 4, 1916, clipping in George Patton, Sr., Scrapbook V, George Patton, Sr., Papers.

51. George S. Patton, Sr., "Progressive Democracy," pp. 1–21, Box 16, George Patton, Sr., Papers.

52. George S. Patton, Sr., "Why Women Should Not Be Given the Vote," *West Coast Magazine* 10 (September 1911): 689–701, in Addendum II, Box 28, Wilson Papers.

53. Men's League Opposed to Suffrage Extension of Los Angeles County to George Patton, Sr., Nov. 6, 1911, Box 3, George Patton, Sr., Papers; *Los Angeles Examiner,* Sept. 24, 1911, clipping in Addendum II, Box 28, Wilson Papers.

54. Speech of Beatrice Ayer Patton at Tufts University, Dec. 7, 1950, pp. 1–2, Box 10, Patton Papers. See also Beatrice Ayer Patton, "A Soldier's Reading," *Armor* 61 (November-December 1952): 10.

55. (London) *Independent,* Aug. 8, 1995; Frank R. Vellutino, "Dyslexia," *Scientific American,* 256 (March 1987): 34–41; Anne Marshall Huston, *Common Sense About Dyslexia* (Lanham, Md.: Madison Books, 1987), pp. 11–27.

56. Julie A. Frost and Michael J. Emery, "Interventions for Children with Reading Disabilities," unpaged handout for National Association of School Psychologists. For the 20 percent figure see Carlo D'Este, *Patton: A Genius for War* (New York: Harper-Collins, 1995), pp. 45–49.

57. Paul D. Harkins, "General Patton," p. 2, Box 103, Douglas Southall Freeman Papers, Manuscript Division, Library of Congress; Reminiscences of Frank McCarthy, pp. 25–31, July 1969, Box 17, Frank McCarthy Papers, George C. Marshall Library, Lexington, Va.

58. See the photos of the children going to school on the first day in Photo Album 282, Numbers 44 and 77, Henry E. Huntington Library, San Marino, Cal. See also Philip Bard to Beatrice Ayer Patton, Baltimore, Aug. 26, 1947, Box 34, Patton Papers, Library of Congress; Stephen Cutter Clark to George Patton, Sr., Pasadena, Feb. 21, 1901, Binder 13, George Patton, Sr., Papers.

59. George Patton, Jr., Report Card, term ending June 28, 1898, Addendum II, Box 21, Wilson Papers; Patton Report Card, term ending Dec. 22, 1899, Binder 12,

George Patton, Sr., Papers; Patton Report Card, term ending Dec. 21, 1900, Binder 13, George Patton, Sr., Papers.

60. *Catalina Islander,* Aug. 12, 1925, in Box 13, Banning Company Papers; Photo Album 282, Numbers 272, 293, and 294, Henry E. Huntington Library, San Marino, Cal.; George Patton, Jr., to George Patton, Sr., Catalina, Summer of 1899, Binder 12, and summer of 1901, Binder 14, George Patton, Sr., Papers.

61. Reminiscences of Hancock Banning, Jr., p. 51, 1971, Oral History Program, University of California at Los Angeles.

62. Beatrice Ayer Patton, "Under the Skin," pp. 1–2, Box 10, Patton Papers; William Banning to Ellen Banning Ayer, Los Angeles, June 23, 1909, June 28, 1909, and July 3, 1909, Box 12, Banning Company Papers; Joseph A. A. Burnquist (ed.), *Minnesota and Its People* (Chicago: S. J. Clarke, 1924), I, 301.

63. Selena Gray Galt Ingram Diary, June 21, 1903, Jan. 6, 1904, Sept. 7, 1904, April 26, 1906, May 15, 1906, and June 10, 1907, Selena Gray Galt Ingram Papers, Henry E. Huntington Library, San Marino, Cal.

64. *The Reminiscences of Frederick Ayer* (Boston: printed privately, 1923), p. 68; Edwin P. Conklin, *Middlesex County and Its People* (New York: Lewis Historical Publishing Company, 1927), III, pp. 85–86; Scott C. Steward, *The Sarsaparilla Kings: A Biography of Dr. James Cook Ayer and Frederick Ayer* (Cambridge, Mass.: n.p., 1993), pp. 9–11.

65. *New York Times,* Jan. 13, 1912, and Feb. 1, 1912; Edward G. Roddy, *Mills, Mansions, and Mergers: The Life of William M. Wood* (North Andover, Mass.: Merrimack Valley Textile Museum, 1982), pp. 70–72, 123; George Patton, Sr., to California Wine Association, Los Angeles, Sept. 12, 1904, and Oct. 10, 1904, Box 3, George Patton, Sr., Papers; William Cahn, *Lawrence 1912: The Bread & Roses Strike* (New York: Pilgrim Press, 1977), p. 150.

66. Photo Album 180, Photo 167, Henry E. Huntington Library, San Marino, Cal.; Poem, 1902, Addendum, Box 13, Banning Company Papers.

67. Frederick Ayer, Sr., to George Patton, Sr., Boston, Nov. 11, 1902, and Dec. 1, 1902, Binder 15, George Patton, Sr., Papers; Ellen Banning Ayer to George Patton, Sr., Glenwood Springs, Colorado, Oct. 16, 1902, Binder 12, George Patton, Sr., Papers.

68. George Patton, Sr., to Sue Shorb, n.p., Jan. 26, 1903, Addendum II, Box 28, Wilson Papers; Henry E. Huntington to George Patton, Sr., n.p., April 26, 1904, Box 110, Henry E. Huntington Papers, Henry E. Huntington Library, San Marino, Cal.; David Lavender, *The Great Persuader* (Garden City, N.Y.: Doubleday, 1970), p. 376.

69. Charles A. Stocking to George Patton, Sr., Woodbury, N.Y., June 10, 1901, Binder 14, George Patton, Sr., Papers; Description and School History of Candidates, August 1904, p. 176, United States Military Academy Archives, West Point.

70. Francis G. Newlands to George Patton, Sr., Reno, Nov. 18, 1902, Binder 15, George Patton, Sr., Papers; James McLachlan to George Patton, Sr., Washington, D.C., Dec. 15, 1902, Binder 15, George Patton, Sr., Papers.

71. George Patton, Sr., to John Mercer Patton, n.p., Feb. 6, 1903, Addendum II, letterbook in Box 28, Wilson Papers.

72. George Patton, Sr., to Francis C. Woodman, n.p., May 2, 1903, Addendum II, letterbook in Box 28, Wilson Papers.

73. George Patton, Sr., to George Hugh Smith, n.p., Nov. 16, 1903, Box 15, George Patton, Sr., Papers.

74. Report on George S. Patton, Jr., Virginia Military Institute, Feb. 15, 1904, Patton Papers.

75. George Patton, Jr., to George Patton, Sr., n.p., Nov. 28, 1903, Patton Papers.

76. Bard to Beatrice Ayer Patton, Baltimore, Aug. 26, 1947, Box 34, Patton Papers, Library of Congress; George Patton, Sr., to George Patton, Jr., San Gabriel, Jan. 19, 1904, Box 1, Patton Papers; L. Harvie Strother to George Patton, Sr., Lexington, Jan. 16, 1904, Box 1, Patton Papers.

77. Description and School History of Candidates, August 1904, p. 176, United States Military Academy Archives; George Patton, Sr., to George Patton, Jr., Los Angeles, March 4, 1904, Patton Papers.

78. George Patton, Jr., to George Patton, Sr., Lexington, March 18, 1904, Patton Papers.

79. George Patton, Jr., to George Patton, Sr., Lexington, March 13, 1904, Patton Papers; George Patton, Sr., to Huntington, May 5, 1904, Box 110, Huntington Papers.

80. Edgar F. Puryear, Jr., *Nineteen Stars* (Orange, Va.: Green Publishers, 1971), p. 1; Martin Blumenson, *The Patton Papers* (Boston: Houghton Mifflin, vol. I, 1972, and vol. II, 1974), I, p. 88. *The Patton Papers,* volume one covering 1885 to 1940 and volume two covering 1940 to 1945, are hereafter cited as Blumenson, followed by volume number and page.

81. Theodore J. Crackel, *The Illustrated History of West Point* (New York: Harry N. Abrams, 1991), pp. 186–192, 196–197, 207–210.

82. Description and School History of Candidates, August 1904, *passim,* United States Military Academy Archives; *Assembly* 16 (Winter 1958): 70–71.

83. George Patton, Jr., to George Patton, Sr., July 10, 1904, and July 17, 1904, Patton Papers.

84. George Patton, Jr., to George Patton, Sr., July 24, 1904, Patton Papers; Hugh S. Johnson, *The Blue Eagle from Egg to Earth* (Garden City, N.Y.: Doubleday, Doran, 1935), pp. 67–68.

85. George Patton, Sr., to Frederick Ayer, Los Angeles, Sept. 12, 1904, and Oct. 10, 1904, Box 2, George Patton, Sr., Papers; Frederick Ayer to George Patton, Sr., n.p., Sept. 2, 1904, and Sept. 26, 1904, Box 2, George Patton, Sr., Papers; George Patton, Jr., to George Patton, Sr., West Point, Sept. 18, 1904, Patton Papers.

86. George Patton, Jr., to George Patton, Sr., n.p., Oct. 30, 1904, Patton Papers; Class and Conduct Report, Nov. 1, 1904, Patton Papers.

87. Puryear, *Nineteen Stars,* pp. 3–5.

88. George Patton, Jr., to George Patton, Sr., n.p., Nov. 12, 1904, Patton Papers; George Patton, Jr., to George Hugh Smith, West Point, Jan. 6, 1905, Box 7, George Patton, Sr., Papers.

89. George Patton, Jr., to George Patton, Sr., n.p., Dec. 17, 1904, Patton Papers.

90. George Patton, Jr., to George Patton, Sr., n.p., March 30, 1905, Patton Papers; Puryear, *Nineteen Stars,* p. 9.

91. Beatrice Ayer Patton, "Under the Skin," pp. 2–3, Box 10, Patton Papers; *Reminiscences of Frederick Ayer,* p. 77; Steward, *Sarsaparilla Kings,* p. 39.

92. George Patton, Jr., to George Patton, Sr., n.p., May 21, 1905, Patton Papers.

93. George Patton, Jr., to George Patton, Sr., n.p., April 9, 1905, Patton Papers.

94. Crackel, *Illustrated History of West Point,* p. 209; Patton Class Reports, March 1905 and April 1905, Patton Papers; Forms D, Class of 1909, Cadet Records, United States Military Academy Archives.

95. George Patton, Sr., to George Patton, Jr., San Gabriel, June 10, 1905, Box 6, Patton Papers, Library of Congress; Roger H. Nye, *The Patton Mind: The Professional Development of An Extraordinary Leader* (Garden City Park, N.Y.: Avery Publishing Group, 1993), p. 16.

96. Selena Gray Gault Ingram Diary, June 19, 1905; George Patton, Jr., to George Patton, Sr., New York, Aug. 28, 1905, Patton Papers.

97. Patton Class Reports, September 1905, Patton Papers; George Patton, Jr., to George Patton, Sr., Oct. 23, 1905, Patton Papers.

98. George S. Patton, Jr., Notebook, p. 6, Patton Papers; Puryear, *Nineteen Stars,* p. 7.

99. Forms D, Class of 1909, Cadet Records, United States Military Academy Archives.

100. Patton Notebook, p. 6; *The Howitzer* 7 (1907):34–35; George Patton, Jr., to Beatrice Ayer, West Point, July 9, 1906, Patton Papers.

101. George Patton, Jr., to Beatrice Ayer, West Point, Aug. 19, 1906, Patton Papers; Puryear, *Nineteen Stars,* p. 7.

102. Patton Notebook, p. 15.

103. George Patton, Jr., to George Patton, Sr., n.p., sometime in 1907, Patton Papers; George Patton, Jr., to Beatrice Ayer, West Point, Aug. 28, 1906, Patton Papers.

104. Selena Gray Galt Ingram Diary, Nov. 4, 1906, Nov. 12, 1906, and Nov. 13, 1906; unidentified clipping in Ingram Diary.

105. George Patton, Jr., to George Patton, Sr., West Point, Oct. 7, 1906, and Nov. 11, 1906, Patton Papers.

106. Blumenson, I, 134; George Patton, Jr., to Anne Wilson, n.p., sometime in 1907, Patton Papers.

107. Forms D, Class of 1909, Cadet Records, United States Military Academy Archives.

108. Selena Gray Galt Ingram Diary, June 28, 1907, July 23, 1907, and Aug. 12, 1907.

109. George Patton, Jr., to George Patton, Sr., Avalon, Aug. 20, 1907, Patton Papers.

110. George Patton, Jr., to Beatrice Ayer, West Point, Nov. 12, 1907, Patton Papers; George S. Patton, Jr., Class and Conduct Report, Nov. 1, 1907, Patton Papers.

111. George Patton, Jr., to Beatrice Ayer, West Point, Feb. 22, 1908, Patton Papers; Circular, Washington's Birthday Ride, Patton Papers.

112. Everett S. Hughes, "Notes on Patton," Box 2, Everett S. Hughes Papers, Manuscript Division, Library of Congress; Beatrice Ayer Patton, "Army Etiquette," p. 3, Box 10, Patton Papers.

113. George Patton, Jr., to Beatrice Ayer, West Point, March 23, 1908, Patton Papers.

114. *National Cyclopedia of American Biography,* vol. XXIV (New York: James T. White, 1935), pp. 13–14, and vol. XXX (New York: James T. White, 1943), p. 400.

115. George Patton, Jr., to Anne Wilson Patton, West Point, April 12, 1908, Box 5, George Patton, Sr., Papers.

116. Selena Gray Galt Ingram Diary, March 18, 1908.

117. Ibid., March 20, 1908.

118. George Patton, Sr., to Huntington, Los Angeles, Oct. 30, 1908, and Dec. 24, 1908, Box 5, George Patton, Sr., Papers.

119. *The Howitzer* 10 (1909): 176; Forms D, Class of 1909, Cadet Records, United States Military Academy Archives.

120. Patton Notebook, p. 10; George Patton, Jr., to Beatrice Ayer, New York, July 8, 1908, Patton Papers.

121. George Patton, Jr., to Beatrice Ayer, West Point, Sept. 9, 1908, Patton Papers; George Patton, Jr., to Ruth Wilson Patton, West Point, Sept. 13, 1908, Patton Papers.

122. George Patton, Jr., to Beatrice Ayer, West Point, Sept. 18, 1908, Patton Papers.

123. George Patton, Jr., to Beatrice Ayer, West Point, Sept. 29, 1908, Patton Papers.

124. George Patton, Jr., to Kate Fowler, West Point, Fall of 1908, George S. Patton, Jr., Papers, United States Army Military History Institute, Carlisle Barracks, Pa.

125. George Patton, Jr., to Kate Fowler, West Point, Nov. 29, 1908, Patton Papers, United States Army Military History Institute. The date is incorrectly given as Oct. 29, 1908.

126. George Patton, Jr., to Beatrice Ayer, West Point, Nov. 25, 1908, Patton Papers.

127. Patton Notebook, p. 10.

128. George Patton, Jr., to George Patton, Sr., West Point, Jan. 17, 1909, Patton Papers.

129. George Patton, Jr., to Mama and Papa, West Point, Jan. 17, 1909, Patton Papers.

130. See *National Cyclopedia of American Biography,* vol. XXIV (New York: James T. White, 1935), pp. 13–14, and vol. XXX (New York: James T. White, 1943), p. 400.

131. *The Howitzer* 10 (1909): 176

132. *The Furlough Book of the Class of 1909,* unpaged, United States Military Academy Archives.

133. George Patton, Jr., to George Patton, Sr., n.p., April 25, 1909, and Gettysburg, May 11, 1909, Patton Papers.

134. Forms D, Class of 1909, Cadet Records, United States Military Academy Archives.

135. Register of Delinquencies, Book 42, p. 317, and Book 43, p. 276, United States Military Academy Archives.

CHAPTER TWO   A DAY AS A LION

1. George S. Patton, Jr., to Beatrice Ayer, n.p., Sept. 13, 1909, George S. Patton, Jr., Papers, Special Collections, United States Military Academy Library, West Point; *Official Army Register for 1911* (Washington, D.C.: Adjutant General's Office, 1910), p. 176.

2. George Patton, Jr., to George S. Patton, Sr., n.p., Sept. 20, 1909, Patton Papers.

3. Patton to Beatrice Ayer, n.p., Sept. 25, 1909, Patton Papers.

4. Patton to Beatrice Ayer, n.p., Oct. 1, 1909, Oct. 3, 1909, and Oct. 4, 1909, Patton Papers.

5. George Patton, Jr., to George Patton, Sr., Fort Sheridan, Dec. 5, 1909, Patton Papers.

6. Patton to Beatrice Ayer, Fort Sheridan, December 13, 1909, Patton Papers.

7. Patton to Beatrice Ayer, Fort Sheridan, March 2, 1910, Patton Papers.

8. Beatrice Ayer Patton, "Army Etiquette," p. 1, Feb. 23, 1943, Box 10, Patton Papers.

9. George Patton, Jr., to George Patton, Sr., n.p., April 4, 1910, and Fort Sheridan, April 16, 1910, Patton Papers.

10. Patton to Beatrice Ayer, Fort Sheridan, May 16, 1910, Patton Papers.

11. Selena Gray Galt Ingram Diary, May 10, 1910, and May 26, 1910, Selena Gray Galt Ingram Papers, Henry E. Huntington Library, San Marino, Cal.; Wedding Invitation, Box 54, George S. Patton, Sr., Papers, Henry E. Huntington Library, San Marino, Cal.; Scott C. Steward, *The Sarsaparilla Kings* (Cambridge, Mass.: n.p., 1993), p. 37.

12. George Patton, Sr., to Henry E. Huntington, Los Angeles, Feb. 26, 1910, and April 27, 1910, Box 5, George Patton, Sr., Papers.

13. *Los Angeles Times,* Jan. 22, 1987; Selena Gray Galt Ingram Diary, Dec. 8, 1911, and Dec. 9, 1911. See also Photo Album Number 282, Photos 220 to 229, Henry E. Huntington Library, San Marino, Cal.

14. *Los Angeles Times,* Jan. 22, 1987.

15. Beatrice Ayer Patton, "Army Etiquette," p. 4; Beatrice Ayer Patton, "Under the Skin," p. 4, Box 10, Patton Papers.

16. Beatrice Ayer Patton, "Under the Skin," p. 4; Beatrice Ayer Patton, "The Army Wife," *Atlantic Monthly* (December 1941): 767–768, in Box 10, Patton Papers.

17. Beatrice Ayer Patton, "The Army Wife," p. 767.

18. George Patton, Jr., to Anne Wilson Patton, Fort Sheridan, Sept. 30, 1910, Miscellaneous Box, Patton Papers; George Patton, Jr., to George Patton, Sr., n.p., Summer of 1910, Box 7, George Patton, Sr., Papers.

19. Beatrice Ayer Patton to George Patton, Sr., Fort Sheridan, Oct. 16, 1910, Box 7, George Patton, Sr., Papers.

20. Selena Gray Galt Ingram Diary, Dec. 8, 1911.

21. Ruth Wilson Patton to George Patton, Sr., n.p., May 9, 1911, Box 7, George Patton, Sr., Papers. This letter is dated 1910, but it is clearly 1911.

22. Ruth Patton to George Patton, Sr., Highland Park, Ill., May 14, 1911, Box 7, George Patton, Sr., Papers.

23. *Los Angeles Examiner,* Sept. 10, 1911, and Sept. 24, 1911, in Addendum II, Box 28, Benjamin D. Wilson Papers, Henry E. Huntington Library, San Marino, Cal.; George S. Patton, "Why Women Should Not Be Given the Vote," *West Coast Magazine* 10 (September 1911): 689–701.

24. George Patton, Jr., to George Patton, Sr., n.p., April 12, 1911, Patton Papers.

25. Quoted in Speech of Douglas Southall Freeman at West Point, August 19, 1950, p. 3, Box 8, Patton Papers.

26. Blumenson, I, 224–225; *New York Times,* Jan. 13, 1912; Samuel Yellen, *American Labor Struggles* (New York: S. A. Russell, 1936), pp. 180–185; *Literary Digest* 45 (Sept. 14, 1912): 407; Edward G. Roddy, *Mills, Mansions, and Mergers: The Life of William M. Wood* (North Andover, Mass.: Merrimack Valley Textile Museum, 1982), pp. 70–72.

27. Roddy, *Mills, Mansions, and Mergers,* pp. 15, 72, 123; *Literary Digest* 64 (January 3, 1920), 17; *New York Times,* May 1, 1919, and Feb. 3, 1926. Around the time of the strike the Reverend Adolf A. Berle of Tufts College condemned the woolen company's owners with the comment: "Somebody is doing a satanic wrong." During the Second World War, Bea described Berle's son, then the assistant secretary of state, as a thick-speeched Jew. Berle's comments are in Roddy, *Mills, Mansions, and Mergers,* pp. 70–71. On the activities of Berger and Gompers see the *New York Times,* Feb. 25, 1912, March 3, 1912, and March 5, 1912.

28. George Patton, Jr., to George Patton, Sr., n.p., January 23, 1912, Patton Papers; Bradford Grethen Chynoweth, *Bellamy Park* (Hicksville, N.Y.: Exposition Press, 1975), p. 65; Bradford G. Chynoweth, "A More Perfect Union," pp. 140–141, Box 3, Bradford G. Chynoweth Papers, United States Army Military History Institute, Carlisle Barracks, Pa.

29. Patton to Frederick Foltz, "Report on Modern Pentathlon," Sept. 19, 1912, pp. 1–2, Box 2, Patton Papers.

30. Ibid., 3; Selena Gray Galt Ingram Diary, July 8, 1912.

31. Patton, "Report on Modern Pentathlon," pp. 3–4; Foltz to Unknown, n.d., Box 2, Patton Papers; unidentified newspaper clippings, Box 2, Patton Papers.

32. Blumenson, I, 233–234; Patton, "Report on Modern Pentathlon," pp. 9–10.

33. George Patton, Sr., to George Patton, Jr., San Gabriel, Sept. 22, 1912, Box 2, Patton Papers. George Patton, Sr.'s comment about the "jew" with the long nose undoubtedly referred to Äsbrink. When General Patton visited Stockholm after World War II, Äsbrink was among those who greeted him. See George S. Patton, Jr., Diary, Nov. 28, 1945, Patton Papers. Now rarely used, the word "sabreur" denotes anyone wielding a large saber.

34. George Patton, Jr., to Beatrice Ayer Patton, n.p., August 23, 1912, Patton Papers.

35. George Patton, Jr., to Beatrice Ayer Patton, n.p., Sept. 7, 1912, and Sept. 28, 1912, Patton Papers.

36. Blumenson, I, 241.

37. *Army and Navy Journal* 50 (October 12, 1912): 174; 50 (Jan. 11, 1913): 569; 50 (Feb. 22, 1913): 761; and 50 (March 15, 1913): 867. See also George S. Patton, Jr., "The Form and Use of the Saber," *Journal of the United States Cavalry Association* 23 (March 1913): 752–759.

38. George Patton, Jr., to George Patton, Sr., Fort Myer, May 19, 1913, Patton Papers.

39. George S. Patton, Jr., "Army Racing and Records for 1913," *The Rasp,* n. v. (1914): 345–353; George Patton, Jr., to Anne Wilson, Fort Myer, May 5, 1913, Patton Papers.

40. George Patton, Jr., to Beatrice Ayer Patton, Frederick, Md., June 25, 1913, and Gettysburg, July 1, 1913, Patton Papers; Speech of Beatrice Ayer Patton to Haverhill Women's Club, Sept. 30, 1943, pp. 3–4, Box 10, Patton Papers.

41. George Patton, Jr., to George Patton, Sr., Saumur, July 22, 1913, Patton Papers; Adna R. Chaffee, Jr., "Living at Saumur: A Few Facts and Figures," *The Rasp,* n. v. (1912): 242. Patton spelled the hotel Budan, Chaffee, later the great advocate of the use of tanks, Budon.

42. Guy V. Henry, "The Cavalry School of Application at Saumur, France," *The Rasp,* n. v. (1912), 223–240.

43. Blumenson, I, 261–262; Beatrice Ayer Patton to Anne Wilson, Saumur, Aug. 28, 1913, Patton Papers.

44. George Patton, Jr., to Beatrice Ayer Patton, n.p., Sept. 29, 1913, and Oct. 2, 1913, Patton Papers; *The Rasp,* n. v. (1913): 249.

45. George Patton, Jr., to Beatrice Ayer Patton, Fort Riley, Oct. 14, 1913, Patton Papers; George Patton, Jr., to George Patton, Sr., Fort Riley, Oct. 16, 1913, Patton Papers.

46. George Patton, Jr., to George Patton, Sr., Fort Riley, Oct. 16, 1913, Patton Papers.

47. Anne Wilson Patton to George Patton, Sr., New York, November 16, 1913, Box 7, George Patton, Sr., Papers.

48. George S. Patton, Jr., "Mounted Swordsmanship," *The Rasp,* n. v. (1914): 162–169.

49. Sue Wilson Shorb to Ruth Patton, San Francisco, Sept. 8, 1914, and Sept. 19, 1914, Addendum, Box 11, Banning Company Papers, Henry E. Huntington Library, San Marino, Cal.; George Patton, Sr., to Beatrice Ayer Patton, Fort Riley, Sept. 22, 1914, Patton Papers.

50. George Patton, Jr., to George Patton, Sr., Fort Riley, Nov. 12, 1914, Patton Papers.

51. Sue Wilson Shorb to Ruth Patton, San Francisco, April 29, 1914, June 14, 1914, and Sept. 8, 1914, Addendum, Box 11, Banning Company Papers; Sue Wilson Shorb to George Patton, Sr., San Francisco, July 23, 1914, and Dec. 22, 1914, Addendum, Box 11, Banning Company Papers.

52. Blumenson, I, 280–281.

53. George Patton, Jr., to George Patton, Sr., Fort Riley, Feb. 11, 1915, Patton Papers.

54. George Patton, Jr., to George Patton, Sr., Fort Riley, Nov. 12, 1914, and Feb. 11, 1915, Patton Papers; Robert H. Patton, *The Pattons: A Personal History of an American Family* (New York: Crown, 1994), pp. 142–143.

55. George Patton, Jr., to Beatrice Ayer Patton, Fort Riley, March 1, 1915, Patton Papers.

56. George Patton, Jr., to George Patton, Sr., Fort Riley, May 16, 1915, Patton Papers; George S. Patton, Jr., "Valor," in Patton Poems, Patton Papers; Carmine A. Prioli (ed.), *The Poems of General George S. Patton, Jr.: The Lines of Fire* (Lewiston, N.Y.: Edwin Mellen Press, 1991), pp. 37–38.

57. Prioli (ed.), *Poems of General George S. Patton, Jr.,* pp. 22–24; Patton, "The Rulers," in Patton Poems; *Official Army Register for 1916* (Washington, D.C.: Adjutant General's Office, 1915), pp. 171–172.

58. Blumenson, I, 293–294.

59. George Patton, Jr., to Beatrice Ayer Patton, n.p., Oct. 13, 1915, and Oct. 26, 1915, Patton Papers.

60. See the Guide to the John J. Pershing Papers, p. 3, Manuscript Division, Library of Congress.

61. Donald Smythe, "Pershing's Great Personal Tragedy," *Missouri Historical Review* 60 (April 1966): 320–324; Frank E. Vandiver, *Black Jack: The Life and Times of John J. Pershing* (College Station and London: Texas A & M University Press, 1977), II, pp. 597–598.

62. Vandiver, *Black Jack,* II, p. 600; George Patton, Jr., to Beatrice Ayer Patton, Hot Wells, Texas, Oct. 29, 1915, Patton Papers.

63. George Patton, Jr., to Beatrice Ayer Patton, n.p., Oct. 30, 1915, and Nov. 1, 1915, Patton Papers; George Patton, Jr., to Anne Wilson, Sierra Blanca, Nov. 1, 1915, Patton Papers.

64. Report of George S. Patton to Commanding General, West Texas Cavalry, Sierra Blanca, Texas, Nov. 25, 1915, Box 3, Patton Papers.; George Patton, Jr., to George Patton, Sr., n.p., Nov. 27, 1915, Patton Papers.

65. George Patton, Jr., to Beatrice Ayer Patton, Fort Bliss, Jan. 31, 1916, Patton Papers.

66. George Patton, Jr., to George Patton, Sr., n.p., March 8, 1916, Patton Papers.

67. George Patton, Jr., to George Patton, Sr., n.p., March 8, 1916, Patton Papers. See also in the Patton Papers at West Point the photo album of the Mexican Expedition.

68. Vandiver, *Black Jack,* II, pp. 604–605.

69. Blumenson, I, 319–320; Vandiver, *Black Jack,* II, p. 607; George Patton, Jr., to George Patton, Sr., n.p., March 12, 1916, Patton Papers.

70. George Patton, Jr., to Beatrice Ayer Patton, Casas Grandes, March 20, 1916, Box 123, George S. Patton, Jr., Papers, Manuscript Division, Library of Congress.

71. George Patton, Jr., to Beatrice Ayer Patton, n.p., March 27, 1916, Box 123, Patton Papers, Library of Congress.

72. Vernon L. Williams, *Lieutenant Patton and the American Army in the Mexican Punitive Expedition, 1915–1916* (Austin: Presidial Press, 1983), p. 60; Vandiver, *Black Jack*, II, p. 634.

73. Haldeen Braddy, *Pershing's Mission in Mexico* (El Paso: Texas Western Press, 1966), pp. 15–18.

74. See *New Orleans Times-Picayune,* April 7, 1916; New York *World,* June 19, 1916.

75. George Patton, Jr., to Beatrice Ayer Patton, n.p., April 13, 1916, Box 123, Patton Papers, Library of Congress. See also Edward Gibbons, *Floyd Gibbons: Your Headline Hunter* (New York: Exposition Press, 1953), p. 57.

76. George Patton, Jr., to George Patton, Sr., n.p., early May 1916, Patton Papers; George Patton, Jr., to Beatrice Ayer Patton, n.p., July 12, 1916, Box 123, Patton Papers, Library of Congress; Curtis G. Chezem, "The Mexican Automobile Battle," *Journal of the West* 30 (October 1991): 47–48; Hugh S. Johnson, *The Blue Eagle from Egg to Earth* (Garden City, N.Y.: Doubleday, Doran, 1935), pp. 67–68.

77. *New York Times,* May 23, 1916; George Patton, Jr., to Pershing, Camp Meade, Md., Sept. 24, 1920, Box 155, Pershing Papers; Pershing to George Patton, Jr., Paris, Nov. 27, 1922, Box 155, Pershing Papers; Reminiscences of Kenyon A. Joyce, pp. 348–349, Box 1, Kenyon A. Joyce Papers, United States Army Military History Institute, Carlisle Barracks, Pa.; George Patton, Jr., to George Patton, Sr., n.p., May 15, 1916, Patton Papers.

78. Donald Smythe, "John J. Pershing: A Study in Paradox," *Military Review* 49 (September 1969): 68–69; Jerome Kearful, "A George Patton Episode," *National Guardsman* 4 (June 1950), 9.

79. Blumenson, I, 315; Smythe, "John J. Pershing," p. 69. See also the photos Patton sent home of football games and cockfights in Photo Album, Box 18, Patton Papers.

80. Interview with Joseph W. Viner, unidentified clipping, Box 7, Patton Papers.

81. George Patton, Jr., to Beatrice Ayer Patton, n.p., May 17, 1916, Box 123, Patton Papers, Library of Congress; *New York Times,* May 23, 1916.

82. Beatrice Ayer Patton to George Patton, Sr., Fort Bliss, May 16, 1916, Box 7, George Patton, Sr., Papers.

83. George Patton, Jr., to Beatrice Ayer Patton, n.p., June 1, 1916, Box 123, Patton Papers, Library of Congress; Martin Blumenson, "Patton in Mexico: The Punitive Expedition," *American History Illustrated* 12 (October 1977): 41.

84. George Patton, Jr., to George Patton, Sr., n.p., June 15, 1916, Patton Papers.

85. George Patton, Jr., to Beatrice Ayer Patton, n.p., July 20, 1916, Box 123, Patton Papers, Library of Congress.

86. George Patton, Jr., to Beatrice Ayer Patton, n.p., July 7, 1916, and July 29, 1916, Box 123, Patton Papers, Library of Congress.

87. George Patton, Jr., to Beatrice Ayer Patton, n.p., July 14, 1916, Box 123, Patton Papers, Library of Congress.

88. George Patton, Jr., to Beatrice Ayer Patton, n.p., July 22, 1916, Box 123, Patton Papers, Library of Congress.

89. George Patton, Jr., to Kate Fowler Merle-Smith, n.p., Aug. 28, 1916, George S. Patton, Jr., Papers, United States Army Military History Institute, Carlisle Barracks, Pa; Richard M. Huber, *Big All the Way Through: The Life of Van Santvoord Merle-Smith* (Princeton, N.J.: n.p., 1952), pp. 31–32.

90. George Patton, Jr., to Beatrice Ayer Patton, n.p., Oct. 7, 1916, Patton Papers; Special Order No. 149, Punitive Expedition, Colonia Dublán, Oct. 9, 1916, Patton Papers.

91. Address of George S. Patton, Sr., Santa Rosa, Cal., Sept. 5, 1916, pp. 27–29, Addendum II, Box 29, Benjamin D. Wilson Papers, Henry E. Huntington Library, San Marino, Cal. See also in Scrapbook I, George Patton, Sr., Papers the following clippings: *San Pedro News*, Sept. 14, 1916; *Anderson News,* Sept. 21, 1916; *Los Angeles Examiner,* Oct. 4, 1916; *Visalia Delta,* Oct. 19, 1916. For the quote on women's suffrage see *Redlands Review,* Oct. 18, 1916, in Scrapbook V, George Patton, Sr., Papers.

92. Anne Wilson Patton to Pershing, Lake Vineyard, Oct. 12, 1916, Box 418, Pershing Papers.

93. *Brawley News,* Nov. 1, 1916, in Scrapbook I, George Patton, Sr., Papers; Winfield Hogaboom, "George S. Patton, Jr., Soldier, Diplomat, Poet," *Los Angeles Graphic,* June 23, 1917, in Scrapbook V, George Patton, Sr., Papers.

94. Anne Wilson Patton to Pershing, Lake Vineyard, Oct. 29, 1916, Box 418, Pershing Papers.

95. Anne Wilson Patton to Pershing, San Gabriel, Nov. 16, 1916, Box 418, Pershing Papers.

96. George Patton, Sr., to Edward M. House, Los Angeles, Nov. 18, 1916, Addendum II, Box 29, Wilson Papers; Charles H. Butler to Lynn Helm, Washington, D.C., Jan. 18, 1917, Box 2, George Patton, Sr., Papers.

97. George Patton, Sr., to Norman Bridge, n.p., Dec. 14, 1916, Box 2, George Patton, Sr., Papers; Bridge to J. A. B. Scherer, n.p., Dec. 12, 1916, Box 2, George Patton, Sr., Papers.

98. George Patton, Jr., to Beatrice Ayer Patton, n.p., Nov. 14, 1916, Patton Papers.

99. George Patton, Jr., to Beatrice Ayer Patton, n.p., Nov. 29, 1916, Patton Papers.; Brady, *Pershing's Mission in Mexico,* pp. 59–60; Vandiver, *Black Jack,* II, p. 662.

100. George Patton, Jr., to Beatrice Ayer Patton, n.p., Nov. 20, 1916, Patton Papers.

101. George S. Patton, Jr., "Notes on Some Faults of the Advance Guard of a Squadron of Cavalry," Box 4, Patton Papers.

102. George S. Patton, Jr., "Cavalry Work of the Punitive Expedition," *Journal of the United States Cavalry Association* 27 (January 1917): 426–433; George Patton, Jr., to Beatrice Ayer Patton, n.p., Dec. 1, 1916, Patton Papers.

103. Clarence C. Clendenen, *The United States and Pancho Villa: A Study in Unconventional Diplomacy* (Ithaca, N.Y.: Cornell University Press, 1961), pp. 293–294; George Patton, Jr., to Beatrice Ayer Patton, n.p., Jan. 28, 1917, Patton Papers. See also the numerous photos of the refugees piled into wagons in the photo album labeled Vol. 18, Patton Papers.

104. George Patton, Jr., to Beatrice Ayer Patton, n.p., Jan. 29, 1917, Patton Papers; Pershing to Anne Wilson Patton, Fort Sam Houston, March 15, 1917, Box 418, Pershing Papers; various unidentified newspaper clippings, February and March 1917, Box 5, Patton Papers.

105. George S. Patton, Jr., to Pershing, n.p., April 11, 1917, Box 155, Pershing Papers; Pershing to George Patton, Jr., Telegram, Fort Sam Houston, May 5, 1917, Box 155, Pershing Papers.

CHAPTER THREE   THE SUICIDE CLUB

1. John J. Pershing to Francis E. Warren, Colonia Dublán, Jan. 20, 1917, Box 426, John J. Pershing Papers, Manuscript Division, Library of Congress.

2. Ruth Wilson Patton to Pershing, Lake Vineyard, April 12, 1917, Box 418, Pershing Papers.

3. George S. Patton, Sr., to George S. Patton, Jr., Lake Vineyard, April 30, 1917, George S. Patton, Jr., Papers, Special Collections, United States Military Academy Library, West Point.

4. Patton to Beatrice Ayer Patton, Washington, May 3, 1917, Patton Papers.

5. Frank E. Vandiver, *Black Jack: The Life and Times of John J. Pershing* (College Station and London: Texas A & M University Press, 1977), II, pp. 686–687, 696–701; George S. Patton, Jr., Diary, May 18, 1917, to May 28, 1917, Patton Papers.

6. Patton Diary, June 6, 1917, to June 13, 1917; Patton to Beatrice Ayer Patton, London, June 12, 1917, Patton Papers.

7. Patton Diary, June 13, 1917; Patton to Beatrice Ayer Patton, Paris, June 14, 1917, Patton Papers. This is the first of two letters of this date.

8. Patton to Beatrice Ayer Patton, Paris, June 14, 1917, Patton Papers. This is the second letter of this date.

9. Patton to Beatrice Ayer Patton, Paris, June 15, 1917, Patton Papers. Patton Diary, June 14, 1917.

10. Pershing to Anne Wilson Patton, Paris, June 23, 1917, Box 418, Pershing Papers.

11. Patton to Beatrice Ayer Patton, Paris, June 24, 1917, June 25, 1917, and June 29, 1917, Patton Papers.

12. Patton to Beatrice Ayer Patton, n.p., July 3, 1917, and July 24, 1917, Patton Papers; Patton Diary, July 13, 1917, and July 14, 1917.

13. Patton to Beatrice Ayer Patton, n.p., July 24, 1917, Patton Papers; Geoffrey Powell, *Plummer: The Soldier's General* (London: Leo Cooper, 1990), p. 269; General Sir Hubert P. Gough, *The Fifth Army* (London: Hodder and Stoughton, 1931), pp. 209–211.

14. Patton to Beatrice Ayer Patton, n.p., July 16, 1917, Patton Papers.

15. Patton to Beatrice Ayer Patton, n.p., July 17, 1917, and Aug. 16, 1917, Patton Papers.

16. Patton to Beatrice Ayer Patton, n.p., Aug. 5, 1917, Aug. 8, 1917, Aug. 16, 1917, and Sept. 13, 1917, Patton Papers.

17. Clara Warren to Francis Warren and Pershing, Washington, D.C., Sept. 23, 1917, Box 425, Pershing Papers.

18. Patton to Beatrice Ayer Patton, n.p., Aug. 24, 1917, Patton Papers.

19. Patton Diary, Aug. 30, 1917; Patton to Beatrice Ayer Patton, n.p., Sept. 2, 1917, Patton Papers.

20. Pershing to Anne Wilson Patton, Chaumont, Sept. 10, 1917, Box 418, Pershing Papers. See also the memorandum of Beatrice Ayer Patton, 1947, Box 82, Douglas Southall Freeman Papers, Manuscript Division, Library of Congress.

21. Patton Diary, Sept. 7, 1917; Patton to Beatrice Ayer Patton, n.p., Sept. 5, 1917, Patton Papers.

22. Patton to Beatrice Ayer Patton, n.p., Sept. 18, 1917, and Sept. 19, 1917, Patton Papers.

23. Patton to Beatrice Ayer Patton, n.p., Sept. 23, 1917, and Oct. 2, 1917, Patton Papers; *Armor* 76 (November–December 1967): 48.

24. *San Gabriel Bulletin,* Oct. 11, 1917, clipping in Box 418, Pershing Papers; Anne Patton to Pershing, Lake Vineyard, Oct. 11, 1917, and Oct. 12, 1917, Box 418, Pershing Papers.

25. Anne Patton to Pershing, Lake Vineyard, Oct. 14, 1917, Box 418, Pershing Papers.

26. Pershing to Anne Patton, Paris, Nov. 5, 1917, Box 418, Pershing Papers.

27. Beatrice Ayer Patton to Pershing, Thomasville, Ga., Nov. 6, 1917, Box 155, Pershing Papers.

28. Pershing to Anne Patton, Paris, Nov. 5, 1917, Box 418, Pershing Papers; Patton to Beatrice Ayer Patton, n.p., Oct. 19, 1917, Patton Papers; George Patton, Jr., to George Patton, Sr., n.p., Nov. 6, 1917, Patton Papers.

29. George Patton, Jr., to George Patton, Sr., n.p., Nov. 6, 1917, Patton Papers.

30. Patton to Beatrice Ayer Patton, n.p., Nov. 9, 1917, and Nov. 10, 1917, Patton Papers.

31. Patton to Beatrice Ayer Patton, n.p., Nov. 18, 1917, and Nov. 20, 1917, Patton Papers; George S. Patton, Jr., "Our Beginnings," *American Legion Post of the Tank Corps Magazine,* p. 1 in Box 7, George S. Patton, Sr., Papers, Henry E. Huntington Library, San Marino, Cal.

32. Patton to Beatrice Ayer Patton, n.p., Nov. 23, 1917, Patton Papers.

33. B. H. Liddell Hart, *The Tanks: The History of the Royal Tank Regiment* (New York: Frederick A. Praeger, 1959), I, pp. 128–134; Patton to Beatrice Ayer Patton, n.p., Nov. 26, 1917, Patton Papers; Field Marshal Lord Carver, *The Apostles of Mobility: The Theory and Practice of Armoured Warfare* (New York: Holmes & Meier, 1979), pp. 28–30; Robert H. Larson, *The British Army and the Theory of Armored Warfare, 1918–1940* (Newark: University of Delaware Press, 1984), pp. 60–61; Colonel H. C. B. Rogers, *Tanks in Battle* (London: Seeley Service & Co., 1965), pp. 48, 50, 68.

34. Patton to Beatrice Ayer Patton, n.p., Dec. 2, 1917, Patton Papers; Liddell Hart, *Tanks,* I, pp. 129–134.

35. Patton, "Our Beginnings," pp. 1–2; Dale E. Wilson, *Treat 'Em Rough!: The Birth of American Armor, 1917–20* (Novato, Cal.: Presidio, 1989), pp. 16–17.

36. Report of Sereno E. Brett, p. 4, Dec. 28, 1918, Sereno E. Brett Papers, Special Collections, United States Military Academy Library, West Point; Rogers, *Tanks in Battle,* p. 68.

37. Wilson, *Treat 'Em Rough!,* pp. 16–23; Patton to Beatrice Ayer Patton, n.p., Dec. 5, 1917, and Dec. 12, 1917, Patton Papers; Carver, *Apostles of Mobility,* pp. 29–30; Liddell Hart, *Tanks,* I, p. 34.

38. Bradford Grethen Chynoweth, *Bellamy Park* (Hicksville, N.Y.: Exposition Press, 1975), p. 91; Patton to Beatrice Ayer Patton, n.p., Dec. 12, 1917, Patton Papers.

39. Patton to Beatrice Ayer Patton, n.p., Nov. 14, 1917, Patton Papers; Henry L. Stimson Diary, Feb. 26, 1918, Henry L. Stimson Papers, Sterling Memorial Library, Yale University, New Haven, Conn.

40. Patton to Beatrice Ayer Patton, n.p., Dec. 18, 1917, Patton Papers.

41. Roger H. Nye, "Whence Patton's Military Genius?" *Parameters* 21 (Winter 1991–1992): 68; Roger H. Nye, "Why Patton?" *Friends of the West Point Library Newsletter,* n. v. (March 1991): 6; Ruth Ellen Patton Totten to Roger H. Nye, South Hamilton, Mass., Oct. 18, 1990, Box 3, Roger H. Nye Papers, Special Collections, United States Military Academy Library, West Point.

42. Nye to Ruth Ellen Patton Totten, Highland Falls, N.Y., Nov. 17, 1990, Box 3, Nye Papers.

43. Roger H. Nye, *The Patton Mind: The Professional Development of an Extraordinary Leader* (Garden City Park, N.Y.: Avery Publishing Group, 1993), pp. 6–7.

44. Ibid., p. 181.

45. Harry H. Semmes, *Portrait of Patton* (New York: Appleton-Century-Crofts, 1955), pp. 38–39.

46. Nye, "Whence Patton's Military Genius?" p. 66; Nye, *Patton Mind,* p. 65.

47. George Patton, Sr., to George Patton, Jr., San Gabriel, June 10, 1905, Box 6, George S. Patton, Jr., Papers, Manuscript Division, Library of Congress.

48. "The Attack," in Patton Poems, pp. 45–47, Patton Papers.

49. "A Dream," in Patton Poems, p. 16, Patton Papers.

50. Patton to Beatrice Ayer Patton, n.p., Dec. 29, 1917, Patton Papers; Patton, "Our Beginnings," pp. 1–2.

51. Patton to Beatrice Ayer Patton, n.p., Jan. 6, 1918, Patton Papers; Liddell Hart, *Tanks,* I, pp. 135, 138–139.

52. Beatrice Ayer Patton, "Dobbs Alumnae Day Speech," pp. 3–4, April 29, 1943, Box 10, Patton Papers.

53. Patton, "Our Beginnings," p. 2; Patton to Beatrice Ayer Patton, n.p., Jan. 16, 1918, and Jan. 17, 1918, Patton Papers.

54. Patton to Beatrice Ayer Patton, n.p., Jan. 30, 1918, Patton Papers; Chynoweth, *Bellamy Park,* pp. 91–92.

55. Patton to Beatrice Ayer Patton, n.p., Feb. 8, 1918, Patton Papers.

56. Patton to Beatrice Ayer Patton, n.p., Feb. 11, 1918, Patton Papers; Stimson Diary, Feb. 26, 1918.

57. Patton to Beatrice Ayer Patton, n.p., Feb. 17, 1918, and Feb. 18, 1918, Patton Papers; Patton, "Our Beginnings," p. 2.

58. Patton, "Our Beginnings," pp. 3–4; Patton to Beatrice Ayer Patton, n.p., Jan. 31, 1918, Patton Papers.

59. Patton to Beatrice Ayer Patton, n.p., Jan. 31, 1918, and Feb. 21, 1918, Patton Papers.

60. Patton to Beatrice Ayer Patton, n.p., Feb. 22, 1918, and Feb. 23, 1918, Patton Papers.

61. Patton to Beatrice Ayer Patton, n.p., March 3, 1918, and March 4, 1918, Patton Papers; *New York Times,* Jan. 21, 1918, and Jan. 22, 1918.

62. Patton to Beatrice Ayer Patton, n.p., March 12, 1918, Patton Papers.

63. Patton to Beatrice Ayer Patton, n.p., March 13, 1918, Patton Papers.

64. George S. Patton, Jr., "Lecture on Discipline," March 18, 1918, Box 48, Patton Papers, Library of Congress.

65. Patton to Beatrice Ayer Patton, n.p., March 22, 1918, Patton Papers; "F. A.," in Patton Poems, p. 31, Patton Papers.

66. See, for example, Scott C. Steward, *The Sarsaparilla Kings: A Biography of Dr. James Cook Ayer and Frederick Ayer* (Cambridge, Mass.: n.p., 1993), p. 47.

67. Patton, "Our Beginnings," p. 4; Patton to Beatrice Ayer Patton, n.p., March 24, 1918, Patton Papers.

68. Personal Experiences Report of First Lieutenant Julian K. Morrison, pp. 83–85, Dec. 10, 1918, Brett Papers.

69. Personal Experiences Report of Captain Newell P. Weed, pp. 1–2, Dec. 11, 1918, Box 47, Patton Papers, Library of Congress.

70. Patton to Beatrice Ayer Patton, n.p., March 26, 1918, March 30, 1918, April 3, 1918, and April 5, 1918, Patton Papers.

71. Patton to Beatrice Ayer Patton, n.p., April 10, 1918, Patton Papers.

72. Patton to Kate Fowler Merle-Smith, Tank Center, April 19, 1918, George S. Patton, Jr., Papers, United States Army Military History Institute, Carlisle Barracks, Pa.

73. Patton to Beatrice Ayer Patton, n.p., April 22, 1918, Patton Papers; Wilson, *Treat 'Em Rough!,* pp. 36–39.

74. Patton to Beatrice Ayer Patton, n.p., May 7, 1918, Patton Papers.

75. George Patton, Jr., to George Patton, Sr., n.p., May 21, 1918, Patton Papers.

76. Unidentified newspaper interview with Joseph W. Viner, 1973, Box 7, Patton Papers.

77. Patton to Beatrice Ayer Patton, n.p., May 25, 1918, Patton Papers.

78. Patton to Beatrice Ayer Patton, n.p., May 26, 1918, Patton Papers.

79. Patton to Beatrice Ayer Patton, n.p., May 28, 1918, May 29, 1918, and June 3, 1918, Patton Papers. See also Blumenson, I, 535–537.

80. Wilson, *Treat 'Em Rough!,* pp. 39–43; unidentified newspaper interview with Joseph W. Viner, Box 7, Patton Papers; Patton to Beatrice Ayer Patton, n.p., June 5, 1918, and June 7, 1918, Patton Papers.

81. Unidentified newspaper interview with Joseph W. Viner, Box 7, Patton Papers.

82. Patton to Beatrice Ayer Patton, n.p., June 12, 1918, June 14, 1918, and June 15, 1918, Patton Papers.

83. Blumenson, I, 544–545; Patton to Beatrice Ayer Patton, n.p., June 19, 1918, and June 23, 1918, Patton Papers.

84. Patton to Beatrice Ayer Patton, n.p., June 30, 1918, and July 1, 1918, Patton Papers.

85. Patton to Beatrice Ayer Patton, n.p., July 7, 1918, and July 14, 1918, Patton Papers.

86. Patton to Beatrice Ayer Patton, n.p., July 18, 1918, and July 22, 1918, Patton Papers.

87. Patton to Beatrice Ayer Patton, n.p., July 12, 1918, and Aug. 15, 1918, Patton Papers.

88. Patton to Beatrice Ayer Patton, n.p., Aug. 15, 1918, Patton Papers; George Patton, Jr. to George Patton, Sr., n.p., Aug. 20, 1918, Patton Papers.

89. George Patton, Jr., to George Patton, Sr., n.p., Aug. 20, 1918, Patton Papers.

90. Patton to Beatrice Ayer Patton, n.p., Aug. 26, 1918, and Sept. 1, 1918, Patton Papers; Donald Smythe, *Pershing: General of the Armies* (Bloomington: Indiana University Press, 1986), p. 173; James J. Cooke, *The Rainbow Division in the Great War, 1917–1919* (Westport, Ct.: Praeger, 1994), p. 144.

91. Patton to Beatrice Ayer Patton, n.p., Aug. 13, 1918, Patton Papers; Rogers, *Tanks in Battle,* pp. 50, 68.

92. Wilson, *Treat 'Em Rough!,* pp. 101–102; Patton Diary, Sept. 9, 1918; Cooke, *Rainbow Division,* pp. 146–148.

93. Patton Diary, Sept. 9, 1918; Major General William R. Kraft, Jr., "The Saga of the Five of Hearts," *Army* 97 (July-August 1988): p. 35; Wilson, *Treat 'Em Rough!,* p. 103.

94. Lieutenant Colonel George S. Patton, Jr., "Special Instructions for the 326 Bn. and 327 Bn.," Sept. 8, 1918, Box 10, Patton Papers, Library of Congress; John F. Wukovits, "Best-Case Scenario Exceeded," *Military History* 9 (November 5, 1992): 62.

95. Timothy K. Nenninger, "The Development of American Armor, 1917–1940: Experience," *Armor* 78 (January–February 1969): 49–50; Captain G. H. Rarey, "American Light Tank Brigade at St. Mihiel," *Infantry Journal* 32 (March 1928): 283; Personal Experiences Report of Major Sereno E. Brett, p. 10, Dec. 14, 1918, Brett Papers.

96. Rarey, "American Light Tank Brigade at St. Mihiel," p. 283; Brett Personal Experiences Report, p. 10.

97. Rarey, "American Light Tank Brigade at St. Mihiel," p. 284; Personal Experiences Report of Captain Harry G. Borland, pp. 42–42, December, 1918, Brett Papers; Personal Experiences Reports of First Lieutenant Don C. Wilson and Second Lieutenant D. M. Taylor, n.p., Dec. 11, 1918, Box 47, Patton Papers, Library of Congress.

98. Cooke, *Rainbow Division in the Great War,* pp. 148, 152, 161; Blumenson, I, 578–579.

99. Cooke, *Rainbow Division in the Great War,* p. 146; Wilson, *Treat 'Em Rough!,* pp. 107–108.

100. George Patton, Jr., to George Patton, Sr., n.p., Sept. 20, 1918, Patton Papers; William Manchester, *American Caesar: Douglas MacArthur, 1880–1964* (Boston & Toronto: Little, Brown, 1978), pp. 101–102.

101. Rarey, "American Light Tank Brigade at St. Mihiel," p. 284–286; George Patton, Jr., to George Patton, Sr., n.p., Sept. 20, 1918, Patton Papers.

102. George Patton, Jr., to George Patton, Sr., n.p., Sept. 20, 1918, Patton Papers.

103. Ibid.; Wilson, *Treat 'Em Rough!,* p. 114.

104. Rarey, "American Light Tank Brigade at St. Mihiel," p. 285.

105. Ibid., p. 286; George Patton, Jr., to George Patton, Sr., n.p., Sept. 20, 1918, Patton Papers.

106. Unidentified newspaper interview with Joseph W. Viner, Box 7, Patton Papers; Wilson, *Treat 'Em Rough!,* pp. 118–119.

107. Rarey, "American Light Tank Brigade at St. Mihiel," p. 287; Blumenson, I, 596.

108. Patton to Beatrice Ayer Patton, n.p., Sept. 20, 1918, Patton Papers.

109. Smythe, *Pershing,* pp. 190–191.

110. Ibid., p. 195; Patton to Beatrice Ayer Patton, n.p., Sept. 25, 1918, Patton Papers.

111. Semmes, *Portrait of Patton,* p. 52.

112. Patton to Beatrice Ayer Patton, n.p., Sept. 25, 1918, Patton Papers; Wilson, *Treat 'Em Rough!,* pp. 133–134.

113. Blumenson, I, 610–615; Patton to Beatrice Ayer Patton, n.p., Sept. 28, 1918, and Oct. 29, 1918, Patton Papers; Captain G. M. Rarey, "American Tank Units in the Forêt D'Argonne," *Infantry Journal* 32 (April 1928): 390–393.

114. Patton to Beatrice Ayer Patton, n.p., Oct. 2, 1918, and Oct. 10, 1918, Patton Papers; Rarey, "American Tank Units in the Forêt D'Argonne," pp. 392–393.

115. Patton to Beatrice Ayer Patton, n.p., Oct. 16, 1918, Oct. 17, 1918, and Oct. 20, 1918, Patton Papers.

116. Patton to Beatrice Ayer Patton, n.p., Oct. 28, 1918, and Oct. 29, 1918, Patton Papers.

117. Patton to Pershing, n.p., Nov. 17, 1918, Box 155, Pershing Papers; Captain G. H. Rarey, "Lessons fron the Use of Tanks by the American Army," *Infantry Journal* 32 (May 1928): 518; Kenneth S. Davis, *Soldier of Democracy: A Biography of Dwight Eisenhower* (Garden City, N.Y.: Doubleday, Doran, 1945), pp. 175–178.

CHAPTER FOUR   LEAVENWORTH AND ALL THAT

1. George S. Patton, Jr., to Anne Wilson Patton, n.p., Oct. 26, 1918, George S. Patton, Jr., Papers, Special Collections, United States Military Academy Library, West Point.

2. Patton to Beatrice Ayer Patton, n.p., Nov. 17, 1918, Patton Papers.

3. Patton to John J. Pershing, n.p., Nov. 17, 1918, Box 155, John J. Pershing Papers, Manuscript Division, Library of Congress.

4. Patton to Beatrice Ayer Patton, n.p., Nov. 17, 1918, Patton Papers.

5. Patton to Beatrice Ayer Patton, n.p., Nov. 18, 1918, Patton Papers.

6. Patton to Beatrice Ayer Patton, n.p., Nov. 20, 1918, Patton Papers.

7. Patton to Beatrice Ayer Patton, Nov. 24, 1918, Nov. 25, 1918, and Nov. 26, 1918, Patton Papers.

8. *New York Times,* Jan. 4, 1919; Patton to Beatrice Ayer Patton, n.p., Dec. 11, 1918, Patton Papers.

9. Pershing to Anne Wilson Patton, Paris, Dec. 27, 1918, Box 418, Pershing Papers.

10. Patton to George S. Patton, Sr., n.p., Jan. 7, 1919, Box 7, George S. Patton, Sr., Papers, Henry E. Huntington Library, San Marino, Cali.

11. Blumenson, I, 668.

12. Patton to Beatrice Ayer Patton, n.p., Jan. 28, 1919, Patton Papers; Patton to George S. Patton, Sr., n.p., Jan. 28, 1919, Box 7, George S. Patton, Sr., Papers.

13. Blumenson, I, 671; Patton to Beatrice Ayer Patton, n.p., Feb. 7, 1919, Box 21, George S. Patton, Jr., Papers, Manuscript Division, Library of Congress.

14. Patton to Beatrice Ayer Patton, n.p., Feb. 9, 1919, Patton Papers.

15. Patton to Beatrice Ayer Patton, n.p., Feb. 10, 1919, Patton Papers.

16. Patton to Anne Wilson Patton, n.p., Feb. 18, 1919, Patton Papers; Patton to Pershing, n.p., Feb. 18, 1919, Box 155, Pershing Papers. The details of the final conversation with the Prince are in " 'Toast to the Ladies' Given by George S. Patton, Jr., at a West Point Dinner in Fort Leavenworth, 1924," Box 5, Patton Papers.

17. Carmine A. Prioli (ed.), *The Poems of General George S. Patton, Jr.* (Lewiston, N.Y.: Edwin Mellen Press, 1991), pp. 70–74; George Patton, Sr., to Patton, Washington, D.C., Feb. 20, 1919, Box 21, Patton Papers, Library of Congress; Bradford Grethen Chynoweth, *Bellamy Park* (Hicksville, N.Y.: Exposition Press), pp. 109–110.

18. George Patton, Sr., to John S. McGroarty, n.p., Aug. 21, 1919, Box 6, George Patton, Sr., Papers; Prioli (ed.), *Poems of General George S. Patton, Jr.,* pp. 65–66.

19. George S. Patton, Jr., Diary, Feb. 23, 1919, Box 21, Patton Papers, Library of Congress; Patton to Pershing, n.p., Feb. 23, 1919, Box 155, Pershing Papers.

20. Patton Diary, Feb. 26, 1919, and Feb. 28, 1919, and March 1, 1919; Patton to Pershing, n.p., March 26, 1919, Box 155, Pershing Papers.

21. Patton to Pershing, n.p., March 26, 1919, Box 155, Pershing Papers.

22. *New York Times,* March 18, 1919; *New York Herald,* March 18, 1919.

23. Beatrice Ayer Patton to George Patton, Sr., Washington, D.C., March 4, 1919, Box 21, Patton Papers, Library of Congress.

24. Speech by Beatrice Ayer Patton, "Dobbs Day Nursery Benefit," pp. 6–7, Nov. 16, 1943, Box 10, Patton Papers.

25. Patton to George Patton, Sr., n.p., April 1, 1919, Patton Papers.

26. Patton to Pershing, Camp Meade, April 3, 1919, Box 155, Pershing Papers.

27. Patrick J. Cooney, "U. S. Armor Between the Wars," *Armor* 99 (March–April 1990): 18.

28. Kenneth S. Davis, *Soldier of Democracy: A Biography of Dwight Eisenhower* (Garden City, N.Y.: Doubleday, Doran, 1945), pp. 174–180; Reminiscences of Lieutenant General John W. Leonard, pp. 1, 14–19, 1980, Oral History Research Office, Columbia University Library, New York City.

29. Davis, *Soldier of Democracy,* p. 185; Leonard Reminiscences, pp. 18–19; Dwight D. Eisenhower, *At Ease: Stories I Tell to Friends* (Garden City, N.Y.: Doubleday, 1967), p. 169.

30. Blumenson, I, 706–707; Patton to George Patton, Sr., Davenport, Iowa, June 2, 1919, Patton Papers.

31. Patton to Pershing, Washington, D.C., June 14, 1919, Box 155, Pershing Papers.

32. Ibid.; Cooney, "U. S. Armor Between the Wars," p. 18.

33. Pershing to Patton, Chaumont, July 7, 1919, Box 155, Pershing Papers.

34. Robert H. Patton, *The Pattons: A Personal History of an American Family* (New York: Crown, 1994), pp. 188–189; Pershing to Patton, Chaumont, July 7, 1919, Box 155, Pershing Papers.

35. Pershing to Anne Wilson Patton, Paris, June 30, 1919, Box 418, Pershing Papers.

36. Patton, *Pattons,* pp. 189–191; Pershing to Patton, Chaumont, July 7, 1919, Box 155, Pershing Papers.

37. Tyler Abell (ed.), *Drew Pearson Diaries, 1949–1959* (New York: Holt, Rinehart and Winston, 1974), pp. 412–413; William Manchester, *American Caesar: Douglas MacArthur, 1880–1964* (Boston: Little, Brown, 1978), pp. 127–129; *Parade,* January 6, 1985, in Patton Vertical File, United States Military Academy Archives, West Point.

38. Patton to Anne Wilson, Washington, D.C., July 11, 1919, Box 21, Patton Papers, Library of Congress.

39. *Catalina Islander,* Aug. 12, 1925, in Box 12, Banning Company Papers, Henry E. Huntington Library, San Marino, Cal.; Reminiscences of Hancock Banning, Jr., p. 81, 1971, Oral History Program, University of California at Los Angeles; *Los Angeles Examiner,* Aug. 8, 1925.

40. Patton to George Patton, Sr., Camp Meade, Sept. 12, 1919, Box 7, George S. Patton, Sr., Papers; Blumenson, I, 710–711.

41. Patton to George Patton, Sr., Camp Meade, Sept. 12, 1919, Box 7, George Patton, Sr., Papers; Bradford G. Chynoweth to George F. Hofmann, Berkeley, Cal., June 30, 1971, Box 2, Bradford G. Chynoweth Papers, United States Army Military History Institute, Carlisle Barracks, Pa.

42. Patton to George Patton, Sr., Camp Meade, Sept. 12, 1919, Box 7, George Patton, Sr., Papers; Patton to Anne Wilson Patton, Camp Meade, Sept. 20, 1919, Box 21, Patton Papers, Library of Congress; Henry L. Stimson Diary, Dec. 8, 1919, Henry L. Stimson Papers, Sterling Memorial Library, Yale University, New Haven, Ct.; Frank R. McCoy to Van S. Merle-Smith, Fort Sheridan, Ill., March 13, 1921, Box 16, Frank R. McCoy Papers, Manuscript Division, Library of Congress.

43. Patton to Anne Wilson, Camp Meade, Sept. 20, 1919, Box 21, Patton Papers, Library of Congress; Patton to George Patton, Sr., Camp Meade, Oct. 3, 1919, Box 7, George Patton, Sr., Papers.

44. Eisenhower, *At Ease,* pp. 169–170; Chynoweth to Hofmann, Berkeley, July 8, 1971, Box 2, Chynoweth Papers.

45. Chynoweth to Hofmann, Berkeley, July 8, 1971, Box 2, Chynoweth Papers.

46. Chynoweth to Hofmann, Berkeley, June 30, 1971, Box 2, Chynoweth Papers; Sidney R. Hinds to W. D. Crittenden, Falls Church, Va., May 30, 1971, Box 2, Chynoweth Papers.

47. Eisenhower, *At Ease,* p. 170.

48. Patton to Ruth Wilson Patton, n.p., Nov. 6, 1919, Box 21, Patton Papers, Library of Congress.

49. Eisenhower, *At Ease,* p. 170; George F. Hofmann, "John Walter Christie," *Dictionary of American Biography, 1941–1945* (New York: Charles Scribner's Sons, 1973), Supplement III, 165–166. Quoted is Chynoweth to Hofmann, Berkeley, June 30, 1971, Box 2, Chynoweth Papers.

50. Dale E. Wilson, *Treat 'Em Rough!: The Birth of American Armor, 1917–20* (Novato, Cal.: Presidio, 1989), pp. 223–224; Eisenhower, *At Ease,* pp. 172–173.

51. Eisenhower, *At Ease,* pp. 170–172.

52. See Patton's comments in C. E. Callwell, *The Life of Sir Stanley Maude* (Boston and New York: Houghton Mifflin, 1920), pp. 114, 122–123, 141, 144, 147, 157, 164, 264, 336, George S. Patton, Jr., Library, Special Collections, United States Military Academy Library, West Point.

53. Patton to Anne Wilson, n.p., Nov. 27, 1919, Box 21, Patton Papers, Library of Congress.

54. Frederick Ayer, Jr., to George Patton, Sr., Boston, Feb. 19, 1920, Box 2, George Patton, Sr., Papers. On the size of Frederick Ayer's estate see Defendant's Answer to Charges, Sept. 8, 1919, in Records, *United States v. James C. Ayer, et al.,* Case Number 2245, United States District Court for Massachusetts, National Archives—Northeast Region, Waltham, Mass.

55. Patton to George Patton, Sr., Camp Meade, April 26, 1920, Box 7, George Patton, Sr., Papers.

56. Patton to George Patton, Sr., n.p., Feb. 19, 1920, Box 7, George Patton, Sr., Papers.

57. George Patton, Sr., to Patton, n.p., March 23, 1923, Box 7, George Patton, Sr., Papers; Patton Income Tax Return, 1923, Box 7, George Patton, Sr., Papers.

58. Ayer to George Patton, Sr., Boston, Feb. 26, 1923, Box 7, George Patton, Sr., Papers; *New York Times,* Aug. 31, 1912, and Nov. 28, 1912.

59. Patton to George Patton, Sr., n.p., Feb. 1, 1920, Box 7, George Patton, Sr., Papers.

60. Patton to George Patton, Sr., Camp Meade, Feb. 11, 1920, Box 7, George Patton, Sr., Papers.

61. Patton to George Patton, Sr., n.p., April 5, 1920, and April 26, 1920, Box 7, George Patton, Sr., Papers.

62. Patton to George Patton, Sr., Camp Meade, June 8, 1920, and June 19, 1920, Miscellaneous Box, Patton Papers.

63. George S. Patton, Jr., "Tanks in Future Wars," *Infantry Journal* 16 (May 1920): 958–962.

64. Dwight D. Eisenhower, "A Tank Discussion," *Infantry Journal* 17 (November 1920): 454–458.

65. Eisenhower, *At Ease,* p. 173.

66. Bradford G. Chynoweth, "A More Perfect Union," pp. 129, 140–143, Box 3, Chynoweth Papers.

67. Chynoweth, *Bellamy Park,* pp. 63, 90–92.

68. Chynoweth to Hofmann, Berkeley, June 30, 1971, Box 2, Chynoweth Papers.

69. Chynoweth to Hinds, Berkeley, January 4, 1972, Box 2, Chynoweth Papers.

70. Bradford G. Chynoweth, "Cavalry Tanks," *Cavalry Journal* 30 (July 1921): 247–251; George S. Patton, Jr., "Comments on 'Cavalry Tanks,'" *Cavalry Journal,* 30 (July 1921): 251–252.

71. Wilson, *Treat 'Em Rough!,* pp. 227–230; Patton to George Patton, Sr., Fort Myer, Oct. 9, 1920, Miscellaneous Box, Patton Papers.

72. Beatrice Ayer Patton to Anne Wilson, n.p., Sept. 29, 1920, Box 21, Patton Papers, Library of Congress.

73. Patton to George Patton, Sr., Fort Myer, Oct. 9, 1920, Miscellaneous Box, Patton Papers; Ayer to George Patton, Sr., Boston, Nov. 22, 1920, Box 2, George Patton, Sr., Papers.

74. Patton to George Patton, Sr., Fort Myer, Nov. 29, 1920, Miscellaneous Box, Patton Papers.

75. Chynoweth, *Bellamy Park,* p. 123.

76. Patton to George Patton, Sr., Fort Myer, Feb. 27, 1921, Box 7, George Patton, Sr., Papers.

77. Patton to Ruth Wilson Patton, n.p., June 13, 1921, Miscellaneous Box, Patton Papers; Eisenhower, *At Ease,* pp. 178–179, 182.

78. Patton to George Patton, Sr., Fort Myer, Oct. 11, 1921, Box 7, George Patton, Sr., Papers.

79. Patton to George Patton, Sr., Fort Myer, Nov. 12, 1921, Box 7, George Patton, Sr., Papers.

80. Patton to George Patton, Sr., Fort Myer, January 16, 1922, Box 7, George Patton, Sr., Papers.

81. George S. Patton, Jr., "Tactical Tendencies," pp. 1–7, Box 7, George Patton, Sr., Papers; Patton to George Patton, Sr., Fort Myer, February 1, 1922, Box 7, George Patton, Sr., Papers; George Patton, Jr., "What the World War Did for Cavalry," *Cavalry Journal* 31 (April 1922): 165–172; Edward Davis, "The British Cavalry in Palestine and Syria," *Cavalry Journal* 31 (April 1922): 123–129.

82. Roger H. Nye, undated memorandum, p. 12, Box 1, Roger H. Nye Papers, Special Collections, United States Military Academy Library, West Point.

83. George Patton, Sr., to John S. McGroarty, n.p., Aug. 21, 1919, Box 6, George Patton, Sr., Papers; "Through a Glass, Darkly," in Patton Poems, pp. 54–56, Patton Papers; Prioli (ed.), *Poems of General George S. Patton,* pp. 118–119, 128–129.

84. Robert H. Patton, *The Pattons: A Personal History of an American Family* (New York: Crown, 1994), pp. 239–240; Ruth Ellen Patton Totten to Roger H. Nye, South Hamilton, Oct. 18, 1990, Nye Papers.

85. Patton, *Pattons,* p. 201; Patton to George Patton, Sr., Fort Myer, Feb. 1, 1922, Miscellaneous Box, Patton Papers.

86. Patton to George Patton, Sr., Fort Myer, March 13, 1922, Miscellaneous Box, Patton Papers.

87. Patton to Beatrice Ayer Patton, Fort Myer, April 17, 1922, Box 21, Patton Papers, Library of Congress.

88. Patton to Beatrice Ayer Patton, Fort Myer, July 4, 1922, and July 5, 1922, Box 21, Patton Papers, Library of Congress.

89. Patton to George Patton, Sr., n.p., Sept. 13, 1922, Miscellaneous Box, Patton Papers.

90. Patton to George Patton, Sr., n.p., Oct. 1, 1922, Box 7, George Patton, Sr., Papers.

91. Ruth Ellen Patton Totten, "Christmas with the Pattons," *Ladycom* 5 (December 1973): 26–31.

92. Beatrice Ayer Patton to George Patton, Sr., Junction City, Kansas, Jan. 18, 1923, Box 7, George Patton, Sr., Papers.

93. Ibid.

94. Patton to George Patton, Sr., n.p., March 20, 1923, Box 7, George Patton, Sr., Papers.

95. Patton to George Patton, Sr., n.p., June 1, 1923, Box 7, George Patton, Sr., Papers.

96. Patton to George Patton, Sr., n.p., June 15, 1923, Miscellaneous Box, Patton Papers.

97. Chynoweth, *Bellamy Park,* p. 121; *Assembly* 45 (December 1986): 155.

98. Chynoweth, *Bellamy Park.* pp. 121–123; Chynoweth to Hofmann, Berkeley, March 8, 1972, Box 2, Chynoweth Papers; *The Command and General Staff School, 1923–1924, Conferences,* pp. 70–71, 75–77, in Combined Arms Research Library, Fort Leavenworth, Kansas; *Address by Brigadier General H. A. Smith at Opening Exercises of the Command and General Staff School, Fort Leavenworth,* p. 6, Combined Arms Research Library.

99. Chynoweth to Hofmann, Berkeley, March 8, 1972, Box 2, Chynoweth Papers; Chynoweth, *Bellamy Park,* pp. 122–123; Louis Morton, *The Fall of the Philippines* (Washington, D.C.: Office of the Chief of Military History, 1953), pp. 578–579.

100. Chynoweth to Hofmann, Berkeley, March 8, 1972, Box 2, Chynoweth Papers.

101. Patton to Floyd L. Parks, Fort Myer, Jan. 28, 1933, Box 8, Floyd L. Parks Papers, Dwight D. Eisenhower Library, Abilene, Kansas.

102. Frank James Price, *Troy H. Middleton: A Biography* (Baton Rouge: Louisiana State University Press, 1974), pp. 89–90.

103. Ruth Wilson Patton to George Patton, Sr., Boston, Dec. 17, 1923, and Dec. 24, 1923, Box 7, George Patton, Sr., Papers. To show the difference in the value of money then and now, the mansion at Prides Crossing, filled, Ruth Patton noted, with servants, was appraised after Frederick Ayer's death at $288,400. See Defendant's Answer to Charges, Sept. 8, 1919, Records of *United States v. James C. Ayer, et al.,* Case Number 2245, United States District Court for Massachusetts, National Archives—Northeast Region, Waltham, Mass.

104. Ruth Wilson Patton to George Patton, Sr., Boston, Dec. 27, 1923, Box 7, George Patton, Sr., Papers.

105. Beatrice Ayer Patton to George Patton, Sr., Boston, late 1923, Box 7, George Patton, Sr., Papers.

106. George S. Simonds to Patton, Washington, n.d., Box 7, George Patton, Sr., Papers; Patton to Anne Wilson, n.p., Jan. 5, 1924, Box 7, George Patton, Sr., Papers; Chynoweth, *Bellamy Park,* p. 106.

107. Patton to George Patton, Sr., Fort Leavenworth, March 23, 1924, Miscellaneous Box, Patton Papers.

108. Patton to George Patton, Sr., Fort Leavenworth, April 30, 1924, Miscellaneous Box, Patton Papers.

109. *Commandants, Staff, Faculty and Graduates, 1881–1939, The Command and General Staff School* (Fort Leavenworth: Command and General Staff School Press, 1939), p. 31, in Combined Arms Research Library; Price, *Middleton,* p. 89; Chynoweth, *Bellamy Park,* p. 55.

110. Blumenson, I, 820–821.

CHAPTER FIVE   THE WARRIOR SOUL

1. George S. Patton, Jr., to George S. Patton, Sr., Boston, July 29, 1924, Miscellaneous Box, George S. Patton, Jr., Papers, Special Collections, United States Military Academy Library, West Point.

2. Patton to George Patton, Sr., Boston, September 22, 1924, Jan. 15, 1925, and Jan. 20, 1925, Miscellaneous Box, Patton Papers.

3. Patton to George Patton, Sr., Boston, Feb. 3, 1925, Box 7, George S. Patton, Sr., Papers, Henry E. Hungtington Library, San Marino, Cal.

4. Sadie L. Patton Hutchinson to George Patton, Sr., Palo Alto, Jan. 27, 1925, Box 5, Patton, Sr., Papers.

5. Patton to George Patton, Sr., Boston, Feb. 10, 1925, Miscellaneous Box, Patton Papers.

6. Patton to George Patton, Sr., Boston, Feb. 17, 1925, Miscellaneous Box, Patton Papers.

7. Patton to Beatrice Ayer Patton, n.p., March 17, 1925, Box 21, George S. Patton, Jr., Papers, Manuscript Division, Library of Congress. This letter is misdated Feb. 17, 1925.

8. Bradford Grethen Chynoweth, *Bellamy Park* (Hicksville, N.Y.: Exposition Press, 1975), p. 109; H. L. Walthall to Bradford G. Chynoweth, Washington, D.C., July 8, 1925, Box 1, Bradford G. Chynoweth Papers, United States Army Military History Institute, Carlisle Barracks, Pa.

9. Patton to Beatrice Ayer Patton, Aboard *Grant,* March 27, 1925, and March 29, 1925, Box 21, Patton Papers, Library of Congress; Patton to Ruth Wilson Patton, Aboard *Grant,* March 27, 1925, Miscellaneous Box, Patton Papers.

10. Chynoweth, *Bellamy Park,* p. 109.

11. Patton to Beatrice Ayer Patton, Schofield Barracks, April 2, 1925, Patton Papers.

12. Omar N. Bradley and Clay Blair, *A General's Life* (New York: Simon and Schuster, 1983), p. 58; Chynoweth to Dwight D. Eisenhower, Camp Gaillard, Canal Zone, April 1, 1926, Box 1, Chynoweth Papers.

13. Patton to Beatrice Ayer Patton, n.p., April 6, 1925, Patton Papers.

14. Patton to Beatrice Ayer Patton, n.p., April 10, 1925, Patton Papers.

15. Chynoweth, *Bellamy Park,* pp. 109–110; Chynoweth to Eisenhower, Camp Gaillard, Canal Zone, April 1, 1926, Box 1, Chynoweth Papers.

16. Patton to George Patton, Sr., Schofield Barracks, July 30, 1925, Miscellaneous Box, Patton Papers.

17. Beatrice Ayer Patton to Ruth Wilson Patton, n.p., July 6, 1925, Box 5, George Patton, Sr., Papers.

18. Thomas C. Major to Frank McCarthy, Portuguese Bay, Cal., July 30, 1965, Box 12, Frank McCarthy Papers, George C. Marshall Library, Virginia Military Institute, Lexington, Va. Major was Scott's son-in-law.

19. Ibid.; James G. Harbord to Patton, New York, March 2, 1926, Box 21, George S. Patton, Jr., Papers, Manuscript Division, Library of Congress.

20. Patton to George Patton, Sr., Schofield Barracks, February 15, 1926, Miscellaneous Box, Patton Papers.

21. Ibid.; Harbord to Patton, New York, March 2, 1926, Box 21, Patton Papers, Library of Congress; Patton to Chynoweth, Schofield Barracks, March 25, 1926, Box 1, Chynoweth Papers.

22. Patton to George Patton, Sr., Schofield Barracks, April 12, 1926, Miscellaneous Box, Patton Papers.

23. Roger H. Nye, *The Patton Mind: The Professional Development of an Extraordinary Leader* (Garden City Park, N.Y.: Avery Publishing Group, 1993), p. 85; Blumenson, I, 798–799.

24. Patton to Eisenhower, n.p., July 9, 1926, Box 91, Dwight D. Eisenhower Pre-Presidential Papers, Dwight D. Eisenhower Library, Abilene, Kansas.

25. Chynoweth, *Bellamy Park,* pp. 121–125; Chynoweth to Patton, Camp Gaillard, Canal Zone, July 16, 1926, Box 1, Chynoweth Papers.

26. Bradley and Blair, *General's Life,* pp. 38, 58–59; Chynoweth, *Bellamy Park,* pp. 126–127.

27. Patton to George Patton, Sr., n.p., Aug. 31, 1926, Miscellaneous Box, Patton Papers. For the athletic achievements of those mentioned see the various issues of the West Point yearbook, *Howitzer,* from 1909 to 1916.

28. See the following in the Records, *United States v. James C. Ayer, et al.,* Case Number 2245, United States District Court for Massachusetts, National Archives— Northeast Region, Waltham, Mass.: George S. Patton, Sr., Answers to Interrogatories, Dec. 4, 1926, pp. 1–4; Defendant's Answer to Charges, Sept. 8, 1919.

29. Edward O. Proctor to George Patton, Sr., Boston, Aug. 17, 1926, Box 2, George Patton, Sr., Papers; Frederick Ayer to George Patton, Sr., Boston, March 28, 1919, Box 2, George Patton, Sr., Papers; unidentified newspaper clipping, Box 54, George Patton, Sr., Papers; *New York Times,* April 25, 1926, and April 6, 1927.

30. Patton to George Patton, Sr., n.p., August 31, 1926, Box 7, George Patton, Sr., Papers; Docket Book, pp. 440–441, Case Number 2245, *U.S. v. James C. Ayer*.

31. Blumenson, I, 304–306.

32. Patton to George Patton, Sr., Schofield Barracks, Feb. 3, 1927, Miscellaneous Box, Patton Papers.

33. Patton to Beatrice Ayer Patton, Lake Vineyard, Feb. 24, 1927, Patton Papers.

34. Patton to Beatrice Ayer Patton, Los Angeles, Feb. 28, 1927, Box 21, Patton Papers, Library of Congress.

35. Patton to George Patton, Sr., Aboard *S.S. President Polk,* March 17, 1927, Miscellaneous Box, Patton Papers.

36. Beatrice Ayer Patton to Floyd L. Parks, Lake Vineyard, n.d. but June 1927, Box 8, Floyd L. Parks Papers, Dwight D. Eisenhower Library, Abilene, Kansas; Inventory and Appraisal, Estate of George S. Patton, Sr., Feb. 28, 1928, Box 50A, George Patton, Sr., Papers.

37. Final Account of the Estate of George S. Patton, Sr., California Superior Court, Oct. 1, 1928, Box 50A, George Patton, Sr., Papers.

38. Patton to Frederick Ayer, Jr., San Gabriel, Feb. 15, 1927, copy, Box 2, George Patton, Sr., Papers; Arvin H. Brown to Patton, n.p., July 29, 1927, Box 50A, George Patton, Sr., Papers; Eltinge T. Brown Company to Patton, Los Angeles, Sept. 19, 1927, Box 50A, George Patton, Sr., Papers.

39. Patton to Arvin Brown, Schofield Barracks, September 2, 1927, Box 50A, George Patton, Sr., Papers. Frida's real name was Kathleen A. Brown.

40. Brown to Patton, n.p., Sept. 19, 1927, Box 50A, George Patton, Sr., Papers.

41. Patton to Beatrice Ayer Patton, Schofield Barracks, Nov. 2, 1926, Patton Papers.

42. Blumenson, I, 811–816.

43. Patton to Brown, Schofield Barracks, Oct. 27, 1927, Box 50A, George Patton, Sr., Papers.

44. Blumenson, I, 819.

45. Lieutenant Colonel Bruce Palmer to Patton, Washington, D.C., Sept. 13, 1927, Box 21, Patton Papers, Library of Congress.

46. Beatrice Ayer Patton, "Hawaii," *Paradise of the Pacific* 41 (May 1928): 5; Ruth Ellen Patton, "Night in Hawaii," *Paradise of the Pacific* 41 (August 1928): 31.

47. Field Marshal Sir William Robertson, *Soldiers and Statesmen, 1914–1918* (New York: Charles Scribner's Sons, 1926), I, 18, 39, 45, 59, 111, 137, 160, in George S. Patton, Jr., Library, United States Military Academy Library, West Point.

48. Nye, *Patton Mind,* p. 90; Hans von Seeckt, "The Armies of Today," *Cavalry Journal* 39 (April 1930): 252–261; George S. Patton, Jr., "Notes on Mechanization, 1928–1929," p. 5, Miscellaneous Box, Patton Papers. One of Seeckt's admirers, Fritz Schaeffer, was instrumental in Patton's removal from command of the Third Army late in 1945.

49. Patton to Brown, Mitchel Field, Aug. 4, 1928, Box 50A, George Patton, Sr., Papers.

50. Reminiscences of John K. Waters, pp. 49–55, April 9, 1980, United States Army Military History Institute, Carlisle Barracks, Pa.

51. Brown to O'Melveny, Tullton and Myers, n.p., Sept. 3, 1929, Box 21, George Patton, Sr., Papers; Telegram, Anne Wilson Patton to Patton, Los Angeles, Oct. 8, 1928, Box 21, George Patton, Sr., Papers.

52. Report of Inheritance Tax Appraiser, State of California, Box 21, George Patton, Sr., Papers; Last Will of Ruth Wilson Patton, August 8, 1924, Box 21, George Patton, Sr., Papers.

53. Brown to Patton, n.p., Aug. 7, 1930, and Sept. 25, 1930, Box 43, George Patton, Sr., Papers; Patton to Brown, Washington, D.C., Sept. 6, 1930, George Patton, Sr., Papers.

54. Patton to Brown, Washington, D.C., May 29, 1930, Box 43, George Patton, Sr., Papers.

55. Anne Wilson Patton to Brown, Aboard Sunset Limited, Oct. 22, 1928, Box 28, George Patton, Sr., Papers.

56. Anne Wilson Patton to Brown, Washington, D.C., Nov. 21, 1928, Box 28, George Patton, Sr., Papers; Konrad F. Schreier, Jr., "U.S. Army Tank Development, 1925–1940," *Armor* 99 (May–June 1990): 25. On the Infantry and Ordnance opposition to Christie and his tanks, see Chynoweth to George F. Hofmann, Berkeley, June 30, 1971, Box 2, Chynoweth Papers.

57. *Cavalry Journal* 38 (January 1929): 129–132, and *Cavalry Journal* 38 (April 1929): 292–297.

58. Nye, *Patton Mind,* p. 85; Blumenson, I, 860.

59. Anne Wilson Patton to Brown, Washington, D.C., Nov. 6, 1928, Box 21, George Patton, Sr., Papers.

60. Patton to Brown, n.p., March 28, 1929, Box 21, George Patton, Sr., Papers; Anne Patton to Brown, Rome, March 6, 1929, Box 23, George Patton, Sr., Papers.

61. Patton to Chynoweth, n.p., May 29, 1929, Box 1, Chynoweth Papers.

62. Chynoweth to Patton, Fort Benning, Georgia, June 26, 1929, Box 1, Chynoweth Papers.

63. Patton to Beatrice Ayer Patton, Fort Bliss, October 12, 1929, Patton Papers; George S. Patton, Jr., "The 1929 Cavalry Division Maneuvers," *Cavalry Journal* 39 (January 1930): 7–15.

64. George S. Patton, Jr., and C. C. Benson, "Mechanization and Cavalry," *Cavalry Journal* 39 (April 1930): 234–240.

65. George S. Patton, Jr., "Motorization and Mechanization in the Cavalry," *Cavalry Journal* 39 (July 1930): 331–348.

66. George S. Patton, Jr., "The Effect of Weapons on War," *Infantry Journal* 37 (November 1930): 483–488.

67. Henry Cabot Lodge, *The Storm Has Many Eyes* (New York: W. W. Norton, 1973), p. 44.

68. Henry L. Stimson Diary, Nov. 16, 1930, and Dec. 13, 1930, Henry L. Stimson Papers, Sterling Memorial Library, Yale University, New Haven, Ct.

69. Anne Wilson Patton to Brown, Washington, D.C., Dec. 15, 1930, and Dec. 23, 1930, Box 33, George S. Patton, Sr., Papers; Stimson Diary, Dec. 13, 1930.

70. Mary A. Crowley to Mary Scally, Washington, D.C., Dec. 14, 1930, Box 15, George Patton, Sr., Papers.

71. Ruth Ellen Patton to Anne Wilson, Dobbs Ferry, N.Y., about 1930, Box 34, George Patton, Sr., Papers.

72. George S. Patton, Jr., "Success in War," *Cavalry Journal* 40 (January 1931): 28. For an earlier version of this paper see "The Secrets of Victory," March 26, 1926, Box 6, Patton Papers.

73. Patton, "Success in War," pp. 26–30.

74. Chynoweth, *Bellamy Park,* p. 133.

75. Ibid., pp. 133–134.

76. Ibid., p. 136.

77. Arvin H. Brown, Executor, Estate of Annie Wilson, Report of Jan. 22, 1934, Box 24, George Patton, Sr., Papers; Annie Wilson Estate Tax Report, May 25, 1934, Box 24, George Patton, Sr., Papers; Brown to S. A. Reed, Los Angeles, June 5, 1934, Box 24, George Patton, Sr., Papers; *New York Times,* Jan. 21, 1934.

78. Patton to Brown, n.p., June 2, 1931, Box 43, George Patton, Sr., Papers; Brown to Reed, Los Angeles, June 5, 1934, Box 24, George Patton, Sr., Papers.

79. Report of Executor, Annie Wilson Estate, pp. 23–24, Box 24, George Patton, Sr., Papers; Anne Wilson Patton to Ethel R. Shorb, San Marino, Dec. 26, 1931, Box 24, George Patton, Sr., Papers; Brown to Patton, n.p., Jan. 27, 1932, and March 21, 1932, Box 24, George Patton, Sr., Papers; Telegram, Patton to Anne Wilson Patton, Washington, Feb. 1, 1932, Box 24, George Patton, Sr., Papers; Anne Wilson Patton to Brown, San Marino, March 30, 1932, Box 24, George Patton, Sr., Papers.

80. Patton to Anne Wilson Patton, Washington, Dec. 30, 1931, Box 24, George Patton, Sr., Papers.

81. George S. Patton, Jr., "The Probable Characteristics of the Next War and the Organization, Tactics and Equipment Necessary to Meet Them," Paper, Army War College, Feb. 29, 1932, Archives, United States Army Military History Institute, Carlisle Barracks, Pa.; Martin S. Blumenson, "George S. Patton's Student Days at the Army War College," *Parameters* 5 (1976): 25–32.

82. Beatrice Ayer Patton to Anne Wilson Patton, Rosslyn, Va., July 4, 1932, Box 34, George Patton, Sr., Papers.

83. Lucian K. Truscott, Jr., *The Twilight of the U.S. Cavalry: Life in the Old Army, 1917–1942* (Lawrence: University Press of Kansas, 1989), pp. 109–110.

84. Beatrice Ayer Patton to Brown, Washington, D.C., May 12, 1932, Box 43, George Patton, Sr., Papers; Telegrams, Beatrice Ayer Patton, Patton, and Anne Wilson Patton to Senators Samuel Shortridge and Hiram W. Johnson, and to Congressman William H. Evans, April 21, 1932, Box 43, George Patton, Sr., Papers.

85. Patton to Anne Wilson Patton, Fort Myer, July 8, 1932, Box 34, George Patton, Sr., Papers.

86. Patton to Anne Wilson Patton, Fort Myer, July 15, 1932, Box 34, George Patton, Sr., Papers.

87. Reminiscences of Raymond P. Brandt, pp. 66–69, Sept. 28, 1970, Oral History Project, Harry S. Truman Library, Independence, Mo.; Truscott, *Twilight of the U.S. Cavalry,* pp. 127–129; *New York Times,* July 30, 1932; William Manchester, *American Caesar: Douglas MacArthur* (Boston and Toronto: Little, Brown, 1978), p. 15.

88. Matthew Josephson, *Infidel in the Temple: A Memoir of the Nineteen-Thirties* (New York: Alfred A. Knopf, 1967), pp. 99–100.

89. Truscott, *Twilight of the U.S. Cavalry,* p. 123; *New York Times,* July 30, 1932.

90. *New York Times,* July 30, 1932.

91. Dwight D. Eisenhower, *At Ease: Stories I Tell to Friends* (Garden City, N.Y.: Doubleday, 1967), pp. 216–217.

92. Anne Wilson Patton to Brown, San Gabriel, April 16, 1932, Box 33, George Patton, Sr., Papers.

93. Brown to Patton, n.p., Oct. 13, 1932, and Nov. 9, 1932, George Patton, Sr., Papers.

94. Stimson Diary, February 23, 1933, February 27, 1933, and March 5, 1933.

95. Patton to Anne Wilson Patton, Fort Myer, March 2, 1933, Box 26, George Patton, Sr., Papers.

96. Truscott, *Twilight of the U.S. Cavalry,* p. 108; Patton to Beatrice Ayer Patton, Fort Myer, July 29, 1933, Patton Papers.

97. Reminiscences of General Kenyon A. Joyce, p. 236, Box 1, Kenyon A. Joyce Papers, United States Army Military History Institute, Carlisle Barracks, Pa.

98. Waters Reminiscences, pp. 54–55.

99. "The Cavalry Maneuvers at Fort Riley, Kansas, 1934," *Cavalry Journal* 43 (July-August 1934): 5–14; Patton to Beatrice Ayer Patton, Fort Riley, May 4, 1934, Patton Papers.

100. Patton to Beatrice Ayer Patton, n.p., May 13, 1934, Patton Papers.

101. Patton to Beatrice Ayer Patton, n.p., July 7, 1934, Patton Papers.

102. Josephson, *Infidel in the Temple,* pp. 258, 274–276.

103. Chynoweth to Hofmann, Berkeley, Jan. 17, 1972, Chynoweth Papers.

104. Patton to Beatrice Ayer Patton, n.p., May 13, 1934, Patton Papers; Blumenson, I, 907.

CHAPTER SIX   "1918 MINDS, ALL"

1. *Washington Star,* April 9, 1935, clipping in Box 155, John J. Pershing Papers, Manuscript Division, Library of Congress.

2. Edward Joesting, *Hawaii: An Uncommon History* (New York: W. W. Norton, 1972), pp. 302–304; Robert Calvert, Jr., "Drum, Drum, I Wish He Would Stop Beating His Own Drum," *Army* 39 (September 1989): 59.

3. Calvert, "Drum, Drum, I Wish He Would Stop Beating His Own Drum," 59; Ladislas Farago, *Patton: Ordeal and Triumph* (New York: Ivan Oblensky, 1964), pp. 116–117.

4. James H. Polk, "Patton: 'You Might As Well Die a Hero,'" *Army* 25 (December 1975): 39–40.

5. Joesting, *Hawaii,* pp. 303–304.

6. Michael Slackman, "The Orange Race: George S. Patton, Jr.'s Japanese-American Hostage Plan," *Biography* 7 (Winter 1984): 17–18; Gavan Dawes, *Shoals of Time: A History of the Hawaiian Islands* (New York: Macmillan, 1968), pp. 307, 383.

7. Slackman, "The Orange Race," p. 18.

8. George S. Patton, Jr., "Plan. Initial Seizure of Orange Nationals! A General Staff Study," Box 3, Hawaiian Department, Adjutant General's Office, Emergency Defense & Mobilization Plans, 1940–1941, Record Group 338, National Records Center, Suitland, Md.; Slackman, "The Orange Race," pp. 1–49; *San Francisco Chronicle,* Feb. 29, 1984.

9. Slackman, "The Orange Race," p. 14.

10. George S. Patton, Jr., "Surprise," June 3, 1937, Miscellaneous Box, George S. Patton, Jr., Papers, Special Collections, United States Military Academy Library, West Point; Blumenson, I, 914–917.

11. Reminiscences of Hancock Banning, Jr., pp. 117–118, 1971, Oral History Program, University of California at Los Angeles.

12. Robert H. Patton, *The Pattons: A Personal History of an American Family* (New York: Crown, 1994), pp. 230–234.

13. George S. Patton, Jr., to John J. Pershing, Fort Shafter, Nov. 12, 1936, Nov. 17, 1936, Feb. 25, 1937, and March 21, 1937, Box 155, John J. Pershing Papers, Manuscript Division, Library of Congress.

14. Kenyon A. Joyce to Patton, n.p., March 16, 1937, Box 1, Kenyon A. Joyce Papers, United States Army Military History Institute, Carlisle Barracks, Pa.; Blumenson, I, 916–917.

15. Blumenson, I, 917–918; Joyce to Patton, n.p., Aug. 30, 1937, Joyce Papers.

16. Patton to Pershing, South Hamilton, Dec. 30, 1937, Box 155, Pershing Papers: Calvert, "Drum, Drum, I Wish He Would Stop Beating His Own Drum," p. 59.

17. Robert W. Grow, "The Ten Lean Years: From the Mechanized Force (1930) to the Armored Force (1940)," *Armor* 96 (May–June 1987); 25, and *Armor* 96 (July–August 1987): 35–38.

18. Grow, "Ten Lean Years" (July–August 1987), pp. 38–39.

19. Ibid., 39; Blumenson, I, 927; Patton to Joyce, Fort Riley, July 12, 1938, Box 1, Joyce Papers.

20. Patton to Joyce, Fort Riley, July 14, 1938, Box 1, Joyce Papers.

21. Joyce to Patton, n.p., July 15, 1938, Box 1, Joyce Papers.

22. Patton to Beatrice Ayer Patton, Fort Clark, July 24, 1938, Patton Papers.

23. Patton to Beatrice Ayer Patton, Fort Clark, August 4, 1938, Patton Papers.

24. Patton to Beatrice Ayer Patton, Fort Clark, August 8, 1938, Patton Papers.

25. Ibid. On night fighting see, for example, Patton's notes in a book Bea gave him for Christmas in 1937: Charles Oman, *A History of the Art of War in the Sixteenth Century* (New York: E. P. Dutton, 1937).

26. Ginger Marshall Martus, "'When and If Becomes Now for Restored Schooner," *Historic Preservation News* (June–July 1994); 15–16, 26, Miscellaneous Box, Patton Papers; Patton to Beatrice Ayer Patton, Fort Clark, Aug. 15, 1938, Patton Papers.

27. Patton to Beatrice Ayer Patton, Fort Clark, Aug. 23, 1938, Patton Papers.

28. Patton to Beatrice Ayer Patton, Fort Clark, Aug. 27, 1938, and Sept. 2, 1938, Patton Papers.

29. Washington Oil Field Contracts, Box 35, George S. Patton, Sr., Papers, Henry E. Huntington Library, San Marino, Cal.; Arvin H. Brown to George S. Patton, Jr., and Anne Wilson Patton, Los Angeles, November 29, 1939, Box 35, George Patton, Sr., Papers.

30. Patton, *Pattons,* p. 243; Patton to Beatrice Ayer Patton, Fort Clark, Aug. 23, 1938, Patton Papers.

31. Grow, "Ten Lean Years" (July–August 1987), pp. 39–41.

32. Joyce to Patton, n.p., Jan. 30, 1939, Box 4, Patton Papers.

33. Joyce to Patton, n.p., May 15, 1939, and Patton to Joyce, n.p., May 22, 1939, Box 4, Patton Papers.

34. Joyce to Patton, n.p., June 2, 1939, Box 4, Patton Papers.

35. Patton to George C. Marshall, Fort Myer, July 20, 1939, Box 79, George C. Marshall Papers, George C. Marshall Library, Virginia Military Institute, Lexington, Va.; Marshall to Patton, n.p., July 24, 1939, Box 79, Marshall Papers; Patton to Beatrice Ayer Patton, Fort Myer, July 27, 1939, Patton Papers.

36. Patton to Beatrice Ayer Patton, Fort Myer, July 29, 1939, Patton Papers.

37. Larry I. Bland (ed.), *George C. Marshall Interviews and Reminiscences for Forrest C. Pogue* (Lexington, Va.: George C. Marshall Research Foundation, 1991) pp. 545–546; Omar N. Bradley and Clay Blair, *A General's Life* (New York: Simon and Schuster, 1983), p. 65.

38. Bland (ed.), *George C. Marshall Interviews and Reminiscences,* p. 607.

39. Edwin H. Randle, "The General and the Movie," *Army* 21 (September 1971): 18.

40. Polk, "Patton: 'You Might As Well Die a Hero,'" pp. 40–41.

41. Patton to Joyce, Fort Myer, Aug. 21, 1939, Box 4, Patton Papers.

42. Joyce to Patton, n.p., Aug. 25, 1939, Box 4, Patton Papers.

43. Grow, "Ten Lean Years" (July-August 1987), pp. 41–42.

44. Patton to Joyce, Fort Myer, Nov. 3, 1939, Box 4, Patton Papers; Joyce to Patton, n.p., Nov. 8, 1939, Box 4, Patton Papers.

45. Bradford Grethen Chynoweth, *Bellamy Park* (Hicksville, N.Y.: Exposition Press, 1975), pp. 126–127; Bradford G. Chynoweth to George F. Hofmann, Berkeley, July 8, 1971, and Feb. 25, 1972, Box 2, Bradford G. Chynoweth Papers, United States Army Military History Institute, Carlisle Barracks, Pa.

46. Chynoweth, *Bellamy Park,* pp. 167–169; *Official Army Register, January 1, 1941* (Washington, D.C.: Government Printing Office, 1941), pp. 165, 238.

47. Chynoweth, *Bellamy Park,* pp. 170–171; Chynoweth to Hofmann, Berkeley, Jan. 17, 1972, Box 2, Chynoweth Papers.

48. Chynoweth to Hofmann, Berkeley, June 30, 1971, and Feb. 25, 1972, Box 2, Chynoweth Papers; Chynoweth, *Bellamy Park,* pp. 171–172.

49. John S. Wood to Hanson W. Baldwin, Reno, Nov. 20, 1964, Series I, Box 20, Hanson W. Baldwin Papers, Sterling Memorial Library, Yale University, New Haven.

50. John Cranston, "1940 Louisiana Maneuvers Lead to Birth of Armored Force," *Armor* 99 (May–June 1990): 32; Patton to Joyce, Fort Myer, Feb. 6, 1940, Box 4, Patton Papers.

51. Joyce to Patton, n.p., Feb. 27, 1940, Box 4, Patton Papers.

52. Cranston, "1940 Louisiana Maneuvers," p. 32; Chynoweth, *Bellamy Park,* p. 172; Wood to Baldwin, Reno, Nov. 20, 1964, Series I, Box 20, Baldwin Papers. See also Doris Kearns Goodwin, *No Ordinary Time: Franklin and Eleanor Roosevelt, The Home Front in World War II* (New York: Simon and Schuster, 1994), pp. 50–51.

53. Chynoweth, *Bellamy Park,* pp. 172–174; Chynoweth to Hofmann, Berkeley, July 8, 1971, Box 2, Chynoweth Papers; Hugh M. Cole, *The Lorraine Campaign* (Washington, D.C.: Department of the Army, 1950), p. 173; *Official Army Register, January 1, 1941,* pp. 775, 893.

54. Cranston, "1940 Louisiana Maneuvers," p. 32; Goodwin, *No Ordinary Time,* pp. 50–51.

55. Basil H. Liddell Hart, "Tank Warfare and Its Future," pp. 5–6, Aug. 29, 1950, Box 1, John S. Wood Papers, George Arents Library for Special Collections, E. S. Bird Library, Syracuse University.

56. Joyce to Patton, n.p., June 28, 1940, Box 4, Patton Papers.

57. Cranston, "1940 Louisiana Maneuvers," p. 32.

58. *Washington Post,* March 20, 1940; Pershing to Beatrice Patton and George Patton, n.p., June 10, 1940, Box 155, Pershing Papers.

59. Bradley and Blair, *General's Life,* p. 97; Patton to Joyce, Fort Myer, July 15, 1940, Box 4, Patton Papers.

60. Patton to Beatrice Ayer Patton, Fort Benning, Aug. 27, 1940, Patton Papers; Blumenson, II, 5.

61. Patton to Beatrice Ayer Patton, Fort Benning, Aug. 31, 1940, Patton Papers.

62. Patton to Beatrice Ayer Patton, Fort Benning, Sept. 3, 1940, Patton Papers; Patton to John K. Herr, Fort Benning, Sept. 10, 1940, John K. Herr Papers, Special Collections, United States Military Academy Library, West Point.

63. Patton to Herr, Fort Benning, Sept. 10, 1940, Herr Papers; Patton to Beatrice Ayer Patton, Fort Benning, Sept. 3, 1940, Patton Papers.

64. Roger H. Nye, *The Patton Mind: The Professional Development of an Extraordinary Leader* (Garden City Park, N.Y.: Avery Publishing Group, 1993), pp. 120–122; Descriptive List of Signed and Annotated Books from the George S. Patton, Jr., Library, unpaged, Patton Papers.

65. Patton to Beatrice Ayer Patton, Fort Benning, Sept. 3, 1940, Patton Papers; George S. Patton, Jr., "Armored Operations in Poland," Box 12, George S. Patton, Jr., Papers, Manuscript Division, Library of Congress; Nye, *Patton Mind,* p. 120.

66. Dwight D. Eisenhower to Patton, Fort Lewis, Wash., Sept. 17, 1940, Box 91, Dwight D. Eisenhower Pre-Presidential Papers, Dwight D. Eisenhower Library, Abilene, Kansas.

67. Patton to Eisenhower, Fort Benning, Oct. 1, 1940, Box 91, Eisenhower Pre-Presidential Papers.

68. Donald E. Houston, *Hell on Wheels: The 2nd Armored Division* (Novato, Cal.: Presidio, 1977), p. 43; "The Second Armored Division Grows Up," *Cavalry Journal* 50 (March–April 1941), 50; General Order 19, Second Armored Division Nov. 16, 1940, Miscellaneous Box, Patton Papers.

69. Henry L. Stimson Diary, Nov. 16, 1940, Henry L. Stimson Papers, Sterling Memorial Library, Yale University, New Haven, Ct.

70. Ibid., Nov. 18, 1940; "The Second Armored Division Grows Up," pp. 50–51.

71. Stimson Diary, Nov. 19, 1940.

72. Albert N. Garland, "From the Papers of Lt. Gen. Raymond S. McLain: They Had Charisma," *Army* 21 (May 1971): 30; William H. Riddle to Fox Film Studios, Oshkosh, Wis., July 23, 1965, Box 12, Frank McCarthy Papers, George C. Marshall Library, Virginia Military Institute, Lexington, Va.

73. Houston, *Hell on Wheels,* pp. 46–47; "Second Armored Division Grows Up," p. 51.

74. Reminiscences of Colonel August E. Schanze, p. 19, n.d., United States Army Military History Institute, Carlisle Barracks, Pa.; *Time* 37 (April 14, 1941), 23.

75. "Company D and the Old Man," *Time* 37 (Feb. 24, 1941): 20–21.

76. Stimson Diary, March 26, 1941.

77. Joyce to Patton, n.p., March 28, 1941, Box 4, Patton Papers.

78. Lawrence Brothers to Patton, San Marino, Cal., April 22, 1941, Box 36, George S. Patton, Sr., Papers. See also the Restrictive Agreement in Box 36, George Patton, Sr., Papers.

79. Brown to Patton, copy, n.p., July 28, 1941, Box 36, George Patton, Sr., Papers; Patton to Brown, Fort Benning, August 2, 1941, Box 36, George Patton, Sr., Papers. In fairness to Patton and to Arvin Brown it should be pointed out that restrictive covenants were common throughout the first half of the twentieth century.

80. Patton to Pershing, Fort Benning, Sept. 24, 1940, Box 155, Pershing Papers.

81. Mrs. John S. Wood to Liddell Hart, Montreux, Switzerland, Feb. 28, 1968, File 1/763, Basil H. Liddell Hart Papers, Liddell Hart Centre for Military Archives, King's College London; *Time* 37 (April 14, 1941): 23–24.

82. Patton to Joyce, Fort Benning, May 5, 1941, Patton Papers; Joyce to Patton, n.p., May 20, 1941, Box 4, Patton Papers.

83. "Address to Officers and Men of the Second Armored Division," p. 4–5, May 17, 1941, Box 5, Patton Papers.

84. Oscar W. Koch, "Second Armored Division Maneuvers in Tennessee," *Cavalry Journal* 50 (September–October 1941), 64–67; Houston, *Hell on Wheels,* pp. 61–68.

85. Benjamin Franklin Cooling, "The Tennessee Maneuvers, June 1941," *Tennessee Historical Quarterly* 24 (Fall 1965): 265–280; Stimson Diary, June 25, 1941, and June 26, 1941.

86. Major George Harrison, "Comments on Maneuvers," Stimson Diary, June 26, 1941.

87. Houston, *Hell on Wheels,* pp. 44, 61, 68–69, 73; Kenneth S. Davis, *Soldier of Democracy: A Biography of Dwight Eisenhower* (Garden City, N.Y.: Doubleday, Doran, 1945), p. 265.

88. Patton to Floyd L. Parks, Fort Benning, Aug. 1, 1941, Box 8, Floyd L. Parks Papers, Dwight D. Eisenhower Library, Abilene, Kansas.

89. Schanze Reminiscences, pp. 19–20.

90. Ibid., 20–21.

91. J. L. Mims, "I Knew General Patton Personally," pp. 6–7, 10–11, Box 7, Patton Papers.

92. Blumenson, II, 40; Patton to Beatrice Ayer Patton, Fort Benning, Aug. 9, 1941, Patton Papers.

93. Patton to Beatrice Ayer Patton, Fort Benning, Aug. 9, 1941, Patton Papers; Reminiscences of General Jacob L. Devers, pp. 96–98, Nov. 18, 1974, Dwight D. Eisenhower Library, Abilene, Kansas.

94. Patton to Brown, Fort Benning, August 2, 1941, Box 36, George Patton, Sr., Papers.

95. Henry Cabot Lodge, *The Storm Has Many Eyes* (New York: W. W. Norton, 1973), p. 76; *Shreveport* (La.) *Times,* Aug. 15, 1941, clipping in Box 19, Walter Krueger Papers, Special Collections, United States Military Academy Library, West Point.

96. Wood to Liddell Hart, Bryn Mawr, Sept. 10, 1946, File 1/763, Liddell Hart Papers; Wood to Baldwin, Reno, Nov. 20, 1946, Series I, Box 20, Baldwin Papers; Charles M. Baily, *Faint Praise: American Tanks and Tank Destroyers During World War II* (Hamden, Ct.: Archen Books, 1983), pp. 13–18.

97. Houston, *Hell on Wheels,* pp. 75–77; Patton to Sherman Miles, Fort Benning, Oct. 23, 1941, Box 3, Nelson A. Miles Family Papers, Manuscript Division, Library of Congress.

98. Houston, *Hell on Wheels,* pp. 79–81; Christopher R. Gabel, *The U. S. Army GHQ Maneuvers of 1941* (Washington, D.C.: Center of Military History, 1992), p. 197.

99. *Corpus Christi* (Texas) *Times,* Sept. 9, 1941, clipping in Box 19, Krueger Papers.

100. Houston, *Hell on Wheels,* pp. 83–86; Gabel, *U. S. Army GHQ Maneuvers of 1941,* p. 96; New York *Times,* Sept. 17, 1941.

101. "The Battle of Bridges," *Cavalry Journal* 51 (January–February 1942): 50–52; Forrest C. Pogue, *George C. Marshall: Ordeal and Hope* (New York: Viking Press, 1966), pp. 162–163; Gabel, *U. S. Army GHQ Maneuvers of 1941,* pp. 96–100.

102. Gabel, *U. S. Army GHQ Maneuvers of 1941,* pp. 103–105; Patton to Miles, Fort Benning, Dec. 3, 1941, Box 3, Miles Family Papers.

103. Houston, *Hell on Wheels,* p. 88; Gabel, *U. S. Army GHQ Maneuvers of 1941,* pp. 106–111.

104. Gabel, *U. S. Army GHQ Maneuvers of 1941,* p. 110; *New York Times,* Sept. 29, 1941, and Sept. 30, 1941.

105. Harry B. Crea to Omar N. Bradley, Memphis, April 16, 1951, Box 6, Omar N. Bradley Papers, Special Collections, United States Military Academy Library, West Point.

106. Patton to Miles, Fort Benning, Oct. 23, 1941, and Dec. 3, 1941, Box 3, Miles Family Papers; *New York Times,* Oct. 1, 1941; Gabel, *U. S. Army GHQ Maneuvers of 1941,* pp. 120–121.

107. Charles L. Scott to Patton, Fort Knox, December 16, 1941, Box 4, Patton Papers; Jacob L. Devers to Patton, Fort Knox, Dec. 16, 1941, Box 4, Patton Papers.

108. Patton to Beatrice Ayer Patton, Fort Benning, Oct. 25, 1941, Patton Papers.

109. Patton to Joyce, Fort Benning, Oct. 29, 1941, Box 4, Patton Papers; Peggy O'Connell Parker, "The *When and If*—Patton's Own," *Army* 28 (February 1978): 34.

110. *New York Times,* Nov. 17, 1941, and Nov. 25, 1941.

111. Houston, *Hell on Wheels,* pp. 93–96.

112. Ibid., pp. 97–98; *New York Times,* Nov. 17, 1941, and Nov. 18, 1941.

113. Houston, *Hell on Wheels,* pp. 98–99; *New York Times,* Nov. 25, 1941.

114. *New York Times,* Nov. 29, 1941; Houston, *Hell on Wheels,* pp. 99–101.

115. Pogue, *Marshall: Ordeal and Hope,* p. 208.

116. Larry I. Bland, ed., *George C. Marshall Interviews and Reminiscences for Forrest C. Pogue* (Lexington, Va: George C. Marshall Research Foundation, 1991), p. 547.

117. Jacob L. Devers to Patton, Fort Knox, Dec. 16, 1941, Box 4, Patton Papers.

118. Bradley and Blair, *General's Life,* pp. 93–95.

119. Ibid., p. 98.

120. Ibid., p. 99.

121. Ibid., p. 99–100.

122. Wood to Liddell Hart, Bryn Mawr, Sept. 10, 1946, and Reno, January 23, 1959, File 1/763, Liddell Hart Papers.

123. Devers to Patton, Fort Knox, Dec. 16, 1941, Box 4, Patton Papers.

124. Joyce to Patton, n.p., Dec. 21, 1941, Box 4, Patton Papers.

CHAPTER SEVEN   FIELD OF HONOR

1. Reminiscences of General John K. Waters, pp. 149–158, April 9, 1980, United States Army Military History Institute, Carlisle Barracks, Pa.

2. Elton F. Hammond, "Signals for Patton," *Signals* 2 (September–October 1947): 5; Reminiscences of Lieutenant General Hobart R. Gay, p. 15, October 4–5, 1980, United States Army Military History Institute, Carlisle Barracks, Pa.

3. George S. Patton, Jr., to James W. Wadsworth, Fort Benning, Jan. 13, 1942, Box 32, James W. Wadsworth Papers, Manuscript Division, Library of Congress.

4. Wadsworth to Patton, n.p., January 14, 1942, Box 12, Wadsworth Papers.

5. *Time,* 39 (Feb. 23, 1942): 49; Bradford Grethen Chynoweth, *Bellamy Park* (Hicksville, N.Y.: Exposition Press, 1975), pp. 170–171.

6. Henry L. Stimson Diary, March 18, 1942, Henry L. Stimson Papers, Sterling Memorial Library, Yale University, New Haven, Conn.; Larry I. Bland (ed.), *George C. Marshall Interviews and Reminiscences for Forrest C. Pogue* (Lexington, Va.: George C. Marshall Research Foundation, 1991), p. 547.

7. George W. Howard, "The Desert Training Center—California-Arizona Maneuver Area," *Journal of Arizona History* 26 (Autumn 1985): 274.

8. Ibid., 274, 277; I. D. White, "Patton—The Man and the Film," *Military Affairs* 34 (December 1970): 138.

9. Beatrice Ayer Patton's Notes, Dec. 7, 1949, Binder 9, George S. Patton, Jr., Papers, Special Collections, United States Military Academy Library, West Point.

10. Howard, "Desert Training Center," pp. 277–278; unidentified newspaper clipping, April 21, 1942, George S. Patton, Jr., Scrapbook, Patton Papers; George S. Patton, Jr., "The Desert Training Corps," *Cavalry Journal* 51 (September–October 1942): 2–5; Roger H. Nye, "Dining-In Comments, School of Advanced Military Studies, Fort Leavenworth," p. 4, May 4, 1991, Box 1, Roger H. Nye Papers, Special Collections, United States Military Academy Library, West Point.

11. Thomas W. Pew, Jr., "On the Way to War," *American West* 22 (November–December 1985): 24–27.

12. Ibid., p. 28.

13. Maxene Andrews and Bill Gilbert, *Over Here, Over There: The Andrews Sisters and the USO Stars in World War II* (New York: Zebra Books, 1993), pp. 139–140.

14. Dwight D. Eisenhower to Patton, Washington, D.C., April 4, 1942, Box 91, Dwight D. Eisenhower Pre-Presidential Papers, Dwight D. Eisenhower Library, Abilene, Kansas; Patton to Eisenhower, Indio, April 13, 1942, Box 91, Eisenhower Pre-Presidential Papers; Alfred D. Chandler (ed.), *The Papers of Dwight D. Eisenhower, The War Years* (Baltimore: Johns Hopkins Press, 1970), I, p. 227.

15. Patton to Eisenhower, Indio, undated but late April 1942, Box 91, Eisenhower Pre-Presidential Papers.

16. Hanson W. Baldwin, " 'P' Wood of the 4th Armored," *Army*, n. v. (January 1968): 48–49.

17. Colonel Arthur P. Nesbit to Mrs. John S. Wood, Columbia, Tenn., April 16, 1967, Box 2, John S. Wood Papers, George Arents Library for Special Collections, E. S. Bird Library, Syracuse University.

18. Reminiscences of General Jacob L. Devers, pp. 100–101, Nov. 18, 1974, Dwight D. Eisenhower Library, Abilene, Kansas.

19. Arvin H. Brown to Patton, Los Angeles, May 8, 1942, Box 36, George S. Patton, Sr., Papers, Henry E. Huntington Library, San Marino, Cal.; Legal Description of Property and Agreements, April 28, 1942, Box 36, George Patton, Sr., Papers; Agreement and Declaration of Race Relations, San Marino Civic Betterment Association, June 1, 1942, Box 36, George Patton, Sr., Papers.

20. Bland (ed.), *George C. Marshall Interviews and Reminiscences for Forrest C. Pogue,* pp. 545–546, 582.

21. Harry C. Butcher, *My Three Years with Eisenhower* (New York: Simon and Schuster, 1946), pp. 4–8; Devers Reminiscences, p. 119; *Time* 40 (Nov. 16, 1942): 25.

22. Patton to Eisenhower, Indio, July 8, 1942, Box 91, Eisenhower Pre-Presidential Papers.

23. George Patton, Jr., to George S. Patton IV, Indio, July 13, 1942, Patton Papers; Beatrice Ayer Patton's Notes, Dec. 7, 1949, Binder 9, Patton Papers.

24. Butcher, *My Three Years with Eisenhower,* pp. 24–30; Beatrice Ayer Patton's Notes, Dec. 7, 1949, Binder 9, Patton Papers.

25. Notes on Patton from Everett S. Hughes Diary, Box 2, Everett S. Hughes Papers, Manuscript Division, Library of Congress; Everett S. Hughes Diary, Aug. 18, 1942, Hughes Papers.

26. Harry C, Butcher Diary, Aug. 9, 1942, Box 165, Eisenhower Pre-Presidential Papers.

27. Patton to Beatrice Ayer Patton, London, Aug. 11, 1942, Box 34, George S. Patton, Jr., Papers, Manuscript Division, Library of Congress.

28. George S. Patton, Jr., Diary, Aug. 11, 1942, and Aug. 15, 1942, Patton Papers.

29. Chandler (ed.), *The Papers of Dwight D. Eisenhower,* I, pp. 469–470; Patton Diary, Aug. 14, 1942, and Aug. 15, 1942.

30. Beatrice Ayer Patton's Notes, Dec. 7, 1949, Binder 9, Patton Papers.

31. Butcher, *My Three Years with Eisenhower,* pp. 62–63; Butcher Diary, Aug. 17, 1942; Fred Cardwell to Walter O. Boswell, New York City, April 30, 1925, and May 25, 1925, Box 57, Patton Papers, Library of Congress.

32. Butcher Diary, Aug. 18, 1942, and Aug. 20, 1942; Beatrice Ayer Patton to Brown, n.p., Sunday, undated but 1942, and Washington, Aug. 23, 1942, Box 43, George S. Patton, Sr., Papers.

33. Patton to Eisenhower, Washington, August 25, 1942, Box 91, Eisenhower Pre-Presidential Papers.

34. Stimson Diary, Aug. 26, 1942.

35. Ibid., Aug. 27, 1942.

36. *I Could Never Be So Lucky Again: An Autobiography by General James H. "Jimmy" Doolittle* (New York: Bantam Books, 1991), pp. 299–300.

37. Lindsey Nelson, *Hello Everybody, I'm Lindsey Nelson* (New York: Beech Tree Books, 1985), pp. 85–86.

38. Beatrice Ayer Patton to Brown, Washington, D.C., Oct. 3, 1942, Box 43, George Patton, Sr., Papers.

39. Samuel Eliot Morison, *Operations in North African Waters, October 1942–June 1943* (History of the United States Naval Operations in World War II, vol. II) (Boston: Little, Brown, 1960), pp. 17, 22–25, 29–34, 39; *Newsweek* 20 (Nov. 16, 1942): 18; *Time* 40 (Nov. 16, 1942): 23–24.

40. Benjamin A. Dickson, "G-2 Journal: Algiers to the Elbe," pp. 14–16, Benjamin A. Dickson Papers, Special Collections, United States Military Academy Library, West Point; George F. Howe, *Northwest Africa: Seizing the Initiative in the West* (Washington, D.C.: Office of the Chief of Military History, 1957), pp. 35, 80.

41. Beatrice Ayer Patton's Notes, Dec. 7, 1949, Binder 9, Patton Papers; Patton Diary, Oct. 6, 1942.

42. Patton Diary, Oct. 6, 1942; Beatrice Ayer Patton's Notes, Dec. 7, 1949, Patton Papers.

43. Reminiscences of Admiral John Lesslie Hall, Jr., pp. 112–113, 1964, Oral History Research Office, Columbia University Library, New York City.

44. Reminiscences of Admiral H. Kent Hewitt, Reel 9, pp. 16–18, and Reel 10, p. 16, 1962, Oral History Research Office, Columbia University Library, New York City.

45. Beatrice Ayer Patton's Notes, Dec. 7, 1949, Binder 9, Patton Papers.

46. Patton Diary, Oct. 21, 1942; Beatrice Ayer Patton's Notes, Dec. 7, 1949, Binder 9, Patton Papers.

47. Reminiscences of Frank McCarthy, pp. 31–32, July 1969, Box 17, Frank McCarthy Papers, George C. Marshall Library, Virginia Military Institute, Lexington; Hewitt Reminiscences, Reel 17, pp. 1–3, and Reel 24, pp. 44–45.

48. Patton Diary, Oct. 21, 1942; Beatrice Ayer Patton's Notes, Dec. 7, 1949, Binder 9, Patton Papers.

49. Beatrice Ayer Patton's Notes, Dec. 7, 1949, Binder 9, Patton Papers.

50. Patton Diary, Oct. 23, 1942; Hewitt Reminiscences, Reel 17, p. 3, and Reel 18, pp. 4–5.

51. Reminiscences of Admiral John Jennings Ballantine, pp. 345–346, 348–349, 1964, Oral History Research Office, Columbia University Library, New York City.

52. Edwin H. Randle, "The General and the Movie," *Army* 72 (September 1971): 18–19.

53. Hewitt Reminiscences, Reel 17, pp. 6–10.

54. Ibid., Reel 17, p. 4; Reel 18, p. 5; and Reel 25, p. 26.

55. Patton to Beatrice Ayer Patton, Aboard *Augusta,* Oct. 29, 1942, and Nov. 2, 1942, Patton Papers.

56. Randle, "The General and the Movie," p. 19.

57. Hewitt Reminiscences, Reel 18, p. 5.

58. Dickson, "G-2 Journal," p. 21–22; *A Sailor's Odyssey: The Autobiography of Admiral of the Fleet Viscount Cunningham of Hyndhope* (New York: E. P. Dutton, 1951), pp. 491–492.

59. Patton Diary, Nov. 7, 1942.

60. Hewitt Reminiscences, Reel 17, pp. 4–5, and Reel 24, p. 44.

61. Dickson, "G-2 Journal," 14; *Time* 40 (Nov. 23, 1942): 34; Hewitt Reminiscences, Reel 17, pp. 4–5, and Reel 18, p. 5; Hall Reminiscences, p. 113.

62. Hobart R. Gay Memoir, p. 1, Dec. 5, 1942, Miscellaneous Box, Patton Papers; Captain Selwyn H. Graham, "We Knew George Patton, Jr., When—," *Shipmate* (October 1988): 21–22, in Box 7, Patton Papers. Captain Graham was aboard the *Augusta*.

63. Gay Memoir, pp. 1–2, Miscellaneous Box, Patton Papers; Patton Diary, Nov. 8, 1942.

64. Ballantine Reminiscences, pp. 356–357; Patton to Charles P. Summerall, Headquarters, Western Task Force, Nov. 23, 1942, Box 5, Floyd L. Parks Papers, Dwight D. Eisenhower Library, Abilene, Kansas.

65. Jack Coggins, *The Campaign for North Africa* (Garden City, N.Y.: Doubleday, 1980), p. 73.

66. Gay Memoir, pp. 2–3, Miscellaneous Box, Patton Papers; Ballantine Reminiscences, pp. 356–357; Hall Reminiscences, pp. 118–120; Hewitt Reminiscences, Reel 19, p. 1.

67. Gay Memoir, p. 3, Miscellaneous Box, Patton Papers; Hewitt Reminiscences, Reel 19, p. 1; Hall Reminiscences, pp. 118–120; Patton Diary, Nov. 11, 1942.

68. "Historical Record of Deception in the War Against Germany & Italy," I, pp. 99–114, CAB 154/100, Public Record Office, Kew, London.

69. Hewitt Reminiscences, Reel 19, p. 7; Gay Memoir, p. 3, Miscellaneous Box, Patton Papers; Howe, *Northwest Africa,* pp. 175–176.

70. Hall Reminiscences, pp. 118–120.

71. Ibid., 121; Patton to Summerall, Headquarters, Western Task Force, Nov. 23, 1942, Box 5, Parks Papers.

72. Stephen W. Sprindis to Frank McCarthy, Danbury, Ct., Sept. 10, 1961, Box 12, McCarthy Papers; Patton to Summerall, Headquarters, Western Task Force, Nov. 23, 1942, Box 5, Parks Papers.

73. Gay Memoir, pp. 3–4, Miscellaneous Box, Patton Papers; Hall Reminiscences, pp. 144–145.

74. Patton Diary, Nov. 14, 1942, and Nov. 15, 1942; Patton to Eisenhower, Casablanca, Nov. 15, 1942, Box 91, Eisenhower Pre-Presidential Papers.

75. Blumenson, II, 118.

76. Patton Diary, Nov. 17, 1942; Patton to Beatrice Ayer Patton, n.p., sometime in November 1942, Box 34, Patton Papers, Library of Congress.

77. Norman Gelb, *Desperate Venture: The Story of Operation Torch, The Allied Invasion of North Africa* (New York: William Morrow, 1992), p. 269; Patton Diary, Nov. 21, 1942.

78. Patton Diary, Nov. 19, 1942; Butcher, *My Three Years with Eisenhower,* pp. 154, 250; Martin Blumenson, *Mark Clark* (New York: Congdon & Weed, 1984), pp. 85–86, 110–111.

79. Patton to Beatrice Ayer Patton, n.p., Dec. 2, 1942, Box 34, Patton Papers, Library of Congress.

80. Butcher Diary, Dec. 10, 1942; Patton to Beatrice Ayer Patton, n.p., Dec. 5, 1942, Box 34, Patton Papers, Library of Congress.

81. Everett S. Hughes, "Notes on a Much Discussed Subject," Dec. 30, 1942, Box 2, Hughes Papers.

82. George S. Patton, Jr., "Wild Boar Hunt, French Morocco," Dec. 6, 1942, Addendum, Box 12, Banning Company Papers, Henry E. Huntington Library, San Marino, Cal.

83. George S. Patton, Jr., "An Account of Lunch with General Noguès," pp. 1–3, Rabat, Morocco, Dec. 8, 1942, Addendum, Box 12, Banning Company Papers.

84. Patton to Beatrice Ayer Patton, n.p., Dec. 5, 1942, Box 34, Patton Papers, Library of Congress; Gelb, *Desperate Venture,* pp. 242, 268, 305; *Time* 40 (Nov. 23, 1942): 31.

85. George S. Patton, Jr., "Visit to Tunisian Front," pp. 1–6, Box 43, George Patton, Sr., Papers; Patton to Beatrice Ayer Patton, n.p., Dec. 15, 1942, Box 34, Patton Papers, Library of Congress; Butcher, *My Three Years with Eisenhower,* pp. 203, 227.

86. Beatrice Ayer Patton to Patton, At K's (Washington, D.C.), Dec. 2, 1942, Patton Papers.

87. Beatrice Ayer Patton to Patton, n.p., Dec. 8, 1942, and Dec. 12, 1942, Patton Papers.

88. Patton to Beatrice Ayer Patton, n.p., Dec. 20, 1942, Patton Papers; Blumenson, II, 140.

89. Hanson W. Baldwin, "Notes on General Eisenhower," p. 3, April 26, 1946, Series III, Box 101, Hanson W. Baldwin Papers, Sterling Memorial Library, Yale University, New Haven, Ct.

90. Butcher, *My Three Years with Eisenhower,* pp. 229–231; Gelb, *Desperate Venture,* pp. 278–280.

91. Patton Diary, Dec. 31, 1942, and Jan. 2, 1943; Patton to Eisenhower, Headquarters, Western Task Force, Jan. 2, 1943, Box 9, Eisenhower Pre-Presidential Papers; Stimson Diary, Jan. 21, 1943.

92. *Time* 40 (Dec. 28, 1942): 32.

CHAPTER EIGHT   "NOT MUCH OF A WAR"

1. Beatrice Ayer Patton to George S. Patton, Jr., Jan. 1, 1943, Jan. 3, 1943, and Jan. 4, 1943, George S. Patton, Jr., Papers, Special Collections, United States Military Academy Library, West Point; *Time* 40 (Nov. 30, 1942): 80.

2. Beatrice Ayer Patton to Patton, n.p., Jan. 23, 1943, Patton Papers; Edward G. Roddy, *Mills, Mansions, and Mergers: The Life of William M. Wood* (North Andover, Mass.: Merrimack Valley Textile Museum, 1982), pp. 70–71.

3. George S. Patton, Jr., Diary, Jan. 6, 1943, Patton Papers; Patton to Beatrice Ayer Patton, n.p., Jan. 9, 1943, Box 43, George S. Patton, Jr., Papers, Manuscript Division, Library of Congress.

4. Field Marshal Viscount Alanbrooke Diary, Jan. 16, 1943, Jan. 17, 1943, and Jan. 18, 1943, Field Marshal Viscount Alanbrooke Papers, Liddell Hart Centre for Military Archives, King's College, London.

5. Patton Diary, Jan. 9, 1943.

6. Reminiscences of Admiral William A. Sullivan, II, pp. 970–971, 1965, Naval History Project, Oral History Research Office, Columbia University Library, New York City.

7. Patton Diary, Jan. 12, 1943.

8. Doris Kearns Goodwin, *No Ordinary Time, Franklin and Eleanor Roosevelt: The Home Front in World War II* (New York: Simon and Schuster, 1994), pp. 402–403; Patton Diary, Jan. 14, 1943.

9. Harry C. Butcher Diary, Jan. 19, 1943, and Jan. 19–20, 1943, Box 166, Dwight D. Eisenhower Pre-Presidential Papers, Dwight D. Eisenhower Library, Abilene, Kansas; Patton Diary, Jan. 15, 1943.

10. Patton Diary, Jan. 16, 1943; Reminiscences of Frank McCarthy, pp. 32–35, July 1969, Box 17, Frank McCarthy Papers, George C. Marshall Library, Virginia Military Institute, Lexington, Va.

11. McCarthy Reminiscences, pp. 32–33. McCarthy may have mistaken "mother" for "wife," for none of the obituaries of Dick Jenson mention his being married.

12. Patton Diary, Jan. 18, 1943; Henry H. Adams, *Harry Hopkins: A Biography* (New York: G. P. Putnam's Sons, 1977), p. 310.

13. Sammy Schulman, *Where's Sammy?* (New York: Random House, 1943), pp. 224–225; Adams, *Harry Hopkins,* p. 312; Patton Diary, Jan. 21, 1943, and Jan. 23, 1943.

14. *The Memoirs of General Lord Ismay* (New York: Viking Press, 1960), p. 289; Roger H. Nye, *The Patton Mind: The Professional Development of an Extraordinary Leader* (Garden City Park, N.Y.: Avery Publishing Groups, 1993), p. 16.

15. Patton Diary, Jan. 24, 1943.

16. Reminiscences of Admiral John Lesslie Hall, Jr., pp. 122–123, 126–127, 1964, Naval History Project, Oral History Research Office, Columbia University Library, New York City.

17. "Historical Record of Deception in the War Against Germany & Italy," I, p. 131, CAB 154/100, Public Record Office, Kew, London; *Time* 41 (Feb. 1, 1943): 26; Everett S. Hughes Diary, Jan. 26, 1943, Box 2, Everett S. Hughes Papers, Manuscript Division, Library of Congress.

18. Henry L. Stimson Diary, Jan. 21, 1943, Henry L. Stimson Papers, Sterling Memorial Library, Yale University, New Haven, Ct.

19. Butcher Diary, Jan. 28, 1943.

20. Benjamin A. Dickson, "G-2 Journal: Algiers to the Elbe," p. 36, Benjamin A. Dickson Papers, Special Collections, United States Military Academy Library, West Point; Patton Diary, Jan. 28, 1943.

21. George S. Patton, Jr., "Visit to Marrakech and Boar Hunt," pp. 1–6, Feb. 1, 1943, Addendum, Box 12, Banning Company Papers, Henry E. Huntington Library, San Marino, Cal.; George S. Patton, Jr., "Visit to Marrakech and Quarzazate," pp. 1–8, Box 43, George S. Patton, Sr., Papers, Henry E. Huntington Library, San Marino, Cal.

22. Patton Diary, Feb. 3, 1943.

23. Patton to Beatrice Ayer Patton, n.p., Feb. 3, 1943, Patton Papers; Patton Diary, Feb. 4, 1943.

24. Patton Diary, Feb. 5, 1943, and Feb. 6, 1943; Hughes Diary, Feb. 12, 1943; Tyler Abell (ed.), *Drew Pearson Diaries, 1949–1959* (New York: Holt, Rinehart and Winston, 1974), p. 238.

25. Patton Diary, Feb. 14, 1943; Patton to Beatrice Ayer Patton, APO 758 New York, Feb. 23, 1943, Patton Papers.

26. Charles Richardson, *Flashback: A Soldier's Story* (London: William Kimber, 1985), p. 137.

27. *London Sunday Times,* August 18, 1974; Rowland Ryder, *Oliver Leese* (London: Hamish Hamilton, 1987), pp. 137, 141.

28. Patton Diary, Feb. 18, 1943.

29. George F. Howe, *Northwest Africa: Seizing the Initiative in the West* (Washington, D.C.: Office of the Chief of Military History, 1957), pp. 48, 522–525; Dickson, "G-2 Journal," pp. 39–40.

30. Dickson, "G-2 Journal," pp. 36–37.

31. Reminiscences of General John K. Waters, pp. 187–188, 589, April 9, 1980, United States Army Military History Institute, Carlisle Barracks, Pa.

32. Ibid., pp. 189–190.

33. Ibid., p. 191.

34. *Time* 41 (March 1, 1943): 16–17; William R. Betson, "Sidi Bou Zid—A Case History of Failure," *Armor* 91 (November–December 1982): 38–40; Martin Blumenson, *Kasserine Pass* (Boston: Houghton Mifflin, 1967), pp. 136–140; Ladislas Farago to Hanson W. Baldwin, Washington, D.C., June 30, 1964, Series I, Box 5, Hanson W. Baldwin Papers, Sterling Memorial Library, Yale University, New Haven, Ct.

35. Dickson, "G-2 Journal," p. 44.

36. Ibid., p. 47.

37. Reminiscences of Admiral Alan Goodrich Kirk, pp. 189–192, 1962, Oral History Research Office, Columbia University Library, New York City.

38. Ibid., pp. 193–194; Patton Diary, Feb. 19, 1943; Patton to Beatrice Ayer Patton, Algiers, Feb. 19, 1943, Patton Papers.

39. Butcher Diary, Feb. 20, 1943.

40. Patton to Beatrice Ayer Patton, APO 758 New York, Feb. 23, 1943, Patton Papers.

41. Butcher Diary, Feb. 23, 1943.

42. Ibid.

43. Patton Diary, March 2, 1943; Howe, *Northwest Africa,* pp. 471–474.

44. Patton to Beatrice Ayer Patton, n.p., March 2, 1943, Patton Papers.

45. Patton Diary, March 4, 1943.

46. Butcher Diary, March 6, 1943, and March 7, 1943; Reminiscences of Brigadier General S. L. A. Marshall, II, pp. 37–38, 1974, United States Army Military History Institute, Carlisle Barracks, Pa. Dickson, "G-2 Journal," pp. 43, 52, noted that when Fredendall evacuated Gafsa, sixty miles south of Kasserine, he allowed the town's prostitutes to come "riding out on the light tanks." When Gafsa was retaken, the houses of prostitution reopened for business.

47. Patton Diary, March 5, 1943.

48. Nigel Nicholson, *Alex: The Life of Field Marshal Earl Alexander of Tunis* (New York: Atheneum, 1973), p. 177; Brian Holden Reid, "Alexander, Field-Marshal Earl Alexander," in John Keegan (ed.), *Churchill's Generals* (New York: Grove Weidenfeld, 1991), p. 114.

49. Nicholson, *Alex,* pp. 177–179; Harry C. Butcher, *My Three Years with Eisenhower* (New York: Simon and Schuster, 1946), p. 273; Howe, *Northwest Africa,* pp. 514–520.

50. Patton Diary, March 6, 1943; Dickson, "G-2 Journal," p. 48.

51. Dickson, "G-2 Journal," p. 44–45, 48.

52. Ibid., pp. 49–50.

53. *Time* 41 (April 12, 1943): 29.

54. Reminiscences of General Omar N. Bradley, p. 52, 1966, Box 30, Omar N. Bradley Papers, United States Military Academy Archives, West Point.

55. Chester B. Hansen Diary, March 26, 1943, Bradley Papers, Special Collections, United States Military Academy Library. Although part of the Bradley Collection, the copies of the Hansen diaries are in Special Collections.

56. Ibid.

57. Ibid., pp. 50–51.

58. Bradley Reminiscences, p. 53.

59. Marshall Reminiscences, pp. 37–38.

60. Bradley Reminiscences, pp. 162–163; Omar N. Bradley and Clay Blair, *A General's Life* (New York: Simon and Schuster, 1983), p. 140.

61. Lindsey Nelson, *Hello Everybody, I'm Lindsey Nelson* (New York: Beech Tree Books, 1985), pp. 86–88.

62. Bradley Memorandum, Box 2, *A General's Life* Files, Bradley Papers.

63. Paul McDonald Robinett, *Armor Command* (Washington, D.C.: McGregor & Werner, 1958), p. 110.

64. Ibid., pp. 198–199.

65. Ibid., pp. 199; *Memoirs of General William T. Sherman* (New York: Da Capo, 1984), II, p. 408.

66. George F. Howe, *The Battle History of the 1st Armored Division: "Old Ironsides"* (Washington, D.C.: Combat Forces Press, 1954), p. 204.

67. Patton to Dwight D. Eisenhower, n.p., March 13, 1943, Box 91, Eisenhower Pre-Presidential Papers.

68. Patton to Beatrice Ayer Patton, n.p., March 11, 1943, Patton Papers; Beatrice Ayer Patton to Arvin H. Brown, Washington, D.C., March 17, 1943, Box 43, George Patton, Sr., Papers.

69. Butcher, *My Three Years with Eisenhower,* p. 47; Patton Diary, March 12, 1943, and March 13, 1943.

70. Patton Diary, March 12, 1943.

71. Ibid., March 14, 1943; Howe, *Northwest Africa,* p. 545.

72. Patton Diary, March 17, 1943.

73. Ibid., March 18, 1943; Howe, *Battle History of the 1st Armored Division,* pp. 208–209; Dickson, "G-2 Journal," p. 51.

74. Robinett, *Armor Command,* p. 202; Howe, *Battle History of the 1st Armored Division,* p. 207.

75. Robinett, *Armor Command,* p. 204; Patton Diary, March 19, 1943.

76. Patton Diary, March 19, 1943; Howe, *Battle History of the 1st Armored Division,* pp. 207–209.

77. Patton Diary, March 19, 1943; Bradley and Blair, *General's Life,* p. 144; Howe, *Northwest Africa,* pp. 550–551.

78. Patton Diary, March 20, 1943.

79. Ibid., March 21, 1943; Howe, *Battle History of the 1st Armored Division,* p. 209.

80. Howe, *Northwest Africa,* p. 553; Dickson, "G-2 Journal," pp. 44, 53; Patton Diary, March 22, 1943.

81. Robinett, *Armor Command,* p. 208.

82. Patton Diary, March 23, 1943; Patton to Beatrice Ayer Patton, APO 758 New York, March 23, 1943, Patton Papers.

83. Bradley Reminiscences, pp. 54–55.

84. Nigel Hamilton, *Master of the Battlefield: Monty's War Years, 1942–1944* (New York: McGraw-Hill, 1983), pp. 185–193; *Time* 41 (April 5, 1943): 16–17.

85. Patton Diary, March 23, 1943; Patton to George C. Marshall, Hqs. II Corps, March 29, 1943, Box 79, George C. Marshall Papers, George C. Marshall Library, Virginia Military Institute, Lexington, Va.; Peter C. Hains III, "Employment of Tank Destroyers," *Cavalry Journal* 53 (May–June 1944): 60–68.

86. Patton Diary, March 24, 1943; Robinett, *Armor Command,* p. 209.

87. Hains, "Employment of Tank Destroyers," pp. 65–66.

88. " 'A' Force Permanent Record File," pp. 39–40, CAB 154/3, Public Record Office, Kew, London.

89. Patton Diary, March 25, 1943.

90. Patton Diary, March 28, 1943; *Time* 41 (April 5, 1943): 14.

91. Bernard Law Montgomery Diary, March 28, 1943, Reel 4, Bernard Law Montgomery Papers, Imperial War Museum, London; W. G. F. Jackson, *Alexander of Tunis as Military Commander* (New York: Dodd, Mead, 1971), p. 182.

92. Patton Diary, March 29, 1943, and March 31, 1943; Jackson, *Alexander of Tunis as Military Commander,* p. 179; Howe, *Northwest Africa,* p. 486.

93. Patton Diary, March 29, 1943; Howe, *Battle History of the 1st Armored Division,* p. 214.

94. Patton Diary, March 30, 1943, and March 31, 1943; Howe, *Battle History of the 1st Armored Division,* p. 215; Howe, *Northwest Africa,* pp. 571–572.

95. *San Francisco Chronicle,* April 4, 1943, clipping in George S. Patton, Jr., Papers, United States Army Military History Institute, Carlisle Barracks, Pa.

96. Bradley and Blair, *General's Life,* p. 147; Patton Diary, April 1, 1943.

97. Patton to Echo Jenson, n.p., April 1, 1943, Patton Papers, United States Army Military History Institute.

98. Reminiscences of General Barksdale Hamlett, p. 8, March 12, 1976, United States Army Military History Institute, Carlisle Barracks, Pa.

99. Beatrice Ayer Patton to Brown, Washington, D.C., April 3, 1943, Box 43, George Patton, Sr., Papers.

100. Vincent Orange, *Coningham: A Biography of Air Marshal Sir Arthur Coningham* (London: Methuen, 1990), pp. 130, 144–145.

101. Ibid., p. 146; Bradley and Blair, *General's Life,* p. 147; Patton Diary, April 1, 1943, and April 2, 1943.

102. Patton Diary, April 3, 1943.

103. Ibid. See also Appendix A to the entry of April 3, 1943, which is Coningham's telegram.

104. Orange, *Coningham,* p. 147; Dickson, "G-2 Journal," p. 54.

105. Patton Diary, April 3, 1943.

106. Orange, *Coningham,* pp. 147–148.

107. Patton Diary, April 4, 1943; Orange, *Coningham,* p. 148.

108. Lord Tedder, *With Prejudice* (Boston: Little, Brown, 1967), p. 411; Bradley and Blair, *General's Life,* p. 148.

109. Howe, *Northwest Africa,* p. 582; Patton Diary, March 25, 1943, and April 3, 1943.

110. Bradley Reminiscences, pp. 154–157.

111. Ernest N. Harmon with Milton MacKaye and William Ross MacKaye, *Combat Commander: Autobiography of a Soldier* (Englewood Cliffs, N.J.: Prentice-Hall, 1970), pp. 123–124.

112. Bradley Reminiscences, p. 51. Noel Monks of the *London Daily Mail* reported that the GIs called Harmon "Gravel voice." See Noel Monks, *Eyewitness* (London: Frederick Muller, 1955), p. 237.

113. Harmon, *Combat Commander,* pp. 125–126; Patton Diary, April 10, 1943; Howe, *Battle History of the 1st Armored Division,* p. 219.

114. Edwin H. Randle, "The General and the Movie," *Army* 21 (September 1973): 19–20; Patton Diary, April 7, 1943.

115. Patton Diary, April 7, 1943.

116. *Time* 41 (April 12, 1943): 28–30.

117. Bradley and Blair, *General's Life,* pp. 53–54, 151–152; Robinett, *Armor Command,* pp. 149, 169, 199, 215.

118. Hamlett Reminiscences, pp. 9–10.

119. Butcher Diary, April 17, 1943; Patton Diary, April 11, 1943, and April 16, 1943; Omar N. Bradley, *A Soldier's Story* (New York: Henry Holt, 1951), pp. 67–68.

120. *Time* 41 (April 12, 1943): 28; Patton Diary, April 11, 1943.

121. Patton Diary, April 11, 1943; Bradley, *Soldier's Story,* p. 68.

122. Patton Diary, April 14, 1943; Butcher Diary, April 17, 1943.

123. Butcher Diary, April 17, 1943.

124. Ibid.

CHAPTER NINE   SICILY ON MY MIND

1. Everett S. Hughes Diary, April 16, 1943, Box 2, Everett S. Hughes Papers, Manuscript Division, Library of Congress.

2. Ibid., April 17, 1943.

3. *A Sailor's Odyssey: The Autobiography of Admiral of the Fleet Viscount Cunningham of Hyndhope* (New York: E. P. Dutton, 1951), pp. 534–537; George S. Patton Jr., Diary, April 22, 1943, George S. Patton, Jr., Papers, Special Collections, United States Military Academy Library, West Point; George S. Patton, Jr., to Dwight D. Eisenhower, APO 758 New York, April 23, 1943, Box 91, Dwight D. Eisenhower Pre-Presidential Papers, Dwight D. Eisenhower Library, Abilene, Kansas; Omar N. Bradley and Clay Blair, *A General's Life* (New York: Simon and Schuster, 1983), pp. 169–171.

4. Reminiscences of Omar N. Bradley, pp. 158–160, 1966, Box 30, Omar N. Bradley Papers, United States Military Academy Archives, West Point.

5. George E. Martin, *Blow, Bugle, Blow* (Bradenton, Fla.: Opuscula, 1986), pp. 95–96.

6. Patton Diary, April 23, 1943.

7. Ibid., April 28, 1943; Hughes Diary, April 28, 1943.

8. Patton Diary, April 29, 1943. See also Carlo D'Este, *Bitter Victory: The Battle for Sicily, 1943* (New York: E. P. Dutton, 1988), pp. 109–117.

9. Hughes Diary, April 29, 1943.

10. Patton Diary, April 30, 1943; Patton to Beatrice Ayer Patton, n.p., May 1, 1943, Patton Papers.

11. Note of Beatrice Ayer Patton attached to Patton to Beatrice Ayer Patton, Mostaganem, May 1, 1943, Patton Papers; Patton Diary, April 27, 1943.

12. Patton Diary, May 3, 1943; D'Este, *Bitter Victory,* pp. 121–122.

13. Patton Diary, May 3, 1943, and May 5, 1943.

14. Ibid., May 7, 1943; Reminiscences of Paul D. Harkins, pp. 18–19, April 28, 1974, United States Army Military History Institute, Carlisle Barracks, Pa.

15. Everett S. Hughes, "Notes on a Much Discussed Subject," May 6, 1943, Box 2, Hughes Papers.

16. Hughes Diary, May 7, 1943, and May 8, 1943.

17. Arvin H. Brown to Patton, Los Angeles, April 3, 1943, Miscellaneous Box, Patton Papers.

18. Patton to Brown, APO 758 New York, May 5, 1943, Box 43, George S. Patton, Sr., Papers, Henry E. Huntington Library, San Marino, Cal.

19. Correspondence Regarding Promotions, Box 1, Records of United States Forces European Theater, Secretary of General Staff, Record Group 338, National Archives II, College Park, Md.; Bernard S. Carter to Louise Hope Thacher Carter, Headquarters I Armored Corps, North Africa, April 4, 1943, and April 9, 1943, Box 2, Bernard S. Carter Papers, Special Collections, United States Military Academy Library, West Point.

20. Bernard Carter to Louise Carter, Headquarters I Armored Corps, Jan. 28, 1943, and APO 758 New York, May 1, 1943, Box 2, Carter Papers.

21. Bernard Carter to Louise Carter, APO 758 New York, May 25, 1943, and June 10, 1943, Box 2, Carter Papers.

22. Larry I. Bland (ed.), *The Papers of George Catlett Marshall* (Baltimore and London: Johns Hopkins Press, 1991), II, pp. 700–701; Ernest N. Harmon with Milton MacKaye and William Ross MacKaye, *Combat Commander: Autobiography of a Soldier* (Englewood Cliffs, N.J.: Prentice-Hall, 1970), p. 143.

23. Bradley Reminiscences, pp. 123–124; Lewis H. Brereton, *The Brereton Diaries* (New York: William Morrow, 1946), p. 186.

24. Hughes Diary, May 10, 1943.

25. Patton to Hughes, n.p., May 12, 1943, Box 5, Hughes Papers.

26. *New York Times,* Feb. 28, 1951; Patton to Kent C. Lambert, Jr., n.p., May 12, 1943, Box 5, Hughes Papers.

27. *Time* 41 (April 12, 1943): 28–30; Patton to Beatrice Ayer Patton, APO 758 New York, May 7, 1943, and May 10, 1943, Patton Papers.

28. Patton Diary, May 13, 1943.

29. Ibid., May 16, 1943; Bradley and Blair, *General's Life,* pp. 158, 169.

30. Patton Diary, May 18, 1943.

31. Bernard Law Montgomery Diary, May 10, 1943, to May 17, 1943, Bernard Law Montgomery Papers, Imperial War Museum, London.

32. Patton Diary, May 20, 1943; Patton to Beatrice Ayer Patton, n.p., May 21, 1943, Patton Papers.

33. Patton to Beatrice Ayer Patton, APO 758 New York, May 5, 1943, Patton Papers; Patton to Fred Ayer, Jr., APO 758 New York, May 5, 1943, Box 43, George S. Patton, Sr., Papers.

34. James M. Gavin, *On to Berlin* (New York: Viking, 1978), p. 10; Bradley and Blair, *General's Life,* p. 173; Samuel W. Mitcham, Jr., and Frederich von Stauffenberg, *The Battle of Sicily* (New York: Orion, 1991, p. 92.

35. Reminiscences of Admiral Richard L. Conolly, p. 155, 1960, Oral History Research Office, Columbia University Library, New York City; John M. Taylor, *General Maxwell Taylor: The Sword and the Pen* (Garden City, New York: Doubleday, 1989), p. 47.

36. Mitcham, Jr., and von Stauffenberg, *Battle of Sicily,* pp. 93–94; Conolly Reminiscences, pp. 139–140; Reminiscences of Admiral Alan Goodrich Kirk, p. 196, 1962, Oral History Research Office, Columbia University Library, New York City.

37. Benjamin A. Dickson, "G-2 Journal: Algiers to the Elbe," pp. 72–73, Benjamin A. Dickson Papers, Special Collections, United States Military Academy Library, West Point.

38. Conolly Reminiscences, pp. 125, 139–140.

39. Reminiscences of Admiral H. Kent Hewitt, Reel 23, p. 11, Oral History Research Office, Columbia University Library, New York City.

40. Conolly Reminiscences, pp. 145–146.

41. Bradley and Blair, *General's Life,* pp. 170, 174; Patton Diary, June 2, 1943.

42. Reminiscences of Frank McCarthy, p. 34, July 1969, Box 17, Frank McCarthy Papers, George C. Marshall Library, Virginia Military Institute, Lexington, Va.

43. Patton Diary, June 2, 1943; Harmon with MacKaye and MacKaye, *Combat Commander,* pp. 142–143; *New York Times,* Feb. 28, 1951.

44. Patton Diary, June 10, 1943.

45. Ernest N. Harmon to Hughes, APO 251 New York, Nov. 20, 1943, Box 5, Hughes Papers.

46. Hughes to Harmon, n.p., Dec. 4, 1943, Box 5, Hughes Papers; *New York Times,* Feb. 28, 1951.

47. John P. Lucas Diary, June 7, 1943, John P. Lucas Papers, United States Army Military History Institute, Carlisle Barracks, Pa.

48. Albert C. Wedemeyer, *Wedemeyer Reports!* (New York: Henry Holt, 1958), p. 221; D'Este, *Bitter Victory,* p. 172.

49. Patton Diary, June 20, 1943, and June 21, 1943.

50. Patton to James W. Wadsworth, APO 758 New York, June 20, 1943, Box 22, James W. Wadsworth Papers, Manuscript Division, Library of Congress; Patton to Wadsworth, APO 758 New York, June 20, 1943, copy, Box 79, George C. Marshall Papers, George C. Marshall Library, Virginia Military Institute, Lexington, Va.; Bessie

Christian to Wadsworth, Washington, D.C., July 24, 1943, Box 22, Wadsworth Papers.

51. Reminiscences of Charles Poletti, pp. 345, 356–358, May 1978, Oral History Research Office, Columbia University Library, New York City.

52. Ibid., p. 343.

53. Ibid., p. 361.

54. Kirk Reminiscences, p. 204; Conolly Reminiscences, pp. 149–150.

55. Reminiscences of Admiral William A. Sullivan, II, pp. 1022–1023, 1965, Naval History Project, Oral History Research Office, Columbia University Library, New York City.

56. Poletti Reminiscences, p. 361.

57. D'Este, *Bitter Victory,* p. 220.

58. Conolly Reminiscences, p. 144.

59. Hewitt Reminiscences, Reel 24, pp. 12–13.

CHAPTER TEN   ATROCITIES AMID THE TRIUMPHS

1. George S. Patton, Jr., Diary, July 6, 1943, George S. Patton, Jr., Papers, Special Collections, United States Military Academy Library, West Point.

2. Samuel Eliot Morison, *Sicily-Salerno-Anzie, January 1943–June 1944* (History of the United States Naval Operations in World War II, Vol. IX), (Boston: Little, Brown, 1960), p. 64.

3. Patton Diary, July 8, 1943.

4. Ibid., July 9, 1943.

5. George S. Patton, Jr., "Incidents Relating to Sicily Campaign," 1, Box 43, George S. Patton, Sr., Papers, Henry E. Huntington Library, San Marino, Cal.

6. Reminiscences of Charles Poletti, p. 432, May 1978, Oral History Research Office, Columbia University Library, New York City.

7. *Time* 42 (July 26, 1943), 27–30.

8. Ibid.; George S. Patton, Jr., "Description of Events," pp. 2–3, July 18, 1943, Box 43, George S. Patton, Sr., Papers.

9. Basil H. Liddell Hart, "Notes for History: Talk with R. B. Bethell and Guy Pollock, 9 September 1943," LH 11/1943/56, Basil H. Liddell Hart Papers, Liddell Hart Centre for Military Archives, King's College, London; Lieutenant-Colonel R. B. Bethell, "Sicily: Report on the Invasion," July 10, 1943, CAB 106/849, Public Record Office, Kew, London. In general, see Carlo D'Este, *Bitter Victory: The Battle for Sicily, 1943* (New York: E. P. Dutton, 1988), pp. 606–608.

10. "Historical Record of Deception in the War Against Germany & Italy," I, pp. 188–189, CAB 154/100, Public Record Office.

11. Reminiscences of Admiral Richard L. Conolly, pp. 157–158, 1960, Oral History Research Office, Columbia University Library, New York City.

12. Patton Diary, July 10, 1943; Conolly Reminiscences, pp. 387–388.

13. Noel Monks, *Eyewitness* (London: Frederick Muller, 1955), pp. 186–188; undated memorandum, Box 3, *A General's Life* Files, Omar N. Bradley Papers, United States Military Academy Archives, West Point.

14. Hobart R. "Hap" Gay Diary, July 11, 1943, Hobart R. Gay Papers, Special Collections, United States Military Academy Library, West Point.

15. Dwight D. Eisenhower to Harold R. L. G. Alexander and George S. Patton, Jr., Malta, July 12, 1943, WO 214/22, Public Record Office, Kew, London; Gay Diary, July 11, 1943.

16. Gay Diary, July 12, 1943; Harry C. Butcher Diary, July 13, 1943, Box 167, Dwight D. Eisenhower Pre-Presidential Papers, Dwight D. Eisenhower Library, Abilene, Kansas.

17. Patton Diary, July 12, 1943.

18. Ibid., July 13, 1943.

19. Joseph M. Swing Memorandum, La Marsa Camp, Tunisia, July 16, 1943, in Gay Diary, July 13, 1943; Vincent Orange, *Coningham: A Biography of Air Marshal Sir Arthur Coningham* (London: Metheun, 1990), p. 163.

20. Patton to John S. Wood, Headquarters 7th Army, October 15, 1943, Box 2, John S. Wood Papers, George Arents Library for Special Collections, E. S. Bird Library, Syracuse University.

21. Omar N. Bradley and Clay Blair, *A General's Life* (New York: Simon and Schuster, 1983), pp. 187–189; Gay Diary, July 13, 1943; Benjamin A. Dickson, "G-2 Journal: Algiers to the Elbe," p. 84, Benjamin A. Dickson Papers, Special Collections, United States Military Academy Library, West Point.

22. Patton Diary, July 13, 1943.

23. Michael Slackman, "The Orange Race: George S. Patton, Jr.'s Japanese-American Hostage Plan," *Biography* 7 (Winter 1984), 7; Butcher Diary, Aug. 9, 1942, and August 17, 1942; George E. Martin, *Blow, Bugle, Blow* (Bradenton, Fla.: Opuscula, 1986), pp. 95–96.

24. Patton Diary, June 16, 1943.

25. Testimony of Colonel Homer W. Jones, p. 30, Washington, Feb. 17, 1944, File 333.9, Box 67, Records of the Office of the Inspector General, Record Group 159, National Archives II, College Park, Md.

26. Patton Diary, June 27, 1943; Testimony of Captain Howard Cry, p. 48, Record of Trial of Captain John T. Compton by General Court-Martial, Oct. 23, 1943, Judge Advocate General's Files, Falls Church, Va.

27. Patton Diary, July 15, 1943.

28. James J. Weingartner, "Massacre at Biscari: Patton and an American War Crime," Historian 52 (November 1989): 29; Testimony of Captain James O. Smith, Compton Trial, pp. 1, 45; Martin, *Blow, Bugle, Blow,* pp. 95–97.

29. Testimony of Sergeant Horace T. West, pp. 68–72, 79, 101–102, Record of Trial of Sergeant Horace T. West by General Court-Martial, September 2–3, 1943, Judge Advocate General's Files, Falls Church, Va.

30. Testimony of Second Lieutenant David T. Duncan, pp. 74, 100–101, and Summary of Trial, pp. 4–5, West Trial, Judge Advocate General's Files.

31. Testimony of Captain Robert C. Dean, pp. 69–71, and Summary of Trial, p. 4, West Trial, Judge Advocate General's Files.

32. Weingartner, "Massacre at Biscari," pp. 32, 39; Martin, *Blow, Bugle, Blow,* p. 97.

33. Basil H. Liddell Hart, "Notes for History: Talk with Alexander Clifford, 4th April 1944," LH 11/1944/29, Liddell Hart Papers. Liddell Hart later had two interviews with Patton in England, but he never brought up what Clifford told him. One reason that these atrocities have been hard to pin down is that Clifford and Lee died at early ages. Try as I might, I have been unable to identify the American correspondent who accompanied Clifford. I suspect it may have been yet another Hearst reporter, for Noel Monks of the *Daily Mail* often traveled about with H. R. Knickerbocker of the Hearst papers.

34. Ibid. Monk Dickson observed: "In Sicily when the Goums battalion captured a community they regarded it their right to loot the town and rape the women. This created a considerable problem for us and caused terror throughout the civilian population." See Memorandum in Box 3, *A General's Life* Files, Bradley Papers.

35. Liddell Hart to Alexander Clifford, Wolverton Park, Buckinghamshire, Nov. 8, 1948, LH 1/175, Liddell Hart Papers.

36. Clifford to Liddell Hart, London, Nov. 17, 1948, LH 1/175/29, Liddell Hart Papers.

37. Liddell Hart to Clifford, Wolverton Park, Buckinghamshire, Nov. 30, 1948, LH 1/175, Liddell Hart Papers.

38. Testimony of Captain Jean Reed, Compton Trial, p. 46.

39. Lucian K. Truscott, Jr., *Command Missions: A Personal Story* (New York: E. P. Dutton, 1954), p. 215; "Sicily: The First Phase of Occupation," File 319.1, Box 72, Records of the War Department General and Special Staffs, Civil Affairs Division, Record Group 165, National Archives II, College Park, Md.

40. "Sicily: The First Phase of Occupation," File 319.1, Box 72, Records of the War Department General and Special Staffs, Civil Affairs Division.

41. Ibid.; Memorandum, May 4, 1944, File 319.1, Box 72, Records of the War Department General and Special Staffs, Civil Affairs Division. Again I should like to thank Professor Joseph Salemi for details.

42. Everett S. Hughes Diary, July 15, 1943, Box 2, Everett S. Hughes Papers, Manuscript Division, Library of Congress.

43. Patton Diary, July 17, 1943; Hughes Diary, July 22, 1943; Truscott, *Command Missions,* p. 222.

44. Hughes Diary, July 18, 1943, and July 20, 1943.

45. Truscott, *Command Missions,* pp. 221–224; Patton Diary, July 19, 1943, and July 20, 1943.

46. Patton Diary, July 19, 1943; Gay Diary, July 20, 1943; Bradley and Blair, *General's Life,* pp. 192–193.

47. Gay Diary, July 20, 1943; D'Este, *Bitter Victory,* pp. 419–422; Patton Diary, July 19, 1943, and July 20, 1943.

48. Gay Diary, July 20, 1943; Truscott, *Command Missions,* pp. 224–227; Patton Diary, July 22, 1943; *Washington Post,* July 24, 1943.

49. Patton Diary, July 22, 1943.

50. Gay Diary, July 21, 1943.

51. Gay Diary, July 23, 1943; Patton Diary, July 24, 1943; Hughes Diary, July 27, 1943.

52. Gay Diary, July 25, 1943; Bernard Law Montgomery Diary, July 25, 1943, Bernard Law Montgomery Papers, Imperial War Museum, London; Nigel Hamilton, *Master of the Battlefield: Monty's War Years, 1942–1944* (New York: McGraw-Hill, 1983), pp. 325–327; D'Este, *Bitter Victory,* pp. 444–447; Patton Diary, July 25, 1943.

53. Gay Diary, July 25, 1943; Patton Diary, July 25, 1943.

54. Henry L. Stimson Diary, July 22, 1943, Henry L. Stimson Papers, Sterling Memorial Library, Yale University, New Haven.

55. Hughes Diary, July 26, 1943.

56. Patton Diary, July 25, 1943.

57. Gay Diary, July 28, 1943; Montgomery Diary, July 28, 1943.

58. *By Quentin Reynolds* (New York: McGraw-Hill, 1963), pp. 292–294.

59. D'Este, *Bitter Victory,* pp. 468–472; Patton Diary, July 31, 1943.

60. Washington newspaper clipping, April or May 1969, Box 7, Patton Papers; *Time* 42 (August 9, 1943): 30–36.

61. Truscott, *Command Missions,* pp. 229–231; Patton Diary, Aug. 1, 1943; Omar N. Bradley, "Amphibious Landings on North Coast of Sicily," p. 1, Memorandum in Box 66, Omar N. Bradley Papers, United States Military Academy Archives, West Point.

62. Patton Diary, Aug. 1, 1943.

63. Reminiscences of Omar N. Bradley, p. 2, 1965, Box 17, Frank McCarthy Papers, George C. Marshall Library, Virginia Military Institute, Lexington, Va.

64. Patton Diary, Aug. 3, 1943.

65. Bradley Reminiscences, pp. 2–3.

66. Bradley, "Amphibious Landings on North Coast of Sicily," p. 1; Truscott, *Command Missions,* pp. 231–234; Albert N. Garland and Howard McGaw Smyth, *Sicily and the Surrender of Italy* (Washington, D.C.: Office of the Chief of Military History, 1965), pp. 363–367.

67. Gay Diary, Aug. 9, 1943; Patton Diary, Aug. 9, 1943; Eisenhower to Alexander, Aug. 5, 1943, Papers of Lord Alexander of Tunis, WO 214/22. Public Record Office, Kew, London.

68. Patton Diary, Aug. 10, 1943; Bradley, "Amphibious Landings on North Coast of Sicily," p. 2; Truscott, *Command Decisions,* pp. 234–235.

69. Truscott, *Command Decisions,* p. 235; Patton Diary, Aug. 10, 1943.

70. Bradley, "Amphibious Landings on North Coast of Sicily," p. 2; "Confidential & Personal Memoir of Omar N. Bradley," 1947, p. 38, Box 38, Bradley Papers.

71. "Confidential & Personal Memoir of Omar N. Bradley," p. 39.

72. Ibid.

73. Bradley, "Amphibious Landings on North Coast of Sicily," pp. 3–4; Patton Diary, Aug. 15, 1943, and Aug. 16, 1943.

74. Patton Diary, Aug. 10, 1943.

75. Colonel F. Y. Leaver to Colonel Richard T. Arnest, APO 758 New York, Aug. 4, 1943, Box 91, Eisenhower Pre-Presidential Papers.

76. Monks, *Eyewitness,* pp. 190, 194–197.

77. Demaree Bess, "Report of an Investigation," pp. 1–5, Aug. 19, 1943, Box 91, Eisenhower Pre-Presidential Papers. See also Donald E. Currier to Arnest, 93d Evacuation Hospital, Aug. 12, 1943, Box 91, Eisenhower Pre-Presidential Papers.

78. Perrin H. Long to Surgeon General North African Theater of Operations, APO 534 New York, Aug. 16, 1943, Box 91, Eisenhower Pre-Presidential Papers.

79. Truscott, *Command Missions,* p. 243; Gay Diary, Aug. 16, 1943, and Aug. 17, 1943; Alexander to Eisenhower, Allied Forces Headquarters, Aug. 17, 1943, WO 214/22, Lord Alex of Tunis Papers.

80. Patton Diary, Aug. 17, 1943; Truscott, *Command Missions,* p. 244.

81. Gay Diary, Aug. 17, 1943.

82. Liddell Hart, "Notes for History: Talk with Lt.-General J. T. Crocker," Oct. 10, 1943, LH 11/1943/65, Liddell Hart Papers.

83. "The Sicilian Campaign: Axis Operations and Evacuation," pp. 251–254, CAB 146/32, Public Record Office, Kew, London.

84. D'Este, *Bitter Victory,* p. 609; Garland and Smyth, *Sicily and the Surrender of Italy,* p. 419.

85. Bradley and Blair, *General's Life,* pp. 199–200.

86. Patton to Beatrice Ayer Patton, APO 758 New York, Aug. 18, 1943, Patton Papers.

87. *By Quentin Reynolds,* pp. 296–297.

88. Harry C. Butcher, *My Three Years with Eisenhower* (New York: Simon and Schuster, 1946), p. 396.

89. Eisenhower to Patton, n.p., Aug. 17, 1943, Box 91, Eisenhower Pre-Presidential Papers; Patton Diary, Aug. 20, 1943.

90. Hughes Diary, Aug. 20, 1943.

91. Bob Hope as told to Pete Martin, *The Last Christmas Show* (Garden City, N.Y.: Doubleday, 1974), pp. 14, 17.

92. Patton Diary, Aug. 21, 1943.

93. Joseph R. Couch, "The Day Gen. Patton Slapped a Soldier," *Washington Post,* June 3, 1979.

94. Hughes Diary, Aug. 21, 1943.

95. Patton Diary, Aug. 22, 1943.

96. Currier to Eisenhower, copy, Sept. 15, 1964, Box 1, Donald E. Currier Papers, United States Army Military History Institute, Carlisle Barracks, Pa.

97. Patton Diary, Aug. 23, 1943; "General Patton's Address to the Officers and Non-Commissioned Officers of the Divisions of the Seventh Army," pp. 1–5, Box 5, Patton Papers.

98. *Parameters* 10 (December 1980), inside back cover.

99. Monks, *Eyewitness,* p. 197.

100. Ibid., 198.

101. Hughes Diary, Aug. 27, 1943.

102. Patton to Beatrice Ayer Patton, APO 758 New York, Sept. 7, 1943, Patton Papers; Patton to Eisenhower, APO 758 New York, Aug. 29, 1943, Box 91, Eisenhower Pre-Presidential Papers.

103. Patton Diary, Aug. 29, 1943; Gay Diary, Aug. 29, 1943.

104. Hughes Diary, Sept. 2, 1943; *Official Army Register, January 1, 1944* (Washington, D.C.: Government Printing Office, 1944), p. 170.

105. Butcher Diary, Sept. 2, 1943; Butcher, *My Three Years with Eisenhower,* pp. 403–404.

106. Chester B. Hansen Diary, Sept. 4, 1943, Omar N. Bradley Papers, Special Collections, United States Military Academy Library, West Point.

CHAPTER ELEVEN   "LOWER THAN WHALE TRACKS"

1. John P. Marquand, "The General," Draft A, p. 1, Folder 676, John P. Marquand Papers, Beinicke Rare Book and Manuscript Library, Yale University, New Haven, Ct.

2. Ibid., pp. 4–5.

3. Ibid., pp. 6–7. On Feb. 4, 1945, Patton wrote in his diary (George S. Patton, Jr., Papers, Special Collections, United States Military Academy Library, West Point): "Stiller is simply too dumb to live. He never does a single thing quite right."

4. Marquand, "The General," p. 7.

5. Ibid., pp. 7–10.

6. Ibid., pp. 11–12.

7. Ibid., p. 14.

8. Ibid., pp. 14–16.

9. Ibid., pp. 17–18.

10. Ibid., 19; Patton Diary, Sept. 9, 1943.

11. Marquand, "The General," pp. 2–3; Millicent Bell, *Marquand: An American Life* (Boston: Little, Brown, 1979), pp. 509–510.

12. Bernard S. Carter to Louise Hope Thacher Carter, Headquarters 7th Army, Sept. 6, 1943, Box 2, Bernard S. Carter Papers, Special Collections, United States Military Academy Library, West Point.

13. Patton Diary, Sept. 6, 1943; Hobart R. Gay Diary, Sept. 6, 1943, Hobart R. Gay Papers, Special Collections, United States Military Academy Library, West Point.

14. Patton Diary, Sept. 7, 1943, to Sept. 11, 1943.

15. Noel Monks, *Eyewitness* (London: Frederick Muller, 1955), pp. 200–201.

16. Patton Diary, Sept. 15, 1943.

17. Basil H. Liddell Hart, "An Interim Reflection on the Italian Campaign," LH 11/1953/59, Basil H. Liddell Hart Papers, Liddell Hart Centre for Military Archives, King's College, London; Barrie Pitt, *The Crucible of War: Western Desert 1941* (London: Jonathan Cape, 1980), pp. 111–116, 174–186.

18. Patton to Beatrice Ayer Patton, APO 758 New York, Sept. 13, 1943, Patton Papers; Irving A. Fein, *Jack Benny: An Intimate Biography* (New York: G. P. Putnam's Sons, 1976), p. 92.

19. Charles Richardson, *Flashback: A Soldier's Story* (London: William Kimber, 1985), pp. 158–159.

20. Patton Diary, Sept. 17, 1943.

21. Ibid., Sept. 18, 1943.

22. Reminiscences of Charles Poletti, pp. 434–436, May 1978, Oral History Research Office, Columbia University Library, New York City.

23. Harry C. Butcher Diary, Sept. 16, 1943, Box 167, Dwight D. Eisenhower Pre-Presidential Papers, Dwight D. Eisenhower Library, Abilene, Kansas.

24. Everett S. Hughes Diary, Sept. 19, 1943, Box 2, Everett S. Hughes Papers, Manuscript Division, Library of Congress.

25. Report of Colonel Herbert Slayden Clarkson, Inspector General's Department, Sept. 18, 1943, Box 91, Eisenhower Pre-Presidential Papers.

26. Patton Diary, Sept. 21, 1943.

27. Ibid., Oct. 14, 1943.

28. Ibid., Oct. 21, 1943.

29. Ibid., Oct. 16, 1943; Hughes Diary, Oct. 8, 1943, and Oct. 18, 1943.

30. Brigadier General G. A. Lincoln, "Memorandum for Secretary of War," Washington, D.C., Feb. 18, 1946, Box 21, Robert P. Patterson Papers, Manuscript Division, Library of Congress.

31. "Historical Record of Deception in the War Against Germany & Italy," II, pp. 17–20, CAB 154/101, Public Record Office, Kew, London.

32. Ibid., pp. 17–21; Patton Diary, Oct. 27, 1943, Oct. 28, 1943, and Oct. 29, 1943.

33. Patton Diary, Oct. 16, 1943, and Oct. 24, 1943; Reminiscences of General Kenyon A. Joyce, pp. 345–346, Box 1, Kenyon A. Joyce Papers, United States Military History Institute, Carlisle Barracks, Pa.

34. Joyce Reminiscences, pp. 350–351.

35. Ibid., pp. 347–348.

36. Ibid., p. 353.

37. Patton Diary, Nov. 3, 1943; Patton to Beatrice Ayer Patton, APO 758 New York, Nov. 7, 1943, Patton Papers.

38. Patton Diary, Nov. 7, 1943; Patton to Beatrice Ayer Patton, APO 758 New York, Nov. 7, 1943, Patton Papers.

39. Harry C. Butcher, *My Three Years with Eisenhower* (New York: Simon and Schuster, 1946), p. 370; Patton Diary, July 20, 1943, and Nov. 8, 1943. For some of the hangings in the Mediterranean Base Section and the North African Theater of Operations for violation of Article of War 92, covering rape and murder, during 1943, see the following cases: 238038, Box 11, vol. 1; 267110, Box 13, vol. 2; 267198, Box 13, vol. 2; 267488, Box 13, vol. 2; and 270659, Box 13, vol. 2, all in Ledger Sheets, Fiscal Years 1943, 1944, and 1945, Records of the Office of the Judge Advocate General, Record Group 153, National Archives II, College Park, Md. The original complaints in some of these can be found in "Murders of Civilians by Allied Soldiers, Region I, Sicily," Box 3743, Records of the Allied Operational and Occupa-

tion Headquarters, World War II, Record Group 331, National Archives II, College Park, Md.

40. Patton Diary, Nov. 9, 1943.

41. Patton to Beatrice Ayer Patton, APO 758 New York, Nov. 18, 1943, Patton Papers; Patton Diary, Nov. 16, 1943; Harry L. Coles and Albert K. Weinberg, *Civil Affairs: Soldiers Become Governors* (Washington, D.C.: Department of the Army, 1964), p. 194.

42. Patton Diary, Nov. 17, 1943, and Nov. 20, 1943.

43. Ibid., Nov. 17, 1943, and Nov. 22, 1943.

44. Butcher Diary, Nov. 23, 1944.

45. Herman Klurfeld, *Behind the Lines: The World of Drew Pearson* (Englewood Cliffs, N.J.: Prentice-Hall, 1968), pp. 69–70; Jack Anderson with James Boyd, *Confessions of a Muckraker: The Inside Story of Life in Washington During the Truman, Eisenhower, Kennedy and Johnson Years* (New York: Random House, 1979), p. 105.

46. Typescript of Seymour Korman Broadcast, pp. 1–4, Nov. 23, 1943, Box 91, Eisenhower Pre-Presidential Papers.

47. Hughes Diary, Nov. 23, 1943.

48. Ibid., Nov. 26, 1943; Larry I. Bland (ed.), *George C. Marshall Interviews and Reminiscences for Forrest C. Pogue* (Lexington, Va.: George C. Marshall Research Foundation, 1991), p. 627.

49. Patton Diary, Nov. 28, 1943.

50. Ibid., Nov. 27, 1943; Hughes Diary, Nov. 29, 1943.

51. Sherman Miles to Beatrice Ayer Patton, Boston, Nov. 27, 1943, Box 33, George S. Patton, Jr., Papers, Manuscript Division, Library of Congress; Beatrice Ayer Patton to Miles, South Hamilton, n.d., Box 3, Nelson A. Miles Family Papers, Manuscript Division, Library of Congress.

52. Nita Patton to Arvin H. Brown, South Hamilton, Dec. 4, 1943, Box 26, George S. Patton, Sr., Papers, Henry E. Huntington Library, San Marino, Cal.

53. Henry L. Stimson Diary, Dec. 8, 1943, Henry L. Stimson Papers, Sterling Memorial Library, Yale University, New Haven, Ct.

54. *New York Daily Mirror,* Dec. 8, 1943.

55. Hughes Diary, Dec. 11, 1943.

56. Patton Diary, Dec. 5, 1943.

57. Ibid., Dec. 7, 1943.

58. Memo, undated, File 8454, President's Personal File, Franklin D. Roosevelt Papers, Franklin D. Roosevelt Library, Hyde Park, New York; Reminiscences of Mark W. Clark, p. 17, 1971, Eisenhower Administration Project, Oral History Research Office, Columbia University Library, New York City.

59. "Historical Record of Deception in the War Against Germany & Italy," II, pp. 20–25, CAB 154/101.

60. Ibid., 25–26; George S. Patton, Jr., "The Flight in Egypt," pp. 14–15, Box 43 George Patton, Sr., Papers; Patton Diary, Dec. 17, 1943, and Aug. 8, 1945.

61. "Historical Record of Deception in the War Against Germany & Italy," II, p. 28, CAB 154/101.

62. Patton to Beatrice Ayer Patton, APO 758 New York, Dec. 23, 1943, Patton Papers; Patton Diary, Dec. 21, 1943.

63. Patton Diary, Dec. 24, 1943; Butcher Diary, Dec. 12, 1943, and Dec. 23, 1943.

64. Patton Diary, Dec. 25, 1943.

65. Ibid., Dec. 27, 1943.

66. Ibid., Jan. 1, 1944.

67. Hughes Diary, Jan. 2, 1944; Patton Diary, Jan. 2, 1944, and Jan. 3, 1944.

68. Hughes Diary, Jan. 5, 1944; Butcher, *My Three Years with Eisenhower,* pp. 461, 463; Reminiscences of General Jacob L. Devers, pp. 176–177, Feb. 4, 1975, Dwight D. Eisenhower Library, Abilene, Kansas.

69. Hughes Diary, Jan. 2, 1944.

70. George S. Patton, Jr., "Trip to Malta, January 4, 1944," pp. 1–2, Addendum, Box 12, Banning Company Papers, Henry E. Huntington Library, San Marino, Cal.; Patton Diary, Jan. 4, 1944.

71. Patton Diary, Jan. 9, 1944, and Jan. 10, 1944.

72. Devers Reminiscences, pp. 179–180, 183.

73. Patton Diary, Jan. 22, 1944; Hughes Diary, Jan. 24, 1944, and Jan. 25, 1944. Quoted is Hughes's diary.

74. Patton Diary, Jan. 26, 1944; Butcher, *My Three Years with Eisenhower,* pp. 480–481.

75. Hughes Diary, Jan. 31, 1944.

CHAPTER TWELVE   WHITHER DESTINY?

1. George S. Patton, Jr., Diary, Jan. 27, 1944, George S. Patton, Jr., Papers, Special Collections, United States Military Academy Library, West Point.

2. George S. Patton, Jr., to Beatrice Ayer Patton, APO 9563 New York, Feb. 5, 1944, Patton Papers; Patton Diary, January 28, 1944, January 29, 1944, and January 31, 1944.

3. Patton to Beatrice Ayer Patton, APO 9563 New York, Feb. 5, 1944, Patton Papers; Patton Diary, Feb. 1, 1944, and Feb. 2, 1944.

4. DeWitt C. Smith, Jr., "Recollections of General Wood and the 4th Armored Division," Jan. 20, 1967, Box 2, John S. Wood Papers, George Arents Library for Special Collections, E. S. Bird Library, Syracuse University.

5. Patton Diary, Feb. 3, 1944.

6. Ibid., Feb. 10, 1944.

7. Ibid., Feb. 11, 1944; Harry C. Butcher, *My Three Years with Eisenhower* (New York: Simon and Schuster, 1946), p. 390.

8. Patton Diary, Feb. 12, 1944; Butcher, *My Three Years with Eisenhower,* p. 491.

9. Patton Diary, Feb. 16, 1944.

10. Ibid.

11. Ibid., Feb. 17, 1944.

12. Ibid., Feb. 18, 1944.

13. Lewis H. Brereton, *The Brereton Diaries: The War in the Air in the Pacific, Middle East and Europe, 2 October 1941–8 May 1945* (New York: William Morrow, 1946),

p. 237; Eric Hammel, *Air War Europa: America's Air War Against Germany in Europe and North Africa, 1942–1945* (Pacifica, Cal.: Pacifica Press, 1994), p. 381; Reminiscences of General Elwood P. Quesada, pp. 41–42, June 1960, Aviation Project, Oral History Research Office, Columbia University Library, New York City.

14. Reminiscences of General Otto P. Weyland, pp. 5–6, June 1960, Aviation Project, Oral History Research Office, Columbia University Library, New York City.

15. Ibid., pp. 1, 6–9.

16. Roger H. Nye, *The Patton Mind: The Professional Development of an Extraordinary Leader* (Garden City Park, N.Y.: Avery, 1993), pp. 88–89, 118, 187–188.

17. Robert H. Larson, *The British Army and the Theory of Armored Warfare, 1918–1940* (Newark: University of Delaware Press, 1984), pp. 205–211; Major K. J. Macksey, *Armoured Commander: A Biography of Major-General Sir Percy Hobart* (London: Hutchinson, 1967), pp. 141–145; Basil H. Liddell Hart, "Tank Warfare and Its Future," p. 5, Aug. 29, 1950, Box 1, Wood Papers. Especially interesting are David Fraser, *Alanbrooke* (New York: Atheneum, 1982), pp. 114–121; Gregory Blaxland, *Destination Dunkirk: The Story of Gort's Army* (London: William Kimber, 1973), pp. 10–12.

18. Liddell Hart, "Tank Warfare and Its Future," pp. 5–6. The Great March Offensive lasted from March 21, 1918, to April 5, 1918.

19. Ibid., p. 7; Basil H. Liddell Hart, "Notes for History—American Forces (February 1944)," pp. 1–2, LH11/1944/7, Basil H. Liddell Hart Papers, Liddell Hart Centre for Military Archives, King's College, London; Macksey, *Armoured Crusader,* pp. 143, 335.

20. Basil H. Liddell Hart, "Notes for History: Talk with Martel, 28th October 1944," LH 11/1944/62, Liddell Hart Papers.

21. Liddell Hart, "Notes for History—American Forces," p. 3.

22. Mrs. John S. Wood to Liddell Hart, Montreux, Switzerland, Feb. 28, 1968, File 1/763, Liddell Hart Papers.

23. Albin F. Irzyk, "The 'Name Enough' Division," *Armor* 96 (August 1986), 20; Bradford G. Chynoweth to George F. Hofmann, Berkeley, July 8, 1971, Box 2, Bradford G. Chynoweth Papers, United States Army Military History Institute, Carlisle Barracks, Pa.

24. Mrs. John S. Wood to Liddell Hart, Montreux, Switzerland, Feb. 28, 1968, File 1/763, Liddell Hart Papers; Reminiscences of General Jacob L. Devers, p. 87, Nov. 18, 1974, Dwight D. Eisenhower Library, Abilene, Kansas. On Abrams's religion see Chester V. Clifton, "A Tribute to Abe," *Assembly* 33 (December 1974), 13.

25. Liddell Hart to John S. Wood, Wolverton Park, Buckinghamshire, Dec. 20, 1948, File 1/763, Liddell Hart Papers.

26. Liddell Hart, "Notes for History—American Forces," pp. 1, 4–5; Devers Reminiscences, p. 69; Chynoweth to Hofmann, Berkeley, July 8, 1971, Box 2, Chynoweth Papers.

27. Liddell Hart, "Notes for History—American Forces," pp. 4–5.

28. Liddell Hart Diary, March 14, 1944, and March 15, 1944, Liddell Hart Papers; Notes on Interview with Patton, March 14, 1944, Doc. 11/1944/14, Liddell

Hart Papers; Liddell Hart, "Note on Two Discussions with Patton, 1944," Feb. 20, 1948, Doc. 11/1944/40, Liddell Hart Papers.

29. Patton to Beatrice Ayer Patton, APO 403 New York, March 16, 1944, Patton Papers.

30. Wood to Liddell Hart, n.p., April 20, 1950, File 1/763, Liddell Hart Papers.

31. Liddell Hart Diary, March 21, 1944; Notes on Conversation with General Omar N. Bradley, March 21, 1944, Doc. 11/1944/15, Liddell Hart Papers.

32. Liddell Hart to Patton, Westmoreland, March 28, 1944, Folder 1/568, Liddell Hart Papers.

33. Liddell Hart to Wood, Westmoreland, March 29, 1944, File 1/763, Liddell Hart Papers.

34. Wood to Liddell Hart, Chippenham, April 28, 1944, File 1/763, Liddell Hart Papers.

35. Patton Diary, March 1, 1944; Patton to Beatrice Ayer Patton, APO 403 New York, March 16, 1944, Patton Papers; Macksey, *Armoured Crusader,* pp. 125–126.

36. Patton Diary, March 1, 1944.

37. Ibid., March 6, 1944.

38. Ibid., March 7, 1944, and March 8, 1944; Frank James Price, *Troy H. Middleton: A Biography* (Baton Rouge: Louisiana State University Press, 1974), pp. 175–176.

39. Patton to Beatrice Ayer Patton, APO 403 New York, February 20, 1944, March 6, 1944, and March 12, 1944. Patton Papers.

40. Patton Diary, March 9, 1944, and March 10, 1944.

41. Ibid., March 14, 1944.

42. Ibid., March 26, 1944, and March 27, 1944.

43. Ibid., March 27, 1944.

44. Everett S. Hughes Diary, March 30, 1944, Box 2, Everett S. Hughes Papers, Manuscript Division, Library of Congress; Patton Diary, March 30, 1944.

45. Blumenson, II, 430–431.

46. Patton Diary, April 4, 1944; Hughes to Major General V. L. Peterson, APO 887 New York, April 7, 1944, File 333.9, Box 67, Records of the Office of the Inspector General, Record Group 159, National Archives II, College Park, Md.

47. Patton to Beatrice Ayer Patton, APO 403 New York, April 4, 1944, Patton Papers.

48. Testimony of Colonel Homer W. Jones, pp. 30–31, Washington, D.C., Feb. 17, 1944, File 333.9, Box 67, Records of the Office of the Inspector General.

49. Testimony of Colonel Forrest E. Cookson, pp. 2–4, 7, Washington, D.C., Feb. 16, 1944, File 333.9, Box 67, Records of the Office of the Inspector General; Lieutenant Colonel William R. Cook, "Report on Investigation," p. 4, File 333.9, Box 67, Records of the Office of the Inspector General. Middleton's role in all of this remains murky. Told by the division chaplain of the murders at Biscari, Middleton's chief of staff, Colonel Martin, went over and saw "three mounds of bodies, stacked like cordwood." Martin, in turn, informed Middleton, who never investigated the matter or again brought it up. What took place between Middleton and Patton is conjecture.

See George E. Martin, *Blow, Bugle, Blow* (Bradenton, Fla.: Opuscula, 1986), pp. 96–97.

50. Patton Diary, April 5, 1944.

51. Hughes to Peterson, APO 887 New York, April 7, 1944, File 333.9, Box 67, Records of the Office of the Inspector General. When Peterson died, Hughes wrote his obituary for the West Point alumni magazine. See *Assembly* 15 (July 1956): 81–82.

52. Cook, "Report on Investigation," pp. 1–4.

53. Patton Diary, April 7, 1944.

54. Reminiscences of John J. McCloy, I, pp. 1, 5, 11–14, 1973, Eisenhower Administration Project, Oral History Research Office, Columbia University Library, New York City.

55. Patton to Hughes, APO 403 New York, April 26, 1944, Appendix 141, Patton Papers.

56. George C. Marshall to Dwight D. Eisenhower, n.p., April 26, 1944, Box 91, Dwight D. Eisenhower Pre-Presidential Papers, Dwight D. Eisenhower Library, Abilene, Kansas.

57. Walter Bedell Smith to Marshall, SHAEF Message, April 27, 1944, Box 91, Eisenhower Pre-Presidential Papers. See also Butcher, *My Three Years with Eisenhower,* pp. 530–531.

58. *Washington Post,* April 29, 1944; Eisenhower to Marshall, Office of the Supreme Commander, April 29, 1944, Box 67, George C. Marshall Papers, George C. Marshall Library, Virginia Military Institute, Lexington, Va.; Marshall to Eisenhower, n.p., April 29, 1944, Box 67, Marshall Papers; Alfred D. Chandler (ed.), *The Papers of Dwight David Eisenhower: The War Years* (Baltimore and London: Johns Hopkins Press, 1970), II, pp. 1836–1838.

59. Henry L. Stimson Diary, May 2, 1944, Henry L. Stimson Papers, Sterling Memorial Library, Yale University, New Haven, Ct.

60. Harry C. Butcher Diary, May 9, 1944, Box 168, Eisenhower Pre-Presidential Papers.

61. Patton Diary, April 30, 1944, and May 1, 1944. On Ike bringing up the Lambert affair, see Chandler (ed.), *Papers of Dwight D. Eisenhower* II, p. 1841.

62. Patton Diary, May 3, 1944.

63. "Some Personal Memoirs of Justus 'Jock' Lawrence, Chief Public Relations Officer, European Theater of Operations," pp. 4, 145–147, Miscellaneous Box, Patton Papers.

64. Butcher Diary, May 11, 1944; Patton to Beatrice Ayer Patton, APO 403 New York, May 3, 1944, Patton Papers.

CHAPTER THIRTEEN   INVASION BLUES

1. George S. Patton, Jr., to Beatrice Ayer Patton, APO 403 New York, May 3, 1944, George S. Patton, Jr., Papers, Special Collections, United States Military Academy Library, West Point.

2. Patton to Beatrice Ayer Patton, APO 403 New York, May 5, 1944, Patton Papers.

3. George S. Patton, Jr., Diary, May 8, 1944, Patton Papers; George S. Patton, Jr., "Tank and Infantry Demonstration," pp. 2, 7–9, May 8, 1944, Box 58, George S. Patton, Jr., Papers, Manuscript Division, Library of Congress.

4. Patton Diary, May 8, 1944, and May 9, 1944.

5. Ibid., May 10, 1944.

6. Ibid., May 12, 1944.

7. "Presentation of Overlord Plans at St. Paul's School, May 15, 1944," WO 219/268, Public Record Office, Kew, London; Reminiscences of General William H. Simpson, pp. 50–54, March 15, 1972, Oral History Research Office, Columbia University Library, New York City; Reminiscences of Admiral John Lesslie Hall, Jr., pp. 165–167, 1964, Oral History Research Office, Columbia University Library, New York City.

8. Hall Reminiscences, pp. 167–168.

9. Bernard S. Carter to Louise Hope Thacher Carter, APO 403 New York, March 26, 1944, Box 3, Bernard S. Carter Papers, Special Collections, United States Military Academy Library, West Point; Bernard Carter to Thomas C. Thacher, APO 758 New York, Sept. 17, 1943, Box 3, Carter Papers.

10. Bernard Carter to Louise Carter, APO 403 New York, April 18, 1944, Box 3, Carter Papers.

11. Bernard Carter to Louise Carter, APO 403 New York, May 12, 1944, Box 3, Carter Papers.

12. Patton Diary, Feb. 5, 1944; Bernard Carter to Louise Carter, APO 403 New York, March 26, 1944, and April 4, 1944, Box 3, Carter Papers.

13. Patton to Beatrice Ayer Patton, APO 403 New York, Feb. 20, 1944, and Feb. 23, 1944, Patton Papers.

14. Bernard Carter to Louise Carter, APO 403 New York, May 16, 1944, Box 3, Carter Papers.

15. George S. Patton, Sr., to Patton, n.p., March 23, 1923, Box 7, George S. Patton, Sr., Papers, Henry E. Huntington Library, San Marino, Cal.

16. *New York Times,* Jan. 2, 1944, and Jan. 4, 1944; Forrest C. Pogue, *George C. Marshall: Organizer of Victory* (New York: Viking, 1973), pp. 349–351; Patton to Beatrice Ayer Patton, APO 403 New York, Feb. 19, 1944, Patton Papers.

17. "Historical Record of Deception in the War Against Germany and Italy," I, p. 102, CAB 154/100, Public Record Office, Kew, London.

18. F. W. Winterbotham, *The Ultra Secret* (New York: Harper & Row, 1974), pp. 121–122.

19. Reminiscences of Admiral Alan Goodrich Kirk, pp. 260–261, 1962, Oral History Research Office, Columbia University Library, New York City; William B. Breur, *The Secret War: Deception, Espionage, and Dirty Tricks, 1939–1945* (Novato, Calif.: Presidio, 1988), pp. 233–234; "Plan 'Fortitude South' (Pas de Calais)," Documents 2A and 9A, WO 219/2223, Public Record Office, Kew, London.

20. Breuer, *Secret War with Germany,* pp. 234–236; William B. Breuer, *Hoodwinking Hitler: The Normandy Deception* (Westport, Ct.: Praeger, 1993), pp. 159–161.

21. "Enemy Reactions to Fortitude-Neptune," Cover & Deception Report No. 6, pp. 2–3, Box 1, Records of the Army Staff, Record Group 319, National Archives II, College Park, Md.

22. Cover & Deception Orders of July 20, 1944, Box 1, Records of the Army Staff, Record Group 319.

23. Breuer, *Secret War with Germany,* pp. 235–236.

24. For May 29, 1944, see the statement of Colonel Theodore J. Krokus, Brooklyn, May 28, 1970, Box 5, Patton Papers. For May 31, 1944, see Gilbert R. Cook Diary, May 31, 1944, Box 4, Gilbert R. Cook Papers, Dwight D. Eisenhower Library, Abilene, Kansas; James A. Huston, *Across the Face of France: Liberation and Recovery, 1944–63* (n.p.: Purdue University Studies, 1963), pp. 107–109; Charles Dornbush (ed.), *Speech of General George S. Patton, Jr., to His Third Army* (Cornwallville, N.Y.: Hope Farm Press, 1963), p. 7; Hobart R. "Hap" Gay Diary, May 31, 1944, Hobart R. Gay Papers, Special Collections, United States Military Academy Library, West Point. For June 5, 1944, see Lynn A. Hoppe to the curator of the Patton Museum at Fort Knox, Boise City, Idaho, Sept. 17, 1976, Box 5, Patton Papers.

25. Reminiscences of Joshua Miner, p. 49, n.d., Oral History Research Office, Columbia University Library, New York City.

26. This account is taken from the sources cited in the previous two footnotes.

27. Harry M. Kemp, *The Regiment, Let the Citizens Bear Arms! A Narrative History of An American Infantry Regiment in World War II* (Austin, Texas: Nortex Press, 1990), pp. 63–65.

28. Gay Diary, May 29, 1944.

29. Patton Diary, June 1, 1944; Chester B. Hansen Diary, June 1, 1944, and June 2, 1944, Omar N. Bradley Papers, Special Collections, United States Military Academy Library, West Point.

30. Patton Diary, June 5, 1944.

31. Ibid., June 6, 1944.

32. Patton to Beatrice Ayer Patton, APO 403 New York, June 17, 1944, Patton Papers.

33. Sir Brian Horrocks with Eversley Belfield and Major-General H. Essame, *Corps Commander* (London: Sedgwick & Jackson, 1977), pp. 3, 10–12.

34. "Magic" Diplomatic Summaries, June 1, 1944, pp. A4-A6, Box 11, Records of the National Security Agency/Central Security Service, Record Group 457, National Archives II, College Park, Md.; Thomas Parrish, *The Ultra Americans: The U.S. Role in Breaking the Nazi Codes* (New York: Stein and Day, 1946), pp. 197–198. See also Carl Boyd, *Hitler's Japanese Confidant: General Ōshima Hiroshi and MAGIC Intelligence, 1941–1945* (Lawrence: University Press of Kansas, 1993).

35. "Magic" Diplomatic Summaries, June 22, 1944, p. 1, Box 11, Records of the National Security Agency/Central Security Service, Record Group 457; Bruce Lee, *Marching Orders: The Untold Story of World War II* (New York: Crown, 1995), pp. 224–225.

36. "Magic" Diplomatic Summaries, June 30, 1944, pp. 1–2, Box 11, Records of the National Security Agency/Central Security Service, Record Group 457.

37. Basil H. Liddell Hart, "Notes for History," p. 1, Doc. 11/1944/39, Basil H. Liddell Hart Papers, Liddell Hart Centre for Military Archives, King's College, London.

38. Ibid., p. 1.

39. Ibid., p. 2.

40. Ibid., pp. 2–3. In what has to be an error in memory, Liddell Hart later claimed that their first meeting convinced Patton to change his mind about tanks. "At any rate," he wrote in 1948, "when I spent another evening with him in June just before he went over to Normandy, he was no longer talking about 1918 methods, but on much bolder lines." Stephen Brooks, the archivist who sorted Liddell Hart's papers, has pointed out that on June 19 Patton reiterated his original views. See Stephen Brooks, "Liddell Hart and His Papers," in Brian Bond and Ian Roy (eds.), *War and Society: A Yearbook of Military History* (New York: Holmes & Meier, 1977), II, p. 138. A guess is that Patton again turned to tanks because of his innate faith in them, plus his long association with tank proponents such as Wood, Grow, Chynoweth, and Cook, to name just a few.

41. Liddell Hart, "Notes for History," pp. 2–3.

42. Ibid.; Bradford G. Chynoweth to George F. Hofmann, Berkeley, Jan. 17, 1972, Box 2, Bradford G. Chynoweth Papers, United States Army Military History Institute, Carlisle Barracks, Pa.

43. Liddell Hart, "Notes for History," p. 3.

44. Ibid., p. 4.

45. Patton Diary, June 30, 1944; Richard Rohmer, *Patton's Gap: An Account of Normandy, 1944* (New York and Toronto: Beaufort Books, 1981), p. 116.

46. Lee, *Marching Orders,* p. 229.

47. "Historical Record of Deception in the War Against Germany & Italy," II, pp. 61–62, CAB 154/101. See also "Plan 'Fortitude South II,' " Folio 6, Doc. 1A, WO 219/2226.

48. "Historical Record of Deception in the War Against Germany & Italy," II, pp. 62–63, 232–233, CAB 154/101.

49. Ibid., p. 63.

50. Ibid.; Anthony Cave Brown, *Bodyguard of Lies* (New York: Harper & Row, 1975), pp. 737–738.

51. "Historical Record of Deception in the War Against Germany & Italy," II, pp. 63–65, CAB 154/101; "Enemy Reactions to Fortitude-Neptune," Cover & Deception Report No. 6, pp. 2–3, Box 1, Records of the Army Staff, Record Group 319.

52. Brigadier A. T. Cornwall-Jones to General Andrew J. McFarland, n.p., Box 367, Records of the United States Joint Chiefs of Staff, 1942–1945, Record Group 218, National Archives II, College Park, Md.

53. Patton Diary, July 6, 1944; George S. Patton, Jr., "Notes on France," p. 1, Aug. 18, 1944, Addendum, Box 12, Banning Company Papers, Henry E. Huntington Library, San Marino, Cal.; Chester B. Hansen Diary, July 2, 1944, and July 6, 1944,

Omar N. Bradley Papers, Special Collections, United States Military Academy Library, West Point.

54. Russell F. Weigley, "From the Normandy Beaches to the Falaise-Argentan Pocket: A Critique of Allied Operational Planning in 1944," *Military Review* 70 (September 1990): 48–49; Reminiscences of General Omar N. Bradley, p. 115, 1966, Box 30, Omar N. Bradley Papers, United States Military Academy Archives, West Point.

55. Winterbotham, *Ultra Secret,* pp. 98, 139–140, 189; William Randolph Hearst, Jr., with Jack Casserly, *The Hearsts Father and Son* (Niwot, Colo.: Roberts Rinehart, 1991), p. 143.

56. Weigley, "From the Normandy Beaches to the Falaise-Argentan Pocket," p. 50; T. Michael Booth and Duncan Spencer, *Paratrooper: The Life of Gen. James Gavin* (New York: Simon and Schuster, 1994), p. 206; Patton Diary, July 6, 1944.

57. Patton Diary, July 7, 1944.

58. Ibid., July 9, 1944.

59. Ibid., July 14, 1944.

60. General Sir Miles Dempsey to Liddell Hart, "Operation Goodwood," 1952, File 1/230/22A, Liddell Hart Papers. See also Basil H. Liddell Hart, *The Tanks: The History of the Royal Tank Regiment* (New York: Frederick A. Praeger, 1959), II, p. 359.

61. Dempsey, "Operation Goodwood," Liddell Hart Papers; Carlo D'Este, *Decision in Normandy* (New York: E. P. Dutton, 1983), pp. 355–356; Operation Goodwood File, WO 205/1121, Public Record Office, Kew, London; Notes of Conversation Between General Miles Dempsey and Lieutenant-Colonel G. S. Jackson, March 8, 1951, pp. 3–5, CAB 106/1061, Public Record Office, Kew, London.

62. Brown, *Bodyguard of Lies,* pp. 736–737; Liddell Hart, *Tanks,* II, p. 370; Harry C. Butcher, *My Three Years with Eisenhower* (New York: Simon and Schuster, 1946), p. 627.

63. Jacob L. Devers to Bradley, Washington, D.C., July 14, 1969, in Letters, vol. 3, p. 16, Box 15, Bradley Papers; Bradley Reminiscences, pp. 115–116.

64. Patton Diary, July 17, 1944, and July 18, 1944; Notes on Meeting between General Patton and Correspondents, July 17, 1944, pp. 1–2, Box 47, Patton Papers, Library of Congress.

65. Patton to Beatrice Ayer Patton, APO 403 New York, July 13, 1944, and July 27, 1944, Patton Papers.

66. Handwritten addendum to Gay Diary, July 26, 1944.

67. "Magic" Diplomatic Summaries, July 10, 1944, pp. 1, 5–6, Box 12, Records of the National Security Agency/Central Security Service, Record Group 457.

68. "Magic" Diplomatic Summaries, July 17, 1944, pp. 2–3, Box 12, Records of the National Security Agency/Central Security Service, Record Group 457.

69. "Magic" Diplomatic Summaries, July 29, 1944, p. A–3, Box 12, Records of the National Security Agency/Central Security Service, Record Group 457.

70. "Magic" Diplomatic Summaries, July 30, 1944, p. 4, Box 12, Records of the National Security Agency/Central Security Service, Record Group 457.

71. Liddell Hart, *Tanks,* II, pp. 361–370.

72. Weigley, "From the Normandy Beaches to the Falaise-Argentan Pocket," pp. 52–53; Liddell Hart, *Tanks,* II, pp. 370–371; Patton Diary, July 23, 1944.

73. Liddell Hart, *Tanks,* II, pp. 370–372; Omar N. Bradley and Clay Blair, *A General's Life* (New York: Simon and Schuster, 1983), pp. 280–281.

74. DeWitt C. Smith, Jr., "Recollections of General Wood and the 4th Armored Division," Jan. 20, 1967, Box 2, John S. Wood Papers, George Arents Library for Special Collections, E. S. Bird Library, Syracuse University.

75. Patton Diary, July 29, 1944.

76. See Martin Blumenson, *Breakout and Pursuit* (Washington, D.C.: Office of the Chief of Military History, 1961), pp. 309–313; *Rolling Review* 12 (July 31, 1967): 2, in File 1/763, Liddell Hart Papers; Wood to Liddell Hart, 4th Armored Division, Aug. 23, 1944, File 1/763, Liddell Hart Papers. For Blumenson's assumption adopted as history, see Russell F. Weigley, *Eisenhower's Lieutenant: The Campaign of France and Germany, 1944–1945* (Bloomington: Indiana University Press, 1981), pp. 172–173.

77. "Confidential & Personal Memoir of Omar N. Bradley," 1947, p. 99, Omar N. Bradley Papers, United States Military Academy Archives, West Point.

78. Wood to Liddell Hart, Vienna, Dec. 5, 1948, File 1/763, Liddell Hart Papers; Basil H. Liddell Hart, "The Liberation of France," I, 9, December 1965, Box 1, Wood Papers. On August 6, Hansen wrote in his diary: "Meanwhile, we aides live in mortal fear that Patton may unjustly grab credit for the breakthrough which was made before he became active."

79. Wood to Liddell Hart, Reno, Aug. 2, 1962, File 1/763, Liddell Hart Papers.

80. Liddell Hart to Wood, Wolverton Park, Buckinghamshire, Dec. 20, 1948, and n.p., Aug. 27, 1962, File 1/763, Liddell Hart Papers.

CHAPTER FOURTEEN   HURRY UP AND WAIT

1. William Randolph Hearst, Jr., with Jack Casserly, *The Hearsts: Father and Son* (Niwot, Colo.: Roberts, Rinehart, 1991), p. 148; Frank James Price, *Troy H. Middleton: A Biography* (Baton Rouge: Louisiana State University Press, 1974), p. 186. Patton's indication that he knew nothing about the taking of Avranches is further proof that he was not involved in the breakout. The latest assertion that he directed the breakout is Carlo D'Este's remarks in John Nelson Rickard, *Patton at Bay: The Lorraine Campaign, September to December, 1944* (Westport, C.: Praeger, 1999), p. xii.

2. George S. Patton, Jr., Diary, Aug. 1, 1944, George S. Patton, Jr., Papers, Special Collections, United States Military Academy Library, West Point.

3. Price, *Middleton,* pp. 184–187.

4. Ibid., pp. 187–188.

5. Ibid.

6. Patton Diary, Aug. 1, 1944.

7. Ibid.

8. Chester B. Hansen Diary, Aug. 2, 1944, Omar N. Bradley Papers, Special Collections, United States Military Academy Library, West Point.

9. Patton Diary, Aug. 1, 1944, and Aug. 2, 1944.

10. Wesley Frank Craven and James Lea Cate (eds.), *The Army Air Forces in World War II* (Washington, D.C.: Office of Air Force History, 1983), III, pp. 246–247; Reminiscences of General Otto P. Weyland, pp. 10–13, June 1960, Aviation Project, Oral History Research Office, Columbia University Library, New York City.

11. Weyland Reminiscences, pp. 10–14.

12. Reminiscences of Colonel Anthony V. Grossetta, pp. 30–31, Sept. 23, 1977, Air Force Project, Oral History Research Office, Columbia University Library, New York City.

13. Ibid., pp. 31–32.

14. Craven and Cate (eds.), *The Army Air Forces in World War II*, III, p. 247.

15. John S. Wood to Basil H. Liddell Hart, Somewhere in Korea, Sept. 15, 1952, File 1/763, Basil H. Liddell Hart Papers, Liddell Hart Centre for Military Archives, King's College, London.

16. Patton Diary, Aug. 1, 1944; Russell F. Weigley, *Eisenhower's Lieutenants: The Campaign of France and Germany, 1944–1945* (Bloomington: Indiana University Press, 1981), pp. 365–366; Wood to Cowper (for Captain Blumenson, who asked), Santa Monica, March 24, 1954, File 1/763, Liddell Hart Papers; Price, *Middleton,* pp. 188–189.

17. Patton Diary, Aug. 1, 1944, and Aug. 4, 1944; Hobart R. "Hap" Gay Diary, Aug. 4, 1944, Hobart R. Gay Papers, Special Collections, United States Military Academy Library, West Point; Hobart R. Gay to Wood, Third Army Headquarters, August 24, 1945, Box 1, John S. Wood Papers, George Arents Library for Special Collections, E. S. Bird Library, Syracuse University.

18. Wood to Cowper, Santa Monica, March 24, 1954, File 1/763, Liddell Hart Papers.

19. Hansen Diary, Sept. 16, 1944, and Sept. 19, 1944; Price, *Middleton,* p. 189; Troy H. Middleton to Wood, Baton Rouge, April 12, 1962, File 1/763, Liddell Hart Papers. See also Forrest C. Pogue, *The Supreme Command* (Washington, D.C.: Center of Military History, 1953), p. 205.

20. Patton Diary, Aug. 7, 1944.

21. Thomas Parrish, *The Ultra Americans: The U.S. Role in Breaking the Nazi Codes* (New York: Stein and Day, 1986), pp. 223–225; Sir Brian Horrocks, with Eversley Belfield and Major-General H. Essame, *Corps Commander* (London: Sedgwick & Jackson, 1977), pp. 38–39.

22. Alan F. Wilt, "Coming of Age: XIX TAC's Roles During the 1944 Dash Across France," *Air University Review* 36 (March–April 1985): 72–73; Craven and Cates (eds.), *Army Air Forces in World War II,* III, pp. 247–250.

23. Parrish, *Ultra Americans,* pp. 225–226; Major Warrack Wallace, "Report on Assignment with Third United States Army," pp. 2–5, SRH 108, Box 30, Records of the National Security Agency/Central Security Service, Record Group 457, National Archives II, College Park, Md.

24. Omar N. Bradley and Clay Blair, *A General's Life* (New York: Simon and Schuster, 1983), p. 293; Horrocks, with Belfield and Essame, *Corps Commander,* pp. 38–39; Pogue, *Supreme Command,* pp. 207–208.

25. Bradley and Blair, *General's Life,* p. 293; Patton Diary, Aug. 7, 1944.

26. Hansen Diary, Sept. 5, 1944.

27. Martin Blumenson, *Breakout and Pursuit* (Washington, D.C.: Office of the Chief of Military History, 1961), pp. 434–437, 497; Hansen Diary, Sept. 5, 1944; Patton Diary, Aug. 8, 1944.

28. George S. Patton, Jr., to Beatrice Ayer Patton, APO 403 New York, Aug. 8, 1944, Patton Papers.

29. William G. Weaver, *Yankee Doodle Went to Town* (Ann Arbor, Mich.: Edwards Brothers, 1959), pp. 122–123. See also Blumenson, *Breakout and Pursuit,* pp. 434–437.

30. Nigel Hamilton, *Master of the Battlefield: Monty's War Years, 1942–1944* (New York: McGraw–Hill, 1983), p. 776.

31. Liddell Hart, "Notes for History: Talk with Jim Rose," Oct. 28, 1944, LH 11/1944/63, Liddell Hart Papers. Quoted is Liddell Hart's version of the conversation.

32. Ibid.; Ronald Levin, *Ultra Goes to War: The Secret Story* (London: Hutchinson, 1978), pp. 112–113.

33. Price, *Middleton,* p. 186; Weyland Reminiscences, pp. 13–15.

34. Patton Diary, Aug. 9, 1944; Weigley, *Eisenhower's Lieutenants,* p. 205.

35. Gay Diary, Aug. 12, 1944; Patton Diary, Aug. 11, 1944, and Aug. 12 1944; Basil H. Liddell Hart, *The Tanks: The History of the Royal Tank Regiment* (New York: Frederick A. Praeger, 1959), II, p. 598.

36. Gay Diary, Aug. 12, 1944; Blumenson, *Breakout and Pursuit,* p. 656.

37. Weaver, *Yankee Doodle Went to Town,* pp. 236–237; Pogue, *Supreme Command,* pp. 209–211.

38. Omar N. Bradley, "Memorandum for the Record: Argentan Falaise Gap Operation," pp. 1–2, Box 66, Omar N. Bradley Papers, United States Military Academy Archives, West Point; Bradley and Blair, *General's Life,* p. 298.

39. Patton Diary, Aug. 13, 1944; Pogue, *Supreme Command,* pp. 213–214.

40. Martin Blumenson, "General Bradley's Decision at Argentan (13 August 1944)," in Kent Roberts Greenfield (ed.), *Command Decisions* (Washington, D.C.: Office of the Chief of Military History, 1960), pp. 441–413; Diary of General Miles C. Dempsey, Aug. 13, 1944, Papers of General Miles C. Dempsey, WO 285/9, Public Record Office, Kew, London.

41. Hamilton, *Master of the Battlefield,* p. 791; Bradley, "Memorandum for the Record," p. 3; Weaver, *Yankee Doodle Went to Town,* p. 236.

42. Bradley and Blair, *General's Life,* pp. 301–302; Patton Diary, Aug. 14, 1944.

43. Patton Diary, Aug. 14, 1944; Gay Diary, Aug. 14, 1944; Michel Dufresne, "Normandy, 14 August 1944: Decisions That Saved the German Armies," *Revue Historique des Armees,* n.v. (June 1993): 47–63. The famous quote is from Sir Walter Scott's *Marmion,* Canto VI, I, 532, written in 1808.

44. Bradley and Blair, *General's Life,* pp. 302–303; Patton Diary, Aug. 15, 1944.

45. Gay Diary, Aug. 15, 1944.

46. Ibid., Aug. 16, 1944; Patton Diary, Aug. 16, 1944, and Aug. 18, 1945.

47. Gay Diary, Aug. 16, 1944.

48. Horrocks, with Belfield and Essame, *Corps Commander,* pp. 47–48; Weaver, *Yankee Doodle Went to Town,* pp. 103–104; Patton Diary, Aug. 17, 1944; Blumenson, *Breakout and Pursuit,* pp. 531, 537.

49. Horrocks, with Belfield and Essame, *Corps Commander,* pp. 49, 52; Reminiscences of General Elwood P. Quesada, pp. 49–50, June 1960, Aviation Project, Oral History Research Office, Columbia University Library, New York City.

50. Blumenson, *Breakout and Pursuit,* pp. 557–558.

51. Horrocks, with Belfield and Essame, *Corps Commander,* p. 53; Bradley, "Memorandum for the Record," p. 3.

52. Weaver, *Yankee Doodle Went to Town,* pp. 108, 237; Patton Diary, Aug. 19, 1944.

53. Weaver, *Yankee Doodle Went to Town,* pp. 236–239.

54. *New York Times,* Aug. 16, 1944, and Aug. 17, 1944.

55. Tyler Abell (ed.), *Drew Pearson Diaries, 1949–1959* (New York: Holt, Rinehart and Winston, 1974), pp. 344–345; Hearst, with Casserly, *Hearsts,* pp. 149–150, 160.

56. Patton to Beatrice Ayer Patton, n.p., Oct. 26, 1918, Patton Papers; Patton Diary, Aug. 19, 1944; Blumenson, I, 629.

57. Weyland Reminiscences, pp. 11–13.

58. Ibid., pp. 17–18.

59. Patton Diary, Aug. 17, 1944, and Aug. 20, 1944; Bradford G. Chynoweth to George F. Hofmann, Berkeley, July 8, 1971, Box 2, Bradford G. Chynoweth Papers, United States Army Military History Institute, Carlisle Barracks, Pa.; Bradford Grethen Chynoweth, *Bellamy Park* (Hicksville, NY: Exposition Press, 1975), pp. 133, 140.

60. Patton Diary, Aug. 20, 1944; Weigley, *Eisenhower's Lieutenants,* pp. 569–570.

61. See especially entries 278017, 278018, and 278173, General Court-Martial Ledger Sheets, Fiscal Year 1945, Box 14, Records of the Office of the Judge Advocate General, Record Group 153, National Archives II, College Park, Md.

62. George S. Patton, Jr., "Notes on France," p. 7, Aug. 18, 1944, Addendum, Box 12, Banning Company Papers, Henry E. Huntington Library, San Marino, Cal.

63. George S. Patton, Jr., "A Few Notes on the Third Army," p. 3, Addendum, Box 12, Banning Company Papers.

64. Patton Diary, Aug. 21, 1944; Patton to Beatrice Ayer Patton, APO 403 New York Aug. 21, 1944, Patton Papers.

65. *New York Times,* Aug. 17, 1944.

66. Gay Diary, Aug. 22, 1944; Patton Diary, Aug. 22, 1944; Bradley and Blair, *General's Life,* p. 310.

67. Gay Diary, Aug. 22, 1944, and Aug. 23, 1944; Patton Diary, Aug. 23, 1944.

68. Gay Diary, Aug. 23, 1944; Patton Diary, Aug. 23, 1944.

69. Gay Diary, Aug. 25, 1944; Patton Diary, Aug. 25, 1944.

70. Gay Diary, Aug. 26, 1944.

71. Notes of Telephone Conversation Between Brigadier General William A. Borden and Major General John S. Wood, pp. 1–3, January 1945, Box 1, John S.

Wood Papers, George Arents Library for Special Collections, E. S. Bird Library, Syracuse University. On German tanks see Blumenson, *Breakout and Pursuit,* pp. 205–206.

72. Patton Diary, Aug. 28, 1944.

73. Ibid.; Basil H. Liddell Hart, "The Liberation of France," II, p. 5, Box 1, Wood Papers.

74. Bradley and Blair, *General's Life,* p. 321; Blumenson, *Breakout and Pursuit,* pp. 690–692.

75. Patton Diary, Aug. 29, 1944.

76. Ibid., Aug. 30, 1944; Liddell Hart, "The Liberation of France," II, p. 50.

77. Patton Diary, Aug. 30, 1944.

78. Reminiscences of Omar N. Bradley with Lieutenant Colonel Charles K. Hanson, Tape One, Interview Two, p. 45, February 1975, Omar N. Bradley Papers, United States Military Academy Archives, West Point.

79. Patton Diary, Aug. 7, 1944.

80. Weaver, *Yankee Doodle Went to Town,* pp. 250–251; Harry C. Butcher, *My Three Years with Eisenhower* (New York: Simon and Schuster, 1946), p. 660; Bradley Reminiscences, p. 45.

81. Bradley Reminiscences, p. 45.

82. Transcript of George S. Patton, Jr., Press Conference, Sept. 7, 1944, p. 10, Box 47, George S. Patton, Jr., Papers, Manuscript Division, Library of Congress.

83. Transcript of George S. Patton, Jr., Press Conference, Sept. 23, 1944, p. 3, Box 47, Patton Papers, Library of Congress.

84. Hugh M. Cole, *The Lorraine Campaign* (Washington, D.C.: Historical Division, Department of the Army, 1950), pp. 2, 20; Blumenson, *Breakout and Pursuit,* pp. 666–668; Patton to Beatrice Ayer Patton, APO 403 New York Aug. 28, 1944, Patton Papers.

85. Patton Diary, Aug. 31, 1944; Blumenson, *Breakout and Pursuit,* pp. 642, 656.

86. Patton Diary, Aug. 31, 1944, and Sept. 1, 1944.

87. Patton to George C. Marshall, APO 403 New York, Sept. 1, 1944, Box 79, George C. Marshall Papers, George C. Marshall Library, Virginia Military Institute, Lexington, Va.

88. Chester Wilmot, "Notes on Conversations with Montgomery," pp. 7–8, CAB 106/1113, Public Record Office, Kew, London.

89. Patton Diary, Sept. 2, 1944.

90. Reminiscences of Brigadier General S. L. A. Marshall, I, p. 13–14, 1974, United States Army Military History Institute, Carlisle Barracks, Pa.

91. Patton Diary, Sept. 3, 1944; Alein Gersten to Frank McCarthy, El Monte, Cal., May 29, 1965, Box 12, Frank McCarthy Papers, George C. Marshall Library, Virginia Military Institute, Lexington, Va.; *New York Times,* Oct. 1, 1944.

CHAPTER FIFTEEN   STUMBLING INTO THE BULGE

1. George S. Patton, Jr., Diary, Sept. 3, 1944, George S. Patton, Jr., Papers, Special Collections, United States Military Academy Library, West Point; Hugh M. Cole,

The Lorraine Campaign (Washington, D.C.: Historical Division, Department of the Army, 1950), p. 52.

2. Bernard Law Montgomery, "Notes on the Campaign in North Western Europe," III, 1–5, Doc. 75/3, Reel 7, Bernard Law Montgomery Papers, Imperial War Museum, London.

3. Ibid.; Omar N. Bradley and Clay Blair, *A General's Life* (New York: Simon and Schuster, 1983), pp. 329–330.

4. Hanson W. Baldwin, "Notes on General Eisenhower," p. 4, April 26, 1946, Series III, Box 101, Hanson W. Baldwin Papers, Yale Manuscripts and Archives, Sterling Memorial Library, Yale University, New Haven, Conn.

5. Baron Ōshima interview with Adolf Hitler and Joachim von Ribbentrop, Sept. 4, 1944, in "Magic" Diplomatic Summaries, Sept. 8, 1944, Box 13, Records of the National Security Agency/Central Security Service, Record Group 457, National Archives II, College Park, Md.

6. Hobart R. "Hap" Gay Diary, Sept. 5, 1944, Hobart R. Gay Papers, Special Collections, United States Military Academy Library, West Point; Cole, *Lorraine Campaign,* pp. 53–54; Patton Diary, Sept. 5, 1944.

7. Gay Diary, Sept. 5, 1944; Bradley and Blair, *General's Life,* p. 325.

8. Patton Diary, Sept. 6, 1944; Gay Diary, Sept. 6, 1944; Cole, *Lorraine Campaign,* p. 63.

9. Patton Diary, Sept. 4, 1944.

10. Transcript of Press Conference, Sept. 7, 1944, Box 47, George S. Patton, Jr., Papers, Manuscript Division, Library of Congress.

11. Gay Diary, Sept. 8, 1944, and Sept. 10, 1944; Patton Diary, Sept. 9, 1944.

12. Patton Diary, Aug. 31, 1944, and Sept. 9, 1944.

13. Reminiscences of General Otto P. Weyland, pp. 14–17, June 1960, Aviation Project, Oral History Research Office, Columbia University Library, New York City; Forrest C. Pogue, *The Supreme Command* (Washington, D.C.: Center of Military History, 1953), pp. 229, 265.

14. Bradley and Blair, *General's Life,* pp. 326–327; Pogue, *Supreme Command,* pp. 278–288.

15. Chester B. Hansen Diary, Sept. 12, 1944, Omar N. Bradley Papers, Special Collections, United States Military Academy Library, West Point; Cole, *Lorraine Campaign,* p. 213.

16. Gay Diary, Sept. 12, 1944; Patton Diary, Sept. 13, 1944.

17. Cole, *Lorraine Campaign,* pp. 84–87, 213, 214.

18. Gay Diary, Sept. 16, 1944; Cole, *Lorraine Campaign,* pp. 214–215; Patton Diary, Sept. 17, 1944.

19. Gay Diary, Sept. 15, 1944; Anthony Kemp, *The Unknown Battle: Metz, 1944* (New York: Stein and Day, 1981), pp. 233–238.

20. Colonel Robert J. Icks, "Metz," March 8, 1953, Box 1, John S. Wood Papers, George Arents Library for Special Collections, E. S. Bird Library, Syracuse University.

21. Cole, *Lorraine Campaign,* pp. 128, 262–264; Icks, "Metz." On Walker's bitterness toward Cole see John Nelson Rickard, *Patton at Bay: The Lorraine Campaign, September to December, 1944* (Westport, Ct.: Praeger, 1999), pp. 136–137.

22. Cole, *Lorraine Campaign,* pp. 263–270; Icks, "Metz."

23. Kemp, *Unknown Battle,* p. 113; Cole, *Lorraine Campaign,* p. 269.

24. Icks, "Metz," *passim;* Cole, *Lorraine Campaign,* pp. 268–269; Gay Diary, Sept. 29, 1944.

25. Basil H. Liddell Hart, "How the Allies Let Victory Slip in 1944," August 8, 1944, pp. 38–39, in CAB 106/1113, Public Record Office, Kew, London.

26. Basil H. Liddell Hart to John S. Wood, n.p., June 4, 1953, File 1/763, Basil H. Liddell Hart Papers, Liddell Hart Centre for Military Archives, King's College, London.

27. Wood to Liddell Hart, Geneva, June 25, 1953, File 1/763, Liddell Hart Papers.

28. Patton Diary, Oct. 7, 1944; Gay Diary, Oct. 8, 1944.

29. Reminiscences of Frank McCarthy, pp. 37–38, July 1969, Box 171, Frank McCarthy Papers, George C. Marshall Library, Virginia Military Institute, Lexington, Va.

30. Michael D. Doubler, *Closing with the Enemy: How GIs Fought the War in Europe, 1944–1945* (Lawrence: University Press of Kansas, 1994), pp. 131–132; Kemp, *Unknown Battle,* pp. 114–116.

31. Patton Diary, Oct. 9, 1944; Kemp, *Unknown Battle,* pp. 123–125; Cole, *Lorraine Campaign,* p. 275; Gay Diary, Oct. 9, 1944.

32. Gay Diary, Oct. 12, 1944; Patton Diary, Oct. 12, 1944; James F. Byrnes, *All in One Lifetime* (New York: Harper & Brothers, 1958), p. 245.

33. Byrnes, *All in One Lifetime,* p. 246.

34. Reminiscences of General William H. Simpson, pp. 61–63, March 15, 1972, Oral History Research Office, Columbia University Library, New York City.

35. Bernard S. Carter to Louise Hope Thacher Carter, APO 403 New York, Oct. 23, 1944, and Oct. 29, 1944, Box 2, Bernard S. Carter Papers, Special Collection, United States Military Academy Library, West Point.

36. Patton Diary, Oct. 17, 1944.

37. Gay Diary, Sept. 19, 1944; Sept. 20, 1944; Sept. 23, 1944; and Sept. 29, 1944.

38. Patton Diary, Oct. 19, 1944; Cole, *Lorraine Campaign,* p. 300.

39. Carlo D'Este, *Decision in Normandy* (New York: E. P. Dutton, 1983), pp. 468–469.

40. Gay Diary, Oct. 22, 1944; Patton Diary, Oct. 22, 1944.

41. Cole, *Lorraine Campaign,* p. 258; Doubler, *Closing with the Enemy,* pp. 134–135; Patton to Arvin H. Brown, APO 403 New York, Oct. 25, 1944, Box 43, George S. Patton, Sr., Papers, Henry E. Huntington Library, San Marino, California; Gay Diary, Nov. 1, 1944, and Nov. 7, 1944; Bradley and Blair, *General's Life,* p. 342.

42. Hansen Diary, Oct. 22, 1944, Oct. 30, 1944, and Nov. 2, 1944; Patton Diary, Oct. 31, 1944.

43. Patton Diary, Nov. 4, 1944; Patton to Beatrice Ayer Patton, APO 403 New York, Nov. 6, 1944, Patton Papers.

44. Patton to Beatrice Ayer Patton, APO 403 New York, Nov. 7, 1944, and Nov. 8, 1944, Patton Papers; Patton Diary, Nov. 5, 1944.

45. Patton to Beatrice Ayer Patton, APO 403 New York, Nov. 8, 1944, Patton Papers.

46. Patton Diary, Nov. 8, 1944; Gay Diary, Nov. 8, 1944; Cole, *Lorraine Campaign,* pp. 321–324, 372–373.

47. Patton Diary, Nov. 9, 1944; Rickard, *Patton at Bay,* pp. 177–179.

48. Gay Diary, Nov. 11, 1944, and Nov. 12, 1944; Cole, *Lorraine Campaign,* pp. 391–394.

49. Gay Diary, Nov. 13, 1944, and Nov. 16, 1944.

50. Pogue, *Supreme Command,* p. 317; Bradley and Blair, *General's Life,* pp. 341–343; Russell F. Weigley, *Eisenhower's Lieutenants: The Campaign of France and Germany, 1944–1945* (Bloomington: Indiana University Press, 1981), pp. 364–365, 416–420.

51. Gay Diary, Nov. 17, 1944, and Nov. 18, 1944; Cole, *Lorraine Campaign,* pp. 323, 452.

52. A. Harding Ganz, "Patton's Relief of General Wood," *Journal of Military History* 53 (July 1989): 265–266.

53. Gay Diary, Nov. 18, 1944; Cole, *Lorraine Campaign,* p. 458; Ganz, "Patton's Relief of General Wood," p. 266.

54. Gay Diary, Nov. 19, 1944. Patton's letter to Wood is attached to Gay's diary entry.

55. Ibid., Nov. 20, 1944; Patton Diary, Nov. 20, 1944.

56. Gay Diary, Nov. 21, 1944, Nov. 22, 1944, Nov. 23, 1944, and Nov. 24, 1944.

57. W. Averell Harriman and Elie Abel, *Special Envoy to Churchill and Stalin, 1941–1946* (New York: Random House, 1975), pp. 373–374; Field Marshal Viscount Alanbrooke Diary, Nov. 24, 1944, Field Marshal Viscount Alanbrooke Papers, Liddell Hart Centre for Military Archives, King's College, London.

58. Weyland Reminiscences, p. 22.

59. Joseph Balkoski, "Patton's 3rd Army: The Lorraine Campaign, 8 Nov.–1 Dec. '44," *Strategy and Tactics,* n.v. (January–February 1980): 10.

60. Weyland Reminiscences, pp. 23–25.

61. Bernard Carter to Louise Carter, APO 403 New York, Nov. 23, 1944, and Nov. 25, 1944, Box 1, Carter Papers.

62. Gay Diary, Nov. 26, 1944; Harriman and Abel, *Special Envoy to Churchill and Stalin,* p. 374; Patton Diary, Nov. 27, 1944.

63. Ganz, "Patton's Relief of General Wood," pp. 270–271; Gay Diary, Dec. 1, 1944.

64. Patton Diary, Dec. 3, 1944.

65. Reminiscences of Brigadier General S. L. A. Marshall, Tape 2, Interview 3, p. 40, Nov. 12, 1973, United States Army Military History Institute, Carlisle Barracks, Pa.

66. Ganz, "Patton's Relief of General Wood," p. 272.

67. Wood to Baldwin, Reno, Jan. 7, 1965, File 1/763, Liddell Hart Papers.

68. Note by General George S. Patton IV attached to Patton Diary, Nov. 18, 1944.

69. Reminiscences of General Jacob L. Devers, pp. 91, 92, 94, Nov. 18, 1974, Dwight D. Eisenhower Library, Abilene, Kansas.

70. Bradford S. Chynoweth to Sidney R. Hinds, Berkeley, Jan. 10, 1972, Box 2, Bradford S. Chynoweth Papers, United States Army Military History Institute, Carlisle Barracks, Pa.

71. Patton to George C. Marshall, Hqs. 3rd Army, Dec. 5, 1944, Box 79, George C. Marshall Papers, George C. Marshall Library, Virginia Military Institute, Lexington, Va; Patton to Gilbert R. Cook, APO 403 New York, Dec. 10, 1944, Box 3, Gilbert R. Cook Papers, Dwight D. Eisenhower Library, Abilene, Kansas.

72. See Alden Hatch, *Ambassador Extraordinary: Clare Boothe Luce* (New York: Henry Holt, 1956), pp. 168–169.

73. Gay Diary, Dec. 6, 1944.

74. Patton Diary, Dec. 6, 1944.

75. Ibid., Dec. 6, 1944, and Dec. 7, 1944.

76. Gay Diary, Dec. 12, 1944, and Dec. 13, 1944; Patton Diary, Dec. 9, 1944.

77. Gay Diary, Dec. 10, 1944, and Dec. 13, 1944; Patton Diary, Dec. 10, 1944; George S. Patton, Jr., "Notes on Bastogne Operations," p. 1, Box 4, Patton Papers.

78. Weyland Reminiscences, pp. 19–21.

79. Reminiscences of General Paul D. Harkins, pp. 28–30, April 28, 1974, United States Army Military History Institute, Carlisle Barracks.

80. Gay Diary, Nov. 12, 1944; Weigley, *Eisenhower's Lieutenants,* p. 420.

81. Weigley, *Eisenhower's Lieutenants,* pp. 416–420; Wood to Liddell Hart, Reno, Dec. 26, 1963, File 1/763, Liddell Hart Papers.

82. Gay Diary, Nov. 25, 1944; Patton Diary, Nov. 25, 1944.

83. Benjamin A. Dickson, "G-2 Journal: Algiers to the Elbe," pp. 169–170, Benjamin A. Dickson Papers, Special Collections, United States Military Academy Library, West Point.

84. Ibid., p. 176.

85. Pogue, *Supreme Command,* pp. 366–370.

86. Dickson, "G-2 Journal," pp. 171–172; Pogue, *Supreme Command,* p. 370.

87. Dickson, "G-2 Journal," pp. 171–172.

88. Ibid., pp. 186–187.

89. Bradley and Blair, *General's Life,* pp. 353–354; Ladislas Farago, *Patton: Ordeal and Triumph* (New York: Ivan Obolensky, 1964), pp. 695–698.

90. Patton Diary, Dec. 16, 1944; Gay Diary, Dec. 16, 1944.

91. Patton Diary, Dec. 17, 1944.

92. Farago, *Patton,* pp. 703–704.

93. Weyland Reminiscences, pp. 24–25.

94. Gay Diary, Dec. 18, 1944.

CHAPTER SIXTEEN   HITS AND ERRORS

1. George S. Patton, Jr., Diary, Dec. 18, 1944, George S. Patton, Jr., Papers, Special Collections, United States Military Academy Library, West Point.

2. Hobart R. "Hap" Gay Diary, Dec. 18, 1944, Hobart R. Gay Papers, Special Collections, United States Military Academy Library, West Point; George S. Patton, Jr., "Notes on Bastogne Operation," pp. 2–3, Box 4, Gilbert R. Cook Papers, Dwight D. Eisenhower Library, Abilene, Kansas; Albin F. Irzyk, "Bastogne: A Fascinating Vignette," *Armor* 95 (March–April 1986): 26.

3. Gay Diary, Dec. 18, 1944. It will be remembered that Churchill talked about the March drive when told that the Germans had broken through French lines in 1940.

4. Patton, "Notes on Bastogne Operation," pp. 2–3, 11; Reminiscences of Karl R. Bendetsen, pp. 129–130, Oct. 24, 1972, Oral History Collection, Harry S. Truman Library, Independence, Mo.

5. Reminiscences of General Anthony C. McAuliffe, p. 121, 1963, Oral History Research Office, Columbia University Library, New York City; Patton Diary, Dec. 19, 1944; Reminiscences of General Paul D. Harkins, pp. 28–30, April 28, 1974, United States Army Military History Institute, Carlisle Barracks, Pa.

6. Gay Diary, Dec. 19, 1944.

7. Harkins Reminiscences, pp. 29–31; Patton Diary, Dec. 20, 1944.

8. Patton Diary, Dec. 20, 1944; Omar N. Bradley and Clay Blair, *A General's Life* (New York: Simon and Schuster, 1983), pp. 362–365; Trevor N. Dupuy, David L. Bongard, and Richard C. Anderson, Jr., *Hitler's Last Gamble: The Battle of the Bulge, December 1944–January 1945* (New York: HarperCollins, 1994), pp. 201–202.

9. Patton Diary, Dec. 20, 1944; Oscar W. Koch with Robert G. Hays, *G-2: Intelligence for Patton* (Philadelphia: Whitmore Publishing Company, 1971), p. 106.

10. Irzyk, "Bastogne," pp. 25–26.

11. Ibid., pp. 26–28.

12. Ibid., pp. 29–30; Patton Diary, Dec. 20, 1944; Gay Diary, Dec. 20, 1944.

13. Patton Diary, Dec. 21, 1944; Nigel Hamilton, *Monty: Final Years of the Field Marshal, 1944–1976* (New York: McGraw-Hill, 1987), pp. 222–228, 308–309.

14. Patton Diary, Dec. 22, 1944; Gay Diary, Dec. 22, 1944; Chester B. Hansen Diary, Dec. 20, 1944, and Dec. 22, 1944, Omar N. Bradley Papers, Special Collections, United States Military Academy Library, West Point.

15. Patton Diary, Dec. 20, 1944; Reminiscences of Lieutenant General John W. Leonard, pp. 50–53, Nov. 5, 1972, Dwight D. Eisenhower Library, Abilene, Kansas.

16. Reminiscences of General Otto P. Weyland, pp. 25–26, 1960, Oral History Research Office, Columbia University Library, New York City; Wesley Frank Craven

and James Lea Cate (eds.), *The Army Air Forces in World War II* (Washington, D.C.: Office of Air Force History, 1983), III, p. 686.

17. Weyland Reminiscences, p. 26; Patton Diary, Dec. 23, 1944.

18. Dupuy, et al., *Hitler's Last Gamble,* pp. 221–222; Bernard Law Montgomery, "Notes on the Campaign in North-Western Europe, 19 December 1944 to 18 January 1945," p. 3, Reel 7, Bernard Law Montgomery Papers, Imperial War Museum, London.

19. Montgomery, "Notes on the Campaign in North-Western Europe," pp. 4–5.

20. Patton Diary, Dec. 25, 1944; Chester Wilmot, "Notes on Conversations with Montgomery," May 18, 1946, p. 10, and March 29, 1949, p. 18, CAB 106/1113, Public Record Office, Kew, London; Hansen Diary, April 12, 1945, Bradley Papers.

21. McAuliffe Reminiscences, pp. 130–131.

22. Ibid., pp. 146–147.

23. Frank S. Johnson, "The Battle of the Bulge Foreshadowed," *Military Review* 75 (December 1994): 112.

24. Gay Diary, Dec. 25, 1944.

25. Dupuy, et al., *Hitler's Last Gamble,* pp. 228–229; Patton Diary, Dec. 26, 1944; McAuliffe Reminiscences, p. 130.

26. Patton, "Notes on Bastogne Operation," pp. 5–6.

27. George S. Patton, Jr., to Thomas T. Handy, Headquarters Third Army, Feb. 6, 1945, Thomas T. Handy Papers, George C. Marshall Library, Virginia Military Institute, Lexington, Va.

28. Dupuy, et al., *Hitler's Last Gamble,* pp. 273–274; Patton Diary, Dec. 26, 1944; Hugh M. Cole, *The Ardennes: Battle of the Bulge* (Washington, D.C.: Center of Military History, 1965), p. 611; Sir Brian Horrocks with Eversley Belfield and Major-General H. Essame, *Corps Commander* (London: Sedgwick & Jackson), 1977), pp. 158, 168.

29. Patton Diary, Dec. 27, 1944; Cole, *Ardennes,* p. 611; Dupuy, et al., *Hitler's Last Gamble,* pp. 274–275.

30. Gay Diary, Dec. 29, 1944; Cole, *Ardennes,* pp. 612–613, 617.

31. Reminiscences of Brigadier General S. L. A. Marshall, I, pp. 13–14, 1974, United States Army Military History Institute, Carlisle Barracks, Pa.

32. Gay Diary, Dec. 30, 1944.

33. Cole, *Ardennes,* p. 647.

34. Charles Sawyer, *Concerns of a Conservative Democrat* (Carbondale and Edwardsville: Southern Illinois University Press, 1968), p. 126; Gay Diary, Feb. 10, 1945.

35. Marshall Reminiscences, I, p. 13.

36. S. L. A. Marshall, *Bringing Up the Rear* (San Rafael, Cal.: Presidio Press, 1979), pp. 133–134.

37. Bernard S. Carter to Louise Hope Thacher Carter, APO 403 New York, May 12, 1944, Box 3, Bernard S. Carter Papers, Special Collections, United States Military Academy Library, West Point.

38. Gay Diary, Dec. 31, 1944; Patton Diary, Jan. 1, 1945; Reminiscences of Lieutenant General James H. Doolittle, pp. 44–45, Sept. 26, 1971, United States Air

Force Academy Library, Boulder, Colo., copy in Oral History Research Office, Columbia University Library, New York City.

39. Gay Diary, Jan. 1, 1945.

40. Ibid., Jan. 3, 1945.

41. Ibid., Jan. 4, 1945.

42. Ibid., Jan. 5, 1945.

43. Patton Diary, Jan. 4, 1945; Cole *Ardennes,* pp. 621, 647.

44. Cole, *Ardennes,* pp. 260–264. See also James J. Weingartner, *Crossroads of Death: The Story of the Malmédy Massacre and Trial* (Berkeley: University of California Press, 1979).

45. Fred Ayer Memorandum, December 1945, Miscellaneous Box, George S. Patton, Jr., Papers, Special Collections, United States Military Academy Library, West Point.

46. Gay Diary, Jan. 6, 1945, and Jan. 7, 1945.

47. Ibid., Jan. 8, 1945, and Jan. 9, 1945.

48. Ibid., Jan. 9, 1945, and Jan. 10, 1945; Charles B. MacDonald, *The Last Offensive* (Washington, D.C.: Office of the Chief of Military History, 1973), pp. 40–41.

49. Gay Diary, Jan. 11, 1945, and Jan. 12, 1945.

50. Dupuy, et al., *Hitler's Last Gamble,* p. 342; MacDonald, *Last Offensive,* p. 43.

51. Patton Diary, Jan. 18, 1945.

52. Gay Diary, Jan. 18, 1945.

53. Patton Diary, Jan. 19, 1945; MacDonald, *Last Offensive,* p. 116.

54. Gay Diary, Jan. 22, 1945; Patton to Beatrice Ayer Patton, APO 403 New York, Jan. 24, 1945, Patton Papers.

55. Gay Diary, Jan. 22, 1945; MacDonald, *Last Offensive,* p. 119.

56. Gay Diary, Jan. 23, 1945; Patton Diary, Jan. 24, 1945.

57. Gay Diary, Jan. 24, 1945; Patton Diary, Jan. 24, 1945.

58. MacDonald, *Last Offensive,* pp. 60–67; Gay Diary, Jan. 27, 1945.

59. Montgomery, "Notes on Campaign in North-Western Europe," pp. 3–5; Harry C. Butcher Diary, Jan. 27, 1945, Box 169, Dwight D. Eisenhower Pre-Presidential Papers, Dwight D. Eisenhower Library, Abilene, Kansas.

60. Gay Diary, Jan. 29, 1945.

61. Ibid., Feb. 1, 1945.

62. Gay Diary, Feb. 2, 1945; Patton Diary, Feb. 2, 1945, and Feb. 3, 1945.

63. Gay Diary, Feb. 5, 1945; Patton to Beatrice Ayer Patton, APO 403 New York, Feb. 6, 1945, Patton Papers.

64. MacDonald, *Last Offensive,* p. 100.

65. Ibid., pp. 101–103; Gay Diary, Feb. 7, 1945; Patton Diary, Feb. 7, 1945.

66. Gay Diary, Feb. 9, 1945; Patton Diary, Feb. 10, 1945.

67. Patton Diary, Feb. 13, 1945; Patton to Beatrice Ayer Patton, APO 403 New York, Feb. 14, 1945, Patton Papers.

68. Patton Diary, Feb. 12, 1945, and Feb. 14, 1945.

69. Harkins Reminiscences, pp. 34–35.

70. Ibid., p. 35; *New York Journal-American,* June 2, 1951.

71. Patton Diary, Feb. 16, 1945.

72. Gay Diary, Feb. 19, 1945; Patton Diary, Feb. 19, 1945; MacDonald, *Last Offensive,* p. 127.

73. Gay Diary, Feb. 20, 1945; MacDonald, *Last Offensive,* pp. 128–129.

74. Patton Diary, Feb. 21, 1945; Gay Diary, Feb. 21, 1945.

75. Gay Diary, Feb. 22, 1945; Patton Diary, Feb. 23, 1945.

76. Patton Diary, Feb. 25, 1945; Gay Diary, Feb. 25, 1945.

77. Patton Diary, Feb. 27, 1945.

78. Gay Diary, Dec. 21, 1944, Dec. 24, 1944, and Dec. 26, 1944.

79. James T. Quirk to His Wife, n.p., Jan. 25, 1945, James T. Quirk Papers, Harry S. Truman Library, Independence, Mo.

80. Hansen Diary, Feb. 22, 1945.

81. Quirk to His Wife, n.p., Feb. 27, 1945, Quirk Papers.

82. Gay Diary, Feb. 16, 1945; Harry C. Butcher, *My Three Years with Eisenhower* (New York: Simon and Schuster, 1946), pp. 773–774.

83. Gay Diary, Feb. 27, 1945; Butcher, *My Three Years with Eisenhower,* pp. 774–775.

84. Butcher, *My Three Years with Eisenhower,* pp. 793, 796–797, 801; Bruce Bairnsfather, *Carry On Sergeant* (Indianapolis: Bobbs-Merrill, 1927), *passim.*

85. Paul R. Allerup, "Patton's Army: Soldiers Were Proud of Outfit," *Los Angeles Times,* Jan. 23, 1973.

86. Patton Diary, Feb. 28, 1945; Roger H. Nye, *The Patton Mind: The Professional Development of an Extraordinary Leader* (Garden City Park, N.Y.: Avery Publishing Group, 1993), pp. 6–7; Roger H. Nye to Ruth Ellen Patton Totten, Highland Falls, N.Y., Nov. 17, 1990, Box 3, Roger H. Nye Papers, Special Collections, United States Military Academy Library, West Point.

87. Patton Diary, March 1, 1945; Patton to Beatrice Ayer Patton, APO 403 New York, March 1, 1945, Patton Papers.

88. Gay Diary, March 3, 1945; Fred Ayer, Jr., to His Family, n.p., March 8, 1945, Miscellaneous Box, Patton Papers; MacDonald, *Last Offensive,* pp. 156–162.

89. Gay Diary, March 4, 1945; MacDonald, *Last Offensive,* pp. 115, 196–197.

90. Gay Diary, March 5, 1945, and March 6, 1945.

91. Ibid., March 6, 1945, and March 7, 1945; Patton Diary, March 7, 1945; George E. Martin, *Blow, Bugle, Blow* (Bradenton, Fla.: Opuscula, 1986), pp. 154–155.

92. Patton Diary, March 13, 1945; Henry J. Taylor, *Men and Power* (New York: Dodd, Mead, 1946), pp. 14, 170–171.

93. Gay Diary, March 9, 1945.

94. Ibid., March 10, 1945.

95. Ibid., March 11, 1945, and March 13, 1945.

96. Taylor, *Men and Power,* p. 156.

97. Ibid., 172.

98. Ibid., 169–170.

99. Gay Diary, March 11, 1945, March 13, 1945, and March 14, 1945.

100. Ibid., March 16, 1945. Major General Patton's comment accompanies Gay Diary, March 17, 1945.

101. Gay Diary., March 17, 1945.

102. Ibid., March 18, 1945; MacDonald, *Last Offensive*, pp. 269–270.

103. Gay Diary, March 19, 1945, and March 20, 1945; Patton Diary, March 20, 1945.

104. Gay Diary, March 20, 1945.

CHAPTER SEVENTEEN   "HAVEN'T YOU LEARNED NOT TO TAKE THIS MAN SERIOUSLY?"

1. Hobart R. "Hap" Gay Diary, March 22, 1945, and March 23, 1945, Hobart R. Gay Papers, United States Military Academy Library, West Point; George S. Patton, Jr., Diary, March 21, 1945, George S. Patton, Jr., Papers, Special Collections, United States Military Academy Library, War Point; John Toland, *The Last 100 Days* (New York: Random House, 1966), p. 259.

2. Patton Diary, March 24, 1945; Gay Diary, March 23, 1945, and March 24, 1945.

3. Patton Diary, March 24, 1945. On the Seine incident see William G. Weaver, *Yankee Doodle Went to Town* (Ann Arbor, Mich.: Edwards Brothers, 1959), pp. 108, 237.

4. James T. Quirk to His Wife, n.p., April 1, 1945, James T. Quirk Papers, Harry S. Truman Library, Independence, Mo.

5. Margaret Bourke-White, *"Dear Fatherland, Rest Quietly": A Report on the Collapse of Hitler's "Thousand Years"* (New York: Simon and Schuster, 1946), pp. 19–31; Quirk to His Wife, n.p., March 29, 1945, Quirk Papers.

6. Quirk to His Wife, n.p., March 29, 1945, Quirk Papers.

7. Patton Diary, March 26, 1945; Gay Diary, March 25, 1945.

8. George S. Patton, Jr., to Beatrice Ayer Patton, APO 403 New York, March 29, 1945, Patton Papers.

9. Gay Diary, Feb. 9, 1945.

10. Harry C. Butcher, *My Three Years with Eisenhower* (New York: Simon and Schuster, 1946), p. 273; Patton to Beatrice Ayer Patton, APO 403 New York, March 29, 1945, Patton Papers.

11. Richard Baron, Abe Baum, and Richard Goldhurst, *Raid! The Untold Story of Patton's Secret Mission* (New York: G. P. Putnam's Sons, 1981), pp. 6–7; *Time* 45 (April 9, 1945); 36; Patton Diary, March 25, 1945; Gay Diary, March 25, 1945; Forrest C. Pogue, *The Supreme Command* (Washington, D.C.: Center of Military History, 1954), p. 424.

12. *Star,* Nov. 15, 1981, in Patton Clippings, Patton Papers; Baron, et al. Raid!, pp. 8–14.

13. Robert Slater, *Warrior Statesman: The Life of Moshe Dayan* (New York: St. Martin's Press, 1991), pp. 91–92.

14. Gay Diary, April 4, 1945; Patton Diary, April 4, 1945; Lieutenant Colonel Frederick E. Oldinsky, "Patton and the Hammelburg Mission," *Armor* 85 (July–August 1976); 13–14; Russell F. Weigley, *Eisenhower's Lieutenants* (Bloomington: Indiana University Press, 1981), p. 655.

15. *Star,* Dec. 22, 1981, in Patton Clippings, Patton Papers.

16. Oldinsky, "Patton and the Hammelburg Mission," p. 18.

17. Charles B. MacDonald, *The Last Offensive* (Washington, D.C.: Office of the Chief of Military History, 1973), pp. 418–419.

18. Reminiscences of Omar N. Bradley, pp. 15–16, Feb. 28, 1975, Omar N. Bradley Papers, United States Military Academy Archives, West Point.

19. *War Reports: A Record of Dispatches Broadcast by the BBC's War Correspondents with the Allied Expeditionary Force, June 6, 1944–May 5, 1945* (London: Oxford University Press, 1946), p. 356.

20. *Time* 45 (April 9, 1945): 33.

21. Gay Diary, April 5, 1945.

22. Ibid., April 4, 1945, and April 5, 1945.

23. Ibid., April 4, 1945; Patton Diary, April 5, 1945.

24. Reminiscences of Bernard Bernstein, p. 113, July 23, 1975, Oral History Project, Harry S. Truman Library, Independence, Mo.

25. Ibid., 114–117.

26. Gay Diary, April 10, 1945.

27. Ibid., April 11, 1945.

28. Bernstein Reminiscences, pp. 118–121.

29. Ibid., pp. 120–121.

30. Ibid., pp. 122–124.

31. Gay Diary, April 12, 1945.

32. Ibid., April 12, 1945, and April 13, 1945.

33. Ibid., April 12, 1945; Patton Diary, April 12, 1945.

34. Patton to Dwight D. Eisenhower, Hqs. 3rd Army, April 15, 1945, Box 91, Dwight D. Eisenhower Pre-Presidential Papers, Dwight D. Eisenhower Library, Abilene, Kansas; Gay Diary, April 14, 1945.

35. Quirk to His Wife, n.p., April 18, 1945, Box 1, Quirk Papers.

36. Quirk to His Wife, n.p., April 20, 1945, Quirk Papers.

37. Patton Diary, April 17, 1945, and April 18, 1945.

38. Everett S. Hughes Diary, April 17, 1945, Box 2, Everett S. Hughes Papers, Manuscript Division, Library of Congress; Patton to Beatrice Ayer Patton, APO 403 New York, March 31, 1945, Patton Papers.

39. Hughes Diary, April 18, 1945.

40. Bernard S. Carter to Louise Hope Thacher Carter, APO 887 New York, April 21, 1945, Box 3, Bernard S. Carter Papers, Special Collections, United States Military Academy Library, West Point.

41. Patton to George C. Marshall, APO 403 New York, March 1, 1945, Box 79, George C. Marshall Papers, George C. Marshall Library, Virginia Military Institute, Lexington, Va.

42. Patton to Gilbert R. Cook, APO 403 New York, April 23, 1945, Box 4, Gilbert R. Cook Papers, Dwight D. Eisenhower Library, Abilene, Kansas; Cook to Patton, Washington, D.C., May 3, 1945, Box 4, Cook Papers.

43. Patton to Cook, APO 403 New York, April 19, 1945, Box 4, Cook Papers.

44. Patton to John S. Wood, Hqs. 3rd Army, May 4, 1945, Box 2, John S. Wood Papers, George Arents Library for Special Collections, E. S. Bird Library, Syracuse University.

45. Holmes E. Dager to Wood, somewhere in Germany, April 20, 1945, and April 21, 1945, Box 1, Wood Papers.

46. Creighton W. Abrams to Wood, somewhere in Germany, May 1, 1945, Box 1, Wood Papers.

47. Gay Diary, April 18, 1945.

48. Ibid., April 19, 1945.

49. Ibid., April 24, 1945; Robert Paul Browder and Thomas G. Smith, *Independent: A Biography of Lewis W. Douglas* (New York: Alfred A. Knopf, 1986), pp. 230–231; Patton to Beatrice Ayer Patton, APO 403 New York, April 25, 1945, Patton Papers.

50. Gay Diary, May 4, 1945.

51. Joseph S. Roucek, "General Patton's Stopped Invasion of Czechoslovakia and the Role of Vlasev," *Ukrainian Quarterly* 13 (June 1957): 114–119; Quirk to His Wife, n.p., May 7, 1945, Quirk Papers.

52. Quirk to His Wife, n.p., May 7, 1945, Quirk Papers.

53. Quirk to His Wife, n.p., May 7, 1945, and May 8, 1945, Quirk Papers.

54. Quirk to His Wife, n.p., May 8, 1945, Quirk Papers.

55. Ibid. See also Larry G. Newman, "Gen. Patton's Premonition," *American Legion Magazine* 73 (July 1962): 12–13, 34.

56. David Sanders, *John Hersey* (New York: Twayne, 1967), pp. 34–37; David Sanders, *John Hersey Revisited* (Boston: Twayne, 1987), pp. 8–9.

57. Beverley M. Bowie and Volkmar Wentzel, "The White Horses of Vienna," *National Geographic Magazine* 114 (September 1958): 401–409; J. J. Hanlin, "The General and the Horses," *American Legion Magazine* 74 (February 1963): 22–23, 43; Patton Diary, May 7, 1945; Henry Morganthau III, *Mostly Morganthau: A Family History* (New York: Ticknor & Fields, 1991), pp. 409–410.

58. Reminiscences of General Anthony C. McAuliffe, p. 150, July 15, 1963, Oral History Research Office, Columbia University Library, New York City.

59. Ibid., 153.

60. Patton to Cook, APO 403 New York, May 15, 1945, Box 4, Cook Papers; Cook to Major General Stephen J. Chamberlin, n.p., June 2, 1945, Box 3, Cook Papers.

61. Henry C. McLean Diary, June 22, 1945, Henry C. McLean Papers, Special Collections, United States Military Academy Library, West Point; Quirk to His Wife, n.p., May 20, 1945, Quirk Papers.

62. Chamberlain to Cook, APO 500, July 8, 1945, Box 3, Cook Papers.

63 Patton Diary, May 2, 1945; Bernard Carter to Louise Carter, APO 887 New York, May 12, 1945, Box 3, Carter Papers.

64. Alden Hatch, *The Wadsworths of the Genesee* (New York: Coward-McCann, 1959), p. 273.

65. Frederick Ayer, "Various and Sundry Memos Concerning Standing of G.S.P. and Other Miscellaneous Data," pp. 3–4, Dec. 27, 1945, Miscellaneous Box, Patton Papers; Patton Diary, May 14, 1945; Bernard Carter to Louise Carter, APO 887 New York, May 12, 1945, Carter Papers; Stephanie Mansfield, *The Richest Girl in the World: The Extravagant Life and Fast Times of Doris Duke* (New York: G. P. Putnam's Sons, 1992), pp. 83, 87, 180–182.

66. Bernard Carter to Louise Carter, APO 887 New York, May 28, 1945, Carter Papers.

67. Patton Diary, May 16, 1945.

68. Ibid., May 17, 1945, and May 18, 1945.

69. Quirk to His Wife, n.p., June 5, 1945, Quirk Papers.

70. Hughes Diary, June 5, 1945, and June 7, 1945.

71. *Time* 45 (June 18, 1945): 15; *Newsweek* 25 (June 18, 1945): 30–31.

72. Reminiscences of Lieutenant General James H. Doolittle, pp. 46–48, Sept. 26, 1971, United States Air Force Academy Library, Boulder, Colo., copy in Oral History Research Office, Columbia University Library, New York City.

73. *Newsweek* 25 (June 18, 1945): 31; *Time* 45 (June 25, 1945): 19.

74. Frank McCarthy to Marshall, Washington, D.C. June 12, 1945, Box 79, Marshall Papers.

75. Henry L. Stimson Diary, June 13, 1945, Henry L. Stimson Papers, Sterling Memorial Library, Yale University, New Haven, Ct.

76. Ibid., June 14, 1945. For the press conference see *New York Times,* June 15, 1945.

77. Frederick Ayer to Hanson W. Baldwin, Boston, Jan. 18, 1962, Series I, Box 1, Hanson W. Baldwin Papers, Sterling Memorial Library, Yale University, New Haven, Ct.

78. Hughes Diary, July 29, 1945.

79. *New York Times,* June 23, 1945.

80. *New York Times,* June 27, 1945.

81. Quirk to His Wife, Paris, June 22, 1945, Quirk Papers.

82. Reminiscences of R. Jay Thomas, pp. 210–213, 1957, Oral History Research Office, Columbia University Library, New York City.

83. Hughes Diary, July 4, 1945.

84. Patton to Beatrice Ayer Patton, n.p., July 17, 1918, Patton Papers; *National Cyclopedia of American Biography,* vol. XXXII (New York: James T. White, 1945), pp. 342–343.

85. Stimson Diary, July 20, 1945; David Marcus to His Wife, Berlin, July 20, 1945, Box 2, David Marcus Papers, Special Collections, United States Military Academy Library, West Point.

86. Memorandum of Stimson on Potsdam Conference, p. 36, July 21, 1945, Reel 128, Stimson Papers.

87. Memorandum of Stimson on Potsdam Conference, pp. 50–54, July 25, 1945, to July 27, 1945, Reel 128, Stimson Papers.

88. Patton to Beatrice Ayer Patton, APO 403 New York, May 24, 1945, Patton Papers; Memorandum of Stimson on Potsdam Conference, pp. 52–53, July 25, 1945, and July 26, 1945, Reel 128, Stimson Papers; Hughes Diary, July 28, 1945.

89. Memorandum of Stimson on Potsdam Conference, p. 55, July 26, 1945, Reel 128, Stimson Papers; Reminiscences of Harvey H. Bundy, p. 288, 1961, Oral History Research Office, Columbia University Library, New York City.

90. Patton to Beatrice Ayer Patton, APO 403 New York, August 8, 1945, Patton Papers.

91. Patton to Beatrice Ayer Patton, APO 403 New York, August 10, 1945, Patton Papers; Patton Diary, Aug. 8, 1945.

92. Patton to Beatrice Ayer Patton, APO 403 New York, August 10, 1945, Patton Papers.

93. Joseph McBride, *Frank Capra: The Catastrophe of Success* (New York: Simon and Schuster, 1992), p. 496.

CHAPTER EIGHTEEN   HEADLONG TOWARD DISASTER

1. Walter L. Dorn, "The Debate Over American Occupation Policy in Germany in 1944–1945," p. 1, n.d., Box 16, Walter L. Dorn Papers, Special Collections, Columbia University Library, New York City; Paul W. Gulgowski, *The American Military Government of United States Occupied Zones of Post World War II Germany in Relation to Policies Expressed by Its Civilian Governmental Authorities at Home During the Course of 1944/45 Through 1949* (Frankfurt am Main: Haag & Herchen, 1983), pp. 30–33.

2. George S. Patton, Jr., Diary, Aug. 18, 1945, George S. Patton, Jr., Papers, Special Collections, United States Military Academy Library, West Point.

3. George S. Patton, Jr., "Memorandum on Military Government," pp. 4–5, n.d., in Patton 201 File, Box 47, George S. Patton, Jr., Papers, Manuscript Division, Library of Congress; Keith Merrill, Untitled Paper Prepared at Frankfurt, Nov. 1, 1945, Box 5, Patton Papers.

4. Reminiscences of General Bruce C. Clarke, p. 113, Jan. 14, 1970, Oral History Collection, Harry S. Truman Library, Independence, Mo.

5. Walter L. Dorn, "Minister President Friedrich Schaeffer and the Tardy De-Nazification of the Bavarian Government," pp. 1–2, Oct. 2, 1945, File 000.1, Box 1, Records of the United States Forces European Theater, Secretary of the General Staff, Record Group 338, National Archives II, College Park, Md. See also John Gimbel, *The American Occupation of Germany: Politics and the Military, 1945–1949* (Stanford, Cal.: Stanford University Press, 1968), pp. 37, 82; Vera Franke Eliasberg, "Political Party Developments," in Gabriel A. Almond (ed.), *The Struggle for Democracy in Germany* (Chapel Hill: University of North Carolina Press, 1949), pp. 221–280; Earl F. Ziemke, *The U.S. Army in the Occupation of Germany* (Washington, D.C.: Center for Military History, 1975), pp. 384–385.

6. *PM,* May 31, 1945, and June 11, 1945, in Pierre M. Purves Collection, Patton Papers. In his report on Schaeffer, Dr. Dorn noted that after Fischer had been removed as minister of the interior, Schaeffer tried to get him the post of governing president of Northern Bavaria.

7. Patton to Dwight D. Eisenhower, Headquarters, Third Army, Aug. 11, 1945, File 000.1, Box 1, Records of the United States Forces European Theater, Secretary of the General Staff; Eisenhower to Patton, n.p., August 25, 1945, File 000.1, Box 1, Records of the United States Force European Theater, Secretary of the General Staff.

8. Patton Diary, Aug. 27, 1945; Patton to Beatrice Ayer Patton, APO 403 New York, Aug. 31, 1945, Patton Papers; Ziemke, *U.S. Army in the Occupation of Germany,* p. 384.

9. Patton to Henry L. Stimson, Third Army Headquarters, Aug. 31, 1945, and Sept. 1, 1945, Reel 113, Henry L. Stimson Papers, Sterling Memorial Library, Yale University, New Haven, Ct.

10. Robert P. Patterson to Patton, n.p., Sept. 10, 1945, Box 21, Robert P. Patterson Papers, Manuscript Division, Library of Congress.

11. Patton to Patterson, APO 403 New York, Sept. 21, 1945, Box 21, Patterson Papers.

12. Walter L. Dorn, "The Unfinished Purge of Germany: A Critical Study of Allied De-Nazification Policy," chapter 8, p. 22, unpublished manuscript, Box 13, Dorn Papers.

13. Ladislas Farago, *The Last Days of Patton* (New York: McGraw-Hill, 1981), pp. 148–159; Dorn, "Unfinished Purge," chapter 7, p. 23; Ziemke, *U.S. Army in the Occupation of Germany,* p. 385.

14. Dorn, "Unfinished Purge," chapter 8, p. 23.

15. Patton Diary, Sept. 29, 1945. Relying on the unreliable account by Patton's nephew, Patton's most recent biographer, who used neither the Dorn Papers at Columbia University nor his report in the National Archives, dismissed Dorn as a "self-righteous professor." See Carlo D'Este, *Patton: A Genius for War* (New York: HarperCollins, 1995), p. 772. Letters in the National Archives show that Bedell was grateful to Dorn and showed his report to leading members of Ike's staff. See Walter Bedell Smith to Generals Harold R. Bull and Willard S. Paul, Office of the Chief of Staff, Oct. 2, 1945, File 000.1, Box 1, Records of the United States Forces European Theater, Secretary of the General Staff.

16. All quotes are from Dorn, "Minister President Friedrich Schaeffer and the Tardy De-Nazification of the Bavarian Government," pp. 1–4. See also Walter L. Dorn, "General Patton and the Third Army in September 1945," pp. 1–2, May 19–20, 1949, Box 16, Dorn Papers; Tom Bower, *The Pledge Betrayed: America and Britain and the Denazification of Postwar Germany* (Garden City, N.Y.: Doubleday, 1982), p. 136. On Christian Weber see Alan Bullock, *Hitler: A Study in Tyranny* (New York: Harper & Row, 1964), pp. 302, 391.

17. *New York Times,* Sept. 20, 1945, and Sept. 21, 1945; Carolyn Woods Eisenberg, *Drawing the Line: The American Decision to Divide Germany, 1944–1949* (New York: Cambridge University Press, 1996), pp. 132–133.

18. Farago, *Last Days of Patton,* pp. 168–171, 201–202; Patton Diary, Sept. 15, 1945; *Time* 46 (October 8, 1945): 30–31.

19. Patton Diary, Sept. 16, 1945.

20. Ibid., Sept. 15, 1945, and Sept. 17, 1945.

21. Ibid., Sept. 18, 1945; Farago, *Last Days of Patton,* pp. 161–162.

22. On Wood and Charles F. Ayer, see Blumenson, II, 760; Farago, *Last Days of Patton,* pp. 135–136; William Cahn, *Lawrence 1912: The Bread & Roses Strike* (New York: Pilgrim Press, 1977), pp. 140, 146, 150; *New York Times,* Aug. 31, 1912, and Nov. 28, 1912.

23. Blumenson, II, 761–762; Farago, *Last Days of Patton,* pp. 178–179; Patton Diary, Sept. 25, 1945.

24. Patton Diary, Sept. 25, 1945.

25. Frank E. Mason to Ernest C. Deane, Leesburg, Va., July 26, 1972, Box 5, Patton Papers; Mason to Roy Howard, Bad Wiessee, Germany, Sept. 26, 1945, Box 9, Frank E. Mason Papers, Herbert Hoover Library, West Branch, Iowa.

26. Frank E. Mason, "Memorandum on General Patton Interview," Bad Wiessee, Sept. 25, 1945, Box 20, Mason Papers; Mason to Howard, Bad Wiessee, Sept. 25, 1945, Box 9, Mason Papers; Mason to Deane, Leesburg, Va., July 26, 1972, Box 5, Patton Papers.

27. Mason to George C. Marshall, Leesburg, Va., Nov. 4, 1945, Box 5, Patton Papers.

28. Deane to Mason, Mexia, Texas, Feb. 22, 1950, Box 5, Patton Papers; Deane to Mason, Fayetteville, Ark., July 30, 1972, Box 5, Patton Papers.

29. Deane to Mason, Mexia, Texas, Feb. 22, 1950, Box 5, Patton Papers.

30. Patton Diary, Sept. 25, 1945.

31. Dorn, "Unfinished Purge," chapter 8, pp. 26, 26A, 27, Box 13, Dorn Papers; Dorn Interview, "General Patton and the Third Army in September 1945," pp. 4–5.

32. Dorn, "Unfinished Purge," chapter 8, p. 27, Box 13, Dorn Papers; Transcript of Walter Bedell Smith Press Conference, September 26, 1945, Box 5, Patton Papers. On Frank see the following: Bradley F. Smith, *Reaching Judgment at Nuremberg* (New York: Basic Books, 1977), pp. 194–196; Saul K. Padover, "What Happened in Bavaria," *Nation* 169 (October 20, 1945), 397. For Bedell's comment on Patton, see *Time* 46 (October 8, 1945): 30–31.

33. Patton Diary, Sept. 29, 1945.

34. Dorn Interview, "General Patton and the Third Army in September 1945," pp. 1, 5–6.

35. Ibid., 6–8.

36. Dorn, "Unfinished Purge," chapter 8, pp. 26, 26A, Box 13, Dorn Papers.

37. Ibid., chapter 8, p. 28.

38. Reminiscences of General James M. Gavin, pp. 23–24, 1972, Oral History Research Office, Columbia University Library, New York City.

39. C. L. Sulzberger, *The Last of the Giants* (New York: Macmillan, 1970), p. 323.

40. Beatrice Ayer Patton to Floyd L. Parks, South Hamilton, Feb. 25, 1946, Box 8, Floyd L. Parks Papers, Dwight D. Eisenhower Library, Abilene, Kansas.

41. Patton to Beatrice Ayer Patton, APO 403 New York, Oct. 4, 1945, Patton Papers; Patton Diary, Oct. 2, 1945.

42. *New York Daily Mirror,* Oct. 5, 1945, and Oct. 6, 1945.

43. *New York Daily News,* Oct. 3, 1945.

44. *New York Daily News,* Oct. 14, 1945.

45. *New York Daily News,* Oct. 4, 1945.

46. Patton Diary, Oct. 7, 1945.

47. See "Sicily: The First Phase of Occupation," File 319.1, Box 72, Records of the War Department General and Special Staffs, Civil Affairs Division, Record Group 165, National Archives II, College Park, Md.

48. Patton Diary, Oct. 8, 1945; Patton to Beatrice Ayer Patton, APO 408 New York, Oct. 10, 1945, Patton Papers.

49. *Stars and Stripes* (So. German edition), Oct. 13, 1945, in Purves Collection.

50. Patton Diary, Oct. 13, 1945.

51. Patton to Beatrice Ayer Patton, APO 408 New York, Oct. 19, 1945, Patton Papers.

52. Patton Diary, Oct. 25, 1945.

53. Blumenson, II, 760; Patton to Beatrice Ayer Patton, APO 408 New York, Oct. 31, 1945, Patton Papers; Patton Diary, Oct. 28, 1945.

54. Patton to Gilbert R. Cook, APO 408 New York, Nov. 11, 1945, Box 3, Gilbert R. Cook Papers, Dwight D. Eisenhower Library, Abilene, Kansas.

55. Patton to Beatrice Ayer Patton, APO 408 New York, Nov. 8, 1945, Patton Papers.

56. Farago, *Last Days of Patton,* pp. 232–233.

57. Patton to Beatrice Ayer Patton, APO 408 New York, Nov. 15, 1945, Patton Papers.

58. Patton Diary, Nov. 23, 1945.

59. Ibid., Nov. 27, 1945, and Nov. 28, 1945.

60. Ibid., Nov. 29, 1945, and Dec. 3, 1945.

61. Farago, *Last Days of Patton,* pp. 240–247; Warren A. Lapp, M.D., "An Ex-Medical Officer's Recollections of the Last Days of General George S. Patton, Jr.," *MSCK Bulletin* 66 (January 1987): 17–19.

62. Lapp, "Ex-Medical Officer's Recollections," pp. 18–19.

63. Blumenson, II, 820–824; Lapp, "Ex-Medical Officer's Recollections," p. 20.

64. Lapp, "Ex-Medical Officer's Recollections," p. 21; Frederick Ayer, Jr., Diary, Dec. 16, 1945, Miscellaneous Box, Patton Papers.

65. Ayer Diary, Dec. 15, 1945.

66. Lapp, "Ex-Medical Officer's Recollections," p. 21.

67. Ayer Diary, Dec. 21, 1945; Albert W. Kenner to Robert B. Hill, n.p., Dec. 27, 1945, Box 1, Albert W. Kenner Papers, United States Army Military History Institute, Carlisle Barracks, Pa.

68. Frederick Ayer, "Various and Sundry Memos Concerning . . . G. S. P., Dec. 27, 1945," p. 2, Miscellaneous Box, Patton Papers.

69. Ayer Diary, Dec. 23, 1945.

70. Ibid., Dec. 24, 1945.

CHAPTER NINETEEN   A DIARY AND A MOVIE

1. Beatrice Ayer Patton to Robert P. Patterson, Washington, D.C., Dec. 29, 1945, Box 21, Robert P. Patterson Papers, Manuscript Division, Library of Congress.

2. Patterson to Lord Archibald P. Wavell, n.p., Feb. 7, 1946, Box 21, Patterson Papers.

3. Patterson to Harry S. Truman, n.p., Dec. 22, 1945, Box 21, Patterson Papers; Truman to Patterson, Washington, D.C., February 4, 1946, Box 21, Patterson Papers.

4. Dwight D. Eisenhower to Hastings L. Ismay, n.p., Jan. 24, 1946, Eisenhower File IV/EIS, Lord Ismay Papers, Liddell Hart Centre for Military Archives, King's College, London.

5. Beatrice Ayer Patton to Sherman Miles, Green Meadows, Fall of 1947, Box 3, Nelson A. Miles Family Papers, Manuscript Division, Library of Congress. Bernard Carter, like Allen a lieutenant colonel on Koch's staff, wrote of Allen: "He's a typical & very coarse-speaking newspaper type, but has a brilliant mind & we get on very well—I'm told he's scared of me which seems unbelievable." See Bernard S. Carter to Louise Hope Thacher Carter, APO 403 New York, Oct. 4, 1944, Box 2, Bernard S. Carter Papers, Special Collections, United States Military Academy Library, West Point.

6. *New York Times,* Aug. 20, 1950.

7. Reminiscences of Admiral John Lesslie Hall, Jr., pp. 183–184, 1964, Oral History Research Office, Columbia University Library, New York City.

8. Bradford G. Chynoweth to George F. Hofmann, Berkeley, Feb. 9, 1972, Box 2, Bradford G. Chynoweth Papers, United States Army Military History Institute, Carlisle Barracks, Pa.

9. Tyler Abell (ed.), *Drew Pearson Diaries, 1949–1959* (New York: Holt, Rinehart and Winston, 1974), pp. 344–345.

10. Ibid., pp. 204, 238.

11. Richard Norton Smith, *The Colonel: The Life and Legend of Robert R. McCormick, 1880–1955* (Boston: Houghton Mifflin, 1997), pp. 512–513.

12. Frank E. Mason to Beatrice Ayer Patton, n.p., April 10, 1952, Box 9, Frank E. Mason Papers, Herbert Hoover Library, West Branch, Iowa.

13. Henry Regnery to Beatrice Ayer Patton, n.p., April 22, 1952, Box 183, Herbert Hoover Post-Presidential Individual Papers, Herbert Hoover Library, West Branch, Iowa.

14. Regnery to Herbert Hoover, Chicago, April 22, 1952, Box 183, Hoover Papers.

15. *New York Journal-American,* July 1, 1952, and July 2, 1952; Abell (ed.), *Drew Pearson Diaries,* p. 344.

16. *New York Times,* Oct. 25, 1952; Anne Wilson Patton to Arvin H. Brown, Sr., Pensacola, Oct. 30, 1952, Box 26, George S. Patton, Sr., Papers, Henry E. Huntington Library, San Marino, Ca.

17. *Milwaukee Journal,* Sept. 30, 1953, in Box 7, George S. Patton, Jr., Papers, Special Collections, United States Military Academy Library, West Point.

18. Ruth Ellen Patton Totten to George Clark Lyon, Carlisle Barracks, Pa., sometime in January 1954, Box 27, George Patton, Sr., Papers.

19. Ruth Ellen Totten to Arvin Brown, Jr., n.p., answering letter of April 28, 1954, Box 27, George Patton, Sr., Papers.

20. George S. Patton IV to Williston B. Palmer, West Point, Sept. 20, 1955, Box 27, George Patton, Sr., Papers.

21. Arvin Brown, Jr., to Ruth Ellen Totten, n.p., July 6, 1956, Box 27, George Patton, Sr., Papers.

22. Ruth Ellen Totten to Arvin Brown, Jr., n.p., July 8, 1956, Box 27, George Patton, Sr., Papers.

23. Arvin Brown, Jr., to William Bancroft Mellor, n.p., Sept. 18, 1956, Box 34, George Patton, Sr., Papers.

24. Arvin Brown, Jr., to George Patton IV, Los Angeles, Jan. 25, 1957, Box 27, George Patton, Sr., Papers.

25. Eisenhower to Ismay, Washington, D.C., Jan. 14, 1959, Eisenhower File IV/EIS, Ismay Papers.

26. Frank McCarthy to John S. Wood, Beverly Hills, Oct. 17, 1961, Box 1, John S. Wood Papers, George Arents Library for Special Collections, E.S. Bird Library, Syracuse University.

27. Wood to Basil H. Liddell Hart, From Korea, Sept. 15, 1952, File 1/763, Basil H. Liddell Hart Papers, Liddell Hart Centre for Military Archives, King's College, London.

28. *New York Herald-Tribune,* June 10, 1964; Wood to Liddell Hart, Reno, June 10, 1964, File 1/763, Liddell Hart Papers.

29. Wood to Hanson W. Baldwin, Reno, Nov. 5, 1964, and Nov. 20, 1964, Series I, Box 20, Hanson W. Baldwin Papers, Sterling Memorial Library, Yale University, New Haven, Ct.

30. Wood to Baldwin, Reno, Jan. 7, 1965, File 1/763, Liddell Hart Papers.

31. Frederick Ayer to Baldwin, Boston, January 18, 1962, Series I, Box 1, Baldwin Papers.

32. Donald E. Currier to William Cunningham, Boston, June 10, 1957, Box 1, Donald E. Currier Papers, United States Army Military History Institute, Carlisle Barracks, Pa.

33. Currier to Fred Ayer, Jr., n.d., Box 1, Currier Papers.

34. Ayer to Currier, Washington, April 18, 1964, Box 1, Currier Papers.

35. Currier to Ayer, Boston, Oct. 5, 1964, Box 1, Currier Papers.

36. Ayer to Currier, Washington, D.C., Oct. 27, 1964, Box 1, Currier Papers.

37. McCarthy to Mellor, n.p., n.d., Box 12, Frank McCarthy Papers, George C. Marshall Library, Virginia Military Institute, Lexington, Va.; McCarthy to Richard Zanuck, n.p., Feb. 3, 1966, Box 11, McCarthy Papers.

38. William H. Riddle to Fox Film Studios, Oshkosh, July 23, 1965, Box 12, McCarthy Papers.

39. William Prochnau, *Once upon a Distant War* (New York: Times Books, 1995), pp. 158, 168, 397; Neil Sheehan, *A Bright Shining Lie: John Paul Vann and America in Vietnam* (New York: Random House, 1988), pp. 284–285.

40. Omar N. Bradley to Francis de Guingand, n.p., March 7, 1970, Box 11, McCarthy Papers.

41. John Eisenhower to McCarthy, Brussels, Belgium, Sept. 2, 1969, Box 12, McCarthy Papers; John Eisenhower to McCarthy, n.p., March 12, 1970, Box 12, McCarthy Papers.

42. Thomas S. Bigland to Bradley, London, May 26, 1970, Box 11, McCarthy Papers.

43. See Ruth Ellen Patton Totten and George S. Patton IV to Frederick Ayer, "Comments on Henry Regnery," July 23, 1958, Box 5, George S. Patton, Jr., Papers, Special Collections, United States Military Academy Library, West Point.

CHAPTER TWENTY   PATTON: A BRIEF ASSESSMENT

1. Roger H. Nye, "Dining-In Comments, School of Advanced Military Studies, Fort Leavenworth," p. 5, May 4, 1991, Box 1, Roger H. Nye Papers, Special Collections, United States Military Academy Library, West Point.

2. Ibid., p. 3.

3. Sidney R. Hinds to Donald E. Houston, Falls Church, Va., April 13, 1971, Box 2, Bradford G. Chynoweth Papers, United States Army Military History Institute, Carlisle Barracks, Pa.

4. Reminiscences of General Omar N. Bradley, p. 61, 1966, Box 30, Omar N. Bradley Papers, United States Military Academy Archives, West Point.

5. See "Sicily: The First Phase of the Occupation," File 319.1, Box 72, Records of the War Department General and Special Staffs, Civil Affairs Division, Record Group 165, National Archives II, College Park, Md.

6. Bradford Grethen Chynoweth, *Bellamy Park* (Hicksville, N.Y.: Exposition Press, 1975), pp. 167–169.

7. Ruth Ellen Patton Totten to Arvin H. Brown, Jr., South Hamilton, n.d. but January 1954, Box 27, George S. Patton, Sr., Papers, Henry E. Huntington Library, San Marino, Cal.

8. Nye, "Dining-In Comments, School of Advanced Military Studies, Fort Leavenworth," p. 13.

9. Arthur H. Blair to Roger H. Nye, College Station, Texas, March 14, 1992, Box 1, Nye Papers.

10. Nye to Blair, n.p., April 20, 1992, Box 1, Nye Papers.

11. Noel Monks, *Eyewitness* (London: Frederick Muller, 1955), pp. 194–195, 199; Chester B. Hansen Diary, December 8, 1944, Omar N. Bradley Papers, Special Collections, United States Military Academy Library, West Point.

12. Everett S. Hughes Diary, Aug. 27, 1943, Box 2, Everett S. Hughes Papers, Manuscript Division, Library of Congress.

13. Frederick Ayer to Hanson W. Baldwin, Boston, Jan. 18, 1962, Series I, Box 1, Hanson W. Baldwin Papers, Sterling Memorial Library, Yale University, New Haven, Ct.

14. *New York Times,* Jan. 13, 1912; Feb. 1, 1912; Nov. 28, 1912; and June 8, 1913.

Manuscripts and Oral Histories Cited

MANUSCRIPTS

Field Marshal Viscount Alanbrooke Papers, Liddell Hart Centre for Military Archives, King's College, London.

Lord Alexander of Tunis Papers, Records of the War Office, Public Record Office, Kew, London.

Hanson W. Baldwin Papers, Sterling Memorial Library, Yale University, New Haven.

Banning Company Papers, Henry E. Huntington Library, San Marino, California.

Omar N. Bradley Papers, United States Military Academy Archives, West Point.

Serene E. Brett Papers, Special Collections, United States Military Academy Library, West Point.

Harry C. Butcher Diary, Dwight D. Eisenhower Pre-Presidential Papers, Dwight D. Eisenhower Library, Abilene, Kansas.

Bradford G. Chynoweth Papers, United States Military History Institute, Carlisle Barracks, Pennsylvania.

Gilbert R. Cook Papers, Dwight D. Eisenhower Library, Abilene, Kansas.

Donald E. Currier Papers, United States Army Military History Institute, Carlisle Barracks, Pennsylvania.

Miles C. Dempsey Papers, Records of the War Office, Public Record Office, Kew, London.

Benjamin A. Dickson Papers, Special Collections, United States Military Academy Library, West Point.

Walter L. Dorn Papers, Special Collections, Columbia University Library, New York City.

Dwight D. Eisenhower Pre-Presidential Papers, Dwight D. Eisenhower Library, Abilene, Kansas.

Douglas Southall Freeman Papers, Manuscript Division, Library of Congress.

Hobart R. Gay Papers, Special Collections, United States Military Academy Library, West Point.

Thomas T. Handy Papers, George C. Marshall Library, Virginia Military Institute, Lexington.

Chester B. Hansen Diary, Omar N. Bradley Papers, Special Collections, United States Military Academy Library, West Point.

Hawaiian Department Records, Adjutant General's Office, Record Group 338, National Records Center, Suitland, Maryland.

Guy V. Henry Papers, United States Army Military History Institute, Carlisle Barracks, Pennsylvania.

John K. Herr Papers, Special Collections, United States Military Academy Library, West Point.

Herbert Hoover Post-Presidential Papers, Herbert Hoover Library, West Branch, Iowa.

Everett S. Hughes Papers, Manuscript Division, Library of Congress.

Henry E. Huntington Papers, Henry E. Huntington Library, San Marino, California.

Selena Gray Galt Ingram Papers, Henry E. Huntington Library, San Marino, California.

Lord Ismay Papers, Liddell Hart Centre for Military Archives, King's College, London.

Kenyon A. Joyce Papers, United States Army Military History Institute, Carlisle Barracks, Pennsylvania.

Albert W. Kenner Papers, United States Army Military History Institute, Carlisle Barracks, Pennsylvania.

Walter Krueger Papers, Special Collections, United States Military Academy Library, West Point.

Basil H. Liddell Hart Papers, Liddell Hart Centre for Military Archives, King's College, London.

John P. Lucas Papers, United States Army Military History Institute, Carlisle Barracks, Pennsylvania.

David Marcus Papers, Special Collections, United States Military Academy Library, West Point.

John P. Marquand Papers, Beinicke Rare Book and Manuscript Library, Yale University, New Haven.

George C. Marshall Papers, George C. Marshall Library, Virginia Military Institute, Lexington.

Frank E. Mason Papers, Herbert Hoover Library, West Branch, Iowa.

Frank McCarthy Papers, George C. Marshall Library, Virginia Military Institute, Lexington.

Frank R. McCoy Papers, Manuscript Division, Library of Congress.

Henry C. McLean Papers, Special Collections, United States Military Academy Library, West Point.

Nelson A. Miles Family Papers, Manuscript Division, Library of Congress.

Bernard Law Montgomery Papers, Imperial War Museum, London.

Roger H. Nye Papers, Special Collections, United States Military Academy Library, West Point.

Floyd L. Parks Papers, Dwight D. Eisenhower Library, Abilene, Kansas.

Robert P. Patterson Papers, Manuscript Division, Library of Congress.

George S. Patton, Jr., Papers, Manuscript Division, Library of Congress.

George S. Patton, Jr., Papers, United States Army Military History Institute, Carlisle Barracks, Pennsylvania.

George S. Patton, Jr., Papers, Special Collections, United States Military Academy Library, West Point.

George S. Patton, Sr., Papers, Henry E. Huntington Library, San Marino, California.

John J. Pershing Papers, Manuscript Division, Library of Congress.

James T. Quirk Papers, Harry S. Truman Library, Independence, Missouri.

Records of the Allied Operational and Occupation Headquarters, World War II, Record Group 331, National Archives II, College Park, Maryland.

Records of the Army Staff, Record Group 319, National Archives II, College Park, Maryland.

Records of the Cabinet, Public Record Office, Kew, London.

Records of the National Security Agency/Central Security Service, Record Group 457, National Archives II, College Park, Maryland.

Records of the Office of the Inspector General, Record Group 159, National Archives II, College Park, Maryland.

Records of the Office of the Judge Advocate General, Record Group 153, National Archives II, College Park, Maryland.

Records of the Trial of Captain John T. Compton by General Court-Martial, October 23, 1943, Judge Advocate General's Files, Falls Church, Virginia.

Records of the Trial of Sergeant Horace T. West by General Court-Martial, September 2–3, 1943, Judge Advocate General's Files, Falls Church, Virginia.

Records of United States Forces European Theater, Secretary of the General Staff, Record Group 338, National Archives II, College Park, Maryland.

Records of the United States v. James C. Ayer, et. al., United States District Court for Massachusetts, National Archives—Northeast Region, Waltham, Massachusetts.

Records of the United States Joint Chiefs of Staff, 1942–1945, Record Group 218, National Archives II, College Park, Maryland.

Records of the War Department General and Special Staffs, Civil Affairs Division, Record Group 165, National Archives II, College Park, Maryland.

Records of the War Office, Public Record Office, Kew, London.

Franklin D. Roosevelt Papers, Franklin D. Roosevelt Library, Hyde Park, New York.

James de Barth Shorb Papers, Henry E. Huntington Library, San Marino, California.

Henry L. Stimson Papers, Sterling Memorial Library, Yale University, New Haven.

United States Military Academy Archives, West Point.

James W. Wadsworth Papers, Manuscript Division, Library of Congress.

Benjamin D. Wilson Papers, Henry E. Huntington Library, San Marino, California.

John S. Wood Papers, George Arents Library for Special Collections, E. S. Bird Library, Syracuse University.

ORAL HISTORIES

Columbia University Library, New York City.
    John Jennings Ballantine
    Harvey H. Bundy
    Mark W. Clark

Richard L. Conolly
James M. Gavin
Anthony V. Grossetta
John Lesslie Hall, Jr.
H. Kent Hewitt
Alan Goodrich Kirk
John W. Leonard
Anthony C. McAuliffe
John J. McCloy
Joshua Miner
Charles Poletti
Elwood P. Quesada
William H. Simpson
William A. Sullivan
Rolland Jay Thomas
Otto P. Weyland

Dwight D. Eisenhower Library, Abilene, Kansas.
Jacob L. Devers
John W. Leonard

George C. Marshall Library, Virginia Military Institute, Lexington.
Omar N. Bradley
Frank McCarthy

Harry S. Truman Library, Independence, Missouri.
Karl R. Bendetsen
Bernard Bernstein
Raymond P. Brandt
Bruce C. Clarke

University of California at Los Angeles Library.
Hancock Banning, Jr.

United States Air Force Academy Library, Boulder, Colorado.
James H. Doolittle

United States Army Military History Institute, Carlisle Barracks, Pennsylvania.
Hobart R. Gay
Barksdale Hamlett
Paul D. Harkins
Guy V. Henry
Kenyon A. Joyce

S. L. A. Marshall
August E. Schanze
John K. Waters

United States Military Academy Archives, West Point.
Omar N. Bradley

Index